**Microsoft**®

# Microsoft® SQL Server™ 2005 Administrator's Companion

*Edward Whalen*
*Marcilina Garcia*
*Burzin Patel*
*Stacia Misner*
*Victor Isakov*

PUBLISHED BY
Microsoft Press
A Division of Microsoft Corporation
One Microsoft Way
Redmond, Washington 98052-6399

Library of Congress Control Number: 2006934391

Printed and bound in the United States of America.

1 2 3 4 5 6 7 8 9    QWT    1 0 9 8 7 6

Distributed in Canada by H.B. Fenn and Company Ltd.

A CIP catalogue record for this book is available from the British Library.

Microsoft Press books are available through booksellers and distributors worldwide. For further information about international editions, contact your local Microsoft Corporation office or contact Microsoft Press International directly at fax (425) 936-7329. Visit our Web site at www.microsoft.com/mspress. Send comments to mspinput@microsoft.com.

**Acquisitions Editor:** Martin DelRe
**Developmental Editor:** Jenny Moss Benson
**Project Editor:** Melissa von Tschudi-Sutton
**Production:** Custom Editorial Productions, Inc.

Body Part No. X12-64017

# Contents at a Glance

# Table of Contents

## Part I
## Introduction to Microsoft SQL Server 2005

Part II

# System Design and Architecture

Part III
# Microsoft SQL Server 2005 Administration

Part IV

# Microsoft SQL Server 2005 Architecture and Features

## Part V
# Microsoft SQL Server 2005 Business Intelligence

## Part VI
# High Availability

Part VII
# Performance Tuning and Troubleshooting

# Acknowledgments

*Edward Whalen*  It is not easy to acknowledge all the people who have made this book possible. I would like to thank the contributing authors, our editors Jenny Moss Benson and Melissa von Tschudi-Sutton, and the technical and copy editors Robert Brunner and Matthew Dewald. Without a strong technical staff, this book would not be possible. Writing a book involves a lot of time and effort. I would like to thank my wife, Felicia, for putting up with the sacrifices necessary to write this book.

*Marcilina Garcia*  I would like to thank the editors for their thorough review and helpful comments. Special thanks to Melissa von Tschudi-Sutton for her quick response to my many inquiries about help on logistical issues, and for her proactive management of the submission and editing process.

*Burzin Patel*  I would like to thank everyone at Microsoft Press who made this book possible, especially Melissa von Tschudi-Sutton, Jenny Moss Benson, Martin DelRe, and the technical and copy editors. Their dedication and thoroughness has a lot to do with the completeness and quality of this book. I would also like to thank my wife Dianne and children, Carl and Natasha, for their untiring support and putting up with my virtually never-ending work schedule.

*Stacia Misner*  I would like to thank fellow authors Ed Whalen, Marci Garcia, Burzin Patel, and Victor Isakov, as well as the Microsoft Press team of Martin DelRe, Melissa von Tschudi-Sutton, and Jenny Moss Benson, for allowing me the opportunity to work with them to produce this book. I also appreciate the efforts of the copy editor and technical reviewer who helped find me find the right words to express complex ideas concisely and accurately. Finally, I especially want to thank my husband and best friend, Gerry Misner, who patiently endured yet another book project.

*Victor Isakov*  I would like to first and foremost thank the thousands of people around the globe I have had the privilege to train over the past decade or so. Your boundless enthusiasm and endless questions have very much inspired me and helped me overcome my "dislike" of writing books. The people at Microsoft Press have been wonderful, as have a number of people in the SQL Server product team. So thanks to all concerned. Finally, and most importantly, to Marc, Larissa, Natalie, and Alex. There is no need for words!

# Contributing Authors

We would like to thank the following authors for contributing to this book:

*Charlie Wancio*    We would like to thank Charlie Wancio for contributing to this book with Chapter 11, "Creating Tables and Views," and Chapter 13, "Enforcing Data Integrity." Charlie has been developing database applications for over 15 years. He has worked with Microsoft SQL Server since version 6.5. His company, Wancio Consulting, Inc., specializes in database applications and legacy data conversions. You can find him at www.wancioconsulting.com.

*Frank McBath*    We would like to thank Frank McBath for contributing to this book with Chapter 27, "Log Shipping and Database Mirroring." Frank is an expert in both SQL Server and Oracle and is currently working at Microsoft in the Oracle-Microsoft Alliance group. He was one of the early adopters of SQL Server 2005 Database Mirroring. You can find his blog at www.databasediskperf.com.

*Arnel Sinchongco*    We would like to thank Arnel Sinchongco for contributing to this book with Chapter 25, "Disaster Recovery Solutions." Arnel is a long-time SQL Server DBA and long-time colleague, who is currently working as a DBA-Manager at Pilot Online in Norfolk, VA.

*Nicholas Cain*    We would like to thank Nicholas Cain for contributing to this book with Chapter 3, "Roles and Responsibilities of the SQL Server DBA." Nic started working as a DBA at the now defunct Microwarehouse and is now working at T-Mobile managing a team of SQL Server and Oracle DBAs.

# Introduction

Microsoft SQL Server 2005 is a major new release of SQL Server with a wealth of new features and enhancements from previous versions that provide improved database scalability, reliability, security, administration, and performance, to name a few. If you are currently a SQL Server database administrator (DBA), you have probably either already made the upgrade to SQL Server 2005 and are learning to use the new tools and features, or you should be in the process of considering the upgrade. Application support for all applications that will run against SQL Server 2005 should be verified and applications should be tested before going into production.

This book will help guide you in the learning curve with SQL Server 2005 and assist with implementing and performing DBA-related tasks. There are a lot of new SQL Server 2005 areas to consider including new and improved user interfaces, new system and database performance analysis tools, new features for database performance, new business intelligence tools, and more. It will take some time and research to get a good handle on SQL Server 2005—but it will be worth the effort. This book is a good place to begin if you are new to SQL Server and a good guide and reference for the current SQL Server 7.0 or 2000 DBA.

## How to Use this Book

*Microsoft SQL Server 2005 Administrator's Companion* is a handy guide and reference for the busy DBA. Look for these helpful elements throughout the book:

 **Real World**  Everyone can benefit from the experiences of others. Real World sidebars contain elaboration on a particular theme or background based on the adventures of other users of SQL Server 2005.

**Note**  Notes include tips, alternate ways to perform a task, and other information highlighted for your benefit.

**Important** Boxes marked Important shouldn't be skipped. (That's why they're called Important.) Here you'll find security notes, cautions, and warnings to keep you and your SQL Server 2005 database system out of trouble.

**Best Practices** Best Practices boxes call attention to the authors' advice for best practices based upon our own technical experience.

**More Info** Often there are excellent sources for additional information on key topics. These boxes point you to additional recommended resources.

**On the CD** On the CD boxes point to additional information or tools that are provided on this book's companion CD.

# What's in This Book

Microsoft SQL Server 2005 Administrator's Companion is divided into seven sections. The first three sections provide the foundation for understanding and designing a SQL Server 2005 database system, from choosing, configuring, and sizing server and storage hardware to installing the database software, creating databases, and database administration. The next two sections build on the foundation to cover more in-depth SQL Server 2005 architectural topics and use of new features. The fifth section is dedicated to business intelligence features. The last two sections cover in-depth high availability solutions, troubleshooting methodologies, and performance tuning topics that every DBA should know. Each section is described further below.

- **Part I: Introduction to Microsoft SQL Server 2005** The first three chapters of this book provide fundamental information for the DBA. This includes an overview of SQL Server 2005 features, information about the editions of SQL Server 2005 and licensing to help you determine which is appropriate for your system, and a review of typical tasks and responsibilities of the DBA.

- **Part II: System Design and Architecture** This section focuses on the underlying hardware architecture for the SQL Server database server. It covers system design topics from server hardware to SQL Server network configuration. This includes choosing between 32-bit and 64-bit systems (regarding hardware, Windows, and SQL Server 2005), choosing disk storage, understanding disk configuration and disk performance, capacity planning, installing SQL Server, and configuring the network for SQL Server.

- **Part III: Microsoft SQL Server Administration**   The administration section of the book provides the foundation for building and maintaining databases. It covers how to create databases, tables, views, and indexes. The very important DBA task of protecting data with backup and restore methods are described. User management, security, and other database maintenance tasks are also covered. This section presents the essential tasks that are the primary responsibility of the SQL Server DBA.

- **Part IV: Microsoft SQL Server 2005 Architecture and Features**   This section covers in greater depth concurrent data access topics including transaction management, understanding transactions, locking, blocking, and isolation levels. The new data partitioning feature, which allows tables and indexes to be horizontally partitioned, is also described.

- **Part V: Microsoft SQL Server 2005 Business Intelligence**   This section covers introductions to each of the business intelligence features for SQL Server 2005. These include SQL Server Integration Services, Analysis Services, Reporting Services, Notification Services, and Service Broker.

- **Part VI: High Availability**   This part of the book provides high availability and disaster recovery solutions for SQL Server 2005. These include database mirroring, log shipping, clustering, and replication.

- **Part VII: Performance Tuning and Troubleshooting**   This part focuses on performance topics to help you monitor, troubleshoot, scale, and tune SQL Server 2005. This may be one of the more interesting parts of the book for advanced DBAs. It covers tuning methodologies, monitoring for performance, system tuning, scaling up/scaling out, database tuning, and query tuning. It covers how to use the tools available in Windows and SQL Server 2005, including the SQL Server Profiler, Database Engine Tuning Advisor, and the new dynamic management views to assist with database tuning.

# About the CD

The companion CD that ships with this book contains a fully searchable electronic version of this book. You can view the eBook on-screen using Adobe Acrobat or Adobe Reader. The CD also contains lengthy code samples from Chapters 24 and 31 for your convenience.

# Computer System Requirements

Be sure your computer meets the following system requirements:

- Windows Server 2003 or Windows XP operating system

- SQL Server 2005 Developer Edition or Enterprise Edition (to use all the features mentioned in this book because many of them are available only in these versions.)

- For minimum hardware requirements for installing SQL Server 2005, see Chapter 8, "Installing and Upgrading Microsoft SQL Server 2005."

# Support

Every effort has been made to ensure the accuracy of this book and companion CD content. Microsoft Press provides corrections for books through the Web at the following address:

*http://www.microsoft.com/learning/support*

To connect directly to the Microsoft Knowledge Base and enter a query regarding a question or issue that you may have, go to the following address:

*http://www.microsoft/learning/support/search.asp*

If you have comments, questions, or ideas regarding the book or companion CD content, or if you have questions that are not answered by querying the Knowledge Base, please send them to Microsoft Press using either of the following methods:

- **E-Mail:**

  mspinput@microsoft.com

- **Postal Mail:**

  Microsoft Press
  Attn: Microsoft SQL Server 2005 Administrator's Companion Editor
  One Microsoft Way
  Redmond, Washington 98052-6399

Please note that product support is not offered through the preceding mail addresses. For support information, please visit the Microsoft Product Support Web site at the following address:

*http://support.microsoft.com*

## Talk to Us

We've done our best to make this book as accurate and complete as a single-volume reference can be. However, SQL Server 2005 is a major upgrade from previous versions with a wealth of new features and enhancements, and as service packs are released some of the details may change. We're sure that alert readers will find omissions and even errors (though we fervently hope not too many of those). If you have suggestions, corrections, or tips, please write or contact us and let us know. You can find the authors' contact information on the About the Authors page in the back of the book. We really do appreciate hearing from you.

# Part I
# Introduction to Microsoft SQL Server 2005

# Chapter 1
# What's New in Microsoft SQL Server

Microsoft SQL Server 2005 is Microsoft's new release of its relational database management system. It has been highly anticipated since SQL Server 2000 and is well worth the wait. Officially released in November of 2005, it is focused on making it easier to create, deploy, and manage enterprise database systems and applications, while increasing scalability, availability, performance, reliability, security, and programmability. SQL Server 2005 is a major new release with many major and minor product changes from earlier editions, such as SQL Server 7.0 and SQL Server 2000. It includes a number of new features and substantial enhancements to existing features that were inspired by customer feedback.

If you are just starting out as a database administrator (DBA) with SQL Server 2005, this book will provide the foundation you need to understand what tasks a DBA is responsible for, how to perform these tasks, and what SQL Server 2005 has to offer. If you are already familiar with SQL 7.0 or 2000, you will have a great foundation on which to build an understanding of the changes in SQL Server 2005 and of the significant ways that its new features can be used to improve your current SQL Server systems. SQL Server 2005 provides many new and enhanced features that you will want to know about, and this book will guide you through the learning curve. For example, the presentation and usability of the database tools and utilities user interfaces have been improved for convenience and productivity. It may take some time to get used to these new interfaces, so plan time for a small learning curve there as well—it is well worth the effort of checking out all the new tools, menus, and options.

This chapter provides an overview of the new features and enhanced support for existing features that SQL Server 2005 offers. This is not a comprehensive list of all the features SQL Server 2005 provides, as there are too many to all be covered in detail in this book. Because this book is focused on the work of the database administrator, it covers the topics that are the most relevant to this audience.

There are numerous enhancements for developers and programmers that will not be covered in this book but are referenced here. These include the ability to program database objects—including triggers, functions, stored procedures, user-defined data types, and user-defined aggregates—in .NET languages, such as Microsoft Visual C# and Visual Basic .NET. The use of .NET languages supports programming with more features and more complex logic than with the Transact-SQL language. The T-SQL language has been extended with several new features and enhancements as well, such as recursive queries and a new xml data type. In addition, the TOP operator now accepts a numeric expression, such as a variable name instead of only an integer, to specify the number of rows to return, and it can be used in INSERT, UPDATE, and DELETE statements and SELECT queries.

---

**More Info**   For information on the new features and enhancements for developers, see the SQL Server Books Online topic "Database Engine Programmability Enhancements."

---

It is important to notice that several new features and enhancements are available only with SQL Server 2005 Enterprise Edition, as noted throughout this chapter and throughout the book. You should be aware of this and consider the features supported by each edition of SQL Server when choosing which one to use. Also, there are many small changes in behavior from previous versions of SQL Server that are referenced below, which are not covered in detail in this book.

---

**More Info**   There are numerous detailed changes within SQL Server 2005 that can affect the behavior of your current SQL Server 7.0 or 2000 applications. See the SQL Server Books Online topic "Behavior Changes to Database Engine Features in SQL Server 2005" for some of these very specific changes in behavior. This article also references several other SQL Server Books Online topics that cover more of these details.

# New Hardware Support

As hardware architecture has continued to improve for better performance and scalability, Windows 2003 Server and SQL Server SQL Server 2005 provide software versions to support these new architectures. Windows and SQL Server provide support for the new Intel and AMD 64-bit hardware platforms and for NUMA systems. Support for these platforms by the combination of Windows Server 2003 and SQL Server 2005 has greatly improved the method and capacity for memory access.

## Native 64-Bit Support

There are specific versions of SQL Server 2005 software that provide support for specific hardware processor architectures. These include support for both the Intel Itanium-2 and the x64 processor architecture (both Intel and AMD provide an x64 architecture) running on the Windows Server 2003 64-bit operating system. Windows Server 2003 for the 64-bit Itanium-2 platform supports running only 64-bit applications, while the Windows 2003 x64 platform supports both 32-bit and 64-bit applications on the same system. There are specific versions of SQL Server 2005 for each of these platforms. The previous version of SQL Server, SQL Server 2000, provides a 64-bit version only for the Itanium or Itanium-2 architecture. There is no version of SQL Server 2000 for the new x64 architecture.

With native 64-bit, the memory access limitations of 32-bit addressing are eliminated. More data can be processed per clock cycle, and much larger amounts of memory can be accessed with direct memory addressing (without AWE memory access overhead). See Chapter 5, "32 Bit versus. 64-Bit Platforms and Microsoft SQL Server 2005," for more details on these platforms, the difference between 32-bit and 64-bit memory access, and AWE.

## NUMA Support

Windows Server 2003 and SQL Server 2005 also support Non-Uniform Memory Access (NUMA) server architecture. This architecture provides a scale out solution by grouping CPU and memory into units, or nodes, that can perform together as one server. Each node has its own CPUs, memory, and system bus, while the individual nodes connect to each other via an external bus to access memory on another node when needed. Windows Server 2003 and SQL Server 2005 have been enhanced to take advantage of this architecture by increasing the ability of a thread running on a CPU within a certain unit to use memory located in that same node, thus avoiding overhead of crossing the external bus.

**More Info**    See the SQL Server Books Online topic "NUMA Support in SQL Server" for a description of the NUMA architecture and how SQL Server is designed to take advantage of NUMA hardware with no database or application changes necessary.

# Data Availability

SQL Server 2005 provides several completely new features that help minimize down time, allow greater and faster data access, and provide additional data protection. These new features include online restore, online index operations, database snapshot, fast recovery, mirrored backups, database mirroring, snapshot isolation, and read committed snapshot. The online index operations, snapshot isolation, and read committed snapshot features are all based on another new feature called row versioning, which is a method of storing a copy of a row of data in memory or *tempdb* so that the data can be read by one process at the same time that it is being modified by another process without causing blocking. These new features are described briefly here and in more detail throughout this book.

## Online Restore

The new online restore feature allows individual files and filegroups to be restored and brought online for access while the remaining files in the database remain offline, thus allowing faster access to restored data. Using online restore, you can restore an individual file or filegroup and then bring that data online and access it while the other files or file-groups remain offline. The data that resides in the restored files can be accessed by users, while the data in the files that remain offline cannot be accessed. When a user attempts to access data that resides in a file that is still offline, SQL Server returns an error message. This allows at least some data to be accessible before the entire database is restored.

You can restore one file or filegroup at a time, bringing each online as soon as the file or filegroup is restored without having to wait for the entire database to be restored. This may be a factor to consider when determining how to place database data within file-groups. See more details on online restore in Chapter 15, "Restoring Data." This feature is available only in SQL Server 2005 Enterprise Edition.

## Online Index Operations

Online index operations is also a new feature that allows greater data accessibility. Without using the online option, underlying table data is locked and thus blocked from user access when an index is created, altered (includes rebuilding the index), or dropped. With the new online option, these operations are performed online so that users can still access the table data and other indexes on the table while the operation is occurring. This feature uses a new process called row versioning to allow table and index data to be accessed while an index on that table is being created, deleted, or altered. This will be an important factor in allowing users greater data access when rebuilding indexes for database maintenance. For more details on indexes and online index building see Chapter 12, "Creating Indexes for Performance." This feature is also available only with SQL Server 2005 Enterprise Edition.

## Database Snapshot

Database Snapshot is a new feature with SQL Server 2005 that provides the ability to create a snapshot of a database, a static view of the database that remains intact and accessible until the snapshot is deleted. A database snapshot can be accessed directly by name, as if it were a separate database. This can be very useful for providing a static view of data for report queries; consistent results are guaranteed because any changes made to the base database from which the snapshot was created are not visible through the database snapshot. A database can also be reverted back to a database snapshot, reverting the base database back to the point in time when the snapshot was created. This can be useful, for example, when data is accidentally deleted or updated and the changes must be undone. In this case, reverting to a database snapshot could potentially be faster than restoring the entire database.

Database Snapshots can also be created from a mirrored database on a standby server, providing a separate read-only database against which reports and queries can be run without using resources or causing contention on the primary database server. The Database Snapshot feature is available only with SQL Server 2005 Enterprise Edition. See Chapter 10, "Creating Databases and Database Snapshots," for details on creating and using database snapshots.

## Fast Recovery

With previous versions of SQL Server, users could not access a database that was in the process of being restored until the entire recovery process was complete, which included both the redo (roll forward) and the undo (rollback) phases. With the new fast recovery feature, the database is made partially accessible to users as soon as the redo phase is complete but before the undo phase completes. This allows earlier access to the database during a restore. Fast recovery is available only in SQL Server 2005 Enterprise Edition. See Chapter 15 for more information about restoring data.

## Mirrored Backups

The new mirrored backup feature allows a backup to be created on more than one device at the same time when a backup is performed. Having mirrored sets of backed up data provides a safety net in case one backup set or a part of the set becomes corrupted or damaged. A backup device from one backup set can be interchanged with the corresponding backup device from a mirrored set, thus allowing more possibilities to ensure successful restores of data. See Chapter 14, "Backup Fundamentals," for details on how to perform a mirrored backup and other data backup topics.

## Database Mirroring

The new database mirroring feature provides a new method for maintaining a standby server that provides failover capabilities. A copy of a principal database can be mirrored to another instance of SQL Server. This is done by SQL Server automatically writing and replaying transaction log records on the mirrored system. There are two modes for database mirroring—synchronous and asynchronous. The mirrored database can be on the same physical server as the principal, but it should reside on a separate physical server in order to serve as a standby server for failover. By having them on separate servers, both the server hardware and the data are protected from failure. It is an alternative to failover clustering, which protects only the server hardware but does not provide a copy of the data. See Chapter 27, "Log Shipping and Database Mirroring" for details on setting up and using database mirroring and how failover works. Database mirroring is fully supported with SQL Server 2005 Enterprise Edition Service Pack 1 and partial support is provided with SQL Server 2005 Standard Edition Service Pack 1 (limited to a single redo thread and safety setting enabled). It is not available with other editions.

## Read Committed Snapshot and Snapshot Isolation

There are two new ways to effect process blocking behavior within SQL Server that provide greater data availability and may also provide performance improvements. They are the new read-committed snapshot option for the read-committed isolation level and the new snapshot isolation level setting. These new locking behaviors are built on the new feature called row-versioning, which stores a consistent view of a row of data in memory or *tempdb* so that users can access that versioned row without blocking on a modification of that same row by another process. This reduces locking contention and reduces the problem of blocked processes waiting for lock resources to modify data. See Chapter 17, "Transactions and Locking," for details on row-versioning and how these two new options work and when to use them.

# Performance

There are several new features and built-in support within SQL Server 2005 that provide potential for improved system performance and for monitoring performance. Data partitioning, the ability to partition table data and indexes into horizontal partitions, can help with performance and manageability of data. There are new query hints and query plan guides available to help improve performance and to improve query plan reuse. There are also new dynamic management system views for monitoring performance information. Each of these is described in the following sections.

## Data Partitioning

Native table and index partitioning capabilities are new for SQL Server 2005 Enterprise Edition only. Partitioning can significantly improve query performance against very large tables by allowing data to be accessed through a part (partition) of the table instead of the whole base table. Partitioning a table divides the data into partitions based on a particular column value, such as date. For example, a table may be partitioned so that each month's worth of data is separated into its own partition. This reduces the amount of data that must be searched to find a particular row or rows. Indexes can be created per partition as well, thus reducing the size of the indexes.

Partitioning also provides for more capabilities in managing table data. For example, many table and index operations (such as index rebuilds) can be performed per partition rather than on the entire table at once, thus reducing the time to complete the operation and the contention on the data. Also, partitions can be moved from one table to another without physically moving the data. This is useful when archiving data from the active table to a history table for example. See Chapter 19, "Data Partitioning," for details on how to partition tables and indexes.

## Plan Guides

Plan guides are a new feature in SQL Server 2005 Standard and Enterprise Editions that provide users a mechanism to inject query hints into a query without having to modify it. This mechanism is very powerful for tuning queries that originate in third-party applications and cannot be trivially modified with the hints directly in the application code. Plan guides can be applied to any SELECT, UPDATE, DELETE, or INSERT...SELECT statement. This feature is explained in detail in Chapter 33, "Tuning Queries Using Query Hints and Plan Guides."

## Forced Parameterization

Forced parameterization is a new feature that can be used to improve performance in cases where repeated compilations of the same SQL statement occur because of nonparameterization. By specifying the FORCED query hint, SQL Server 2005 attempts to force parameterization of the query, thereby effectively reusing an existing compiled plan and eliminating the need to compile different invocations of the same query with differing parameter values. The FORCED parameterization query hint is covered in Chapter 33.

## Dynamic Management Views

Dynamic management views, also called DMVs, are new in SQL Server 2005. They provide a new method for accessing a wide range information on database performance and resource usage and allow greater visibility into the database than previous versions of SQL Server, providing easier and more substantive monitoring of database health, diagnosing problems, and tuning performance. See Chapter 31, "Using Dynamic Management Views," for details on the available DMVs and examples of how to use them.

# Enhancements to Existing Features

SQL Server 2005 has many enhancements to existing features that improve ease of use and manageability. These include enhancements for data access, failover clustering, replication, indexed views, and full-text search.

## SNAC

SQL Native Client (SNAC) is a new data access technology in Microsoft SQL Server 2005. SNAC is a stand-alone data access application programming interface (API) library that combines the SQL OLE DB provider and the ODBC driver, which were previously available via the Microsoft Data Access Components (MDAC) library, into one native dynamic-link library while also providing new functionality above and beyond what is supplied by MDAC.

SQL Native Client introduces a simplified architecture by way of a single library (SQLN-CLI.DLL) for all the APIs and can conceptually be viewed as a conglomerate of four components: ODBC, OLEDB, TDS Parser plus Data Access Runtime Services, and SNI functionality.

## Failover Clustering

SQL Server 2005 failover clustering, as with previous versions of SQL Server, is a high availability solution built on Windows Clustering Services to provide protection from a database server failure. New with SQL Server 2005, clustering support has been extended to include Analysis Services, Notification Services, and SQL Server replication. The number of nodes supported in Enterprise Edition has also been increased to eight, and the Standard Edition of SQL Server 2005 supports up to a 2-node cluster. (Standard Edition of previous versions of SQL Server did not support clustering at all.) See Chapter 26, "Failover Clustering–Installation and Configuration," for a detailed description of failover clustering and the process of implementing a SQL Server 2005 cluster.

# Replication

There are many new enhancements to replication that improve manageability, scalability, security, and availability. Some examples include a new Replication Monitor, the ability to initialize transactional subscriptions from a backup of the database, the ability to make schema changes to published tables, and improved support for non-SQL Server subscribers.

One of the major enhancements to transactional replication is the new peer-to-peer transactional replication capability. This allows two-way replication that works well for situations in which a subset of the data can be modified on one SQL Server while a different subset of the data is modified on the other SQL Server, such that each server can act as a publisher and subscriber to the other without running into many update conflicts, yet still maintaining the full data set on both servers. A similar capability in SQL Server 2000 was known as bi-directional transactional replication, which had to be implemented manually. See Chapter 20, "Replication," for more on the different types of replication.

# Indexes

Several index-related enhancements have been made to improve index and query performance. These include a new database option to update statistics asynchronously (both indexed and nonindexed column statistics), the ability to include non-key columns as part of a nonclustered index, new options to control index locking granularity, the ability to index an XML data type column, and improved usage of indexed views by the query optimizer to resolve queries. For details on indexing topics see Chapter 12.

# Full-Text Search

There have been several enhancements to full-text indexing and search capabilities in the areas of programmability, manageability, and performance. These include the following:

- The ability to back up and restore full-text catalogs without having to repopulate the data

- The preservation of full-text catalogs with the database data when a database is detached and re-attached

- Support for full-text indexes on and full-text queries against XML data

- The use of Microsoft Search technology to build the new Microsoft Full-Text Engine for SQL Server (MSFTESQL) service, providing significantly improved performance during full-text index population

- A dedicated instance of MSFTESQL for each SQL Server 2005 instance

These capabilities make managing full-text catalogs a much easier task than with previous versions of SQL Server. To find details on these and additional programmability enhancements to full-text see the SQL Server Books Online topic "Full-Text Search Enhancements."

# Tools and Utilities

Enhancements have been made to many of the SQL Server administration tools and utilities. The previous Enterprise Manager has been replaced with the SQL Server Management Studio, Query Analyzer replaced with Query Editor (part of SQL Server Management Studio), and the osql command line utility with sqlcmd. In addition, the new configuration utility called SQL Server Configuration Manager rolls three previous tools—Server Network Utility, Client Network Utility, and Service Manager—into one. Also, the previous Index Tuning Wizard has been replaced by the new Database Engine Tuning Advisor tool. The SQL Profiler tool still exists but with several enhancements and a different look, and there is a new tool called SQL Server Surface Area Configuration. There is also a new utility called tablediff for comparing the data in two tables. These tools and utilities are briefly described here and in more detail throughout the book. It may take some time to become familiar with these new tools and utilities.

## SQL Server Management Studio

The SQL Server Management Studio replaces the previous Enterprise Manager and more. From the Management Studio you can access all of the other utilities. SQL Server Management Studio is used in examples throughout this book and its uses for tuning are covered in Chapter 30, "Using Profiler, Management Studio, and Database Tuning Advisor."

## Query Editor

Query Editor is the replacement for the previous Query Analyzer. It is a graphical interface used to write, open, save, and execute T-SQL statements, and to view the results. Query Editor is built into the SQL Server Management Studio; it is not a separate console, such as Query Analyzer.

## SQL Configuration Manager

The SQL Configuration Manager tool is new for SQL Server 2005 and replaces the three previous tools—Server Network Utility, Client Network Utility, and Service Manager—by rolling them all into one tool. This tool allows you to manage all operating system services for SQL Server services and networking. See Chapter 9, "Configuring Microsoft SQL Server 2005 on the Network," for details on using the SQL Configuration Manager.

## Surface Area Configuration

The Surface Area Configuration tool is new for SQL Server 2005. It provides the capability to enable, disable, stop, or start services (including SQL Server, SQL Server Agent, Reporting Services, and more), features (including Database Engine, Analysis Services, and Reporting Services features), and remote connectivity. Disabling or stopping unused services or components helps to reduce the "surface area" of SQL Server 2005 and, thus, helps to secure the system by keeping tighter control of what services or processes are running on the server. Some features, services, and connections are disabled by default on installation and must be explicitly enabled. See Chapter 8, "Installing and Upgrading Microsoft SQL Server 2005," and Chapter 9, " Configuring Microsoft SQL Server 2005 on the Network" for information about using this tool.

## SQL Server Profiler

The SQL Server Profiler remains a separate tool with SQL Server 2005, as with previous versions. It has been enhanced with a different interface and lots of new features. The Profiler tool can be used to trace numerous events that occur on the server along with data relating to the event. For example, T-SQL batches or stored procedure events that are executed on the server can be traced, and data can be collected about the event such as the user name, how many reads and writes were performed, and how long the execution took. The Profiler allows you to save that data to a file or a database table for further analysis and sorting. See Chapter 30, "Using Profiler, Management Studio, and Database Tuning Advisor," for information about using the SQL Profiler for monitoring database activity and tuning.

## Database Engine Tuning Advisor

The Database Engine Tuning Advisor is a new tuning tool that replaces the previous Index Tuning Wizard and provides more capabilities. This tool allows you to analyze a workload file or table (a Profiler trace saved to a table) and provides tuning recommmendations that can include indexing, partioning data, and using non-key columns in a nonclustered index. See Chapter 30 for details on using the Database Tuning Advisor.

## SQL Server Upgrade Advisor

The Upgrade Advisor tool is a free downloadable tool that can be run on any SQL Server 7.0 or SQL Server 2000 system to analyze the effort and issues that may be encountered when upgrading to SQL Server 2005. The tool outputs a report of the findings, warnings, and recommendations, and how to resolve or further research the potential issues encountered. This tool should be run before upgrading to SQL Server 2005 and the results analyzed to help point out issues that need to be addressed before upgrading.

## sqlcmd Utility

The sqlcmd utility replaces the command line utilities isql and osql and allows T-SQL commands and a set of specific sqlcmd commands to be executed. When run by command line, sqlcmd uses the OLE DB provider. (The previous osql utility used ODBC.) When running sqlcmd via the SQL Server Management Studio in sqlcmd mode, the .NET SqlClient is used. Note that because these two connectivity methods have different default options, it is possible to get different results from executing the same query by command line versus through Management Studio.

## tablediff Utility

The new tablediff utility can be run by command line or in a batch file and is used to compare the data in two tables. This is particularly useful in replication topologies where there is a need to verify consistent data between the publisher and one or more subscribers. There are many options for this tool, such as specifying a row-by-row comparison or only a row count and schema comparison.

# Business Intelligence Features

Many of the business intelligence capabilities of SQL Server 2000 have been improved in SQL Server 2005, and in some cases these capabilities have been completely re-architected. (SQL Server 2005 Enterprise Edition is required to support most of the advanced functionality.) An important new feature is the addition of Business Intelligence Development Studio, which supplies a set of templates for developing business intelligence projects in an integrated development environment. Integration Services replaces Data Transformation Services with better performance, greater flexibility and portability, and improved support for complex data management and integration activities. While Analysis Services did not undergo a name change, it did get quite an architectural make-over to support a wider variety of analytical requirements, as well as to provide more options for managing data latency. Of all the business intelligence features in SQL Server 2005, Reporting Services has changed the least from its counterpart in SQL Server 2000, but there are plenty of new features that make the transition well worth the relatively minimal effort required to upgrade to SQL Server 2005, whether you're responsible for developing reports, administering a report server, or accessing Reporting Services as an end user. Notification Services in general conforms to the application principles introduced in Notification Services 2.0, a downloadable add-in for SQL Server 2000, but it has been improved to simplify development and administrative tasks and to boost performance and scalability. Lastly, Service Broker is a new feature included with SQL Server 2005 as a framework for the development and management of asynchronous messaging applications.

## Business Intelligence Development Studio

Because tasks related to developing a business intelligence solution are quite different from tasks required to administer those solutions in production, SQL Server 2005 provides two separate environments for each set of tasks—Business Intelligence Development Studio for development and SQL Server Management Studio for administration. Business Intelligence Development Studio is, in fact, a version of Microsoft Visual Studio 2005 that you use to create Integration Services, Analysis Services, or Reporting Services projects. If you're already using Visual Studio 2005 for application development, the business intelligence templates are simply added to your existing version. You can learn about using this integrated development environment in Chapter 21, "Integration Services," Chapter 22, "Analysis Services, and Chapter 23, "Reporting Services."

## Integration Services

Integration Services is not an enhanced version of Data Transformation Services (DTS) from SQL Server 2000 but a completely redesigned set of tools you can use to develop scalable, flexible, and high performing data integration solutions. In Chapter 21, you learn how Integration Services compares to Data Transformation Services. You also learn the basic processes required to build, monitor, and manage packages that extract data from a variety of sources, optionally transform that data, and then load the results into one or more destinations.

## Analysis Services

Analysis Services in SQL Server 2005 frees developers of online analytical processing (OLAP) solutions from traditional, rigid cube structures by enabling flexible designs that support a variety of analytical requirements. After reading Chapter 22, you'll understand how Analysis Services in SQL Server 2005 differs from Analysis Services in SQL Server

2000 and how to build a simple database to explore the new features in the current version of the product.

## Reporting Services

In SQL Server 2005, Reporting Services includes new interactive features that can be implemented by report authors, additional management tools available to report server administrators, and ad hoc report writing capabilities for nontechnical users, to name a few. You can learn about these new capabilities in Chapter 23.

## Notification and Broker Services

Notification Services is a platform for developing and maintaining messaging applications used to send alerts to subscribers, typically in the form of an e-mail message, when specific events occur or on a scheduled basis. Service Broker is also a messaging application platform, but one which facilitates the asynchronous exchange of messages between applications. See Chapter 24, "Notification and Broker Services," for an introduction to these two technologies.

## Summary

This chapter provided an overview of the major new features and enhancements of SQL Server 2005 that will be most interesting to the DBA. References to information for developer topics were provided, as there are many new features for development which are not covered in this book. This book focuses on installation, configuration, administration, high availability, scalability, business intelligence capabilities, and performance topics for SQL Server 2005, as well as how to use some of the new features that will be important for the DBA.

# Chapter 2
# Microsoft SQL Server 2005 Editions, Capacity Limits, and Licensing

Much like its predecessors, Microsoft SQL Server 2005 is available in a number of editions that can be installed on a variety of hardware platforms using different licensing models. Evaluating the needs of your environment and deciding on the appropriate edition, platform architecture, and licensing model are the first steps to getting started with SQL Server 2005 and are crucial to ensuring long-term success.

This chapter introduces you to the different SQL Server 2005 editions and provides examples of the environments for which each is best suited. It also compares the editions based on features and platforms supported. In addition, you will learn about the various capacity limits and the considerations for high availability. Lastly, it provides detailed information about the SQL Server 2005 licensing models, including multicore processor and high-availability licensing considerations, and presents example scenarios in which each is best suited.

# SQL Server 2005 Editions

This section explains each of the six editions of SQL Server 2005 and typical usage scenarios in which each is best used. Details about the editions, including the features, platforms supported, and capacity limits, are presented later in this chapter.

## Mobile Edition

As the name suggests, SQL Server 2005 Mobile Edition is a compact database with a very small footprint (2 MB) designed specifically for mobile devices. This edition is a successor to the CE Edition that shipped with SQL Server 2000.

Mobile Edition supports a subset of the features supported by other editions of SQL Server 2005, such as replication (subscriber only) and transaction support, and has the advantage of supporting a subset of the same popular T-SQL language you may already be familiar with from using other editions of SQL Server. This familiar development platform can help you leverage your existing skills. Mobile Edition integrates with the Microsoft .Net Compact Framework using Microsoft Visual Studio 2005, making application development easier and more efficient. It also integrates with SQL Server Management Studio, which simplifies the process of building, deploying, and managing the SQL Server 2005 Mobile databases. SQL Server Management Studio is explained in detail in Chapter 31 "Dynamic Management Views." Overall, SQL Server 2005 Mobile Edition provides you with a powerful database that enables simple access to enterprise data for devices that are intermittently or continuously connected to the master SQL Server database system. SQL Server 2005 Mobile Edition can be used on any device that runs Microsoft Windows CE 5.0, Microsoft Windows XP Tablet PC Edition, Windows Mobile 2003 Software for Pocket PC, or Windows Mobile 5.0.

Because Mobile Edition is a specialized edition intended just for mobile devices, it will not be covered in detail in this book.

---

**More Info**   For more information about SQL Server 2005 Mobile Edition, refer to *http://www.microsoft.com/sql/editions/sqlmobile*.

---

## Express Edition

SQL Server 2005 Express Edition is a free, easy-to-use, and redistributable version of SQL Server 2005 that offers developers a robust database for building reliable applications. Although there are some capacity limits, SQL Server Express is a full-fledged and powerful database offering many of the same features as the other SQL Server 2005 editions explained later, including support for transactions, replication (subscriber only), OSQL command-line tool and Common Language Runtime (CLR). It also has the ability to serve as a witness in SQL Server 2005 database mirroring, as explained in Chapter 27, "Log Shipping and Database Mirroring."

SQL Server Express can make use of only a single processor and 1 GB of RAM. In addition, it has a database size limit of 4 GB, which limits its use for larger business applications. Unlike its predecessor, Microsoft SQL Server Desktop Edition (MSDE) that shipped with SQL Server 2000, SQL Server Express does not use a workload governor to degrade performance if there are more than five concurrent batch workloads executing simultaneously. This is a huge benefit over MSDE, as it makes the performance predictable and scalable.

SQL Server 2005 Express Edition is primarily targeted to developers looking to embed a redistributable database engine in their application. These developers no longer need to develop their own data repository and can rely on the powerful set of features, performance, and the well-defined T-SQL programming language offered by SQL Server Express. This edition is also well-suited for supporting basic Web sites.

## Workgroup Edition

SQL Server 2005 Workgroup Edition is an ideal entry-level database targeted at small organizations that need a database with no limits on database size or number of users. It is a fast, easy-to-use, and affordable database solution that provides most of what you need to run applications.

The Workgroup Edition supports most of the features in Standard Edition, explained in the following section, but does not include Analysis Services, Reporting Services or Notification Services. In addition, it is limited to being able to use only two processors and 3 GB of memory. This limitation means that even if the system contains more than two processors and greater than 3 GB of memory, Workgroup Edition will not be able to make use of the additional capacity.

SQL Server 2005 Workgroup Edition is best suited for departmental or branch office operations. It includes the core database features of SQL Server and can be upgraded directly to Standard Edition or Enterprise Edition.

## Standard Edition

SQL Server 2005 Standard Edition is targeted for departmental usage in medium-sized businesses and infrastructures that require a highly available data management and analysis platform. In SQL Server 2005, Standard Edition moves into the higher end of the spectrum with support for high-availability features such as two-node failover clustering, database mirroring, and, in theory, support for an unlimited amount of memory. It also offers enhanced business intelligence functionality and SQL Server Integration Services, SQL Server Analysis Services, and SQL Server Reporting Services.

Standard Edition is ideal for users looking for an affordable enterprise-class database. It is one of the most popular editions of SQL Server.

## Enterprise Edition

Enterprise Edition is the most robust edition of SQL Server 2005 and is best suited for critical enterprise online transaction processing (OLTP) workloads, highly complex data analysis, and data warehousing workloads in large organizations with complex requirements. This edition supports the complete set of enterprise data management and business intelligence features and offers the highest level of availability with full support for database mirroring and failover clustering. Enterprise Edition provides user-ready advanced business intelligence and reporting features, making it a very competitively priced comprehensive enterprise solution.

SQL Server 2005 Enterprise Edition is the most expensive edition, making all the features of SQL Server available for use. It is targeted to the larger customers with more critical and complex processing requirements and includes enhanced features such as advanced business analysis, proactive caching, scale-out report servers, and data-driven subscriptions.

## Developer Edition

SQL Server 2005 Developer Edition includes all of the features and functionality of the Enterprise Edition but is designed for individual database developer or tester use solely for the purpose of building and testing applications. The special development and test license agreement for this edition disallows users from using it in a production environment. Developer Edition can be directly upgraded for production use to SQL Server 2005 Standard or Enterprise Edition, providing users with an easy upgrade path. Using the SQL Server Developer Edition is also an excellent way for developers to sample the complete set of features and functionality of Enterprise Edition and prepare to deploy it.

Unlike the other editions, SQL Server 2005 Developer Edition is licensed to individual users and is solely for development and test purposes.

### Real World    What About SQL Server 2005 Datacenter Edition?

I have often come across customers who want to purchase SQL Server 2005 Datacenter Edition to meet their mission-critical and high-availability needs. This search is futile because there is no such SQL Server edition. What these customers are often looking for and referring to is the Windows Server Datacenter Edition operating system.

Users looking for the highest levels of scalability and reliability should consider using Windows Server 2003 Datacenter Edition with SQL Server 2005 Enterprise Edition. This is the recommended solution for all mission-critical database applications, ERP (Enterprise Resource Planning) software, high-volume, and real-time transaction processing applications.

# Understanding Windows Platform Support

The Windows operating system comes in several variants, each targeted towards a particular size and type of business. Understanding and determining the most appropriate one for your SQL Server 2005 deployment is almost as important as selecting the correct edition of SQL Server 2005.

SQL Server 2005 can be installed and run on Windows 2000, Windows 2003, and Windows XP. These three operating systems are described briefly in the following list:

■ Windows 2000

   Windows 2000, also referred to as Win2K, W2K, or Windows NT 5.0, was released in February 2000 as a successor to Windows NT 4.0. It is designed to work with uniprocessor and Symmetric Multi Processor (SMP) systems, with editions targeted specifically for the desktop and server systems. SQL Server 2005 is supported on four versions of Windows 2000: Professional, Server, Advanced Server, and Datacenter Server (IA-32 only).

   Windows 2000 has since been succeeded by Windows Server 2003 (described later in this list), which has many feature and performance enhancements, including a better I/O and TCP/IP stack. Whenever possible, I recommend you use one of the editions of Windows Server 2003 instead of Windows 2000.

   > **More Info**   More information about Windows 2000 can be found at *http://www.microsoft.com/windows2000.*

■ Windows XP

   Windows XP is a general-purpose operating system intended for use primarily with notebook, desktop, and business computer systems. It was released in October 2001 and ships in four editions: Home, Professional, Tablet, and Media Center. While some of the SQL Server 2005 editions, like Standard Edition, are supported on Windows XP, I recommend you use this operating system only for development and test activity and light database workloads.

> **More Info**    More information about Windows XP can be found at *http://www.microsoft.com/windowsXP*.

■  Windows Server 2003

The successor to Windows 2000, Windows Server 2003 is currently Microsoft's flagship server operating system. It was released in April 2003, and is the only operating system to support the IA-32 as well as the IA-64 and x64 platforms. Windows Server 2003 boasts enhanced security, increased reliability, simplified administration, higher scalability, and better performance and is ideally suited for large mission-critical applications. Windows Server 2003 ships in four editions: Web, Standard, Enterprise, and Datacenter. It is the preferred operating system for running SQL Server 2005 databases.

> **More Info**    More information about Windows Server 2003 can be found at *http://www.microsoft.com/windowsserver2003*.

> **Note**    Windows Small Business Server 2003 is not a separate operating system; it is a Windows bundle that includes Windows Server 2003 and other technologies to provide a small business with a complete technology solution. The technologies are integrated to enable a small business with targeted solutions that are easily deployed. SQL Server 2005 is supported on the Windows Small Business Server 2003 Standard and Premium Editions.

> **More Info**    More information about Windows Small Business Server 2003 can be found at *http://www.microsoft.com/windowsserver2003/sbs*.

The SQL Server 2005 support for these operating systems varies based on four factors:

1. Edition of SQL Server 2005 (Express, Workgroup, Standard, Enterprise, or Developer)
2. Operating system version (Windows 2000, Windows XP, Windows Server 2003, or Windows Small Business Server 2003)
3. Edition of the operating system version (Standard, Enterprise, Datacenter, and so on)
4. Platform (IA-32, IA-64, or x64)

The supported combinations of the Windows versions for the five different SQL Server 2005 32-bit (IA-32) editions are presented in Table 2-1.

> **More Info**    WOW64 in Table 2-1 refers to the Windows on Windows 32-bit subsystem of a 64-bit (x64) server. For additional information on WOW64, refer to the MSDN article "Running 32-bit Applications" at *http://msdn.microsoft.com/library/default.asp?url=/library/en-us/win64/win64/running_32_bit_applications.asp*.

**Table 2-1    Supported Operating Systems for SQL Server 2005 (IA-32) Editions**

| Operating System | Enterprise Edition (IA-32) | Developer Edition (IA-32) | Standard Edition (IA-32) | Workgroup Edition (IA-32) | Express Edition (IA-32) |
|---|---|---|---|---|---|
| Windows 2000 Professional Edition SP4 | No | Yes | Yes | Yes | Yes |
| Windows 2000 Server SP4 | Yes | Yes | Yes | Yes | Yes |
| Windows 2000 Advanced Server SP4 | Yes | Yes | Yes | Yes | Yes |
| Windows 2000 Datacenter Edition SP4 | Yes | Yes | Yes | Yes | Yes |
| Windows XP Home Edition SP2 | No | Yes | No | No | Yes |
| Windows XP Professional Edition SP2 | No | Yes | Yes | Yes | Yes |
| Windows XP Media Edition SP2 | No | Yes | Yes | Yes | Yes |
| Windows XP Tablet Edition SP2 | No | Yes | Yes | Yes | Yes |
| Windows Server 2003 Server SP1 | Yes | Yes | Yes | Yes | Yes |
| Windows Server 2003 Enterprise Edition SP1 | Yes | Yes | Yes | Yes | Yes |
| Windows Server 2003 Datacenter Edition SP1 | Yes | Yes | Yes | Yes | Yes |
| Windows Server 2003 Web Edition SP1 | No | No | No | No | Yes |

**Table 2-1    Supported Operating Systems for SQL Server 2005 (IA-32) Editions (continued)**

| Operating System | Enterprise Edition (IA-32) | Developer Edition (IA-32) | Standard Edition (IA-32) | Workgroup Edition (IA-32) | Express Edition (IA-32) |
|---|---|---|---|---|---|
| Windows Small Business Server 2003 Standard Edition SP1 | Yes | Yes | Yes | Yes | Yes |
| Windows Small Business Server 2003 Premium Edition SP1 | Yes | Yes | Yes | Yes | Yes |
| Windows Server 2003 64-Bit x64 Standard Edition SP1 | WOW64 | WOW64 | WOW64 | WOW64 | WOW64 |
| Windows Server 2003 64-Bit x64 Datacenter Edition SP1 | WOW64 | WOW64 | WOW64 | WOW64 | WOW64 |
| Windows Server 2003 64-Bit x64 Enterprise Edition SP1 | WOW64 | WOW64 | WOW64 | WOW64 | WOW64 |

Table 2-2 lists the supported combinations of Windows versions and editions for the three SQL Server 2005 (IA-64) 64-bit editions used with the Intel Itanium-based servers. The 64-bit platform is explained in detail in Chapter 5, "32-Bit versus 64-Bit Platforms and Microsoft SQL Server 2005."

**Table 2-2    Supported Operating Systems for SQL Server 2005 (IA-64) Editions**

| | Enterprise Edition (IA64) | Developer Edition (IA64) | Standard Edition (IA64) |
|---|---|---|---|
| Windows Server 2003 64-Bit Itanium Datacenter Edition SP1 | Yes | Yes | Yes |
| Windows Server 2003 64-Bit Itanium Enterprise Edition SP1 | Yes | Yes | Yes |

Table 2-3 lists the supported Windows versions and editions for the four SQL Server 2005 editions for x64 (EM64T and Opteron) systems. The x64 platform is explained in detail in Chapter 5.

**Table 2-3  Supported Operating Systems for SQL Server 2005 Editions for x64 Systems**

|  | Enterprise Edition (x64) | Developer Edition (x64) | Standard Edition (x64) | Express Edition (IA-32) |
|---|---|---|---|---|
| Windows Server 2003 64-Bit x64 Standard Edition SP1 | Yes | Yes | Yes | WOW64 |
| Windows Server 2003 64-Bit x64 Datacenter Edition SP1 | Yes | Yes | Yes | WOW64 |
| Windows Server 2003 64-Bit x64 Enterprise Edition SP1 | Yes | Yes | Yes | WOW64 |

SQL Server 2005 Express Edition does not have an x64 version; however, you can use the IA-32 version running in WOW64 mode, implying that it will run on the Windows 32-bit sub-system of the 64-bit server.

# Understanding Processors and Memory Limits

Each SQL Server 2005 edition has different limits for the number of processors and amount of memory it supports. After you have completed sizing your environment as explained in Chapter 6, "Capacity Planning," and have a reasonably accurate estimate of the number of processors and the amount of memory you will need in the database server, you should determine which SQL Server 2005 edition best fits your needs using the following tables.

Table 2-4 lists the maximum amount of memory supported by each of the SQL Server 2005 editions for both the 32-bit (IA-32) and the 64-bit (IA-64 and x64) platforms.

**Table 2-4  Maximum Amount of Memory Supported**

| SQL Server 2005 Edition | Maximum Memory Supported (IA-32) | Maximum Memory Supported (IA-64 and x64) |
|---|---|---|
| Enterprise Edition | OS maximum | OS maximum |
| Developer Edition | OS maximum | 32 terabytes |

Table 2-4   Maximum Amount of Memory Supported (continued)

| SQL Server 2005 Edition | Maximum Memory Supported (IA-32) | Maximum Memory Supported (IA-64 and x64) |
|---|---|---|
| Standard Edition | OS maximum | 32 terabytes |
| Workgroup Edition | 3 GB | Not applicable |
| Express Edition | 1 GB | Not applicable |

The cells that state "OS maximum" indicate that the maximum amount of memory supported by the particular SQL Server 2005 edition is based on what the underlying operating system supports. For example, SQL Server 2005 Standard Edition (IA-32) running on Windows Server 2003 Enterprise Edition (IA-32) will support 32 GB of memory, while the same edition of SQL Server 2005 running on Windows Server 2003 Standard Edition (IA-32) supports only 4 GB of memory because Windows Server 2003 Standard Edition (IA-32) supports only 4 GB of memory. The Workgroup and Express Editions are not natively supported on the 64-bit platform, and therefore, the values are listed as "Not applicable."

Table 2-5 lists the maximum number of processors supported by each of the SQL Server 2005 editions for both the 32-bit (IA-32) and the 64-bit (IA-64 and x64) platforms.

Table 2-5   Maximum Number of Processors Supported

| SQL Server 2005 Edition | Number of Processors Supported (IA-32) | Number of Processors Supported (IA-64 and x64) |
|---|---|---|
| Enterprise Edition | OS maximum | OS maximum |
| Developer Edition | OS maximum | OS maximum |
| Standard Edition | 4 | 4 |
| Workgroup Edition | 2 | Not applicable |
| Express Edition | 1 | Not applicable |

For SQL Server 2005 Enterprise Edition, the "OS maximum" implies that the number of processors supported by SQL Server 2005 is based on what the underlying operating system supports. For example, SQL Server 2005 Enterprise Edition (32-bit) running on Windows Server 2003 Standard Edition (IA-32) supports a maximum of four processors, while the same SQL Server edition running on Windows Server 2003 Enterprise Edition (IA-32) supports a maximum of eight processors.

# Factoring in Head-Room

I strongly recommend that you factor in some room for growth for both the number of processors and the amount of memory when selecting your SQL Server 2005 edition. For example, if your sizing reveals that SQL Server 2005 requires 3 GB of memory and two processors to run your application, you should select the SQL Server 2005 Standard Edition, budget permitting, instead of the Workgroup Edition. This choice will ensure that the deployment will not be at its limits from the start and will provide you some flexibility to add more memory or additional processors if your sizing estimates were not perfectly accurate or your application workload grows, both of which are very probable.

# Comparing SQL Server 2005 Editions

In addition to considering the amount of memory supported, the number of processors supported, and so on, also consider the features that are supported by the SQL Server 2005 edition to make sure they meet your needs. The features supported vary based on the SQL Server 2005 edition and, in some cases, the platform (IA-32, IA-64, or x64), but they are independent of the underlying operating system on which SQL Server 2005 runs.

The following sections present the key differences for the Database Engine, Analysis Services, Reporting Services, Notification Services, Integration Services, and Replication features supported by the various editions of SQL Server 2005.

> **Note**    Components that are common across the editions are not listed. For a complete list of differences, refer to: *http://msdn2.microsoft.com/en-us/library/ms143761.aspx.*

## Database Engine Features

Table 2-6 lists the differences in the database engine features supported by SQL Server 2005 Enterprise Edition (IA-32, IA-64, and x64), Developer Edition (IA-32, IA-64, and x64), Standard Edition (IA-32, IA-64, and x64), and Workgroup Edition (IA-32).

## Analysis Services

Table 2-7 lists the differences in the SQL Server Analysis Services (SSAS) features supported by SQL Server 2005 Enterprise Edition (IA-32, IA-64, and x64), Developer Edition (IA-32, IA-64, and x64), Standard Edition (IA-32), and Standard Edition (IA-64, and x64).

**Table 2-6   Database Engine Feature Comparison by Edition**

| Feature | Enterprise Edition (IA-32, IA-64, and x64) and Developer Edition (IA-32, IA-64, and x64) | Standard Edition (IA-32, IA-64, and x64) | Workgroup Edition (IA-32) |
| --- | --- | --- | --- |
| Microsoft .NET Framework | Yes | Yes | No |
| Failover clustering | Yes | 2-node only | No |
| Multi-instance support | 50 | 16 | 16 |
| Database snapshot | Yes | No | No |
| Database mirroring | Yes | Safety FULL only | No |
| Dynamic AWE | Yes | No | No |
| Database available during recovery undo | Yes | No | No |
| Highly-available upgrade | Yes | No | No |
| Hot-add memory | Yes | No | No |
| Mirrored backup media | Yes | No | No |
| Online index operations | Yes | No | No |
| Online page and file restore | Yes | No | No |
| Parallel index operations | Yes | No | No |
| Updateable distributed partitioned views | Yes | No | No |
| Enhanced read-ahead and scan | Yes | No | No |
| Table and index partitioning | Yes | No | No |
| VIA support | Yes | No | No |
| Parallel DBCC | Yes | No | No |

**Table 2-7   Analysis Services Feature Comparison by Edition**

| Feature | Enterprise Edition (IA-32, IA-64, and x64) and Developer Edition (IA-32, IA-64, and x64) | Standard Edition (IA-32) | Standard Edition (IA-64 and x64) |
|---|---|---|---|
| Failover clustering | Yes | Yes | No |
| Multi-instances | 50 | 16 | 16 |
| Parallelism for model processing | Yes | No | No |
| Parallelism for model prediction | Yes | No | No |
| Text-mining Term Extraction Transformation (SSIS) | Yes | No | No |
| Text-mining Term Lookup Transform (SSIS) | Yes | No | No |
| Data Mining Query Transformation (SSIS) | Yes | No | No |
| Data Mining Processing Destination (SSIS) | Yes | No | No |
| Algorithm Plug-in API | Yes | No | No |
| Advanced configuration and tuning options for Data Mining algorithms | Yes | No | No |
| Account intelligence | Yes | No | No |
| Cross-database/cross-server linked measures and dimensions | Yes | No | No |
| Metadata translations | Yes | No | No |
| Perspectives | Yes | No | No |
| Semi-additive measures | Yes | No | No |
| Writeback dimensions | Yes | No | No |
| Create cubes without database | Yes | Yes | No |
| Auto-generate staging and data warehouse schema | Yes | Yes | No |
| Auto-generate DTS packages for updating data warehouse data | Yes | Yes | No |

**Table 2-7    Analysis Services Feature Comparison by Edition (continued)**

| Feature | Enterprise Edition (IA-32, IA-64, and x64) and Developer Edition (IA-32, IA-64, and x64) | Standard Edition (IA-32) | Standard Edition (IA-64 and x64) |
|---|---|---|---|
| Proactive caching | Yes | No | No |
| Auto parallel partition processing | Yes | No | No |
| Partitioned cubes | Yes | No | No |
| Distributed partitioned cubes | Yes | No | No |

## Reporting Services

Table 2-8 lists the differences in the SQL Server Reporting Services (SSRS) features supported by SQL Server 2005 Enterprise Edition (IA-32, IA-64, and x64), Developer Edition (IA-32, IA-64, and x64), Standard Edition (IA-32, IA-64, and x64), and Workgroup Edition (IA-32).

**Table 2-8    Reporting Services Feature Comparison by Edition**

| Feature | Enterprise Edition (IA-32, IA-64, and x64) and Developer Edition (IA-32, IA-64, and x64) | Standard Edition (IA-32, IA-64, and x64) | Workgroup Edition (IA-32) |
|---|---|---|---|
| Support for remote and nonrelational data sources | Yes | Yes | No |
| MHTML, CSV, XML, and Null rendering extensions | Yes | Yes | No |
| E-mail and file share delivery extensions | Yes | Yes | No |
| Custom data processing, delivery, and rendering extensions | Yes | Yes | No |
| Report caching | Yes | Yes | No |
| Report history | Yes | Yes | No |
| Scheduling | Yes | Yes | No |
| Subscriptions | Yes | Yes | No |

**Table 2-8  Reporting Services Feature Comparison by Edition (continued)**

| Feature | Enterprise Edition (IA-32, IA-64, and x64) and Developer Edition (IA-32, IA-64, and x64) | Standard Edition (IA-32, IA-64, and x64) | Workgroup Edition (IA-32) |
|---|---|---|---|
| Data-driven subscriptions | Yes | No | No |
| User-defined role definitions | Yes | Yes | No |
| Report model item security | Yes | Yes | No |
| Support for infinite clickthrough in ad hoc reports | Yes | No | No |
| Report server scale-out deployment | Yes | No | No |

## Notification Services

SQL Server Notification Service is supported only in SQL Server 2005 Enterprise and Standard editions. The key difference between these two editions is that the Notification Services in Enterprise Edition is more scalable because it supports parallelism, multicast, and distributed deployments.

## Integration Services

Table 2-9 lists the differences in the SQL Server Integration Services (SSIS) features supported by SQL Server 2005 Enterprise Edition (IA-32, IA-64, and x64), Developer Edition (IA-32, IA-64, and x64), Standard Edition (IA-32, IA-64, and x64), and Workgroup Edition (IA-32).

**Table 2-9  Integration Services Feature Comparison by Edition**

| Feature | Enterprise Edition (IA-32, IA-64, and x64) and Developer Edition (IA-32, IA-64, and x64) | Standard Edition (IA-32, IA-64, and x64) | Workgroup Edition (IA-32) |
|---|---|---|---|
| SSIS Service | Yes | Yes | No |
| All other source and destination adapters, tasks, and transformations, except for those listed below | Yes | Yes | No |
| Data Mining Query Transformation | Yes | No | No |

**Table 2-9    Integration Services Feature Comparison by Edition (continued)**

| Feature | Enterprise Edition (IA-32, IA-64, and x64) and Developer Edition (IA-32, IA-64, and x64) | Standard Edition (IA-32, IA-64, and x64) | Workgroup Edition (IA-32) |
|---|---|---|---|
| Data Mining Model Training Destination Adapter | Yes | No | No |
| Fuzzy Grouping transformation | Yes | No | No |
| Fuzzy Lookup transformation | Yes | No | No |
| Term Extraction transformation | Yes | No | No |
| Term Lookup transformation | Yes | No | No |
| Slowly Changing Dimension transformation and wizard | Yes | IA-32: yes IA-32: no | No |
| Dimension Processing destination adapter | Yes | No | No |
| Partition Processing destination adapter | Yes | No | No |

# Replication

Table 2-10 lists the differences in Replication features supported by SQL Server 2005 Enterprise Edition (IA-32, IA-64, and x64), Developer Edition (IA-32, IA-64, and x64), Standard Edition (IA-32, IA-64, and x64), and Workgroup Edition (IA-32).

**Table 2-10    Replication Feature Comparison by Edition**

| Feature | Enterprise Edition (IA-32, IA-64, and x64) and Developer Edition (IA-32, IA-64, and x64) | Standard Edition (IA-32, IA-64, and x64) | Workgroup Edition (IA-32) |
|---|---|---|---|
| Merge replication | Yes | Yes | Limited* |
| Transactional replication | Yes | Yes | Limited* |
| Non-SQL Server Subscribers | Yes | Yes | No |
| Oracle publishing | Yes | No | No |
| Peer-to-peer transactional replication | Yes | No | No |

* An unlimited number of subscriptions to snapshot publications, 25 subscriptions to all merge publications, and 5 subscriptions to all transactional publications are supported when Workgroup Edition is used as a publisher.

# SQL Server 2005 Capacity Limits

Although rare, every once in a while you may encounter a SQL Server 2005 component preset capacity limit. The most common capacity limits are "maximum number of columns per index" and "maximum number of indexes/statistics per table." There will also be times when you have questions about the maximum number of rows you can have in a table or the number of database instances you can host on a single system. Table 2-11 helps answer these questions by listing the maximum values for various SQL Server database engine objects.

Table 2-11   Maximum Capacity Limits for SQL Server 2005

| SQL Server 2005 Database Engine Object | Maximum Values |
| --- | --- |
| Batch size | 65,536 × Network Packet Size |
| Bytes per short string column | 8,000 |
| Bytes per GROUP BY, ORDER BY | 8,060 |
| Bytes per index key | 900 |
| Bytes per foreign key | 900 |
| Bytes per primary key | 900 |
| Bytes per row | 8,060 |
| Bytes in source text of a stored procedure | The lesser of batch size or 250 MB |
| Bytes per varchar(max), varbinary(max), xml, text, or image column | $2^{31} - 1$ |
| Characters per ntext or nvarchar(max) column | $2^{30} - 1$ |
| Clustered indexes per table | 1 |
| Columns in GROUP BY, ORDER BY | Limited only by number of bytes (see Bytes per GROUP BY, ORDER BY) |
| Columns or expressions in a GROUP BY WITH CUBE or WITH ROLLUP statement | 10 |
| Columns per index key | 16 |
| Columns per foreign key | 16 |
| Columns per primary key | 16 |
| Columns per base table | 1,024 |
| Columns per SELECT statement | 4,096 |
| Columns per INSERT statement | 1,024 |

**Table 2-11** Maximum Capacity Limits for SQL Server 2005 (continued)

| SQL Server 2005 Database Engine Object | Maximum Values |
| --- | --- |
| Connections per client | Maximum value of configured connections[*] |
| Database size | 1,048,516 terabytes |
| Databases per instance of SQL Server | 32,767 |
| Filegroups per database | 32,767 |
| Files per database | 32,767 |
| File size (data file) | 16 terabytes |
| File size (log file) | 2 terabytes |
| Foreign key table references per table | 253 |
| Identifier length (in characters) | 128 |
| Instances per computer | 16 (50 for Enterprise Edition) |
| Length of a string containing SQL statements (Batch size) | 65,536 × network packet size |
| Locks per connection | Maximum locks per instance of SQL Server |
| Locks per instance of SQL Server | IA-32: up to 2,147,483,647 |
|  | IA-64, ×64: limited only by memory |
| Nested stored procedure levels | 32 |
| Nested subqueries | 32 |
| Nested trigger levels | 32 |
| Non clustered indexes per table | 249 |
| Parameters per stored procedure | 2,100 |
| Parameters per user-defined function | 2,100 |
| REFERENCES per table | 253 |
| Rows per table | Limited only by available storage |
| Tables per database | Limited by number of objects in a database |
| Partitions per partitioned table or index | 1,000 |
| Statistics on nonindexed columns | 2,000 |
| Tables per SELECT statement | 256 |
| Triggers per table | Limited by number of objects in a database |
| UNIQUE indexes or constraints per table | 1 clustered and 249 nonclustered indexes |
| XML indexes | 249 |

[*] The maximum value of configured connections can be set using the *sp_configure* stored procedure or using SQL Server Management Studio.

The capacity limits are the same for all editions of SQL Server 2005 and for all the platforms (IA-32, IA-64, and x64). The only exceptions are "instances per computer," which is different for Enterprise Edition, and "Locks per instance of SQL Server," which is different for 32-bit (IA-32) and 64-bit (IA-64 and x64) systems, as noted in Table 2-11.

# Understanding SQL Server 2005 Licensing

I have often found the SQL Server licensing models to be plagued by confusion and very poorly understood. Recent changes in processor technology, including the introduction of hyperthreading and multicore technologies, have further complicated matters. This section attempts to explain the licensing considerations for SQL Server 2005 deployments in simple terms.

SQL Server 2005 can be deployed using one of three distinct licensing models:

1. **Server plus user client access licensing**   Requires a license for the system running SQL Server 2005 and a client access license (CAL) for each user that connects to the SQL Server instance.

2. **Server plus device client access licensing**   Requires a license for the system running SQL Server 2005 and a CAL for each device that connects to the SQL Server instance.

> **Note**   A client access license (CAL) is a legal document granting a device or user access to the SQL Server software. A single user CAL can grant access to multiple servers for one user. Similarly, a single device CAL can grant access to multiple servers for one device. Unlike earlier versions, SQL Server 2005 does not require you to specify the licensing model and CAL details during the SQL Server installation process.

3. **Processor licensing**   Requires a license for each physical processor in the operating system environment running SQL Server 2005.

These licensing considerations apply only to SQL Server 2005 Enterprise, Standard, and Workgroup Editions. SQL Server 2005 Express Edition is available as a free download and, therefore, exempt from the licensing considerations. Also, SQL Server 2005 Developer Edition is intended solely for development and test purposes and licensed per individual developer or tester and, therefore, the three licensing models mentioned previously do not apply to it.

The following subsections explain the licensing models for the Enterprise, Standard, and Workgroup Editions and provide example scenarios for which each is best suited.

## User Client Access Licensing

The user client access licensing model requires users to have a server license for every operating system environment on which SQL Server 2005 or any of its components are running, plus a license for each user who connects to SQL Server 2005. Figure 2-1 depicts an environment that uses this licensing model. In this example a server is installed with the SQL Server 2005 Standard Edition database as well as Analysis Services and is accessed by seven users. Four of these users access only the database engine while the other three access, the database as well as Analysis Services.

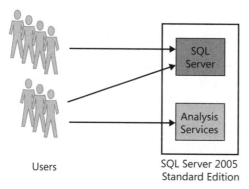

Users            SQL Server 2005
                 Standard Edition

**Figure 2-1**    User client access licensing model.

For this configuration a SQL Server 2005 Standard Edition server license is required for the operating system environment on which SQL Server 2005 is installed. In addition, seven user CALs are required for the users who access SQL Server and Analysis Services. Note that there is no differentiation in the CALs for the users who connect to SQL Server and those who connect to SQL Server and Analysis Services; a single user CAL grants the user access to any of the installed SQL Server 2005 components. If the client access license package comes with a server license and five user CALs, you will have to purchase two additional CALs separately to meet the total requirement of seven CALs.

Server licenses are specific to particular SQL Server 2005 editions; this means that you will need different server licenses for the Enterprise, Standard, and Workgroup Editions. However, user CALs are common and can be used to connect to any of the three editions. The only exception is the special Workgroup user CAL, which, unlike the regular CAL, can be used only for users to connect to a SQL Server system running Workgroup Edition.

The user client access licensing model is best suited for deployments where there are a few users who connect to the SQL Server 2005 server from multiple devices. For example, a user may connect to the server from her office desktop during office hours, from her laptop after–hours, and from her mobile device while she is traveling. Because the user CAL is associated with a user, only one CAL is required in this case even though the user accesses the server from three different devices.

## Device Client Access Licensing

Similar to the user client access licensing model, the device client access licensing model requires you to have a server license for every operating system environment on which SQL Server 2005 or any of its components are running and a license for each device that connects to SQL Server 2005. Figure 2-2 depicts an environment that uses this licensing model. In this example, a server is installed with the SQL Server 2005 Workgroup Edition database in a department store and is accessed by five point-of-sales devices.

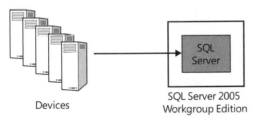

**Figure 2-2**   Device client access licensing model.

For this configuration, a SQL Server 2005 Workgroup Edition server license is required for the operating system environment on which SQL Server 2005 is installed. In addition, five device CALs are required for the five point-of-sales devices that will connect to SQL Server.

Device CALs are common to the Enterprise, Standard, and Workgroup Editions and can be used to connect any device to any of these three editions. The only exception to this is the special Workgroup device CAL, which, unlike the regular CAL, can be used only to connect to a SQL Server system running Workgroup Edition.

The device client access licensing model is best suited for scenarios where there are multiple users that connect to the server via a few devices. A classic example of this is a department store that is open around the clock and has a handful of sales registers (devices) connected to an application that uses a SQL Server database at the back end.

In this department store, different cashiers use these sales registers during the shift, and there are three such shifts every day. With the device user CAL licensing model, the department store is required to have a server license only for the operating system environment running SQL Server 2005 and device CALs for each of the devices. This licensing model could potentially be much cheaper than the user client access licensing model because it is not dependent on the individual users accessing the database, only the devices that access it. If the department store has five point-of-sales registers and twenty-five employees operating those registers throughout the day, this model requires the department store to purchase only five device client access lncenses. In this case, the device client access licening model is also simpler to adopt because it does not require detailed tracking of the different department store personnel who use the sales registers.

---

**Important**    When using the user or device client access licensing model, the number of individual licenses required is determined by the number of distinct users or devices that connect directly or indirectly to the SQL Server software. This implies that any hardware or software multiplexing through which multiple distinct users or devices are aggregated such that they appear as fewer users or devices to SQL Server software does not exempt them from requiring individual CALs. For example, consider a three-tier (Web tier, application tier, and database tier) customer relationship management (CRM) application that uses SQL Server as the back-end data store and uses a single user login for the application tier to connect to the database tier. If this application supports a thousand unique, named users and uses the SQL Server user client licensing model, it will require a thousand user CALs even though only one user login effectively connects to SQL Server software.

## Processor Licensing

The per processor-based licensing model is the simplest to understand and adopt, but it can often be expensive for smaller deployments. In this model, a processor license is required for each processor installed on each operating system environment running a SQL Server 2005 database or any of its components such as Reporting Services, Analysis Services, and so on. With this licensing model, an unlimited number of users or devices can connect to the system and use any of the database services. Processor licenses are based on only the number of physical processors in the system and are independent of the other system resources such as memory or number of disks. Unlike the user and the device client access licensing models explained previously, no additional CALs are required for the individual users that connect to the server. Different processor licenses are available for the SQL Server 2005 Enterprise, Standard, and Workgroup Editions.

The processor licensing model is best suited for scenarios in which a large number of users using different devices need to occasionally access the database components for short durations of time. For example, an e-commerce site that uses a back-end SQL Server database may have hundreds or even thousands of unique users connecting via their individual computers to the e-commerce site. In a scenario such as this, the user or device client access licensing models would require CALs for each of the occasionally connected users or devices and would most likely become more expensive very quickly. It would also be very difficult to track individual users or device CAL requirements. The processor licensing model is a perfect fit for such applications, especially if the number of users and devices is large.

Most processors of the current generation are hyperthreaded or have multiple cores. *Hyperthreading* technology provides thread-level parallelism on each processor, resulting in more efficient use of processor resources, higher processing throughput, and improved performance. *Multicore* processors, on the other hand, combine multiple independent processors and their respective caches and cache controllers onto a single silicon chip. SQL Server 2005 does not differentiate these processors and considers both–processors built with hyperthreading technology and processors with multiple cores–as a single processor. For example, all three processors–single-core, dual-core, and quad-core–shown in Figure 2-3 are considered as a single processor by SQL Server 2005 and require only one processor license.

Processor licensing is not dependent on any processor attributes such as the architecture (IA-32, IA-64, x64), processor speed, or processor cache size.

The way SQL Server 2005 defines a processor and enforces licensing is actually an advantage for the user, who can get more throughput from a more powerful multicore processor-based system without incurring additional costs for SQL Server licensing.

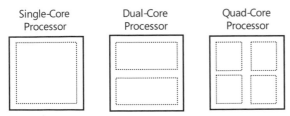

**Figure 2-3**   Multicore processors: single-core, dual-core, and quad-core.

**Important**   If you are executing any of the other SQL Server 2005 components, such as Analysis Services, Reporting Services, and so on, on systems other than the system where the SQL Server database server is running, you will require additional server or processor licenses. Additional server licenses are necessary for each server where a component of SQL Server is running if you are using the user or device client access licensing model. Additional processor licenses are necessary for each processor of the systems where the SQL Server components are running if you are using the processor licensing model.

# Licensing Considerations for High-Availability Environments

High availability with SQL Server 2005 involves configuring two or more servers so that if one of them fails, one of the others can pick up the workload and continue processing. SQL Server 2005 offers three types of solutions for achieving high-availability: failoverclustering, database mirroring, and backup log shipping, all of which are explained in detail in Chapter 27, "Failover Clustering Installation and Configuration," and Chapter 28. Each of these solutions uses one or more standby or "passive" servers, which hold a replica of the main "active" database. During normal processing, the workload is directed to the "active" server, as shown in Figure 2-4a. In the event of a failure of the "active" server, the processing is transferred to the passive server and it becomes the active server, as shown in Figure 2-4b.

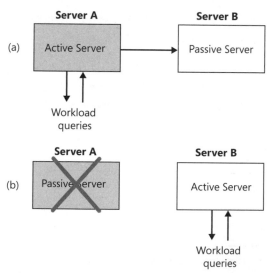

**Figure 2-4**   Workload processing in an active-passive server setup.

In such an active-passive high-availability setup, SQL Server 2005 licensing does not require you to license the passive node as long as all the following are true:

- The number of processors in the passive node is equal to or less than the number of processors in the active node.

- No workload is processed on the passive node during normal operation.

- When the active node failsover to the passive node, it does not continue processing any workload.

- The passive node assumes the duties of the active node for a period of only 30 days or fewer.

If any of these points is not true, then the passive node needs to be licensed in addition to the active node.

In SQL Server 2005, you can create a database snapshot on a passive node of a mirrored database, which is explained in Chapter 28, and run reports of it, as shown in Figure 2-5.

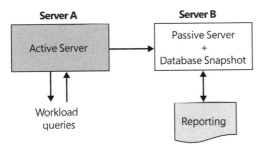

**Figure 2-5**   Active-passive server setup with reporting on the passive node.

If you plan to use this configuration, you will also need SQL Server licenses for the passive node since you are effectively executing a workload on the passive node as well.

# SQL Server 2005 Pricing

The price for the SQL Server software is highly dependent on the configuration of the system, the licensing model, and the SQL Server 2005 edition you select. In addition, the price may also vary based on reseller discounts or any volume licensing discounts you secure. Table 2-12 lists the retail prices in the spring of 2006 for the processor licensing and the user or device client access licensing model in United States Dollars (USD) for the Enterprise, Standard, and Workgroup Editions. (See *http://www.microsoft.com/sql/ howtobuy*.) This Web site also contains information about volume discounting and how to obtain copies of the SQL Server 2005 software.

**Table 2-12    SQL Server 2005 Retail Pricing in USD**

| SQL Server 2005 Edition | Retail Pricing (USD) | |
| --- | --- | --- |
| | **Processor License** | **Server Plus User/Device CALs** |
| Workgroup Edition | $3,899 | $739 with 5 Workgroup CALs |
| | | $146 per additional Workgroup CAL* |
| Standard Edition | $5,999 | $1,849 with 5 CALs |
| | | $162 per additional CAL* |
| Enterprise Edition | $24,999 | $13,969 with 25 CALs |
| | | $162 per additional CAL* |

*Example pricing per Microsoft Corporation.

The retail price for Microsoft SQL Server 2005 Developer Edition, which may be installed and used by only one user, is USD$49.95.

The licensing models are independent of the platform (IA-32, IA-64, or x64) the SQL Server software runs on. This implies that a processor license for an Itanium processor-based system costs the same as a processor license for a Pentium IV processor-based system.

# Summary

The first step toward a successful deployment is selecting the SQL Server 2005 edition that best meets your needs. The rich set of features, enhanced capacity limits, multiple platform support, and flexible licensing can make the selection task in SQL Server 2005 a lot more difficult than in earlier versions, but overall, it is almost always a good challenge to face.

In this chapter we learned about the six different SQL Server 2005 editions and compared them based on the features available. We also learned about the various capacity limits and the supported Windows operating systems and platforms. Lastly, we took a detailed look at the different SQL Server 2005 licensing models and the implications of multicore and hyperthreaded processors and licensing requirements for servers used in redundant high-availability configurations.

# Chapter 3

# Roles and Responsibilities of the Microsoft SQL Server DBA

## Different Kinds of DBA

A database administrator (or DBA) has many possible roles, depending on his or her environment. A DBA might be part of a large team or might be a single person responsible for more than just the database components of the system, including other applications. In larger environments, the DBA might be assigned a single function, such as developing stored procedures and SQL statements, or might be in charge of maintaining the production environment. This chapter introduces you to the different roles of DBAs and duties that these DBAs might perform. Remember that no two companies are the same and no two environments are the same.

### The Prime Directive of the DBA

Regardless of the responsibilities you have as DBA, your ultimate goal should be to maximize the stability and protection of the database. Today's corporate data is the lifeblood of our companies. Protecting this data from intrusion and being prepared for disasters, both natural and man-made, is our top priority. The DBA is the person ultimately charged with this responsibility, and it should not be taken lightly.

## Production DBA

The *production DBA* is responsible for the day-to-day operation and maintenance of a production database. Production DBAs take care of all changes in the production environment, perform the backups and restores, and concern themselves with the database and server performance.

Being a production DBA is probably one of the most challenging jobs. Under normal operating conditions, the job is demanding, and during emergency situations, such as a system crash, the job can be very stressful. The production DBA must be constantly concerned with backups, security, and system performance. In addition, the production DBA must be very careful since even a minor mistake could cause system downtime.

### A DBA Wears Both a Belt and Suspenders

I was in a class many years ago when the instructor was speaking to us about how careful a production DBA must be at all times. Referring to checks and double checks, he said, "A DBA is someone who wears both a belt and suspenders. He may look funny, but his pants never fall down."

## Development DBA

The *development DBA* is usually tied to a team of developers and is responsible for the team's development systems. The development DBA handles all matters concerning non-production systems, including providing development guidance to the team. The development DBA provides an early opportunity to tune performance in all aspects of new database applications being created. The knowledge that the development DBA brings will help him or her recognize early on potential issues with stored procedure function and indexes that might need to be placed to be sure of performance in production. Conversely, the development DBA should be in a position to recognize when new indexes should not be created due to performance problems created with bulk loads of new data.

In addition to assisting with development efforts and providing guidance to the development team, the development DBA is often responsible for the creation of all installation scripts for changes between environments. If a new database, stored procedure, table definition change, or new element is ready to move into test or production, it is a best practice for the development DBA to create the scripts for the changes. Doing this allows the DBA to recognize early possible problems with an install script or accurately define the order in which change scripts are applied and pass that information along to the DBA who will actually make the changes. The ability to work hand-in-hand with the production DBA to provide the best service at all levels is critical.

## Architect DBA

The *architect DBA* plays a critical role in the development of applications. The architect DBA provides the knowledge and expertise to build database solutions. Logical and physical database design, normalization and de-normalization methods, and stored procedure development are all critical aspects the architect DBA brings to the table. Frequently, an architect DBA works closely with the development team. The architect DBA invariably works with data analysts and project managers in creating database models so that the logical models fit the business need. For this reason, the architect DBA needs to have skills in database creation, logical layout, and design, as well as the ability to transform business requirements into a finished product.

Often the architect DBA helps to create stored procedures and complex queries and provides design solutions for potential problem areas such as reporting structures or archival procedures. The architect DBA works closely with the development DBA to create databases, tables, procedures, and queries that perform well and meet coding standards that are agreed upon by all parties in an organization.

Ultimately, the business application, once implemented, will succeed or fail based upon the model created by the architect DBA, so long-term experience with modeling is frequently an essential prerequisite for moving into this role. This position has the ability to directly influence how customers perceive any application based on SQL Server. Without a good database model in place, a production DBA can certainly work on performance improvements, but bear in mind, a poorly designed database can be tuned only so much.

## ETL DBA

The *ETL DBA* provides the knowledge and expertise in ETL (Extract, Transform, Load) methods. This includes retrieving data from various data sources—whether it is from another DBMS plain text files, or other sources—and then transforming this data and loading into SQL Server (or extracting data from SQL Server into a separate destination). Expertise in *SSIS* (SQL Server Integration Services, the replacement for DTS) is critical in this role to ensure that data is loaded optimally.

You could have a situation in which there is a large data warehouse running SQL Server 2005 Analysis Services. The data stored here is comprised of a subset of your OLTP data that you keep in SQL Server 2005. To be able to use the data in the data warehouse, you must first get it there. This is where SSIS comes into play. You can take data from SQL Server 2005 and port it into Analysis Services. You are not limited to doing a straight data migration, but you can perform advanced logic upon the data that you are transferring and perform transformations. This could be something as simple as changing the data so that it is all upper case or as complex as calculating averages within a dataset.

You are not limited to moving data within SQL Server 2005 components, however. You are able to access and work with a wide variety of data sources, and even multiple sources within a single package, using OLE DB providers and ODBC drivers for database connectivity. In addition, you can also extract data from text files, Excel spreadsheets, and even XML documents.

The same storage components that can be the source of data for loading into SQL Server 2005 can also act as a destination, allowing you to provide small data subsets for reporting, uploading to ftp sites, or sending in an e-mail message to users. The ability to schedule an SSIS package means that you can set data loads to run during off-hour periods, and with Notification Services integration you will receive notifications on the status of the package, including details of possible failures.

SSIS is not limited to the loading and unloading of data. It is also a critical tool from a management perspective for the DBA. The DBA can create and schedule with SSIS to perform administration functions. If you have the need to rebuild indexes or statistics on a frequent basis, you can create a package which runs the scripts to accomplish those tasks. A package that loops through all of your servers, executes a full backup of all of your databases, and lets you know which ones, if any, experienced a problem could prove invaluable.

In SQL Server 2000, DTS packages were a massively powerful tool that allowed the DBA to bring data into and out of SQL Server and performed administrative functions. SSIS in SQL Server 2005 has improved this function by providing containers for workflow repetition—packages that can repeat or direct workflow based on information passed in at run time. SSIS is one of the most powerful tools that you will see. More and more there will be a critical need to have a DBA dedicated to SSIS and to manage the flow of data.

## OLAP DBA

Microsoft SQL Server 2005 Analysis Services (SSAS) provides *OLAP*, or Online Analytical Processing, and data mining functionality. Aggregated data is contained within multidimensional structures and constructed from a variety of data sources using data mining algorithms. Designing, creating, and managing these structures falls within the realm of the OLAP DBA. The OLAP DBA works with large data sets helping to drive direction within the company by maintaining cubes for critical business decision support.

Rather than work in SQL, the queries on an SSAS OLAP system are run in MDX (SQL; Multidimensional Expressions), XMLA (XML for Analysis), or Data Mining Extensions (DMX). To manage the objects within SSAS, Analysis Services Scripting Language (ASSL) can be used.

Invariably, the OLAP DBA will work with extremely large datasets and bring data from a variety of sources. From these sources a single data model is created and provided to end users. The data model can be queried directly, provided in reports, or used as the data source for custom Business Intelligence applications. The amalgamation of data allows business users to mine through the data to look for trends or specific patterns. Rarely used in smaller companies, the OLAP DBA works closely with the ETL DBA (or in some cases is the same person) to load the data from the large number of possible sources available.

# Basic Duties of a DBA

A SQL Server DBA must wear many hats to provide a full level of service. The requirements for the DBA will vary from company to company depending upon the typical business needs or budget. The DBA might be required to perform all tasks from installation and configuration to performance tuning and guiding purchases. Conversely, the DBA might have responsibility for a single particular task such as managing backups and restores, performance optimization, or ETL tasks.

Whatever your DBA responsibilities, there are some core, basic duties that should become second nature to all DBAs.

## Installation and Configuration

The SQL Server DBA is the primary source for completing installations of SQL Server in the environment. Depending on the company structure, the DBA might be providing guidelines for configurations, or the DBA might be doing a full system implementation including the operating system. It is the responsibility of the DBA to ensure that the system is configured so that it performs optimally with SQL Server.

### Software Installation

The DBA must be involved in all aspects of the SQL Server installation. This means also being involved in the installation and configuration of Windows Server 2003 and other software components such as third-party backup utilities, reporting services, and notification services. There are many components added to Windows Server 2003 default installations that might not be appropriate for a server that is purely used as a SQL Server database server, for example, IIS, and printing services. Each of these items will add to the server overhead and ultimately affect performance.

Creating a document that identifies the components that will be installed on the system helps prevent unwanted items, which in turn improves performance and ensures consistency among all of your installations. This will also assist with troubleshooting any potential problems by providing a baseline against which you can confirm Windows services and system components.

In addition to documenting and assisting with the Windows installation, the DBA is responsible for the proper installation of SQL Server 2005. It is important that the correct choices are made at the time of installation to prevent later problems and avoid a reinstall of the software to fix unwanted problems. A document that provides information about the components to be installed and the location of the binaries and the default location of the data files should be written so that, as with the operating system, consistency is achieved across installations.

As with all software, you should first complete an install on a test system. This ensures that your methods for setting up the OS and SQL Server 2005 can be followed as directed and that there are no problems that will affect your production systems.

## Hardware and Software Configuration

Generally, the DBA does not configure server hardware, although this may be required in some circumstances. Even if you are not in a position to configure the hardware, it is your responsibility to provide guidance and specifications so that the configuration provides the best level of performance, scalability, and growth to the system within the budgetary constraints. Because the DBA is ultimately responsible for the performance of the system and will be the first line of contact in the event of a slow system or when the system is running out of capacity, you must understand the hardware you are working with. This topic is covered in both Chapter 4, "I/O Subsytem Planning and RAID Configuration" and Chapter 6, "Capacity Planning."

As with the installations, documenting the configuration is critical. It is worthwhile to document all aspects of the system setup. This can mean everything from the type of RAID used to the number of drives involved in that RAID configuration, as well as the BIOS version of the RAID controller. It is also important to document the types of HBAs used for connectivity to a Storage Area Network (SAN) alongside the driver revisions. You will also want to know how much memory is in the system, how that memory is configured, how much extra capacity can be added, and whether you need to remove all the memory and replace it with a higher density memory to increase capacity. You also need to know the CPUs in the server. Microsoft licensing for SQL Server 2005 can be based on a per-processor model. Given recent advancements in technology, you can have a dual core system. Windows Server 2003 reports the number of cores in the system; however, this can be on fewer processors, which can save you a significant amount of money when it comes to purchasing the license because Microsoft charges per processor rather than per core. For example, a single processor dual core system will show two CPUs, but you need to purchase a license for only a single processor.

A large amount of data is accessible only by restarting the server and accessing the BIOS. Therefore, documenting all system settings prevents potential downtime to a production system that is required to verify the RAID configuration. It is important that you also include in your documentation the reasons for making the configuration choices that you did. For example, you configured the drives as a RAID-5 array because high write performance was not critical on the machine and maximizing the disk capacity was. Providing these reasons for the configuration choices helps other DBAs understand and validate your decisions.

## Service Packs and Security Updates

Microsoft will introduce service packs and security updates for SQL Server 2005 (and for Windows) as the tool evolves. Bugs will be identified, performance improvements will be introduced, and even new features will find their way into the product. Proper security update management becomes a vital task for ensuring that systems remain stable, supportable, and secure.

The DBA must be aware of any new release that could make an improvement to or resolve a recognized problem of SQL Server. New functionality and performance improvements tend to come in the form of service packs, whereas security updates tend to be fixes for bugs and security problems. These fixes are then rolled up into service packs so that all items are updated at the same time.

Understanding the service packs and security updates and implementing them through a phased approach—by testing through development and QA, or quality assurance, before migrating into production—is critical, as is keeping an accurate document identifying the exact revision of SQL Server on a given system. Imagine a situation in which you applied a new security update into production to address a problem before you applied it in a QA/UAT (User Acceptance Testing) environment. Suddenly, the functionality you have come to expect is gone, or performance has dropped to a level unacceptable to the user community. You now have to double your downtime to roll back the security update. It can be far worse than that. You may even have to go back and restore the system databases to get SQL Server in the state prior to the application of the security update, which means extended downtime for your systems and major impact to your users.

In addition to identifying and managing SQL Server 2005 service packs and security updates, the DBA should also be an integral part of managing the service packs and security updates for the Windows Server 2003 operating system. Any change to the operating system can seriously impact SQL Server in many ways, from major performance problems to connectivity issues and even failures in the SQL services themselves. Microsoft frequently introduces security enhancements for the operating system. The DBA should work with the system engineer to identify those that are critical and that should be applied. These changes should then go through the self same QA/UAT procedures as the SQL Server 2005 security updates to provide assurances of system stability and performance.

# Security

The DBA is ultimately responsible for the data stored within the databases. All of the work that a DBA does in configuring systems for performance, scalability, and reliability does not compare to the critical function of maintaining proper levels of security for the data. Managing security is vital for ensuring that sensitive data is not provided to unauthorized users, be they internal or external, and for maintaining the integrity of the data.

## User Accounts and Permissions

The primary area of focus for a DBA is user-level access to SQL Server. User accounts are created to provide access to the server and then down to the database. This user access can be further limited through the use of stored procedures to provide access to only a single column in a single table or even to a single value in a single table. User access should be provided only when authorized by the data owner. This access should also be as restrictive as possible so to provide the maximum level of protection to the data.

There is often a temptation to provide complete access to a database to simplify administration tasks. Avoid this whenever possible because it can lead to disaster. When you are managing a large number of users and you have common objects that require access, it is best to create and use database roles. This allows you to grant the role access to a particular object. You can then add to that role any users that require the same permissions. Doing this simplifies administration and still maintains a strong level of secure access.

Users can gain access by one of two methods: SQL Server authentication or Windows authentication. Windows authentication makes use of Active Directory user management and integrates the user access with their domain account. This means that the user only has to log in to his or her workstation. These credentials are then passed down to SQL Server 2005, which then provides the user with the relevant levels of access that have been set up by the DBA. SQL Server authentication requires more direct management at the DBA level. For these logins, you create a separate login for each user who requires access to SQL Server 2005. You can assign a password to each user requesting access. New to SQL Server 2005, you can also allow users to change their passwords and enforce password policies through tools such as the password strength and an expiration date that prompts users to change their passwords frequently. This is something that is not available in SQL Server 2000, where the DBA must manually manage all user accounts and passwords.

## Server Security

The DBA might not have responsibility for the system where SQL Server is installed. However, the DBA must be able to help manage the system's security access and help make sure that the operating system is accessible only to authorized personnel. It is not productive to lock down SQL Server only to find that all users have administrative rights on the operating system and the ability to make any and all changes to SQL from there, including retrieving database backup files. A well locked down operating system helps prevent the loss or theft of data.

## Security Auditing

Having strong security policies in place is critical to keeping data safe. However, it is also important to be aware of who is accessing the system and to check that users are not receiving escalated privileges and that changes are being made only by authorized personnel. There are many new auditing options within SQL Profiler that allow you to audit all changes to your database. These changes can include schema changes, insert, update, and delete operations and events related to permissions changes or new logins created. This data can be stored in a separate SQL Server installation and queried (either manually or automatically) to look for security changes or unauthorized database changes.

The DBA also needs to be familiar with the Windows Server 2003 event logs. These event logs allow the DBA to recognize logins local to the system, trap system, and application events. Correlating all of this information may seem a daunting task, but it is important to keep the integrity of your data intact.

# Operations

Once installation is complete on a system and the configuration is optimal, the DBA is also responsible for day-to-day operations, maintaining data integrity, and making sure that there is a level of recoverability for the data in the event of a severe hardware problem or other disaster.

## Backup and Restore

It is commonly recognized that backup and restore operations are the most crucial tasks that the DBA performs. As a DBA, it is your responsibility to ensure that all databases are backed up on a regular basis to allow for a restore should there be a major problem. There are different kinds of backups: full, differential, partial, and transaction log, as described in Chapter 14, "Backup Fundamentals." Each one of these can be used depending upon the level of recovery required for the data on the server. With SQL Server 2005, you can also password protect a backup to prevent unauthorized restores. Backup procedures in themselves are quite simple to master; however, frequent tests of backups can help you greatly down the road. Similarly, testing restores of these backups is very important. After all, what good is a backup if you can never restore it? Test all kinds of restores that you might encounter, and test them frequently by performing those restores to a backup system. If you do so, you will be prepared if a disaster occurs, and you can feel confident that you know what to do.

### Change Management

As the DBA, you should make any changes to SQL Server 2005, to the databases, or to the schemas contained therein. If these changes are handled by a developer, for example, you cannot verify the code that is going in or confirm what was changed and why. How can you maintain the integrity of the database when you allow others to make any changes? Changes should always go through a QA/UAT process to confirm that they do not break accessing applications and receive a sign off before being moved into production. When you make the production changes, always document what is being done and by whom. Implement a true change management system along with bug tracking, and use a tool like Visual SourceSafe to retain older copies of procedures and schema changes. Finally, before you implement any change, be sure that you have a rollback strategy in case of any problems. After all, it's the DBA that the users will come to when they are unable to access their data.

## Service Levels

The DBA is responsible for providing an appropriate level of service to the customer or to the data consumer. This might be in the form of a contracted Service Level Agreement (SLA) or an agreement between departments. In either case, the DBA is held accountable for providing the highest level of service through server uptime and performance.

## System Monitoring

Routinely monitoring the system allows you to recognize problems early and deal with potential issues before they affect the customer directly. This could be from monitoring locks and blocks within the database to recognizing when CPU levels are rising or when a failure of a network card that eliminates redundancy within the system occurs. It is imperative that both SQL Server 2005 and the operating system are monitored. For example, you might get a call from a user stating that a query is running particularly slowly, but you find no locking conditions within the database to account for that. When you look at performance counters on the operating system, you see that CPU levels are running at 98 percent, severely affecting the user's ability to perform tasks. Likewise, that user might complain later in the day of the same problem. This time the CPU levels are low at 20 percent, but investigation within the database shows that there is a blocking process preventing the query from running.

Pulling all of this information together helps to fix problems, but knowing your system can also help you to prevent problems by notifying users of queries that are using mass amounts of CPU on the system or returning huge result sets that are eating up network bandwidth. A good DBA is able to prevent problems with early identification and has routines in place to monitor these items. In addition, the better notes that you take, and the better documentation you create, the easier it might be to solve the problem.

---

**Note**   By setting up your own knowledge base, you can easily find answers to problems you have already encountered. I use SharePoint to keep a knowledge base of problems and solutions that I have run into. This way I can easily find something that I don't remember, and additionally, I can share these solutions with my co-workers.

---

You can use System Monitor to identify resource issues and SQL Server Management Studio Activity Monitor for limited internal SQL performance information. In addition, several third-party utilities are available, which can provide a complete overview of the system, including CPU utilization, memory usage, I/O statistics, processes, lock escalations, blocking, and buffer cache usage. Some of these tools will also trend the information and can be configured to provide alerts when certain events occur or certain thresholds are surpassed.

One of the best indicators of how a system is performing is to gather regular feedback from the user base accessing the data. You can send out feedback forms to gather information about how the users feel the system is responding and work to identify potential problems from the information that they provide.

## Performance Tuning

System monitoring helps you recognize when there are problems. Performance tuning helps you eliminate those problems and prevent them from occurring. Monitoring long-running queries helps you identify areas where you can make improvements, such as adding an index, rewriting a query, or de-normalizing data. You might also find that performance is suffering from a lack of memory, so you can adjust the amount of memory available to SQL Server or add more memory to the machine. You might recognize that all queries are performing as well as they can and that the user load has just increased to a point where you need to make system modifications to improve performance. A DBA needs to be able to provide solutions for problems and to provide these solutions proactively. Working hard to tune all aspects of SQL Server and the system could save thousands of dollars in hardware upgrades that were not required and at the same time identify where upgrades really are required.

## Routine Maintenance

In order for your system to perform as it should, regular maintenance must be performed. A large portion of this can be automated. However, keep a close eye on the systems to make sure that users are not negatively affected.

Regular maintenance tasks include the following:

- **Index Rebuilds** Much improved in SQL Server 2005, as indexes can be built without locking tables, although performance will drop as the index is rebuilt

- **Compressing data files** Frees up some disk space on your system, especially if you run frequent insert/delete statements

- **Updating Statistics** Makes sure that SQL Server is using the up-to-date statistics to create its execution plans, ensuring high query performance

- **Database Consistency Checks** Check for corruption within databases/tables/indexes

These items can be run within Maintenance Plans and can be set up with the assistance of a wizard. You might want to run other maintenance routines such as data purges, which can be set up manually.

## Reliability

Keeping SQL Server 2005 reliable and available means keeping the customer happy and the DBA relaxed. It takes some advanced planning and work to create an environment in which you feel you have control over the data and can support your customers in even the most dire circumstances.

## Disaster Recovery

Where do you stand in the event of a server failure? What if you lost an entire datacenter? How much data can you stand to lose in either event? What are the business needs and requirements? Who will pay for it all?

These are all question that a DBA must ask. Provided that you run regular backups and have tested your restores, then you will be able to recover from most situations. However, you still may lose a day's worth of business, and for some companies that could be millions of dollars. If the business says that you have the funds for true disaster recovery, both geographically local and diverse, there are options that you can implement with SQL Server 2005 to ensure that you keep the systems available.

### Clustering

Clustering is a method for having multiple servers connected by shared disk. Each node within the cluster is capable of running SQL Server 2005, although only a single node at a time can own a SQL Server 2005 instance. This gives you great hardware redundancy within a datacenter. If you have a two-node cluster running a single instance of SQL Server 2005 and the primary hardware fails, SQL Server automatically fails over to the second node. Normally, this happens in under 20 seconds. There is no loss of data and user impact—a loss of connection for the duration of the failover—is minimal.

## Log Shipping

Log shipping is a method for keeping consistent copies of a database separate to the primary instance. This is the primary method for maintaining external copies of a database outside the local datacenter, so that in the event of a loss to the datacenter itself, you still have a working copy offsite. With log shipping, you restore a backup of the primary database in STANDBY or NORECOVERY mode on a secondary server. You then create regularly scheduled dumps of the transaction log from the primary database. These logs are then shipped over and applied on the secondary machine. While you are not getting instant failover with no loss of data, you can minimize any potential data loss by scheduling the logs to be dumped, copied, and loaded frequently. Log shipping works very well and is reliable, and you can delay transaction being applied on the secondary node, which is useful as a backup scenario for those times when you are making significant database changes or want to have a window of data recovery for any changes. Log shipping creates an exact duplicate of the primary database and includes all logged transactions that take place (including schema changes).

## Database Mirroring

Database mirroring is a new form of log shipping. Like log shipping, database mirroring is a copy of the primary database that is kept in recovery mode. Unlike log shipping, rather than waiting on the transaction log to be backed up, a copy of the live transaction log is kept on the mirror. As entries are made into the primary transaction log, they are sent to the standby as well. In this manner, the standby is kept up-to-date with the primary. This is covered in detail in Chapter 27, "Log Shipping and Database Mirroring."

## Replication

Replication is a method of providing data to a reporting server. You can have real time or near real time transactions applied to a secondary server. This is particularly useful for keeping a reporting environment with current data that does not affect the hardworking primary server. However, replication has its drawbacks as it is a copy of the data and not a copy of the database.

# Planning and Scheduling Downtime

Even the best, most stable system will at some point need some downtime, whether to install a service pack or security update, to introduce some new code, or to support an application change. These changes should be scheduled well in advance and communicated to the users. If possible, set up regularly scheduled downtimes for the system during which you can apply security update if necessary, or just perform maintenance tasks. This way, the users are always aware that the system will be down at a specific date and time, and if for some reason there is no work to do, the system remains up.

# Capacity Planning

In addition to planning disaster recovery scenarios and downtime, you must be able to determine the capacity for the system and implement improvements when necessary. To do this, schedule regular capacity planning tasks, for example, monitoring the size of databases and ensuring that there is sufficient disk space to host the required amount of data. Working with the development team and determining requirements early on for new applications will help you size any system accordingly from a processor, memory, disk, and network standpoint.

# Documentation

Documentation was discussed previously in this chapter, and it is worth reiterating because of the vital need of both the DBA and the business to know exactly what is running, where it is running, and what it is running on. In addition to securing your system, your documentation should be secured as well. This documentation could contain sensitive system information.

## Configuration Documentation

Configuration documentation should contain all information about the installation and configuration of a SQL Server 2005 instance and the hardware and operating system that support the installation. This documentation will be your reference when someone asks about the CPU revision, the current build level of SQL Server, or whether you have the logs on a RAID-5 or RAID-10 volume, for example. Having this information on hand saves you a lot of work in the long term.

## Design Documents

How do you design a system? What criteria do you use for making the decisions about installing SQL Server 2005 or configuring the operating system? How do you decide which RAID level to use for each volume? By creating a document that describes the decision-making process, you explain your methodology and justify your decisions.

## Operational Information

Who is your customer? If a database becomes unavailable, who needs to know, who is affected, and what is the Service Level Agreement (SLA) for a resolution? What jobs run against the database, and what happens to the data that is imported or exported to it? The operational information document should contain all of this information and anything else important to the everyday operation of your environments. You will save a great deal of time by being aware who is affected when there is a problem, understanding the interactions of different systems, and being able to easily identify possible problem code when there is an issue.

# Development and Design

Some smaller companies require the DBA's role to expand to include code development and database design. Even if this is not the case in your environment, you should always be aware of development efforts and be in a position to provide guidance when necessary, and to recognize good or bad design or coding to prevent production problems.

## Database Design

Database design is usually carried out by a database architect. However, if you can provide guidance about the physical layout of a database, you can provide early assistance and prevent the database from being backed into a corner when issues of scalability arise later.

## Data Modeling

*Data modeling* is a critical part of design. The data model includes table relationships, referential integrity, and the logical layout of the database. There are several third-party utilities that can assist with creating a model, but you can also use the Database Designer that comes with SQL Server Management Studio. This is a very powerful tool but one that you should be careful using to avoid accidentally introducing changes into your environment. If possible, use this tool on the development or test environment.

## Procedure and SSIS Development

You might be required to create stored procedures to perform certain functions within SQL Server 2005, such as performing insertions, updates, and deletions or implementing some kind of advanced business logic that provides data sets to customers or that feeds data out to a Web page. Stored procedures have two major advantages over standard queries. First, from a security perspective, a user who is given access to execute a stored procedure can do only that and work with only the results of the procedure. This limits the damage that can be done. Second, SQL Server stores the execution plan of the procedure in its cache. This has major performance benefits because extra time is not spent in SQL Server identifying the best way to execute the procedure.

SQL Server Integration Services (SSIS) is the replacement for DTS in SQL Server 2000. SSIS projects are designed and built to provide true ETL functionality to SQL Server 2005. As discussed earlier in the chapter, ETL is an acronym for the following terms.:

**Extract** Extracting data from a source, whether a database or a file

**Transform** Changing that data, applying logic, and formatting

**Load** Loading the data into a destination, whether a database or a file

With ETL you can load data into SQL Server from other relational databases such as Oracle or Sybase, from files created by spreadsheet software, or from plain text files. Conversely, you can also export data from SQL Server to any of those destinations and to many others.

## Scalability

What good is your installation if you can't scale as your enterprise grows? A good DBA plans ahead and recognizes areas where you might need to grow the database. This could mean adding extra instances to an existing box or providing a separate reporting server so that your main OLTP databases do not become overwhelmed.

## Replication

Replication can be used for several purposes and in different ways. Snapshot replication allows you to take a snapshot of the data and load it into another database. This is extremely useful when you have a relatively small table with data that changes rarely and you wish to move it for reporting purposes. Transactional replication is used for making incremental changes to a secondary server. Changes to the primary, or publishing, table are applied over at the secondary, or subscribing, table, which allows you to report against OLTP environments without affecting your main systems. Merge replication allows you to have separate publishing databases and the ability to sync data between them. This ability is especially useful, for example, if you have many sales offices and want to keep a central repository of all sales made while allowing each individual office to maintain its own copy of the data independently.

## Named Instances

In smaller shops in which there isn't sufficient funding for many servers, but there is a need for separate installs of SQL Server, you can use named instances. A named instance is a complete installation of SQL Server. You can host multiple instances of SQL on a single piece of hardware, and each instance is an independent entity running its own processes with its own databases and security settings. Bear in mind that these instances share server resources. It's very useful for occasions when you want to run a QA and training environment without purchasing extra hardware and when you want to install in a cluster because instances allow you to have multiple actives nodes.

# DBA Tips, Guidelines, and Advice

There is a lot more to being a good DBA than just administering the databases. This section provides some additional information including tips, guidelines, and advice about being a better DBA and handling extreme situations.

## Know Your Operating System

Understanding the inner workings of Windows Server 2003 is not critical to the function of a DBA. However, knowing the operating system well enough to assist in the configuration and being able do advanced troubleshooting to solve problems can save you a great deal of time and difficulty when problems exist. At the very least, you should be able to recognize and understand that basic configuration of Windows and be able to perform basic troubleshooting steps to provide the best possible service to your customers. After all, why wait an hour for an on-call Windows administrator to determine why users can't access the database when you can look and see for yourself that the service has stopped?

## Help Desk

From time to time, you may be asked to assist with help desk functions. Getting face-to-face (or phone-to-phone) interaction with a customer can be an invaluable experience. You can see the kinds of frustrations a user is having with your databases, or you might be called to provide assistance with building a query. Developing a customer-orientated focus helps others to see your role as valuable, which is helpful when you need to get something done.

## Purchasing Input

Who better knows what you need to run your database than the DBA? Certainly providing input into the servers that are purchased is important, but it goes further than that. For example, if your department is evaluating new storage solutions, what's going to work best for you? What about third-party tools and utilities? Certainly they might provide huge benefits. Getting involved in purchasing decisions at even the lowest level helps prevent problems for you later on and also gives you the feeling of really owning your environment.

## Know Your Versions

Which version of SQL Server 2005 should you be using? There are five to choose among (not including Mobile), each with a different cost, its own choices and benefits, and its own limitations. The following editions are available:

- **Enterprise Edition** The ultimate in scalability and performance for large organizations

- **Standard Edition** Ideal for small- to- medium-sized organizations; does not scale as well as Enterprise Edition

- **Workgroup Edition** Provides only core components; ideal for departmental or office use

- **Developer Edition** Fully functional and licensed for development or test use

- **Express Edition** Free, easy to use, but limited in performance and connectivity

## Don't Panic

Mistakes can often make a bad situation worse. The key to handling a problem such as a broken system is being prepared and handling the situation calmly and efficiently. A DBA is only human. A DBA can stay awake for only a certain number of hours before making really big mistakes. Even though a situation looks very bad, you cannot keep working forever. If you need to take a break, take it. Here are some tips for handling extreme DBA experiences:

- **Get rest when you need it.** You can't work without a break.

- **Call in help when you need it.** Even if you don't normally use outside consulting help, it's not a bad idea to pre-qualify some extra help in case you need it. Some companies specialize in helping out in times of disaster.

- **Keep the user community and management well informed.** If you schedule regular updates, such as every half hour, they won't keep bugging you for information.

- **Have a plan.** When developing your disaster recovery system, include a document that states how and when to implement the disaster plan.

- **Test and then follow your plan.** By following your plan, which has been tested, you increase your likelihood of success.

- **Be confident in yourself and in the decisions that you make.** For better or worse, others will judge you in part on appearance. Showing confidence in the face of a pressure situation speaks volumes to users and to management.

Be careful and follow the first rule of medicine: Do no harm. Be sure that you are not making things worse by taking your time and getting help if you need it.

### Real World   "The Red Book"

When putting together a disaster recovery system (I prefer the term "disaster survival system"), create documentation that describes how and when to implement the plan. I prefer to put this into a bright red binder that I refer to as "The Red Book." The Red Book has precise implementation steps for how and when to implement the disaster recovery plan and copies should be kept at multiple key locations, such as the primary site, the disaster recovery site, the IT director's office, and so on. What do I mean by "when"? It is not always obvious when the Disaster Recovery system should kick in.

Because most disaster recovery plans are difficult to reset, such as putting the primary database instance back to the primary data center, the decision to implement disaster recovery must be manual. If the primary data center loses power, you must determine how long it will be without power. If the plan is to be back online in 30 minutes, you might decide to wait rather than implement the disaster recovery plan.

## Summary

While this chapter provides an overview of the duties and responsibilities of the SQL Server DBA, it can't describe all of your possible responsibilities. Some companies have a single DBA working on all aspects of server maintenance and working to keep SQL Server up and performing. Other companies have hundreds of DBAs scattered nationwide or even worldwide, each responsible for a single machine or a single aspect of SQL administration.

As a DBA, you might focus on performance, on engineering database solutions, on developing the backend for new applications, or on loading data from various sources into a data warehouse. Your duties depend on the needs of your company and upon the skills that you possess. As you acquire new skills and your experience grows, you become more valuable to your company and the customers you support.

# Part II
# System Design and Architecture

# Chapter 4
# I/O Subsystem Planning and RAID Configuration

In this chapter, you'll learn how to properly design and configure the I/O subsystem. In order to properly configure the I/O subsystem for both space and performance, it is necessary to understand some of the fundamentals of I/O processing and RAID configuration. Knowledge of the fundamentals of I/O performance will allow you to size and configure your system properly.

The term I/O stands for Input/Output, but in recent years the term has really evolved to mean the storage subsystem. Technically, there is I/O going on with the network, the CPU bus, memory, and so on, but this term usually refers to storage. The term "storage" has replaced disk drives because today's storage subsystems are really much more than disk drives (although they use disk drives). Storage today consists of disks, Storage Area Networks (SANs), Network Attached Storage (NAS), and hybrids. In this book, I/O refers to the act of transferring data to and from the storage subsystem.

This chapter begins by describing the functionality and performance of the fundamental component of the I/O subsystem: the disk drive. Disk arrays, or RAID, is then explained, and advanced features such as caching and elevator sorting are covered. In addition, monitoring and benchmarking the I/O subsystem is discussed. Finally, this chapter will present some of the I/O requirements of SQL Server and show how to configure your SQL Server system properly for optimal I/O performance and functionality. After you complete this chapter, you will be able to properly size and configure the I/O subsystem for space, redundancy, and performance.

# I/O Fundamentals

In order to understand why I/O sizing is important, we will begin by detailing the performance characteristics of the fundamental building block of the I/O subsystem: the disk drive. Since most I/O subsystems are made up of one or more disk drives, it is important to understand how they work and what properties they have.

Disk drives are important because they provide persistent storage. *Persistent storage* is storage that exists in the absence of an external power source. There are two reasons why disk storage is important. First, disk drives provide the most storage for your money. Disk drives are significantly less expensive than memory. Second, disk drives do not lose their data in the event of a power failure. If you have ever experienced a power outage, you'll appreciate that feature.

The disk drive, also often called the hard disk, is one of the fundamental components of the computer system. The mechanics of disk drives have not changed much in the last 20 years. Disk drives are much more reliable and faster than they originally were, but they are fundamentally the same today as then. From a performance standpoint, disk drives are one of the most important hardware components to optimize. Even though you don't typically tune a disk drive by setting parameters, by knowing its performance characteristics and limitations and by configuring your system with those limitations in mind, you are, in effect, tuning the I/O subsystem.

In the last few years the size of disk drives has grown dramatically. For example, just a few years ago an 8-gigabyte (GB) disk drive was the standard. Now, it is not uncommon to have a system made up of 146-GB disk drives, or even larger. The problem from a database standpoint is that while disk drives are more than 15 times larger, they are roughly twice as fast as they were a few years ago. The problem comes in when a large number of smaller drives are replaced by one larger drive, leaving the I/O subsystem underpowered. Thus, an underperforming I/O subsystem is one of the most common SQL Server performance problems.

## Disk Drive Basics

The data storage component of a disk drive is made up of a number of disk platters. These platters are coated with a material that stores data magnetically. Data is stored in tracks, which are similar to the tracks of a record album (or CD, for those of you who don't remember records). Each track, in turn, is made up of a number of sectors. As you get farther from the center of the disk drive, each track contains more sectors. Figure 4-1 shows a typical disk platter.

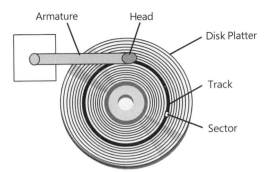

**Figure 4-1**   Disk platter.

Instead of having just one platter, a disk drive is often made up of many disk platters stacked on top of each other, as shown in Figure 4-2. The data is read by a magnetic head. This head is used both to read data from and write data to the disk. Because there are many platters, there are also many disk heads. These heads are attached to an armature that moves in and out of the disk stack, much like the arm that holds the needle on a record player. The heads and armatures are all connected; as a result, all heads are at the same point on all platters at the same time. Because disks operate in this manner, it makes sense for all heads to read and write at the same time; thus, data is written to and read from all platters simultaneously. Because the set of tracks covered by the heads at any one time resembles a cylinder, we say that data is stored in cylinders, as shown in Figure 4-2.

**Figure 4-2**   Disk cylinders with cylinder highlighted.

Disk drives can be made up of as few as one disk platter or more than six platters. The density of the data on the platters and the number of platters determine the maximum storage capacity of a disk drive. Some lines of disk drives are almost identical except for the number of disk platters. A popular line of disk drives has a 36GB disk drive with two disk platters and an otherwise identical 73-GB disk drive with four disk platters.

# Disk Drive Performance Characteristics

Now that you understand the physical properties of disk drives, let's look at the performance characteristics of the disk drive. There are three main performance factors related to disk drive performance: rotational latency, seek time, and transfer time.

## Rotational Latency

Many high-performance disk drives spin at 10,000 revolutions per minute (rpm). If a request for data caused the disk to have to rotate completely before it was able to read the data, this spin would take approximately 6 milliseconds (ms), or 0.006 seconds. This is easy to understand, as a rotational speed of 10,000 rpm equates to 166.7 rotations per second. This, in turn, translates to 1/166.7 of a second, or 6 ms, per rotation.

For the disk heads to read a sector of data, that sector must be underneath the head. Because the disk drive is always rotating, the head simply waits for that sector to rotate to the position underneath it. The time it takes for the disk to rotate to where the data is under the head is called the *rotational latency*. The rotational latency averages around 3 ms but can be as long as 6 ms if the disk has to rotate completely.

The rotational latency is added to the response time of a disk access. When you are choosing disk drives for your system, it is extremely important from a performance standpoint that you take into consideration the length of the disks' rotational latency. As you have just seen, for a 10,000-rpm disk drive, the average rotational latency is around 3 ms. Older generation disk drives spin at 7,200 rpm or even 5,400 rpm. With the 7,200 rpm disk drive, one rotation takes 8.3 ms, and the average rotational latency is about 4.15 ms. This length of time might not seem like a lot, but it is about 38 percent longer than that of the 10,000-rpm disk drive. As you will see later in this chapter, this longer response time can add a lot to your I/O times.

## Disk Seeks

When retrieving data, not only must the disk rotate under the heads that will read the data, but the head must also move to the track where the data resides. The disk armature moves in and out of the disk stack to move the heads to the cylinder that holds the desired data. The time it takes the head to move to where the requested data resides is called the *seek time*. Seek time and rotational latency are represented in Figure 4-3.

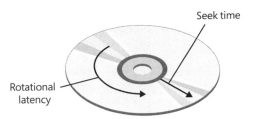

**Figure 4-3**   Rotational latency and seek time.

The time it takes for a seek to occur depends mainly on how far the disk heads need to move. When the disk drives are accessing data sequentially, the heads need to move only a small distance, which can occur quickly. When disk accesses are occurring all over the disk drive, the seek times can get quite long. In either case, by minimizing the seek time, you improve your system's performance.

Seek time and rotational latency both add to the time it takes for an I/O operation to occur, and thus they worsen the performance of a disk drive. Rotational latency is usually around 3 ms for 10,000-rpm disks. The seek time of the disk varies depending on the size and speed of the disk drive and the type of seek being performed.

## Track-to-Track Seeks

Track-to-track seek time is the time the heads take to move between adjacent tracks. This type of seek is used when performing sequential I/O operations. A typical 10,000-rpm, 73-GB disk drive has a track-to-track seek time of around 0.3 ms, although it varies for reads and writes. As you can see, for disks with a track-to-track seek time of only 0.3 ms, the rotational latency of approximately 3 ms is the larger factor in the disk drive performance. If the I/O operations are submitted to the disk drive quickly enough, the disk drive will be able to access adjacent tracks or even read or write an entire track at a time. However, this is not always the case. In some cases, the I/O operations are not requested quickly enough, and a disk rotation occurs between each sequential access. Whether this happens typically depends on the design and the speed of the disk controller.

## Average Seek Time

The average seek time is the time the heads take on average to seek between random tracks on the disk. According to the specification sheet of an average 10,000-rpm disk drive, the seek time for such a disk is around 5 ms. Because almost all of the I/O operations that SQL Server generates are random, your disk drives will be performing a lot of random I/O.

> **Note**    I mentioned in the text that almost all SQL Server I/O operations are random. There are several reasons for this. In an online system, one user might be performing a table scan, which is a sequential operation. At the same time, however, you may have hundreds of other users who are doing their own operations on the I/O subsystem. From the I/O subsystem's perspective, the multiple sequential accesses performed by different users mimic a random access pattern. In a batch system, the same effect is caused by parallelism. The only way to truly achieve sequential access is to have only one user on the system, disable parallelism, and perform a table scan. This achieves the effect of sequential disk access, but at what cost?

The maximum seek time of this type of disk can be as long as 10 ms. The maximum seek occurs from the innermost track of the platter to the outermost track, or vice-versa. This is referred to as a *full-disk seek*. However, the seeks will not normally be full-disk seeks, especially if the disk drive is not full.

### Transfer Time

The transfer time is the time it takes to move the data from the disk drive electronics to the I/O controller. Typically the transfer time of the disk drive is so much higher than the seek time and rotational latency that it does not fit into the performance equations, but it can be problematic at times.

### You Get What You Pay For

Lately some storage vendors have begun to offer the option of including Serial ATA drives in their storage subsystems. Because the transfer time of Serial ATA drives is so much slower than SCSI or Fibre Channel drives, you can potentially experience significant performance problems. Even though the potential throughput of SAN storage might be very high, it is only as fast as its slowest component. By saving a few dollars on disk drives, you might lose a lot more performance than you are counting on.

## Disk Drive Specifications

In this section, you will see how quickly a disk drive can perform various types of I/O operations. To make these calculations, you must have some information about the disk drive. Much of this information can be found by looking at the specifications of the disk drive that the manufacturer provides. The sample specifications in this chapter are for a 10,000-rpm, 73-GB disk drive. Other specifications for a sample disk drive are shown in Table 4-1. These statistics are taken from of a major disk drive vendor's Web site.

Table 4-1    Disk Drive Specifications

| Specification | Value | Description |
|---|---|---|
| Disk capacity | 73 GB | The unformatted disk capacity |
| Rotational speed | 10,000 rpm | Speed at which the disk is spinning |
| Transfer rate | 320 MBps | Speed of the SCSI bus |
| Average seek time | 4.7 ms (read) 5.3 ms (write) | Average time it takes to seek between tracks during random I/O operations |
| Track-to-track seek time | 0.2 ms (read) 0.5 ms (write) | Average time it takes to seek between tracks during sequential I/O operations |
| Full-disk seek time | 9.5 ms (read) 10.3 ms (write) | Average time it takes to seek from the innermost sector to the outermost sector of the disk, or vice versa |
| Average latency | 3 ms | Average rotational latency |
| Mean time between failures (MTBF) | 1,400,000 hours | Average disk life |

As you will see, these types of specifications can help you determine the performance of the disk drive.

## Disk Drive Performance

Several factors determine the amount of time it takes for an I/O operation to occur:

- The seek time required (for the heads to move to the track that holds the data)

- The rotational latency required (for the data to rotate under the heads)

- The time required to electronically transfer the data from the disk drive to the disk controller

The time it takes for an I/O operation to occur is the sum of the times needed to complete these steps, plus the time added by the overhead incurred in the device driver and in the operating system. Remember, the total time for an I/O operation depends mainly on whether the operation in question is sequential or random. Sequential I/O performance depends on track-to-track seeks. Random I/O performance depends on the average seek time.

## Sequential I/O

Sequential I/O consists of accessing adjacent data in disk drives. Because track-to-track seeks are much faster than random seeks, it is possible to achieve much higher throughput from a disk when performing sequential I/O. To get an idea of how quickly sequential I/O can occur, let's look at an example.

It takes approximately 0.3 ms to seek between tracks on a typical disk drive, as mentioned earlier. If you add the seek time to the rotational latency of 3 ms, you can conclude that each I/O operation takes approximately 3.3 ms. Theoretically, this speed would allow us to perform 303 track-to-track operations per second (because each second contains 303 intervals of 3.3 ms). How much data per second this is and how many SQL Server I/Os per second this is really depend on how many logical I/Os there are in a track.

In addition, other factors come into play with sequential I/O, such as the SCSI bus throughput limit of 320 megabytes per second (MBps) for Ultra320 SCSI and operating system components such as the file system and the device driver. That overhead factors into the maximum rate of sequential I/O that a drive can sustain, which is around 250 operations per second (depending on how big the operations are). As you will see in Chapter 6, "Capacity Planning," if you run a disk drive at more than 75 percent of its I/O capacity, queuing occurs; thus, the maximum recommended I/O rate is 225 operations per second.

## Random I/O

Random I/O occurs when the disk heads must read data from various parts of the disk. This random head movement results in reduced performance. Again, let's look at the sample disk we covered earlier. Now instead of taking approximately 0.3 ms to seek between adjacent tracks on the disk, the heads must seek random tracks on the disk. This random seeking takes approximately 5 ms on average to complete, which is more than 16 times longer than average track-to-track seeks. A typical random I/O operation requires approximately 5 ms for the heads to move to the track where the data is held and 3 ms in rotational latency, for a total of 8 ms, giving a theoretical maximum of 125 I/O operations per second (because each second contains 125 intervals of 8 ms). Thus, using the same rule as earlier, if you run a disk drive at more than 75 percent of its capacity, queuing occurs. Therefore, the maximum recommended I/O rate is 94 I/O operations per second. If you follow a rule of thumb that takes into account overhead in the controller, you would want to drive these disk drives at no more than 94 I/O operations per second.

## Real World    You Can't Argue with Mathematics

The fundamentals of disk drive performance are explained by simple mathematics. As described above, you can push a disk drive only so hard before queuing occurs and latencies rise. This is one of the most common problems that I run into as a performance consultant. With larger and larger disk drives, the problem is only getting worse. Today it is possible to create and run a terabyte database on four disk drives (or even one). The database might fit, but it certainly won't perform well unless you have a terabyte of RAM. I have heard many times "The salesman told me that since it is a SAN I can do 40,000 I/Os per second." Well, you might be able to do that if you have 400 disk drives attached, but not four. Remember to perform the fundamental calculations.

When a disk drive performs random I/O, a normal latency (the time it takes to perform individual I/O operations) is 8 ms. When a drive is accessed more quickly than it can handle, queuing will occur and the latency will increase, as shown in Figure 4-4. As you can see, the closer the number of operations per second gets to the disk's recommended maximum rate, the longer the latencies get. In fact, if you get to 100 percent, queuing will certainly occur and performance will degrade dramatically.

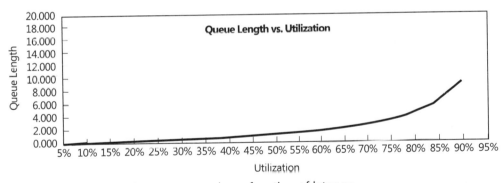

**Figure 4-4**   I/O operations per second as a function of latency.

As you will learn later in this book, SQL Server, like all other relational database management systems, is highly sensitive to I/O latencies. When I/O operations take excessive amounts of time to complete, the performance of SQL Server degrades, and problems such as blocking and deadlocks might occur. When a thread is waiting on an I/O operation, it might be holding locks. The longer the operation takes to complete, the longer the locks are held, thus causing these types of problems.

## Solutions to the Disk Performance Limitation Problem

So how do we solve the problem of disk performance limitations? It is actually quite straightforward. By following these guidelines, you should be able to design an I/O subsystem that performs optimally:

- **Isolate sequential I/O operations**   By isolating components that are sequential in nature on their own disk volume, you can maintain that sequential nature. The transaction log is an example of a sequentially accessed file. If you place more than one sequentially accessed file on the same disk volume, the I/O operations will become random because the disk must seek between the various sequential components.

- **Distribute random I/O operations**   Because the I/O operations are random in nature, you can alleviate the load by adding disk drives. If you build a system with enough disk drives to handle the random I/O load, you should not experience any problems. How many disks to use and how to configure them will be addressed later in this chapter and in Chapter 6.

# Redundant Array of Independent Disks (RAID)

Before the turn of the twenty-first century, we had to manage the use of multiple disk drives by spending significant time balancing data files among all of these disks. This process could be very time-consuming but not very effective. In addition, the lack of fault-tolerance left the system nonfunctional in the event of the loss of even a single disk drive. Many years ago a solution was introduced to solve this problem: RAID.

### Real World   A Little Bit of Personal History

I was working at Compaq Computer Corporation when they introduced their first RAID controller. It was very exciting because it gave them an opportunity to better support the emerging server market. This array controller supported up to eight IDE drives and several RAID levels. At the same time, they introduced their first multiprocessor system. Things have certainly changed a lot since then.

RAID (Redundant Array of Independent Disks) allows you to create a collection of disk drives that appears to the operating system as a single disk. You can implement RAID by using software and existing I/O components, or you can purchase hardware RAID devices. In this section, you will learn what RAID is and how it works.

As the name implies, RAID takes two or more disk drives and creates an array of disks. To the operating system, this array appears as one *logical disk*. This logical disk is also known as a *disk volume* because it is a collection of disks that appears as one. If hardware RAID is used the array appears as one disk to the user, the application, and the operating system. In many cases, however, this single logical disk is much larger than any disk you could purchase. Not only does RAID allow you to create large logical disk drives, but most *RAID levels,* configurations of RAID, provide disk fault tolerance as well. Fault tolerance allows the RAID logical disk to survive, or tolerate, the loss of one or more individual disk drives. In the next few sections, you will learn how this is possible and the characteristics of various RAID levels.

As mentioned earlier, RAID can be implemented using software; in fact, Windows 2003 comes with RAID software. However, this chapter is concerned mostly with hardware-based RAID because of the additional features that it provides, although software and hybrid (hardware and software combination) striping can be effective. In the next two sections, you will learn about some of these features and the characteristics of the various RAID levels.

> **Note**   A hardware stripe presents itself to the OS as a disk drive. Since there are limitations on the number of drives that can be in a LUN (based on your brand of hardware) often you will have multiple LUNs to use with SQL Server. I have found that it is more efficient to stripe within SQL Server using diskgroups, rather than using software striping.

## RAID Basics

The main characteristic of a RAID array is that two or more physical disk drives are combined to form a logical disk drive, which appears to the operating system (and Performance Monitor) as one physical disk drive. A logical disk drive can be as large as terabytes, even though terabyte disk drives are not mainstream (yet!).

### Striping

Most of the RAID levels that will be described here use data striping. *Data striping* combines the data from two or more disks into one larger RAID logical disk, which is accomplished by placing the first piece of data on the first disk, the second piece of data on the second disk, and so on. These pieces are known as *stripe elements,* or *chunks.* The size of the stripe is determined by the controller. Some controllers allow you to configure the stripe size, whereas other controllers have a fixed stripe size. The individual piece of data on each disk is referred to as a stripe or chunk, but the combination of all of the chunks across all disk drives is also referred to as the stripe, as shown in Figure 4-5.

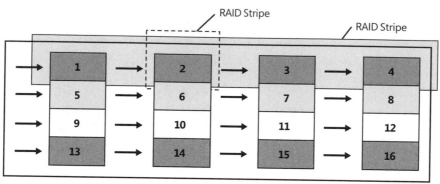

**Figure 4-5**   RAID stripes.

---

**Note**   The term *stripe* can be used to describe the piece of data on a specific disk drive, as in the *disk stripe,* or to refer to the set of related data, as in the *RAID stripe.* Keep this in mind as you read this chapter and others that refer to RAID.

## Redundancy

The RAID level identifies the configuration type and therefore the characteristics of a RAID array other than internal or external logic. One of the most important of these characteristics is fault tolerance. *Fault tolerance* is the ability of a RAID system to continue to function after a disk drive has failed. Fault tolerance is the primary purpose of RAID controllers. Because your data is valuable, you must protect it against a disk failure.

# RAID Levels

In this section, you will learn about the most common RAID levels: how they work, what fault tolerance they provide, and how quickly they perform. There are other RAID levels that are rarely used; only the most popular ones will be mentioned.

## RAID-0

RAID-0 is the most basic RAID level, offering disk striping only. A chunk is created on each disk drive, and the controller defines the size of the chunk. As Figure 4-6 illustrates, a round-robin method is used to distribute the data to each chunk of each disk in the RAID-0 array to create a large logical disk.

Although RAID-0 is considered a RAID level, technically, there is no redundancy at this level. Because there is no redundancy, there is no fault tolerance. If any disk fails in a RAID-0 array, all data is lost. The loss of one disk is similar to losing every fourth word in this book. With this portion of the data missing, the array is useless.

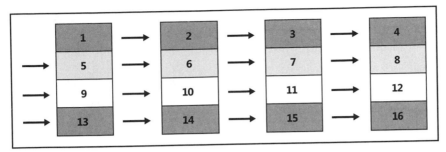

**Figure 4-6**   RAID-0.

### RAID-0 Recommendations

RAID-0 is not normally recommended for storing SQL Server data files. Because the data in the database is so important to your business, losing that data could be devastating. Because a RAID-0 array does not protect you against a disk failure, you shouldn't use it for any critical system component, such as the operating system, a transaction log, or database files.

---

**Note**    A disk drive spins at a high rate and operates at a high temperature. Because the disk is a mechanical component, it eventually will fail. Thus, it is important to protect SQL Server data files from that failure by creating a fault-tolerant system and by performing proper backups.

---

## Real World   Long Live the Disk Drive

According to our specifications above, our typical 73-GB disk drive has a MTBF of 1,400,000 hours. My first question to the disk drive vendors is "How can you tell?" My next question is "Who is going to run a disk drive for 159 years?" I guess my 10-year-old 5 MB (yes MB) disk drive should still be useful. Check back in 149 years, and I'll let you know if it's still working.

The problem is that this average arises from the fact that most disk drives will never fail, but some will fail during the first few days of operation. My experience is that most failures occur during the first few weeks of operation or when the drives have been running for a long time and are shut down for a few days. In cases in which disk drives are running for long periods of time, I don't recommend shutting them down for any reason.

## RAID-1 and RAID-10

RAID-1 is the most basic fault-tolerant RAID level. RAID-1, also known as mirroring, duplicates your data disk. As Figure 4-7 shows, the duplicate contains all of the information that exists on the original disk. In the event of a disk failure, the mirror takes over; thus, you lose no data. Because all the data is held on one disk (and its mirror), no striping is involved. Because RAID-1 uses the second disk drive to duplicate the first disk, the total space of the RAID-1 volume is equal to the space of one disk drive. Thus, RAID-1 is costly because you must double the number of disks but you get no additional disk space in return. However, you do get a high level of fault tolerance.

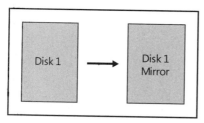

Figure 4-7   RAID-1.

For a RAID-1 volume, an I/O operation is not considered complete until the controller has written data to both disk drives. Until that happens, a "fault" (disk failure) cannot be tolerated without loss of data. Once that data has been written to both disk drives, the data can be recovered in the event of a failure in either disk. This means that if writing the data to one disk takes longer than writing the same data to the other disk, the overall latency will equal the greater of the two latencies.

---

**Note**   There are variations on how RAID-1 and RAID-10 are implemented. Some vendors allow triple mirroring, where there are two mirrored copies of the data. Another variation allows parts of disk drives to be mirrored. The fundamental concept is the same; a duplicate of the data is kept.

---

The fact that the write goes to both disks also reduces the performance of the logical disk drive. When calculating how many I/O operations go to the array, you must multiply the number of writes by two, because the write must go to both disk drives in the mirror. Reads occur on only one disk. Disks might perform at different rates because the heads on one disk might be in a position different than the heads on the other disk; thus, a seek might take longer. Because of a performance feature of RAID-1 known as split seeks, the disks' heads might be in different positions.

*Avg. reads per disk per second = reads to the array per second / 2 (drives in the array)*

*Avg. writes per disk per second = writes to the array per second * 2 (RAID overhead) / 2 (drives in the array)*

*Split seeks* allow the disks in a RAID-1 volume to read data independently of each other. Split seeks are possible because reads occur on only one disk of the volume at a time. Most controller manufacturers support split seeks. Split seeks increase performance because the I/O load is distributed to two disks instead of one. However, because the disk heads are operating independently and because they both must perform the write, the overall write latency is the longer latency between the two disks.

RAID-10 is a combination of RAID-0 and RAID-1. RAID-10 involves mirroring a disk stripe. Each disk will have a duplicate, but each disk will contain only a part of the data, as Figure 4-8 illustrates. This level offers the fault tolerance of RAID-1 and the convenience and performance advantages of RAID-0.

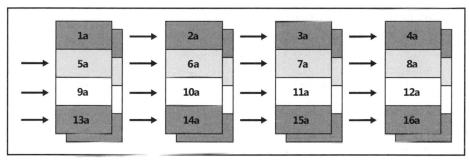

**Figure 4-8**   RAID-10. The "mirrors" behind the disks represent the B drives.

As with RAID-1, each RAID-10 write operation will incur two physical I/O operations—one to each disk in the mirror. Thus, when calculating the number of I/O operations per disk, you must multiply the writes to the array by two because the write must be written to both drives in the mirror. As with RAID-1, the RAID-10 I/O operation is not considered completed until both writes have been done; thus, the write latency might be increased. But, as with RAID-1, most controllers support split seeks with RAID-10.

*Avg. reads per disk per second = reads to the array per second / number of drives in the array*

*Avg. writes per disk per second = writes to the array per second * 2 (RAID overhead) / number of drives in the array*

## RAID-10 by Any Other Name

RAID-10 is the RAID level with the most different names. This RAID level is sometimes known as RAID-0+1, RAID-1+0, RAID-1/0, RAID-1_0, and so on. Some people claim that if the 0 comes first, the array is striped and then mirrored, and thus it is less tolerant to failures. You should do your own research based on the brand of array controller you have purchased, but I have found that regardless of the naming convention, the basic concept of a disk drive or disk drive piece is duplicated on another disk. Vendors design their RAID-10 for maximum fault tolerance and performance.

RAID-10 offers a high degree of fault tolerance. In fact, the array can survive even if more than one disk fails. Of course, the loss of both sides of the same mirrored data cannot be tolerated (unless the mirror consists of more than two drives). If the mirror is split across disk cabinets, the loss of an entire cabinet can be tolerated.

## RAID-1 and RAID-10 Recommendations

RAID-10 offers high performance and a high degree of fault tolerance. RAID-1 or RAID-10 should be used when a large volume is required and more than 10 percent of the I/O operations are writes. RAID-1 should be used when the use of only two disk drives can be justified. RAID-1 and RAID-10 recommendations include the following:

- Use RAID-1 or RAID-10 whenever the array experiences more than 10 percent writes. This offers maximum performance and protection.

- Use RAID-1 or RAID-10 when performance is critical. Because RAID-1 and RAID-10 support split seeks, you get premium performance.

- Use write caching on RAID-1 and RAID-10 volumes. Because a RAID-1 or RAID-10 write will not be completed until both writes have been done, performance of writes can be improved through the use of a write cache. Write caching is safe only when used in conjunction with battery–backed up caches.

RAID-1 and RAID-10 are the best fault-tolerant solution in terms of protection and performance, but this protection comes at a cost. You must purchase twice the number of disks than are necessary with RAID-0. If your volume is mostly read, RAID-5 might be acceptable.

## RAID-5

RAID-5 is a fault-tolerant RAID level that uses parity to protect data. Each RAID stripe creates parity information on one disk in the stripe. Along with the other disks in the

RAID stripe, this parity information can be used to re-create the data on any of the other disk drives in the stripe. Thus, a RAID-5 array can tolerate the loss of one disk drive in the array. The parity information is rotated among the various disk drives in the array, as Figure 4-9 shows.

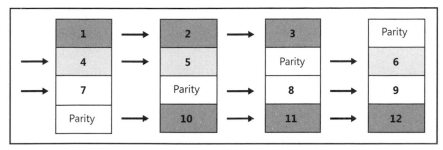

**Figure 4-9**   RAID-5.

The advantage of RAID-5 is that the space available in this RAID level is equal to $n-1$, where $n$ is the number of disk drives in the array. Thus, a RAID-5 array made up of 10 disk drives will have the space of 9 disks, making RAID-5 an economical, fault-tolerant choice.

Unfortunately, there are performance penalties associated with RAID-5. Maintaining the parity information requires additional overhead. When data is written to a RAID-5 array, both the target disk stripe and the parity stripe must be read, the parity must be calculated, and then both stripes must be written out.

A RAID-5 write actually incurs four physical I/O operations (two reads and two writes) for each write to the array. This is important to sizing, where you must design enough disk drives that you do not exceed 125 I/Os per second per disk drive. This has been mentioned in this chapter, and will be covered in more detail in Chapter 6, "Capacity Planning." Specifics are provided in a few paragraphs.

*Avg. reads per disk per second = reads to the array per second / number of drives in the array*

*Avg. writes per disk per second = writes to the array per second \* 4 (RAID overhead) / number of drives in the array*

## RAID-5 Parity

In RAID-5, a parity bit is created on the data in each stripe on all of the disk drives. A parity bit is an additional piece of data that, when created on a set of bits, determines what the other bits are. This parity bit is created by adding up all of the other bits and determining which value the parity bit must contain to create either an even or odd number.

The parity bit, along with all of the remaining bits, can be used to determine the value of a missing bit.

Let's look at an example of how parity works. For this example, we will consider a RAID-5 system with five disk drives. Each disk drive essentially contains bits of data, starting from the first part of the stripe on the disk and ending at the end part of the stripe on the disk. The parity bit is based on the bits from each disk drive.

In this example, we will consider the parity to be even; thus, all of the bits must add up to 0. If the first bit on the first disk drive is 0, the first bit on the second drive is 1, the first bit on the third drive is 1, and the first bit on the fourth drive is 1, the parity must be 1 in order for these bits to add up to an even number, as Table 4-2 shows.

**Table 4-2    An Example of RAID Parity**

| Disk 1 | Disk 2 | Disk 3 | Disk 4 | Disk 5 | |
|--------|--------|--------|--------|--------|--------|
| Bit 1 | Bit 1 | Bit 1 | Bit 1 | Parity Bit | Sum of Bits |
| 0 | 1 | 1 | 1 | 1 | 4 (even) |

Think of the parity as being created on single bits. Even though the disk stripe contains many bits, you make the data recoverable by creating a parity on the single bits.

As you can see from Table 4-2, the parity is actually created on individual bits in the stripes. Even though the disk drives are broken up into chunks or stripe pieces that might be 64 KB or larger, the parity can be created only at the bit level, as shown here. Parity is actually calculated with a more sophisticated algorithm than that just described.

For example, suppose Disk 3 fails. In this case, the parity bit plus the bits from the other disk drives can be used to recover the missing bit from Disk 3 because they must all add up to an even number.

*Creating the Parity*    As you have seen in this section, the RAID-5 parity is created by finding the sum of the same bits on all of the drives in the RAID-5 array and then creating a parity bit so that the result is even. Well, as you might imagine, it is impractical for an array controller to read all of the data from all of the drives each time an I/O operation occurs. This would be inefficient and slow.

When a RAID-5 array is created, the data is initially zeroed out, and the parity bit is created. You then have a set of RAID-5 disk drives with no data but with a full set of parity bits.

From this point on, whenever data is written to a disk drive, both the data disk and the parity disk must be read, then the new data is compared with the old data, and if the data for a particular bit has changed, the parity for that bit must be changed. This is accomplished with an exclusive OR (XOR) operation. Thus, only the data disk and the parity disk, not all of the disks in the array, need to be read. Once this operation has been completed, both disk drives must be written out because the parity operation works on entire stripes. Therefore, for each write to a RAID-5 volume, four physical I/O operations occur: two reads (one from data and one from parity) and two writes (back to data and back to parity). However, with a RAID-5 array, the parity is distributed, so this load should be balanced among all the disk drives in the array. This process consists of the following steps:

1. Write to the RAID-5 array occurs.

2. Current data is read from the disk.

3. Current parity is read from the disk.

4. Exclusive Or (XOR) operation is performed on data and new parity is calculated.

5. Data is written out to the disk.

6. Parity is written out to the disk.

As you can see, RAID-5 incurs significant overhead on writes. However, reads do not incur any additional overhead (unless a drive has failed).

### RAID-5 Recommendations

Because of the additional I/O operations incurred by RAID-5 writes, this RAID level is recommended for disk volumes that are used mostly for reading. Because the parity is distributed among the various disks in the array, all disks are used for read operations. Because of this characteristic, the following suggestions are recommended:

■ **Use RAID-5 on read-only volumes** Any disk volume that does more than 10 percent writes is not a good candidate for RAID-5.

■ **Use write caching on RAID-5 volumes** Because a RAID-5 write will not be completed until two reads and two writes have occurred, the response time of writes can be improved through the use of a write cache. (When using a write cache, be sure that it is backed up by battery power.) However, the write cache is not a cure for overdriving your disk drives. You must still stay within the capacity of those disks.

As you can see, RAID-5 is economical, but you pay a performance price. You will see later in this chapter how high that price can be.

# RAID Performance

To properly configure and tune your RAID system, you must understand the performance differences between the various RAID levels, which the previous section outlined.

By understanding how the RAID system works and how it performs under various conditions, you can better tune your I/O subsystem. This section compares in detail the various performance characteristics that you have seen in the previous section.

## Read Performance

The RAID level you choose will not significantly affect read performance. When read operations are performed on a RAID volume, each drive contributes to the volume's performance. Because random I/O operations are typically the most problematic, they are covered here. You can maximize sequential performance by isolating the sequential I/O operations on their own volume. Let's look at random-read performance under the various RAID levels:

- RAID-0 volumes spread data evenly among all the disks in the array. Thus, random I/O operations should be spread equally among all the disk drives in the system. If we estimate that a particular disk drive can handle 150 random I/O operations per second, a RAID-0 array of 10 disk drives should be able to handle 1500 I/O operations per second.

- RAID-1 volumes support split seeks, so both disk drives perform read operations. Thus, a RAID-1 volume can support twice the number of reads that a single disk can, or 250 I/O reads per second. If reads occur more frequently than that, performance will suffer.

- RAID-10 arrays, like RAID-1 arrays, support split seeks. Therefore the maximum read performance is equal to the number of disk drives multiplied by 150 I/O operations per second. You might be able to initiate I/O operations more frequently, but they will not be completed as quickly as you request them.

- RAID-5 arrays spread the data evenly among all of the disk drives in the array. Even though one disk drive is used for parity in each stripe, all drives are typically used because the I/O operations are random in nature. Thus, as with the RAID-0 array, the read capacity of a RAID-5 array is 150 I/O operations per second multiplied by the number of disk drives in the array. An array running at more than that will reduce SQL Server performance.

As you can see, calculating the read capacity of a RAID array is fairly straightforward. By adding enough disk drives to support your I/O requirements and staying within these limitations, you will optimize your system's performance.

## Write Performance

The type of RAID controller you use dramatically affects write performance. Again, because random I/O operations are typically the most problematic, they are covered here. You can maximize sequential performance by isolating the sequential I/O operations on their own volume or volumes. Let's look at random-write performance under the various RAID levels:

- RAID-0 is the level most capable of handling writes without performance degradation, but you forfeit fault tolerance. Because RAID-0 does not mirror data or use parity, the performance of RAID-0 is simply the sum of the performance of the individual disk drives. Thus, a RAID-0 array of 10 disk drives can handle 1,500 random writes per second.

- RAID-1 arrays must mirror any data that is written to the array. Therefore, a single write to the array will generate two I/O operations to the disk drives. So a RAID-1 array has the read capacity of two disks or 300 I/O Operations Per Second (IOPS) drives but the write capacity of a single disk drive, or 150 IOPS.

- RAID-10 has the same write characteristics as the RAID-1 array does. Each write to the RAID-10 volume generates two physical writes. Thus, the capacity of the RAID-10 array is equivalent to the capacity of one-half of the disk drives in the array.

- RAID-5 arrays are even slower for write operations. A write to a RAID-5 array generates two reads from the disks and two writes to the disks. A write to a RAID-5 array generates four physical I/O operations to the disks. Thus, the write capacity of a RAID-5 array is equivalent to the capacity of one-fourth of the disk drives in the array.

As you can see, calculating the write capacity of a RAID array is a fairly complex operation. By adding enough disk drives to support your I/O requirements and staying within these limitations, you will optimize your system's performance. The next section describes how to calculate the number of I/O operations per disk under various circumstances.

## Disk Calculations

To determine how much load is being placed on the individual disk drives in the system, you must perform some calculations. If you are using a hardware RAID controller, the number of I/O operations per second that Performance Monitor displays is the number of I/O operations that are going to the array. Additional I/O operations that are generated by the controller for fault tolerance are not shown. In fact, Windows 2003 doesn't register that they are occurring, but you must be aware of them for determining the necessary number of disk drives required for optimal performance. The formulas in the following sections can help you determine how many I/O operations are actually going to each disk in the array.

## RAID-0

The rate of I/O operations per disk drive in a RAID-0 array is calculated by adding up all the reads and writes to the array and dividing by the number of disks in the array. RAID-0 requires only the following simple and straightforward equation:

*operations per disk = (reads + writes) / number of disks*

## RAID-1

- With RAID-1, the calculation becomes a little more complicated. Because the number of writes is doubled, the number of I/O operations per disk per second is equal to the number of reads plus two times the number of writes, divided by the number of disk drives in the array (two for RAID-1). The equation is as follows:

  *operations per disk = (reads + (2 * writes)) / 2*

  RAID-1 is slower on writes but offers a high degree of fault tolerance.

## RAID-10

RAID-10 is slow on writes, as is RAID-1, but RAID-10 offers a high degree of fault tolerance. The calculation for RAID-10 is the same as that for RAID-1. Because writes are doubled, the number of I/O operations per disk is equal to the number of reads plus two times the number of writes, divided by the number of disk drives in the array. The equation is as follows:

*operations per disk = (reads + (2 * writes)) / number of disks*

## RAID-5

RAID-5 offers fault tolerance but has a high level of overhead on writes. RAID-5 reads are distributed equally among the various disk drives in the array, but writes cause four physical I/O operations to occur. To calculate the number of I/O operations occurring on the individual disk drives, you must add the reads to four times the number of writes before dividing by the number of disk drives. Thus, the equation for RAID-5 is as follows:

*operations per disk = (reads + (4 * number of writes)) / number of disks*

# RAID Comparison

Let's compare the RAID levels directly. This might better help you to determine which RAID level is best for your system. When you compare I/O performance across RAID levels, one of the most important factors is the read-to-write ratio. The various RAID levels perform comparably when performing reads; only the write rates differ. You should also consider whether your system needs to be fault tolerant. Finally you should be aware of the various cost-to-space ratios. Table 4-3 summarizes the various RAID levels.

Table 4-3   RAID Levels Comparison

| RAID Level | Performance | Fault Tolerance | Cost |
| --- | --- | --- | --- |
| RAID-0 | Best | No fault tolerance | Economical |
| RAID-1 | Good | Good | Expensive |
| RAID-10 | Good | Good | Expensive |
| RAID-5 | Fast reads, slow writes | OK | Most economical with fault tolerance |

As you can see, your best choice really depends on your requirements. To see the difference between RAID-5 and RAID-10 at different read/write ratios, look at the following table. Table 4-4 represents 500 I/O operations per second across 10 disk drives with varying read/write ratios.

Table 4-4   RAID-5 and RAID-10 Comparison

| Read/Write Ratio | RAID-5 I/O Operations (Reads + (4 * Writes)) / Disks | RAID-10 I/O Operations (Reads + (2 * Writes)) / Disks |
| --- | --- | --- |
| 100% reads | (500 + 0) / 10 | (500 + 0) / 10 |
| 0% writes | 50 I/O operations per disk | 50 I/O operations per disk |
| 90% reads | (450 + 200) / 10 | (450 + 100) / 10 |
| 10% writes | 65 I/O operations per disk | 55 I/O operations per disk |
| 75% reads | (375 + 500) / 10 | (375 + 250) / 10 |
| 25% writes | 87.5 I/O operations per disk | 62.5 I/O operations per disk |
| 50% reads | (250 + 1000) / 10 | (250 + 500) / 10 |
| 50% writes | 125 I/O operations per disk | 75 I/O operations per disk |
| 0% reads | (0 + 2000) / 10 | (0 + 1000) / 10 |
| 100% writes | 200 I/O operations per disk | 100 I/O operations per disk |

As you can see, at about 90 percent reads and 10 percent writes, the disk usage is about even. For higher percentages of writes, RAID-5 requires much more overhead.

# Which RAID Level Is Right for You?

Which RAID level is right for you? The answer to this question depends on several factors.

- What are your fault tolerance requirements? Depending on your requirements, based on company policy or legal requirements, you might have more or fewer restrictions that normal.

- What is your budget? Many times compromises are made based on the available budget for your I/O subsystem.

- What are your performance requirements? Often performance requirements outweigh budget requirements if you have strict service level agreements. Your needs will determine your requirements.

Now that you have an overview of how I/O works, let's look at SQL Server I/O requirements.

# SQL Server I/O Overview

SQL Server is especially sensitive to I/O latencies because of the concurrency of transactions within the SQL Server engine. Under normal conditions, tens or hundreds of applications are running against a SQL Server database. To support this concurrency, SQL Server has a complex system of row, page, extent, and table locks, as you will see throughout this book. When a piece of data or a SQL Server resource is locked, other processes must wait for that data or resource to be unlocked.

If I/O operations take excessive amounts of time to complete, these resources will be held for a longer-than-normal period, further delaying other threads processing in the system. In addition, this could lead to a greater chance of deadlocks. The longer the I/O takes to complete, the longer the locks are held, and the potential for problems increases. As a result, individual delays can multiply in a way that could cripple the system.

In addition, query processing will be significantly slower. If long table scans are running on your system, for example, hundreds of thousands or even millions of rows will often need to be read in order to complete the task. Even slight variations in performance become dramatic when applied to a million I/O operations. One million operations at 10 ms each will take approximately 2.8 hours to complete. If your system has overloaded the I/O subsystem and each I/O operation is taking 40 ms, the time to complete this query will increase to more than 11 hours.

As you can see, SQL Server performance can be severely degraded by a poorly sized or poorly configured I/O subsystem. By designing your I/O subsystem to work within the capacity of the individual components, you will find that your system's performance is optimal.

Let's look at what affects SQL Server I/O and why it is important to tune the SQL Server I/O subsystem. We will begin by looking at reads, then writes, and then the transaction log I/Os. Finally, we will look briefly at backup and recovery.

## SQL Server Reads

When a user session wants to read data from the database, it will read either directly from the SQL Server buffer cache, or, if the buffer cache does not have the data that is requested, the data will be read into the buffer cache and then from the buffer cache. If the requested data is in the buffer cache, then it is referred to as a *buffer hit*. If the data is not in the buffer cache it is referred to as a *buffer miss*. The ratio of buffer hits to total buffer requests is called the buffer *cache hit ratio*. For optimal performance the buffer hit ratio should be as close to 100 percent as you can get.

---

**Note**   When a read is made from the database, it is called a logical read since it could be a read from memory or a read from disk. A read from the disk drive is called a physical read. A read from memory takes approximately 100 nanoseconds, while a read from disk will take approximately 8 milliseconds or more.

---

The important point about SQL Server read operations is that the user session will wait on reads to complete before their request will complete. When selecting data from the database, the user will wait on the complete operation including all of the physical reads.

The time it takes to select from the database depends on how much data will be read and how long it takes for those reads to occur. Even with cache reads, the time it takes to read a large amount of data can be significant. With physical reads, the time can be even longer.

SQL Server users actually wait on reads to complete before their SQL statement has completed. As you will see in the next section, SQL Server users will not wait on writes to complete.

## SQL Server Writes

SQL Server writes by the user sessions occur only in the buffer cache. When a change is made, the buffer is modified in the buffer cache. If the data is not already in the cache, it will be read into cache from disk. As a change is made and a COMMIT operation is executed, a log write will occur specifying the changes that have been made, and then the COMMIT operation will complete. The user session will not wait on that data to be written out to disk before proceeding. The changed data will be written out at a later time via either the lazy writer process or the checkpoint process. Checkpoints and the lazy writer will be discussed in more detail in Chapter 14, "Backup Fundamentals ."

User sessions never wait on database writes to complete. The exception is the transaction log. In other words, users wait on reads but not on writes. Therefore, read performance is more important than write performance for the user community's usability experience.

## Transaction Log

The transaction log is used primarily for restoring the database in the event of a data failure and to recover in the event of an instance failure. Whenever a commit operation has been initiated, a commit record must be written into the transaction log before that statement can complete. For this reason, the write performance (mostly sequential) of the transaction log is very important.

## Backup and Recovery

Perhaps the most commonly overlooked I/O considerations for SQL Server are backup and recovery. With most SQL Server systems there is only a small window of opportunity for performing backups. This time must be optimized. Earlier in this chapter you saw illustrations of how a slow I/O subsystem can cause SQL query performance problems. In addition, when performing backups, you must consider not only the I/O performance of the SQL Server database but the network performance and the performance of the disk partition to which you are backing up. The performance of the disk partition to which you are backing up is often overlooked, which can cause backup performance problems. In addition, network throughput can also be an issue. These issues will also be covered in Chapter 14 and Chapter 15, "Restoring Data."

# Planning the SQL Server Disk Layout

As you saw earlier in this chapter, you should configure your I/O system properly to avoid overloading it. Overloading the I/O subsystem causes the I/O latency to increase and degrade SQL Server performance. In this section, you will learn how to build a SQL Server system that can perform within the limitations of your subsystem. The first part of this configuration exercise shows you how to determine the I/O requirements of your system. Then you will plan and create your system.

## Determine I/O Requirements

Determining the I/O requirements of a system that exists as only a concept can be difficult if not impossible. However, if you can't determine the I/O requirements from hard data, you might be able to gather enough data to make an educated guess. In either case, building an I/O subsystem that cannot expand is not a good idea. Always leave some room for required increases in capacity and performance because sooner or later you will need them.

You should design your system to meet a set of minimum requirements based on the amount of space that you need for data storage and on the level of performance you need. In the next sections, you will see how to determine how many disks these factors require.

## Space

Determining the space required by your SQL Server database is easy compared to determining the performance requirements. The amount of space is equal to the sum of the following:

- Space required for data
- Space required for indexes
- Space required for temporary data
- Space required for the transaction log

The space required for data must include enough space to handle data that is added to your database. Your business and your customers will dictate, to a large degree, the amount by which your database will grow. To determine your system's growth rate, check your existing database on a regular basis and calculate the size differences in the amount of space used in it. Calculate this growth rate over several months to determine trends. You might be surprised by the rate at which your data is growing.

In a system without any history, you can estimate the amount of growth by taking the number of product orders, inventory items, and so on, and multiplying that by the estimated row size. Doing this for several periods (perhaps months or years) will give you a rough idea of the rate at which the data files will grow. This will not tell you how much your indexes will grow. The amount of index space per data row depends on how the index is constructed and on the amount of data. A complex index takes more space per row of data than a simple index. It is then up to you and your management to determine whether your system should be able to handle growth for two years, five years, or longer. This will allow you to determine how to configure your I/O subsystem for space.

Once you have determined the amount of data in the database, the size of the indexes, the amount of temporary database space required, and the rate of growth, you can determine how much disk space is required. You must then take into account the effects of using RAID fault tolerance. Remember, RAID-1 or RAID-10 (data mirroring) takes up half the disk space of the physical disk drives. RAID-5 takes up the disk space of one disk of the array. Remember also that the disk size that the manufacturer provides is unformatted space. An unformatted disk drive that is labeled as a 9.1-GB disk is actually an 8.6-GB disk when formatted. Once you have calculated the amount of space currently required and estimated the amount of growth space required, you must then move to the next step: performance. It is necessary to calculate both space and performance requirements and configure your I/O subsystem accordingly.

## Performance

It is not sufficient to simply configure your system to meet the space requirements. As you have seen throughout this chapter, how you configure the I/O subsystem can significantly enhance or severely degrade the performance of your system. However, determining the performance requirements of your I/O subsystem is not nearly as easy as determining the space requirements.

The best way to determine performance requirements is to look at a similar application or system. This data can give you a starting point for estimating future requirements. You will learn much more about this in Chapter 6. Assuming that you find a similar system, you can then use data gathered from that system and the information earlier in this chapter to determine the number of disk drives required. Remember to take into account the RAID level that will be used on that I/O subsystem. The next steps are planning the SQL Server disk layout and then implementing the solution.

# Plan the Disk Layout

Planning the layout involves determining where the data will be positioned and then creating SQL scripts to create the database. The advantage of creating databases with SQL scripts, rather than through SQL Server Enterprise Manager, is that you can reuse a script, modifying it if necessary.

The script should take into account the number of logical volumes that your system has and the number of physical disks in those volumes. It is important to balance the database so that each disk drive will handle roughly the same number of I/O operations per second. An unbalanced system suffers the performance experienced by the slowest volume. You should make sure that the transaction log and the data files are distributed across the disk drives in a way that supports optimal performance.

## Planning the Log

The process of planning where to put the transaction log is fairly simple. Using only one data file for the transaction log is often the best approach. If you must add more log files to the database, be sure to place them on a RAID-1 or RAID-10 volume. Also, be sure to isolate the transaction log from data or other transaction logs.

## Planning the Data Files

The easiest way to configure the I/O subsystem for the data files is to configure each volume with a similar number of similarly sized disk drives. In many cases, you don't need to split the I/O subsystem into multiple volumes. In fact, you might be perfectly happy with one logical volume that spans the entire controller. However, you shouldn't use Windows 2003 striping to span multiple controllers because it adds too much overhead.

---

**Note**   For your data files, span as many disk drives per controller as you can. This allows the controller to distribute the data among multiple disks. Do not use OS striping to span multiple controllers. This incurs too much CPU overhead.

---

If you use multiple controllers, you should simplify the configuration by using similar striping with the same number of disk drives on each controller. If you can't use the same number of disk drives on each of your controllers, you can use proportional filling to properly populate the database.

For example, if you use two volumes, one with 20 disk drives and the other with 10 disk drives, you should create a filegroup with two data files. The first data file should go on the 20-disk volume and be twice as big as the data file on the 10-disk volume. As data is loaded, SQL Server will load twice as much data into the first data file as it loads into the second data file. This should keep the I/O load per disk drive approximately the same.

## Implement the Configuration

Once you have developed your SQL scripts to create the database, it is necessary only to run them and to view the result. If you made a mistake and the database was not created as planned, now is the time to fix it, not after the data has been loaded and users are accessing the system. The use of SQL scripts allows you to modify the scripts and to run them again and again as necessary. An example of a script that uses multiple files within a filegroup to spread the database among several controllers is shown here.

This script will create a database across several drive letters, D, E, and F. With this design, E and F will get twice as many I/Os as D. This design would be used if E and F have twice as many disk drives as D. The L drive is used for the transaction log.

```
CREATE DATABASE demo
ON
PRIMARY ( NAME = demo1,
   FILENAME = 'd:\data\demo_dat1.mdf',
   SIZE = 100MB,
   MAXSIZE = 200,
   FILEGROWTH = 20),
( NAME = demo2,
   FILENAME = 'e:\data\demo_dat2.ndf ',
   SIZE = 200MB,
   MAXSIZE = 200,
   FILEGROWTH = 20),
( NAME = demo3,
   FILENAME = 'f:\data\demo_dat3.ndf ',
   SIZE = 200MB,
```

```
    MAXSIZE = 200,
    FILEGROWTH = 20)
LOG ON
( NAME = demolog1,
    FILENAME = 'l:\data\demo_log1.ldf ',
    SIZE = 100MB,
    MAXSIZE = 200,
    FILEGROWTH = 20) ;
GO
```

The information in this section and throughout the chapter should help you create an optimal I/O subsystem for your SQL Server system.

## Summary

In this chapter you have been introduced to the fundamentals of I/O and performance characteristics of disk drives and RAID. Because I/O performance is so important to SQL Server, you must carefully plan and design the SQL Server System. This has been briefly covered here and will be covered in future chapters as well. It is important that the I/O subsystem be monitored and tuned as necessary. In Chapter 6, you will see how to monitor and benchmark the storage system to plan for the future.

This chapter provided the fundamentals and basics of I/O performance. The chapter started with the fundamentals of disk drive performance. These fundamentals are important since the disk drive is the basic building block of most I/O subsystems. By exceeding the capacity of these components, the response time or latency of the I/O subsystem will increase. This will cascade into poor SQL Server performance, potential blocking, or even deadlocks. In addition to disk drives, the RAID level that you select can also adversely influence the performance of your I/O subsystem. Careful design and planning can help alleviate some of these problems. Determining how much hardware you actually need is the act of sizing and is discussed in Chapter 6. A properly sized system will provide for good performance and flexibility for changes over time. Remember the fundamentals, and add capacity as necessary.

# Chapter 5

# 32-Bit Versus 64-Bit Platforms and Microsoft SQL Server 2005

## CPU Basics

The CPU, or central processing unit, is the brains of the computer system. The *CPU* handles the processing of the commands that run the operating system, SQL Server, and user programs. The CPU chip includes the processing system and some memory that can be used for instructions and data. The CPU that most of us use on a regular basis is known as the x86 processor.

The x86 processor has been around since the late 70's, and we have come a long way in that time. Today's PCs and servers are based on the Intel 8086 processor. The 8086, introduced in 1978, marked the beginning of the x86 architecture. The 8086 was a 16-bit processor. This was soon followed by the 80186 and 80286 processors, which were also 16-bit. However, with new technology, the 80286 was actually able to access up to 16 megabytes (MB) of RAM. This was quite an accomplishment in those days, but who would ever be able to use an entire 16 MB of RAM anyway?

The Intel 80386 processor, introduced in 1986, was the third generation of x86 chips. The 80386 was also known as the i386. The i386 introduced us to 32-bit processing. With 32-bit processing and a virtual memory architecture, it was now possible to address up to 4 gigabytes (GB). With virtual memory, it was possible for the operating system to actually address up to 4 GB of RAM (2 GB for user and 2 GB for operating system) even though nobody would actually ever have an actual computer system with 4 GB of actual RAM in it.

In contrast with this quick 8-year succession from the 16-bit processor to the 32-bit processor, it took an amazing 20 years for the mainstream introduction of 64-bit processors. This is not to say that there weren't 64-bit processors available during that time; there most certainly were, as you will see later in this chapter. However, in 2006 the 64-bit processor is finally becoming mainstream and starting to replace the 32-bit systems.

# 64-Bit Versus 32-Bit Addressing

The introduction of the Intel *EM64T processor* and the *AMD Opteron* (AMD64) processors have brought 64-bit technology to the mainstream. The primary advantage of the 64-bit architecture is its ability to access larger amounts of data. With 32-bit systems, both virtual and physical memory is limited. There are some workarounds to allow for more physical memory, but the virtual memory limitation cannot be overcome with 32-bit processors.

## Virtual Memory

When physical memory was limited to 64 kilobytes and was very expensive, virtual memory was introduced. *Virtual memory* is a technique by which a process in a computer system can address memory whose size and addressing is not coupled to the physical memory of the system. This allows multiple processes to take full advantage of the system even though there is not enough memory to fully accommodate all of them at the same time.

Virtual memory works in conjunction with paging. With paging, memory is moved between physical memory and a paging area on disk. This allows data to be moved out of physical memory to make room for other processes, while keeping that data available for the process that is using it.

When virtual memory was first introduced, it seemed unlikely that the amount of physical memory would exceed the virtual address space. The microprocessor's early developers may have assumed that the 32-bit architecture would not last 20 years without being replaced. Yet, several years ago, 32-bit systems began shipping with more than 4 GB of memory.

This introduced a dilemma. The systems can have more than 4 GB of memory, but the virtual memory address space, or the amount of memory a single process can address, is still limited to 4 GB. With the addition of *PAE* (Page Address Extension) and *AWE* (Address Windowing Extension), SQL Server can use more than 4 GB of memory. However, this memory can be used only for the SQL Server buffer cache. This memory cannot be used for connection memory or procedure cache.

### Real World    Virtual Memory Can Be a Problem

With large numbers of user connections, it is possible to reach the limits on available SQL Server connections. It has been my experience that connection problems occur with a large number of SQL Server sessions. These problems typically occur with between 4,000 and 5,000 users, depending on what the users are doing. This is a virtual memory problem, not a physical memory problem. Regardless of the amount of physical memory in the system, because SQL Server runs as one process, it is limited to 2 GB (3 GB with the /3-GB flag) for virtual memory. It is this memory that causes connection problems. Hence, physical memory is not the only problem.

With the introduction of 64-bit processors, these limitations are for now no longer an issue. With 64-bit processors, both the virtual and physical memory limitations are much higher than with 32-bit processors. Although SQL Server has been running on 64-bit systems since SQL Server 6.0 on Alpha, PowerPC, and MIPS platforms, the new EM64T and Opteron processors are now making 64-bit processing mainstream. Currently, with SQL Server 2005, Microsoft supports SQL Server on x86, x86 64, and Itanium 2 platforms.

The EM64T and Opteron processors can access up to 256 *terabytes* of virtual memory ($2^{48}$ bytes). The architecture allows this limit to be increased to a maximum of 16 *exabytes* ($2^{64}$ bytes). Although this is suitable for today's computing power, it might or might not be sufficient in another 20 years.

### Physical Memory

Currently, 32-bit systems using PAE and AWE can support up to 64 GB of physical memory. This is sufficient for many databases, but with databases getting larger and larger, soon this will be insufficient. With 64-bit systems, the amount of physical memory has greatly increased. However, it will probably be quite a while before systems will actually support this much memory.

The initial wave of systems that support the EM64T and Opteron processors can currently address up to 1 terabyte of virtual memory ($2^{40}$ bytes). The architecture allows this limit to be increased to a maximum of 4 petabytes ($2^{52}$ bytes). This should be sufficient for the foreseeable future.

## Hardware Platforms

SQL Server 2005 is supported on three platforms: the x86 platform, the x86-64 (or x64) platform, and the Itanium platform. The x86 platform is 32-bits, and the x64 and

Itanium platforms are 64-bit. These platforms are all generally available from various vendors. The x86 and x64 chips are very similar, and the Itanium uses a different architecture. This section provides a brief overview of the different chip architectures.

## x86

As discussed earlier in this chapter, the x86 architecture is the product of an evolution that started with the 8086 processor back in 1978. The architecture has been enhanced and clock speeds have been increased, but it is still compatible with operating systems and programs that run on the 80386 chipset. With later versions of the x86 chips, systems can support up to 64 GB of RAM using PAE and AWE. Recently, both Intel and AMD have introduced processors that support both the x86 and x64 architectures on the same system. In fact, all x64 systems are also x86 systems, depending on what operating system you are running. The x86 architecture is summarized in Table 5-1.

**Table 5-1   x86 Architecture Memory Summary**

|                  | Value         | Notes                                             |
| ---------------- | ------------- | ------------------------------------------------- |
| Physical memory  | 4 GB / 64 GB  | > 4 GB requires PAE                               |
| Virtual memory   | 4 GB          | 3 GB for user memory*<br>1 GB for kernel memory*  |

* Although the x86 architecture can use 3 GB for user and 1 GB for kernel memory, the default is 2 GB and 2 GB for user and kernel. The operating system must flag the CPU that it wants to use 3 GB for user memory. In Windows, this is done with the /3 GB flag.

Although the x86 has been around for a long time, it is still the mainstream processor used worldwide. In the next few years, however, I expect to see the x64 architecture take over.

## x64

The x64 platform is very flexible in that it is both a 32-bit processor and a 64-bit processor, depending on what operating system you install. If you install a 32-bit version of Windows Server 2003 on it, the system works as an x86 processor including PAE and AWE support. If you install Windows Server 2003 x64 on any x86-64 system, it will run as a 64-bit system.

One of the primary advantages of the x64 architecture is that when you are running a 64-bit version of Windows, 32-bit programs run perfectly well. There is no loss of performance, nor are there for the most part any compatibility problems. However, if you are going to run the 64-bit version of Windows Server 2003, it is recommended that you run the 64-bit version of SQL Server 2005. The x64 architecture is summarized in Table 5-2.

**Table 5-2   x64 Architecture Memory Summary**

|  | Value | Notes |
|---|---|---|
| Physical memory | 1 terabyte | Later will be increased to 4 petabytes |
| Virtual memory | 256 terabyte | Architecture supports 16 exabytes |

> **Note**   The x64 architecture summary table refers to the x64 architecture running in 64-bit mode.

Because of the flexibility and performance of the x64 architecture, I expect to see the industry moving to 64-bit very quickly. In fact, most server systems are currently shipping with this processor.

## Itanium

The Itanium architecture is also known as the IA-64 architecture. This architecture was developed in 1989 when HP collaborated with Intel to develop a replacement for its PA-RISC line of processors. Microsoft has ported versions of Windows XP, Windows 2000, and Windows 2003 for the Itanium processor, and SQL Server is supported on Windows 2000 and Windows 2003 Itanium 2 platforms. The Itanium 2 processor is fairly popular, and there are many SQL Server implementations on Itanium 2.

### Itanium 2 Versus x86-64

My opinion is that the x86-64 processor will very soon become the platform of choice for 64-bit SQL Server. Because of its flexibility, price, and the fact that it has already replaced all i386 chips for the server, I believe that the Itanium 2 platform will soon be used only for large Unix servers. There will still be a few companies that prefer the Itanium 2 platform, but they will be a small minority.

The Itanium 2 processor is a 64-bit processor that can run some Windows 32-bit programs in a 32-bit emulation mode. This emulation mode is not very efficient, and 32-bit programs are not known to work very well on the Itanium 2 platform. This is why it is recommended that 64-bit SQL Server be run on this platform. There is a version of SQL Server 2000 for Itanium 2, but only the server components are available. All management must be done from a 32-bit system. The Itanium 2 architecture is summarized in Table 5-3.

**Table 5-3    Itanium 2 Architecture Memory Summary**

|  | Value | Notes |
| --- | --- | --- |
| Physical memory | 1 petabyte | Physical addressing is 50-bits. |
| Virtual memory | 16 exabytes | This is the full 64-bit address. |

One key advantage of the Itanium 2 processor is that it is typically found in higher-end systems. While you are most likely to find the EM64T and Opteron processors in 2 through 8 CPU systems, you might see high-end systems support up to 128 Itanium processors in a single system. This is an advantage for high-end customers. These systems are usually very high-end with exceptional levels of support, I/O bandwidth, and expandability.

# Windows Versions

There are a number of Windows Server versions available that accommodate SQL Server 2005. Each of these systems has its own advantages and limitations. This section provides an overview of the various choices.

## Windows 2000

Windows 2000 is available in both an x86 and an Itanium version. Windows 2000 includes many improvements over Windows NT. Advancements include an improved memory management system and improved networking capabilities, as well as improvements in the domain administration and functionality.

Windows 2000 is available in Server, Advanced Server, and Datacenter Server Editions. The Server Edition is more limited than the Advanced Server Edition in both the number of CPUs supported and the amount of RAM supported. Datacenter Server Edition is enhanced in support of processors and memory as well as in the enhanced technical support that it is available for it. Because Windows 2000 has been rendered obsolete by Windows Server 2003, it will not be covered in detail in this book.

**Note**    The limits of SQL Server 2005 depend on both the version of Windows that you are running and the version of SQL Server.

# Windows Server 2003

At the time of this book's publication, Windows Server 2003 is the most current version of Windows available. Windows Server 2003 is available in an x86, an x64, and an Itanium version. Windows Server 2003 includes many improvements over Windows 2000, including Active Directory.

From a purely SQL Server point of view, the most important features that were provided in Windows Server 2003 were the x64 support and the enhanced PAE support for x86. In addition, clustering was greatly improved in Windows Server 2003. Like Windows 2000, Windows Server 2003 comes in a variety of editions, including Standard Edition, Enterprise Edition, and Datacenter Edition. The features of the Windows Server 2003 32-bit editions are shown in Table 5-4.

**Table 5-4   Windows Server 2003 32-Bit Editions**

| Feature | Standard Edition | Enterprise Edition | Datacenter Edition |
| --- | --- | --- | --- |
| Maximum RAM | 4 GB | 64 GB | 64 GB |
| Maximum number of CPUs | 4 | 8 | 32 |
| Clustering | No | Yes | Yes |

The variety allows you to choose what you need and avoid purchasing software that you don't need.

# Windows Server 2003 64-Bit editions

Windows Server 2003 is also available in 64-bit editions for both the x64 and Itanium platforms. As with Windows Server 2003 for the x86 platform, these platforms also come in several different editions. SQL Server 2005 is available for both the x64 and Itanium versions of Windows Server 2003. The features of the Windows Server 2003 64-bit editions are shown in Table 5-5.

**Table 5-5   Windows Server 2003 64-Bit Editions**

| Feature | Standard Edition | Enterprise Edition | Datacenter Edition |
| --- | --- | --- | --- |
| Maximum RAM | 32 GB | 1 TB | 1 TB |
| Maximum number of CPUs | 4 | 8 | 64 |
| Clustering | No | Yes | Yes |

**Note**   The Itanium Edition of Windows Server 2003 is available only in Enterprise and Datacenter Editions.

## Windows Comparison

The version of Windows that you choose depends on the number of CPUs that you require and the amount of memory that you want to utilize. This must be chosen in conjunction with the version of SQL Server. In order to utilize a 64-bit version of SQL Server, you must be running a 64-bit version of Windows. The 64-bit version of SQL Server can be very useful when large databases are being supported.

# SQL Server 2005 Options

Like Windows, SQL Server also comes in a variety of editions. These editions allow you to choose the features and functionality that you need and avoid paying for features that you don't need. SQL Server 2005 is available in Express, Developer, Mobile, Workgroup, Standard, and Enterprise Editions. This book is geared more towards the server market, so we won't cover Express, Developer, Mobile, and Workgroup Editions in this chapter. Some of the key differences between the editions are shown in Table 5-6.

**Table 5-6   SQL Server 2005 Editions**

| Feature | Standard Edition | Enterprise Edition |
| --- | --- | --- |
| Maximum RAM | OS maximum | OS maximum |
| Maximum number of CPUs | 4 | Unlimited |
| Partitioning | No | Yes |
| Parallel index operations | No | Yes |
| Indexed views | No | Yes |
| Mirroring and clustering | Yes | Yes |
| Online indexing and restore | No | Yes |
| Integration Services  Advanced Transforms | No | Yes |

Of course, there are many more features, most of which work on both Standard and Enterprise Editions. This table shows only some of the key features. Chapter 8, "Installing and Upgrading Microsoft SQL Server 2005," provides a more complete discussion of the differences.

## SQL Server 32-Bit Edition

The differences between SQL Server 2005 32-bit edition and SQL Server 2005 64-bit edition have been presented throughout this chapter. SQL Server 32-bit edition can be installed on either a 32-bit or 64-bit version of Windows, but there are a few issues to consider when selecting the appropriate installation.

## Running 32-Bit SQL Server 2005 on 32-Bit Windows 2003 Server

The most common choice for SQL Server 2005 32-bit is to run on 32-bit Windows Server 2003. If you are running Windows Server 2003 32-bit, then SQL Server 2005 32-bit is your only choice. With the 32-bit version of the operating system and the database, you are limited by all of the 32-bit limitations mentioned above. By taking advantage of PAE and AWE, you can take advantage of memory above 4 GB for SQL Server data buffers only.

### 32-Bit SQL Server on 64-Bit Windows

It is possible to run SQL Server 2005 32-bit on Windows Server 2003 64-bit. This can be a good solution if you are planning to upgrade to SQL Server 2005 64-bit at a later time because you will be required only to upgrade SQL Server at a later time. Having the 64-bit version of Windows Server 2003 does not provide a noticeable performance difference over the 32-bit version of Windows. If you want to use more than 4 GB of RAM, you still must use AWE enabled, and other 32-bit limitations are in effect.

When installing the 32-bit version of SQL Server 2005 on the x64 version of Windows Server 2003, SQL Server uses the Windows on Windows 64 subsystem (WOW64). The WOW64 subsystem is the compatibility mode that allows 32-bit programs to run natively in 32-bit mode on the 64-bit operating system. SQL Server operates in 32-bit mode even though the underlying operating system is 64-bit. This is one of the biggest advantages of x64 over Itanium.

**Note**   The x86 32-bit version of SQL Server 2005 is not supported on the Itanium platform.

## SQL Server 64-Bit

In order to run the 64-bit version of SQL Server 2005, you must have the 64-bit version of Windows Server 2003. With this combination, you can benefit from all of the advantages of running in a 64-bit environment. With the 32-bit version of SQL Server, you have the option of Windows Server 2003 32-bit or 64-bit version, but with SQL Sever 2005 64-bit, your only option is to run on a 64-bit version of Windows Server 2003. Remember, there are two options for 64-bit Windows 2003: Itanium and EM64T/Opteron processor families.

**Note**   You cannot run the 64-bit version of SQL Server 2005 on a 32-bit version of Windows Server 2003.

# Taking Advantage of 64-Bit SQL Server

In this chapter you have learned about the limitations of the 32-bit architecture. These drawbacks limit both virtual memory and physical memory. Both of these limits have been known to cause problems with SQL Server users. The virtual memory limitation can restrict the number of connections into SQL Server because of running out of virtual memory. The physical memory limitation can restrict the amount of SQL Server buffer cache and procedure cache. For large databases you might require large amounts of SQL Server cache in order to perform optimally.

### Real World    Size Matters

The amount of SQL Server memory that is allocated is very important, especially as databases increase in size. Years ago, the standard practice was to size the buffer cache as 20 percent of the size of the database. Thus for a 100-GB database, the amount of memory allocated for SQL Server is 10 GB. As databases reached terabytes in size, that became impractical. Today's rule of thumb is 5 percent to 10 percent of the database size. In order to achieve this value, 64-bit memory addressing is probably essential.

If you are using SQL Server in an environment with a relatively small number of users and a fairly small database, you still might consider using the 32-bit version of Windows Server 2003 and SQL Server 2005. However, in the next few years, I believe that the 32-bit versions will begin to be phased out. It might become difficult to find server systems that are not 64-bit capable. I have yet to find any real downsides to running a 64-bit capable processor in 64-bit mode rather than in 32-bit mode.

> **Important**    Even though SQL Server 2005 x64 should be considered equivalent to the 32-bit (with enhancements), you should use the version that is recommended by your application software vendor. If the software vendor has not certified with the 64-bit version, you might not be supported by them even if 64-bit isn't the problem.

Here are a few guidelines on when SQL Server 2005 64-bit is recommended:

- **The number of sessions is very large.**    If your concurrent user count and sessions are in the thousands, you are a candidate for 64-bit.

- **The database is medium to large.**    If your database is over 100 GB, then you are a candidate for 64-bit.

- **The database will experience heavy growth.**    If the growth of either of the first two items is significant, then consider 64-bit.

- **You want to stay ahead of the curve.**    Eventually the 32-bit versions of SQL Server 2005, or later, will be phased out. Eventually you will not be able to purchase Windows for 32-bit, just like you cannot run Windows on 16-bit processors. 64-bit is here to stay.

In the meantime, there is still a significant number of users who are not yet ready to throw out all of their hardware and go to 64-bit platforms. The next section discusses the simple steps necessary to take advantage of upper memory on 32-bit systems.

## Utilizing Large Memory with the 32-Bit Version of SQL Server 2005

To enable 32-bit memory on the 32-bit version of SQL Server 2005, there are only two steps:

1. Set the SQL Server configuration parameter "awe enabled" to 1. This parameter is set to 0 by default. This parameter enables AWE mode, which allows the use of memory > 4 GB.

2. Set the max server memory parameter to a number greater than 4 GB.

In SQL Server 2005, the amount of AWE is dynamic and the memory allocated for SQL Server is somewhere between "min server memory" and "max server memory." In earlier versions of SQL Server, AWE memory was not dynamic.

---

**Note**    In order to utilize AWE memory, the user account under which SQL Server runs must be granted the Lock Pages In Memory option.

---

It is a big improvement that AWE memory is now dynamic. With Windows 2000, AWE memory was fixed. Whenever you started up SQL Server, the amount of memory configured in "max server memory" was allocated by SQL Server. This memory was not released until SQL Server is shut down.

---

**Important**    Do not allow SQL Server to use too much memory. This could cause paging in Windows. Always try to leave at least 1 to 2 GB for the operating system.

## Utilizing Large Memory with the 64-Bit Version of SQL Server 2005

With the 64-bit version of SQL Server, it is not necessary to make any operating system or SQL Server configuration changes. Simply set the initialization parameters "min server memory" and "max server memory," and SQL Server will dynamically allocate memory within that range. It is possible to enable the awe enabled flag to guarantee that the memory allocated for SQL Server is not swappable. In earlier versions of SQL Server, the parameter "set working set size" indicated that SQL Server memory was not swappable. This flag has been depreciated.

## Summary

In this chapter you have seen the advantages of running SQL Server in 64-bit mode. There are only a few advantages, including virtual and physical memory increases. However, these advantages are significant. Whether you can take advantage of the features of 64-bit or not really depends on your configuration and your database size.

If your database is fairly small (less than 10 GB) and you are not experiencing any performance problems due to I/O and memory issues, then 32-bit SQL Server might be right for you. However, if you have a large database and you are doing extensive I/O, you will probably benefit from more memory and increased efficiency.

### Real World    Memory Won't Solve All of Your Problems

If you are in an environment in which you are doing a significant number of I/O operations and are experiencing I/O problems, you might benefit from more memory. However, keep in mind that it won't eliminate all I/O problems from occurring. Regardless of how much buffer cache you have, checkpoints always generates significant I/O operations. The transaction log generates the same amount of I/O operations regardless of the amount of memory, and backups will be the same.

The benefits of 64-bit are significant when you have large databases and when you can benefit from an increased cache-hit ratio. The rule of thumb is to set "max server memory" sufficiently high so that the buffer cache is 5 to 10 percent of the database size. This might be achievable with 32-bit, but if you are going to use more than 4 GB of RAM and you already have the hardware, I recommend that you try 64-bit.

# Chapter 6
# Capacity Planning

Two of the biggest challenges in the IT world are sizing and capacity planning. Sizing and capacity planning are related tasks which involve determining how much hardware and software is needed in order to optimally run your applications. A system that is oversized is a waste of money. A system that is undersized could perform poorly and cost you a large amount of money and business. Sizing and capacity planning involve mathematics, skill, and instinct, and even then you can get it wrong. In this chapter, you will learn some of the fundamentals of sizing and capacity planning.

As with many database tasks, sizing and capacity planning are not an exact science. In order to be successful at capacity planning, you must be imaginative and willing to take a risk. It is not uncommon for a full-blown production system not to behave as expected when the capacity planning exercise was done. Not everything is predictable. In this chapter you will learn about sizing and capacity planning, service level agreements, and some techniques for monitoring and benchmarking and load testing your system.

# Principles of Capacity Planning

Capacity planning is the activity that results in an estimate of resources that are required to run your system optimally. Capacity planning is a crucial activity in planning both hardware and software resources. The process has two distinct operations: *Sizing* is the act of determining the resources required for a new system; *capacity planning* is the act of determining what resources are required to be added to your existing system in order to meet future load requirements.

## Capacity Planning Versus Sizing

Capacity planning and sizing each serve a similar purpose: to determine the amount and types of resources necessary to meet future load requirements. The difference is in the amount and type of data that is available to determine the future load. With capacity planning you have available to you performance data that can be gathered from an existing system. This data can be used as a basis of calculations that can be extrapolated to the future load. For example, if you are currently running a SQL Server system with 500 concurrent users, you can use this data to extrapolate the load that will be generated by the addition of 250 concurrent users. This calculation might not be simple, but at least you have a starting point.

When sizing a system that currently has no baseline data associated with it, there can be no extrapolation. For example, if you are migrating from an ERP system that is Oracle-based to a SQL Server-based ERP system, you can get some data from the existing system, but in general the performance data from the Oracle system is not helpful when performing a SQL Server sizing. However, any data is better than no data. Whether you are sizing a system or performing a capacity planning exercise, you must use the data available to you, calculate estimated workloads, do your research, and add in a little bit of guesswork.

The desired result of a capacity planning or sizing exercise is to accurately determine what hardware and software are needed in order to meet your service level agreement, which is explained in the following section, based on a predetermined workload. You should design the system to be able to handle peak workloads and to perform as required. You should sufficiently size the system to meet the requirements without over-designing the system. If you over-design the system, you will end up spending more money than is required without significantly improving system performance. If you under-design the system, the service level agreement will not be met, and you will get angry phone calls.

# Service Level Agreements

The *service level agreement* (SLA) is a contract, either formal or informal, between the IT organization and the customer defining the level of service that will be provided to them. The customer might be the end users, the call center, or another organization within your company. The SLA might specify a number of different items that guarantee uptime, response times, phone wait times, and other requirements. Some of the things that might be included in an SLA include the following:

- **Average response time**  Specifies the average response time for each transaction, query, and operation that the user might perform; will be an "average not to exceed" specification

- **90 percent response time**  Specifies a value that 90 percent of all transactions, queries, and operations must achieve

- **Maximum response time**  Specifies a value that 100 percent of all transactions, queries, and operations must achieve

- **Uptime requirement**  Specifies how much the system must be up and available for users and should include a window for performing regularly scheduled tasks

- **Disaster recovery time**  Specifies how soon the system must be back online at the disaster recovery site in the event of a catastrophic failure

The SLA should be written in such a way that both the customer and the IT department are protected. The IT department should only join into a contract that it can fulfill and include clauses that require the customer to inform it of changes to the system load.

Let's look at an example of some specific items that might be in an SLA, shown in Figure 6-1.

***

**Note**  The example shown in Figure 6-1 illustrates a simple SLA with general terms. An actual SLA would be more detailed and comprehensive.

**Real World   Service Level Agreements: Protect Yourself**

It is important that an SLA is not a one-sided agreement. You should make sure that you protect yourself by specifying what parameters the agreement covers. For example, if you specify guaranteed response times, you should specify that this is for a specific user load. If the customer were to double the user load from 500 concurrent users to 1,000 concurrent users without informing you, this should violate the SLA. Thus, you should specify the user count for which the agreement is valid, and you can consider specifying how much notice you should be given for an addition of new users, as shown in the sample SLA in Figure 6-1. This notice gives you time to add hardware if necessary. Create an agreement that you can live up to.

You should make sure that the SLA is something that you can meet and exceed. You must then develop metrics and processes for measuring your system in order to validate that the SLA is being met.

The following operations must meet the following response time criteria during the hours of 6 a.m. and 10 p.m. Monday through Friday:

| Operation | Avg. Response Time | 90 Percent Response Time | Max Response Time |
|---|---|---|---|
| Customer account query | 2 seconds | 3 seconds | 5 seconds |
| Add new customer | 1 second | 2 seconds | 4 seconds |
| Monthly sales report | 5 minutes | 7.5 minutes | 10 minutes |

- The database must be available during the hours of 4 a.m. to 11 p.m. Monday through Friday.

- The system will be unavailable due to maintenance during the hours of 1 a.m. to 6 a.m. every Saturday.

This agreement is valid for up to 500 concurrent users. The customer will give the IT department notice 60 days before the addition of concurrent users in excess of 500.

Figure 6-1   An example service level agreement.

## Mathematics of Capacity Planning

The fundamentals of sizing and capacity planning are based on queuing theory. *Queuing theory* is the mathematics that governs the effects of multiple entities all using the same resources. For those of you hoping that you would never have to do mathematics again, I apologize. Sizing, capacity planning, and performance tuning are all about mathematics.

The concept of queuing theory is quite straight-forward. Before jumping into queuing theory we will start by defining two terms: *service time* and *wait time,* or *queue time.* Service time is the time that the action that you are measuring takes to complete. Wait time, or queue time, is the time that the action that you are measuring is waiting for all of the jobs ahead of it to complete. The response time of your job is equal to the service time plus the queue time, as this formula shows:

```
response time = service time + queue time
```

For example, the time it takes you to make a deposit at the bank is the sum of the time it takes to make the deposit, plus the time you have spent waiting in line. Total task time is measured in the same way with almost every operation in your computer hardware and software.

The amount of time spent queuing depends on the capacity of the resource used. In some cases there is no queuing, and in other cases there is significant queuing. In Figure 4-4 in Chapter 4, "I/O Subsystem Planning and RAID Configuration," you saw how latencies increased as you neared the capacity of the disk drive. This is true throughout the computer system. A lightly used resource might experience no queuing, but the closer you get to the capacity of the resource, the higher the chance of queuing. When you reach the capacity of a device you are guaranteed to queue.

For example, if there are four bank tellers, and four customers arrive at the bank at the same time, there is a chance that you won't have to wait in line (if there is nobody already in line). However, if five people arrive in line at exactly the same time, then there is a 100 percent probability that someone will have to wait. If there is one teller, if it takes one minute for each transaction, and if there are 10 people arriving over a 10-minute period, there is a chance that they won't have to wait (if they arrive at exactly one-minute intervals).

Thus, the closer you get to the maximum capacity of any resource, such as bank tellers, disk drives, CPU, and so on, the more chance you have of queuing. When you reach the maximum capacity of the resource, you have a 100 percent chance of queuing, and then queuing increases as the utilization increases. The chance of having to wait depends on how close you are to the capacity of the resource, as Figure 6-2 shows.

Queuing theory, as it pertains to sizing and capacity planning, has two components:

1.  The chance of queuing increases exponentially as you near the capacity of the resource.

2.  The response time is equal to the sum of the service time plus the queue time.

The rest of this chapter will use these concepts to explain capacity planning and sizing.

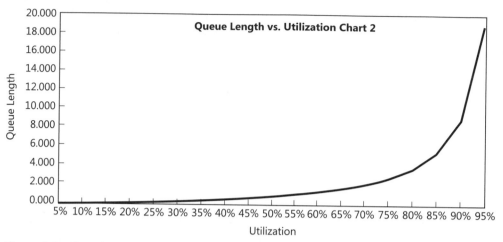

**Figure 6-2**  Queuing vs. utilization.

You can see in the first graph in Figure 6-2 how the chance of queuing changes the slope of the curve at about 80 percent. We try to size for this area, called the knee of the curve, when determining the amount of resources that we want to allocate when sizing a system. As you learned in Chapter 4, we will try to do no more than 100 I/Os per second (IOPS) per disk drive because this number is approximately 75 percent of the capacity of the disk drive. This is true of I/O, CPU, and network.

# CPU Capacity Planning

The CPU performance is a finite entity within the computer system. There are a finite number of CPUs in a system, and each CPU has a finite number of CPU cycles that can be used per second. Fortunately for us, there are CPU counters available in the Windows Performance Monitor, or perfmon. These CPU counters provide utilization information based on 100 percent utilization. In this section we will look at sizing CPUs and monitoring CPU utilization.

## Sizing CPUs

Sizing CPUs is the process of allocating a sufficient number and type of CPUs so that normal On-Line Transaction Processing systems operate at less than or equal to 75 percent CPU utilization. This is so excessive CPU queuing does not occur and response times are reasonable. This might seem like a fairly easy thing to do, but with newer and faster CPUs being introduced every day, how can you determine what number will be? This isn't an easy question to answer. Read the specifications on the processors and try to understand the different features of the chips. Some factors that affect performance and scalability are the following:

- **CPU cache** The larger the CPU cache, the more scalability you will get in a multi-processor system.

- **Dual (or Quad or more) core chips** A dual core processor actually has two CPUs in one. However, they may or may not be sharing the same cache.

- **Hyperthreading** This technique takes advantage of normally idle CPU cycles. It looks like an additional CPU to the OS, but it really isn't one and doesn't provide the performance of an additional CPU.

- **CPU bus bandwidth** The more bandwidth available to the CPU the better. As you have more and more CPUs, the change of having collisions on the bus increases (since the bandwidth is finite). A higher bandwidth bus allows more processing to take place without bus contention.

As this list shows, there are many factors to take into account, but I'm sorry to say there is no magic formula to calculate the number of CPUs. The way to size CPUs is to take whatever data you have today and extrapolate the effect of your changes.

Typically, CPU scalability with SQL Server is in the range of 60 to 80 percent. Adding a CPU to a one-CPU system should give you 60 to 80 percent more performance. However, depending on your application, your performance will vary. The features identified above all have an effect on CPU scalability.

You might be wondering why I mentioned that this applies to OLTP systems. In OLTP systems we are concerned about response time and the user experience. Thus, we are concerned that we do not see excessive queuing that leads to increased response times. In batch systems the concern is for throughput (how much work is being done) and not response time. Therefore, it is acceptable to be at 100 percent CPU utilization since the response times might be in minutes or hours.

## Monitoring CPU Usage

A quick and easy way to see how much CPU is being utilized in the system is via the Windows Task Manager. Task Manager provides a graphical view of the percentage of CPU being used by all the processors in the system. The CPU and memory performance views are selected by clicking on the Performance tab in Windows Task Manager. The CPU and memory view of Task Manager is shown in Figure 6-3.

---

**Note** CPU and memory are somewhat unique in that they both have a finite value. Both CPU and memory can reach 100 percent utilization. When CPU reaches 100 percent utilization, tasks queue up waiting for the CPU to become available. When memory reaches 100 percent utilization, other memory is paged out. However, both cause performance problems.

In Figure 6-3, you can see the CPU utilization in the top left box with the CPU history (for each CPU, core, or hyperthread CPU) to the right. Below that is the Page File utilization with its history to the right. Underneath are additional data for the following:

- **Totals**   This provides a quick view of processes, handles, and threads.

- **Physical Memory**   This is the actual RAM in the system and includes total, how much is available and how much is used for system cache.

- **Commit Charge**   How much memory has been allocated to the operating system and to programs. This includes the total, peak, and how much the memory is limited (RAM plus paging file).

- **Kernel Memory**   The memory used by the operating system kernel is shown as a total and how much is paged and nonpaged memory.

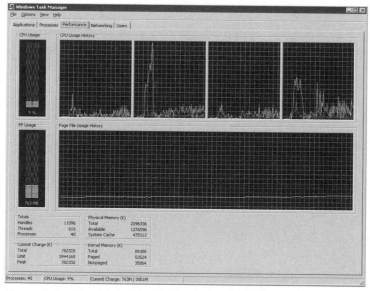

**Figure 6-3**   The performance view of Task Manager.

In addition, CPU utilization can be measured from the processor performance object within perfmon. Perfmon is the Windows Performance Monitor and is invoked from the Start menu by selecting Administrative Tools, then Performance. Perfmon is made up of objects, such as Processor, Processes, Physical Disk, etc., and counters such as the ones listed here. The actual CPU utilization is measured via the following counters:

- **Percent processor time**   The total percentage of time that the CPU is active based on the total capacity of the CPU

- **Percent user time**   The total CPU utilization for user programs; represents work done on behalf of user programs

- **Percent privileged time**   The CPU utilization for the Windows operating system; includes the operating system functions as well as device drivers (except for interrupt processing)

- **Percent interrupt time**   The percentage of CPU time spent servicing interrupts

- **Percent idle time**   The percentage of time that the CPU isn't doing anything

---

**Note**   When selecting counters, you can always click the Explain button. This will provide a description of what that counter information is providing.

Windows CPU counters are shown in Figure 6-4.

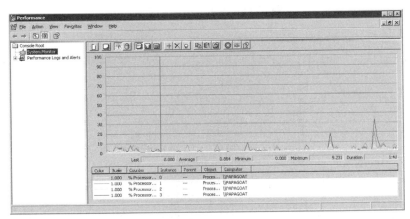

**Figure 6-4**   Perfmon CPU counters.

Perfmon is a powerful and useful tool that can be used to help with system and SQL Server tuning, sizing, and capacity planning. In addition, you can get a limited amount of CPU information from SQL Server itself. The @@CPU_BUSY function within SQL Server provides information on how much CPU time SQL Server itself has used. This is a cumulative counter in ticks. Multiply by @@timeticks to get the number of milliseconds. By setting up timers and finding the number of milliseconds of CPU time and the elapsed time you can get a good indication of how much CPU percentage is being used. To get the milliseconds of CPU time used, use this syntax:

```
SELECT @@CPU_BUSY * @@timeticks;
```

This can be valuable information and perfmon data.

Perfmon data can be saved directly into a SQL Server database. This information can be extremely valuable since it can be saved for a long period of time. While a day's worth of CPU data from perfmon might be mildly useful for future planning, a year's worth is very useful, as shown in Figure 6-5.

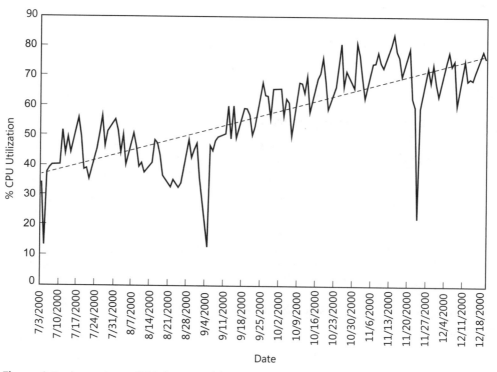

**Figure 6-5** Long-term CPU data used for capacity planning.

Figure 6-5 illustrates how long-term data can identify trends that you might not see by looking at perfmon on a daily basis. As you can see, the major dips in the chart represent holidays where the activity on the system was reduced. You can use this chart to anticipate when you might run out of power and need to upgrade your hardware. By looking only at short time samples, this would be missed. This technique can be applied to several areas, such as user counts, memory utilization, and disk space.

Keep in mind that the quality of your capacity planning or sizing exercise is directly related to the quality of the data that you have to work with. The better your the data, the better the result of your calculations.

# Memory Capacity Planning

Memory does not act in the same way as CPU, network, and I/O because there are no collisions involved in allocating memory. What you do get is the need to move objects out of memory in order to make room for other data that needs to be moved into memory. Windows Server 2003 is a virtual memory operating system. The ramifications of a virtual memory operating system have changed in the last few years.

Originally the virtual memory operating system was designed to allow you to use more memory than is actually in the system by fooling the programs into thinking that there is more memory than there actually is. In fact, with a 32-bit architecture a program or a single process can access up to 4 GB of memory even if you don't have that much physical memory. If you use more memory than is available in physical memory, some of it is copied out to disk until it is needed again. This is known as paging.

> **Best Practices** Paging is a very expensive operation, and if excessive paging is occurring, then any other tuning work will not be effective. If paging is occurring, fix this problem first and then move on to other performance problems. It is always better to reduce SQL Server memory allocation in order to reduce paging. So, if you are experiencing paging, stop and fix the problem.

## Real World  Don't Over-Allocate Memory

Occasionally I've run into the situation in SQL Server 2000 where the "Max Server Memory" has been configured too high and causes paging to occur. This is much less likely to occur with SQL Server 2005 since memory, including AWE memory, dynamically reduces itself if it has been over-allocated.

When the 32-bit processor was introduced, nobody expected that these processors would still be around with systems that had more than 4 GB of RAM. This has introduced an entirely new problem. With 32-bit systems that have more than 4 GB of RAM, a single process can still address only 4 GB of RAM. Multiple processes can use up this memory, but a single process cannot. A workaround called PAE and AWE enables SQL Server to use this memory for buffer pages but not for normal processing. This was covered in detail in Chapter 5, "32-Bit Versus 64-Bit Platforms and Microsoft SQL Server 2005."

## Sizing Memory

When sizing memory, it is important to have sufficient memory to achieve a high cache-hit ratio. The cache-hit ratio is the percentage of time that requested data is found in memory rather than on disk. Typically, the larger the database, the more memory is needed to achieve this cache-hit ratio. The amount of memory available and its effectiveness depends on your hardware and whether you are running a 32-bit or 64-bit operating system.

The amount of memory allocated to SQL Server should be significantly high so that a cache-hit ratio of more than 98 percent is achieved. However, you should not make the memory so high that paging occurs or other processes are starved for memory. Careful monitoring should be done so that these do not occur. In the next section, we'll discuss how to monitor memory.

One way to improve the cache-hit ratio is to add more memory and increase the SQL Server memory allocation (other ways are to tune queries and good application design). This is usually effective in most situations; however, you might need a significant amount of memory in order to make an effect. In addition, if you are running on a 32-bit system, the memory in excess of 4 GB must be allocated using PAE and AWE. (See Chapter 5 for more information.) Adding memory in excess of 4 GB is much more efficient when running SQL Server 2005 on a 64-bit Windows system.

### Real World   The Importance of Sizing

Assuming that the database is large, adding memory to a SQL Server system almost always provides a benefit. The value of sizing is in determining how much memory is required and what value it provides. Although the price has dropped in the past few years, memory can still be very expensive. In addition, the larger the memory module, the more expensive it can be. In order to put 32 GB or 64 GB of RAM in your system, you might have to purchase very large modules.

Since data is stored in 8-KB pages both on disk and in memory, you might have a problem with page allocation. The number of pages in the buffer cache is equal to the amount of memory divided by the page size (which is 8 KB). Although data is stored in the buffer cache in pages, it is usually used in rows. By keeping together rows that are used together, you can more effectively use the buffer cache.

For example, if you have 800 MB of memory allocated to the SQL Server buffer cache, this equates, at 8 KB per page, to 102,400 pages in memory. If you are only using one row per page, this gives you 102,400 rows in memory. If you can actually use an average of 10 rows per page, then you have 1,024,000 useful rows in memory. Since data is typically sorted into clustered indexes, it is important that you cluster on a useful cluster key that might result in efficient memory usage.

## Monitoring Memory

As discussed in the previous section, Windows Server 2003 Task Manager can be a convenient tool for displaying the amount of memory used and available in the system. The memory utilization can be found in the "Performance" tab of Task Manager, as shown previously in Figure 6-3.

Memory can also be monitored effectively in perfmon. One of the most important perfmon counters is the *Pages/sec* counter under the *Memory* object. This counter tells you whether you are experiencing excessive paging. It is okay to have some paging, but if this number is 100 or greater, you have a big problem. In addition, the *Percent Usage* and *Percent Usage Peak* counters in the *Paging File* performance object can also indicate excessive paging in the operating system. Memory counters include the following:

- **Pages/sec**  Found under the *Memory* object, this counter provides information on the amount of paging that is happening in the system. This is a key counter that indicates memory is over-allocated.

- **Available Mbytes**  Also found under the *Memory* object, this counter indicates how much memory is available for programs to use.

- **Percent Usage**  Found under the *Paging File* object, this counter indicates the percentage of the paging file that is currently used. Significant usage indicates serious paging.

- **Percent Usage Peak**  Also found under the *Paging File* object, this counter indicates the highest percentage of the paging file that has been used. This can indicate whether you have ever had a significant amount of paging.

These important Windows memory counters are shown in Figure 6-6.

The SQL Server cache-hit ratio can be monitored in perfmon via the buffer cache-hit ratio counter, available through the Buffer Manager performance object. Your goal should be 100 percent; however, anything above 98 percent is acceptable. If you are consistently seeing a much lower cache-hit ratio, you should take steps to attempt to improve this.

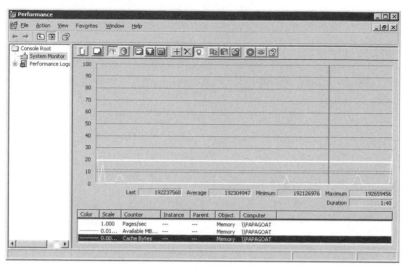

**Figure 6-6**   Perfmon memory counters.

Achieving this goal should be your target, however, it is not always possible to reach a 98 percent cache-hit ratio. With very large databases that are performing large queries, you might not achieve this; however, you should still strive for it.

# I/O Capacity Planning

One of the most common performance problems that we experience in the field is an undersized I/O subsystem. However, unlike CPU and memory sizing, it is fairly easy to add more I/O capacity. The I/O subsystem should be monitored constantly, and more capacity should added as needed. As with any sizing and capacity planning exercise, care should be taken to carefully monitor and assess your changing needs. Unlike CPU, Memory, and Network, the I/O subsystem problems leave a very specific indication within perfmon counters. This will be discussed later in this section.

## Sizing the I/O Subsystem

As you have seen in earlier in this chapter, a disk drive can handle only a finite number of IOPS (I/Os per second). By monitoring the I/O subsystem and applying the techniques and mathematics that were covered in Chapter 3, I/O sizing is a fairly exact science. The end goal is to limit the number of IOPS per disk drive to 100 or fewer. If your system exceeds this, then more disk drives should be added. Be sure to account for the additional I/Os that are generated by the RAID overhead.

### Real World    Disk Drive Performance

It is getting more and more common to run into undersized I/O subsystems because of the adoption of very large disk drives. In the past, when disk drives were 2 GB (remember them?) to support the size of your database, you were forced to have a sufficient number of disk drives so that performance wasn't an issue. Later when we had 9-GB disk drives, you were usually still okay. However, when 18-GB, 36-GB, 73-GB, and 200-GB+ disk drives were introduced, we began seeing more and more I/O performance issues. Now it is possible to put a 1-terabyte volume on four disk drives. This can lead to extreme performance issues, since the number of I/Os per second that you can do depends on the number of disk drives in your array. Combine this with a very low-end storage system, and you could be heading for trouble.

Unfortunately, not all I/O problems are solved by adding more disk drives. This is why it is recommended that hardware should be added only after the application, indexes, and SQL statements have been tuned. The reason for this is that unnecessary I/Os cannot be compensated for by simply adding hardware.

For example, if a system with a 100-GB database is configured with 500 MB of SQL Server cache, it is unlikely that the cache-hit ratio will be very good, causing most of the data reads to go to disk. Even if the I/O subsystem is optimal, a random read will take 6 milliseconds (ms). Thus adding more disk drives will not reduce the I/O latencies to fewer than 6 ms. Adding more memory, increasing the cache-hit ratio, and reducing the number of physical I/Os are much more effective than adding more disks in this case.

In addition, by tuning indexes and SQL statements, you might be able to further reduce the number of IOPS. In fact, index tuning is really all about reducing the number of I/O operations, both physical and logical. So, your goal should be to reduce the number of I/Os before adding more disk drives. Once you have reduced the I/O operations as much as possible, then it is time to add more I/O capacity.

## Monitoring the I/O Subsystem

One of the best tools for determining how I/O is performing is perfmon. There are other tools available within Windows Server 2003, such as Task Manager, but for I/O, the best tool is perfmon. In this chapter, we will focus on perfmon as it relates to I/O performance.

Perfmon has two main objects that pertain to I/O: *LogicalDisk* and *PhysicalDisk*. The main difference between the *PhysicalDisk* object counters and *LogicalDisk* object counters is how they are split up. The *LogicalDisk* counters look at drive letters only; the *PhysicalDisk* counters look at the entire drive. So, if the first drive in your system is divided into drive letters, or partitions, C and D, the *LogicalDisk* object shows two counters but the *PhysicalDisk* object shows only the physical disk. For this reason, I prefer to use the *PhysicalDisk* object rather than the *LogicalDisk* object.

The following counters are very useful for measuring physical I/Os:

- *Disk Reads/sec*   The read IOPS (I/Os Per Second) for the disk drive or drives
- *Disk Transfers/sec*   The total (read plus write) IOPS for each disk drive
- *Disk Writes/sec*   The write IOPS for each disk drive
- *Avg. Disk sec/Read*   The disk read latency, or average time for a read operation, (in seconds); this counter and the next counter are probably the most important I/O counters
- *Avg. Disk sec/Write*   The disk write latency, or average time for a write operation, in seconds

Some of Windows I/O counters are shown here in Figure 6-7.

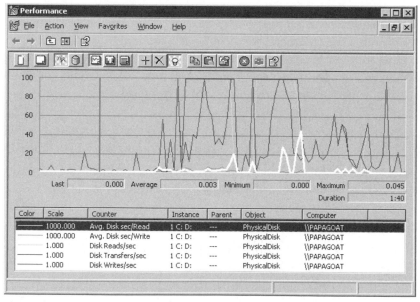

**Figure 6-7**   Perfmon I/O counters.

As mentioned earlier in this section, the I/O subsystem has very specific indications that it is being overloaded. These are in the *Avg. disk sec/Read* and *Avg. disk sec/Write* counters that are available in the *PhysicalDisk* or *LogicalDisk* performance objects. These counters show the disk latencies on reads and writes. The read and write latencies should be 5 to 10 ms (0.005 to 0.010 seconds) for an optimal I/O subsystem. If the latencies exceed 20 ms (0.020 seconds), you might be experiencing an I/O problem. Latencies above 30 ms (0.030 seconds) are completely unacceptable. Of course, use common sense. If you experience high latencies only during backups or other batch operations, the effect on users might not be significant.

# Network Capacity Planning

The network is a slightly different case than the components discussed above. Network performance is important, but it affects SQL Server 2005 in a different manner than the other components. When executing a SQL statement, the CPU, memory, and I/O subsystems are all used extensively to execute that operation. Unless you are performing a distributed transaction or a query that includes a linked server, you will be accessing the network only during the beginning phase, when the query is submitted to the SQL Server database engine, and during the final phase, when the results are returned to the client. Thus, the execution of the query is not affected by a slow network.

## Sizing the Network

The network is probably easier to size than some of the other components, but it is harder to increase its performance. You cannot simply add on another network card into the same subnet and get more network performance. Increasing the network capacity might be very difficult and require working with your network administration team and making changes to your subnet and network topology. This assumes, of course, that you are not already using the fastest network speed and topology available.

On the client side there is still the possibility that poor network performance can cause performance problems. This can happen when large amounts of data are transmitted to the client as a result of your SQL statement. If you are transmitting large amounts of data and the network is slow (for example, 10baseT), you can experience performance problems. There is no standard formula for calculating the required network bandwidth, but standard sizing mathematics is in effect. Thus, you should size in order to avoid exceeding 80 percent of the network bandwidth. Also, remember that most networks specify bandwidth in bits per second, not bytes per second. So, a gigabit network can handle a theoretical maximum of 125 MB/sec.

It is recommended that a gigabit or faster network be used between database servers, application servers, and other support servers such as backup servers and network attached storage (NAS) systems. After using the fastest network hardware available, the next option for increasing network throughput is using multiple network connections and segmenting the network. If you are using NAS storage, this should be on a dedicated network. Connectivity between the database server and the backup server also should be on a dedicated network.

### Real World    Client Network Problems Do Occur

Several years ago I was working on a performance tuning consulting job. I discovered that the core problem was that the application was actually receiving 64 MB of data from the SQL Server database, however, the GUI that the users saw displayed only a small amount of this data. In addition, even though the data center was using 100baseT network connections (this was before gigabit), the customer was unaware of the amount of data that was being downloaded to the client and forwarded the problem over to the developers. Because of the effort and cost needed to upgrade the network to 100baseT, that option could not be done at the time. Unfortunately, the client had to live with this until the developers could make a change to reduce the amount of data returned.

## Monitoring the Network

The network can be monitored both via perfmon and Windows Task Manager. Task Manager contains a Network tab. This tab provides a nice view of the network speed and the percentage of network bandwidth used. By clicking the View drop-down list and selecting columns, you can add additional columns to this graph.

Windows Task Manager network monitoring is shown in Figure 6-8.

In addition to Task Manager, there are a number of network counters available in perfmon. They can be very useful for monitoring the network and include the following counters in the *Network Interface* performance object:

- **Bytes Received/sec**  The number of bytes received through the network adapter
- **Bytes Sent/sec**  The number of bytes sent out of the network adapter or adapters
- **Bytes Total/sec**  The total traffic through the network adapter or adapters
- **Current Bandwidth**  The estimated speed of the network card or cards in bits/sec
- **Output Queue Length**  Indicates whether queuing is occurring and the network is overloaded; a value greater than 2 indicates a network delay

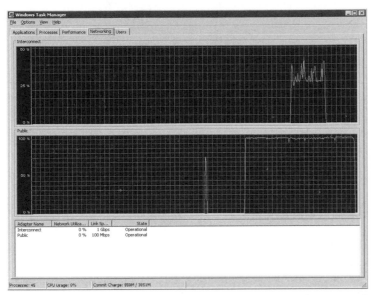

Figure 6-8   Windows Task Manager used to monitor the network.

Some Windows network counters are shown in Figure 6-9.

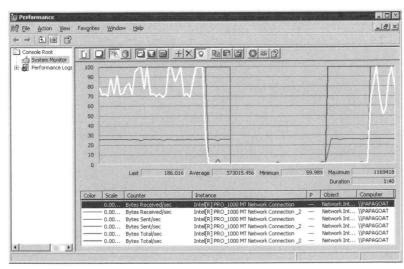

Figure 6-9   Perfmon network monitoring.

---

**Note**   There are additional network counters under the *TCPv4* and *TCPv6* performance objects.

---

Sizing the system for CPU, memory, I/O, and network is a combination of monitoring, analysis, mathematics, and skill. Sizing and capacity planning is not an exact science but an art. When in doubt, it is best to size for the worst-case scenario and oversize the system. It is better to have a slightly oversized system that has awesome performance than to have an undersized system that you get complaints about.

# Growth Considerations

When sizing a system and performing a capacity planning exercise, accounting for future growth is crucial. In fact, capacity planning is all about system growth. But as with the previous sections in this chapter, the calculations needed to calculate future growth depend heavily on the data that you put into these calculations. If you are not given sufficient information to anticipate the system growth, then you will be completely unable to anticipate system problems.

For this reason, it is important that the IT staff communicates with its customer. This customer might be the accounting group, the call center, or another user community. Your customer must provide you with a projection of future system usage. If your system grows from 500 online users to 1,000 online users and you are not prepared, it is very possible that the SLA will be violated. If the IT department doesn't communicate with its customer, then it is at fault for not anticipating the growth.

## Calculating Growth

In its simplest form, the growth of the system can be associated with the number of users in the system, both distinct users and sessions. If you have collected this data over a long period of time, it can be correlated and used, in conjunction with CPU and I/O performance counters, for your growth calculations.

Using user count as a performance metric is demonstrated in Figure 6-10.

By keeping track of the user count on a daily basis, you can see trends in the activity on the system. This chart was created by sampling the database using a select from sysprocesses and counting the number of users. This data was inserted into a database. After a few months, the data was very useful.

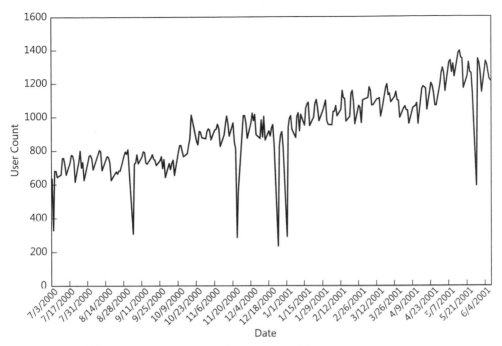

**Figure 6-10**  Using user count as a performance metric.

By having both CPU utilization and user counts as performance metrics, you can calculate the average and maximum CPU utilization per user. The CPU count is gathered from sysprocesses, and the CPU utilization is gathered from @@CPU_BUSY. With this value you can extrapolate the CPU utilization with additional users as shown here[.]:

```
CPU per user = CPU Utilization / User Count
New CPU utilization = User Count * CPU per user
```

This calculation provides a rough estimate of the resources needed when additional users are added.

## Planning for Future Growth

Planning for future growth should start early and be addressed on a regular basis. Long-term performance monitoring should be done and the results of this monitoring should be analyzed on a monthly basis. In addition, you should conduct regular discussions with your customers in order to plan for additional users and changes in the application.

Keep in mind that changes to applications are not always improvements. A significant number of performance tuning activities are initiated by the need to tune a new version of an application that does not perform as well as the current version. This is a very common problem. This is somewhat solved by using load-testing application revisions, but the majority of applications are put into production with no load testing.

# Benchmarking and Load Testing

One way to help plan your system and to validate changes to your system is done via benchmarking and load testing. Benchmarking and load testing are similar in nature and just slightly different in usage. A *benchmark* is a performance test used to compare the performance of different hardware or software. A benchmark can be an industry standard test or a custom test used to measure a particular configuration or program. There are many companies that publicly publish benchmarks results. These results can be used to compare systems and are usually used by the publishing companies as marketing material. There are several organizations that are used to develop and facilitate standardized benchmarks. One of the best known of these is the TPC (Transaction Processing Performance Council; *www.tpc.org*). The TPC was founded in 1988.  Its mission is to create standards and regulate the publication of database benchmarks. Microsoft is an active and leading member of the TPC.

## Real World   TPC Experience

Three of the co-authors of this book—Edward Whalen, Marci Garcia, and Burzin Patel—worked as SQL Server benchmarking engineers at one time in their careers. Edward Whalen chaired the TPC-C subcommittee for several years, and all three have been involved in publishing record-breaking TPC results on SQL Server in the past.

A *load test* is the practice of modeling the characteristics of a program or system by simulating a number of users accessing that system or program. When used to test a system operating at more than normal usage to the point of maximum capacity, it is called a *stress test*. There is really not much difference between a load test and a benchmark. Typically, a benchmark is used to compare various products, whereas a load test is used to characterize a single product.

In either case, load testing and benchmarking can be used to characterize the performance of your system and to determine how future activity will affect your performance. In addition, by load testing your application each time changes are made to it, potential performance problems can be found before the application is introduced to the user community.

## Load Testing the Application

Load testing your application is a critical piece of your overall performance management plan. By simulating the user community, you can accurately measure the performance of your system on a regular basis. In addition, it is a useful tool in validating that changes have made things better (or worse). This information and the load testing scripts can be used each time a change is made to the application in order to validate the changes. Validation tests can include the following:

- **Performance changes** Performance changes that you make to the application can be validated. These changes could be index improvements, code changes, or parameter changes.

- **Functional changes** New features can be validated and performance tested. It is not uncommon for functional changes to cause blocking problems or general performance problems in the system.

- **Load changes** The number of simulated users can be increased in order to find out at what point the SLA is violated.

- **Hardware changes** It is important to load test new hardware before it goes into production to validate that it has been correctly configured and sized.

Load testing can be done on both a system-wide basis as described here, or load testing and benchmarking can be performed on a specific component such as the I/O and network subsystems.

## Benchmarking the I/O Subsystem

The I/O subsystem is one of the most important components of your system, and one that can cause significant performance problems if it is not configured and sized properly. Any I/O subsystem is made up of finite components that have finite performance characteristics. Unfortunately, the DBA is not usually the person responsible for the I/O subsystem and must sometimes must prove that this component is a problem before any changes can be made. In this section you will learn how to gather that evidence.

**Real World "The I/O Subsystem Can't Be a Problem. It's a SAN."**

I have heard the statement that the I/O subsystem can't be a bottleneck because the company has spent tens of thousands of dollars buying a SAN. This is a myth. Any I/O subsystem can be a performance bottleneck, and often it is. On more than one occasion, I have used Iometer, an open-source software project, to demonstrate to a client that the I/O subsystem is limited and exactly where that limit is.

A free tool that you can use to benchmark IO performance is Iometer. Iometer was originally developed by Intel but was distributed to the open source community several years ago. Iometer is an excellent benchmarking tool, and you can't beat the price.

Using Iometer can be very useful for discovering and documenting performance problems. It is easy to use if you understand the basic principles on which it works. This section is not a complete tutorial on using Iometer, but here are some of the key issues you might encounter when using it.

## Getting Iometer

Iometer is an open-source software project originally created by Intel that is available free of charge at *www.iometer.org*. At this Web site, you can easily find and download Iometer. Once you have installed it on your system, you are ready to start load testing your I/O subsystem.

## Using Iometer

Iometer is easy to start up and use, and it consists of two parts. The Dynamo is a program that actually generates I/Os. The GUI, known simply as Iometer, is used for configuration, management, and presentation of data. Iometer is very configurable and can be used in a number of ways, but the basic concept is this: a work load is generated against the I/O subsystem, and the result of that workload is measured and presented.

To run Iometer, complete the following steps:

1.  Create a disk target. This is one of the most important steps. If you create a disk target that is too small, the test will not generate significant random I/Os to properly exercise the I/O subsystem. If necessary (for example, if SAN or NAS storage is very large), create a very large disk target file. A minimum size of 5 GB is recommended.

2.  Configure workers. The workers allow you to specify how many outstanding I/Os to issue to the disk target at a time. This also is very important because a disk can do approximately 100 IOPS at 6 ms. If you are issuing only one I/O at a time (in other words, each I/O waits for the previous one to complete), the latency will be 6 ms and your throughput will be 100 IOPS. In order to simulate a SQL Server system that has many active users, you must issue at least four to six outstanding I/Os per disk target. Try varying workers per target and see your results.

3.  Create or modify an access specification. The access specification determines the mix and properties of the I/Os. In order to simulate SQL Server I/Os, use an 8-KB block size, specify mostly random access (80 to 90 percent) and mostly reads (75 to 90 percent). You can collect perfmon data to determine the percentage of reads to writes on your system. In addition, you can run perfmon and Iometer concurrently and see how your system performs under stress.

4. Run the test. You can run the test for as long as you want. You can also set it up to perform many tests in sequence.

5. Evaluate the results. The results displayed within Iometer tell you the throughput and the latency. This data can be very valuable for sizing and capacity planning purposes.

Take the time to try Iometer to see what kind of performance results you can achieve on your disk subsystem. You might be surprised by what you find.

## Benchmarking the Network

The network can be benchmarked and load tested with a program that is available on the Windows Server 2003 product CD-ROM, in the Valueadd\Msft\Net\Tools folder. TTCP, or Test TCP, is a standard program that is available to test the maximum throughput of your network. TTCP has been around for several years and is available on Windows Server 2003 and other platforms. TTCP can be found on the Windows Server 2003 CD in the Valuadd\Msft\Net\Tools folder. The TTCP program can also be found at the Microsoft Download Center. You should check there for the latest version. This program can be used to test both TCP and UDP traffic. Testing network connections is especially important if you are using replication, log shipping, or database mirroring to a remote site.

### Using TTCP

TTCP allows you to determine the throughput of your network. This information can be used to validate that you are getting the throughput that you need and to allow you to debug problems. You cannot assume that if you have gigabit network cards, you are getting gigabit throughput. There are many components involved in a network, including routers, firewalls, proxy servers, and more, that can cause additional overhead, reducing network throughput and increasing latencies.

By using TTCP you can actually test the real components. You are not simulating the production environment in a test environment. This provides the absolute best type of data since it represents the actual performance of your network.

---

**Important**   TTCP will saturate your network. This means that everybody else on this network is affected while you are doing your test. Be careful when running this so that you don't cause problems that might affect your employment.

---

TTCP is run on two different machines that represent the test environment. On one system you run TTCP in receive mode; on the other system you run TTCP in transmit mode. At the end of the test a report that tells you how much throughput was achieved is produced automatically. TTCP has a number of optional parameters that allow you to configure the packet size, the protocol (TCP or UDP), and the amount of data to send across the network.

To run TTCP, invoke it in receive mode on the receive system by running ttcp −r −s. On the driving system, invoke ttcp in transmit mode by running ttcp −t −s *recveiving_system*. The results show you the network throughput between the two systems.

You will find this tool very useful, and the data it provides can be invaluable for finding network performance problems. As with any tool that saturates the network, be careful when you run it so that you don't affect others on the network.

## Using MOM for Capacity Planning

The Microsoft Operations Manager (MOM) product can also provide useful information for capacity planning and sizing. MOM stores perfmon data for long periods of time so that it can be analyzed and used for purposes such as tuning, sizing, and capacity planning. You can configure both the amount of data that MOM collects and the duration for which it stores the data.

It is desirable to keep this kind of data as long as possible, but keeping it indefinitely is impractical. Determine which metrics are important for you, and configure MOM appropriately. By saving data such as CPU utilization, user counts, and I/O utilization for a significant amount of time, you can extrapolate future usage. MOM can also be used to validate that you have met your SLA.

## Summary

In this chapter, you have learned the fundamentals of sizing and capacity planning. You have reviewed some mathematics that you probably hope you'll never use again. In addition, you have learned how to size a system for CPU, memory, I/O, and network capacity. This chapter has also introduced you to some new tools that are useful for benchmarking and load testing both the I/O subsystem and the network. You will find these tools and concepts important not only for sizing and capacity planning, but for performance tuning as well.

Chapter 7

# Choosing a Storage System for Microsoft SQL Server 2005

The most common performance problems found in Microsoft SQL Server database systems involve the disk storage system, where SQL Server data and log files are stored. Selecting the appropriate storage system to store your SQL Server files and configuring that storage properly can have a huge effect on the performance of your database system. This is because SQL Server performance is extremely dependent on I/O performance, as accessing database data is all about performing I/O—reads and writes.

Chapter 4, "I/O Subsystem Planning and RAID Configuration," describes in detail how disks drives work and perform, what the various RAID levels mean, how to lay out SQL Server files for best performance at the disk level, and how to monitor and analyze disk performance. The disk and RAID principles in Chapter 4 hold true independent of which storage system you choose. Bad I/O performance is often a result of the disk storage sizing and configuration rather than the type of storage system being used, although the different storage system types also have factors that affect performance, which will be discussed in this chapter. This chapter explains the different storage systems available and the suggested uses of each, while Chapter 4 discusses size and configuration of disks within a storage system for best SQL Server database performance. Together, these two chapters offer a holistic view of using storage with SQL Server.

There are various types of storage systems to choose from, each with its own set of features and benefits. With so many choices and acronyms for them, it may be hard to understand what they mean, how they differ from each other, and for what environment each type is best suited. The variety of options for connecting servers to storage further adds to the complexity. In order to help clarify the storage possibilities, this chapter provides descriptions of each of the common storage technologies and connectivity methods that are currently available on the market, along with terminology, concepts, benefits, differences from other storage types, and examples of when to use each.

After reading this chapter, you will understand the difference between SAN, NAS, and DAS storage; understand the characteristics of fibre channel, SCSI, iSCSI, and Ethernet technologies as related to storage devices; understand storage concepts and terminology; and understand bandwidth as it relates to performance.

## TMA = Too Many Acronyms

There are several acronyms used repeatedly throughout this chapter. They will all be described in more detail in the following sections, but here is a one-stop shop of definitions to help give you a jump-start on the topics covered:

- **DAS (direct attached storage)** DAS is a storage system that utilizes any storage controller that is not part of a network. The server host is directly attached to the storage device, whether internal or external storage, as opposed to attaching to a storage device via a network as with NAS and SAN.

- **NAS (network attached storage)** NAS is a storage device that is available to servers via an IP (Internet Protocol) local area network (LAN).

- **SAN (storage area network)** SAN is storage system that allows a network of systems to access storage over a dedicated storage network. This network could be an IP network (iSCSI SAN) or a fibre channel network (FC SAN).

- **FC (fibre channel)** A serial data transfer technology designed for very high bandwidth data transfers across longer distances than SCSI.

- **FCP (fibre channel protocol)** A data transfer protocol that maps the SCSI-3 protocol to implement serial SCSI over FC networks; transferring data at the block level.

- **SCSI (small computer system interface)** A parallel interface standard for attaching peripheral devices (including storage, printers, tape drives, etc.) to computers.

- **iSCSI (Internet SCSI)** An IP-based standard for linking hosts to storage devices over a network and transporting data by SCSI commands encapsulated in TCP/IP packets over the network.

- **HBA (host bus adapter)** Refers in this chapter to an I/O adapter card used to connect a host computer to a storage device; performs low-level interface functions to minimize the impact on host processor performance.

# Interconnect and Protocol Technologies

In order to understand how to choose a storage system, you should first have some knowledge about the various interconnect technologies that can be used to connect servers to storage devices. We will start with a description of these interconnect types as a foundation for the later sections. If you are already familiar with these, you may want to skip to the "Storage Systems" section later in this chapter for details on SAN, NAS, and DAS storage.

There are four common types of interconnect and protocol combinations used to connect servers with storage: SCSI, TCP/IP over Ethernet, FCP over FC, and iSCSI over Ethernet. For the purposes of this chapter, we use the term *interconnect* to refer to the physical cable connection and the term *protocol* to refer to the communication method that runs over the interconnect. We will define the various interconnect types and the protocols on which they are based, the storage types with which they can interact, and the benefits and limitations of each. At the end of this section we will provide a comparison chart that summarizes the differences among these interconnect technologies. This serves as a foundation for the later section on storage systems so that you will have a better understanding of how to choose a storage system and interconnect type appropriate for your requirements. A particular interconnect type may be used with more than one storage system type, as you will see.

## Understanding Data Transfer: Block Form Versus File Format

There are two major forms in which data is transported and accessed: block form and file form. Data is always stored in block form on disk without any file formatting of the data. This is true whether the data originates from the application in blocks of data, such as with SQL Server data, or the data originates as a formatted file. Databases are the largest example of applications that perform direct block-level data access, meaning that data is accessed in block form, or in its "raw" form, just as it is stored on disk. Examples of file-level data access include word processing and spreadsheet applications. Data can be transported between servers and storage in its original block form, or it can be read from disk, file formatted, and transported in file form.

For networked Windows platforms, file-formatted data is sent using SMB/CIFS transfer protocols (server message block/common Internet file system). For Unix/Linux platforms, other protocols are used, such as NFS (network file system). One major difference regarding performance between block and file-level data access is that file formatting protocols incur overhead since data is in block form on disk. Block-level data is sent using a family of SCSI protocols. If an application requires data in block form, because data is in block form on disk, a block-level transport would be more efficient than a file-level transport in that case. If an application requires file-based I/O, then data from disk must be converted to the file format, thus a file-level transport would be sufficient.

Thus, for SQL Server, which requires data in block form, it is more efficient to transfer that data in its original block form. Since the SCSI and iSCSI protocols transfer data in block form (over various interconnect types) to the storage device, these are the best choices for SQL Server data for I/O performance. This topic will be discussed throughout the chapter as it relates to the different interconnects, protocols, and storage systems. SAN storage provides block I/O access, similar to having a server directly attached to a local disk (DAS). NAS devices provide file system I/O by redirecting file requests over a network to a storage device. The back end data on disk is stored in block format, so a file formatting protocol must be used to transform the data into the appropriate format. These storage types will be described in more detail later in this chapter.

Table 7-1 shows the various protocols and their interconnects with the form of data transport supported and the corresponding type of storage system.

**Table 7-1   Data Transport Forms by Protocol/Interconnect Type**

| Protocol/Interconnect | Storage Attach-ment Type | File Form | Block Form |
|---|---|---|---|
| TCP/IP over Ethernet | NAS | Yes | No |
| SCSI over parallel SCSI | DAS | No | Yes |
| SCSI-3 over FC (FCP) | SAN | No | Yes |
| iSCSI over Ethernet | SAN | No | Yes |

## SCSI Protocol over Parallel SCSI Interconnect

The *SCSI (small computer system interface)* protocol has been around for many years—the first true SCSI standard was published in 1986. It has evolved over the years with various SCSI standards including SCSI-1, SCSI-2, and SCSI-3. For each set of standards, there are various data transfer modes and feature sets such as Ultra2 SCSI, Ultra3 SCSI, Wide Ultra2 SCSI, and so on. There are two types of SCSI interconnects: parallel and serial (which includes FC). We will discuss the parallel SCSI interconnect in this section. Serial SCSI is discussed in the section "Fibre Channel (FC) Interconnect."

The SCSI interconnect is used to attach peripheral devices to computers. With parallel SCSI, data is transmitted in chunks of either one or two bytes (8 or 16 bits) at a time depending on the type of SCSI, rather than serially in individual bits. This transmission occurs across multiple data lines via a SCSI cable with multiple wires inside, thus the term "parallel." The SCSI protocol, whether over parallel or serial interconnect, is a block-based protocol, meaning that data is transferred in block form, not in file format. Thus, there is no overhead for file system formatting of data.

SCSI is not limited to connecting disk storage devices, although that will be our focus here. Historically, other SCSI devices include printers, tape drives, CD/DVD writers, CD-ROMS, and scanners, for example, although many of these devices are connected via USB or Ethernet today.

Because not all SQL Server database administrators (DBAs) are familiar with or have an opportunity to explore the hardware, the next few paragraphs provide background information about the hardware components involved with SCSI. We will not get into details on the entire family of SCSI standards and all the transfer modes and features. This foundational information is intended to clarify the basic physical characteristics of SCSI that determine its limitations and benefits.

---

**More Info**   To find more detailed information on SCSI and the various standards, search on *www.google.com* for "SCSI protocol" or "SCSI standards."

---

For disk storage devices—which could be a single hard disk drive or a set of disk drives in an internal or external disk enclosure or cabinet—a SCSI disk controller resides inside the server and handles the transfer of data to and from the disk, among other I/O-related functions. In other words, I/O is managed by the SCSI controller inside the server. The disk storage device connects directly to the SCSI controller via a SCSI cable that plugs into a channel on the controller at one end and into the storage device on the other end. SCSI disk controllers may have more than one channel, thus allowing more than one storage device to be connected to one controller and providing more disk storage on the system.

---

**Note**   With SCSI storage, the disk controller always resides inside the server itself, whether the disks are internal or external to the server. This means that every server that attaches to SCSI storage will need its own disk controller(s). A SCSI controller may also be a RAID controller, when RAID configurations are supported by the controller. The disk controller location is one key difference from SAN storage, where the disk controllers reside inside the SAN, which is outside the server.

---

With SCSI, disk storage can be connected internally to a server and externally using internal and external cables. See Figure 7-1 for examples of SCSI cables and SCSI controllers.

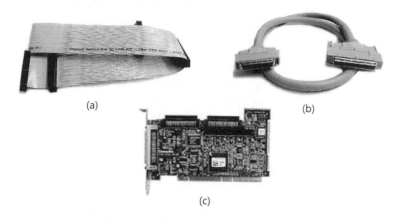

(a)

(b)

(c)

**Figure 7-1**   Examples of SCSI cables and controllers: (a) internal SCSI cable, (b) external SCSI cable, and (c) SCSI controller.

## Clustering with SCSI

SCSI storage can be used in a Windows cluster with SQL Server 2005 failover clustering as the shared storage for the cluster nodes. There are some limitations with using SCSI for clustering, such as a limited number of shared disks that can be configured, a limited number of nodes, limited scalability, and limited management capabilities. Also, the SCSI disk controller write cache must be turned off with this type of clustering, which when turned on provides a performance benefit for writes to the database. Therefore, SCSI connected storage for clustering does not provide good storage and host flexibility and expandability as the servers are direct attached to the storage, nor does it provide the best performance in cases where high writes occur on the data because the controller write cache cannot be used.

The outstanding difference between SCSI and iSCSI (discussed in a later section) is that iSCSI is a SCSI protocol designed specifically to transport data across IP networks. This allows servers to access storage via a network card and Ethernet interconnect rather than using a SCSI controller.

## Advantages of SCSI

One of the main advantages of using SCSI attached devices is their low cost. Servers generally come with built-in SCSI storage for the internal disk drive(s). If the system needs more disks for storage space or for performance and there are slots available in the server, you can purchase an additional SCSI controller(s), external disk cabinet, and disks. This is a less expensive way to add disks to one server than, for example, buying a SAN storage system and the components necessary for connecting the server to the SAN only to add disks to one server.

Another advantage of SCSI is that it can provide high bandwidth (high data transfer rates). The most recent SCSI standard, as of writing this book, is SCSI-3, and Ultra320 SCSI is the latest transfer mode. Used together, they provide a maximum bandwidth of 320MB/second. That is the largest bandwidth currently available with SCSI. Table 7-2 shows the latest SCSI types and various maximums they support. The number of devices includes the SCSI adapter (or disk controller) itself. For example, for Ultra320 the maximum number of devices is 16. Those are the disk controller and 15 disk drives.

**Table 7-2  Parallel SCSI Maximums**

| SCSI Transfer Modes | Bus Width in Bits (8 bits = 1 Byte) | Maximum Bandwidth or Throughput in MB/sec | Maximum Number of Devices | Maximum Cable Length in Meters* |
|---|---|---|---|---|
| Ultra2 SCSI | 8 | 40 | 8 | 12 |
| Wide Ultra2 SCSI | 16 | 80 | 16 | 12 |
| Ultra3 and Ultra160 SCSI | 16 | 160 | 16 | 12 |
| Ultra320 SCSI | 16 | 320 | 16 | 12 |

* Assuming maximum number of devices attached.

**Note** The maximum cable length listed in the table is 12 meters. This is the practical maximum. If you have only two devices on the SCSI chain, that cable length can be increased up to 25 meters maximum.

Another advantage with SCSI is that when using a disk controller with multiple channels, each channel provides the above throughput because each channel is completely independent and all channels run in parallel. Note that each channel counts as a device. Hence, a four-channel disk controller will provide up to four times the throughput and four times the number of devices as a single channel. With a four-channel Ultra320 controller, for example, you can connect up to 16 devices per channel. This gives you a total 64 devices, minus four devices for the four channels, leaving 60 other devices available.

**Note** The SCSI protocol also runs over a FC interconnect, and with iSCSI it runs over an Ethernet interconnect.

## Disadvantages of SCSI

One major limitation of SCSI connectivity is the limited length of the SCSI cables and the limited number of devices per channel. Electrical limitations are inherent to parallel data transfer on a parallel SCSI cable. Thus, parallel SCSI has the most limited data transfer distances of all the interconnect types. At best, the maximum SCSI cable length is 25 meters, and even this length is possible only when two devices are attached. If you have only one server and a few disks, this limitation might not be an issue, but it can become a problem in an enterprise datacenter environment with many servers and storage devices that may be spread across longer distances.

In addition, the fact that SCSI-cabled storage is directly attached to a server, which by definition is DAS, does not allow for flexibility or manageability when moving storage between servers or adding storage to the server. As you will see later in this chapter, SAN storage provides the best flexibility and manageability of storage with servers.

# Ethernet Interconnect

Networking enables computers to send and receive data to and from other computers. Ethernet is a network standard, used in LANs and metropolitan area networks (MANs) to provide connectivity between computers. A MAN is a network that may span buildings within the same city or metropolitan area tens of kilometers in size, but not across cities, which is a wide area network (WAN). Ethernet cables, either optical fiber cable or copper cable, are used to physically connect computers to a network. The cable connects on one end to a network card in the computer and on the other end to a network port connecting the computer to an IP network infrastructure, which likely includes network switches and/or hubs.

Data is transferred over IP networks in file format (with the exception of iSCSI). Thus, data is formatted by the operating system file system protocols.

In addition to connecting computers to each other on a network, Ethernet technology can be used to connect storage devices to the network as well. This is known as network attached storage (NAS). Computers can access storage on NAS devices via the IP network infrastructure. For example, a SQL Server system can be connected to a NAS device, and the data and log files can be stored on that device. When transferring the SQL Server data between the NAS device and the server (on the Windows platform, of course), the Server Message Blocking protocol is used to format the data into file format, which adds some overhead and latency to the data transfer. For more information, see the section on NAS later in this chapter.

There are different data transfer rates available with Ethernet connectivity, as shown in Table 7-3. The most widely used is 100 Mbps for desktop and notebook computers and 1 Gbps for application, web, and database servers. Higher network bandwidth to and from the database server particularly allows more efficient communication with multiple clients sending requests to the server. The largest throughput with Ethernet, 10 Gbps, using the 10GbE technology over fiber cable, is the most recently introduced, in 2002, and is even suitable for some wide area networks (WAN). 10GbE over copper cable was introduced in 2004. This technology is not yet common or widespread as research and development are still under way.

---

**Important**   Gbps is gigabits per second (Gb/sec), not gigabytes per second (GB/sec). Mbps is megabits per second (Mb/sec), not megabytes per second (MB/sec).

---

**Table 7-3   Ethernet Throughput**

| Ethernet Type | Bandwidth or Throughput | Converted to MB |
|---|---|---|
| 10BaseT | 10 Mbps | 1.25 MB/sec |
| 100BaseT | 100 Mbps | 12.5 MB/sec |
| 1GbE | 1 Gbps | 125 MB/sec |
| 10GbE | 10 Gbps | 1250 MB/sec |

## Advantages of Ethernet

One of the advantages of using Ethernet to attach storage devices is the low cost of implementation. You need only a network card in the computer to connect to the storage device. No special hardware, such as a disk controller or a host bus adapter, is needed. Network cards are less expensive than these other types of cards, and the existing network card in the computer and the existing network may be used in most cases.

iSCSI over Ethernet is also an excellent low-cost option for using Ethernet to connect servers with storage. iSCSI is described in detail in a later section of this chapter.

## Disadvantages of Ethernet

When using Ethernet networks to connect to a storage device, the file system formatting of data for transport adds overhead, thus adding to the total time it takes to perform an I/O (known as *I/O latency*). Although iSCSI also utilizes Ethernet interconnects, it has an advantage because it eliminates the file formatting overhead, as seen in the next section.

> **Note**   The time it takes to transfer, queue, and process I/O requests is called I/O latency.

# iSCSI

*iSCSI*, or Internet SCSI, is a standard that enables SCSI commands to be sent over an IP network using the TCP/IP protocol to establish connections between IP-based storage devices and clients. It is basically a protocol that encapsulates SCSI commands in TCP/IP packets. You will also see it called iSCSI over Ethernet. iSCSI is quickly gaining popularity because of the cost benefits it offers by communicating over standard IP networks. Like SCSI, iSCSI is also a block-based protocol—data is transferred in blocks without file system formatting. It is a cost-effective alternative to FC solutions for applications that require block-based instead of file-level storage, such as SQL Server.

> **What Is iSCSI?**   iSCSI is not a completely new protocol in itself; rather, it is a protocol designed to send SCSI commands over Ethernet using TCP/IP to provide a more cost-effective way of connecting servers with storage devices. iSCSI uses the common IP network infrastructure, making it easier to add existing servers to a storage device without additional server hardware components. Only a network card and IP network infrastructure are needed.

## Advantages of iSCSI

iSCSI allows both common network messaging traffic and block-based data transfers to IP-based storage devices over an existing IP network, as opposed to having to install a separate FC network for storage access. Currently, FC still offers higher data transfer throughput than iSCSI, but 1-Gbps Ethernet is already making iSCSI a rival in small-to-medium business environments. As 10-Gbps Ethernet becomes more popular, iSCSI may become more widely used, although higher bandwidth does not always equal faster I/O performance, depending on the amount of data being transferred.

iSCSI also overcomes the distance limitations of SCSI to equal that of Ethernet and allows multiple host servers to access the same iSCSI storage device. The main benefit of iSCSI is that it eliminates the need for an FC infrastructure—no HBAs and FC switches and cables are needed—and is therefore less expensive than using FC. It also provides for storage flexibility, scalability, and easy-to-use storage management.

Usually, no new hardware is required for the servers to use iSCSI protocol. All that is needed are network cards, Ethernet cables, and the IP network infrastructure. An additional network card (or HBA) and network switch may be needed, however, because it is important to configure a dedicated network between servers and iSCSI storage, isolating the I/O traffic from other network traffic to avoid contention and maintain acceptable I/O performance.

Microsoft began support for iSCSI in 2000 and developed a driver specific for iSCSI: the Microsoft iSCSI driver for Windows 2000 or Windows 2003. This driver can be downloaded for free and must be installed on each server that will use the iSCSI protocol to access iSCSI storage. Storage systems that support iSCSI have their iSCSI driver built-in; the storage devices are known as the target. iSCSI storage devices have Ethernet RJ45 connectors for the front-end connectivity.

> **Note**   The Microsoft Windows iSCSI initiator (driver) can be downloaded for free off the Microsoft web site following the link at *www.microsoft.com/ windowsserver2003/technologies/storage/iscsi/msfiSCSI.mspx*. This must be installed on each server that will access an iSCSI storage device.

One difference between iSCSI and FC that potentially could affect performance is the maximum bandwidth. iSCSI currently has a maximum bandwidth of 1 Gbps using 1GbE, whereas FC has a current maximum bandwidth of 2 Gbps. The lower bandwidth with iSCSI might result in lower performance compared with FC in cases where the amount of data being transferred per second approaches the bandwidth limitations, such as when performing backups and restores, streaming video, and scanning large amounts of data for reports. Bandwidths of 4 Gbps and 10 Gbps are under development for FC, as well as 10 Gbps for Ethernet, so these two interconnects are close in the bandwidth race.

### Disadvantages of iSCSI

There is some built-in overhead incurred with iSCSI from encapsulating the SCSI commands in TCP/IP packets that is not present in the basic SCSI protocols. This overhead can add to the overall I/O latency, or time it takes to complete an I/O. Some tests have shown that as much as 30 percent of processing power can be consumed by iSCSI overhead. That is, of course, just a general number that depends on several factors, including the amount of I/O activity on the system and the server and network configuration. iSCSI HBA's are available from some storage networking hardware vendors, such as Qlogic, with TOE (TCP Offload Engines) to offload that processing overhead from the system processor and onto the HBA. This type of HBA takes the place of the network card in the server for connectivity to the iSCSI storage device.

## Fibre Channel (FC) Interconnect

*Fibre Channel* is a high-speed technology used primarily for transferring SCSI commands serially (as opposed to in parallel) between computers and SAN disk arrays. This is the context in which we use it in this chapter. It was originally developed to overcome performance barriers of legacy LANs. Fibre Channel Protocol (FCP) maps the SCSI-3 protocol to implement serial SCSI over FC networks, and thus, transfers data at the block level. FCP can be run over different physical mediums including optical cable, coaxial cable, and twisted pair (telephone cable). Optical cable supports greater distances, of up to 10 km. Because it uses a serial wiring technology, it eliminates the electrical limitations found in parallel SCSI technology.

FC networks use dedicated host bus adapters (HBAs) to deliver high-performance block I/O transfers between servers and storage. The FC protocol most often runs on fibre optic cables, which currently provide up to 2 Gbps of bandwidth, and soon to reach 4 Gbps. It can also run on copper wire cabling, but distance is more limited. Fibre optic cabling allows data transmissions of up to 10 km or more.

---

**Note**    The "Fibre" in "Fibre Channel" is purposely spelled with "-re" on the end to differentiate the FC interconnect standard from the "fiber" used in other fiber optic applications.

## Advantages of Fibre Channel

There are several advantages of using fibre channel interconnects and the FCP protocol (SCSI-3 over fibre). Data transfer rates, now at up to 2 Gbps and soon to reach 4 Gbps, are the highest available for SAN storage, and FCP has the lowest transmission overhead of the data transfer protocols. Thus, an FC SAN system provides high performance for large data transfers, such as for large databases that are heavily accessed, backups, restores, image data transfers, and real-time computing, for example.

Another benefit of FC over SCSI is the relatively longer distance achieved—10 km with fibre optic cable. This allows servers and storage to be more easily racked and set up in the datacenter without being limited to using short cables. It also supports transferring data over fibre optic cable between two sites within 10 km of each other, such as for a standby or disaster recovery data site. Other network infrastructure is used to achieve data transfers across longer distances, such as over T-1, T-3, or OC-3 lines that are leased from service providers.

## Disadvantages of Fibre Channel

There may be a cost disadvantage when using FC if you want to implement it, but do not yet have an FC network infrastructure. All server hosts that need to attach to the storage using FC must contain one or more HBA's (fibre channel cable for connectivity). Also, an FC switch, or switches for redundancy, are needed. These may have to be purchased. Once this infrastructure is in place, more hosts can be added easily, they each still need an HBA and cables.

In addition, FC SAN systems provide optional software that allows snapshots, clones, and mirroring of data, for example. These also are add-on costs. However, for a system storing large amounts of business critical data, this is likely necessary.

# Interconnect Bandwidth Comparison

To give a consolidated view of how these interconnect types compare with each other based solely on bandwidth, Table 7-4 lists the connectivity types we have discussed and the current practical maximum bandwidths of each. Take into account that this is changing as 4 Gbps and 10 Gbps FC and 10 Gbps Ethernet will be available in the future. Interconnect bandwidth alone should not be the sole determining factor in choosing a storage subsystem. Many other factors must be considered, such as flexibility, expandability, manageability, and cost. See the "Speed Versus Bandwidth" sidebar below for a description of data transfer speed as related to bandwidth.

**Table 7-4   Connection Bandwidth Comparison**

| Protocol/Interconnect | Physical Cable Type | Current Maximum Bandwidth |
|---|---|---|
| SCSI over Parallel SCSI | Ultra320 SCSI cable | 320 MB/sec |
| iSCSI over Ethernet | 10/100BaseT Ethernet cable | 100 Mbps = 12.5 MB/sec |
| | 1 Gigabit Ethernet cable (1GbE) | 1 Gbps = 125 MB/sec |
| TCP/IP over Ethernet | 10/100BaseT Ethernet cable | 100 Mbps = 12.5 MB/sec |
| | 1 Gigabit Ethernet cable (1GbE) | 1 Gbps = 125 MB/sec |
| FCP (SCSI-3-based protocol) | 1 Gigabit Fibre Optic cable | 1 Gbps = 125 MB/sec |
| | 2 Gigabit Fibre Optic cable | 2 Gbps = 250 MB/sec |

## Speed Versus Bandwidth

A common misconception is that data transfer bandwidth equates to data transfer speed, or I/O performance. For example, you may hear that a 2 Gbps (250 MB/sec) FC interconnect will be "faster" than a 160 MB/sec SCSI interconnect. This is not necessarily true, although it could appear to be, depending on the scenario. Bandwidth does not refer to transfer speed, but rather the size or amount of data that can be transferred at once (at the same speed).Suppose the largest amount of data that an application attempts to transfer concurrently is only 10 MB. Whether you have a 1 Gbps or 2 Gbps optical fiber interconnect, they both transfer data at the speed of light. So the difference in bandwidth alone will not make a difference in the speed of the transfer since the maximum bandwidth is never approached. 10 MB of data will travel just as quickly across a 1Gbps interconnect as a 2 Gbps interconnect. It is only when the size of data being transferred approaches the bandwidth limitations that a higher bandwidth interconnect will perform faster. For example, if the amount of data that needs to be transferred is 10 GB (such as with a large data file import), then a 2 Gbps (250 MB/sec) interconnect will complete the data transfer twice as fast as a 1 Gbps (125 MB/sec) interconnect. The 2 Gbps interconnect would allow twice as much data to be transferred per second. This analysis is similar for the performance of Ethernet networks at 10 Mbps, 100 Mbps, and 1 Gbps. For example, when backing up a large file that is gigabytes in size, a higher throughput interconnect enables the file to be backed up in less time.

---

**Note**   When bandwidth is not a bottleneck, meaning the bandwidth limits are not approached, then there will be no performance gain from simply increasing bandwidth.

# Storage Systems

There are three major categories of storage systems: DAS, NAS, and SAN. These terms describe the method by which server hosts are attached to and access storage devices. We will describe each type in the following sections. These storage types and the interconnects that can be used with them are not independent of each other, and they can be integrated in various ways, as you will see in the following sections.

## DAS

*DAS* stands for direct attached storage. This means that a server is directly connected physically to a storage device. That storage device can be either internal or external disk storage. This is the most basic and most widely used type of storage. The physical interconnect runs directly from the server to the storage device, so there are no switches or hubs between the server and the storage, as there are with NAS and SAN. DAS can include different types of external storage and different types of interconnects.

Parallel SCSI connected storage is always DAS whether the disks are internal to the server or external in a disk enclosure. See Figure 7-2. With a FC SAN storage device, if the hosts are connected directly to the device instead of connecting through an FC switch as shown in Figure 7-3, then this is also considered DAS. The determining factor for DAS is the direct physical connection between server and storage.

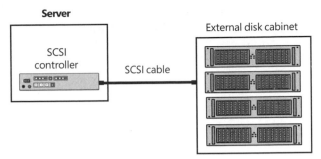

**Figure 7-2**   Parallel SCSI DAS system.

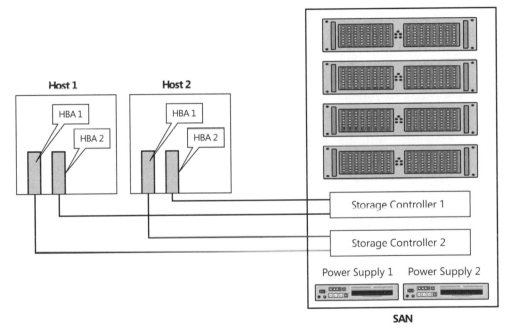

**Figure 7-3**   FC SAN cabled directly as DAS.

## Can an FC SAN Also Be DAS?

Servers can be directly connected to either SCSI storage or FC SAN storage by SCSI or FC interconnects. Thus, with FC SAN storage, the system is also considered DAS if you do not have an FC switch between the server host or hosts and the storage device. So the answer is "Yes, an FC SAN can be categorized as DAS." You can directly attach a limited number of server hosts to an FC SAN storage device depending on the number of front-end ports on the device. FC SAN becomes true

SAN and not DAS when one or more switches are added so that a larger number of hosts can be connected to the storage. In this case, it becomes a true storage area network (SAN). See the SAN section later in this chapter for more information.

DAS might be used for a FC SAN device that will host only a couple of servers and will not be expanded for some time. Otherwise, going with a pure FC SAN with FC switches from the beginning makes it much easier to add server hosts to the storage device later without having to take the existing hosts offline.

DAS is appropriate for small SQL Server database systems, servers that do not need access to large amounts of disk space, or that serve static content, such as Web servers. For a small business environment with only one SQL Server database server, running a small database, for example, DAS, is appropriate. This is the most commonly used storage technology for small SQL Server systems.

DAS systems using either SCSI connected storage or FC SAN storage can be clustered using Windows 2003 Cluster Services and SQL Server 2005 failover clustering for high availability. With SCSI connected storage, there is a maximum of two nodes in a cluster. For FC SAN storage, the maximum number of nodes is equivalent to the Windows operating system maximum, eight nodes with Windows 2003 Enterprise and Datacenter Editions and SQL Server 2005 Enterprise Edition. The limit is two nodes for SQL Server 2005 Standard Edition.

**More Info**    For more information on clustering topics, see *http://msdn2.microsoft.com/enus/library/ms189134(SQL.90).aspx.*

## SAN

The most common storage subsystem used for database storage in medium-to-large business environments, is the *storage area network (SAN)*. This is because of the benefits that SAN provides for flexibility, scalability, storage consolidation, and centralized storage management among a large number of server host machines. SANs provide the largest amounts of consolidated storage and the largest number of server hosts that can be connected to the storage device. The hosts can be of different operating systems as well.

The SAN system itself basically consists of the disk controllers, also called storage processors, which are powered by their own CPUs; the disk cabinets, or disk enclosures; and the disk drives. A SAN generally comes with two controllers and one cabinet of disks. Although you may be able to get just one controller, it is not recommended. The controllers have their own cache memory for caching reads and writes of data. More disk cabinets can be added for more disks up to the maximum for the SAN model. One point to note about SAN is the disk controllers/processors are built into the SAN rather than residing in the host server.

Each SAN model supports a limited number of host machines and a limited number of disk drives. Make sure that you know these limitations before choosing a model to fit your current needs and future growth.

A SAN can be based on either the FC or the iSCSI interconnect standards. The one you choose depends on the needs of your system. We describe both options in the following sections.

## FC SAN

FC SANs are well-designed for mission-critical and I/O-intensive applications where high performance and high availability are essential. This is the top-of-the-line choice in storage solutions for performance and expandability, but it is also the most costly, requiring dedicated FC equipment in the server hosts and for the FC network infrastructure. FC networks are more complicated to configure and manage than IP networks and demand a high level of expertise to configure the network and storage correctly. FC networks with dedicated fibre optic cable can extend to 10 km, thus connecting data centers in local or metropolitan areas. However, this distance is a limitation for sites spread across the country. This is where IP networks have an advantage. Protocols that allow fibre channel traffic to be transported over IP are currently being developed to overcome the 10 km distance limitation.

Host servers communicate I/O requests to the SAN through an HBA in each server. The HBA is connected to the SAN with an FC cable either directly to the SAN or through an FC switch. With directly attached host servers to the SAN (which is actually DAS), the number of possible hosts is limited by the number of ports on the SAN. With an FC switch, the number of hosts can be much greater. The maximum number depends on the SAN model. If you are unsure of system growth needs, it's best to configure the FC switch or switches into the solution up front to allow for easier addition of more server hosts later. Alternatively, hosts can connect via Ethernet to a NAS gateway or an iSCSI bridge that then connects to the SAN via FC, eliminating the need for HBAs in the host servers and reducing costs. However, this adds to I/O latency and thus degrades I/O performance.

Figure 7-4 shows an example of a SAN system with three host servers connected to the storage via an FC switch. Each of the three hosts is assigned to its own logical disk unit(s) that are configured on the SAN. The disk configuration and assignment to hosts is done through the SAN management software.

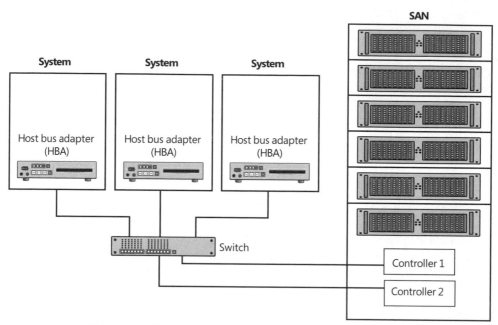

**Figure 7-4** FC SAN with three hosts and single HBAs.

To configure a SAN for high availability, you must ensure that each component within the I/O system is redundant, meaning there are two of each component so that one of the pair will take over if the other fails. This is called a *fully redundant SAN* system and is the recommended configuration for high availability of both the storage system and the data transfer paths between servers and storage. For a fully redundant system, the following components are needed:

- Two HBAs per host server

- Two fibre channel switches

- Two disk controllers (also called storage processors) inside the SAN

- Two power supplies in the SAN

Figure 7-5 shows an example of a fully redundant SAN system with three hosts.

By cabling and configuring the SAN and server hosts properly with fully redundant components, the I/O system is protected from a single point of failure, such as an HBA or a switch failure, by providing two possible paths from the host server to the SAN.

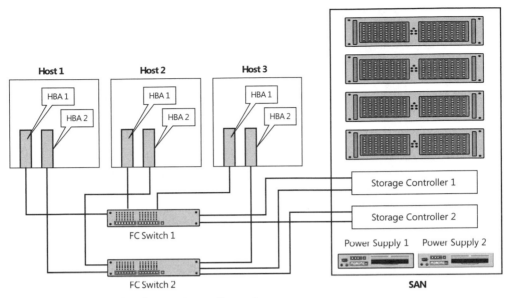

**Figure 7-5**   Fully redundant SAN configuration.

**Note**   If your system is critical and you need this level of redundancy, then ask your hardware vendor for a fully redundant SAN solution up front, or the dual components may be overlooked on the hardware order.

In addition to the fault tolerance benefits of redundant components, having dual data access paths between the servers and the SAN (dual HBAs, cables, and switches) provides the possibility of using *multipath I/O* (MPIO). With MPIO, both paths can be used simultaneously to access the storage to provide load balancing of I/O traffic for greater performance. The storage vendor normally provides the multipath driver necessary for your SAN.

## Real World   SCSI DAS vs. FC SAN Performance

In the field, I've seen cases in which there were misconceptions about expected performance of SAN as compared with direct attached SCSI storage. It is often thought that by moving from a SCSI DAS storage system to an FC SAN system, I/O performance will automatically and noticeably improve. However, there are many factors that affect performance aside from the SAN itself, such as the number of disk drives, the amount of data being transferred per second, controller cache settings, and others. For example, if you have a direct attached SCSI array with 10 disk drives, then move that to a SAN with only six disk drives, you may not see any performance gain from the SAN and may even see a degradation. Having a fewer number of drives can hurt performance. In many cases with SQL Server database activity, which most often consists of random and small sized I/O's, you will hit a physical disk bottleneck before hitting a throughput bottleneck. A SCSI direct connection at 320 MB/sec provides greater throughput than a 1-Gbps or 2-Gbps (125-MB/sec or 250-MB/sec, respectively) FC connection. On the other hand, the SAN provides other significant benefits, such as a much larger I/O cache than a SCSI disk controller, although this cache is then shared by all hosts on the SAN. Therefore, simply moving to a SAN does not in itself equate to faster I/O performance. The SAN must be configured properly and with enough disk drives to handle the I/O needs of the system. Generally, you should configure at least the same number of disks, if not more, for a particular host when moving from a SCSI DAS system to SAN. If possible, test the I/O performance of the SAN with a benchmark or load test before implementing into production to determine the best disk configuration. See Chapter 4 for more information on disk I/O performance.

## iSCSI SAN (or IP SAN)

iSCSI makes SAN more affordable for small-to-medium-sized organizations that cannot afford an FC network. With an iSCSI SAN, a network attached iSCSI storage device allows multiple hosts to access the device over an IP network. iSCSI SAN is the best alternative to FC SAN because of its lower cost of implementation and ability to transfer data over much greater distances than FC. No HBAs or FC network infrastructure are required as with FC SAN configurations, and it is easier to install and support than FC SAN. See Figure 7-6. iSCSI HBAs are available, though, for offloading the iSCSI processing from the system processors to the HBA itself.

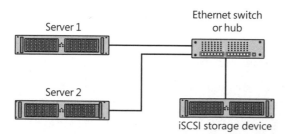

**Figure 7-6**  iSCSI storage with two hosts on Ethernet network.

iSCSI bandwidth between a server host and the storage is dependent upon the type of Ethernet and IP network bandwidth, for example, 100 Mbps or 1GbE. To avoid hitting bandwidth limitations, the highest available bandwidth for all network components such as cables, switches, and network cards should be used, and a dedicated network should be configured in order to completely isolate the server-to-storage-device data transfers from other network traffic.

The data transport latency is higher with iSCSI than with FC because of the overhead incurred by encapsulating the SCSI commands in TCP/IP packets. Also, the entire network infrastructure must be taken into account regarding bandwidth. For example, the Ethernet cabling may be at 1GbE, but if a network switch is overloaded with heavy network traffic from multiple servers, this can cause network congestion and further increase latencies.

**More Info** Refer to the Microsoft article "Microsoft Support for iSCSI" for more information about how iSCSI works and the Microsoft iSCSI Initiator package with the iSCSI driver at *download.microsoft.com/download/a/6/4/a6403fbb-8cdb-4826-bf8f-56f79cb5a184/MicrosoftSupportforiSCSI.doc*.

## iSCSI Bridge to FC SAN

Data that is passed through an iSCSI bridge is translated from iSCSI to FC, allowing an iSCSI host to be connected to an FC SAN storage back end. This enables servers on an existing IP network infrastructure to access storage on an FC SAN without having to add an HBA and FC interconnect to that server. Again, this incremental step adds some overhead and latency to data transfers between the host and the storage compared with direct FC connectivity.

# NAS

*NAS* stands for network attached storage, storage that is connected using an IP-based network, not, for example, an FC network. A NAS storage device consists of disk storage and management software and is completely dedicated to serving files over the network. This differs from DAS in that NAS relieves the server from the overhead of file sharing responsibilities. Servers access data on NAS devices via standard Ethernet connectivity.

A NAS device is a file server that attaches to the LAN like any other client or server in the network. Rather than containing a full-blown operating system, the NAS device uses a slimmed-down microkernel specialized for handling only file reads and writes supporting CIFS/SMB, NFS, and NCP file protocols, for example.

## When to Use NAS

NAS is not recommended for SQL Server data storage because of the overhead incurred by protocols used for file-level data access (SMB/CIFS). Block-level data access is much more efficient for SQL Server. Also, the NAS is subject to the variable behavior and overhead of a network that may contain thousands of users. A dedicated network is therefore necessary to eliminate contention as well as for the obvious security benefits. Therefore, although it is possible to store SQL Server files on NAS storage, it is not commonly used and not generally recommended because of slower performance.

NAS is most commonly and most appropriately used for basic file storage and sharing of data such as reference data, images, audio and video, Web content, and archives. It also provides storage access to systems with different operating systems.

### NAS Gateway to FC SAN

A NAS gateway provides a way to connect servers to a SAN using an Ethernet network card in the server. A server connects to a NAS gateway by Ethernet, and the NAS gateway then connects to an FC SAN by FC. The NAS gateway converts file-formatted data into block-level data for storage on the SAN. This eliminates the need for FC infrastructure for the servers, thus, also eliminating the purchase of HBAs and FC switches for the server hosts. Again, this is not a recommended solution for SQL Server data because of the performance degradation with the data conversion. A good purpose for the NAS gateway is using your SAN storage for both file and block data storage. (The file data is converted to block by the gateway.) Therefore, you could have SQL Server data stored on the SAN and accessed via an FC network and also have other files stored on the SAN accessed via the NAS gateway by hosts on the Ethernet LAN.

---

**Note** One example of how these protocols and storage devices can intermingle is Netapp, which provides a single storage device that simultaneously supports FC SAN, iSCSI SAN, and NAS capabilities. All three types of storage access can be performed at the same time against the storage via the different interconnect types. Some hosts can access storage on the device via pure TCP/IP over IP network, some can connect via iSCSI over IP network, and others can access via FPC over FC network. This allows different access needs to be met from the same storage device.

---

# Storage Considerations for SQL Server 2005

Now let's put all the previous information together and relate it specifically to SQL Server storage needs. Knowing the type of data to be stored, whether shared files, archives, or SQL Server data, for example, will help you determine what system is best. SQL Server performance is very dependent on I/O performance. In other words, read and write latencies greatly affect SQL Server performance. Therefore, for the very best I/O performance with SQL Server you would choose a block-based data transport protocol, either

SCSI, iSCSI, or FCP. NAS, which transports data in file form, is not really a viable choice for SQL Server data.

To determine whether to select less costly SCSI DAS or more expandable and flexible SAN storage, consider the following:

- How big will the size of the database or databases be?

- How many users will access the database, and what type of activity will they be performing, including OLTP, reports, batch jobs, and others?

- How many disk drives will be needed for storage space, including backups, and how many spindles will be needed for best practice for performance? For example, to physically separate log files from data files.

- At what rate will the data grow?

- At what rate will users be added to the system?

- Are there/ will there be other servers added to the environment that will need storage and thus could utilize the SAN as well?

- What are the organization's high-availability, scalability, and disaster-recovery requirements?

If only one SQL Server suffices for your entire business and the database and number of users accessing it (or the amount of database activity) are somewhat small, then a SCSI DAS solution might be appropriate. "Small" could be between one and 50 users with a database size of 100 MB to 1 GB, for example. A database this size could easily fit into the SQL Server buffer cache in memory on the server, and reduce the amount of disk I/O, thus requiring a small number of disk drives on the system. Keep in mind that high availability can be covered by clustering with SCSI storage, and disaster recovery can be accomplished using database mirroring or other solution as described in Chapter 26, "Disaster Recovery Solutions".

If the SQL Server application or applications run on a medium- to large-sized database system, if there are multiple servers in the environment that need more storage, if the application performs intense I/O activity, if there is a need to consolidate existing servers' storage to manage it more easily then consider SAN storage. SAN storage also provides more options for high availability and disaster recovery through SAN based software solutions, such as database snapshots or clones and mirrored databases across storage, including local or remote mirrors. You may also want to start with a smaller, less expensive SAN system that supports a smaller number of disks and a smaller number of host servers if it will meet your current needs. This approach still provides opportunity for growth and upgrade later if more storage or server hosts need to be added. If you know that you will need room for growth, plan for that up front and go with the bigger SAN to reduce downtime and the risk involved with upgrades. A SAN upgrade will involve downtime.

Table 7-5 shows a comparison of storage types and the type of data appropriate for each.

**Table 7-5   Storage Comparison Chart**

| Protocol | Data Transport | Best Used for | Benefits/Drawbacks |
| --- | --- | --- | --- |
| SCSI DAS (SCSI over Parallel SCSI) | Block-based | SQL Server files; data that is mainly accessed by the direct-attached server (not a file share server) | Good performance, low flexibility |
| NAS (TCP/IP over Ethernet) | File-based | File servers, file sharing, archive, static data | Lowest performance and high data accessibility between servers, but not optimal for SQL Server data |
| iSCSI SAN (iSCSI over Ethernet) | Block-based | SQL Server files and any other data, although more data transport overhead than FC SAN | Possibly a less expensive option than FC SAN. Good performance, good flexibility |
| FC SAN (SCSI-3 based protocol over FC) | Block-based | SQL Server files, I/O intensive data, and any other data | Highest performance/flexibility combined. Given the appropriate budget, probably can't go wrong with FC SAN for SQL Server data |

# Summary

Choosing a storage system for SQL Server 2005 data and log files is very important for overall I/O performance, storage flexibility, manageability, and scalability. We have discussed the different types of data transport interconnects that are available—SCSI, Ethernet, and FC—and the various data transfer protocol types—SCSI, iSCSI, FCP, and TCP/IP—and how they interact with the three main storage system configurations, DAS, NAS, and SAN. There are many factors to consider when choosing a storage system for SQL Server data. Although it is more expensive than DAS or NAS, SAN storage also provides the greatest features and benefits, so you may have to make a trade-off between cost, performance, and features. Identifying those trade-offs will help you make the best decision.

# Chapter 8

# Installing and Upgrading Microsoft SQL Server 2005

Now that you have a good understanding of the different editions of Microsoft SQL Server 2005 Server, the platforms on which it can be run, and capacity planning and storage configuration concepts, let's get to the next most important step: installing SQL Server 2005.

This chapter provides a detailed look at the planning necessary before installation and the step-by-step installation process using the graphical user interface and the command line. You will also learn how to upgrade to SQL Server 2005 from earlier versions, how to configure SQL Server features and services using the new SQL Server Surface Area Configuration tool, and how to uninstall SQL Server 2005 components.

## Preinstallation Planning

Before installing SQL Server 2005, it is extremely important that you plan the installation process well and have all the relevant information necessary for the installation process. This will help ensure a smooth installation experience and prevent unnecessary postinstallation changes.

This section explains some of the important configuration options you need to have decided on before starting the installation. While the graphical user interface-based installation method is relatively easy and many users like to adopt a "discover-as-you-go" approach, I have found time and again that this is not the most productive approach. The time supposedly saved by not planning out the installation is spent either cancelling and restarting the installation, or debugging and resolving incorrect configuration options after the installation is complete. Both of these cases are undesirable. I highly recommend that you read the following sections to understand the various planning considerations and then decide which ones are applicable and important to your deployment.

## Minimum Hardware Requirements

SQL Server 2005 has a well-defined set of minimum hardware requirements that need to be met for SQL Server 2005 installation. These requirements are listed in Table 8-1. These are only the bare minimum requirements for SQL Server 2005 installation; they do not guarantee good performance. Refer to Chapter 6, "Capacity Planning," to determine the appropriate hardware resources required for your particular deployment.

**Table 8-1   Minimum Hardware Requirements**

| Resource | Requirement |
| --- | --- |
| Monitor | At least 1024 × 768 pixel resolution (SVGA) if using graphical tools |
| Pointing device | Microsoft mouse or compatible pointing device |
| DVD drive | Only required if installing from DVD media |
| Network card | Only required if accessing via the network |
| Processor | **32-bit systems:**<br>• Processor type: Pentium III-compatible or higher<br>• Processor speed: 600 MHz minimum<br>**64-bit systems:**<br>• Processor type (IA64): Itanium processor or higher<br>• Processor type (x64): AMD Opteron, AMD Athlon 64, Intel Xenon with Intel EM64T support and Intel Pentium IV with EM64T support<br>• Processor speed: 1 GHz minimum |
| Memory (RAM) | Minimum 512 MB, recommended 1 GB |

During installation, the System Configuration Checker (SCC) will display an error message and terminate the installation if the system does not meet the minimum processor type requirements. SCC will issue a warning if the minimum processor speed or the recommended memory requirements are not met.

> **Note** If you have 1 GB of memory in the system, the SQL Server 2005 installation wizard may incorrectly flag a warning stating that the current system does not meet the recommended hardware requirements. This is an anomaly in the installer. If you're sure that system does meet the minimum requirements, you can ignore this message.

The disk space requirements for the SQL Server executables and samples vary based on the components selected for installation. Table 8-2 lists the disk space utilized by the different SQL Server 2005 components.

**Table 8-2   SQL Server 2005 Disk Space Requirements**

| Feature | Disk Space Required |
| --- | --- |
| Database engine, replication, and full-text search | 150 MB |
| Analysis Services | 35 KB |
| Reporting Services and Report Manager | 40 MB |
| Notification Services engine, client, and rules components | 5 MB |
| Integration Services | 9 MB |
| Client Components | 12 MB |
| Management Tools | 70 MB |
| Development Tools | 20 MB |
| SQL Server Books Online and SQL Server Mobile Books Online | 15 MB |
| Samples and sample databases | 390 MB |

The maximum disk space required if all of the components and samples are selected is approximately 750 MB.

## Selecting the Processor Architecture

As mentioned in Chapter 2, "SQL Server 2005 Editions, Capacity Limits, and Licensing," each SQL Server 2005 edition is available on the 32-bit (IA-32), 64-bit (IA64), and 64-bit (x64) platforms. To make sure that the software installs correctly and performs well, make sure that you install the correct executables SQL Server 2005 platform version for your operating system and hardware. While combinations such as installing the IA64 SQL Server 2005 software on a 32-bit system will simply not install and result in an error message, some combinations like 32-bit software on the x64 platform may work but not perform properly.

# Installing Internet Information Services

If you plan to install Microsoft SQL Server 2005 Reporting Services, you will require Internet Information Services (IIS) 5.0 or later installed on the server before SQL Server 2005 setup is started. You can install IIS using the following steps:

1. Click Start, then select Control Panel (or select Settings and then Control Panel), and then double-click Select Add or Remove Programs in Control Panel.

2. In the left pane, click Add/Remove Windows Components.

3. Select Application Server in the Windows Components Wizard that opens, and then select Details.

4. Select the check box next to Internet Information Services (IIS) in the Application Server dialog box that appears, then click OK, and then click Next.

5. You may be prompted to insert your Windows media CD, so you may want to have this available during installation.

In general, having IIS installed on your server is not recommended unless it is absolutely required. If you do not plan to use Reporting Services on your server, I'd recommend you do not install IIS and ignore the warning messages that are displayed during the installation process.

# Components to Be Installed

Unlike earlier versions of SQL Server, which required invoking separate installation processes for the different components, SQL Server 2005 has a fully integrated setup through which all the components can be installed together via a single installation process. You can select any combination of the following components for installation:

- SQL Server Database Services
- Analysis Services
- Reporting Services
- Notification Services
- Integration Services
- Workstation components, books online, and development tools

Depending on the Microsoft SQL Server components you choose to install, the following 10 services are installed:

1. **SQL Server Main**   SQL Server database engine

2. **SQL Server Agent**   Used for automating administrative tasks, executing jobs, alerts, and so on

3. **SQL Server Analysis Services**   Provides online analytical processing (OLAP) and data mining functionality for Business Intelligence (BI) applications

4. **SQL Server Reporting Services**   Manages, executes, renders, schedules, and delivers reports

5. **SQL Server Notification Services**   Platform for developing and deploying applications that generate and send notifications

> **Note**   When you install SQL Server Notification Services, a service is not installed by default and will not appear under Services in the Control Panel. The service is configured only when you build an application and register a service to run that application.

6. **SQL Server Integration Services**   Provides management support for Integration Services package storage and execution

7. **SQL Server Full Text Search**   Enables fast linguistic searches on content and properties of structured and semistructured data by using full-text indexes

8. **SQL Server Browser**   Name resolution service that provides SQL Server connection information for client computers

9. **SQL Server Active Directory Helper**   Publishes and manages SQL Server services in Windows Active Directory

10. **SQL Server VSS Writer**   Allows backup and restore applications to operate in the Volume Shadow-copy Service (VSS) framework

I recommend that you be selective and install only the components you actually plan to use. This will limit the number of unnecessary services that run on your server and prevent them from consuming precious server resources like disk space, memory, processor, and so on.

## Service Accounts

All SQL Server 2005 services require a login account to operate. The login account can be either a local service account, a domain user account, a network service account, or a local system account.

■ **Local Service account**   This is a built-in account that has the same level of access as members of the users group. This low-privileged access limits the damage that can be done in case the service gets compromised. This account is not effective for use with services that need to interact with other network services since it accesses network resources with no credentials.

- **Domain User account**   As the name suggests, this account corresponds to an actual domain user account. This account is preferred when the service needs to interact with other services on the network.

- **Network Service account**   This account is similar to the Local Service account, except that services that run as the Network Service account can access network resources with the credentials of the computer account.

- **Local System account**   The Local System account is a highly privileged account and should be used very selectively. You should be careful not to confuse this account with the Local Service account. With respect to privileges, they are at opposite ends of the spectrum.

---

**Best Practices**   You should always configure a service to run with the lowest effective privileges that can be used.

Table 8-3 lists the default accounts for each of the 10 SQL Server services. You can change these as required, but always consider the limitations and security exposures explained previously.

**Table 8-3   SQL Server Service Default Accounts**

| SQL Server Service | Default Account |
|---|---|
| SQL Server | Domain User |
| SQL Server Agent | Domain User |
| SQL Server Analysis Services | Domain User |
| SQL Server Reporting Services | Domain User |
| SQL Server Notification Services | N/A |
| SQL Server Integration Services | Network Service |
| SQL Server Full-Text Search | Same account as SQL Server |
| SQL Server Browser | Domain User |
| SQL Server Active Directory Helper | Network Service |
| SQL Server VSS Writer | Local System |

Before you start installation, make sure that all domain accounts required to configure the services during setup have been created and are available for use.

## Multiple Instances and Side-by-Side Installation

Microsoft SQL Server 2005 supports multiple instances of the database engine, Analysis Services, and Reporting Services to be installed side-by-side on the same computer. Side-by-side installations are completely separate instances and not dependent on each other in any way. You can choose to have any combination of side-by-side installs of SQL Server 7.0, SQL Server 2000, or SQL Server 2005 listed as supported in Table 8-4.

**Table 8-4   Supported Side-by-Side Installations**

| Side-by-Side Install | SQL Server 2000 (32-bit) | SQL Server 2000 (64-bit) | SQL Server 2005 (32-bit) | SQL Server 2005 (IA64) | SQL Server 2005 (x64) |
|---|---|---|---|---|---|
| SQL Server 7.0 | Yes | No | Yes | No | No |
| SQL Server 2000 (32-bit) | Yes | No | Yes | No | Yes |
| SQL Server 2000 (64-bit) | No | Yes | No | Yes | No |
| SQL Server 2005 (32-bit) | Yes | No | Yes | No | Yes |
| SQL Server 2005 (IA64) | No | Yes | No | Yes | No |
| SQL Server 2005 (x64) | Yes | No | Yes | No | Yes |

If you already have an instance of SQL Server installed on your system, you should decide before starting the installation process whether you'd like to upgrade it (as explained later in this chapter) or install a new SQL Server 2005 instance on the side.

## Licensing Mode

As explained in Chapter 2, SQL Server 2005 can be installed using a per-processor licensing model, a user client access license (user CAL) licensing model, or a device client access license (device CAL) licensing model. Before starting the installation process, you should determine the licensing model you plan to use and secure the required licenses.

## Collation

A *collation* determines the rules by which character data is sorted and compared. SQL Server 2005 has two groups of collations: Windows collations and SQL collations. SQL collations are provided primarily as a compatibility option with earlier versions of SQL Server. You should use these if you plan to use replication with databases on earlier versions of SQL Server or if your application requires a specific SQL collation of an earlier SQL Server version. For all other cases, you should use the Windows collation.

---

**Best Practices**   You should decide on an organization-wide collation and use it for all your SQL Server 2005 servers so you're assured of consistency for all server-to-server activity.

---

The collation specified during the installation process becomes the SQL Server instance's default collation. This collation is used for all the system databases and any user databases that do not explicitly specify a collation.

## Authentication Modes

SQL Server supports two authentication modes: Windows authentication mode and mixed mode.

- **Windows authentication mode**    This authentication mode permits users to connect only by using a valid Windows user account. With Windows authentication, SQL Server validates the account credentials using information from the Windows operating system. The Windows authentication mode optionally provides password policy enforcement for validation for strong passwords, support for account lockout, and password expiration. The sa user ("sa" is short for "system administrator") is disabled when Windows authentication is selected.

- **Mixed mode**    This authentication mode permits users to connect using either Windows authentication or SQL Server authentication. Users who connect through a Windows user account are validated by Windows, while users who connect using SQL Server login are validated by SQL Server. The sa user is enabled when mixed mode is selected and a password prompt appears during the installation process.

---

**Best Practices**    Never use a blank or weak password for the sa account.

It is recommended that you use strong passwords for all users who will log in to SQL Server 2005. A strong password must be six or more characters long and have at least three of the following types of characters:

- Uppercase letters
- Lowercase letters
- Numbers
- Non-alphanumeric characters

Although Windows authentication is the recommended authentication mode and more secure than mixed mode, many applications require mixed mode authentication. You should evaluate your application needs and select the authentication based on that.

## Security Considerations

A large part of the long-term security of your server environment is dictated by some relatively simple and inexpensive best practices you can adopt during the planning and installation phase. To make your SQL Server installation as secure as possible, the following are recommended:

- Physically secure the server and make it accessible only to authorized personnel.
- Have at least one firewall between the server and the Internet.

- Enforce strong passwords for all SQL Server accounts and enable password policies and password expiration.

- Create service accounts with least privileges.

- Run separate SQL Server services under separate Windows accounts to prevent one compromised service from being used to compromise others.

- Use NTFS instead of a FAT file system.

- Disable all unnecessary protocols, including NetBIOS and server message block (SMB), on the servers.

> **Note**   Disabling the NetBIOS protocol may cause connectivity problems if you're using DHCP. You may want to check with your system administrator before disabling any protocols.

# Installing SQL Server 2005

Once you've completed the preinstallation planning and have all the required information available, you are ready to install SQL Server 2005. SQL Server 2005 can be installed on your local server using either the SQL Server 2005 Installation Wizard or the command prompt installation. If you're new to SQL Server or plan to install just a couple of servers, I recommend you use the Installation Wizard. The command prompt-based installation is often slightly trickier and better suited to experienced users who need to perform multiple similar installations and want to automate the process. SQL Server also provides the option of installing just the SQL Native Access Client (SNAC) connectivity libraries on the server; this process is explained in detail later in this chapter. This is particularly useful for client systems that need to use SNAC to connect to the SQL Server 2005–based server. All of these installation methods are explained in detail in the following sections.

> **Note**   Installing to a remote server, which was possible in earlier versions of SQL Server, is not supported in SQL Server 2005. To install SQL Server 2005 onto a remote server, you need to log in remotely to the server and run the setup program, or remotely execute the command prompt installation on the remote server.

## Installing SQL Server 2005 Using the Installation Wizard

The SQL Server 2005 Installation Wizard is a Windows installer-based program that interactively guides you through the entire installation process. The Installation Wizard has built-in tools for performing appropriate configuration and error checking and provides meaningful warning and error messages.

The following steps explain how to install a new nonclustered SQL Server 2005 instance on your local server. If you already have an instance of SQL server installed on your server, some of the windows shown in the figures may not be presented or may be slightly different. This is because the Installation Wizard reuses the information already available on the system; for example, the Registration dialog box (step 8) will not prompt you for the PID if you've already installed the same version of SQL Server 2005 on the system before.

1. Log in to the system as Administrator or as a user who has administrator privileges on the server.

> **Note**    The SQL Server 2005 Setup program can be invoked in many ways. In most cases, the program automatically starts when the SQL Server 2005 DVD media is inserted into the DVD drive or when a remote network share is mapped onto the server. If the program is not automatically loaded, you can navigate to the Servers directory and double-click the Splash.hta program. With either of these approaches, the Start dialog box, shown in Figure 8-1, appears.

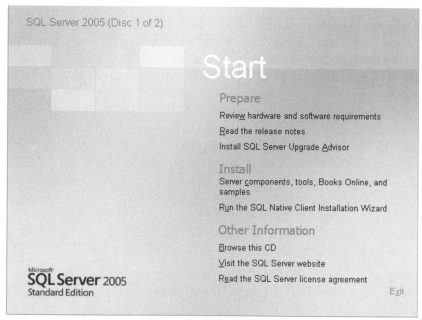

**Figure 8-1**    SQL Server Setup—Start window.

2.  The Start window presents options to prepare and install the server as well as access other information. To install SQL Server 2005, click the "Server components, tools, Books Online, and samples" option in the Start window.

3.  The End User License Agreement (EULA) window appears. Read the agreement and select the I Accept the Licensing Terms and Conditions check box. Selecting the check box will activate the Next button. Select Next.

4.  The Installing Prerequisites dialog box, shown in Figure 8-2, appears, and the software components required prior to installing SQL Server 2005 are installed. Select Install. This step may take several minutes to complete.

> **Note**   You may see a different list in Figure 8-2 if some of the components have already been installed via a previous install, or by some other application.

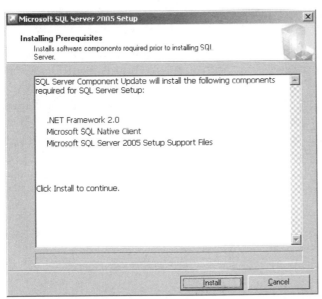

**Figure 8-2**   SQL Server Setup—Installing Prerequisites dialog box.

5.  The Welcome page for the Installation Wizard appears. Select Next.

6.  The System Configuration Check (SCC) page appears. At this point, the Installation Wizard scans the system for conditions that do not meet the minimum requirements and displays the status for each action with a message for the errors and a warning, as shown in Figure 8-3.

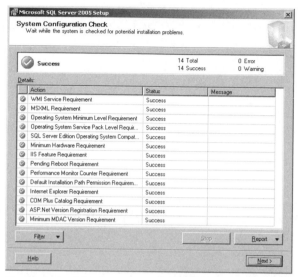

**Figure 8-3** SQL Server Setup—System Configuration Check page.

7. Once the SCC has completed scanning the computer, the Filter button in the lower-left corner is activated and can be used to filter the output to Show All Actions, Show Errors, Show Successful Actions, or Show Warnings in the window. You can only view the actions that are relevant, for example if there are no errors the Show Errors option is not activated. Correspondingly, the Report button in the lower-right corner can be used to view a report in a report format, save the report to a file, copy the report to the Clipboard, or send the report as e-mail. Once SCC completes the configuration check, click Next to continue with the setup.

> **Note**  If the SCC determines a pending action that must be completed before proceeding, for example a pending reboot operation, it will block the setup by not activating the Next button and force you to complete the pending actions.

8. The setup performs some additional checks that may take a few minutes and then displays the Registration Information page. On the Registration Information page, enter information in the Name, Company, and Product Key text boxes. Select Next to continue.

9. The Components To Install page displays, as shown in Figure 8-4. On this page, select the components to be installed that you identified during the preinstallation planning.

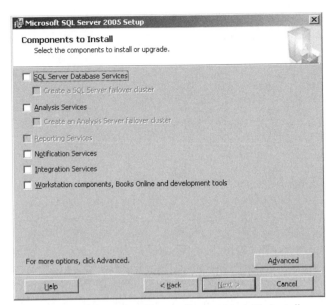

**Figure 8-4**   SQL Server Setup—Components To Install page.

10. To select specific subcomponents for any of the components, you can select the Advanced button on the lower-right side of the page, which will display the Feature Selection dialog box as shown in Figure 8-5.

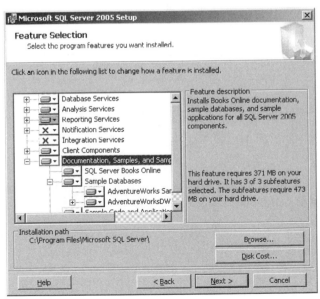

**Figure 8-5**   SQL Server Setup—Feature Selection dialog box.

In this dialog box, you can select the Will Be Installed On Local Hard Drive option to install the feature but not all the subcomponents of the feature, select the Entire Feature Will Be Installed On Local Hard Drive option to install the feature and all the subcomponents of the feature, or select the Entire Feature Will Be Unavailable option to not install the feature. Once you have selected the appropriate services, select Next to continue.

---

**Note**    The sample databases and sample code and applications are not installed by default even when the Documentation, Samples, and Sample Databases feature is selected. To install these, select the Advanced button and explicitly select them for installation, as shown in Figure 8-5, or select the Entire Feature Will Be Installed On Local Hard Drive option for the Documentation, Samples, And Sample Databases feature.

---

11.  The Instance Name page, shown in Figure 8-6, appears. On this page, you can select the instance to be either a Default Instance or a Named Instance. If you select Named Instance, the text box in which you need to enter a valid instance name is activated. You can select the Installed Instances button in the lower right of the page to view the instances already installed on the system. If a default or named instance is already installed on the server and you select it, the setup will upgrade it and present you the option of installing additional components. This is explained in the section on upgrading to SQL Server 2005 later in this chapter. Click Next to continue.

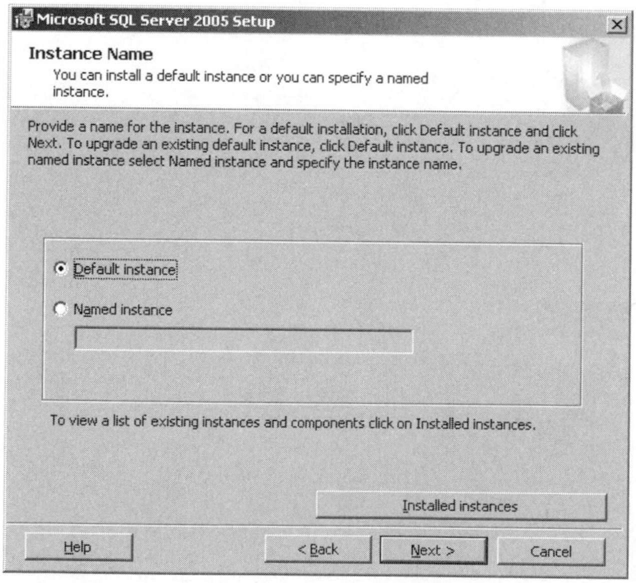

**Figure 8-6**    SQL Server Setup—Instance Name page.

> **Note**   A server can have only one default instance of SQL Server. This implies that if you have SQL Server 2000 installed on your server as a default instance and you do not want to upgrade it, you should install the SQL Server 2005 as a named instance.

12.   The Service Account page, shown in Figure 8-7, is displayed. This page is used to specify the accounts the services use to log in. You can either specify the same account for all the services installed or select the Customize For Each Service Account check box and specify the login accounts for each service selected for installation individually. You can then select the login account to use one of the built-in system accounts (Local Service, Network Service, or Local System) by clicking on the Use The Built-in System Account radio button and selecting the appropriate account from the drop-down list, or you can specify a domain user by selecting the Use A Domain User Account radio button and entering a domain user name, password, and domain. In the Start Services At The End Of Setup section, you can select the check boxes next to the services you would like to start automatically every time the system is started. Click Next to continue.

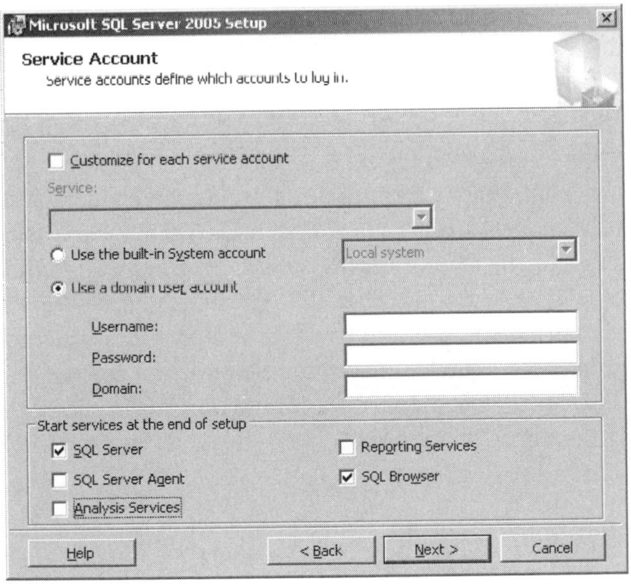

**Figure 8-7**   SQL Server Setup—Service Account page.

13.  The Authentication Mode page, shown in Figure 8-8, appears. On this page, click the appropriate radio button to select either Windows Authentication Mode or Mixed Mode (Windows Authentication And SQL Server Authentication). If you use the mixed mode, you will need to enter and confirm the login password for the sa user. Click Next to continue.

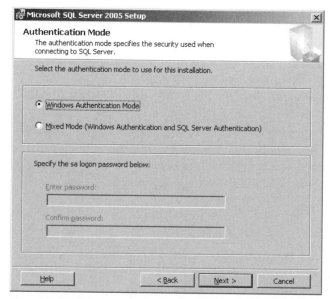

**Figure 8-8**   SQL Server Setup—Authentication Mode page.

14.  The Collation Settings page, shown in Figure 8-9, appears. On this page you can choose to customize the collation for each individual service being installed using the Customize For Each Service Account check box, or you can use the same collation for all the services. For the collation, you can select either Collation Designator And Sort Order or SQL Collations (Used For Compatibility With Previous Versions Of SQL Server) using the radio buttons. If you are using the collation designator and sort order, select the language (for example, Latin1_General for the English language) from the drop-down list and the appropriate check boxes below. If you are using the SQL Collations, select the desired one from the scrollable list below the radio button. Click Next to continue.

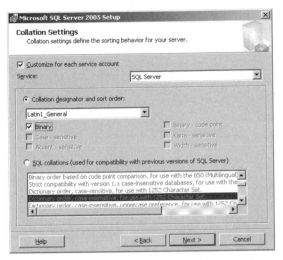

**Figure 8-9**   SQL Server Setup—Collation Settings page.

15. If you selected to install Reporting Services, the Report Server Installation Options page, shown in Figure 8-10, appears. You can use the radio buttons on this page to choose to Install The Default Configuration for Reporting Server or Install But Do Not Configure The Server. You can select the Details button located in the upper right of the page to view the details of the Report Server installation information. If a Secure Sockets Layer (SSL) certificate has not been installed on the server, a warning message is displayed. Since reports often contain sensitive information, it is recommended that you use SSL in most installations. Select Next to continue.

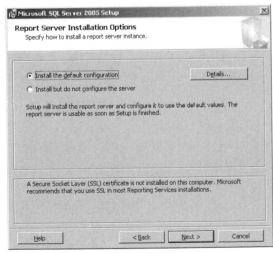

**Figure 8-10**   SQL Server Setup—Report Server Installation Options page.

16. The Error And Usage Report Settings page, shown in Figure 8-11, appears. On this page, you can select the two radio buttons, Automatically Send Error Reports For SQL Server 2005 To Microsoft Or Your Corporate Error Reporting Server and Usage Data For SQL Server 2005 To Microsoft, to set the desired default action. This data is collected for information purposes only, and selecting either of these options will not have any adverse effects on the performance of your system. Select Next to continue.

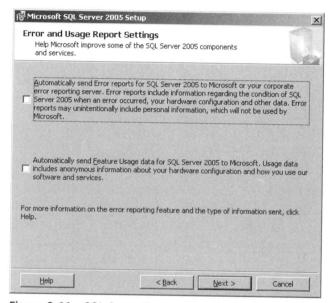

**Figure 8-11**   SQL Server Setup—Error And Usage Report Settings page.

17. The Ready To Install page, shown in Figure 8-12, appears. You can review the summary of features and components selected for installation. To make any changes, select the Back button and go back in the installation process until the relevant page appears. For the most part, the installation process will retain your selections so that you don't have to re-enter all of the information after backtracking through the pages. Select Install to continue.

18. The Setup Progress page, shown in Figure 8-13, appears. At this point in the installation process, the selected services are actually installed and configured on your system. This step may take a while to complete and is dependent on the speed of your processor and the disk being installed to. The page continuously updates the progress bar to reflect the installation status of the individual components and will reset for each component being installed. To view the log file for the component installation status, you can click the component name. When all of the steps are completed, select Next to continue.

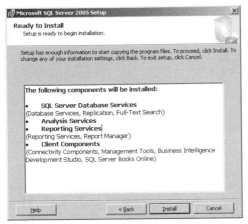

**Figure 8-12**   SQL Server Setup—Ready To Install page.

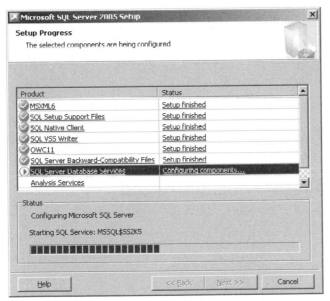

**Figure 8-13**   SQL Server Setup—Setup Progress page.

19. The Completing Microsoft SQL Server 2005 Setup page, shown in Figure 8-14, appears. On this page, you view the summary log. You can also select the Surface Area Configuration Tool to configure SQL Server 2005 as explained in the Surface Area Configuration section that follows. Click Finish to complete the installation.

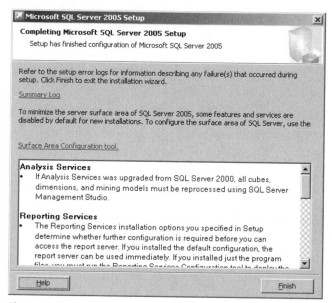

**Figure 8-14**    SQL Server Setup—Completing Microsoft SQL Server 2005 Setup page.

20.    Restart the system if the setup prompts you to do so.

---

**Note**    If you need to add or remove components to a default or named instance of SQL Server 2005, you can do so by selecting Add Or Remove Programs in Control Panel, selecting the SQL Server 2005 instance you want to modify, and then clicking the Change or Remove buttons.

## Installing SNAC Using the Installation Wizard

1.    Log in to the system as Administrator or as a user who has administrator privileges on the server.

---

**Note**    The SQL Server 2005 Setup program can be invoked in many ways. In most cases, the program will start automatically when the SQL Server 2005 DVD media is inserted into the DVD drive or when a remote network share is mapped onto the server. If the program is not automatically loaded, you can navigate to the Servers directory and double-click the Splash.hta program.

2.    The Start window appears, similar to what is shown in Figure 8-1. Select Run The SQL Native Client Installation Wizard.

3.    The Welcome page of the wizard appears. Click Next to continue.

4.  The License Agreement page appears. Read and accept the terms in the license agreement and click Next.

5.  The Registration Information page appears. Enter your name and the name of your organization in the text fields and click Next.

6.  The Feature Selection page, shown in Figure 8-15, appears. Select the program features you want to install and click Next.

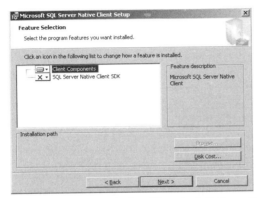

**Figure 8-15**   SQL Native Client Installation—Feature Selection page.

> **Note**   The Client Components contain the SNAC network library files and should be selected if you are installing SNAC on a client for connectivity.

7.  The Ready To Install The Program page appears. Click Install.

8.  After the installation process completes, click Finish.

## Installing SQL Server 2005 Using the Command Prompt

Unlike earlier versions, SQL Server 2005 does not have an unattended install recorder and playback mechanism. Instead, it ships with a powerful command prompt installation option, which can be used to install, modify, or uninstall SQL Server components and perform certain maintenance tasks. With command prompt installation, you can choose either to specify all the input parameter directly on the command line or to pass them in using a settings (.ini) file.

The syntax for a command prompt installation is shown in the following example.

```
Start /wait <DVD Drive>\Servers\setup.exe /qb INSTANCENAME=MSSQLSERVER
ADDLOCAL=SQL_Engine SQLACCOUNT=advadmin SQLPASSWORD=Pa55wD
AGTACCOUNT=advadmin AGTPASSWORD=Pa55wD SQLBROWSERACCOUNT=advadmin
SQLBROWSERPASSWORD=Pa55wD
```

In this example, the SQL Server 2005 database engine is installed as a default instance using the account advadmin and password Pa55wd.

---

**Important** Since the password is clearly visible in the code, it presents a potential security risk and should be used carefully. Do not leave any references to a password such as this in an unprotected script file.

---

The command prompt installation can be used to customize every option in the installation process. Table 8-5 lists the command prompt installation options and gives a brief description of each.

**Table 8-5  Command Prompt Installation Options**

| Command Prompt Option | Description |
|---|---|
| /qb | Installation is done in quiet mode with basic GUI information displayed, but no user interaction is required. |
| /qn | Installation is done in quiet mode with no GUI displayed. |
| Options | This parameter is for the Registration Information dialog box and must be specified when using a settings file. |
| PIDKEY | This parameter is used to specify the registration key. [Note: Do not specify the hyphens (-) that appear in the key.] |
| INSTALLSQLDIR | This parameter is used to specify the installation directory for the instance specific binary files. |
| INSTALLSQLSHAREDDIR | This parameter is used to specify the installation directory for Integration Services, Notification Services, and Workstation components. |
| INSTALLSQLDATADIR | This parameter is used to specify the installation directory for the SQL Server data files. |
| INSTALLASDATADIR | This parameter is used to specify the location for the Analysis Services data files. |
| ADDLOCAL | This parameter is used to specify the components to install. ADDLOCAL=ALL installs all the components. Setup fails if ADDLOCAL is not specified. (Note: Feature names are case sensitive.) |
| REMOVE | This parameter specifies which components to uninstall. The INSTANCENAME parameter must be used in conjunction with this parameter. |

**Table 8-5   Command Prompt Installation Options (continued)**

| Command Prompt Option | Description |
| --- | --- |
| INSTANCENAME | This parameter specifies the name of the instance. MSSQLSERVER is used to represent the default instance. This parameter must be specified for instance-aware components. |
| UPGRADE | This parameter is used to specify which product to upgrade. The INSTANCENAME parameter must be used in conjunction with this parameter. |
| SAVESYSDB | This parameter can be used during uninstall to specify not to delete system databases. |
| USESYSDB | This parameter is used to specify the root path to the system databases data directory during upgrade. |
| SQLACCOUNT, SQLPASSWORD, AGTACCOUNT, AGTPASSWORD, ASACCOUNT, ASPASSWORD, RSACCOUNT, RSPASSWORD | These parameters are used to specify the service accounts and passwords for the services. A service account and password need to be provided for each service selected for installation. |
| SQLBROWSERAUTOSTART, SQLAUTOSTART, AGTAUTOSTART, ASAUTOSTART, RSAUTOSTART | These parameters are used to specify the startup behavior of the respective service. When set to 1, the service will start automatically; when set to 0, the service must be started manually. |
| SECURITYMODE and SAPWD | SECURITYMODE=SQL is used to specify mixed mode authentication. SAPWD is used to specify the password for the sa account. |
| SQLCOLLATION and ASCOLLATION | These parameters are used to set the collations for SQL Server and Analysis Services, respectively. |
| REBUILDDATABASE | This parameter is used to rebuild the master database. |
| REINSTALLMODE | This parameter is used to repair installed components that may be corrupted. |
| REINSTALL | This parameter is used to specify the components to reinstall and must be specified when using REINSTALLMODE. REINSTALL parameters use the same values as ADDLOCAL parameters. |
| RSCONFIGURATION | This parameter is applicable only if Reporting Services or Report Manager is installed. It is used to specify whether to configure the service. |
| SAMPLEDATABASESERVER | This parameter is used to specify the server and instance name to which the sample databases should be attached. |

**Table 8-5**   **Command Prompt Installation Options** (continued)

| Command Prompt Option | Description |
|---|---|
| DISABLENETWORKPROTOCOLS | This parameter is used to set up the start-up state of the network protocols. |
| ERRORREPORTING | This parameter is used to configure SQL Server to send reports from any fatal errors directly to Microsoft. |

**More Info**   For a complete list of parameters and their possible values, refer to the SQL Server Setup Help by double-clicking

<DVD Drive>\Servers\Setup\help\1033\setupsql9.chm and searching for 'How to: Install SQL Server 2005 from the Command Prompt'.

In the next few sections, we will see how these parameters can be used in combination to perform a variety of operations such as installing a default instance with all the components, installing a named instance with mixed mode authentication, adding components to an existing instance, and using a settings file to pass in the installation parameters.

## Installing a Default Instance

This is one of the most commonly used command prompt–based installation scenarios. The following command installs all of the SQL Server 2005 components in a default instance (MSSQLSERVER) on the local server. A Windows administrator account called advadmin with a password of Pa55wD is used for all the services.

```
start /wait <DVD Drive>\Servers\setup.exe /qb INSTANCENAME=MSSQLSERVER
ADDLOCAL=ALL SAPWD=Pa55wD SQLACCOUNT=advadmin SQLPASSWORD=Pa55wD
AGTACCOUNT=advadmin AGTPASSWORD=Pa55wD ASACCOUNT=advadmin ASPASSWORD=Pa55wD
RSACCOUNT=advadmin RSPASSWORD=Pa55wD SQLBROWSERACCOUNT=advadmin
SQLBROWSERPASSWORD=Pa55wD
```

**Best Practices**   If you plan to store these commands as script files, you should make sure to store them in a secure location with the correct permissions, since they contain unencrypted passwords.

## Installing a Named Instance with Mixed Authentication

The following command installs database engine and management tools components on a named instance of SQL Server 2005 called SS2K5 with mixed authentication and the

Latin1_General_BIN collation. A Windows administrator account called advadmin with a password of Pa55wD is used for all the services.

```
start /wait <DVD Drive>\Servers\setup.exe /qb INSTANCENAME=SS2K5
ADDLOCAL=SQL_Engine,SQL_Data_Files,Client_Components,Connectivity,SQL_Tools9
0 SECURITYMODE=SQL SQLCOLLATION=Latin1_General_Bin SQLAUTOSTART=1
AGTAUTOSTART=1 SAPWD=Pa55wD SQLACCOUNT=advadmin SQLPASSWORD=Pa55wD
AGTACCOUNT=advadmin AGTPASSWORD=Pa55wD SQLBROWSERACCOUNT=advadmin
SQLBROWSERPASSWORD=Pa55wD
```

## Adding Components to an Existing Instance

The command prompt installation method can also be used to add components to an existing SQL Server 2005 instance. The following command adds the Analysis Server components with the Latin1_General_Bin collation setting to an existing instance named SS2K5. Once again, a Windows administrator account called advadmin with a password of Pa55wD is used for all the services.

```
start /wait <DVD Drive>\Servers\setup.exe /qb INSTANCENAME=SS2K5
ADDLOCAL=Analysis_Server,AnalysisDataFiles ASCOLLATION=Latin1_General_Bin
SAPWD=Pa55wD ASACCOUNT=advadmin ASPASSWORD=Pa55wD
```

## Installing Using a Settings (.ini) File

All the command prompt installation examples we've seen so far have specified the setup options directly on the command line. This approach works well but is not very easy to use given that the commands are usually rather long and prone to typos. Also, the commands need to be re-typed for each use and cannot be easily persisted across sessions. To circumvent these problems, SQL Server 2005 allows you to use a settings file with which you can pass in the desired command prompt options. A settings file is a text file which contains a list of setup parameters.

The following example settings file specifies the options that can be used to install all SQL Server 2005 components using the mixed mode authentication and the Latin1_General_BIN collation for both SQL Server database as well as Analysis Server.

```
[Options]
USERNAME=Mike
COMPANYNAME=Microsoft

PIDKEY=ADDYOURVALIDPIDKEYHERE


ADDLOCAL=ALL


INSTANCENAME=MSSQLSERVER
```

```
SQLBROWSERACCOUNT=advadmin
SQLBROWSERPASSWORD=Pa55wD

SQLACCOUNT=advadmin
SQLPASSWORD=Pa55wD

AGTACCOUNT=advadmin
AGTPASSWORD=Pa55wD

ASACCOUNT=advadmin
ASPASSWORD=Pa55wD

RSACCOUNT=advadmin
RSPASSWORD=Pa55wD

SQLBROWSERAUTOSTART=1
SQLAUTOSTART=1
AGTAUTOSTART=1
ASAUTOSTART=0
RSAUTOSTART=0

SECURITYMODE=SQL
SAPWD=Pa55wD

SQLCOLLATION=Latin1_General_BIN
ASCOLLATION=Latin1_General_BIN

DISABLENETWORKPROTOCOLS=2
```

---

**Note**   A sample template file (Template.ini) listing all the configurable parameters is provided with the SQL Server media and can be found in the same directory as the Setup.exe program.

The settings file is specified using the /settings option of the command prompt installation. For example, the following command passes in the SqlInstall.ini file containing the setup parameters to the setup program.

```
start /wait <DVD Drive>\Servers\setup.exe /qb /settings C:\SqlInstall.ini
```

**Best Practices**   Since the settings files contain logins, passwords, and product keys, you should always store them in a secure location with the appropriate file permissions.

# Upgrading to SQL Server 2005

If you have an existing installation of SQL Server, you can choose to upgrade it to SQL Server 2005 instead of installing a new instance. SQL Server 2005 supports direct upgrade paths from SQL Server 7.0 with SP4 and SQL Server 2000 with SP3 or later versions. Table 8-7 lists the versions of SQL Server and the possible direct upgrade path to the corresponding SQL Server 2005 edition. Before upgrading from one edition to another, you should always verify that all the functionality you are currently using is supported in the edition being upgraded to.

**Table 8-7   Supported Upgrade Paths to SQL Server 2005**

| Upgrade from | Supported Upgrade Paths |
| --- | --- |
| SQL Server 7.0 Enterprise Edition SP4 | SQL Server 2005 Enterprise Edition |
| SQL Server 7.0 Developer Edition SP4 | SQL Server 2005 Enterprise Edition |
| | SQL Server 2005 Developer Edition |
| SQL Server 7.0 Standard Edition SP4 | SQL Server 2005 Standard Edition |
| | SQL Server 2005 Enterprise Edition |
| SQL Server 7.0 Desktop Edition SP4 | SQL Server 2005 Standard Edition |
| | SQL Server 2005 Workgroup Edition |
| SQL Server 7.0 Evaluation Edition SP4 | Upgrade not supported |
| SQL Server Desktop Engine (MSDE) 7.0 SP4 | SQL Server 2005 Express Edition |
| SQL Server 2000 Enterprise Edition SP3 or later versions | SQL Server 2005 Enterprise Edition |
| SQL Server 2000 Developer Edition SP3 or later versions | SQL Server 2005 Developer Edition |
| SQL Server 2000 Standard Edition SP3 or later versions | SQL Server 2005 Enterprise Edition |
| | SQL Server 2005 Developer Edition |
| | SQL Server 2005 Standard Edition |
| SQL Server 2000 Workgroup Edition | SQL Server 2005 Enterprise Edition |
| | SQL Server 2005 Developer Edition |
| | SQL Server 2005 Standard Edition |
| | SQL Server 2005 Workgroup Edition |

Table 8-7    Supported Upgrade Paths to SQL Server 2005 (continued)

| Upgrade from | Supported Upgrade Paths |
|---|---|
| SQL Server 2000 Personal Edition SP3 or later versions | SQL Server 2005 Standard Edition |
| | SQL Server 2005 Workgroup Edition |
| | SQL Server 2005 Express Edition |
| SQL Server 2000 Evaluation Edition SP3 or later versions | SQL Server 2005 Evaluation Edition |
| SQL Server Desktop Engine (MSDE) 2000 | SQL Server 2005 Workgroup Edition |
| | SQL Server 2005 Express Edition |
| SQL Server 2000 IA-64 (64-bit) Enterprise Edition | SQL Server 2005 IA-64 (64-bit) Enterprise Edition |
| SQL Server 2000 IA-64 (64-bit) Developer Edition | SQL Server 2005 IA-64 (64-bit) Enterprise Edition |
| | SQL Server 2005 IA-64 (64-bit) Developer Edition |
| SQL Server 2005 Developer Edition | SQL Server 2005 Enterprise Edition |
| | SQL Server 2005 Standard Edition |
| | SQL Server 2005 Workgroup Edition |
| SQL Server 2005 Standard Edition | SQL Server 2005 Enterprise Edition |
| | SQL Server 2005 Developer Edition |
| SQL Server 2005 Workgroup Edition | SQL Server 2005 Enterprise Edition |
| | SQL Server 2005 Developer Edition |
| | SQL Server 2005 Standard Edition |
| SQL Server 2005 Evaluation Edition | SQL Server 2005 Enterprise Edition |
| | SQL Server 2005 Developer Edition |
| | SQL Server 2005 Standard Edition |
| | SQL Server 2005 Workgroup Edition |
| | SQL Server 2005 Express Edition |
| SQL Server 2005 Express Edition | SQL Server 2005 Enterprise Edition |
| | SQL Server 2005 Developer Edition |
| | SQL Server 2005 Standard Edition |
| | SQL Server 2005 Workgroup Edition |
| SQL Server 2005 IA-64 (64-bit) Developer Edition | SQL Server 2005 IA-64 (64-bit) Enterprise Edition |
| | SQL Server 2005 IA-64 (64-bit) Standard Edition |
| SQL Server 2005 x64 (64-bit) Developer Edition | SQL Server 2005 x64 (64-bit) Enterprise Edition |
| | SQL Server 2005 x64 (64-bit) Standard Edition |
| SQL Server 2005 IA-64 (64-bit) Standard Edition | SQL Server 2005 IA-64 (64-bit) Enterprise Edition |
| | SQL Server 2005 IA-64 (64-bit) Developer Edition |

**Table 8-7   Supported Upgrade Paths to SQL Server 2005 (continued)**

| Upgrade from | Supported Upgrade Paths |
| --- | --- |
| SQL Server 2005 x64 (64-bit) Standard Edition | SQL Server 2005 x64 (64-bit) Enterprise Edition |
| | SQL Server 2005 x64 (64-bit) Developer Edition |
| SQL Server 2005 IA-64 (64-bit) Evaluation Edition | SQL Server 2005 IA-64 (64-bit) Enterprise Edition |
| | SQL Server 2005 IA-64 (64-bit) Developer Edition |
| | SQL Server 2005 IA-64 (64-bit) Standard Edition |
| SQL Server 2005 x64 (64-bit) Evaluation Edition | SQL Server 2005 x64 (64-bit) Enterprise Edition |
| | SQL Server 2005 x64 (64-bit) Developer Edition |
| | SQL Server 2005 x64 (64-bit) Standard Edition |

A SQL Server 2000 32-bit instance running on the 32-bit subsystems of an x64 system cannot be upgraded to run on the 64-bit subsystem directly. If you require converting your 32-bit SQL Server instance to SQL Server 2005 (64-bit), you will need to install SQL Server 2005 on the 64-bit server as a new instance and then move the database over. You can move the databases either by backing them up from the 32-bit system and restoring them on the 64-bit system, or by detaching the databases from the 32-bit system, copying them over to the 64-bit system and attaching them to the 64-bit system. In either case, you will need to do some additional housekeeping tasks such as recreating logins, reconfiguring replication, and so forth on the new 64-bit server instance.

English-language versions of SQL Server can be upgraded to an English-language or any other localized version of SQL Server 2005. However, localized versions of SQL Server can be upgraded only to localized versions of SQL Server 2005 of the same language. In addition, SQL Server 2005 does not support cross-version instances, implying that all the components (for example, Database Engine, Analysis Services, and Reporting Services) within a single instance must be the same.

## SQL Server Upgrade Advisor

SQL Server Upgrade Advisor is a stand-alone tool that can help you analyze your SQL Server 7.0 or SQL Server 2000 database for possible incompatibilities before being upgraded to SQL Server 2005 and help you proactively resolve them. Although most well-designed SQL Server databases should be seamlessly upgradeable to SQL Server 2005, there are some scenarios in which SQL Server 2005 has tightened up on checking for compliance with SQL standards and disallows certain nonstandard code constructs. The Upgrade Advisor is a great way to quickly and easily check for such cases.

The following sections explain the steps to install and use the Upgrade Advisor.

## Installing SQL Server Upgrade Advisor

The SQL Server Upgrade Advisor is a stand-alone tool that must be installed via a separate installation process. To install SQL Server Upgrade Advisor:

1. Log in to the system as Administrator or a user who has administrator privileges on the server.

---

**Note**   The SQL Server 2005 Setup program can be invoked in many ways. In most cases, the program will automatically start when the SQL Server 2005 DVD media is inserted into the DVD drive or when a remote network share is mapped onto the server. If the program does not load automatically, you can navigate to the Servers directory and double-click the Splash.hta program.

---

2. From the Start window, from the Prepare section, select Install SQL Server Upgrade Advisor.

3. On the Welcome page, click Next.

4. The License Agreement page appears. Read and accept the terms of the license agreement by selecting the radio button, and then click Next.

5. The Registration Information page appears. Enter your name and the name of your organization and click Next.

6. The Feature Selection page appears. On this page, leave the Upgrade Advisor feature selected. You can change the directory to which Upgrade Advisor will be installed by using the Browse button. You can also view the disk cost by using the Disk Cost button. Click Next to continue.

7. The Ready To Install The Program page appears. Click Install.

8. The Setup Wizard will install the Upgrade Advisor and should report a successful completion message. Click Finish to complete the installation.

## Using SQL Server Upgrade Advisor

The Upgrade Advisor is built from two components: the Upgrade Advisor Analysis Wizard and the Upgrade Advisor Report Viewer.

- **Upgrade Advisor Analysis Wizard**   This tool helps analyze the SQL Server 7.0 or SQL Server 2000 instance for issues that can cause the upgrade to fail or your application to falter after the upgrade. The wizard does not modify the instance in any way and can be run as many times as you like.

■ **Upgrade Advisor Report Viewer**    This tool is used to view the list of issues found by the Analysis Wizard.

The typical sequence of events when using the Upgrade Advisor includes executing the Update Advisor, gathering the recommendations, taking the recommended corrective actions, and rerunning Upgrade Advisor to verify the changes. While this process can be completed in a single pass, I have often found it to require a couple of iterations before all the issues are resolved.

The following steps explain the process of using the SQL Server Upgrade Advisor Analysis Wizard and viewing the report using the Upgrade Advisor Report Viewer:

1.  To open SQL Server 2005 Upgrade Advisor click the Start button, and then point to All Programs, then Microsoft SQL Server 2005, and then select SQL Server 2005 Upgrade Advisor. The Upgrade Advisor Start window appears, as shown in Figure 8-16.

2.  Select Launch Upgrade Advisor Analysis Wizard. The Welcome page appears. Click Next.

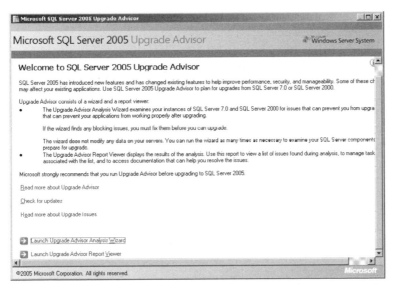

**Figure 8-16**   SQL Server 2005 Upgrade Advisor—Start window.

3.  The SQL Server Components page appears, as shown in Figure 8-17. Enter the name of the server you want to run Upgrade Advisor against. You can choose to query the server and automatically populate the appropriate check boxes for the components by clicking on Detect, or you can choose to manually select the check boxes. Click Next to continue.

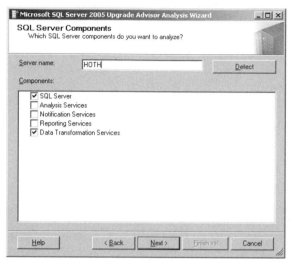

**Figure 8-17** SQL Server 2005 Upgrade Advisor—SQL Server Components page.

4. The Connection Parameters page, shown in Figure 8-18, appears. Select the instance name (select MSSQLSERVER for the default instance), select the authentication mode, and enter the login credentials if using the SQL Server authentication mode. Click Next.

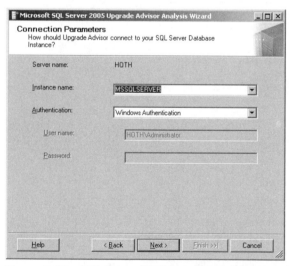

**Figure 8-18** SQL Server 2005 Upgrade Advisor—Connection Parameters page.

5. The SQL Server Parameters page appears, as shown in Figure 8-19. Select the check boxes for the databases to be analyzed. Additionally, if you want to analyze trace files and SQL batch files, select the appropriate check boxes as well. Click Next.

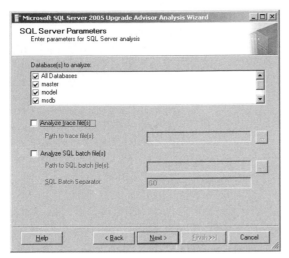

**Figure 8-19**   SQL Server 2005 Upgrade Advisor—SQL Server Parameters page.

6.  Based on the components you selected for analysis in step 3, the appropriate component parameter page displays. Enter the requested information for each, and then click Next.

7.  The Confirm Upgrade Advisor Settings page appears, as shown in Figure 8-20. Review the information and click Run to execute the analysis process. You can select the Send Reports To Microsoft check box if you want to submit your upgrade report to Microsoft. Re-executing the Upgrade Advisor process causes any previous reports to be overwritten.

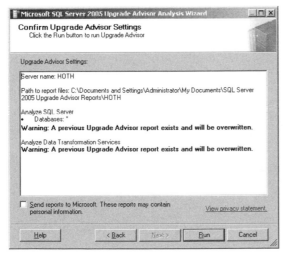

**Figure 8-20**   SQL Server 2005 Upgrade Advisor—Confirm Upgrade Advisor Settings page.

8. The Upgrade Advisor Progress page appears, as shown in Figure 8-21. The analysis may take several minutes to complete and is dependent on the number of components selected. Once the analysis is completed, you can select Launch Report to view the report that was generated or exit the wizard by clicking Close.

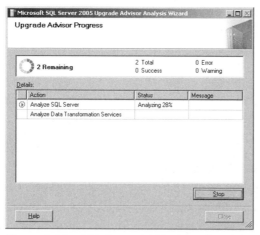

**Figure 8-21** SQL Server 2005 Upgrade Advisor—Upgrade Advisor Progress page.

9. When you select Launch Report in step 8 or the Launch Upgrade Avisor Report Viewer option shown in Figure 8-16, the window shown in Figure 8-22 appears. From this window, you can choose to view all the issues for all the components together or filter the view using the Instance Or Component and Filter By drop-down lists. Clicking on the + next to a line item expands the display to show a more detailed description. You also can use the This Issue Has Been Resolved check box on each line item to mark the task resolved, which will then delete it from the current report.

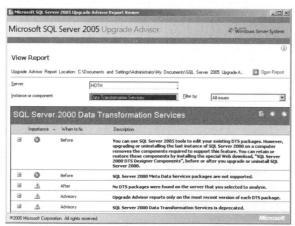

**Figure 8-22** SQL Server 2005 Upgrade Advisor—View Report window.

## Upgrade Procedure

The procedure to upgrade an earlier version of SQL Server to SQL Server 2005 is very similar to the procedure for a new SQL Server 2005 installation. To upgrade a version of SQL Server 7.0 or SQL Server 2000, start with steps 1 through 9 listed in the section "Installing SQL Server 2005 Using the Installation Wizard." Then follow these steps:

1.  When the Instance Name page appears, select the default or named instance to upgrade. To upgrade a SQL Server default instance already installed on your system, click Default Instance, and then click Next to continue. To upgrade a SQL Server named instance already installed on your system, click Named Instance, and then enter the instance name in the text field below, or click the Installed Instances button, select an instance from the Installed Instances list, and click OK to automatically populate the instance name text field. After you have selected the instance to upgrade, click Next to continue.

    ---

    **Note**    If you want to do an upgrade, make sure you specify the name of the existing default or named instance correctly. If the instance specified does not exist on the system, the Installation Wizard will install a new instance instead of performing an upgrade.

    ---

2.  The Existing Components page, shown in Figure 8-23, appears. On this page, you can select the check boxes next to the components you want to upgrade (the list of components is based on the SQL Server instances and versions installed on your system and, therefore, may be different than what is shown in Figure 8-23). You can also view the details of the listed components by clicking on the Details button in the lower-right corner. Click Next to continue with the upgrade.

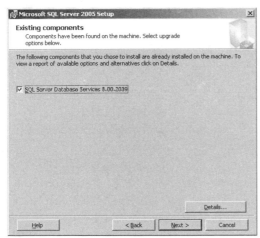

**Figure 8-23**    SQL Server Upgrade—Existing Components page.

> **Troubleshooting**   You should make sure that the SQL Server 2005 edition to which you're trying to upgrade is listed in Table 8-7 as a valid upgrade path. If not, the setup process will block the upgrade by graying out the component selection check boxes.

3. The Upgrade Logon Information page appears. On this page, click the appropriate radio button to select either the Windows Authentication Mode or the Mixed Mode (Windows Authentication and SQL Server Authentication). If you select to use the mixed mode, you will need to enter and confirm login password for the sa user. Click Next to continue.

4. The upgrade process will analyze the instance and then display the Error And Usage Report Settings page. On this page, you can select one of two radio buttons to Automatically Send Error Reports To Microsoft Or Your Corporate Error Reporting Server, or to Automatically Send Feature Usage Data For SQL Server 2005 To Microsoft, to set the desired default action. This data is collected for information purposes only, and selecting either of these options will not have any adverse effects on the performance of your system. Click Next to continue.

5. On the Ready To Install page, review the components selected for upgrade, and then click Install to upgrade them.

## Post-Upgrade Steps

The procedure explained previously upgrades the SQL Server database executables to SQL Server 2005; however, this may not be sufficient to ensure optimal performance and functioning of your application. In addition to upgrading to SQL Server 2005, you will need to complete the following tasks manually to upgrade your individual databases and do some housekeeping tasks:

1. **Register servers**   After upgrading to SQL Server 2005, you must reregister your servers.

2. **Set database compatibility to 90**   After an upgrade, SQL Server 2005 automatically sets the database compatibility level for each database to the level of the previous SQL Server version. For example, if you upgrade SQL Server 2000 to SQL Server 2005, the database compatibility level for all the upgraded user databases will be set to 80 (SQL Server 2000). You should change the database compatibility level for each of your databases to SQL Server 2005 (90) by executing the *sp_dbcmptlevel* stored procure command shown below from one of the SQL Server tools like SQL Server Management Studio.

```
sp_dbcmptlevel
```

**Best Practices**   You should always run your databases in the 90 compatibility level for SQL Server 2005 and avoid setting the compatibility level to an earlier version to permanently work around any incompatibilities you encounter after an upgrade.

3. **Execute update statistics**   You should update statistics on all tables. This ensures that the statistics are current and help optimize query performance. You can use the *sp_updatestats* stored procedure to update the statistics on all user tables in your database.

4. **Update usage counters**   You should run DBCC UPDATEUSAGE on all upgraded databases to correct any invalid row or page counts, for example DBCC UPDATE-USAGE ('AdventureWorks').

5. **Configure the surface area**   You should enable the required SQL Server 2005 features and services using the SQL Server 2005 Surface Area Configuration tool explained later in this chapter.

6. **Repopulate full-text catalogs**   The upgrade process disables full-text on all databases. If you plan to use the full-text feature, you should repopulate the catalogs. You can do this using the *sp_fulltext_catalog* stored procedure.

# Reading the SQL Server 2005 Setup Log Files

SQL Server 2005 setup has a significantly enhanced logging mechanism wherein all actions performed by setup are logged in an easy-to-read format. The master log file for the setup process is named Summary.txt and is located under: %ProgramFiles%\Microsoft SQL Server\90\Setup Bootstrap\LOG\. This file contains a summary for each component being installed. The following is a typical Summary.txt log file fragment.

```
Microsoft SQL Server 2005 9.00.1399.06
==============================


OS Version     : Microsoft Windows Server 2003 family, Enterprise Edition
Service Pack 1 (Build 3790)
Time           : Thu Jan 12 22:38:12 2006
```

```
Machine         : HOTH
Product         : Microsoft SQL Server Setup Support Files (English)
Product Version : 9.00.1399.06
Install         : Successful
Log File        : C:\Program Files\Microsoft SQL Server\90\Setup
Bootstrap\LOG\Files\SQLSetup0003_HOTH_SQLSupport_1.log
--------------------------------------------------------------------------
Machine         : HOTH
Product         : Microsoft SQL Server Native Client
Product Version : 9.00.1399.06
Install         : Successful
Log File        : C:\Program Files\Microsoft SQL Server\90\Setup
Bootstrap\LOG\Files\SQLSetup0003_HOTH_SQLNCLI_1.log
--------------------------------------------------------------------------
Machine         : HOTH
Product         : Microsoft Office 2003 Web Components
Product Version : 11.0.6558.0
Install         : Successful
Log File        : C:\Program Files\Microsoft SQL Server\90\Setup
Bootstrap\LOG\Files\SQLSetup0003_HOTH_OWC11_1.log
--------------------------------------------------------------------------
...
```

You can use the Summary.txt file to examine the details of a component installation process by referring to the log file name listed on the respective Log File line. This is particularly useful when a component fails to install and the installation process needs to be debugged. The individual component log files are created in text format and stored in the %ProgramFiles%\Microsoft SQL Server\90\Setup Bootstrap\LOG\Files directory.

# Uninstalling SQL Server 2005

Similar to the installation process, SQL Server 2005 can be uninstalled using either an uninstall wizard or the command prompt. The following sections explain both of these methods in detail.

## Uninstalling SQL Server 2005 Using the Uninstall Wizard

1. To begin the uninstall process, click the Start button, select Control Panel (or select Settings and then Control Panel), and then in Control Panel, double-click Add Or Remove Programs.

2. In the left pane, click Add/Remove Windows Components.

3. Select the SQL Server 2005 component to uninstall. The Change and Remove buttons are then displayed. Click Remove. This starts the SQL Server 2005 Uninstall Wizard.

4. The Component Selection page, shown in Figure 8-24, is displayed. On this page, you can select the installed instance and common components you'd like to uninstall. You can select the Report button to view the list of SQL Server 2005 components and features installed on your computer. The report displays the versions, the editions, any updates, and the language information for each installed component and feature. Click Next.

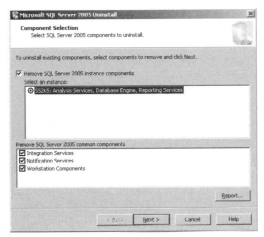

**Figure 8-24**   SQL Server 2005 Uninstall—Component Selection page.

5. The Confirmation page is displayed. Review the list of components and features that will be uninstalled.

6. Click Finish to uninstall the selected components. The Setup Progress window appears and displays the uninstall status for each component. When the uninstall process is completed, the window will close automatically.

---

**Note**   The Add Or Remove Programs window may continue to display some of the components as installed even though they've been uninstalled. This is because the Add Or Remove Programs window does not auto-refresh. The easiest way to refresh the window is to close it and then click Add Or Remove Programs in the Control Panel again.

# Uninstalling SQL Server 2005 Using the Command Prompt

As mentioned earlier, SQL Server 2005 can be uninstalled from the local server by specifying the REMOVE option in command prompt. When the option is specified with the ALL parameter, all the instance aware components are uninstalled. For example, the following command uninstalls all components from an instance called SS2K5 on the local server.

```
start /wait <DVD Drive>\Servers\setup.exe /qb REMOVE=ALL INSTANCENAME=SS2K5
```

**Note**   To uninstall the default instance, specify INSTANCENAME=MSSQLSERVER.

The command prompt can also be used to selectively uninstall specific components of a SQL Server 2005 instance. For example, the following command uninstalls the Analysis Server components from the default instance of SQL Server on the local server in silent mode with no GUI displayed (/qn).

```
start /wait <DVD Drive>\Servers\setup.exe /qn REMOVE=
Analysis_Server,AnalysisDataFiles INSTANCENAME=MSSQLSERVER
```

**Note**   The REMOVE option can also be used in conjunction with the ADDLOCAL option. While these two are seemingly orthogonal actions, they can be used very effectively to simplify the installation command. For example, to install all the components of SQL Server 2005 except Notification Services, you can install all the components (ADDLOCAL=ALL) and use the REMOVE option to exclude Notification Services, as shown in the following example query:

```
start /wait <DVD Drive>\Servers\setup.exe /qn ADDLOCAL=ALL
REMOVE=Notification_Services INSTANCENAME=MSSQLSERVER
```

An alternative is to specify all the components of SQL Server 2005 except Notification Services individually as comma-separated parameters to the ADDLOCAL option.

These commands do not uninstall the SQL Native Access Client (SNAC) component from the server. To uninstall SNAC, execute the command (where C is the boot drive).

```
start /wait C:\Windows\System32\msiexec /qb /X <DVD
Drive>\Servers\setup\sqlncli.msi
```

# Using SQL Server Surface Area Configuration

SQL Server 2005 by default disables some features, services, and connections for new installations in order to reduce the attackable surface area and, thereby, help protect your system. This security scheme is new in SQL Server 2005 and is very different from earlier versions, which by default always enable all installed components.

The SQL Server Surface Area Configuration tool is a new configuration tool that ships with SQL Server 2005 and can be used to enable, disable, start, or stop features, services, and remote connectivity. This tool provides a single interface for managing Database Engine, Analysis Services, and Reporting Services features and can be used locally or from a remote server.

The following steps list the process used to invoke and use the SQL Server Surface Area Configuration tool:

1. Click the Start button and point to All Programs. Point to Microsoft SQL Server 2005, select Configuration Tools, and then select SQL Server Surface Area Configuration.

2. The SQL Server Surface Area Configuration start window, shown in Figure 8-25, appears. From this window, you can specify the server you want to configure by selecting the link adjacent to Configure Surface Area For Localhost. In the Select Computer dialog box that appears, select Local Computer or Remote Computer and enter the name of the remote computer in the text box if necessary. Click OK to continue.

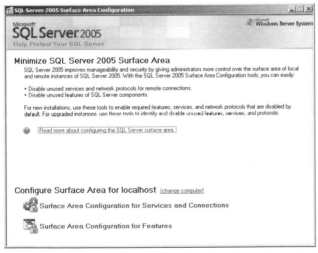

**Figure 8-25**   SQL Server Surface Area Configuration—Start window.

3. Click the Surface Area Configuration For Services And Connections link to enable or disable Windows services and remote connectivity or the Surface Area Configuration For Features link to enable or disable features of the Database Engine, Analysis Services, and Reporting Services.

4. Click the Surface Area Configuration for Services and Connections link to set the startup state (Automatic, Manual, or Disabled) for each of the installed services and Start, Stop, or Pause the respective service. In addition, you can use this link to manage the connectivity options by specifying whether local connections only or local and remote connections are permitted, as shown in Figure 8-26.

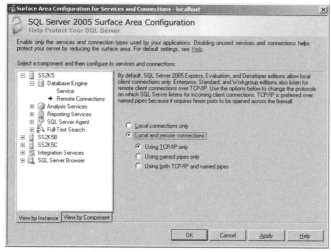

**Figure 8-26**   Surface Area Configuration For Services And Connections dialog box.

## Real World    Error While Connecting Remotely

I have found that one of the most common problems for folks using SQL Server 2005 Express, Evaluation, or Developer Editions is not being able to connect to the server from a remote system. The error message returned when trying to connect remotely is as follows:

"An error has occurred while establishing a connection to the server. When connecting to SQL Server 2005, this failure may be caused by the fact that under the default settings SQL Server does not allow remote connections. (provider: SQL Network Interfaces, error: 28 - Server doesn't support requested protocol) (Microsoft SQL Server, Error: -1)"

As mentioned earlier, SQL Server 2005 by default disables several network proto-cols to reduce the possible attack surface area. In line with this principle, the SQL Server 2005 Express, Evaluation, and Developer Editions disallow remote connec-tions to the server, and that is why you cannot connect to the server remotely. You can easily remedy the situation by using the SQL Server Surface Area Configuration tool, selecting Remote Connections, and then selecting the Local And Remote Con-nections and Using Both TCP/IP /IP And Named Pipes options.

5. Click the Surface Area Configuration For Features link. The window shown in Fig-ure 8-27 appears. This window provides a single interface for enabling or disabling the installed components listed in Table 8-6.

> **Note**    To configure a component, the component has to be running. If the component is not running, it will not be displayed as shown in Figure 8-27.

**Table 8-6    Surface Area Configuration for Features**

| Component | Configurable Feature |
| --- | --- |
| Database Engine | Ad hoc remote queries |
| | CLR integration |
| | DAC |
| | Database Mail |
| | Native XML Web Service |
| | OLE Automation |
| | SQL Server Service Broker |
| | SQL Mail |
| | Web Assistant |
| | xp_cmdshell |
| Analysis Services | Ad hoc data mining queries |
| | Anonymous connections |
| | Linked objects |
| | User-Defined Functions |
| Reporting Services | Scheduled Events and Report Delivery |
| | Web Service and HTTP Access |
| | Windows Integrated Security |

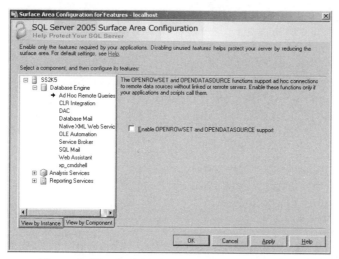

**Figure 8-27**   Surface Area Configuration for Features window.

---

**Best Practices**   These days security is a major concern for almost all deployments. To reduce the surface area for a possible attack, be selective about the features you enable and have a policy for enabling only those that you plan to use. It is also worthwhile to use the SQL Server Surface Area Configuration tool periodically and disable features that you are no longer using.

## *sac* Utility

The *sac utility* can be used to import or export Microsoft SQL Server 2005 surface area settings. This utility is very useful in cases where the same surface area configuration needs to be replicated on multiple servers. To configure multiple servers with the same setting, you can configure the surface area on one server using the graphical SQL Server Surface Area Configuration tool and then use the *sac* utility to export the setting to a file. This file can then be used to import the setting into remote servers using the same utility. The *sac* utility (Sac.exe) is located under the directory:

```
%Program Files%\Microsoft SQL Server\90\Shared
```

The following command can be used to export the surface area configuration settings for all default instance settings of a server named HOTH into an XML-formatted file called sacSetting.txt.

```
sac out C:\sacSettings.txt –S HOTH –U sa –P Pa55wD –I MSSQLSERVER
```

This file can then be imported into some other server using the in option. The following command imports the sacSettings.txt file into a server called NABU.

```
sac in C:\sacSettings.txt -S NABU
```

> **More Info**    The *sac* utility is very powerful and provides the flexibility of export-
> ing and importing settings for specific services as well as Features and Network
> settings. The entire list of options for this utility can be found at *http://
> msdn2.microsoft.com/en-us/library/ms162800.aspx*.

# Summary

Installing the software is the first step towards using SQL Server 2005. Although it is a relatively easy task, it is important to do preinstallation planning, select the correct installation options, and perform all of the postinstallation configuration steps to ensure an optimal installation and to avoid having to make repairs or patches postinstallation.

In this chapter, you've learned about the Installation Wizard and command prompt-based options available for installing the SQL Server 2005 components. You also learned about the new SQL Server 2005 Upgrade Advisor and how it can assist you in ensuring a smooth upgrade process, and how the SQL Server Surface Area Configuration tool and *sac* utility can be used to configure SQL Server 2005.

# Chapter 9
# Configuring Microsoft SQL Server 2005 on the Network

Once you've installed Microsoft SQL Server 2005, the next step is to configure the network components so that it is accessible via the network. This is an important step in ensuring connectivity to the database system and has a large influence on the overall performance. SQL Server 2005 introduces many changes in the way the network components are configured as well as a new network library that makes the task of configuring easier in some ways, given the simplified configuration tools and libraries, but more complex in other ways, given all of the new concepts and tools introduced.

In this chapter, we will start by looking at the SQL Server 2005 network architecture. Using this as a foundation, you will learn about the various network libraries, application programming interfaces (APIs), and the new SNAC (SQL Native Client) library. You will also learn about the SQL Server Browser service, ODBC DSNs (Data Source Name), and the configuration of network protocols. Lastly, you will learn how to monitor network and performance, how to identify possible network bottlenecks, and how to resolve performance problems.

# Understanding the SQL Server Network Services

SQL Server 2005 uses many well-defined protocol layers to enable communication between the server and clients. Figure 9-1 schematically depicts the three communication layers for SQL Server 2005:

- Application Protocol layer
- SQL Network Interface (SNI) layer
- Hardware layer

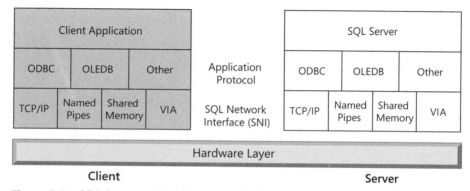

**Figure 9-1**   SQL Server network communication layers.

A request for data originates on the client side by a client application like SQL Server Management Studio (SSMS) or a custom SQL Server application. Client applications use APIs such as ODBC and OLE DB to access the data. The client request is sent down the stack to the SNI layer and serviced by either TCP/IP, named pipes, shared memory or VIA network libraries based on the status (enabled/disabled) and the configured priority order. The APIs and network libraries are explained in detail in the following sections. The SNI layer then sends the request to the hardware layer. The hardware layer uses a communication protocol like Ethernet to transmit the data across the wire to the server system.

At the server side, the request goes up the network stack from the hardware layer, through the SNI layer, and to the database engine as shown in Figure 9-1. The database engine then services the request and sends the requested data back to the client through the same layers in reverse order.

While Figure 9-1 depicts the client and server network stacks separately, this is only a logical representation of the client and server side network stacks. In reality, both of these stacks can reside on the same computer system. However, even when the network stacks reside on the same system, the communication still has to pass through the different network layers; the only layer that can be minimized is the hardware layer.

## SQL Server APIs

To communicate with SQL Server, an application must speak SQL Server's language. One means of communication is to use one of the tools provided with SQL Server, such as command-line sqlcmd, or the SQL Server Management Studio. These tools can be useful for executing ad-hoc queries, but they are not useful for day-to-day application processing. For example, the people who process inventory, accounts payable, and accounts receivable can work more productively using specialized applications rather than extracting the data by keying in SQL statements. In fact, most users of such applications don't know SQL.

SQL Server provides a number of APIs like ODBC, OLEDB and JDBC which developers can use to write applications that connect to SQL Server and execute various database functions. This section describes some common APIs.

### ODBC Connectivity

Pronounced as separate letters, ODBC is short for Open DataBase Connectivity, a standard database access method developed by the SQL Access group in 1992. The goal of ODBC is to make it possible to access any data from any application. SQL Server 2005 fully supports the ODBC protocol via the MDAC (Microsoft Data Access Components) library and the newer SNAC library, both of which are explained later in this chapter.

The ODBC API has the same form regardless of the relational database management system (RDBMS) making it well-suited for applications that require supporting multiple back-end data sources. In fact, it is one of the most popular protocols and used by more than 70 percent of industry applications.

---

**More Info**   For more information on ODBC refer to: *http://msdn.microsoft.com/library/default.asp?url=/library/en-us/odbc/htm/dasdkod bcoverview.asp.*

---

## Real World   ODBC Connection Pooling—What Is It?

The ability to pool connections from within an application was introduced with ODBC 2.x. Normally, an application creates an additional connection from the application layer to the database each time a different user logs in to the application.

This process can be inefficient because establishing and maintaining a connection to the database involves quite a bit of overhead.

A connection pool allows other threads within an application to use existing ODBC connections without requiring a separate connection. This capability can be especially useful for Internet applications that make repeated connections to the database. Applications that require connection pooling must register themselves when they are started. Connection pooling can be enabled when creating or configuring the DSN, as explained later in this chapter.

When an application requests an ODBC connection, the ODBC Connection Manager determines whether a new connection will be initiated or an existing connection reused. This determination is made outside the control of the application. The application thread then works in the usual manner. Once the thread has finished with the ODBC connection, the application makes a call to release the connection. Again, the ODBC Connection Manager takes control of the connection. If a connection has been idle for a certain amount of time, the ODBC Connection Manager will close it.

While connection pooling can help save resources and possibly even increase performance, careful consideration should be given to factors like security and application functionality before enabling it. I recommend that you consult your application configuration manual to determine whether connection pooling is well-suited for your application.

## OLE DB

Object Linking and Embedding (OLE DB; DB refers to databases) is the strategic system-level programming interface for accessing data and the underlying technology for ADO as well as a source of data for ADO.NET. OLE DB is an open standard for accessing all kinds of data, both relational and nonrelational, including mainframe ISAM/VSAM and hierarchical databases; e-mail and file system stores; text, graphical, and geographical data; and custom business objects, making it conceptually easier for extracting data from heterogeneous sources.

OLE DB provides consistent, high-performance access to data and can support a variety of development needs, including the creation of front-end database clients and middle-tier business objects using live connections to data in relational databases and other stores. OLE DB is commonly used when building Visual BASIC applications and is closely tied to ADO. As of SQL 7.0, it works with COM and DCOM. Unlike ODBC, OLE DB does not require that you set up a DSN.

> **More Info** For more information on OLE DB refer to
> *http://msdn.microsoft.com/library/default.asp?url=/library/en-us/oledb/htm/das*
> *dkoledboverview.asp.*

## What Is MDAC?

MDAC is a common abbreviation for Microsoft Data Access Components, which is a group of Microsoft technologies that interact together as a framework, allowing programmers a uniform and comprehensive way of developing applications for accessing data. MDAC is made up of various components: ActiveX Data Objects (ADO), OLE DB, and Open Database Connectivity (ODBC).

The MDAC architecture may be viewed as three layers: a programming interface layer, a database access layer, and the database itself. These component layers are all made available to applications through the MDAC API.

MDAC is integrated with Microsoft Windows and ships with the operating system. The latest version as of January 2006 is MDAC 2.8 SP1. Additional information about MDAC can be found at *http://msdn.microsoft.com/data/mdac.*

## JDBC

Microsoft first released a JDBC (Java Database Connectivity) driver a couple of years back and supported connectivity from Java applications to SQL Server. Prior to this release, customers wanting to access SQL Server from Java application were forced to use third-party JDBC drivers such as those from DataDirect (*www.datadirect.com*).

SQL Server 2005 introduces an updated version of this driver. The SQL Server 2005 JDBC Driver download is available to all SQL Server users at no additional charge and provides access to SQL Server 2000 and SQL Server 2005 from any Java application, application server, or Java-enabled applet. This is a Type 4 JDBC driver that is JDBC 3.0 compliant and runs on the 1.4 JDK and higher. The SQL Server 2005 JDBC driver supports Java-based desktop applications and server applications using Java 2 Enterprise Edition (J2EE). It has been tested against all major application servers including BEA WebLogic, IBM Web-Sphere, JBoss, and Sun, and runs on Linux and Solaris in addition to Windows.

> **More Info** The new JDBC Driver is also freely redistributable for registered partners. Additional information about the driver and redistribution license can be found at *http://msdn.microsoft.com/data/jdbc/default.aspx.*

## Other APIs

A number of other APIs are also available to enable your applications to communicate with SQL Server. These APIs include SQL Management Objects (SMO), DBLib, SQL-Distributed Management Framework (SQL-DMF), and SQL-Namespace (SQL-NS). In general, each of these protocols supports a specific function or market segment that requires its own programming interface.

---

**Note**   SQL Server 2005 does not ship the DBLib driver, but it still supports the API. This means that any DBLib-based application is supported with SQL Server 2005 but needs to have the DBLib library separately installed on the client systems.

---

# SQL Server Network Libraries

As discussed earlier, SQL Server supports a number of net-libraries: Named Pipes, TCP/IP, shared memory and VIA at the SNI layer. Each network library corresponds to a different network protocol or set of protocols. All SQL Server commands and functions are supported across all network protocols; however, some protocols are faster than others. This section provides a brief overview of each network library.

## Named Pipes

Named pipes is a protocol developed for local area networks. With named pipes a portion of memory is used by one process to pass information to another process, so that the output of one is the input of the other. The second process can be on the same computer as the first or on a remote networked computer.

Named pipes is the default client protocol and one of the default network protocols on Windows systems. Although named pipes is an efficient protocol, it is not usually used for large networks because it does not support routing and gateways. It is also not preferred for use with a slower network because it requires significantly more interaction between the server and the client than do other protocols, such as TCP/IP.

## Shared Memory

In SQL Server 2005 the shared memory protocol is implemented as local named pipes and runs in kernel mode, making it extremely fast. Clients using the shared memory protocol can connect only to a SQL Server instance running on the same computer. This limits the usefulness of this protocol and makes it well-suited only for applications that run locally on the database server system and for troubleshooting cases where you suspect that the other protocols are configured incorrectly.

## TCP/IP

TCP/IP is one of the most popular network protocols because of the number of platforms on which it runs, its acceptance as a standard, and its high speed. TCP/IP is also the most common network protocol used for Internet traffic, includes standards for routing network traffic, and offers advanced security features. The TCP/IP net-library's rich feature set coupled with its high performance makes it a good choice.

The TCP/IP protocol provides many settings to fine tune its performance, which often makes configuration a complex task. Most of the key settings can be altered via SQL Server Configuration Manager, as explained later in this chapter. Other settings not exposed via SQL Server Configuration Manager can be altered using the Windows registry. You should refer to your Microsoft Windows documentation for details about these settings and best practices when making changes directly to the Windows registry.

## VIA

The Virtual Interface Adapter (VIA) is a high-performance protocol that requires specialized VIA hardware and can be enabled only with this hardware. It is recommended that you consult your hardware vendor for information about using the VIA protocol.

# Selecting a Network Library

Since the shared memory protocol can connect only to a SQL Server instance running on the same computer, its usefulness is limited. On the other hand, the VIA protocol, while high-performing, requires specialized hardware which usually makes it an expensive option and limits its use. This leaves the choice between the named pipes and TCP/IP protocols for most applications.

In a fast local area network (LAN) environment, TCP/IP and named pipes clients are comparable in terms of performance. However, the performance difference between the two becomes apparent with slower networks, such as across wide area networks (WANs) because of the different ways the interprocess communication (IPC) mechanisms communicate.

For named pipes, network communications are typically more interactive. A server does not send data until the client asks for it using a read command. A network read typically involves a series of peek named pipes messages before it begins to read the data. These can be very costly in a slow network and cause excessive network traffic.

With TCP/IP, data transmissions are more streamlined and have less overhead. Data transmissions can also take advantage of TCP/IP performance enhancement mechanisms such as windowing and delayed acknowledgements, which can be very beneficial in a slow network. Depending on the type of applications, such performance differences can be significant. TCP/IP also supports a backlog queue, which can provide a limited smoothing effect compared to named pipes that may lead to pipe busy errors when attempting to connect to SQL Server.

In general, TCP/IP is preferred in slow LAN, WAN, or dial-up networks, whereas a named pipe is a better choice when network speed is not an issue because it offers more functionality and ease of use.

---

**Note**  The Multiprotocol, NWLink IPX/SPX, AppleTalk and Banyan VINES protocols, which were supported with earlier versions of SQL Server, are no longer supported with SQL Server 2005.

---

# SQL Native Client (SNAC)

SQL Native Client, also known as SNAC (pronounced to rhyme with "lack"), is a data access technology new in Microsoft SQL Server 2005. SNAC is a stand-alone data access application programming interface (API) that combines the SQL OLE DB provider and the ODBC driver into one native dynamic-link library (SQLNCLI.DLL) while also providing new functionality above and beyond that supplied by the Microsoft Data Access Components (MDAC).

It is a common misconception that the SQL Native Client replaces MDAC. This is absolutely not true; MDAC is still fully supported. The big difference between SNAC and MDAC is that unlike earlier editions, SQL Server 2005 does not distribute the MDAC library. Instead, it ships the SNAC library, which is backward compatible with MDAC to a large extent but not one hundred percent. The MDAC distribution is now owned by the Windows operating system, and the SQL Server-specific features are frozen at the SQL Server 2000 level, with MDAC 2.8 being the last common version. This change provides SQL Server with a better version of the story going forward, in a way eliminating the dependence on Windows and providing the flexibility to introduce new features and changes that are SQL server specific. SNAC is supported only on Windows 2000 with Service Pack 4 (or higher), Windows XP with Service Pack 1 (or higher), and Widows 2003 with or without Service Packs.

SQL Native Client introduces a simplified architecture by way of a single library (SQLNCLI.DLL) for all the APIs and can conceptually be viewed to be built up of four components: ODBC Functionality (based on SQLSRV32.DLL), OLEDB Functionality (Based on SQLOLEDB.DLL), TDS Parser plus Data Access Runtime Services, and SNI Functionality (based on DBNETLIB.DLL), as shown in Figure 9-2.

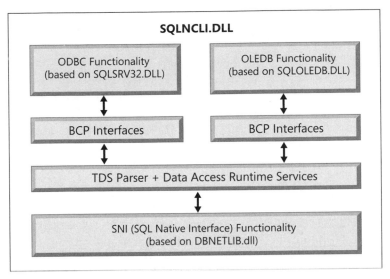

**Figure 9-2**   SQL Native Client architecture.

SNAC is built on a completely restructured code base and has improved serviceability and performance. While your application workload may exhibit different performance characteristics, some benchmark tests using artificial workloads have exhibited performance comparable to MDAC for the OLEDB provider and up to 20 percent faster for ODBC.

## Using SQL Native Client

SQL Native Client can be used for new applications or can be substituted for MDAC to enhance existing applications that need to take advantage of new SQL Server 2005 features. SQL Server 2005 features that require SNAC include the following:

- Database mirroring
- Asynchronous operations
- New data types (XML data types, user-defined data types, large value data types)
- Multiple Active Result Sets (MARS)
- Query notifications
- Password change/expiry
- Snapshot isolation (this does not apply to Read Committed Snapshot Isolation)
- Encryption without validation

> **More Info**   You can find more information about these features by referring to the "Features of SQL Native Client" topic at *http://msdn.microsoft.com/data/sqlnative/default.aspx.*

SQL Server 2005 applications that utilize features like the new large value data-types (for example, VARCHAR(MAX)) that require SNAC get down-leveled to the corresponding SQL Server 2000 equivalent (for example, TEXT) when MDAC is used. Client applications using SNAC can access SQL Server 2000 and SQL Server 7.0, but as can be expected some new features, such as MARS, are not available for use.

There is another misconception that MDAC support is being deprecated by SQL Server, and all applications should immediately adopt SNAC. This again is not true. While only SNAC will be shipped with future versions of SQL Server, support for MDAC is not going away anytime in the foreseeable future. If your application does not need to use any of the new SQL Server 2005 features that require SNAC, you can continue using the MDAC library and upgrade to SNAC when you have a good reason to do so.

Converting an application to use SNAC is easy and can be achieved by performing the following steps:

1. **Change the application connection string.**  This usually involves an application code change but can also be done without one in cases where the application uses a configuration file to specify the connection string.

2. **Create a new SNAC based ODBC DSN for applications that require a DSN.**  The procedure to do this is explained in the "Creating an ODBC DSN" section later in this chapter.

3. **Test the new configuration exhaustively.**  Although step 1 is necessary to be able to use features such as the new large value data types, many of the features such as read committed snapshot isolation can be used by simply performing steps 2 and 3.

   I'd recommend you use SNAC for new applications or applications being redesigned while continuing to use MDAC for stable, mature, and deployed applications. Existing applications that need to exploit SQL Server 2005 capabilities should convert to use SQL Native Client.

## Tracing and Debugging

Tracing and debugging client access problems are significantly easier with SNAC. SNAC contains a rich, flexible, built-in data trace facility called BID (Built-In Diagnostics) tracing which can be used to trace all client components like OLE DB, ODBC, TDS Parser, and SNI (Netlibs). BID tracing is fairly easy to use and can help with cursory analysis and detailed under-the-cover investigation of the exact sequence of operations at the network library level.

---

**More Info**    For additional information about BID tracing refer to *http://msdn.microsoft.com/library/default.asp?url=/library/en-us/dnadonet/html/ tracingdataaccess.asp*. This article contains a good overview of the trace architecture, demonstrates how you can perform cursory trace file analysis, and looks at simple trace use-cases.

---

SNAC is installed with SQL Server 2005. Client systems that need to connect to SQL Server 2005 using SNAC need SNAC to be installed on each client system individually. You can do this using the procedure outlined in Chapter 8, "Installing and Upgrading Microsoft SQL Server 2005."

# Configuring Network Protocols

SQL Server 2005 by default disables certain network protocols to enhance the security of the server. Table 9-1 presents the default protocol status for each SQL Server 2005 edition.

**Table 9-1    Default Network Protocol Configurations**

| SQL Server 2005 Edition | Shared Memory | TCP/IP | Named Pipes | VIA |
| --- | --- | --- | --- | --- |
| Express | Enabled | Disabled | Enabled for local connections, disabled for remote connections | Disabled |
| Workgroup | Enabled | Enabled | Enabled for local connections, disabled for remote connections | Disabled |
| Standard | Enabled | Enabled | Enabled for local connections, disabled for remote connections | Disabled |
| Enterprise | Enabled | Enabled | Enabled for local connections, disabled for remote connections | Disabled |
| Developer | Enabled | Disabled | Enabled for local connections, disabled for network connections | Disabled |

If an instance of SQL Server is being upgraded to SQL Server 2005, the network configuration settings from the previous installation are preserved. This does not apply for cases where a previous version of SQL Server exists on the server but is not being upgraded. SQL Server 2005 treats such cases the same as a new install and configures the network protocols as per Table 9-1.

The network protocols can be enabled using the SQL Server Surface Area Configuration utility explained in Chapter 8 or using the SQL Server 2005 Network Configuration mode of SQL Server Configuration Manager, as explained in the next section.

---

**Important**    The VIA (Virtual Interface Architecture) protocol is generally used for heavy-duty high-end workloads and requires special network adapters. It is disabled by default, and you should not enable it unless you have the correct network adapters and plan to use this protocol.

# Configuring Server and Client Protocols

In SQL Server 2005, successfully establishing connectivity between a client application and the SQL Server instance requires both the server protocols on the system hosting the SQL Server 2005 instance and the client protocols on the client system to be configured correctly. Although you can configure these servers and client protocols using various tools and utilities, I've found the SQL Server Configuration Manager to be the simplest to use.

SQL Server Configuration Manager is a tool that is installed by SQL Server 2005 setup. It can be used to configure:

- SQL Server 2005 Services

- SQL Server 2005 Network Protocols for each instance of SQL Server installed on the system

- SQL Native Client Configuration

The sections below explain each of these in detail.

## SQL Server 2005 Services

SQL Server Configuration Manager can be invoked by selecting Programs from the Start menu, then selecting Microsoft SQL Server 2005, then Configuration Tools, and then SQL Server Configuration Manager. When invoked, the window shown in Figure 9-3 is displayed.

You can use the SQL Server 2005 Services pane to start, stop, pause, resume, or restart any of the services installed on the local system by right-clicking on the respective service name. You can also configure the properties, such as the login account, the startup mode, the startup parameters, etc., by right-clicking the respective service name and selecting the Properties option.

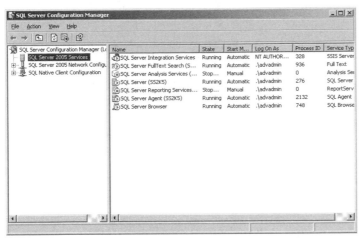

Figure 9-3    SQL Server Configuration Manager.

## SQL Server 2005 Network Protocols

Expanding the SQL Server Network Configuration lists the protocols for each installed SQL Server instance. Selecting a protocol for a particular instance results in the protocols being displayed on the right-hand pane and their current status, as shown in Figure 9-4.

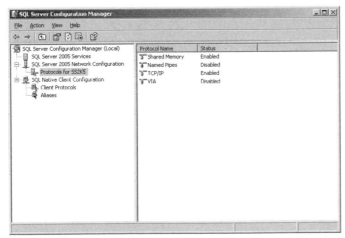

Figure 9-4    SQL Server Configuration Manager—SQL Server Network Configuration.

Each of these protocols can be enabled or disabled by right-clicking the respective protocol and selecting the appropriate action. In addition, certain protocol properties can also be set by right-clicking on the respective protocol and selecting the Properties option.

The options that can be set for each of the four protocols are as follows:

1. **Shared Memory**   Shared Memory Properties dialog box can be used to enable or disable the shared memory protocol. Shared memory has no configurable settings.

2. **Named Pipes**   The Named Pipes Properties dialog box can be used to enable and disable the protocol or change the named pipe to which Microsoft SQL Server listens. To change the named pipe, type the new pipe name in the Pipe Name box and then restart SQL Server. By default SQL Server listens on \\.\pipe\sql\query for the default instance and \\.\pipe\MSSQL$<instancename>\sql\query for a named instance. This field is limited to 2,047 characters.

---

> **Best Practices**   Since sql\query is well-known as the named pipe used by SQL Server you should change the pipe name to help reduce the risk of malicious attacks.

3. **TCP/IP**   The TCP/IP Properties dialog box has two tabs: Protocol and IP Addresses. The Protocol tab can be used to configure the following parameters:

   ❑ **Enabled**   This parameter is used to specify whether the TCP/IP protocol is enabled (Yes) or disabled (No).

   ❑ **Keep Alive**   SQL Server 2005 does not implement changes to this property.

   ❑ **Listen All**   When this parameter is set to Yes, SQL Server listens on all of the IP addresses that are bound to network cards on the system. When set to No, you must configure each IP address separately using the Properties dialog box for each IP address. Unless you have a specific need to bind individual IP addresses, you should leave this set to Yes, which is the default value.

   ❑ **No Delay**   SQL Server 2005 does not implement changes to this property.

   The IP Addresses tab can be used to configure the following parameters for each of the IP addresses (IP ):

   ❑ **Active**   Indicates whether SQL Server is listening on the designated port (Yes) or not (No). This option cannot be set for IPAll.

   ❑ **Enabled**   This parameter is used to enable (Yes) or disable (No) the connection. This option cannot be set for IPAll.

   ❑ **IP Address**   This parameter is used to specify the IP address used by the connection. This option cannot be set for IPAll.

❑ **TCP Dynamic Ports**  This parameter is used to specify whether dynamic ports are used. Setting to 0 enables dynamic ports. If no value is specified, dynamic ports are not enabled.

❑ **TCP Port**  This parameter is used to specify a static port on which SQL Server listens. The SQL Server database engine can listen on multiple ports on the same IP address. To enable SQL Server to listen on multiple ports on the same IP address, list multiple ports separated by a comma in this field, for example, 1428,1429,1430. However, you should only specify ports that are not already being used. This field is limited to 2,047 characters. To configure a single IP address to listen only on the specified ports, the Listen All parameter must also be set to No on the Protocols Tab of the TCP/IP Properties dialog box.

4. **VIA** The VIA Properties dialog box can be used to enable or disable the VIA protocol as well as set the following parameter values:

❑ **Default Port**  This parameter is used to set the default port. The values are specified in the format <network interface card number>:<port number>, for example, 0:1433.

❑ **Enabled**  This parameter is used to specify whether the protocol is enabled (Yes) or disabled (No).

❑ **Listen Info**  This parameter is specified in the format <network interface card number>:<port number>. Multiple ports can be specified by separating them with commas. This field is limited to 2,047 characters.

The SQL Server 2005 service must be restarted to apply the changes to any of the protocols. With SQL Server 2005, configuring the network protocols incorrectly causes the SQL server service to fail to start up. For example, enabling the VIA protocol on a system that does not have the correct VIA hardware configured prevents the SQL Server service from starting up and results in error messages similar to the following being reported in the SQL Server error log:

```
2006-03-04 09:32:39.85 Server

    Error: 17182, Severity: 16, State: 1.

2006-03-04 09:32:39.85 Server

    TDSSNIClient initialization failed with error 0x7e, status code 0x60.

2006-03-04 09:32:39.89 Server

    Error: 17182, Severity: 16, State: 1.

2006-03-04 09:32:39.89 Server

    TDSSNIClient initialization failed with error 0x7e, status code 0x1.

2006-03-04 09:32:39.89 Server
```

```
        Error: 17826, Severity: 18, State: 3.
```

2006-03-04 09:32:39.89 Server

   Could not start the network library because of an internal error in the network library. To determine the cause, review the errors immediately preceding this one in the error log.

2006-03-04 09:32:39.89 Server

```
        Error: 17120, Severity: 16, State: 1.
```

2006-03-04 09:32:39.89 Server

   SQL Server could not spawn FRunCM thread. Check the SQL Server error log and the Windows event logs for information about possible related problems.

---

**Note**   The SQL Server error log is located under the MSSQL\LOG directory of the particular instance of SQL Server, for example, C:\Program Files\Microsoft SQL Server\MSSQL.1\MSSQL\LOG\.

## SQL Native Client Configuration

SQL Server 2005 client programs communicate with SQL Server 2005 servers using the protocols provided in the SNAC library file. The SQL Native Client Configuration settings can be used to specify the status (enabled/disabled) and the order of the protocols for the client programs running on the system. These settings do not affect client programs connecting to earlier versions of SQL Server.

The Client Protocols under the SQL Native Client Configuration can be used to manage the client protocols. When Client Protocols is selected, the window shown in Figure 9-5 appears.

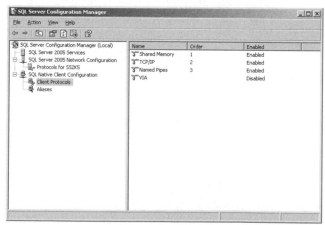

**Figure 9-5**   SQL Server Configuration Manager—Client Protocols.

To change the status of a client protocol, you can right click on the respective protocol name on this window and select Enable or Disable.

You can also manage the order in which the client protocols are selected by right-clicking any of the protocols and selecting Order. Doing so results in the Client Protocols Properties window, shown in Figure 9-6, appearing.

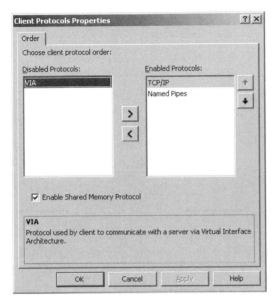

**Figure 9-6**   SQL Server Configuration Manager—Client Protocols Properties.

In this window you can enable or disable the client protocols by selecting the respective protocol and then using the ">" or "<" button. Once enabled, you can change the order of the protocols using the up and down arrows in the right-hand pane of the window. As discussed earlier, when enabled the shared memory protocol is always tried first and therefore, on this window, this protocol can only be enabled or disabled using the Enable Shared Memory Protocol check box located towards the bottom of the window.

The properties for the client protocols can be managed by selecting Client Protocols in the console pane, right-clicking the desired protocol in the details pane, and selecting Properties. The configured properties are used by all client programs on the system connecting via the respective protocol. You can set the properties for the four different protocols as follows:

1. **Shared Memory**   Shared memory has no configurable settings. The only property you can set is whether the protocol is enabled (Yes) or disabled (No).

2.  **Named Pipes**   The named pipes properties can be used to set whether the proto-
    col is enabled (Yes) or disabled (No) and to set the default pipe the Named Pipes
    Net-library uses to attempt to connect to the target instance of SQL Server. By
    default, SQL Server listens on \\.\pipe\sql\query which is specified as sql/query
    in the Default Pipe text box.

3.  **TCP/IP** The TCP/IP Properties can be used to set the following four properties:

    ❑ **Default Port**   The default port specifies the port that the TCP/IP Net-library
      uses to attempt to connect to the target instance of SQL Server. The port for
      the default SQL Server instance is 1433, which is used when connecting to a
      default instance of Database Engine. If the default instance has been config-
      ured to listen on a different port, you will need to change this value to that
      port number. This does not apply when connecting to named SQL Server
      instances because the SQL Server Browser service is used to dynamically
      determine the port number.

    ❑ **Enabled**   This parameter is used to specify whether the protocol is enabled
      (Yes) or disabled (No).

    ❑ **Keep Alive**   TCP/IP is a connection-oriented protocol, implying that the
      connection between the client and the server is maintained even during
      instances when there is no data being communicated back and forth. The
      Keep Alive parameter specifies how often TCP attempts to verify that an idle
      connection is still intact by sending a KEEPALIVE packet. The parameter is
      specified in milliseconds and has a default value of 30,000 milliseconds. For
      majority of the deployments the default value should work fine. You should
      change this setting only if you're trying to resolve a specific TCP/IP-related
      connection problem.

    ❑ **Keep Alive Interval**   If a KEEPALIVE packet is not acknowledged by the
      server, the client retransmits it. The Keep Alive Interval is used to determine
      the interval separating the retransmissions until a response is received. The
      default is 1,000 milliseconds, which should work fine for a majority of the
      deployments.

4.  **VIA** The VIA Properties can be used to set the following three settings:

    ❑ **Default NIC**   This parameter indicates to which Network Interface Card
      (NIC) the VIA protocol is bound. NICs are numbered starting at zero. Com-
      puters with only one NIC always indicate 0.

❑ **Default Server** This parameter specifies the VIA port on which VIA is listening when accepting connections from VIA clients. The default port is: 0:1433.

❑ **Enabled** This parameter is used to specify whether the protocol is enabled (Yes) or disabled (No).

# Using ODBC Data Source Names (DSN)

An ODBC Data Source Name (DSN) is a symbolic name that represents an ODBC connection and is used to provide connectivity to a database through an ODBC driver. A DSN stores the connection details such as database name, database driver, user identifier, password, and so on , saving you the trouble of having to remember and specify all the details when making a connection. While ODBC applications can access the database directly and do not necessarily require a connection through a DSN, using an ODBC DSN is preferred because of its transparency, flexibility, and ease of use. Once you create an ODBC DSN you can reference it in your application to retrieve data from the database.

Depending on the requirements of your application you can create one of three types of DSNs:

■ **System DSN** This type of DSN has a system-wide scope, implying that it is visible and accessible by all users and Windows services that log in to the system. The connection parameters for a system DSN are stored in the Windows registry. This is the most commonly used DSN type.

■ **User DSN** This type of DSN is limited to having a user-wide scope, implying that only the user who created the DSN can view and use it. Similar to System DSNs, the information for User DSNs is stored in the registry. User DSNs are very useful in shared development and test environments where multiple users may need to share a common system and use it in differing ways. In such environments each user of the system can create his or her own User DSN which is not viewable to anyone else, thereby eliminating any confusion and limiting unintentional modifications to a DSN created by some other user.

■ **File DSN** A File DSN is very similar to a System DSN, the only difference being that the parameter values are stored in a file instead of the Windows registry. File DSNs are text files that have a .DSN extension and are stored under: %Program Files%\Common Files\ODBC\Data Sources. File DSNs have the advantage of being easy to backup since all you need to do is back up the .DSN files.

---

**Best Practices**    When using the mixed mode authentication, File DSNs store the SQL Server user ID and password in plain text. Therefore, you should always secure these files.

---

All three DSNs are functionally equivalent. The only difference lies in their scope and the location where the parameter values are stored. DSNs are created on the client system. If there are multiple client systems that need the same DSN, you will have to create it multiple times on each of the client systems. Multiple DSNs can point to the same SQL Server database.

## Creating an ODBC DSN

Creating an ODBC DSN is simple. The steps below explain the procedure that can be used to create a System DSN. User and File DSN can be created using the same basic steps by selecting the User and File options as appropriate:

1. Open the ODBC Data Source Administrator by selecting Programs from the Start menu, then Control Panel, then Administrative Tools, Data Sources (ODBC), and then select the System DSN tab. The ODBC Data Source Administrator window appears, similar to the one shown in Figure 9-7.

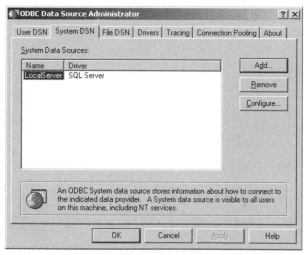

**Figure 9-7**    ODBC Data Source Administrator.

2. Select the Add button. The Create New Data Source window appears, as shown in Figure 9-8.

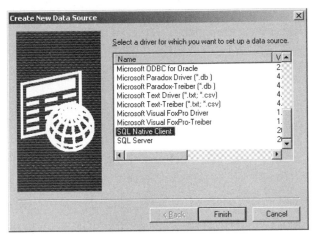

**Figure 9-8**   Create New Data Source.

3.  To create a System DSN using the new SNAC driver, scroll down to the bottom of the list, select SQL Native Client, and click Finish. The first page of the Create a New Data Source to SQL Server Wizard appears, as shown in Figure 9-9.

> **Note**   To use the MDAC driver, select SQL Server from the list shown in Figure 9-8.

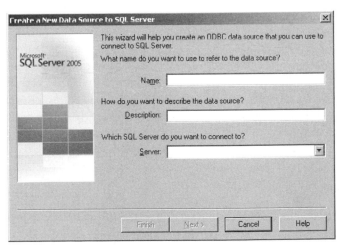

**Figure 9-9**   First page of the Create a New Data Source to SQL Server Wizard.

4.  Enter the Name of the DSN (for example, **MyTestDSN**), a description for the DSN (for example, **My Test Data Source Name**), and the server instance hosting the

database you want to connect to by selecting the name from the drop-down list, specifying the server name and instance name (for example, **HOTH\SS2K5**), or specifying the server IP address and instance name (for example, **192.168.1.101\SS2K5**). Click Next. The second page of the Create A New Data Source To SQL Server Wizard appears, as shown in Figure 9-10.

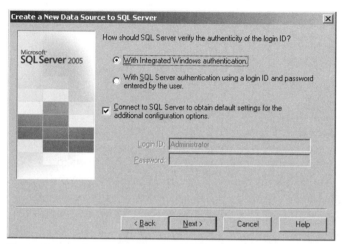

**Figure 9-10**    Second page of the Create A New Data Source To Sql Server Wizard.

5.  Select the authentication mode and enter the login ID and password if using the SQL Server authentication mode. It is recommended that you leave the check box next to Connect To SQL Server selected in order to obtain default settings for the additional configuration options, as this enables the wizard to connect to the SQL Server instance and provides you with the list of selectable options in the successive pages of the wizard. You can clear this check box if you're creating a DSN to a database that is not online or if you already know all the required parameter values and prefer to not query the database for the same. Select Next to continue. The third page of the Create A New Data Source To SQL Server Wizard appears, as shown in Figure 9-11.

---

**Best Practices**    It is a SQL Server best practice to use Integrated Windows authentication mode. However, some applications specifically require the use of the mixed mode (SQL Server) authentication, for example the PeopleSoft-Oracle Financials application. For all such applications, it is acceptable to use the mixed mode authentication.

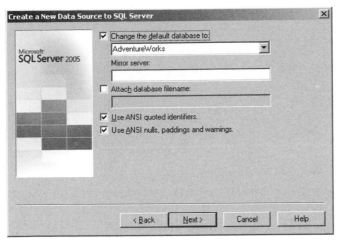

**Figure 9-11**   Third page of the Create A New Data Source to SQL Server Wizard.

6. Select the Change The Default Database To check box if required, and specify the name of the name of the database to which you'd like the DSN to connect. If using database mirroring, explained in detail in Chapter 28, "Log Shipping and Database Mirroring," you can specify the name of the mirror server in the text box provided. You can also chose to attach a database by selecting the Attach Database Filename check box, specifying the database name in the Change The Default Database to textbox, and specifying the complete path to the database filename (for example, %Program Files%\Microsoft SQL Server\MSSQL.1\MSSQL\Data\TestDB.mdf) in the text box below the Attach Database Filename check box. Select the Use ANSI Quoted Identifiers and the Use Ansi Nulls, Paddings And Warnings check boxes as required. Select Next to continue. The fourth page of the Create A New Data Source To SQL Server wizard appears, as shown in Figure 9-12.

7. On this page of the Create A New Data Source To SQL Server Wizard, you can choose to change the language of SQL Server system messages; use strong encryption for data; perform translation of character data; use regional settings when outputting currency, numbers, dates, and times; save queries that take more than a preset amount of time to a log file; and log ODBC driver statistics to a log file. For most DSNs, leaving the setting to the default works fine.

8. Click Finish to continue. The ODBC Microsoft SQL Server Setup window appears, as shown in Figure 9-13. Use this window to test the data source by clicking Test Data Source.

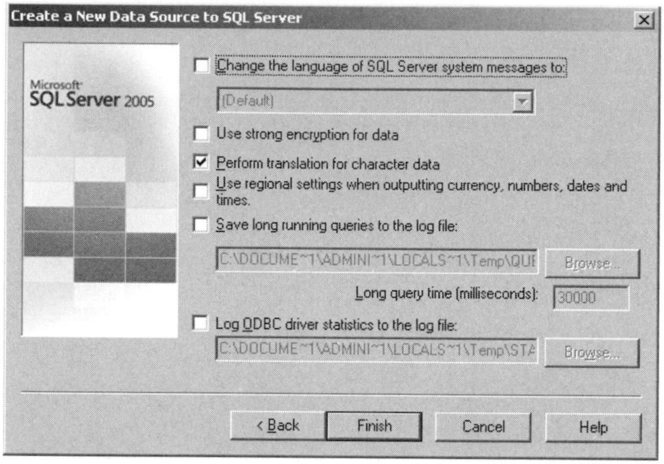

**Figure 9-12**   Fourth page of the Create A New Data Source To SQL Server Wizard.

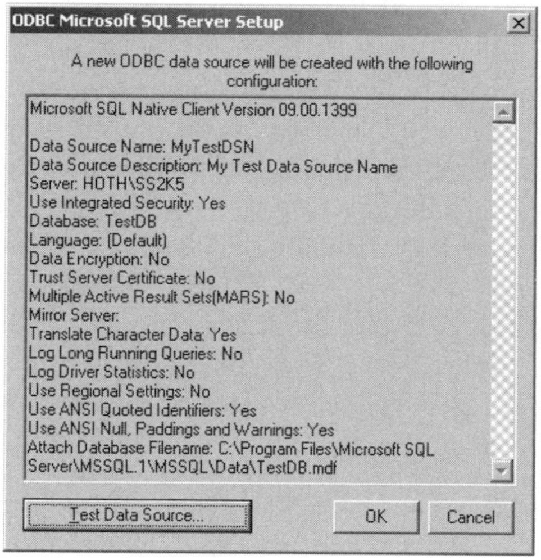

**Figure 9-13**   ODBC Microsoft SQL Server Setup.

A successful completion of the test results in the window is shown in Figure 9-14. Click OK to exit the test window, and then click OK to confirm the data source name creation. You can also select Cancel if you need to backtrack in the creation process and change any of the parameters. This brings you back to the ODBC Data Source Administrator window, and you will see the newly created DSN listed there, as shown in Figure 9-15.

**Figure 9-14**    SQL Server ODBC Data Source Test.

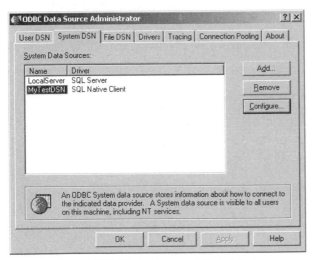

**Figure 9-15**    ODBC Data Source Administrator.

---

**Note**    Once a DSN has been created, you can choose to change any of the parameter values by clicking the Configure button and going through the configuration process again.

## Using Aliases

As we saw in the previous section, you can connect to a SQL Server instance by specifying the system name or TCP/IP address and the instance name for nondefault instances, or the named pipe. However, there are times when you must refer to the SQL Server instance by an alternate name, for example, if the name of your database instance is HOTH\SS2K5 but your application can accept only eight-letter database names in its connection string. For all such cases you can use an alias for the database instance and connect using that.

An alias is a named entity that contains all of the information required to connect to a particular SQL Server instance. Aliases are created on the client system. If there are multiple client systems that need the same alias name, you will have to create the alias multiple times, once on each of the client systems. Multiple aliases can point to the same SQL server instance.

The steps below explain the procedure for creating an alias for a database using the TCP/IP protocol:

1. Open SQL Server Configuration Manager by selecting Programs from the Start menu, then Microsoft SQL Server 2005, then Configuration Tools, and then SQL Server Configuration Manager.

2. In SQL Server Configuration Manager, expand SQL Native Client Configuration as shown in Figure 9-16.

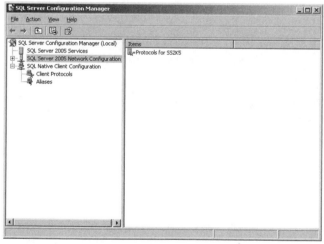

**Figure 9-16**    SQL Server Configuration Manager—SQL Native Client Configuration.

3. Right-click Aliases and select New Alias. The Alias – New window appears, as shown in Figure 9-17. In this dialog box, enter the alias name (for example, **MyTestAlias**),

the TCP/IP port number associated with the SQL Server instance (for example, **1029**)[1], leave the Protocol as TCP/IP since you're creating an alias for the TCP/IP protocol, and enter the name in the Server Name text box or the TCP/IP address of the system hosting the SQL server instance. Click OK to create the alias. The new alias entry appears in the pane at the right side of SQL Server Configuration Manager, as shown in Figure 9-18.

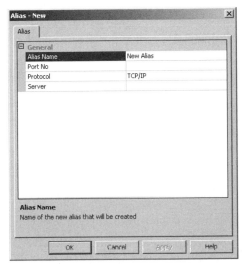

**Figure 9-17**    Alias – New window used to create a new SQL Server 2005 server alias.

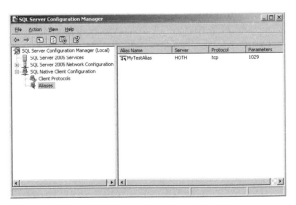

**Figure 9-18**    SQL Server Configuration Manager.

---

1  The TCP/IP port number can be identified by viewing the value of the "TCP/IP Dynamic ports" for the TCP/IP protocol in SQL Server Configuration Manager or by checking the port specified for the ipv4 protocol in SQL Server error log, for example, Server is listening on [ 'any' <ipv4> 4475].

# SQL Server Browser Service

SQL Server 2005 introduces a new program called the SQL Server Browser (sql-browser.exe), which is used to provide information about SQL Server instances installed on the system. For those of you who are familiar with SQL Server 2000, the SQL Browser service replaces the SQL Server Resolution Service which operated on UDP port 1434 and provided a way for clients to query for network endpoints of SQL Server instances. SQL Server Browser service is installed with the first instance of SQL Server 2005 installed on the system. There is always only one SQL Browser service installed and running on any system. This is true even for systems that host multiple instances of SQL Server 2005 or instances of previous versions of SQL Server (SQL Server 7.0 and SQL Server 2000). The SQL Server Browser service is configured to start automatically for upgraded, clustered, and named instances. For new default instances it is set to start manually. The start-up mode (automatic, manual, or disabled) is configured using the Surface Area Configuration tool, SQL Server Configuration Manager, or the Services utility under Administrative Tools in the Control Panel.

The SQL Server Browser service provides the instance name and the version number for each instance of the database engine and SQL Server Analysis Service installed on the system. However, it is not necessary to have this service running to communicate with the server. If the SQL Server Browser service is not running on the system, you can still connect to the particular instance of SQL Server by specifying the protocol, server name and port number, or named pipe directly in the connection string, for example, tcp:HOTH,1429.

---

**Note**   The SQL Server Browser service is not required when a request is made for resources in the default SQL Server instance. This is because there is always only one default instance of SQL Server on a system, and by default it is always configured to listen to TCP/IP network requests on port 1433 and named pipe network requests using the pipe \sql\query.

---

# SQL Browser Working

Every instance of SQL Server[2] with the respective protocol enabled has a unique port number or specific named pipe assigned that is used to communicate with client applications. For named instances, these ports are dynamically assigned when the SQL Server instance is started (this doesn't apply to the default instance installed on the system since that is always configured to use port 1433 and the pipe \sql\query). Since the ports are

---

2   This applies to all editions of SQL Server including SQL Server Express.

assigned dynamically, the client applications have no way of determining to which port to connect. This is where SQL Server Browser comes to the rescue.

When SQL Server Browser service starts, it identifies all SQL Server instances installed on the system and the port numbers and named pipes associated with each using the information stored in the Windows registry. Multiple port numbers and named pipes are returned for SQL Server instances that have more than one port number or named pipe enabled. SQL Server Browser then begins listening to network requests on UDP port 1434.

When a SQL Server 2000 or SQL Server 2005 client needs to request SQL Server resources, the client network library initiates the request by sending a UDP message using 1434. SQL Server Browser, which is listening on port 1434, responds to the request and returns the TCP/IP port or named pipe associated with the requested SQL Server instance. The client application then sends the request for information to the server, using the respective port or named pipe of the respective instance, which then services the request and returns the requested data.

The SQL Server Browser program is installed to %Program Files%\Microsoft SQL Server\90\Shared\sqlbrowser.exe. For debugging purposes it is sometimes helpful to start the program via the command line instead of as a service. To do so you can use the following command:

```
%Program Files%\Microsoft SQL Server\90\Shared\sqlbrowser.exe  -c
```

## Understanding "Login Failed" (Error 18456) Error Messages

If SQL Server 2005 encounters an error that prevents a login from succeeding, it returns the following error message to the client:

```
Msg 18456, Level 14, State 1, Server <server name>, Line 1
Login failed for user '<user name>'
```

Unlike other error messages that are descriptive and help you to quickly drill-down into the exact cause, the message for error 18456 has been intentionally kept fairly nondescript to prevent information disclosure to unauthenticated clients. In particular, the error 'State' is always reported as '1' regardless of the nature of the failure. There is no way to determine additional information about the error at the client level.

For cases where you need to debug the exact cause of the failure, a user with administrative privileges can find additional information from the SQL Server errorlog where a corresponding entry will be recorded provided the audit-level is set to log failures on login (default value). For example, an entry such as the following may be recorded in the error log corresponding to an 18456 error.

```
2006-02-27 00:02:00.34 Logon    Error: 18456, Severity: 14, State: 8.

2006-02-27 00:02:00.34 Logon    Login failed for user '<user name>'. [CLIENT:
<ip address>]
```

The important information presented in the entry in the SQL Server error log is the 'State' information which, unlike the error returned to the client, is set to correctly reflect the source of the problem. Some of the common error states include:

| Error State | Error Description |
| --- | --- |
| 2 or 5 | Userid is not valid |
| 6 | Attempt to use a Windows login name with SQL Server Authentication |
| 7 | Login disabled and the password is incorrect |
| 8 | Password is incorrect |
| 9 | Password is not valid |
| 11 or 12 | Valid login but server access failure |
| 13 | SQL Server service is paused |
| 18 | Password change required |

Based on this information you can determine that the error in the above message (State = 8) was caused by a password mismatch.

# Hiding a SQL Server 2005 Instance

When the SQL Server Browser service is running by default, all instances of SQL Server are exposed. However, there may be cases when you would like to hide a particular SQL server instance while continuing to expose others. SQL Server 2005 provides you this flexibility by providing an instance-specific option to hide the identity.

The following steps explain the process of hiding an instance of SQL Server using SQL Server Configuration Manager:

1.  Open SQL Server Configuration Manager by selecting Programs from the Start menu, then Microsoft SQL Server 2005, then Configuration Tools, and then SQL Server Configuration Manager.

2.  In SQL Server Configuration Manager, expand SQL Server 2005 Network Configuration, as shown in Figure 9-16. Right-click the Protocols for *<instance name>* and

select Properties. The Protocols for *<instance name>* Properties window appears, as shown in Figure 9-19.

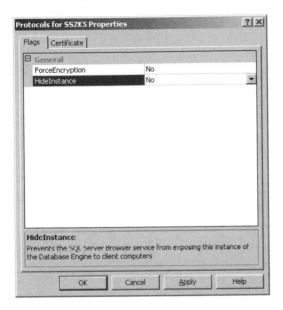

**Figure 9-19**   SQL Server Configuration Manager—Protocols for <instance name> Properties.

3.  On the HideInstance box in the Flags pane, select Yes to hide the instance. Click OK to apply the changes and close the dialog box. You do not need to restart your server to make this change effective. Once you click OK, the setting change is immediately applied and new connections will not be able to connect to the instance via the SQL Browser service. A connection can still be made to the SQL Server instance by specifying the protocol, server name (or TCP/IP address), and port number, or the named pipe directly, for example:

```
tcp:192.168.1.101,1429
```

# Network Components and Performance

The network can be divided broadly into two layers: the software layer, which houses the network protocols, and the hardware layer, which includes the network interface cards (NIC), cables, and so on. Each network layer has its own characteristics and performance considerations. There are several reasons for choosing a particular protocol or network hardware component. Usually, this choice is made based on your business rules and how each system is connected to the other systems in your network. In this section we'll examine the software and hardware related factors that affect SQL Server performance.

## The Software Layer

With the newer versions of the Windows operating system and SQL Server 2005, the software layer of the networking stack autoconfigures itself for a majority of the cases requiring little or no user intervention. However, there may be times when you may experience connectivity problems. If you experience problems connecting a SQL Server client to a SQL Server 2005 server, you may want to the check the following:

- Make sure that the SQL Server service is enabled and running.

- Make sure that the SQL Server 2005 instance has been enabled to accept remote connections.

- Make sure that the correct protocols have been configured on the client and SQL Server systems.

- Try connecting the client to the server system in some other manner, for example by using Windows Explorer. If you cannot connect via Windows Explorer, your problem probably relates to some hardware issue or network adapter configuration.

- If connecting to a named SQL Server instance, make sure that the SQL Server Browser service is running. In addition, if using a firewall, make sure that the UDP port 1434 is not blocked.

While SQL Server 2005 network stack exposes many user configurable settings, these hardly ever need to be changed to enhance performance. In my experience the network performance is good with just the default settings as long as the hardware layer is configured and operating correctly.

## The Hardware Layer

The amount of throughput the network can handle depends on both the type and the speed of the network. The networking hardware you choose largely determines the performance of the network. While in many organizations the hardware infrastructure team takes care of the hardware layer, it is important that you as a database administrator understand the hardware layer to determine where network performance problems are occurring.

At the hardware layer the fundamental and most important metric to consider is the network bandwidth. The *network bandwidth* measures the amount of data that a network can transmit in a specified amount of time. Network bandwidth is sometimes stated in the name of the network hardware itself, as in 100BaseT, which indicates a 100-megabit per second (Mbps) bandwidth.

**Note**  Network bandwidth is stated in megabits per second (Mbps), not mega-bytes per second (MBps).

This rated network throughput, for example 100BaseT, can sometimes be deceiving because the rating is calibrated from perfect work conditions in a lab environment. The effective network bandwidth realized by real-world applications like SQL Server is often far less because of the overheads associated with transmitting data. In addition, the rate at which a particular network adapter can transmit data decreases as the size of the transmission decreases because each network transmission takes a certain amount of overhead, which results in suboptimal use of fixed-size network packets. For example, the amount of network bandwidth and overhead required to transmit 200 bytes of data is approximately the same as the amount necessary to transmit 1,200 bytes of data. This is because each data transmission is encapsulated in a fixed-size TCP/IP packet of 1,500 bytes, which is the default TCP/IP transmission packet size, or 9,000 bytes, which is the "jumbo-frame" packet size for TCP/IP (and is rarely used). Since applications like SQL Server typically deal with transmissions of small amounts of data, the amount of throughput that your server can handle might be smaller than the bandwidth of the network hardware. In my experience I have usually seen the actual realized bandwidth to be about 35 to 50 percent of the rated bandwidth, imply-ing that a 100BaseT network can provide an effective bandwidth of about 35 to 50 Mbps, or about 4.4 to 6.2 MBps.

The most popular and widely used network hardware is still 100BaseT Ethernet, although Gigabit (1000BaseT) network hardware has become very affordable and increasingly prevalent. 10BaseT is still an available and supported option, though not rec-ommended given the availability of the 100BaseT and 1000BaseT. Table 9-2 presents the maximum rated transmission bandwidths of commonly used network hardware. It also lists the maximum effective bandwidths I have seen being realized with SQL Server work-loads.

**Table 9-2  Maximum Network Bandwidths**

| Network | Maximum Bandwidth | |
|---|---|---|
| | **Rated** | **Effective** |
| 10BaseT | 10 Mbps | 3.5 to 5 Mbps |
| 100BaseT | 100 Mbps | 35 to 50 Mbps |
| Gigabit Ethernet or 1000BaseT | 1000 Mbps | 350 to 500 Mbps |

As much as possible you should use Gigabit Ethernet to provide connectivity throughout your environment, or at least between the SQL Server system and all client systems that connect to it. This maximizes the probability of the network not becoming a bottleneck and provides you flexibility to grow your workload in the future without having to redo the network infrastructure. While the price differential between 100BaseT and Gigabit used to be significant, this has been drastically reduced recently, making Gigabit Ethernet a more easily adoptable solution. When using Gigabit Ethernet you need to make sure that in addition to the network adapters the rest of your infrastructure, like the network switches, cables, and so on, also supports Gigabit Ethernet.

# Network Monitoring

The type and speed of the network hardware you choose can affect the overall performance of your database system. If you try to transmit more data than your network can handle at one time, data transmissions will queue up and be delayed. This delay will, in turn, slow down the entire system.

The first step in finding network problems is to periodically monitor and log the network performance so that you can gauge the network utilization as a percent of the maximum effective bandwidth, as listed in Table 9-2. You can then use this data to determine whether your network is a bottleneck and also gauge the magnitude of the problem.

## Monitoring Network Performance

Monitoring the network performance is often not as straightforward a task as monitoring some of the other components of the system, such as memory and processors. This is primarily because the network usually involves multiple systems communicating with each other and utilizes multiple network interface cards, network cables, and network drivers. Tools like Windows Perfmon, which is explained in Chapter 29, "Concepts of Tuning," help you view some of the key networking metrics but have some inherent inaccuracies built in to them because they present data only for the system on which it's running and not the actual underlying network. While these coarse-gain measurements are acceptable for measuring performance of most SQL Server systems, at times it may be necessary to purchase additional network monitoring hardware or software for more accurate measurements. Monitoring the network performance using specialized software or hardware is outside the scope of this book and will not be explained.

When using Windows Perfmon to measure network performance, the most important metric to monitor is "Bytes Total/sec." This metric, when compared to the effective bandwidth of your select network infrastructure, helps you determine the utilization of your network. For example, if your server is configured with 100BaseT network gear and the Bytes Total/sec measured over a period of time is, say, 4,000,000 (32 Mbps), your network may be running close to the maximum permissible network bandwidth possible by the network infrastructure.

# Finding Solutions to Network Problems

You can solve bandwidth problems in a number of ways, depending on the specific problem. You might be able to solve the problem by purchasing more or different hardware, segmenting the network, or even redesigning the application.

One way to resolve the network utilization problem is to increase the network's bandwidth. Upgrading the network hardware from 100BaseT to 1000BaseT increases the bandwidth tenfold. This solution is simple, but it can be expensive. Let's look at alternatives.

If you are seeing too much traffic on the network, it might be the right time to divide the network into subnets based on departments or workgroups. By subnetting, you can create a network for each office or department instead of having the entire company on the same network. This process reduces the number of systems on a single network and thus reduces the traffic. Sometimes, the network grows slowly over a long period of time, and you might not notice additional traffic until a problem occurs. The use of subnets might be an easy solution to alleviate network congestion.

Another solution is looking at the network usage from a functional standpoint. Is the network being used for good reasons? Are the applications returning too much data? It is always a good idea to look at the SQL Server client applications to be sure that they are not requesting more data than what is actually needed. Using queries that return the minimum number of rows is an easy way to reduce network traffic if you have many users.

As you can see, there can be a variety of problems and, thus, a variety of solutions. Don't be afraid to look at all the possibilities. Logic errors in applications can sometimes manifest themselves as network bandwidth problems. Scheduling problems can also arise—for example, it's not a good idea to back up your data across the network during the busiest time of day.

# Summary

Configuring the SQL Server network components correctly is an essential step in ensuring that users and applications are able to connect to the SQL Server database reliably and realize good performance.

SQL Server 2005 introduces several changes to the network components by way of new tools and libraries as well as configuration management. In this chapter we took an in-depth look at some of these, like SQL Server Configuration Manager and SQL Native Client, and the applicability of these to particular usage scenarios. We also took a look at the procedure to create ODBC DSNs, configuring network protocols as well as analyzing and troubleshooting network performance.

# Part III
# Microsoft SQL Server 2005 Administration

# Chapter 10
# Creating Databases and Database Snapshots

A database's manageability and performance is largely determined by its structure and configuration. A well-designed database provides you with flexibility in managing day-to-day operations and helps streamline I/O operations to maximize the effectiveness of the storage subsystems.

In Chapter 4, "I/O Subsystem Planning and RAID Configuration," you learned about the fundamentals of I/O subsystems. Chapter 7, "Choosing a Storage System for SQL Server 2005," explained the factors to consider when choosing a particular storage solution. This chapter builds on those fundamentals and shows you how to design, create, and configure a database for optimal manageability and performance. We will also take an in-depth look at Database Snapshots, a new feature introduced in SQL Server 2005 that permits you to create a point-in-time read-only snapshot of a database.

After reading this chapter, you will understand the structure of a SQL Server database and the purpose of the five system databases. You will learn how to create, configure, and alter a user database; see example real-world application databases; and learn some useful best practices. You will also learn about Database Snapshots along with valuable insights into their working, common uses, is limitations, and the methods used to create, use, and delete them.

# Understanding the Database Structure

A database in SQL Server 2005 can conceptually be viewed as a named collection of objects that hold data and metadata. The data component relates to actual user information stored in the database, for example, information about employees for a human resources application, while metadata is the data that describes how the database handles and stores the data, for example, table definitions, indexes, and so on. Each database file is mapped onto an operating system file that resides on an NTFS or FAT file system. The operating system files are then organized into filegroups for manageability purposes.

## Database Files

Every SQL Server database always has one primary data file and one transaction log file. A database can also have additional transaction log files and one or more secondary data files.

### Primary Data File

The primary data file is the most important file in the database. It is used to store the start-up information and metadata for the database. It contains the system tables of the database, like sysindexes, syscolumns, user data, and so on, user data and holds information about the other files in the database. The primary data file usually has an .mdf file name extension.

### Transaction Log File

The transaction log is an integral part of the database and is used to recover a database in the event of a failure. Every database operation that modifies the state of the database is stored in the transaction log file. A database must have at least one transaction log file, and they can have more for manageability and data distribution purposes. If there is more than one physical log file for a database, the log grows through the end of each physical file before circling back to the first physical file, assuming that that part of the transaction log is free. If the physical transaction log file is completely full and auto-growth is enabled, the size of the file or files is increased. The minimum size for a single transaction log is 512 KB, though it's a good practice to create it with at least 3 MB. The transaction log files usually have an .ldf extension.

### Secondary Data File

A SQL Server database can also have secondary data files. The secondary data files are used to store user data like tables, indexes, views, and stored procedures. Secondary data files are used to spread the user database across multiple disks for manageability and performance reasons. The secondary data files usually have an .ndf file name extension.

---

**Note**  The .mdf, .ldf, and .ndf file name extensions are recommended standard naming conventions; however, they are not required nor explicitly enforced by SQL Server 2005.

---

### Naming Database Files

Every SQL Server 2005 database file has two names: a physical file name and a logical file name. The physical file name is the complete name of the physical file including the directory path and is used to identify the file on the disk. Physical names must conform to the operating system's file naming convention. The logical file name is used to refer to the file in T-SQL statements and needs to conform to the SQL server 2005 identifier naming conventions.

## Database Filegroups

A database filegroup is a logical grouping of data files used primarily for manageability and allocation purposes. In SQL Server 2005 there can be two types of filegroups: primary and user-defined filegroups:

- **Primary filegroup**  Every SQL Server 2005 database always has a primary filegroup, which contains the primary data file (.MDF). The primary filegroup may also contain zero or more secondary data files (.NDF).

- **User-defined filegroup**  A user defined filegroup is explicitly created by the user. A database can have zero or more user-defined filegroups, and each user-defined filegroup can have zero or more secondary data files associated with it.

SQL Server 2005 has the concept of a default filegroup, which, as the name suggests, is the default filegroup for all secondary data files created without an explicit filegroup assignment. The primary filegroup is initially assigned to be the default filegroup; however, this can be changed to be any other user-defined filegroup by a db_owner using SQL Sever Management Studio or the T-SQL ALTER DATABASE command  (T-SQL was introduced in Chapter 1, "Overview of New Features and Enhancements"):

```
ALTER DATABASE <database_name> MODIFY FILEGROUP <new_filegroup_name> DEFAULT;
```

For example:

```
ALTER DATABASE TestDB MODIFY FILEGROUP NewFG DEFAULT ;
```

At any given point in time, only one filegroup can be designated as the default filegroup.

A secondary data file can be a part of only one filegroup. Once a data file has been created as part of a particular filegroup, you cannot move it directly to another filegroup. If you want to move the file to another filegroup, you must first empty it by relocating any data present in that file to other files in the same filegroup using the command:

```
DBCC SHRINKFILE (<data_file>, EMPTYFILE);
```

For example:

```
DBCC SHRINKFILE (TestDB_2, EMPTYFILE);
```

Once emptied, you can delete the file and recreate it on the other filegroup.

Even though there can be more than one transaction log file, the transaction log files are never a part of a filegroup and cannot be placed individually. All transaction log files utilized sequentially in a circular fashion to store the logical log records.

While filegroups are simply containers for the data files that don't intrinsically help improve performance, in some cases performance gains are realized by appropriate placement of tables and indexes on specific disks. This is particularly true for complex workloads where the data access patterns are well understood, and there are gains to be realized by appropriate placement of the tables. For example, if an application has a huge volume of data continuously being inserted into, for example, a case-history information table, it may make sense to separate this table into its own filegroup. Filegroups also help you partition large tables across multiple files to distribute the I/O throughput. They can also be used effectively to store indexes and *text, ntext,* and *image* data type columns on files other than where the table itself is stored.

---

**Note**   SQL Server 2005 permits a database to have 32,767 data files and filegroups; however, this limit is almost never expected to be reached. In real world deployments, the number of files and filegroups in a database is usually less than a half dozen, and many of the small and lightly accessed databases have just a single data and transaction log file. The one exception to this is when data partitioning is used. In this case the database could very easily have upwards of 250 filegroups and files. You will learn more about this in Chapter 20, "Data Partitioning."

---

# Understanding System Databases

Every SQL Server 2005 instance contains five system databases—*master, model, msdb, tempdb,* and *resource*—that are used for the server initialization, housekeeping, and temporary storage required for application data. In addition, SQL Server 2005 also optionally installs two sample databases: *AdventureWorks* and *AdventureWorksDW*. The purpose of all these databases is described in the sections below.

## master

The *master* is by far the most important system database in SQL Server 2005. It contains a set of system tables that serve as a central repository for the entire instance and maintaining information about login accounts, other databases, file allocations, system configuration setting, disk space, resource consumptions, endpoints, linked servers, and so on. Unlike earlier versions of SQL Server, the *master* database in SQL Server 2005 does not store system objects; the system objects are now stored in the *resource* database, which is explained later.

The *master* database records the initialization information for SQL Server 2005, and therefore it is absolutely critical to the SQL Server instance. It is a recommended best practice to locate the *master* database on a fault-tolerant disk drive and always have a current backup to protect against the event that it gets completely destroyed and has to be restored from a backup media. You should always back up the *master* database after creating, modifying, or deleting a user database; changing the server or any database configuration; and modifying or adding user accounts.

> **More Info**   In the absolute worst-case scenario when the *master* database is destroyed and no backup is available, you can rebuild it to its state when the instance was installed using the REBUILDDATABASE option available in the unattended setup. This operation should be performed very selectively and after careful consideration as it wipes out your entire server-wide configuration including all logins, forcing you to redo everything from scratch. Search for "Rebuild *master* database" in SQL Server Books Online for information on how to rebuild the *master* database.

## model

The *model* database servers as a template for all new databases created in the SQL Server 2005 instance. When the CREATE DATABASE command is executed to create a new user database or when the *tempdb* database (explained later) is initialized, SQL Server 2005 simply copies the contents of the model database to the new database. In cases where you want to create every new database with a table, stored procedure, database option, permission, and so on, you can add it to the model database, and it will be added to every new database that is created from there on.

## msdb

The *msdb* database is used by the SQL Server instance, primarily by *SQL Server Agent*, to store scheduled jobs, alerts, and backup/restore history information. All the information stored in it is viewable via the SQL Server tools, so other than backing up this database, there is little need for you to access or directly query this database.

---

**Note** The *master*, *model*, and *msdb* databases have the following restrictions:

- Cannot add, rename, or delete any file or filegroup
- Cannot be renamed or dropped
- Cannot be set to READ_ONLY or OFFLINE
- Cannot change default collation
- Cannot change database owner
- Cannot drop guest user from the database
- Cannot participate in database mirroring
- Cannot create full-text catalog, full-text index, or triggers

## resource

The *resource* database, introduced in SQL Server 2005, is a read-only database that contains all of the system objects, such as system stored procedures, system extended stored procedures, system functions, and so on. The *resource* database provides a means of quick version upgrades and the ability to easily roll back service packs. In previous versions of SQL Server, upgrading the SQL Server version involved the lengthy process of dropping and creating the system objects. However, since the *resource* database now contains all the system objects, it is sufficient simply to copy a single *resource* database file onto the server. The same mechanism is used when a version of SQL Server needs to be rolled back.

The *resource* database does not contain any user data or metadata, so you do not need to include it in your regular backup/restore scheme. Instead, it should be treated as code and should have a backup/restore plan similar to what's used for the other SQL Sever executables. The *resource* database is hidden and does not show up in the SQL Server Management Studio or the *sp_helpdb* output. Only its data (mssqlsystemresource.mdf) and log (mssqlsystemresource.ldf) files can be seen in the SQL Server Data directory (for example, C:\Program Files\Microsoft SQL Server\MSSQL.1\MSSQL\Data).

# tempdb

The *tempdb* database is an instance-wide temporary workspace that SQL Server 2005 uses for a variety of operations. Some of the common uses include the following:

- Storage for private and global temporary variables, regardless of the database context

- Work tables associated with ORDER BY clauses, cursors, GROUP BY clauses, and HASH plans

- Explicitly created temporary objects such as stored procedures, cursors, tables, and table variables

- Versions of updated records for the snapshot isolation feature when enabled

- Results of temporary sorts from create or rebuild index operations if SORT_IN_TEMPDB is specified

The *tempdb* database is the only system database in SQL Server 2005 that is recreated every time SQL Server is started, implying that it always starts with a clean copy and no information is persisted across SQL Server restarts. Operations in *tempdb* are always minimally logged (SIMPLE recovery model) so that sufficient information is stored to allow roll back of an in-flight operation if needed. Since *tempdb* is reinitialized when SQL Server 2005 starts, there is no need for the ability to recover or redo the database.

---

**Note**   Since there is a single *tempdb* database across the entire SQL Server instance, it is a potential bottleneck if there are many databases that utilize it heavily running on the instance. While I have never encountered a situation like this, it is worth keeping in mind. If this were to ever become a problem, you may consider installing multiple instances of SQL Server 2005 on the same server and splitting up the databases between the two or more instances. Since each instance will have its own *tempdb*, it will effectively help distribute the utilization.

---

While *tempdb* is initially installed in the same location as the other system databases, it is often a good idea to relocate it to a high-performing disk subsystem. This is particularly important for applications that make heavy use of *tempdb*.

Relocating *tempdb* involves a slightly different procedure than other databases because it is recreated when SQL Server starts. To move *tempdb*:

1. Determine the current location of *tempdb* files (Tempdb.mdf and Tempdb.ldf), for example, in C:\Program Files\Microsoft SQL Server\MSSQL.1\MSSQL\Data.

2. Relocate the files using the ALTER DATABASE commands:

```
ALTER DATABASE tempdb
MODIFY FILE (NAME = tempdev, FILENAME = 'X:\TempdbData\tempdb.mdf') ;
GO
ALTER DATABASE tempdb
MODIFY FILE (NAME = templog, FILENAME = 'Y:\TempdbLog\templog.ldf') ;
GO
```

where X and Y are the new drives on which *tempdb* is relocated.

3. Restart SQL Server 2005. This will create new *tempdb* data and log files under the new directories.

4. Verify the new locations of *tempdb* using the command:

```
sp_helpdb tempdb ;
```

5. Delete the files identified in Step 1 to avoid any confusion and free up space.

   *The tempdb* database is a global resource that is available to all users operating on the particular instance of SQL Server. All users can create temporary objects (those starting with # or ##) in *tempdb*.

---

**Note**   For detailed steps on moving the *tempdb* master file, search for "Rebuild *master* database" in SQL Server Books Online and refer to the "Moving *tempdb* to a new location" topic.

---

For high-throughput and large applications, it is a recommended best practice that you create multiple *tempdb* data files. Multiple *tempdb* data files minimize contention on the IAM and SGAM pages and results in better performance. A general rule of thumb I like to use is to create *tempdb* files equal in number to the processor cores in the server. In other words, for a 4-processor dual-core server, I'd create 8 *tempdb* data files. The files should all be the same size and located on a high-performing disk subsystem (RAID-10), as explained in Chapter 4. You should also make sure that the *tempdb* master file has been relocated to the high-performing disk subsystem and is the same size as the other files.

---

**Note**   The *tempdb* database's performance in SQL Server 2005 has been significantly optimized. Many of the internal points of contention that existed in earlier versions of SQL Server have been resolved. If you used trace flag 1118 (-T1118) on your server to get around SGAM single page allocation contention, as explained in Microsoft Knowledge Base article 328551, FIX: Concurrency enhancements for the tempdb database, "*http://support.microsoft.com/kb/328551*" with SQL Server 2000, you may want to test your application without this trace flag to see if the problem you originally encountered has been resolved by design in SQL Server 2005. There is a high likelihood that it is. If not, you can continue to use trace flag -T1118.

## *AdventureWorks* and *AdventureWorksDW*

The *AdventureWorks* and *AdventureWorksDW* are two new sample databases introduced in SQL Server 2005 that are based on a fictitious "Adventure Works Cycles" company. The *AdventureWorks* database is an online transaction processing (OLTP) sample database while the *AdventureWorksDW* is a data warehousing sample database. These databases replace the *pubs* and *Northwind* databases that used to ship with earlier versions of SQL Server. However, some of the tables are similar in structure and can continue to be used for old sample queries.

---

**More Info**   You can search for the "*AdventureWorks* to *pubs* Table Comparison" and "*AdventureWorks* to *Northwind* Table Comparison" topics in SQL Server Books Online for a comparison between the *AdventureWorks* and *pubs* and *Northwind* tables.

---

Both of these sample databases are not installed by default and have to be manually selected during SQL Server 2005 installation. (Refer to Chapter 8, "Installing and Upgrading Microsoft SQL Server," for details on installing these databases.) These databases have no involvement in the operation of SQL Server and are used solely for example purposes. Since they are standard databases and most users have access to them, I have found that they serve as an effective base for creating and sharing samples. For example, if I want to demonstrate a certain operation to a customer, I just create a sample based on the *AdventureWorks* database and send it to the customer with instructions on how to execute it. Most of the samples in the SQL Server Books Online are also based on these two databases.

---

# Creating User Databases

Unlike system databases that are always installed by default, you need to create and configure all user databases manually. The sections below explain the processes involved in creating, altering, viewing, and deleting user databases.

# Creating a Database

In SQL Server 2005 user databases can be created using either SQL Server Management Studio or the CREATE DATABASE command. Creating a database using either method is a relatively straight-forward operation that can be done fairly quickly. However, setting the various database options correctly requires detailed understanding of the databases requirements and anticipated usage characteristics.

SQL Server Management Studio is the easier of the two options and presents a graphical user interface for the database creation and configuration. The CREATE DATABASE command, on the other hand, requires the user to know the format of the command and the parameters but has the advantage of being able to save the T-SQL.

### Real World    A Hybrid Method to Create a Database

I have found that a hybrid approach using SQL Server Management Studio to create the database and then the SCRIPT DATABASE AS option to script it and save it to a file, as explained in Chapter 31, "Using Profiler, Management Studio, and Database Tuning Advisor," is easiest and works well. With this approach you realize the best of both worlds: an easy creation process and the ability to save the process to a file for backup purposes and possible reuse.

## Creating a Database Using SQL Server Management Studio

The following steps explain the process of creating a user database using SQL Server Management Studio:

1.  To start SQL Server Management Studio, click the Start button, point to All Programs, select Microsoft SQL Server 2005, and then select SQL Server Management Studio.

2.  Log in to the instance you want to use, and then wait until the server finishes processing the login and the Object Explorer pane appears on the left side of the window. If the Object Explorer pane does not appear, you can display it by selecting Object Explorer from the View menu.

3.  Click on the + sign next to the server name to expand the instance, as shown in Figure 10-1.

4.  Right-click Databases and then select New Database from the shortcut menu.

5.  Select the General tab and enter the database name, for example, *TestDB*. You will notice that the logical name column is automatically filled in with the name of the database, as shown in Figure 10-2.

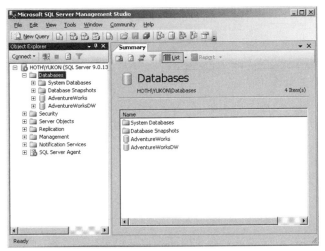

**Figure 10-1**   SQL Server Management Studio—Object Explorer.

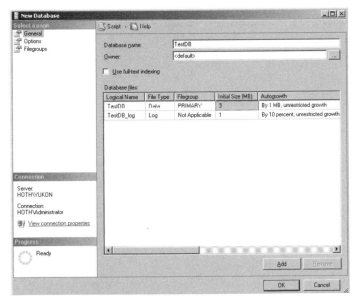

**Figure 10-2**   New Database—General tab.

6. If you would like to keep all of the other database options at their default values, click OK, and your database will be created with the default settings. If you'd like to change any of the default database settings, continue with the following steps.

7. If you'd like to change the owner of the database, click on the ... button next to Owner and select the desired login from the Browse list. Leaving the Owner value as *<default>* will make the logged in user for the session the owner of the database.

8. Select the Use Full-Text Indexing check box if you want to enable full-text search on the database.

---

**Note** Full-text search allows fast and flexible searching of text data stored in the database and can operate on words as well as phrases based on rules of a particular language. While a very powerful feature, this option should be enabled only if you plan to actually use it as there is overhead associated with maintaining the full-text indexes.

---

**Note** SQL Server Management Studio creates all databases with a primary data file (.mdf) and one transaction log file (.ldf). These two files appear in the database files grid. Both of these files have default logical names assigned to them, but they can be changed to any valid SQL Server identifier name by selecting the cell and typing in the new name.

---

9. You can add additional files by clicking the Add button in the lower-right corner of the New Database screen. This adds another row with default values to the database files grid.

10. Enter the Logical Name for the file in the new row that is created in the database files grid. All of the other database file options can be left at their default settings or configured as explained in the following list:

   ❑ **File type** This drop-down list option is used to select whether the file is a data or log file. However, the file types for the auto-created primary data file and transaction log files cannot be changed.

   ❑ **Filegroup** The filegroup option applies only to data files and is used to select the filegroup to which the file belongs. The main database file always belongs to the primary filegroup. The additional data files created can belong to either the primary or a new filegroup created using the <new filegroup> option in the drop-down list. In this screen, shown in Figure 10-3, you can specify the name of the filegroup and set the filegroup to be read-only if required. You can also make the filegroup the default, implying that all successive new file creations will by default be added to this filegroup.

   ❑ **Initial size (MB)** This option sets the initial size for each of the files. It is recommended that you create the database with sufficient space to prevent unnecessary and excessive auto-grow operations.

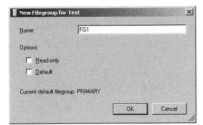

**Figure 10-3**   New Filegroup window.

❑ **Autogrowth**   Autogrowth is a very powerful option in SQL Server through which the size of a database file is automatically increased if it fills up. The autogrowth options can be changed by selecting the ... button and setting the values in the Change Autogrowth screen, as shown in Figure 10-4.

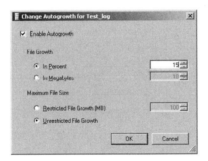

**Figure 10-4**   Change Autogrowth window.

---

**Best Practices**   For production databases it is best to configure the database file sizes slightly larger than the maximum size you antici-pate so that you do not trigger the auto-growth mechanism. Because the database engine needs to acquire a schema lock when the size of the database is extended to prevent transactions from progressing, it is best to treat the Autogrowth option as a worst-case insurance pol-icy and not rely on it to do the appropriate file-sizing job for you.

---

❑ **Path**   This option is used to specify the location of the physical file.

❑ **File name**   This option cannot be set. The physical file name is automatically set to the same value as the corresponding logical file name with the appro-priate file name extensions (.mdf, .ldf, .ndf) added.

Figure 10-5 shows a database named *TestDB* configured with two new file-groups (FG1 and FG2), two additional files (TestDB_data2 and TestDB_data3), and the autogrowth value changed to 15 percent.

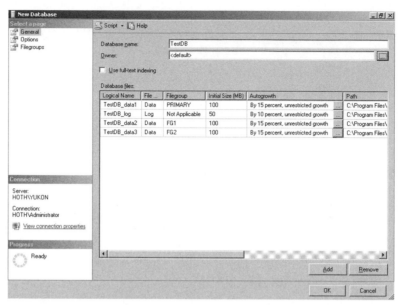

**Figure 10-5**   New Database window for database TestDB.

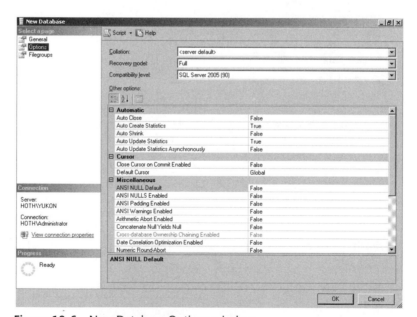

**Figure 10-6**   New Database Options window.

11.  Select the Options tab from the left pane, as shown in Figure 10-6, and set the appropriate database options. The various database options are explained in detail in the Database Options section that follows.

12.  Select the Filegroups tab from the pane at left, as shown in Figure 10-7. This screen is used to create new filegroups.

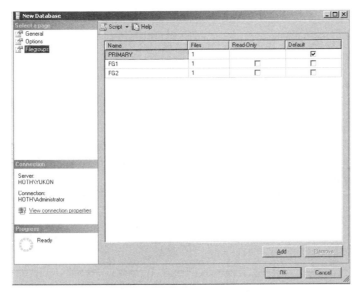

**Figure 10-7**   New Database Filegroups window.

13.  To add a new filegroup, select Add in the lower-right corner and enter the name of the filegroup in the Name cell. You can also select the filegroup to be read-only or set it to be the default filegroup for the database.

14.  Click OK to create the database. The database creation will take between a few seconds to several minutes depending on the number and sizes of the database files created. Once completed, a new entry for the database appears in the Object Explorer of SQL Server Management Studio, as shown in Figure 10-8.

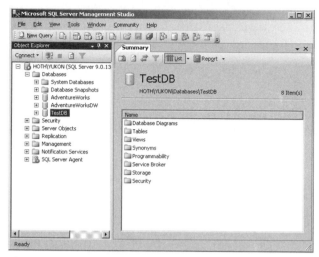

**Figure 10-8**    SQL Server Management Studio Object Explorer with new database TestDB.

## Creating a Database Using the T-SQL Command

You can use the CREATE DATABASE T-SQL command to create a new database and the required database files and filegroups. In its simplest form the CREATE DATABASE command simply needs to specify the name of the database and the name and locations of the primary data file and transaction log file, as shown in the command below.

```
CREATE DATABASE EasyDB

ON PRIMARY

 ( NAME = N'EasyDB_data',

   FILENAME = N'C:\EasyDB_data.mdf')

 LOG ON

 ( NAME = N'EasyDB_log',

   FILENAME = N'C:\EasyDB_log.ldf') ;

GO
```

> **Note**    The "N" before the strings is used to specify them as Unicode strings.
> Additional information about Unicode strings can be found by searching for
> "Unicode [SQL Server], constants" in SQL Server Books Online.

As you can imagine, this simple command is of little use to all but the simplest of databases. The code below presents a more real-world example of a database created with one primary and two secondary files all placed on separate filegroups that are also created by the command. The command also changes the database collation to Latin1_General_BIN2.

```
CREATE DATABASE TestDB
 ON  PRIMARY
 ( NAME = N'TestDB_data1',
   FILENAME = N'C:\TestDB_data1.mdf',
   SIZE = 102400KB,
   MAXSIZE = UNLIMITED,
   FILEGROWTH = 15%),
 FILEGROUP [FG1]
 ( NAME = N'TestDB_data2',
   FILENAME = N'C:\TestDB_data2.ndf',
   SIZE = 102400KB,
   MAXSIZE = UNLIMITED,
   FILEGROWTH = 15%),
 FILEGROUP [FG2]
 ( NAME = N'TestDB_data3',
   FILENAME = N'C:\TestDB_data3.ndf',
   SIZE = 102400KB,
   MAXSIZE = UNLIMITED,
   FILEGROWTH = 15%)
 LOG ON
 ( NAME = N'TestDB_log',
   FILENAME = N'C:\TestDB_log.ldf',
   SIZE = 51200KB ,
   MAXSIZE = 2048GB ,
   FILEGROWTH = 10%)
 COLLATE Latin1_General_BIN2 ;
GO
```

The attributes of the database that are not a part of the CREATE DATABASE command are set using the ALTER DATABASE command after the database has been created. The sample commands below change the PARAMETERIZATION option to FORCED, ARITH-ABORT to ON, and QUOTED_IDENTIFIER to ON for the *TestDB* database:

```
ALTER DATABASE TestDB SET PARAMETERIZATION FORCED ;

GO

ALTER DATABASE TestDB SET ARITHABORT ON ;

GO

ALTER DATABASE TestDB SET QUOTED_IDENTIFIER ON ;

GO
```

The other attributes that can be modified using ALTER DATABASE are explained in the following section. The ALTER DATABASE command can also be used to add, remove, or modify the files and filegroups associated with the database after it has been created.

---

**Note**   SQL Server 2005 introduces a new feature that instantly initializes files and helps speed up the process of creating a database, restoring a database, or adding or increasing the size of a data file. Instant file initialization is realized by reclaiming used disk space without filling the space with zeros; instead, the previous data is overwritten directly by the new data. In some cases, instant file initialization may pose a security risk because the previously deleted disk contents are not initialized and might be accessed by an unauthorized user or service. If such a security issue is of concern, you can disable instant file initialization for the instance of SQL Server by revoking SE_MANAGE_VOLUME_NAME privilege from the SQL Server service account.

## Setting Database Options

This section briefly describes the various database options that can be set during database creation , or be changed via SQL Server Management Studio by right-clicking on the database name, selecting Properties, and then selecting Options. The names in the parenthesis correspond to the corresponding database option that can be configured via the ALTER DATABASE command. For example, to change the database collation via the ALTER DATABASE command, you need to use the COLLATE option.

### Collation (COLLATE)

Collations specify the rules by which character data is compared and sorted. Each SQL Server collation specifies the sort order to use for non-Unicode and Unicode character data types (*char, varchar, text, nchar, nvarchar* and *ntext*), which are discussed in detail in Chapter 11, "Creating Tables and Views," and the code page used to store non-Unicode character data. Collations specified for Unicode data do not have specific code pages associated with them.

Every SQL Server instance has a default collation, which is the collation with which the instance was installed. This collation is used for all the system databases and is assigned to all new databases when the <server default> default option in SQL Sever Management Studio, or the COLLATE option in the ALTER DATABASE command, is not explicitly set.

A common collation used by many applications for the English language is Latin1_General_BIN. In this collation the "Latin1_General" corresponds to the English language (code page 1252) while "BIN" corresponds to a binary sort order. Similarly, "Latin1_General_CS_AS_KS_WS" corresponds to the English language with a case-sensitive, accent-sensitive, kana-sensitive, and width-sensitive sort order.

---

**Note**    Given a choice, select the binary sort order. I have often found this to perform slightly better than the other sort orders, though not by much.

---

**More Info**    Additional information about database collations can be found by searching for "Collations [SQL Server]" in SQL Server Books Online.

## Recovery Model (RECOVERY)

The recovery model determines how database transactions are logged and what the exposure to data loss is. In SQL Server 2005, three recovery models are available:

- **Full**    The full recovery model does the most extensive logging and allows the database to be recovered to the point of failure. This recovery model presents the highest protection against data loss. You should always configure all production databases to use full recovery.

- **Bulk-logged**    The bulk-logged recovery model fully logs transactions but only minimally logs most bulk operations, such as bulk loads, *SLECT INTO*, and index creations. Bulk-logged recovery model allows the database to be recovered to the end of a transaction log backup only when the log backup contains bulk changes. Recovery to the point of failure is not supported.

- **Simple**    The simple recovery model minimally logs most transactions, logging only the information required to ensure database consistency after a system crash or after restoring a database backup. With this model the database can be recovered only to the most recent backup. This recovery model has the maximum exposure to data loss and should not be used where data loss in the event of a crash cannot be tolerated.

## Compatibility Level

The compatibility level of a database specifies the SQL Server version compatibility and can be set to SQL Server 7.0 (70), SQL Server 2000 (80), or SQL Server 2005 (90). When set to a value other than SQL Server 2005 (90), the compatibility level makes the database behavior compatible with that version of SQL Server. It is highly recommended that you use the SQL Server 2005 (90) compatibility level. The other compatibility levels are provided primarily to help quickly address upgrade time incompatibilities and provide you with time to work through the issues. The compatibility level cannot be set using the ALTER DATABASE command; you need to use the *sp_dbcmptlevel* stored procedure instead. For example, the following command sets the database compatibility level for the *TestDB* database to SQL Server 2000.

```
sp_dbcmptlevel TestDB, 80 ;
```

---

**More Info**   For a detailed list of differences between the different compatibility levels, you may want to refer to the "Behavioral Differences Between Level 60 or 65 and Level 70, 80, or 90" section in the *sp_dbcmptlevel* help topic in SQL Server Books Online.

## Auto Close (AUTO_CLOSE)

You can use this option to control whether the database will be automatically closed when not in use. When this option is set to TRUE in SQL Server Management Studio, or to ON when using the ALTER DATABASE command, SQL Server closes the database whenever the last user disconnects from it, freeing up the associated resources. When a user tries to use the database again, the database is reopened. The closing and reopening process is completely automatic and transparent.

---

**Best Practices**   Usually a SQL Server instance has only a few user databases, but it is possible for it to have several hundred databases, for example, being a hosting provider that hosts many small user databases on a single server instance. For database instances with hundreds of databases that are infrequently accessed, it is recommended to set the database's AUTO_CLOSE option to TRUE. Setting this option forces the database to be closed when all the database processes complete and all users disconnect from the database, thereby freeing up server resources. The AUTO_CLOSE option is not recommended for frequently accessed databases.

## Auto Create Statistics (AUTO_CREATE_STATISTICS)

Accurate optimization of some queries often requires column statistics on specific columns that may not already have statistics created on them. Setting the Auto Create Statistics option to TRUE in SQL Server Management Studio, or to ON when using the

ALTER DATABASE command, permits SQL Server to create statistic on a table columns automatically as needed. You should always leave this option set to TRUE unless you have a very good reason to turn it off.

---

**Note**   Statistics that are automatically generated by SQL Server always have the prefix "_WA_Sys_" and end in a hexadecimal number. For example, _WA_Sys_ProcessID_2CD08213 is an auto-created statistic on column ProcessID. You can view all auto- and manually created statistics using the *sp_autostats* *<table name>* command. For example, you can check on the statistics for the Persons table in the *AdventureWorks* database using the command *sp_autostats* *'Person.Address'*.

## Auto Shrink (AUTO_SHRINK)

You can use this option to control whether the database files will be automatically shrunk. When this option is set to TRUE in SQL Server Management Studio, or to ON when using the ALTER DATABASE command, the database data and log files are shrunk when more than 25 percent of the file contains unused space. The files are shrunk to a size where 25 percent of the file is unused space, or to the size of the file when it was created, whichever is larger. In most cases it is advisable to leave this option set to FALSE.

## Auto Update Statistics (AUTO_UPDATE_STATISTICS)

You can use this option to control whether statistics will be updated automatically. SQL Server uses a cost-based optimizer that is extremely sensitive to the accuracy of the statistical information available to it. To ensure that relatively accurate statistics are always available, it employs the auto update statistics mechanism.

You should always leave the Auto Update Statistics database option set to TRUE for all user databases. If there is an exceptional situation where you believe that this option needs to be disabled for a particular table, you should disable it only for the particular table using the *sp_autostats* command. Disabling this option at the database level can have some nasty long-term performance implications.

**Real World   Auto Update Statistics—Is It Really Needed?**

I have often seen customers turn the auto update statistics option off and justify the action with the following claims:

- The update mechanism performs extensive table scans and is particularly detrimental to performance when the database contains large tables.

- It unnecessarily chews up precious server resources.

- It gets triggered too frequently.

- It is not needed because the database has been running for several days and all the statistics have already been auto-updated.

All of these arguments are flawed. While update statistics may take a while to run against large tables with millions of rows, the auto-update process does not scan the tables. Instead, it uses a sophisticated algorithm that dynamically computes the number of rows to be sampled and the frequency with which the operations should be triggered. Also, the shape of the data in any production database is constantly changing. Even if the tables themselves are not growing, data could be being updated, causing the statistics on the table to change significantly. Having the auto update statistics mechanism enabled helps present a representative image of the data to the optimizer, enabling it to better optimize queries, and the increased likelihood of generating better query execution plans far outweighs the relatively small overhead in server resources.

## Auto Update Statistics Asynchronously (AUTO_UPDATE_STATISTICS_ASYNC)

When a query encounters an out-of-date statistic and the update statistic thresholds have been met, it issues an update statistic call and waits for the operation to complete before compiling the query execution plan and executing the query. This can sometimes lead to long and unpredictable response times.

To address this problem, SQL Server 2005 introduces this new option to update statistics asynchronously. When set to TRUE in SQL Server Management Studio or ON when using the ALTER DATABASE command, this option causes the query to not wait for an out-of-date statistic to be recomputed; instead it uses the out-of-date statistics and issues a background request to recompute the statistic. This option may cause the query optimizer to choose a suboptimal query plan based on the out-of-date statistics and should therefore be used with caution.

You may want to enable this option if your database has large tables where the data isn't excessively skewed. Databases that have large batch-type queries that operate on large tables that are frequently inserted to and deleted from should use this option selectively. It is best to experiment with this option and check for yourself if your particular workload will benefit. If there is no measurable gain, I'd recommend keeping it set to FALSE.

## Close Cursor on Commit Enabled (CURSOR_CLOSE_ON_COMMIT)

You can use this option to control whether a cursor is closed when a transaction is committed. When set to TRUE in SQL Server Management Studio or ON when using the

ALTER DATABASE command, any open cursors are closed on commit or rolled back in compliance with the SQL-92 standard. It should be left at the default setting, FALSE, unless your application specifically requires this functionality to be enabled.

### Default Cursor (CURSOR_DEFAULT)

You can use this option to set the scope of the cursor type to global or local. When you set it to global and the cursor is not explicitly defined as local during creation, the cursor will be created with a global scope and be referenced by any stored procedure or batch executed by the connection. Conversely, when you set this option to local and the cursor is not explicitly defined as global during creation, the cursor is created with a local scope and can only be referenced by local cursor variables in the batch, trigger, stored procedure, or a stored procedure *OUTPUT* parameter.

### ANSI NULL Default (ANSI_NULL_DEFAULT)

You can use this option to determine the default value of a column, alias data type, or CLR user-defined type for which the nullability, which is discussed in more detail in Chapter 11, is not explicitly defined. When set to TRUE in SQL Server Management Studio or ON when using the ALTER DATABASE command, the default value is NULL, and when set to FALSE, the default value is NOT NULL. Connection-level settings override the default database-level setting. Similarly, columns that are defined with explicit constraints follow constraint rules regardless of this setting.

### ANSI NULL Enabled (ANSI_NULLS)

You can use this option to determine how NULL values are compared. When set to TRUE in SQL Server Management Studio or ON when using the ALTER DATABASE command, all comparisons to a null value evaluate to UNKNOWN. When set to FALSE, comparisons of non-UNICODE values to a null value evaluate to TRUE if both values are NULL. Connection-level settings override the default database setting.

---

**Note**   ANSI NULL Enabled should be set to TRUE when creating or manipulating indexes on computed columns or indexed views.

---

### ANSI Padding Enabled (ANSI_PADDING)

You can use this option to control the padding of strings for comparison and insert operations. When set to TRUE in SQL Server Management Studio or ON when using the ALTER DATABASE command, all strings are padded to the same length before conversion or insertion into a *varchar* or *nvarchar* data type. Trailing blanks in character values inserted into *varchar* or *nvarchar* columns and trailing zeros in binary values inserted into *varbinary* columns are not trimmed. When set to FALSE, trailing blanks for *varchar* or *nvarchar*, and zeros for *varbinary* are trimmed. Connection-level settings that are set by using the SET statement override the default database setting. In general, it is recommended you keep this option set to TRUE.

> **Note**   ANSI Padding Enabled should be set to TRUE when creating or manipulating indexes on computed columns or indexed views.

## ANSI Warnings Enabled (ANSI_WARNINGS)

You can use this option to determine the behavior of certain exception conditions. When set to TRUE in SQL Server Management Studio or ON when using the ALTER DATABASE command, errors or warnings are issued when conditions such as divide-by-zero occur or null values appear in aggregate functions. When set to FALSE, no warning is raised, and instead a NULL value is returned. Connection-level settings that are set by using the SET statement override the default database setting.

> **Note**   ANSI Warnings Enabled should be set to TRUE when creating or manipulating indexes on computed columns or indexed views.

## Arithmetic Abort Enabled (ARITHABORT)

You can use this option to determine the behavior of certain exception conditions. When set to TRUE in SQL Server Management Studio or ON when using the ALTER DATABASE command, a query is terminated when divide-by-zero error or overflow occurs during query execution. When set to FALSE, a warning message is displayed when one of these errors occurs, but the query, batch, or transaction continues to process as if no error occurred.

> **Note**   Arithmetic Abort Enabled should be set to TRUE when creating or manipulating indexes on computed columns or indexed views.

## Concatenate Null Yields Null (CONCAT_NULL_YIELDS_NULL)

You can use this option to control the concatenation rules for NULL operators. When set to TRUE in SQL Server Management Studio or ON when using the ALTER DATABASE command, the result of a concatenation operation is NULL when either operand is NULL. When set to FALSE, NULL values are treated as an empty character string, implying that a concatenation of the strings "xyz" and NULL will yield "xyz."

> **Note**   Concatenate Null Yields Null should be set to TRUE when creating or manipulating indexes on computed columns or indexed views.

## Cross-Database Ownership Chaining Enabled (DB_CHAINING)

Cross-Database Ownership Chaining Enabled is a security feature that controls whether the database can be accessed by external resources, such as objects from another database. When set to TRUE in SQL Server Management Studio or ON when using the ALTER DATABASE command, the database can be the source or target of a cross-database ownership chain. Setting the option to FALSE prevents participation in cross-database ownership chaining. This option is effective only when the instance-wide cross db ownership chaining server option is set to 0. When the cross db ownership chaining option is enabled via SQL Server Management Studio or set to 1 via the *sp_configure* stored procedure, this option is ignored and all databases in the server can participate in cross database ownership chaining.

## Date Correlation Optimization Enabled (date_correlation_optimization_option)

This option controls the date correlation optimization. The date correlation optimization improves performance of queries that perform an equijoin between two tables that specify a date restriction in the query's WHERE clause predicate, and whose datetime columns are linked by a foreign key constraint.

Setting the Date Correlation Optimization Enabled to TRUE directs SQL Server to maintain correlation statistics between any two tables in the database that are linked by a FOREIGN KEY constraint and have datetime columns. Setting this option to FALSE disables date correlation.

---

**Note**   Tables that can benefit from enabling this optimization are typically part of a one-to-many relationship and are used primarily for decision support, reporting, or data warehousing purposes.

---

## Numeric Round-Abort (NUMERIC_ROUNDABORT)

This option determines the behavior when an operation results in a loss of precision. When set to TRUE in SQL Server Management Studio or ON when using the ALTER DATABASE command, an error is generated when loss of precision occurs in an expression. When set to FALSE, losses of precision do not generate error messages and the results are rounded to the precision of the column or variable storing the result.

---

**Note**   Numeric Round-Abort should be set to FALSE when creating or manipulating indexes on computed columns or indexed views.

## Parameterization (PARAMETERIZATION)

Parameterizing SQL queries enables the database optimizer to reuse a previously compiled query plan, thereby eliminating the need for recompiling it for successive invocations of the same query with differing parameter values. If a nonparameterized SQL statement is executed, SQL Server 2005 internally tries to parameterize the statement to increase the possibility of matching it against an existing execution plan. This mode of parameterization is referred to as simple parameterization. SQL Server 2005 also introduces a new parameterization mode called forced parameterization. With forced parameterization, all nonparameterized SQL statements, subject to certain limitations, are force parameterized, and unlike simple parameterization the likelihood of SQL Server 2005 parameterizing those statements is far higher.

You can use this option to control whether the queries in the database will be simple or forced parameterized. When PARAMETERIZATION is set to SIMPLE, SQL Server will try to parameterize queries using the simple scheme unless a query hint has been specified for a particular query to force parameterize it. Conversely, when PARAMETERIZATION is set to FORCED, all queries will be force parameterized unless a query hinto has been specified for a particular query to parameterize it using the simple scheme.

> **Note** SIMPLE parameterization in SQL Server 2005 is the same as auto-parameterization in SQL Server 2000.

## Quoted Identifier Enabled (QUOTED_IDENTIFIER)

This option controls the interpretation of double quotation marks by the parser. When set to TRUE in SQL Server Management Studio or ON when using the ALTER DATABASE command, double quotation marks can be used to enclose delimited identifiers, for example, FirstName = "Mike". When set to FALSE, identifiers cannot be in quotation marks and must follow all T-SQL rules for identifiers.

## Recursive Triggers Enabled (RECURSIVE_TRIGGERS)

This option controls the behavior of recursion of AFTER triggers. When set to TRUE in SQL Server Management Studio or ON when using the ALTER DATABASE command, recursive firing of AFTER triggers is permitted. When set to FALSE, direct recursive firing of AFTER triggers is not allowed.

> **Note** Only direct recursion is prevented when Recursive Triggers Enabled is set to FALSE. To disable indirect recursion, you must also set the nested triggers server option to 0 using the *sp_configure* command.

## Trustworthy (TRUSTWORTHY)

You can use this option to control access to resources outside the database. When set to TRUE in SQL Server Management Studio or ON when using the ALTER DATABASE command, database modules like user-defined functions and stored procedures that use an impersonation context can access resources outside the database. When set to FALSE, database modules that use an impersonation context cannot access resources outside the database.

> **Note** The *model* and *tempdb* databases always have TRUSTWORTHY set to FALSE, and the value cannot be changed for these databases. The *master* database by default has TRUSTWORTHY set to TRUE.

## Page Verify (PAGE_VERIFY)

You can use this option to determine the mechanism used to discover damaged database pages caused by disk I/O path errors.

When set to Checksum, a checksum over the contents of the whole page is calculated and the value stored in the page header when a page is written to disk. When the page is later read from disk, the checksum is recomputed and compared to the checksum value stored in the page header. If the values do not match, an error is reported.

When set to TornPageDetection, a specific bit for each 512-byte sector in the 8-kilobyte (KB) database page is saved and stored in the database page header when the page is written to disk. When the page is read from disk, the torn bits stored in the page header are compared to the actual page sector information. Unmatched values indicate that only part of the page was written to disk, a condition called a torn page.

When set to None, the database will not generate or verify a checksum or torn page detection bits.

> **Best Practices** The default page verification mechanism in SQL Server 2005 is *Checksum*. It is recommended that you use this option because even though the TornPageDetection option may use fewer resources, it provides only a minimal subset of the checksum protection. It is not advisable to set this option to None.

## Database Read-Only (READ_ONLY or READ_WRITE)

You can use this option to control whether updates are allowed on the database. When set to TRUE in SQL Server Management Studio or ON when using the ALTER DATABASE command, users can only read from the database and are not permitted to modify data. When set to FALSE, the read and write operations are permitted on the database. To change the state of this option, you must have exclusive access to the database.

## Database State (DB_STATE_OPTION)

You can use this option to control the state of the database. When set to NORMAL, the database is fully operational and available for use. When the database is set to CLOSED, the database is shut down cleanly and marked offline. The database cannot be accessed or modified while in this state. When set to EMERGENCY, the database is marked READ_ONLY, logging is disabled, and access is limited to members of the sysadmin fixed server role. The EMERGENCY database state is used primarily for troubleshooting purposes.

## Restrict Access (DB_USER_ACCESS_OPTION)

You can use this option to control access to the database. In MULTIPLE mode all users are allowed to connect to the database as long as they have the appropriate permissions. Conversely, in the SINGLE mode only one user is permitted to access the database at a time. In the RESTRICTED mode only members of the db_owner, dbcreator, and sysadmin roles can connect to the database.

---

**Note**   Connection-level settings take precedence over the database-level settings, implying that if a database option is set at the database level and also is specified at the connection level, the connection-level setting is utilized.

---

# Viewing Database Details

The details of a database, such as the size, collation, filegroups, database options, and so on, can be viewed via SQL Server Management Studio or using the *sp_helpdb* stored procedure.  The process used to do this is explained in the sections below.

## Viewing Database Details with SQL Server Management Studio

The following steps explain the process of viewing the details of a database via SQL Server Management Studio:

1. Click the Start button, point to All Programs, select Microsoft SQL Server 2005, and then select SQL Server Management Studio.

2. Log in to the instance you want to use, and then click on the + sign next to Databases to expand the list of databases.

3. Select a database, right-click it, and then select Properties from the shortcut menu. The window shown in Figure 10-9 is displayed. You can then select the appropriate page from the left pane to view the required details.

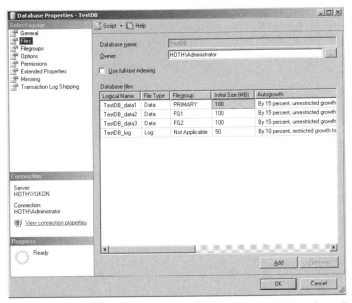

**Figure 10-9**   SQL Server Management Studio—View Database Details.

# Viewing Database Details with the *sp_helpdb* Command

The *sp_helpdb <database_name>* command lists the details of the database, as shown in Figure 10-10.

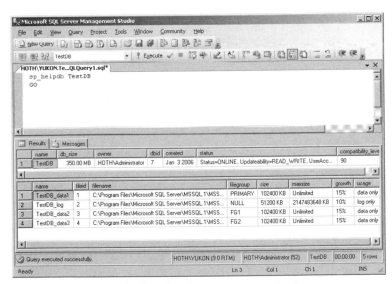

**Figure 10-10**   sp_helpdb <database_name> *output.*

If no database name is provided to the *sp_helpdb* command, the high-level details of all the databases in the instance get listed. In addition the command:

```
sp_dboption <database_name>
```

can be used to list all of the options that have been set for the database.

# Deleting a Database

A database can be deleted via SQL Sever Management Studio, or via the DROP DATA-BASE command. Listed below are some important points to consider when dropping a database:

- A database cannot be deleted if it is in use.

- Dropping a database deletes the database from an instance of SQL Server and deletes the physical disk files used by the database. The only exception is when the database or any one of the files is offline. In this case, the disk files are not deleted and must be deleted manually from the file system.

- A database can be deleted regardless of its state: offline, read-only, suspect, and so on. However, once deleted it can be re-created only by restoring a backup.

- Only users having CONTROL permission on the database can delete it.

- If a database participates in log shipping, the log shipping needs to be removed before deleting the database.

## Deleting a Database Using SQL Server Management Studio

The following steps explain the process of deleting a database via SQL Server Management Studio:

1. Click the Start button, point to All Programs, select Microsoft SQL Server 2005, and then select  SQL Server Management Studio.

2. Log in to the instance you want to use, and then click the + sign next to Databases to expand the list of databases.

3. Right-click the database you want to delete and select Delete from the shortcut menu.

4. Based on your requirements, select the check boxes to delete backup and restore history information for databases and to close existing connections, as shown in Figure 10-11. Click OK to complete the operation.

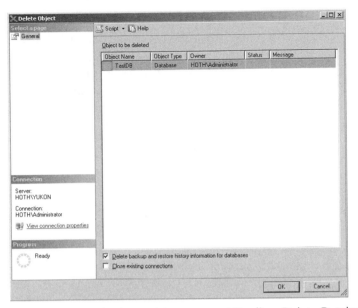

Figure 10-11   SQL Server Management Studio—Delete Database.

## Deleting a Database Using the DROP DATABASE Command

The DROP DATABASE command can be used to drop one or more databases or database snapshots, for example.

```
USE master ; -- make sure the current conext is not set to <database_name>

GO

DROP DATABASE TestDB ;

GO
```

When executing this command the current context cannot be set to the database being dropped. The DROP DATABASE command cannot be executed as part of an implicit or explicit transaction.

# Real-World Database Layouts

Now that we've covered the fundamentals of databases, let's pull all of the concepts together and apply them to define the structure of the databases for three applications—simple, moderately complex, and complex—given a fixed number of disk drives, a set of application characteristics, and a set of requirements.

## Simple Application Workload

**Scenario**: In this scenario a user has a very simple application that utilizes a backend SQL Server 2005 database as a data repository for a small application. The maximum database size is estimated to be 8 GB with the data access somewhat evenly distributed across all the tables, with an average 95 percent read and 5 percent write data access ratio. The user would like to protect the database against single disk failures but has a tight budget and can afford only eight disk drives.

**Solution**: A mirrored (RAID-1) disk is created (C:) and used to store all five system databases and SQL Server executables. This addresses the user's requirement for protection against single disk failures for the system database and executables.

---

**Best Practices**    Storing the *master*, *model*, *msdb*, *tempdb*, and *resource* database and SQL Server executables on a mirrored disk is also a recommended best practice.

---

Since in any database the data access is almost always random in nature, while the transaction log access is primarily sequential, it is best to separate out the data and transaction log files onto separate disks.

---

**Best Practices**    Separating out the data and transaction log files onto separate disks is another recommended best practice.

---

To do this and meet the protection against single disk failure requirement, the remaining six disks are configured into two sets, one set of four disks configured as RAID-5 to hold the primary data file, and the other as a two-disk mirrored (RAID-1) pair used to hold the transaction log. Since the data access distribution is heavily skewed towards read activity, the RAID-5 disk configuration will yield better performance than a RAID 10 because the disk stripe size is wider and only 5 percent of the queries will encounter the double write overhead imposed by RAID-5. RAID-1 is not the most optimal configuration for the log file, but since the user has a very limited number of disks available and again only 10 percent of the workload involves writes, the RAID-1 choice is acceptable. Ideally, if more disks were available, it would have been best to configure both the data (D) and the transaction log (L:) disks as RAID-10. The final database layout along with the filegroup and data file details is shown in Figures 10-12.

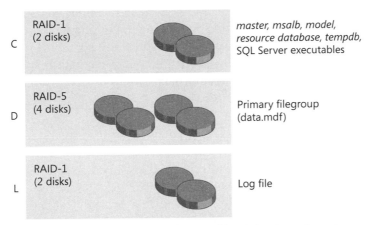

**Figure 10-12** Simple application workload database layout.

## Moderately Complex Application Workload

**Scenario**: In this scenario the user has a moderately complex application that utilizes a backend SQL Server 2005 database as a data repository for the entire application. The maximum database size is estimated to be 35 GB with a fairly even split between read and write type transactions. While the read transactions access the entire database, the write activity is primarily targeted to a single large CaseLog table which is heavily inserted into. The application has a high transactions/second throughput with a mix of very simple transactions that are executed in high volumes as well as large complex queries that involve multiple table joins and sort operations that are executed less frequently. The user has 28 disk drives available for the database and would like to maximize performance while protecting the database against single disk failures.

**Solution**: A mirrored (RAID-1) disk is created (C) and used to store the *master*, *msdb*, *model*, and *resource* databases as well as the SQL Server executables. This addresses the user's requirement for protection against single disk failures for the system database and executables. Since the application has a sizable amount of write activity, the database transaction log is created on a RAID-10 disk (L) utilizing six disk drives. Given the size of the database and the presence of large complex T-SQL queries that could possibly utilize *tempdb*, the *tempdb* database is created with eight data files on a six-drive RAID-10 disk (T). The remaining 14 drives are split into two RAID-10 disks with eight drives (D) and six drives (E). D is used to store the primary filegroup consisting of the primary data file (data.mdf) as well as filegroup FG1 which contains a single secondary data file. FG1, with the single secondary data file (data1.ndf), is created primarily for manageability purposes given the size of the database and the need to be able to move the data around at a later time. All the database tables, except the CaseLog table, are stored on this disk

(D). The E drive holds filegroup FG2, which consists of a single secondary data file (data2.ndf), and is used to store the CaseLog table. Separating the CaseLog table out into its own filegroup helps keep the heavy write activity from interfering with the read activity on the other database tables. This is particularly important given that the application executes a high transaction per second. The final database layout along with the filegroup and data file details is shown in Figures 10-13.

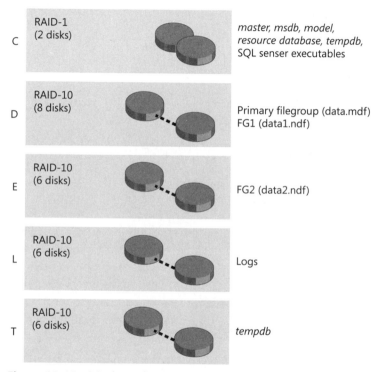

C   RAID-1 (2 disks)   *master, msdb, model, resource database, tempdb,* SQL senser executables

D   RAID-10 (8 disks)   Primary filegroup (data.mdf) FG1 (data1.ndf)

E   RAID-10 (6 disks)   FG2 (data2.ndf)

L   RAID-10 (6 disks)   Logs

T   RAID-10 (6 disks)   *tempdb*

**Figure 10-13**   Moderately complex application workload database layout.

# Complex Application Workload

**Scenario**: In this scenario the user has a complex application that utilizes a backend SQL Server 2005 database to store all its data and metadata. The maximum database size is projected to be 100 GB with a growth of 10 percent every year. The application is characterized by a wide range of transaction types. The usual online transaction processing workload executes relatively light, primarily read type transactions on the database throughout the day. In addition, there is also a set of heavy-duty batch jobs that are executed every 12 hours. These batch jobs execute some very complex queries, involving multiple table joins and perform a large number of insert and delete operations. The user has a 42 disk drives available for the database and would like the database to perform well for both online and batch workloads, be highly available and protected against single disk failures.

**Solution**: A mirrored (RAID-1) disk is created (C) and used to store the *master, msdb, model,* and *resource* databases as well as the SQL Server executables. This addresses the user's requirement for protection against single disk failures for the system database and executables. Since the batch jobs perform large amounts of inserts and deletes, the database transaction log is created on dedicated RAID-10 disk (L) utilizing eight disk drives. Given the size of the database and the presence of large complex queries that could possibly utilize *tempdb* to hold the results of operations that cannot be held in memory, *tempdb* is created on a RAID-10 disk (T) with another eight drives.

The remaining 24 drives are configured as a single RAID-10 disk (D) and used to store the primary filegroup consisting of the primary data file (Data.mdf) and filegroup FG1, containing a single secondary data file (Data2.ndf) that is created for manageability purposes. This database layout is chosen because of the wide variations in the application database's usage characteristics. The reason for having just one large 24-disk stripe is that both the online transaction processing and the batch workloads that execute only once in a while can benefit from all of the disks. There will undoubtedly be some interference when the online and batch workloads execute concurrently, but this should be far outweighed by the extra disk drives available to both types of workloads. The final database layout along with the filegroup and data file details is shown in Figures 10-14.

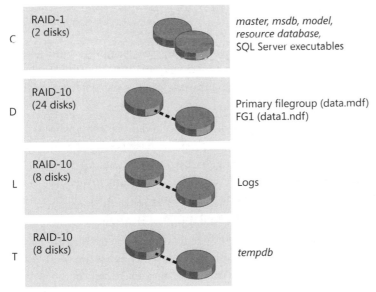

**Figure 10-14**   Complex application workload database layout.

> **Note**   You will notice that in all three examples above, multiple disks were used to store the databases even though in most cases a single or a couple of disks could have been adequate from a database size perspective. This was done intentionally for performance reasons. Having the data distributed across multiple drives reduces the disk seek latencies as explained in Chapter 4, and thereby increases performance. Given the relatively low costs of disks these days, this is usually acceptable. If needed, you can utilize the free disk space to store some hot backup of the database or some other data. However, care should be taken not to store any heavily accessed data that would affect the performance of the main database.

# Using Database Snapshots

*Database Snapshots* is a new feature introduced in SQL Server 2005 which enables you to take a point-in-time, read-only snapshot of a database. A database snapshot can be queried as if it were just another user database and can exist for as long as needed. When you're done using it, the database snapshot can be deleted or restored back onto the source database.

> **Note**   Database Snapshots are in no way related to snapshot backups, snapshot replication, or the new snapshot transaction isolation level.

## How Database Snapshots Work

When a database snapshot is created, a view of a source database is captured as it exists at that point in time while eliminating any changes made by uncommitted transactions. Therefore, a database snapshot can be considered a transactionally consistent snapshot of a database.

Database Snapshots operate at the database page level. Once a database snapshot is created, a copy of the original version of a page in the source database is copied to the database snapshot using a copy-on-write mechanism before being modified for the first time. Subsequent updates to data contained in a modified page do not affect the contents of the snapshot. As can be expected, the database snapshot stores only copies of the source database pages that have been changed since the snapshot was created.

The snapshot mechanism uses one or more sparse files to store the copied source database pages. The sparse file starts off as an empty file and grows as pages are updated in the source database. The sparse files initially take very little disk space but can grow very large for database snapshots created from source databases that have had a significant number of updates since the database snapshot was created.

When a query accesses a database snapshot, SQL Server internally checks whether the page containing the data has been modified since the snapshot was created. If it has, SQL Server uses the original source database page stored in the sparse file. If the page containing the data has not been modified, SQL Server accesses the page directly from the source database.

When a snapshot is deleted, the copies of the original pages that were stored in the sparse file are deleted. On the other hand, if the database snapshot is reverted back to the source database, the original pages are copied back onto the source database.

# Managing Database Snapshots

Database snapshots can be created, viewed, deleted, or reverted using T-SQL commands. SQL Server Management Studio can be used as well, but only to view and delete the snapshots.

## Creating Database Snapshots

A database snapshot can be created using the CREATE DATABASE command with the AS SNAPSHOT OF option specified. For example, a database snapshot of the TestDB database can be created using the following command:

```
CREATE DATABASE TestDB_ss_122805 ON

( NAME = TestDB_data1,

   FILENAME = 'C:\Program Files\Microsoft SQL
Server\MSSQL.1\MSSQL\Data\TestDB_data1_1800.ss' ),

( NAME = TestDB_data2,

   FILENAME = 'C:\Program Files\Microsoft SQL
Server\MSSQL.1\MSSQL\Data\TestDB_data2_1800.ss' ),

( NAME = TestDB_data3,

   FILENAME = 'C:\Program Files\Microsoft SQL
Server\MSSQL.1\MSSQL\Data\TestDB_data3_1800.ss' )

AS SNAPSHOT OF TestDB ;

GO
```

Since multiple database snapshots can exist on the same source database, it is important to use a meaningful naming convention. The recommended best practice is to use a concatenation of the original database name (*TestDB*), some indicator that the name relates to a database snapshot (*ss*), and a timestamp or some other unique identifier to distinguish multiple snapshots on the same source database (*122805*).

## Viewing Database Snapshots

Database snapshot details can be viewed using the *sp_helpdb* command just like any regular database. Example:

```
sp_helpdb TestDB_ss_122805 ;
```

SQL Server Management Studio can also be used to view the details using the following steps:

1.  In SQL Server Management Studio, log in to the instance you want to use.

2.  Expand the server in the Object Explorer pane on the left.

3.  Expand the list of databases and then click the **+** sign next to Database Snapshots to expand the list of database snapshots. You may have to right-click Database Snapshots and select Refresh in order to view any database snapshots that were created after SQL Server Management Studio was started.

4.  Right-click the database snapshot you wish to view details of and select Properties from the shortcut menu. The database snapshot properties are displayed as shown in Figure 10-15.

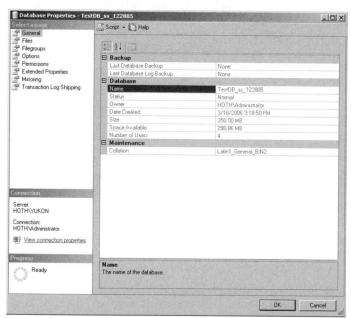

**Figure 10-15**    SQL Server Management Studio—View details of Database Snapshot.

5.  Click OK to continue.

## Deleting a Database Snapshot

A database snapshot can be selected using the DROP DATABASE command. Example:

```
DROP DATABASE TestDB_ss_122805 ;
```

SQL Server Management Studio can also be used to delete a database snapshot using the following steps:

1. In SQL Server Management Studio, log in to the instance you want to use.

2. Expand the server in the Object Explorer pane on the left.

3. Expand the list of databases and then click the + sign next to Database Snapshots to expand the list of database snapshots. You may have to right-click Database Snapshots and select Refresh in order to view any database snapshots that were created after SQL Server Management Studio was started.

4. Right-click the database snapshot you want to delete and select Delete from the shortcut menu.

5. The Delete Object dialog box is displayed, as shown in Figure 10-16.

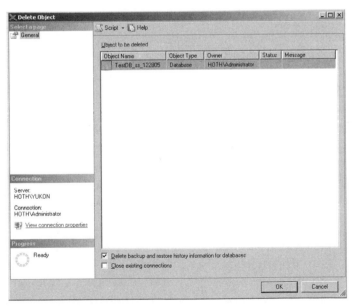

**Figure 10-16** SQL Server Management Studio—Delete Database Snapshot dialog box.

6. Click OK to delete the database snapshot.

## Reverting a Database

A database snapshot can be used to revert the source database to the state it was in when the snapshot was created. Reverting a database overwrites all updates made to the original database since the snapshot was created by copying the copy-on-write pages from the sparse files back into the database.

A database can be reverted using the RESTORE DATABASE command. For example, the command below reverts the snapshot TestDB_ss_122805 onto the source *TestDB* database:

```
RESTORE DATABASE TestDB FROM

DATABASE_SNAPSHOT = 'TestDB_ss_122805' ;

GO
```

Before a database can be reverted, make sure that no other database snapshots exist on the source database, that the source database does not contain any read-only or compressed filegroups, and that all the filegroups that were online when the snapshot was created are online.

# Common Uses

SQL Server 2005 Database Snapshots is a very powerful feature that can be effectively used for a wide range of scenarios. Some common uses include the following:

- **Safeguarding against administrator and user errors** You can take a database snapshot before any major operation is performed on the database. In the event of an error or unexpected event, you can use the snapshot to revert the original database to the point in time when the snapshot was taken. You can also take multiple database snapshots during the course of a complex operation. If one of the intermediate steps resulted in an error, you can roll back the database state to an appropriate database snapshot save-point.

- **Report generation on historical data** You can create a database snapshot at a particular point in time, for example, at the end of the financial year, and use it to run year-end reports on.

- **Offloading reporting tasks from the main database server** In this scenario the database snapshot is used in conjunction with database mirroring. As explained in Chapter 28, "Log Shipping and Database Mirroring," database mirroring provides a mechanism to maintain a mirrored replica of the database on another server. Since the mirror copy of the database is by design not directly accessible, reporting jobs cannot be directly run against it. To work around this limitation, you can create a database snapshot on the mirror and run your reports against the database snapshot.

### Database Snapshot Performance

The existence of one or more database snapshots negatively affects the performance of the main database because it has to perform additional tasks when the
data is accessed and updated. This is particularly true for database snapshots that
exist on source databases that have been heavily updated since the database snapshot was created.

While multiple database snapshots are permitted on the same database, the multiple copy-on-write operations for the multiple snapshots can adversely affect performance. I have found that a couple of concurrently existing database snapshots on
a source database that is infrequently updated has relatively minimal impact on performance.

## Database Snapshots Limitations

The following limitations apply to database snapshots:

- Database snapshots are read-only and can be created only on the same server
  instance that the source database resides on.

- The specifications of the database snapshot files cannot be changed. The only way
  to accomplish this is to drop and recreate the database snapshot.

- Database snapshot files cannot be deleted, backed-up, or restored, nor can they be
  attached or detached.

- If a snapshot runs out of disk space or encounters some other error, it is marked as
  suspect and must be deleted.

- Snapshots of the *model*, *master*, and *tempdb* system databases are not permitted.

- You cannot create snapshots on a FAT32 file system or on RAW partitions.

- Full-text indexing is not supported on database snapshots.

- A database snapshot inherits the security constraints of its source database at the
  time it was created. Permission changes made to the source database after the database snapshot was created are not reflected in existing snapshots.

- Reverting a database snapshot to a compressed or read-only filegroup is not supported.

- Once a database snapshot has been created, the underlying database cannot be
  dropped, detached, or restored.

**Note** If a source database goes into a RECOVERY_PENDING state, its database snapshots may become temporarily inaccessible. However, after the issue on the source database is resolved, the snapshots should become available again.

# Summary

In this chapter, you've learned about the structure of a SQL Server 2005 system and user database including database files, filegroups, various configuration options, and methods for creating, altering, viewing, and deleting databases. You've also learned about the new database snapshot feature including its working, common uses, limitations, and the methods used to create, view, and delete them.

# Chapter 11
# Creating Tables and Views

Tables are the foundation of a relational database. Every database consists of one or more tables that store the data, or information in the database. The first part of this chapter covers the fundamentals of tables and demonstrates how to create, modify, and drop tables. Before you begin to create tables, you'll need to make some decisions about the type of data that will be stored in each table, the structure of each table (including the data type of each column), and the relationships of the different tables to one another. We will cover the structure of tables in this chapter, while table relationships are covered in Chapter 13, "Enforcing Data Integrity." After tables, this chapter covers fundamentals of views, types of views, and how to create and manage them.

The last part of the chapter covers the useful new system views for SQL Server 2005. These are a collection of views designed to provide access to metadata information, and they take the place of querying system tables in SQL Server 2000. The specific category of system views called dynamic management views are covered in much detail in a chapter of their own, Chapter 31, "Dynamic Management Views."

## Table Fundamentals

A table is an object in a database that stores data in a collection of rows and columns. A column defines one piece of data stored in all the rows. Columns in a table are frequently called fields. You can think of a table as a grid of columns and rows like a spreadsheet. A single table in a SQL Server 2005 database can have up to 1,024 columns, and there can be up to two billion tables in a database. The maximum row size is 8,060 bytes, except for variable length data types. The number of rows and total size of the table are limited only by the available storage.

Following are the basic rules for table and column names (identifiers). These same rules apply to all SQL Server objects, such as views, indexes, triggers, and procedures:

- The first character must be a letter (either uppercase or lowercase) as defined in the Unicode standard (which includes letters from other languages), or an underscore (_).

- Subsequent characters can be letters from the Unicode standard (again, either uppercase or lowercase), digits (0-9), the "at" sign (@), the dollar sign ($), the number sign (#), or an underscore (_).

- The length must be at least one and up to 128 characters (except for local temporary tables, which can have a maximum of 116 characters for the table name).

- Spaces and other symbols may be used if delimited by double quotation marks or brackets, [], for example, "First Name" or [First Name]. This is not recommended as the quotation marks or brackets must always be used when referencing that name.

- SQL Server reserved words can be used, but should not be for the same reason—they must be delimited by quotation marks or brackets.

There are several design decisions that should be made before getting into the details of creating tables. This will help provide consistency, accuracy, and efficiency throughout your database. These decisions include the following:

- What data will each table contain?

- How will you name each table and column? Do you have a standard naming convention to follow? If not, should you develop one?

- What data type should be used for each column? How many characters or what range of numbers is needed in the data type?

- Which columns should and should not be allowed to contain null values?

- Which columns should have a default value?

- How will each table relate to other tables, if applicable?

- What column(s) will be used as a primary key or foreign key?

- How will the data be accessed? What column(s) will be good candidates for indexes? What columns will be used in the JOIN or WHERE clauses when retrieving data?

# Data Types

A *data type* is an attribute that specifies the type of data that the column can store. Choosing the correct data type for each column is important when creating tables. The following guidelines should help you make a good decision on the data type for each column:

- Try to use the smallest-sized data type for data. Not only will this save storage space, but it will also increase your performance. The smaller the storage size, the faster SQL can retrieve, sort, write, and transfer the data.

- Use *char* when the data values in a column are expected to be consistently close to the same size. *Char* has a maximum of 8,000 characters.

- Use *varchar* when the data values in a column are expected to vary considerably in size or contain a lot of NULL values. (A *char(50)* field will take up 50 bytes of storage even if the value is NULL.) *Varchar* also has a maximum of 8,000 characters.

- Use a numeric data type for columns used to store only numbers. A *char* or *varchar* data type will work, but numeric types generally take up less storage space, and an index on a numeric column will have better performance for searches and joins. Be careful with something like ZIP codes or social security numbers, as they may always consist of numbers, but they also can have leading zeros. These must be stored in character fields to avoid losing any leading zeros.

- Do not use the Unicode *nchar* and *nvarchar* data types unless you need to store Unicode data. The Unicode character set takes twice as much space to store as the *char* and *varchar* counterparts. Unicode types are designed to include characters appearing in non-English languages, including Chinese, Japanese, and others.

## System Data Types

SQL Server provides two types of data types: system data types and user-defined data types. System data types are the built-in data types provided by SQL Server and are described in Table 11-1. The table is first divided into different categories of data types and then in order of storage size.

SQL Server 2005 introduces a few new data types: *varchar(max)*, *nvarchar(max)*, *varbinary(max)*, and *xml*. For the variable data types, the *(max)* data types are known as large value data types. They can store up to 2 GB of data. In previous versions of SQL Server, you needed to use the (now depreciated) data types *text*, *ntext*, or *image*. An advantage of the new large value data types is that you can use Transact-SQL functions on them, you can use them as variables, and you can use them as parameters to procedures and functions.

For example, here is a simple function created using the T-SQL CREATE FUNCTION command in which you can pass a large value data type, and perform a couple of string functions on the parameter:

```
CREATE FUNCTION first_line(@large_text  varchar(max))

RETURNS varchar(100) AS

BEGIN

   RETURN 'First Line: ' + SUBSTRING(@large_text, 1,
80)

END
```

The other new data type is *xml*. This data type allows you store XML documents and fragments of XML documents natively, which means the database engine takes into account the XML nature of the documents you are storing. In the previous version of SQL Server, there were less direct ways of storing and manipulating XML in the database. Now that *xml* is a built-in data type, SQL Server 2005 adds a number of new features to support XML data storage and manipulation.

**Table 11-1  System Data Types in SQL Server 2005**

| Data Type | Description | Storage Size |
|---|---|---|
| **Character Strings** | | |
| *char[(n)]* | Fixed-length, non-Unicode character data with length of *n* characters (1 non-Unicode character = 1 byte), where *n* is a value from 1 through 8,000. | *n* bytes |
| *varchar[(n)]* *varchar(max)* | Variable-length non-Unicode character data with a length of *n* characters, where *n* is a value from 1 through 8,000, or *max*. *max* indicates a maximum storage size of $2^{31}-1$ bytes. (*varchar(max)* is preferred over the use of the depreciated *text* data type.) | Actual length of data entered + 2 bytes |
| **Unicode Character Strings** | | |
| *nchar[(n)]* | Fixed-length Unicode character data of *n* characters, where *n* is a value from 1 through 4,000. | $2 \times n$ bytes |
| *nvarchar[(n)]* *nvarchar[(max)]* | Variable-length Unicode data of *n* characters, where *n* is a value from 1 through 4,000, or *max*. *max* indicates a maximum storage size of $2^{31}-1$ bytes. (*nvarchar(max)* is preferred over the use of the depreciated *ntext* data type.) | $2 \times$ the actual length of data entered + 2 bytes |

**Table 11-1   System Data Types in SQL Server 2005 (continued)**

| Data Type | Description | Storage Size |
|---|---|---|
| **Exact Numerics** | | |
| *Bit* | Integer data type that can be a value of 1, 0, or NULL. Note: *bit* columns can not have indexes on them. | 1 byte for up to eight *bit* columns, 2 bytes for a table with nine through 16 *bit* columns, and so on |
| *Tinyint* | Integer data from 0 through 255. | 1 byte |
| *Smallint* | Integer data from $-2^{15}$ ($-32,768$) through $2^{15} - 1$ (32,767). | 2 bytes |
| *integer* or *int* | Integer (whole number) data from $-2^{31}$ ($-2,147,483,648$) through $2^{31}-1$ (2,147,483,647) | 4 bytes |
| *Bigint* | Integer data from $-2^{63}$ ($-9,223,372,036,854,775,808$) through $2^{63}-1$ (9,223,372,036,854,775,807) | 8 bytes |

| Data Type | Description | Precision | Storage |
|---|---|---|---|
| *decimal[(p,[s])]* or *numeric[(p,[s])]* | Fixed-precision and fixed-scale numbers. (The data type *numeric* is functionally equivalent to *decimal*.) Precision (*p*) specifies the total number of digits that can be stored, both to the left and to the right of the decimal point. Scale (*s*) specifies the maximum number of digits that can be stored to the right of the decimal point. Scale must be less than or equal to precision. The minimum precision is 1, and the maximum precision is 38, with a default of 18. | 1–9 10–19 20–28 29–38 | 5 bytes 9 bytes 13 bytes 17 bytes |

| Data Type | Description | Storage Size |
|---|---|---|
| *Smallmoney* | Monetary data values from *−214,748.3648* through *214,748.3647*, with accuracy to one ten-thousandth (.0001) of a monetary unit. | 4 bytes |
| *Money* | Monetary data values from (*−922,337,203,685,477.5808*) through *922,337,203,685,477.5807*), with accuracy to one ten-thousandth (.0001) of a monetary unit. | 8 bytes |

**Table 11-1   System Data Types in SQL Server 2005 (continued)**

| Data Type | Description | | | Storage Size |
|---|---|---|---|---|
| **Approximate Numerics** | | | | |
| *float[(n)]* | Floating-point numerical data that can range from *−1.79E +308 to −2.23E–308, 0, and 2.23E–308 to 1.79E+308.* The value *n* is the number of bits used to store the mantissa of the float number in scientific notation, and can range from 1 to 53. For 1<= *n* <=24, SQL Server treats *n* as 24. For 25<=*n*<=53, *n* is treated as 53. The default for *n* is 53. | **n** <br> 1–24 <br> 25–53 | **Precision** <br> 7 digits <br> 15 digits | **Storage** <br> 4 bytes <br> 8 bytes |
| *Real* | Floating-precision numerical data that can range from *−3.40E + 38 to −1.18E –38, 0, and 1.18E –38 to 3.40E + 38* <br><br> . The synonym for *real* is *float(24)*. | | | 4 bytes |
| **Date and Time** | | | | |
| *Smalldatetime* | Date and time data from January 1, 1900, through June 6, 2079, with accuracy to the minute. It is stored in two 2-byte integers. The first stores the number of days past January 1, 1900 and the second stores the number of minutes past midnight. | | | 4 bytes |
| *Datetime* | Date and time data from January 1, 1753, through December 31, 9999, with accuracy to 3.33 milliseconds. It is stored in two 4-byte integers. The first stores the number of days before or after January 1, 1900 and the second stores the number of milliseconds after midnight. | | | 8 bytes |
| **Binary** | | | | |
| *binary[(n)]* | Fixed-length binary data of *n* bytes, where *n* is a value from 1 through 8,000 | | | *n* bytes |
| *varbinary[(n)]* <br> *varbinary[(max)]* | Variable-length binary data of *n* bytes, where *n* is a value from 1 through 8,000, or *max. max* indicates a maximum storage size of 2^31–1 bytes. (*varbinary(max)* is preferred over the use of the depreciated *image* data type.). | | | Actual length of data entered + 2 bytes |

Table 11-1    System Data Types in SQL Server 2005 (continued)

| Data Type | Description | Storage Size |
|---|---|---|
| **Other Data Types** | | |
| Timestamp | A *timestamp* column is updated automatically with a unique binary number every time a row is inserted or updated. Each table can have only one *timestamp* column. | 8 bytes |
| Cursor | A reference to a cursor. Can be used only for variables and stored procedure parameters. | Not applicable |
| *unique identifier* | Stores a 16-byte binary value that is a globally unique identifier (GUID). | 16 bytes |
| sql_variant | Allows values of various data types. The data value and data describing that value—its base data type, scale, precision, maximum size, and collation—are stored in this column. The following types of values are not allowed with *sql_variant – text, ntext, image, timestamp, xml, varchar(max), nvarchar(max), varbinary(max), sql_variant*, and user-defined data types. | Size varies. Maximum length of 8,016 bytes |
| Table | Similar to using a temporary table—the declaration includes a column list and data types. Can be used to define a local variable or for the return value of a user-defined function. | Varies with table definition |
| Xml | Stores XML data. | Size of data. Maximum of 2 GB |

## Real World    Appropriate Use of Data Types

In the field I have seen data types misused such that the type selected could cause unexpected results when inserting data or comparing data. If the appropriate data type had been selected, these problems could have been avoided. Following are some examples.

One case of misused data types that I've seen is the use of a number data type, such as *int*, for a column that stores Social Security numbers or ZIP code numbers. If the number entered has a leading 0, such as the ZIP code for Boston (02110), as a number data type the leading 0 is dropped and the number is stored as 2110. The same applies for Social Security numbers. For these types of numbers, the character data type should be selected. Social Security number could be *char(9)*, and ZIP code might be *char(5)* or *char(10)* to include the dash and four-digit extension.

Another misuse case is selecting the character data type for a column that will store dates. This allows non-date data to be entered, such as "3/25/2005" including the slashes, or invalid data such as "ABC." These entries cannot be compared in a greater-than-or-equal-to date comparison and would provide incorrect results if sorted. For date values, the *smalldatetime* and *datetime* data types should be used.

To determine the correct data type, consider what the possible values may be and how the values will be used in queries, such as in equality comparisons, greater-than-or-less-than comparisons, or in the ORDER BY clause, for example.

## Aliases and Common Language Runtime User-Defined Data Types

SQL Server 2005 allows you to define your own data types in T-SQL (or Management Studio) or in the Microsoft .NET Framework. There are two classes of user-defined data types—alias types and common language runtime (CLR) user-defined types. First let's talk about alias types; they are the most simple to create.

### Creating Alias Data Types

Alias data types are system data types that have been customized. An alias data type is based on a single system data type, but it provides a mechanism for applying a more descriptive name to a data type. Alias data types allow you to refine system data types further to ensure consistency when working with common data elements in different tables. This is especially useful when there are several tables that must store the same type of data in a column. This can make it easier for a programmer or database administrator to understand the intended use of any object defined with the data type. When creating an alias you must supply the alias name, the system data type upon which it will be based, and the *nullability* (whether NULL is allowed as a value or not).

Here is an example showing good use of an alias type. Suppose your database contains phone number data that may be used in a variety of columns in a table (for example, home, work, cell, and so on) and/or in a number of different tables. You could create an alias data type named *phone_number,* which could be used for all columns (in all tables) that contain phone number data. The *phone_number* data type could be defined as **varchar(12) null**. Then, when creating tables, you do not need to remember if you used **varchar(12), char(15) or varchar(50)**. Just use the alias data type and all of your phone number columns will be consistent.

Here is the T-SQL syntax for creating an alias or CLR user-defined data type.

```
CREATE TYPE [ schema_name. ] type_name
{
    FROM base_type
    [ ( precision [ , scale ] ) ]
```

```
    [ NULL | NOT NULL ]
  | EXTERNAL NAME assembly_name [ .class_name ]
}
```

Here is the T-SQL CREATE TYPE command to create a *phone_number* alias data type that can hold up to 12 characters, per the example above:

```
CREATE TYPE phone_number FROM varchar(12) NULL
```

To do this using SQL Server Management Studio Object Explorer, follow these steps:

1. Start SQL Server Management Studio. In Object Explorer view, connect to the server instance of your choice, and then expand the server's Management Databases folder.

2. Expand your database and expand Programmability.

3. Right-click Types, select New, and then select User-Defined Data Types on the shortcut menu.

4. Enter the Schema, Name, Data Type, Size, and Nullability. In our example, these are, respectively, *dbo, phone_number, varchar,* and 12, a nullability is checked to allow nulls.

   Your screen should be similar to the one shown in Figure 11-1.

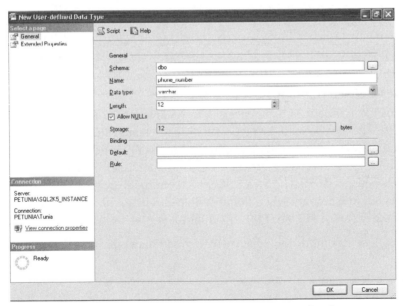

**Figure 11-1**   Creating an alias type using Management Studio.

5. Click OK to save the new data type.

### Creating CLR User-Defined Data Types

New for SQL Server 2005, CLR user-defined data types obtain their characteristics from methods and operators of a class that you must create using one of the programming languages supported by the .NET Framework—including Microsoft Visual C# and Microsoft Visual Basic .NET. A user-defined type must first be coded as a class or structure, compiled as a dynamic-link library (DLL), and then loaded into SQL Server 2005. This can also be accomplished through Microsoft Visual Studio. Following are the basic steps for creating a CLR user-defined type:

1. Code the user-defined type as a class or structure using a supported Microsoft .NET Framework programming language.

2. Compile the class or structure to build an assembly using the appropriate compiler.

3. Register the assembly in SQL Server 2005 using the CREATE ASSEMBLY statement.

4. Create the data type that references the assembly using the CREATE TYPE statement.

The ability to execute CLR code is disabled by default in SQL Server 2005. To enable CLR code execution, enable the following option using the *sp_configure* stored procedure as shown here:

```
sp_configure 'clr enabled', 1
reconfigure ;
```

Because CLR is more of a developer topic than a DBA topic, we refer you to the page entitled "CLR User-Defined Types" in SQL Server Books Online for more information and links to examples of coding CLR user-defined types and registering them with SQL Server 2005.

### Dropping User-Defined Data Types

Both alias and CLR user-defined data types can be renamed, but the data type itself cannot be modified. The user-defined data type can only be created and dropped, and it can be dropped only if it is not currently in use by a table or another database object. With CLR user-defined types, the ALTER ASSEMBLY statement can be used to modify an assembly that is registered as a type with SQL Server, but there are several considerations that must be taken into account when doing so that can be found in SQL Server Books Online under the topic "ALTER ASSEMBLY (Transact-SQL)."

Here is the T-SQL syntax for dropping any user-defined data type:

```
DROP TYPE [ schema_name. ] type_name
```

For example, this command drops the alias type we created previously.

```
DROP TYPE phone_number
```

**Note**  Previous versions of SQL Server used *sp_addtype* and *sp_droptype* to perform these functions. They can still be used, but they should be avoided because they will be obsolete in future versions.

To drop or rename any user-defined type from the Object Explorer, follow these steps:

1.  In Object Explorer view, connect to the server instance of your choice, and then expand the server's Databases folder.

2.  Expand the database name and then expand Programmability.

3.  Expand Types, and then expand User-Defined Data Types.

4.  Right-click the user-defined data type you want to use, and then select Delete or Rename on the shortcut menu.

5.  If you are deleting the type, a Delete Object dialog box appears. Click OK to confirm the deletion. If you are renaming the type, just enter the new name and click Enter.

**Note**  Renaming a user-defined data type automatically renames the data type for all columns using this data type.

**Note**  All user-defined data types (both alias and CLR types) that are created in the *model d*atabase will be available in all databases that are subsequently created. User-defined types that are created within a database are available only to that database.

# Nulls

A null value is an unknown or missing value that is referred to as NULL. The nullability of a column refers to the ability of the column to accept or reject null values. A null value in a column usually indicates that no entry has been made or an explicit NULL was supplied for that column for a particular row of data. Null values are neither empty values nor 0 values; their true values are unknown—thus, no two null values are equal.

It is best to avoid allowing the use of null values as much as possible, and only allow nulls when necessary and truly appropriate. When possible, use default values to be used when no value is supplied instead of allowing null values for a column. With null values, more complexity is incurred in queries and updates, coding can be more complicated when dealing with the possibility of null values, and unexpected results can occur if not taken into consideration when coding. Keep in mind that the PRIMARY KEY constraint and the IDENTITY property can not allow null values as well.

## IDENTITY Column

Use the IDENTITY property to create a column that contains system-generated sequential values to identify each row inserted into a table. This value is based on a seed value and an increment value. The seed is a value that will be the identity value for the first row inserted into the table. The increment is the amount by which SQL Server will increase the identity value for successive inserts. The default seed value is 1, and the default increment value is 1. This means that the value on the first row inserted will be 1, the value on the second row inserted will be 2, and so on. An identity column is commonly used as a primary key constraint in the table to uniquely identify a row. (See Chapter 13 to learn about primary key constraints.)

Some things to keep in mind about the IDENTITY property include:

- There can be only one identity column per table.

- Null values are not allowed.

- It can be used only with the following data types: *tinyint*, *smallint*, *int*, *bigint*, or *numeric/decimal* with a scale of zero.

---

**Note** The IDENTITY column does not enforce the uniqueness of records. This will need to be done using a unique index.

---

When you insert into a table with an identity column you do not put a value into the identity column. For example, let's create myTable with three columns, making the first column an IDENTITY column, using the following CREATE TABLE statement:

```
CREATE TABLE myTable
(myID int IDENTITY (1,1),
firstName varchar(30),
lastName varchar(30) );
```

The following INSERT statements to insert rows into myTable are correct:

```
INSERT INTO myTable(firstName, lastName) VALUES ('Ben', 'Franklin')
INSERT INTO myTable(firstName, lastName) VALUES ('Paul' , 'Revere')
INSERT INTO myTable(firstName, lastName) VALUES ('George' , 'Washington');
```

Now select all the rows from myTable:

```
SELECT * FROM myTable;
```

The results will show the identity value that was inserted in the myID column for each row as follows:

```
myID     firstName        lastName
------   -----------      -----------

1        Ben              Franklin

2        Paul             Revere

3        George           Washington
```

The myID column was automatically populated with the next value in the sequence. You will get an error if you try to fill in a value for an identity column.

If you need to know the value of the identity column of the last row inserted, you can use the built-in function @@IDENTITY. After the three insert statements in the previous example, you can add the following statement to see the identity value that was last inserted.

```
SELECT @@IDENTITY
```

This will return a 3, as that was the last identity value inserted into myTable.

SQL Server does not guarantee sequential gap-free values in identity columns. If records are deleted, SQL Server will not back fill the missing values. By the same token, if you delete all the records from a table, it will not reset the identity. The next identity number will be the next number in sequence. After the following code is executed in the myTable example, you will see that the identity column sequence picks up where it last left off. First we delete a row from the table with this DELETE statement:

```
DELETE FROM myTable WHERE lastName = 'Revere'
```

Then we insert a new row:

```
INSERT INTO myTable(firstName, lastName) VALUES ('Abe' , 'Lincoln')
```

Then we select all rows from the table to see the identity values now:

```
SELECT * FROM myTable
```

The rows returned show that the next identity value of 4 was used for the inserted row and the previously used identity value of 2 is now deleted from the table and will not be used again. Here are the results:

```
myID     firstName        lastName
------   ----------       -----------

1        Ben              Franklin

4        Abe              Lincoln

3        George           Washington
```

There is a way to set the value of an identity column explicitly when you are inserting a record. This is accomplished by first setting the IDENTITY_INSERT property to ON, then inserting the row:

```
SET IDENTITY_INSERT myTable ON
INSERT myTable (myID, firstName, lastName) Values(2, 'John', 'Hancock')
SET IDENTITY_INSERT myTable OFF
```

The identity value of 2 was allowed to be explicitly inserted into myTable. Now select all rows to see the values:

```
SELECT * FROM myTable
```

The new results for the table are as follows:

| myID | firstName | lastName |
| ------ | ---------- | ----------- |
| 1 | Ben | Washington |
| 4 | Abe | Lincoln |
| 2 | John | Hancock |
| 3 | George | Washington |

---

**Note**    Only one table in a session can have the IDENTITY_INSERT property set to ON. It is a good practice to turn it on to use it and then immediately turn it back off.

---

# Creating, Modifying, and Dropping Tables

When you create a table, you must specify the table name, column names, and column data types. Column names must be unique to a table, but the same column name can be used in different tables within the same database. The column name can be omitted for columns that are created with a *timestamp* data type, in which case the column name will default to "timestamp."

## Creating Tables

You should adopt standards when naming your tables and columns. Making good use of uppercase and lowercase letters and using underscores to separate words will help make the table and columns easier to read and understand. Try to keep the names short but still long enough to be descriptive. If you use the same column in different tables, try to use the same name. This consistency helps avoid confusion when creating and using queries.

Below is the basic T-SQL syntax for creating a table. Not all of the arguments for creating a table are listed here. Refer to SQL Server Books Online for the complete CREATE TABLE syntax:

```
CREATE TABLE
    [ database_name . [ schema_name ] . | schema_name . ]
table_name
    (
    column_name <data_type>
    [ NULL | NOT NULL ]
    [ DEFAULT constant_expression ]
    [ IDENTITY [ ( seed ,increment ) ]
    [ ,...n ]
    )
```

Below are descriptions of the CREATE TABLE arguments listed in the above syntax:

- *database_name* Optional. Name of the database in which the table will be created. Defaults to the current database.

- *schema_name* Optional. Name of the schema to which the new table belongs. Defaults to dbo.

- *table_name* Required. Name of the new table.

- *column_name* Required. Name of the column.

- *data_type* Required. System or user-defined data type including arguments (precision, scale, max, and so on) if applicable.

- *nullability* Optional. Indicates whether null values are allowed in the column. Simply state NULL or NOT NULL. NOT NULL is the SQL Server default, but the server defaults can be changed. It is best to specify the nullability of a column when creating a table.

- DEFAULT Optional. The value you want to be used for the column for any row that is inserted without explicitly supplying a value for that particular column.

- IDENTITY Optional. Indicates that the column is an identity column. The (seed, increment) values will default to (1, 1) if not specified.

The following is a T-SQL example creating a table using some of the optional arguments:

```
CREATE TABLE Employees
(
    Employee_ID     smallint        NOT NULL IDENTITY(1000,1),
    SSN             char(9)         NOT NULL,
    FName           varchar(50)     NOT NULL,
    Middle          char(1)          NULL,
    LName           varchar(50)     NOT NULL,
    BirthDate       smalldatetime   NULL,
    Salary          smallmoney      NULL,
    Department_ID   smallint        NOT NULL,
    Active_Flag     char(1)         NOT NULL    DEFAULT 'Y'
)
```

This script creates a table named Employees with eight columns. *Smallint* was used for the Employee_ID column because the number of employees may be more than 255 (*tiny-int*) but fewer than 32,767 (*int*). The IDENTITY property will automatically assign an incremental integer to this column starting with 1,000, incrementing by 1 for each new row. The first name and last name fields are NOT NULL, meaning values are required at the time the record is created. The *Active_Flag* field will default to a value of *y* for each record inserted, unless otherwise specified.

To create a table using SQL Server Management Studio from the Object Explorer, follow these steps:

1. In Object Explorer view, connect to the server instance of your choice, and then expand the server's Databases folder.

2. Expand the database name, right-click Tables, and then select New Table on the shortcut menu. A grid displays to allow you to enter all the columns.

3. Type column names, choose data types, and choose whether to allow nulls for each column.

---

**Note**   In addition to the options in the grid, a column properties page will be displayed at the bottom of the window that has some additional column settings.

---

4. On the File menu, select Save *table name* or hit CTRL-S to save table.

5. In the Choose Name dialog box, type a name for the table and click OK.

Figure 11-2 shows our example Employee table.

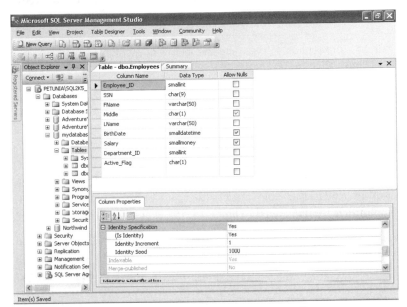

**Figure 11-2**   Creating a table using Management Studio.

# Modifying Tables

After a table is created and even if data already populates the table, you can rename the table or add, modify, or delete columns.

---

**Important**   Caution should be taken when renaming a table or column because it may cause existing queries, views, user-defined functions, stored procedures, or programs that refer to the original table or column name to become invalid and return errors.

---

The data type of an existing column can be changed only if the table is empty (in other words, has no rows) or the existing data in the column can be implicitly converted to the new data type.

For example, you can not change a varchar(50) column to an *int* data type if the column contains first names. If the varchar(50) column contained only numbers, like ZIP codes (without the dashes), it can be converted to an int column. (Any leading zeros are lost.)

For data types where the length of the data type is specified, such as *binary*, *char*, *nchar*, *varbinary*, *varchar*, and *nvarchar*, the length can be increased or decreased. If you decrease the length, all values in the column that exceed the new length will be truncated. For example, changing a varchar(50) column to varchar(5) will truncate all of the data in the column exceeding five characters.

---

**Note**   There is an exception to changing the length of a column as described above—you cannot change the length of a column that has a PRIMARY KEY or FOREIGN KEY constraint. Thus, the constraint would have to be dropped in order to change the column length.

---

There is a bit more to the adjustment of the data types *decimal* and *numeric*. There is a precision value and a scale value for these types. If the scale value is decreased, any digits to the right of the decimal exceeding the new size of the scale value will be rounded to the new scale number of digits. For example, assume a column is defined as data type *numeric(9,4)*, and one row in the table has a value of 1234.5678 for that column. If the data type of the column is then changed to *numeric(9,2)*, that value is adjusted to 1234.57.

The same is not true for the precision. The whole number part of the value cannot be changed when altering a column. If you adjust the precision smaller and there is a value in your column that is already larger than that precision, SQL Server will not allow you to alter the column. For example, assume a column currently has data type *numeric(9,4)* and one row in the table has a value of 1234.5678 for that column. You will not be able to change the column to data type *numeric(7,4)*. You can, however, change the column's data type to *numeric(8,4)* since that covers the eight digits in the number.

To modify an existing table using T-SQL, you use the ALTER TABLE command. Refer to SQL Server Books Online for the complete ALTER TABLE syntax.

Here are some examples of ways to modify the Employees table that we created in the previous CREATE TABLE example. This first example adds a new column to a table and demonstrates using the user-defined data type that we created earlier:

```
ALTER TABLE Employees
ADD Home_phone   phone_number
```

This example removes a column from a table:

```
ALTER TABLE Employees
DROP COLUMN SSN
```

This example modifies the size of an existing column. The LName column was originally created as varchar(50):

```
ALTER TABLE Employees
ALTER COLUMN  LName   varchar(100)  NOT NULL
```

After running the above statements, the columns in the Employees table, if viewed in Management Studio, appear as shown in Figure 11-3.

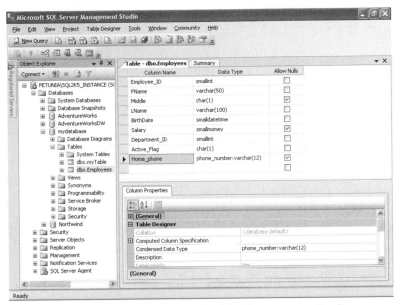

**Figure 11 3**   Modified table viewed with Management Studio.

It is easy to make modifications to your table using SQL Server Management Studio. Here's how to do so from the Object Explorer:

1.  In Object Explorer view, connect to the server instance of your choice, and then expand the server's Databases folder.

2.  Expand the database name and expand Tables.

3.  Right-click the table you want to work with, and then select Modify on the shortcut menu. A grid  showing all the current columns of the table is displayed, as shown above in Figure 11-3.

4.  Name or data type changes can be done in place. Right-click any row and select Insert Column or Delete Column on the shortcut menu, if desired.

---

**Note**   You can change the order of the columns by clicking your left mouse button on the grid arrow to the left of the column and dragging the column up or down to the desired position.

---

**Note**   In addition to the options in the grid, a column properties page with some additional column settings is displayed at the bottom of the window.

---

5.  To save changes, select Save *table name* on the File menu or enter Ctrl-S.

# Dropping Tables

When you drop a table, all data, indexes, constraints, and permission specifications for that table are deleted from the database. Dropping a table is not the same action as either the TRUNCATE TABLE or the DELETE command. The TRUNCATE TABLE and DELETE commands are used to remove data only from a table, not to remove the entire table itself. More on these two commands is discussed at the end of this section.

> **Note**  System Tables can not be dropped.

To delete a table using T-SQL, you use the following command:

```
DROP TABLE < table_name >
```

The following is an example that drops the Employees table:

```
DROP TABLE Employees
```

> **Note**  If the table is referenced by a FOREIGN KEY constraint, the referencing constraint or the referencing table must be dropped first.

To drop a table using SQL Server Management Studio from the Object Explorer, follow these steps:

1.  In Object Explorer view, connect to the server instance of your choice, and then expand the server's Databases folder.

2.  Expand the database name and expand Tables, and then right-click the table you want to delete.

3.  Select Delete on the shortcut menu and click OK to confirm the deletion.

If you want to remove only the data in a table, use either the TRUNCATE TABLE or DELETE command. The DELETE statement removes all rows in a table or removes only a subset of rows if you use the conditional WHERE clause. All rows deleted are recorded in the transaction log. The TRUNCATE TABLE statement always removes all rows from a table. It does not record the deleted rows in the transaction log, and a WHERE clause cannot be used. TRUNCATE TABLE is much faster than DELETE when the desired result is the removal of all of the rows from a table. Both statements release the space occupied by the deleted rows for the storage of new data.

# Views

There are two basic types of *views* in SQL Server 2005: standard views and indexed views. A standard view is a virtual table based on the result set of a SELECT statement. A view contains rows and columns just like a real table. The fields in a view are fields from one or more real tables or other views in the database. You can add T-SQL arguments to a view definition as with any SELECT statement, such as WHERE, JOIN, and UNION, to present the data as if the data was coming from a single table. In a standard view, the database does not store the view data. The view is actually a predefined SQL statement that the database engine executes and retrieves dynamically when the view is referenced. A view can be used inside a query, a stored procedure, or another view.

> **Note**   Although a view is not a real table, the data in the base tables can still be manipulated, with some limitations, through the view as if it were a real table.

An *indexed view* is like a standard view except that it has a unique clustered index created on it. This causes the data of the view to be stored physically on disk, just like a table. Not only does the view now take up disk space, but there is also the additional overhead of maintaining the view when the data in the base tables changes. Because of this, there are limited reasons to use indexed views. The reason for creating an indexed view is to achieve better performance for queries using the view, as with table indexes. Indexed views work best for queries that aggregate many rows or have joins that cause the response time of the standard view to be slow, and where the data in the underlying tables is not frequently updated.

> **Note**   Secondary, nonclustered indexes can also be created on an indexed view to provide additional query performance. They will also be stored physically on a disk like the clustered index.

Performance must be considered when deciding whether to use an indexed view. If the indexed view is using base tables that are frequently inserted into, deleted from, or updated via a front-end application, that application may become noticeably slower. This occurs because each time a user changes the data in the base tables, the base table indexes are updated. In addition, the indexed view will need to be updated. Indexes can certainly increase the query performance of the view, but you need to find the right balance of the indexes and maintenance overhead to meet your needs. With read-only or mostly-read access of the table data, the update overhead problem will not be an issue.

---

**Note**   *Partitioned views* are included in SQL Server 2005 for backward compatibility purposes only and are in the process of being depreciated. They are being replaced by partitioned tables. See Chapter 19, "Data Partitioning," to learn more.

---

Indexed views can be created with any version of SQL Server 2005, but the query optimizer automatically considers using the indexed view only with Enterprise Edition. With other editions of SQL Server, the table hint WITH (NOEXPAND) must be specified in order for the indexed view to be considered for the execution plan. This hint is placed after the indexed view name in the SELECT statement that references the indexed view.

## Advantages of Views

Views can hide the complexity of database tables and present data to the end user in a simple organized manner.

Views can be created to do any or all of the following:

- Allow access to a subset of columns. Display only the columns needed by the end-user and hide columns with sensitive data.

- Rename columns. User-friendly column names can be used instead of the base table column names.

- Allow access to a subset of rows. Display only the rows needed by the end-user by using a conditional WHERE clause.

- Join two or more tables. Frequently used complex joins, queries, and unions can be coded once as a view, and the view can be referenced for simplicity and consistency of coding.

- Aggregate information. Sums, counts, averages, and so on can be calculated in a view to simplify coding when those aggregates will be referenced multiple times.

## Data Security with Views

Views can be used for security, allowing users access to certain data through the view without granting the user permission to directly access the underlying base tables. A view can be used to allow only harmless data to be available while hiding sensitive information. For example, a view may display a subset of columns only, such as an employee's name, e-mail address, and phone number, while hiding the employee's salary. With the WHERE clause, you can also limit the access to only certain rows.

## Creating, Modifying, and Dropping Views

The creator of the view must have access to all of the tables and columns referenced in the view. A view, like a table, can have up to 1,024 columns. Views can be built on other views and nested up to 32 levels.

**Note**   If you define a view with a SELECT * statement and then alter the structure of the underlying tables by adding columns, the new columns will not appear in the view. To see the new columns in the view, you must alter the view.

Use the following to create a view using T-SQL Syntax:

```
CREATE VIEW [ schema_name . ] view_name [ (column [ ,...n ] ) ]
[ WITH { [ ENCRYPTION ] [ SCHEMABINDING ] [ VIEW_METADATA ] }
[ ,...n ] ]
AS select_statement
[ WITH CHECK OPTION ]
```

Here is a description of the arguments for the CREATE VIEW statement:

- *schema_name* Optional. Name of the schema to which the view belongs. Defaults to dbo.

- *view_name* Required. Name of the view.

- *column* Optional. Names of all of the columns in the view. The column names are required if the column value is derived from a function, an expression, or a constant, or if two or more columns in the *select_statement* have the same name, as is typical with table joins. If column names are stated, there must be a one-to-one correlation to the columns in the *select_statement*. If omitted, the column names in the view will be the same as the column names in the *select_statement*.

- ENCRYPTION Optional. Encrypts the actual SQL source code for the view. The view cannot be modified. To change the view, the view must be dropped and then recreated from the original source code of the view.

- SCHEMABINDING Optional. Binds the columns of the view to the schema of the underlying table or tables. The base table or tables cannot be modified in a way that would affect the view definition.

- VIEW_METADATA Optional. SQL Server will return the metadata information about the view instead of the underlying tables to the DB-Library, ODBC and OLE DB APIs. This metadata enables the client-side APIs to implement updatable client-side cursors.

- *select_statement* Required. The SQL SELECT statement that defines the view. This can be from a single table, multiple tables, or other views, optionally using functions. Multiple SELECT statements separated by UNION or UNION ALL can also be used.

- CHECK OPTION Optional. Ensures that any data modification through the view complies with the WHERE condition of the view. CHECK OPTION cannot be specified if TOP is used anywhere in *select_statement*.

The SELECT clauses in a view definition cannot include the following:

- COMPUTE or COMPUTE BY clauses

- An ORDER BY clause, unless there is also a TOP clause in the select list of the SELECT statement

- The *INTO* keyword

- The OPTION clause

- A reference to a temporary table or a table variable

---

**Note**    It is a good idea to use a naming convention when creating views. Popular conventions include the prefix *v_* or the suffix *_v* to the name (for example, *employees_v*).

---

The following T-SQL example demonstrates how to create a view to show employees from a single department, how to join multiple tables, and how to rename a few columns:

```
CREATE VIEW dept_101_employees_view

AS

SELECT  emp.FName AS First_Name,

        emp.LName AS Last_Name,

        hire.Hire_Date,

        dept.Description AS Department_Name

FROM    Employees emp

INNER JOIN Employment hire ON emp.employee_id =
hire.employee_id

INNER JOIN Departments dept ON dept.department_id =
emp.department_id

WHERE   dept.department_id = 101

WITH CHECK OPTION
```

The CHECK OPTION specified here will allow only INSERTS or UPDATES to this view for employees in department 101. For example, you cannot insert an employee into department 200 using this view, nor can you update the department for an employee in this view to another department.

When a user queries SELECT * from this view, the user sees more specifically named columns ("Department_Name" instead of "Description"), the sensitive data is hidden (for example, the salary column is hidden and cannot be selected), and the number of rows returned is limited to only one department. The complexity of the join is also hidden from the user. The user will not know that the data is actually coming from three tables.

The columns can also be renamed at the beginning of the statement, as displayed in the following example. This example also shows the use of an aggregate function and encryption of the view so that the source cannot be viewed by others:

```
CREATE VIEW dept_101_employee_vacation_view

(First_Name, Last_Name, EmployeeNumber, Hire_Date,
Avg_Vacation_Remaining)

WITH ENCRYPTION, SCHEMABINDING

AS

SELECT  emp.FName,

        emp.LName,

        emp.EmployeeNumber,

        hire.Hire_Date,

        AVG(emp.vac_days_remaining)

FROM    Employees emp

INNER JOIN Employment hire ON emp.employee_id =
hire.employee_id

INNER JOIN Departments dept ON dept.department_id =
emp.department_id

WHERE   dept.department_id = 101

GROUP BY emp.FName, emp.LName, emp.EmployeeNumber,
hire.Hire_Date
```

> **Note** Be careful using ENCRYPTION. You will not be able to retrieve the source (the actual SQL) of the view from the database. You must keep a copy of the view in a separate file in order to maintain it.

To allow this view to become an indexed view, we included the SCHEMABINDING option in the CREATE VIEW statement. To create the unique clustered index, run the following T-SQL. (See Chapter 12, "Creating Indexes for Performance," to learn more about creating indexes.)

```
CREATE UNIQUE CLUSTERED INDEX v_ind_dept_101_employee_vacation ON
dept_101_employee_vacation_view (EmployeeNumber);
```

To create a view from the Object Explorer:

1.  In Object Explorer view, connect to the server instance of your choice, and then expand the server's Databases folder.

2.  Expand the database name and then right-click Views and select New View on the shortcut menu. This opens a window that asks you to select the base source for your view. For multiple sources, you can click the Add button after each selection, or use Ctrl-Click to select several sources, and then click the Add button.

3.  Click Close when you are finished.

4.  You can create joins by dragging a column from one source to another. Select inner or outer joins by right-clicking the box in the middle of the join line.

5.  Select all of the columns you want in your view by clicking the check box next to the field. The alias name for each column can be entered in the grid below the diagram.

6.  You can enter the WHERE clause of the SQL in the Filter and Or columns of the grid.

7.  You can also add or modify the SQL in the SQL window displayed below the grid.

8.  When you are finished, select Save *view name* on the File menu, or enter Ctrl+S.

If you created our example *dept_101_employees_view* view, your screen should look similar to Figure 11-4.

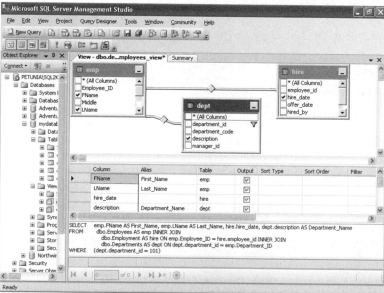

**Figure 11-4   Creating a view using Management Studio.**

# View Source

The source definition for your view can be seen by accessing system views. System views are the new method in SQL Server 2005 used to access information about database metadata. The following T-SQL command shows how to select the view definition from system view INFORMATION_SCHEMA.VIEWS (see the section later in this chapter 'System Views'). The system stored procedure to view text of an object, *sp_helptext*, is still available with SQL Server 2005 as well. Here is the T-SQL using both methods to retrieve the CREATE VIEW statement definition we used to create our example view *dept_101_-employees_view* in *mydatabase*:

```
SELECT VIEW_DEFINITION FROM mydatabase.INFORMATION_SCHEMA.VIEWS
WHERE table_name = 'dept_101_employees_view';
```

--OR

```
use mydatabase
```

```
go
```

```
sp_helptext dept_101_employees_view;
```

> **Note**   You will not be able to view the source of the example view *dept_101_employee_vacation_view* because it was created using WITH ENCRYPTION. The *text* field will contain NULL.

# Modifying Views

The T-SQL Syntax for modifying a view is basically the same as the syntax for creating the view, except ALTER is used instead of CREATE:

```
ALTER VIEW [ schema_name . ] view_name [ (column [ ,...n ] ) ]
[ WITH { [ ENCRYPTION ] [ SCHEMABINDING ] [ VIEW_METADATA ] }
[ ,...n ] ]
AS select_statement
[ WITH CHECK OPTION ]
```

Using SQL Server Management Studio Object Explorer:

1. In Object Explorer view, connect to the server instance of your choice, and then expand the server's Databases folder.

2. Expand the database name and expand Views.

3. Right-click the view you want to work with, and then select Modify on the shortcut menu.

4. You can modify the view using similar steps as with creating the view. Right-click in the Diagram pane to bring up a menu of additional modification options such as Add Table.

5. Once you have made the desired changes, select Save *view name* on the File menu, or enter Ctrl-S to save the changes.

---

**Note**   You will notice that any views created with the encryption option will display a small lock in the icon next to the view name. You will not be able to modify an encrypted view as the modify menu item is shaded and not selectable.

---

## Dropping Views

To delete a view, use the DROP VIEW command. The T-SQL Syntax to do this is as follows:

```
DROP VIEW [ schema_name . ] view_name [ ...,n ]
```

This T-SQL example drops the view we created earlier:

```
DROP VIEW dept_101_employees_view
```

Using SQL Server Management Studio Object Explorer:

1. In Object Explorer view, connect to the server instance of your choice, and then expand the server's Databases folder.

2. Expand the database name and expand Views.

3. Right-click the view you want to delete, and then select Delete on the shortcut menu.

4. Click OK to confirm the deletion.

# System Views

System views are new for SQL Server 2005. They are designed to expose instance and database related metadata in an organized and useful method. Some system tables from SQL Server 2000 are now implemented in SQL Server 2005 as system views for backward compatibility. Although the SQL Server 2000 system tables can still be queried by name, SQL Server 2005 features and related metadata will not be seen. Thus, the results may be different from those when querying the corresponding new system view. See the example later in this section.

Using the new system views is the recommended method for viewing metadata and system information. There are many SQL Server 2005 system tables that do not have system views for accessing data from them, such as the backup and restore history tables. In those cases, the data must be accessed by querying the system table itself.

System base tables are the underlying tables that actually store metadata for a specific database. These base tables are used within SQL Server 2005 Database Engine and are not intended for customer user. Therefore, the system views are provided for accessing that metadata without accessing the base tables. All of the system objects referenced by the system views are physically persisted in the system base tables stored within the read-only system database called Resource. This database is not visible to users and does not appear in SQL Server Management Studio. Users cannot use or connect to it, unless in single-user mode, which is only recommended to allow Microsoft Customer Support Services to assist in troubleshooting and support issues.

All system views are contained in either the INFORMATION_SCHEMA or the sys schemas. Both schemas logically appear in every database.

There are six collections of system views: catalog, compatibility, dynamic management, information schema, replication, and notification services. There are numerous categories of system views within each collection. Following are descriptions of each of the collections:

- **Catalog views**   Return information that is used by the Database Engine, such as information on objects, databases, files, security, and more. (They do not contain information about backups, replication, database maintenance plans, or SQL Server Agent catalog data.)

- **Compatibility views**   Provided for backward compatibility only with SQL Server 2000 system tables. They do not expose any SQL Server 2005 new feature metadata, such as partitioning. Use the new catalog views instead.

- **Dynamic management views (DMVs)**   Return information on server state or database state that can be used for monitoring the health of a server instance and databases, and diagnose performance problems. DMVs can be identified by their name, which begins with "dm_," plus an abbreviation of what category the DMV is a part, then a description of what the view returns. For example, dm_db_file_space_usage is part of the database category of DMVs and returns information on file space usage.

- **Information schema views**   These are system views that are part of a separate schema, called INFORMATION_SCHEMA. Returns metadata for database objects in a particular database. All other system views are part of the sys schema.

- **Replication views**    Return information about replication. They are created when a database is configured as a publisher or subscriber, and different views are created in the different databases: *msdb*, *distribution*, publisher database, and subscriber database. Otherwise, these views will not exist. Using replication stored procedures is still a good way to access replication metadata.

- **Notification services views**    Return instance and application data specifically related to Notification Services; designed to help with debugging, tracking, or troubleshooting.

---

**More Info**    Dynamic management views are covered in detail in Chapter 31

---

To display the system views for a database from the Object Explorer, perform the following steps:

1. In Object Explorer view, connect to the server instance of your choice, and then expand the server's Databases folder.

2. Expand the database name and expand Views.

3. Expand System Views. The example in Figure 11-5 shows the INFORMATION_ SCHEMA.VIEWS system view expanded and the columns in that view displayed in the right pane (by highlighting the Columns folder).

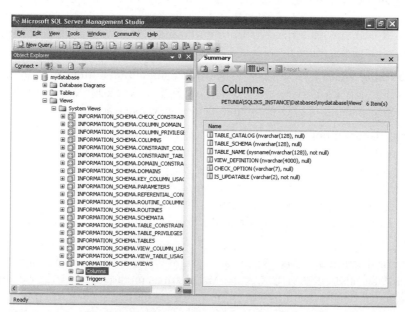

**Figure 11-5**    Displaying system views using Management Studio.

**More Info**   To find out which system views belong to each collection category, visit the topic "System Views' in SQL Server Books Online. There you will find all of the views listed and what data columns they include. There is also a mapping of SQL Server 2000 system tables to their new system views found in the topic "Mapping SQL Server 2000 System Tables to SQL Server 2005 System Views."

When retrieving data from the system views, the schema name and view name must both be specified—such as sys.databases or INFORMATION_SCHEMA.VIEWS. To access the sys.tables view and the INFORMATION_SCHEMA.TABLES view for example, run the following T-SQL:

—catalog view

```
SELECT * FROM sys.tables;
```

—information schema view

```
SELECT * FROM INFORMATION_SCHEMA.TABLES;
```

The output from both queries is shown in Figure 11-6. Notice the output is different for each of these views—although they have the same name, they are contained in different schemas. The first set of output from sys.tables has many columns (not all shown in the figure), while the second set of output has only the four columns.

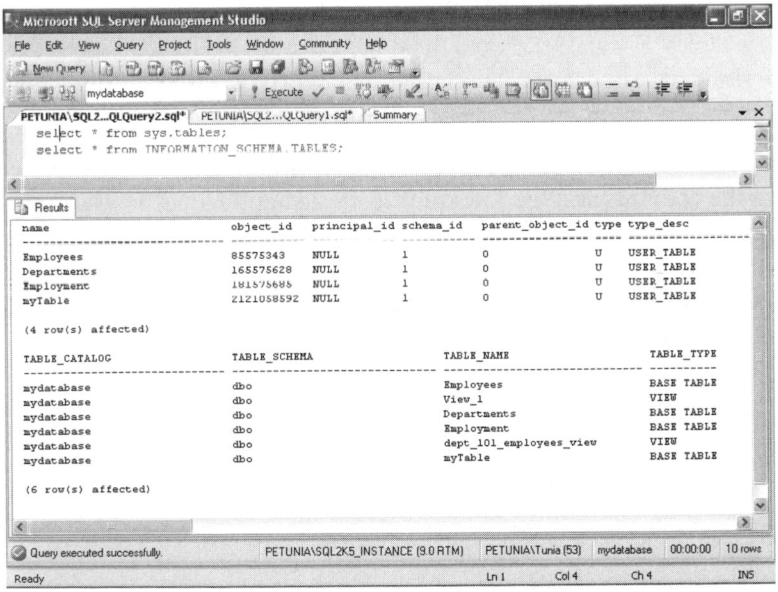

**Figure 11-6**   System view output example.

Now let's compare the output from querying the SQL Server 2000 system table sysdatabases, which is really a view in SQL Server 2005 for backward compatibility, and the new system view sys.databases. Run the following T-SQL:

—new SQL Server 2005 System view

```
SELECT * FROM sys.databases;
```

—compatibility view of the SQL Server 2000 system table sysdatabases

```
SELECT * FROM sysdatabases;
```

The output from the two queries above will be different—the sys.databases view exposes all of the SQL Server 2005 feature information and includes additional columns, while the SQL Server 2000 backward compatibility view results exclude that information and only show results as they appeared in SQL Server 2000 when querying the sysdatabases table.

To display the definition of a system view, you can run the system stored procedure sp_helptext, as in the following two T-SQL examples:

```
sp_helptext 'sys.tables';

exec sp_helptext 'INFORMATION_SCHEMA.TABLES';
```

## Summary

Tables are the basis of a relational database. In this chapter, we have learned how to create, modify, and delete tables. We have explored the different system data types provided by SQL Server 2005, along with how to create user-defined data types. We described how to define tables including the use of NULL values and the IDENTITY property.

Views are virtual tables that look and act like database tables to the end user. Views can be used to limit both the columns and the rows to provide a simplified view for the end user, to simplify coding for the database developer, and to increase data security. In this chapter we have learned how to create, modify, and delete views. We have also learned about indexed views. A clustered index is created on a view and the result set is stored physically in the database. This can speed up slow-running queries but at a cost of disk space and increased table update times.

System views provide a new metadata access method for SQL Server 2005. There are numerous system views that allow users to access metadata information and server and database state information without accessing the underlying system base tables.

# Chapter 12
# Creating Indexes for Performance

Indexes are a Microsoft SQL Server feature designed to speed access to data in the database. Indexes are similar to the index of this book. By using indexes, you can quickly find specific data without having to read through all of the data in the table. In this chapter, you will learn what indexes are, how they work, and what you can do to improve performance on your system by using indexes. In addition, you will learn about the new index features in SQL Server 2005.

## Index Fundamentals

Indexes are an optional structure that is designed to help you access table data more quickly and efficiently. Indexes are not required, and not having indexes will not affect the functionality of your queries, only the performance of those queries. However, this performance difference can be dramatic and can affect the overall performance of your system. The performance of queries is improved by reducing the amount of work needed to find the desired data. Without indexes, the entire table must be searched, causing a full table scan that must read all of the data in a table. Within SQL Server there are several different types of indexes and different ways that they can be configured, but the fundamentals of the index apply to all index types.

An index speeds access to data by allowing you to take shortcuts to find a specific piece of data. Like an index in a book, the SQL Server index helps you quickly find data by a series of choices. Let's look at an illustration of how the index works using "Last Name" and "First Name" as our selection criteria. Say I want to find the telephone number of Mr. John Smith. Following is an illustration of the steps SQL Server uses to find Mr. Smith using an index:

1.  Open the first page in the index. You will see a list of names and pointers to other pages in the index as shown here:

    Aaberg, Jesper-Furse, Kari—Go to index page 2

    Gabel, Ron-Lysaker, Jenny—Go to index page 3

    Ma, Andrew-Rytt, Christian—Go to index page 4

    Sacksteder, Lane-Zwilling, Michael—Go to index page 5

2.  Open index page 5, where you will see the following list:

    Sacksteder, Lane-Severino, Miguel—Go to index page 12

    Sloth, Peter-Spanton, Ryan—Go to index page 13

    Speckmann, Melanie-Tham, Bernard—Go to index page 14

    Thirunavukkarasu, Ram-Tupy, Richard—Go to index page 15

    Turner, Olinda-Zwilling, Michael—Go to index page 16

3.  Since you are still looking for John Smith, open page 13. On this page, you will again find the page that further refines your search criteria. This will again point to another page, perhaps full of Smiths.

4.  In this final page, there will be an entry for Smith, John that points to the page in the database that has his phone number.

The result of this process is that with five page reads in the database, you have found John Smith's telephone number. The other alternative, known as a table scan, involves reading every page in the table and comparing the data in the table to the search criteria. A table scan can be a very slow operation, and it usually should be avoided.

**Real World   It's All About the I/O**

Indexes are really all about the I/O. You use indexes to decrease the number of I/O operations that you perform. When you perform a table scan, thousands or even millions of I/Os are generated. These operations are expensive. Using an index finds your data faster because there are fewer reads necessary in order to find your data. By performing fewer I/Os, performance is increased and resource utilization is reduced.

The index is created with one or more *index keys*. The index key is the column or columns in the table that define what is indexed. This is the value that will be used to find the data in the table quickly. It can be character strings, integers, floats, and so on. Because these keys are used as the criteria for finding the data in the table and because you don't always look for data using the same columns in your WHERE clause of your query, multiple indexes are allowed. The exception is the clustered index, which is discussed later in this chapter. You can have only one clustered index per table.

> **Note**   The index key column does not support the following data types: *image*, *ntext*, and *text* data types.

Since indexes are created on index keys, you must include the leading key values in the WHERE clause of your SQL statement in order to use an index. If you do not include the index key in the WHERE clause, that index won't be used to find your data. Specifically, the leading side of the index must be included in the WHERE clause of the SELECT statement. In addition, there are a few other restrictions that are described later in this chapter.

An index that has been defined with only one key column is called a *simple index*. An index that has more that one key column is called a *composite index*. More than one column should be used in the index key if it makes the index more unique or gives it greater *selectivity*. The more unique the index, the better the index since it allows for fewer rows to be retrieved within the queries. As you will learn later in this chapter, indexes should be created to be as unique as possible, but very wide indexes with lots of key values are less efficient in terms of space and modification performance.

> **Note**   The benefit of an index is that you can find your data with as few reads as possible. The wider the index, the more index pages that it consumes, and thus it takes more space and more pages are needed to find the desired data. As a

result, there is always a give-and-take between creating more unique indexes and creating smaller indexes.

An index can be either unique or non-unique. With a unique index, there can be only one index key value; with a non-unique index, you can have duplicate index key values. For example, if the unique index were created on Lastname, Firstname, there could be only one entry for each name, a duplicate entry would be refused and an error issued. A unique index has the highest level of selectivity that an index can have, since each key value is associated with only one row, or each row has a unique key value. Any attempt to insert a duplicate index key value into a unique index will result in a failure. A set of columns that is designed to uniquely define each row in the table is called the *Primary Key (PK)*, as mentioned in Chapter 13, "Enforcing Data Integrity." The primary key is usually associated with a constraint and often is a very good candidate for a clustered index. Unfortunately, a table cannot always be defined with a primary key since it might be impossible to uniquely identify a row. There can be only one primary key per table, and the primary key cannot contain NULL values. When the primary key is defined, a unique index that is used to enforce uniqueness is created.

## Real World    Artificial Primary Keys Are Not Always Good

The statement that I made in the preceding paragraph is not entirely true. You can always create a primary key by adding a unique column to a table, such as an identity column. However, even though you can do it, it is not always a good idea to do it. This should be done with care and only when absolutely necessary. As you will see in Chapter 20, "Replication," you sometimes need to add a primary key. When not needed, you should not artificially create a Primary Key just for the sake of having one. This can cause undo overhead that is not necessary.

The index structure resembles an inverse tree (like a directory structure). This tree begins with the first page of the index which is known as the *root node*. The root node contains ranges of key values and pointers to other pages in the index. These intermediate pages are known as *branch nodes*. The branch nodes also contain key values and pointers to lower branch nodes and eventually to *leaf nodes*. The leaf node is the lowest-level page in the index and contains key values and either a rowid that points to the data itself (in a table) or a cluster key value (in a clustered index table). The index tree structure is shown here in Figure 12-1.

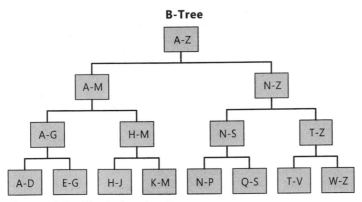

**Figure 12-1**   The index structure.

As you can see, the index is built in a tree-like structure. The tree-like structure used in an index is known as a B-tree. The index structure is built from the root node to the leaf node via the branch nodes as shown above. Although this example shows an index as a single character, the index pages are actually made up of values of the entire index key. How many pages the index takes depends on how wide the index is. The *index width* is determined by how many columns are in the index keys and how big those columns are. The number of rows in an index page is determined by how wide the index is.

The branch nodes are described in terms of branch levels. A *branch level* is the set of branch nodes that are the same distance from the root node, as shown in Figure 12-2.

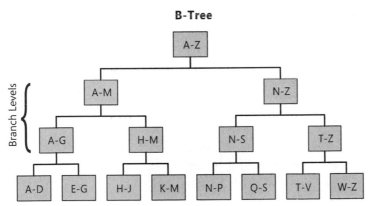

**Figure 12-2**   The index branch levels.

The number of I/Os required to retrieve the data that is requested depends on the number of branch levels that must be traversed to reach the leaf node. This directly affects the performance of retrieving the requested data. The number of branch levels depends on the width of the index (number of key columns and their sizes) and the number of rows in the table. Theoretically, in a very small table, the root node and leaf node can be in the same page. In this case, the index itself usually incurs more overhead than a table scan would.

When using an index, the root node is read and, based on the value of index key that you are using, the decision of which branch node is read is made. The branch nodes then allow you to quickly zoom in on your data by following the trail and decisions made by the branch nodes. Eventually, you will reach the leaf node and either a rowid or a key value for a clustered index lookup will be supplied. In some cases, you might reach a series of leaf nodes. At this point you will either retrieve your data directly or traverse a clustered index (bookmark lookup) in order to retrieve your data. There will be more on exactly how this works once you have been introduced to clustered indexes.

Depending on how you create the index, the index is sorted in either ascending or descending order. Because the index provides the sort order, you can often avoid having to execute a sort when the ORDER BY clause in the SQL statement is the same as the order of the index (assuming this index is used). This provides an additional advantage by reducing sorting in the database. However, this is not always the case.

## How to Optimally Take Advantage of Indexes

In order to take advantage of indexes, the index key must be referenced in the WHERE clause of your SQL statement. In a multicolumn index, the leading edge of the index must be supplied in the WHERE clause of your SQL statement. This must be the leading edge of the index since the data in the index is sorted on the first index key value and then subsequent key values.

For example, if an index is created on the columns *last_name* and then *first_name*, the data is sorted first by *last_name* and then within each last name the *first_name* data is sorted. Figure 12-3 shows an example that illustrates this point.

**Figure 12-3**   Example of using an index.

Since the values in the second key column in the index are scattered throughout the entire index, you can benefit from using this index only if the first key column also exists in the WHERE clause. Therefore, if an index is created on *last_name* and *first_name* as shown above, the index can be accessed very effectively in the following SQL statement:

```
SELECT PhoneNumber
FROM myTable
WHERE last_name = 'smith'
AND first_name = 'john' ;
```

Furthermore, this index can be somewhat useful with the following query since it reduces the number of rows retrieved. However, there will possibly be many Smiths retrieved.

```
SELECT PhoneNumber
FROM myTable
WHERE last_name = 'smith' ;
```

However, the following query will not use this index at all (unless it has no choice since it is a clustered index) since the last names are held together but the first names are scattered throughout the index. In this case, a table scan will be used.

```
SELECT PhoneNumber
FROM table
WHERE first_name = 'john' ;
```

As you will see later in this chapter, the index keys and the values that you use in the WHERE clause will together determine how beneficial the index is for improving the performance of your query. In addition, the type of index also determines its effectiveness.

# Index Types

SQL Server has a number of different index types such as clustered indexes, nonclustered indexes, included column indexes, indexed views, full-text indexes, and XML indexes, each with their own purpose and characteristics. By understanding how indexes work, you will be better able to create and tune indexes. Based on the type of index, the way it works might be different.

## Clustered Index

A *clustered index* stores the table data in sorted order in the leaf page of the index based on the index key. Because of the requirement that the clustered index store the data in sorted order, there is the need to constantly rearrange pages in the index. As data is inserted into the database, space might be needed to add these new pages into the index.

If new entries are added to the database, a new page is also added and a page split occurs. This page split can cause significant overhead but is unavoidable since a clustered index must store the data in sorted order. A clustered index is shown in Figure 12-4.

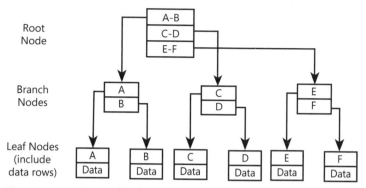

**Figure 12-4**   Example of a clustered index.

The data is actually stored in the leaf node of the index. Because of this, data that is stored in a clustered index must be accessed through the index structure. There is no other way to access this data but via the index. Because the data is stored in the index itself, it cannot be accessed directly. The leaf nodes are linked together via pointers. There is a pointer in each leaf node to the node before it and the node after it. This is known as a linked list. Since the leaf nodes of the index are connected via a linked list, the leaf nodes in the index are read in sequence during a table scan.

An index can be defined on either a table or a clustered index. When a nonclustered index is used to find data in a clustered index, the leaf nodes of the nonclustered index supply the index keys to the clustered index, and the underlying clustered index is scanned. This step is known as a *bookmark lookup*. The bookmark lookup is either a row access by rowid (no clustered index) or an index seek using the clustered index key (clustered index). This is why the effectiveness of the clustered index is so important.

## Real World   A Bad Clustered Index Is Worse Than No Index

I have occasionally run across good nonclustered indexes that point to a very bad clustered index. For example, suppose that we have a table that represents everybody in the country. Furthermore, let's say that we create a clustered index for the respective states in which everybody lives. In addition, we create nonclustered indexes on last name, first name, and state. Upon performing an index lookup on last name, first name, and state, the nonclustered index, the bookmark key is returned in only a few page selects. In this example, the very fast nonclustered index lookup returns a specific state, say, Texas, as the key to the bookmark lookup. Unfortunately, the bookmark lookup to the clustered index requires an index scan that pulls in so many rows that a table scan is invoked. The table scan is required to find a few rows or one row because of the clustered index. In this case, the clustered index is so bad that every lookup invokes a table scan. If the clustered index is created on a better index key, such as social security number, the fast non-clustered index seek is then directed to an efficient clustered index seek. Thus, if an index is a bad index in general, it is much worse as a clustered index.

It is very important that the clustered index be as effective as possible. A unique index or a primary key is an excellent candidate for a clustered index.

## Nonclustered Index

A *nonclustered index* is both logically and physically independent of the table data. This index is similar to the clustered index with the exception that the table data is not stored in the leaf node of the index. Instead, the leaf node contains either the cluster key, for an index pointing to a clustered index, or a row id that points directly to the table data when there is no clustered index.

Nonclustered indexes can be defined as either unique or non-unique. In addition, a nonclustered index can be used as a primary key index, although it is often recommended to cluster on the primary key index. You can have 249 nonclustered indexes defined on a table. These indexes can be defined on various combinations of columns (up to 16 columns and 900 bytes). The more indexes there are, the better various queries can become. However, more indexes mean more overhead. Whenever data is inserted, updated, or deleted, all of the indexes affected by that row must also be updated. As a result, the number of indexes grows, and the update, insert, and delete operations become slower.

A *covering index* is an index that includes enough information that performing the bookmark lookup is not necessary. This tool works in conjunction with a *covering query*. If the selected criteria are included on the trailing end of the index and if the leading end of the index is used in the WHERE clause of a query, the index itself can return the data to the user. For example, the following query can be issued if an index is created on *last_name*, *first_name*, and *social_security_number*:

```
SELECT social_security_number
FROM myTable
WHERE last_name = 'smith'
AND first_name = 'john' ;
```

Since the social security number is available in the index, that value is returned without having to perform the bookmark lookup. In SQL Server 2005 the Index with Included Columns is provided specifically to provide covering indexes.

## Included Columns Index

The included columns index is an index where additional column values that are not used in the key values of the index are included in the index. This allows for smaller indexes that can provide a covering function. Since the size and number of key columns determine the number of index levels, there is a benefit in keeping them as small as possible. If the addition of another key column does not make the index any more selectable, then it is not worth adding it to the keys unless it can be used in a covering fashion.

With the included columns index these included columns are not part of the index key but are stored in the leaf node of the index, similar to a clustered index. The included columns index offers several advantages over the clustered index, including the following:

- Unlike a clustered index, more than one included columns index can be defined on a table or clustered index.

- The included columns index must contain only the columns necessary for covering.

- The nonkey columns can be column types not supported as key columns such as image or text.

- The bookmark lookup can be avoided.

As you can see, the included columns index offers the flexibility of the covering index without the extra overhead of adding it to the index keys.

## Indexed Views

An ordinary view is simply a SQL statement that is stored in the database. When the view is accessed, the SQL statement from the view is merged with the base SQL statement, forming a merged SQL statement. This SQL statement is then executed.

When a unique clustered index is created on a view, this view is materialized. This means that the index actually contains the view data, rather than evaluating the view each time it is accessed. The indexed view is sometimes referred to as a *materialized view*. The result set of the index is stored actually in the database like a table with a clustered index. This can be quite beneficial because these views can include joins and aggregates, thus reducing the need for these aggregates to be computed on the fly.

Another advantage of an indexed view is that it can be used even though the view name is not expressly named in the WHERE clause of the SQL statement. This can be very advantageous for queries that are extensive users of aggregates. The indexed view is automatically updated as the underlying data is updated. Thus, these indexes can incur significant overhead and should be used with care. Only tables that do not experience significant update, insert, and delete activity are candidates for indexed views.

## Full-Text Index

The full-text index is very different from a B-tree index and serves a different function. The full-text index is built and used by the Full-Text Engine for SQL Server, or MSFT-ESQL. This engine is designed to perform searches on text-based data using a mechanism that allows searching using wildcards and pattern recognition. The full-text index is designed for pattern searches in text strings.

The full-text index is actually more like a catalog than an index, and its structure is not a B-tree. The full-text index allows you to search by groups of keywords. The full-text index is part of the Microsoft Search service; it is used extensively in Web site search engines and in other text-based operations. Unlike B-tree indexes, a full-text index is stored outside the database but is maintained by the database. Because it is stored externally, the index can maintain its own structure. The following restrictions apply to full-text indexes:

- A full-text index must include a column that uniquely identifies each row in the table.

- A full-text index also must include one or more character string columns in the table.

- Only one full-text index per table is allowed.

- A full-text index is not automatically updated, as B-tree indexes are. That is, a B-tree index, a table insert, update, or delete operation will update the index. With the full-text index, these operations on the table will not automatically update the index. Updates must be scheduled or run manually.

The full-text index has a wealth of features that cannot be found in B-tree indexes. Because this index is designed to be a text search engine, it supports more than standard text-searching capabilities. Using a full-text index, you can search for single words and phrases, groups of words, and words that are similar to each other.

## XML Index

XML indexes are used to speed access to XML data. XML data is stored as BLOB data in the database. Unlike B-tree indexes, the XML index is designed to work with the exists statement. XML indexes are defined as either primary XML indexes or secondary XML indexes.

A primary XML index is a shredded and persisted representation of the XML BLOB in the *xml data type* column. For each row in the BLOB, the index creates several rows. The number of rows in the index is roughly equivalent to the number of nodes in the XML BLOB.

In order to have a secondary XML index, you must first have a primary XML index. The secondary XML indexes are created on *PATH*, *VALUE*, and *PROPERTY* attributes of the XML BLOB data.

# Designing Indexes

Designing indexes is critical to achieving optimal performance from the indexes in the system. Creating an index is only half of the story—if the index is not actually used, then you have done nothing more than add overhead to the system. An effective index derives its effectiveness from how well it is designed *and* from how it is used.

## Index Best Practices

The lack of indexes and poorly designed clustered indexes cause many of the performance problems that you might experience in a SQL Server system. Designing optimal indexes can make the difference between a poorly performing system and an optimally performing system. There is a delicate balance between having too many indexes, which slows down update performance, and too few indexes, which slows down query performance. Choosing the right columns to index on and the appropriate type of index to use are also both very important. In this section you will learn some techniques and tips for creating optimal indexes.

There are a number of best practices that should be followed when creating indexes. These practices help you create the most optimal indexes for your system. The following list of best practices includes both general and specific recommendations, and items are not listed in any particular order:

- **Create indexes with good selectivity, or uniqueness**   An index with good selectivity has very few or no duplicates. A unique index has ultimate selectivity. If a non-clustered index does not have good selectivity, it most likely will not be chosen. A clustered index with poor selectivity causes poor performance on bookmark lookups and is worse than no clustered index because more reads are required. This is because you would have to suffer the overhead of both the nonclustered index lookup and the clustered index lookup (bookmark lookup).

- **Create indexes that reduce the number of rows**   If a query selects a few rows from a large table, indexes that help facilitate this reduction of rows should be created.

- **Create indexes that select a range of rows**   If the query returns a set of rows that are similar, an index can facilitate the selection of those rows.

- **Create clustered indexes as unique indexes if possible**   The best candidates for clustered indexes are primary keys and unique indexes. However, it is not always a good idea to make the primary key index the clustered index if it is too big. In some cases it is better to make the primary key index nonclustered and use a smaller clustered index.

- **Keep indexes as narrow as possible**   An index that is created on one or a few small columns is called a *narrow index*, and an index with many large key columns is called a *wide index*. The fewer the columns in the index the better, but you must have enough columns to make it effective.

- **Use indexes sparingly on tables that have a lot of update activity**   You can create more indexes on tables that do not have much update activity.

- **Don't index very small tables**   With very small tables there is more overhead than benefit involved with the index. Since an index adds pages that must be read, a table scan might sometimes be more efficient.

- **Create covering indexes when possible**   Covering indexes are greatly enhanced with the introduction of included columns indexes.

- **Index views where appropriate**   Indexed views can be very effective with aggregates and some joins.

By following these guidelines your indexes become more effective and, therefore, are more likely to be used. An ineffective index is not likely to be used and thus just adds unnecessary overhead on the systems. Indexes, especially clustered indexes, should be carefully designed and used sparingly since indexes add overhead and reduce the performance on data updates.

## Index Restrictions

There are a number of restrictions on the various index types. These restrictions are shown in Table 12-1.

**Table 12-1   Index Restrictions**

| Index Restriction | Value |
| --- | --- |
| Number of clustered indexes per table | 1 |
| Number of nonclustered indexes per table | 249 |
| Number of XML indexes per table | 249 |

**Table 12-1**  Index Restrictions (continued)

| Index Restriction | Value |
|---|---|
| Number of key columns per index. (Note: This does not included additional nonkey columns in an index with included columns.) | 16 |
| Maximum index key record size. (Note: This does not include additional nonkey columns in an index with included columns.) | 900 bytes |

In addition, there are a few design considerations related to the type of data that can be used in an index key column:

- **Computed Columns**  The computed columns data type can be indexed.

- **LOB (Large Object)**  LOB data such as *image*, *ntext*, *text*, *varchar(max)*, *nvarchar(max)*, and *varbinary(max)* cannot be indexed.

- **XML**  XML columns can be indexed only in an XML index type.

As you learned earlier in this chapter, it is also important to consider the order of the index key columns in addition to their data type, since the order of the key columns could determine how effectively the index is used.

# Using the Index Fill Factor

As discussed earlier in this chapter, the index is sorted based on the index keys. In order to keep the indexes sorted, some rearranging of data constantly occurs. Under normal conditions adding a new entry to the index involves simply adding rows to the leaf pages of the indexes. When there is no more space available in these pages, a new page is created and approximately half of the rows from the existing page are moved into this new index page. This is known as a *page split*.

With the page now split into two pages, the new row is inserted into the appropriate page in the index. This page split is quite an expensive operation. The number of page splits per second is a counter in the *Access Methods* object in perfmon and should be occasionally monitored. This page split is quite an expensive operation due to high IOs and page allocations required.

If you know that your index will have constant updates or insertions, you can reduce the number of page splits that occur by leaving some extra space in the leaf pages of the index. This is done via the index *fill factor*. The fill factor specifies how full the index should be when it is created.

By specifying the fill factor, additional rows are left empty in the index pages, thus leaving room for new rows to be added. The fill factor specifies the percentage of the index to fill and can take an integer value from 1 to 100. Setting the fill factor to 75 fills the index 75 percent, leaving 25 percent of the rows available.

The disadvantage of setting the fill factor is that the indexes will be larger and less efficient than a tightly packed index. The advantage of setting the fill factor is that page splits can be reduced. The fill factor setting appropriate for you really depends on your configuration and the load on the system. Remember that indexes, like all data, are stored both on disk and in memory in 8K pages. Setting the fill factor of an index to 50 causes the index to take up twice as many pages as a fill factor of 100. Keep this in mind when setting the fill factor.

## Partitioned Indexes

Partitioned indexes are indexes that are partitioned either on the underlying partitioned table or independently of the underlying partitioned table. The basic underlying function and structure of the partitioned index is the same as with a nonpartitioned index, but the partitioning column is always included in the index keys. Partitioned indexes are discussed in Chapter 19, "Data Partitioning."

---

**Note**   Partitioning is supported only in the Enterprise and Developer editions of SQL Server 2005.

---

# Creating Indexes

Indexes can be created either via SQL Server Management Studio using the graphical user interface (GUI) or via command line tools. SQL Server Management Studio is convenient because of its ease of use. The GUI can generate a script that you can then modify and reuse. However, I prefer to create indexes using the command line option because these scripts can be reused and modified to create other similar indexes. In addition, these scripts are an excellent way to document your database. If there is a problem with indexes and you needed to recreate them, these scripts can be used to create all indexes in the database. One way to do this is to use the GUI to create the first index, have the GUI generate a script, and then modify and reuse that script.

Indexes are created with the CREATE INDEX command. The CREATE INDEX command supports many options and is used for all of the various index types. The syntax of the CREATE INDEX command is as follows:

```
CREATE [ UNIQUE ] [ CLUSTERED | NONCLUSTERED ] INDEX index_name
    ON <object> ( column [ ASC | DESC ] [ ,...n ] )
    [ INCLUDE ( column_name [ ,...n ] ) ]
    [ WITH ( <relational_index_option> [ ,...n ] ) ]
```

```
     [ ON { partition_scheme_name ( column_name )
         | filegroup_name
         | default
         }
     ]
  [ ; ]
```

The parameters for the CREATE INDEX statement are as follows:

- The *UNIQUE* parameter specifies that the index to be created is unique.

- The *CLUSTERED* parameter specifies that the index is a clustered index.

- The *NONCLUSTERED* parameter specifies that this is a nonclustered index. This is the default type of index.

- The object information specifies on what table and columns the index is created.

- The *INCLUDE* parameter specifies included nonindexed columns.

- Partitioning option parameters specify how the index is partitioned.

## Index Creation Examples

Now that you've seen how to create an index using the CREATE INDEX statement, let's look at a few examples of how to create some indexes. As mentioned earlier in this section, the index can be created either via SQL Server Management Studio or with SQL statements. To create an index with the Management Studio, follow these steps:

1. Expand the database, and then expand the table.

2. Right-click on the Indexes icon and select New Index. This will invoke the new index utility as shown in Figure 12-5.

3. The New Index utility is used to create indexes. Fill in the Index Name and pull down the Index Type from the top part of the screen and check Unique if you want to create a unique index.

4. Next, select the Add button. This will invoke the Select Column tool. Here you can select the columns to be included in the index. This tool is shown in Figure 12-6.

5. Once you have selected the columns to include in the index, click on the OK button to return to the New Index utility, where you can move columns up and down

using the Move Up and Move Down buttons. You can remove a column if you so desire.

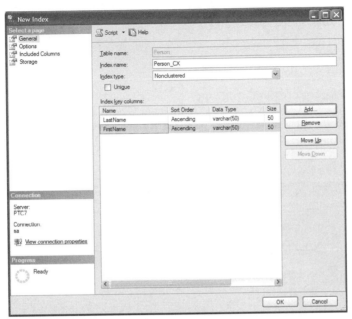

**Figure 12-5**   The New Index utility.

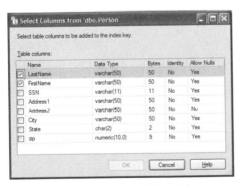

**Figure 12-6**   The Select Table Columns tool.

6.  After you choose the index columns and order, you can either click OK to create the index or choose other index options.

7. In order to set advance index options, click on the Options page selection button. The options page allows you to set advanced options such as:

   ❑ Drop Existing Index (if index is existing)

   ❑ Rebuild Index (if index is existing)

   ❑ Automatically compute statistics

   ❑ Use row locks or page locks

   ❑ Use *tempdb* for the creation of the index

These options are advanced and should be used with some caution. The Options page is shown in Figure 12-7.

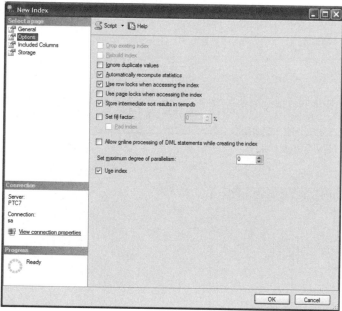

**Figure 12-7** The Options page of the New Index utility.

8. The third choice is the Included Columns page. Here you can choose to Add or Remove included columns to or from this index. This is shown in Figure 12-8.

9. The final option is the Storage page, shown in Figure 12-9. Here you can select the filegroup or partition scheme to use for this index. Usually the PRIMARY filegroup is sufficient, but you can change it if necessary.

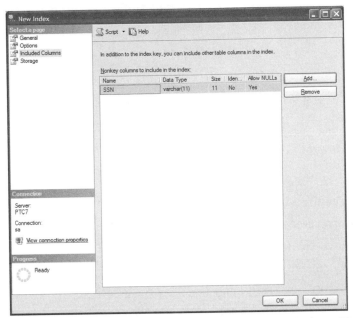

**Figure 12-8**   The Included Columns page of the New Index utility.

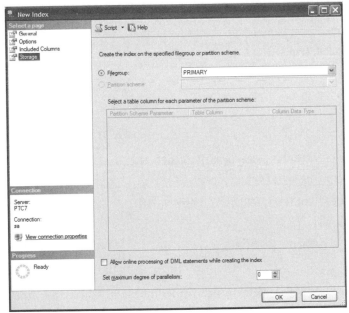

**Figure 12-9**   The Storage page of the New Index utility.

This same index can be created via SQL Statements. The SQL statement that will create the identical index is shown here:

```
USE [Production]
GO
CREATE NONCLUSTERED INDEX [Person_ix] ON [dbo].[Person]
(
        [LastName] ASC,
        [FirstName] ASC
)
WITH (STATISTICS_NORECOMPUTE  = OFF,
    SORT_IN_TEMPDB = OFF, DROP_EXISTING = OFF,
    IGNORE_DUP_KEY = OFF, ONLINE = OFF,
    ALLOW_ROW_LOCKS  = ON,
    ALLOW_PAGE_LOCKS  = OFF) ON [PRIMARY] ;
GO
```

The same index with an included column (SSN) is shown in this example:

```
USE [Production]
GO
CREATE NONCLUSTERED INDEX [Person_IX] ON [dbo].[Person]
(
        [LastName] ASC,
        [FirstName] ASC
)
INCLUDE ( [SSN]) WITH (STATISTICS_NORECOMPUTE  = OFF,
    SORT_IN_TEMPDB = OFF, DROP_EXISTING = OFF,
    IGNORE_DUP_KEY = OFF, ONLINE = OFF,
    ALLOW_ROW_LOCKS  = ON,
    ALLOW_PAGE_LOCKS  = OFF) ON [PRIMARY] ;
GO
```

Whether you use the GUI or SQL statements, the outcome is the exact same index.

## Normal Index Creation Logging

During normal index operations a large amount of transaction log information is generated. This can affect performance and cause additional maintenance. This log information is used to recover after a system failure. Because indexes are independent of the data in the database and can be reproduced easily, some of these operations can be performed without full logging.

## Minimally Logged Operations

A number of index operations can be performed with a reduced amount of logging. This is known as a *minimal logged operation*. These minimal logged operations generate less transaction log information but are not recoverable and must be re-run if they fail. Minimal logged operations are not available when running in full logged mode. When running in bulk logged and simple logged modes, minimal index logging can be performed.

Whether you choose to run in minimally logged mode is ultimately up to you the DBA. There is some risk involved because long-running operations cannot be recovered, but the advantage is that logging can be significantly reduced. The choice is up to you.

> **Important**    Running in a logging mode other than Full can be risky and lead to loss of data under certain conditions. I only recommend running in Full logging mode.

When running in full logging mode, there is additional overhead involved in creating transaction log entries and in backing up the transaction log, but this mode provides the ability to recover from a system failure.

If you choose to run in minimally logged mode, the overhead involved in logging operations is reduced. However, in the event of a system failure all minimally logged operations are lost, cannot be recovered, and must be redone.

# Index Maintenance and Tuning

Maintaining indexes is an ongoing operation. Because of factors such as page splits and updates to index branch and leaf pages, the index often becomes fragmented. Even though the data is stored in a logically contiguous manner, with time it is no longer physically contiguous. Thus, the indexes should be reorganized occasionally. In this section, you will learn some of the fundamentals for discovering information about indexes and how to maintain indexes.

# Monitoring Indexes

Monitoring Indexes might be a slight misnomer. It really is more of a task of investigating indexes, determining their effectiveness, and determining whether these indexes are being used. Whether an index is used really depends on how effective it is compared to other indexes and to the clustered index. The optimizer then decides whether or not to use the index.

Because indexes are an auxiliary structure and used only when the optimizer determines that they can improve query performance, it is often the case that an index is not used. It is also very possible to create indexes that are never used. This is a very common occurrence.

The factors affecting whether indexes are used include the following:

- **The compatibility between the index columns and the WHERE clause of the query**    If the leading edge of the index columns doesn't match with the WHERE clause, the index will not be used. For example, if the index is created on *last_name* and *first_name* but the WHERE clause includes only *first_name*, the index will not be used.

- **The selectivity of an index**    If an index is highly selectable, it is more likely to be used than indexes with less selectivity. The more unique the index is, the more likely it is to be used.

- **Covering indexes**    If the index covers a query, it is likely to be used.

- **Join usage**    If the index is defined on a join column, it might be used.

In order to determine the effectiveness of an index, the command DBCC SHOW_STATISTICS can be used. Table 12-2 lists the output of DBCC SHOW_STATISTICS.

**Table 12-2   Output of SHOW_STATISTICS**

| Value | Notes |
| --- | --- |
| Name | The name of the statistic |
| Updated | The date and time that statistics on this object were last gathered |
| Rows | The number of rows in the table |
| Rows sampled | The number of rows sampled for statistics gathering |
| Steps | The number of distribution steps |
| Density | The selectivity of the first key column in the index |
| Average key length | The average length of the key columns |
| String index | An indication that the index includes a string summary index if the value is Yes |

Other information from DBCC SHOW_STATISTICS is returned if DENSITY_VECTOR is specified in the DBCC SHOW_STATISTICS command. Table 12-3 lists this information.

**Table 12-3 Output of SHOW_STATISTICS with DENSITY_VECTOR**

| Value | Notes |
| --- | --- |
| All density | The selectivity of a set of index column prefixes |
| Average length | The average length of a set of index column prefixes |
| Columns | Names of the index column prefixes that are displayed in the all density or average density displays |

Other information from DBCC SHOW_STATISTICS is returned if HISTOGRAM is specified in the DBCC SHOW_STATISTICS command. This information is included in the following Table 12-4.

**Table 12-4 Output of SHOW_STATISTICS with HISTOGRAM**

| Value | Notes |
| --- | --- |
| RANGE_HI_KEY | The upper bound of the histogram step |
| RANGE_ROWS | The estimated number of rows that fall within this step, excluding the upper bound |
| EQ_ROWS | The estimated number of rows that are equal to the upper bound value of the histogram step |
| DISTINCT_RANGE_ROWS | The estimated number of distinct values that fall within the histogram step, excluding the upper bound |
| AVG_RANGE_ROWS | Average number of duplicate values within the histogram step, excluding the upper bound |

The output of DBCC SHOW_STATISTICS can be valuable for determining whether an index is good. It will also help you determine which indexes might be used and which indexes will probably not be used. An example of DBCC SHOW STATISTICS is shown in Figure 12-10.

To the experienced professional, this information can be valuable for viewing the effectiveness of an index. The density is an indication of the number of distinct rows. A column that is unique will have a density of 1. The more duplicate values, the lower the number of the density value.

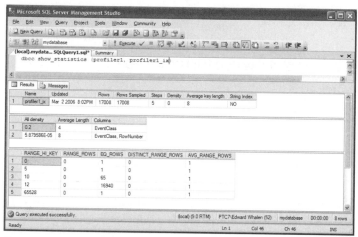

Figure 12-10    DBCC SHOW STATISTICS output.

# Rebuilding Indexes

If you have worked with previous versions of SQL Server, you are probably familiar with the process of rebuilding indexes. When data is added to or updated in the index, page splits occur. These page splits cause the physical structure of the index to become fragmented. In order to restore the structure of the index to an efficient state, the index needs to be rebuilt. The more fragmented the index, the more performance improvement will result from rebuilding the index.

With SQL Server 2005 you can view the fragmentation in an index via the *sys.dm_db_index_physical_stats* function. If the percentage of index fragmentation is less than or equal to 30 percent, Microsoft recommends correcting this with the ALTER INDEX REORGANIZE statement. If the percentage of fragmentation is greater than 30 percent, Microsoft recommends using the ALTER INDEX REBUILD WITH (ONLINE = ON) statement.

With SQL Server 2005, there are additional methods of rebuilding and reorganizing indexes that have been added. Table 12-5 lists these Index maintenance operations.

Table 12-5    Index Operations

| Index Operation | Notes |
| --- | --- |
| ALTER INDEX REORGANIZE | Reorganizes the index by reordering the leaf pages of the index. It will also repack the leaf pages. This should be used if fragmentation is not too great. This is an online operation that makes the DBCC INDEXDEFRAG statement obsolete. |

Table 12-5    Index Operations (continued)

| Index Operation | Notes |
| --- | --- |
| ALTER INDEX REBUILD | Drops the index and recreates it. This is a much more significant operation that the REORGANIZE statement and consumes more resources, but it produces a better result. With the ONLINE = ON qualifier, this online operation replaces the DBCC DBREINDEX statement. |
| CREATE INDEX WITH DROP_EXISTING=ON | Creates a new index while dropping the existing index of the same name, thus rebuilding the index. This statement is usually used to modify the definition of the index. |
| DBCC INDEX DEFRAG | Replaced by ALTER INDEX REORGANIZE.* |
| DBCC INDEX REBUILD | Replaced by ALTER INDEX REBUILD.* |

*These statements are provided in SQL Server 2005 for compatibility reasons and will not be supported in future versions. You should discontinue the use of these statements whenever feasible. An example of the REBUILD INDEX statement is shown here:

```
ALTER INDEX [uniquet_ix]

ON [dbo].[unique_t]

REBUILD WITH ( PAD_INDEX  = OFF,

    STATISTICS_NORECOMPUTE  = OFF,

    ALLOW_ROW_LOCKS  = ON, ALLOW_PAGE_LOCKS  = OFF,

    SORT_IN_TEMPDB = OFF,

    IGNORE_DUP_KEY  = OFF, ONLINE = OFF ) ;
```

A simpler form is shown here:

```
ALTER INDEX [uniquet_ix]

ON [dbo].[unique_t]

REBUILD ;
```

These operations are part of ongoing index maintenance. Without rebuilding indexes, occasional fragmentation can cause severe index performance problems.

# Disabling Indexes

With SQL Server 2005 you can now disable an index. An index is disabled via the ALTER INDEX DISABLE command. This allows you to deny access to an index without removing the index definition and statistics. With a nonclustered index or an index on a view, the index data is removed when the index is disabled. Disabling a clustered index also disables access to the underlying table data, but the underlying table data is not removed.

Disabling an index allows you to try various new indexes without worrying about a better specific index being used instead. Disabling all other indexes on a table guarantees that only the existing index will be used, if possible. This command is useful for testing since it does not require existing indexes to be rebuilt after the test.

In order to re-enable access to the index, and underlying data if it is a clustered index, run the command ALTER INDEX REBUILD or CREATE INDEX WITH DROP EXISTING. These commands recreate the index data, enable the index, and allow user access to that data. In essence, the disable index command allows you to delete an index but retain its definition. An example of this is shown here:

```
ALTER INDEX profiler1_ix ON profiler1 DISABLE ;
```

Perform tests ...

```
ALTER INDEX profiler1_ix ON profiler1 REBUILD ;
```

## Tuning Indexes

Tuning indexes is typically an iterative process in which indexes are analyzed, rebuilt, and monitored. The DBCC SHOW_STATISTICS command can assist you with determining the selectivity of the index. In addition, you can run your own SQL statements to determine which columns might make good candidates for indexing. You can try a SQL statement such as the following:

```
SELECT col1, COUNT(*)
FROM myTable
GROUP BY col1
ORDER BY COUNT(*) DESC ;
```

This statement can give you a fairly good indication of the selectivity of the index on that column. However, remember that this query can be quite intense and can utilize significant system resources.

Tuning indexes typically involves a thorough knowledge of your application. Index tuning often comes from viewing profiler output and starting with the SQL statements that are performing the most read operations. Because the main benefit of indexes is reducing the number of I/O operations necessary to retrieve data, starting with SQL statements that perform lots of read operations is usually very efficient.

## Online Index Operations

With SQL Server 2005 you can now create, rebuild, and drop indexes online. By using the ONLINE qualifier of the CREATE INDEX and ALTER INDEX statements, concurrent access to the index can happen while the underlying table data is being accessed. So now an index can be rebuilt while other users are updating the underlying table data. Prior to

SQL Server 2005, when you were rebuilding an index, the underlying table was locked, and other users were prohibited access to that data.

# Summary

As you have seen in this chapter, indexes can be very helpful for reducing the number of I/Os required to retrieve data and for speeding access to that data. This chapter has offered many tips and guidelines for creating and using indexes effectively. As a review of some of those, here again are some index best practices:

- Use indexes only when necessary.
- Index large tables.
- Create indexes as narrowly as possible.
- Use covering queries and indexes or included columns indexes where possible.

By creating indexes and properly maintaining these indexes, the system performance can be optimized. Indexes can be quite beneficial, but beware that poorly clustered indexes can do more harm than good.

# Chapter 13
# Enforcing Data Integrity

Chapter 11, "Creating Tables and Views," discussed the fundamentals of designing and creating tables. Before finalizing your table design, you must consider what data values should and should not be allowed into each column of a table and determine how the data across tables in a database may be related. Identifying valid values that can be inserted into a table and maintaining consistency among tables that have related data are the essence of data integrity. Data integrity is enforced as a means to guarantee that data is valid and consistent throughout the database tables.

This chapter discusses the various categories of data integrity and how to enforce data integrity using the built-in capabilities of Microsoft SQL Server 2005. Using SQL Server to enforce data integrity, rather than coding an application to enforce this, is the recommended choice.

In this chapter we will cover what data integrity means and how to enforce integrity with constraints, and we will describe the use of SQL Server built-in capabilities for enforcing data integrity, including PRIMARY KEY constraints, FOREIGN KEY constraints, UNIQUE constraints, CHECK constraints, NULL and NOT NULL constraints, and DEFAULT definitions.

## What Is Data Integrity?

*Data integrity* refers to the accuracy, consistency, and correctness of the data. Rules are set up in the database to help ensure the validity of the data. Data integrity falls into the following categories:

*Domain integrity*, also known as column integrity, specifies a set of data values that are valid for a column. This can be defined by the data type, format, data length, nullability, default value, and range of allowable values.

*Entity integrity*, also known as table or row integrity, requires that all of the rows in a table have a unique identifier, enforced by either a PRIMARY KEY or UNIQUE constraint.

*Referential integrity* ensures that the relationships between tables are maintained. Every FOREIGN KEY value in the referencing table must either be NULL, match a PRIMARY KEY value, or match a UNIQUE key value in an associated referenced table. The referenced row cannot be deleted if a FOREIGN KEY refers to the row, nor can key values be changed if a FOREIGN KEY refers to it. Also, you cannot insert or change records in a referencing table if there is not an associated record in the primary referenced table.

*User-defined integrity* lets you define business rules that do not fall under one of the other integrity categories, including column-level and table-level constraints.

# Enforcing Integrity with Constraints

Constraints are an ANSI-standard method used to enforce the integrity of the data in the database. They are rules that SQL Server Database Engine enforces for you. There are various types of constraints, each of which enforces a specific rule. All of the built-in constraints are enforced before a data change is made to the database so that if a constraint is violated, the modification statement is not executed. This way, there is no rollback of data necessary if the constraint is violated.

SQL Server 2005 provides the following types of constraints:

- PRIMARY KEY constraints
- UNIQUE constraints
- FOREIGN KEY constraints
- CHECK constraints
- DEFAULT definitions
- NULL/NOT NULL constraints

The following sections will describe each of these to help you determine when to use each type of constraint. You will also see how to create, modify, and delete the constraints using Transact-SQL syntax and using SQL Server Management Studio.

## PRIMARY KEY Constraints

The ability to uniquely identify a row in a table is fundamental to relational database design. This is accomplished using a PRIMARY KEY constraint. The primary key is a column or set of columns that uniquely identifies a row in a table. The PRIMARY KEY column or columns can never be NULL, and there can be only one primary key on a table. A PRIMARY KEY constraint on a table guarantees that every row in the table is unique. If an attempt is made to insert a row of data with a duplicate value or a NULL value for the primary key, an error message will result and the insert is not allowed. The database will not allow a column defined as nullable to be part of a primary key. This will prevent a NULL value from being inserted into any of the primary key columns.

When a PRIMARY KEY constraint is defined for a column or a set of columns, SQL Server 2005 Database Engine automatically creates a unique index on the PRIMARY KEY column or columns to enforce the uniqueness requirement of the PRIMARY KEY constraint. If a clustered index does not already exist on the table or a nonclustered index is not explicitly specified, a unique, clustered index is created by default.

An existing table may already have a column or set of columns that meet the conditions for a primary key. This key is known as a *natural key*. In some cases, you may need to add an additional column to act as your primary key. This is known as a *surrogate key*. A surrogate key is an artificial identifier that is unique. This is most often a system-generated sequential number. SQL Server supplies an IDENTITY column that is a very good candidate for a primary key. See Chapter 11 for more information on using IDENTITY columns.

Even if you have a natural key in your table, it is sometimes more practical to use a surrogate key. The natural key may be very long or consist of many columns. Using a surrogate key in this case may be simpler, especially if the primary key will be referenced by a foreign key in another table. Performance might be another reason to use a surrogate key, but it is purely a database design decision.

---

**Note**   If you create a numeric surrogate column in your table to use as a key field, a popular naming convention to use is a suffix of "ID" so it can be easily recognized as a PRIMARY KEY column.

---

A table can also have several columns or sets of columns that each could serve as the PRIMARY KEY. These are called *candidate keys*. They all may be candidates for the PRIMARY KEY, but only one can be chosen. Unique indexes can still be used on the other candidate keys to preserve uniqueness in that column or set of columns. Selecting a specific candidate key to be the PRIMARY KEY is a database design decision. After the PRIMARY KEY is selected, the other candidate keys are then known as *alternate keys*.

The PRIMARY KEY constraint can be created either when you first create a table, or it can be added later by modifying a table. When using CREATE TABLE, use the keyword CONSTRAINT to define the constraint, as the following example illustrates. (Refer to SQL Server Books Online for the complete CREATE TABLE syntax.)

Here is the partial T-SQL syntax:

```
CONSTRAINT constraint_name
    PRIMARY KEY [CLUSTERED | NONCLUSTERED]
    {column(,...n)}
```

The following example shows how to create a PRIMARY KEY constraint within the CRE-
ATE TABLE statement:

```
CREATE TABLE Employees
(
    Employee_ID     smallint        NOT NULL IDENTITY(1000,1),

    SSN             char(9)         NOT NULL,
    FName           varchar(50)     NOT NULL,
    Middle          char(1)         NULL,
    LName           varchar(50)     NOT NULL,
    BirthDate       smalldatetime   NULL,

    Salary          smallmoney      NULL,

    Department_ID   smallint        NOT NULL,

    Active_Flag     char(1)         NOT NULL DEFAULT 'Y',

    CONSTRAINT PK_Employees_Employee_ID PRIMARY KEY CLUSTERED

        ( Employee_ID   ASC )

)
```

The CONSTRAINT clause in the previous statement creates a PRIMARY KEY constraint
named *PK_Employees_Employee_ID* on column *Employee_ID*. The index created, which
has the same name as the constraint, is a clustered index on the *Employee_ID* column
arranged in ascending order.

To add a PRIMARY KEY constraint to an existing table, use the ALTER TABLE command:

```
ALTER TABLE Employees

ADD CONSTRAINT PK_Employees_Employee_ID PRIMARY KEY CLUSTERED

    ( Employee_ID   ASC )
```

SQL Server 2005 Database Engine will validate the key to guarantee that the key meets
the following rules for primary keys:

- The column or columns do not contain and will not allow NULL values.  If using
  SQL Server Management Studio, the column or columns will be automatically converted to NOT NULL when the key is created.

- There are no duplicate values.

If these rules are not met, an error will be returned and the primary key will not be
created.

To create a PRIMARY KEY constraint using SQL Server Management Studio, follow these steps from the Object Explorer:

1. In Object Explorer view, connect to the server instance of your choice, and then expand the server's Databases folder.

2. Expand Tables, right-click the table you want to work with, and then select Modify on the shortcut menu.

3. Click the row selector for the column you want to define as the primary key. For multiple columns, hold down the CTRL key while you click the row selectors. Each column will be highlighted as you select it.

4. Right-click the row selector for the column and select Set Primary Key on the shortcut menu.

5. A primary key symbol (a key) icon will be displayed in the row selector of the column(s) of the primary key, as shown in Figure 13-1.

6. Save the changes (CTRL+S). A primary key index, named "PK" followed by the table name, is automatically created in the background.

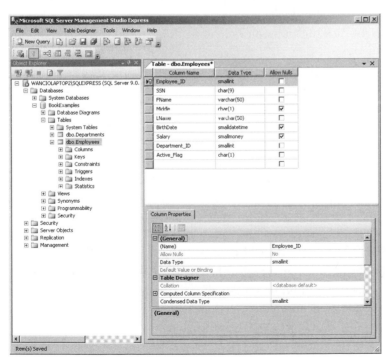

**Figure 13-1**   Setting a PRIMARY KEY constraint.

To drop a PRIMARY KEY constraint, use the ALTER TABLE command. Only the constraint name is necessary. For example, to drop the constraint we created previously, use the following statement:

```
ALTER TABLE Employees
DROP CONSTRAINT PK_Employees_Employee_ID
```

A PRIMARY KEY constraint cannot be dropped if it is referenced by a FOREIGN KEY constraint in another table. First, you must delete the FOREIGN KEY constraint; then you will be able to delete the PRIMARY KEY constraint. In addition, a PRIMARY KEY constraint cannot be dropped if there is a PRIMARY XML index applied to the table. The index would have to be deleted first.

---

**Note**   To change an existing PRIMARY KEY constraint, you must first drop the constraint and then create the new constraint. Both of these tasks can be accomplished using the ALTER TABLE command as shown in the previous T-SQL examples.

---

To drop a PRIMARY KEY constraint using SQL Server Management Studio, follow these steps from the Object Explorer:

1. In Object Explorer view, connect to the server instance of your choice, and then expand the server's Databases folder.

2. Expand Tables, right-click the table you want to work with, and then select Modify on the shortcut menu.

3. Right-click the row selector for the column of the current primary key, and then select Remove Primary Key on the shortcut menu.

4. Save the changes (CTRL-S).

## UNIQUE Constraints

Like the PRIMARY KEY constraint, the UNIQUE constraint ensures that a column or a set of columns will not allow duplicate values. But unlike the PRIMARY KEY constraint, the UNIQUE constraint will allow NULL as one of the unique values—only one NULL value is allowed per column as it is treated like any other value and must be unique. There can also be more than one UNIQUE constraint on a table. Both PRIMARY KEY and UNIQUE constraints can also be referenced by a FOREIGN KEY constraint.

SQL Server 2005 enforces entity integrity with the UNIQUE constraint by creating a unique index on the selected column or set of columns. Unless a clustered index is explicitly specified, a unique, nonclustered index is created by default.

The UNIQUE constraint can be created either when you create or modify a table. When using CREATE TABLE, use the keyword CONSTRAINT to define the constraint. (Refer to SQL Server Books Online for the complete CREATE TABLE syntax.)

Here is the partial T-SQL syntax:

```
CONSTRAINT constraint_name
    UNIQUE [CLUSTERED | NONCLUSTERED] {column(,...n)}
```

The following example shows how to create a UNIQUE constraint within the CREATE TABLE statement:

```
CREATE TABLE Employees
(
    Employee_ID     smallint        NOT NULL IDENTITY(1000,1),

    SSN             char(9)         NOT NULL,
    FName           varchar(50)     NOT NULL,
    Middle          char(1)         NULL,
    LName           varchar(50)     NOT NULL,
    BirthDate       smalldatetime   NULL,

    Salary          smallmoney      NULL,

    Department_ID   smallint        NOT NULL,

    Active_Flag     char(1)         NOT NULL DEFAULT 'Y',

    CONSTRAINT PK_Employees_Employee_ID PRIMARY KEY CLUSTERED

        ( Employee_ID ASC ),

    CONSTRAINT IX_Employees UNIQUE NONCLUSTERED

        ( SSN ASC )

)
```

The last CONSTRAINT clause in the previous SQL statement will create a UNIQUE constraint named *IX_Employees*, on column *SSN*. The index created will be nonclustered with *SSN* in ascending order.

To add a UNIQUE constraint to an existing table, use the ALTER TABLE command. If the Employees table already exists, we can add the UNIQUE constraint as follows:

```
ALTER TABLE Employees

ADD CONSTRAINT IX_Employees UNIQUE NONCLUSTERED

    ( SSN ASC )
```

To create a UNIQUE constraint using SQL Server Management Studio, follow these steps from the Object Explorer:

1.  In Object Explorer view, connect to the server instance of your choice, and then expand the server's Databases folder.

2. Expand Tables, right-click the table you want to work with, and then select Modify on the shortcut menu.

3. Right-click the table grid anywhere and select Indexes/Keys on the shortcut menu. The Indexes/Keys dialog box will be displayed, as shown in Figure 13-2.

4. Click the Add button.

5. Highlight Columns in the General section of the properties grid on the right and then click the ellipsis button (…), and then select all the columns and the sort order for the Unique index.

6. Click OK when finished to close dialog box.

7. For Type, select Unique Key from the drop-down list, as shown in Figure 13-3.

8. Click Close to close the Indexes/Keys dialog box.

9. Save the changes (CTRL-S). This will create the constraint.

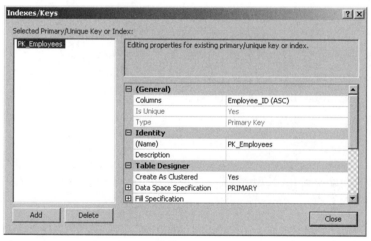

**Figure 13-2**    Indexes/Keys dialog box.

To drop a UNIQUE constraint, you will also use the ALTER TABLE command. Again, only the constraint name is necessary:

```
ALTER TABLE Employees
```

```
DROP CONSTRAINT IX_Employees
```

Similar to a PRIMARY KEY constraint, a UNIQUE constraint cannot be dropped if it is referenced by a FOREIGN KEY constraint in another table. First, you must delete the FOREIGN KEY constraint, and then you can delete the UNIQUE constraint.

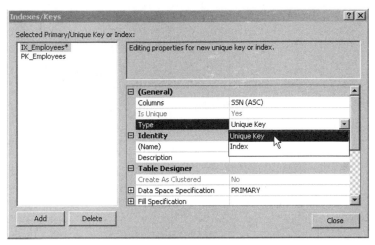

**Figure 13-3**  Creating a UNIQUE constraint.

---

**Note**  To change an existing UNIQUE constraint, you must first drop the constraint and then create the new constraint. Both of these tasks can be accomplished using the ALTER TABLE command, as shown in the previous examples.

---

To drop a UNIQUE constraint using SQL Server Management Studio, follow these steps from the Object Explorer:

1.  In Object Explorer view, connect to the server instance of your choice, and then expand the server's Databases folder.

2.  Expand Tables, right-click the table you want to work with, and then select Modify on the shortcut menu.

3.  Right-click anywhere on the table grid and select Indexes/Keys on the shortcut menu. The Indexes/Keys dialog box will be displayed, as shown previously in Figure 13-2.

4.  Select the desired unique key index name to drop, and click the Delete button.

5.  Click Close to close the dialog box.

6.  Save the changes (CTRL-S). This will drop the constraint.

## FOREIGN KEY Constraints

A FOREIGN KEY (FK) is a column or set of columns that is used to establish a relationship between two tables. The FOREIGN KEY constraint governs the link between the parent, or referenced, table and the child, or referencing, table. This constraint enforces data referential integrity (DRI) between tables. The number and data type of the column or columns in the parent table key must match the number and data type of the column or columns in the child table.

Generally, the link is between the PRIMARY KEY of the parent table and the FOREIGN KEY of the child table. The column or columns from the parent table are not required to be the PRIMARY KEY; the column or columns can be from another alternate key or any other column or set of columns that have a UNIQUE constraint.

The relationship does not have to be between two separate tables. The FOREIGN KEY constraint can be defined on the same table that it references. A table may have a column that is a FOREIGN KEY linked back to the same table's PRIMARY KEY or UNIQUE KEY. This is known as a *self-referencing relationship*. For example, assume there was a "Manager_ID" column in the example Employees tables. The Manager_ID column would contain the Employee_ID value of the manager of the current employee record. A FOREIGN KEY constraint would be defined on the Manager_ID of the Employees table (child), to the Employee_ID of the Employees table (parent).

---

**Note** The FOREIGN KEY column or columns are not required to be the same name as in the parent table, although this is a good convention to follow to help eliminate confusion. This is not possible in a self-referencing relationship.

---

Once the FOREIGN KEY constraint is created, rules are enforced by the database engine to ensure data referential integrity. When a row is inserted into the child table with the FOREIGN KEY constraint, the values to be inserted into the column or columns defined as the foreign key are checked against the values in the key of the referenced, or parent, table. If no row in the referenced table matches the values in the foreign key, the row cannot be inserted. The database engine will raise an error. A NULL value is allowed in the FOREIGN KEY column or columns if the columns themselves allow NULLs (even though NULLs are not allowed in the PRIMARY KEY of the parent table). In the case of a NULL value, the database engine will bypass the verification of the constraint.

If a key value in either the parent or child table is changed, the FOREIGN KEY constraint enforces validation of the change before it is made. For example, if an attempt is made to change the current child value, the new value must exist in the parent table. If an attempt is made to change or delete the current parent value, the current value must not exist in a child table. A FOREIGN KEY constraint does not allow you to delete or update a row from the parent table if the value exists as a FOREIGN KEY in the child table unless you are using the CASCADE action, shown below. All rows with matching values must first be deleted or changed in the child table before those rows can be deleted in the parent table.

An exception to this rule is if the FOREIGN KEY constraint is created using the ON UPDATE and/or ON DELETE options. These options have the following four referential actions:

- **NO ACTION**   The default action; the FOREIGN KEY constraint is strictly enforced so that an error is raised if the parent row is deleted or updated to a new value and the value exists in the child table.

- **CASCADE**   The database engine automatically deletes or updates all rows in the child table with the matching foreign key values which correspond to the rows affected in the parent table. There are no errors or messages in this case, so be sure this behavior is what you expect.

- **SET NULL**   The database engine automatically sets all of the matching foreign key values in the child table to NULL.

- **SET DEFAULT**   The database engine automatically sets all of the matching foreign key values in the child table to the DEFAULT value for the column.

> **Note**   FOREIGN KEY constraints, unlike PRIMARY KEY constraints, are not automatically indexed by the database engine. They are excellent candidates for an index if the constraint is often validated by modification statements, or used in joins, and should therefore be explicitly indexed.

The FOREIGN KEY constraint can be created either when you create or modify a table. When using CREATE TABLE, use the keyword CONSTRAINT to define the constraint. (Refer to SQL Server Books Online for the complete CREATE TABLE syntax.)

Here is the partial T-SQL syntax:

```
CONSTRAINT constraint_name
    FOREIGN KEY [column(,...n)]
    REFERENCES ref_table[(ref_column(,...n))]
    [ ON DELETE { NO ACTION | CASCADE | SET NULL | SET DEFAULT
} ]
    [ ON UPDATE { NO ACTION | CASCADE | SET NULL | SET DEFAULT
} ]
```

The following example will create a *Departments* table with a PRIMARY KEY constraint and an *Employee* table with a FOREIGN KEY constraint:

```
CREATE TABLE Departments
(
    Department_ID    smallint      NOT NULL IDENTITY(10,1),
    Dept_Name        varchar(150)  NOT NULL,
```

```
        CONSTRAINT PK_Departments_Department_ID PRIMARY KEY CLUSTERED

            ( Department_ID ASC )

)
CREATE TABLE Employees
(
        Employee_ID      smallint        NOT NULL IDENTITY(1000,1),

        SSN              char(9)         NOT NULL,
        FName            varchar(50)     NOT NULL,
        Middle           char(1)         NULL,
        LName            varchar(50)     NOT NULL,
        BirthDate        smalldatetime   NULL,

        Salary           smallmoney      NULL,

        Department_ID    smallint        NOT NULL,

        Active_Flag      char(1)         NOT NULL DEFAULT 'Y',

        CONSTRAINT PK_Employees_Employee_ID PRIMARY KEY CLUSTERED

            ( Employee_ID ASC ),

        CONSTRAINT FK_Employees_Departments FOREIGN KEY ( Department_ID )

            REFERENCES  Departments ( Department_ID )

            ON UPDATE CASCADE

            ON DELETE NO ACTION

)
```

The last CONSTRAINT clause in the previous SQL statement will create a FOREIGN KEY constraint between the *Employees* table (the referencing, or child, table) and the *Departments* table (the referenced, or parent, table). The ON UPDATE and ON DELETE options are also specified. With the ON UPDATE CASCADE option, if the *Department_ID* is modified (updated to new values) in the *Departments* table, all matching foreign keys in the *Employees* table will also be changed to the new value. With the ON DELETE NO ACTION option, if an attempt is made to delete a row in the *Departments* table, and a row with a matching value in the FOREIGN KEY column exists in the child table, then an error occurs and the DELETE statement will not be executed. Business rules must be well-defined to determine what action should be taken in these cases. This is just an example.

The FOREIGN KEY constraint can also be created on existing tables using the ALTER TABLE command. By default, the SQL Server 2005 database engine will validate the data in the FOREIGN KEY when the constraint is created. There is an option to bypass this check by specifying WITH NOCHECK in the ALTER TABLE command. Using WITH NOCHECK will allow existing rows that do not meet the foreign key criteria to remain intact, and any rows thereafter that are added, deleted, or inserted will be validated against the constraint.

Here is an example of using ALTER TABLE to add a FOREIGN KEY constraint:

```
ALTER TABLE Employees WITH NOCHECK
ADD CONSTRAINT FK_Employees_Departments FOREIGN KEY ( Department_ID )
  REFERENCES  Departments ( Department_ID )
   ON UPDATE CASCADE
   ON DELETE NO ACTION
```

To create a FOREIGN KEY constraint using SQL Server Management Studio, follow these steps from the Object Explorer:

1.  In Object Explorer view, connect to the server instance of your choice, and then expand the server's Databases folder.

2.  Expand Tables, then expand the table you want to work with.

3.  Right-click Keys and select New Foreign Key on the shortcut menu.

4.  The Foreign-Key Relationships dialog box will be displayed as shown in Figure 13-4.

5.  The relationship appears in the Selected Relationship list with a system-provided name in the format FK_<tablename>_<tablename>, where tablename is the name of the foreign key table.

6.  Select the new relationship name in the Selected Relationship list.

7.  Click on Tables And Columns Specification in the grid, then click the ellipsis (...) to the right of the property. This will bring up the Tables And Columns dialog box as shown in Figure 13-5.

8.  In the Primary key table drop-down list, select the table that will be on the primary-key side of the relationship.

9.  In the grid beneath, select the column or columns contributing to the table's primary or unique key.

10. In the adjacent grid cell to the right of each column, select the corresponding FOR-EIGN KEY column of the FOREIGN KEY table. See Figure 13-5.

11. Table Designer suggests a name for the relationship. To change this name, edit the contents of the Relationship name text box.

12. Click OK to close the dialog box, then click Close to close the Relationship window.

13. Save changes (CTRL+S). A Save dialog box will be displayed asking for confirmation to save changes to both tables (parent and child), as shown in Figure 13-6. Click Yes. This will create the relationship.

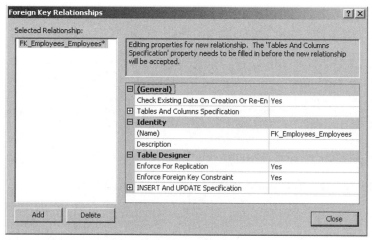

**Figure 13-4** Foreign-Key Relationships dialog box.

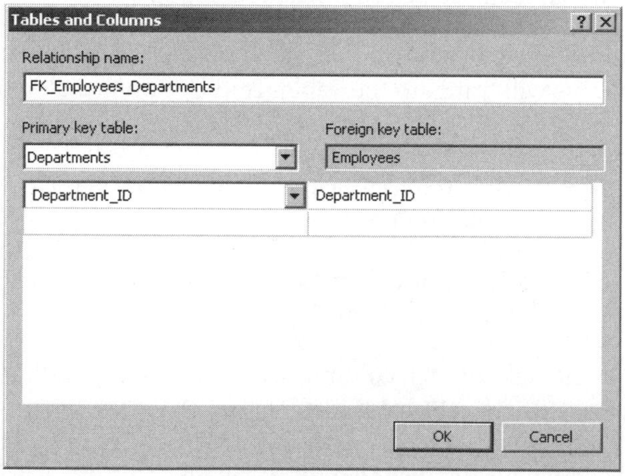

**Figure 13-5** Foreign Key Tables And Columns dialog box.

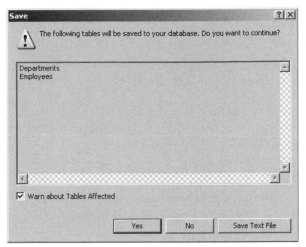

**Figure 13-6**   Foreign Key Save dialog box.

To drop a FOREIGN KEY constraint, you will also use the ALTER TABLE command; only the constraint name is necessary:

```
ALTER TABLE Employees

DROP CONSTRAINT FK_Employees_Departments
```

> **Note**   To change an existing FOREIGN KEY constraint, you must first drop the constraint and then create the new constraint. Both of these tasks can be accomplished using the ALTER TABLE command as shown in the previous examples.

To drop a FOREIGN KEY constraint using SQL Server Management Studio, follow these steps from the Object Explorer:

1. In Object Explorer view, connect to the server instance of your choice, and then expand the server's Databases folder.

2. Expand Tables, then expand the table you want to work with.

3. Expand Keys.

4. Right-click the desired relationship name and select Delete from the shortcut menu.

5. In the Delete Object dialog box, click OK to confirm delete.

An existing FOREIGN KEY constraint can also be enabled or disabled. Disabling a constraint keeps the constraint defined on the table, but the data is no longer validated on inserts, updates, or deletes. At some point when the constraint is enabled, you can specify whether you want the database to validate the existing data. The default for enabling a constraint is not to validate the data (WITH NOCHECK). The ALTER TABLE command is used with an argument of CHECK CONSTRAINT to enable a constraint and NOCHECK CONSTRAINT to disable an existing constraint.

Now why would you want to create a constraint just to disable it? Consider the case when a more complicated set of operations must be followed in which a PRIMARY KEY is affected, something that the basic FOREIGN KEY constraint is not capable of handling. For example, assume that a row will be deleted from the parent table, and other tables aside from the child table should be checked for some value before action is taken. A FOREIGN KEY constraint cannot perform action on tables outside of the table on which the constraint is defined. In this and other cases, you will have to create a trigger, write code in the application, or code a stored procedure to perform the checks on the other tables. But if the effect of these checks is in essence to maintain a FOREIGN KEY relationship, then it is helpful to see that relationship defined (although disabled) on the those tables as well when looking at the table properties, if only as an indication that the relationship is being validated even though this validation does not happen through the FOREIGN KEY constraint. It is used just for clarity.

Another reason you may want to disable a FOREIGN KEY constraint is to temporarily allow changes that would otherwise violate the constraint. The constraint can then be re-enabled using WITH NOCHECK to enforce the foreign key once again.

---

**Note** It is best practice and more efficient to use FOREIGN KEY constraints for referential integrity where possible rather than coding through triggers or other methods. Constraints are checked before modifications are executed, thus avoiding unnecessary rollback of the data modification if the constraint is violated.

---

The following ALTER TABLE statement disables the constraint:

```
ALTER TABLE Employees
    NOCHECK CONSTRAINT FK_Employees_Departments
```

This statement enables the constraint and checks that existing values meet the constraint criteria.

```
ALTER TABLE Employees
    CHECK CONSTRAINT FK_Employees_Departments
    WITH CHECK
```

To enable or disable a FOREIGN KEY constraint using SQL Server Management Studio, follow these steps from the Object Explorer:

1.  Start SQL Server Management Studio. In Object Explorer view, connect to the server instance of your choice, and then expand the server's Databases folder.

2.  Expand Tables, then expand the table you want to work with.

3.  Expand Keys.

4.  Right-click the desired FOREIGN KEY constraint name and select Modify on the shortcut menu. The Foreign-Key Relationships dialog box will be displayed as previously shown in Figure 13-4.

5.  For the property Enforce Foreign Key Constraint in the grid, select Yes to enable or No to disable.

6.  Click Close to close the dialog box.

7.  Save changes (CTRL-S).

## CHECK Constraints

The CHECK constraint is used to enforce domain integrity by restricting the values allowed in a column to specific values. CHECK constraints contain a logical (Boolean) expression, similar to the WHERE clause of a query, that causes the database to evaluate whether the value of an inserted or updated record fits the criteria of the CHECK constraint. If the expression evaluates to *false* (meaning the value is not within the allowed set of values), the database does not execute the modification statement, and SQL Server returns an error.

A CHECK constraint can be created with any logical expression that returns *true* or *false* based on the logical operators. You can use any of the logical operators in your expression such as =, <>, >, <, <=, >=, IN, BETWEEN, LIKE, IS NULL, NOT, AND, OR, and so on. You can also use built-in functions, reference other columns, and even use a subquery. You can apply multiple CHECK constraints to a single column, and you can apply a single CHECK constraint to multiple columns by creating it at the table level.

---

**Note**   CHECK constraints are validated only during INSERT and UPDATE statements, not during DELETE statements.

---

The CHECK constraint can be created when you either create or modify a table. When using CREATE TABLE, use the keyword CONSTRAINT to define the constraint. (Refer to SQL Server Books Online for the complete CREATE TABLE syntax.)

Here is the partial T-SQL syntax:

```
CONSTRAINT constraint_name
    CHECK ( logical_expression )
```

The following example creates a table with a CHECK constraint:

```
CREATE TABLE Employees
(
    Employee_ID     smallint        NOT NULL IDENTITY(1000,1),

    SSN             char(9)         NOT NULL,
    FName           varchar(50)     NOT NULL,
    Middle          char(1)         NULL,
    LName           varchar(50)     NOT NULL,
    BirthDate       smalldatetime   NULL,

    Salary          smallmoney      NULL,

    Department_ID   smallint        NOT NULL,

    Active_Flag     char(1)         NOT NULL DEFAULT 'Y',

    CONSTRAINT PK_Employees_Employee_ID PRIMARY KEY CLUSTERED

        ( Employee_ID ASC ),

    CONSTRAINT IX_Employees UNIQUE NONCLUSTERED

        ( SSN ASC ),

    CONSTRAINT CK_Employees_Salary

        CHECK (Salary > 0 AND Salary <= 1000000)
)
```

The last CONSTRAINT clause in the previous SQL statement will create a CHECK constraint named *CK_Employees_Salary* that restricts the value of the *Salary* field to a value greater than zero and less than or equal to one million.

To add a CHECK constraint to an existing table, use the ALTER TABLE command. When you add a CHECK constraint, existing values in the table are by default checked for compliance with the constraint, and if there are values that violate the constraint, an error is returned. The WITH NOCHECK option can be specified to bypass validation of existing data.

Assuming the *Employees* table already exists, we can add the CHECK constraint as follows:

```
ALTER TABLE Employees

ADD CONSTRAINT CK_Employees_Salary

    CHECK (Salary > 0 AND Salary <= 1000000)
```

To create a CHECK constraint using SQL Server Management Studio, follow these steps from the Object Explorer:

1. In Object Explorer view, connect to the server instance of your choice, and then expand the server's Databases folder.

2. Expand Tables, then expand the table you want to work with.

3. Right-click Constraints and select New Constraint on the shortcut menu. The Check Constraints dialog box will be displayed as shown in Figure 13-7.

4. A new relationship appears in the Selected Check Constraints list with a system-provided name in the format CK_<*tablename*>.

5. Click on Expression in the grid, then click the ellipsis (...) to the right of the property. The Check Constraints Expression dialog box will be displayed as shown in Figure 13-8.

6. Enter your logical expression. For example: (Salary > 0 AND Salary <= 1000000).

7. Click OK to close the Expression dialog box, then click Close to close the Check Constraints dialog box.

8. Save changes (CTRL-S). This will create the CHECK constraint.

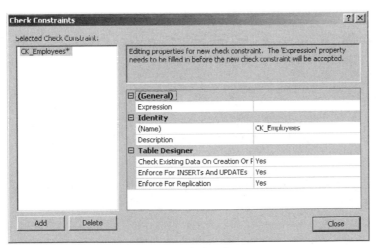

**Figure 13-7**   Check Constraints dialog box.

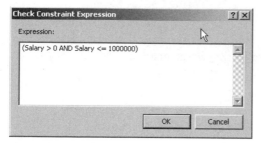

**Figure 13-8**   Check Constraints Expression dialog box.

To drop a CHECK constraint, use the ALTER TABLE command; only the constraint name is necessary:

```
ALTER TABLE Employees
DROP CONSTRAINT CK_Employees_Salary
```

---

**Note**   Previous versions of SQL Server allowed defining rules for similar functionality to CHECK constraints, using the CREATE RULE and DROP RULE commands. These are deprecated commands that will not be supported in future versions of SQL Server.

---

To drop a CHECK constraint using SQL Server Management Studio, follow these steps from the Object Explorer:

1.  In Object Explorer view, connect to the server instance of your choice, and then expand the server's Databases folder.

2.  Expand Tables, then expand the table you want to work with.

3.  Expand Constraints.

4.  Right-click on the desired constraint name and select Delete from the shortcut menu.

5.  The Delete Object dialog box will be displayed as shown in Figure 13-9. Click OK to confirm deletion.

---

**Note**   To change an existing CHECK constraint, you must first drop the constraint and then create the new constraint. You can use the ALTER TABLE command as shown in the previous examples.

---

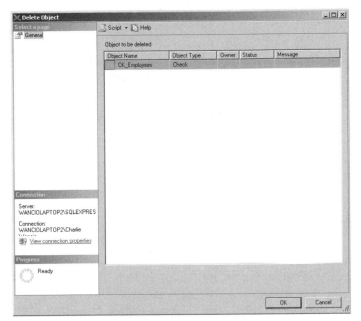

**Figure 13-9** Delete Object dialog box.

An existing CHECK constraint can also be enabled or disabled, just like a FOREIGN KEY constraint. Disabling a constraint keeps the constraint defined on the table, but the data is no longer validated on inserts and updates. When the constraint is enabled, you have the option of specifying whether you want the database to validate the existing data. The default for enabling a constraint is not to validate the data (WITH NOCHECK). The ALTER TABLE command is used with an argument of CHECK CONSTRAINT to enable the constraint, and NOCHECK CONSTRAINT to disable the existing constraint.

This statement disables the constraint:

```
ALTER TABLE Employees
    NOCHECK CONSTRAINT CK_Employees_Salary
```

This statement enables the constraint and validates the existing data:

```
ALTER TABLE Employees WITH CHECK
    CHECK CONSTRAINT CK_Employees_Salary
```

To enable or disable a CHECK constraint using SQL Server Management Studio, follow these steps from the Object Explorer:

1. In Object Explorer view, connect to the server instance of your choice, and then expand the server's Databases folder.

2. Expand Tables, then expand the table you want to work with.

3. Expand Constraints.

4. Right-click the desired constraint name and select Modify on the shortcut menu. The Check Constraints dialog box will be displayed as previously shown in Figure 13-7.

5. For the property Enforce for INSERTs and UPDATEs in the grid, select Yes to enable or No to disable.

6. Click Close to close the dialog box.

7. Save changes (CTRL-S).

## NULL and NOT NULL Constraints

The NULL and NOT NULL constraints are used on a column in a table to allow or prevent null values from being inserted into that column. A NULL constraint allows NULL values, and a NOT NULL constraint does not allow NULL values in the column. This type of constraint is used to enforce domain integrity, or what values are allowed in a column.

You should use NOT NULL instead of NULL whenever possible because operations that deal with null values, such as comparisons, require more processing overhead. It is better to use a DEFAULT (discussed in the next section), when possible, than to allow null values.

---

**Note**   You should always define a column explicitly as NULL or NOT NULL. NOT NULL is the SQL Server default, but the server defaults can be changed and different environments may have different values. It is recommended to use NOT NULL where possible or create a DEFAULT instead of allowing a null value.

---

The NULL and NOT NULL constraints can be created either when you create or modify a table. When using CREATE TABLE, use the keyword NULL or NOT NULL when specifying a column to define the constraint. (Refer to SQL Server Books Online for the complete CREATE TABLE syntax.)

Here is the partial T-SQL syntax:

```
CREATE TABLE
    table_name
    (
        column_name <data_type> [ NULL | NOT NULL ]
    )
```

To change the constraint of an existing column, use the ALTER TABLE - ALTER COLUMN command.

Here is the partial T-SQL syntax:

```
ALTER TABLE table_name
    ALTER COLUMN column_name <data_type> [ NULL | NOT NULL ]
```

> **Note**   The data type of the column must be specified when you are changing the NULL or NOT NULL constraint. If the data type is to remain the same, simply specify the current column data type.

NOT NULL can be specified in ALTER COLUMN only if the column currently contains no null values. The null values must be updated to some value before you can use the ALTER COLUMN with NOT NULL. A table update could be executed that updates all existing null values to some default value to accomplish this.

Refer to Chapter 11 for more details on creating tables using NULL and NOT NULL columns.

## DEFAULT Definitions

A DEFAULT definition on a column provides automatic entry of a default value for a column when an INSERT statement does not specify the value for that column. DEFAULT constraints enforce domain integrity as well. A DEFAULT definition can assign a constant value, the value of a system function, or NULL to a column. DEFAULT can be used on any column except IDENTITY columns and columns of data type *timestamp*.

The DEFAULT constraint applies only to INSERT statements, and the value is applied to the column only if a value is not explicitly set for the column in the INSERT statement.

> **Note**   Specifying a NULL value for a column within an INSERT statement is not the equivalent of leaving the column value unspecified. The database engine will not use the column DEFAULT in that case, but rather a NULL value will be entered in the column.

The DEFAULT definition can be created when you either create or modify a table. When using CREATE TABLE, use the keyword DEFAULT when specifying a column to define the constraint. (Refer to SQL Server Books Online for the complete CREATE TABLE syntax.)

Here is the partial T-SQL syntax:

```
CREATE TABLE
    table_name
    (
        column_name <data_type> [ DEFAULT constant_expression ]
    )
```

The following example has several columns using a DEFAULT definition. Some use constants, one uses NULL, and one uses a system function:

```
CREATE TABLE Employees
(
    Employee_ID    smallint        NOT NULL IDENTITY(1000,1),

    SSN            char(9)         NOT NULL DEFAULT '000000000',
    FName          varchar(50)     NOT NULL,
    Middle         char(1)         NULL DEFAULT NULL,
    LName          varchar(50)     NOT NULL,
    HireDate       smalldatetime   NOT NULL DEFAULT GETDATE(),

    Salary         smallmoney      NULL DEFAULT 0,

    Department_ID  smallint        NOT NULL,

    Active_Flag    char(1)         NOT NULL DEFAULT 'Y'
)
```

To change the DEFAULT of an existing column, use the ALTER TABLE - ALTER COLUMN command.

Here is the partial T-SQL syntax:

```
ALTER TABLE table_name
    ALTER COLUMN column_name <data_type> [ DEFAULT constant_expression ]
```

---

**Note** The data type of the column must be specified when changing the DEFAULT definition. If the data type will remain the same, simply specify the current column data type.

---

NOT NULL can be specified in ALTER COLUMN only if the column currently contains no null values. The null values must be updated to some value before you can use the ALTER COLUMN with NOT NULL.

> **Note**  Previous versions of SQL Server used the CREATE DEFAULT and DROP DEFAULT commands for the creation and deletion of defaults. These are deprecated commands that will not be supported in future versions of SQL Server.

Refer to Chapter 11 for more details on creating tables and setting DEFAULT values for columns.

## Summary

In this chapter, we have learned the importance of database integrity and how to use the built-in capabilities of SQL Server 2005 to help ensure that the data in a database remains accurate and correct. The use of database constraints to enforce data integrity is the preferred method.

Domain, entity, and referential integrity are enforced with the various constraint types available in SQL Server:

- PRIMARY KEY Constraints

- UNIQUE Constraints

- FOREIGN KEY Constraints

- CHECK Constraints

- NULL and NOT NULL Constraints

- DEFAULT Definitions

All of these constraints were described in this chapter along with examples of how to create and modify each, using T-SQL and using SQL Server Management Studio. Following is a consolidated example of a table creation script displaying the use of all the constraints discussed in this chapter:

```
CREATE TABLE Departments
(
    Department_ID    smallint        NOT NULL IDENTITY(10,1),

    Dept_Name        varchar(150)    NOT NULL,

    CONSTRAINT PK_Departments_Department_ID PRIMARY KEY CLUSTERED

        ( Department_ID ASC )

)
CREATE TABLE Employees
(
    Employee_ID      smallint        NOT NULL IDENTITY(1000,1),
```

```
SSN            char(9)           NOT NULL,
FName          varchar(50)       NOT NULL,
Middle         char(1)           NULL,
LName          varchar(50)       NOT NULL,
BirthDate      smalldatetime     NULL,

Salary         smallmoney        NULL,

Department_ID  smallint          NOT NULL,

Active_Flag    char(1)           NOT NULL DEFAULT 'Y',
CONSTRAINT PK_Employees_Employee_ID PRIMARY KEY CLUSTERED

    ( Employee_ID ASC ),

CONSTRAINT FK_Employees_Departments FOREIGN KEY ( Department_ID )

    REFERENCES  Departments ( Department_ID )

    ON UPDATE CASCADE

    ON DELETE NO ACTION,

CONSTRAINT IX_Employees UNIQUE NONCLUSTERED

    ( SSN ASC ),

CONSTRAINT CK_Employees_Salary

    CHECK (Salary > 0 AND Salary <= 1000000)
)
```

There are more detailed options available for most of these constraints that were not covered in this chapter.

---

**More Info**   Refer to SQL Server Books Online for further options that can be used with these constraints.

# Chapter 14
# Backup Fundamentals

One of the most important roles of a DBA is performing regular backups of SQL Server data. Creating backups of critical business data should be one of the foremost concerns of a database administrator (DBA) because backups provide a way to restore data that otherwise could be completely lost. The DBA should also be concerned with performing occasional tests of restoring the database to ensure the process goes as planned without any glitches. When you have to restore a database because of a real loss of data, you don't want to find out that your strategy was incorrect.

There are many options and types of backup methods available for backing up transaction logs and database data. In order to design a good backup strategy for your particular needs, you must first understand how backups work and what you must do to protect all of your data. In this chapter you will learn about the reasons backups are necessary, the relationship between the transaction log and recovery, the differences among the recovery models, the various backup types and options, backup history tables, backing up system databases, and new backup features in SQL Server 2005.

There are several new features in SQL Server 2005 that provide enhanced backup and restore capabilities. These features provide more options, flexibility, and reliability for your backup process. The new or enhanced backup features that are discussed throughout this chapter include backing up to mirrored media, partial backups, copy-only backups, and full-text catalog backups.

# Why Perform Backups with a Highly Available System?

You may wonder whether backups are always necessary, particularly if your system is designed for high availability with redundant components, such as with disks drives protected by RAID fault tolerance (see Chapter 4, "I/O Subsystem Planning and RAID Configuration"), servers that are clustered for failover (with Microsoft Cluster Services and SQL Server 2005 Failover Clustering), and a fully redundant SAN storage system (see Chapter 7, "Choosing a Storage System for Microsoft SQL Server 2005"). These high-availability methods provide protection or failover capabilities only for certain software and hardware component failures, such as a power failure for one clustered server node or a single disk drive failure. However, they do not provide protection from all possible causes of data loss. Problems such as a user accidentally deleting data from the database, unexpected data corruption from a software or hardware failure, or an entire disk cabinet failure are not protected by typical high-availability or fault-tolerance methods. In addition, a disaster such as flooding, fire, or hurricane can also destroy your entire datacenter, including your data. In all of these cases, backups are necessary for recovering your data. In a disaster situation, the backups must also be stored at another site or they will also be destroyed. See Chapter 25, "Disaster Recovery Solutions," for more information on this topic.

> **Note**   Even if you have a fully redundant and highly available hardware system, you absolutely need to perform database backups of your critical business data. There is no substitute for database backups.

Backups are also useful in other cases not related to system failures and data loss. You could use a backup to set up database mirroring or to restore a database to a development or test system. You may also archive backup files over months or years so they are accessible if they are needed for an audit.

# System Failures That Require Backups

To to help you better understand when and why backups are required, we will discuss specific types and examples of failures from which data can be restored only if there is a backup of the database. One assumption made in this section is that there is no disaster recovery site, a secondary datacenter to which all data is replicated so that it could take over in the event of failure at the primary datacenter. You might conclude that you can always use the disaster recovery site as a " backup" site if you keep it up-to-date, but you should still always create backups of your data in case even the disaster recovery systems incur any of the failures we discuss below as well.

## Hardware Failures

As we've mentioned, you can protect your data from many hardware failures using high-availability solutions such as disk RAID and server clustering, but this does not cover all hardware failures. The following are possible hardware failures that require a database backup in order to restore the lost data:

- **Disk failure with no RAID** If you do not have RAID fault tolerance configured or if you are using RAID-0 for the disk drives where the SQL data and/or log files reside, then the failure of any disk drive causes data loss. In this case, the failed disk must be replaced and configured into the system, and the database must be restored from backups.

- **Catastrophic event** If a disaster occurs at the datacenter and the system hardware is damaged or destroyed, all data can be lost. In this case, an entirely new system would have to be built, and the data would have to be restored onto it from back-ups.

- **Multiple component failures** If more than one component fails at a time, such as multiple disks of a RAID array or the entire disk cabinet resulting in the array being unable to recover data by simply replacing disks, then a backup is needed to restore the data.

- **Security breach** There is the possibility that someone could purposely damage a system as an act of sabotage and destroy data.

There can be other unexpected scenarios that can cause data loss, such as data corruption on a disk caused by disk subsystem failures. All of these can be recovered only by restoring a database backup.

# Software Failures

In addition to hardware failure, there are possible software failures that require restoring data from a backup in order to recover your system. Software failures are not as common as hardware failures but can be more disastrous than them. The following are possible software failures for which you need backups for recovery:

- **Operating system failure**  If an operating system failure occurs relating to the I/O system, data can be corrupted on disk. Don't be alarmed because not all operating system failures cause data corruption. This is quite rare.

- **SQL Server failure**  Same as above, in that a database application failure can potentially cause data corruption but does not commonly do so.

- **Other application failure**  Another application on the server that would cause data to be corrupted on the disks could fail.

- **Accidental data deletion or modification**  For example, an administrator or developer could accidentally run a delete or update command on the production system that was meant to be run on a development system and corrupts data.

- **Security breach**  A person could purposely breach security to access data and make modifications that should not be made. In this case it might be easier to restore the database rather than trying to isolate the modifications.

The above scenarios are not common but are definitely possible. It's best to be sure you can recover from any unexpected failure by always having recent backups.

# Purpose of the Transaction Log

One very important component for performing proper backups and restores is the SQL Server transaction log. Every database has its own transaction log, which is implemented as one or more log files that reside on physical disk. The transaction log is used to record all transactions and the modifications that those transactions make to the database. The data in the log file is referred to as log records.

In general, the term transaction refers to a logical unit of work that can consist of queries and modifications to data. When referring to the transaction log, the term transaction refers specifically to data modifications only, for example, an UPDATE, INSERT, or DELETE operation, or a database schema change operation. Records of read-only queries performed by SELECT statements are not stored in the transaction log since they do not make any changes to data. Only transactions that perform data modifications are recorded in the log. Throughout this section as we discuss the transaction log, we use the term transaction to refer to one or more data modification operations.

Storing log records of transactions makes data recovery possible, which is the main purpose of the transaction log. There are also other uses for the transaction log that are discussed throughout this book, such as database mirroring, transactional replication, and log shipping.

To understand how the transaction log works, let's step through the process of a transaction. A single transaction can result in multiple changes to data, such as an update that modifies many rows in a table, and one transaction can therefore generate multiple log records. As a transaction occurs, changes to the associated database data pages (in the data files) are not immediatley written to disk. First, each page that will be modified is read into in the SQL Server buffer cache in memory, and the changes to that page(s) are made in memory. At this point, a log record is created in the log buffer in memory. (See Chapter 18, "Microsoft SQL Server 2005 Memory Configuration," for details about memory buffers.) As the log buffer fills or when the transaction commits, the log record or records for that transaction are written out to the log file on disk. If the transaction did commit, then the commit record is written out to the log disk as well. Note that when a transaction has committed, it is not considered complete in SQL Server until the commit record has been written to the log file on disk.

Whether a transaction has committed in the log file yet or not, once a data modification record is written to the log file for that transaction, then any changes that are made to associated data pages in memory during the transaction may now be written to disk (to the data files). These pages are known as dirty pages because they have been modified in memory but not on disk, thus the data is not yet "permanent." The modified data pages will be actually written to disk at a later time as they are flushed out from the data buffer in memory through various SQL Server automatic operations. Once the dirty pages are written to disk, the data is now "permanent" in the database. If the transaction rolls back rather than committing, then these data changes on disk are rolled back as well by using the records in the log file to reverse the effects of the transaction.

In other words, there can be uncommitted transaction records in the log file if records are flushed from the log buffer before the transaction has committed. The records are considered uncommitted, or active, until the entire transaction finishes and the commit record is written to the log file. The uncommitted records are stored in order to allow SQL Server to perform data recovery or rollback when necessary, as discussed in the next section. Active, uncommitted transactions cannot be truncated from the log file such that large, long-running transactions are often a source of excessive log file growth.

**Note**  SQL Server requires that a transaction is written to the log file on disk first, before any data file changes are written to disk. Thus, the SQL Server transaction log is known as a write-ahead log. This guarantees that no data is written to disk until its associated log record is written to disk. Once the data is written to disk, it is made "permanent" in the database.

Since data changes are not written to disk immediately, the transaction log file is the only means by which transactions can be recovered in the event of a system failure. Any data in memory, including the data buffer cache and the log buffer cache, are lost in the event of system failure and therefore cannot be used for recovery. There are two ways in which the transaction log may be used for data recovery: through automatic recovery performed by SQL Server and through restoring backups of the transaction logs.

**Note**  Transaction log backups are required in order to recover a damaged database up to the point of failure. If SQL Server automatic recovery will not suffice and if you have only data backups without transaction log backups, then you can recover data only up to the last data backup. Therefore, be sure to perform transaction log backups for critical databases that allow modifications. If a database is read-only, then you do not need transaction log backups and can set the database to the simple recovery model as described later in the chapter.

# Microsoft SQL Server Automatic Recovery

SQL Server uses the records stored in the transaction log to perform automatic data recovery in the case of a power failure or an unclean shutdown of SQL Server in which data is not damaged or corrupted in any way. In this case, backups are not needed to recover the database. This is normal SQL Server operation. Automatic recovery occurs per database every time SQL Server starts up and occurs with all of the recovery models—simple, bulk-logged, or full—discussed in the next section. SQL Server always logs enough data in the transaction log to be able to perform automatic recovery when necessary, even with the simple recovery model.

When a system failure such as a power loss occurs, there may be transactions in flight, or active, that have uncommitted records written to the log file. There may also be committed transactions whose records were written to the log file with a commit record but whose associated changes to the data files have not yet been written. To resolve these inconsistencies and maintain data integrity, SQL Server performs automatic recovery on each database upon  restart. No user intervention is required other than restarting SQL Server.

During automatic recovery, transactions that were committed in the log file but whose data changes were not yet written to the data files are rolled forward, meaning that by reading the committed transaction records from the log and replaying those records (in other words, rolling forward the transaction), the appropriate data changes are written to the data files on disk and thus made permanent in the database. Any transactions that were not committed yet and have uncommitted records in the transaction log are rolled back, meaning the changes to the data files made by those records are reversed as if the transaction never started. This leaves each database in a consistent state.

# Recovery Models and Logging

Each database is configured with a particular SQL Server recovery model that determines the manner in which transaction logging and SQL Server recovery are handled. When you create a database, the recovery model for that database is set to the recovery model of the system *model* database. If you do not change the model database recovery model setting after SQL Server installation, then all user databases are created with the Full recovery model setting, the default of the model database. The recovery model can be changed using the Management Studio or T-SQL commands.

The following sections describe the three possible recovery models: simple, full, and bulk-logged. For all three recovery models, data backups must be taken to ensure that data can be recovered when automatic recovery will not suffice. The main difference between the types is the method in which transaction logs are managed and backed up.

## Simple Recovery Model

The simple recovery model provides the fewest capabilities for restoring data. You cannot restore data to a point in time with simple recovery, and only data backups, including differential backups, can be restored. This is because transaction log backups are not taken and are not even allowed with simple recovery model. This method requires the least administration and simplest restore method but provides no possibility to recover beyond the restore of the latest data backup.

When a database is set to use the simple recovery model, the transaction log for that database is automatically truncated after every database checkpoint and after every data backup. (Checkpoints occur automatically and are described in Chapter 18.) Truncating the log means that the inactive log records are simply dropped without any backup of them and that log space is freed up for reuse. Using simple recovery model also provides a log of the minimum information required for automatic recovery, so log space used is minimized. The information logged is just enough for SQL Server to be able to perform automatic recovery in case of a system crash, and to recover the database after a data restore. Thus, no explicit transaction log or log file space management is needed by the DBA.

Simple recovery model is useful in a variety of cases. First, databases that do not store critical business data such as development or test databases are a good candidate for simple recovery. These types of databases can be easily recreated as needed by restoring a backup of production data. You might not be concerned about recording data changes to the development database if you will not need to restore those changes for any reason. Usually, a development database is periodically refreshed from production instead.

Other good candidates for simple recovery are databases that store all or mostly read-only data, so that even if a small number of data changes do occur between data backups, these can easily be reproduced manually. If the database is completely read-only, then there are no data changes to be written to the log anyway.

On the other hand, if the database data is read-write and data is modified often, and if the data is critical such that you do not want to risk losing changes, then log backups are necessary. In this case, one of the other two recovery models must be chosen, full or bulk-logged.

## Full Recovery Model

The full recovery model provides the highest level of recovery capabilities: the ability to recover data to a specific point in time. To achieve this, data backups must be performed regularly and transaction log backups must be performed continuously, without gaps, between data backups. Each time the log file is backed up, the inactive log records are truncated, freeing up space to be reused. If no log backups are taken, the log will continue to grow, potentially until the disk is full. Therefore, you must set up log backups when using the full recovery model. With this model, all transactions are fully logged, including all bulk and index operations, making this the only model that allows full point-in-time recovery capabilities.

> **Note** To achieve the full capabilities of point-in-time recovery of data, the full recovery model must be used.

With full recovery model, log backups must be set up explicitly to run on a regular schedule, which is most commonly done by creating a database maintenance plan in SQL Server Management Studio or through a third-party backup management software.

> **Note**   Simply setting a database to full recovery model is not, in itself, enough
> to protect your data. You must create and schedule data and log backups to
> occur regularly. This is not done automatically by setting the full recovery model.

## Bulk-Logged Recovery Model

The bulk-logged recovery model is similar in behavior and capabilities to the full recovery model, and it also requires data and log backups for recovery. Bulk-logged model is a special case that is intended for use in conjunction with the full recovery model. It provides unique logging behavior for large bulk operations that cause a large number of transaction records to be written to the log file, which takes up significant disk space if performed under the full recovery model. With bulk-logged model, bulk operations are minimally logged, but all other transactions are still fully logged. Minimal logging of bulk operations provides better performance and greatly reduces the amount of space used in the log file.

Bulk operations that are minimally logged with bulk-logged recovery model include the following:

- Bulk imports of data using the bcp utility, OPENROWSET, or BULK INSERT
- SELECT INTO
- WRITETEXT or UPDATETEXT (note that these are deprecated commands in SQL Server 2005 and exist for backward compatibility)
- CREATE INDEX
- ALTER INDEX REBUILD (formerly known as DBCC DBREINDEX)
- DROP INDEX (when it causes a new heap rebuild such as when a clustered index is dropped)

There are two main benefits and purposes of setting the recovery model to bulk-logged before the above operations are performed. One benefit is an improvement in the performance of the operation itself and other activity on the system because of the reduced activity and reduced contention on the log file. The second benefit is a reduction of log file growth. Excessive log growth can be an issue when rebuilding or defragmenting indexes on large tables or when bulk loading data.

The ideal usage of the bulk-logged recovery model is to enable it just before a bulk operation will occur and then return to full recovery model when the operation is completed.

Switching between full and bulk-logged as needed is the recommended solution. See SQL Server Books Online for steps to take when switching between these two recovery models.

---

**Note**    The database mirroring feature requires that the database always remain in the full recovery model. Do not switch to bulk-logged in this case.

---

The main difference between log backups with bulk-logged versus full model is that with bulk-logged model any log backup that contains bulk-logged records must be restored completely to the end of that log backup file; you cannot restore in this case to a point in time within that log backup. So if bulk-logged recovery model is set and there is a database failure that requires data restoration, you cannot restore to a point in time within any of the log backups that contain bulk-logged records. You probably would not want to restore to a point in time during a bulk-logged operation anyway, as it might leave the database in an inconsistent or unknown state.

## Viewing and Changing the Recovery Model

The recovery model can be configured on a per-database basis. When a user database is created, it inherits the same recovery model as the SQL Server model database, the template for all user-created databases. The model database has full recovery model set by default when you install SQL Server. You can change the model database setting so all future user databases that are created inherit the new model database setting. You can also change the recovery model at any time per database without changing the model database setting. Be sure you understand the behavior and implications of each recovery model before selecting one.

---

**Note**    When you create a new user database, the recovery model is set to that of the model database. You can change the setting for the model database to affect all subsequently created user databases; the change will not affect the setting of any currently existing databases.

---

To change the recovery model using SQL Server Management Studio, perform the following steps:

1. Start SQL Server Management Studio. In Object Explorer view, connect to the server instance of your choice, and then expand the server's Databases folder.

2. Right-click the database name, and then click Properties on the shortcut menu.

3. Click Options in the left pane to view the Options page.

4. Select the Recovery Model from the drop-down list.

5. Click OK to save.

Figure 14-1 shows the Database Properties window with the Options page selected.

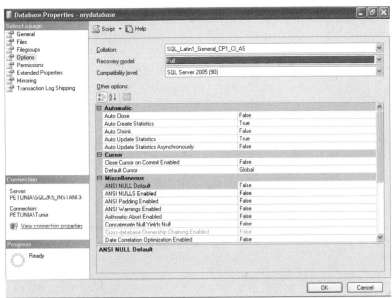

**Figure 14-1**   Recovery model on the Options page.

Here is the T-SQL code to set the recovery model to full for *mydatabase*:

```
USE master

ALTER DATABASE mydatabase SET RECOVERY FULL ;
```

Read SQL Server Books Online for more information about options associated with the ALTER DATABASE statement and for important steps regarding transaction log backups when switching between recovery models.

# Types of Backups

We've already discussed several topics involving transaction log backups, but of course transaction log backups cannot be used to restore a database by themselves. To restore a database, you must have a base backup of the data files. You can choose to back up only parts of a database at a time, such as a file or filegroup, or an entire database. The many different types of backups available can be confusing, so I will try to simplify them by highlighting when you might want to use each type. The different backup categories—data, differential, and log—and the types within each category are described in the following sections.

---

**Note**    Backups are an online process. When SQL Server performs a backup, the database being backed up remains online for users to access. Backups generate additional load on the system and can block user processes, so you absolutely want to schedule them during off-peak hours if possible to reduce overhead and contention as much as possible.

---

## Data Backups

The first major category of backups we will discuss is data backups. A data backup includes an image of one or more data files and enough log record data to allow recovery of the data upon restore. Data backups include the following three types:

- **Full database backup**    Includes all data files in the database; a complete set of data. A complete set of file or filegroup backups can be equivalent to a full database backup.

- **Partial backup**    New for SQL Server 2005; includes the primary filegroup and any read-write filegroups; excluding any read-only filegroups by default.

- **File or filegroup backup**    Includes only the file or filegroup specified.

### Full Database Backup

The full database backup is sometimes referred to simply as the "full backup." I prefer to call it "full database backup" to avoid confusion with a "full file backup" or "full filegroup backup." A full database backup is a backup of the entire database that contains all data files and the log records needed to recover the database to the point in time when the backup completed. Full database backups should be part of the backup strategy for all business-critical databases.

A full database backup contains the complete set of data needed to restore and recover a database to a consistent state—so it can be thought of as a baseline. Other backups may be restored on top of a restored full database backup—such as differential backups, partial backups, and log backups. However, all other backup types require a full database backup to be restored before they can be restored. You cannot restore only a differential, partial, or log backup by themselves.

## Real World   Create Useful T-SQL Backup/Restore Scripts from Management Studio

If you are working in Management Studio, you can easily create T-SQL scripts of the work you are performing or want to perform through the GUI. If you have a window such as a Properties window or a Task window open, click the Script button at the top of the window. You can pull down the Script menu to select where the script should be created—to a new query window, to the clipboard, to a file, or to a SQL Server job. For some Properties windows, you may have to make a change to a property before creating a script. For example, here is how to script a backup operation of the *Adventureworks* database:

1. Start SQL Server Management Studio. In Object Explorer view, connect to the server instance of your choice, and then expand the server's Databases folder.

2. Right-click the database name and select Tasks on the shortcut menu then Backup on the submenu. The Back Up Database window will appear as shown in Figure 14-2.

3. Set all of the appropriate backup options within the window.

4. Click the Script button to script to a new query window, or select another option from the Script drop-down list.

5. If you do not want to execute the backup at this time, click the Cancel button to close the Back Up Database window. If you click OK, the backup will be executed.

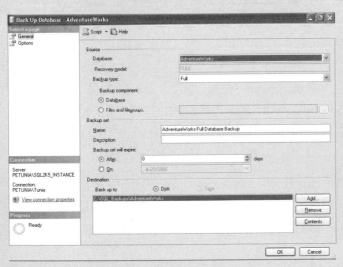

**Figure 14-2**   Scripting a backup operation.

## Partial Backup

The partial backup capability is new for SQL Server 2005. Partial backup is entirely different than a differential backup, which we describe later in this chapter. Partial backup is mainly intended for use with read-only databases that use the simple recovery model; however, it also works with full and bulk-logged recovery models. The partial backup always backs up both the primary filegroup and any filegroups that are read-write. A read-write filegroup allows data modifications to the files in that filegroup, in contrast with a read-only filegroup, which allows only reads of that filegroup. Read-only filegroups are not backed up with a partial backup unless they are explicitly specified in the backup command. Note too that the primary filegroup cannot be individually set to read-only. To force the primary filegroup to read-only, you can set an entire database to read-only.

---

**Important** The partial backup feature is intended for use with read-only databases using the simple recovery model. It is not the same as a differential backup. Partial backup still backs up entire filegroups, not just the changes, as the differential backup does.

---

The main purpose of the partial backup is to provide a faster and smaller backup for databases with one or more read-only filegroups that have been backed up at least once within a full database backup or a full file backup and that have had no changes made to them (since they are read-only). Thus, those filegroups do not need to be backed up again. Therefore, once you have a full database backup, you can use the partial backup to back up only those filegroups that have changed. When you restore, you first restore the full database backup, then restore the partial backups.

Since we are on the topic of read-only filegroups, here is how to set a filegroup to read-only using Management Studio:

1. Start SQL Server Management Studio. In Object Explorer view, connect to the server instance of your choice, and then expand the server's Databases folder.

2. Right-click the database name and select Properties on the shortcut menu.

3. Under Select a Page on the left, click Filegroups.

4. You will see a check box in the Read-Only column for filegroups other than Primary. Select the check box to set that filegroup to read-only, as shown in Figure 14-3.

5. Click OK to save the changes and close the Properties dialog box.

If a filegroup is set to read-only, all the files in that filegroup are read-only. Use the following steps to set an entire database to read-only using Management Studio:

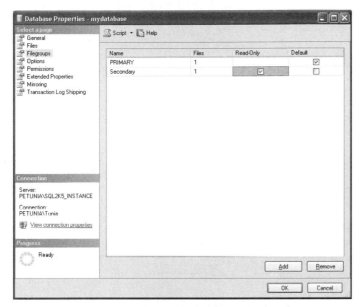

**Figure 14-3**    Setting a filegroup to read-only.

1. Start SQL Server Management Studio. In Object Explorer view, connect to the server instance of your choice, and then expand the server's Databases folder.

2. Right-click the database name and select Properties on the shortcut menu.

3. Under Select a Page at left, click Options.

4. Scroll down to the State section.

5. On the drop-down list next to Database Read-Only, select True to set the database to read-only, as shown in Figure 14-4.

6. Click OK to save changes and close the Properties dialog box.

If the entire database is set to read-only, then it is appropriate to use the simple recovery model and perform a full database backup without performing differential or parital backups because no data is modified.

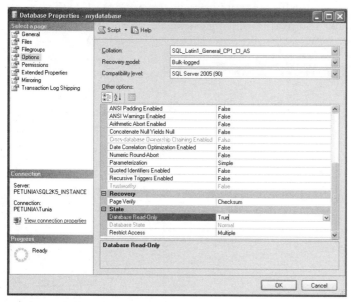

**Figure 14-4**   Setting a database to read-only.

## File and Filegroup Backup

As an alternative to performing a full database backup of the entire database at once, you can choose to backup only one file or filegroup at a time. This assumes that there are mutliple filegroups in the database (in addition to the primary filegroup). An individual file within a filegroup may be backed up, or an entire filegroup, which includes all the files within that filegroup, can be backed up. File or filegroup backups can be necessary when a database is so large that back up must be done in parts because it takes too long to back up the entire database at one time.

Another potential benefit of having a file backup is that if a disk on which a particular file resides fails and is replaced, just that file can be restored, instead of the entire database. This is not a common scenario, but it can happen. See Chapter 10, "Creating Databases and Database Snapshots," for more discussion about database file layout on disk.

To ensure that you can restore a complete copy of the database when needed, you must have either a full database backup as a baseline or a complete set of full backups for each of the files and/or filegroups in the database. A complete set of file or filegroup backups is equivalent to a full database backup. If you do not have a full database backup and do not have a complete backup set of all files, then you will not be able to restore the entire database.

In addition, when performing file or filegroup backups with full or bulk-logged recovery models, you must still back up transaction logs as well. When restoring, the logs must be applied after restoring a file or filegroup backup to roll forward transactions and maintain data consistency with the rest of the database. Only transactions that apply to the file or filegroup being restored are applied from the transaction log backups.

If a database is using the simple recovery model, only read-only filegroups are supported for filegroup backup because there are no log backups taken with simple recovery model. Therefore, if a filegroup in the database is read-write, there must be a full database backup taken so that the entire database can be restored if necessary. When restoring the data in this case, there are no transaction logs to restore, just the data backups.

As you may have guessed by now, one drawback of performing file or filegroup backups is that more administration and care are required with both the backup and restore strategy than with complete full database backups. You must be sure you always have a complete set of file or filegroup backups and the transaction log backups to go with them in order to recover from a full database failure. Complications also arise when you are restoring from multiple copies of file backups and possibly file differential backups. (Differential backups are covered in the next section.) On the other hand the benefits include faster backup times for a single filegroup backup versus an entire database backup. So in the case of a large database that takes too long to backup all at once, filegroup backups are a good option.

## Differential Backups

A differential backup backs up only the data that has changed since the last base backup. A differential backup is not a stand-alone backup—there must be a full backup that the differential is based on, called the base backup. Differential backups are a means of backing up data more quickly by backing up only changes in data that occurred since the last base backup, resulting in a smaller backup than a full backup. This may allow you to perform differential backups more frequently than you could perform full backups. A differential backup can be created on the database, partial, file, or filegroup level. For smaller databases, a full database differential is most common. For much larger databases, differential backups at the file or filegroup level might be needed to save space and to reduce backup time and the associated system overhead.

In addition to being faster and smaller than a full backup, a differential backup also makes the restore process simpler. When you restore using differentials, you must first restore the full base backup. Then, you restore the most recent differential backup that was taken. If multiple differentials were taken, you need to restore only the most recent one, not all of them. No log backups need to be restored between the full and differential backups. After the differential has been restored, then any log backups taken after the differential can be restored.

You may want to schedule differential backups often between full database backups to avoid having to restore lots of transaction log backups in the case of a failure. For example, you might take full database backups on the weekend and take a differential database backup every week night. Throughout the day, you perform log backups at shorter intervals, such as every 30 minutes. This is a common strategy and fairly simple to execute and recover from.

## Log Backups

We have already covered a lot about log backups in the previous sections (see the section "Purpose of the Transaction Log"), so we will provide just a recap here. Log backups are required when a database uses the full or bulk-logged recovery models, or else the log file will grow continually until the disk is full. Simple recovery model does not allow log backups because the log file is truncated automatically upon database checkpoints.

The transaction log contains records of transactions (in other words, modifications) that are made to the database. A backup of the log is necessary for recovering transactions between data backups. Data may be recovered to a point in time within the log backup as well, with the exception of log backups that contain bulk-logged records—these must be restored to the end of the backup. Without log backups, you can restore data only to the time when a data backup was completed. Log backups are taken between data backups to allow point-in-time recovery. For read-only databases, log backups are not needed, and you may set the database to use the simple recovery model in this case.

There is one special type of log backup, called the tail-log backup, that we have not yet defined. This is a log backup taken immediately upon a system failure. Assuming the log disks are intact and accessible, a last tail-log backup can be taken before attempting to restore data. This is the best case scenario because it allows you to recover up to the point of failure. You must not forget to take the tail-log backup before you start restoring data, or the transactions that were in the log at the time of failure will be lost. Also, attempting a restore without first taking the tail-log backup will result in an error unless you use the WITH REPLACE or WITH STOPAT clause. For information on the options for the BACKUP command when taking a tail-log backup, see the SQL Server Books Online topic "Tail-Log Backups."

---

**Important**    In the event of a failure on the system, if possible, immediately take a log backup, called the tail-log backup, to help you restore to the point of failure.

## Copy-Only Backups

Each time a backup occurs, SQL Server stores information about the backup to keep track of the restore sequence. (See Chapter 15, "Restoring Data.") Each data backup, for example, serves as a base backup for any differential backups taken later, so by default, backups affect other backups and how they will be restored. In other words, each backup affects future backup and restore procedures.

There may be a situation in which you would like to create a backup of a file or database but do not want to affect the current backup and restore procedures. You can do this using a new backup type in SQL Server 2005 called a copy-only backup. It will leave the current backup and restore information intact in the database and will not disturb the normal sequence of backups that are in process.

---

**Note** To use copy-only backups, you must use T-SQL scripts with the BACKUP and RESTORE commands. Copy only backups are not an option in SQL Server Management Studio.

---

## Full-Text Catalog Backups

SQL Server 2005 provides a new feature to backup full-text catalog data. The full-text data is backed up by default with a regular backup. It is treated as a file and is included in the backup set with the file data. A full-text catalog file can also be backed up alone without the database data. Use the BACKUP command to perform a full-text catalog backup. See SQL Server Books Online for more options, such as differential and file backup options, with full-text catalog backups.

---

# Backup and Media Fundamentals

Information about backup history, backup devices, and media sets are stored in the system *msdb* database. This information is extremely useful in helping to understand and manage backups, such as to determine what databases and files have been backed up, what type of backups have been performed, and which backup sets are available for restore. Basic backup set and media set terminology are unchanged since SQL Server 2000, and the information in the backup history tables of both is similar, but with SQL Server 2005 there are some additional columns in the tables and one completely new table, called backupfilegroup.

The following system tables within the *msdb* system database store history information about backups:

- **Backupfile**   For each backup event that occurs, this table stores a row for each data and log file in the database, including a column, *is_present*, that indicates whether that file was backed up as part of the backup set.

- **Backupfilegroup**   This table is new for SQL Server 2005. It contains a row for each filegroup in a database at the time of a backup. This table does not indicate whether that filegroup was backed up. See the *backupfile* table to find that information.

- **Backupset**   This table contains one row for each backup set. A new backup set is created for each backup event.

- **Backupmediaset**   This table contains one row for each backup media set to which backup sets are written.

- **Backupmediafamily**   This table contains one row for each media family, or if part of a mirrored media set, one row for each mirror in the set.

## Understanding Backup Devices and Media Sets

To understand the information provided in these tables, there are several concepts and terms that we must define first. Backups are written to either a location on disk (a file) or to a tape device or devices. A backup device is a logical name that is given to a tape or disk file to which a backup can be written. All of the backup data stored on a single backup device, which could contain data from multiple backups, is known as a media family. A media set is made up of a fixed type and number of backup devices used to store one or more backup sets. A media set cannot include both disk and tape devices; it must be all one type of device or the other. There can be multiple backup devices within a media set such as multiple disk locations or multiple tape devices. When this is the case, then each backup written to that media set is written evenly across all the devices in that set.

For example, if a backup is written to two disk backup devices (for example, two files on disk), then those two files together make up one media set. The T-SQL example below shows how to take a full database backup of a database named Mydatabase by writing it to two files on separate disk drives or disk arrays: C:\SQL_Backups\mydb1.bak and D:\SQL_Backups\mydb2.bak. At this point, these files have not been identified as a specific backup device yet. We will show how to do this below:

```
BACKUP DATABASE mydatabase
TO DISK = 'C:\SQL_Backups\mydb1.bak ',
DISK = 'D:\SQL_Backups\mydb2.bak '
WITH MEDIANAME = 'mydb_disk_media' ;
```

In this example, a full database backup is written across the two files listed. See Figure 14-5. Half of the backup is stored on C drive and half on D drive. The media set, consisting of the two files, is named Mydb_disk_media. If this is the first time this media set is used, it is formatted with a media header and initialized by default. If a backup has been written to the media set before, then by default (the default is WITH NOINIT) the backup is appended to the media set. To force an overwrite of all existing backups on the media set without reformatting the media header, specify the WITH INIT option. See SQL Server Books Online for the many options available to the BACKUP command.

Now let's talk about creating backup devices for these two files, which we could have done before executing the BACKUP command. Unofficially, the two files used above are considered backup devices, but they do not yet appear under the Management Studio Server Objects/Backup Devices. You can explicitly create a backup device name for each file or tape that will be used for backups even if you have already backed up to that file or tape before the backup device is created, and you may decide to do so for a couple of reasons. One reason is so that you can view its properties and media contents within Management Studio. Another reason is so you can use that backup device name instead of the full physical file name when performing backups. If you do not explicitly create backup device names for these files, you will not see their information in Management Studio under Server Objects/Backup Devices nor will there be a backup device option in the Backup window when you perform a backup through Management Studio. You will instead have to select the physical file name.

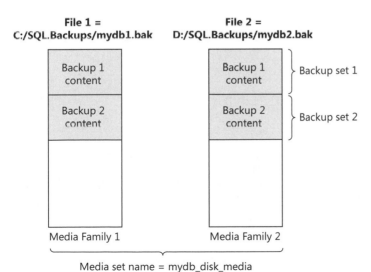

**Figure 14-5**   Logical view of backup across two files.

To view backup devices in Management Studio, follow these steps:

1. Start SQL Server Management Studio. In Object Explorer view, connect to the server instance of your choice.

2. Expand the Server Objects folder.

3. Expand the Backup Devices folder. Any existing backup devices will appear as shown in the example in Figure 14-6.

You can create the backup device either using Management Studio or by using the *sp_addumpdevice* stored procedure. Using Management Studio, follow the previous steps to view backup devices, then right-click in the white space in the pane on the right and select New Backup Device. If the new device does not yet exist, it will not yet have media contents to view. If you create a device with the same name and location as a file or tape to which you have already written a backup or backups, the object will appear and all of its media contents will automatically be visible in the Management Studio. Let's go through an example of this scenario.

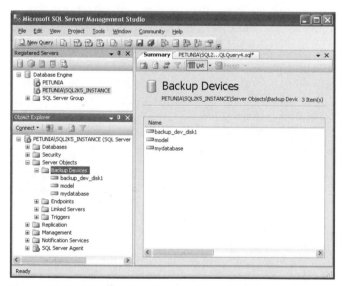

**Figure 14-6** Viewing backup devices.

Using the BACKUP command example above, we backed up to two files: located on C:\SQL_Backups\mydb1.bak and D:\SQL_Backups\mydb2.bak. Before you have explicitly created these as backup devices, they will not be visible in Management Studio even though the files do exist once we executed the BACKUP command above. To make them visible in Management Studio, follow these steps:

1.  Follow the previous steps for viewing backup devices.

2.  Right-click in the white space in the right pane and select New Backup Device.

3.  Enter a name for the device.

4.  Enter the destination as the same name and path that we gave it above. For example, Figure 14-7 shows the creation of a backup device to identify the file C:\SQL_Backups\mydb1.bak with a name of mydb1_dev.

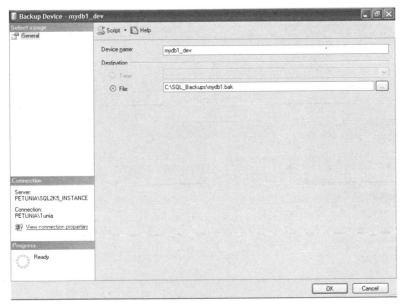

**Figure 14-7**   Creating a backup device.

To create this same device using T-SQL instead, use the following command:

```
EXEC sp_addumpdevice 'disk', 'mydb1_dev', 'C:\SQL_Backups\mydb1.bak' ;
```

To create a backup device for the second file, use the following command:

```
EXEC sp_addumpdevice 'disk', 'mydb2_dev', 'D:\SQL_Backups\mydb2.bak' ;
```

Now the backup devices, which we called mydb1_dev and mydb2_dev, appear in the Backup Device window. These backup device names serve as the logical names for the physical backup files C:\SQL_Backups\mydb1.bak and D:\SQL_Backups\mydb2.bak. To view the media contents of a backup device, perform the following steps:

1. Start SQL Server Management Studio. In Object Explorer view, connect to the server instance of your choice.

2. Expand the Server Objects folder.

3. Expand the Backup Devices folder.

4. Right-click a backup device name and select Properties.

5. Click Media Contents in the left panel. For example, information about the existing backup on the device we created above is shown in Figure 14-8.

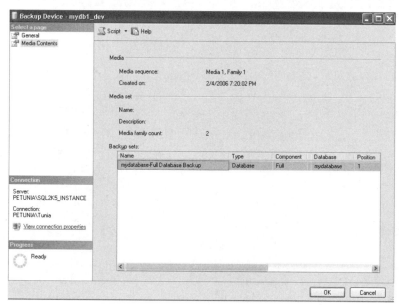

**Figure 14-8**   Viewing the contents of a backup device—media family 1.

Since this backup device is part of a media set that includes two backup devices (mydb1_dev and mydb2_dev), you will see Family 1. For the second device in the media set you will see Family 2.

When you perform a backup, you will now be able to select the backup device name in Management Studio, or you can use it as the logical name in the BACKUP command instead of the physical file name.

## Mirrored Media Sets

SQL Server 2005 provides a new feature, called mirrored media sets, that allows you to back up data to more than one media set at a time. Having more than one copy of your backup increases reliability in case one set of media has a failure during restore, such as if a tape is damaged. In that case, one of the other mirrored media sets can be used.

You can create up to four mirrors of a backup, or a total of four copies. All of the mirrored media sets must have the same number of backup devices, and the backup devices must be equivalent—such as disk type or the same type of tape device. Here is an example of backing up to three mirrored media sets, each set made up of two tape devices:

```
BACKUP DATABASE mydatabase

TO TAPE = '\\.\tape0' , TAPE = '\\.\tape1'

MIRROR TO TAPE = '\\.\tape2' , TAPE = '\\.\tape3'

MIRROR TO TAPE = '\\.\tape4' , TAPE = '\\.\tape5'

WITH MEDIANAME = 'mydb_mirrored_media_set' ;
```

Another benefit of mirrored sets it that you can substitute a media family from one mirrored media set for another. Using the BACKUP example above, there are two media families, or backup devices, per mirrored media set. If tape1, which contains media family 2, is damaged, you can restore media family 2 from either tape 3 or tape 5, which each contain mirrors of media family 2. In other words, you can restore a particular media family from any one of the mirrored media sets. All you need is one good, complete set of the media families to restore.

## Overview of Backup History Tables

To find information about the backups that have occurred, you can query the system tables mentioned above. We'll give some examples that will help understand what you can find out from these tables. The backup_set_id column of the backupfile table can be used to determine which backed up files are in a backup set. The media_set_id column tells you to which media set the backup belongs.

For example, run the following query:

```
USE msdb

SELECT a.backup_set_id, a.media_set_id, a.database_name,

    b.logical_name, b.file_type

FROM backupset a, backupfile b

WHERE  a.backup_set_id = b.backup_set_id ;
```

The backup_set_id relates a group of files that existed as part of the database when the backup was taken. Whether it was a full database backup or a file backup, all files in the database are listed. This number increases sequentially for each backup set to represent the position of each in the media set. For example, the highest number represents the most recent backup set. This allows you to identify a specific backup set to restore.

Here is a sample result set from running the query above:

| backup_set_id | media_set_id | database_name | logical_name | file_type |
|---------------|--------------|---------------|--------------|-----------|
| 1 | 1 | AdventureWorks | AdventureWorks_Data | D |
| 1 | 1 | AdventureWorks | AdventureWorks_Log | L |
| 2 | 1 | AdventureWorks | AdventureWorks_Data | D |
| 2 | 1 | AdventureWorks | AdventureWorks_Log | L |
| 3 | 1 | AdventureWorks | AdventureWorks_Data | D |
| 3 | 1 | AdventureWorks | AdventureWorks_Log | L |
| 4 | 1 | AdventureWorks | AdventureWorks_Data | D |
| 4 | 1 | AdventureWorks | AdventureWorks_Log | L |
| 9 | 3 | mydatabase | mydatabase_file1_primary | D |
| 9 | 3 | mydatabase | mydatabase_log | L |
| 10 | 3 | mydatabase | mydatabase_file1_primary | D |
| 10 | 3 | mydatabase | mydatabase_log | L |
| 10 | 3 | mydatabase | mydb_file2_primary | D |
| 11 | 3 | mydatabase | mydatabase_file1_primary | D |
| 11 | 3 | mydatabase | mydatabase_log | L |
| 11 | 3 | mydatabase | mydb_file2_primary | D |
| 12 | 3 | mydatabase | mydatabase_file1_primary | D |
| 12 | 3 | mydatabase | mydatabase_log | L |
| 12 | 3 | mydatabase | mydb_file2_primary | D |

In the output above, we see that there have been four backups taken of *mydatabase* with backup_set_id = 9, 10, 11, and 12. The first backup set with id = 9 consisted of only one data file and one log file, Mydatabase_file1_primary and Mydatabase_log. After that backup was taken, another file, mydb_file2_primary, was added to the database. Thus, subsequent backup sets (10, 11, and 12) list all 3 files, including the new file, in the database.

The value in the media_set_id column relates to the media set to which a backup is written. In the above output, the media set = 1 was used for backups of the *AdventureWorks* database, and media set = 3 was used for *mydatabase*. Each of the backups taken were appended to the media set. The backup_set_id indicates the position of each backup set within the media set.

The file_type column has either a "D" for data, "L" for log, or "F" for full-text catalog. These indicate whether the file in that row is a data file or a log file.

There is another really interesting column in the backupfile table that we look at in this next example. The following T-SQL statement queries three backup sets (with id's 16,17, and 18) and the is_present and type columns. The is_present column identifies whether the specific file is part of the backup set. A value of 0 indicates that it is not part of the backup set, and a 1 indicates that it is part of the backup set. For a log backup, for example, all the files in the database are part of the backup set because transactions from the log are backed up for all files. Therefore, all files appear with is_present = 1 for a log backup. This does not mean that all the files were completely backed up. For a file backup, both the file and the portion of the log that relates to that file are backed up, so both the data file and the log file have is_present = 1. For a differential database backup, all files are contained in the backup. For a differential file backup, only the specified file and its portion of the log are contained in the backup. The example below demonstrates this.

In our example, the type column identifies the type of backup that was performed for each backup set. Possible backup types are "D" (database), "I" (database differential), "L" (log), "F" (file or filegroup), "G" (file differential), "P" (partial), and "Q" (partial differential).

Here is the T-SQL example for querying this information:

```
USE msdb
SELECT a.backup_set_id, b.logical_name, b.file_type,
    b.is_present, a.type
FROM backupset a, backupfile b
WHERE a.backup_set_id = b.backup_set_id
    AND b.backup_set_id IN (16,17,18) ;
```

Here is a set of sample results:

| backup_set_id | logical_name | file_type | is_present | type |
| --- | --- | --- | --- | --- |
| 16 | mydatabase_file1_primary | D | 1 | L |
| 16 | mydatabase_log | L | 1 | L |
| 16 | mydb_file2_primary | D | 1 | L |
| 17 | mydatabase_file1_primary | D | 0 | F |
| 17 | mydatabase_log | L | 1 | F |
| 17 | mydb_file2_primary | D | 1 | F |
| 18 | mydatabase_file1_primary | D | 1 | D |
| 18 | mydatabase_log | L | 1 | D |
| 18 | mydb_file2_primary | D | 1 | D |

The fourth row of the sample results shows a file that is not part of the backup set for backup set 17 (because is_present = 0 for that file). Only the Mydatabase_log and Mydb_file2_primary files are contained in the backup set. This indicates that a file backup (type "F") was taken of Mydb_file2_primary and the portion of the log relating to that file was backed up with it by design.

For backup_set_id = 16, all three files are contained in this backup set, and it has a type of log backup (type = "L"). For a log backup, the entire transaction log is backed up, which contains transactions for all files in the database. Therefore, all database files have is_present = 1 for a log backup.

For backup_set_id = 18, all three files are again contained in the backup set, as this was a full database backup (type = "D"). This is a complete database backup of all files in the database.

## Viewing Backup Sets in Management Studio

When using SQL Server Management Studio to restore a complete database, the most recent full database backup set, along with any corresponding differential and log backups, are presented by default in the Restore Database dialog box. To open this dialog box, follow these steps:

1. Start SQL Server Management Studio. In Object Explorer view, connect to the server instance of your choice, and then expand the server's Databases folder.

2. Right-click the database name and select Tasks from the menu, then select Restore and Database from the submenus.

3. Select From Database as the source for restore and you will see only the most recent set of backups for restoring the database, as shown in Figure 14-9. Previous database backups will not be seen by default. (For file or filegroup restores, a history of files backed up is presented by default in Management Studio, not just the most recent one.)

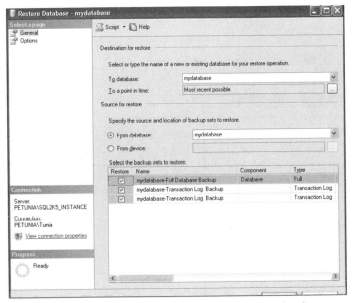

**Figure 14-9** Restoring the most recent database backup.

To restore from a different backup device or to see previous backups that exist on a backup device, complete the following steps from within the Restore Database dialog box (opened in previous steps):

1. Select From Device as the source for restore.

2. Click the ellipsis and then select Backup Device from the drop-down Backup Media pull-down list.

3. Click the Add button.

4. Select the backup device you would like to view from the drop-down list, and click the OK button, as shown in Figure 14-10.

5. Click the Contents button.

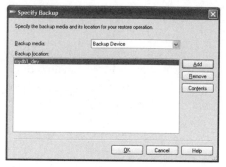

**Figure 14-10**   Selecting a backup device.

All of the backups on that device will be presented as shown in Figure 14-11.

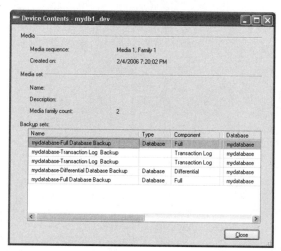

**Figure 14-11**   Viewing all contents on a device.

More information on performing data restores is presented in Chapter 15, "Restoring Data."

## Backup Strategy

Designing solid backup and restore strategies for each critical user and system database is very important for protecting your data. Backup types and backup schedules may be different for various databases and database servers. When planning a backup strategy, consider the following factors:

- How critical is the data to the success of the business? Will you lose money if the data is lost or unavailable?

- Is the data read-only or is it read-write? Read-only data may not need to be backed up more than once.

- Is there an off-peak time when backups can be taken to minimize the performance overhead? For example, if users are not on the system during weekend nights, this might be a good time to perform full database backups.

- How big is the database and how long does it take to perform various types of backups? Is this time acceptable? For example, if the database is very large and backups take a lot of time, you may need to perform full database backups only once every other week and perform differential backups in between.

- To what media will the backups be written? Backing up first to disk and then copying the backup files off to tape or DVD is a common strategy. Taking the tapes or DVD's offsite is a minimal strategy for disaster recovery that should be seriously considered.

- Will you want to mirror the backup to have two or more copies for protection? Mirroring the backup to more than one media set provides protection in case one of the media sets becomes corrupt and cannot be restored from.

---

**Important**    You should not write backups to the same disks that store the source data or log files. If you lose the source data because of a disk failure or data corruption, you could also lose the backup. Backups should be written to disks physically separate from the database files.

---

Off-peak time is a time period during which a minimal amount of user activity occurs on the system. Backing up data from the production database is an online process, but the overhead can affect performance of other activity on that database or other databases on that server. During a backup operation, high reads are performed on the database and high writes are performed to the backup destination. The performance impact to other activity on the system varies depending on several factors.

One option for reducing the impact of backups on performance is to perform a snapshot backup, which is a backup that requires cooperation from third-party independent hardware or software vendor solutions. A typical snapshot backup solution is accomplished by mirroring data onto separate physical disks so that the mirror can be split at some point in time, creating an almost instantaneous copy of the database and thus eliminating the need for a backup of the production database. This is a costly solution, but it is beneficial for very large, critical databases.

---

**Important** SQL Server 2005 does not allow you to back up a mirror database (the mirror copy in a database mirroring scenario) because it is not in a recovered state, nor does it allow backing up any kind of SQL Server database snapshot. This capability may be an enhancement in a future release of SQL Server.

---

As of the writing of this book, SQL Server 2005 does not allow taking a backup of a mirror database because it is in a state of no recovery. A database must be in a recovered, online state in order to be backed up. A database snapshot, or SQL Server snapshot, can be taken of a mirror database. Such a snapshot can be accessed only in a read-only manner, such as for reporting, but like a mirror database, database snapshots cannot be backed up.

Generally, backups should be performed regularly and frequently for all critical databases that allow data modifications. The more often modifications are made and the more critical the data, the more frequently backups should occur. Less critical databases, such as development and test systems, may need to be backed up only occasionally or not at all. A clear plan for backing up all user databases and pertinent SQL Server system databases (discussed in the next section) should be developed.

### Real World    Common Backup Strategy

Although there are many options for backup strategies and types of backups that can be taken, the majority of cases are well suited to a simple strategy that is easy to restore from. The following is an example of such a common backup strategy for backing up critical user databases.

1. Perform a full database backup every Saturday night

2. Perform a differential database backup every Wednesday night

3. Perform continual transaction log backups every 30 minutes

This can be scheduled to run automatically using the Database Maintenance Plan Wizard.

The Real World example shows a common backup strategy scenario, and specific days and times may vary. Such a schedule is very beneficial because it is simple to implement, understand, and restore from. However, if your database is very big or if user activity requires continuous uptime and optimal performance, this schedule may not be possible. File or filegroup backups may be necessary in these cases, although administration complexity is increased. Here is a sample strategy for backing up a very large database, assuming it has only two filegroups (Filegroup1, the primary filegroup, and Filegroup2, a secondary filegroup):

1. Full filegroup backup of Filegroup1 on Saturday night (provides the base)

2. Full filegroup backup of Filegroup2 on Sunday night (provides the base)

3. Differential filegroup backup of Filegroup1 on Tuesday night

4. Differential filegroup backup of Filegroup2 on Wednesday night

5. Differential filegroup backup of Filegroup1 on Thursday night

6. Differential filegroup backup of Filegroup2 on Friday night

7. Continual transaction log backups every 30 minutes

This backup plan allows recovery of the database by following these steps:

1. Restore the two filegroup base backups (from steps 1 and 2 above).

2. Restore the most recent differential backup of Filegroup1 (from step 5 above).

3. Restore the transaction logs backups taken since Filegroup1 differential backup.

4. Restore the most recent differential backup of Filegroup2 (from step 6 above).

5. Restore the transaction log backups taken since Filegroup2 differential backup.

The differential backups from steps 3 and 4 do not need to be restored because all of the changes since the base backup are incorporated into the most recent differential backup. Nor do any log backups taken before the most recent file differential backups need to be restored. Taking differential backups reduces the number of transaction log backups that must be restored.

A common and easy way to set up straight-forward SQL Server backups is to use the Database Maintenance Plan Wizard in SQL Server Management Studio. See Chapter 17 for details on how to set up database maintenance plans.

---

**Important**   You absolutely should test restoring from your backups (onto a test system) to verify your backup and restore strategy work as expected. Perform these restore tests regulary, such as every few months or more often.

# Backing Up System Databases

In addition to user databases, it is also important to back up pertinent system databases. You do not need to back up all of them, only the critical ones. Here is a list of all the system databases and optional sample databases:

- **master**   Stores SQL Server system-level information, such as logon accounts, server configuration settings, existence of all other databases, and the location of the files

- **model**   Contains a database template used when creating new user databases

- **msdb**   Stores information and history on backup and restore operations, SQL Agent jobs, and replication

- **tempdb**   Provides temporary space for various operations, and is recreated every time SQL Server is restarted

- **distribution**   Exists only if the server is configured as the distributor for replication

- **Resource**   Contains all the system objects that are included in SQL Server 2005 but does not contain any user data or user metadata. This is a new system database for SQL Server 2005 that is read-only.

- **AdventureWorks and AdventureWorksDW**   Provide sample data. These can optionally be selected for installation during SQL Server installation and are provided for use in testing and experimentation

Of the system databases, you should back up the two most critical and informative system databases, *master* and *msdb*, regularly. They usually back up in seconds, so you may want to back these up every night. You might want to also backup the *model* database occasionally if you make changes, such as adding user-defined data types, that you would like to preserve for future user databases to use as their template.

*tempdb* never needs backed up because it does not store permanent data. In fact, SQL Server does not even allow you to back it up. It is recreated every time SQL Server restarts and all data is permanently deleted from it when SQL Server shuts down.

The *distribution* database, which is used in replication, should be backed up regularly. The method to backup and restore this database depends on the type of replication configured—transactional, snapshot, and merge. See SQL Server Books Online for details regarding backup and restore procedures with replicated databases.

The *Resource* database is read-only and does not contain user data or metadata and therefore does not need backed up. This database is used to make upgrading to new versions of SQL Server easier and faster and to make roll backs of service packs easier. It is intended for access only by Microsoft Customer Support Services when supporting and trouble-shooting customer issues.

The *AdventureWorks* and *AdventureWorksDW* sample databases do not need to be backed up unless you have a special reason you want to save them. They can even be deleted if you do not want to use them.

## Summary

In this chapter, we covered the foundations of transaction logging and database recovery models in order to help you better understand backups. We also covered the various types and categories of backups that can be performed on a database. Understanding backups and performing them properly are essential parts of database maintenance and data recoverability. Without backups, your data can be lost regardless of how much fault tolerance is configured at the hardware or software level. Do not get caught without a good backup, or you may risk losing your job along with the data. Always perform back-ups and test restoring from them on occasion to verify that you can restore the database and data when necessary.

# Chapter 15
# Restoring Data

In Chapter 14, "Backup Fundamentals," we discussed taking backups of critical database data and their importance for data protection because they provide the ability to recover from system or disk failures which could cause data loss. In addition to taking backups, another one of the most important roles of a database administrator (DBA) is being able to restore data that has been backed up. Taking backups is just one side of the story. Successfully restoring that data is the other side.

In this chapter we discuss the fundatmentals of the restore process and define terminology and concepts. Then we discuss the different ways to restore data, how to perform restores, and the new options for restoring data with Microsoft SQL Server 2005. These new options include online restore, fast recovery, and piecemeal restore.

# Practicing and Documenting Restore Procedures

Before getting into the details of restoring data, here is some important advice. Knowing how to restore data and practicing the restore process to ensure that it works as expected are important tasks that a DBA should not avoid. Often this is not considered a priority, but it really should be. If there is not a system available with enough disk space to test restoring a full database backup, then try a test with a smaller database or one of the sample databases using the same backup and restore method and the same backup types as used for the production database.

One backup method, for example, could be to perform a backup to disk first and then to copy the backup file to tape. In this case, practice performing a restore from the backup on disk and a restore from the tape backup so that if the disk backup is erased or corrupted, you also know how to restore from the tape. Understanding where the tapes are stored, how to retrieve them, how to identify what is on them, and how long it takes to retrieve them are all important to know when you need to retrieve data quickly. The steps for restoring data using both methods should be well-documented, and that documentation should be kept in a place where appropriate parties can access it in the case when the DBA is not accessible.

# Restore and Recovery Concepts

In order to better understand how to restore data, it helps to know the terminology and concepts behind the restore process. This section defines terms that are used throughout the chapter and explains the phases of the restore process.

There are three possible phases in a restore operation: the data copy, redo, and undo phases. The term *restore* is used here in a more specific way to describe the first two phases of a restore operation: the data copy and redo (roll forward) phases. *Recovery* is the term used to describe the phase that performs undo (roll back) and brings the database online to a recovered state. The following are descriptions of these three phases, which are summarized in Table 15-1:

- **Data Copy Phase**   The process of copying the data, index, and log pages from the backup media to the database files. Copies data from data backups, and optionally differential backups, to the database files. No log backups nor any log information in the data backups are applied in this phase.

- **Redo Phase**   This phase replays logged changes to the data by processing log backups. It begins by replaying any logged data stored within the data backups themselves, and then if any log backups are restored, it continues by replaying transactions from each restored log backup.

- **Undo Phase**   This phase occurs only if there are changes to data from uncommitted transactions in the restored data at the recovery point. (Log records may include transaction records of transactions that had not been committed at the time of backup.) These changes are rolled back, so the database will be in a state as if those uncommitted transactions never occurred. After the undo phase, no more data can be restored to the database. This phase occurs when a database is restored with recovery. At the end of this phase the database is brought online for use, or recovered. If there were no uncommitted transactions to handle, then undo is skipped and the database is recovered.

**Table 15-1   Restore Operation Phases and Descriptions**

| Restore | Phase 1<br>Data copy phase | Copies data from data backups to the database files; no logs are restored in this phase |
|---|---|---|
| | Phase 2<br>Redo phase (roll forward) | Replays logged records of transactions, first from any logged data in the data backups themselves and then from any log backups restored |
| Recovery | Phase 3<br>Undo phase (roll back)and data set online | Rolls back any data changes from uncommitted transactions that were replayed in the redo phase and brings the data set online |

The terms "restore" and "recovery" are used in more general ways as well. The single term "restore" is often used to refer to the entire process of restore and recovery. The term "recovery" is used in the sense of recovering lost data, which can also refer to the entire process of restoring and recovering data. "Recovery" is also used to refer to the SQL Server automatic recovery process, also known as startup recovery. (Automatic recovery and recovery models are explained in Chapter 14.) Depending on the context, these terms can be used in a more general or more specific way.

Recovery point is the specified point in time to which a set of data is restored. In other words, the data set is restored to its state at that point in time. A recovery point is the point to which the data set is rolled forward. This data set is called the roll forward set. If there are uncommitted transactions at the recovery point, then undo, or roll back, occurs to bring the data to a consistent state such that there are no data changes in the database from transactions that were not committed. The undo process is skipped if there are no uncommitted transactions in the roll forward set.

**Important**   Backups created using SQL Server 2005 cannot be restored to a previous version of SQL Server.

**Important**   Backups created using SQL Server 7.0 or SQL Server 2000 can be restored to a SQL Server 2005 server, but the system databases—*master*, *model*, and *msdb*—cannot be restored. (An interesting exception is that a log backup taken using SQL Server 7.0 cannot be restored to SQL Server 2000 or 2005 if that log backup contains a CREATE INDEX operation.) Backups from SQL Server 6.5 or earlier versions cannot be restored to SQL Server 2005; the backup format is incompatible. A data export and import must be performed instead.

A *restore sequence* is a set of RESTORE statements used to perform the restore steps described above: data copy, roll forward, roll back, and bring data online. This might be only one RESTORE statement or a series of RESTORE statements in the correct order. For example, a restore sequence to restore a complete database to a point of failure might include statements that first restore a full database backup, then a differential database backup, then multiple log backups, and finally a tail-log backup that also recovers the database (using the RECOVERY option described in the following section).

A *recovery path* is any complete sequence of data and log backups that can be restored to bring a database to a point in time. As data backups are being taken on a database, a recovery path is created from the point at which the base backup or backups begin. Whenever data is restored and recovered, a new recovery path is created at that recovery point. If the recovery point is up to a point of failure (as recent as possible) and a database backup is then taken again, a new single recovery path begins with that complete backup (not a forked path). On the other hand, if data is restored to a point in time that is earlier than the current database state, the database is used from that point, and log backups continue, then the current recovery path is forked into two paths so that there are now two possible recovery paths from which to restore. (An example of this follows.) If you always restore data to the most recent point in time or to the point of failure when possible with a tail-log backup, then you will not have forked recovery paths.

For example, assume a full database backup is taken, followed by three log backups, and later the database is restored using the full database backup and only two of the three log backups, thus bringing the database back to an earlier point in time than the current point. If the database continues to be used, then a second recovery path is forked from the first recovery path at that recovery point, which was the end of the second log restore. See Figure 15-1 for a diagram of this scenario. Now if log backups continue on a regular schedule (log backups four and five in Figure 15-1) once the database is recovered, then there are two possible recovery paths that could be used for restoring data. In our example, the following are the two possible restore sequences that could be restored based on the two recovery paths:

1. Recovery Path 1: Restore full database backup, log backups one, two, and three

2. Recovery Path 2: Restore full database backup, log backups one, two, four, and five

---

**Best Practices**    It is best practice to avoid creation of multiple recovery paths for ease of management of your backup and restore processes.

---

Having forked recovery paths is neither correct or incorrect, but the downside is that it can be a bit complex to figure out which path to take when restoring data again. It is a best practice to avoid creating multiple recovery paths either by performing a full backup of the database as soon as possible after a restore to a point in time or by restoring the database to the point of failure using the tail-log backup or to the most recent point possible. See Figure 15-2 for examples of these. (The types of backups are covered in Chapter 14.)

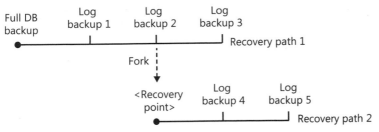

**Figure 15-1**   Forked recovery path example.

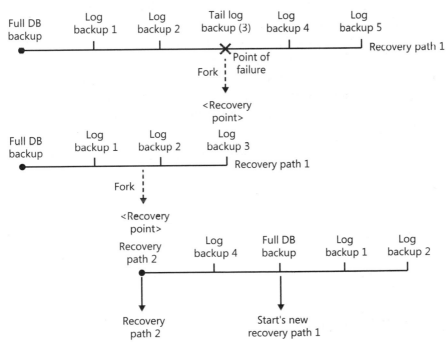

**Figure 15-2**   Avoiding forked recovery paths.

# Restoring Data from Backups

You may need to restore data for various reasons. The most critical reason is to restore lost data, which may be a factor in the success or failure of a business. Here are some common scenarios in which you may restore data:

- To restore data lost or corrupted because of a system failure
- To restore a database onto a development system for use by application developers while developing and testing new code
- To restore a database onto a test system to load test your applications or to test the use of certain database features in a controlled environment
- To restore a database onto a separate server as a read-only database that can be accessed by users to perform queries, such as for reports.

There are several ways to restore data, depending on the types of backups taken and the purpose of the restore. These are described in the following sections.

## Complete Database, Differential Database, and Log Restores

A complete database restore is performed by restoring a full database backup. It restores all the files that existed in the database at the time of the backup. A differential database restore can be applied after its base complete database restore is performed with the NORECOVERY option. If multiple differential database backups have been taken since the full database backup, only the most recent differential backup needs to be restored. This is because each differential backup contains all changes since the base backup, not since the last differential backup. (In some cases there may not be a differential backup to apply, only log backups.)

The following is the basic T-SQL syntax for a complete database restore or a differential restore operation:

```
RESTORE DATABASE <database_name>
FROM <backup_device>
WITH FILE = n, [RECOVERY | NORECOVERY];
```

The following is the basic T-SQL syntax for a log restore operation:

```
RESTORE LOG <database_name>
FROM <backup_device>
WITH FILE = n, [RECOVERY | NORECOVERY];
```

There are many options to both the RESTORE DATBASE and RESTORE LOG statements that may be of interest. For example, when performing a restore in a command prompt or with Query Editor, the "STATS = *percentage*" option will print the progress of the restore as the indicated percentage completes. The default is 10 percent. Please see SQL Server Books Online for usage of all possible arguments and options for the RESTORE command.

A log restore applies a log backup by rolling forward transaction records. Multiple log backups may be applied one after the other as long as the NORECOVERY option is specified. When the last log backup will be applied, use the RECOVERY option to recover the database and bring it online.

Instead of using the logical backup device name in the FROM clause, you can list the physical file or files or tape drive path with "DISK=" or "TAPE=" options. The file number determines which backup file to apply. (Some methods for getting the file number follow.) If not specified in the WITH clause, the default is RECOVERY, meaning that the undo phase will occur, if necessary, and the database will be brought online. If the RECOVERY option is included but SQL Server determines that more data is needed to recover (such as a log backup when restoring a file that has changed since it was backed up), an error occurs and the database or file remains offline in a restoring state. Once the data has been successfully recovered (roll back has occurred and the data brought online), then no more backups can be applied. If the data has already been recovered, then to allow further backups to be applied you have to start the entire restore sequence again. Therefore, use the WITH NORECOVERY option if you need to apply other backups after restoring the database, such as a full database differential backup or log backups.

The file number can be found by looking in the Management Studio Restore Database window in the Position column, as shown in Figure 15-3. To open the Restore Database window, complete the following steps:

1. In Object Explorer view, connect to the server instance of your choice, and then expand the server's Databases folder.

2. Right-click the appropriate database name.

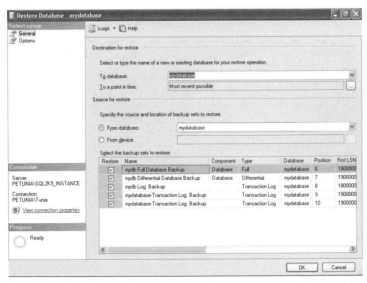

**Figure 15-3** Viewing file numbers in Management Studio (position column).

3. Select Tasks, then Restore, and then Database.

4. Click OK to restore the database immediately, or click on the Script drop-down menu at the top of the window to script the restore statements.

Another method of retrieving the file number for a set of backups is by running the following SELECT statement on the *backupset* history table. (The backup history tables are introduced in Chapter 14).

```
USE msdb ;
SELECT backup_set_id, media_set_id, position, name, type
FROM backupset ;
```

The following are sample results from this query:

| backup_set_id | media_set_id | position | name | type |
| --- | --- | --- | --- | --- |
| 36 | 10 | 6 | mydb Full Database Backup | D |
| 37 | 10 | 7 | mydb Differential Database Backup | I |
| 38 | 10 | 8 | mydatabase-Transaction Log Backup | L |
| 39 | 10 | 9 | mydatabase-Transaction Log Backup | L |
| 40 | 10 | 10 | mydatabase-Transaction Log Backup | L |

Below is an example of restoring the full database backup, differential database backup, and three log backups listed in the query output above by specifying the file numbers in the correct order in the restore sequence. (This could also be done by using Management Studio and selecting the appropriate files to restore, as shown in Figure 15-3.) Notice that NORECOVERY is specified in the first four restore statements so that further backups can be applied before recovering the database:

```
USE master ;
--restore full database backup
RESTORE DATABASE [mydatabase]
FROM  mydb1_dev, mydb2_dev
WITH  FILE = 6,  NORECOVERY ;

--restore differential db backup
RESTORE DATABASE [mydatabase]
FROM  mydb1_dev, mydb2_dev
WITH  FILE = 7,  NORECOVERY ;

--restore log backup 1
RESTORE LOG [mydatabase]
FROM  mydb1_dev, mydb2_dev
WITH  FILE = 8,  NORECOVERY ;
```

```
--restore log backup 2
RESTORE LOG [mydatabase]
FROM  mydb1_dev, mydb2_dev
WITH  FILE = 9,  NORECOVERY ;

--restore log backup 3 and recover database and bring online
RESTORE LOG [mydatabase]
FROM  mydb1_dev, mydb2_dev
WITH  FILE = 10, RECOVERY ;
```

Notice that NORECOVERY was explicitly specified in the first four restore statements to allow further data to be restored. The last restore log statement specifies RECOVERY. After that log backup is restored, the database is brought online, and no more data can be restored (rolled forward) at that point.

## Point-in-Time Restore

When using full or bulk-logged recovery models, and thus taking regular log backups, it is possible to recover to a point-in-time during a log backup. The exception is that with bulk-logged recovery model, if a particular log backup does contain bulk-logged records, then the entire log backup must be restored and point-in-time restore is not possible within that log backup. Whereas with bulk-logged, a log backup can be restored to a point in time if that log backup does not contain bulk-logged records. Point-in-time restore recovers only the transactions that occurred before the specified time within a log backup.

Point-in-time recovery can be accomplished using Management Studio or the RESTORE statement with the STOPAT option. When using the RESTORE command in a restore sequence, you should specify the time to stop with each command in the sequence, so you don't have to identify which backups are needed to restore to that point. SQL Server determines when the time has been reached and does not restore records after that point but does recover the database. For example, here is a restore sequence using STOPAT to restore up to 1:15 p.m. and recover the database (even though we do not know within which backup the records up to 1:15 p.m. reside):

```
--restore db backup stopping at 1:15PM
RESTORE DATABASE [mydatabase]
FROM  mydb1_dev, mydb2_dev
WITH STOPAT = 'May 17, 2006 1:15 PM', NORECOVERY ;

--restore records from log backup 1
RESTORE LOG [mydatabase]
FROM  mydblog_dev1
WITH  STOPAT = 'May 17, 2006 1:15 PM', NORECOVERY ;
```

```
--restore records from log backup 2
RESTORE LOG [mydatabase]
FROM   mydblog_dev2
WITH   STOPAT = 'May 17, 2006 1:15 PM', RECOVERY ;
```

There are many scenarios to consider when using the RESTORE statement. See SQL Server Books Online for more specifics about using the STOPAT option.

If the time specified falls beyond the log backup that is restored, then the database is not recovered, thus allowing further log backups to be applied. If you made a mistake specifying the time and meant to stop at an earlier time, then the restore sequence must be restarted.

To use Management Studio to select a point-in-time to recover to, follow these steps:

1. In Object Explorer view, connect to the server instance of your choice, and then expand the server's Databases folder.

2. Right-click the database name.

3. Select Tasks, then Restore, and then Database.

4. Click the ellipses for the To A Point In Time: field. The Point in Time Restore window opens, as shown in Figure 15-4. There you can specify an exact time up to which to restore.

5. Click OK if you want to restore the database now, or click on the Script drop-down menu at the top of the window to script the restore statements.

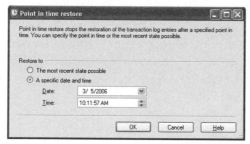

**Figure 15-4**   Point-In-Time Restore dialog box.

If that time occurs before the interval captured by a log backup, then the point-in-time restore fails and no data is rolled forward. If the time occurs after the log backup, then the entire log backup is restored, but the database is not recovered. If the time is within the log backup, then the point-in-time restore succeeds and the database is recovered.

# File and Filegroup Restore

A file or filegroup restore is applicable only for databases that contain multiple filegroups (one or more filegroups in addition to the default PRIMARY filegroup). An individual file can be restored or an entire filegroup can be restored, including all the files within that filegroup.

> **Note**   When creating a database with multiple files and filegroups, it is recommended to place user data files on a secondary filegroup or filegroups (setting one of them as the default filegroup instead of primary) so that the primary filegroup contains only the system tables and objects, not user database files. This allows for more flexibility when performing filegroup backups and online restores.

With multiple filegroups in a database, files and filegroups can be backed up and restored individually. If all database files were in the primary filegroup, there would be little benefit of having individual file backups, since the online restore capability applies only to filegroups other than the primary filegroup. (See the section Online Restore later in this chapter.) The main benefit of being able to restore one file individually is that it can reduce the time for restoring data in the case where only one file is damaged or affected by accidental data deletion. That file can be restored individually instead of restoring the entire database.

If the filegroup to which a file belongs is read-write, then you must have the complete chain of log backups since the file was backed up, plus the tail-log backup, in order to recover the file to a state consistent with the rest of the database. Only the changes in the log backups that affect that particular file are applied. If the file is read-only or if that file has not had any data changes made to it, then it can be successfully restored and recovered without applying log backups.

When creating file or filegroup backups, make sure to get a complete set of backups of each of the filegroups so that you could restore the entire database by filegroup if needed. It is best to get a full database backup as a safety net in case you need to restore the entire database.

If using simple recovery model, only read-only filegroups can be backed up using file or filegroup backup. Read-write filegroups cannot be backed up when using the simple recovery model because there are no log backups taken with this model, and therefore the data cannot be recovered to be consistent with the database.

> **Important**   A tail-log backup must be taken before restoring a file backup because it is needed to recover the file to a state consistent with the rest of the database. If you cannot get a tail-log backup, then you cannot restore an

individual file or filegroup backup alone but must restore the entire database. Otherwise, the database would not be consistent. The exceptions to this are if the filegroup for that file is read-only or if no data changes were made to that file since it was backed up.

Differential file and filegroup backups may be restored as well. Before restoring a differential file or filegroup backup, the base file or filegroup backup must be restored first. Any transaction log backups, including the tail-log backup, must also be applied if the file has changed since the differential backup. The following is a T-SQL example of restoring a full file backup (the base), a differential file backup, and log backups, including the tail-log backup:

```
USE master ;
--restore base file backup
RESTORE DATABASE mydatabase
FILE = 'mydb_file3_on_secondary_fg'
FROM  mydb1_dev, mydb2_dev WITH  FILE = 21, NORECOVERY ;

--restore differential file backup
RESTORE DATABASE mydatabase
FILE = 'mydb_file3_on_secondary_fg'
FROM  mydb1_dev, mydb2_dev WITH  FILE = 22, NORECOVERY ;

--restore log backup
RESTORE LOG mydatabase
FROM  mydb1_dev, mydb2_dev WITH  FILE = 23, NORECOVERY ;

--restore tail log backup
RESTORE LOG mydatabase
FROM  mydb1_dev, mydb2_dev WITH  FILE = 24, RECOVERY ;
```

To restore all files in a filegroup from a filegroup backup rather than individual files, you can use the "FILEGROUP=" syntax, as in the following example:

```
USE master ;
--restore filegroup backup
RESTORE DATABASE mydatabase
FILEGROUP = 'SECONDARY_FG'
FROM  mydb_secondary_fg_backup_dev
WITH NORECOVERY ;
```

```
--restore log backup
RESTORE LOG mydatabase
FROM  mydb_log_backup_dev
WITH  FILE = 26, NORECOVERY ;

--restore tail-log backup
RESTORE LOG mydatabase
FROM  mydb_log_backup_dev
WITH  FILE = 27, RECOVERY ;
```

Log backups taken since the filegroup was backed up and the tail-log backup must be restored in order to recover the filegroup unless the filegroup was read-only when backed up.

## Page Restore

Page restores are possible only for databases using the full or bulk-logged recovery models, not with the simple recovery model, and only available with SQL Server 2005 Enterprise Edition. This capability is provided in order to recover a corrupted data page that has been detected by checksum or a torn write. SQL Server 2005 has improved page-level error detection and reporting.

To restore a page, the file ID number and the page ID number are both needed. Use the RESTORE DATABASE statement to restore from the file, filegroup, or database that contains the page, and the PAGE option with <fileID:pageID>. The following example restores four data pages (with IDs 89, 250, 863, and 1049) within file ID = 1. Note that to complete the page restores, a log backup must be taken and then restored at the end of the restore sequence:

```
USE master ;
RESTORE DATABASE mydatabase
PAGE = '1:89, 1:250, 1:863, 1:1049'
FROM file1_backup_dev
WITH NORECOVERY ;

RESTORE LOG mydatabase  FROM log_backup_dev1
WITH NORECOVERY ;

RESTORE LOG mydatabase FROM log_backup_dev2
WITH NORECOVERY ;

BACKUP LOG mydatabase TO current_log_backup_dev
RESTORE LOG mydatabase FROM current_log_backup_dev
WITH RECOVERY ;
```

There are a number of ways to identify the file and page ID of corrupted pages, including viewing the SQL Server error log, and there are several limitations and considerations that you should know before performing page restores that are described in detail in SQL Server Books Online under the topic "Performing Page Restores."

## Partial and Piecemeal Restore

As an enhancement to partial restores in SQL Server 2000, SQL Server 2005 allows piecemeal restores from not only a full database backup but also from a set of individual filegroup backups. The purpose of a piecemeal restore is to provide the capability to restore and recover a database in stages or by pieces, one filegroup at a time. As each filegroup is restored, it is brought online for access. Filegroups that have not been restored yet are marked offline and are not accessible until they are restored or simply recovered. If the filegroup is read-only and data is not damaged, it can be recovered without having to restore data. Restoring a database in stages at different times is possible because the piecemeal restore performs checks during the process to ensure that data is consistent in the end.

The piecemeal restore sequence recovers data at the filegroup level. The primary filegroup must be restored in the first stage as a partial restore (optionally along with any other secondary filegroups) using the PARTIAL option of the RESTORE command, which indicates the beginning of a piecemeal restore. When the PARTIAL option is specified in the command, the primary filegroup is implicitly selected. If you use PARTIAL for any other stage in the restore sequence, the primary filegroup is implicitly selected and a new piecemeal restore scenario begins. Therefore, PARTIAL must be used only in the very first restore statement of the sequence.

Assume *mydatabase* contains three filegroups that are all read-write: *primary*, *secondary_fg_1*, and *secondary_fg_2*. Here is an example of a restore sequence that begins a piecemeal (partial) restore and restores only the primary filegroup and one of the read-write secondary filegroups, and recovers those two filegroups only. The third filegroup will be marked offline and will not be accessible until it is restored and brought online. But in the meantime, the first two filegroups are made available:

```
USE master ;
--first create the tail-log backup
BACKUP LOG mydatabase TO mydb_taillog_backup ;

--begin initial stage of a piecemeal restore with primary filegroup restore
RESTORE DATABASE mydatabase
FILEGROUP='PRIMARY'
FROM mydbbackup
WITH PARTIAL, NORECOVERY ;
```

```
--restore one of the secondary read-write filegroups
RESTORE DATABASE mydatabase
FILEGROUP='SECONDARY_FG_1'
FROM secondary_fg_backup
WITH NORECOVERY ;

--restore unbroken chain of log backups
RESTORE LOG mydatabase
FROM mydb_log_backup_dev1
WITH NORECOVERY ;

RESTORE LOG mydatabase
FROM mydb_log_backup_dev2
WITH NORECOVERY ;

RESTORE LOG mydatabase
FROM mydb_taillog_backup
WITH RECOVERY ;
```

After the primary filegroup is restored, it is brought online and any other filegroups that were not restored are automatically marked offline and placed in a state of recovery pending. Any filegroups that are not damaged and are read-only may be brought online without restoring the data. Subsequent restore sequences can be performed in stages at any time after the PARTIAL restore sequence. Each stage in itself is a complete restore sequence that restores a piece of the database and brings that piece online. If the filegroup being restored is read-write, then an unbroken chain of log backups must also be applied. If the restored filegroup is read-only, the log backups do not need to be applied and are automatically skipped if included as part of the restore sequence.

Following the previous example, which shows the first stage of a piecemeal restore, the second stage can be run at a later time to restore the remaining read-write secondary filegroup, *secondary_fg_2*. Here is what that second restore sequence looks like:

```
USE master ;
--second stage - restore the remaining secondary read-write filegroup
RESTORE DATABASE mydatabase
FILEGROUP='SECONDARY_FG_2'
FROM secondary_fg_backup2
WITH NORECOVERY ;

--restore unbroken chain of log backups because this is a read-write
--filegroup
RESTORE LOG mydatabase
FROM mydb_log_backup_dev1
WITH NORECOVERY ;
```

```
RESTORE LOG mydatabase
FROM mydb_log_backup_dev2
WITH NORECOVERY ;

RESTORE LOG mydatabase
FROM mydb_taillog_backup
WITH RECOVERY ;
```

Now all three filegroups are online and available.

Piecemeal restores are applicable only for databases with multiple filegroups. With both offline and online piecemeal restores, the first stage is the same. After the intial stage, the primary filegroup and any other specified filegroups are restored and brought online and made available. At that point, all unrestored filegroups are marked offline. The difference between offline and online piecemeal restore is that with offline, when additional restore stages are performed after the first stage, the database must be brought offline for these additional restore stages, whereas with online restore, the database can remain online while subsequent filegroups are restored.

---

**Note**    Online piecemeal restore is supported only with SQL Server 2005 Enterprise Edition. All other editions support only offline piecemeal restore.

### Real World    Most Common Backup and Restore Procedures

In the real world, the least complicated backup and restore procedures are the most often implemented. That is, full database, differential database, and log backups are taken regularly. For example, a full database backup might be taken once a week, a differential database backup each night, and log backups every 20 minutes. These types of backups are very easy to understand and restore. Individual file and filegroup backups are much less commonly implemented as they are more complex to restore and may not be necessary. These backups are useful when a database is too big to backup all at once because of time and/or the overhead incurred during backups, which can adversely affect performance of the system for any other processes that need to run.

## Revert to Database Snapshot

Database snapshots are available only with SQL Server 2005 Enterprise Edition. A database snapshot is a read-only, static view of a source database that can be accessed for reporting purposes (read-only access). If a database snapshot has been taken of a database, then reverting back to it is similar but not equivalent to a database restore in that it restores the database to the state it was in when the snapshot was taken. This involves overwriting any updates that were made to the source database pages since the snapshot was taken with the copy-on-write pages that were saved for the snapshot (the original source data pages that were copied when the source page was updated). For example, if a snapshot is taken at one point in time and after that a table is accidentally dropped, then reverting to the snapshot is one method of getting the dropped table back.

A database snapshot should never be considered a replacement for a backup. If certain data in the source database that is also part of the snapshot is corrupted, then both the database and snapshot contain corrupted data. If a copy-on-write page in the snapshot is corrupted, then reverting to it includes the corrupted data. Snapshots are not intended for use in place of solid database backups. They are a better fit for use as a reporting database or for a safety net from administrative or user errors, such as a dropped table. It may be quicker to revert to a snapshot than to perform a data restore. See Chapter 10, "Creating Databases and Database Snapshots," for more details on creating database snapshots.

Once the database has been reverted to a snapshot, no data can be rolled forward. The snapshot revert operation automatically rebuilds the log, overwriting the old log file, so a full database backup or file backup must be taken before log backups can begin again. Before reverting to a particular snapshot, you must drop any other snapshots that may also exist. You can accomplish this either using the *DROP DATABASE <snapshot_name>* statement or through Management Studio. Now you can revert to the one snapshot that is left. Dropping a snapshot does not affect the source database. During the revert process, both the source database and the snapshot are unavailable.

The RESTORE command is used to revert to a database snapshot that was taken. Here is the basic syntax for the T-SQL command to revert to a database snapshot:

```
RESTORE DATABASE <database_name>
FROM DATABASE SNAPSHOT = <database_snapshot_name>;
```

# Onine Restore

Online restore is a new feature with SQL Server 2005 Enterprise Edition. This allows a database to remain online during certain restore operations, permitting users to access some filegroups in the database while other filegroups may be offline. For a database to be online, at least its primary filegroup must be online. The entire database is not online during a restore, only certain filegroups at a time. If a file is being restored, the entire filegroup that it belongs to will be offline during the restore, but the primary filegroup and any other filegroups may remain online and users may access data in those online filegroups. Data in a filegroup that is being restored is offline and not accessible, and an error is returned if an attempt to access that data is made. File restores are automatically performed as online restores (by default).

---

**Note**   Online restore capabilities are available only with SQL Server 2005 Enterprise Edition.

---

## Fast Recovery

Fast recovery is a new feature supported only in SQL Server 2005 Enterprise Edition that allows a database to be available during the undo (rollback) phase of the restore process. In previous versions of SQL Server, a database could not be accessed until the undo phase was complete. When recovering from a crashed system, the undo phase can potentially take minutes or hours to complete. Fast recovery eliminates the need for users to wait while uncommitted transactions are rolled back. This is accomplished by SQL Server acquiring appropriate locks on data for the transactions that are being rolled back. This is an automatic feature.

---

**Note**   Fast recovery is also available only with SQL Server 2005 Enterprise Edition.

---

## Summary

In this chapter we covered the concepts of restoring and recovering data. There are various methods for restoring that are based on the type of backups that are taken. Data can be restored to any point in time or to the point of failure if backups are taken properly. Therefore, the strategy chosen for backup and restore is extremely important for protecting critical business data. Documenting restore procedures and putting them in a known location that the appropriate people can access is also very important.

There were several features mentioned in this chapter that are available only with SQL Server 2005 Enterprise Edition: online restores, fast recovery, and database snapshots. Be careful when choosing your edition to make sure you get the features you are expecting.

# Chapter 16

# User and Security Management

In addition to backup and recovery, the tasks of user and security management are probably the most important tasks that SQL Server DBA must perform. In the last few years, the job of security management has become much more important. In this chapter, you will be introduced to the basic concepts of SQL Server user and security management: logins, user IDs, schemas, permissions, and roles.

The SQL Server login is the method that allows users to connect in to the SQL Server instance. The login is the connection to the outside world. Within each database are user ids that provide a way of regulating access at the database level. Logins are mapped into user IDs at the database level. In addition, schemas are used for ownership of objects. Permissions allow users to perform specific tasks or access specific objects, and roles are a way of creating permissions on a pseudo-entity, which in turn is assigned to users.

Effective security is necessary to ensure that only authorized personnel or businesses are able to access your SQL Server database. In many cases, there are laws that specify the level of security that must be placed on your system. In the event of a security breach, you can lose data that can result in disastrous consequences and significant liability. Thus, security and user management are key parts of the SQL Server DBA's job.

The areas of user and security management have been enhanced in SQL Server 2005. In addition to users and logins, the concept of a schema has been introduced in this version of SQL Server. A schema now owns SQL Server objects. Since a schema can be owned by a role, now multiple users can have administrative rights over SQL Server objects. This allows you to drop individual users without having to change the ownership of the underlying objects.

The schema is covered later in this chapter. The chapter begins with the concepts of user login and user ID. The *user login* is the way that a user is identified to SQL Server. A *user*

*ID* is used to assign user permissions to specific objects within a database. In addition, with SQL Server 2005 a schema can also be used to assign specific permissions to database objects.

With SQL Server 2005, security is managed hierarchically. This hierarchy is made up of principals (users, groups, and processes that can access SQL Server objects) and securables (the objects that are being managed), and permissions, which can be granted to either principals or securables. In addition to the enhancements to the permissions hierarchy, all permissions are now grantable via the GRANT statement, thus simplifying management.

# Principals

Principals are the entities that can request access to SQL Server resources and consist of its own hierarchy. This hierarchy is made up of different levels that have progressively smaller scopes and consists of the following principals:

- Windows principals
- Domain logins
- Windows local logins
- SQL Server principals
- SQL Server login
- Database principals
- Database user
- Database role
- Application role

The higher you are in the hierarchy, the more influence you have on the scope of your security influence.

## Logins

The user login is the way that a user is identified to SQL Server. It is important that each user be uniquely identified so that the user can be tracked, if necessary, and so that individual permissions or group permissions can be applied. A login can be managed either via Windows Server 2003 or within SQL Server 2005. When SQL Server is configured, you can select to manage its security either via Windows authentication or mixed mode. With mixed mode authentication the user can log in with either Windows or SQL Server authentication.

There are both advantages and disadvantages of each method. The primary advantage of using Windows logon is that security can be maintained and monitored on an enterprise-wide basis, and it is generally considered to be a more secure method. Users log on to the domain and no further authentication is required. The disadvantage of Windows logons is that there is a necessary amount of coordination between the database administrators and the system administrators. Typically, the database administrators don't have authorization to create and manage domain accounts.

## Windows Authentication

With Windows authentication, SQL Server 2005 relies on Windows Server 2003 to provide the logon security. When a user logs on to Windows Server 2003, the user's account identity is validated. SQL Server verifies that the user was validated by Windows and allows access based on that authentication. SQL Server integrates its login security process with the Windows logon security process to provide these services. Network security attributes are validated through a sophisticated encryption process provided by Windows. Because the SQL Server login and Windows logon security processes are integrated when this mode is used, no further authentication methods are required for you to access SQL Server once you are authenticated by the operating system. The only password you need to supply to log in to SQL Server is your Windows password.

Windows authentication is considered a better security method than mixed mode authentication because of the additional security features it provides. These features include secure validation and encryption of passwords, auditing, password expiration, minimum password length, and automated account lockout after a certain number of unsuccessful logon attempts.

## Mixed Mode Authentication

With mixed mode authentication, users can access SQL Server by using either Windows authentication or SQL Server authentication. When mixed mode authentication is used, SQL Server authenticates a login made from an insecure system by verifying whether a SQL Server login account has been set up for the user requesting access. SQL Server performs this account authentication by comparing the name and password provided by the user attempting to connect to SQL Server with login account information stored in the database. If a login account has not been set up for the user or if the user does not provide the correct name and password, SQL Server access is denied.

Web applications require SQL Server Authentication (through Microsoft Internet Information Server) because users of these applications are most likely not within the same domain as the server and thus cannot rely on Windows security. Other applications that require database access might require SQL Server authentication as well. Some application developers prefer to use SQL Server security for their applications because it simplifies the security of their applications. When applications use SQL Server security within a trusted network, application developers do not have to provide security authentication within the application itself, which simplifies their job.

## Creating Logins

The method for creating logins varies depending on the type of login you wish to create. If you are using Windows authentication, the logins are created through either the domain administration console or the local system administration console, depending on whether you are creating a domain or local user account.

Creating a SQL Server login is done within SQL Server. You can create a login either via SQL Server Management Studio or with SQL statements from within the sqlcmd tool. SQL Server Management Studio provides an easy way to quickly create a SQL Server login; however, creating logins through SQL scripts provides a self-documenting method for creating repeatable scripts.

In order to create a login through SQL Server Management Studio, use the following steps:

1. Start SQL Server Management Studio. In Object Explorer view, connect to the server instance of your choice, and then navigate to logins security, as shown in Figure 16-1.

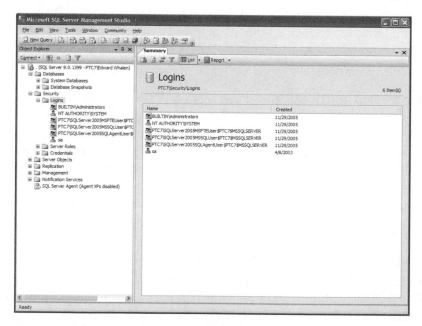

**Figure 16-1**    SQL Server Management Studio.

2. Right-click either the logins identifier in the navigation pane or an item in the logins list on the right side, and then select New Login. This invokes the Login – New utility, shown in Figure 16-2.

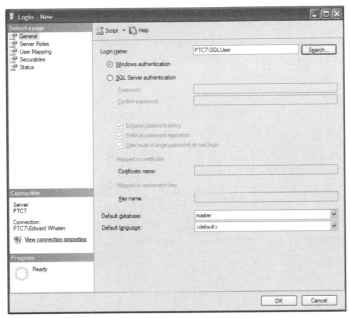

**Figure 16-2**   The SQL ServerLogin – New utility.

3. From this utility, there are a number of pages that allow you to create and identify the new login that can be selected using the icons in the upper left of the window. These pages include the following:

- ❑ **General**   This page allows you to define the authentication type, default database, and default language.

- ❑ **Server roles**   This page allows you to select which roles are assigned to this login. Roles are covered later in this chapter.

- ❑ **User Mapping**   This page is used to define the databases to which the login has access.

- ❑ **Securables**   The securables page is used to assign permissions to securables for this login.

- ❑ **Status**   The status page is used to grant permissions to this login and to disable the login if desired.

4. Once you have configured the user, click the OK button to create the login. Once the login has been created, the Login – New utility closes and the new login is visible in the login list.

Alternately, you can create SQL Server logins by using the CREATE LOGIN command. CREATE LOGIN requires the parameter *login_name*. The *login_name* parameter is the name by which the new login will be identified, and it must be unique in the database. The optional parameters include *<option_list1>* and *<sources>*. The available options and their descriptions are presented here:

```
CREATE LOGIN login_name { WITH <option_list1> | FROM <sources> }

<option_list1> ::=
    PASSWORD = 'password' [ HASHED ] [ MUST_CHANGE ]
    [ , <option_list2> [ ,... ] ]

<option_list2> ::=
    SID = sid
    | DEFAULT_DATABASE = database
    | DEFAULT_LANGUAGE = language
    | CHECK_EXPIRATION = { ON | OFF}
    | CHECK_POLICY = { ON | OFF}
    [ CREDENTIAL = credential_name ]

<sources> ::=
    WINDOWS [ WITH <windows_options> [ ,... ] ]
    | CERTIFICATE certname
    | ASYMMETRIC KEY asym_key_name

<windows_options> ::=
    DEFAULT_DATABASE = database
    | DEFAULT_LANGUAGE = language
```

The parameters to CREATE LOGIN are divided into two sets. The first set of parameters only applies to SQL Server logins. The second set applies to Windows logins. Here are the SQL Server login parameters:

- Specifying PASSWORD sets the password for this new login.

- Optionally, specifying HASHED indicates that the password is already hashed or encoded and will not be hashed. This allows you to export and import a login without having to know its password.

- The optional parameter MUST_CHANGE forces the user to change his or her password on first login. If this is set, both CHECK_EXPIRATION and CHECK_POLICY must be set to on.

- The SID parameter allows you to manually assign the GUID for the SQL Server user. If this is not specified, one will be assigned automatically by SQL Server.

- CHECK_EXPIRATION specifies whether the password expiration policy is applied to this login. The default value is OFF.

- CHECK_POLICY specifies that the Windows password policy is applied to this login. The default value is ON.

- CREDENTIAL is the name of the credential associated with the SQL Server login.

The following parameters apply to a login that is mapped to a Windows login.

- WINDOWS specifies that this login is mapped to a Windows account.

- CERTIFICATE is the name of the certificate, located in the *master* database, that is associated with this login.

- ASYMMETRIC KEY is the name of the asymmetric key, located in the *master* database, that is associated with this login.

The following parameters apply to logins that use either SQL Server or Windows authentication:

- The DEFAULT DATABASE parameter allows you to assign a default database for this login.

- DEFAULT_LANGUAGE allows you to specify the default language for this login.

Here are a few examples of creating logins using the CREATE LOGIN command:

1. Create a simple login with forced password change on first connect and whose default database is *users*.

   ```
   CREATE LOGIN edw WITH PASSWORD = 'abcd1234' MUST_CHANGE,
   CHECK_POLICY=ON, CHECK_EXPIRATION=ON, DEFAULT_DATABASE=users ;
   ```

2. Create login from the guest account of Windows.

   ```
   CREATE LOGIN [ptc7\Guest] FROM WINDOWS ;
   ```

Logins are an important part of your security policy. If you use Windows authentication, the SQL Server logins use the same security policy as your Windows system.

In addition to the CREATE LOGIN statement, there is a DROP LOGIN statement that is used to delete a login and an ALTER LOGIN statement that is used to modify logins. These two statements are used to manipulate already existing logins.

### Real World    Real World  How Do I Move Logins?

How do you move a login from one system to another? How do you preserver the password when you do this? Microsoft Support has developed and published via support.microsoft.com [in ital] a stored procedure called sp_help_revlogin, which allows you to script the creation of logins, including the retention of passwords. Search support.microsoft.com [ital] for sp_help_revlogin. The stored procedure for SQL Server 2005 is slightly different from the one for SQL Server 2000.

## Users

Whereas logins provide a method of authenticating and mapping user accounts, users allow us to map specific permissions to users. The logins that were covered in the previous section are a database-wide account that allows us to connect into the database. Within each database is a set of users who have permissions associated with those user accounts and the database. This is how permissions are assigned to individual logins. By default, a SQL Server login does not have any database permissions associated with it.

A SQL Server user can be created when a SQL Server login is created, or it can be created separately. Typically, a SQL Server user is created when you create the login, and it can be done within the Login – New utility available in SQL Server Management Studio by selecting the User Mapping page and clicking OK. In addition to adding the SQL Server user, you can also specify the login's default schema, as shown in Figure 16-3. If you don't specify a default schema, dbo is used. Schemas are described later in this section.

In addition to creating a user with SQL Server Management Studio, either as part of the login creation process or by creating the user directly, you can also create a user using the CREATE USER command. Follow these steps to create a user in SQL Server Management Studio:

1.  In Object Explorer view, connect to the server instance of your choice, and then expand the server's Databases folder.

2.  Select and expand your database, and then expand the Security folder.

3.  Right-click Users in either the navigation pane or in the main pane. This invokes the Database User – New utility. This utility allows you to create a user, associate that user with a login, and assign roles and securables. This is what allows the actual login to be associated with specific database objects and permissions, as shown in Figure 16-4.

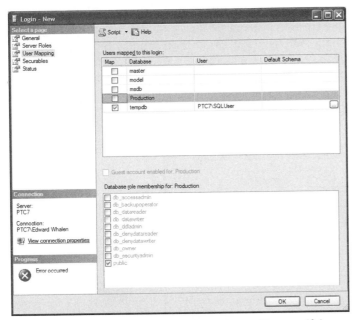

Figure 16-3    The SQL Server Login – New utility specifying user.

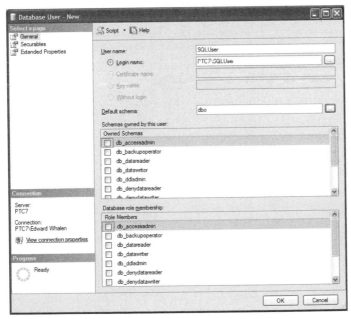

Figure 16-4    The Database User – New utility.

The User – New utility also allows you to select securables that have permissions granted to new users, as shown in Figure 16-5. In order to assign securables to the new user, select the Securables page and click the Add or Remove button to either add or remove securables permissions on the user. The Add button invokes a pop-up that asks you what type of securable you want to add. Select the type from specific objects, objects of a type, or all objects belonging to a specific schema. Once this has been selected, you can then modify individual securable permissions, as shown in Figure 16-5.

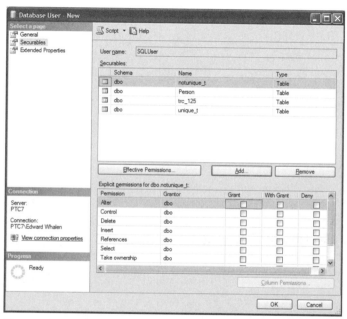

**Figure 16-5**    The Securables page of the Database User – New utility.

The final page is the Extended Properties page. From this page, you can add custom properties to a database.

In addition to using SQL Server Management Studio, you can also create a user from the command line using the CREATE USER command. The CREATE USER command allows you to create a SQL Server user without having to create a login at the same time. The CREATE USER command has the following syntax:

```
CREATE USER user_name
    [ { { FOR | FROM }
      {
        LOGIN login_name
```

```
        | CERTIFICATE cert_name
        | ASYMMETRIC KEY asym_key_name
    }
    | WITHOUT LOGIN
]
[ WITH DEFAULT_SCHEMA = schema_name ]
```

The parameters are as follow:

- *user_name* specifies the name of the user that you are creating.

- LOGIN specifies the login name with which this user is associated.

- CERTIFICATE is the name of the certificate, located in the *master* database, that is associated with this user.

- ASYMMETRIC KEY is the name of the asymmetric key, located in the *master* database that is associated with this user.

- WITH DEFAULT_SCHEMA specifies the first schema that should be searched when objects are resolved for this user.

- WITHOUT LOGIN specifies that this user is not associated with a specific SQL Server login.

A user must be associated with a login for a login to be able to access objects. Once the login and user have been established, permissions can be granted.

## Roles

As you will see later in this chapter, each login and user must be granted permissions in order to perform tasks in the database. The type of permission varies based on both function and whether the permission is granted to the login or the user. A login is granted system permissions, such as create database, bulk copy, and so on. These permissions are assigned to roles, specifically the fixed server roles, which are in turn assigned to logins.

Roles are used to help ease the burden of security management. Rather than applying specific permissions to each user and object, roles allow you to assign specific permissions to a pseudo user or role and then assign this role to users. So, instead of applying specific permissions for all of the users in the accounting group, you can create an accounting role, set the permissions for that role, and then assign the rights of that role to other users.

There are two different types of permissions. The server permissions provide server-wide permissions such as shutdown, checkpoint, create database, and so on (see SQL

Server Books Online for a complete list). In addition to the server roles, there are database permissions. The database permissions are used to provide permissions to database objects.

Server permissions can be assigned via the fixed server roles. The fixed server roles consist of the roles shown in Table 16-1.

**Table 16-1   Fixed Server Roles**

| Role | Permissions |
| --- | --- |
| Bulkadmin | Granted the ADMINISTER BULK OPERATIONS permission |
| Dbcreator | Granted the CREATE DATABASE permission |
| Diskadmin | Granted the ALTER RESOURCES permission |
| Processadmin | Granted the ALTER ANY CONNECTION and ALTER SERVER STATE permissions |
| Securityadmin | Granted ALTER ANY LOGIN permission |
| Serveradmin | Granted the ALTER ANY ENDPOINT (used for network communication), ALTER RESOURCES, ALTER SERVER STATE, ALTER SETTINGS, SHUTDOWN, and VIEW SERVER STATE permissions |
| Setupadmin | Granted the ALTER ANY LINKED SERVER permission |
| Sysadmin | Granted the CONTROL SERVER permission with GRANT option |

These permissions are described later in this chapter.

**Note**   The GRANT option allows the user to grant this permission to other users.

## Fixed Database Roles

Similar to the server permissions and roles, database roles are created to make managing database permissions easier. The database permissions are used to grant access to specific objects. As with server permissions, there are pre-created database roles that help administer permissions of users on objects. You can use these predefined, fixed database roles, or you can create your own roles. The fixed database roles are listed in Table 16-2.

**Table 16-2   Fixed Database Roles**

| Role | Permissions |
| --- | --- |
| db_accessadmin | Granted the ALTER ANY USER and CREATE SCHEMA permissions and granted the CONNECT permission with GRANT option. |
| db_backupoperator | Granted the BACKUP DATABASE, BACKUP LOG and CHECKPOINT permissions. |

**Table 16-2   Fixed Database Roles (continued)**

| Role | Permissions |
|------|-------------|
| db_datareader | Granted the SELECT permission |
| db_datawriter | Granted the INSERT, UPDATE, and DELETE permissions |
| db_ddladmin | Granted the ALTER ANY ASSEMBLY, ALTER ANY ASYMMETRIC KEY, ALTER ANY CERTIFICATE, ALTER ANY CONTRACT, ALTER ANY DATABASE DDL TRIGGER, ALTER ANY DATABASE EVENT NOTIFICATION, ALTER ANY DATASPACE, ALTER ANY FULLTEXT CATALOG, ALTER ANY MESSAGE TYPE, ALTER ANY REMOTE SERVICE BINDING, ALTER ANY ROUTE, ALTER ANY SCHEMA, ALTER ANY SERVICE, ALTER ANY SYMMETRIC KEY, CHECKPOINT, CREATE AGGREGATE, CREATE DEFAULT, CREATE FUNCTION, CREATE PROCEDURE, CREATE QUEUE, CREATE RULE, CREATE SYNONYM, CREATE TABLE, CREATE TYPE, CREATE VIEW, CREATE XML SCHEMA COLLECTION, and REFERENCES permissions |
| db_denydatareader | Denied the SELECT permission |
| db_denydatawriter | Denied the INSERT, UPDATE, and DELETE permissions |
| db_owner | Granted the CONTROL permission with GRANT option |
| db_securityadmin | Granted the ALTER ANY APPLICATION ROLE, ALTER ANY ROLE, CREATE SCHEMA, and VIEW DEFINITION permissions |

These roles can be used to provide permissions on specific objects in the database. In order to create your own role, follow these steps:

1. In Object Explorer view, connect to the server instance of your choice, and then expand the server's Databases folder.

2. Select and expand your database, and then expand the Security folder.

3. Right-click Roles in the navigation pane or in the main pane.

4. Then select either New Database Role or New Application Role from the shortcut menu. If you select Database Role, you will see the Database Role – New utility, as shown in Figure 16-6. This utility allows you to create a new role, select users for this role, select schemas that the role owns, and select securables and extended types.

> **Note**   An application role is a principal that allows an application to run with user-like permissions. A database role is a role that is applied to users in the database. Every database user is part of the public role, which provides default permissions for each user that has access to the database.

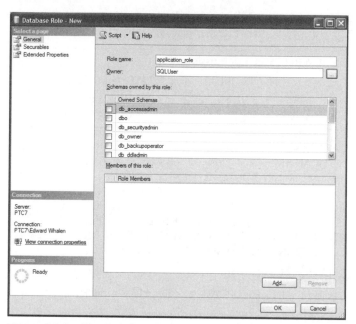

**Figure 16-6** The Database Role – New utility.

The first step is to give the role a name and an owner. In addition, in the General window you can also select schemas owned by this role, and select other roles that this role is a member of.

Selecting the securables page allows you to select securables that this role has permissions to access and select those permissions. The Add button invokes a pop-up window that asks you what type of securable you want to add. Select the type from specific objects, objects of a type, or all objects belonging to a specific schema. Once this has been selected, you can then modify individual securable permissions, as shown in Figure 16-7.

In addition to the general and securables page, there is an extended properties page. The final page is the extended properties page. From this page you can add custom properties to a role.

Creating an application role is similar to creating a database role, but you must supply the password that the application uses to access the application role. The introduction of the application role allows you to connect applications to the database without having to create users for each individual application user. This simplifies application management.

In addition to creating a role, the SQL Server Management Studio provides a nice feature that lets you script role creation. By right-clicking an existing role and selecting Script

Database Role, then Create To or Script Database Role, and then Drop To, you are provided with the SQL to create or drop the role. This script can then be modified to create roles like this role. In addition to creating roles, you can also modify or delete a role.

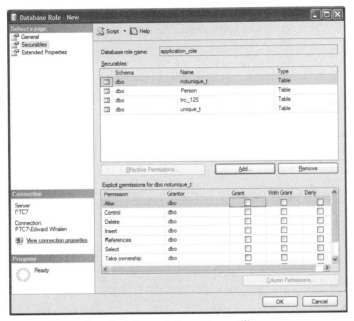

**Figure 16-7**   The Database Role – New utility.

***

**Note**   Most utilities in the SQL Server Management Studio include a "Script" button. Clicking this button displays the SQL code that will be performing the Management Studio tasks.

As with other tasks in SQL Server, the act of creating a role can be done with SQL statements. Creating a role is accomplished with the CREATE ROLE statement. The CREATE ROLE statement does not have very many parameters. The syntax for this statement is as follows:

CREATE ROLE role_name [ AUTHORIZATION owner_name ]

The *role_name* is the name of the role, and the *owner_name* is the database user or role that owns this role. Once the role has been created, permissions and securables can be assigned to this role. In addition to the CREATE ROLE statement, there is a DROP ROLE and ALTER ROLE statement.

# Securables

Securables are the resources to which the SQL Server database engine regulates access, or secures. As with the entire SQL Server security system, there is a hierarchy. The securables are made up of three scopes, which in turn contain other securables. The three scopes are server, database, and schema. These scopes in turn contain the following securables:

- Server securable scope
  - ❑ Endpoint
  - ❑ Login
  - ❑ Database
- Database securable scope
  - ❑ User
  - ❑ Role
  - ❑ Application role
  - ❑ Assembly
  - ❑ Message type
  - ❑ Route
  - ❑ Service
  - ❑ Remote service binding
  - ❑ Fulltext catalog
  - ❑ Certificate
  - ❑ Asymmetric key
  - ❑ Symmetric key
  - ❑ Contract
  - ❑ Schema
- Schema securable scope
  - ❑ Type
  - ❑ XML schema collection
  - ❑ Object

Within the securables, the user, role, and schemas are treated equally. The schema has changed in SQL Server 2005 in order to ease administration of objects.

# Schemas

A schema is a collection of objects that form a unique namespace. The schema is intended to reduce some of the issues associated with having all objects owned by a user. In the past, when a user was dropped from SQL Server, ownership of all associated objects had to be transferred to another user, or they were deleted and had to be recreated if they were again needed. The reason is that in SQL Server 2000 and earlier versions, the schema and the user were coupled.

In SQL Server 2000, for example, if my username is joe and I create a table called inventory in the database *mydb* on ptc7 (my system name), the fully qualified ownership of the table is ptc7.mydb.joe.inventory. The schema name is joe. In SQL Server 2000, the schema name and the owner of the object cannot be decoupled easily, so any change in joe's status causes additional work to change the ownership of the object.

With SQL Server 2005, the schema can now be decoupled from the username. When creating a table, you now have a choice to create the table with a schema associated with the login or a schema that is decoupled from the login. With this enhancement you can now detach the ownership of the object from the underlying user.

In SQL Server 2005, for example, if my username is joe and I create a table called inventory in the database *mydb* on ptc7 (my system name) specifying the apps schema, the fully qualified name of the table is ptc7.mydb.apps.inventory. The ownership of the schema can be either a user or a role. By assigning the ownership of a schema to a role, multiple users can own the objects in that schema. Benefits of using schemas include the following:

- By assigning the ownership of a schema to a role, multiple users can own a schema. If a user is deleted, the ownership of objects doesn't necessarily need to be changed.

- Dropping database users is simplified.

- Multiple users can share the same schema, providing for uniform name resolution of objects among users.

- Fully qualified names now contain the schema rather than just the user name. Fully qualified names are server.database.schema.object.

The use of independent schemas is recommended in SQL Server 2005. Schemas can be created within the SQL Server Management Studio using the following steps:

1. In Object Explorer view, connect to the server instance of your choice, and then expand the server's Databases folder.

2. Select and expand your database, and then expand the Security folder.

3. Right-click Schemas in either the navigation pane or the main pane to open the Schema – New window, as shown in Figure 16-8.

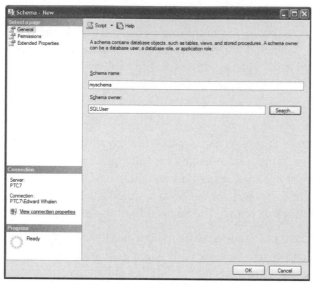

**Figure 16-8**    The Schema – New utility.

4. Select to set permissions for this schema. You can add users that have permissions on this schema and add explicit permissions on each of those users. This is shown in Figure 16-9.

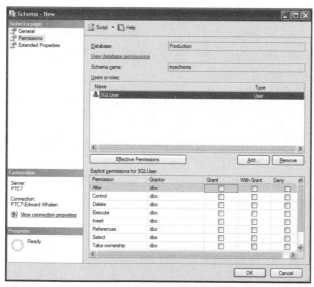

**Figure 16-9**    The Permissions page of the Schema – New utility.

5.  In addition to the General and Permissions pages in this utility, there is also an Extended Properties page. The final page is the Extended Properties page. From this page, you can add custom properties to a schema.

A schema can also be created with the CREATE SCHEMA statement. The CREATE SCHEMA statement has the following syntax:

```
CREATE SCHEMA schema_name_clause [ <schema_element> [ , ...n ] ]

<schema_name_clause> ::=
    {
        schema_name
    | AUTHORIZATION owner_name
    | schema_name AUTHORIZATION owner_name
    }

<schema_element> ::=
    {
        table_definition | view_definition | grant_statement
        revoke_statement | deny_statement
    }
```

The following parameters are provided:

- *schema_name* is the name of the schema to be added.

- AUTHORIZATION provides the database principal that owns the schema.

- *table_definition* is a table create statement that creates a table within the schema.

- *view_definition* is a view create statement that creates a view within the schema.

- *grant_statement* is a grant on any securable except this new schema.

- *revoke_statement* is a revoke on any securable except this new schema.

- *deny_statement* is a deny on any securable except this new schema.

The schemas are covered by permissions, which are described in the next section.

# Permissions

*Permissions* are used to control access to database objects and schemas and to specify which users can perform certain database actions. You can set both server and database permissions. *Server permissions* are used to allow DBAs to perform database administration tasks. *Database permissions* are used to allow or disallow access to database objects and statements. In this section, we'll look at the types of permissions and how to allocate them.

## Server Permissions

Server permissions are assigned to DBAs to allow them to perform administrative tasks. These permissions are defined on the fixed server roles. User logins can be assigned to the fixed server roles, but these roles cannot be modified. (Server roles are explained in the section "Using Fixed Server Roles" earlier in this chapter.) Server permissions include SHUTDOWN, CREATE ANY DATABASE, ALTER SERVER SETTINGS, and ALTER SETTINGS. Server permissions are used only for authorizing DBAs to perform administrative tasks and do not need to be modified or granted to individual users.

## Database Object Permissions

Database object permissions are a class of permissions that are granted to allow access to database objects. Object permissions are necessary to access a table or view by using SQL statements such as SELECT, INSERT, UPDATE, and DELETE. An object permission is also needed to use the EXECUTE statement to run a stored procedure. You can use SQL Server Management Studio or SQL commands to assign object permissions.

### Using SQL Server Management Studio to Assign Object Permissions

To use SQL Server Management Studio to grant database object permissions to a user, follow these steps:

1.  In Object Explorer view, connect to the server instance of your choice, and then expand the server's Databases folder.

2.  Select and expand your database, and then expand the Security folder.

3.  Expand the Users folder and then right-click a user name in the main pane and choose Properties from the shortcut menu to display the Database User window, as shown in Figure 16-10. From this window you can assign schemas and role membership.

4.  Click the Securables button to display the Securables page, shown in Figure 16-11. On this page, you manage the permissions assigned to this user.

5.  Click the Add button to display the Add Objects utility, as shown in Figure 16-12.

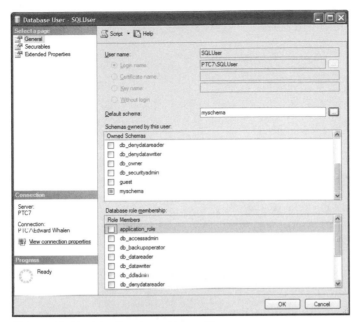

**Figure 16-10**    The Database User utility.

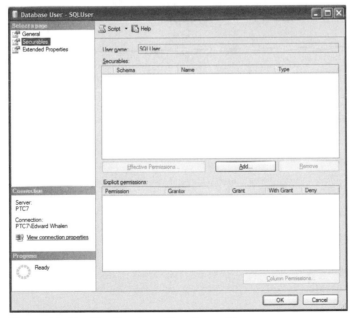

**Figure 16-11**    The Database User Securables page.

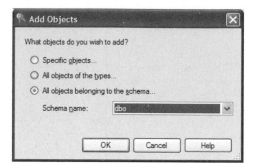

**Figure 16-12** The Add Objects utility.

6. Select the object type from the list of Specific Objects, All Objects of Type, or All Objects Belonging to the Schema. For this example, I chose all objects belonging to schema [dbo] and was returned to the Securables page, as shown in Figure 16-13.

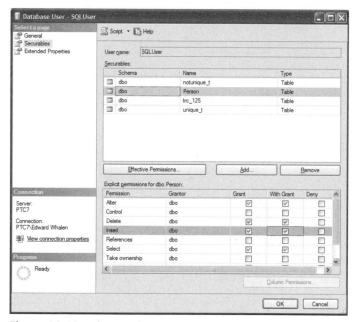

**Figure 16-13** The Database User Securables page.

7. From this page, select a securable from the list and check the explicit permissions from the boxes below.

8. Select the desired permissions and then click OK.

**Note** On each permission, you have the option of Grant, which gives you that permission, With Grant, which gives you permissions to grant this permission to others, and Deny, which denies this permission on the object.

## Using SQL to Assign Object Permissions

To use SQL to assign object permissions to a user, you run the GRANT statement. The GRANT statement has the following syntax:

```
GRANT { ALL [ PRIVILEGES ] }
    | permission [ ( column [ ,...n ] ) ] [ ,...n ]
    [ ON [ class :: ] securable ] TO principal [ ,...n ]
    [ WITH GRANT OPTION ] [ AS principal ]
```

The parameters are as follow:

- ALL means to assign a number of permissions depending on whether the securable is a database, a table, a view, a stored procedure, and so on as described here. See SQL Server Books Online for more details.

    ❑ If the securable is a database, "ALL" means BACKUP DATABASE, BACKUP LOG, CREATE DATABASE, CREATE DEFAULT, CREATE FUNCTION, CREATE PROCEDURE, CREATE RULE, CREATE TABLE, and CREATE VIEW.

    ❑ If the securable is a scalar function, "ALL" means EXECUTE and REFERENCES.

    ❑ If the securable is a table-valued function, "ALL" means DELETE, INSERT, REFERENCES, SELECT, and UPDATE.

    ❑ If the securable is a stored procedure, "ALL" means EXECUTE.

    ❑ If the securable is a table, "ALL" means DELETE, INSERT, REFERENCES, SELECT, and UPDATE.

    ❑ If the securable is a view, "ALL" means DELETE, INSERT, REFERENCES, SELECT, and UPDATE.

- PRIVILEGES is provided for SQL-92 compliance. The keywords ALL and ALL PRIVILEGES are synonymous.

- *permission* is the name of the permission.

- *column* is the name of the column in a table to which to apply the permission.

- *class* specifies the class of the securable.

- TO *principal* specifies to which principal to grant the permission.

- WITH GRANT OPTION gives the principal the right to grant this permission to others.

- AS *principal* specifies the principal from which the grantor derives its rights.

---

**Note**    Using the GRANT OPTION keyword allows the user or users specified in the statement to grant the specified permission to other users. This can be useful when you grant permissions to other DBAs. However, the GRANT option should be used with care.

---

The AS *principal* option specifies whose authority the GRANT statement is run under. To run the GRANT statement, a user or role must have been specifically granted authority to do so.

Here is an example of how to use the GRANT statement:

```
GRANT SELECT ON [dbo].[Person] TO [SQLUser] WITH GRANT OPTION ;

GRANT INSERT ON [dbo].[Person] TO [SQLUser];

GRANT UPDATE ON [dbo].[Person] TO [SQLUser];

GRANT DELETE ON [dbo].[Person] TO [SQLUser];
```

The AS myuser option is used because the *myuser* user has permissions to grant permissions on the test1 table. The WITH GRANT OPTION keyword allows the *edw* user to grant these permissions to other users.

## Using SQL to Revoke Object Permissions

You can use the SQL REVOKE statement to revoke a user's object permissions. This is useful when a user's role has changed and you want to take away permissions that you have previously granted. The syntax of the REVOKE statement is shown here:

```
REVOKE [ GRANT OPTION FOR ]
     {
       [ ALL [ PRIVILEGES ] ]
       |
               permission [ ( column [ ,...n ] ) ] [ ,...n ]
     }
```

```
[ ON [ class :: ] securable ]
{ TO | FROM } principal [ ,...n ]
[ CASCADE] [ AS principal ]
```

The parameters to REVOKE are similar to GRANT. An example of REVOKE is shown here:

```
REVOKE DELETE ON [dbo].[Person] TO [SQLUser] CASCADE;
```

---

**Note**  The CASCADE option specifies that when the permission is revoked from this user it is revoked from all users that this user has granted the permission to. Thus, the entire chain of grants is revoked.

---

In addition, the DENY statement can be used to Deny permissions to users. The syntax of the DENY statement is as follows:

```
DENY { ALL [ PRIVILEGES ] }
    | permission [ ( column [ ,...n ] ) ] [ ,...n ]
    [ ON [ class :: ] securable ] TO principal [ ,...n ]
    [ CASCADE] [ AS principal ]
```

The parameters to DENY are similar to REVOKE. An example of DENY is shown here:

```
DENY ALTER ON [dbo].[Person] TO [SQLUser] CASCADE;
```

## Statement Permissions

In addition to assigning database object permissions, you can assign permissions for particular types of operations. Object permissions enable users to access existing objects within the database, whereas statement permissions authorize them to create database objects, including databases and tables and do not reference a particular object. Some of the most commonly used statement permissions are listed here:

- BACKUP DATABASE allows the user to execute the BACKUP DATABASE command.

- BACKUP LOG allows the user to execute the BACKUP LOG command.

- CREATE DATABASE allows the user to create new databases.

- CREATE DEFAULT allows the user to create default values that can be bound to columns.

- CREATE PROCEDURE allows the user to create stored procedures.

- CREATE RULE allows the user to create rules.

- CREATE TABLE allows the user to create new tables.

- CREATE VIEW allows the user to create new views.

You can assign statement permissions by using either SQL Server Management Studio or SQL.

## Using SQL Server Management Studio to Assign Statement Permissions

To use SQL Server Management Studio to grant database object permissions to a user, follow these steps:

1. In Object Explorer view, connect to the server instance of your choice, and then expand the server's Databases folder.

2. Right-click a database name in the main pane or the database name in the navigation pane and then choose Properties from the shortcut menu to display the Database Properties utility, as shown in Figure 16-14.

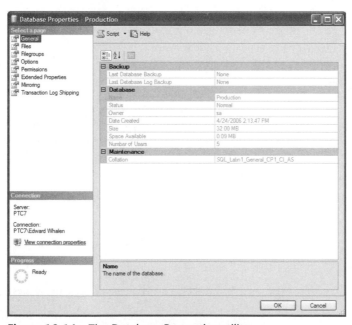

**Figure 16-14** The Database Properties utility.

3. Select the Permissions page, shown in Figure 16-15. Here you can assign statement permissions to the users and roles that have access to this database. The upper window contains the list of users and roles that have access to this database.

4. Highlight a user or role and then select the permissions in the lower window. The columns containing check boxes define the statement permissions that can be assigned, assigned with grant option, or denied.

---

**Note**   A permission can be granted with or without the grant option, however, for the grant option to be assigned, the permission must also be assigned. You cannot check the With Grant column without checking the Grant column.

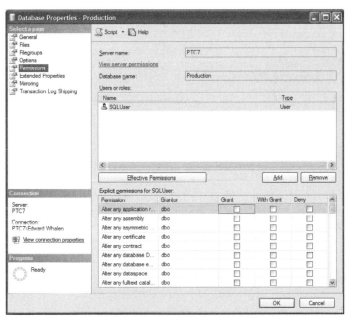

**Figure 16-15**   The Database Properties Permissions page.

## Using SQL to Assign Statement Permissions

To use SQL to assign statement permissions to a user, you use the GRANT statement (as shown earlier). The GRANT statement has the following syntax:

```
GRANT { ALL [ PRIVILEGES ] }
    | permission [ ( column [ ,...n ] ) ] [ ,...n ]
```

```
[ ON [ class :: ] securable ] TO principal [ ,...n ]
[ WITH GRANT OPTION ] [ AS principal ]
```

Some of the most common statement permissions that can be assigned to a user are BACKUP DATABASE, BACKUP LOG, CREATE DATABASE, CREATE DEFAULT, CREATE FUNCTION, CREATE PROCEDURE, CREATE RULE, CREATE TABLE, and CREATE VIEW, as described earlier. Please check SQL Server Books Online for a complete list and description. For example, to add the BACKUP DATABASE, CREATE TABLE and CREATE VIEW statement permissions to the user account SQLUser, use the following command:

```
GRANT BACKUP DATABASE, CREATE TABLE, CREATE VIEW

TO [SQLUser]

WITH GRANT OPTION;
```

Permissions should be granted and revoked with care. Be sure to keep records of permissions that have been added in case you need to redo these GRANTS.

## Using SQL to Revoke Statement Permissions

You can use the SQL statement REVOKE to remove statement permissions from a user account. The REVOKE statement has the following syntax:

```
REVOKE [ GRANT OPTION FOR ]
    {
      [ ALL [ PRIVILEGES ] ]
      |
              permission [ ( column [ ,...n ] ) ] [ ,...n ]
    }
    [ ON [ class :: ] securable ]
    { TO | FROM } principal [ ,...n ]
    [ CASCADE] [ AS principal ]
```

For example, to remove just the CREATE VIEW statement permissions from the user account edw, use the following command:

```
REVOKE CREATE VIEW

FROM [edw]

CASCADE
```

As you can see, removing statement permissions from a user account is not a complex process, but it should be done with care.

# Summary

In this chapter you have learned about the principals of user and security management. SQL Server 2005 is similar to SQL Server 2000 in many ways, but the handling of user schema separation is one difference. Keep in mind that the tasks of user and security management are probably among the most important tasks that the SQL Server DBA must perform. This is often an ongoing task for most DBAs because employees join, leave, and change roles within an organization on a regular basis.

Effective security is necessary for ensuring that only authorized personnel or businesses are allowed access to your SQL Server database. Thus, security and user management are key parts of the SQL Server DBA's job. SQL Server Security has been made easier with the SQL Server Management Studio, and the ability to script commands. Scripting commands allows you to save the SQL statements used to execute the command, thus documenting what was done, and also the ability to modify and reuse the command. Security and user management should not be taken lightly and should be done with care.

# Part IV
# Microsoft SQL Server 2005 Architecture and Features

# Chapter 17
# Transactions and Locking

In this chapter, we discuss the fundamentals and concepts relating to transactions and locking in Microsoft SQL Server 2005, including a description of the various transaction modes, isolation levels, process blocking, and deadlocking. Many of the transaction and locking concepts are similar to those in SQL Server 2000. The major new and exciting feature in SQL Server 2005 relating to transaction behavior is the new snapshot capability that comes in the form of two new isolation levels—read-committed snapshot and snapshot isolation—that utilize the new row versioning feature. In this chapter, we discuss what a transaction is, what properties SQL Server requires for valid transactions, what the different transaction modes are, how to specify the beginning and the end of a transaction, and how to commit and roll back transactions. We'll also look at the types and modes of locking that SQL Server uses, the use of locking hints in Transact-SQL code, and the effect on locking behavior of using the various transaction isolation levels.

## What Is a Transaction?

A transaction is one or more database operations that must be executed in their entirety as one logical unit of work. If one of a series of operations fails or does not complete, then all operations within that transaction should be rolled back, or undone, so that none of them complete. If the transaction is a single operation that performs modifications to multiple rows of data and it does not complete, then all of the changes made should be rolled back so the operation is not left partially done; rather, all or nothing is done. Transactions allow SQL Server to ensure data integrity, consistency, and recoverability.

The transaction log of each database keeps a record of all data modifications that a transaction performs on the database (such as an insert, update, delete, or schema change), and it marks the beginning and end of the transaction's records. SQL Server uses this transaction log to recover data in case of errors or system failures. How the transaction log works is discussed in more detail in Chapter 14, "Backup Fundamentals."

SQL Server provides various ways to explicitly begin and end transactions via application programming interface (API) functions or T-SQL statements, which we will discuss throughout this chapter. Therefore, the integrity of a transaction depends in part on the developer. The developer must know when to start and end the transaction and how to sequence data modifications to ensure logical consistency and meaningfulness of data. In addition, performance of the system may also depend on how transactions are handled. For example, locking behavior (and therefore the potential for process blocking) must be taken into consideration with transactions, which vary depending on the isolation level in effect. A long-running transaction can potentially hold locks for extended periods of time, thus blocking other users. These topics are covered throughout this chapter.

# ACID Properties

Now that you know generally what a transaction is, let's take a look at the properties that must be met for a transaction to be considered valid. These are not specific to SQL Server transactions, but to transactions in general. SQL Server supports these properties, which have not changed from previous versions of SQL Server. A logical unit of work must exhibit four properties, called the atomicity, consistency, isolation, and durability (*ACID*) properties, to qualify as a valid transaction. SQL Server provides mechanisms to help ensure that a transaction meets each of these requirements.

## Atomicity

SQL Server ensures either that all data modifications in a transaction are completed as a group if the transaction is successful or that none of the modifications occur if the transaction is not successful. In other words, SQL Server ensures the atomicity of your transactions. The transaction must be performed as an atomic unit—thus the term "atomicity." For a transaction to be successful, every step, or statement, in the transaction must succeed. If one of the steps fails, the entire transaction fails and any modifications made after the transaction started will be undone. SQL Server provides a transaction management mechanism that automatically determines whether a transaction has succeeded or failed, and undoes data modification, as necessary, in the case of a failure.

## Consistency

SQL Server also ensures the consistency of your transactions. Consistency means that all data remains in a consistent state—that the integrity of the data is preserved—after a transaction finishes, regardless of whether the transaction succeeded or failed. Before a transaction begins, the database must be in a consistent state, which means that the integrity of the data is upheld and that internal structures, such as B-tree indexes and doubly linked lists, are correct. Likewise, after a transaction occurs, the database must be in a consistent state—a new state if the transaction succeeded or its pre-transaction state if the transaction failed.

Consistency is also a transaction management feature provided by SQL Server. If your data is consistent and your transactions maintain logical consistency and data integrity, SQL Server will ensure the consistency of the data after a transaction. When you are using data replication in a distributed environment, various levels of consistency can be achieved, ranging from eventual transactional convergence, or latent consistency, to immediate transactional consistency. The level of consistency depends on the type of replication you use.

## Isolation

The "I" in ACID stands for isolation. Isolation means that the effects of each transaction are the same as if the transaction was the only one in the system; in other words, modifications made by a concurrent transaction must be isolated from the modifications made by any other concurrent transaction. In this way, a transaction will not be affected by a value that has been changed by another transaction until the change is committed. A transaction either recognizes data in the state it was in before another concurrent transaction modified the data, or it recognizes the data after the second transaction has completed; however, it does not recognize the data in an intermediate state. This is referred to as serializable isolation because it results in the ability to have a common starting set of data reloaded and to replay a series of transactions to end up with the data in the same state no matter how many times it is performed. If a transaction fails, its modifications will have no effect because the changes will be rolled back. SQL Server enables you to adjust the isolation level of your transactions according to what is acceptable for business needs; serializable is not the only option. A transaction's isolation behavior depends on the isolation level you specify. Levels of isolation are covered in more detail in a later section.

## Durability

The last ACID property is durability. Durability means that once a transaction is committed, the effects of the transaction remain permanently in the database, even in the event of a system failure. The SQL Server transaction log and your database backups provide durability. If SQL Server, the operating system, or a component of the server fails, the database will automatically recover when SQL Server is restarted. SQL Server uses the transaction log to replay the committed transactions that were affected by the system crash and to roll back any uncommitted transactions.

If a data drive fails and data is lost or corrupted, you can recover the database by using data backups and transaction log backups. Proper recovery planning is essential in any database system. With proper backups, you should always be able to recover from a failure. Unfortunately, if your backup drives fail and you lose the backup that is needed to recover the system, you might not be able to recover your database. See Chapter 14 and Chapter 15, "Restoring Data," for details about backing up and restoring your database and transaction logs.

## Committing Transactions

Now that you understand the properties of a valid transaction, let's look at the mechanisms SQL Server provides to manage transactions with both the default SQL Server behavior and via programmable transaction management. The key to transactions is the commit process.

Committing transactions—in essence, committing the data changes made by transactions—is an integral part of data integrity, locking, and consistency. A commit is an operation that conceptually saves all changes to the database made since the start of a transaction. A commit guarantees that all of the transaction's modifications, first written to the buffer cache in memory, will be permanent in the database. When a transaction is committed, it means any changed records are written to the log file and, eventually also written to the data files (if not already). If the changes were not yet written to the data files at the point of the commit, then the changes will be written when the SQL Server background processes, such as the lazy writer or checkpoint, writes them out. A commit also frees resources such as locks, which are held by a transaction.

Starting and ending transactions appropriately to enforce logical consistency of data is the responsibility of the application developer and/or the DBA who writes SQL code or stored procedures. A transaction may need to include multiple data modification statements that must be part of a single unit in order to maintain data integrity and consistency in the database. If one of those statements fails, the other statements must not complete either or the data will be left inconsistent. SQL Server cannot determine on its own when a logical unit of work should begin or end—only a developer who knows the business logic can determine that—but SQL Server does provide the mechanisms needed to manage transactions.

## Transaction Commit Modes

There are three basic transaction modes in which SQL Server operates to begin transactions and commit data: autocommit, explicit, and implicit modes. In addition to these, there is a new transaction mode in SQL Server 2005 that is only applicable for multiple active result sets (MARS), called batch-scoped transaction mode. The default transaction mode for SQL Server 2005 is autocommit.

Using API functions and T-SQL statements, a transaction can be started in one of the three basic modes. The transaction mode can be set to either autocommit or implicit for a SQL Server connection, or a transaction can be started explicitly through coding. Let's take a look at how each of these modes works and how to use them.

### Autocommit Mode

In autocommit mode, the SQL Server default mode, each T-SQL statement (select, insert, update, delete, schema changes, and so on) is committed when it finishes or is rolled back when it fails. No explicit T-SQL statements or application code is necessary to control transactions with this mode. Each transaction consists of just one T-SQL statement. Autocommit mode is useful when you are executing statements by interactive command line, using the sqlcmd utility or Query Editor, because you do not have to explicitly start and end each transaction. Each statement is treated as its own transaction by SQL Server and is committed as soon as it is finished. Every connection to SQL Server uses autocommit mode until you start an explicit transaction by using BEGIN TRANSACTION or until you specify implicit mode. Once the explicit transaction is ended (with a commit or rollback) or implicit mode is turned off, SQL Server automatically returns to autocommit mode. Autocommit is also the default mode for ADO, OLE DB, ODBC, and DB-Library.

### Explicit Mode

An explicit transaction is one in which you explicitly define both the start and the end of the transaction. Explicit mode is used most often in application programming, in stored procedures, and T-SQL scripts. When you are executing a group of statements to perform a task, you might need to determine at what points the transaction should start and end so that either the entire group of statements succeeds or the entire group's modifications are rolled back, such is the case when multiple tables with related data must be modified together in order for a particular business function to complete properly and to maintain consistent data between those tables. For example, a bank deposit transaction may require an update to the customer balance and an insert into a historical table that stores a record with information about the deposit, such as the time and place it occurred.

When you explicitly identify the beginning and the end of a transaction, you are using explicit mode, and the transaction is referred to as an explicit transaction. You specify an explicit transaction by using either T-SQL statements or API functions. This section explains only the T-SQL method, as the specific API functions are a more detailed developer topic and are beyond the scope of this book (For more information, see *Inside Microsoft SQL Server 2005: T-SQL Programming*, by Itzik Ben-gan, Dejan Sarka, and Roger Wolter, published by Microsoft Press.). It is very important that the application developer also understands the implications of starting and ending transactions within the application.

## Using Explicit Transactions

Let's look at a situation in which you would need to use an explicit transaction to start and end a task. Suppose we have a stored procedure that handles the database task of creating a customer's order for an item. The steps in this procedure include selecting the customer's current account information, entering the new order ID number and the item ordered, calculating the price of the order plus taxes, and updating the customer's account to reflect payment due for the order.

We want either all of these steps to be completed together or none of them to be completed so that the data will remain consistent in the database. To achieve this, we will group the statements that handle these tasks into an explicit transaction. If we do not group the statements into a transaction, we could end up with inconsistent data in the database. For example, if the network connection from the client to the server is interrupted after the new order number is entered but before the customer account is updated with the payment due, the database will be left with a new order for the customer but no charge on the customer's account. Without an explicit transaction, SQL Server would commit each statement as soon as it finished using autocommit mode, leaving the stored procedure half-completed at the time of the network disconnect. However, if the steps are defined within one explicit transaction, SQL Server automatically rolls back the entire transaction upon disconnection, and the client can later reconnect and execute the procedure again.

Using explicit transactions when your task consists of several steps is also beneficial because, whether or not you specify your own ROLLBACK statements, SQL Server will automatically roll back your transactions when a severe error occurs, such as a break in communication across the network, a database crash, a client system crash, or a deadlock. (Deadlocks are covered in the section "Blocking and Deadlocks" later in this chapter.)

The T-SQL statement used to start a transaction is BEGIN TRANSACTION (BEGIN or BEGIN TRAN are equivalent; see the syntax that follows). You specify the end of an implicit or an explicit transaction by using either COMMIT TRANSACTION or

ROLLBACK TRANSACTION. You can optionally specify a name for a transaction in the BEGIN TRANSACTION statement. You can then refer to the transaction by name in the COMMIT TRANSACTION or ROLLBACK TRANSACTION statement, although the name is useful only for human readability of code and for no other reason; SQL Server ignores the name if one is provided. The name helps readers identify to which BEGIN TRANSACTION a COMMIT or ROLLBACK belongs. The syntax for these three statements is shown here:

```
BEGIN {TRAN|TRANSACTION}
    [transaction_name | @tran_name_variable]
    [WITH MARK ['description']]

COMMIT {TRAN | TRANSACTION}
    [transaction_name | @tran_name_variable]

ROLLBACK {TRAN|TRANSACTION}
    [transaction_name | @tran_name_variable
    | savepoint_name | @savepoint_name_variable]
```

The BEGIN TRANSACTION statement has an option WITH MARK. This marks the transaction so that the transaction name gets written to the transaction log, marking the transaction so that a log can be restored to the point in the log where that transaction occurred.

> **Note**  COMMIT WORK is the equivalent of COMMIT TRAN, except the former does not accept a user-defined transaction name. ROLLBACK WORK is the equivalent of ROLLBACK TRAN, except the former also does not accept a user-defined transaction name. Use the statements in the example syntax if you want to define a transaction name for coding clarity.

Generally, all resources used by a transaction, such as locks, are released when the transaction commits (except for nested transactions, which are discussed in the "Creating Nested Transactions" section later in this chapter). Note that the way in which locks are managed during a transaction also depends on the isolation level. For example, when using the READCOMMITTED isolation level, shared locks for SELECT statements are released during a multi-statement transaction as soon as the SELECT completes, they are not held until the end of the transaction. See the section "Isolation Levels" later in this chapter for more details.

A transaction commits successfully if each of its statements is successful. For example, here is the T-SQL to run a single statement explicit transaction, named update_marital_status, that updates the MaritalStatus column value to "M" in the Employee table for a particular EmployeeID:

```
USE AdventureWorks;
BEGIN TRAN update_marital_status;
    UPDATE HumanResources.Employee
    SET MaritalStatus='M'
    WHERE EmployeeID=8;
COMMIT TRAN update_marital_status;
```

The transaction name update_marital_status is ignored by SQL Server; it serves simply as an aid to the programmer for identifying which transaction is being committed. This is useful in the case of nesting transactions as seen in the next section. In this previous example, since only one data modification statement makes up the entire transaction, the same can be accomplished without an explicit transaction, but instead using the SQL Server default autocommit mode as follows:

```
USE AdventureWorks;
UPDATE HumanResources.Employee
SET MaritalStatus='M'
WHERE EmployeeID=8;
```

In autocommit mode, the UPDATE statement begins a transaction which is committed as soon as the update completes.

When a transaction includes multiple modification statements that must be executed as a unit or not at all, an explicit transaction or implicit mode is necessary instead of using autocommit mode (see section "Implicit Mode" later in this chapter). For an example of creating an explicit transaction, let's expand on the previous update transaction by adding another update that changes a woman's title to correspond to her marital status that should be part of the unit of work. Here is the code to do this:

```
USE AdventureWorks;
BEGIN TRAN update_marital_status;
    UPDATE HumanResources.Employee
    SET MaritalStatus='M'
    WHERE EmployeeID=8;
    UPDATE Person.Contact
    SET title = 'Mrs.'
    FROM HumanResources.Employee e JOIN Person.Contact p
    ON e.ContactID =  p.ContactID
    WHERE e.EmployeeID = 8;
COMMIT TRAN update_marital_status;
```

Now if there is a failure during processing, the entire transaction rolls back so that the updated marital status is not updated without the title also being updated. Therefore, that these pieces of information will be consistent—either as they were before the transaction started or as updated by the transaction.

## @@TRANCOUNT Variable

The built-in SQL Server variable @@TRANCOUNT keeps track of the number of active transactions for each user connection. When no active transactions are present, @@TRANCOUNT is 0. Each BEGIN TRANSACTION statement increases @@TRANCOUNT by 1. Each COMMIT statement decreases @@TRANCOUNT by 1. If a ROLLBACK statement is executed within the outer transaction or any inner nested transactions, @@TRANCOUNT is set to 0, unless a savepoint is specified, in which case @@TRANCOUNT is not affected. Remember, you should commit each inner transaction so that @@TRANCOUNT can be decremented properly. You can test the value of @@TRANCOUNT to determine whether any active transactions are present by running the following query:

```
SELECT @@TRANCOUNT
```

If @@TRANCOUNT has a value of 1 when a COMMIT is encountered, then the transaction is committed and all its modifications are made a permanent part of the database. If @@TRANCOUNT is greater than 1 when a COMMIT is encountered, then @@TRANCOUNT is simply decremented by 1 and no transactions are actually committed—the outer transaction stays active. This is important for nesting transactions, as seen in the next section.

## Creating Nested Transactions

SQL Server allows nested transactions, or transactions that begin within another transaction. The first transaction to begin is called the outer transaction, and any nested transactions that start within that outer transaction are all referred to as inner transactions. A common example of this is when one stored procedure begins a transaction (outer) and then makes a call to another stored procedure that also begins a transaction (inner). (This case is also something to be careful of to avoid locks being held unnecessarily.) With nested transactions, you must explicitly commit each inner transaction so SQL Server can maintain the correct value for @@TRANCOUNT. When inner transactions are committed with a COMMIT statement, their resources are not released and their changes are not actually committed until the outer transaction finally commits. Although SQL Server does not commit inner transactions upon encountering their COMMIT statements, it does update the @@TRANCOUNT, decreasing it by 1 for each COMMIT encountered. Therefore, the COMMIT statements for inner transactions are necessary so that @@TRANCOUNT can be properly decremented such that it equals 1 when the outer transaction reaches its COMMIT statement.

If the outer transaction or any of the inner transactions fails, then none of the transactions will commit and the outer transaction and all inner transactions will be rolled back. If the outer transaction commits, all inner transactions commit. In other words, SQL Server basically ignores any COMMIT statements within inner nested transactions, in the sense that the inner transactions do not commit, and instead wait for the final commit or rollback of the outer transaction to determine the completion status of the outer and all inner transactions.

Also, in nested transactions, if a ROLLBACK statement is executed within the outer transaction or any of the inner transactions, the outer and all inner transactions are rolled back. It is not valid to include an inner transaction name with a ROLLBACK statement—if you do, SQL Server returns an error. Include the name of the outermost transaction, no name at all, or a savepoint name. Savepoints are explained in the "Savepoints" section later in this chapter.

Let's look at an example of a nested transaction by beginning a transaction and then calling a stored procedure that also begins a transaction. Therefore, the transaction started within the stored procedure becomes a nested inner transaction. The following code shows an example of creating a stored procedure and then starting a transaction that calls the stored procedure, building from the previous examples. First, here is the T-SQL code to create the stored procedure:

```
USE AdventureWorks;

GO

CREATE PROCEDURE update_marital_status(@new_status char(1),

    @emp_id smallint, @new_title char(4))
    AS

    BEGIN TRAN update_status_tran;

        UPDATE HumanResources.Employee

        SET MaritalStatus=@new_status

        WHERE EmployeeID=@emp_id;

        UPDATE Person.Contact

        SET title = @new_title

        FROM HumanResources.Employee e JOIN Person.Contact p

        ON e.ContactID =  p.ContactID

        WHERE e.EmployeeID = @emp_id;

    COMMIT TRAN update_status_tran;

GO
```

Now, here is the T-SQL that starts a transaction (outer) and calls the above stored procedure, which also starts a transaction (inner):

```
BEGIN TRAN outer_tran;
    EXEC update_marital_status 'M', 8, 'Mrs.';
    GO
COMMIT TRAN outer_tran;
GO
```

The first BEGIN TRAN above increments @@TRANCOUNT to 1. The BEGIN TRAN within the stored procedure then increments @@TRANCOUNT to 2. Therefore, the COMMIT TRAN within the stored procedure must be present to decrement @@TRAN-COUNT to 1. Otherwise, the above COMMIT TRAN outer_tran statement would not be able to commit the two transactions, as @@TRANCOUNT would still be 1, not 0.

To view the results of the stored procedure, run the following query:

```
SELECT e.MaritalStatus, p.title
FROM HumanResources.Employee e join Person.Contact p
ON e.ContactID =  p.ContactID
WHERE e.EmployeeID = 8;
```

The above update_status_tran  transaction must have a COMMIT statement within the stored procedure to mark the end of that transaction, but it will not actually commit until the outer_tran transaction commits. Whether update_status_tran is committed or rolled back depends entirely on whether outer_tran commits and vice versa. If either outer or inner transaction fails, then both are automatically rolled back. By explicitly defining the start and end of the transaction within the stored procedure, it is guaranteed that any time that stored procedure is called from an application program, the code within the stored procedure is always executed as a transaction, whether the application code has started a transaction or not. Therefore, the developer does not have to code the transaction start and end in the application code itself. This is a good way to protect transactions.

---

**Note**  For explicit transactions that use BEGIN TRAN, you must commit each transaction explicitly. When you use nested transactions, SQL Server is not able to commit the outermost or innermost transactions until all the inner transactions have been explicitly committed with a COMMIT statement.

## Implicit Mode

In implicit transaction mode, SQL Server automatically starts a new transaction upon encountering certain T-SQL statements. After the current transaction is explicitly committed or rolled back, a new transaction begins again the next time one of the key statements is encountered. You do nothing to delineate the start of a transaction, but you must execute a COMMIT TRAN or ROLLBACK TRAN to end an implicit transaction. If an implicit transaction is active and the user is disconnected, it is rolled back automatically just like an auto-commit or explicit transaction. The following T-SQL statements automatically begin a new transaction in implicit mode if a transaction is not already open:

- ALTER TABLE
- CREATE
- DELETE
- DROP
- FETCH
- GRANT
- INSERT
- OPEN
- REVOKE
- SELECT
- TRUNCATE TABLE
- UPDATE

When one of these statements is used to begin an implicit transaction, the transaction continues until it is explicitly ended, even if another of these statements is executed within the transaction. After the transaction has been explicitly committed or rolled back, the next time one of these statements is used, a new transaction is started. This process continues until implicit mode is turned off. The instance keeps generating a chain of implicit transactions until implicit mode is turned off. To enable or disable the implicit transaction mode, you can use the following T-SQL command:

```
SET IMPLICIT_TRANSACTIONS {ON | OFF}
```

ON enables implicit mode, and OFF disables it. When implicit mode is turned off, auto-commit mode becomes the default again. Implicit transaction mode can also be turned on through the application code using features of both the OLE DB and ODBC API's. By default, implicit mode is off. ADO does not support implicit mode, but only autocommit and explicit.

**More Info**   For details on how to program this, see SQL Server Books Online topic "API Implicit Transactions."

> ### Real World   Using Implicit Transactions
>
> I have witnessed a scenario in which implicit transaction mode was inadvertently set by a user as the default for user connections via Query Editor. The effect was that when the user opened a window and performed one of the statements that starts a transaction in implicit mode, the locks were held until the user closed the window—thus ending the connection—because the user did not explicitly run the COMMIT command to commit the transaction. This was causing random and long blocking issues within SQL Server. The fix was to disable the implicit transaction mode as the default connection option for all new connections, via Options under the Tools menu in Management Studio, thus reinstating autocommit as the default mode.

Implicit transactions are useful when you are running scripts that perform data modifications that need to be protected within a transaction. You can turn on implicit mode at the beginning of the script, perform the necessary modifications, and then turn off implicit mode at the end. To avoid concurrency problems, disable implicit mode after making data modifications and before browsing through data. If the next statement after a commit is a SELECT statement, it starts a new transaction in implicit mode, and the resources are not released until that transaction is committed (also dependent on the isolation level used).

**Important**   Be very careful when using implicit mode to make sure transactions are committed as soon as possible so that you avoid holding locks for excessive periods of time, thus potentially causing blocking problems.

## Transaction Performance

Consideration must be taken in order to code transactions for best performance. The appropriate transaction mode (implicit, autocommit, or explicit) must be used to fit the need. Transactions should be made as short as possible so that the resources are held for as little time as possible to avoid locking contention with concurrent users.

Any variable assignment, conditional logic, browsing data, or other related preliminary data analysis should be done outside of transactions, not inside them. Also, a transaction should not be started within an application and then placed on hold while waiting for user input. User input should always be done outside of a transaction. Otherwise, locks may be held unnecessarily long while waiting for the user input, potentially blocking other concurrent users. Perform data analysis or get user input before starting the transaction.

Always be consistent with the method for beginning and ending transactions. If you start a transaction with the OLE DB API functions, for example, then the same method should be used to end the transaction. If the transaction is instead committed using the T-SQL COMMIT statement, the OLE DB driver does not recognize that the transaction has been committed. Mixing methods for a transaction can lead to undefined results.

It is good practice to encapsulate transactions within stored procedures where possible. Using stored procedures helps to limit multiple roundtrips of communication between the client application and SQL Server to perform a transaction, thus reducing the network time and total transaction execution time. Starting and ending transactions within stored procedures also avoids some of the other issues mentioned above, such as user input during a transaction and consistency starting and ending transactions.

To reduce blocking problems when reading data, consider the read-committed snapshot isolation level, new for SQL Server 2005. See the section "Isolation Levels" later in this chapter for more details.

# Transaction Rollbacks

The opposite of a commit is a rollback. A rollback reverses any changes made by a transaction that has not been committed. A rollback can occur in one of two ways: as an automatic rollback by SQL Server or as a manually programmed rollback. In many scenarios, such as restoring data or a client connection being interrupted during a transaction, SQL Server performs automatic rollback for you.

## Automatic Rollbacks

If a transaction fails because of a severe or fatal error, such as a loss of network connection while the transaction is being run or a failure of the client application or server, SQL Server automatically rolls back the transaction. A rollback reverses all database modifications the transaction performed and frees up any database resources the transaction used.

The manner in which SQL Server rolls back a transaction can be set to two different behaviors. With the SQL Server default setting, if a run-time statement causes an error, such as a constraint or rule violation, SQL Server automatically rolls back only the particular statement in error, not the entire transaction. To change this behavior, you can use the SET XACT_ABORT statement. Setting XACT_ABORT to ON tells SQL Server to automatically roll back a transaction in the event of a run-time error. This technique is useful when, for instance, one statement in your transaction fails because it violates a foreign key constraint and—because that statement failed—you do not want any of the other statements to succeed. By default, XACT_ABORT is set to OFF.

SQL Server also uses automatic rollback during recovery of a server. For example, if you have a power loss while running transactions and the system is rebooted, SQL Server performs automatic recovery when it is restarted. Automatic recovery involves reading from the transaction log information to replay committed transactions that did not get written to disk and to roll back transactions that were in flight (not committed yet) at the time of the power loss.

## Programmed Rollbacks

You can specify a point in a transaction at which a rollback occurs by using the ROLL-BACK statement. The ROLLBACK statement terminates the transaction and reverses any changes that were made up to that point. It also frees all resources held by that transaction and decrements @@TRANCOUNT to 0. If a rollback occurs in the middle of a transaction, the rest of the transaction is ignored. If the transaction encapsulates an entire stored procedure, for example, and the ROLLBACK statement occurs within the stored procedure, the stored procedure is rolled back and processing resumes at the next statement in the batch after the stored procedure call (assuming the transaction was not a nested transaction).

A transaction cannot be rolled back after it commits. For an explicit rollback of a single transaction (with no nested transactions) to occur, a ROLLBACK statement must be executed before the COMMIT statement. In the case of nested transactions, once the outermost transaction has committed (which causes the inner transactions to commit also), none of the transactions can be rolled back. As mentioned previously, you cannot roll back individual inner transactions; instead, the entire outer transaction and all inner transactions are rolled back together. When the ROLLBACK statement is executed within a nested transaction, it is rolled back to the very first BEGIN TRANSACTION that started the outer transaction. So, if you include a transaction name in the ROLLBACK statement, it must be the outermost transaction's name, otherwise you will receive an error from SQL Server.

Below is an example of performing a ROLLBACK within a nested transaction based on the previous examples. We have added a ROLLBACK within the stored procedure, CRE-ATE TABLE and INSERT statements in the outer transaction to use as a test for ROLL-BACK and to show the effect on the outer transaction, and some print statements of @@TRANCOUNT:

```
USE AdventureWorks;

GO

IF EXISTS (SELECT name FROM sys.objects
    WHERE name = N'update_marital_status')
    DROP PROC update_marital_status;
```

```
GO

CREATE PROCEDURE update_marital_status(@new_status char(1),
    @emp_id smallint, @new_title char(4))
    AS
    DECLARE @tran_count tinyint;
    BEGIN TRAN update_status_tran;
        UPDATE HumanResources.Employee
        SET MaritalStatus=@new_status
        WHERE EmployeeID=@emp_id;
        UPDATE Person.Contact
        SET title = @new_title
        FROM HumanResources.Employee e JOIN Person.Contact p
        ON e.ContactID =  p.ContactID
        WHERE e.EmployeeID = @emp_id ;
        SELECT @tran_count = @@TRANCOUNT;
        PRINT 'inside proc tran_count = ';
        PRINT @tran_count;
        IF (SELECT COUNT(*) from Test_Table) <> 0
            ROLLBACK TRAN;
        ELSE
            COMMIT TRAN update_status_tran;
GO


DECLARE @tran_count tinyint;
BEGIN TRAN outer_tran;
IF EXISTS (SELECT name FROM sys.objects
    WHERE name = N' Test_Table ')
    DROP TABLE Test_Table;
GO
    CREATE TABLE Test_Table (ColA int, ColB char(1));
    INSERT INTO Test_Table VALUES (1, 'A');
```

```
SELECT @tran_count = @@TRANCOUNT;
PRINT 'before proc tran_count = ';
PRINT @tran_count;
EXEC update_marital_status 'M', 8, 'Mrs.';
SELECT @tran_count = @@TRANCOUNT;
PRINT 'after proc tran_count = ';
PRINT @tran_count;
IF @@TRANCOUNT = 1
    COMMIT TRAN outer_tran;
GO
```

Running the above code creates the stored procedure and then executes the batch (starting at the DECLARE statement) that creates the table Test_Table, inserts one row in it, executes the stored procedure that calls a rollback because the condition for the IF statement is true, and then continues with the batch. The PRINT statements show this. Because the ROLLBACK is executed, the outer transaction is rolled back as well, so at the end of the batch, the Test_Table table does not exist because the CREATE TABLE and INSERT statements are rolled back as well. To see these transactions commit, simply change the following line in the stored procedure:

```
IF (SELECT COUNT(*) from Test_Table) <> 0
```

Change to the following:

```
IF (SELECT COUNT(*) from Test_Table) = 0
```

You should then be able to view the Test_Table with one row inserted.

Also note that because the ROLLBACK occurs at a different level from the BEGIN TRAN with which it corresponds (it corresponds to the outer transaction BEGIN TRAN, as we have discussed for nested transactions), SQL Server returns an error message 266. This message is expected and can be ignored, and it does not affect execution. It occurs whenever @@TRANCOUNT at the beginning of a stored procedure is different at the end of the stored procedure. If the ROLLBACK is in the outer transaction, this does not occur.

> **More Info** For ways to avoid or work around this message, see the topic "Rollbacks and Commits in Stored Procedures and Triggers" in SQL Server Books Online.

There is a way to avoid having to roll back an entire transaction, which allows you to keep some of the modifications. This is done using savepoints.

## Using Savepoints

Savepoints offer a way to roll back just a portion of a transaction. All modifications up to the savepoint remain in effect and are not rolled back, but the statements that are executed after the savepoint and up to the ROLLBACK statement are rolled back. You must specify the savepoint in the transaction. After a roll back to a savepoint occurs, the statements following the ROLLBACK statement then continue to be executed. If you roll back the transaction without specifying a savepoint, all modifications are reversed to the beginning of the transaction as usual. The entire transaction is rolled back, even if you have previously executed a savepoint rollback. Note that when a transaction is being rolled back to a savepoint, SQL Server does not release locked resources. They are released when the transaction commits or upon a full-transaction rollback.

Savepoints are useful in situations in which an error is unlikely to occur, such that a roll back to savepoint does not occur very often.  For example, instead of checking for validity of an update before executing the update, use a savepoint to roll back part of a transaction in the case of an error, assuming that such an error is an infrequent occurrence. This can be more efficient than coding to test the validity of each update before executing it.  This is most effective when the probability of encountering an error is low, and the cost of checking the validity of the update is relatively high.

To specify a savepoint in a transaction, use the following syntax:

```
SAVE {TRAN|TRANSACTION}
    {savepoint_name | @savepoint_name_variable}
```

Position a savepoint in the transaction at the location to which you want to roll back. To roll back to the savepoint, use ROLLBACK TRAN with the savepoint name, as shown here:

```
ROLLBACK TRAN savepoint_name
```

You can have more T-SQL statements after the ROLLBACK to a savepoint statement to continue the transaction. Remember to include a COMMIT statement or another ROLLBACK statement after the first ROLLBACK to savepoint statement in order for the entire transaction to be completed. Here is an example using ROLLBACK to a savepoint:

```
USE AdventureWorks;
GO
BEGIN TRAN update_marital_status;
    UPDATE HumanResources.Employee
    SET MaritalStatus='S'
    WHERE EmployeeID=8;
    SAVE TRAN first_update_only;
    UPDATE Person.Contact
    SET title = 'Ms.'
    FROM HumanResources.Employee e JOIN Person.Contact p
    ON e.ContactID =  p.ContactID
    WHERE e.EmployeeID = 8;
    ROLLBACK TRAN first_update_only;

    SELECT e.MaritalStatus, p.title
    FROM HumanResources.Employee e JOIN Person.Contact p
    ON e.ContactID =  p.ContactID
    WHERE e.EmployeeID = 8 ;

COMMIT TRAN update_marital_status;
GO
```

If you look at the output from the SELECT statement, you can see that the first update succeeded but only the second update was rolled back by the ROLLBACK first_update_only statement.

# Transaction Locking

SQL Server uses an object called a lock to allow synchronized access by multiple users that attempt to access the same piece of data at the same time. Locking helps to ensure logical integrity of transactions and data. Locks are managed internally by SQL Server lock manager and are acquired on a per-user-connection basis. When a user connection acquires (or owns) a lock on a resource, the lock indicates that the user has the right to use that resource. Resources that can be locked by a user include a row of data, a page of data, an extent (eight pages), a table, a file, or an entire database. For example, assuming the default isolation level of read committed is used, if the user holds a lock on a data page, another user cannot perform operations on that page that affect the operations of the user owning the lock. Therefore, a user cannot update a data page that is currently locked for reading or for modification by another user. Nor can a user acquire a lock that conflicts with a lock already held by another user. For instance, two users cannot both have locks to update the same page at the same time. The same lock cannot be used by more than one user.

SQL Server's locking management automatically acquires and releases locks, according to users' actions. No action by the DBA or the programmer is needed to manage locks. However, you can use programming hints to indicate to SQL Server which type of lock to acquire when performing a particular query or database modification; these are covered in the section "Locking Hints" later in this chapter.

In this section, we'll look at the levels of granularity of locks and options for locking modes. But first, let's examine some of the locking management features that enhance SQL Server performance.

## Locking Management Features

SQL Server supports row-level locking—the ability to acquire locks on a row in a data page or an index page. Row-level locking is the finest level of locking granularity that can be acquired in SQL Server. This lower level of locking provides many online transaction processing (OLTP) applications with more concurrency. Row-level locking is especially useful when you are performing row inserts, updates, and deletes (their corresponding indexes are also affected).

In addition to providing the row-level locking feature, SQL Server provides ease of administration for lock configuration. It is not necessary to set the "locks" configuration option manually to determine the number of locks available for SQL Server use. By default, this value is 0, which means that as more locks are needed, SQL Server dynamically allocates more, up to a limit set by SQL Server memory. If locks have been allocated but are no longer in use, SQL Server deallocates them.

SQL Server is also optimized to dynamically choose which types of locks to acquire on a resource—for example, row-level locking for single row inserts, updates, and deletes; page locking for partial scans of table data; and table locking for full table scans. There can be multiple lock types held in a lock hierarchy as well. The next section explains the levels of locking in more detail.

# Lockable Resources

Locks can be acquired on a number of resources; the type of resource determines the granularity level of the lock. Table 17-1 lists the resources that SQL Server can lock—also known as lock types.

**Table 17-1  Lockable Resources**

| Resource | Type of Locking | Description |
|---|---|---|
| RID (Row ID) | Row level | Locks an individual row of data in a table |
| Key | Row level | Locks an individual row of data in an index |
| Page | Page level | Locks an individual 8-KB page of data or index |
| Extent | Extent level | Locks an extent, a group of eight contiguous data pages, or index pages |
| Table | Table level | Locks an entire table |
| HOBT | Heap or B-tree index level | Locks an index or a heap of table data (for a table with no clustered index) |
| File | File level | Locks a database file |
| Application | Application resource | Locks an application-specified resource |
| Metadata | Metadata level | Locks pages of metadata |
| Allocation unit | Allocation unit level | Locks allocation unit |
| Database | Database level | Locks an entire database |

As the granularity level becomes coarser (or larger), data access concurrency decreases. For example, locking an entire table with a certain type of lock can block that table from being accessed by any other users, but lock overhead decreases because fewer locks are used. As the granularity level becomes finer (or smaller)—such as with page-level and row-level locking—concurrency increases because more users are allowed to access various pages or rows in the same table at one time. In this case, overhead also increases because more locks are required when many rows or pages are being accessed individually.

SQL Server automatically chooses the type of lock appropriate for the task while minimizing the overhead of locking. SQL Server also automatically determines a lock mode for each type of lock; these modes are covered in the following section.

# Lock Modes

A lock mode specifies how a locked resource can be accessed by concurrent users (or concurrent transactions). Each type of lock mentioned previously is acquired in one of these modes. There are seven different lock modes used by SQL Server 2005: shared, update, exclusive, intent, schema, bulk update, and key-range. These lock modes are the same as in SQL Server 2000.

## Shared

Shared lock mode is used for read-only operations such as operations you perform by using the SELECT statement. This mode allows concurrent transactions to read the same resource at the same time, but it does not allow any transaction to modify that resource. Shared locks are released as soon as the read is finished, unless the isolation level has been set to repeatable read or higher or unless a locking hint that overrides this behavior is specified in the transaction.

## Update

Update lock mode is used when an update might be performed on the resource. Only one transaction at a time can obtain an update lock on a resource. If the transaction makes a modification (because, for example, the search condition found rows to modify), the update lock is converted to an exclusive lock (described next); otherwise, it is converted to a shared lock. This type of lock helps avoid deadlocks for concurrent updates in the case when repeatable read or serializable isolation levels are used. See the section "Isolation Levels" later in this chapter for descriptions of these levels.

## Exclusive

Exclusive lock mode is used for operations that modify data, such as updates, inserts, and deletes. When an exclusive lock is held on a resource by a transaction, no other transaction can read or modify that resource (others may read the data without blocking on the exclusive lock if a locking hint, read uncommitted isolation level, or read committed snapshot isolation are used). This lock mode prevents the same data from being updated at the same time by concurrent users, which otherwise could potentially cause inconsistent or incorrect data.

## Intent

Intent lock mode is used to establish a locking hierarchy. There are different types of intent locks, as described below. The purpose of the intent lock is to protect the lower-level resource locks, such as page and row locks that may be needed by a transaction, from being exclusively locked by another transaction through a higher-level resource lock, such as a table lock. For example, an intent lock at the table level acquired by a transaction indicates that SQL Server intends to acquire a lock on a resource lower in the hierarchy, such as on one or more pages or rows in that table. The intent lock on the table is acquired before any lower level locks are acquired, signaling the intention to lock a lower-level resource in the locking hierarchy. This prevents a second transaction from acquiring an exclusive lock on that same table, which would block intended page-level or row-level access by the first transaction. See the section "Viewing Locks" later in this chapter for an example of intent lock usage.

Using intent locks provides better performance for SQL Server as it allows SQL Server to check only at the table level for intent locks to determine whether a lock can be acquired on an entire table, rather than having to check every page-level and row-level lock on the table.

There are six categories of intent lock modes, as follows:

- **Intent shared (IS)**   Indicates that a transaction intends to acquire or holds a shared lock on a resource, and protects shared locks on some resources lower in the hierarchy.

- **Intent exclusive (IX)**   Indicates that a transaction intends to acquire or holds an exclusive lock on a resource and protects exclusive locks on some resources lower in the hierarchy.

- **Shared with intent exclusive (SIX)**   Indicates that a transaction intends to acquire or holds a shared lock on some resources and an exclusive lock on other resources. The SIX also protects shared locks on all resources lower in the hierarchy and intent exclusive locks on some resources lower in the hierarchy.

- **Intent update (IU)**   Acquired only on page resources, indicates that a transaction intends to or holds an update lock on a resource. The IU lock is converted to an IX if the update operation occurs.

- **Shared intent update (SIU)**   A combination of acquiring both a shared and intent update lock on the same resource and holding them simultaneously within a transaction.

- **Update intent exclusive (UIX)**   A combination of acquiring both an update and intent exclusive lock on the same resource and holding them simultaneously within a transaction.

## Schema

There are two categories of schema lock mode: schema modification and schema stability. Schema modification (Sch-M) lock mode is used when a table data definition language (DDL) operation is performed, such as the addition of a column to a table or deletion of a table, or when certain data manipulation language (DML) operations are performed, such as truncating a table. While this lock is held, no users can access the table.

Schema stability (Sch-S) lock mode is used when queries are being compiled. When a query is compiled, other transactional locks are not blocked, including exclusive locks, but DDL and DML statements that use a schema modification (Sch-M) lock cannot be executed on the table while there is a schema stability lock.

### Bulk Update

Bulk update lock mode is used when you are bulk copying data into a table with either the TABLOCK hint specified or when the table lock on bulk load option is set by using the *sp_tableoption* stored procedure. The purpose of the bulk update lock is to allow multiple threads to bulk copy data concurrently into the same table while preventing access to that table by any processes that are not performing a bulk copy.

### Key-Range

Key-range lock mode is used to lock index rows in order to fulfill the requirement for transactions using the serializable isolation level—that any query executed during the transaction will retrieve the same set of rows if executed more than once during the transaction. By locking the index rows of the index keys accessed for the duration of the transaction, no rows whose key falls within the range of the locked index keys can be inserted, updated, or deleted. This protects the rows so that the transaction can read repeatable data later in the transaction. This prevents the scenario called phantom read, which could otherwise occur when a transaction reads a range of rows, and then a second transaction inserts or deletes rows in that same range. Then the first transaction then reads the range of rows a second time, resulting in a different result set than with the first query. Phantom rows "appeared" or "disappeared" during the first transaction.

# Viewing Locks

You can view current locks held by selecting from the system view sys.dm_tran_locks. (The *sp_lock* procedure used to view locks in previous versions of SQL Server is supported for backward compatibility only.) To show an example of locking, run the following T-SQL that creates a test table and inserts two rows for our test:

```
USE AdventureWorks;

CREATE TABLE test1(col1 int);

INSERT INTO test1 VALUES (1);

INSERT INTO test1 VALUES (2);
```

To create the ability to capture the specific lock information for this example, we open three connections to the server via Management Studio Query Editor. We will run an update on test1 in one window with a time delay before the transaction commits, perform a query on test1 in the second window, and view the lock information in the third window. To accomplish this, in the first Query Editor window, run the following explicit transaction with an UPDATE and a WAITFOR DELAY statement as follows:

```
Use AdventureWorks;
BEGIN TRAN
    UPDATE test1 SET col1=999 WHERE col1=1;
    WAITFOR DELAY '00:00:15';
COMMIT;
```

Immediately from the second connection, run the following SELECT statement, using default autocommit transaction mode:

```
USE AdventureWorks;
SELECT * FROM test1;
```

The SELECT should block on the UPDATE for 15 seconds (time for the WAITFOR DELAY command to complete and then the UPDATE to commit). Immediately go to the third window and run the following query to view the current locks held:

```
SELECT resource_type, request_mode, request_status, request_session_id
FROM sys.dm_tran_locks
```

The results will look similar to the following, where request_session_id is the server process identifier (SPID) for the connection, assuming no other processes are running on the server:

| resource_type | request_mode | request_status | request_session_id |
| --- | --- | --- | --- |
| DATABASE | S | GRANT | 53 |
| DATABASE | S | GRANT | 52 |
| RID | X | GRANT | 52 |
| RID | S | WAIT | 53 |
| PAGE | IS | GRANT | 53 |
| PAGE | IX | GRANT | 52 |
| OBJECT | IS | GRANT | 53 |
| OBJECT | IX | GRANT | 52 |

The resource_type column shows the type of resource on which the lock is held, the request_mode column shows the lock mode, and the request_status column shows the status for the lock request. For resource_type, OBJECT is equivalent to table. You can see from the above output that SPID 53 (the SELECT) was blocked by SPID 52 (the UPDATE), shown by its request_status of WAIT—it is waiting for a shared lock on the RID resource which is currently locked by SPID 52 with an exclusive lock (request_status is GRANTED). These lock types are not compatible, so SPID 53 must wait on, and is thus blocked by, SPID 52. Once the UPDATE completes and the transaction is committed, then the SELECT completes.

Also from this output you can see how intent locks are acquired on the higher-level resources. For SPID 52 (the UPDATE), intent exclusive locks on both the PAGE and OBJECT level were acquired because it acquired an exclusive lock on the row. For SPID 53, intent shared locks were acquired at the PAGE and OBJECT level because it acquired a shared lock on the row. This shows how intent locks are acquired at the higher level. Both SPID 52 and 53 hold shared locks at the database level. This is true of every connection into a database.

# Locking Hints

Locking hints are T-SQL keywords that can be used with SELECT, INSERT, UPDATE, and DELETE statements to direct SQL Server to use a preferred type of locking behavior for locks on a particular table or view. Locking hints on views are propagated to all the tables and/or views that are referenced by that view. You can use locking hints to override the default transaction isolation level. You should use this technique only when absolutely necessary because if you're not careful, you could cause blocking or deadlocks.

The following list describes the available table-level locking hints:

- **HOLDLOCK**   Holds shared locks until the completion of a transaction rather than releasing them as soon they are no longer needed. Equivalent to using the SERIALIZABLE locking hint. Cannot be used with a SELECT query that includes the FOR BROWSE option.

- **NOLOCK**   Applies only to the SELECT statement. Does not obtain shared locks for reading data and does not honor exclusive locks, such that a SELECT statement is allowed to read data that is exclusively locked by another transaction, and will not block other locks requested on the same data. Allows for reads of uncommitted data (known as dirty reads). Equivalent to READUNCOMMITTED.

- **PAGLOCK**   Acquires page locks where either a single table lock or individual row or key locks would normally be used.

- **READCOMMITTED**   The default isolation level for SQL Server. Applies to read operations, such that shared locks are acquired as data is read and released when the read operation is complete. This behavior changes if the option

READ_COMMITTED_SNAPSHOT is ON. (This option is new for SQL Server 2005.) In this case, locks are not acquired and row versioning is used. (See more on this in the "Isolation Levels" section of this chapter.)

- **READCOMMITTEDLOCK**   New for SQL Server 2005. Equivalent to READCOMMITTED, but will apply whether the setting for READ_COMMITTED_SNAPSHOT is ON or OFF, allowing you to override that setting.

- **READPAST**   Applies to read operations; skips reading rows that are currently locked by other transactions so that blocking does not occur. The results are returned without these locked rows as part of the result set. Can be used only with transactions running at the READ COMMITTED or REPEATABLE READ isolation levels. Applies to SELECT, DELETE, and UPDATE statements but is not allowed in the INTO clause of INSERT statements.

- **READUNCOMMITTED**   Equivalent to NOLOCK.

- **REPEATABLEREAD**   Performs a scan with the same locking behavior as that of a transaction using the repeatable read isolation level.

- **ROWLOCK**   Acquires row locks when page or table locks are normally taken.

- **SERIALIZABLE**   Equivalent to HOLDLOCK. Performs a scan with the same locking behavior as that of a transaction using the SERIALIZABLE isolation level.

- **TABLOCK**   Uses a shared lock on a table, rather than page or row locks, that is held until the end of the statement.

- **TABLOCKX**   Uses an exclusive lock on a table. This hint prevents other transactions from accessing the table.

- **UPDLOCK**   Uses update locks that are held until the end of the transaction.

- **XLOCK**   Acquires exclusive locks that are held until the end of the transaction.

Let's look at a situation where using a locking hint could be useful. Suppose you are using the default read committed isolation level serverwide for all transactions. With read committed, when a transaction performs a read, a shared lock is held on the resource only until the read is completed, and then the shared lock is released. Therefore, if a transaction reads the same data twice during a transaction, the results might differ between reads because another transaction could have obtained a lock and updated the same data between the first and second read.

To avoid getting different data from the two reads, you could specify the serializable isolation level for the connection, but doing so causes SQL Server to use that isolation level for all statements within the transactions for that connection and holds all shared locks from all SELECT statements for the duration of each transaction. If you do not want to enforce serializability on all the statements for that connection, you can instead add a locking hint to a specific query.

The HOLDLOCK locking hint in a SELECT statement instructs SQL Server to hold all shared locks for the table on which the hint is specified until the end of the transaction, overriding whatever the current isolation level is. Thus, if the transaction performs a repeated read, the results returned are consistent with the first read.

---

**Note** SQL Server Database Engine query optimizer almost always chooses the optimal locking types and modes for a query. Locking hints should be used only if they are well understood and only when absolutely necessary, as they might adversely affect concurrency by causing unintended blocking or deadlocks.

---

You can also combine compatible locking hints, such as TABLOCK and REPEAT-ABLEREAD, but you cannot combine conflicting hints, such as REPEATABLEREAD and SERIALIZABLE. To indicate a table locking hint, include the keyword WITH and the hint name within parentheses after the table name in the T-SQL statement. The following statement is an example of using the NOLOCK hint in a SELECT statement:

```
USE AdventureWorks;
SELECT COUNT(*)
FROM Production.Product WITH (NOLOCK);
```

The above NOLOCK hint directs SQL Server not to acquire shared locks and not to honor exclusive locks on the Product table. Although this hint ensures the transaction will not block on locked table data, it also allows dirty reads of the table data.

The keyword WITH is not required for most of the table hints and can be omitted, but it is always safe to include it. If more than one hint is specified, the WITH keyword must be used, and the hints should be separated by a comma within the parentheses, such as in the following example, which specifies both TABLOCK and REPEATABLEREAD hints. This example demonstrates a successful repeatable read scenario. Run the first transaction (an explicit transaction) in one Query Editor window and the second transaction (an autocommit transaction) in a second window immediately after the first, as follows.

From Query Editor window one, run the following:

```
USE AdventureWorks;
BEGIN TRAN;
    SELECT SafetyStockLevel
    FROM Production.Product WITH (TABLOCK, REPEATABLEREAD)
```

```
    WHERE ProductID = 1;
    WAITFOR DELAY '00:00:15';
    SELECT SafetyStockLevel
    FROM Production.Product
    WHERE ProductID = 1;
COMMIT;
```

From the second window immediately run the update:

```
USE AdventureWorks;
UPDATE Production.Product SET SafetyStockLevel = 800
WHERE ProductID = 1;
```

The first transaction returns the same value for each of the two SELECT statements because of the REPEATABLEREAD locking hint. The TABLOCK hint causes a shared lock on the entire table to be acquired instead of just a row or page lock. The UPDATE in the second transaction blocks waiting for the first transaction to finish, after which it completes and changes the value of SafetyStockLevel to 800. To see the locks held during these transactions, query the system view sys.dm_tran_locks.

As seen in this example, the second transaction was blocked by the first because of the locking hint REPEATABLEREAD. Locking hints should be used only when the implications of doing so are well understood and when necessary for a specific desired behavior, as you can cause blocking that would not typically occur with the default locking behavior.

---

**Note**    Notice in the above example that an UPDATE statement was blocked by a SELECT statement, thus showing that a SELECT statement can cause blocking, not just be blocked. This is why you want to be careful when using locking hints.

# Blocking and Deadlocks

Blocking and deadlocks are two events that can occur with concurrent transactions. Sometimes they are desirable because they help maintain data consistency, and sometimes they are not desirable because of possible performance degradation for users. Blocking and deadlocks both relate to locking.

Blocking occurs when one transaction is holding a lock on a resource and a second transaction requires a conflicting lock type on that resource. The second transaction must wait for the first transaction to release its lock—in other words, it is blocked by the first transaction. If a transaction holds a lock for an extended period, it can cause a chain of blocked transactions that are waiting for the first transaction to finish so they can obtain their required locks, a condition referred to as chain blocking. Figure 17-1 shows the concept of blocking.

**Chain Blocking"**

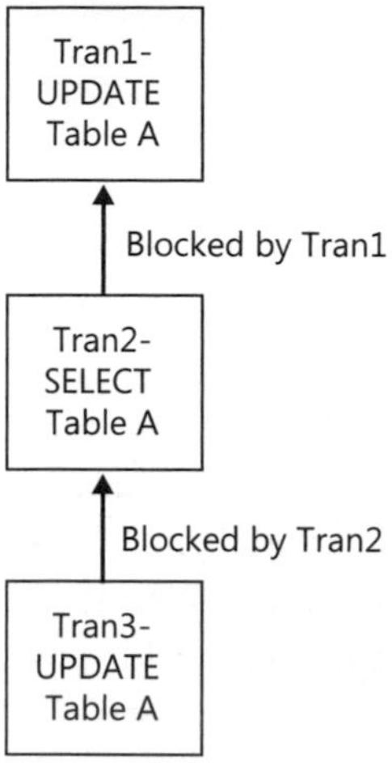

**Figure 17-1**   Blocking.

A deadlock differs from a blocked transaction in that a deadlock involves two blocked transactions, each of which is waiting for the other to release a lock. For example, assume that one transaction is holding an exclusive lock on Table1 and a second transaction is holding an exclusive lock on Table2. Before either exclusive lock is released, the first transaction requires a lock on Table2 and the second transaction requires a lock on Table1. Now each transaction is waiting for the other to release its exclusive lock, yet neither transaction will release its exclusive lock until a commit or rollback occurs to complete the transaction. Neither transaction can be completed because it requires a lock held by the other transaction in order to continue. Thus, the two transactions are in a deadlock. Figure 17-2 illustrates a deadlock scenario. When a deadlock occurs, SQL Server chooses to terminate one of the transactions, called the victim, and that transaction will have to be run again.

If transactions are long running, then locks on the data may also be held for the duration of the transaction. For example, a single UPDATE statement that updates a large number of rows in a table can take considerable time to complete, thus holding locks for that entire transaction duration. For another example, assume a transaction consists of multiple update and insert statements. In this case, the locks on all data modifications are held for the duration of the transaction, so the more work performed during the transaction, the more locks will be held and the longer it will take. This can cause blocking and deadlocking with other processes. Therefore, it is important to keep transactions as short and quick as possible to avoid long blocking times.

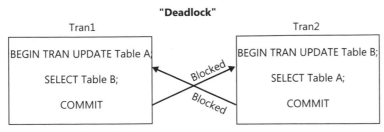

**Figure 17-2**   Deadlock.

As already mentioned in this chapter, there are several factors that affect blocking, including using locking hints and setting isolation levels. Isolation levels are discussed in the next section.

---

**More Info**   For information about how to code to avoid deadlocks, look up the "Minimizing Deadlocks" topic in SQL Server Books Online.

---

# Isolation Levels

SQL Server 2005 supports five isolation levels that affect the way locking behavior for read operations is handled.  There is one new isolation level and one new option to an existing isolation level for SQL Server 2005 that are intended to enhance concurrency for online transaction processing (OLTP) applications: snapshot isolation and read committed snapshot. These depend on a new feature called row versioning that can be used to avoid reader-writer blocking scenarios.

The transaction isolation level determines the level at which a transaction is allowed to read inconsistent data—that is, the degree to which one transaction is isolated from another. A higher isolation level increases data accuracy, but it can reduce the number of concurrent transactions. On the other hand, a lower isolation level allows more concurrency but results in reduced data accuracy. These isolation levels are set at the SQL Server session, or connection, level and last for the duration of the session. Note that some of them correspond directly to locking hints, which can be set at the statement level. (See the previous section "Locking Hints.") The isolation level you specify for a SQL Server session, or the default if you do not specify a level, determines the locking behavior for all SELECT statements performed during that session until the isolation level is modified.

The five levels of isolation, plus one new database option affecting isolation, are as follows:

- **Read uncommitted**   Lowest level of isolation. At this level, transactions are isolated just enough to ensure that physically corrupted data is not read. Dirty reads are allowed because no shared locks are held for data reads, and exclusive locks on data are ignored. See the section below for a description of dirty reads. (Corresponds to the NOLOCK and READUNCOMMITTED locking hints.)

- **Read committed**   Default level for SQL Server. At this level, reads are allowed only on committed data, so a read is blocked while the data is being modified. Shared locks are held for reads, and exclusive locks are honored. Thus, dirty reads are not allowed. There is a new database option that determines the behavior of read committed, called read committed snapshot. By default the read committed snapshot option is off, such that the read committed isolation level behaves exactly as described here. (See next bullet.)

- **Read committed snapshot (database option)**   New for SQL Server 2005, this is actually a database option, not a stand-alone isolation level. It determines the specific behavior of the read committed isolation level. When this option is on, row versioning is used to take a snapshot of data. Provides data access with reduced blocking in a manner similar to read uncommitted isolation, but without allowing dirty reads. See the section "Read Committed Snapshot" later in this chapter.

- **Repeatable read**   Level at which repeated reads of the same row or rows within a transaction achieve the same results. Until a repeatable read transaction is completed, no other transactions can modify the data because all shared locks are held for the duration of the transaction. (Corresponds to REPEATABLEREAD locking hint.)

- **Snapshot isolation**   New for SQL Server 2005. This isolation level uses row versioning to provide read consistency for an entire transaction while avoiding blocking and preventing phantom reads. There is a corresponding database option that must also be set to use this isolation level. See the section below titled "Snapshot Isolation" for more information.

- **Serializable**   Highest level of isolation; transactions are completely isolated from each other. At this level, the results achieved by running concurrent transactions on a database are the same as if the transactions had been run serially (one at a time in order) because it locks entire ranges of keys, and all locks are held for the duration of the transaction.

# Concurrent Transaction Behavior

To better understand isolation levels, we will look at three types of behaviors that can occur when you are running concurrent transactions. These behaviors are as follows:

- **Dirty read**   A read that contains uncommitted data. A dirty read occurs when one transaction modifies data and a second transaction reads the modified data before the first transaction has committed the changes. That data is not yet a permanent part of the database and could possibly be rolled back.

- **Non-repeatable read**   When one transaction reads a row, then a second transaction modifies the same row, and then the first transaction reads that row again, getting different results. Because the first transaction's repeated reads retrieve different data, the results are not repeatable within that transaction.

- **Phantom read**   A read that occurs when a transaction attempts to retrieve a row that does not exist when the transaction begins but that is inserted by a second transaction before the first transaction finishes. If the first transaction again looks for the row, it will find that the row has suddenly appeared. The same situation could occur with a row delete; a row that was existing later disappears. This is called a phantom row.

Table 17-2 lists the types of behaviors each isolation level allows. As you can see, read uncommitted is the least restrictive isolation level, and serializable is the most restrictive. As mentioned previously, the default SQL Server isolation level is read committed. As the level of isolation increases, SQL Server holds more restrictive locks and holds locks for longer periods of time. Since the isolation level affects the locking behavior for SELECT statements, isolation affects the locking mode used on data that is being read.

**Table 17-2   Isolation Level Behaviors**

| Isolation Level | Dirty Read | Non-repeatable Read | Phantom Read |
|---|---|---|---|
| Read uncommitted | Yes | Yes | Yes |
| Read committed without snapshot | No | Yes | Yes |
| Read committed with snapshot (statement level) | No | Yes | Yes |
| Repeatable read | No | No | Yes |
| Snapshot (transaction level) | No | No | No |
| Serializable | No | No | No |

# Row Versioning

To implement the new snapshot isolation level behaviors—via read committed snapshot and snapshot isolation—a new feature called row versioning is used. These two snapshot options are different in that the read committed snapshot affects only statement-level locking behavior, while snapshot isolation affects an entire transaction.Both use row versioning as a means to create snapshots of modified data by storing a copy of the data image as it was before the modification (in tempdb), so that a consistent snapshot view of the data can be accessed from tempdb without blocking on writes to the actual table data and without locking the actual table data.

Row versioning is a framework that is always enabled in SQL Server 2005 because it is used by default for purposes other than for isolation levels, such as for supporting online index building, modifications made in triggers, and modifications made by multiple active result sets (MARS) sessions. For the locking behavior options being discussed here, row versioning can be enabled or disabled depending on the isolation level and database options set.

Sizing the *tempdb* system database is a very important consideration with SQL Server 2005, as it is used for several enhanced features, such as for row versioning. With row versioning, snapshot versions of modified rows are stored in *tempdb* as needed to support the various operations that utilize row versioning. This space used in *tempdb* is called the version store. There are actually two version stores, an online index build store and a common store for all other uses.  The versioned rows are stored until they are no longer needed by the transaction or operation, and then they are released for removal by a background thread that executes once per minute. If a transaction is short and versioned rows are not needed for very long, the modified row or rows may not be stored beyond the buffer cache in memory, and thus may not be written to *tempdb* on disk. (All data is written to memory first before going to disk.) It is not required that a versioned row get written to disk. If the row is not needed for long, it may be flushed out of the buffer cache before getting written to tempdb; thus, the disk write overhead is avoided.

When a row-versioning based isolation level is enabled for a database, then all data modifications for that database are row versioned, even if there are no active transactions using that isolation level. This causes an increase in resource usage for data modifications. *Tempdb* must have sufficient space allocated to hold the version stores as well. It is better to allocate file space initially for *tempdb* than to allow the file to automatically grow, as the auto grow process can cause heavy overhead and performance degradation. *Tempdb* may have to be very large, depending on the rate of data modifications within each database that is enabled for row-versioning isolation. If disk space becomes full and the *tempdb* file therefore does run out of space, the Database Engine automatically attempts to shrink the version store. This is not a desirable condition and incurs over-head and possible transaction errors if the shrink attempt is not successful.

> **More Info**    See SQL Server Books Online topic "Row Versioning Resource Usage" for details on the shrink process.

Note that *tempdb* holds the version stores for all databases for an instance of SQL Server. So if there are multiple databases in an instance, and multiple are configured for row-versioning based isolation, consider the *tempdb* size for all of those database's version stores. If *tempdb* runs out of available disk space, then row versions are no longer generated by modification statements, and queries that try to access versioned data roll back.

In addition to space in *tempdb*, row versioning can add up to 14 bytes of information to the user database data file(s) for each affected row of data. This information is added the first time a row is modified and when any of the row-versioning features are being utilized (features mentioned above). It contains the transaction sequence number of the transaction that committed the current version, plus a pointer to the versioned row in the version store. Extra space in the data files should be allocated to support this overhead.

> **More Info**    See the topic "Troubleshooting Insufficient Disk Space in tempdb" in SQL Server Books Online for information on analyzing the space used in tempdb.

## Read Committed Snapshot

Read committed snapshot is a database option that can be turned on or off at the database level only and is used in conjunction with the read committed isolation level. When this database option is enabled (ON) and read committed isolation level is used, row versioning is used to provide read consistency at the statement level. A stored version, or snapshot, of the row or rows is taken as it existed at the beginning of the statement, so that it can be read while another process is updating that data. This avoids a reader blocking on a writer. Also, since the reader does not hold shared locks on the table data being read, writers are not blocked by readers.

To enable read committed snapshot for a database, you must turn on the database option using the ALTER DATABASE T-SQL command. The command will succeed only when there are no other connections into the database but the one running the command. If there are other connections, this command will run in a wait state until they are disconnected. It should complete in just a few seconds. Here is an example of turning on read committed snapshot for the *AdventureWorks* database:

```
ALTER DATABASE AdventureWorks
SET READ_COMMITTED_SNAPSHOT ON;
```

To show how this isolation level works, we'll use a variation of a previous example with the test1 table. First we drop and recreate the table and insert two rows, using Query Editor as follows:

```
USE AdventureWorks;
DROP TABLE test1;
CREATE TABLE test1(col1 int);
INSERT INTO test1 VALUES (1);
INSERT INTO test1 VALUES (2);
```

In the same Query Editor window, begin this update transaction with a 15-second delay before committing. This update normally blocks a query of the same data when read committed isolation is used without the snapshot option. This will show what happens when the snapshot option is enabled:

```
BEGIN TRAN;
    UPDATE test1 SET col1=999 WHERE col1=1;
    WAITFOR DELAY '00:00:15';
COMMIT;
```

From a second Query Editor window, immediately run this query on the test1 table, which explicitly sets the transaction isolation level to read committed, the default. Read committed isolation level must be used for the transaction in order for read committed snapshot to have an effect and for versioned rows to be read by the query. (Autocommit transaction mode is on, so we do not have to explicitly begin and end a transaction since there is only one SELECT statement in this transaction.):

```
USE AdventureWorks;
SET TRANSACTION ISOLATION LEVEL READ COMMITTED;
SELECT * FROM test1;
```

With read committed snapshot isolation enabled in the database, the above SELECT does not block on the UPDATE but reads the versioned rows that have the values 1 and 2. After the UPDATE commits, you will see the new values—999 and 2 if you rerun this SELECT.

To see the default behavior, let's turn read committed snapshot off:

```
ALTER DATABASE AdventureWorks
SET READ_COMMITTED_SNAPSHOT OFF;
```

Now if you rerun the UPDATE and SELECT, changing the updated value as follows, the SELECT blocks and does not return data until the UPDATE has committed. Run the following in one Query Editor window:

```
Use AdventureWorks;
BEGIN TRAN;
    UPDATE test1 SET col1=1 WHERE col1=999;
    WAITFOR DELAY '00:00:15';
COMMIT;
```

Run the following in a second window:

```
USE AdventureWorks;
SET TRANSACTION ISOLATION LEVEL READ COMMITTED;
SELECT * FROM test1;
```

One effect of using read committed snapshot isolation is that reads do not block on writes. This is similar to using the NOLOCK table hint on the SELECT or the READ UNCOMMITTED isolation level for the transaction, except that with those options dirty reads are possible. With read committed snapshot, dirty reads never occur. The data is read before the data is modified or after a modification is committed, but not if the modification is not yet committed (dirty read). Another effect is that reads also do not take shared locks on the table data, as with NOLOCK and READ UNCOMMITTED.

> **Important**   Read committed snapshot isolation can help reduce blocking contention, as do the NOLOCK hint and the READ UNCOMMITTED isolation level, but with the added benefit that it does not allow dirty reads. Whether or not dirty reads should be allowed should depend on business data access requirements regarding concurrent users.

### Advantages of Read Committed Snapshot

One of the main benefits of the read committed snapshot database option used with read committed isolation level is that potential lock contention (blocking) can be avoided in many cases, as seen in the above example. In addition, a consistent version of data can be read without blocking on a current modification of that data, such that dirty reads are not allowed. Read committed snapshot provides a new option to the NOLOCK hint and READ UNCOMMITTED isolation level commonly used in previous versions of SQL Server to reduce blocking.

### Disadvantages of Read Committed Snapshot

The main disadvantage of using read committed snapshot is the overhead incurred in the row versioning process. When the read committed snapshot option is enabled for a database, then all data modifications must be row versioned in the *tempdb* database, in spite of whether any read committed transactions are accessing that data. There is also a background process which runs once per minute to remove versioned rows that are no longer needed. *Tempdb* space also becomes an issue; there must be sufficient space to hold the version stores, and *tempdb* disk performance is critical. When reading or writing a versioned row, there is overhead of reading or maintaining a chained link list, linking one or multiple versions of a row. Thus, overhead is incurred during data modifications as row versions are stored and during reads as the appropriate row version is determined and read.

The potential performance benefits of using read committed snapshot depend on several factors, including the rate of data modifications in the database, the I/O performance of the *tempdb* disk(s), and the amount of SQL Server blocking that occurred before read committed snapshot is enabled. If there are frequent and long blocks occurring within the system, then read committed snapshot may give a significant performance improvement.  If there are no blocking problems in the system, then overall performance may show degradation by turning read committed snapshot on. If there were once blocking problems in the system and those have already been reduced or eliminated by using NOLOCK and READ UNCOMMITTED, then using read committed snapshot may show performance degradation or no difference in performance since there is no blocking problem to fix. If NOLOCK and READ UNCOMMITTED are removed and replaced with read committed snapshot, you may also see performance degradation, but you will eliminate the potential for dirty reads. Evaluating the appropriate method really depends on the data access requirements of each particular environment.

## Snapshot Isolation Level

Snapshot isolation is a new isolation level for SQL Server 2005 that also uses row versioning. It is different than other isolation levels in that it must be used in conjunction with a new database option called ALLOW_SNAPSHOT_ISOLATION. Once the database option is turned on, then row versioning is enabled for the database, and all data modifications are versioned. This allows transactions to use the isolation level SNAPSHOT. The database option and the isolation level work together: one at the database level to enable row versioning and the other at the transaction level to use the versioned rows. By default, ALLOW_SNAPSHOT_ISOLATION database option is set OFF for user databases.

The main difference between read committed snapshot and SNAPSHOT isolation is that SNAPSHOT ensures a consistent view of the data for the entire duration of a transaction, not just for a statement, so all reads during the transaction access a view of the data as it was last committed before the transaction started. The locking behavior is just like that of read committed snapshot; read operations acquire no shared locks on data and do not block on data modifications.

To use SNAPSHOT isolation, first the database option must be turned on as follows:

```
ALTER DATABASE AdventureWorks

SET ALLOW_SNAPSHOT_ISOLATION ON;
```

If you do not turn on the database option ALLOW_SNAPSHOT_ISOLATION and try to use SNAPSHOT isolation level, Error 3952 is returned and the transaction will not execute. Let's run through an example of using SNAPSHOT isolation now with the database option enabled. First, run the following T-SQL in one Query Editor window, which refreshes the data in test1 table, sets the isolation level to SNAPSHOT, and then begins a transaction with the same query run twice with a 15-second delay in between:

```
USE AdventureWorks;

TRUNCATE TABLE test1;

INSERT INTO test1 VALUES (1);

INSERT INTO test1 VALUES (2);

SET TRANSACTION ISOLATION LEVEL SNAPSHOT;

BEGIN TRAN

    SELECT * FROM test1;

    WAITFOR DELAY '00:00:15';

    SELECT * FROM test1;

COMMIT;
```

Immediately run the following in a second window, to see the UPDATE complete and commit without blocking.

```
Use AdventureWorks;

BEGIN TRAN

    UPDATE test1 SET col1=999 WHERE col1=1;

COMMIT;
```

The second SELECT statement above finishes after the UPDATE has completed, but it does not read the updated value 999. This is because the SNAPSHOT isolation level reads from the version store so that the data read is the same as it was at the beginning of the snapshot transaction. Therefore, both SELECT statements return the same data. These results are the same as if the REPEATABLE READ isolation level were used, but the method of achieving the results is quite different with SNAPSHOT isolation, which uses row versioning instead of holding shared locks.

### Advantages of Snapshot Isolation

One of the advantages of using snapshot isolation is the reduction in lock contention, as with read committed snapshot. With snapshot isolation, an entire transaction can read consistent data for its duration (via the version store) without preventing data modifications and without holding shared locks. This is especially beneficial in certain read-only cases, for example, when reports must be run against a set of consistent data while data is being continually updated by other users. The data modifications are not blocked by the snapshot transaction reads, and the reads are not blocked by the data modifications.

### Disadvantages of Snapshot Isolation

The disadvantages of snapshot isolation are similar in concept to those of read committed snapshot in that it uses *tempdb* for the version store, entails row versioning maintenance overhead, and adds up to 14 bytes to each data row modified (see the previous section, "Disadvantages of Read Committed Snapshot"). However, the overhead and performance degradation may be much greater with snapshot isolation. More *tempdb* space is needed because versions of rows must be saved in *tempdb* for the duration of entire transactions, not just for a statement. This means the version store can grow much larger since rows may not be removed as often.

Another disadvantage is that there can be a situation where an update conflict occurs and the snapshot transaction must be rolled back. This happens when the following order of events occurs: a snapshot transaction begins and reads some data, a second transaction updates that same data, and the snapshot transaction then tries to update that same data. This causes an update conflict, and the snapshot transaction is terminated and automatically rolled back.

Consider using database snapshots as an alternative to snapshot isolation where data does not have to be kept up-to-date, such as for daily, weekly, or monthly reporting queries.

## Viewing Snapshot Database Options

To view whether the snapshot database options are enabled (1) or disabled (0) for all databases, run the following query:

```
SELECT name, snapshot_isolation_state, is_read_committed_snapshot_on
FROM sys.databases
```

In the sample results shown below, snapshot isolation is turned on for *master*, *msdb*, and *AdventureWorks*, and read committed snapshot is turned off for all databases. Snapshot isolation is on by default only for *master* and *msdb*, and it cannot be disabled for these system databases. Read committed snapshot is off for all databases by default, and it cannot be turned on for the system databases *master*, *msdb*, and *tempdb*.

| name | snapshot_isolation_state | is_read_committed_snapshot_on |
|------|--------------------------|-------------------------------|
| master | 1 | 0 |
| tempdb | 0 | 0 |
| model | 0 | 0 |
| msdb | 1 | 0 |
| AdventureWorksDW | 0 | 0 |
| AdventureWorks | 1 | 0 |
| mydatabase | 0 | 0 |
| Northwind | 0 | 0 |

# Summary

In this chapter, you've learned about transactions, how they are managed by default by SQL Server, and how you can explicitly manage them. We covered topics including the ACID properties of a transaction, the transaction modes that can be used to specify the beginning and the end of a transaction, how resource locks are used to protect data consistency, and the different ways to control transactions and locking behavior. We've also taken a look at blocking, deadlocks, and the isolation levels, including the new read committed snapshot, snapshot isolation database option, and the new snapshot isolation level. These concepts of transactions, locking, blocking, and isolation are critical to understand and must be used appropriately in order for concurrent transactions to access data with the proper locking behavior that suits the business data requirements.

Chapter 18

# Microsoft SQL Server 2005 Memory Configuration

Internal memory management for Microsoft SQL Server 2005 has changed in many ways since SQL Server 2000. Configuring memory on the system has remained very similar, though. This chapter covers the configuration topics. Configuring memory effectively can greatly improve database performance, so it is important to understand the options database admistrators have in this area. This chapter focuses on the basics of buffer cache management and memory configuration settings and options in SQL Server 2005 to allow you to make informed decisions about SQL Server memory configuration for performance. This chapter explains several important SQL Server memory-related internal processes that will help you better understand memory usage in your system. It does not get into the details of internal SQL Server caches. For details on the internal caches, see the book by Microsoft Press titled *Inside Microsoft SQL Server: The Storage Engine*. Also, see Chapter 4, "I/O Subsystem Planning and RAID Configuration," for details on physical disk performance and RAID topics, which go hand-in-hand with memory relating to performance.

## Buffer Cache

Caching data in this context refers to the process of storing data from disk in memory. When data is read from disk into memory, that data "gets cached" or it is "in cache." Because data access is much faster when the data can be found in memory, you want SQL Server to have enough memory to achieve a high cache hit ratio.

The SQL Server buffer cache is the largest cache in SQL Server memory—it stores all data and index pages. Each instance of SQL Server maintains a singly linked list, called the *free list*, that contains the addresses of pages in the buffer cache that are free, or available for storing data. When SQL Server first starts up, as pages are allocated for the buffer cache they are initially free for use. As threads begin accessing data and SQL Server reads a page from physical disk, that page is stored in the first free page in the free list. If that thread or another thread must read or modify the same page, it can read the page from or modify it in the buffer cache, instead of performing physical I/Os to the disk. The buffer cache significantly speeds read and write performance by accessing the pages in memory, which is a less resource-expensive operation than accessing pages on disk.

Each buffer page contains header information about the page. This header holds a reference counter and an indicator of whether the page is dirty. A *dirty* page is one that has been modified in the buffer cache but whose changes have not yet been written to disk. Each time a page is referenced in the buffer cache by a SQL statement, its reference counter is incremented by one. Periodically, the buffer cache is scanned and the reference counter is divided by four, with the remainder discarded. If the result of the division is zero, the page has been referenced fewer than three times since the last scan, and the dirty page indicator is set for that page. This indicator signals that the page can be added back to the free list. If the page has been modified, its modifications are first written to disk before the page is freed; otherwise, if the page had been only read but not modified, then it will simply be freed without being written to disk. Basically, as more buffer pages are needed for new data pages to be read in, the least frequently referenced pages will be freed.

When SQL Server is running on Windows 2000, Windows Server 2003, or Windows XP, the work of scanning the buffer cache is performed by individual worker threads during the time interval between the scheduling of an asynchronous read operation and the completion of that read. The worker threads also write dirty pages to disk and add pages to the free list. These write operations are also performed asynchronously so they do not interfere with the thread's ability to complete other operations.

## Lazy Writer Process

There are two other built-in automatic mechanisms SQL Server uses to scan the buffer cache and write out dirty pages: the lazy writer and the checkpoint processes. The *lazy writer* periodically checks to ensure that the free buffer list does not fall below a specific size (depending on the size of the buffer cache). If the free list has fallen below that size, the lazy writer scans the cache, reclaims unused pages, and frees dirty pages with a reference counter set to zero. When running SQL Server on Windows 2000, Windows Server 2003, and Windows XP, most of this work is done by the individual threads mentioned above, so typically the lazy writer does not have much work to do. However, in very I/O-intensive systems, the lazy writer is needed to help maintain the free list. The *checkpoint process* also writes out modified buffer pages to disk but does not free those pages; see the following section, "Checkpoint Process," for details on how and when the checkpoint process runs.

# Checkpoint Process

A *checkpoint* is a SQL Server operation that synchronizes the physical data with the current state of the buffer cache by writing out all modified data pages in buffer cache to disk. It does not put the pages back on the free list as the lazy writer does. The checkpoint also forces any pending transaction log records in the log buffer to be written to the log file on disk. This assures a permanent copy of the data on disk at the point in time when the checkpoint process completes. SQL Server has a thread dedicated to checkpoints. Performing checkpoints also reduces the necessary recovery time in the event of a system failure in cases where automatic recovery by SQL Server is possible. This is because by writing data out to disk, checkpoints minimize the number of transactions that must be rolled forward (transactions that completed but are not written to disk yet).

The time needed to recover the database is determined by the time since the last fully completed checkpoint and the number of dirty pages in the buffer cache. So decreasing the checkpoint interval—the amount of time between checkpoints (discussed in the next section)—reduces the recovery time, but with some cost. The checkpoint process incurs some overhead because it may perform a large number of writes, depending on the number of modified pages that must be written to disk. These writes could potentially interfere with and slow the user transaction response times. This is typically not a problem but potentially could be in systems that experience heavy data modifications.

The checkpoint operation involves a number of steps, including the following:

- **Writing out all dirty data to disk**   A *dirty* page is one that has been modified in the buffer cache or log cache, but has not yet been written to disk.

- **Writing a list of outstanding, active transactions to the transaction log**   This step notifies SQL Server of which transactions were in progress when the checkpoint occurred, so that in the case of an automatic recovery, SQL Server knows to go back further in the log than the checkpoint in order to recover those transactions.

- **Storing checkpoint records in the log**   A record marking the start and the end of each checkpoint is written to the log.

Checkpoints occur per database, so, for example, if you are connected to SQL Server using the *master* database and manually run the checkpoint command, the checkpoint operation runs only on the *master* database. However, when SQL Server performs automatic checkpoints, a checkpoint is run on all databases. Checkpoints occur in the following cases:

- Whenever you issue a manual CHECKPOINT command, a checkpoint operation is executed against the current database in use.

■ Whenever you shut down SQL Server, a checkpoint operation is executed on all databases. Using the SHUTDOWN WITH NOWAIT command skips the checkpoint. This may cause the subsequent restart to take much longer to recover the databases and is not recommended.

■ When the ALTER DATABASE command is used to add or remove a database file, a checkpoint occurs.

■ When a minimally logged operation such as a bulk-copy is performed and the database is in bulk-logged recovery model, a checkpoint occurs.

■ When a change going from the bulk-logged or full recovery models to the simple recovery model is made, a checkpoint occurs.

■ Before a database backup is performed, a checkpoint is executed on that database.

■ By design, for databases using the full or bulk-logged recovery models, checkpoints are periodically run on all databases as specified by the recovery interval server setting (recovery interval is discussed in a later section).

■ With simple recovery model, checkpoints are run automatically either when the log becomes 70 percent full or based on the recovery interval setting as above, whichever comes first in this case. For simple recovery model, the log is truncated after checkpoints occur.

## Checkpoint Duration

The CHECKPOINT command has a new option with SQL Server 2005. You can specify a checkpoint duration, which is a number, in seconds, that you can request for SQL Server to complete the checkpoint. In SQL Server 2000, this was not directly configurable but was calculated from the recovery interval option. The following command performs a checkpoint on the *AdventureWorks* database and requests that SQL Server complete the checkpoint in 60 seconds:

```
USE ADVENTUREWORKS;

CHECKPOINT 60;
```

By default, SQL Server 2005 adjusts the frequency of writes that are performed during a checkpoint in order to minimize impact on the system. Setting the checkpoint duration to less time in seconds than the time the checkpoint would automatically take (assuming similar write activity) increases the frequency of writes during the checkpoint by having SQL Server dedicate more resources to it, and it will finish faster. On the other hand, setting the checkpoint duration to a longer time decreases the frequency of writes, and thus the checkpoint takes longer to complete but incurs less resources. Typically, checkpoints are best left as automatic.

## Recovery Interval

The *checkpoint interval*, which is the time between the beginnings of consecutive checkpoints, is determined by the *recovery interval* option and the number of records in the transaction log, not by the system time or size of the log. The recovery interval option is set for an entire SQL Server instance, not for each database, but checkpoints do occur on a per-database basis. The recovery interval value is the number of minutes that you choose to allow SQL Server for automatic recovery per database in case of a system failure. SQL Server uses an algorithm to determine when it should perform the next checkpoint for each database based on the recovery interval. For example, if recovery interval is set to five minutes, then SQL Server performs checkpoints per database often enough that in the event of a system failure, no database recovery will take more than five minutes when SQL Server is restarted (assuming the failure is of a type from which SQL Server can recover automatically).

The number of transactions in the log file also affects the checkpoint interval. The more records in the transaction log, the shorter the checkpoint interval will be, which means the checkpoint executes more often. As more data modifications occur, more records are inserted into the transaction log and, consequently, SQL Server writes those changes to disk more often. If few or no changes are made to the database, the transaction log contains only a few records, and the checkpoint interval is longer. If a database is read-only, there are no checkpoints. For example, if the recovery interval is set to five minutes but only a few modifications have been written to the log in the hour since the last checkpoint, then another checkpoint might not occur for an entire hour. This is because the few modifications made will take only a number of seconds to recover, and SQL Server has up to five minutes. On the other hand, if many modifications have occurred in the database and many log records written, the SQL Server checkpoints that database more often.

The default value for recovery interval is 0, which instructs SQL Server to determine the checkpoint interval automatically—usually less than one minute, which is quite often. For systems that have a large amount of memory and a lot of insert, delete, or update activity, this default setting might cause too many checkpoints to occur such that the writes interfere with the other activity on the system. In that case, you might want to set the option to a larger value. If you can tolerate a 10-minute recovery in the event of a system failure, for example, you might see better transaction performance by setting recovery interval to 10, as checkpoints will be performed less often. How you change this option depends on how long you can wait for a recovery in case of a failure, the frequency of failures, and whether performance is affected.

Recovery interval is an advanced option—Show Advanced Options must be set to 1 in order to view it. To set recovery interval using Transact-SQL, use the *sp_configure* stored procedure, as shown here:

```
sp_configure "recovery interval", 10;
RECONFIGURE WITH OVERRIDE;
```

This option does not require restarting SQL Server to take effect, but the change does not become active until you run the RECONFIGURE WITH OVERRIDE command. The RECONFIGURE command signals SQL Server to accept the configuration changes as the run value.

To ensure that the setting you have made is actually in effect, use the following T-SQL statement and verify the run value column shows the value you entered:

```
sp_configure "recovery interval";
```

> **Important**   The recovery interval option is an advanced option and should be changed only after careful planning. Increasing the recovery interval setting increases the time necessary for SQL Server to perform automatic database recovery.

# SQL Server Memory Allocation

Memory management in SQL Server 2005 requires little or no user intervention, and by default memory is allocated and deallocated dynamically by SQL Server as needed for optimal performance, according to the amount of physical memory available. You can override this dynamic behavior if necessary using the configuration options described in this section.

## Dynamic Memory Allocation

With SQL Server 2005, memory allocation is by default dynamic, even when AWE is enabled. (AWE is applicable only on 32-bit operating systems and is explained in detail in Chapter 5, "32-Bit Versus 64-Bit Platforms and SQL Server 2005.") The exception to this is when running SQL Server 2005 on Windows 2000 32-bit operating system with AWE enabled. In this case, the memory allocation is not dynamic but rather static, the same as it was previously with SQL Server 2000 Enterprise Edition 32-bit running on either Windows 2000 or Windows Server 2003 32-bit operating systems. For this exception, the memory is all allocated at SQL Server startup and is not released until SQL Server is shut down.

Store #: 31          Reg: 24 Wiese, Nikki
3300 Finley Road                    96770
Downers Grove, IL 60515
PHN:(630) 390-2100    FAX:(630) 390-2118

INVOICE#: 2625115
MERCHANT: 172188028994              F6 M2
xxxxxxxxxxxxx8834  VISA
BROZOVICH/JOE P
SALE: $64.34 36068B 0601917
5218897 AC SQL SERVER 2    1 @      59.99
        AC SQL SERVER 2005          DJ T
        0735621985
        MICROSOFT PRESS
        BURZIN, PATE

            SUBTOTAL             59.99
    SALES TAX @ 7.25%             4.35
            TOTAL DUE            64.34

VISA xxxxxxxxxxxxx8834               64.34

        TOTAL TENDER             64.34
              CHANGE DUE           0.00

ITEM COUNT 1

INV#: 2625115   Wed Nov 14 20:16:33 2007

THANK YOU FOR CHOOSING FRY'S ELECTRONICS
      SEE BACK FOR RETURN POLICY.
    YOUR BEST BUYS ARE ALWAYS AT FRY'S!

7. If the product returned has any data or information stored on a memory or storage device, Fry's shall not be responsible for the transfer of such data or information to another product given to the customer as an exchange, or for the loss of any data or information or to maintain the confidentiality of any data or information still residing on the returned product.

8. Computer software, video games, audio CDs, VHS videos, and DVD videos are returnable only if unopened.

9. Defective computer software, video games, audio CDs, DVD videos, and pre-recorded videos will be exchanged for the exact same item only.

10. Product using accessories such as laser toner or ink cartridge toner, media, batteries, film, etc. must be returned with the accessory in factory-sealed condition or will require a deduction for a replacement.

11. Refunds will be issued as follows: (1) Check purchases by check (2) Credit card purchases by credit issued to the credit card used in the original purchase transaction (3) Cash purchases by cash, unless the refund is over $500, which will then be refunded by a check mailed from Fry's Home Office.

12. Refund checks are mailed the 10th day from the date merchandise is returned.

13. Service, delivery, and installation charges are non-refundable once performed.

14. Special order items and cut cable/wire are non-returnable.

Rev. B

# Fry's ELECTRONICS
## RETURN / EXCHANGE PRIVILEGES

1. For a refund or exchange, most products may be returned within 30 days of original purchase date. Some other products, such as notebook computers, memory, microprocessors, network-attached storage, CD and DVD recorders, camcorders, digital cameras, air conditioners, and wireless phones may be returned within 15 days of original purchase date. *See store management for specific information.*

2. Original receipt must accompany any product to be returned / exchanged.

3. Product must be in original box with original accessories, packaging, manuals, and registration card in undamaged, clean, and brand-new condition.

4. Products returned within policy with the UPC Code missing from the box may only be accepted back as an exchange for the exact same item.

5. Product that is returned incomplete, damaged, or has been used – – if accepted – – will require a deduction. This deduction is final. Subsequent return of missing items will not reverse the deduction.

6. Product returned with serial number missing or tampered with will NOT BE ACCEPTED BACK FOR RETURN.

7. If the product returned has any data or information stored on a memory or storage device, Fry's shall not be responsible for the transfer of such data or information to another product given to the customer as

**Note**    Support for AWE is available only with SQL Server 2005 Standard, Enterprise, and Developer Editions, and applies only when running on 32-bit operating systems.

SQL Server 2005 manages memory dynamically based on either the default memory settings or settings that you specify. Dynamic memory management means that SQL Server automatically acquires and releases memory for its memory pool as necessary. At startup, SQL Server acquires only the memory that is needed at that point. As users connect and access data, SQL Server allocates memory to the memory pool as needed to support the workload. It allocates memory from the available physical memory in the system if there is any available. SQL Server can also deallocate memory from the memory pool, freeing it for other applications to use. If no other applications are requesting memory, however, SQL Server maintains its memory pool at the current size even if there are unused pages; it deallocates memory only if it is needed by another process.

To avoid excessive paging by the operating system (some minimal paging is normal), SQL Server maintains its virtual memory space at less than available physical memory, so it is never bigger than physical memory. This allows SQL Server to have the largest memory pool possible while preventing SQL Server pages from swapping to the page file on disk. The page file should not be utilized for SQL Server pages. If the leftover available memory in the system is consumed by some other application, SQL Server deallocates more of its memory pool to keep some physical memory free on the system at all times. If the application then releases some memory and SQL Server needs it, SQL Server reallocates the memory. With Windows 2000, the amount of free physical memory was kept between 4MB and 10MB, and with Windows Server 2003 a memory notification API is used to determine when SQL Server should release or allocate memory.

With dynamic memory allocation, if additional applications running on the same machine as SQL Server require memory, SQL Server releases memory for them from its memory pool. Thus, other applications might attempt to steal memory from SQL Server's total memory pool. This is why it is a best practice to dedicate a system for SQL Server and not run other applications alongside it.

**Note**    It is highly recommended that you dedicate the database server to SQL Server only and do not run user applications on the same system. This helps avoid paging problems and avoids other applications stealing memory from SQL Server, as discussed above.

## Static Memory Allocation

There are two cases in which SQL Server maintains a static amount of memory. One was mentioned above, when SQL Server 2005 (32-bit edition of Standard, Enterprise, or Developer) is run on Windows 2000 32-bit, with AWE enabled. The other case is when the memory settings are set to the same value. With static memory allocation, once the maximum amount of memory is allocated to SQL Server, it will not release the memory, even if another process may need it. In this case, paging of the other applications could occur if there is not enough memory in the system to support SQL Server and any other applications.

### Real World    *Don't Forget AWE Enabled*

I have seen cases in which a client has a 32-bit server with 8 GB of RAM running on 32-bit Windows operating system, and they are experiencing poor performance with indications of a memory bottleneck. The first thing I evaluate are the memory configuration options and run System Monitor to identify exactly how much memory SQL Server is actually allocating. (With AWE enabled, the Task Manager does not accurately show the AWE memory allocated to SQL Server.) Many times I have found that even though there was 8 GB of physical RAM in the system, SQL Server was only using about 1.6 GB! After checking the awe-enabled option, I found that it had been overlooked and had not been changed to 1 (enabled). After enabling this option, SQL Server is then able to see about 6GB of memory. This typically provides a huge improvement in performance.

## Setting Max and Min Server Memory

There are two configuration options in SQL Server that allow you to configure memory settings: min server memory and max server memory. There is a third option that must be set if AWE will be used, called awe-enabled. All of these are advanced options, so to view them with *sp_configure*, you must first set show advanced options to 1 and reconfigure, as follows:

```
sp_configure "show advanced options", 1;

RECONFIGURE;
```

To enable the use of AWE memory with SQL Server (where applicable), set the awe-enabled option to 1, (1 = enabled; the default of 0 = disabled) as follows:

```
sp_configure "awe enabled", 1;
```

You must restart the instance of SQL Server for the awe-enabled option to take effect.

To achieve dynamic memory allocation, you can leave the default settings for both min server memory (0) and max server memory (2147483647), which allows SQL Server to acquire as much memory as is available in the system as needed, or you can set those options to other limits. SQL Server dynamically aquires and releases memory between the amounts specified for min and max server memory settings.

The default of min server memory, 0, also allows other applications to force SQL Server to release memory to a low amount. To limit the minimum amount of memory that SQL Server should maintain, you can set a minimum size for the memory pool by configuring the min server memory option, so that SQL Server does not release memory if doing so causes the pool to fall below that size. For example, to ensure that SQL Server always has at least 256 MB of memory, set min server memory to 256, as follows:

```
sp_configure "min server memory", 256;
```

```
RECONFIGURE;
```

You might also want to put a maximum limit on the SQL Server memory pool by setting the max server memory option to a value so that other applications are ensured a certain amount of memory that cannot be used by SQL Server. For example, to tell SQL Server not to use more than 1,000 MB of memory, set max server memory to 1,000, as follows:

```
sp_configure "max server memory", 1000;
```

```
RECONFIGURE;
```

These options only require the RECONFIGURE in order to take effect; they do not require a restart of SQL Server.

When other applications are running on the same system as SQL Server, avoid configuring SQL Server memory settings in a manner that causes excessive paging on the system. For example, if you set the min server memory option too high, other applications might have to page as there may not be enough physical memory left over. Use System Monitor in the Windows 2003 Performance console to view the Memory, Pages/sec counter to determine how much paging is occurring on the system. A low number of occasional pages per second is normal, but a continuously high number of pages per second indicates a paging problem that is slowing down the performance of your system. If you cannot avoid excessive paging by adjusting the SQL Server memory options, you may need to add physical memory in the machine. First, be sure that your memory settings are configured correctly. Remember to enable the awe-enabled option if using 32-bit and there is more than 4 GB RAM in the system in order to allow SQL Server to utilize more than 4 GB.

Microsoft recommends that you allow SQL Server to configure its memory usage dynamically by leaving these two memory options at their defaults. Again, this is best when you have a dedicated machine for SQL Server such that it will not have to release memory for other applications. When other applications demand memory on the server, you might need to adjust these options. But even with a minimum or maximum memory size configured, SQL Server dynamically adjusts memory as needed without violating the upper or lower limits.

To force SQL Server to allocate a fixed amount of memory, set the *min server memory* and *max server memory* options to the same value. SQL Server allocates memory as needed up to the maximum configured value (or actually, up to the maximum memory available, yet not exceeding the max server memory setting). SQL Server then does not release memory below the min server memory value. Again, you do not want to cause paging on the system, so do not set the fixed memory size too large for your system. Leave some memory free for other applications when necessary.

---

**Note**   If you change a configuration value for an option that does not require SQL Server to be restarted, you must run the RECONFIGURE statement for the new value to take effect as the *run value* (the value SQL Server uses while running).

---

Again, Microsoft recommends that you allow SQL Server to configure memory dynamically by leaving the memory options set to their default values if you have a server dedicated to SQL Server. This memory management strategy is designed to improve SQL Server memory usage and to relieve the database administrator (DBA) of memory configuration worries.

# Summary

This chapter focused on the memory configuration settings that a DBA will need to understand and may need to adjust. SQL Server 2005 performs dynamic memory allocation and deallocation by default in all cases but one—when it is run on 32-bit Windows 2000 with AWE enabled. The configuration options may be manually set to adjust dynamic memory allocation minimum and maximum limits or to configure a static memory size for SQL Server. Using these settings appropriately is very important to SQL Server performance.

# Chapter 19
# Data Partitioning

*Data partitioning* is the process of dividing, or partitioning, a table into smaller, more manageable pieces. Data partitioning exists in two forms: horizontal partitioning and vertical partitioning. *Horizontal partitioning* is where a table with a large number of rows is split into multiple partitions, each with the same number of columns but fewer rows. *Vertical partitioning* is where a table with a large number of columns or very large columns is split into multiple partitions, each with the same number of rows but fewer columns.

Vertical partitioning appears in two forms. The first form is known as normalization. *Normalization* is the standard RDBMS practice of taking redundancy out of rows in a table by storing redundant data once and then referencing that data in a lookup table. For example, a table of banking transactions need not have the full extent of customer information in each row. Each row contains a customer ID that points to the customer table which contains the customer ID and information about the customer.

The second form of vertical partitioning is row splitting. *Row splitting* involves taking a row and dividing it into two or more tables. Each table contains the same number of rows; however, a pointer in the first part of the table identifies the remaining row piece in another table. This allows the size of a table to be reduced by splitting off pieces of it.

Normalization is a regular part of database design and has been around for many years. Row splitting is also a fairly common practice, although not as common as normalization. Although these are important concepts, this chapter focuses on the new SQL Server feature of data partitioning that is introduced in SQL Server 2005. SQL Server data partitioning is a horizontal partitioning feature.

Data partitioning has existed in a very limited form since SQL Server 7.0 and then became a little more advanced in SQL Server 2000 using the UNION ALL view. With the UNION ALL view, multiple tables were created, each with the same data structure, and were joined together with a view that was a UNION ALL between all partitions. With SQL Server 7.0, you could not update this view, but with SQL Server 2000, you could. However, the full power of partitioning was not available until native partitioning was introduced in SQL Server 2005.

In this chapter, you will learn about the fundamentals of data partitioning in SQL Server 2005, why you would want to use data partitioning, and how it can benefit your database. You will also learn how to create, modify, and monitor partitions. In addition, this chapter will provide information on how to maintain partitioned tables and indexes and additional tips and techniques for using partitions effectively. Data partitions can be a powerful tool when created and used correctly.

---

**Note**    Data partitioning is available only in SQL Server 2005 Enterprise Edition and Developer Edition. It is not available in Standard Edition.

---

# Partitioning Fundamentals

Data partitioning does one thing and only one thing. It divides the data in a table (or index) into smaller, more manageable pieces, known as *partitions*. By dividing data into smaller pieces, performance can be greatly improved. In the next few sections you will begin to see why partitioning is so important. Later in the chapter you will learn how to use partitioning to optimize your database.

## Data Partitioning Basics

With SQL Server 2005, the data partitioning option allows you to divide a table or index into smaller, more manageable parts (up to 1,000). This is done by creating a partitioning function and a partitioning scheme. The partitioning function defines how the data is divided up within the partitions. The partitioning scheme defines how and to what type of storage the partitions are allocated. Finally, when creating the table or index, the column that the data is partitioned on is defined. This is sometimes known as the *partition column*.

---

**Note** SQL Server 2005 considers all tables and indexes to be partitioned. If you do not explicitly create partitions, the table or index will be considered a single partition.

---

The partition column is similar to an index key in an index. Like a key in an index, if the column is not defined in the WHERE clause of your SQL statement, partitioning will not be effective. Unlike an index, where the lack of the index key causes the index not to be used, the lack of a partition column causes all partitions to be used. This defeats the purpose of the partition. However, unlike an index—where using an index inappropriately can cause more I/Os to be done than in a table scan—with partitioning, you will read all partitions if you don't take advantage of the partitioning. This is no different than not partitioning at all. There is no improvement, but there is no penalty either. As you will see later in this chapter, how you design and create your partitions is important.

# Partitioning Benefits

The primary purpose of partitioning is to divide data in a table into manageable pieces. This has two main advantages. The first is a reduction in the amount of data that must be accessed during certain operations, such as aggregates or table scans. The second is the ability to more closely control the location and type of storage used for your table data.

## Partitioning for Data Manageability

When large SQL Server databases are in production, some management and maintenance tasks can take a very long time to complete. I'm referring specifically to operations such as index rebuilds, index defragmentations, and index creations, which were covered in Chapter 12, "Creating Indexes for Performance." Occasionally, indexes need to be rebuilt in order to repack them and to reduce fragmentation. Fragmentation occurs when data is inserted into, updated, or removed from a table, thus changing the index and causing page splits. If an index is never changed, it never needs to be rebuilt.

Under many circumstances, only a portion of your data is actually changing in a table. For example, in most financial systems, transaction data is stored with a timestamp. As new data is added, it is identified as new by the timestamp. It might be rare for historical data to change. So, if data is partitioned by date, it is necessary only to rebuild the partitions that have changed. This allows you to actively maintain a much smaller data set, while not having to touch the older data.

**Real World   Size Matters**

When rebuilding or defragmenting an index, the size of the index and its underlying data will proportionally affect how long this operation takes to complete. Although there are a number of factors that affect these operations, such as size of the data cache, speed of the I/O subsystem, and the speed of the CPUs, it is a fact that larger indexes take longer to rebuild than smaller indexes because all table data must be read in order to rebuild the index. Thus, by using partitions, you can keep the size of the partition small, reducing the time it takes to maintain that partition.

By partitioning the table so that more manageable pieces can be maintained, the time it takes to complete these operations is minimized. Rebuilding indexes is a fact of life in SQL Server systems, and unfortunately, there are some databases where the indexes cannot be maintained properly because of the sheer size of the table data. By partitioning, the time necessary to complete tasks is minimized and reasonable.

**Note**   Both the ALTER INDEX REBUILD and the DBCC INDEXDEFRAG (which is obsolete) statements support partition operations.

### Partitioning for Storage Resource Utilization

Although storage has become much less expensive in the last few years, it still can be costly for large databases. Rather than sizing the I/O subsystem for space as was previously done, you are most likely sizing your I/O subsystem for performance, which was discussed in both Chapter 4, "I/O Subsystem Planning and RAID Configuration," and Chapter 6, "Capacity Planning." Partitioning can help to maximize both performance and budget.

Many systems maintain a large amount of data but use only a smaller subset of that data under normal conditions. For example, most financial systems must maintain seven years of data in the database, but most data processing is interested in only the latest year's data. In this situation, you can partition the tables into different filegroups. Read-only historical data can be placed on RAID-5 storage and current read-write data can be placed on faster RAID-10 storage.

## Performance Benefits of Partitioning

In addition to maintenance and storage considerations, partitioning can greatly enhance the performance of both queries and transactions in your database. There are often conditions where indexes are not effective. Specifically, indexes are ineffective when large amounts of data are selected from a table. This might be due to aggregates or to table scans caused by other reasons.

## Partitions Versus Indexes

If a data access touches more than five to 10 percent of the rows in a table, it is better to do a table scan than to access the data because of all the extra overhead incurred by going through the branch pages of the index. In addition, if the index access is via a nonclustered index, the resulting bookmark lookup causes additional overhead.

The result of partitioning is that now table scans can be much cheaper because a table scan has now turned into a set of partition scans, which can potentially be performed in parallel. The partition scans consist of a table scan on one or more partitions. This scan accesses far fewer rows than a full table scan across all of the data would access, thus improving performance.

> ### Real World    My Opinion on Data Partitioning
>
> In my opinion, the primary value of partitioning is the ability to reduce the amount of data accessed from SQL statements. This will reduce I/Os and the amount of buffer cache used, thus improving overall system performance. Others might promote the benefit of separating partitions into different filegroups, but this is secondary. With SAN or NAS storage, chances are that you might be accessing logical disks that share the same disk drives regardless of how you split up the partitions. If your I/O subsystem is optimally configured, the real value of data partitioning is data reduction.

With the introduction of data partitioning it is now possible to avoid indexes that you otherwise might not have any choice but to create.

## Partitions Versus Bad Indexes

Prior to SQL Server 2005, it was often necessary to create indexes that were suboptimal simply because you have no other choice. Usually, this takes the form of an index on a *datetime* field. Although indexes on *datetime* fields can be effective in some cases, it's usually not a good idea because the indexes are very unbalanced. Indexes like to be created on columns that are fairly unique so that the modified branch pages can be spread out somewhat among the index pages.

A *datetime* data type is stored as two 4-byte integers. The first 4-byte integer is the number of days before or after the base date of January 1, 1900. The second 4 bytes represent the number of milliseconds since midnight. A *smalldatetime* data type is stored as two 2-byte integers. The first 2-byte integer is the number of days after January 1, 1900. The second 2 bytes are the number of minutes since midnight.

### Real World    Don't Index *datetime*

Since the first part of the *datetime* or *smalldatetime* data types is days, it is conceivable that many entries are made into the table during the same day. Thus, sections of the index that are close to each other will be accessed, causing excessive page splits. In addition, it is unlikely that the WHERE clause of a SQL statement will specify milliseconds or even minutes, thus causing index scans. For this reason, I do not recommend indexing on *datetime* fields, especially now that we have partitions.

# Designing Partitions

Just as with indexes, partitions should be designed carefully in order to be effective. As with indexes, in order to take advantage of data partitioning, you must provide the partitioning column in the WHERE clause of your SQL statements for the partitioning scheme to be evaluated and utilized. Consider the following criteria to design partitions effectively:

- How will this data be used? Are there criteria that are regularly used in the WHERE clause of your SQL statement?

- How is data aggregated? Do reports look at data for each month, quarter, or year?

- Is data separated by account? Do accounts mix, or do you always look at one account at a time?

- Are there common SELECT criteria? Is there some data that is always used in the WHERE clause of your SQL statements?

By understanding the data and finding criteria that data is divided on, you can better develop a partitioning design that is optimal. What and how to partition is decided at the design stage of the database development. The designer, who is intimately familiar with the data and the application, should be able to pick natural partitions for data. For example, since the designer knows that end-of-month processing will select an entire month's worth of data, this might indicate that partitioning on month is natural.

> **Note**   Not only does partitioning allow you to reduce the amount of data accessed in aggregates and table scans, but it allows join data to be reduced as well. When designing your database for performance, keep in mind both indexes and partitions and choose the option more appropriate for your environment.

## Partitioning Design Fundamentals

In order to effectively design partitions, you should consider the following criteria:

- Partition large tables where most data is not regularly used.

- Partition on objects where data can be easily segmented and where data is used together.

- Partition objects that are used in aggregates based on ranges of data such as dates, accounts, and so on.

- Partition where data is segmented but where indexes aren't effective because of the large number of rows normally selected.

Each application and database is different. How you partition will depend on exactly what your application is doing and how your database is designed. These are only guidelines to help with that process.

To sum up the design project, there are two main questions that must be answered:

1. What column will be partitioned?

2. How will that column be partitioned?

Once these questions have been answered, the rest is only mechanics. However, these questions might not always be easy to answer.

# Creating Partitions

Creating partitions is a three-step process. In the first step, a partition function is created. This function defines how the partitions will be formed by specifying how data is divided. The second step is creating the partition scheme. The partition scheme is used to define how the partitions will be physically defined in the database. The third and final step is creating the table or index that uses the partition scheme that you have developed.

## Create the Partition Function

The partition function is used to define the criteria for dividing the data into the individual partitions. A partitioned table or index can be made up of as few as one partition (all objects are considered partitioned now) or as many as 1,000 partitions. These partitions are actually ranges of data. The ranges can be either left-bound (less than or equal to) or right-bound (less than).

The partition function is created with the CREATE PARTITION FUNCTION command. The syntax of the CREATE PARTITION FUNCTION command is as follows:

```
CREATE PARTITION FUNCTION partition_function_name ( input_parameter_type )
AS RANGE [ LEFT | RIGHT ]
FOR VALUES ( [ boundary_value [ ,...n ] ] )
[ ; ]
```

The parameters for the CREATE PARTITION FUNCTION are as follows:

- The *partition_function_name* must fall within the specifications for SQL Server identifiers to , be unique within the database.

- The *input_parameter_type* specifies the data type for the partition column. Valid data types are all data types except *text*, *ntext*, *image*, *xml*, *timestamp*, *varchar(max)*, *nvarchar(max)*, *varbinary(max)*, and *alias* data types, or CLR user-defined data types.

- The *boundary_value* is a list of boundaries that define the partitions. If no value is specified, the partition maps the entire table. It is a constant value against which column values in a table or index are compared.

- The LEFT or RIGHT qualifier specifies the side of the boundary value to which the partition belongs.

---

**Note**   A *SQL Server identifier* is a name of a SQL Server object, such as a table, index, partition function, and so on. It must start with the letters a-z, A-Z or _ (underscore), @, or # and can be made up of the characters, numbers, @, _ (underscore), #, or $. An identifier cannot be a SQL Server reserved key word.

---

The LEFT and RIGHT boundaries define which side of a boundary the data belongs to. For example, if you are partitioning by date the value "4/1/2005," you probably want to use right partitioning to include any data on and after April 1, 2005. If you are partitioning on "12/31/2005," you probably want to use left partitioning. With left partitioning, any data after December 31, 2005 is included in the partition. December 31, 2005 is not included in this partion.

Thus, left and right partitioning allow you to accommodate different partition types. For example, using the LEFT boundaries allow you to use partitions such as years where you might partition as ("12/31/2003," "12/31/2004," "12/31/2005"). This is convenient because the year always ends on December 31. However, if you are partitioning by month, February will end on a different day of the month. Therefore, right partitioning is more appropriate because the month always starts on the first day of the month.

Let's look at a few examples of creating partition functions. The following is a very basic partition based on a set of values:

```
CREATE PARTITION FUNCTION partfunc1 (int)

AS RANGE

FOR VALUES (1000, 2000, 3000, 4000, 5000);
```

This partition function creates the partitions shown in Table 19-1.

**Table 19-1 Partition Example 1**

| Partition | Lower Bound | Upper Bound |
| --- | --- | --- |
| 1 | | < = 1000 |
| 2 | > 1000 | <= 2000 |
| 3 | > 2000 | <= 3000 |
| 4 | > 3000 | <= 4000 |
| 5 | > 4000 | |

Another example of a partition is partitioning by dates. In this example, the partitioning is done by quarter. Because the quarters start on the first days of January, April, July, and October, this partition can be created as a right partition:

```
CREATE PARTITION FUNCTION partdatefunc1 (datetime)

AS RANGE RIGHT

FOR VALUES ('1/1/2003', '4/1/2003',
      '7/1/2003', '10/1/2003',
      '1/1/2004', '4/1/2004',
      '7/1/2004', '10/1/2004',
      '1/1/2005', '4/1/2005',
      '7/1/2005', '10/1/2005');
```

This partition function creates the partitions in Table 19-2. Only a subset of the example above is shown in this table.

**Table 19-2 Partition Example 2**

| Partition | Lower Bound | Upper Bound |
| --- | --- | --- |
| 1 | | < '1/1/2003' |
| 2 | >= '1/1/2003' | < '4/1/2003' |

**Table 19-2    Partition Example 2 (Continued)**

| Partition | Lower Bound | Upper Bound |
|---|---|---|
| 3 | >= '4/1/2003' | < '7/1/2003' |
| 4 | >= '7/1/2003' | < '10/1/2003' |
| 5 | >= '10/1/2003' | < '1/1/2004' |

The partitioning continues on to October 1, 2005. This partitioning function is suitable for right partitioning, while the example that precedes it is more suitable for left partitioning.

Once the partitioning function is created, the partition scheme maps the partition function to filegroups, as discussed in the next section.

## Create the Partition Scheme

The partition scheme is used to map to filegroups the partitions defined in the partition function. The partition scheme can map partitions individually to filegroups or it can map all partitions to the same filegroup. The syntax for the CREATE PARTITION SCHEME command is as follows.

```
CREATE PARTITION SCHEME partition_scheme_name
AS PARTITION partition_function_name
[ ALL ] TO ( { file_group_name | [ PRIMARY ] } [ ,...n ] )
[ ; ]
```

The parameters for the CREATE PARTITION SCHEME are as follows:

- The *partition_scheme_name* must fall within the specifications for SQL Server identifiers, be unique within the database, and be the name of the partition scheme.

- The *partition_function_name* specifies the name of the partition function with which to associate this partition scheme.

- The *file_group_name* is a list of filegroups with which the scheme is associated, or PRIMARY is used to associate all partitions with the primary filegroup. The keyword ALL specifies that all partitions go to this filegroup.

Here are a few examples of creating the partition schemes. The first example simply creates a partition scheme using the primary filegroup for all partitions and uses the partition function created earlier:

```
CREATE PARTITION SCHEME partscheme1

AS PARTITION partfunc1

ALL TO ( 'PRIMARY' );
```

To separate the partitions into different filegroups, use the following syntax:

```
CREATE PARTITION SCHEME partscheme1

AS PARTITION partfunc1

TO ( fg1, fg2, fg3, fg4, fg5, fg6 );
```

---

**Note**  The filegroups specified in the CREATE PARTITION SCHEME statement must already exist.

---

To create a partition scheme for the second example above, use the following syntax:

```
CREATE PARTITION SCHEME partdatescheme1

AS PARTITION partdatefunc1

ALL TO ( 'PRIMARY' );
```

Once you have created the partition function and partition scheme, the partitioned table or index can be created using the partition scheme created here.

## Create the Partitioned Table

Once the partition function and partition scheme are in place, the partitioned table can be created. The partitioned table is created with the CREATE TABLE statement. The pertinent subset of the CREATE TABLE statement syntax is slightly different with partitioned tables, as shown here. The full CREATE TABLE statement is covered in Chapter 11, "Creating Tables and Views."

```
CREATE TABLE
    [ database_name . [ schema_name ] . | schema_name . ] table_name
        ( { <column_definition> | <computed_column_definition> }
        [ <table_constraint> ] [ ,...n ] )
    [ ON { partition_scheme_name ( partition_column_name ) | filegroup
        | "default" } ]
    [ { TEXTIMAGE_ON { filegroup | "default" } ]
[ ; ]
```

The major difference for partitioned tables is the addition of the *partition_scheme_name ( partition_column_name )* qualifier. This allows you to specify which column the table is partitioned on. The *partition_column_name* must correspond to a column with the column type specified in the partition function.

Once you have created the partition function and partition scheme, creating the partitioned table is the easy part. The following examples show how to create the two partitioned tables used in the previous examples. You will notice that even though the partition functions and partition schemes are different in the two examples, the CREATE TABLE statements are identical; only the names have changed:

```
CREATE TABLE parttable1
(
    col1 int,
    col2 int,
    col3 int
)
ON partscheme1 (col1);
```

The second example is as follows:

```
CREATE TABLE parttable2
(
    col1 int        NULL,
    col2 int        NULL,
    col3 int        NULL,
    col4 datetime NULL
)
ON partdatescheme1(col4) ;
```

As you can see, the CREATE TABLE statement is very straightforward for partitioned tables. In addition to partitioned tables, you can also create partitioned indexes.

## Create the Partitioned Index

By default, if you create an index on a partitioned table, it will be partitioned on the underlying partition scheme of the table itself. A partitioned index is created with the CREATE INDEX statement. The pertinent subset of the syntax of the CREATE INDEX statement is as follows. The full CREATE INDEX syntax is shown in Chapter 12:

```
CREATE [ UNIQUE ] [ CLUSTERED | NONCLUSTERED ] INDEX index_name
    ON <object> ( column [ ASC | DESC ] [ ,...n ] )
    [ INCLUDE ( column_name [ ,...n ] ) ]
    [ WITH ( <relational_index_option> [ ,...n ] ) ]
    [ ON { partition_scheme_name ( column_name )
```

```
        | filegroup_name
        | default
        }
    ]
[ ; ]
```

As with the partitioned table, the main difference between the traditional CREATE INDEX statement and the partitioned index statement is the ON ( *partition_scheme_name* ( *column_name* ) qualifier:

```
CREATE INDEX ix_parttable2
ON parttable2(col1);
```

---

**Note**    The index is created on col1, but the table and index are partitioned on col4.

It is possible, and sometimes beneficial, to partition the index differently than the underlying table. This is done by creating a different partition function and partition scheme and referencing this partition scheme in the CREATE INDEX statement, as shown here:

```
CREATE INDEX ix2_parttable2
ON parttable2 (col1)
ON partscheme1 (col2);
```

As you can see, creating a partitioned index can be a little confusing given the multiple use of the ON qualifier. As discussed, with respect to creating tables, the creation of the index is the easy part after the partition function and partition scheme have been created.

# Viewing Partition Information

One of the first things that many people like to do when creating partitions is to test them. It is easy to insert data into a partitioned table because partitioning is automatic. Since partitioning is native to SQL Server 2005, the data is automatically inserted into the correct partition. However, if you want proof that partitioning is working, you can use some of the queries that you will learn in this chapter. Partition information can be found with both SQL statements and SQL Server Management Studio.

## Viewing Partition Information with SQL Statements

If you are like me, you'd like some sort of proof or indication that partitioning is really working. The following example demonstrates how you can create a partitioned table, insert data into it, and see how partitioning has worked:

```
CREATE PARTITION FUNCTION partfunc1 (int)
AS RANGE
FOR VALUES (1000, 2000, 3000, 4000, 5000);

CREATE PARTITION SCHEME partscheme1
AS PARTITION partfunc1
ALL TO ( 'PRIMARY' );

CREATE TABLE parttable1
(
    col1 int,
    col2 int,
    col3 int
)
ON partscheme1 (col1);

INSERT INTO parttable1 VALUES (10, 10, 10);
INSERT INTO parttable1 VALUES (999, 10, 10);
INSERT INTO parttable1 VALUES (1000, 10, 10);
INSERT INTO parttable1 VALUES (2000, 10, 10);
INSERT INTO parttable1 VALUES (3000, 10, 10);
INSERT INTO parttable1 VALUES (5000, 10, 10);
INSERT INTO parttable1 VALUES (6000, 10, 10);
INSERT INTO parttable1 VALUES (7000, 10, 10);
INSERT INTO parttable1 VALUES (9000, 10, 10);
INSERT INTO parttable1 VALUES (993, 10, 10);
INSERT INTO parttable1 VALUES (6000, 10, 10);
INSERT INTO parttable1 VALUES (5000, 10, 10);
INSERT INTO parttable1 VALUES (7000, 10, 10);
INSERT INTO parttable1 VALUES (6600, 10, 10);
INSERT INTO parttable1 VALUES (8200, 10, 10);
```

```
INSERT INTO parttable1 VALUES (8900, 10, 10);
INSERT INTO parttable1 VALUES (17000, 10, 10);
INSERT INTO parttable1 VALUES (61600, 10, 10);
INSERT INTO parttable1 VALUES (81200, 10, 10);
INSERT INTO parttable1 VALUES (18900, 10, 10);
INSERT INTO parttable1 VALUES (10, 10, 10);
INSERT INTO parttable1 VALUES (999, 10, 10);
INSERT INTO parttable1 VALUES (1000, 10, 10);
INSERT INTO parttable1 VALUES (2000, 10, 10);
INSERT INTO parttable1 VALUES (3000, 10, 10);
INSERT INTO parttable1 VALUES (5000, 10, 10);
INSERT INTO parttable1 VALUES (6000, 10, 10);
INSERT INTO parttable1 VALUES (7000, 10, 10);
INSERT INTO parttable1 VALUES (9000, 10, 10);
INSERT INTO parttable1 VALUES (1993, 10, 10);
INSERT INTO parttable1 VALUES (16000, 10, 10);
INSERT INTO parttable1 VALUES (15000, 10, 10);
INSERT INTO parttable1 VALUES (17000, 10, 10);
INSERT INTO parttable1 VALUES (16600, 10, 10);
INSERT INTO parttable1 VALUES (18200, 10, 10);
INSERT INTO parttable1 VALUES (15000, 10, 10);
INSERT INTO parttable1 VALUES (17000, 10, 10);
INSERT INTO parttable1 VALUES (16000, 10, 10);
INSERT INTO parttable1 VALUES (12000, 10, 10);
INSERT INTO parttable1 VALUES (11000, 10, 10);
```

You can use the following query to see a count of the rows in a table divided into partitions:

```
SELECT o.name, p.partition_number, p.rows
FROM sys.objects o
JOIN sys.partitions p ON ( o.object_id = p.object_id )
WHERE o.type = 'U' AND o.name = 'parttable1';
```

The following is the result of this query:

```
name                     partition_number rows
--------------------     ---------------- --------------------

parttable1               1                7

parttable1               2                3

parttable1               3                2

parttable1               4                0

parttable1               5                3

parttable1               6                25
```

```
(6 row(s) affected)
```

To see even more details or to check boundary conditions, use the following query to display every row in a partitioned table along with the partition to which it belongs:

```
SELECT $PARTITION.partfunc1(col1) AS Partition,

col1 AS [data] FROM parttable1

ORDER BY Partition ;
```

The following is the result of this query:

```
Partition   data
----------- -----------

1           10

1           999

1           1000

1           993

1           10

1           999

1           1000

2           2000

2           2000

2           1993

3           3000

3           3000

5           5000
```

| | |
|---|---|
| 5 | 5000 |
| 5 | 5000 |
| 6 | 6000 |
| 6 | 7000 |
| 6 | 9000 |
| 6 | 6000 |
| 6 | 7000 |
| 6 | 6600 |
| 6 | 8200 |
| 6 | 8900 |
| 6 | 17000 |
| 6 | 61600 |
| 6 | 81200 |
| 6 | 18900 |
| 6 | 6000 |
| 6 | 7000 |
| 6 | 9000 |
| 6 | 16000 |
| 6 | 15000 |
| 6 | 17000 |
| 6 | 16600 |
| 6 | 18200 |
| 6 | 15000 |
| 6 | 17000 |
| 6 | 16000 |
| 6 | 12000 |
| 6 | 11000 |

```
(40 row(s) affected)
```

With *datetime* partition functions, the same statements can be used, and similar results are returned to the user. Examples of these queries are shown here:

```
SELECT $PARTITION.partdatefunc1(col4) AS Partition,
    COUNT(*) AS [COUNT] FROM parttable2
```

```
GROUP BY $PARTITION.partdatefunc1(col4)
ORDER BY Partition ;


SELECT $PARTITION.partdatefunc1(col4) AS Partition,
    col4 AS [data] FROM parttable2
ORDER BY Partition ;
```

This function can show you that partitioning is actually functioning correctly.

In addition, SQL Server 2005 includes a number of sys tables that will allow us to view information on the configurations of the partitions. The following query can be used to view your current partitions:

```
SELECT f.name, f.type_desc, f.fanout, p.boundary_id, p.value
FROM sys.partition_functions f
JOIN sys.partition_range_values p ON ( f.function_id = p.function_id ) ;
```

This query will return information similar to what is shown here on the partition functions that were created and modified in the examples in this chapter:

```
name          type_desc fanout  boundary_id value
------------- --------- ------- ----------- ------------------------

partdatefunc1 RANGE      9       1           2005-01-01 00:00:00.000

partdatefunc1 RANGE      9       2           2005-04-01 00:00:00.000

partdatefunc1 RANGE      9       3           2005-07-01 00:00:00.000

partdatefunc1 RANGE      9       4           2005-10-01 00:00:00.000

partdatefunc1 RANGE      9       5           2006-01-01 00:00:00.000

partdatefunc1 RANGE      9       6           2006-04-01 00:00:00.000

partdatefunc1 RANGE      9       7           2006-07-01 00:00:00.000

partdatefunc1 RANGE      9       8           2006-10-01 00:00:00.000

partfunc1     RANGE      6       1           1000

partfunc1     RANGE      6       2           2000

partfunc1     RANGE      6       3           3000

partfunc1     RANGE      6       4           4000

partfunc1     RANGE      6       5           5000


(13 row(s) affected)
```

**Note**    Depending on what other partitions have been created in your database, the output of this query might look different.

This can be very useful when modifying partitions. You first need to make sure that the partitions are created as you think they are before you can modify them.

## Viewing Partition Information with SQL Server Management Studio

With the first release of partitioning in SQL Server 2005, there is not a lot of information that can be viewed from SQL Server Management Studio, but some can be. In order to view partitioning configuration information, follow these steps:

1.  Start SQL Server Management Studio. In Object Explorer view, connect to the server instance of your choice, and then expand the server's Databases folder.

2.  Select and expand the target database's folder, expand the Storage folder, and expand either the Partition Schemes or the Partition Functions folder to view the appropriate schema or functions, as shown in Figure 19-1.

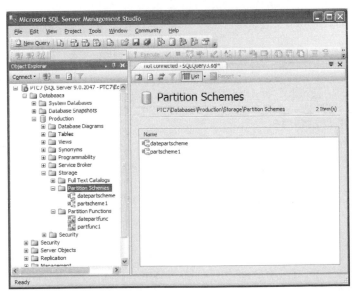

**Figure 19-1**    Viewing Partition Schemes in SQL Server Management Studio.

3.  Right-click the desired partition scheme or function and select Script Partition Function As, or Script Partition Scheme As, select CREATE TO, and then select New

Query Editor Window. This opens a Query Editor window in SQL Server Management Studio, with the SQL statement that can be used to recreate the partition function or scheme. This allows you to see the boundary values and the configuration. This output is shown in Figure 19-2.

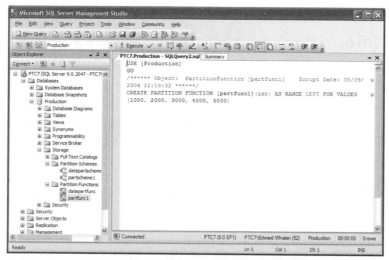

**Figure 19-2**   Query Editor window in SQL Server Management Studio.

As you can see, partitioning integration into Management Studio is fairly limited at this time. However, it is a primarily manual task to partition, so this is not much of a limitation.

# Maintaining Partitions

Maintaining partitions can be a challenge. Over time, as your data changes and the values of the partition columns change, you may need to add, remove, or migrate partitions. One of the benefits of partitioning is that older partitions can be quickly deleted as necessary, partitions can be moved to slower storage, and partitions can be archived to other tables. In this section, we will see how these actions can be done easily and efficiently.

## Adding Partitions

One of the most common tasks that you will perform is adding partitions. As your data grows over time, you will need to increase the number of partitions defined on your partitioned table. You do this by modifying the partition function using the ALTER PARTITION FUNCTION command. The syntax of the ALTER PARTITION FUNCTION command is as follows:

```
ALTER PARTITION FUNCTION partition_function_name()
{
    SPLIT RANGE ( boundary_value )
    | MERGE RANGE ( boundary_value )
} ;
```

Splitting a partition allows you to turn one partition into two partitions. Merging a partition takes two partitions and collapses them into one partition. With the split range function, a new boundary is added to the partition function. The merge range function takes an existing boundary value as its parameter and removes that boundary, thus merging the partitions that share the boundary value.

Here is an example of splitting a partition:

```
ALTER PARTITION FUNCTION partfunc1 ()
SPLIT RANGE (6000);
```

The partitioning information query (shown above) yields the following results both before and after the split:

| Before Split | | | After Split | | |
|---|---|---|---|---|---|
| name | partition_number | rows | name | partition_number | rows |
| parttable1 | 1 | 7 | parttable1 | 1 | 7 |
| parttable1 | 2 | 3 | parttable1 | 2 | 3 |
| parttable1 | 3 | 2 | parttable1 | 3 | 2 |
| parttable1 | 4 | 0 | parttable1 | 4 | 0 |
| parttable1 | 5 | 3 | parttable1 | 5 | 3 |
| parttable1 | 6 | 25 | parttable1 | 7 | 22 |
| | | | parttable1 | 6 | 3 |

(6 row(s) affected)          (7 row(s) affected)

A partition can be merged with the following SQL statement:

```
ALTER PARTITION FUNCTION partfunc1 ()
MERGE RANGE (3000);
```

This yields the following results:

```
name            partition_number rows

-------------   ---------------- -----

parttable1      1                7

parttable1      2                3

parttable1      3                2

parttable1      4                3

parttable1      6                22

parttable1      5                3


(6 row(s) affected)
```

If you are using separate filegroups for each partition, as in our first example, it is necessary to alter the partition scheme using the ALTER PARTITION SCHEME command. The syntax of the ALTER PARTITION FUNCTION command is as follows:

```
ALTER PARTITION SCHEME partition_scheme_name
NEXT USED filegroup_name ;
```

The filegroup identified by *filegroup_name* must exist before you can alter the partition. If it doesn't already exist, the filegroup must be done prior to the altering of the partition scheme. What you are actually doing is taking a partition, usually the last one, and splitting it into two partitions. An example of adding a partition and then splitting off a new partition to use that filegroup is shown here:

```
ALTER PARTITION SCHEME partscheme1

NEXT USED fg7;


ALTER PARTITION FUNCTION partfunc1()

SPLIT RANGE ( 7000 );
```

Think of the first and last partitions as holding all additional data that doesn't fit into your defined partitions. If you want to add a partition to either the beginning or end of your table, simply split the partitions.

## Archiving Partitions

As partitions become old, assuming historical data, moving the older data to slower storage is often acceptable. This can free up the faster storage for other tasks that can take advantage of the performance. In addition, you might want to move data from one table to another. Archiving and moving partitions involve the same mechanism and are covered together.

There are many reasons that you might want to move partitions. In many cases, applications have a built-in mechanism for looking for data in current and archive data tables. By using partitioning, the process of moving data into archive tables is simplified. Moving partitions is done by using the ALTER TABLE statement. The relevant portion of the ALTER TABLE statement is shown here:

```
ALTER TABLE [ database_name . [ schema_name ] . | schema_name . ] table_name
{
...
    SWITCH [ PARTITION source_partition_number_expression ]
        TO [ schema_name. ] target_table
        [ PARTITION target_partition_number_expression ]
}
[ ; ]
```

The SWITCH qualifier allows you to move the partition from the source table (the table being altered) to a destination table and partition. You can use the query on page 525 to identify the partition number, and you can use a query such as this to verify the identification:

```
SELECT $PARTITION.partfunc1(col1) AS "Partition #", *
FROM parttable1
WHERE $PARTITION.partfunc1(col1) = 1;
```

This query selects just the data from partition 1. Once you are certain of the partition number, you are free to move the data. There are several options for ALTER TABLE SWITCH, including the following:

- Move data from a nonpartitioned table to a partition in a partitioned table.
- Move a partition from a partitioned table to a nonpartitioned table.
- Move a partition from a partitioned table to a different partitioned table.

**Note**  In order to switch partitions, both tables must reside in the same filegroup.

Here is an example of how to move data from a partitioned table to a nonpartitioned table:

```
CREATE PARTITION FUNCTION partfunc3 (int)
AS RANGE
FOR VALUES (1000, 2000, 3000, 4000, 5000);


CREATE PARTITION SCHEME partscheme3
AS PARTITION partfunc3
ALL TO ( 'PRIMARY' );


CREATE TABLE parttable3
(
    col1 int,
    col2 int,
    col3 int
)
ON partscheme3 (col1);
```

This creates the partitioned table. At this point you can add data to this test table. When you are ready to move a partition to a nonpartitioned table, use the ALTER TABLE SWITCH statement, as shown here:

```
CREATE TABLE nonparttable1
(
    col1 int,
    col2 int,
    col3 int
);
ALTER TABLE parttable3
SWITCH PARTITION 1
TO nonparttable1;
```

The table *nonparttable1* is a nonpartitioned table even though you have moved a partition into it. This function is useful for archiving and moving data.

# Deleting Partitions

Deleting partitions can be part of a regular maintenance operation. As data ages, it is necessary to prune it from the tables. Performing this operation using the DELETE statement and specifying the data to be deleted in the WHERE clause can be quite time-consuming and sometimes dangerous since a slight mistake in the WHERE clause could remove more data than you desire.

At this time there is no mechanism in SQL Server 2005 for deleting or dropping a partition. However, here is a workaround to perform this task. The method to drop a partition and its data is as follows:

1. Create a nonpartitioned table with the same structure as the table that you want to prune.

2. Move the partition to be removed to the new table.

3. Drop the new table and all of its data.

This workaround is very easy to do, and it can facilitate the removal of old data. This method is much faster than using DELETE. Following is an example using parttable1.

As a refresher, the current partition distribution in the sample table parttable1 is viewed with the following query:

```
SELECT o.name, p.partition_number, p.rows
FROM sys.objects o
JOIN sys.partitions p ON ( o.object_id = p.object_id )
WHERE o.type = 'U' AND o.name = 'parttable1'
ORDER BY p.partition_number;
```

This query yields the following results:

| name | partition_number | rows |
| --- | --- | --- |
| parttable1 | 1 | 6 |
| parttable1 | 2 | 5 |
| parttable1 | 3 | 2 |
| parttable1 | 4 | 3 |

```
parttable1    5                3
parttable1    6                22
```

```
(6 row(s) affected)
```

In addition, let's look at the first two partitions:

```
SELECT $PARTITION.partfunc1(col1) AS Partition,
    col1 AS [Data] FROM parttable1
WHERE col1 < 3000
ORDER BY Partition ;
```

This yields the following data:

```
Partition   Data

----------- -----------

1           10
1           999
1           1000
1           993
1           10
1           999
1           1000
2           2000
2           2000
2           1993
```

```
(10 row(s) affected)
```

First, create a new table using the following SQL statements:

```
CREATE TABLE nonparttable1
(
    col1 int,
    col2 int,
    col3 int
) ;
```

This creates a new nonpartitioned table with the same column definitions as the partitioned table. Once the new table has been created, switch the first partition to the new table as shown here:

```
ALTER TABLE parttable
    SWITCH PARTITION 1 TO nonparttable ;
```

Let's look at the data in both the partitioned and nonpartitioned table after the partition switch:

```
SELECT $PARTITION.partfunc1(col1) AS Partition,
    col1 AS [Data] FROM parttable1
WHERE col1 < 3000
ORDER BY Partition ;
```

This yields the following results:

```
Partition    Data
-----------  -----------
2            2000
2            2000
2            1993


(3 row(s) affected)
```

To get information from the partitioned table, we run this SQL statement.

```
SELECT $PARTITION.partfunc1(col1) AS Partition,
    col1 AS [Data] FROM nonparttable1
WHERE col1 < 3000
ORDER BY Partition ;
```

The statement yields the following data:

```
Partition    Data
-----------  -----------
1            10
1            999
1            1000
1            993
```

| 1 | 10 |
| 1 | 999 |
| 1 | 1000 |

```
(7 row(s) affected)
```

Now that the data has been moved to the nonpartitioned table, the entire nonpartitioned table can be dropped with the following SQL statement:

```
DROP TABLE nonparttable1 ;
```

At this point, the data from what used to be partition one in the partitioned table is gone. For very large tables, this process can be much faster than the DELETE statement.

## Repartitioning Tables

If you want to repartition a table, you have several options. The first option is splitting the partitions as shown above. The other option is converting the partitioned table into a nonpartitioned table (see the following section) and then converting it back to a partitioned table.

## Partitioning a Nonpartitioned Table

There are several methods for partitioning a nonpartitioned table. The first method is creating a partitioned clustered index on the table using CREATE INDEX. This partitioned clustered index has the effect of partitioning and clustering the table. If there is already a partitioned clustered index on this table, you can create a new partitioned clustered index with the DROP EXISTING = ON clause.

The second method is using the ALTER TABLE SWITCH statement and moving the nonpartitioned table to a partitioned table of the same data definitions. Once this has been accomplished, the ALTER PARTITION FUNCTION command can be used to split the partitioned table into the desired new partitions.

## Unpartitioning a Table

Converting a partitioned table into a nonpartitioned table simply involves using the ALTER PARTITION FUNCTION statement with the MERGE RANGE argument to remove all of the partitions. In essence, this leaves you with a partitioned table with one partition, which is essentially a nonpartitioned table with a partition function. Technically, you can then move the remaining partition of the partitioned table to a nonpartitioned table using the ALTER TABLE SWITCH statement.

## Dropping Partition Functions and Schemes

If a partition function and partition scheme are no longer being used, they can be dropped either by using SQL Server Management Studio or by using SQL statements. The scheme can be dropped with the DROP PARTITION SCHEME statement, and the partition function can be dropped with the DROP PARTITION FUNCTION statements. Both statements take the scheme or function name as a parameter. If any partitioned objects are using these functions or schemes, they cannot be dropped.

# Using Partitions

As with indexes, partitions require proper usage. In this section, you will learn how to best take advantage of partitions and how to properly use partitions. Later in this chapter, you will also be presented with a number of scenarios in which partitioning is useful and can help improve the performance of your system.

## Inserting Data into Partitioned Tables

Inserting data into a partitioned table is completely automatic. The data is routed to the correct partition without any intervention by the SQL Server engine. Simply insert data into the table.

## Selecting Data from Partitioned Tables

Selecting data from a partitioned table is as simple as inserting data into the partitioned table. As with insertion, data is automatically selected from the appropriate partition or partitions. As with an index, if no partition column is mentioned in the WHERE clause of the SQL statement, all partitions will be used, thus bypassing the primary benefit of the partitioned table.

## Selecting Data from a Specific Partition

It is possible to select data from a specific partition by using the $PARTITION function. However, this serves the same purpose as simply putting the proper WHERE clause into the query. Hence, partitioning is essentially automatic. In order to view information about the partitions and their configuration, see the earlier sections of this chapter.

**Real World   Include the Partition Column**

I once consulted for a client using a third-party application intended for a hosted environment. The application vendor built partitioning into every table because of this model. For all of their pre-built queries and stored procedures, the partition column was included. The issue occurred when ad-hoc users began querying the database by using another reporting tool. Some of the users did not include the partition column in their queries, thus causing the partition and sometimes the indexes to be bypassed, causing queries to run much more slowly than they should have run. So, remember to include the partition column in your query.

# Partitioning Scenarios

As discussed earlier in this chapter, there are a number of good reasons for using partitioning. This section presents a few scenarios of where and how partitioning can be especially beneficial.

## Scenario 1: Partitioning Historical Data

In the first scenario, we will look at how partitioning can benefit systems by partitioning based on historical data. This is probably the most beneficial type of partitioning because most financial systems include data that has a date attached to it. As mentioned earlier in this chapter, I generally do not recommend indexing on date fields.

Probably the most effective method of partitioning a financial database is on date. Not all tables include date fields, but the largest tables (for example, general ledger and sales) have date fields. Remember, earlier in the chapter you were told that the following two questions must be answered when partitioning a table:

1. What column will be partitioned?

2. How will that column be partitioned?

The answer to the first question is that the general ledger table will be partitioned on date. Depending on the exact table definition of your general ledger table, this is based on how dates are stored.

The answer to the second question depends on the size of your database and how queries are run. In addition, any performance problems that you are experiencing should be included in the decision process. The more granular the partitioning, the more effective the partitioning will be when you take advantage of it.

In many cases, database administrators decide to partition financial systems by quarter, both to simplify the partitioning itself and to accommodate the end-of-quarter processing. Queries that involve aggregates by day, week, or month might benefit from more granular partitioning, but a balance must be struck between managing many partitions and query benefits.

In summary, a financial system can benefit from partitioning sales and general ledger data by date. The granularity of the partitioning depends on your particular needs. In addition, other large table such as customers can benefit from additional partitioning on region and so on.

## Scenario 2: Storage Partitioning

Partitioning for storage is becoming less and less necessary as storage systems improve. However, there are still benefits of packing older, historical data on slower storage. This is purely for cost savings. If you have sufficient disk capacity, both space and performance, there is really no need to physically separate the partitions into different filegroups. However, you will see a benefit from partitioning based on the reduction in I/Os that SQL Server must do in order to perform some operations.

## Scenario 3: Partitioning for Maintenance Optimization

Partitioning for maintenance can be very beneficial. Let's look at Scenario 1 above. In most financial systems, you must keep data for a specified period of time for tax reporting or Sarbanes-Oxley compliance. In some cases, this is seven years or more. Prior to partitioning, old data must be removed by using the DELETE statement and putting the range of data to be deleted into the WHERE clause. This pruning of data can be a very expensive and time-consuming operation. As shown above, in the section on deleting partitions, SQL Server partitioning can greatly speed this operation. A workaround for deleting a partition can be done quickly and easily, as described earlier in this chapter.

This allows you to easily and quickly prune a table. This is possible because you have used partitioning on the historical data in the database.

## Scenario 4: Spatial Partitioning

Often data is stored spatially in a database. For example, data might be stored by region or state. If there is a large amount of data in this database, you can benefit by partitioning by city, state, region, and so on. An example of partitioning by region is shown here:

```
CREATE PARTITION FUNCTION partfunc4 (char(2))

AS RANGE

FOR VALUES ('E', 'N', 'NE', 'NW', 'S', 'SE', 'SW', 'W');


CREATE PARTITION SCHEME partscheme4
```

```
AS PARTITION partfunc4
ALL TO ( 'PRIMARY' );


CREATE TABLE parttable4
(
    col1 int,
    col2 int,
    col3 int,
    region char(2)
)
ON partscheme4 (region);
```

> **Note** The partition function has to have the values of the partitioning column in alphabetical order, due to a SQL Server 2005 requirement. It might look a little strange here, but it works.

As with all partitioning, once the partitions have been created, they can then be used in an automatic manner. The key to partitioning is in the partitioning column.

## Scenario 5: Account Partitioning

In this scenario, let's look at a table which stores data related to a large number of accounts. Partitioning an account table that has only one row per account is very inefficient, but a sales or other data table with a large number of rows per account that is queried or aggregated by account is very effective. By splitting up this aggregated data, you reduce the amount of time necessary for processing the data and the number of I/O operations.

## Scenario 6: Join Partitioning

In the final scenario, let's look at how join performance can be improved. Join performance can be a large issue in many SQL Server systems because equijoins on columns often involve full table scans. Although table scans might not be avoidable, some of the join performance can be improved through partitioning.

By joining two tables that are partitioned on the same column and that include the same number of partitions, the query optimizer actually joins the tables on a partition-by-partition basis, thus improving performance. To make sure that the tables use the same partitioning methodology, use the same partition function and partition scheme on both tables. This ensures that the join performance is improved.

## Scenario Summary

The scenarios in this section focus on partitioning on one type of data. However, partitioning a database should not be limited to one partitioning type. For example, the financial system will benefit from partitioning on dates because the typical general ledger has data stored by date. However, other tables in the same financial database might benefit from partitioning on account or region.

Don't be held to one particular partitioning method. Consider each database individually, and partition each table as appropriate. In addition, keep in mind that join performance can be improved by joining on partition columns.

## Summary

In this chapter, you learned about SQL Server 2005 table and index partitioning. This partitioning works on a range of values and will store the data in the proper partition based on the contents of the partition column. SQL Server 2005 partitioning benefits the database in several ways. By working in conjunction with SQL Server Query Optimizer, only the necessary partitions will be accessed. This helps with the primary goal of performance tuning—reducing the amount of data being accessed.

Data partitioning has existed in a primitive form since SQL Server 7.0 and SQL Server 2000 using the UNION ALL view. As mentioned earlier, the UNION ALL view multiple tables are created, each with the same data structure, and are joined together with a view that is a UNION ALL between all partitions. This method works but is not optimal. It simply works better with SQL Server 2005 native partitioning.

In this chapter, you learned about the fundamentals of data partitioning in SQL Server 2005, why you would want to use data partitioning, and how it can benefit your database. You also learned how to create, modify, and monitor partitions. Data partitions can be a powerful tool when created and used correctly. In order to use them correctly, they must be both designed and accessed correctly. This chapter gives information and tips on how to do both.

Keep in mind that partitioning, like indexing, is very specific to the database and the data in the database. You have been provided with a number of scenarios in which partitioning might help, but as with most things, individual circumstances may vary. As the database administrator, you must decide how to partition based on your database, what it does, and what the data is like. The better you know your database, the better you can partition and take advantage of this powerful new feature.

# Part V
# Microsoft SQL Server 2005 Business Intelligence

# Chapter 20
# Replication

Replication is one of the best features of Microsoft SQL Server 2005. SQL Server replication is a very mature product and is very stable and high-performing. SQL Server replication is used primarily to distribute data between multiple locations within your business. Replication can also be used for many other purposes, including:

- Creating read-only reporting servers, thus relieving some of the load from the OLTP server

- Distributing pricing data

- Combining sales data

---

**Note**  Occasionally, replication has been used to create a pseudo-disaster recovery server; however, replication is not the best solution for disaster recovery because replication does not guarantee that the subscriber database has not changed from the primary database.

In this chapter, you will learn about the fundamentals of SQL Server replication, ways to use SQL Server replication, the different types of replication, and how to configure, manage, and tune replication.

### Real World    The Best Things About SQL Server

I am often asked what I like best about SQL Server, and I always give the same response: the SQL Profiler and SQL Server replication. I have helped many clients implement replication with great success. In one instance, we helped replicate a call center database so that reporting functions could be offloading, thus allowing better performance and faster response times.

I have also helped implement replication for a large grocery store chain. Communication between the main office and stores is done via transactional replication. Each morning, pricing data is replicated out to the stores, and each night, sales data is replicated back to the main office. Replication provides an easy to use and reliable transport mechanism for moving data.

Because transactional replication keeps track of which transactions have been replication, it is unnecessary to implement complicated handshaking mechanisms. If the communication link between publisher and subscriber goes down for a while, replication will catch up when the link is reestablished.

I am a fan of SQL Server replication, but especially of transactional replication. Transactional replication incurs very little overhead on the publisher, is fast, and is easy to use. The reliability and flexibilty makes SQL Server replication one of my favorite things about SQL Server.

# Replication Fundamentals

SQL Server replication is designed to replicate or copy data from one system to another. Replication allows you to replicate as little as a single table or as much as all of the tables in the database. It is very flexible and configurable.

With SQL Server replication technology, the task of distributing and copying data is automated (once it has been configured and tested). No user intervention is needed to replicate data once replication has been set up and configured. Since the replication data and processing is carried out within a SQL Server database, there is additional stability and recoverability. As with any SQL Server transaction, if a failure were to occur, operations resume at the point of failure once the problem was fixed. Because of this, many people prefer replication over other methods of moving data between systems.

Depending on your configuration options, replication can be set up in a number of different ways. For example, you can specify how much or how little data will be replicated, you can specify whether the replicated copies will be read-only or can be modified, and you can specify how often the data is replicated. We'll explore these options and others in the section "Configuring Replication" later in this chapter.

# Uses of Replication

There are a number of applications for replication, including sales data distribution and collection, pricing distribution, offloading of reports, and more. Since replication takes a database or subset of a database and keeps it up-to-date on another server, the uses are quite extensive. Uses of replication can include:

- Scaling out applications
- Data warehousing
- Distributing and consolidating data from satellite locations
- Offloading report processing

Let's look at some of these uses of replication.

## Scaling Out Applications

Application scaling is usually defined as either *scale up* or *scale out*. Scale up refers to a single server that can support larger and more processors. As you add more resources to the server, the performance increases. An example of scale up is replacing a 2-CPU 1-GHz system with an 8-CPU 3-GHz system. This provides for more performance and capacity, but does not allow for redundancy.

Scale out refers to distributing an application such as SQL Server to several systems, thus allowing for both increased capacity and some redundancy. In addition, the servers can be tuned for a specific function or type of activity. Scale out requires some sort of application or tools in order to distribute and maintain the application in a distributed environment.

SQL Server replication can be used to scale out applications by providing copies of the database or parts of the database on multiple systems. By distributing the database, the workload from the users can be distributed, allowing for a high degree of parallelism and scalability. Although this can be effective, it does not work with all applications.

# Data Warehousing

Data warehousing typically involves extracting data from an online transactional processing (OLTP) database and inserting it into a data warehouse database. This task often involves manipulating that data as it is being transferred between databases. In fairly simple cases where there is not much transformation of data and where that transformation is not very complex, replication can be used. In more sophisticated cases, you might find that SQL Server Integration Services is a more appropriate tool. SQL Server Integration Services is covered in Chapter 21, "Integration Services."

If the transformation between the OLTP system and the data warehouse is basic enough, replication can be the right tool for the job. Replication is easy to set up and maintain. By configuring the agents, you can schedule updates to the subscriber to meet your needs.

# Distributing and Consolidating Data

Since SQL Server replication is designed to move data from a central location (the database) to one or more subscribers, it is ideal for replicating data that is used at satellite locations. In addition, data at the satellite location can be replicated back to the central location. This can be pricing data, sales data, inventory, and so on. By using replication, these tasks can be automated.

### Real World    Replicating Store Data

In one of my consulting jobs, I worked on a replication system that took pricing information and replicated it out to over 100 stores. The application was designed so that daily pricing data was copied into a table on the publisher and replicated to all of the stores during the night. Thus, the main system was configured as the publisher, the pricing table was configured as a publication, and each store was configured as a subscriber.

In addition, each day's sales data was taken from every store and replicated into the master database in the home office. Thus, each store had a table that was configured as a publication and replicated to a single table on the main system. Replication was configured to add the store name to a column in this table. The same system that was configured as a subscriber for pricing data was configured as a publisher for sales data.

This system was very effective and is still working well. The only major issue that we ran into was network bandwidth. At the time, some of the stores were configured with only a 64-K link. This proved to be the bottleneck in our system.

## Offloading Report Processing

One of the most common uses of replication is for offloading reports. Systems where both OLTP and reporting functions co-exist can sometimes experience performance problems because of the tendency of the reporting functions to consume most of the resources in the system, leaving the OLTP users to suffer poor performance.

By offloading the reporting functions, which are primarily read-only, using transactional replication, the OLTP users can experience better performance, while at the same time multiple reporting servers offer better reporting performance for those users.

**Real World    Reporting Servers**

I have personally been involved in many cases where we have offloaded reporting using transactional replication. This typically results in much better performance for both the OLTP and reporting users. The OLTP system can be replicated to one or many reporting servers, depending on the frequency and amount of reporting. Because transactional replication creates very little overhead on the source system, performance can be improved without adding additional load to the system.

# Replication Concepts

Before jumping into configuring and using replication, let's look at a few replication concepts. First we'll look at the "publish and subscribe" metaphor and the three types of replication, then we'll examine replication data and data propagation, and last we'll discuss replication agents.

## Replication Components

SQL Server 2005 replication is based on the "publish and subscribe" metaphor first used to implement replication in SQL Server 6.0 and enhanced in SQL Server 7.0 and SQL Server 2000. This metaphor is built on the concepts of publishers, subscribers, and distributors. A *publisher* is a database that makes data available for replication. A *subscriber* is a server that receives replicated data and stores the replicated database. A *distributor* is the server that contains the distribution database or metadata used to maintain and manage the replication.

### Publishers

The publisher is the system that provides the data to be replicated. Depending on the type of replication chosen, the publisher may do some work involved in the replication or do very little work. The publisher consists of a Windows server running a SQL Server 2005 database. This database offers data to be replicated to other systems. In addition, the SQL Server database keeps track of which data has changed so that it can be effectively replicated. The publisher also maintains information about which data is configured for replication.

A replicated environment can contain multiple subscribers, but any given article can have only one publisher. Having only one publisher for a particular set of data does not imply that the publisher is the only system that can modify the data. If configured to do so, both publishers and subscribers can modify data. However, this can get a little tricky as you will see.

The data to be replicated is grouped in an object called a publication. This publication is made up of one or more articles as described here.

### Publications

A *publication* is created in order to publish data to other systems. A publication is a logically related set of one or more articles. Once you have created a publication, it is configured and maintained for distribution to other systems. This is much easier than having to maintain each individual table since most replication activities involve either an entire database or at least a substantial portion of it.

### Articles

An *article* is an individual component of data that is to be replicated. An article can be an entire table, specific columns in a table, specific rows in a table, or a stored procedure. Articles can be configured by using filters, as described below.

## Distributors

The distributor is the server that contains the distribution database and stores metadata, history data, and other information. The publisher and the distributor are not required to be on the same server. In fact, it is usually recommended that you have a dedicated distributor for replication. Each publisher must be assigned a distributor.

---

**Note**   Metadata is data about data. In this case, metadata is the data that keeps track of the current state of the replication. It is also the data that is propagated to other members of the replication set, including information about the properties of data, such as the type of data in a column (numeric, text, and so on) or the length of a column, and information about the structure of data.

---

## Subscribers

Subscribers are the database servers that store the replicated data and receive updates. Beginning with SQL Server 7.0, updates can be made by subscribers and publishers. In

SQL Server 2005 this has been enhanced to include peer-to-peer replication. It's also possible for a subscriber to serve as a publisher to other systems.

### Subscription

A *subscription* is a request by a subscriber to receive a publication. The subscription defines what published data will be sent to the subscriber. This subscription defines what and how the replication occurs on the subscriber side.

# Types of Replication

SQL Server 2005 replication offers three types of replication: snapshot, transactional, and merge. These replication types offer varying degrees of data consistency within the replicated database, as well as different levels of overhead.

## Snapshot Replication

Snapshot replication is the simplest and most straightforward of the replication types. With snapshot replication, a picture, or snapshot, of the database is taken and propagated to the subscribers. The main advantage of snapshot replication is that it does not involve continuous overhead on the publishers and subscribers. The main disadvantage is that the database on the subscriber is only as current as when the snapshot was taken.

In many cases, as you will see later in this chapter, snapshot replication is sufficient and appropriate—for example, when the source data is modified only occasionally, you should perform replication only occasionally. Applications such as phone lists, price lists, and item descriptions can easily be handled using snapshot replication. These lists can be updated once per day during off hours.

## Transactional Replication

Transactional replication can be used to replicate both tables and stored procedures. With transactional replication, any changes made to the articles are captured from the transaction log and propagated to the distributors continuously and automatically. Using transactional replication, you can keep the publisher and the subscriber in almost exactly the same state, depending on how you configure the replication.

Transactional replication should be used when it is important to keep all of the replicated systems current. Transactional replication uses more system overhead because each transaction that changes data in the system must be individually applied to the replicated system, but it keeps the systems in a more consistent state.

## Merge Replication

Merge replication is similar to transactional replication in that it keeps track of the changes made to articles. However, instead of propagating transactions that have made changes, merge replication periodically transmits all changes that have been made to the database. These changes can be batched and sent as necessary. Merge replication is something like a combination of transactional and snapshot replication because changes are sent as a batch.

# Components of Replication

Replication is made up of the replication data as well as the processes, or agents, that actually execute the replication functions. These components are what makes replication function so well. In this section, we will examine the various components that make up replication.

## Replication Data

The replicated data is made up of collections of articles known as publications. These articles can be tables, subsets of rows, subsets of columns, or even stored procedures.

### Articles

As previously discussed, an article is a table or a subset of a table that is being replicated. Subsets are created by using filters. A filter that is used to create a subset of rows is called a *horizontal filter*. A filter that is used to create a subset of columns is called a *vertical filter*. Horizontal and vertical filters are covered in more detail later in this chapter.

---

**Note**    Filters are defined and work differently in merge replication than they do for snapshot and transactional replication.

---

### Publications

A publication is a set of articles grouped together as a unit. Since a database typically consists of multiple tables, publications enable this grouping to be maintained. For example, to replicate a database, it is preferable to group all articles together and replicate the entire database in one publication rather than individually replicating each article. Publications provide the means of replicating logical groupings of articles as one replication object.

A publication can consist of a single article, but it almost always contains more than one article. However, a subscriber can subscribe only to publications, not to articles. Therefore, if you want to subscribe to a single article, you must configure a publication that contains only that article and then subscribe to that publication.

# Push and Pull Subscriptions

Replicated data can be propagated in a number of ways. All propagation methods are based on either push subscriptions or pull subscriptions. A subscriber can support a mixture of push and pull subscriptions simultaneously.

## Push Subscriptions

When using a push subscription, the publisher is responsible for providing updates to the subscribers. Updates are initiated without any request from the subscriber. A push subscription is useful when centralized administration is desired because the replication is controlled and administered by the publisher rather than by multiple subscribers. In other words, the initiation of the replication and the scheduling of the replication is handled on the publisher.

Push subscriptions allow a lot of flexibility for when changes are propagated. Push subscriptions can be configured to keep the replication close to real time or to perform updates on a regular schedule. You'll learn more about these options in the section "Configuring Replication" later in this chapter.

## Pull Subscriptions

Pull subscriptions allow subscribers to specify when changes are propagated, or they can be based on periodic updates (without subscribers knowing when changes have occurred). Pull subscriptions are useful when you have a large number of subscribers and when the subscribers are not always attached to the network. Because pull subscriptions are initiated by subscribers, subscribers not always connected to the network can periodically connect and request replication data. The initiation of the replication is done on the subscriber system, not the distributor.

# Replication Agents

Several agents are used to perform the subscription actions: the Snapshot Agent, the Log Reader Agent, the Distribution Agent, the Merge Agent, and the Queue Reader Agent. In this section, you'll learn what these agents are, what they do, and how to manage them.

## The Snapshot Agent

The Snapshot Agent is used for creating and propagating the snapshots used in snapshot replication. The Snapshot Agent prepares the original replication data and creates the information that is used by the Distribution Agent to propagate that data. The Snapshot Agent stores the snapshot on the distributor or anywhere else that you specify. The Snapshot Agent is also responsible for keeping information about the synchronization status of the replication objects; this information is stored in the distribution database.

The Snapshot Agent is dormant most of the time, and it periodically awakens to perform its tasks based on the schedule that you have configured. Each time the Snapshot Agent runs, it performs the following tasks:

1. The Snapshot Agent establishes a connection from the distributor to the publisher. If a connection is not available, the Snapshot Agent will not proceed with the snapshot. Once the connection has been established, the Snapshot Agent locks all of the articles in the replication to ensure that the snapshot is a consistent view of the data. (For this reason, it is not a good idea to schedule snapshots during peak times.)

2. The Snapshot Agent establishes a connection back from the publisher to the distributor. Once this connection has been established, a copy of the schema for each article is written to the distributor.

3. The Snapshot Agent takes a snapshot of the actual data on the publisher and writes it to a file on the distributor. If all systems involved in the replication are SQL Server systems, the file is stored as a native bulk copy program. If mixed types of systems are involved in the replication, the data is stored in text files. At this point, synchronization information is set.

4. After the data has been copied, the Snapshot Agent updates information in the distribution database.

5. The Snapshot Agent releases the locks on the articles and logs the snapshot into the history file.

As you can see, the Snapshot Agent is responsible only for creating the snapshot but not for distributing it to the subscribers. These tasks are performed by other agents. There are only a few cases in which the snapshot needs to be refreshed. These cases include the following:

- The snapshot should be refreshed prior to initiating snapshot replication on a subscriber. Beware of copying old snapshots to a subscriber. If the data in the publication database never changes, the snapshot does not need to be refreshed. How often it needs to be refreshed depends on the frequency of changes to the database.

- The snapshot should be refreshed before the initial snapshot for transactional and merge replication.

**Note** When transactional or merge replication is being used but is not frequently refreshed, it is unnecessary to refresh the snapshot.

### The Log Reader Agent

The Log Reader Agent is used for transactional replication. The Log Reader Agent moves information from the transaction log on the publisher to the distribution database. Each database that is using transactional replication has its own Log Reader Agent on the publisher.

### The Distribution Agent

The Distribution Agent propagates snapshots and transactions from the distribution database to the subscribers. The Distribution agent works with snapshot and transactional replication. Each publication that is set up for immediate propagation has its own Distribution Agent. Publications that are not set up for immediate distribution share Distribution Agents. If you are using a push subscription, the Distribution Agent runs on the distributor. If you are using a pull subscription, the Distribution Agent runs on the subscriber.

### The Merge Agent

The Merge Agent is used for merge replication and reconciles, or merges, incremental changes that have occurred since the last reconciliation. When you use merge replication, there is no Distribution Agent or Snapshot Agent—the Merge Agent communicates with both the publisher and the distributor. There is one merge agent for each merge subscription.

### The Queue Reader Agent

The Queue Reader Agent is used with transactional replication with the queued updating option. This is a distributor system-based agent, and it takes changes that have occurred at the subscriber and applies them to the publisher. There is only one Queue Reader Agent per database.

# Configuring Replication

Replication is configured from SQL Server Management Studio. There are several major steps that must be followed in order to configure replication. These steps are:

- Configure the distributor
- Configure the publication
- Configure one or more subscribers

Without a distributor, you cannot configure replication. The distributor can be on the same system as the publisher, the same system as the subscriber, or on its own system. Let's look at these steps in some detail.

## Configure the Distributor

The distributor is configured from SQL Server Management Studio:

1. In Object Explorer view, connect to the server instance of your choice, and then expand the server's Databases folder.

2. In the navigation pane, right-click Replication and select Configure Distribution. This invokes the Configure Distribution Wizard. You are greeted with the Configure Distribution Server Welcome page (not shown). Click Next.

3. You will now see the Distributor page, as shown in Figure 20-1. On the Distributor page, select whether you want to create a new distributor or to configure replication to use an existing distributor. Click Next.

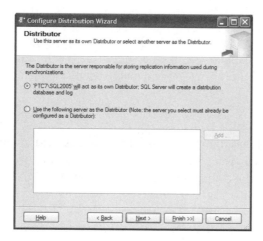

**Figure 20-1**   The Distributor page.

4. Since the SQL Server Agent is required for replication, you are prompted to set it to start automatically in the SQL Server Agent Start page, as shown in Figure 20-2, (if it is not configured to start automatically). Click Next.

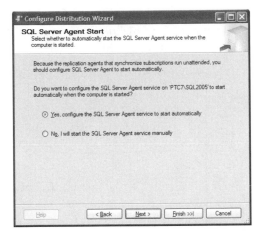

**Figure 20-2**    The SQL Server Agent Start page.

5. Next, you are prompted to set the snapshot folder in the Snapshot Folder page, as shown in Figure 20-3. This page allows you to set the snapshot location. This value can be changed later if you decide to change the snapshot location, or you can use the default location, which is usually fine. Microsoft recommends that you use a network folder for the snapshot location. This network location should be accessible by all systems using this snapshot.

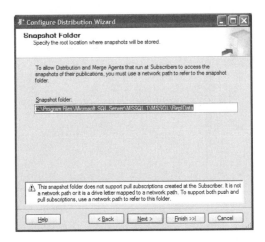

**Figure 20-3**    The Snapshot Location page.

6. If you have chosen to create a new distribution database, the next page, the Distribution Database page, allows you to set the name and file locations for the distribution database, as shown in Figure 20-4. This must be a local drive. Once you have completed this, click Next.

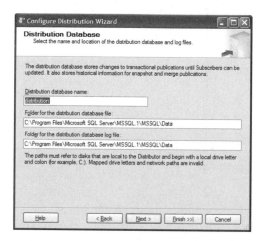

**Figure 20-4** The Distribution Database page.

7. Next, you are prompted to select publishers that can use this distribution database. You can select as many publishers as you want. The Publishers page is shown in Figure 20-5. You can add publishers by clicking the Next button and selecting the publisher. Click Next to proceed.

**Figure 20-5** The Publishers page.

8. The Wizards Action page (not shown) gives you the option of configuring distribution, saving a script to configure distribution with SQL statements, or both. If you want to document the distribution configuration, you can save the script, which can be used again, or modified for slightly different configurations. Click Next to proceed.

9. Finally, you will see the Complete The Wizard page, shown in Figure 20-6. This page allows you to indicate whether to continue or cancel the configuration. When you click Finish, the configuration of the distributor begins.

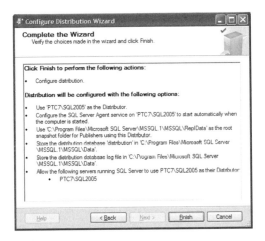

**Figure 20-6**   The Complete The Wizard page.

10. Once you are satisfied and click Finish, the distribution configuration process begins. You will see progress in the Configuration Progress page, as shown in Figure 20-7. If any errors occur, you will see them on this screen. Once it has completed, you have the option of viewing a report on the screen, saving the report to a file, or e-mailing the report. If everything succeeded, there is no need to save the report.

11. Once this has completed successfully, you are notified and are then ready to start creating publications. Click Close to exit the wizard.

## Configure Publications

To create a publication using SQL Server Management Studio, follow these steps from the Object Explorer:

1. In Object Explorer view, connect to the server instance of your choice, and then expand the server's Databases folder.

2. Navigate to Replication then Local Publications. Right-click Local Publications and select New Publication. This invokes the New Publication Wizard.

**Figure 20-7**    The Configuration Progress page.

3.  The first page of the New Publication Wizard welcomes you to the wizard (not shown). Click Next to proceed.

4.  The Publication Databases page allows you to pick the database from which the publication will be selected. In this example, there are six databases: *Production, Test, DBADB* (every DBA should have a database for storing performance information, testing SQL, and so on), *profile* (where I store profiler traces) and, of course, *AdventureWorks* and *AdventureWorksDW*. Select the database that will be the source of the publication. A publication can originate in only one database, although it can consist of one or more objects in that database. In this example, *AdventureWorks* has been selected. This is shown in Figure 20-8. Click Next to continue.

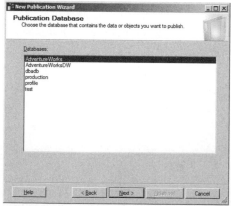

**Figure 20-8**    Choose A Publication Database page.

5. Once you select the source database, you are prompted to select the replication type. The following are the choices for the publication type:

❑ Snapshot publication

❑ Transactional publication

❑ Transactional publication with updatable subscriptions

❑ Merge publication

These publication types were all described earlier in this chapter. Choose the desired type of publication. For this example, transactional has been chosen, as shown in Figure 20-9. Click Next to continue.

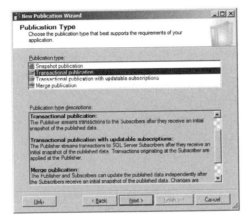

**Figure 20-9** The Publication Type page.

6. After you select the type of publication, the Articles page appears. This page allows you to select the objects, such as tables, stored procedures, views, and so on, that will be part of this publication. As you see in this walkthrough, I have created a table in the *AdventureWorks* database that is not eligible for replication. This is because transactional replication requires a primary key on each article table. By clicking on this table, text is shown that explains that this table is not a candidate for replication because it does not have a primary key defined, as shown in Figure 20-10. The other tables in this database have been selected to be included in this article, as shown in Figure 20-10. Click Next to continue.

**Note** The *AdventureWorks* database does not have a table that is lacking a primary key. I added this table specifically for this example.

Some of the *AdventureWorks* tables do not work with replication. For this example I have chosen only a few tables so that the example works.

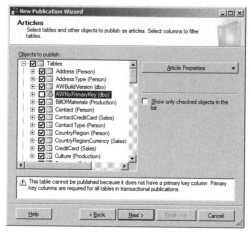

**Figure 20-10**   The Articles page.

7. In addition to selecting the articles to be included into this publication, you can set specific article properties either by highlighting the article and clicking the Article Properties button and selecting Set Properties of Highlighted Table Article, or by selecting Set Properties of All Table Articles. The latter invokes the Article Properties page, as shown in Figure 20-11. Here you can set many article properties. There is typically no need to change these properties. Click OK to exit this box.

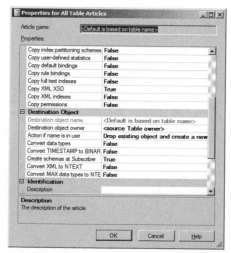

**Figure 20-11**   The Article Properties page.

8. If you have chosen transactional publication with updating subscribers, you will see the Article Issues page as shown in Figure 20-12. This informs you and prompts you for verification that a unique identifier column needed to be added to the tables. This is a requirement of updating subscribers. If you have chosen this option, click Next to continue.

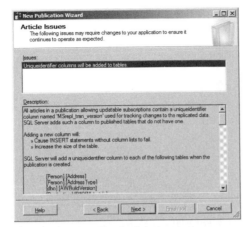

**Figure 20-12** The Article Issues page.

9. Once you have selected the Articles, you will see the Filter Table rows page. As mentioned earlier in this chapter, a table can be either vertically or horizontally filtered. The Filter Table Rows page allows you to either continue on or to click on the Add, Edit, or Delete buttons to add or modify row filters. This is shown in Figure 20-13. Clicking the Add button allows you to add a filter. Clicking Next continues to the next page.

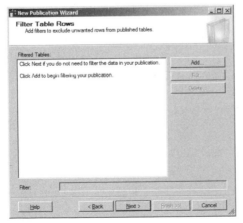

**Figure 20-13** The Filter Table Rows page.

10. By clicking Add, you see the Add Filter page. This page allows you to add a WHERE clause to the replication filter to select only specific rows. In most cases, you will not want to filter the table rows; instead, you will replicate the entire table. The Add Filter page is shown in Figure 20-14. Select the table, modify the WHERE clause for all tables that you want to filter, and click OK when you are done.

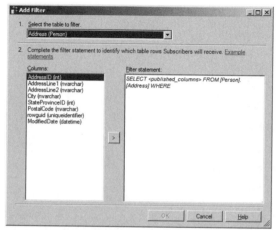

**Figure 20-14**   The Add Filter page.

11. If you have added filters, you are returned to the Filter Table Rows page, but the new filter is visible. Otherwise, the Filter Table rows page stays the same.

---

**Note**   Multiple filters can be added to the same publication.

---

12. Once you have created the filter and selected the Next button, the Snapshot Agent page appears. On this page, you can indicate that the snapshot should run immediately, on a regular schedule, or neither, as shown in Figure 20-15. The Change button allows you to schedule the agent. This invokes the Job Scheduler Properties page that you have seen several times in this book. Click Next to continue.

13. In the Agent Security page, you must specify the security account for each of the agents that will be running. This example uses a Transactional publication. Therefore, it is necessary to supply credentials for the Snapshot Agent and the Log Reader Agent, as shown in Figure 20-16. If we had chosen a Transactional publication with updatable subscriptions, it would have been necessary to supply credentials for the

Snapshot Agent, the Log Reader Agent, and the Queue Reader Agent. Select the Security Settings button to set the security of each agent.

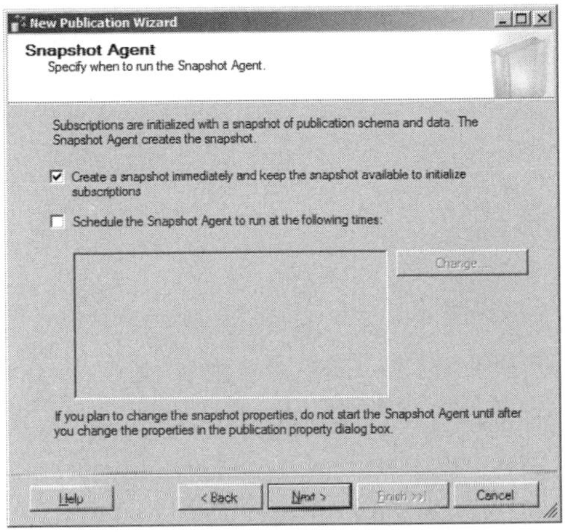

**Figure 20-15**    The Snapshot Agent page.

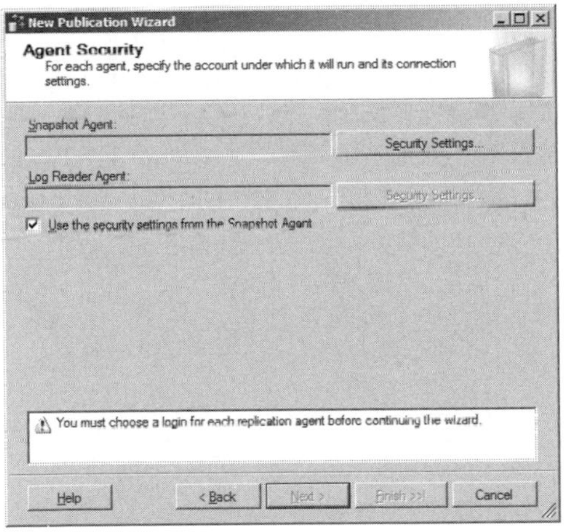

**Figure 20-16**    The Agent Security page.

14. Each of the Agent security pages is slightly different from the others but contains basically the same information as the Snapshot Agent security page, as shown in Figure 20-17. Select the security appropriate for your needs and configuration. Select OK when you have completed the security settings.

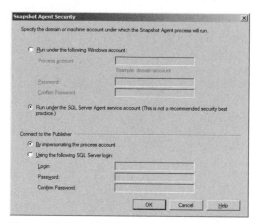

**Figure 20-17** The Snapshot Agent Security page.

15. The Shapshot Agent Security page includes both the Snapshot Agent security settings for the process on the distributor and the security settings for the account running against the publisher. Once you have set all of the security settings, you are returned to the agent security page. However, this time the security settings are filled in. Click Next to continue.

16. When you have completed all of the agent specification pages, you will see the Wizard Actions page. This page allows you either to create the publication or to script the steps necessary to create the publication. It is a good idea to keep a copy of the steps necessary to create the publication by scripting them. In the event that you need to recreate the publication, you can run the script. If you choose to script the publication, the Script File Properties page prompts you for the filename and type of the script file.

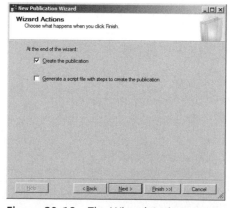

**Figure 20-18** The Wizard Actions page.

17. Once you have completed all of these steps, you will be presented with the Complete The Wizard page. This page allows you to review all of your choices, name the publication, and to create the publication. If you find problems at this stage, you can use the Back button, or you can select Finish in order to create the publication. Click Finish in order to create the publication. You are now informed of the progress of the publication creation process and its success. It is also possible to create the publication using SQL statements. The statements used to create the example in this section are shown in the following example.

# Creating a Publication with SQL Statements

The following is an example that shows the creation of the publication shown above using SQL statements, rather than the wizard.

The following stored procedures are used:

- *sp_replicationdboption* sets database options for replication.
- *sp_addpublication* creates and configures the publication.
- *sp_addpublication_shapshot* creates the snapshot agent.
- *sp_addarticle* will add the various articles to the publication.

The example is shown here:

```
use [AdventureWorks]
exec sp_replicationdboption @dbname = N'AdventureWorks',
@optname = N'publish', @value = N'true'
GO
use [AdventureWorks]
exec sp_addpublication @publication = N'AWPub',
@description = N'Transactional publication of database' 'AdventureWorks' 'from
Publisher' 'PTC9' '.',
@sync_method = N'concurrent', @retention = 0,
@allow_push = N'true', @allow_pull = N'true', @allow_anonymous = N'true',
@enabled_for_internet = N'false', @snapshot_in_defaultfolder = N'true',
@compress_snapshot = N'false',
@ftp_port = 21, @ftp_login = N'anonymous',
@allow_subscription_copy = N'false', @add_to_active_directory = N'false',
@repl_freq = N'continuous', @status = N'active', @independent_agent = N'true',
```

```
@immediate_sync = N'true', @allow_sync_tran = N'false', @autogen_sync_procs =
N'false', @allow_queued_tran = N'false',

@allow_dts = N'false', @replicate_ddl = 1,

@allow_initialize_from_backup = N'false',

@enabled_for_p2p = N'false', @enabled_for_het_sub = N'false'
GO
exec sp_addpublication_snapshot @publication = N'AWPub',

@frequency_type = 1, @frequency_interval = 0,

@frequency_relative_interval = 0, @frequency_recurrence_factor = 0,

@frequency_subday = 0, @frequency_subday_interval = 0,

@active_start_time_of_day = 0, @active_end_time_of_day = 235959,

@active_start_date = 0, @active_end_date = 0,

@job_login = null, @job_password = null,

@publisher_security_mode = 1
use [AdventureWorks]
exec sp_addarticle @publication = N'AWPub', @article = N'Address',

@source_owner = N'Person', @source_object = N'Address',

@type = N'logbased', @description = null,

@creation_script = null, @pre_creation_cmd = N'drop',

@schema_option = 0x000000000803509F,

@identityrangemanagementoption = N'manual',

@destination_table = N'Address', @destination_owner = N'Person',

@vertical_partition = N'false',

@ins_cmd = N'CALL sp_MSins_PersonAddress',

@del_cmd = N'CALL sp_MSdel_PersonAddress',

@upd_cmd = N'SCALL sp_MSupd_PersonAddress'
GO
```

---

**Note**  This step repeats for all tables that were selected as articles for replication.

```
use [AdventureWorks]
exec sp_addarticle @publication = N'AWPub',

@article = N'WorkOrderRouting',

@source_owner = N'Production', @source_object = N'WorkOrderRouting',

@type = N'logbased', @description = null,
```

```
@creation_script = null, @pre_creation_cmd = N'drop',
@schema_option = 0x000000000803509F,
@identityrangemanagementoption = N'manual',
@destination_table = N'WorkOrderRouting', @destination_owner = N'Production',
@vertical_partition = N'false',
@ins_cmd = N'CALL sp_MSins_ProductionWorkOrderRouting',
@del_cmd = N'CALL sp_MSdel_ProductionWorkOrderRouting',
@upd_cmd = N'SCALL sp_MSupd_ProductionWorkOrderRouting'
GO
```

Once the publication has been created, you are ready to start configuring one or more subscribers. Regardless of whether subscribers are created, replication commences as soon as the publications are configured.

## Configure Subscribers

Once publications have been created, subscriptions can be created. For each publication, you can have as many subscriptions as the performance of the system can support. The distributor is very efficient, but the number of publishers and subscribers that can be supported depends on the number of CPUs and amount of memory configured in that system.

### Real World   The Distributor Is Very Efficient

One of the first replication systems that I did took me by surprise. We were replicating an enormous amount of data, and yet the distributor was not working very hard. The replication agents are extremely efficient; the transactions being done within the distribution database are fairly lightweight, thus not creating much of a load. I wish that I could give you the magic calculation for sizing the distributor, but there isn't one. The load varies based on how many transactions, how many articles, and how many subscribers there are. My recommendation is to get something that you can upgrade if you need to, but don't oversize the distributor.

To create subscriptions using SQL Server Management Studio, navigate to Replication and then to Local Subscriptions. Then follow these steps:

1. Right-click Local Subscriptions and select New Subscriptions. This invokes the New Publication Wizard. This wizard begins with the standard welcome screen, not shown. Click Next to proceed.

2. The first step in configuring a subscription is to select the publication that will be used for this subscription. If there is more than one publication, select the one that you want to use for this subscription, as shown in Figure 20-19. Click Next.

3. Once you have selected the publication to be replicated, you are prompted to select the location where the Distribution Agents will run. It is possible for the Distribution Agent to run at either the distributor or the subscriber, depending on whether this is a push or pull subscription. Select push or pull at the Distribution Agent Location page, as shown in Figure 20-20. Click Next.

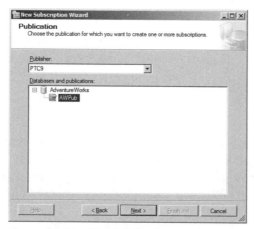

**Figure 20-19**    The Publications page.

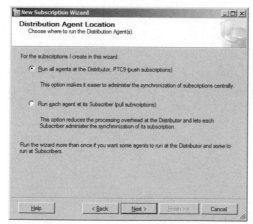

**Figure 20-20**    The Distribution Agent Location page.

4. Once you have selected the Distribution Agent location, you then select the subscriber system and database. Here you can select the system and the database, or

you can choose to create a new database. First, select the box by the SQL Server instance to which you want to subscribe. If you don't see the one that you want, select the Add Subscriber button and connect to the SQL Server instance. Once you have selected the instance, select the database using the dropdown or create a new database (by selecting New Database as the database selection) to use as the subscription database, as shown in Figure 20-21. When you have selected all of the subscriber databases, click Next.

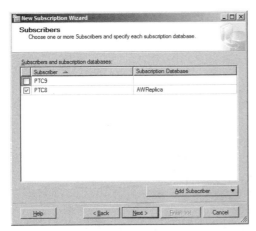

**Figure 20-21** The Subscribers page.

5. As with the New Publication Wizard, the New Subscription Wizard also requires you to set the security connection to both the distributor and the subscriber. This is done on the Distribution Agent Security page, as shown in Figure 20-22.

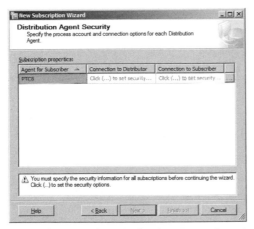

**Figure 20-22** The Distribution Agent Security page.

6. In order to set the security accounts click the ellipses button. This invokes another Distribution Agent Security page. Here you are required to set the security connection to both the distributor and the subscriber, as shown in Figure 20-23. This page is similar to the one seen earlier in this chapter when configuring the publication. Click Next to continue.

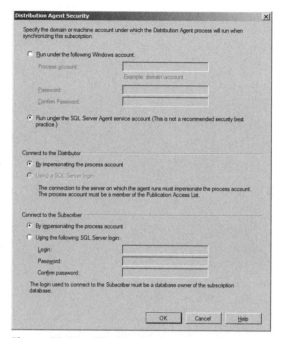

**Figure 20-23**   The Distribution Agent Security page.

7. Once you have completed setting the security accounts for these connections, you will again see the original Distribution Agent Security page with the security information now set. Click Next to continue.

---

**Important**   These examples have used the SQL Server Agent service account for distribution security. This was done for convenience, but it is not recommended. It is recommended that a domain account be used for SQL Server replication.

---

8. Next you are prompted to set the Synchronization Schedule. The following are options for synchronizing replication:

   ❑ **Run Continuously**   Here the agents are constantly running.

❑ **Run on Demand Only**    With this option, the agent runs only when manually initiated.

❑ **Define Schedule**    This invokes the New Job Schedule page where you can
set your own schedule.

The Synchronization Schedule page is shown in Figure 20-24. Click Next to
continue.

**Figure 20-24**    The Synchronization Schedule page.

9. If you are creating an updatable transactional subscription, you are prompted to
select to update subscriptions simultaneously or to queue updates to be committed when possible. This is done on the Update Subscriptions page. With updatable subscriptions, you must additionally provide a login to the publisher in
order to make changes on the publisher. This is a login on the publisher and must
be a SQL Server login. Once you have filled out this screen (if applicable), click
Next to continue.

> **Note**    If you are subscribing to a Transactional Subscription with Updat-
> able Subscriptions you will be prompted to selected an existing linked
> server or to create a new linked server connection. The subscriber must be
> linked to the publisher in for this type of subscriber.

10. Select either Immediately or At First Synchronization from the drop-down list to
specify when to initialize the subscription. The Initialize Subscriptions page is
shown in Figure 20-25.

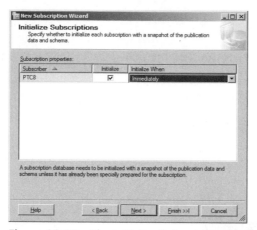

**Figure 20-25** The Initialize Subscriptions page.

11. When you have completed all of the agent specification pages, you will see the Wizard Actions page. This page allows you to either create the subscription or to script the steps necessary to create the subscription. It is a good idea to keep a copy of the steps necessary to create the subscription by scripting them. In the event that you need to recreate the subscription, you can run the script. If you choose to script the subscription, the Script File Properties page prompts you for the filename and type of the script file.

12. Once you have completed all of these steps, you are presented with the Complete The Wizard page, as shown in Figure 20-26. This page allows you to review all of your choices and to create the subscription. If you find problems at this stage, you can click the Back button, or you can click Finish to create the publication.

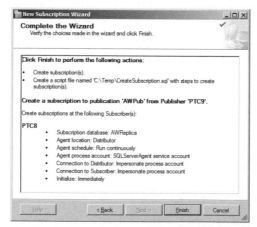

**Figure 20-26** The Complete The Wizard page.

When you click Finish, the Creating Subscriptions page appears and begins to inform you of the progress of the subscription creation and its success.

It is also possible to create the publication using SQL statements. The statements used to create the example in this section are shown in the following sections.

# Creating a Subscription with SQL Statements

The following is an example that shows the creation of the publication shown above using SQL statements, rather than the wizard.

The following stored procedures are used:

- *sp_addsubscription* stored procedure adds a subscription to a publication and sets the subscriber status. The stored procedure runs on the publication database on the publisher.

- *sp_addpushsubscription_agent* stored procedure adds a new scheduled agent job. This job is used to synchronize a push subscription to a transactional publication. It is also executed on the publisher on the publication database.

The example is shown here:

```
----------------BEGIN: Script to be run at Publisher 'PTC9'----------------
use [AdventureWorks]
exec sp_addsubscription @publication = N'AWPub',
@subscriber = N'PTC8', @destination_db = N'AWReplica',
@subscription_type = N'Push', @sync_type = N'automatic',
@article = N'all', @update_mode = N'read only',
@subscriber_type = 0
exec sp_addpushsubscription_agent @publication = N'AWPub',
@subscriber = N'PTC8', @subscriber_db = N'AWReplica',
@job_login = null, @job_password = null, @subscriber_security_mode = 1,
@frequency_type = 64, @frequency_interval = 0,
@frequency_relative_interval = 0, @frequency_recurrence_factor = 0,
@frequency_subday = 0, @frequency_subday_interval = 0,
@active_start_time_of_day = 0, @active_end_time_of_day = 235959,
@active_start_date = 20060722, @active_end_date = 99991231,
@enabled_for_syncmgr = N'False',
```

```
@dts_package_location = N'Distributor'

GO

-----------------END: Script to be run at Publisher 'PTC9'-----------------
```

Replication begins immediately or when scheduled, depending on some of the decisions that you have made in the previous example. Once replication has begun, you can move on to the stage of managing and tuning replication.

# Configuring an Oracle Publication

As mentioned earlier in this chapter, it is possible to replicate an Oracle publication to Microsoft SQL Server 2005. This is a several step process. In order to create an Oracle publication, the following steps must be performed:

1. Create a replication administrative user. This is done with a SQL Script that Microsoft provides. This script is *<drive>*:\\Program Files\Microsoft SQL Server\*<InstanceName>*\MSSQL\Install\oracleadmin.sql. Run this script from the Oracle sqlplus tool:

   ```
   cd <Install Directory>\<Instance>\MSSQL\Install

   sqlplus system/password@inst @oracleadmin.sql
   ```

   This is shown in the following example:

   ```
   C:\Program Files\Microsoft SQL Server\MSSQL.1\MSSQL\Install>sqlplus
   system/ptc12
   3@orcl @oracleadmin


   SQL*Plus: Release 10.2.0.1.0 - Production on Sun Jul 23 07:36:43 2006


   Copyright (c) 1982, 2005, Oracle. All rights reserved.


   Connected to:

   Oracle Database 10g Enterprise Edition Release 10.2.0.1.0 -
   ProductionWith the Partitioning, OLAP and Data Mining options


   User to create for replication: sqlrep

   Replication user passsword:

   Default tablespace: system
   ```

```
old   1: CREATE USER &&ReplLogin IDENTIFIED BY &&ReplPassword DEFAULT
TABLESPACE

&&DefaultTablespace QUOTA UNLIMITED ON &&DefaultTablespace

new   1: CREATE USER sqlrep IDENTIFIED BY sqlrep DEFAULT TABLESPACE
system QUOTA

 UNLIMITED ON system

User created.
old   1: GRANT CREATE PUBLIC SYNONYM TO &&ReplLogin
new   1: GRANT CREATE PUBLIC SYNONYM TO sqlrep


Grant succeeded.


old   1: GRANT DROP PUBLIC SYNONYM TO &&ReplLogin
new   1: GRANT DROP PUBLIC SYNONYM TO sqlrep


Grant succeeded.


old   1: GRANT CREATE SEQUENCE TO &&ReplLogin
new   1: GRANT CREATE SEQUENCE TO sqlrep


Grant succeeded.


old   1: GRANT CREATE PROCEDURE TO &&ReplLogin
new   1: GRANT CREATE PROCEDURE TO sqlrep


Grant succeeded.


old   1: GRANT CREATE SESSION TO &&ReplLogin
new   1: GRANT CREATE SESSION TO sqlrep


Grant succeeded.


old   1: GRANT CREATE TABLE TO &&ReplLogin
new   1: GRANT CREATE TABLE TO sqlrep


Grant succeeded.


old   1: GRANT CREATE VIEW TO &&ReplLogin
new   1: GRANT CREATE VIEW TO sqlrep
```

```
Grant succeeded.

old   1: GRANT CREATE ANY TRIGGER TO &&ReplLogin
new   1: GRANT CREATE ANY TRIGGER TO sqlrep

Grant succeeded.
Disconnected from Oracle Database 10g Enterprise Edition Release
10.2.0.1.0 - Production

With the Partitioning, OLAP and Data Mining options
```

2. Next, grant SELECT access to the newly created Oracle user on all tables that you want to replicate. This is done with the Oracle GRANT command as follows:

   GRANT SELECT on *object* TO *user*;

   For this example, we will use the scott schema and its objects:

```
SQL> GRANT SELECT ON scott.emp TO sqlrep;

Grant succeeded.

SQL> GRANT SELECT ON scott.dept TO sqlrep;

Grant succeeded.

SQL> GRANT SELECT ON scott.bonus TO sqlrep;

Grant succeeded.

SQL> GRANT SELECT ON scott.salgrade TO sqlrep;

Grant succeeded.
```

3. Next, configure the required Oracle software on the SQL Server distributor. This includes the OLE DB provider and Oracle client software.

4. Next, include Oracle for publication and create publications and articles. To create an Oracle publication using SQL Server Management Studio, navigate to Replication. Right-click Replication and select Distributor Properties.

5.  From the Distributor Properties page, select the Publishers tab. From the Publishers tab, click the Add button and select Add Oracle Publisher. This will invokes the Add Server dialog box.

6.  Fill in information on the Oracle net service name, the user name of the SQL Server replication account that we just created, and its password. This is shown in Figure 20-27. Click Connect when done.

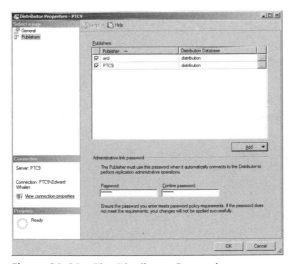

**Figure 20-27**    The Add Server dialog box for Oracle.

7.  You will now see the Distributor Properties page, but with an Oracle publisher listed along with the SQL Server publisher(s). This is shown in Figure 20-28.

**Figure 20-28**    The Distributor Properties page.

8. To create an Oracle publisher using SQL Server Management Studio, navigate to Replication. Right-click Replication and select New, then Oracle Publication. This invokes the New Publication Wizard. Of course, it starts with the welcome page (not shown). Click Next to continue.

9. The Oracle Publisher page allows you to select an Oracle publisher that you have previously configured or to configure a new Oracle publisher. Clicking the Add Oracle Publisher button invokes the same Distributor Properties page that we just used. Select the Oracle publication as seen in Figure 20-29 and click Next.

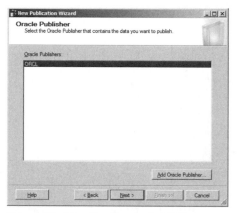

**Figure 20-29**   The Oracle Publisher page.

10. The next page allows you to select snapshot or transactional replication. These are the only options available when replicating from Oracle to SQL Server. For this example, I've selected transactional replication, as shown in Figure 20-30. Click Next to proceed.

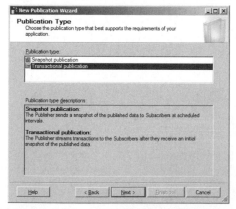

**Figure 20-30**   The Publication Type page.

11. The Articles page lets you select tables just like with a SQL Server publication. As with SQL Server, if a table is not eligible for replication, you will be informed. The articles page is shown in Figure 20-31.

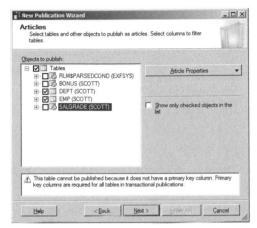

**Figure 20-31**    The Articles page.

12. The remaining pages are the same as with a SQL Server publication and include the Filter Table Rows page, the Snapshot Agent page, the Agent Security page, the Wizard Actions page, and the Complete The Wizard page.

Once you have created the publication, the publication can be subscribed to in the same way that you would subscribe to a SQL Server publication.

**Real World    Oracle and SQL Server Interoperability**

Replication between Oracle and SQL Server is a great step forward in interoperability between Oracle and SQL Server. In addition to replication, it is now possible to monitor Oracle using a plug-in for Microsoft Operations Manager. This interoperability allows you to manage your entire operation from one console, thus easing the administration burden.

# Managing Replication

Replication is managed from SQL Server Management studio or via SQL statements. Once replication has been configured, it requires regular monitoring and maintenance.

Maintenance tasks can be performed either via SQL Server Management Studio or via SQL statements. In order to invoke many of the replication maintenance tasks, right-click Replication.

On the menu that appears, you can select from the following utilities:

- **Publisher Properties**    Used to change properties of the publisher. From this page you can add or remove databases as a publication. Available replication types are transactional and merge.

- **Distributor Properties**    Used to view and change properties of the distributor.

- **Disable Publishing and Distribution**    Used to disable publishing, distribution, or both.

- **Launch Replication Monitor**    Used to invoke the Replication Monitor, with which you can both monitor and manage replication. The Replication Monitor is covered in this and the following section.

- **Generate Scripts**    Used to create scripts for rebuilding the publisher and/or distributor.

- **Update Replication Passwords**    Used to update replication passwords throughout the replication system. This keeps you from having to update passwords in multiple locations.

- **New**    Used to invoke an additional list of options, including New Publication, New Oracle Publication, and New Subscriptions.

- **Refresh**    Used to refresh the replication objects.

These utilities are described in more detail in the following sections.

## Publisher Properties

This utility iis used to change properties of the publisher. From this page you can add or remove databases as a publication. Available replication types are transactional and merge. This doesn't seem like much, but it can have a huge impact on the functionality of replication.

---

**Important**    Clearing the publication permissions box on a database deletes all publications and subscriptions on that database.

---

## Distributor Properties

This utility is used to view and change properties of the distributor. Here you can set options, such as the retention policy and the history retention. The General window of the Distributor Properties utility is shown in Figure 20-32. A new distribution database can be created by clicking the New button.

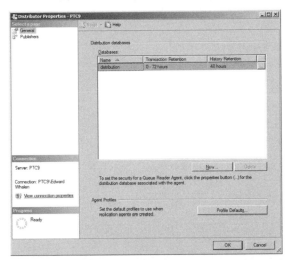

**Figure 20-32**   The Distributor Properties General window.

By clicking on the ellipses button, you can configure the transaction retention period and the history retention periods for the selected database from the Distribution Database Properties window. In addition, the security for the Queue Reader Agent can be set by clicking the Security Settings button. The Distribution Database Properties window is shown in Figure 20-33.

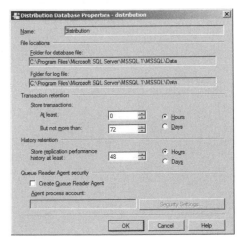

**Figure 20-33**   The Distribution Database Properties window.

From the Main Distributor Properties window, you can modify agent properties by clicking the Profile Defaults button. This invokes the Agent Profiles window. This window gives you the option of modifying agent properties and tuning the replication agents, as shown in Figure 20-34. Tuning agents is covered in the next section of this chapter.

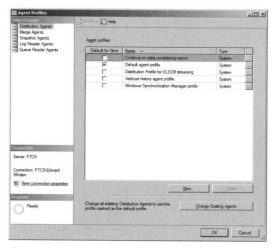

**Figure 20-34**    The Agent Profiles window.

The Publishers window of the Distributor Properties utility allows you to change or add publishers to the distributor. You can add either a SQL Server or an Oracle publisher to the distributor. In addition, you can set the administrative link password that is used by the publisher to connect to the distributor. This window is shown in Figure 20-35.

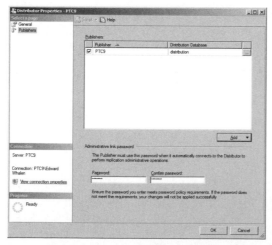

**Figure 20-35**    The Distributor Properties Publishers window.

## Disable Publishing and Distribution

The Disable Publishing and Distribution Wizard walks you through the steps of disabling publishing, distribution, or both. Within the wizard, you can select specific publications to disable, or you can choose to disable all publications. In addition, you can disable distribution and remove the distribution database from the system. This wizard is easy to use.

## Launch Replication Monitor

This utility invokes Replication Monitor, with which you can monitor and manage replication. Replication Monitor is useful for monitoring replication agents and viewing the replication configuration. Replication Monitor allows you to invoke several administrative tasks that are also available through SQL Server Management Studio directly. The initial window of Replication Monitor is shown in Figure 20-36. Replication Monitor is described in more detail in the next section of this chapter.

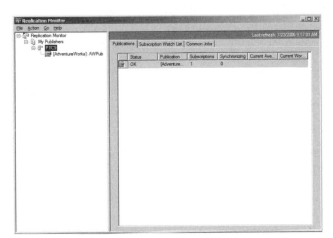

**Figure 20-36**    Replication Monitor.

## Generate Scripts

This very useful utility helps you to create scripts that can be used to manage the publisher and distributor. From the Generate SQL Script tool, shown in Figure 20-37, there are many options for generating scripts associated with creating or dropping the distributor or selected publications. This can also be a very good tool for documenting your configuration and copying it to another system.

**Figure 20-37**   The Generate SQL Script window.

## Update Replication Passwords

This utility updates replication passwords throughout the replication system. This keeps you from having to update passwords in multiple locations. The Update Replication Passwords window is shown in Figure 20-38.

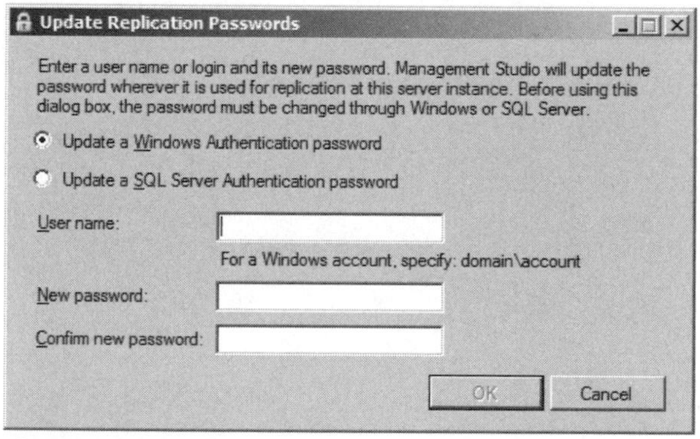

**Figure 20-38**   The Update Replication Passwords window.

This utility can save you a lot of work and help you avoid mistakes by updating all passwords from one utility.

## New

This option invokes an additional list of options including New Publication, New Oracle Publication, and New Subscriptions. These utilities were covered earlier in this chapter, in the "Configuring Replication section."

## Refresh

This utility refreshes the replication objects.

Other replication tasks involve monitoring and tuning replication. This is an important part of managing replication and should be done on a regular basis. Monitoring and tuning replication is covered in the following section.

# Monitoring and Tuning Replication

In some ways, tuning replication involves the normal tuning that you do with any SQL Server system. In other ways, tuning replication involves tuning the specific replication agents. In this section you will see some standard replication tuning tips and techniques, along with specific tasks that must be done in order to tune specific replication types.

## Monitoring Replication with perfmon

The SQL Server agents can be monitored via the Windows performance monitor tool (perfmon). Perfmon can be invoked by selecting it from the Start menu, then All Programs, Administrative Tools, and then Performance, or by selecting Run from the Start menu and typing **perfmon**. From the performance monitor, the SQLServer: Replication Agents object provides a count of the number of agents of each type running on the system. The following are the agents that can be selected:

- Distribution
- Logreader
- Merge
- Queuereader
- Snapshot

The previous counters are not particularly useful for tuning—only for making sure that the required components are up and running.

While some counters are not useful for monitoring performance, other counters are very useful for monitoring performance. For all replication types, it is useful to monitor the following performance objects:

- **PhysicalDisk** These counters are very useful since many performance problems related to snapshot, transactional, and merge replication are I/O related.

- **Processor** It is always a good idea to monitor the system processors. CPU usage might be critical because the reason for doing replication in many cases is to offload reports or data warehouses.

- **System** This counter gives you a good overview of the entire system. Counters such as context switches, processes, and threads can be useful information.

The following are things to watch for:

- **I/O bottlenecks** Are I/O rates too high? Look for I/Os per second and seconds per I/O.

- **Network bottlenecks** It is difficult to find a network bottleneck, but you may be able to determine if you have one by calculating the network throughput and comparing that with the snapshot replication time.

- **CPU time** If the CPU time is too high, especially on the distributor, you might want to add another CPU.

By looking for I/O and network problems and solving them if they exist, you will be able to improve snapshot replication performance.

## Monitoring Replication with the Replication Monitor

SQL Server 2005 has added the Replication Monitor. With the Replication Monitor you can monitor, configure, and even tune replication. The Replication Monitor can be invoked by right-clicking Replication in the SQL Server Management Studio and selecting Launch Replication Monitor. The Replication Monitor is shown earlier in this chapter in Figure 20-36.

The main window of the Replication Monitor, shown in Figure 20-36, lists the publications and their status. This gives you a quick view of how publishing is running.

The Subscription Watch List tab lists the subscriptions associated with this replication system. All of the subscriptions for each type are listed, as shown in Figure 20-39.

By right-clicking the subscription, you can select View Details, Start Synchronization (if stopped), Stop Synchronization (if started), Reinitialize Subscription, Properties, and Agent Profile.

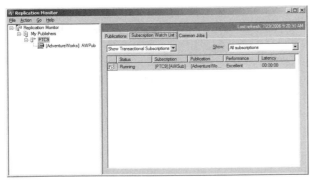

**Figure 20-39**   The Replication Monitor Subscriptions Watch List window.

The View Details page shows the agent status and some history. This window may provide your first indication of a problem with the Distribution Agents. The Distributor to Subscriber History is shown first simply because of where it has been invoked. This window is shown in Figure 20-40.

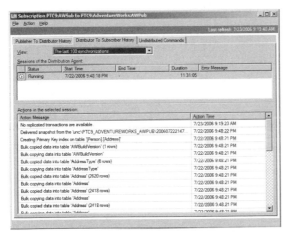

**Figure 20-40**   The Replication Monitor Distributor to Subscriber Details window.

If you select the Publisher to Distributor History tab, you will see the log reader history.

The third tab in the View Details page is Undistributed Commands. This window provides information on commands that have been issued but not applied to the subscriber.

These pages provide status and error information on the various agents and tasks that are taking place in the replicated system. The Replication Monitor is a very good place to find how replication is performing and whether there are errors.

By further expanding the Replication Monitor so that the publications are visible (by clicking +) and selecting a publication, you will see its subscriptions. This window shows the subscriptions, the performance, and the latency of the subscription. This information can indicate issues with the subscription and how well it is performing. The latency describes how long a change takes to propagate from the publisher to the subscriber. The default replication tuning parameters usually result in a change taking 10 to 20 seconds to propagate. If the latency is too high (greater than 40 seconds or so), you might have a problem that you need to investigate. Of course, if you have tuned replication to propagate faster, these values will change.

The Tracer Tokens window allows you to artificially insert a token into the replication stream and time its application. This allows you to periodically test replication and its performance. The Tracer Token is a great way to test replication. This window is shown in Figure 20-41.

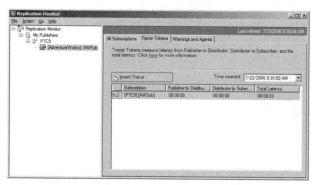

**Figure 20-41**　The Replication Monitor Tracer Tokens window.

The final tab brings up the subscriptions Warnings and Agents window. This is where you can configure alerts . This window is shown in Figure 20-42.

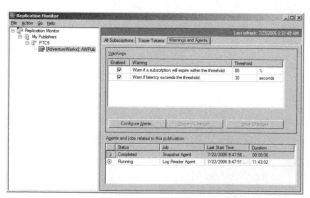

**Figure 20-42**　The Replication Monitor Warnings and Agents window.

In the next few sections, you will see how to tune replication for each replication type. As you will see, snapshot, transactional, and merge replications are tuned differently.

# Tuning for Snapshot Replication

The snapshot replication system is different from the other replication methods in that the entire replication task takes place at once. With transactional and merge replication, a snapshot is propagated to the subscribers, and then replication is constantly being applied to these systems. Snapshot replication is a full refresh of the database and is therefore much more straight-forward.

Since snapshot replication essentially takes an existing database and copies it to the distributor, then to the subscriber, the limiting performance factor in snapshot replication is the ability to move large amounts of data. Factors that can limit snapshot data include the following:

- **I/O performance on the publisher**   Since the entire database, or parts of it, is copied from the publisher, the performance of the I/O subsystem on the publisher can be a limiting factor. The snapshot task is more I/O intensive than CPU intensive, thus CPU power is not usually a factor.

- **I/O performance on the distributor**   As with the publisher, the distributor receives large amounts of data at one time and at some later time distributes that data. A slow I/O subsystem bogs down transactional replication.

- **I/O performance on the subscriber**   As with the other components, the distributor will attempt to distribute a database or subset of a database to the subscriber in one shot. If the I/O subsystem is inadequate, replication performance will suffer.

- **The bandwidth of the network between the publisher, distributor, and subscriber**   Since large amounts of data are being transferred, the network can easily become a bottleneck. Make sure that your network does not limit replication performance.

As you can see, there are several factors that can limit performance. By reducing the effect of these factors by properly sizing and configuring the snapshot replication system, performance will be optimal.

## Monitoring the Snapshot System

Monitoring the snapshot system is done via the Windows performance monitor, perfmon. Within perfmon, there are a number of objects that are added when SQL Server replication is present. In addition there are a number of standard perfmon objects that are useful for monitoring snapshot replication. These objects include:

- *SQLServer:Replication Agents*    Provides counts of each type of agent that is running.

- *SQLServer:Replication Dist*    Provides information on distribution latency.

- *SQLServer:Replication Snapshot*    Provides information on snapshot performance.

These counters give you a fairly good idea of how much activity is occurring in the agent. In addition, the Snapshot Agent Status page can be a good place to find information about how the snapshot performed. In SQL Server Management Studio expand Replication, then Local Publications. Right-click on the publication that you want to monitor and select View Snapshot Agent Status. This is shown in Figure 20-43.

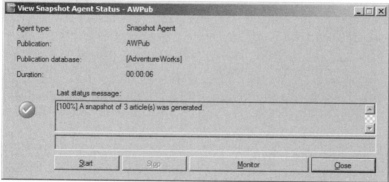

**Figure 20-43**    The Snapshot Agent Status window.

## Tuning the Snapshot System

Tuning the snapshot system usually just involves proper configuration, as mentioned above. The critical things to look for during snapshot replication are I/O and network problems. In order to determine if you are network bound, you should look at the performance of the network and then determine if that network is sufficient for your replication needs. Let's look at an example.

Suppose you have a database that is 5 GB in size. Using a 10baseT network, there is a theoretical maximum bandwidth of 10 megabit per second, which is approximately 1 MB (megabyte) per second. Thus, a 5 GB database will take 5,120 seconds, or 1.4 hours (5 GB x 1,024 (Mbyte/Gbyte)) / 1 (Mbyte/sec), to replicate this database. In contrast, a 100baseT network can perform the same replication in 8.3 minutes. In addition, a Gigabit network can do this same task in 51 seconds. The network comparison is summarized in the following table:

**Table 20-1  Network Speed Comparison**[*]

| Network Speed | Theoretical Time to Perform a Snapshot of a 5 GB database |
| --- | --- |
| 10baseT | 5,120 seconds or 85.3 minutes or 1.4 hours |
| 100baseT | 516 seconds or 8.3 minutes |
| Gigabit | 51 seconds |

*This table uses a theoretical maximum bandwidth of the published network speed. Your actual speed will be much less than the theoretical maximum.

As you can see, the size of your network really does count. By performing calculations like this, you should get a good idea of how long the replication should take. If these tasks are taking much longer, you probably are experiencing a bottleneck somewhere else.

The Snapshot Agent can be tuned by setting the Snapshot Agent properties. The Snapshot Agent Configuration window can be invoked from the Distributor Properties window. In SQL Server Management Studio, right-click Replication and select Distributor Properties. In the Distributor Properties General window, select Default Profiles. Here you can create or modify agent profiles. There are only a few parameters that can be set in the Snapshot Agent Default Configuration window, shown in Figure 20-44.

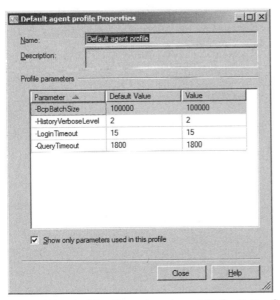

**Figure 20-44**   The Snapshot Agent Default Configuration window.

Once you have created a new profile, you can use the Replication Monitor in order to set that profile to be used by each agent. Right click the publication or the subscription and select Agent Profile. Here you can select the profile to run for each agent.

Snapshot is the most straightforward of the replication types, but in many ways, the most performance challenging (because all tuning issues are in the hardware), since everything is copied at once. This requires a great deal of I/O and network bandwidth.

## Tuning the Distributor

In order to tune the replication system, it is necessary to tune the distributor. The distributor is a SQL Server database that is used as a repository of replication data as well as metadata. This data is held in a SQL Server database for several reasons. These reasons include the following:

- **Performance**   SQL Server performance is ideal for the distributor because the job of the distributor is to acquire, hold, and then distribute data. What better performing repository for data is there than SQL Server itself?

- **Reliability**   Because SQL Server supports a high level of recoverability, the replication data cannot have a better place to reside. Using the transaction log, SQL Server is able to recover from system failures without losing any data.

- **Ease of use**   Because SQL Server replication communicates directly to the distributor via SQL Server communications protocols, setting up and configuring the distributor is very easy to do.

As mentioned above, the distributor uses a SQL Server database to process replication information. Thus, the distributor must be configured and tuned like any other SQL Server database. The default distribution configuration may work for smaller replication systems, but based on the amount of work being done, you will most likely want to configure the distributor manually.

### Configuring the Distributor

Since the distributor uses a SQL Server database, it is necessary to configure this database for optimal performance. By default, the SQL Server Replication Wizard will not place the SQL Server transaction log and data files optimally. This is up to you to do.

Depending on the frequency of modifications to your database, the amount of activity in the distributor can be quite high. Since the distributor uses a SQL Server database, all modifications to the distributor must be logged in the transaction log. Keeping these in mind, you should optimally configure the distribution database and log to be large enough to perform the work required and fast enough to perform it efficiently. These topics were covered in detail in Chapter 4, "I/O Subsystem Planning and RAID Configuration." Here are a few guidelines for configuring the distribution database:

- **Use a RAID controller on the distribution database system.**  By using a hardware RAID controller, the fault-tolerance features that are needed will be performed in hardware, thus more efficiently that using software RAID.

- **Configure the distribution database's transaction log on a RAID-1 volume.**  The transaction log should be isolated in order to allow for the higher performance that is achieved with sequential I/Os.

- **Configure the transaction log large enough so that it is not necessary to constantly backup the transaction log.**  Depending on your needs, it may be possible to run all day without backing up the transaction log and performing that task at night.

- **Never run in truncate log on checkpoint mode.**  The distribution database is critical to replication and must be safeguarded from system failures.

- **Configure the distribution database on a RAID-1 or RAID-10 volume.**  RAID-5 is not appropriate due to the high number of writes to the distribution database.

- **Configure the distribution database to be large enough to hold extra replication data.**  If a subscriber were to fail, you may have to hold several days worth of replication data.

- **Tune the distribution database as you would any other SQL Server database.**  By optimally configuring the distribution database in the beginning, you may be able to avoid costly performance problems later.

## Tuning the Distributor

As mentioned earlier, the distributor is tuned in the same manner as any other SQL Server systems. There are, however, a few differences that you should keep in mind. When snapshot replication is running, including the initial snapshot for other replication types, a large number of I/Os will occur at one time. Since so much data is being written to the distributor, it is possible that the I/O subsystem may become overloaded. If this is the case, the time it takes to perform this snapshot increases. Therefore, it is a good idea to specifically monitor the system during the snapshot.

Performance of the distributor can be enhanced by proper sizing, although as you have seen earlier in this book, sizing is not always an easy task. In the case of the distributor, it may be better to give it a little extra capacity. The distributor is the link between the publishers and the subscribers, and it should be optimally configured so that it is not a bottleneck. Some tips on configuring and tuning the distributor include the following:

- **Tune the I/O subsystem.**    It is important that there be sufficient I/O performance capacity for the distributor, just as any other SQL Server system.

- **CPU power is not usually a problem.**    In most cases, the type of operations that are involved in being a distributor are not extremely CPU-intensive. It is, however, advisable that a multiprocessor system with at least 2 CPUs be used. This allows concurrent operations to take place.

- **Tune Windows.**    Typically there is not much Windows tuning that is necessary. However, there are a few things that can be done. Configure the Server service to maximize throughput for network applications. This configures the memory system to favor applications over file services. This is configured within the Network Connections application within the control panel. Also, remove any unnecessary services that won't be used, such as FTP services.

- **Tune SQL Server.**    Using the techniques and guidelines given within this book, tune the SQL Server system.

By properly configuring and tuning, the distributor replication will be enhanced.

# Tuning for Transactional Replication

In this section, you will learn how to configure and tune a transactional replication system for optimal performance. Transactional replication is different from snapshot replication in that each transaction is replicated from the publisher, to the distributor, and then to the subscriber in small chunks, rather than all at once. Transactional replication begins with a snapshot; however, once this snapshot has been completed, replication is continuous. This section begins with a review of the attributes of transactional replication followed by configuration, monitoring, and tuning guidelines.

## Attributes of Transactional Replication

Transactional replication starts with a snapshot that is copied to the distributor (or snapshot location) and then to the subscriber. Once the snapshot has been completed, the Log Reader Agent reads the transaction log of the publisher, either on a continual basis or on a regular schedule. This is determined by how you configure the Log Reader Agent.

This is the only additional overhead that is incurred on the publisher. The Log Reader Agent itself runs on the distributor and connects to the publisher in order to read the transaction log. On the distributor, the transactions that are read from the transaction log on the publisher are put into the distribution database. These transactions are then eventually sent to the subscribers. Factors that can limit snapshot data include the following:

- **I/O performance on the publisher's transaction log**   The transaction log on the publisher is read in order to determine what changes have been made. Because the transaction log is now being read and written, the sequential nature of the transaction log may be disrupted. This may cause a bottleneck if it is not carefully configured.

- **Performance of the distributor**   Depending on how much replication is being done and how many publishers are using the distributor, a performance problem may develop. Earlier in this chapter, you learned how to configure and tune the distributor.

- **Performance of the subscriber**   Depending on what activity is occurring on the subscriber, a performance problem may develop. Normal SQL Server tuning should be done.

As you can see, there are several factors that can limit performance. By reducing the effect of these factors by properly sizing and configuring the systems involved, performance will be optimal.

## Configuring for Transactional Replication

As discussed in the previous section, the transaction log on the publisher may be experiencing additional overhead. Tuning of the publisher, distributor, and subscriber mainly involves proper configuration of the I/O subsystem on these systems. There are, however, some configuration choices that can make a great deal of difference when configuring snapshot replication. Here are some guidelines for configuring transactional replication system:

- **Configure sufficient I/O capacity**   Follow general I/O capacity guidelines as presented in Chapter 4. In addition, there are some specific I/O changes that should be made on the publisher.

- **Increase the commit batch size on the distributor Tune the Log Reader**   Let's look at each of these configuration guidelines.

### Configure Sufficient I/O

By configuring sufficient I/O capacity, the performance of the entire replication process may be enhanced. As with any SQL Server system, the transaction log should be located on its own RAID-1 volume for data protection. The data files should be located on one or more RAID-10 or RAID-5 volumes. Unlike snapshot replication, there are only minor I/O considerations on the publisher, distributor, and subscriber because of transactional replication. Those considerations are described here in the upcoming sections.

### Configure the I/O Subsystem on the Publisher

In general, the publisher should follow normal SQL Server configuration guidelines as shown throughout this book. In addition to the normal configuration guidelines, you may need to increase the I/O capacity of the transaction log. Normally it is recommended that the transaction log be configured on a RAID-1 volume. If necessary and depending on how busy your system is, you may need to use more disk drives in a RAID-10 volume. RAID-5 is not appropriate for the transaction log.

*Configuring the I/O Subsystem on the Distributor*    The distributor should be configured so that the distribution database has its transaction log on a dedicated RAID-1 disk volume. This allows the distribution database to achieve maximum transaction log performance, thus improving the performance of the distributor.

*Configuring the I/O Subsystem on the Subscriber*    Transaction replication does not specifically call for any special I/O configuration on the subscriber. Simply follow general sizing and configuration guidelines as shown throughout this book.

### Increase the Commit Batch Size on the Distributor

The commit batch size on the distributor determines how many replication transactions are committed in a single batch. While the distribution database is being updated, there are locks held on the distribution tables. Increasing the batch size causes more rows to be committed at a time, thus increasing the time that those locks are held. Decreasing the batch size causes fewer rows to be committed at a time, thus giving other processes a chance to access the distribution database.

If there is a large amount of activity on the distribution database from several different sources (in other words, the publisher and several subscribers), you may want to try reducing the batch size. If the Log Reader Agent is running on a periodic schedule and has a lot of transactions to insert into the distribution database, you may benefit from a larger batch size. There may actually be no need to change it, but if you do, compare the impact of both increasing and decreasing the batch size in order to determine which is better.

The commit batch size can be configured through SQL Server Management Studio (or the Replication Monitor) by selecting the properties of the Distribution Agent. In SQL Server Management Studio, select Distributor Properties. In the Distributor Properties window click Profile Defaults button, as shown earlier in this chapter. Here you can set the agent properties.

In the Replication Monitor, this is found under Agent Profiles. Here you can choose a different agent profile or select to modify the currently selected profile, which in this case is the Default Profile, as shown in Figure 20-45.

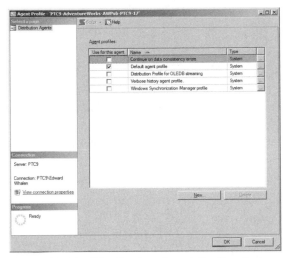

**Figure 20-45**    Distribution Agent Profile window.

Click the ellipses button to modify the Distributor Default Profile, as shown in Figure 20-46. Here you can change parameters such as the polling interval and batch size.

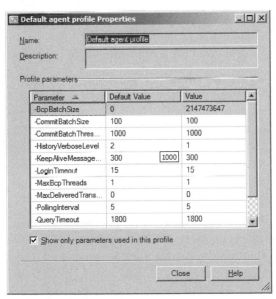

**Figure 20-46**    Distribution Agent Default Configuration window.

---

**Best Practices**   Never change the default profile. Always create a new profile if you wish to change a parameter. Leave the default profile as it is.

---

## Tune the Log Reader

By configuring the log reader, you may be able to reduce its effect on the publisher's transaction log. There are several ways to make the log reader process more efficient. One way is to use a caching controller for the log drive volume. Since log reader Agent reads from the log drive, a cache on a controller allows the read to take place from the cache, rather than causing a random I/O to occur.

Another way to tune the log reader is by modifying the frequency that it runs. The log reader can run on a continuous basis, or it can be configured to run periodically. On a system that is not experiencing a large amount of update activity, it may be acceptable for the log reader to run continuously, but on systems where the transaction log is busy, configuring the log reader to run less frequently can improve performance of the publisher. You are not reading from the transaction log as often, thus allowing the transaction log I/Os to remain sequential. Reads from the transaction log tends to randomize the otherwise sequential I/Os.

Tuning the log reader to run periodically is done through the scheduling of the agent. If the log reader is scheduled to run continuously, you can set the polling interval, which sets how often the Log Reader Agent checks the transaction log. The default value of five seconds is usually sufficient; however, if you cannot accept a five-second delay, this number can be tuned down to a lower value. The polling interval on Log Reader Agent and on the Distribution Agent determines the time that a change could take to propagate through the system.

Another way to make the Log Reader Agent more efficient in heavily used systems is to increase the read batch size. This specifies how many transactions are read from the transaction log and copied to the distributor at a time. In heavily used systems, increasing this parameter can improve performance. In addition, when increasing the polling interval, it may be useful to increase the batch size. If you increase the read batch size on Log Reader Agent, it is advisable to increase the commit batch size on the distributor to correspond to the new read batch size.

The Log Reader Agent can also be configured through SQL Server Management Studio (or the Replication Monitor) by selecting the properties on Log Reader Agent. In SQL Server Management Studio, this is found through the Distributor Properties tool under Agent Profiles and the Profile Defaults button. In the Replication Monitor, this is found under Agent Profiles. Here you can choose a different agent profile or select to modify the currently selected profile, which in this case is the Default Profile (if you haven't changed it), as shown in Figure 20-47.

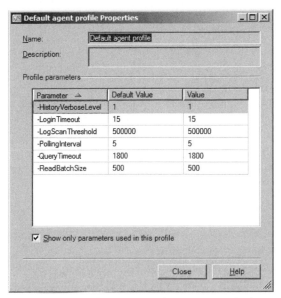

**Figure 20-47**   The Log Reader Agent Default Configuration page.

## Monitoring the Transactional Replication System

As with the other replication types, monitoring transactional replication is done via the Windows performance monitor (perfmon). Within perfmon there are a number of objects that are added when SQL Server replication is present. These objects include the following:

- **SQLServer:Replication Agents**   Gives counts of each type of agent that is running.

- **SQLServer:Replication Dist**   Provides information on distribution latency. Long latencies can be a sign that the distributor is overloaded.

- **SQLServer:Replication Logreader**   Provides data on Logreader activity and latency. Look for long latencies, which can be an indication that there is a problem reading the transaction log on the publisher. Also watch the number of Delivered Transactions per second. If this is high, you may need to add more I/O capacity to the transaction log disk volumes.

By using the Windows performance monitor and monitoring these values, you can sometimes determine if there is a performance problem in the Log Reader Agent or in the distributor. This perfmon data provides a lot of valuable information but may not always identify problems.

In addition to monitoring with perfmon, the Replication Monitor is a good place to see how replication is doing. This can be done by looking at the replication latency output as well as through the use of tracer tokens.

## Tuning the Transactional Replication System

The main steps in tuning the transactional replication system are to properly configure the system and monitor it as shown above. In addition, after the system is in production and you can monitor it, you may need to modify the read batch size and the polling interval. The default value of 10 seconds is usually pretty good. By increasing the polling interval (making it smaller), you replicate transactions faster at the expense of more overhead on the transaction log. By decreasing the polling interval (making it longer), you reduce the overhead on the transaction log but leave transactions in the log longer before they are replicated.

In update intensive systems, you may need to increase the read batch size. This will let the Log Reader Agent read more transactions out of the transaction log at a time. By increasing this value and leaving the polling interval at 10 seconds, you are able to replicate more transactions with less additional overhead.

As with snapshot replication, it is also necessary to monitor and increase the capacity of the network if necessary. If your system appears to be performing optimally, such as CPU and I/O usage within their capacity limits, yet the replication process seems to be taking too long, you may have a network problem. Unfortunately, network problems cannot be diagnosed via perfmon. A network monitor such as SMS (System Management Server) should be used. Look for network usage near the capacity of the network card. In addition to these tuning guidelines, remember that the publisher, distributor, and subscribers are SQL Server systems just like any other SQL Server system.

## Tuning Transactional Replication with Updating Subscriptions

If you are running transactional replication with updating subscriptions, you will have the additional task of monitoring the Queue Reader Agent. As with the other agents, the Queue Reader Agent also has a polling interval. As with the other agents, the Queue Reader Agent polling interval can be changed.

The Queue Reader Agent can also be configured through SQL Server Management Studio (or the Replication Monitor) by selecting the properties on the Queue Reader agent. In SQL Server Management Studio, this is found through the Distributor Properties tool under Agent Profiles and the Profile Defaults button. In the Replication Monitor, this is found under Agent Profiles. Here you can create a new agent profile or modify the currently selected profile, which in this case is the Default Profile, as shown in Figure 20-48.

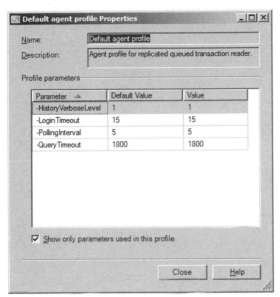

**Figure 20-48**   The Queue Reader Agent Default Configuration window.

Under normal circumstances, the Queue Reader Agent properties should not be changed.

# Monitoring and Tuning the Merge Replication System

In this section, you will learn how to configure and tune a merge replication system for optimal performance. This section begins with a review of the attributes of merge replication, followed by configuration, monitoring, and tuning guidelines. Unlike transactional replication and snapshot replication (except for updating subscribers), merge replication is not a one-way replication. Modifications can be made on either the publisher or any number of subscribers. Another difference is that where transactional replication is done external to the normal operations of SQL Server by reading the transaction log, merge replication triggers are created on the replicated tables in order to track changes to them. In this way, merge replication is very different.

## Attributes of Merge Replication

Merge replication begins with a snapshot, but since it occurs only once, it is not extremely important to tune this snapshot. The merge system creates tables both on the publisher and distributor in order to perform the replication. In addition, a new column is added to every replicated table that holds a unique row identifier. This is used to uniquely identify each row so that the replication agent can effectively track changes.

When a row is inserted or modified, the trigger marks that row as needing replication. At a later time when the Merge Agent runs, it collects all of these rows and sends them to the distributor for replication. At the same time, the Merge Agent modifies any rows on the publisher that have been modified on the subscriber system or systems. In this way, two way replication is accomplished.

## Real World  Merge Replication Overhead

I have been using and implementing replication with SQL Server for many years. Because of the additional overhead incurred involved with a trigger-based replication system, I always recommend transactional replication or transactional replication with updating subscribers before I recommend merge replication. Transactional replication incurs much less overhead on the publisher than merge; thus, I like it better.

## Configuring for Merge Replication

As with transactional replication and snapshot replication, the I/O subsystem and network are very important. In addition to configuring sufficient I/O for merge replication, it is also possible to improve merge replication by configuring the merge batch size. By increasing the batch size, you have fewer batches that are larger and therefore more efficient. In addition to the merge batch size, you may want to tune snapshot replication, as described above. However, the snapshot occurs only once, so this step can be skipped. I/O configuration and the other considerations are described here in the following sections.

### Configure Sufficient I/O

By configuring sufficient I/O capacity, the performance of the entire replication process may be enhanced. As with any SQL Server system, the transaction log should be located on its own RAID-1 volume for data protection. The data files should be located on one or more RAID-10 or RAID-5 volumes. Like transactional replication, there are only minor I/O considerations on the publisher, distributor, and subscriber because of merge replication.

*Configuring the I/O Subsystem on the Publisher*   In general, the publisher should follow normal SQL Server configuration guidelines as shown throughout this book. Unlike transactional replication, no additional load is put on the transaction log, so just follow normal tuning guidelines.

*Configuring the I/O Subsystem on the Distributor*   The distributor should be configured such that the distribution database has its transaction log on a dedicated RAID-1 disk volume. This allows the distribution database to achieve maximum transaction log performance, thus improving the performance of the distributor.

*Configuring the I/O Subsystem on the Subscriber*    Since merge replication is multidirectional, the subscriber and publisher are similarly tuned. As with merge replication, just follow general sizing and configuration guidelines as shown throughout this book.

### Configure the Merge Batch Size

In busy systems, it is possible to improve merge replication performance by configuring the merge batch size. The merge batch size determines how many changed rows at a time are copied to the distributor. By increasing the batch size, fewer batches that are larger are sent, which may be more efficient.

The Merge Agent can also be configured through SQL Server Management Studio (or the Replication Monitor) by selecting the properties on the Merge Agent. In SQL Server Management Studio, this is found through the Distributor Properties tool under Agent Profiles and the Profile Defaults button. In the Replication Monitor, this is found under Agent Profiles. Here you can choose a different agent profile or select to modify the currently selected profile, which in this case is the Default Profile (if you haven't changed it), as shown in Figure 20-49.

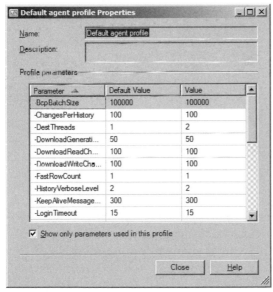

**Figure 20-49**    Merge Agent Default Configuration page.

## Monitoring the Merge Replication System

Monitoring the distributor is done via the Windows performance monitor (perfmon). Within perfmon there are a number of objects that are added when SQL Server replication is present. These objects are the following:

- **SQLServer:Replication Agents**   Gives counts of each type of agent that is running.

- **SQLServer:Replication Merge**   Provides data on Merge rates. This provides information on conflicts per second, uploads per second, and downloads per second. This information provides rate information but does not really help with tuning merge replication.

The SQL Sever merge replication counters are not extremely helpful for determining performance problems. The best way to tune a merge replication system is to simply tune the SQL Server system as normal and pay special attention to the network. Look for normal performance bottlenecks, and follow the guidelines in this chapter to determine if the distributor is overloaded.

As with the other replication types, merge replication can also be monitored from the SQL Server Management Studio. Right-click Replication and select Replication Monitor. Select the Merge Replication subscription. This shows you information about merge subscriptions, as shown in Figure 20-50. Look for things like Delivery Rate, Duration and when it was last synchronized. This can indicate problems.

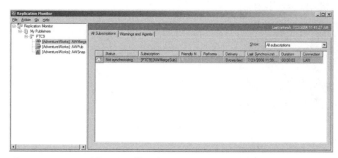

**Figure 20-50**   The Replication Monitor and Merge Subscriptions window.

## Tuning the Merge Replication System

The main steps in tuning the merge replication system are properly configuring the system and monitoring it as shown above, with a special emphasis on I/O and network performance. Once you have put the system into production, you can monitor it via perfmon, but you will not find very useful merge data. Instead, you must rely on other SQL Server counters and Windows counters to tune the system.

As mentioned earlier, you may want to modify the BCP (Bulk Copy Program) and batch sizes if your system is doing a lot of updates. By increasing the BCP size, you increase the performance of the original snapshot. By increasing the batch sizes, you move more changes at a time, which may be more efficient. By moving more changes at a time, you affect the system fewer times, but each time you do, you perform more work, thus causing a larger effect on the system.

In addition to those changes mentioned above, it is also possible to change the polling interval. It is recommended that this not be changed. The default polling interval usually works fine. Before tuning the polling interval, try changing the batch sizes instead. If you feel that you need merge replication to run more or less frequently, then change the polling interval.

Merge Agent can also be configured through SQL Server Management Studio (or the Replication Monitor) by selecting the properties on Merge Agent. In SQL Server Management Studio, this is found through the Distributor Properties tool under Agent Profiles and the Profile Defaults button. In the Replication Monitor, this is found under Agent Profiles. Here you can create a new agent profile or modify the currently selected profile, which in this case is the Default Profile, as shown in Figure 20-51.

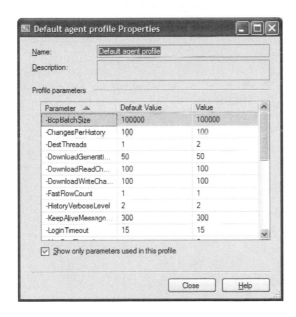

**Figure 20-51** The Merge Agent Default Configuration window.

As with other replication types, it is also necessary to monitor and increase the capacity of the network if necessary. If your system appears to be performing optimally, such as

CPU and I/O usage within their capacity limits, and if the replication process seems to be taking too long, you may have a network problem. Perfmon does not have a counter that will show you network problems. A network monitor such as SMS (System Management Server) should be used. Look for network usage near the capacity of the network card. What can you do if you are near the capacity of your network? Either purchase faster network cards, or add a private network for replication and/or backup and recovery to use. In addition to these tuning guidelines, remember that the publisher, distributor, and subscribers are SQL Server systems just like any other SQL Server system and follow the same tuning guidelines given throughout this book.

## Summary

In this chapter, you have been introduced to SQL Server 2005 replication. You have seen what replication can be used for, what makes up a replicated system, and the different types of replication. You have also learned the basics of configuring, managing, and tuning replication. It might seem difficult at first, but once you have set up replication a few times, you will see that it isn't as hard as it first seems.

Although replication appears at first to run itself and doesn't need any administration, it is important to monitor it regularly. Check the logs regularly, look for errors or problems, and correct them as soon as possible. Be sure to monitor the network and I/O subsystem as well as space on the publisher, distributor, and subscriber.

# Chapter 21
# Integration Services

Moving data between data stores can sometimes be a challenging task, especially when multiple data structures are involved or data needs to be changed before it's placed in a new location. The goal of SQL Server 2005 Integration Services, also known as Integration Services or SSIS, is not only to simplify such data transfer task but also to provide rich functionality in support of more complex extract, transform, and load (ETL) requirements for data warehousing. The goal of this chapter is to introduce you to the key concepts of Integration Services. We'll explore how to build basic packages using the new design environment and how to use some of this product's features to monitor, troubleshoot, and log package execution. We'll also take a look at the administrative tasks associated with Integration Services.

# What Is Integration Services?

Integration Services is the data integration component of SQL Server 2005. Data integration activities can be as simple as moving data between data sources or as complex as consolidating large volumes of data from multiple data sources in different formats, applying rules to modify or cleanse data content, and loading the resulting data into data warehouses designed for reporting and analytical applications. Even if you're not responsible for creating and maintaining a data warehouse, you'll find the features in Integration Services quite useful for routine database administration tasks and any activities requiring you to move data in any form.

# Integration Services Versus Data Transformation Services

Integration Services is the successor to Data Transformation Services (DTS), a data utility first introduced in SQL Server 7.0. DTS simplified the process of migrating data between database systems and was even used as an ETL tool in many data warehouse implementations. Despite its extensive capabilities, DTS had some limitations in performance, portability, and manageability that led Microsoft to develop an entirely new architecture for improved data integration functionality in SQL Server 2005.

## Some Important Enhancements

Ask ten DBAs who have started using Integration Services which enhancements are the most important, and you're likely to get ten different lists. The official comprehensive list of enhancements can be found in the SQL Server Books Online topic, "Integration Services Enhancements." In this section, we'll limit the discussion to the features that typically get strong positive reactions from DBAs during their introduction to Integration Services.

If you were already satisfied with DTS, you're going to be happier with Integration Services. For example, during the development cycle, you can take advantage of the debugging capabilities to monitor package execution more efficiently. If you're part of a team, you can use source control, such as Microsoft Visual SourceSafe, for your data integration projects to manage collaboration within the group. Building complex workflows that included loops or conditional branches was not impossible in DTS, but it was challenging; now Integration Services provides special components to handle these workflow requirements. When you're ready to move your work from one server to another, such as migrating from development to production, you'll find deployment is much simpler in Integration Services. Of course, there are many other features, discussed later in this chapter, which you'll also appreciate.

If, on the other hand, the limitations of DTS kept you from making use of this tool, now's the time to see how Integration Services measures up to your data integration requirements. The biggest improvement is the new architecture of Integration Services replacing the DTS Data Pump with an engine optimized to process and transport large data volumes more efficiently and much faster. Another important new feature is the checkpoint support, which allows you to restart data integration processes from a specific checkpoint rather than the beginning of the package. You also have more options for responding to events during execution and for logging results during execution.

## Migration from DTS to Integration Services

Several key concepts and terminology applicable to DTS still exist in Integration Services. A *package*, for example, is still an executable unit of work that encapsulates the objects that connect to data sources, perform tasks, transform data, and manage workflows. However, because the new architecture of Integration Services has replaced or eliminated

DTS objects, you need to recreate your packages in Integration Services to benefit from its scalability and performance features. To support backward compatibility, all SQL Server 2005 editions (except Express) include the SQL Server 2000 DTS run-time engine. Consequently, you can use Integration Services to develop new packages, convert those DTS packages that will benefit most from the performance enhancements of Integration Services, and then selectively convert the remaining DTS packages at your convenience.

---

**Important**   If you need to edit DTS packages after upgrading the server to Integration Services but before converting the packages, download the Microsoft SQL Server 2000 DTS Designer Components available at *http://www.microsoft.com/downloads/details.aspx?familyid=D09C1D60-A13C-4479-9B91-9E8B9D835CDC&displaylang=en.* There are several items available for download. Search for SQLServer2005_dts.msi to locate the applicable download link.

---

To convert DTS packages, use the Package Migration Wizard. This utility does its best to create an Integration Services package that matches the original DTS package, but changes to the underlying object model and the run-time engine in Integration Services mean that any DTS object model references as well as certain tasks cannot be converted. Before you use the Package Migration Wizard, review the information in this section to understand both what it will and what it won't do.

The following list outlines the DTS tasks that are replaced by Integration Services tasks without requiring additional package modifications:

- *ActiveX*[1]
- *Bulk Insert*
- *Copy SQL Server Objects*[2]
- *Data Mining Prediction*[3]
- *Execute Package*[4]
- *Execute Process*
- *Execute SQL*
- *File Transfer Protocol*
- *Message Queue*
- *Send Mail*

---

1   ActiveX script converts successfully only if it contains no references to the DTS object model.
2   *Transfer SQL Server Objects* in SSIS
3   *Data Mining Query* in SSIS
4   *Execute DTS 2000 Package* in SSIS

- *Transfer Databases*
- *Transfer Error Messages*
- *Transfer Jobs*
- *Transfer Logins*
- *Transfer Master Stored Procedures*

For DTS tasks that cannot be migrated at all, described in the following list, the Package Migration Wizard inserts an *Execute DTS 2000 Package Task* to encapsulate the functionality for backward compatibility which you can replace with Integration Services tasks or leave as is:

- *Analysis Services Processing*[5]
- *Custom*
- *Data Pump*
- *Data Driven Query*
- *Dynamic Properties*
- *Parallel Data Pump*
- *Transform Data*

You need to modify the migrated package to provide replacement functionality for the deprecated DTS tasks described here:

- **Data Driven Query**    Consider replacing with a *Conditional Split Transformation*, an *OLE DB Command Transformation*, or a *Slowly Changing Dimension Transformation*.
- **Dynamic Properties**    Use property expressions or package configurations.
- **Transform Data**    Create a *Data Flow Task* with any data flow components that replicate the transformation.

Several package-specific items won't migrate. For example, even though SQL Server 2005 allows you to use package passwords with the *Execute DTS 2000 Package Task*, the package password on the DTS package migrates only to the Execute DTS Package tasks and does not migrate to the Integration Services package itself. If you have a package that does not contain *Execute DTS 2000 Package Tasks* after migration, the original package password is not migrated. (In all cases, you will be prompted for the package password before you can migrate the package.) Therefore, if you want a package password on the migrated package, you must manually add the new password to the

---

5  The SSIS *Analysis Services Execute DDL Task* and *Analysis Services Processing Task* cannot interact with an Analysis Services 2000 database.

*PackagePassword* package property. Also, if you've added annotations, package logging, or error handling to your DTS package, you'll need to add them manually using Integration Services features.

There is no absolute rule you can apply to determine whether you should rebuild your DTS packages manually or try the migration. If your packages are relatively straightforward, you can get much accomplished by choosing migration. To use the Package Migration Wizard, follow these steps:

1. Click the Start button, and then point to All Programs. Point to Microsoft SQL Server 2005, and then click SQL Server Business Intelligence Development Studio.

2. On the File menu, point to New, and then click Project.

3. Ensure that the Project Type is set to Business Intelligence Projects, which is the default selection, and then click the Integration Services Project template.

4. Type a name for the project, specify a folder used for storing project-related files, and then click OK.

5. In the Solution Explorer window, right-click the SSIS Packages folder, click Migrate DTS 2000 Packages, and then click Next on the Welcome page of the wizard.

---

**Note** To launch the Package Migration Wizard from SQL Server Management Studio, connect to the Database Engine, expand the Management folder and then the Legacy folder, right-click the Data Transformation Services folder, and then click Migration Wizard.

---

6. On the Choose Source Location page of the wizard, specify the storage location of the package. If the package is stored in SQL Server 2000, provide a server name and, if required, SQL Server credentials. If the package is stored as a Structure Storage File, select this option in the Source drop-down list and provide the location of the package.

7. Click Next to display the Choose Destination Location page, and then specify a location where the wizard will store the converted package.

8. Click Next to display the List Packages page, and then select the check box next to each package to convert. You can provide a new name for each selected package by typing the name in the Destination Package column.

9. Click Next to display the next page of the wizard. If the original package does not require a password, continue to the next step. If, on the other hand, the package requires a password, you see the Package Authentication page of the wizard. Select

the package in the Encrypted Packages list, and then click Password. Type the package owner password in the Package Password dialog box, and then click OK. Click Next to continue the wizard.

10. On the Specify A Log File page, specify a location for the log file.

11. Click Next to display the Complete The Wizard page, and then click Finish. The status of the package migration displays in the Migrating The Packages page of the wizard. Click Close.

12. The new package appears in the Solution Explorer window. Double-click the package name to open the package in the development environment.

Review the workflow to locate tasks that might not have converted successfully and tasks that have been stored in *Execute DTS 2000 Package Task*. You'll need to decide on a task-by-task basis how to resolve these migration issues.

## Integration Services Fundamentals

Integration Services shares some common characteristics with DTS. These characteristics are common in name only because the underlying architecture of these objects have been redesigned. A package is still the main container of objects defining which operations, known as *tasks*, should be performed. The sequence of operations is defined by *precedence constraints*. Optionally, you can use a *container*, a new object in Integration Services, to group tasks and other containers.

Each of these objects—containers, tasks, and precedence constraints—is an element of the *control flow* architecture new to Integration Services which manages the run-time activities of each package. The Integration Services run-time engine also provides services to each package, such as connection management, transaction commitment, debugging, logging, event handling, and variable management. We'll take a closer look at these services later in this chapter.

Another key component in the Integration Services architecture is the *data flow* engine, also known as the *data pipeline*. Data flow activities are encapsulated within the *Data Flow Task*, an object for which the control flow engine merely provides operational support and to which precedence constraints are applied just like any other task. For its execution, however, the *Data Flow Task* relies on a separate engine that performs the data extractions, manipulates the data according to defined transformations, and then deposits the resulting data set into a destination.

To achieve maximum performance, the data flow engine uses buffers to manipulate data in memory. Source data—whether it's relational, structured as XML data, or stored in flat files like spreadsheets or comma-delimited text files—is converted into a table-like structure containing columns and rows and then loaded directly into buffers without staging the data first in temporary tables. *Transformations* are data flow objects that operate on the buffered data, by sorting, merging, modifying, or enhancing the data before sending it to the next transformation or to its final destination. By avoiding the overhead of reading from and writing to disk, the processes required to move and manipulate data can operate at optimal speed. Integration Services can even provide data directly to an application by storing it in an ASP.NET DataReader. Using this method, you don't have to place the data in a persistent data store, an important step towards enabling near-real-time data delivery.

# Integration Services Components Overview

Integration Services includes several components, tools, and utilities for developing, deploying, and managing packages. The following list introduces these items, many of which are explained in more detail later in this chapter:

- **Integration Services Service**   Manages storage of packages in .dtsx files or in the MSDB database and monitors their execution

- **Integration Services Runtime**   Saves package layout, applies configurations, executes packages, manages connections and transactions, and supports logging and debugging

- **Integration Services Runtime Executables**   Includes package, containers, tasks, custom tasks, and event handlers

- **Integration Services Data Flow**   Manages data sources, data destinations, transformations, and any custom components you add to a *Data Flow Task*, and provides the in-memory buffers used to transport data from source to destination

- **Business Intelligence Development Studio**   Supports the development and testing of Integration Services packages; supports collaboration with source code management and version control; provides debugging tools such as breakpoints, variable watches, and data viewers; and includes the SQL Server Import and Export Wizard to jumpstart package development

- **SQL Server Management Studio**   Provides access to the Execute Package utility, imports and exports packages to and from available storage modes (MSDB database or SSIS Package Store), and monitors running packages

- **SQL Server Import and Export Wizard**   Copies data from one location to another

- **Package Migration Wizard**   Converts SQL Server 2000 DTS packages to Integration Services packages

- **Package Installation Wizard**   Deploys an Integration Services project prepared by a deployment utility

- **Execute Package Utility (dtexecui)**   Provides a user interface for preparing packages for execution as well as executing packages

- **dtexec**   Runs a package at the command prompt

- **dtutil**   Provides package management functionality at the command prompt to copy, move, or delete packages or to confirm a package exists

- **Integration Services Object Model**   Includes application programming interfaces (APIs) for customizing run-time and data flow operations and automating package maintenance and execution by loading, modifying, and executing new or existing packages programmatically

# Designing Packages

Whether you're migrating a DTS package or creating a new Integration Services package, you use SQL Server Business Intelligence Development Studio. This development environment is rich with features that can initially seem overwhelming but is much easier to navigate once you understand how package objects are classified and how they fit together to achieve a data integration goal. In this section, we'll focus on commonly used components and important features of the development environment.

## The Development Environment

SQL Server Business Intelligence Development Studio is the graphical interface you use to design, test, and execute a package. While Business Intelligence Development Studio appears to be a distinct application, it's actually just a shortcut to Microsoft Visual Studio 2005. If you already use Visual Studio, then the installation of Integration Services integrates the business intelligence *designers* with your existing development environment. A designer is a collection of design tools, including a workspace, toolbox, dialog boxes, and various windows, used to build a project.

### Starting an Integration Services Project

When you work in Visual Studio, you work in the context of a solution and a project. A solution is simply a container for one or more projects. Each project can be a different type. For example, you can have a single solution that contains an Integration Services project that includes all of the packages used to perform the ETL processes for a data warehouse, an Analysis Services project that uses data from that data warehouse, and a Reporting Services project with all reports used to present Analysis Services data. You organize projects into solutions to make it easier to save and retrieve files that might be related.

An Integration Services project contains four folders: Data Sources, Data Source Views, SSIS Packages, and Miscellaneous. At a minimum, you'll add one or more package files to the SSIS Packages folder, but the other folders are optional. To add a new package to the SSIS Packages folder, follow these steps:

1.  Start SQL Server Business Intelligence Development Studio.

2.  On the File menu, point to New, and then click Project.

3.  Ensure that the Project Type is set to Business Intelligence Projects, and then click the Integration Services Project template.

4.  Type a name for the project, **My Package**, change the location for the project to a folder of your choice, and confirm the Create Directory For Solution check box is selected.

5.  Click OK to continue to create the package in the Integration Services package designer, as shown in Figure 21-1.

**Figure 21-1**   A new package in the Integration Services package designer.

The main Visual Studio windows you'll use during package development are described in the following list:

- **Solution Explorer**   By default, this window displays in the upper right corner of your screen. When you add a new package to your project, you'll see a file like Package.dtsx added to the SSIS Packages folder. You can rename this file, but be sure to keep the .dtsx extension or your package won't work.

- **Properties**   This window displays in the bottom right corner of your screen by default. If you select an object added to your package, you can view and modify its properties in this window.

- **Toolbox**   This windows displays by default on the left side of your screen. The contents of the toolbox change according to the current workspace visible in the designer.

- **Integration Services Package Designer**   The designer is the main window that represents your workspace. There are five tabs in the designer window that you use while building and testing your package: (Only four of these tabs are shown in Figure 22-1 because the fifth tab, Progress, appears only after you execute the package.)

- **Control Flow**   Use this tab to manage tasks, containers, and precedence constraints in the package workflow.

- **Data Flow**   Use this tab to define the flow of data between sources and destinations, as well as any transformations applied to the data during transfer.

- **Event Handlers**   Use this tab to add tasks that execute only when specific events have occurred, such as a task failure.

- **Package Explorer**   Use this tab to review package objects in a tree view and to access object properties.

- **Progress**   Use this tab during or after executing a package within the development environment to review the status of executables, the duration of completed executables, and any errors or warnings generated during package execution. This tab appears only when you execute the package.

## Using Data Sources

A *data source* is a file that contains the connection string and credentials used by Integration Services to connect to a data store. Right-click the Data Sources folder and click New Data Source to start the Data Source Wizard which steps you through building a data source. When you have many packages that extract or load data into the same data store, you can use a data source to define the connection once and reuse it many times. If you modify the connection string in the data source, the connection managers are similarly updated. The data source is used only during development and is not saved with the package when you put it into production. Instead, the value of the connection string defined by the data source when the package is saved is stored in the connection manager.

## Using Data Source Views

A *data source view* (DSV) is a file that shows selected tables or views from a data source in your project. Right-click the Data Source Views folder and click New Data Source View to start the Data Source View Wizard, which steps you through the selection of a data source and specification of the database objects you want to include in the DSV. You can add relationships between tables or add custom expressions to the DSV to create derived columns, which is handy if you don't have permissions to change the data structure at the source. When you use the DSV with a data flow component, the package designer translates the relationships and custom expressions into an SQL statement that is stored with the component.

## Using the SQL Server Import and Export Wizard

The SQL Server Import and Export Wizard is designed to copy data from one database to another or to load data into SQL Server databases from flat files, spreadsheets, and OLE DB sources when an ETL solution is not required. To use the SQL Server Import and Export Wizard for building an Integration Services package, follow these steps:

1. To follow this example, you must complete the steps described in the previous example. Right-click the SSIS Packages folder, and then click SSIS Import And Export Wizard.

2. Click Next to bypass the Welcome page and to display the Choose A Data Source page.

3. Select a data source from the Data Source drop-down list. The default data source is SQL Native Client. For this example, select *AdventureWorks* in the Database drop-down list. Click Next.

   You can choose from the following additional data source options:

   - ❑ .NET Framework Data Providers (ODBC, Oracle, and SQL Server)
   - ❑ Flat File Source
   - ❑ Microsoft Access
   - ❑ Microsoft Excel
   - ❑ Microsoft OLE DB Providers (Analysis Services 9.0, Data Mining Services, OLAP Services 8.0, Oracle, and SQL Server)

---

**Note**   You might see additional Microsoft OLE DB Providers listed if you have applications installed on your machine that include an OLE DB provider, such as Microsoft Project 9.0, for example.

---

❑   SQLXMLOLEDB and SQLXMLOLEDB 4.0

When you select a different data source, the Choose A Data Source page changes to prompt you for options required to connect to the selected data source. For example, the .NET Framework Data Provider for ODBC requires you to provide a connection string, a Data Source Name (DSN), and the name of the ODBC driver to use.

4.  On the Choose A Destination page, you select a destination for the data you're importing from the selected data source. The data destination options are the same as the types that you can choose as a data source. You can even choose a destination that doesn't exist yet. When you create a new database, you can specify options for Data File Size and Log File Size, which are explained in more detail in Chapter 10, "Creating Databases and Database Snapshots." In this example, we'll specify a new database, *MyAdventureWorks*. Click the New button, type **MyAdventureWorks** in the Name text field, and then click OK.

5.  Set the authentication type applicable to your server configuration: Windows or SQL Server authentication. If you use SQL Server authentication, you must type a SQL Server username and password in the appropriate text box. Click Next.

6.  On the Specify Table Copy Or Query page, you choose how you want to define which data to extract from the data source. Select Copy Data From One Or More Tables Or Views when you want all data from tables and views that you select on a subsequent page of the wizard. If you need only a subset of data, such as fewer rows or fewer columns, select the Write A Query To Specify The Data To Transfer option. For this example, leave the default option, Copy Data From One or More Tables Or Views, selected. Click Next.

---

**Note**   Users of SQL Server 2000 DTS notice right away that the option Copy Objects And Data Between SQL Server Databases is missing from this page of the wizard. Instead, open SQL Server Management Studio, right-click the database to copy, point to Tasks, and then click Copy Database to start the Copy Database Wizard.

---

7.  On the Select Source Tables And Views page, you choose the tables or views to copy from the source by selecting the corresponding check boxes in the Source column, and then choose the table into which data is to be loaded by selecting

it from the drop-down list in the Destination column. Alternatively, you can type a name to create a new table in the data destination. You can resize columns or the dialog box itself to improve your view of available objects. You can also click the Preview button to confirm you will be copying the correct data. For this example, select the *[AdventureWorks].[HumanResources].[Department]* table in the Source column.

8. Click the Edit button in the Mapping column of the selected row to display the Column Mappings dialog box. Here you can apply transformations to the data during the import by specifying conversion of null values or changing the precision. If the destination table already exists, you can choose to delete rows from the table before loading the copied data or to append rows to the table.

9. If the destination table is new, click Edit SQL if you need to modify the CREATE TABLE statement. Click OK to close the Column Mappings dialog box, and then click Next to display the Complete The Wizard page. The package is saved as a .dtsx file in the folder specified for the current Integration Services project and is not executed immediately.

10. Click Finish to create and save the package, and then click the Close button to close the wizard. Your package is now visible in the package designer, as shown in Figure 21-2.

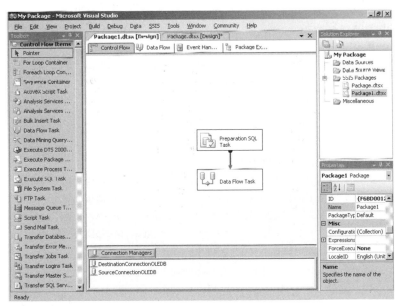

**Figure 21-2**   The Integration Services package designer.

By creating and saving a package to copy data from one location to another, you can repeat the data transfer quickly and easily at a later time as many times as you wish or you can make changes to this package to meet your needs more specifically.

> **Note**   Alternatively, by launching the wizard in SQL Server Management Studio, you can use this tool simply to copy data without producing a package.

## Adding Documentation to a Package

The Integration Services package designer includes two features that you can use to document your packages for easier reading as described here:

■ **Name property**   Either right-click the object to rename in the package designer, click Rename, and then type a new name for the object, or select the object in the designer, and type a name in the Name box in the Properties window. The object name is completely visible in the designer and is included in logs when you enable package logging.

> **Note**   Establish a consistent naming convention by including the type of task or transformation and a description of the object's function in the name.

■ **Annotation**   Right-click the designer work surface, click Add Annotation, and then type an annotation in the new text box. Annotations do not automatically wrap within the text box, so press Ctrl+Enter to force a new line, or drag the handles to resize the text box as needed. To change the font, font style, size, or color, right-click the annotations box, and click Set Text Annotation Font. Use *annotations* in a data source view to describe the tables and relationships it contains or on any package designer work surface—control flow, data flow, or event handler (components described later in this chapter)—to explain the overall objective of the package or describe the business rules being applied by package objects. Annotations are not included in package logs.

## Executing a Package in Visual Studio

While your package is still in development, you can use Visual Studio to run the package. During execution, you can watch the progress of the package as each task executes, and the success or failure of each task is indicated by color. If a task is yellow, it is currently running. A green task has completed successfully, while a red task has failed. To execute a package and review execution results in Visual Studio, follow these steps:

1. To follow this example, you must complete the steps described in the previous sections. Right-click the package in the SSIS Packages folder in Solution Explorer and then click Execute Package. The results of package execution display in the package

designer, as shown in Figure 21-3. Notice the package in Figure 21-3 also illustrates renamed objects and an annotation as described in the previous section.

> **Note** There are several other ways to execute a package. You can choose Start Debugging on the Debug menu, press F5, or click the Start Debugging button on the Debug toolbar. However, if you have other packages or other projects included in your solution, Visual Studio might attempt to build a project or execute a package other than the package you are viewing.

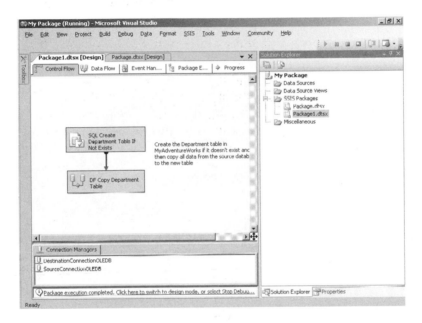

**Figure 21-3** The results of package execution on control flow shown in the package designer.

2. Click the Data Flow tab of the package designer to view the number of rows copied to the destination, as shown in Figure 21-4.

3. Click the Progress tab of the Integration Services package designer to view information related to package execution, such as the start and finish time of package execution and the elapsed time for the package and each step, as shown in Figure 21-5. The Progress tab is useful for troubleshooting packages when a step fails because the error message will be available on this tab.

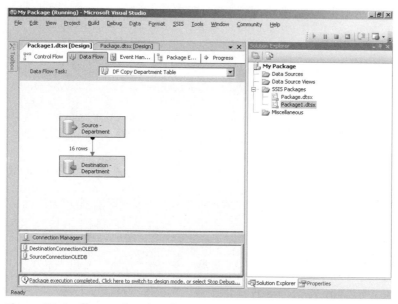

**Figure 21-4**    The results of package execution on data flow shown in the Integration Services package designer.

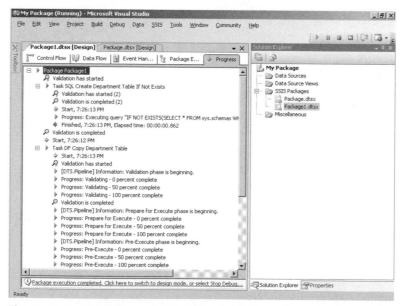

**Figure 21-5**    The progress information for package execution shown in the package designer.

4.  In Visual Studio, the debugger remains active even when the package execution has ended. You won't be able to edit or close the package until you stop the debugger using one of the following methods: Choose Stop Debugging on the Debug menu, press Shift+F5, click the Stop Debugging button on the Debug toolbar, or, at the bottom of the package designer click the link Package Execution Completed. Click Here To Switch To Design Mode, Or Select Stop Debugging From The Debug Menu.

# Control Flow Components

Now that we've created a simple package and briefly explored the development environment, let's take a closer look at the components you can use to manage the control flow of tasks in a package. As mentioned, there are three basic types of control flow components: tasks, containers, and precedence constraints. A set of tasks can optionally be organized into a logical grouping called a container. The order of operations in which each task or container is executed is determined by the sequence in which these objects are linked together by using precedence constraints.

## Tasks

When you view the Control Flow tab of the Integration Services package designer, the Visual Studio Toolbox contains a wide variety of tasks you can add to your package. In the following list, tasks are grouped by function:

- **Extract, transform, and load data task**
  - *Data Flow Task*   encapsulates a set of data flow components used to extract data from a source, optionally perform transformations, and load data into a destination

- **Execute SQL Server tasks**
  - *Bulk Insert Task*   performs high-speed copying of data into a SQL Server database
  - *Execute SQL Task*   runs single or multiple SQL statements or stored procedures; you must optimize queries elsewhere as Integration Services will not do it for you; you can use parameterized queries and map the results to a variable.
  - *Transfer Database Task*   transfers a database between two SQL Server instances. Either instance can be SQL Server 2000 or SQL Server 2005
  - *Transfer Error Messages Task*   transfers user-defined messages (with identifier greater than or equal to 50,000) between SQL Server instances

- ❑ *Transfer Jobs Task*  transfers one or more SQL Server Agent jobs between SQL Server instances

- ❑ *Transfer Logins Task*  transfers one or more logins (except sa) between SQL Server instances

- ❑ *Transfer Master Stored Procedure Task*  transfers one or more user-defined stored procedures between master databases in separate SQL Server instances

- ❑ *Transfer SQL Server Objects Task*  transfers one or more objects—tables, views, stored procedures, user-defined functions, defaults, user-defined data types, partition functions, partition schemes, schemas, assemblies, user-defined aggregates, user-defined types, or XML schema collections—between SQL Server instances

- **Prepare data**

  - ❑ *File System Task*  creates, moves, or deletes directories or files or sets attributes on directories or files

  - ❑ *FTP Task*  downloads or uploads files or manages directories on an FTP server

  - ❑ *Web Service Task*  executes a web service method

  - ❑ *XML Task*  retrieves XML documents, applies operations using Extensible Stylesheet Language Transformations (XSLT) documents or XPATH expressions, merges documents, or validates, compares, or saves updated documents to files or variables

- **Communicate with other processes**

  - ❑ *Execute Package Task*  runs another package as part of the current package workflow

  - ❑ *Execute DTS 2000 Package Task*  runs a package developed for SQL Server 2000

  - ❑ *Execute Process Task*  runs a command-line application or batch file

  - ❑ *Message Queue Task*  sends or receives messages between packages or applications using Microsoft Message Queuing

  - ❑ *Send Mail Task*  sends an e-mail message

  - ❑ *WMI Data Reader Task*  runs a Windows Management Instrumentation (WMI) query to return information about a computer

  - ❑ *WMI Event Watcher Task*  watches for and responds to WMI events

- **Extend package functionality with scripts**
  - ❑ *ActiveX Script Task*   runs ActiveX script—included for backward compatibility only; new script should be developed in Script Task
  - ❑ *Script Task*   runs custom code for functions not available in built-in tasks or transformations

- **Work with Analysis Services objects**
  - ❑ *Analysis Services Processing Task*   processes Analysis Services cubes, dimensions, or mining models
  - ❑ *Analysis Services Execute DDL Task*   runs an XML for Analysis command encapsulating an Analysis Services Scripting Language (ASSL) DDL statement
  - ❑ *Data Mining Query Task*   runs a prediction query based on an Analysis Services data mining model

- **Maintain database objects**
  - ❑ *Back Up Database Task*   backus up one or more SQL Server databases
  - ❑ *Check Database Integrity Task*   checks the allocation and structural integrity of objects in one or more databases
  - ❑ *Execute SQL Server Agent Job Task*   runs a SQL Server Agent Job
  - ❑ *Execute T-SQL Statement Task*   runs a Transact-SQL statement. Use the *Execute SQL Statement Task* instead if you need to run a parameterized query or save the result to a variable
  - ❑ *History Cleanup Task*   deletes entries in these tables: backupfile, backupfilegroup, backupmediafamily, backupmediaset, backupset, restorefile, restorefilegroup, and restorehistory
  - ❑ *Notify Operator Task*   sends a notification message to SQL Server Agent operators
  - ❑ *Rebuild Index Task*   rebuilds indexes in tables or views in one or more SQL Server databases
  - ❑ *Reorganize Index Task*   reorganizes indexes in tables or views in one or more SQL Server databases
  - ❑ *Shrink Database Task*   shrinks database and log files for one or more SQL Server databases
  - ❑ *Update Statistics Task*   updates statistics for one or more SQL Server databases

To add the Execute SQL Task to the control flow, follow these steps:

1. To follow this example, you must complete the steps described in the previous sections, beginning with "Starting an Integration Services Project." Click the Control Flow tab if it's not already open, and locate the task to be added in the Toolbox.

---

**Note**   If the Toolbox isn't visible, choose Toolbox on the View menu.

---

2. Drag the task to the control flow work surface. For this example, drag the *Execute SQL Task* to the designer, as shown in Figure 21-6. The red icon that appears in the task box indicates further configuration is required. In this case, the task requires a connection.

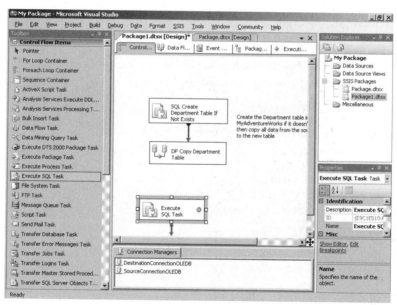

**Figure 21-6**   Adding a task to the control flow.

Each task has properties you configure to define its behavior when the package executes. To configure the *Execute SQL Task* properties, follow these steps:

1. Right-click *Execute SQL Task*, and then click Edit to display the Task Editor.

2. Type **Truncate Table** in the Name box, select *DestinationConnectionOLEDB* in the Connection drop-down list (or create one by selecting <New Connection> in the Connection drop-down list and completing the OLE DB Connection Manager

configuration). Type **truncate table HumanResources.Department** in the SQL-Statement box, as shown in Figure 22-7. For longer statements, you might find it easier to click the ellipsis button in the SQLStatement box and then type the statement in the Enter SQL Query dialog box.

An *Execute SQL Task* requires a connection manager, explained in more detail later in this chapter, and a SQLStatement. You can type directly in the SQLStatement box as shown in this example, you can click Build Query to open the Query Builder window, or you can click Browse to locate a SQL file and import its contents as a SQLStatement. You can use multiple SQL statements terminated by semicolons here, and you can insert a GO command between statements to create multiple batches.

Another option is to change the SQLSourceType property from the default, Direct Input, to FileConnection to specify a SQL file in the FileConnection property (which appears when you change SQLSourceType) if you want to maintain the SQL Statement externally from the package. Yet another option is to select Variable as the SQLSourceType and provide a SourceVariable that will contain one or more SQL statements at package run-time.

**Figure 21-7**   Configuring properties of an Execute SQL Task.

3.  Click OK to close the editor.

Each task has its own set of properties that you configure in the task editor or by changing the property value in the Properties window. While only some tasks will require you to specify a connection, all tasks have a page where you can associate an expression with a task property—an advanced feature that makes Integration Services very flexible.

## Containers

You can group related tasks into containers. Because you can collapse or expand a container, using a container just for grouping makes it easier to navigate a package workflow that contains many tasks. Add a container to the control flow of a package just as you add a task. Drag other tasks or other containers into the newly added container. There are three different types of containers, as described here:

- **For Loop Container**   This type of container creates a workflow that repeats the tasks in the container until the *EvalExpression* defined for the container evaluates as false. You also must assign a value to the container's InitExpression which is a starting value used for items like a counter, and is incremented according to the container's AssignExpression.

- **ForEach Loop Container**   This type of container creates a workflow that repeats the tasks in the container for each item found in a collection, such as rows in a table, files in a folder, objects in a variable, among others. When configuring this container, you specify the type of collection and configure the location of the items in the collection.

- **Sequence Container**   This type of container groups tasks together as a single unit in the workflow.

## Precedence Constraints

Use precedence constraints to link tasks or containers, also known as *executables*, together into an order of operations. In addition to defining the sequence of operations, you define the conditions under which each subsequent step in the workflow is executed. To add a precedence constraint, click the first executable, and then drag the green arrow that appears at the base of the executable to a second executable so that the two objects are connected by the arrow, as shown in Figure 21-8.

By default, adding a precedence constraint between two executables causes the second object to execute only if the first object executes successfully. You can change the constraint to cause the second executable to run only if the first executable fails. This option is useful for handling error conditions within a package and could be as simple as sending an email to an administrator when a task fails. A third option is to define the constraint to run the second executable after the first executable runs, regardless of success or failure. To change the constraint, right-click the connector, and select Success, Failure, or Completion as necessary.

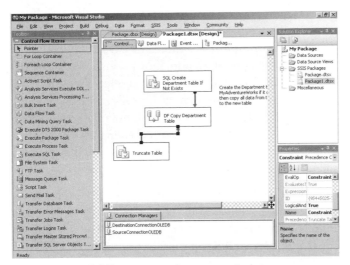

**Figure 21-8** Adding a precedence constraint.

You can also create a complex precedence constraint based on the evaluation of an expression or on both the execution result of the preceding executable as well as the expression's result. For example, let's say that you want to run a second executable only if the first executable completes successfully and some condition is true, such as the existence of a file on a network share. You could use a Script Task to check for the existence of the file and set the value of a variable to True, and then require the precedence constraint to evaluate the variable's value. To add a complex precedence constraint, follow these steps:

1. To follow this example, you must complete the steps described in the previous sections, beginning with "Starting an Integration Services Project." Right-click the connector between the *Data Flow Task* and the *Execute SQL Task* and then click Edit to display the Precedence Constraint Editor dialog box, as shown in Figure 21-9.

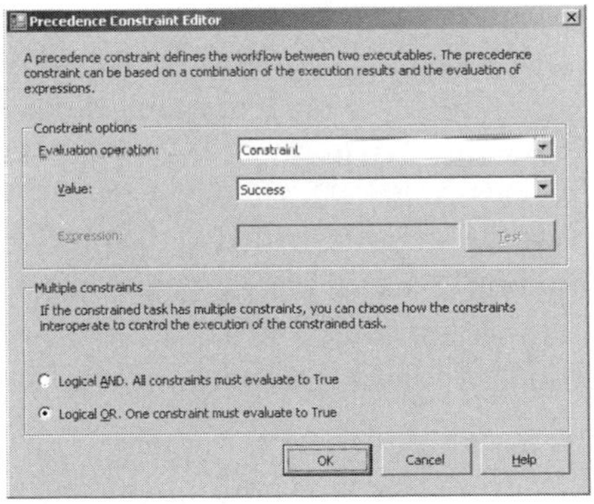

**Figure 21-9** The Precedence Constraint Editor.

Possible values for Evaluation Operation are Constraint, Expression, Expression And Constraint, and Expression Or Constraint. Thus, you can specify one or the other condition, or both conditions, to control whether the next executable in the workflow executes. When you select an option that includes Constraint, you must specify a Value of Success, Failure, or Completion. When you select an option that includes Expression, you must define an expression in the editor. To continue the example requiring the existence of a file, you prefix the variable name with @; if your variable name is FileFound, use this expression: `@FileFound == True`. Your expression must also include a logical operator and a comparison value in the expression and must evaluate as a Boolean data type.

When an executable has multiple constraints placed on it—that is, when two or more worfkflow connectors lead to a single executable—be sure to specify in the Precedence Constraint Editor whether both constraints must evaluate as True for that executable to run (Logical AND), or whether either one of the constraints must be True (Logical OR). This setting is ignored if there is only one constraint on the executable.

2. Select Logical OR. One Constraint Must Evaluate To True, as shown in Figure 22-9, and then click OK.

## Connection Managers

A connection manager is an Integration Services object that contains the information required to create a physical connection to data stores and the metadata describing the structure of the data. In the case of a flat file, a connection manager contains the file path, file name, and metadata identifying rows and columns. A connection manager for a relational data source contains the name of the server, the name of the database, and the credentials for authenticating access to the data. Connection managers are the bridge between package objects and physical data structures, used by tasks that require a connection (such as the Execute SQL Task), by data adapters that define sources and destinations, and by transformations that perform lookups to a reference table. To add and configure an OLE DB connection manager, follow these steps:

1. To follow this example, you must complete the steps described in the previous sections, beginning with "Starting an Integration Services Project." Right-click the Connections Manager tray at the bottom of the Control Flow, Data Flow, or Event Handlers tab of the package designer, and click New OLE DB Connection.

2. Select a defined connection in the Configure OLE DB Connection Manager dialog box, or click New to define a new connection in the Connection Manager dialog box. For this example, click New.

3.  Select a provider in the Provider drop-down list and specify a server name and authentication credentials. You can type a database name or select a database in the Select Or Enter A Database Name drop-down list. For this example, type **localhost** in the Server Name box and select *AdventureWorks* in the Select Or Enter A Database Name drop-down list, as shown in Figure 22-10. (If you're working with a SQL Server on a separate server, replace localhost with the applicable server name.)

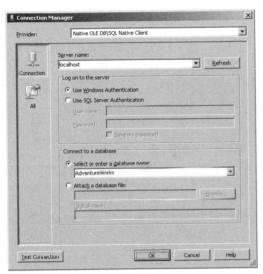

**Figure 21-10**   The Connection Manager dialog box.

4.  Click OK twice to close each dialog box.

## Data Flow Components

So far, we've seen how control flow components get things done in package, but the real power of Integration Services is the data flow engine. Now we're ready to examine the components used by the data flow engine. To work with data flow components, you first add a *Data Flow Task* to the control flow, then define one or more sources as the beginning of one or pipelines within the data flow. A single *Data Flow Task* could manage multiple pipelines if the order of operations doesn't matter. Each pipeline will run in parallel, more or less. (The degree of parallelism depends on system resources and the data volumes in each pipeline). Otherwise, you'll need to create multiple *Data Flow Tasks* and use precedence constraints to manage sequencing.

It's helpful to think of the data flow pipeline as a physical pipeline with discrete start and end points and with individual channels running through this pipeline, as shown in Figure 21-11. Each channel corresponds to a column in the row of data currently in the pipeline. As columns are removed during transformations, the number of channels in the pipeline is reduced downstream. Conversely, as new derived columns are added to the pipeline, the number of channels downstream is increased. Both the data type and the size of the data traveling through a particular channel must stay constant unless a transformation like Data Conversion modifies the channel metadata. While the pipeline is a useful metaphor, in actuality the data is placed in a buffer and transformed in place; only certain transformations physically move data from one buffer to another.

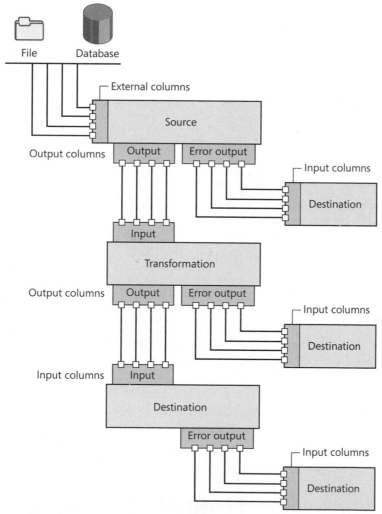

**Figure 21-11**   The data flow pipeline.

## Data Sources and Data Destinations

Every data flow path starts with a source and usually ends with a destination. Data sources and data destinations are data flow components that sit between the physical connection to the data storage and the buffers created in memory to transport the data to another location. In most cases, the type of data storage accessed as a source can also be accessed as a destination. The direction the data flows out of or into this type of object determines whether it is a data source or a data destination. There are, however, some special data destinations for which there is no corresponding data source. As you work with these objects, you'll notice that a data source has two outputs, one for normal data flow and one for error output. By contrast, a data destination has only one input and one error output. Table 21-1 lists the available data adapters and their use as source, destination, or both.

**Table 21-1   Available Data Adapters and Their Uses**

| Data Adapter | Source | Destination |
| --- | --- | --- |
| Data Mining Model Training | — | √ |
| DataReader | √ | √ |
| Dimension Processing | — | √ |
| Excel | √ | |
| Flat File | √ | √ |
| OLE DB | √ | √ |
| Partition Processing | — | √ |
| Raw File | √ | √ |
| Recordset | — | √ |
| Script Component | √ | √ |
| SQL Server | — | √ |
| SQL Server Mobile | — | √ |
| XML | √ | — |

If you're already responsible for accessing data in a variety of structures, you'll likely have no trouble applying what you know to the configuration of data sources and data destinations. Some of these objects, however, warrant further explanation:

■ **Data Mining Model Training**   You can automate the process of training an Analysis Services data mining model by using this destination. Before using this destination, be sure you understand the content and structural requirements of the data mining model.

■ *DataReader*   As a destination, the *DataReader* destination can expose the data in the pipeline to applications than can access the ADO.NET DataReader interface. Using this approach, for example, you can load data directly into a Reporting Services report without persisting the data in a file or relational table.

■ *Dimension Processing*   Use this destination to automate updating dimension objects in Analysis Services databases. Dimension processing is explained in Chapter 22, "Analysis Services."

■ *Partition Processing*   This destination is used to load fact table data into an Analysis Services partition, which is also explained in Chapter 22.

■ *SQL Server*   This destination type can be used only if the package executes on the same server hosting the target database in SQL Server 2005. Because this destination actually sends data to the database directly from memory without requiring a connection, performance can be up to 25 percent faster than using an OLE DB connection.

---

**Note**  If you're loading data to a SQL Server destination on another server, use the OLE DB destination. In the OLE DB Destination Editor, select Table Or View–Fast Load or select Table Name Or View Name Variable–Fast Load in the Data Access Mode drop-down list to get the best performance.

To start a data flow and add a data source adapter to the data flow, follow these steps:

1. To follow this example, you must complete the steps described in the previous sections, beginning with "Starting an Integration Services Project." On the Control Flow tab of the package designer, open the Toolbox window if necessary and drag the *Data Flow Task* to the design surface, and add a precedence constraint between the *Execute SQL Task* and the *Data Flow Task*.

2. Double-click the new task to open the corresponding Data Flow tab, as shown in Figure 21-12. Notice the contents of the Toolbox window change to show only sources, destinations, and transformations instead of the tasks it contains when the Control Flow tab is open.

3. Drag the *OLE DB Source* from the Toolbox onto the design surface, and then double-click the data adapter to open the OLE DB Source Editor.

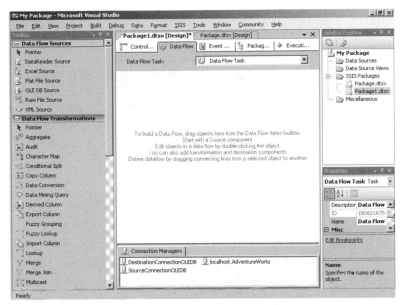

**Figure 21-12**   The Data Flow tab of the package designer.

4.  Select a connection in the OLE DB Connection Manager drop-down list, or click the New button to configure a new connection manager to use with this data source. Specify a Data Access Mode. The default is Table Or View which you select in the Name Of The Table Or The View drop-down list. To continue the example, select the *localhost.AdventureWorks* connecton manager and select the *[HumanResources].[Department]* table, as shown in Figure 21-13.

    Instead, you could choose to get the the name of a table or a view from a variable, in which case you select Table Name Or View Name Variable as the data access mode and then specify the name of the variable in the Variable Name drop-down list. Other options include getting the name from executing a SQL command that you include in the data source adapter as SQL Command Text (when you choose the SQL Command data access mode) or getting the table or view name from a variable that contains a SQL command (when you choose the SQL Command From Variable data access mode).

5.  Click Columns in the left pane of the dialog box to display the column mappings between the data store and the output columns used to send data to the next data flow component, as shown in Figure 21-14. Configuring error output will be explained later in this chapter. Click OK.

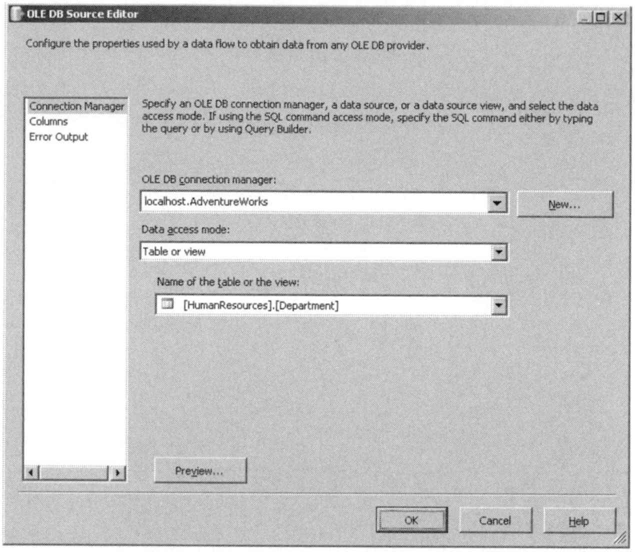

**Figure 21-13** The OLE DB Source Editor dialog box.

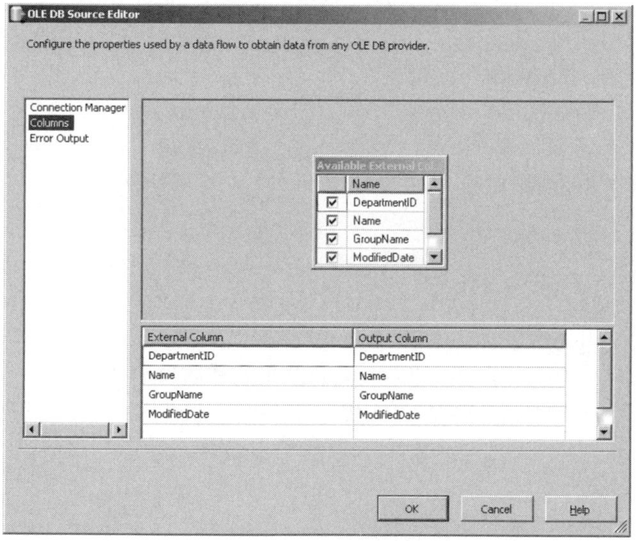

**Figure 21-14** The OLE DB Source Editor's column mappings.

The External Column and Output Column mappings generate automatically.

---

**Note**   You should clear the selection of any column in the Available External Columns box that won't be used downstream to prevent memory from being unnecessarily allocated to the column.

---

If your goal is to copy data directly from a source to a destination, your next step is to add a destination to the data flow. On the other hand, if you need to transform the data before loading it into the destination, you must add each transformation object to the data flow first because the buffer structures created for the data flow are dependent on the definition of upstream objects.

## Transformations

Transformations are data flow objects that operate on data in the data flow pipeline. Most transformations have one input, one regular output, and one error output. Some transformations have multiple inputs to consolidate data from separate pipelines, and some transformations have multiple outputs to separate data into separate pipelines. Not all transformations have error output.

The type of transformations in the pipeline affect the data flow engine's management of buffers. Row transformations, like Data Conversion or Derived Column, are very efficient at reusing existing buffers. Multiple rows are received into the buffer from an upstream component in batches, data in the buffer is manipulated on a row-by-row basis, and then these rows in the buffer are operated on by the next component. This process continues until all rows from the source have been transformed.

Other transformation types must create new buffers to store output before allowing the next component access to the data, and they will consequently place the greatest demands on system resources. Transformations operating on rowsets, like Aggregate or Sort, must read all input before creating any output. Transformations that combine input, such as Merge or Union All, are somewhere in between the other transformation types, reading some input before creating output, but they do copy that output to a different buffer and thus have greater resource requirements. The available transformations and the relationship between input and output rows are described here:

- **Row transformations**

    - *Character Map*   applies string functions, commonly *Uppercase* or *Lowercase*, to character data in a column and overwrites the column with the new string or adds a column to the output row

    - *Copy Column*   creates new columns in the output row from existing columns in the input row for subsequent transformation

❑ *Data Conversion* applies data conversion functions to change data type, column length, or precision and scale to an input column and adds a column with the new data to the output row

❑ *Derived Column* applies expressions to an input column to create a new value for a new column in the output row or as a replacement value for the existing column

❑ *Script* runs custom code against data in the pipeline

❑ *OLE DB Command* runs a SQL statement (optionally parameterized) against each row in the pipeline

■ **Rowset transformations**

❑ *Aggregate* applies an aggregate function (for example, *Sum*, *Minimum*, *Maximum*, and so on) to grouped records and produces new output records from aggregated results; output records contain only the columns used for grouping and the aggregated values

❑ *Sort* applies an ascending or descending sort to one or more columns and optionally removes rows with duplicate values in the sort columns

❑ *Percentage Sampling* creates a random sample set of output rows by selecting a specified percentage of input rows; commonly used for data mining

❑ *Row Sampling* creates a random sample set of output rows by selecting a specified number of input rows; used primarily for testing packages with a subset of representative data

❑ *Pivot* reduces normalization in a normalized data set by pivoting on a column value, producing a smaller dataset

❑ *Unpivot* increases normalization in a denormalized data set by creating multiple output rows from a single input row based on a common column value

■ **Split and Join Transformations**

❑ *Conditional Split* separates input rows into separate output pipelines based on a Boolean expression configured for each output; a single input row is passed to the first output row which the condition is true or to a default output defined for rows which meet no conditions

❑ *Multicast* copies all input rows to two or more outputs

❑ *Merge* combines two sorted datasets with the same column structure into a single output

- ❑ *Merge Join*   combines two sorted datasets using a FULL, LEFT, or INNER join to produce output rows with more columns than the input rows from either dataset

- ❑ *Union All*   combines two or more datasets with the same column structure into a single output

- ❑ *Lookup*   joins input rows with columns in a reference dataset (from a table, view, or SQL statement) that match exactly to add one or more columns to the output row

- **Data quality transformations**
  - ❑ *Fuzzy Lookup*   finds close or exact matches between one or more columns (*DT_WSTR* and *DT_STR* data types only) in the input row and a row in a reference table; adds selected columns from the matched row and columns for fuzzy matching metrics

  - ❑ *Fuzzy Grouping*   finds close or exact matches between input rows based on one or more columns and adds columns to the output identifying matches and similarity scores

- **Data mining transformations**
  - ❑ *Data Mining Query*   runs a prediction query based on an Analysis Services data mining model against the input rows and creates output rows from the query result set

  - ❑ *Term Extraction*   extracts nouns or noun phrases (or both) from an input column containing English text, places the extracted terms into a column in the output row, and adds another column for the score; multiple output rows per input row are created when multiple terms are extracted from an input column

  - ❑ *Term Lookup*   matches text in an input column with a reference table, counts the number of occurrences of the term in the dataset, and adds a term and frequency column to the output row; as with Term Extraction, multiple output rows per input row can be created

- **Special transformations**
  - ❑ *Export Column*   reads a file name from an input column and inserts data from another column in the same row into the specified file.

  - ❑ *Import Column*   reads a file name from an input column and inserts data from the specified file into a new output column for the same row

  - ❑ *Audit*   adds the value of a system variable, such as MachineName or ExecutionInstanceGUID, to a new output column

❑ *Row Count*    counts the number of rows currently in the data flow and stores the value in a variable

❑ *Slowly Changing Dimension*    manages inserts and updates in a data warehouse

### Real World    Metadata Validation

You can add one or more transformations to the design surface of a data flow, but you cannot configure a transformation until you connect it to the regular or error output of an upstream component. Because metadata about the pipeline is maintained in the pipeline connections (the red and green arrows between components) and transformations, you must add transformations in the correct sequence or you will encounter validation errors that must be resolved before you can execute the package. Similarly, if you delete columns, change a column's data type, change a string column's length, or change a numeric column's precision or scale, you will encounter errors in downstream components. Sometimes, if you double-click the first downstream component, a message displays to indicate a metadata problem exists and offers to fix the problem automatically. Click Yes, and continue this process with each subsequent component in the pipeline. You can override metadata validation by setting a transformation's ValidateExternalMetadata property to False, but property applies only during design time. Metadata problems prevent packages from executing.

## Error Output Configuration

When data cannot be passed into the regular output of a data source or a transformation, you ignore the error completely, redirect the row to the component's error output, or fail the component. To configure error output, follow these steps:

1. To follow this example, you must complete the steps described in the previous sections, beginning with "Starting an Integration Services Project." Drag a destination component, such as the *OLE DB Destination* to follow this example, from the Toolbox to the data flow design surface, click the *OLE DB Source*, and then drag the red connector to the destination to complete the connection.

2. In the Configure Error Output dialog box, select a value in the Error drop-down list and in the Truncation drop-down list for a specific column. For example, select Ignore Failure in the Error drop-down list for the ModifiedDate column and select Redirect Row in the Truncation drop-down list, as shown in Figure 21-15. Click OK.

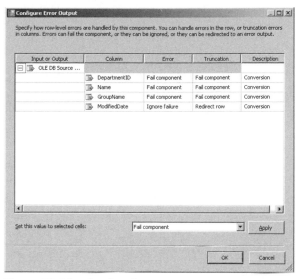

**Figure 21-15** Configuring error output.

3. Double-click the destination to open the *OLE DB Destination Editor*, select a connection to a data source to which you want to send the error rows (or click New to create a new connection), select a data access mode, and provide a table name or applicable property value based on the selected data access mode. For this example, select *DestinationConnectionOLEDB* in the OLE DB Connection Manager drop-down list.

4. Click New to create and execute a script for a new table. You can modify this script by changing the default name or by changing column names. The script is generated from the metadata associated with the input to the destination. Click OK to return to the OLE DB Destination Editor, as shown in Figure 21-16. To continue this example, replace [OLE DB Destination] with **[DepartmentErrors]**. When you use the fast load option, you can set options such as keeping identity values from the source data, keep null values, lock the table for loading, check constraints during the load, and specify batch sizes.

5. Click Mappings in the left pane of the dialog box to display the column mappings between the input columns and the output columns used to send data to the destination. Click OK.

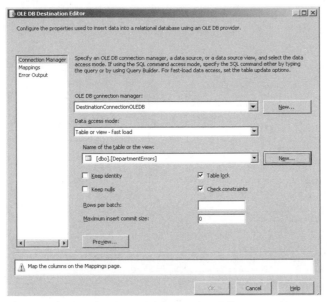

**Figure 21-16**   The OLE DB Destination Editor.

# Debugging Tools

Sometimes you need to step through execution of a package to troubleshoot a problem or to confirm that tasks or transformations are behaving as you intend. The difference between architectures in the control flow engine and the data flow engine requires different tools for debugging control flow and data flow. They all allow you to pause the action and review the current state of information about the package.

## Control Flow Breakpoints

In Control Flow, you can use *breakpoints* to pause package execution and review information in Visual Studio debug windows. You can define a breakpoint before control flow begins or after it ends, as well as before or after an executable runs within the control flow. You can even add or delete breakpoints while debugging. To add a breakpoint, follow these steps:

1.  To follow this example, you must complete the steps described in the previous sections, beginning with "Starting an Integration Services Project." On the Control Flow tab of the package designer, right-click anywhere in the design surface, and

then click Edit Breakpoints. Select the Break When The Container Receives The OnPreExecute Event check box, as shown in Figure 21-17. Click OK to close the Edit Breakpoints window.

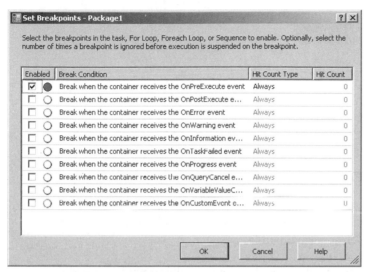

**Figure 21-17** The Set Breakpoints dialog box.

You can set a breakpoint for *events* raised by executables, which are simply tasks, containers, and even packages. Events are essentially messages like "I'm starting," "I'm done now," and "I had a problem."

2. In Solution Explorer, right-click the package and click Execute Package to start debugging. The Visual Studio windows change, but nothing happens yet because your breakpoint stopped the action before it even got started. However, this pause gives you the opportunity to add another breakpoint. Right-click a component, such as the first *Data Flow Task* created by the SSIS Import and Export Wizard in a previous example, click Edit Breakpoints, and then select the Break When The Container Receives The OnPostExecuteEvent check box. This breakpoint will stop the action when this task finishes. Click OK.

3. Press F5 or click the Continue button in the Debug toolbar. Notice the breakpoint symbol on the *Data Flow Task* to indicate the point where execution has paused, as shown in Figure 21-18.

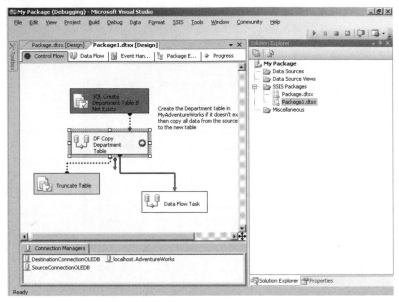

**Figure 21-18**   Debugging Control Flow.

Now you can go exploring. Here are some of the things you can do:

❑ Open the Data Flow for this task to see how many rows were transferred.

❑ Open the Progress tab to view warning or error messages as well as status information on completed tasks or tasks in progress.

❑ Open other debugging windows. Choose Output on the View menu or point to Windows on the Debug menu and then choose one of the following windows: Breakpoints, Watch, Locals, Call Stack, or Threads. Multiple debug windows can be open simultaneously.

4. Press Shift+F5 or click the Stop Debugging button in the Debug toolbar to end package execution. You don't have to run a package through all tasks before stopping.

5. Choose Delete All Breakpoints on the Debug menu when you have completed your debugging activities.

---

**Important**   If you choose to delete all breakpoints, configured data viewers (discussed in the next section) are also deleted from the data flow. You can selectively clear breakpoints on the Debug menu by pointing to

Windows and choosing Breakpoints. In the Breakpoints window, you can clear the check box for individual breakpoints.

## Data Flow Data Viewers

You can add a *data viewer* to the pipeline to monitor the rows passing through it. It's like having a window into your pipeline; you can see actual data rows before and after a transformation by placing a data viewer on either side of the transformation. For large volumes of data, viewing each row might be impractical, so you have other data viewers that can consolidate the information into a histogram, scatter plot, or column chart. Experiment with each viewer to discover how each best meets your needs. To add a data viewer, follow these steps:

1. To follow this example, you must complete the steps described in the previous sections, beginning with "Starting an Integration Services Project." Click the Data Flow tab of the package designer. In the Data Flow Task drop-down list at the top of the package designer, select the first *Data Flow Task* (which contains the *Source–Department* and *Destination–Department* objects) created in a previous example in the Data Flow Task drop-down list.

2. Right-click on the connector between two component objects, and then click Data Viewers.

3. In the Data Flow Path Editor, click Add to open the Configure Data Viewer dialog box, as shown in Figure 22-19. Click OK. If you want to limit the columns you see in the data viewer, click the Grid tab and remove columns from the Displayed Columns list.

4. Click OK to return to the Data Flow Path Editor. You can continue adding other data viewers to this path. Each data viewer displays in a separate window during debugging. Click OK. The Data Flow work surface now includes an icon to indicate a data viewer has been added.

5. In Solution Explorer, right-click the package and click Execute Package. The data viewer acts as a breakpoint and stops when it receives input, as shown in Figure 22-20. You might need to resize the data viewer window.

6. Scroll through the contents of the window to view columns by row. When you are finished, click the green arrow button at the top of the data viewer to continue package execution. The package will stop at any additional breakpoints in the package, or run to completion.

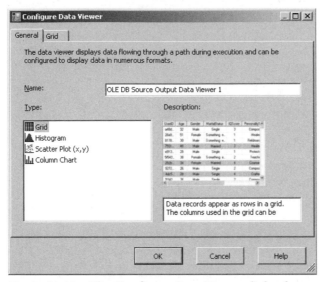

**Figure 21-19**   The Configure Data Viewer dialog box.

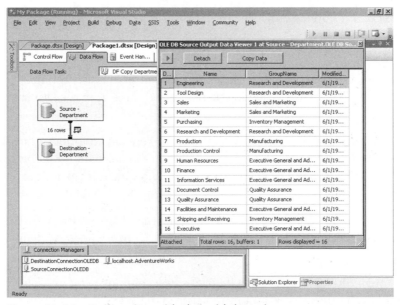

**Figure 21-20**   Debugging with the grid data viewer.

# Logging

As shown in the previous section, you have several options for monitoring the progress of package execution during the development cycle, but these options are useful only when you are executing the package manually. Once you place a package into production, however, you need a different way to monitor the results. Integration Services provides a variety of formats for logging and allows you to configure the level of detail to be logged at the package, container, and task levels. You can configure logging to one or more providers, as described here:

- **Text** Saves as CSV file with .log extension; easy to view package results using this format
- **SQL Server Profiler** Writes trace file with .trc extensions; useful for monitoring package execution time over a period of time
- **SQL Server** Writes data to a sysdtslog90 table in a specified database; easy to query with SQL
- **Event Log** Writes to the Application Log in the Windows Event log; good for use in conjunction with Microsoft Operations Manager
- **XML File** Writes data to file with .xml extension; with XSLT, easy to share as web page and to consolidate log files from multiple sources

To configure logging, follow these steps:

1. To follow this example, you must complete the steps described in the previous sections, beginning with "Starting an Integration Services Project." In the package designer, choose Logging on the SSIS menu. Select a log provider, such as SSIS Log Provider for SQL Server, in the Provider Type drop-down list. Click Add.

2. Next, associate the log provider with one or more executables. For this example, select the Package1 check box and then select the newly added log in the Select The Logs To Use For The Container. By default, all child executables are selected.

3. To configure the log provider, select a connection manager in the Configuration drop-down list, such as DestinationConnectionOLEDB, as shown in Figure 21-21.

4. Click the Details tab and select the events to be logged. For this example, select OnError and OnPostExecute, as shown in Figure 22-22. If you click Advanced, you can select or clear specific columns to be logged by event, such as Computer, Operator, MessageText, and others. All available columns are selected by default. Click OK.

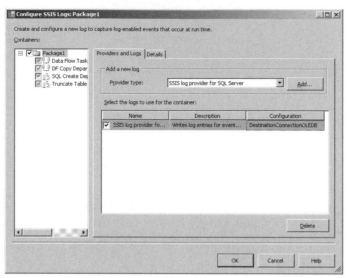

**Figure 21-21**    Configuring package logging.

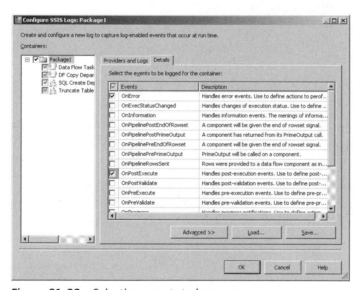

**Figure 21-22**    Selecting events to log.

5.  Run the package, and then use SQL Server Management Studio to view the contents of the sysdtslog90 in the target database specified in the connection you associated with the log provider.

> **Important**   Keep in mind that logging adds overhead to package execution and can tax system resources.

# Advanced Integration Services Features

There are so many features available in Integration Services, but there is so little space to discuss all of them in detail. In this section, we'll review a few other features you should be familiar with but which you may not need to implement right away if your data integration needs are still relatively simple.

## Variables

Variables are the means by which you can add infinite flexibility to your packages. The subject of variables was introduced previously in this chapter in the context of passing a variable value as a parameter in a SQL statement used in an Execute SQL Task. Variables can also be used in expressions, most commonly for changing an executable's properties at run-time. There are two kinds of variables available in Integration Services, as described in the following list:

- **System variables** Defined by Integration Services on creation of a package, container, task, or event handler. You cannot add or update a system variable. You can access the value of a variable only at run-time. For example, you can read the MachineName and then change properties of other tasks to modify package behavior when executing on a specific machine.

- **User variables** Defined by the package developer. You can use this type of variable to dynamically set values and control processes during package execution. You can assign a literal value to the variable or derive a value by evaluating an expression. As explained in a previous example, you can test for the existence of a file, store the result as True or False in a variable, and then test the variable in a precedence constraint before allowing an executable to run.

> **Note**   Variable names are case sensitive in Integration Services.

## Event Handlers

An event handler is a special type of container—think of it as a mini-package that has its own tasks and containers. An event handler executes only in response to the event for which it is configured. The following list provides a few examples of how you might use an event handler.

- Delete a file on a network share after its presence has been detected and has caused an executable to run.

- Determine if the computer has enough memory to run a package.

- Send an e-mail message to you when an error causes a component to fail.

### Checkpoints

Using *checkpoints* allows you to restart a package restart from a point of failure instead of the beginning of package. This capability allows you to save a lot of time, particularly when you're extracting large volumes of data from another server or processing Analysis Services objects. As the package executes, information about its progress is written to a checkpoint file. If the package fails, the checkpoint file is read by Integration Services to determine the point at which the package should be restarted.

An important concept to understand, however, is the relationship between nested containers and checkpoints if a package is restarted, for example, if you use a loop container that in turn holds other containers. If failure occurs before all loops of the parent container are complete, then the loop starts at the beginning even if tasks in the child containers completed successfully before the failure.

# Deploying Packages

Once you've developed and tested your package, what's next? You probably don't want to run the package manually in Visual Studio on a regular basis. In this section, we'll review package configuration options, deployment and security considerations when moving packages into production, and tasks related to package management after deployment.

## Package Configuration

Package configurations allow you to customize how a package runs in different circumstances. For example, when you run the package on a development server, you might want to connect to sample databases for extracting and loading data, but when you run the package on a production server, you want to connect instead to real data sources. You aren't limited to changing connection information; by using variables and expressions liberally when configuring properties for executables and data flow components, you can manage run-time values externally. These values can be stored as environment variables, registry entries, or SQL Server tables, or passed from a parent package to a child package as a variable. While the possibilities seem limitless, the most common reason for using package configuration is to change the connection string when moving the package to another server. To define package configuration, follow these steps:

1. To follow this example, you must complete the steps described in the previous sections, beginning with "Starting an Integration Services Project." In the package designer, choose Package Configurations on the SSIS menu. Select the Enable Package Configurations check box, and then click Add to start the Package Configuration Wizard. Click Next on the Welcome page of the wizard to display the Select Configuration Type page

2. Select an item in the Configuration Type drop-down list, such as XML Configuration File. Your selection changes the boxes in this page of the wizard that define the location of the configuration information. In this example, we'll use an XML file because it's easy to view and change later. Type **MyConfig.dtsConfig** in the Configuration File Name box, as shown in Figure 21-23. Click Next.

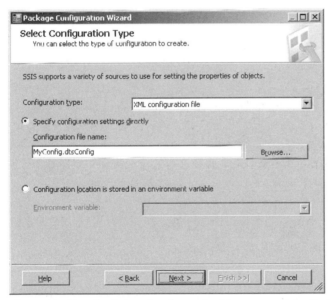

**Figure 21-23**  The Select Configuration Type page of the Package Configuration Wizard.

3. On the Select Properties To Export page of the wizard, as shown in Figure 21-24, you can select as many properties of executables, connection managers, log providers, the package itself, and package variables as you want to manage externally in the configuration file. For this example, scroll up to locate the Connection Managers folder, expand the SourceConnectionOLEDB and the Properties folders, and

then select the ConnectionString property. The current attributes associated with the selected property display in the dialog box. Click Next.

4. Type a Configuration Name such as **Source ConnectionString**, and then click Finish. The configuration is now listed in the Package Configurations Organize, as shown in Figure 21-25. You can create multiple configurations for a single package. When you later deploy the package, you can control which configurations to apply at run-time. Click Close.

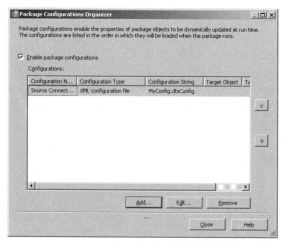

**Figure 21-24**    The Package Configurations Organizer.

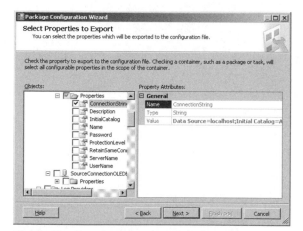

**Figure 21-25**    The Select Properties To Export page of the Package Configuration Wizard.

Now that a package configuration exists, you can open the configuration container, which in this case is an XML file, and edit the contents directly. For example, you can change the value of the connection string to have the package connect to a different server when you use this configuration the next time the package executes.

# Package Deployment

Integration Services makes it very easy to deploy your package to an Integration Services server. Use Visual Studio's Build command to create a manifest file and a set of package and configuration files from your Integration Services project which you can then move to the new server. After moving the files, you launch the Package Installation Wizard by double-clicking the manifest file. The wizard steps you through the process of selecting a target server and a storage method for your package. If you have a package configuration, the wizard also allows you to change configured values before the package is installed on the server. To deploy a package, follow these steps:

1. To follow this example, you must complete the steps described in the previous sections, beginning with "Starting an Integration Services Project." Right-click the project name in the Solution Explorer window and then click Properties. In the Property Pages dialog box for your project, click Deployment Utility. Set the CreateDeploymentUtility property to True. If you want to allow package configuration changes on deployment, be sure the value of the AllowConfiguration-Changes property is True. Also, take note of the DeploymentOutputPath. This is the folder where your utility will be stored. Click OK.

2. Right-click the project in the Solution Explorer window again, but this time click Build. If the deployment utility is built successfully, the status bar at the bottom of the screen will display Build Succeeded.

3. Using Windows Explorer, navigate to the solution folder for your project and then navigate to the folder specified by DeploymentOutputPath in Package Properties. Here you will find the copies of your packages (the .dtsx files), a copy of the configuration file (with extension .dtsConfig), and a special SSISDeploymentManifest file. This file details the files to be deployed together to the new server.

4. To install your packages on a new server, copy the contents of the Deployment folder to a location on the other server. For this example, you can just leave the files where they are and continue as if the files were relocated. Double-click the SSISDeploymentManifest file to start the Package Installation Wizard, and then click Next on the Welcome page.

5. On the Deploy SSIS Packages page of the wizard, select SQL Server Deployment, which is the recommended option. Regardless of the deployment option you

choose, you can optionally validate your package after deployment to ensure it still works after being copied and transferred. Click Next.

6.  Provide a target server name and credentials if you're using SQL Server authentication. You can optionally choose to apply SQL Server security by selecting Rely On Server Storage For Encryption on this page. Click Next.

7.  Note the default folder to which the package is installed. Click Next twice to start installation.

8.  On the Configure Packages page of the wizard, you can change the value of properties you included in the package configuration file. For this example, you can keep the current value. Click Next, and then click Finish to complete the wizard.

9.  To confirm the package is installed on the server, open SQL Server Management Studio. Choose Connect Object Explorer on the File menu, select Integration Services in the Server Type drop-down list, change the Server Name if necessary, and then click Connect.

10. Expand the Stored Packages and MSDB folders to view a list of the installed packages. If you previously selected the file system for installation, your packages will be visible in the File System folder.

# Package Security

There are several ways to use Integration Services security to protect sensitive data, such as passwords and property values defined in a package, and data produced by the package, such as configurations, checkpoints, and logs. The key points about security are outlined in this section.

## Protecting Data

Integration Services considers some component properties to be sensitive. That is, the values supplied for those properties should be treated as confidential, such as a connection string or a password. Whether you provide this value directly to the property or by using a variable to pass in a value at run-time, Integration Services will detect the components with sensitive properties and then suppress or encrypt the values based on the protection level defined for the package. You can use different protection levels for each environment in which the package exists. For example, on your development computer, you might use a different level of protection than you configure for a package deployed to the server. To set the protection level of a package in Visual Studio, click anywhere on the Control Flow tab, select the package in the drop-down list at the top of the Properties window. Change the Protection Level to an appropriate value, as described in the following here:

- **DontSaveSensitive**   Marks sensitive information when the package is saved and replaces the information with blanks if a different user opens the package

- **EncryptSensitiveWithUserKey**   Encrypts sensitive information with a key based on the user and replaces the information with blanks if a different user opens the package; package execution fails for a different user

- **EncryptSensitiveWithPassword**   Encrypts sensitive information with the PackagePassword value and replaces the information with blanks if a different user opens the package and cannot supply the password; any user providing the password can execute the package.

- **EncryptAllWithPassword**   Saves the PackagePassword value with the encrypted package; any user providing the password can open the package in the package designer or execute the package using dtexec

- **EncryptAllWithUserKey**   Encrypts the package with a key based on the user creating or exporting the package; only that user can open the package in the package designer or execute the package using the dtexec utility

- **ServerStorage**   Uses SQL Server database roles to protect the package, only when the package is saved to the SQL Server MSDB database

The content of a package isn't the only information you might need to protect. You also may need to protect configuration files, checkpoint files, and log files. You should use the SQL Server Configuration Type for package configurations and the SQL Server log provider for logging so you can apply database security to this information. If you must save any information to a file, then configure operating system security on the folder where the configuration, checkpoint, or log file is stored.

## Using Digital Signatures

A package that has been digitally signed and later modified cannot be executed. You must update the digital signature if you later need to change the package. You won't be able to sign a package without a digital certificate available on your computer. Once you have a certificate, choose Digital Signing from the SSIS menu in the package designer, click Sign, and select the certificate. When the package is deployed to the server, you can specify an execution option to require validation of the signature.

## Protecting Packages

Packages installed in the MSDB database on a SQL Server 2005 instance can be associated with a reader role and a writer role. In SQL Server Management Studio, connect to

Integration Services, right-click a package in the MSDB folder, and click Package Roles. As shown in Figure 22-26, you can select one or more database-level roles for each package role. In addition, be aware the Windows administrators on the server can view and stop all packages currently running while SQL Server administrators can view and stop only those packages they started.

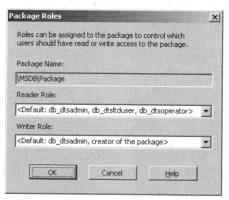

**Figure 21-26**    The Package Roles dialog box.

## Package Execution

To manually start package execution, you can use the dtexec command prompt utility, but this method requires that you know the syntax for the command, which can be tricky if you want to specify additional execution options such as a change in connection string or property value. This utility gives you one more way to manage package execution without using configuration files. However, it's easiest to build the command and arguments for the dtexec utility by using the Execute Package Utility (also known as the dtexecui utility), which provides a graphical interface for specifying run-time options.

To start this utility in SQL Server Management Studio, you connect to Integration Services, right-click a package in either the File System or MSDB folder, and click Run Package. You can also run dtexecui from the command-line. In the Execute Package Utility dialog box, you navigate through each page and select execution options. For example, click Configurations to select a different configuration file. This file doesn't have to be stored on the same server, but it does need to be in a location accessible by Integration Services during package execution. When you have finished selecting options, click Command Line to view the command line string generated, as shown in Figure 22-27. If you select different options in the Execute Package Utility dialog box, the command line string will not match this example.

**Note** You can copy the command line string and append it to the dtexec command to create a job step in a SQL Server Agent job when you want the package to run on a regular schedule.

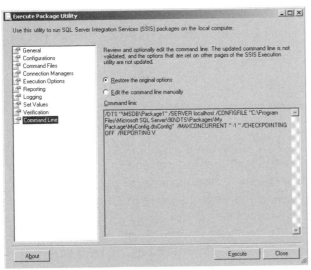

**Figure 21-27** The Command Line page of the Execute Package Utility.

## Package Management

There are several places where you can store packages for use by Integration Services. You can register a package with the Integration Services service by storing it in either the MSDB database or the SQL Server Package Store, but you can also reference a package file on the file system without registering it. In that case, you simply have to supply a path and package name. In SQL Server Management Studio, you can review the registered packages in the Stored Packages folder list, which is further divided into two folders, File System and MSDB. The File System folder contains packages that have been placed in the <SQL Server install directory>\90\DTS\Packages folder during package deployment. The MSDB folder lists packages that are stored in the sysdtspackages90 table of the *MSDB* database. The usual method of storing packages in this location is to use the package deployment utility, but you can also use the Import Package command (by right-clicking on the File System or MSDB folder) to locate, register, and store packages in the respective storage mode.

## Monitoring Packages

Use the Running Packages folder to view a list of packages currently executing. When you click this folder in the Object Explorer window and then click the Report button in the Summary page toolbar, general information about running packages displays, such as the amount of time a package has been running. Refresh the folder to view the most recent information because it does not refresh automatically. If you click a specific package on the Summary page, you can view additional information about the package such as its version and description. To stop a package, right-click the package and then click Stop.

# Summary

In this chapter, you've learned a lot about Integration Services, from fundamental concepts to designing and managing packages. Far from being a complete reference for Integration Services, this chapter introduced you to the most important things you need to know to start building basic packages and to put packages into production. Some advanced features were also briefly discussed so you can consider their usefulness for more complex data integration projects you tackle once you gain more experience. As data continues to proliferate in organizations, there will be plenty of opportunities to expand your data integration skills and take full advantage of the flexibility that Integration Services offers.

# Chapter 22
# Analysis Services

Business systems capture data from ongoing operations, whether the data is entered by a human being or generated by an automated process, and often store this data in a relational database. As a database administrator, you're already familiar with the virtues of a relational database for supporting business operations. You've also likely encountered its limitations when people want to start using the relational database as a source for analysis. At its simplest, the preparation of data for analysis requires summarization of detailed transaction data. However, data preparation becomes more difficult when you need to support analysis of data over time, such as year-over-year growth, or to discover patterns, such as the characteristics of people who are likely to buy a particular product.

SQL Server 2005 Analysis Services, also known as Analysis Services, enables you to easily implement an infrastructure that supports a wide range of analytical capabilities, from ad hoc queries to data mining. Because there are too many features to cover in-depth in a single chapter, we'll focus instead on the basic Analysis Services concepts required to build a functional database. We'll also review important administrative activities to manage a database after it is placed in production.

## What Is Analysis Services?

Analysis Services is the SQL Server 2005 component that provides two very different, but complementary, analytical capabilities: *online analytical processing (OLAP)* and *data mining*. An OLAP engine is popular for enabling fast ad hoc queries by end users. A user can interactively explore data by *drilling, slicing and dicing*, or *pivoting*. By drilling, a user can navigate from summarized data into successively more detailed data when querying an OLAP database to narrow the focus of analysis. A user slices and dices by placing data in a cross tab report with categories on both rows and columns to see the intersecting values. A user pivots by switching categories between rows and columns or by moving categories from the cross tab into a filter or out of the report altogether. A data mining engine, on the other hand, is more often used behind-the-scenes by technical specialists and subject matter experts to uncover hidden patterns in corporate data. These patterns can be used to develop profiles of people or events which can then be used to support decisions, such as which prospects to target in a marketing campaign or which products to promote together. Data mining can also be used for prediction, such as determining which customers are likely to stop using your products or services.

# Analysis Services 2005 Versus Analysis Services 2000

Analysis Services 2005 is the next generation of Analysis Services 2000, which itself was based on technology first introduced in SQL Server 7.0 as Microsoft OLAP Services. Data mining capabilities were added in Analysis Services 2000, hence the change in the component name in the SQL Server 2000 release. While conceptually the types of analysis supported by Analysis Services 2000 and Analysis Services 2005 are similar, the Analysis Services 2005 architecture is much different to support a broader array of analytical requirements than Analysis Services 2000.

## A Selective Look at New Features

The new architecture of Analysis Services provides a rich set of features that support more complex design models, enhance manageability, and improve scalability. Whether your job is to build or to maintain an Analysis Services database, there are a number of enhancements that simplify your efforts. You can find a complete list of these new features in the SQL Server Books Online topic "Analysis Services Enhancements." Let's briefly review the most important changes to understand as you get familiar with Analysis Services.

Experienced Analysis Services developers and administrators immediately notice the separation of the development and administration environments. Developers now use an integrated development environment, SQL Server Business Intelligence Development Studio, in which they can switch easily between different types of database objects, debug complex calculations, and manage team development using a source control application such as Microsoft Visual SourceSafe. Integration with the .NET Framework enables developers to embed Analysis Services functionality into custom applications or to create stored procedures as better-performing replacements for user-defined functions. Administrators can access a variety of tools in a single management environment, SQL Server Management Studio, where they can configure and manage multiple servers, develop and execute XML for Analysis (XMLA) scripts to automate routine tasks, and configure properties for database objects. Importantly, the security model has been improved in Analysis Services so you can limit the administrative tasks that can be performed by specific users to certain databases or even selected database objects.

Developers of Analysis Services databases now have several new considerations for designing a *dimension*, a key component of an Analysis Services database. Dimensions add context to numerical data under analysis by providing labels to describe the time, place, or people involved in a transaction or event. Analysis Services 2000 imposed certain restrictions on the size, structure, and content of dimensions that have been eliminated in Analysis Services 2005. For example, now that dimension data is no longer stored in memory, you can work with very large dimensions without impacting server memory and without developing workarounds for the limit of 64,000 children per parent.

Another significant difference in the structure of dimensions is the shift from a hierarchy-driven design to an attribute-driven design. If you used member properties in Analysis Services 2000, for example, you'll now use attributes to present this data. More importantly, however, this new approach enables queries to support summarizations of values by arbitrary groupings, easily done in SQL queries against relational data but problematic when querying traditional OLAP structures. As a result, Analysis Services now blurs the line between relational and multidimensional reporting.

You also have new options for managing data integrity. While ETL processes should prevent data integrity issues in your source data, you can now gracefully accommodate orphaned records in the fact table for which a dimension reference does not yet exist by using a placeholder member. By taking advantage of this feature, you can ensure the values in the OLAP database always match the values in the source system. If, on the other hand, this behavior is not desirable, you can either force an error or ignore the error. If you force an error, you can fix the problem before the database is available for querying. While ignoring the error is a valid option, it's not recommended unless you're working on a prototype and are focused on getting the correct design before resolving data integrity issues.

Dimensions are still organized into a multidimensional structure called a *cube*, but there are some important conceptual differences between Analysis Services 2000 and Analysis Services 2005. In Analysis Services 2000, a single database can contain multiple cubes. Each cube corresponds to one, and only one, fact table in a relational data mart or warehouse. You can combine multiple cubes by creating a virtual cube when you need to analyze data across one or more fact tables. A common use for a virtual cube is to compare daily level actual sales with monthly level budgeted sales. In Analysis Services 2005, you can still create multiple cubes within one database, but best practice is to create one cube. This single cube contains one or more *measure groups*, each of which corresponds to one fact table. Thus, a measure group is analogous to a cube in Analysis Services 2000, and an Analysis Services 2005 cube is analogous to a virtual cube.

If you had to deal with *semiadditive measures* in Analysis Services 2000, you'll appreciate the new aggregate functions available in Analysis Services 2005. A semiadditive measure is a numerical value that you can add up across any dimension except time. A very commonly encountered semiadditive measure is Inventory Count, a value representing the number of units currently in inventory at a specific point in time. Because you can add inventory values across products but not across time, this numerical value is considered semiadditive. Handling semiadditive measures in Analysis Services 2000 requires you to add special calculations to a cube, but now there are several aggregate functions you can use in Analysis Services 2005, including *FirstChild, LastChild, FirstNonEmpty, LastNon-Empty, AverageOfChildren*, and *ByAccount.*

After putting an Analysis Services 2000 database into production, you must schedule periodic processing to include new records added to the data warehouse since the last update. In Analysis Services 2005, you can still manage processing on a scheduled basis, but you also have the option to use *proactive caching* to trigger processing only when the source data changes. By using proactive caching, you can manage the latency of the data and keep data available for queries during processing. If the time required to reprocess a cube is longer than the configured latency period, queries can be resolved directly from the relational source systems.

If you've used the data mining features in Analysis Services 2000, or even if you're new to data mining, you'll really enjoy working with the new modeling tools and data mining algorithms included in Analysis Services 2005. In addition to the Decision Trees and Clustering previously available, you now have access to Linear Regression, Logistic Regression, Naive Bayes, Neural Network, Sequence Clustering, and Time Series algorithms. The data mining tools in Analysis Services are easy to implement, but you should take care to appropriately prepare your data for the type of data mining you want to do and to understand which algorithm is applicable to the business problem you want to solve.

---

**More Info**    Take the time to read *Data Mining with SQL Server 2005* by ZhaoHui Tang and Jamie MacLennan for a good comparison of the algorithms and practical examples.

## Migration from Analysis Services 2000

Because Analysis Services 2005 includes a new architecture for dimensions and cubes, you can't continue to use your existing Analysis Services 2000 databases with the Analysis Services 2005 server. You must rebuild the database objects from scratch, or you can use the Analysis Services Migration Wizard to recreate database objects in Analysis Services 2005. The wizard merely reconstructs these objects using equivalent (or near-equivalent) Analysis Services 2005 objects and doesn't attempt to implement an optimal design. You can, of course, make changes to the migrated database objects. In this section, we'll review the migration process.

---

**More Info** For a thorough explanation of cube design issues that can impact migration and mapping of features before and after migration, refer to "Analysis Services 2005 Migration" at *http://www.microsoft.com/technet/prodtechnol/sql/ 2005/asmigrtn.mspx.*

---

To use the Analysis Services Migration Wizard, follow these steps:

1. Start SQL Server Management Studio. In the Connect to Server dialog box, select Analysis Services in the Server Type drop-down list. In the Server Name drop-down list, select the instance to host the migrated databases, right-click the server in the Object Explorer window, and then click Migrate Database. On the Welcome page of the wizard, click Next.

2. On the Specify Source And Destination page of the wizard, type the name of the Analysis Services 2000 server hosting the databases to migrate. Notice you can choose Script File as an alternate destination if you want to generate an XMLA script to perform the migration another time. For this example, we'll perform the migration now. Click Next.

3. On the Select Databases To Migrate page of the wizard, all available databases on the source server are selected. Clear the selection of any databases that you don't want to migrate now. You can also change the Destination Database name on this page, if desired. Click Next.

4. On the Validating Databases page of the wizard, a validation log is generated. This log lists any warnings or errors that could affect migration, as shown in Figure 22-1. In this example, the migration of the Foodmart 2000 sample database (included with Analysis Services 2000) is validated, but warnings indicate that virtual dimensions will be renamed. You can click View Log to filter the validation log to show

only errors, warnings, or successes. You can also click Save Log to save the results as a text file. Click Next.

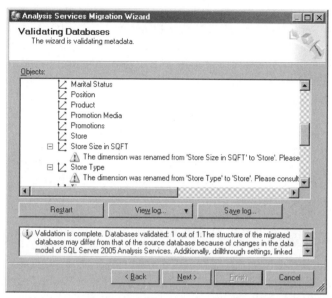

**Figure 22-1** The Validating Databases page of the Analysis Services Migration Wizard.

5. On the Migrating Databases page of the wizard, you monitor the progress of the migration. When migration is complete, click Next.

6. The final page of the wizard displays a view of the database objects in the migrated database. Click Finish to complete the wizard.

Only metadata is migrated by the Analysis Services Migration Wizard. You still must load data into the cubes, but first you should make any necessary modifications to the database design. You make design changes by creating a project in SQL Server Business Intelligence Development Studio and importing the database object definitions into the project. To import an Analysis Services database into the development environment, follow these steps:

1. Start SQL Server Business Intelligence Development Studio. On the File menu, point to New, and then click Project.

2. Ensure that the Project Type is set to Business Intelligence Projects, and then click the Import Analysis Services 9.0 Database template. Type a name for the project, change the location for the project to a folder of your choice, and confirm that the Create Directory For Solution check box is selected.

3. Click OK to start the Import Analysis Services 9.0 Database Wizard, and then click Next to bypass the Welcome page.

4. On the Source Database page of the wizard, type the name of the Analysis Services server and select the migrated database in the Database drop-down list, click Next, and then click Finish. The project now contains files corresponding to each database object in the selected database.

5. To open a particular file, double-click the file name in the Solution Explorer window.

Later in this chapter, we'll review some of the more important features of the main database objects and how to make changes to the object definitions.

## Analysis Services Fundamentals

Before you start building an Analysis Services database, it's helpful to have a general understanding of OLAP concepts. There are many vendors that sell products labeled as OLAP, but unfortunately there is no consistent definition of OLAP that encompasses all these products. In 1993, E.F. Codd, of relational database fame, published a paper that spelled out twelve rules for OLAP. Because the paper was sponsored by a vendor and wasn't a true research paper, these rules were never broadly accepted. A couple of years later, *FASMI* was introduced in The OLAP Report (*www.olapreport.com/fasmi*) and is now commonly cited in explanations of OLAP.

FASMI is the acronym for a collection of rules—Fast Analysis of Shared Multidimensional Information. In this section, we'll explain the most important things you need to know about how Analysis Services satisfies these rules.

Fast is defined by The OLAP Report as a response in five seconds or less. Ideally, an ad hoc query should return a result in subseconds. To achieve this quick response time, most OLAP products, including Analysis Services, use *aggregations*. Aggregations are summarized values derived from detailed source data and stored on the server. If aggregations are designed correctly, then queries against OLAP aggregations are faster than queries against a relational aggregate table. Analysis Services makes it easy to design and maintain aggregations for enabling fast query performance.

An OLAP product should support analysis by providing the results of complex business calculations without requiring the end user to learn a programming language to access those results. An Analysis Services cube encapsulates business logic and stores calculations in a single location for easy access by users. Not only does use of an Analysis Services cube ensure everyone uses the same calculation definition every time, Analysis Services is specifically designed for performing sophisticated analytical calculations on large volumes of data, such as time series analysis, currency conversions, and budget allocations, to name a few. Analysis Services also supports *key performance indicators* (KPIs), which are measurements over time that compare actual business results to predefined goals, and includes several data mining algorithms for more advanced statistical analysis.

A shared OLAP solution must support access to data by many users in two important ways. First, sensitive data must be secured adequately. Analysis Services not only includes security to control access to specific databases but also supports securing data at more granular level, such as limiting access to selected dimensions, sections of a dimension, or even particular cells in a cube. Second, users must be able to write data back to the cube. Analysis Services provides support for write-back, often a requirement for budgeting solutions, but you'll need to use a client application that also supports write-back to take advantage of this feature.

Multidimensionality is the one rule that must absolutely be met for a product to be accepted as OLAP compliant. Where a relational database is a two-dimensional representation of data stored in tables containing rows and columns, an OLAP database stores data in a multidimensional structure called a cube. Unlike the geometrical cube which is limited to three dimensions, an OLAP cube can have *n* dimensions. In practice, a cube requires at least one dimension but usually has seven to twelve dimensions. This range is considered only a design guideline to avoid confusing users with too much information. A *dimension* is a set of logically related labels that give context to the values you analyze. Often, you can recognize a dimension when you see or hear the word "by" used in the description of a request for information. For example, when I want to get sales by year by product, I would create a query with two dimensions—Time and Product. (Technically, Sales is in a third dimension for measures, but that's a special type of dimension that is designed differently.)

Dimensions have *members*, which represent the labels that are presented during analysis. For example, the result of the query to get sales by year by product might return 2003, 2004, and 2005, each of which is a member of the Time dimension. Likewise, Bikes, Accessories, and Clothing are members of the Product dimension. Whereas a dimension comes from one or more related tables, members come from the same column in the dimension table, which is defined as an *attribute* in Analysis Services. Traditionally, OLAP products organize members of a dimension into a *hierarchy* that contains multiple *levels*. In the Time dimension, days roll up to months, months roll up to quarters, and quarters roll up to years. Days, Months, Quarters, and Years are levels of the hierarchy which each contain its own set of members.

In Analysis Services 2000, you build dimensions by mapping dimension columns to hierarchy levels. Analysis Services breaks with tradition by mapping dimension columns to attributes that can then be organized into a *user hierarchy*. A user hierarchy might be a natural grouping of attributes, like *Day*, *Month*, *Quarter*, and *Year*, in which an attribute has a many-to-one relationship with one other attribute in the hierarchy. Or a user hierarchy could be a grouping that users find helpful for analysis, regardless of the cardinality of the relationship between attributes. For example, if a user hierarchy includes *Color* and *Size* attributes in the *Product* dimension, the size L could be related both to Blue and to Red, although of course the values associated with Blue L products could be different from Red L products.

Lastly, the Information rule in FASMI refers to the volume of data that an OLAP product can support. Of course, an OLAP product's ability to manage large data volumes is dependent to a significant degree on available hardware resources, such as RAM and disk space. Analysis Services has been architected specifically for scalability. You can select the physical storage mode appropriate for the data volumes you must support and create partitions to locate data on separate drives or even separate servers as well as to minimize the time required to add new data.

Once you have built an Analysis Services database and made it available for users to query, you need to implement processes for keeping cube data up-to-date with minimal downtime. Analysis Services provides several options for managing updates, such as incremental processing to load only the newest data and limit the time required to recalculate aggregations. Analysis Services can even be configured to respond to queries while data is being updated.

## Integration with SQL Server 2005 Components

After you define the dimension and cube structures during the development phase of an Analysis Services database, you must run processes to read the source data and load it into storage on a regular basis, although certain types of storage don't require physically moving and restructuring the data. It's generally not practical to run these processes manually. You can use Integration Services to access source data, prepare new storage structures if necessary, and then *process* database objects to add new records or to refresh dimensions and cubes. Use SQL Server Agent to schedule execution of Integration Services on a periodic basis. After processing, the cube is ready for browsing by end users. A cube can also be a data source for reports developed for use with Reporting Services and a source for a Notification Services event provider to send information when a defined condition is met.

## Analysis Services Components Overview

Analysis Services includes several tools for developers and administrators to use when designing, deploying, processing, and managing Analysis Services databases and related objects. Analysis Services also includes client components to send commands and queries from user applications to the Analysis Services server. Many of these components are discussed in more detail later in this chapter. For now, review the following list of Analysis Services components to get a general idea of each component's purpose:

- **Analysis Services Service** Manages database object metadata and server resources, processes transactions, creates aggregations, stores data, and responds to client application queries.

- **Unified Dimensional Model (UDM)** Combines relational and dimensional models of one or more underlying data sources to centralize common business calculations and other business logic and to support ad hoc queries while shielding end users from the technical details about the data sources

- **Business Intelligence Development Studio** Supports the development, testing, and deployment of the UDM

- **SQL Server Management Studio** Provides administrative support for Analysis Services servers, databases, and database objects

- **SQL Server Profiler** Supports debugging, auditing, and playback of Analysis Services activities

- **Analysis Services Deployment Wizard** Automates deployment of an Analysis Services database to a specified server

- **Synchronize Database Wizard** Copies metadata and cube data from a source server database to a destination server database

- **Migration Wizard** Converts an Analysis Services 2000 database to an Analysis Services 2005 database

- **Analysis Management Objects (AMO) Object Model** Includes application programming interfaces (APIs) for creating, changing, or deleting Analysis Services database objects, applying security, or processing objects

- **XML for Analysis (XMLA) protocol for client applications** Sends commands and queries to an Analysis Services server and receives responses

- **Local Cube Engine (Msmdlocal.dll)** Supports the use of local cubes and local mining models on client workstations

# Designing Analysis Services Projects

You perform all design work using SQL Server Business Intelligence Development Studio, which is introduced in Chapter 21, "Integration Services." If you skipped that chapter, you should turn back to review one section, "The Development Environment," for an overview of this integrated development environment. First-time users of this environment are often initially confused by the many windows to work in and by the number of properties associated with each database object. With practice comes familiarity, so be patient. It won't take long to learn how to navigate the interface effectively to build rich analytical solutions. Unfortunately, space doesn't permit a thorough explanation of all features in this interface, but you will learn enough in this section to build a basic solution and begin experiencing some of the benefits that Analysis Services has to offer.

---

**More Info**    For a solid introduction to Analysis Services using hands-on tutorials, refer to *Microsoft SQL Server 2005 Analysis Services Step by Step*, by Reed Jacobson, Stacia Misner, and Hitachi Consulting, Microsoft Press, 2006. A deeper discussion of Analysis Services, with an emphasis on developing applications based on Analysis Services, is available in *Applied Microsoft Analysis Services 2005* by Teo Lachev, Prologika Press, 2005. To learn how to integrate Analysis Services into a complete data warehousing architecture using Microsoft technology, take a look at *The Microsoft Data Warehouse Toolkit: With SQL Server 2005 and the Microsoft Business Intelligence Toolset* by Joy Mundy, Warren Thornthwaite, and Ralph Kimball, Wiley, 2006.

---

# Data Preparation

An OLAP database is often built as an extension of a data warehouse. In fact, Analysis Services 2000 requires data to be structured as a star schema or snowflake schema, two types of schemas commonly used in a data warehouse. Both schemas include fact tables and dimensions tables. A *fact table* is a table that contains detailed data, such as sales transactions, with one or more numeric columns for *measures* like counts, dollars, or units. A fact table also has foreign key columns that relate to primary keys in one or more dimension tables. A *dimension table* contains descriptive information about the measures in the fact table, such as the date or time of a transaction, the customer who made the purchase, or the product sold.

Rather than build an Analysis Services database directly on top of a star schema or snowflake schema, you build a *Unified Dimensional Model* (UDM) as an intermediate layer between the data source and the Analysis Services database. With this layer in place, you can work on the design of database objects without maintaining a connection to the source while you work. You still need tables that resemble fact tables or dimension tables, but you are no longer limited to using either of the schema structures required by Analysis Services 2000.

## Starting an Analysis Services Project

To build an Analysis Services database, you work in the context of solutions and projects just like developers using Microsoft Visual Studio to build applications in C# .NET or Visual Basic .NET, as explained in Chapter 21. In fact, Business Intelligence Development Studio *is* Visual Studio; it simply has a different name listed in the Microsoft SQL Server 2005 program group. An Analysis Services project contains eight folders: Data Sources, Data Source Views, Cubes, Dimensions, Mining Structures, Roles, Assemblies, and Miscellaneous. To start a new Analysis Services project, follow these steps:

1. Start SQL Server Business Intelligence Development Studio. On the File menu, point to New, and then click Project.

2. Ensure that the Project Type is set to Business Intelligence Projects, and then click the Analysis Services Project template. Type a name for the project, such as **My Adventure Works** to follow the examples in this chapter. Change the location for the project to a folder of your choice, and confirm that the Create Directory For Solution check box is selected.

3. Click OK to create the project in Visual Studio, as shown in Figure 22-2.

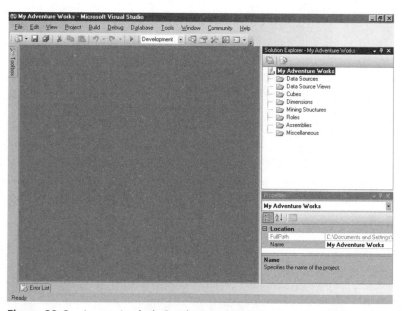

**Figure 22-2**   A new Analysis Services project in Business Intelligence Development Studio.

You'll use several Visual Studio windows during project development, as described in the following list:

- **Solution Explorer**  By default, this window displays in the upper-right corner of your screen. When you add a new object to your project, you'll see a file added to the object's folder. You can rename this file, but be sure to keep the assigned file extension (such as .dim or .cube) or your Analysis Services database won't work.

- **Properties**  This window displays in the lower-right corner of your screen by default. If you select an object in one of the designers, you can view and modify its properties in this window.

- **Designers**  A designer is a collection of design tools, including a workspace, dialog boxes, and various windows used to create database objects. Business Intelligence Development Studio includes the following Analysis Services designers:

  - ❏ **Data source view designer**  Add or remove tables and views to the Data Source View, make structural changes by adding named calculations or named queries and by creating logical keys or logical relationships between tables, organize tables into diagrams, and explore source data.

  - ❏ **Cube designer**  Add or delete measure groups and measures, change property values, associate dimensions with measure groups, add calculations, build KPIs, design actions, create partitions, design aggregations, add perspectives, include translations, and browse a cube.

  - ❏ **Dimension designer**  Add or delete dimension attributes, work with user hierarchies, change property values, add translations, and browse dimension members by attribute hierarchy or by user hierarchy.

  - ❏ **Data mining designer**  Add, change, or delete mining structures; manage and process mining models; and browse or query a mining model.

  - ❏ **Role designer**  Secure databases, cubes, dimensions, dimension members, or cells by user role.

## Using Data Sources

A data source created for an Analysis Services project is much like an Integration Services data source, as discussed in Chapter 21. It's just a file that contains the connection string and credentials used to browse data when exploring the data store or to read data from the source when processing an Analysis Services database object. Typically, the data source refers to the database hosting a data warehouse that contains the dimension and fact tables you use to build an Analysis Services database. However, you could use any relational data source or even another Analysis Services database. To create a Data Source, follow these steps:

1. If necessary, create or open an Analysis Services project in Visual Studio as described in the previous section. Right-click the Data Sources folder in the Solution Explorer window, and then click New Data Source. The first time you start the Data Source Wizard, you see the Welcome page. You can permanently disable this page by selecting the Don't Show This Page Again check box. Click Next.

2. On the Select How To Define The Connection page of the wizard, select a data connection if you have data connections already defined on your workstations, or click New if you need to create one. Alternatively, you can choose Create A Data Source Based On Another Object if you are working with multiple Analysis Services projects and want to keep the current project synchronized with a data source in another project. In this example, we'll assume you have no connections created yet and want to create a new one, so click New to continue.

3. In the Connection Manager dialog box, you can select a different provider. The default provider is SQL Native Client, which you can use to access data in any version of SQL Server. You can choose from the following provider options:

   ❑ .NET Framework Data Providers (Oracle and SQL Server)

   ❑ Microsoft OLE DB Providers (Jet 4.0, Analysis Services 9.0, Data Mining Services, DTS Packages, Indexing Service, Microsoft Directory Services, MSDataShape, OLAP Services 8.0, Oracle, Simple Provider, SQL Server, and SQL Server Replication for DTS)

   ---

   **Note**   You might see additional Microsoft OLE DB Providers listed if you have applications installed on your machine that include an OLE DB provider, such as Microsoft Project 9.0 for example.

   ---

   ❑ SQL Native Client

   ❑ SQLXMLOLEDB, and SQLXMLOLEDB 4.0

   If you have another type of data source that cannot be accessed with these providers, you can develop your own .NET managed provider. This should be considered a last resort, however, as best practice dictates the use of an OLE DB provider whenever possible.

4. Type a server name or select the server name from the drop-down list, select an authentication method (Windows or SQL Server), and select a database. For this example, select the *AdventureWorks* database, which is a sample database that ships

with SQL Server 2005. The authentication method and any credentials you specify here are used to connect to the data source when browsing relational data in the Visual Studio environment.

> **Note** To follow the examples provided in this chapter, it's helpful to use the SQL Server 2005 sample databases. They don't install by default, however. During installation, you must click Advanced and select Documentation, Samples, and Sample Databases on the Components To Install page. After installation, the *AdventureWorks* and *AdventureWorksDW* databases will be available for use. *AdventureWorks* is a sample online transaction processing (OLTP) system and *AdventureWorksDW* is a sample data warehouse. For more information, refer to Chapter 8, "Installing and Upgrading Microsoft SQL Server 2005."

5. Click OK to return to the Data Source Wizard. With the new data source selected, click Next. On the Impersonation Information page of the Data Source Wizard, shown in Figure 22-3, you need to assign credentials for Analysis Services to use when processing database objects.

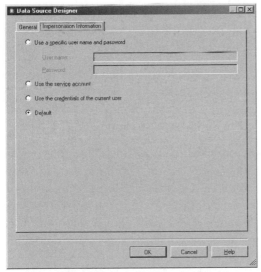

**Figure 22-3** The Impersonation Information page of the Data Source Wizard.

> **Important** Not all impersonation options are applicable to all tasks that might be executed by Analysis Services. For example, neither Use A Specific User Name And Password nor Use The Credentials Of the Current User can be used when Analysis Services processes database objects. Choose

Default to allow Analysis Services to determine when to use the service account credentials or the current user. It's also a best practice to assign a domain account to the Analysis Services service to avoid problems authenticating when connecting to a data source on a separate server.

6. Select Default, click Next, change the Data Source Name if desired, and then click Finish.

## Using Data Source Views

A data source view (DSV), first introduced in Chapter 21, is a central component of the UDM. At minimum, it provides an abstracted layer of the source data structures so you can work on your Analysis Services project without maintaining a connection to the source as previously mentioned. Typically, however, you enhance the DSV to provide user-friendly names, enforce business rules, and create relationships between tables for referential integrity. Some people consider it a best practice to perform these enhancements back in the source database, but the DSV gives you the flexibility to make changes when you don't have the appropriate permissions in the database. To create and modify a DSV, follow these steps:

1. To follow this example, you must complete the steps described in the previous sections of this chapter. In Solution Explorer, right-click the Data Source Views folder, click New Data Source View, and then click Next if the Welcome page displays.

2. Select an available data source. Notice you have the option to create a data source now by clicking New Data Source if you started the Data Source View Wizard before creating a data source. To continue the example from the previous section in which you create a data source, select *AdventureWorks* and then click Next.

3. Double-click a table or view to add it to the Included Objects list. Alternatively, you can select one or more tables and then click the arrow buttons to add to the list. You can also add a table and then click the Add Related Tables button to automatically add tables that have a foreign key relationship with the selected table. For this example, add the following tables: *Production.Product*, *Production.ProductCategory*, *Production.ProductSubcategory*, and *Sales.SalesOrderDetail*, as shown in Figure 22-4. When you are finished, click Next.

---

**Note**    As discussed previously, an OLAP database is often created using tables from a data warehouse, and that's still the preferred approach when a data warehouse exists. However, you might want to work directly with an OLTP schema while you're prototyping the Analysis Services database objects or when you want to take advantage of near-real-time analysis of

OLTP data. We're using *AdventureWorks* in this example to illustrate this point.

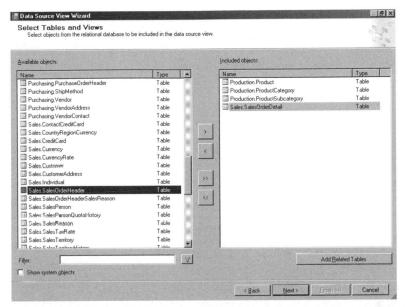

**Figure 22-4**   The Select Tables And Views  page of the Data Source Wizard.

4. Change the DSV name if desired, and then click Finish.

5. Right-click the table header for the *SalesOrderDetail* table, point to Replace Table, and then click With New Named Query. A *named query* is similar to a view in a relational database. You use a Transact-SQL statement to construct a result set that produces a subset of the original data, adds derived columns to concatenate data or compute new values, or combines data from multiple tables. The DSV must have at least one table or view added before you can create a named query.

> **Note**   If you plan to add only a derived column, another option is to create a named calculation. Right-click a table header in the data source view, click New Named Calculation, and provide an expression in the SQL syntax applicable for the data source. There are no performance differences between a named query and a named calculation.

6. Above the diagram pane, you see the Query Definition toolbar. The last button on this toolbar is the Add Table button. Click the Add Table button, double-click

*SalesOrderHeader (Sales)* to add it to the query, and then click Close. You don't need to add a table to the DSV before you include it in a Named Query.

7.  In the *SalesOrderHeader (Sales)* table, select *OrderDate*, *DueDate*, and *ShipDate* to add these columns to the query. You might need to scroll through the table to locate all columns. You can, of course, add expressions to the SELECT statement in addition to, or instead of, adding columns. Click OK to create the named query. Notice the icon that appears in the *SalesOrderDetail* header to indicate this object is a named query instead of a table.

    You will use this named query as a fact table for the cube you build later in this chapter. It contains all the necessary components of a fact table—foreign key columns and numeric columns. However, it's not currently related to any dimensions. You need to add a relationship between the named query and a dimension table.

8.  Locate the *Product* table, drag *ProductID* from the *SalesOrderDetail* named query and drop on *ProductID* in the *Product* table.

    When you create a relationship between two objects in the DSV, you should start with the object that has the foreign key column and then connect it to the object containing the primary key column. If you reverse this process, the Edit Relationship dialog box displays a warning message and gives you the option to reverse the direction of the relationship.

# Dimension Design

As you learned in a previous section of this chapter, a dimension is a logical grouping of labels for numerical values being analyzed. A dimension often describes a person, place, or thing—such as a customer, a sales territory, or a product. In Analysis Services, each dimension is a collection of attributes corresponding to columns in one or more tables. Analysis Services supports several different dimensional models, but we'll limit our examination of dimensions in this section to two types—a standard normalized structure and a server-based time dimension.

## Using the Dimension Wizard

After you create the DSV, you can use the Cube Wizard to automatically create the definitions for the dimensions and cube from the DSV. However, you'll likely find building dimensions one-by-one using the Dimension Wizard is a more productive approach. The Dimension Wizard lets you take either a top-down approach or a bottom-up approach to building a dimension. Following the top-down approach, such as when you're prototyping a business intelligence solution, you define the dimension design first and then generate a schema for you to load with data later. More often, though, you'll use the bottom-up method to design a dimension based on an existing relational schema. To create a dimension, follow these steps:

1. To follow this example, you must complete the steps described in the previous sections of this chapter. In Solution Explorer, right-click the Dimensions folder, click New Dimension, and then click Next on the Welcome page of the wizard.

2. On the Select Build Method page of the wizard, keep the default selections, Build The Dimension Using A Data Source , Auto Build, and Create Attributes And Hierarchies, and then click Next. Selecting Auto Build means that the Dimension Wizard reviews the data in the tables you specify on a subsequent page of the wizard to create attributes and hierarchies.

---

**Note** For absolute control over your dimension, you can disable Auto Build and then create attributes and hierarchies manually. You can also build a dimension without a data source if you want to prototype a structure first and then create a schema later. You can even use a template to help you build the dimension model.

---

3. Click the *Adventure Works* DSV if it is not already selected. The tables used to build the dimension must be included in the DSV. Click Next.

4. Keep the default option, Standard Dimension, in this example. You'll learn more about the other options later in this chapter. Click Next.

   The Main Table defaults to *Production.Product* since it is first alphabetically in the list of tables contained in the data source view. On this page of the wizard, you select the table that represents the *leaf level* of the dimension. The leaf level is the table with the most atomic data. In other words, it's the table that will join to the fact table when the data is loaded into the cube.

5. On the Select The Main Dimension Table page of the wizard, you also need to select the key column or columns that uniquely identify each dimension member, which in this example is *ProductID*. It's selected for you because the key column was defined in the DSV. By default, a dimension uses the same column for the key column and name column, but you can override this behavior by selecting a different name column. Because *ProductID* isn't particularly meaningful to end users, select *Name* in the Column Containing The Member Name (Optional) drop-down list, as shown in Figure 22-5. Click Next.

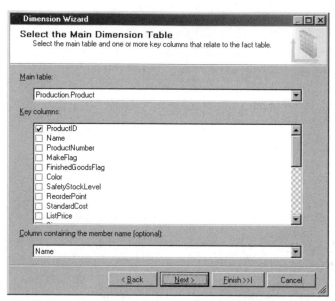

**Figure 22-5**    The Select The Main Dimension Table page of the Dimension Wizard.

6.  The *Production.ProductCategory* and *Production.ProductSubcategory* tables are already selected as related tables because they are related to the main table, *Production.Product*, in the DSV. Data in these two tables should be considered for attributes and hierarchies in the dimension, so you should keep the default selection of these tables on this page. Click Next.

7.  On the Select Dimension Attributes page of the wizard, clear the check boxes next to the following attributes, which all appear together at the bottom of the attribute list on the Select Dimension Attributes page of the wizard: *Name, Product Subcategory – Rowguid, Product Subcategory – Modified Date, Product Category – Name, Product Category – Rowguid,* and *Product Category – Modified Date.*

    All columns from the main table and related tables are selected as dimension attributes by default. You can eliminate any attributes that aren't appropriate for your analytical solution, such as the Rowguid and Modified Date columns that are used to manage data in the OLTP but aren't useful at all for analysis.

8.  To better view the contents of the dropdown lists on this page of the wizard, maximize the dialog box. Locate the row for *Product Subcategory*, and then select *Production.ProductSubcategory.Name* in the Attribute Name Column drop-down list. Next, locate the row for *Product Category*, and then select *Production.ProductCategory.Name* in the corresponding Attribute Name Column drop-down list. Just as the

main table can have a key column and name column defined, you can also distinguish between key columns and name columns for other attributes in a dimension. Click Next.

---

**Note** You can also change the name of the attribute on this page of the wizard. For example, you might want to simplify *Product Category* and *Product Subcategory* to *Category* and *Subcategory,* respectively. Just click in the Attribute Name column and type a more desirable name. You can also rename the attributes later by modifying the attribute's *Name* property directly in the dimension designer.

---

9. On the Specify Dimension Type page of the wizard, the default dimension type is Regular. Some client applications can use dimension types to display information a certain way. For example, a dimension type of Geography might be used by a mapping application to overlay Analysis Services data on maps. For this example, keep the default setting for this dimension. Click Next to continue.

10. On the Define Parent-Child Relationship page, you do not need to make changes since the tables with which you are working do not contain self-referencing tables required for a parent-child relationship. (Refer to the books recommended at the beginning of this chapter for more information about parent-child relationships.) Click Next to continue to the next step of the wizard.

11. After the Detecting Hierarchies task is complete, click Next to review the hierarchies automatically created by the wizard. You can only remove levels from a hierarchy on this page. You can make all other changes to the hierarchies, such as adding levels or renaming levels, in the dimension designer. Click Next to continue.

12. Change the name of the dimension if desired, and then click Finish. When the wizard completes, *Product.dim* is added as a new object in the Dimensions folder of the Solution Explorer window. In the main window of Visual Studio, you see the dimension designer, shown in Figure 22-6. The dimension designer has three tabs: Dimension Structure, Translations, and Browser.

    The Dimension Structure tab displays a list of dimension attributes and a diagram of each table in the DSV used to build the dimension. If you click an attribute in the list, you can view the attribute's properties in the Properties window in the lower right corner.

13. In the Hierarchies and Levels pane of the Dimension Structure tab, right-click *Product Category − Product Subcategory*, click Rename, and then type **Category**. The

Dimension Wizard automatically creates this user hierarchy based on the relationships between the three tables selected for this dimension.

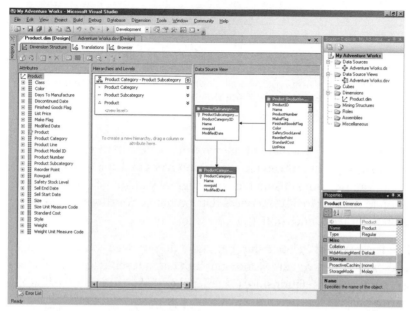

**Figure 22-6**   The Dimension Designer.

## Using the Dimension Browser

You can review the members in each attribute and each user hierarchy on the Browser tab of the dimension designer. However, before you browse the dimension, you must process the dimension, which requires you first to deploy the dimension definition to the Analysis Services server and then process the entire Analysis Services database. Details about deployment and processing are explained later in this chapter. To deploy and browse a dimension, follow these steps:

1. To follow this example, you must complete the steps described in the previous sections of this chapter. Click the Browser tab. Because the dimension in this case has not yet been deployed to the Analysis Server, an error message displays to indicate the dimension is unavailable for browsing.

2. Right-click the project in the Solution Explorer window, and then click Deploy.

---

**Note**   The default target server for deployment is the local server. To deploy to a different server, right-click the project in the Solution Explorer

window, click Properties, click Deployment in the Configuration Properties
tree, and then change the Server property to the correct server.

3. When deployment is complete, click the Reconnect button in the Browser toolbar.
   Any change to an object in an Analysis Services project requires a deployment of
   those changes to the server. Afterwards, you always use the Reconnect button in the
   Browser tab of a designer to reestablish the client-server connection.

4. Notice *Category* is automatically selected in the Hierarchy drop-down list. .Click the
   plus sign to the left of the All member in the Category hierarchy tree to view the
   members of this user hierarchy, as shown in Figure 22-7. You can also view each
   attribute hierarchy, which consists of an All member on the top level and distinct
   attribute members on the leaf level.

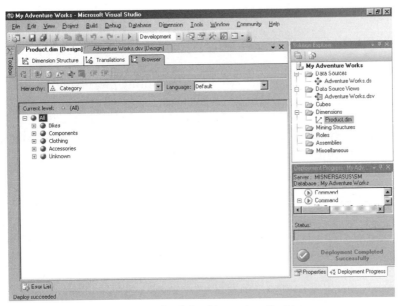

**Figure 22-7**   The Browser tab of the Dimension Designer.

## Building a Server Time Dimension

If your source database is not a standard data warehouse and if the fact table also contains a datetime column, you can create a Server Time Dimension to facilitate analysis by
time. To create a Server Time Dimension, follow these steps:

1. To follow this example, you must complete the steps described in the previous sections of this chapter. In Solution Explorer, right-click the Dimensions folder, click

New Dimension, and then click Next three times (or twice if you have disabled the Welcome page of the wizard). These steps might seem counterintuitive because you really don't have a data source, but your goal is to get to the Select The Dimension Type page of the wizard. Here you select Server Time Dimension, and then click Next.

---

**Note**   If you do, in fact, have a time dimension table available in a data warehouse, it's considered best practice to build an Analysis Services dimension from that table. Instead of selecting Server Time Dimension on the Select the Dimension Type page of the wizard, you select Time Dimension and choose the specific table in the available drop-down list. Whether you create a Server Time Dimension or a Time Dimension, it's important to note that these dimension types are different from any other dimension because they relate to time. Analysis Services has several features that depend on the existence of a correctly typed Time dimension, such as special calculation functions and aggregation behaviors.

---

2.  Set values for First Calendar Day and Last Calendar Day on the Define Time Periods page of the wizard. The date range you specify here must include all dates found in the fact table, or an error will be raised during processing. In the *AdventureWorks SalesOrderHeader* table, the earliest *OrderDate* is July 1, 2001, and the latest *OrderDate* is July 31, 2004, so set First Calendar Day and Last Calendar Day to these dates, respectively. Click the arrow in the drop-down list to set specific dates using a calendar control.

3.  In the Time Periods list, select Year, Quarter, and Month. Date is automatically selected because it's required to create the dimension. Click Next.

4.  The Select Calendars page of the wizard gives you an opportunity to choose other calendars for alternate reporting purposes, such as Fiscal Calendar or Manufacturing Calendar. For more information about these calendar types, refer to the topic "Time (SSAS)" in SQL Server Books Online. To continue this example, you won't select any additional calendars. Click Finish twice to complete the wizard. Take a moment to review the new dimension, as shown in Figure 22-8.

# Cube Design

When you build a cube, you select measures from one or more fact tables and define the type of relationships present between fact tables and dimension tables. For example, a regular relationship between a fact table and dimension table includes properties to specify the key columns in each table that are related. This relationship type will likely satisfy your design requirements most of the time, but you can also define Data Mining, Fact,

Many-To-Many, and Reference relationships. (You can learn more about defining these relationships by reading "Dimension Relationships (SSAS)" in SQL Server Books Online.) Start cube design by using the Cube Wizard to establish the basic definition of the cube, and then make changes using the cube designer. As you work, you can periodically deploy and process the Analysis Services project to test your design by browsing the cube.

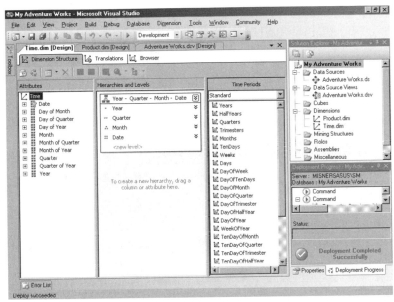

Figure 22-8   A Server Time Dimension.

## Using the Cube Wizard

The Cube Wizard steps you through the process of identifying tables and selecting measures. The wizard also examines the DSV to determine how tables are related so that initial dimension relationships can be added to the cube definition. To create a cube, follow these steps:

1.  To follow this example, you must complete the steps described in the previous sections of this chapter. In Solution Explorer, right-click the Cube folder, and then click New Cube to launch the New Cube Wizard.

2.  Click Next until you reach the Identify Fact And Dimension Tables. Clear the *Production.ProductCategory* and *Production.ProductSubcategory* check boxes, as shown in Figure 22-9.

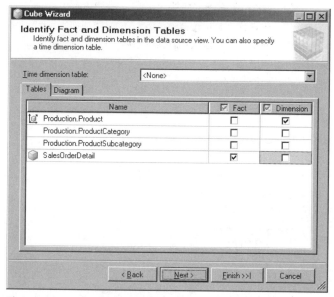

**Figure 22-9**   The Identify Fact And Dimension Tables page of the Cube Wizard.

The wizard requires the selection of one related dimension table for each selected fact table. This requirement is met only when the DSV includes a foreign key relationship between the two tables.

3.   Click Next, and then click >> to move all available dimensions—*Product* and *Time*—to the Cube Dimensions list, and then click Next.

4.   Select the top check box to clear the default selection of all measures, and then select the check boxes to the left of *Order Qty* and to the left of *Line Total*. Type **Order Quantity** as a new name for *Order Qty* and **Sales Amount** for *Line Total*. You can also type a new name of the measure group here if you wish, or you can edit the name in the cube designer.

5.   Click Next twice, change the cube name to **My Adventure Works**, and then click Finish to view the cube designer, as shown in Figure 22-10.

The Cube Structure tab provides access to properties of measure groups, measures, and dimensions in the cube. When you click an object on this tab, you can view its properties in the Properties window and make any necessary changes. You can, for example, rename an object by typing a new name in the Name property box if you missed this step while using the Cube Wizard.

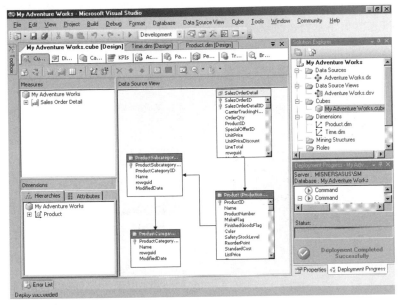

**Figure 22-10**   The Cube Designer.

6. Expand a measure group, such as *SalesOrderDetail* in this example, in the Measures pane to view its measures. To access properties for a measure group or for a measure, such as *Order Quantity*, right-click the object in the Measures pane and then click Properties. The Properties window displays all properties associated with the selected object. The first property you should change for each measure is the *FormatString* property so that measures display properly in the cube browser. You can use standard format strings by selecting a value in the *FormatString* property drop-down list, or you can type a custom format string into the box. For example, you might want to replace the Currency format with $#,# if you want to exclude decimal places in currency values. To continue this example, change the *FormatString* property for *Order Quantity* to **#,#** and change this property for *Sales Amount* to **$#,#**.

> **Note**   Not all cube browsers use the *FormatString* property. Before you spend a lot of time adjusting this property, be sure you know whether the users' client applications will use this property to format values.

7. Notice the *Time* dimension is not visible in the Dimensions pane in the lower left corner of the Cube Structure tab. Because the Cube Wizard didn't recognize which datetime column to use with this dimension, you must manually relate the Server Time dimension with the measure group. Right-click anywhere in the Dimensions pane, click Add Cube Dimension, click *Time*, and click OK.

8. Click the Dimension Usage tab (the second tab in the cube designer), click the intersection of *Time* and *Sales Order Detail*, and then click the ellipsis button that displays in the intersection, as seen in Figure 22-11.

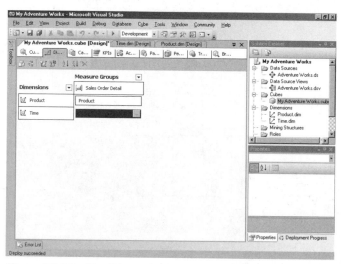

**Figure 22-11** The Dimension Usage tab of the Cube Designer.

9. In the Define Relationship dialog box, select Regular in the Select Relationship Type drop-down list, click *Date* in the Granularity Attribute drop-down list, and then click *OrderDate* in the Measure Group Columns drop-down list, as shown in Figure 22-12. Click OK. By defining the relationship type, the data in the measure group can be correctly analyzed by the *Time* dimension.

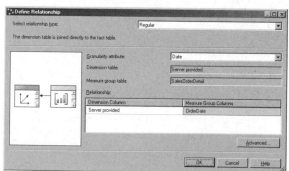

**Figure 22-12** The Define Relationship Dialog Box.

10. Right-click the project in the Solution Explorer window, and then click Deploy.

## Using the Cube Browser

As with dimensions, you must deploy a cube before you can browse it. Visual Studio deploys and processes only those changes made to the database design since the last deployment. It has no way of recognizing whether changes to underlying data have been made, so you will need to manually start processing if you know data has changed but there are no design changes to trigger processing.

The Browser tab of the cube designer includes a Microsoft Office Web Components (OWC) pivot table control with a special metadata pane not available in standard OWC. The metadata pane organizes database objects—measure groups, measures, and dimensions—in a tree view, as shown in Figure 22-13.

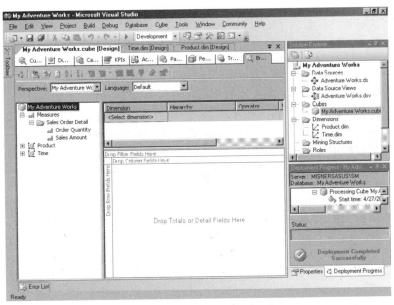

**Figure 22-13**   The Browser tab in the Cube Designer.

You can select items in the metadata tree to do any of the following tasks:

- Drag measures together or individually to the pivot table section labeled Drop Totals or Detail Fields Here to view aggregated values.

- Drag one or more attributes or user hierarchies to Drop Row Fields Here or Drop Column Fields Here to slice and dice, or drill between levels of a user hierarchy or from one attribute to another attribute on the same axis (rows or columns). To pivot, you can move an attribute to the opposite axis, such as from rows to columns.

- Filter aggregated values by dragging one or more attributes to Drop Filter Fields Here.

- Create a *subcube*, which is a subset of a cube based on a filter defined at the top of the Cube Browser. By reducing the scope of data to query from a full cube to a subcube, you can improve query performance.

---

**Note**    Each time you drag a database object into or out of the pivot table control or the subcube filter, you execute a new query. If you are working with a cube containing a large amount of data, you might find performance improves if you create a subcube first and then create your query. Incidentally, the subcube filter included on the Cube Browser tab issues a CREATE SUBCUBE statement. This statement is new to the multidimensional expressions (MDX) language used to query and model Analysis Services. It's not supported by the standard OWC pivot table control. This control has been adapted for use with the cube browser in Visual Studio and SQL Server Management Studio.

---

## Reviewing Advanced Cube Design Features

There is much, much more you can do to enhance the design of a cube that you can learn about in any of the books referenced at the beginning of this chapter. You can also study the design of Microsoft's sample database and use the SQL Server 2005 Analysis Services Tutorial in SQL Server Books Online to learn more about the more advanced design features you can use. You must explicitly install the sample databases during installation of SQL Server, as explained earlier in this book. Using Visual Studio, open the Adventure Works solution located in the %Program Files%\Microsoft SQL Server\90\Tools\Samples\AdventureWorks Analysis Services Project\Enterprise folder. Double-click the Adventure Works.cube file in Solution Explorer to open the cube designer, and then navigate to each of the tabs described in the following list to study the implemented design techniques:

- **Dimension usage**    Shows which dimensions are associated with which measure groups. If an icon exists, it indicates a special relationship type, such as Many-To-Many. Click the intersection of a dimension and measure group, and then click the ellipsis button in the intersection to view the columns used to define the relationship between tables.

- **Calculations**    Lists the MDX calculations used to add new measures, new dimension members, and sets to the cube. These calculations may be visible to end users for use in a query, or they may be hidden if used as an intermediate step in a more complex calculation. You can view all calculations in the form of a complete MDX script if you click the Script View button in the toolbar. When using Script View, you can use Visual Studio's debugging feature to step through the script and monitor the changes to the cube values as each calculation is executed.

> **Note**   A good resource for getting started with MDX is *Fast Track to MDX Second Edition* by Mark Whitehorn, Robert Zare, and Mosha Pasumansky, Springer, 2005. MDX unleashes the power of Analysis Services cubes and is well worth the effort to learn if you are responsible for cube development.

- **KPIs**   Lists the KPI calculations added to a cube. You must use a client application that supports Analysis Services KPIs to enable end user access to the results of these calculations.

- **Actions**   Lists commands that execute in the context of the user's current position in the cube. This feature requires a client application that supports Analysis Services actions to drillthrough to underlying source data, open a related Reporting Services report, or execute a generic action. For example, an action can navigate to a specific URL (defined by the object the user clicked to launch the action) using Microsoft Internet Explorer.

- **Partitions**   Lists the partitions, storage methods, and aggregation design for each measure group. You can also work with partitions using SQL Server Management Studio as explained later in this chapter.

- **Perspectives**   Organizes measure groups and dimensions into smaller sets of database objects to simplify the user experience.

- **Translations**   Defines the translated captions for database objects, such as measures, calculations, dimensions, and so on.

# Managing Analysis Services

If you're responsible for maintaining a cube once the development phase is complete, the remainder of this chapter should be of high interest to you. Now it's time to switch to a new environment, SQL Server Management Studio, to review its features for managing Analysis Services servers, including server configuration and deployment options for moving Analysis Services databases between servers. We'll also review your options for managing scalability with partitioning, storage modes, and aggregations. Then, we'll take a look at the various processing methods available for keeping cubes as up-to-date as possible and at security for managing access to cube data. Finally, we'll briefly examine the use of SQL Server Profiler and the Windows Performance Tool for monitoring and troubleshooting Analysis Services.

## Analysis Server Configuration

There are many Analysis Services server properties you can configure to manage the behavior of the server. Using SQL Server Management Studio, you can change settings that define folder locations for storing Analysis Services databases, specify server security rules, or manage memory, network connectivity, or availability of data mining algorithms, to name a few uses. To configure an Analysis Services server, follow these steps:

1. Start SQL Server Management Studio. In the Connect to Server dialog box, select Analysis Services in the Server Type drop-down list. In the Server Name drop-down list, select the Analysis Server instance to configure. Click OK.

2. In Object Explorer, right-click the Analysis Server instance and then click Properties. To make changes, you type a new value in the Value column. An example of a change you might want to make is the default port on which the server is listening for client requests. The Port property is accessible when you select the Show Advanced (All) Properties check box.

   As the Restart column shown in Figure 22-14 indicates, certain properties require the server to restart. Other properties are in effect when you click OK to close the Analysis Server Properties dialog box.

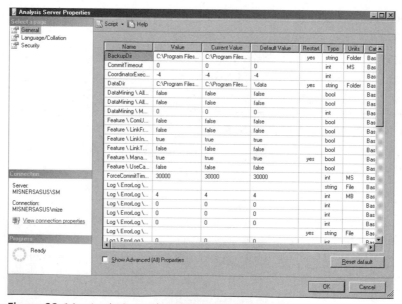

**Figure 22-14**   Analysis Services Server Properties.

# Deployment Options

The development cycle of an Analysis Services project is usually an iterative process in which database objects are designed in Visual Studio on a client workstation, the definition of these objects is copied to the Analysis Services server, and then the objects are processed on a development server to create the physical structure of these objects and load the structures with data. When the development cycle is complete, you need to move the database to a production server. In this section, we'll show you three different ways that you can move a database from one server to another.

> **Note**   You can work directly with the database objects on the server if you select Open from the File menu in Visual Studio and then select Analysis Services Database. In the Connect To Database dialog box, specify a server and database name. Visual Studio creates a project, but your changes are applied to the server object as soon as you save its definition file and usually require reprocessing the object. Reprocessing can impact users if the database is in production.

> **Best Practices**   Nothing prevents two developers from making changes to the same object and overwriting each other's work. Therefore, it's recommended that you work in the disconnected design mode, which is the default mode when you create a new Analysis Services project in Visual Studio. Development teams can check out objects when using source control to ensure that only one person at a time is working on a particular object definition.

## Using the Analysis Services Deployment Wizard

You can configure project properties in Visual Studio to specify a target server for deployment and then deploy directly from the design environment. However, once an Analysis Services database is in production, there is a risk that your project definition files no longer match the current definitions on the server because an administrator might modify partitions or security using SQL Server Management Studio. Fortunately, you have the option to use the Analysis Services Deployment Wizard which asks you whether to maintain or replace existing partition, security, and configuration settings. You can run this wizard in either of two modes:

- **Interactive deployment**   Use this mode to run deployment immediately on completion of the wizard.

- **Script deployment**   Use this mode to define deployment properties and generate a script to run deployment later. The script can be executed manually in SQL Server Management Studio or scheduled as part of a SQL Server Agent job.

Before using the deployment wizard, you need to create a set of input files for the wizard. Just right-click the project in Visual Studio's Solution Explorer, and click Build. A set of four XML files—Analysis Services Database Deployment Contents, Analysis Services Database Deployment Configuration Settings, Analysis Services Database Deployment Options, and Analysis Services Database Deployment Targets—are created and placed in your project's bin folder. You can leave these files in place or move them to another server that has Analysis Services components installed. When you start the Analysis Services Deployment Wizard, you provide the path to these files.

If you prefer to use interactive deployment, you can access the Deployment Wizard from the Microsoft SQL Server 2005/Analysis Services program group. As you step through the wizard, you are prompted for the path to the database file, the target server and database name, options for replacing or ignoring partition and security settings as shown in Figure 22-15, configuration changes such as the data source or data source impersonation information, and processing options.

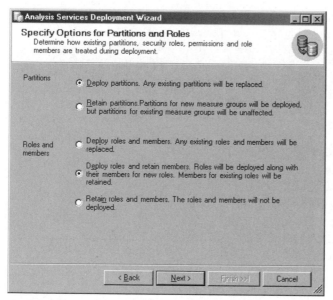

**Figure 22-15**   The Specify Options For Partitions And Roles page of the Deployment Wizard.

The wizard builds the necessary structures on the target Analysis Services server and load data into these structures. If the database already exists on the target server, the wizard deploys updates, just as deployment from Visual Studio behaves. The wizard then determines which objects require processing and processes these objects in sequence.

## Using the Synchronize Database Wizard

An alternative to rebuilding and reprocessing structures on another server is synchronizing data. When you synchronize databases, only the changed objects are affected. Users can continue to query the original version of the database, and then the Analysis Services server gracefully replaces the original version with the synchronized version when synchronization is complete. To start the Synchronize Database Wizard, connect to the target server in SQL Server Management Studio, right-click the Databases folder, and then click Synchronize. After you specify the source server and database, you choose the extent to which security should also be synchronized. You can synchronize all security settings, synchronize roles without membership, or bypass security synchronization altogether. Another important optional setting in the wizard is Use Compression When Synchronizing Databases, which can reduce the impact of send large data volumes across your network. As with the Deployment Wizard, you can run the synchronization when you finish the wizard, or you can generate a script to use later.

## Backing Up and Restoring a Database

Certainly, making regular backups should be a standard administration task, but it's also one more way to move a database from one server to another. In SQL Server Management Studio, connect to Analysis Services, right-click the Analysis Services database, and click Back Up. When you create a backup, both the data and the metadata are stored in a single file. There is no restriction on the size of the database. When you create the backup, you can control whether an existing backup can be overwritten, specify whether the backup file should be compressed, or encrypt the backup file with a password by selecting the applicable options, as shown in Figure 22-16.

> **Note** You can automate this process by using SQL Server Agent. In the Backup Database dialog box, click Script in the toolbar and select Script Action To Clipboard. Create a new SQL Server job and then create a new step. (For more information about creating and automating jobs, refer to the SQL Server Books Online topic, "Creating Jobs.") Change the Type to SQL Server Analysis Services Command and then paste the script into the Command box.

When you need to restore the backup, right-click the Databases folder for the Analysis Services instance in SQL Server Management Studio, provide a name for the database, and provide the path to the backup file. You can specify whether to overwrite an existing database and whether to restore security information from the backup. If you encrypted the database during backup, you'll need the password to restore it.

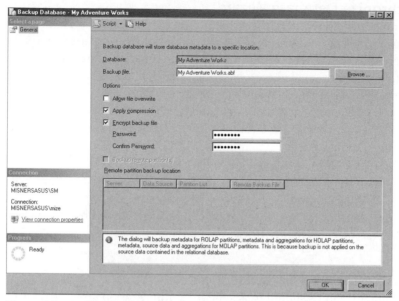

Figure 22-16    The Backup Database dialog box.

# Partitions

Every Analysis Services cube has one *partition* for each measure group by default. If the fact table on which a measure group has fewer than 50 million rows, you don't need to worry about adding more partitions. However, for larger fact tables, partitioning is a critical strategy for managing physical storage, minimizing processing time, and boosting query performance. While you can use Developer Edition to design and implement partitions on a development server, you must use Enterprise Edition for your production server.

## Creating a Partition

You can design partitions on the Partitions tab of the cube designer in Visual Studio, but once a database is in production you'll likely use SQL Server Management Studio to create, modify, or delete partitions. Both environments use the Partition Wizard to create a new partition. To use the Partition Wizard in SQL Server Management Studio, follow these steps.

1. In SQL Server Management Studio, connect to Analysis Services, and then expand the following folders: Databases, Adventure Works DW, Cubes, Adventure Works, Measure Groups, Internet Sales, and Partitions. There are four existing partitions for the Internet Sales measure group, as shown in Figure 22-17.

> **Note** To follow this example, deploy the sample Adventure Works solution using the Analysis Services Deployment Wizard which is described in the previous section of this chapter. The location of the database file is <drive>:\<SQL Server install directory>\90\Tools\Samples\AdventureWorks Analysis Services Project.

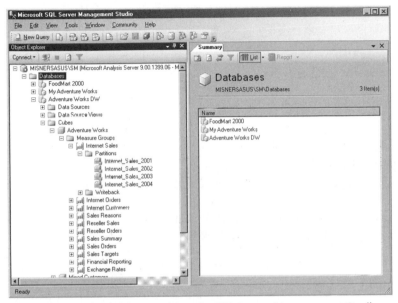

**Figure 22-17** Reviewing partitions in SQL Server Management Studio.

You can double click a partition in Object Explorer to open the Partition Properties dialog box. Each of the Internet Sales partitions is configured identically, except the source data for each partition is based on a different query which separates the fact table into four sets of sales transactions, one for each year of data.

2. Right-click the Partitions folder, click New Partition, and then click Next on the Welcome page. Select the fact table associated with the measure group, which in this case is dbo.FactInternetSales, and then click Next.

3. On the Restrict Rows page of the Partition Wizard, you define which data will be selected from the fact table and loaded into the partition. If you maintain separate fact tables for each partition, you're done with the wizard and can click Finish. However, if you plan to create multiple partitions from a single fact table, you need to create a SELECT statement with a WHERE clause to specify which data should be loaded into this partition. Select the Specify A Query To Restrict Rows check box.

The Query box is automatically populated with a SELECT statement that includes all columns in the fact table as defined in the Data Source View.

4.  Scroll to bottom of the Query box and type **orderdatekey > 1280** after WHERE to add a filter to the SELECT statement. This query is now modified to include data for sales occurring after the last date included in the Internet_Sales_2004 partition. In your own partition, you should use a WHERE clause that specifies both a beginning and ending range. Click the Check button to confirm the query parses correctly, and then click Next.

---

**Important**   Be very careful when defining the WHERE clause here. There will be no warning if rows selected by this query overlap with rows in another partition's source query.

---

5.  On the Processing And Storage Locations page of the Partition Wizard, you can override the default settings and specify a different location for the partition. It could be in a different location than the existing partitions or even on a different server. Before you decide to implement remote partitions, however, be sure to read "Creating and Managing a Remote Partition" in SQL Server Books Online to verify that you can meet the requirements. Click Next.

6.  Change the name of the partition, and select Design Aggregations Later. (You'll learn more about aggregations in a later section of this chapter.) You can optionally process the partition at this point. Since there is no data in the fact table that meets the criteria you specified in the query, you can skip processing. Click Finish.

The new partition displays in the Partitions folder. At this point, you've defined only which data from which fact table will be loaded into the partition. You can also use SQL Server Management Studio merge partitions if you want to combine data from multiple partitions into a single partition, but you'll need to redefine the source query for the final partition because the query won't change automatically. You can change the source query in the partition's Partition Properties dialog box.

## Specifying a Storage Mode

With each partition, you need to consider how the data will be stored physically. Conceivably, if you had three partitions in a cube, each partition could be designed with a different storage mode. Both dimensions and partitions can be designed to use one of the following three storage modes:

- **Multidimensional OLAP (MOLAP)**   Keeps detailed data and aggregations in a multidimensional compressed proprietary structure. With this method, the relational source is accessed only during processing, and queries are resolved entirely from the multidimensional store. It provides the fastest query performance, but it requires a periodic refresh to stay consistent with the relational data. On average, the amount of space required to maintain a copy of detailed data into the MOLAP store is about 20 percent more than the space required for the relational source (without indexes). The query performance gained by using MOLAP more than compensates for additional space required.

- **Hybrid OLAP (HOLAP)**   Keeps aggregations only in the multidimensional store and leaves detailed data in the relational source. Processing is faster than MOLAP because the activities are limited to calculating and storing the aggregations. Queries that require detailed data are slower than queries that can be resolved using aggregations. This option may be best for historical data that is infrequently accessed.

- **Relational OLAP (ROLAP)**   Keeps detailed data and aggregations in the relational source. Queries run more slowly as a consequence and processing runs more slowly when aggregations are involved. The most common reason to use ROLAP is to support real-time analysis when the source database is continually updated.

> **Note**   Unless you have a good reason not to, you should always use the MOLAP storage mode. It's optimized specifically for best performance and processing and provides efficient storage, all important characteristics for an OLAP product.

To configure the storage mode of a partition in SQL Server Management Studio, follow these steps:

1. In SQL Server Management Studio, connect to Analysis Services, expand the Databases folder, expand any database folder, expand the Cubes folder, and then expand the appropriate Measure Groups and Partitions folders. Right-click a partition, click Properties, and then click Proactive Caching.

2. Move the slider to a different storage setting, as shown in Figure 22-18. Here you have many more options than the three storage modes explained at the beginning of this section, but they are simply variations on the same theme. Each of

the MOLAP modes corresponds to a different processing option, which will be explained later in this chapter. Click OK.

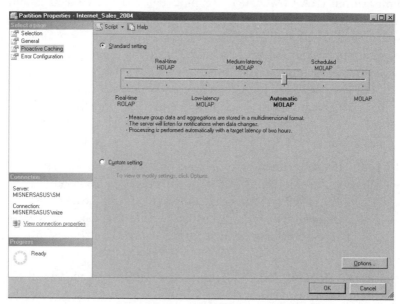

**Figure 22-18**   The Proactive Caching page of the Partition Properties dialog box.

## Designing Aggregations

We mentioned previously that one important benefit of partitioning is the ability to design aggregations differently for each partition. Proper design aggregation is a balancing act between the impact on processing, the additional storage required for aggregations, and the effect on query performance. From a practical perspective, you don't need to worry much about aggregations if you don't have data large enough to require adding partitions to your cube. For large data volumes, aggregations help Analysis Services respond to queries more quickly. As an example, if I ask for yearly sales data and if an aggregated value for each year is already stored, Analysis Services can return those values rather than compute the sum of each year at query time.

Analysis Services uses a special algorithm to factor the number of attributes against the number of rows in a partition so that it can weigh the cost of calculating and storing the aggregation against the benefit of having the aggregation ready to respond to a query. You use the Aggregation Design Wizard to provide counts by partition and by attribute as input values for the algorithm. You can start this wizard on the Partitions tab of the cube designer in Visual Studio, or you can start it from the Partitions folder in SQL

Server Management Studio. To design aggregations in SQL Server Management Studio, follow these steps:

1. Start SQL Server Management Studio, and connect to Analysis Services. In the Object Explorer of SQL Server Management Studio, expand the Cubes folder in any database, and then expand one of the nested Measure Groups. Right-click the Partitions folder, and then click Design Aggregations. Click Next to skip the Welcome page of the wizard.

2. On the Select Partitions To Modify page of the wizard, select the partitions for which you want to design aggregations. Click Next.

---

**Note**   Because you can design both storage mode and aggregations using this wizard, any storage settings you might have previously defined for the selected partitions are replaced by the storage mode you select on the next page of the wizard.

---

3. Change the storage setting if desired, and then click Next.

4. On the Specify Object Counts page of the wizard, click Count. The wizard counts rows in the fact table and in the partition. You can also enter an Estimated Count or a Partition Count directly. Estimated Count is the default count for the partition, but if you type a Partition Count, the number you provide is used instead of Estimated Count. The wizard won't design aggregations if both counts are zero. Click Next.

---

**Note**   There is considerably more to learn about working with counts on this page of the wizard to design efficient aggregations. This example produces a reasonable design but perhaps not the most optimal one that could be created for your data volumes. Refer to the books recommended at the beginning of this chapter for more complete coverage of this topic.

---

5. On the Set Aggregation Options page of the wizard, click Performance Gain Reaches, change the corresponding percentage value if desired, and then click Start. The wizard reviews all possible aggregations that are expected to produce the specified performance gain (unless you click Stop). Usually, the default performance gain setting of 30% percent is adequate. You can repeat this process with different percentages and test the cube by running queries to gauge the effect of adding or decreasing aggregations. When the wizard finishes its calculations, the number of aggregations that have been designed displays at the bottom of the page, as shown in Figure 22-19 in which the default value of 30 was retained. Click Next.

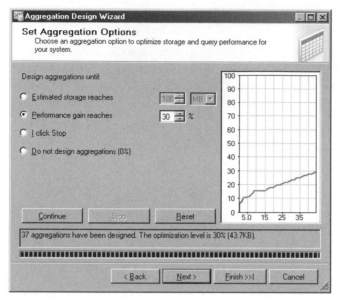

**Figure 22-19**   The Set Aggregation Options page of the Aggregation Design Wizard.

6. You can choose to process the partition now, which includes calculating and storing the aggregations, or you can save the aggregation design if you want to defer processing to a later time. Click Finish.

---

**Note**   If you have C# .NET installed in Visual Studio 2005, you can open the AMOBrowser sample application included by Microsoft. To launch the samples installer, click Microsoft SQL Server 2005 Samples in the Microsoft SQL Server 2005/Documentation and Tutorials/Samples program group. Then, using Visual Studio, open the AMOBrowser.sln in the <drive>:\Program Files\Microsoft SQL Server 2005 Samples\AnalysisServices\Programmability\AMO\AmoBrowser\CS folder.

### Real World   Usage-Based Optimization

The Aggregation Design Wizard uses a mathematical algorithm to determine optimal aggregations based on data density, but it's entirely possible that end users create queries that never use the resulting aggregation. Of course, that defeats the whole purpose of using processing time and disk storage space in the first place. You want aggregations that help user queries run faster, but there's no way to know in advance what those queries might be. Consequently, the Aggregation Design Wizard is merely an interim step so that you have some aggregations that might help some queries and, if you're lucky, most aggregations will help many queries.

To take aggregation design to the next step, you need to know what kind of queries are executing. Fortunately, Analysis Services provides two tools to help you improve aggregations based on actual user activity. First, there is a query log that you must activate on the server to store information about queries. Second, you use the Usage-Based Optimization Wizard to analyze the query log and redesign aggregations accordingly.

To activate the query log, follow these steps:

1. Open SQL Server Management Studio, connect to Analysis Services, right-click the Analysis Server in the Object Explorer window, and then click Properties.

2. Change the Log \ QueryLog \ CreateQueryLogTable property in the Value column to True.

3. Type a server name in the Log \ QueryLog \ QueryLogConnectionString property, specify authentication, and provide a database name. A table will be added to this database for storing query details when you close the Properties dialog box. Notice that the Log \ QueryLog \ QueryLogTableName property defaults to OlapQueryLog. You can change this name if you like.

4. Optionally, you can change Log \ QueryLog \ QueryLogSampling property if you want a different sampling rate for queries. You probably don't need to capture each and every query, but you do want to capture enough to be representative of normal user activity.

You should allow sufficient time for data to build up in the query log. Every situation is different, but a week should be the minimum amount of time that you capture data for the query log. Usually a month provides a better sampling of queries. Be sure to deactivate the query log by changing the sampling rate to 0 when you have finished redesigning aggregations because query sampling just adds unnecessary overhead. You can launch the Usage-Based Optimization Wizard in either Visual Studio or SQL Server Management Studio, just like the Aggregation Design Wizard. Simply right-click the Partitions folder or a specific partition, and then click Usage Based Optimization. You'll first use the Usage Analysis Wizard, which allows you to select the logged queries to analyze and then launches the Aggregation Design Wizard. In the Usage Analysis Wizard, you select criteria to filter the queries for optimization by any or all of the following criteria: Beginning Date, Ending Date, Users, and Most Frequent Queries. If you change the design of any dimension object, you should manually clear out the query log and start a new sampling session to ensure the optimizations apply only to the most current design.

## Processing Data

Recall our earlier discussion of MOLAP, which pointed out that partition data does not stay synchronized with the relational source data. You must process the partitions manually or on a scheduled basis to refresh the data. Whether this occurs nightly, weekly, or even less frequently depends on how often the relational source changes and how current the information needs to be for users. To manually process an object, just right-click the object in Visual Studio or SQL Server Management Studio, click Process, and then choose your processing options. You can also use Integration Services to schedule processing of individual database objects, such as dimensions or partitions, as well as entire databases. As a third alternative, you can generate XMLA scripts that you schedule for execution using SQL Server Agent. One more approach, which we'll explain more fully later in this section, is to use Proactive Caching to process automatically when the relational data source changes.

### Processing Options

Once you have determined when processing should occur, you need to think about what data will be processed. The easiest approach is to do a full process each time, which rebuilds the physical structures and reloads all data from the partition's source table or source query. If any problems occur during processing, the database is rolled back to its original state. Performing a full process is a perfectly reasonable approach if you have small data volumes or if you need to process relatively infrequently.

Another approach particularly well-suited for partitioned cubes is incremental processing. As with full processing, you can use an Integration Services task or scripting to manage incremental processing. If your partitions are filtered by time slices, such as by year or by month, you need only to load data into the most current partition and process that partition independently. Although you can do a full process of the single partition, you can optimize processing performance by configuring an incremental process to use a query that selects records for loading into the partition. Typically, this query returns a relatively small number of records that can be easily appended to existing records in the partition. Aggregations are also updated during processing. The most important thing to know about incremental processing is that you must be extremely careful not to duplicate data already in the partition.

---

**More Info**    There are several more processing options available. A good reference describing these options and the impact of processing on dependent objects is available at *http://msdn.microsoft.com/library/default.asp?url=/library/en-us/dnsql90/html/sql2k5_asprocarch.asp.*

## Proactive Caching

In most organizations, using scheduled processing remains the preferred approach for most analytical solutions that are strategic in nature and therefore more concerned with high-quality historical data. As hardware and software improvements enable faster access to, transformation of, and delivery of information, the demand for real-time analytical solutions that rely on operational data without first storing information in a data warehouse is rising. Proactive caching provides an alternative to scheduled processing by "listening" for changes to the relational source systems and processing the affected object soon afterwards. As an administrator, you need to decide how Analysis Services is notified about changed data and how queries are answered while processing is underway. You can configure proactive caching for individual partitions as well as for dimensions. To configure Proactive Caching for a partition, follow these steps:

1. Start SQL Server Management Studio and connect to Analysis Services. In Object Explorer, expand the Cubes folder in any database, and then expand the appropriate Measure Groups and Partitions folders.

2. Right-click a partition, click Properties, and then click Proactive Caching.

3. Move the slider to Automatic MOLAP, and then click Options to view the Storage Options dialog box, shown in Figure 22-20. If you select either of the other two MOLAP options, Medium-Latency MOLAP or Low-Latency OLAP, and then click Options, you see the same dialog box with different selections configured. You can, of course, override the settings here regardless of which MOLAP option you selected on the slider.

   Proactive Caching must be selected on this page to configure Cache Settings. The following list outlines the effect of the main settings:

   ❑ **Silence interval**   The amount of time to wait after updates to the data source have stopped. Once this period of time has elapsed, processing begins.

   ❑ **Silence override interval**   The amount of time to wait before processing starts if updates are still streaming into the relational source. In other words, if changes to the source are detected and activity is still ongoing after the period specified by the Silence Override Interval, Analysis Services will take a snapshot to isolate the records to include in the update process and plunge forward with processing.

   ❑ **Drop outdated cache**   The amount of time to wait before blocking access to the multidimensional store that is now outdated. If processing takes a long time, you can keep the outdated cache available to respond to user queries meanwhile. However, at some point, you might want to have the queries resolved directly from the relational source. Dropping the cache does just that. Use this option when having fresh data is more important than having queries that run quickly. Keep this option disabled if you want to continue to provide the older data from the cache.

❏ **Update the cache periodically**   The amount of time to rebuild the multidimensional store if no changes have been detected in the relational source. This option is typically used independently of the other options to force a periodic refresh of data without using other scheduling methods.

4. Click the Notifications tab, shown in Figure 22-21, to change settings as desired. The notification options define how Analysis Services is notified about data changes in the relational source. The default value is SQL Server, which applies to SQL Server 2000 or higher. Any dimension and fact tables used for the current partition are monitored for changes, but you can also specifically identify tables to be monitored. Alternatively, choose Client Initiated if a client application can send notification of changes, or choose Scheduled Polling if your relational source is not a SQL Server database. For more information about polling queries, refer to SQL Server Books Online.

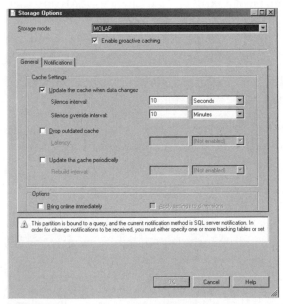

**Figure 22-20**   The General tab of the Storage Options dialog box.

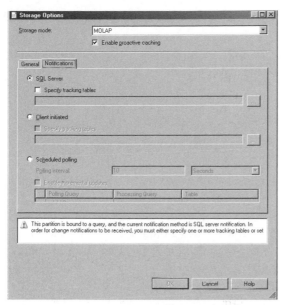

**Figure 22-21**   The Notifications tab of the Storage Options dialog box.

> **Note**   If you use a named query in the data source view, you must explicitly specify tracking tables when using SQL Server notification or use Scheduled Polling instead.

## Security Management

Analysis Services integrates with Windows authentication and then uses a role-based security model to authorize access to a database and its objects. Security can be applied at either the macro or micro level, giving you a degree of control over what people can do or see that should satisfy any security requirement you might have. There are two role types used by Analysis Services to manage security—a server role and a database role. You must add Windows users and groups to one or both of these roles before they can access Analysis Services.

When Analysis Services is installed, all local and domain administrators are enrolled as members of the server role. They are granted server-wide permissions to perform any task on that server. The server role is a fixed role that cannot be renamed or deleted. To manage the server role, connect to Analysis Services in SQL Server Management Studio, right-click the Analysis Services server, click Properties, and then click Security. Here you can add or remove Windows users or groups to the server role. Members of this role can perform the following tasks:

- Create or delete database objects and set properties for these objects using SQL Server Management Studio or Visual Studio.

- Execute programs using AMO to perform administrative tasks.

- Add, change, or delete database roles.

- Use SQL Server Profiler to run traces against Analysis Services.

---

**Note**    You must also be a member of a database role and have process permissions to run traces for processing events.

---

As mentioned, a member of the server role creates a database role for users who need access to objects for processing or users who need to view data. You can even grant a database role member permissions to manage security for a specific database. Adding a member to a database role gives that member access only to the server. You must explicitly grant permissions to the database cubes and dimensions before the member can browse data. To create a database role in SQL Server Management Studio, follow these steps:

1. Start SQL Server Management Studio and connect to Analysis Services. In Object Explorer, expand the Databases folder, expand the database for which you want to create a role, right-click the Roles folder, and then selectclick New Role.

2. On the General page of the Create Role dialog box, provide a name for the role and an optional description. If this role should have some administrative permissions, you can select one or more of the following database permissions:

   - **Full control (administrator)**    As the name implies, the role is granted complete access to all objects in the database.

   - **Process database**    Members of a role limited to this permission can process the database but can't view its data using any client application (including SQL Server Management Studio) unless they belong to another role granting read access.

   - **Read definition**    Members of a role limited to this permission can access metadata but can't view data.

---

**Note**    When a user belongs to more than one role with different permissions, the user is granted all permissions from each role.

---

3.  Click Membership. On this page, you add or remove Windows users or groups.

4.  Click Data Sources. By default, roles are not granted access to the data source since users query the data in the cube. Notice you can grant Read Definition permissions here.

5.  Click Cubes. A new role has no access to cubes in the database by default. When you grant cube access to a role, you need to specify whether access is read only or read/write (for users of writeback applications only). You can also grant permissions for the role to use drillthrough and, optionally, to create a local cube for offline analysis. The role can also have permissions to process specific cubes, but this should be limited to a small number of users.

6.  Click Dimensions. When you grant a role Read or Read/Write access to a cube, then you automatically grant Read access to each dimension in the cube. You can modify permissions here if you need to prevent access to certain dimensions. If you grant permissions here without granting cube permissions, the role members will not be able to view data. Click OK to save the role and close the dialog box.

Most security requirements can be satisfied by controlling access to databases, cubes, and dimensions. To implement security at a more granular level, refer to the topic "Permissions and Access Rights (Analysis Services)" in SQL Server Books Online.

# Performance Management

If you're working with small databases, you're not likely to experience performance problems. As noted several times throughout this chapter, Analysis Services is designed to perform well. As databases get larger, you use partitioning to compensate for the growing data volumes, which in effect makes many smaller cubes that should perform well collectively. You may have to fine-tune your partitioning strategy to get the best performance. To help measure the impact on the server as you work through performance tuning activities, you can use SQL Server Profiler and the Performance Monitor. In this section, we'll explore a few ways you can use these tools to gain a better understanding of what's happening "under the covers."

# SQL Server Profiler

You can use SQL Server Profiler to capture Analysis Services events, whether you just want to monitor activity or you need to troubleshoot performance. Instructions for using SQL Server Profiler are provided in Chapter 30, "Using Profiler, Management Studio, and Database Engine Tuning Adviser." In this section, we'll explain the types of events you can monitor with this tool.

Your operating system includes Windows Management Instrumentation (WMI) to raise events. An *event* provides information about running processes. SQL Server Profiler can listen for events and display them for your review. The following list describes the event categories specific to Analysis Services:

- **Command events**   Tasks that perform an action on the server, such as deployment, processing, and other database administrative activities, whether performed interactively or through scripting

- **Discover events**   Queries to retrieve metadata, such as a list of attribute members in a dimension

- **Discover server state events**   Queries to determine the current state of the server, such as locks on objects or current sessions

- **Errors and warnings events**   Information about error conditions, such as severity level and the application causing the error

- **Notification events**   Information about tasks performed automatically, such as detection of changed data for proactive caching

- **Progress reports events**   Information about the current state of an activity, such as processing a dimension or building aggregations

- **Queries events**   MDX queries received by the server, including execution time

- **Security audit events**   Login and logout information

- **Session events**   Session start and session end information

A particularly handy tool that you can use with SQL Server Profiler is the Flight Recorder. The Analysis Services server has a property, Log \ FlightRecord \ Enabled, that is True by default. When enabled, the Flight Recorder updates a file, FlightRecorderCurrent.trc, in the <SQL Server installation directory>\MSSQL.2\OLAP\Log folder. You can open this file in SQL Server Profiler and replay the trace by pressing F5. SQL Server Profiler simulates the state of the server at the time the trace was captured, which can be helpful for troubleshooting failed queries or processes.

## Performance Counters

Another way to monitor activity on the Analysis Services server is to use performance counters available in the Windows Performance tool. You can use this tool interactively to select specific performance counters and monitor the current values in a graph, or you configure the performance tool to update a log with performance counter values over a period of time. At the time of this writing, Analysis Services performance counters are not documented in SQL Server Books Online.

> **Note**    A Microsoft TechNet white paper, "Microsoft SQL Server 2000 Analysis Services Performance Guide," contains performance counter information and guidelines that are still applicable to Analysis Services 2005. You can find this information at *http://www.microsoft.com/technet/prodtechnol/sql/2000/maintain/ansvcspg.mspx*. All Analysis Services 2005 counters begin with MSAS 2005. You might have to explore different counter groups to find the Analysis Services 2005 equivalent for an Analysis Services 2000 counter.

To start using the Windows Performance tool, follow these steps:

1. In SQL Server Profiler, click the Performance Monitor button.

   > **Note**    Alternatively, in Windows 2003, select Administrative Tools from the Start menu, and then click Performance.

2. Click the New Counter Set button in the toolbar.

3. Right-click anywhere in the graph, and then click Add Counters.

4. Click Use Local Computer Counters, and then, in the Performance Object drop-down list, select a category, such as MSAS 2005: Connection.

5. In the Select Counters From List, select a counter, such as Current User Sessions, and then click Add.

   > **Note**    Click Explain to view a description of the selected counter. You can leave this message box open while you click on other counters.

6. Click Close to close the Add Counters dialog box. Refer to your operating system's help file for more information about using this tool.

# Summary

In this chapter, you've learned about the key features of Analysis Services and how to develop a basic database using the Dimension Wizard and the Cube Wizard. You also learned how to configure server properties, manage large databases through partitioning, keep databases up-to-date, secure Analysis Services databases, and monitor server performance. You should now have a good understanding of how Analysis Services works and how you might use this SQL Server component to expand the data management capabilities of your organization.

# Chapter 23
# Reporting Services

Information locked away in relational or OLAP databases does little to help people make decisions. Although many business applications include reports to present data captured by those applications, these reports have limited value because they don't integrate information with other business applications and because they don't always satisfy the day-to-day business questions that arise. To address these information requirements, organizations often have a team of analysts who are trained to query databases and package the results, whether in a hard-copy report, an Excel spreadsheet, or a professional polished report.

Microsoft SQL Server 2005 Reporting Services, also known as Reporting Services, makes these process easier by providing integrated tools for these analysts to share results across organizations and by enabling non-analysts to develop ad hoc reports. Reporting Services provides an infrastructure for developing, managing, and sharing reports across any size enterprise. More than an application, it's a development platform as well. In this chapter, we'll focus on the basics to show you how to create simple reports and manage the reporting environment.

## What Is Reporting Services?

Reporting Services is the SQL Server 2005 component that uses the Microsoft .NET Framework to support both a Web service and an application programming interface (API) to provide an end-to-end reporting solution for any environment. By end-to-end reporting solution, we mean this component fully supports the *reporting life cycle,* a three-stage process which begins with report authoring, continues with report management, and concludes with delivery of the report to the user community. Many organizations use Reporting Services as a set of applications quite satisfactorily without customization or add-ons. Others use Reporting Services as a development platform to create third-party commercial applications, integrate in-house applications that require reporting, or extend the standard features of Reporting Services with additional capabilities to meet specific requirements of the organization.

# Reporting Services 2005 Versus Reporting Services 2000

Compared to other SQL Server 2005 components, Reporting Services has changed the least because it was added to the SQL Server 2000 platform in 2004. On the surface, nothing looks much different. The architecture and the functionality remains the same, but there are several important changes to the product that affect report developers, Report Server administrators, and the user community. In this section, we'll look at a few of the more significant enhancements. You can find more in-depth information in the SQL Server 2005 Books Online topic, "Reporting Services Enhancements."

## Reporting Services 2005 Enhancements

Let's start our review of Reporting Services 2005 enhancements with changes that affect report authoring. Report developers will notice several new data source options. While Reporting Services 2000 allows you to connect to an Analysis Services 2000 database, you must use an OLE DB provider and then type the query statement using the Multidimensional Expression (MDX) language. Reporting Services 2005 includes a Microsoft SQL Server Analysis Services provider, which has a special query builder interface to eliminate the need to write MDX. Another new data source is an Integration Services package. Instead of persisting transformed data in a data warehouse, you can leverage the Integration Services engine to extract and transform data efficiently and on demand only, and then display the results directly in a report. Also, newly available is the ability to create a dynamic connection that uses an expression to generate the connection string at run-time based on conditions you define in the expression.

During report development, it's common to enhance data retrieved from source systems by adding expressions that perform calculations or set properties of items in the report. The Expression Editor in the Report Designer is much improved, including Intellisense features that provide context-sensitive information about functions, help complete statements, and validate syntax directly within the editor. Report developers also commonly add flexibility to reports by using parameters. Reporting Services 2005 now supports multivalue parameters, enabling users to select one or more values for a single parameter, and adds a calendar control for parameters with a *DateTime* data type.

Report developers can also choose to add new interactive features to a report. For a report that requires scrolling to view all data on a page, a report developer can lock column or row headers in place to enhance the report's readability. Another useful feature is interactive sorting, which allows the user to easily change sort direction of data in the entire report or within a specific data structure while viewing a report.

A significant new feature in Reporting Services 2005 is the ad hoc report authoring tool named Report Builder. This tool is intended for use by users who don't know how to develop queries for relational or OLAP data but do know what information they need to answer a question. Often, information technology staff can't keep up with the requests for more reports, so Report Builder is intended to alleviate the resulting bottleneck and empower users to get quick answers on their own. To support this capability, you must first build a report model that packages the data structures and table relationships in a user-friendly way. Users can then drag and drop items from the report model into a simple report design layout and then run the report to execute the resulting query and view the data.

Looking at the management features of Reporting Services 2005, we find additional tools to simplify administrative tasks. In Reporting Services 2000, you use the Report Manager Web application, command-line utilities, and configuration files to manage server resources and performance. Those tools still exist in Reporting Services 2005, but you can choose to perform many of the same functions with a different tool. First, there is the Reporting Services Configuration tool you can use to configure a local or remote Report Server. In addition, you can use SQL Server Management Studio to access one or more Report Servers within a single interface and perform any of the administrative functions available to you in Report Manager. Next, the SQL Server Surface Area Configuration tool allows you to change the current status of the Report Server Window service, disable scheduling and delivery of reports, disable the Report Server Web service, or disable Windows integrated security for external data sources. Lastly, the SQL Server Configuration Manager provides access to the Windows service properties. You'll find some functionality overlaps between tools, but you benefit by having access to management tools in the environment in which you most frequently work.

## Migration from Reporting Services 2000

Migrating from Reporting Services 2000 is quite simple, and much of the work is done automatically if you upgrade an existing instance. The upgrade procedure changes the definitions of reports on the server, both published reports and report snapshots, to conform to the latest version of Microsoft's Report Definition Language (RDL) schema. If you have report definitions stored elsewhere, such as in a source control system, you can open them in Report Designer, where you are prompted whether to upgrade. Alternatively, if you publish or upload a Reporting Services 2000 report definition directly to a Reporting Services 2005 server, the report definition is automatically upgraded. Once upgraded, the report definition file can no longer be used with Reporting Services 2000.

---

**Important**    If your Reporting Services 2000 implementation uses written custom scripts or applications, you need to test them again to confirm they still work in Reporting Services 2005. Enhancements to the Report Definition Language have also led to changes in the APIs used for scripting or custom development that may require you to rewrite existing applications. For example, the implementation of multivalue parameters has resulted in new methods and properties and rendered others obsolete.

## Reporting Services Fundamentals

As mentioned, Reporting Services provides a platform to fully support authoring, managing, and delivering reports. In this section, we'll introduce important Reporting Services concepts to help you understand how the subcomponents of Reporting Services fit together to provide an end-to-end reporting solution.

Reporting Services supports two types of report authoring—enterprise reporting and ad hoc reporting. Regardless of type, the output of an authoring session is a *report definition* file, with fie extension .rdl, which describes the data, layout, and properties of a report using RDL. RDL is an open schema developed by Microsoft to support the exchange of report definitions between applications creating reports and applications displaying reports. You could manually or programmatically produce the RDL, but the Report Designer is a much easier way.

With enterprise reporting, you can access data from a wide variety of sources, from relational online transactional processing (OLTP) systems and data warehouses to online analytical processing (OLAP) systems like Analysis Services. Enterprise reporting often requires precise layout, use of standard formatting, and insertion of images. While a report could be limited to a single data structure such as a table, an enterprise report quite often combines a table or matrix with a chart. If a report will be distributed primarily in print, page layout and pagination are critical features supported by Reporting Services. If, on the other hand, a report will typically be accessed online, the ability to add interactive features is important. To name just a few interactive features: Reporting Services supports navigation within a report and between reports, parameter selection to filter report contents or change report behavior, and dynamic visibility to switch between a hidden and visible state of selected report items.

Reporting Services supports management activities by providing tools for publishing content to a Report Server and for performing other administrative tasks. Such tasks include setting report properties, managing report execution, and applying security. You can change data content of a report by changing its properties, such as the data source to which it connects or the value of parameters used to filter content. To effectively manage server and network resources, you can control when and how reports execute—on demand or on a scheduled basis—and whether users access the reports directly or from a cache. Security management includes controlling not only what people can see when viewing the catalog of available reports, but also what tasks they can perform, such as adding or deleting reports, changing report properties, or using subscriptions.

Finally, Reporting Services supports all activities related to distributing reports from a central location to the user community. Some users might access reports directly online, others might receive reports as e-mail attachments on a scheduled basis as a subscription, and yet another group might retrieve a collection of reports saved to a network file share. These reports can be selectively rendered in many formats, such as HTML, Microsoft Excel, and Adobe Portable Document Format (PDF), among others. Users can also maintain a private folder called My Reports to organize specific reports of interest for easier access.

Although most users will likely access enterprise reports, power users will make frequent use of the ad hoc reporting capabilities to quickly obtain information not available in enterprise reports. Report Builder is a significantly simpler development environment than Report Designer. In Report Builder, the user works with only one data source, either a SQL Server database or an Analysis Services database, and can use only one data structure: a table, a matrix, or a chart. Rather than construct a SQL or MDX query to retrieve data from the source database, the ad hoc report author selects items from a report model, which is prepared in advance by someone with a strong technical understanding of the source data. Even within this limited environment, the ad hoc report author can add expressions, apply formatting, and insert filter or sorts to produce useful reports which can even be saved to the Report Server for distribution to others.

## Reporting Services Components Overview

Review the following list of Reporting Services components to get a general idea of each component's purpose:

- **Report Server** Receives and responds to client requests and activates applicable subcomponents to handle data processing, report rendering, security management, scheduling, and report delivery

- **Report Manager** Provides a Web-based user interface for the user community to access and interact with reports online and for administrators to manage content and configure report execution and subscription options

- **HTML Viewer** Adds interactive capabilities through a Report Manager toolbar for navigating between pages of a report, searching a report for a text string, refreshing a report, exporting the report to a different format, and adjusting magnification, among other capabilities

- **Report Builder**   Supports ad hoc report development based on a predefined report model

- **Business Intelligence Development Studio**   Includes the Report Server Project Wizard to accelerate the report development process, a report designer for developing, testing, and deploying enterprise reports, and a model designer to develop, tune, and deploy report models used for ad hoc reporting

- **SQL Server Management Studio**   Provides administrative support for Report Servers and SQL Server databases used as a common repository for Reporting Services

- **Reporting Services Configuration Tool**   Provides a user interface for configuring local or remote Reporting Services instances

- **Command-line utilities (Rsconfig, Rskeymgmt, and Rs)**   Support routine administrative tasks on local or remote Report Servers

- *ReportServer* and *ReportServerTempDB* **databases**   Provide centralized storage for reports, cached reports, and report-related information, such as security, data sources, parameter values, and schedules

- **Reporting Services programmability**   Includes several application programming interfaces (APIs) for building custom reporting or report management applications, or for extending the capabilities of the Reporting Services platform

# Authoring Reports

Enterprise reports are developed using SQL Server Business Intelligence Development Studio, introduced in Chapter 21, "Integration Services." This integrated development environment is simply Visual Studio with business intelligence templates. The Report Server Project template provides many tools you can use to build feature-rich reports, but we can provide only a brief introduction of the possibilities in this chapter.

---

**More Info**   For more hands-on tutorials covering the complete enterprise reporting life cycle, refer to *Microsoft SQL Server 2005 Reporting Services Step by Step* by Stacia Misner and Hitachi Consulting, Microsoft Press, 2006. *Professional SQL Server 2005 Reporting Services* by Paul Turley, Todd Bryan, James Counihan, George McKee, and Dave DuVarney, Wrox Press, 2006, explains Reporting Services from a developer's perspective and provides a variety of examples of standard and customized solutions. You can learn how Reporting Services fits into a data warehousing architecture by reading *The Microsoft Data Warehouse Toolkit: With SQL Server 2005 and the Microsoft Business Intelligence Toolset* by Joy Mundy, Warren Thornthwaite, and Ralph Kimball, Wiley, 2006.

# Enterprise Reports

An *enterprise report* is formatted information that is formally distributed within a workgroup, to all employees in an organization, or even to external recipients such as customers or shareholders. This type of report is typically accessible from a central location with security applied, but it may also be distributed on a regular schedule via e-mail or added as a link to a corporate portal. The key tasks related to authoring an enterprise report include defining the queries used to retrieve data for the report, organizing the data into a specific layout, and formatting the report to enhance its appearance.

## Starting a Reporting Services Project

When you start a new project in Visual Studio, you select the Report Server Project template in the Business Intelligence Projects folder and provide a name and location for your project. A Report Server Project provides several windows for report development, as shown in Figure 23-1, which illustrates a report you develop using examples in this section. The windows you use while building this report are described in the following list:

- **Solution Explorer**  By default, this window displays in the upper right corner of your screen. As you add data sources and reports to your project, a corresponding file is added to the applicable folder in this window. You can rename this file, but be sure to keep the assigned file extension (such as .rds or .rdl), or they won't work.

- **Properties**  This window displays in the bottom right corner of your screen by default. If you select an object added to your report, you can view and modify its properties in this window.

- **Toolbox**  This window contains all of the items that you can add to a report, such as a table, an image, or a freestanding textbox, for example.

- **Datasets**  This window displays a tree view of all data fields that you can add to your report as placeholders for actual data during report development.

- **Report Designer**  This window is the main workspace in which you will work to develop a report. The report designer separates your work activities into the following three tabs.

  - **Data**  On this tab, you define which data will be included in the report, including its current location.

❑ **Layout** Here you organize the report data into structures, such as tables or charts, and add enhancements to control appearance and behavior by changing report item properties.

❑ **Preview** You use this tab to test the report before deploying it to the Report Server.

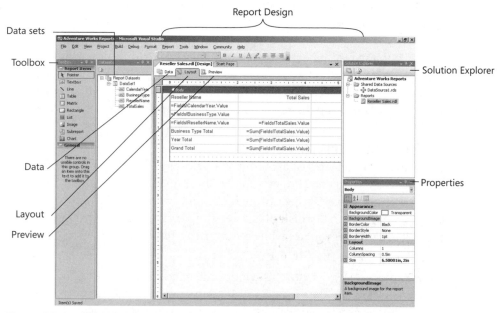

**Figure 23-1** A Report Server project in Visual Studio.

> **Note** There are two other project templates applicable to Reporting Services: Report Server Project Wizard and Report Model Project. If you choose Report Server Project Wizard, you step through a wizard to build a basic table or matrix report using a single data source. This wizard is useful for jumpstarting report development. Using the Report Model Project template is explained later in this chapter.

## Defining Queries

To define a query for a report, you create a data source and a dataset to identify the location of the data and to specify which data to retrieve from the source.

### Creating a Data Source

A data source can be embedded into a report or can be defined as a separate project item for sharing among many reports. In either case, it includes the connection string and credentials used by Reporting Services to connect to a data store. It may be tempting to reuse a data source created for Integration Services or Analysis Services, but at the time of this writing you must create and use data sources specifically for Reporting Services. To create a new shared data source, follow these steps:

1. Start SQL Server Business Intelligence Development Studio. On the File menu, point to New, and then click Project.

2. Ensure that the Project Type is set to Business Intelligence Projects, and then click the Report Server Project template. Type a name for the project, such as Adventure Works Reports in this example, change the location for the project to a folder of your choice, and confirm that the Create Directory For Solution check box is selected. Click OK to create the project in Visual Studio.

3. Right-click the Shared Data Sources folder in the Solution Explorer window, and then click Add New Data Source.

4. Type a new name for the data source if desired, select a data source type, and then type a connection string such as the following, which connects to the *Adventure Works DW* database on a local server:

```
Data Source=(local);Initial Catalog=AdventureWorksDW
```

The specific connection string you use depends on the data source types you choose. Supported data source types include the following:

- ❑ **Microsoft SQL Server**   Connects to SQL Server 7.0 or later

- ❑ **OLE DB**   Connects to SQL Server 6.5 or earlier, SQL Server 2000 Analysis Services, or any data source supporting an OLE DB provider

- ❑ **Microsoft SQL Server Analysis Services**   Connects to SQL Server 2005 Analysis Services

- ❑ **Oracle**   Connects to Oracle only if Oracle client tools are installed on the report author's workstation and the report server

- ❑ **ODBC**   Connects to data sources using native ODBC drivers

- ❑ **XML**   Connects to XML documents, Web services, or applications accessed with a URL using a syntax applicable to the data source

- ❑ **Report Server Model**   Connects to a report server to which as report model has been published and uses the syntax:

```
server=http://<machinename>/reportserver;
datasource=/<folderpath>
```

where *<machinename>* is the server hosting Reporting Services and *<folderpath>* is the path to the report model from the Home folder and the model name, such as / Models/Adventure Works Model.

On the General tab of the Shared Data Source dialog box, you can click the Edit button to access the Connection Properties dialog box for all data source types except XML or Report Server Model. Using this interface, you can make selections to build a connection string automatically. If you plan to use Windows or SQL Server authentication, you don't need to change settings on the Credentials tab of the Shared Data Source dialog box.

5. Click the Credentials tab to specify an authentication method, and then click OK to close the Shared Data Source dialog box. As shown in Figure 23-2, the following four types of credentials are available:

   ❑ **Use Windows Authentication (Integrated Security)**   Recommended for data sources that use Windows authentication when Kerberos is enabled or the database server is in the same domain as the report server

   ❑ **Use A Specific Name And Password**   Used for data sources that depend on database security to authenticate users

   ❑ **Prompt For Credentials**   Used only for reports that run on demand and require access to confidential data; Reporting Services prompts the user to supply credentials before the report executes

   ❑ **No Credentials**   Not generally recommended, but available for databases for which there are no security requirements

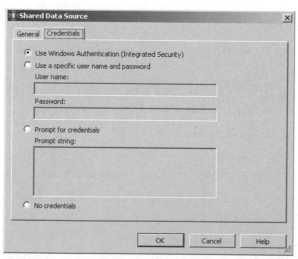

**Figure 23-2**   The Credentials tab of the Shared Data Source dialog box.

**Best Practices**  It's a best practice to use a shared data source because you can make changes, such as using a different server or different authentication method, in one place rather than open each report individually to adjust report-specific data sources.

## Creating a Dataset

A *dataset* is a collection of several items—a pointer to a data source, a query that defines how to retrieve data for the report, and a set of fields created to describe each column returned by the query. When you create a new dataset, you select an existing shared data source or create a new report-specific data source, and then provide a query. Whereas a shared data source is created outside the context of a specific report, a dataset is always associated with a specific report and cannot be shared by many reports. To create a new report and add a dataset, follow these steps:

1.  In Visual Studio, start a new Report Server Project and add a data source as described in the previous example.

2.  Right-click the Reports folder in the Solution Explorer window, point to Add, and then click New Item.

> **Note**  When you right-click the Reports folder, you have the option to click Add New Report, which starts the same wizard launched when you select the Report Server Project Wizard template for a new project.

3.  In the Add New Item dialog box, click the Report template. Replace the default report name, Report.rdl, with a more suitable name, such as Reseller Sales.rdl in this example, and then click Add.

> **Note**  The name of the report you provide here will be the report name the user sees when navigating through the list of available reports. Report names should be user-friendly and should provide information about the contents of the report. You can use spaces to separate words in the report name. Be sure to keep the file extension!

4.  On the Dataset toolbar located on the Data tab of the Report Designer, select New Dataset in the drop-down list. In the Dataset dialog box, replace the default name of the dataset, DataSet1, with a more meaningful name if desired. You can create a report-specific data source for the report by selecting New Data Source in the Data Source drop-down list. For this example, select the shared data source created in the previous example.

---

**Note** The dataset name cannot include a space. If your report will use only one dataset, the name isn't important, but when you have many datasets in the same report, it's helpful to choose a name that distinguishes the current dataset from others.

---

5. You can type directly in the Query String box of the Dataset dialog box, or you can click OK to type a query string on the Data tab of the Report Designer. For simple reports, you do not need to access the other tabs in this dialog box. For more information about using this dialog box, refer to the related SQL Server Books Online topic, such as "Dataset (Fields Tab, Report Designer)," or the books recommended at the beginning of this chapter. To continue this example, click OK without providing a query string here.

6. Click Generic Query Designer, the fourth button on the Dataset toolbar, to toggle from the Generic Query Designer to the Query Builder. When the Query Builder is available, the Data tab contains the following four panes:

   ❑ **Diagram pane** In this pane, you can add or remove tables, select columns from tables, or create joins between tables, among other tasks, by using a graphical interface.

   ❑ **Grid pane** Use this pane to modify columns, such as adding an alias, specifying a sort order, or applying a filter.

   ❑ **SQL pane** You use this pane to view the SQL statement created from the selections made in the Diagram or Grid panes or to modify the statement directly.

   ❑ **Results pane** This pane shows you the query results if you click the Run button in the Dataset toolbar to execute the query.

7. Modify the statement in the SQL pane to produce a statement like the following:

```
SELECT

DimTime.CalendarYear, DimReseller.BusinessType, DimReseller.ResellerName,
SUM(FactResellerSales.SalesAmount) AS TotalSales

FROM

FactResellerSales

INNER JOIN

DimReseller ON FactResellerSales.ResellerKey = DimReseller.ResellerKey
INNER JOIN

DimTime ON FactResellerSales.OrderDateKey = DimTime.TimeKey
```

```
GROUP BY DimTime.CalendarYear, DimReseller.BusinessType,
DimReseller.ResellerName
```

> **Note**  Use a view or a stored procedure for easier maintenance of the
> business logic producing the report data. To use a stored procedure, you
> need to switch to the Generic Query Designer, select StoredProcedure in
> the Command Type drop-down list, and then type the name of the stored
> procedure in the Query pane.

8. Click Run, the button represented as an exclamation point on the Dataset toolbar,
   to validate the query syntax and view the result set, as shown in Figure 23-3. The
   result set is not stored with the report definition but is available here simply to confirm you get the data you expect. Each column in the Result pane is added to the
   Fields collection for the dataset. The data type of each column is also included in
   this collection.

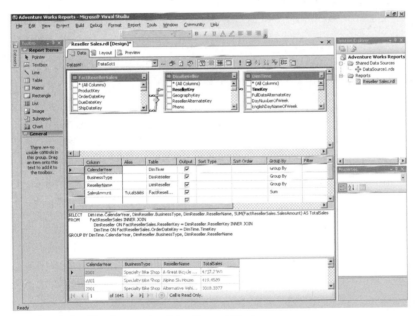

**Figure 23-3**  The Data tab of the Report Designer.

> **Note**  Because the data type of each column is also included in the
> dataset's Fields collection, you need to take extra steps to update the
> report definition if the data type of any column changes later. The easiest

way to update data types is to open the dataset on the Data tab of the Report Designer, and then click the Refresh button on the Dataset toolbar.

## Organizing Data

After using the Data tab of the Report Designer to define the data fields and data types of each query's result set, you use the Layout tab to organize the fields into structures called *data regions*, such as a table, matrix, list, or chart. A field can also be used in a *report item* such as free-standing textboxes. A report item is anything that can be added to a report, which can be a data region or a textbox as mentioned, a graphical element such as an image or a line, or a container such as a rectangle or subreport. In this section, we'll focus only on adding a table to a report because it's the most common data region type and because the same basic steps apply to each data region. To add a table to the report layout, follow these steps:

1. In Visual Studio, open the Adventure Works Reports Report Server Project created and updated in the previous two examples. In Solution Explorer, double-click the Reseller Sales.rdl to open the Report Designer.

2. In the Report Designer, click the Layout tab. The design grid of the report's body is visible in the window. There are horizontal and vertical rulers to help you position report items as you add them to the report body.

> **Note** The size of the report body defaults to 6.5 inches wide and 2 inches high, but you can adjust the default size. One way to reset the size is to select Body in the drop-down list at the top of the Properties window, expand the Size category, and then type new values for the Width and Height properties. Alternatively, you can drag the bottom or right edges of the body to a different size. If you add a report item requiring more space than is currently available, the height and width will increase to accommodate the new item.

3. Double-click Table in the Toolbox window to add it to the report body. You can also drag the item from the window onto the report body for greater control over its position.

> **Note** By default, the Toolbox window displays on the left side of your screen. If the Autohide feature for this window has been enabled, then you will see a Hammer and Wrench icon over which you can hover the cursor pointer to open the window. Otherwise, you can click Toolbox on the View menu to display the Toolbox window.

A *table* is a collection of textboxes organized into a structure with a fixed number of columns and a variable number of rows based on the query result set. Each textbox can contain either static text or an expression that refers either to a field from a dataset or a more complex calculation. When you add a table to the report layout, it contains three columns and three rows. The first and last rows are the table header and table footer respectively, which appear only once in the table, and the middle row is a detail row which repeats for each row in the dataset's result set.

4. In the Datasets window, which by default displays on the left side of your screen, expand the dataset you created, and then drag a field into a textbox in the table. To continue the previous example, drag ResellerName to the first cell of the detail row. When you add a field to the table, its name is also automatically placed in the table header textbox of the same column. Notice the expression added to the detail row looks like this: `=Fields!ResellerName.Value.` This expression refers to the Fields collection that belongs to the dataset from which you selected the field. When the report is processed, the expression is evaluated for each row produced by the dataset query and is replaced with the value in the ResellerName column.

> **Note** If you don't see the Datasets window, click Datasets on the View menu.

5. In the Datasets window, drag TotalSales to the second cell of the detail row.

6. Now drag TotalSales to the textbox in the second column of the table footer, as shown in Figure 23-4. The Report Designer automatically adds a *Sum* function to the field expression when you drag a field to a table header or table footer. These rows should contain only aggregated numeric values. If you don't use an aggregate function with the field expression, the value from the first row in the result set is used to evaluate the expression.

7. Click the first textbox of the table footer, and then type **Grand Total**. In addition to using expressions in a textbox, you can use a constant value such as a text string.

8. Click the Preview tab to view your report, as shown in Figure 23-5. You can see one row for the table header and one detail row for each row in the query's result set. Click the Next Page button in the Preview toolbar to continue to the next page, where you can see additional table rows, or click the Last Page button to view the table footer containing the Grand Total at the bottom of the page.

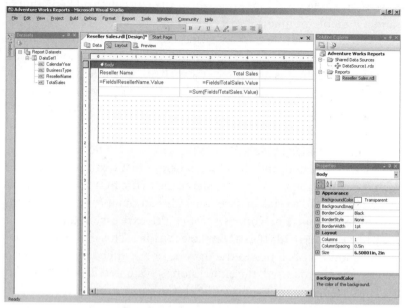

**Figure 23-4**   A table on the Layout tab of the Report Designer.

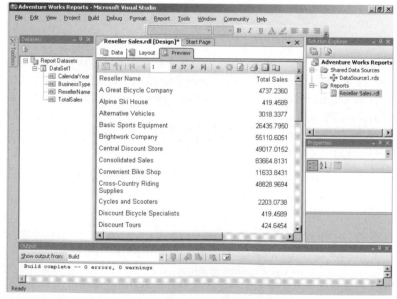

**Figure 23-5**   A report on the Preview tab of the Report Designer.

When a report has many detail rows, it is often useful to organize the detail rows into groups. A *group* is a set of detail rows that are related to a common value, which can be a field or an expression. To add two groups to the table created in the previous example, follow these steps:

1. Click the Layout tab, click the table if necessary to display the row and column handles. The row and column handles are the gray borders added to the left and top edges of a table. Right-click the row handle at the left edge of the detail row (containing the icon with three horizontal bars), click Insert Group to display the Grouping And Sorting Properties dialog box, click the first Expression drop-down list to view available values, and then select =Fields!CalendarYear.Value, as shown in Figure 23-6. Each item in the list is an expression formed from each field in the dataset. Notice the default selection of the group header and group footer, which you can clear if desired. There are also several tabs available in this dialog box to manage properties, such as filters and sorts, for the group.

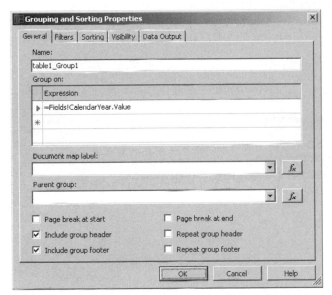

**Figure 23-6** The Grouping and Sorting Properties dialog box.

2. Click OK, right-click the row handle at the left edge of the detail row, click Insert Group, select =Fields!BusinessType.Value in the first Expression drop-down list, and then click OK.

> **Note** The position of a new group depends on which row you right-click in the table. When you right-click a detail row to insert a new group, the group is added between any existing groups and the detail row. When you

select an existing group, the new group is placed between the selected group and other existing groups or between the selected group and the detail row if no other groups exist.

3. Drag CalendarYear from the Datasets window to the first textbox in the first group header row, which is the row just below the table header row. Drag BusinessType to the first textbox in the second group header row, which is the row just above the detail row. By adding fields to the group header rows, you provide context to the set of detail rows within each group. Instead of using a field expression in the group header, you can use static text or an expression that includes a reference to a field. Usually, group headers include the same expression used to define the group, but you might use an expression to concatenate a field value with static text.

4. Type **Year Total** in the first textbox of the group footer row corresponding to the first group, which is the row just above the table footer. Drag TotalSales from the Datasets window to the second textbox in the same row. As with the table footer row, you use aggregate functions in the group header or footer row to create subtotals. Although *Sum* is the default aggregate function, you can use other familiar functions, such as *Avg*, *Min*, *Max*, or *Count*. Complete the table so that it looks like the one shown in Figure 23-7 by adding text for Business Type Total and adding an expression to sum TotalSales to the appropriate textboxes on the applicable group footer row.

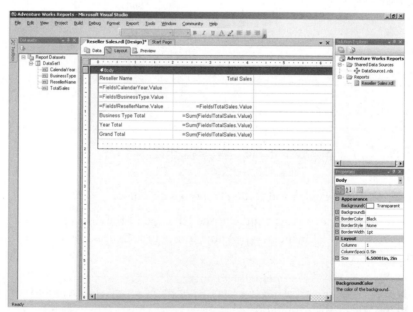

**Figure 23-7** A table with two groups and one detail row in the report layout.

5.  To resize a column, position the cursor pointer on the column handles (the gray area above the table's textboxes) at the right edge of the column and drag to widen or narrow the column. For this example, widen the first column to 2 inches.

6.  Click the Preview tab to see how the table will appear when deployed to the Report Server. The report is rendered as HTML by default, as shown in Figure 23-8, but you can export to other formats for testing. Designing a report for online viewing doesn't always produce a report that renders nicely in another format, so be sure to test the formats users are likely to select for rendering. You can also click the Print Layout button on the Preview toolbar to test the printed version of the report.

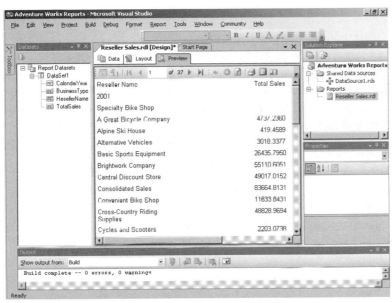

**Figure 23-8**   Preview of a report with table grouping.

Your report is now complete, but you can continue to refine it by adding other data regions, images, or freestanding textboxes. For example, you can drag the table to a lower position in the report body and then add a textbox into which you could type a static title or create an expression for a title that changes according to current report conditions. You can also add a subreport to embed an existing report into the current report to employ a "build once, reuse many times" strategy. Even though the number of report items you can use in a report is relatively small, they can be combined and nested in very creative ways to produce an amazing variety of report styles.

## Adding Report Enhancements

After creating a data set and organizing data in the report, you might enhance the report by setting properties to control behavior and appearance. At minimum, you'll use properties to apply formatting. You can select one textbox individually or select multiple textboxes to apply the same property settings to the selected textboxes (although not all properties support this technique). However, there are several properties available to control behavior as well, such as visibility, interactive sorting, and actions for navigation. For a complete review of your options, refer to the topics "Designing the Report Layout" and "Adding Interactive Features" in SQL Server Books Online. When you have finished authoring a report, you publish the report definition to the report server, as described later in this chapter.

# Ad Hoc Reports

An *ad hoc report* is simpler than an enterprise report because the emphasis is on answering a specific question rather than on rich data content and presentation. Many ad hoc reports might be created, but only a few are saved for sharing with others. In Reporting Services, a report model must be created before a user can develop an ad hoc report. Once the report model is available on a report server, the user can then organize items from the model into a table, matrix, or chart, and add formatting or basic interactive features as needed.

## Report Model Projects

A *report model* insulates users from the technical details about the tables and columns found in a data source. Whereas a report definition is stored as an RDL file, a report model is stored as an SMDL (Semantic Model Definition Language) file. Like RDL, SMDL is an open XML schema that can be used by another application to eventually produce a report. When the user of such a client application selects items from the report model to build a report, the client application constructs a query based on the placement of these objects in a report layout designer. To create a new model based on a SQL Server data source, follow these steps:

1. Start SQL Server Business Intelligence Development Studio. On the File menu, point to New, and then click Project.

2. Ensure that the Project Type is set to Business Intelligence Projects, and then click the Report Model Project template. Type a name for the project, such as Adventure Works Model in this example, change the location for the project to a folder of your choice, and confirm that the Create Directory For Solution check box is selected. Click OK to create the project in Visual Studio.

3. Right-click the Data Sources folder in Solution Explorer, click Add New Data Source to open the Data Source Wizard, click Next to go past the Welcome page, and then click New.

4. In the Connection Manager dialog box, type the server name or select the server in the Server Name drop-down list, select a source database (*AdventureWorksDW* in this example) in the Select Or Enter A Database Name drop-down list, and then click OK. To finish the wizard, click Next and then click Finish.

   A data source for a report model project is similar to a data source for a report project because it defines the connection and authentication information required to retrieve data from the source, but a data source created for a report project can't be added to a report model project. Furthermore, a data source for a report model project can use the SQL Server provider only at the time of this writing.

5. Right-click the Data Source Views folder in Solution Explorer, and then click Add New Data Source View to open the Data Source View Wizard. Click Next to bypass the Welcome page, click *Adventure Works DW* in the Relational Data Sources list if it isn't already selected, and then click Next.

6. Move the following tables from the Available Objects list to the Included Objects list: *DimGeography*, *DimReseller*, *DimTime*, and *FactResellerSales*. Click Next, and then click Finish to close the wizard.

7. Double-click Adventure Works DW.dsv in Solution Explorer to open the data source view. Notice that the existing foreign key relationships defined in the relational database are indicated by connecting related tables in the data source view, as shown in Figure 23-9. The data source view also includes a key icon to identify the primary key in each table.

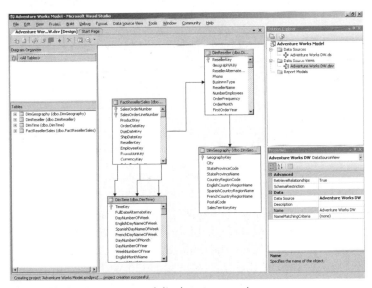

**Figure 23-9**  A report model's data source view.

8.  Right-click the Report Models folder in Solution Explorer, and then click Add New Report Model. Click Next on the Welcome page of the wizard, click Adventure Works DW.dsv on the Select Data Source Views page if it is not already selected, and then click Next.

9.  Keep the default selections on the Select Report Model Generation Rules page, and then click Next. Since you just created a data source view, the statistics in that file are current. Click Next to continue the wizard.

---

**Note**    You can learn more about the purpose of each rule at *http://msdn2.microsoft.com/en-us/library/ms183622.aspx*.

10. Name the model **Adventure Works Reseller Sales**, click Run to generate the report model, and then click Finish when the button is enabled. If a message box displays to indicate the file has been modified outside the source editor, click Yes. The report model is now ready to deploy to the Report Server, but usually the report model requires some adjustments to maximize its usefulness to ad hoc reporting community.

---

**Note**    You can also generate models using SQL Server Management Studio or Report Manager. In fact, the only way to generate a report model from an Analysis Services cube is to use one of these management tools after you have added an Analysis Services data source to the report server. For details about adding a data source, refer to the SQL Server Books Online topics, "How to: Create, Delete, or Modify a Shared Data Source (Report Manager)" and "Connecting to a Data Source." In SQL Server Management Studio, connect to Reporting Services, right-click an existing data source, and then click Generate Model. In Report Manager, open a shared data source, and then click Generate Model. The report model is automatically deployed to the report server after it is generated. To edit a report model based on a SQL Server database, you can download it from the report server and use the report model designer to make any desired changes. However, you can't edit a report model based on an Analysis Services cube.

The report model designer, as shown in Figure 23-10, has two views: Tree View and Detail View. The Tree View on the left side of the designer contains a list of *entities*. One entity is created for each table in the data source view. To the right of the Tree View, the Detail View displays the objects associated with the entity currently selected in the Tree View, which in this example is Fact Reseller Sale.

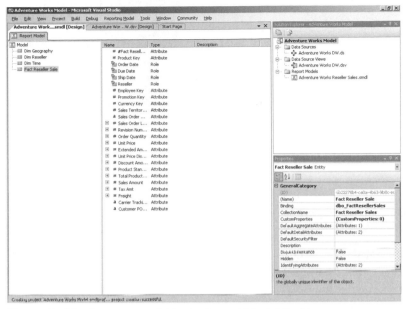

**Figure 23-10**   A report model in the Report Model Designer.

Each entity contains a collection of *attributes* corresponding to the collection of columns in the related table as well as special attributes not found in the data source view, such as expressions or aggregations. For each numeric attribute in the model, the Report Model Wizard creates *Total*, *Avg*, *Min*, and *Max* numeric aggregations. In addition, year, quarter, month, and day variations, as well as a first and last aggregation, are created for date attributes. These additional attributes add flexibility to the report model and reduce the amount of work required to produce the desired results in a report. A symbol in front of each attribute indicates its data type, as described in the following list:

- **a**   a string data type
- **#**   decimal, float, or integer data types
- **Calendar icon**   date time data type
- **Check box icon**   Boolean data type

An entity might also contain a *role* to define a relationship between entities. A role indicated by a multilayer icon defines a one-to-many relationship between the two tables. When two tables have a one-to-one relationship, a single-layer icon is used for the role.

11. To publish a report model to a local report server, use Visual Studio's Deploy command, located on the Build menu, or right-click the report model project in Solution Explorer and click Deploy. If the report server is not local, before you deploy, right-click the project in Solution Explorer, click Properties, and change the TargetServerURL to http://<servername>/ReportServer.

A report model that you create from the management tools, either Report Manager or SQL Server Management Studio, is automatically deployed after it's generated. Once a report model has been deployed, you'll need to apply security to restrict access to the report model to authorized users. Reporting Services security is explained later in this chapter.

A report model is rarely ready to be used immediately after it's created. The following list describes tasks you might perform before deploying a report model which makes it available to users:

- **Rename entities, attributes, and roles**   Change the name of the object either by changing its (Name) property value in the Properties window or by renaming it directly in the designer.

- **Adjust the DefaultAggregateAttribute property for a numeric attribute**   This property determines which aggregate a Report Builder user will see first when browsing the attributes associated with a specific entity.

- **Modify object properties to change default behavior, such as formatting and sorting**   For example, you can update the Format property of numeric attributes using the same Visual Basic .NET formatting strings you use in the Report Designer.

---

**More Info**   For more information, refer to the topic "Attribute Object (Model Designer)" in SQL Server Books Online.

---

- **Rearrange objects to make it easier for users to find and use the report model objects**   You can rearrange and reorganize objects using one of the following methods:

  ❑ **Create folders to group similar objects together**   Right-click an item, such as an entity or even the Model object, in the Tree View, point to New, and then click Folder. After creating a folder, you can then drag items from any Detail View to the new folder.

  ❑ **Create a perspective to focus the model on commonly used entities and attributes**   Right-click Model in the Tree View, point to New, and then click Perspective. In the Edit Perspective dialog box, you can clear entities, roles, and attributes to exclude from the perspective.

❏ **Change the sequence of objects by placing frequently used objects at the top of a list**   Right-click an item in the Detail View for any entity and then click Move Up or click Move Down to reposition the item.

❏ **Delete any unwanted objects**   Right-click an object in Tree View or Detail View, and then click Delete.

❏ **Add expressions**   Right-click an entity in Tree View, point to New, and then click Expression. In the Define Formula dialog box, you double-click fields, operators, and functions to create an expression that performs logical operations, manipulates strings or dates, converts data types, or aggregates numerical data.

---

**Note**   If new columns are added to a table in the underlying data source, you can update the report model by manually adding source fields that correspond to these new columns or by regenerating the report model. However, any objects you deleted previously are added to the report model again if you regenerate the report model.

## Report Builder

Once a report model has been deployed to a report server, then users can build ad hoc reports using Report Builder. This ClickOnce application can be accessed directly from Report Manager or from a URL (*http://<servername>/reportserver/reportbuilder/ reportbuilder.application* or *http://<servername>/reportserver/reportbuilder/reportbuilder- localintranet.application* depending on the trust level under which Report Builder runs). If you are working on a local machine, you can use localhost instead of a specific server name in the URL. Report Builder allows you to navigate through the report model by selecting an entity to review its attributes, which you can add to the report layout, or by selecting a role to view attributes for a related entity. To use Report Builder with the report model created and deployed in the previous example, follow these steps:

1. In Internet Explorer, open Report Manager at *http://localhost/Reports* (or specify a server name if you are working with a Reporting Services instance that is not located on your computer), click Report Builder on the Report Manager toolbar, and then click Run if the Application Run – Security Warning dialog box displays. This dialog box appears only the first time the Report Builder application is launched on a client workstation.

2. In the Source of Data list in the right-hand pane, select a model, such as the Adventure Works Model created in the previous example. If a perspective exists, you can expand the parent report model and then select the perspective. On this screen,

you also select the report layout, which by default is a table, but you can instead choose to create a matrix or a chart. When you click OK to continue, you have access to three panes in the Report Builder window, as shown in Figure 23-11.

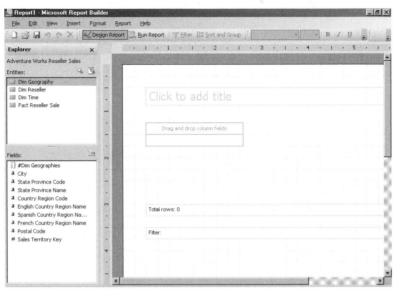

**Figure 23-11    A new report in Report Builder.**

The Explorer pane on the left displays two lists. At the top of the Explorer pane, you see a list of entities and folders in the report model. The Fields list, below the Entities list, displays the attributes for the currently selected object in the Entities list. The largest pane in the Report Builder window is the design area in which you define the report layout.

3.  In the Entities list, click Dim Time. To add an attribute to the report, you can double-click the attribute in the Fields list or drag it to the desired location in the report layout. When you add a field to a detail table, two rows are created in the new column—a header row to display the field name and a detail row to display the field value. For this example, double-click Calendar Year in the Fields list.

4.  Click a role to navigate from entity to entity within a model. Remember from the previous section that a role relates a foreign key in one table with a primary key in another table. To continue this example, in the Entities list click Fact Reseller Sales and then click Reseller. In the Fields list, double-click Business Type.

5.  Double-click Total Sales Amount in the Fields list.

> **Note**  Subtotals are automatically added to the table for each numeric field. To disable this behavior, right-click the column header or the column's detail row and clear the Show Group Subtotals selection.

6.  To add a title, double-click the textbox above the table, and then type the report title, such as **Reseller Sales By Year**.

7.  Click Run Report on the toolbar to generate the report, as shown in Figure 23-12. Report Builder constructs a query to retrieve data from the source based on the attributes and their relationships defined in the report model.

**Figure 23-12**    A report executed in Report Builder.

8.  Double-click the cell immediately below the Total Sales Amount column heading in the 2001 Specialty Bike Shops row to view details for the selected cell, as shown in Figure 23-13. You can identify a field that supports clickthrough when the cursor changes to a hand as you hover the pointer over a cell.

    By using the clickthrough feature of Report Builder, you can generate report after report to see progressively more detailed reports. The number of relationships between entities and the fields contributing to the cell you select for clickthrough determines how many new reports can be created. As long as the information retrieved by clickthrough is related to multiple records in the source database,

Report Builder displays the information in a table. When you clickthrough to a single record, Report Builder displays a list of attributes for the selected record. Because you don't have access to the clickthrough report layout to fix formatting, take the time to review the formatting of each attribute in the report model during its design, and adjust as needed.

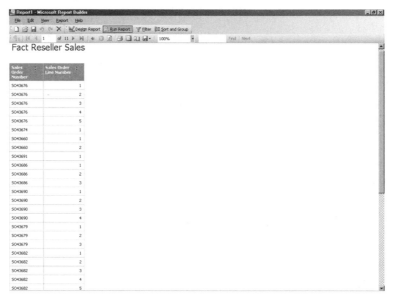

**Figure 23-13**    A clickthrough report in Report Builder.

**Note**    Clickthrough is available only with SQL Server Enterprise edition.

9. Optionally, you can save an ad hoc report for future reference or for sharing with others. To do this, click Save on the toolbar, name the report, and then click Save in the Save Report dialog box. You can place the report in the Home folder. If other folders have been created on the report server, you can place the report in any other folder to which you have access.

After building an ad hoc report, you can add a variety of enhancements. Report Builder includes a formatting toolbar for you to select a different font, font size, font color, and other standard formatting options. You can also type different text in the column headings or total rows to replace the default text. In addition, you can add a filter, which adds a WHERE clause to the query generated by Report Builder, to make it easy to create different versions of the same report. Finally, you can add new fields to the field list by creating a formula, although it's considered a best practice to include any commonly used calculations in the report model to ensure consistency.

# Managing Reporting Services

System administrators are typically responsible for configuring and tuning the report servers for optimal performance. Along with certain power users, they may be responsible for managing content on the server, such as publishing reports, setting report properties, or applying security. In this section, we'll review the key administrative tasks required by Reporting Services to set up and maintain the report server and to manage reports and other resources in a production environment.

## Report Server Configuration

For many Reporting Services implementations, the default configuration of each subcomponent is adequate, but you have several tools available to tune the configuration following installation. The Reporting Services Configuration tool is an easy way to reconfigure report servers, but you can also use command line utilities, such as Rsconfig and Rskeymgmt, about which you can learn more in SQL Server Books Online. Although this configuration tool allows you to set many important report server properties, you might need to edit configuration files directly. We'll review both the configuration tool and configuration files in this section.

### Reporting Services Configuration Tool

Before you can publish reports to the server, you must identify the report server database to be used for storing content and create a virtual directory for accessing the server and for using Report Manager. Use the Reporting Services Configuration tool, located in the Microsoft SQL Server 2005 program group in the Configuration Tools folder, to define these settings after installation and to change properties for components of Reporting Services if the reporting environment changes later. When you start Reporting Services Configuration, you specify the report server instance you want to configure, which can be local or remote.

---

**Note**    You must have local system administrator access to the report server instance you plan to configure.

---

The Reporting Services Configuration tool includes several pages described in the following list:

- **Report Server Status**    On this page, you can start or stop the Report Server Windows service and view the server's initialization status.
- **Report Server Virtual Directory Settings**    The virtual directory used by applications to access Reporting Services is created on the Default Web Site in Internet

Information Services (IIS) at installation, but you can use this page to choose a different Web Site defined in IIS. You can also use this page to secure data sent to browser or client applications with Secure Sockets Layer (SSL) encryption, but you must first install an SSL certificate.

- **Report Manager Virtual Directory Settings** Just like the Report Server virtual directory, you can reconfigure the virtual directory used to launch the Report Manager application.

- **Windows Service Identity** Use this page to update the password for the service account or to change the account used to run the service.

- **Web Service Identity** Use this page to update the security identity or application pool for the Web service if the operating system for the report system is Windows Server 2003. For Windows XP or Windows 2000, you must use the ASP.NET security identity and cannot edit the security identity here.

- **Database Connection** Select a local or remote SQL Server instance that will host the Reporting Services database and specify an account to be used by Reporting Services to connect to this database at run time. The account can be the Report Server Windows service account, a domain user account, or a SQL Server login. These credentials are encrypted and stored in an Reporting Services configuration file.

- **Encryption Key** Manage the symmetrical key used to encrypt and decrypt the connection string and credentials used to connect to the Reporting Services databases, the credentials used to run unattended reports, and stored credentials for selected data sources.

---

**Important** If you move the ReportServer database to a different instance, the symmetric key is invalidated and Reporting Services cannot decrypt the connection strings or credentials. The symmetric key is also invalidated when you rename the server or change the service account that runs the Report Server Windows service. If you lose the backup of the encryption key (or forget the password) and the symmetric key is invalidated, use the Reporting Services Configuration tool to delete the encrypted data in the ReportServer database. You'll then need to use this tool to add the database credentials back to the Report Server configuration file. In addition, for each report and shared data source that uses stored credentials, you'll need to update the credentials individually in one of the management tools, Report Manager or SSMS, and you'll need to open and save each subscription. To avoid all this extra work, take care to back up the symmetric key! Simply making a backup of the symmetric key to a local drive is not sufficient protection, however. You should move the symmetric key backup to a secure, off-site location.

- **Initialization** View the initialization status of a report server. Initialization is required before encrypted data can be stored or to configure a scale-out deployment.

- **E-mail Settings** Specify the name of the e-mail server and the sender address that Reporting Services should use for e-mail delivery of reports generated by a subscription.

- **Execution Account** Define an account to be used by Reporting Services when connecting to a data source that doesn't require credentials or to retrieve resources, such as image files, from another server.

## Reporting Services Configuration Files

Reporting Services uses four configuration files stored as XML files that you can edit as needed. You can find the configuration files in subfolders located in the default installation folder for the Reporting Services instance, such as Program Files\Microsoft SQL Server\MSSQL.3\Reporting Services. The configuration files, and the subfolders in which each is located, are described in the following list:

- **Rsreportserver.config (in the ReportServer subfolder)** Configures the Report Server engine used by the Report Server Web service and Report Server windows service, stores the encrypted connection string for the ReportServer database, and contains settings for thread and memory management, timeout values, the SMTP server, and the number of open connections allowed for a single user. This file also contains configuration settings for delivery, rendering, data, and security extensions.

- **ReportingServicesService.exe.config (in the ReportServer\bin subfolder)** Controls the trace log files, including the amount of detail in these files. To disable logging, change the value of the DefaultTraceSwitch to 0. Other valid values range from 1 for minimal logging to 4 for the most verbose logging. In addition, you can change the number of days for which trace logs are kept. There are four trace logs, stored by default in the %Program Files%\Microsoft SQL Server 2005\MSSQL.3\Reporting Services\LogFiles folder, as described here:

  - **ReportServerService_main_*timestamp*.log** Records activities of the Report Server Windows and Web services, such as server resource allocation and initialization of the services

  - **ReportServerService_*timestamp*.log** Logs information about service operations, such as initialization and the status of polling activities related to schedules, subscriptions, and delivery notifications

  - **ReportServerWebApp_*timestamp*.log** Stores details about Report Manager operations, such as HTTP headers, stack trace information, SOAP envelopes, and exceptions

❏ **ReportServer_*timestamp*.log**   Captures exceptions and warnings generated by the Report Server or calls to perform actions like processing reports, creating folders, or deleting items

■ **RSWebApplication.config (in the ReportManager subfolder)**   Contains information used by Report Manager to manage open connections and to display a default delivery extension and default rendering formats for each delivery extension

■ **RSReportDesigner.config (in the Program Files\Microsoft Visual Studio 8\Common 7\IDE\PrivateAssemblies folder)**   Contains information about extensions used by Visual Studio's Report Designer when previewing reports

---

**Important**   Be sure to review configuration properties carefully in SQL Server Books Online. If you make an invalid change, Reporting Services logs an error to the Windows application log and either fails to start the service or reverts to the default value.

---

# Content Management

Tasks related to content management range from placing resources on the report server to organizing content already on the server, configuring report properties, and applying security. To perform these tasks, you must be granted Content Manager permissions, explained later in this chapter, or be a local system administrator.

## Publishing Content

Before you can manage a report on the report server, you must publish the report. There are three ways to publish a report, as described here:

■ **Deploy from Visual Studio**   First, define deployment properties for each project to be deployed, choose what you want to deploy—the solution, specific projects, or selected reports—and then use Visual Studio's Deploy command. Deployment properties, accessible when you right-click a project in Solution Explorer and choose Properties, are described here:

■ **OverwriteDataSources**   Controls whether shared data sources in the project will be published to the server if the data source file already exists. By default, a shared data source is deployed to the server only if the data source doesn't already exist.

■ **TargetDataSourceFolder**   The folder in which the data source will be placed. This folder will be created if it does not already exist.

- **TargetServerURL**    *A* valid URL to the report server, such as *http://<servername>/ ReportServer* where <servername> is the name of the computer hosting Reporting Services which can be localhost if you are working with a local Reporting Services instance. The URL will not be validated until you try to deploy. If you have multiple instances of Reporting Services on a server, use the following syntax for the URL: *http://<servername>/ReportServer$<instancename>* .

- **TargetReportFolder**    The folder in which the deployed items are placed. This folder is created if it does not already exist.

---

  **Important**    If you redeploy a report that already exists in the TargetRe-portFolder, the report on the server will be replaced without warning.

---

- **Upload files using Report Manager**    Navigate to the target folder on the report server, and then click the Upload File button on the Report Manager toolbar. You can upload one file at a time—a report or any other file, such as a Microsoft Word document. If the file already exists in the current folder, an error message displays when you click OK unless you select the Overwrite Item If It Exists check box.

- **Execute the RS utility**    The RS utility uses an input file with an .rss file extension written in Microsoft Visual Basic .NET to execute commands on the Report Server. To use this utility, you need to provide at least two arguments, the name of the input file and the URL for the Report Server, like this: rs -i *inputfile* -s *Report-ServerURL*. You can optionally include arguments to pass a specific user name and password. For more information, refer to the SQL Server Books Online topic "rs Utility" or the recommended books mentioned at the beginning of this chapter.

---

  **Note**    For an example script, review the PublishSampleReports.rss file located in the %Program Files%\Microsoft SQL Server 2005 Sam-ples\ReportingServices\Script Samples folder. This script is available only if you first install the Microsoft SQL Server 2005 Samples from the Samples program group, which is located in the Documentation and Tutorials pro-gram group of Microsoft SQL Server 2005. Alternatively, if you choose to install samples when installing Reporting Services, you can find this script in the %Program Files%\Microsoft SQL Server\90\Samples\Reporting Ser-vices\Script Samples folder.

---

To publish the report created in the examples in the previous sections of this chapter, follow these steps:

1. Start SQL Server Business Intelligence Development Studio. On the File menu, point to Open, and then click Project/Solution. Navigate to the folder containing

the solution file (with file extension .sln) for the Report Server Project described earlier in this chapter. Select the solution file in the Open Project dialog box, and then click Open.

2. In Solution Explorer, right-click the Adventure Works project, and then click Properties.

3. In the Adventure Works Property Pages dialog box, change the TargetReport-Folder property value to **AdventureWorks Sample Reports** and change the TargetServerURL property value to the URL for your Reporting Services instance, such as **http://localhost/ReportServer**. Click OK to close the dialog box.

4. In Solution Explorer, right-click the Adventure Works project, and then click Deploy. When the report is published successfully to the server, you see Deploy Succeeded in the status bar at the bottom of the Visual Studio window.

## Organizing Content

Use folders to organize reports and resources on the server and to apply security to items in a folder as a group. Using Report Manager, you can perform the following tasks to manage folders:

- **Create a folder**   Navigate to a folder to become the parent folder (or navigate to the Home page if the folder will not be nested), click the New Folder button in the Report Manager toolbar, and then provide a name, and optionally a description.

- **Change folder properties**   Navigate to the folder, and then click the Properties tab. You can rename the folder, add a description, hide the folder name from the list view in Report Manager, or modify security to the folder here.

- **Move a folder**   Click the Show Details button on the Report Manager toolbar, select the check box for the folder, click the Move button on the toolbar, and select a new folder from the tree view of available folders.

    **Note**   You can use this same technique to move a report to a different folder.

- **Delete a folder**   Click the Show Details button on the Report Manager toolbar, select the check box for the folder, and then click the Delete button on the toolbar. All folder contents are also deleted, so be careful.

    **Note**   Reserved folders—Home, My Reports, and Users Folders—cannot be moved, renamed, or deleted. The latter two folders are created only if you enable My Reports on the Report Server. To enable My Reports in Report Manager, click Site Settings in the upper right corner of the browser, select the Enable My Reports To Support User-Owned Folders For Publishing And Running Personalized Reports check box, and then click Apply.

## Working with Report Properties

When you author a report, you are focused on data and layout, but when you publish a report, you must consider how the report will be used and how to optimize report properties for people who will access the report. In Visual Studio, you can define the data source properties, but you have many more properties for the report that you can set in Report Manager (or SQL Server Management Studio). These properties are managed entirely on the server and are not overwritten if you later republish the report definition to the report server. To modify report properties in Report Manager, navigate to the report and click the Properties tab. You can then select the appropriate page for the properties you want to set, as described in this section.

### General

The General page displays information about who created or modified the report definition and when. In addition, this page allows you to change the report name, add a description, or access and update the report definition. From this page, you can use the links and buttons described in the following list:

- **Edit link**   Saves the report definition to the file system for read-only purposes; any edits you make to this file do not change the report definition used by the Report Server until you republish the report.

- **Update link**   Replaces report definition used by the Report Server with a specified file.

- **Create Linked Report button**   A *linked report* uses the same report definition as the report on which it is based, but it can have its own execution, parameter, security, and subscription properties.

  > **Important**   If you delete the base report, all linked reports are also deleted.

- **Change Link button**   Available only for linked reports; allows you to associate the current report with a different report definition.

- **Delete button**   Deletes the current report from the current folder and associated subscriptions, schedules, or history.

- **Move button**   Allows you to move the linked report from the current folder to another location in the Report Server's folder hierarchy.

## Parameters

You can view and change parameter values on this page if the report design includes parameters. Parameters either modify a query or filter a result set after the query executes. You can change parameter values when you create a linked report to create multiple versions of the same report, which can then be individually secured. You can also clear the Prompt User check box, as shown in Figure 23-14 which illustrates the AdventureWorks Sales sample report bundled with Reporting Services, to prevent users from changing a parameter value when viewing the report.

---

**Note** To view this report on your machine, you need to install the Microsoft SQL Server 2005 Samples which you can launch from the Microsoft SQL Server 2005/Documentation and Tutorials program group. Using Visual Studio, open the AdventureWorks Sample Reports.sln and then deploy the project as described in the previous section, "Publishing Content."

---

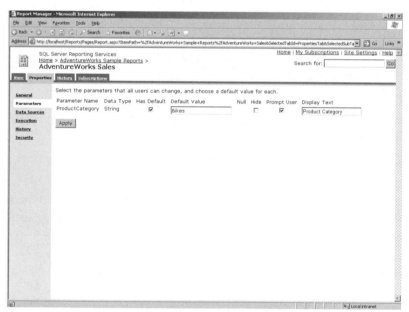

**Figure 23-14** The Parameters properties page of a report in Report Manager.

## Data Sources

On this page, you can update a report's data source properties, including connection type, connection string, and credentials. The OverwriteDataSources property for the project in Visual Studio controls whether republishing a report replaces any changes you make here. Commonly, report development is performed using a data source connecting to a development database, and a published report's data source properties are modified to use a data source connecting to a production database. Importantly, you use this page to configure a report to use stored credentials. You must use stored credentials with a data source if a report is to be executed as an unattended process, such as for a scheduled snapshot or a subscription. Stored credentials are stored in reversible encryption in the ReportServer database and are not stored in the report definition itself.

### Execution

Use the Execution properties page, as shown in Figure 23-15, to control when queries execute, to control whether reports are cached, and to build a history of reports on a manual or scheduled basis. When users need data that is relatively recent and the report query can execute and return results in a reasonable amount of time, use the On Demand execution options. For users who need access to historical data or if a report takes a long time to process, consider using Scheduled execution options.

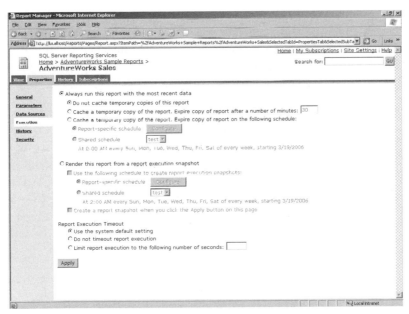

**Figure 23-15**   The Execution properties page of a report in Report Manager.

An overview of execution options is provided in the following list:

- **On Demand—Not Cached**   By default, Reporting Services processes a report on demand each time a user requests the same report, which results in a new query for each request. To improve performance, Reporting Services uses session management. A session starts when a user requests a report. The *intermediate report,* a version of the report created after query execution but before rendering, is placed in the session cache and is retrieved each time the user requests the report until the user closes the browser or client application. If the report definition changes while a user is viewing it in an active session, the user will not see the updated version of the report until manually refreshing the report, which retrieves the current version from the ReportServer database.

■ **On Demand—Cached**    A cached instance of a report is similar to a report placed into the session cache except the same intermediate report can be shared between multiple users. This intermediate report is flagged as a cached instance and is rendered on demand until the cached instance expires on a regular interval or according to a specific schedule. You configure the expiration method applied to the cached instance on the report's Execution properties page. If a report uses query parameters, the query parameters are applied when the cached instance is created. If a user selects a different parameter value, a new cached instance is created but only if a cached instance with that parameter value doesn't already exist. By contrast, a filter based on a report parameter value is applied to the existing cached instance and doesn't create a new cached instance. A cached instance is configured to expire at regular intervals or according to a schedule. The report's data source must be configured to use stored credentials.

■ **Scheduled Snapshot**    When you configure a report as a scheduled snapshot, Reporting Services executes the query and creates an intermediate report before a user opens the report. You can create a snapshot manually or on a scheduled basis. Query parameters are applied when the snapshot is created and can't be changed later because a snapshot is not an interactive report. However, report parameter values used as filters are applied against the snapshot during browsing. Because only one snapshot can exist at a time, each new snapshot of a report replaces the previous one. You must configure the report to use a data source with stored credentials.

---

**Note**    Before you can begin scheduling reports, you must define a schedule. You can create a schedule for each report or create a shared schedule to be used by several activities, such as cache expiration or subscription delivery. To create a shared schedule, click the Site Settings link on any page of Report Manager, click the Manage Shared Schedules link, click the New Schedule button, and then enter schedule details. Before you add a schedule, however, be sure SQL Server Agent is running. If not, you'll receive an error when you try to save the schedule.

■ **Report History**    Snapshots can be saved for future reference if you enable a report's history properties. Each new snapshot also adds the snapshot to report history whether you create the snapshot manually or on a schedule. Because the report is executed as a snapshot, the report must use a data source that draws on stored credentials. You have the option of specifying a maximum limit of accumulated snapshots, or you can keep an unlimited number of snapshots in report history. You can also delete individual snapshots in report history manually.

# Security Management

Reporting Services uses a role-based security system in which Windows groups or users are assigned to *roles* which define groups of activities by function. There are 16 predefined user activities, or *tasks,* and nine predefined system tasks. To associate a specific list of tasks with a role, you can create a *role definition.* Reporting Services includes five predefined item role definitions and two predefined system role definitions. While you can't add or delete tasks, you can change the available role definitions or create your own. To implement security, you can use either Report Manager or SQL Server Management Studio.

## Adding an Item Role Assignment

A *role assignment* is the assignment of a specific user or a group to a role for a specific item on the report server. For any one item, a user or group can have only one such role assignment, but a user can be a member of a group with a role assignment for the same item, in which case the user has permissions for all the tasks in both role definitions. To add a role assignment to the Home folder, follow these steps:

1. Open Report Manager in Microsoft Internet Explorer at *http://<servername>/ Reports.*

2. Click the Properties tab. The default role assignment for the Home folder is Content Manager, to which the local system administrators group, BUILTIN\Administrators, is assigned.

3. Click New Role Assignment on the Report Manager toolbar.

4. Click the Browser link to view the tasks in the role definition, as shown in Figure 23-16. A full description of each task is available on this page. You can add or remove tasks from the role definition by selecting or clearing each task as appropriate. When finished, click OK to apply the changes. Any changes you make here are applied server-wide.

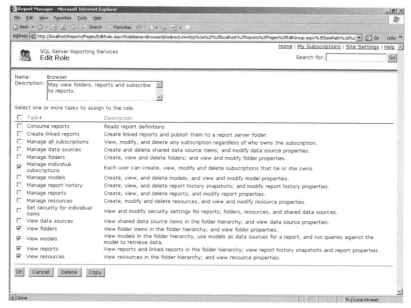

**Figure 23-16** The Edit Role page for the Browser role in Report Manager.

---

**Note** You can also reach this page to add a new role or edit an existing role at any time by using the Site Settings link at the top of any Report Manager page. Follow the Configure Item-Level Role Definitions link to access the Item-Level Roles page.

---

5. On the New Role Assignment page, type a valid Windows group or user name in the Group Or User Name box, and then select the check box for each role to assign. To assign all roles to the specified group or user, select the Role check box above the list of roles.

---

**Note** It's easiest to manage security at the folder level. Each item within the folder inherits the role assignments specified for the parent folder. You can override security inheritance for any nested folders or for individual reports within the parent folder. All users must be granted at least Browser access to the Home folder in order to access other folders.

---

The following table shows the default association of tasks by role in order from most restrictive security on the left to least restrictive security on the right:

**Table 23-1  Default Assignments by Role**

| Default Task | Browser | Report Builder | My Reports | Publisher | Content Manager |
|---|---|---|---|---|---|
| Consume reports | | ✓ | | | ✓ |
| Create linked reports | | | ✓ | ✓ | ✓ |
| Manage all subscriptions | | | | | ✓ |
| Manage data sources | | | ✓ | ✓ | ✓ |
| Manage folders | | | ✓ | ✓ | ✓ |
| Manage individual subscriptions | ✓ | ✓ | ✓ | | ✓ |
| Manage models | | | | ✓ | ✓ |
| Manage report history | | | ✓ | | ✓ |
| Manage reports | | | ✓ | ✓ | ✓ |
| Manage resources | | | ✓ | ✓ | ✓ |
| Set security for individual items | | | | | ✓ |
| View data sources | | | ✓ | | ✓ |
| View folders | ✓ | ✓ | ✓ | | ✓ |
| View models | ✓ | ✓ | | | ✓ |
| View reports | ✓ | ✓ | ✓ | | ✓ |
| View resources | ✓ | ✓ | ✓ | | ✓ |

## Adding a System Role Assignment

A *system role assignment* associates a Windows user or group with a system role to define who can perform administrative tasks on the Report Server, such as managing schedules. System role assignments are independent of item role assignments. For example, if a user is assigned only to a system role and is not a local system administrator, the user can't view folders or reports on the Report Server. Reporting Services has two default system roles: System User and System Administrator. The System User role allows access to the Site Settings page for viewing server properties and shared schedules, which is required if a user needs to use a shared schedule. The System Administrator role includes tasks for viewing and editing server properties, shared schedules, system role assignments, and role definitions. This role can also manage running jobs. To configure system roles, follow these steps:

1. In Report Manager, click the Site Settings link at the top-right corner of the Home page. This link is available only if you have a system role assignment that includes View Report Server Properties or Manage Report Server Properties.

2. Click the Configure Site-Wide Security link. The default system role assignment of the local system administrators group, BUILTIN\Administrators, is System Administrator. You'll always need at least one System Administrator role assignment. Even if you delete the BUILTIN\Administrators system role assignment, however, local system administrators always have access to security settings.

3. Click New Role Assignment on the Report Manager toolbar and type a user or group name. You can assign a user or group to multiple roles.

The following table shows the default association of system tasks by role:

**Table 23-2   Default System Assignments**

| Default Task | System Administrator | System User |
|---|:---:|:---:|
| Execute report definitions | ✓ | ✓ |
| Generate events | | |
| Manage jobs | ✓ | |
| Manager report server properties | ✓ | |
| Manage report server security | ✓ | |
| Manage roles | ✓ | |
| Manage shared schedules | ✓ | |
| View report server properties | | ✓ |
| View shared schedules | | ✓ |

## Performance Management

In this section, you'll discover several ways you can monitor activity on a report server and techniques you can use to proactively manage the resources on your server. You'll also learn how Reporting Services uses SQL Server databases and which tables to monitor for growth. Lastly, you'll learn how to implement execution logging to get a detailed perspective of activity on the report server.

## Performance Counters

You can use the Windows Performance tool, described in more detail in Chapter 6, "Capacity Planning," to monitor Reporting Services activity. Counters associated with MSRS 2005 Windows Service can help you monitor both interactive and scheduled activity on the server. Review the counters associated with MSRS 2005 Web Service to monitor activity initiated by a scheduled operation. Details about the performance counters themselves are in SQL Server Books Online. The following list describes some performance counters you might monitor regularly:

- **Active Sessions**   Counts active browser sessions

- **Reports Executed/Sec**   Volume of successful report execution

- **Total Processing Failures**   Number of failures since the service started

- **Total Requests**   Number of requests since the service started

## Server Resource Management

To manage server resources, you must be able to prevent certain activities from consuming too much memory or running too long. Sometimes you need to temporarily suspend activities for server maintenance or troubleshooting problems. Some common management tasks related to resource management are described in the following list:

- **Source Query Timeout**   Each dataset in a report has its own query timeout setting which you can edit only within Visual Studio. To change this setting, open a report in Visual Studio, click the Data tab of the report designer, select a dataset in the Dataset drop-down list, click the Edit Dataset button to the right of the drop-down list, and type a value in the Timeout box. If the query doesn't finish before the query timeout is exceeded, the report execution will fail. Use a source query timeout to protect against unexpectedly long-running queries.

- **Report Execution Timeout**   Each report's execution properties include a timeout setting which you can use to override the global timeout. Alternatively, you can change the global timeout, which by default is 1,800 seconds, on the Site Settings page of Report Manager.

- **Cancel Jobs**   From the Site Settings page in Report Manager, you can access the Manage Jobs page to view jobs currently executing. Here you can cancel one or more jobs, but be aware you may also need to kill the corresponding process in the source database.

- **Disable a Shared Data Source**   In Report Manager, open a data source and clear the Enable This Data Source check box when you need to temporarily prevent reports or subscriptions from executing.

- **Pause a Shared Schedule**   On the Site Settings page of Report Manager, click Manage Shared Schedules, select the check box for each shared schedule to pause, and then click the Pause button on the Report Manager toolbar. When you pause a shared schedule, all related jobs, such as report executions and subscriptions, are suspended. Use the Resume button when you're ready for jobs to execute on schedule.

## Reporting Services Databases

Reporting Services requires two SQL Server 2005 databases to operate. The *ReportServer* database is used to store report definitions, configuration information, security assignments, and schedules. The *ReportServerTempDB* database is used to store data only temporarily, such as session and caching information. In general, the tables in each database don't require much space. The exception is the ChunkData table in the *ReportServer* database. This table contains the intermediate reports for snapshots and report history. Because an intermediate report includes all report data, it requires more disk space than other items stored in the same database. The ChunkData table in the *ReportServerTempDB* database also contains intermediate reports for the session cache and the cached instances, so it also requires a large amount of disk space relative to other tables but doesn't persist this data over the long-term. Each Reporting Services implementation is unique in its disk space requirements, so we can't provide you with a specific formula to use for estimating disk space. However, the following list identifies the items that will have an impact on disk space consumption:

- Total number of reports

- Total number of snapshots

- Total number of snapshots saved in report history

- Total size of intermediate reports (which include report data) in snapshots and report history

- Total number of cached instances resulting from different combinations of report parameters

- Total number of users affecting session cache

- Session cache timeout length

> **Note**   Be sure to back up the *ReportServer* database regularly along with the *master* and *msdb* databases. User accounts for Reporting Services are stored in the *master* database and *msdb* stores scheduled jobs. You need

only back up the *ReportServerTempDB* database one time for disaster recovery since it contains cached data that can be recreated as users browse reports later.

## Real World    Execution Logs

A great way to monitor report server usage is to implement execution logging. You can review the duration and success rate of report executions and uncover bottlenecks in report execution. The information stored in the ExecutionLog table of the *ReportServer* database isn't useful for direct reporting and analysis, but you can periodically export and transforms records in this table to load into your own logging database. Use the Site Settings page in Report Manager to start or stop execution logging at any time. By default, execution logging is enabled, but log records are kept for only 60 days. To implement execution logging, follow these steps:

1.  Start SQL Server Management Studio and connect to the Database Engine.

2.  Create a new SQL Server database, as described in Chapter 10, "Creating Databases and Database Snapshots," named *RSExecutionLog*.

3.  On the File menu, point to Open, and then click File. Navigate to the %Program Files%\Microsoft SQL Server\90\Samples\Reporting Services\Report Samples\Server Management Sample Reports\Execution Log Sample Reports folder, and open the Createtables.sql file. When you open this file, you'll be prompted to connect to the Database Engine.

4.  Select *RSExecutionLog* in the Available Database drop-down list on the SQL Server Management Studio SQL Editor toolbar, and then click Execute on the same toolbar.

5.  In Windows Explorer, double-click the RSExecutionLog_Update.dtsx file in the %Program Files%\Microsoft SQL Server\90\Samples\Reporting Services\Report Samples\Server Management Sample Reports\Execution Log Sample Reports folder to start the Execute Package Utility. There are several pages you can review in the Execute Package Utility dialog box, but you do not need to make any changes for this example. Click Execute to start running the package, and then click Close twice when package execution completes.

6.  Using Visual Studio, open the Execution Log Sample Reports.rptproj file in the %Program Files%\Microsoft SQL Server\90\Samples\Reporting Services\Report Samples\Server Management Sample Reports\Execution Log

Sample Reports folder. The shared data source in this solution assumes the database is on the local server, but you can edit the data source if you need to reference the database on a different server.

7. Right-click the ExecutionLog project, and then click Deploy. When the project successfully deploys, open the Home page in Report Manager, and navigate to the Execution Log Reports folder. In this folder, you can find several reports that present execution logging information: Execution Status Codes, Execution Summary, and Report Summary. You can, of course, modify these reports to suit your needs more specifically or develop new reports.

## Summary

This chapter introduced the use of Reporting Services throughout to support the reporting life cycle. Basic report authoring techniques were discussed for both enterprise and ad hoc reports, and you learned how to build a report model to support ad hoc report development in Report Builder. You also learned how to perform administrative tasks to manage report server content, control report server behavior, and monitor performance. With this foundation, you have enough knowledge to begin using Reporting Services for delivering information easily throughout your organization.

# Chapter 24

# Notification Services and Service Broker

Transferring data, preparing data for analysis, and sharing data in reports are important information management activities that Microsoft SQL Server 2005 supports. But wait, there's more! SQL Server 2005 can also help you share information across, or even beyond, the organization with notification and asynchronous messaging applications. Using Notification Services, you can run applications that deliver messages when events of interest occur or on a scheduled basis. Service Broker is also involved in the delivery of messages but instead acts as the central clearinghouse for applications that are unable to communicate directly. In this chapter, we'll introduce the basic functionality of these two technologies for you to evaluate the possibilities they enable in your data environment.

## What Is Notification Services?

Notification Services is a bundled component of SQL Server 2005 Enterprise, Standard, and Developer editions used to create and run *notification applications*. A notification application delivers a *notification*, typically in the form of an e-mail message or a file, to a subscriber. A *subscriber* is an individual who receives notifications on a scheduled basis or when an event occurs. An *event* is something of interest that happened, such as a change in a key performance indicator tracked in an Analysis Services cube or new data available in a transactional database meeting certain conditions. Each subscriber has one or more *subscriptions* that define the rules for generating a notification.

To use Notification Services, you first build the application components, which can be as simple or as sophisticated as you need. You use XML files or the Notification Services application programming interface to define the database object structures and the rules for generating notifications. The definitions and rules you create are used by Notification Services to build a pair of databases for storing events, subscribers, and subscriptions when you instantiate the application. You can optionally build applications using managed code to collect events and to add or update subscribers and subscriptions, or you can create stored procedures to perform these activities.

## Notification Services 2005 Versus Notification Services 2.0

Microsoft SQL Server Notification Services 2.0 was introduced in 2002 as a downloadable add-on component to SQL Server 2000. Now a newer version of Notification Services is officially bundled with SQL Server 2005. This newer version includes several performance improvements, support for high availability, and new features to simplify the development and management of notification applications.

To start, let's consider how Notification Services 2005 improves upon certain features in Notification Services 2.0. As one example, the *Notify()* function in Notification Services 2.0 used stored procedures to load notification data into the application database, which sometimes had a negative effect on performance. Now, you need to write your own Transact-SQL statements to insert data into a view for notifications, but this process is much more efficient comparatively. As another example, the *vacuuming* process, which periodically removes stale data from the application database, runs as much as 150 percent faster than it did in 2.0. Finally, if you need high availability, you can now configure failover clustering for Notification Services independently from other cluster resource groups, including the database engine.

Performance and availability improvements are great, but you'll also like the new features for building and managing notification applications in Notification Services 2005. Instead of using command-line utilities to create, start, or stop instances of Notification Services, you can perform these and other administrative tasks using a graphical interface in SQL Server Management Studio. Alternatively, you can use the new management object model to create custom applications for building and maintaining Notification Services applications. Furthermore, you can integrate the Notification Services engine into your custom applications rather than use a Windows service for running Notification Services components.

Regardless of whether you work with custom applications, you'll find that working with the Notification Services 2005 databases is simpler than working with Notification Services 2.0

databases because there are new views available for inserting data for events, subscriptions, and notifications and for writing queries to monitor events and generate notifications. You can also take advantage of condition actions to give subscribers the ability to define a WHERE clause for the subscription query, thereby enabling more complex subscription rules. Finally, you can build an application that monitors events in an Analysis Services cube by using a new event provider to send Multidimensional Expression (MDX) queries to the cube and storing the results as events.

---

**Note**   After you upgrade an existing SQL Server 2000 instance to SQL Server 2005, you can use SQL Server Management Studio or a command-line utility to upgrade the Notification Services instances. You can migrate Notification Services 2.0 running on SQL Server 2000 Standard Edition to either SQL Server 2005 Standard or Enterprise Edition, but you can migrate Notification Services running on SQL Server 2000 Enterprise Edition only to SQL Server 2005 Enterprise Edition. You can find instructions explaining how to migrate a Notification Services 2.0 instance in the SQL Server Books Online topic "Migrating Notification Services Instances."

## Notification Services Fundamentals

Notification Services is not itself an application but a platform for the development and management of notification applications. Each notification application repeats a similar cycle. Using an interface that you create, subscribers and subscriptions are defined. Events are collected by Notification Services in batches by periodically executing queries and inserting the results into a view for that type of event. Notification Services then attempts to match events and subscriptions. When a match is found, Notification Services generates and formats a notification for each subscriber with a subscription for the matched event. Lastly, Notification Services sends the formatted notification to a delivery service, which in turn sends the notification to the subscriber's specified device, such as an e-mail account or a PDA device.

A Notification Services *instance* is a host for one or more applications. The instance has a configuration shared by all applications, such as the same SQL Server instance for instance and application databases. Each application has its own collection of database objects used to store information required to collect events and generate notifications. When you build a Notification Services application, you define the instance configuration, the structure of the application's database objects, and the rules for matching events to subscriptions and sending notifications.

You can run the Notification Services engine on the database server when your notification application is small and used internally. On the other hand, if you have a large application, you should use a dedicated server to take advantage of the scalability and high availability features of SQL Server 2005. For example, if notifications require complex formatting, you might consider using a dedicated Notification Services server to manage this process rather than requiring your application to compete for resources with a database engine installed on the same server.

## Notification Services Components Overview

Notification Services includes many components for you to build and maintain applications. The following list provides an overview of each component:

- **Event providers**   Adds events to the Notification Services application database and monitors external data sources for changes using built-in event providers, such as the file system watcher to monitor directories, the SQL Server event provider to monitor SQL Server databases, the Analysis Services event provider to monitor Analysis Services databases, or custom event providers you create to monitor other types of data sources

- **Generator**   Looks for matches between events and subscriptions on a periodic basis using a T-SQL query defined by the application developer, creates a notification when a match is detected, and creates a batch of notifications for the distributor

- **Distributor**   Receives a batch of notifications from the generator, formats each notification using an XML style sheet (XSLT) defined by the application developer to render output for specific device and sends the notification to a delivery channel

- **Delivery channel**   Sends formatted notifications to a specific device using a custom delivery protocol created by the application developer or a built-in protocol, such as the SMTP protocol, File protocol, or HTTP protocol

- **Notification Services engine**   Runs the event provider, generators, and distributors as a Windows service or as a custom application or process

- **SQL Server Management Studio**   Provides administrative support for Notification Services and the SQL Server databases used to manage data used by Notification Services

- **Nscontrol utility**   Creates, registers, repairs, and updates Notification Services applications at the command prompt

- **Instance and application databases**   Stores event, subscriber, subscription, and notification data as well as application metadata

- **Notification Services Management Objects (NMO)**   Includes application programming interfaces (APIs) for adding subscribers, managing subscriptions, collecting events, and delivering notifications

# Developing Notification Services Applications

If you're an application developer, you might prefer to build a notification application using the .NET Framework 2.0 and the Notification Services Management Objects, an API for Notification Services. Even if you're not an application developer, you can easily build an application using XML and T-SQL. In this chapter, we'll focus exclusively on the latter approach to show you how to build an instance configuration file (ICF) and an application definition file (ADF). The *ICF* contains information about the instance used to run the application, the SQL Server hosting the instance, the path to files used by the application, and parameters you can use to build an application once but reuse many times by changing parameter values. The *ADF* contains information describing the structure of database objects related to events, subscriptions, and notifications, in addition to information about components used to run the application.

In the following sections, we'll review the sections of an ICF and ADF file individually and then show you how to construct these files to build a simple Notification Services application that sends notifications to subscribers interested in monitoring the sales activity of customers in a specific sales territory. This notification application monitors all sales transactions and records events when sales are made. When a subscription matches any of these events, the application generates a notification, applies formatting to the notification, and sends it to the subscribing sales representative.

> **More Info**   For more in-depth information about Notification Services, read
> *Microsoft SQL Server 2005 Notification Services*, by Shyam Pather (Sams, 2006).

## Creating an Instance Configuration File

Each application must be associated with a Notification Services instance, so that's where we begin our development. When you build an application using XML, the Notification Services instance requires an ICF to define the name of the instance, identify and configure the databases hosting the instance, specify the applications to manage within the instance, and provide configuration settings for protocols and delivery channels used by the instance.

> **On the CD**   The following sections illustrate the code required to develop an
> ICF. You will find a complete sample ICF file, SalesActivityICF.xml, on the book's
> companion CD in the \Scripts\Chapter 24 folder.

## Starting a New Instance Configuration File

An ICF file describes a single instance of Notification Services in a valid, well-formed XML file, which means it must contain one or more elements, with the root element containing all other elements. The root element of an ICF file is *NotificationServicesInstance*. Additionally, the ICF must conform to the ConfigurationFileSchema which is included as a default namespace in the file. Here is the code to begin a new ICF, to which we'll add required elements later in this chapter:

```xml
<?xml version="1.0" encoding="utf-8"?>

<NotificationServicesInstance

  xmlns:xsd="http://www.w3.org/2001/XMLSchema"

  xmlns:xsi="http://www.w3.org/2001/XMLSchema-instance"

  xmlns="http://www.microsoft.com/MicrosoftNotificationServices/
ConfigurationFileSchema">
        <!-- Insert required elements here -->

</NotificationServicesInstance>
```

> **Note** Rather than type each section and element directly into the file, you can find a basic template to use as a starting point for developing an ICF in the topic "Minimal ICF Template" in SQL Server Books Online. A template that includes all optional sections is available in the "Complete ICF Template" topic. If you type the code rather than use a template, take care not to add white space to the text on any line.

## Adding an Instance Name

Each SQL Server instance can host one or more Notification Services instances. Accordingly, each Notification Services instance requires a unique name. By default, the instance name is also used as the name of the Windows service for the instance and as part of the name for the database used to store instance data. For this reason, you must conform to certain naming guidelines when specifying a name for the Notification Services instance. Specifically, the length of the name cannot exceed 64 characters and cannot contain quotation marks. Standard naming rules for object identifiers also apply. Here is the syntax for an instance named *SalesActivity*, using the required element *InstanceName*:

```xml
<InstanceName>SalesActivity</InstanceName>
```

## Defining the Host SQL Server Instance

Instance metadata and subscriber data is stored in a database for a specific Notification Services instance. Each application also has its own metadata as well as event, subscription, and notification data that must be stored in a database. Here is the syntax for the required element *SqlServerSystem* using a parameter instead of a specific value:

```
<SqlServerSystem>%_DBEngineInstance_%</SqlServerSystem>
```

In this example, `%_DBEngineInstance_%` is a parameter for which you can optionally define a default value in the *ParameterDefaults* section of the ICF, as explained later in this chapter. By including an underscores in the parameter name, you separate the name from the percent symbols and can therefore more easily read the name. You can also override the default value when you deploy the instance on the Notification Services server.

---

**Note**    Whether you add the SQL Server instance here or specify an instance as a parameter value elsewhere, be sure to use the SQL Server instance name, not its alias or IP address. If the SQL Server instance is in a failover cluster, use the virtual server name.

---

## Defining the Instance Database

Typically, Notification Services creates databases to host the instance and application databases described in the previous section. The *Database* section of the ICF is optional. If you omit this section from the ICF, Notification Services creates a database named *<InstanceName>NSMain</InstanceName>* using the *model* database as a template. The name you provide in the *InstanceName* element of the ICF becomes part of the database name, such as *SalesActivityNSMain* to continue the previous example. If you prefer a different name, you must include the *Database* section and add the *DatabaseName* and *SchemaName* elements to this section. You can also use additional elements to specify database properties, such as filegroups and log files, if the *model* database properties are not sufficient for your application's needs. As an alternative, you can use the *Database* section of the ICF to specify the name and schema of an existing database in which Notification Services will create instance objects.

---

**More Info**    For more information about using elements to define the instance database, refer to the topic "Database Element (ICF)" in SQL Server Books Online.

---

## Defining Hosted Applications

A single Notification Services instance can host one or more applications. Each application hosted by one instance shares subscribers and delivery channels to simplify and centralize administration. Using the ICF, you use the *Applications* section to identify which applications are hosted by the instance by providing a name for the *ApplicationName* element, a path to the ADF using the *ApplicationDefinitionFilePath* element, and a path to the directory containing supplemental files for the application using the *BaseDirectoryPath* element. You can provide this information directly in the ICF, or you can use parameters to reuse this ICF in other environments. Here is the syntax for the *Applications* section of the ADF for the *TerritorySales* application using parameters for the paths:

```
<Applications>

    <Application>

        <ApplicationName>TerritorySales</ApplicationName>

        <BaseDirectoryPath>%_InstancePath_%</BaseDirectoryPath>

        <ApplicationDefinitionFilePath>
%_InstancePath_%\TerritorySales\TerritorySalesADF.xml
        </ApplicationDefinitionFilePath>

    </Application>

</Applications>
```

In this example, `%_InstancePath_%` is another parameter for which you can provide a value in the *ParameterDefaults* section or when you create the instance. When you create the ADF, you must place the file in the path specified here, or the application will fail.

## Defining Delivery Channels

A *delivery channel* is an endpoint to which Notification Services delivers notifications using a specified protocol. A Notification Services instance can support multiple delivery channels. When a subscriber creates a subscription, a device is associated with the subscription, such as an e-mail account. The selection of the device determines which delivery channel will be used to send notifications to that subscriber. Each delivery channel requires a unique name and is associated with a delivery protocol. If the delivery protocol requires arguments, you must also include values for these arguments in the ICF. Notification Services includes two built-in delivery protocols, SMTP Delivery and File Delivery. Here is the syntax for using the File Delivery protocol, including an argument to specify the file name receiving notifications:

```
<DeliveryChannels>

    <DeliveryChannel>

        <DeliveryChannelName>FileChannel</DeliveryChannelName>

        <ProtocolName>File</ProtocolName>

        <Arguments>

            <Argument>

                <Name>FileName</Name>

                <Value>
                %_InstancePath_%\TerritorySales\Notifications\FileNotifications.htm
                </Value>

            </Argument>

        </Arguments>
```

```
    </DeliveryChannel>
</DeliveryChannels>
```

Notice this example sends notifications to a file in a subdirectory of the instance path, but you can certainly define any directory and file name that meets your needs. You must grant the Notification Services engine write permissions to the defined directory, as explained later in this chapter.

---

**Note**   You can find instructions for defining a delivery channel using SMTP Delivery in the SQL Server Books Online topic, "Defining an SMTP Delivery Channel."

---

You can also use custom delivery protocols if you include the definition in a *Protocols* section of the ICF. This section is normally omitted when you use only the built-in delivery protocols.

## Adding Parameter Default Values

By using parameters in an ICF, you can make your applications more portable and flexible. For example, in the previous examples, %_InstancePath_% is used to define the path once. The same path can then be used as a value for multiple elements. When you need to change the instance path, you need only to change the parameter value once, but the change applies to many values in the ICF. You can use parameters without including default values in the ICF, but instance deployment is made easier if you do include parameter defaults. Even if you include them, you can override the default values when you deploy the instance. Here is the syntax for assigning a default value, C:\NS, to the %_InstancePath_% parameter:

```
<ParameterDefaults>

    <Parameter>

        <Name>_InstancePath_</Name>

        <Value>C:\NS</Value>

    </Parameter>

</ParameterDefaults>
```

## Creating an Instance Configuration File by Using Visual Studio

You can use your favorite XML editor or Visual Studio to create a new ICF. You can also edit an ICF by opening the file in SQL Server Management Studio. To begin a new ICF using Visual Studio, follow these steps:

1.  Using Windows Explorer, create a directory for your Notification Services instance and applications, such as **C:\NS**. If you prefer a different location or name, be sure to change the default parameter value for %_InstancePath_% in the ICF.

2. Click Start, point to All Programs, point to Microsoft SQL Server 2005, and then click SQL Server Business Intelligence Development Studio. Despite its name in the Microsoft SQL Server 2005 program group, this item is actually a shortcut to Visual Studio.

3. Insert the CD-ROM provided with this book into your CD-ROM drive.

4. On the File menu, point to Open, and then select File.

5. In the Open File dialog box, navigate to the CD-ROM drive, open the Scripts\Chapter 24 folder, select the SalesActivity.ICF file, and then click Open. Here is the code in the file:

```xml
<?xml version="1.0" encoding="utf-8"?>.

<NotificationServicesInstance

  xmlns:xsd="http://www.w3.org/2001/XMLSchema"

  xmlns:xsi="http://www.w3.org/2001/XMLSchema-instance"

  xmlns="http://www.microsoft.com/MicrosoftNotificationServices/ConfigurationFileSchema">

    <InstanceName>SalesActivity</InstanceName>

    <SqlServerSystem>%_DBEngineInstance_%</SqlServerSystem>

    <Applications>

        <Application>

            <ApplicationName>TerritorySales</ApplicationName>

<BaseDirectoryPath>%_InstancePath_%</BaseDirectoryPath>

            <ApplicationDefinitionFilePath>

%_InstancePath_%\TerritorySales\TerritorySalesADF.xml

            </ApplicationDefinitionFilePath>

            <Parameters>

                <Parameter>

                    <Name>_DBEngineInstance_</Name>

                    <Value>%_DBEngineInstance_%</Value>

                </Parameter>

                <Parameter>

                    <Name>_InstancePath_</Name>

<Value>%_InstancePath_%\TerritorySales</Value>

                </Parameter>
```

```
            </Parameters>
        </Application>
    </Applications>
    <DeliveryChannels>
        <DeliveryChannel>

<DeliveryChannelName>FileChannel</DeliveryChannelName>
            <ProtocolName>File</ProtocolName>
            <Arguments>
                <Argument>
                    <Name>FileName</Name>
                    <Value>
%_InstancePath_%\TerritorySales\Notifications\FileNotifications.htm
                    </Value>
                </Argument>
            </Arguments>
        </DeliveryChannel>
    </DeliveryChannels>
    <ParameterDefaults>
        <Parameter>
            <Name>_InstancePath_</Name>
            <Value>C:\NS</Value>
        </Parameter>
    </ParameterDefaults>
</NotificationServicesInstance>
```

6. On the File menu, select Save SalesActivityICF.xml As. In the File Name dialog box, type **C:\NS\SalesActivityICF.xml**, and then click Save. Your ICF file is now complete.

# Creating an Application Definition File

The ADF is the main file used to describe the events, rules, subscriptions, and rules for notification that comprise a Notification Services application. As previously mentioned in this chapter, Notification Services uses a SQL Server database to manage the tasks performed by the application and to store associated data. The ADF defines the schema of the database objects and the queries used to collect events, match events to subscriptions, and generate notifications. You can optionally add indexes to improve application performance.

A basic ADF file includes definitions for an event class, a subscription class, a notification class, one or more providers, a generator, distributors, and application execution settings. Specific information about each of these definitions is provided in the following sections in which we walk you through the process of building an ADF. By default, Notification Services creates a database for the application named *<InstanceName><ApplicationName>* using the *model* database as a template. You can override this default behavior by including a *Database* section in the ADF, just as you can in the ICF. In the example application we're building, we'll let Notification Services create a database, so we'll omit this section and focus only on the basic requirements.

> **Note**   For more information about using elements to define the application database, refer to the topic "Database Element (ADF)" in SQL Server Books Online.

> **On the CD**   The following sections illustrate the code required to develop an ADF. You will find a complete sample ADF file, TerritorySalesADF.xml, on the book's companion CD in the \Scripts\Chapter 24 folder.

## Starting a New Application Definition File

An ADF is an XML file just like the ICF, so you can use any XML editor or Visual Studio to create and edit the file. You can also edit the file using SQL Server Management Studio. The root element for an ADF file is *Application*. An ADF must conform to the ConfigurationFileSchema, which is included as a default namespace in the file. Here is the code to begin a new ADF, to which we'll add required elements later in this chapter:

```
<Application

    xmlns:xsd="http://www.w3.org/2001/XMLSchema"

    xmlns:xsi="http://www.w3.org/2001/XMLSchema-instance"

    xmlns="http://www.microsoft.com/MicrosoftNotificationServices/ApplicationDefinitionFileSchema">

    <!-- Insert required elements here -->

</Application>
```

> **Note**   As with the ICF templates, you can find two templates in SQL Server Books Online to help you build an ADF more rapidly. Locate the topics "Minimal

ADF Template" and "Complete ADF Template" to find templates you can copy into your ADF file.

## Adding an Event Class

First, you need to understand how to collect events from a source. A Notification Services *event provider* allows you to query a data source and return the results as events to your application. If the source data is in an XML format or in a relational database, you can use the built-in providers to access the data for insertion into the Notification Services databases. Otherwise, you need to develop a custom provider and include it in your application.

Next, you define an *event class* to describe the properties of the tables, views, basic indexes, and stored procedures used to store and manage events in the application database. If you need to track different types of events within a single application, you can create separate event classes. An event class has several elements:

- **EventClasses**   Contains one or more *EventClass* elements to define event classes

- **EventClass**   Contains several child elements to define a single event: *EventClass-Name, Schema, FileGroup, IndexSqlSchema, ChronicleRule,* and *Chronicles*

- **EventClassName**   Defines the name of table and view objects in the application database related to an event; must be unique and must conform to standard naming rules for database objects

- **Schema**   Contains *Field* elements used for a single event

- **Field**   Contains several elements defining a column in tables and views used for storing and displaying information about an event: *FieldName, FieldType,* and *Field-TypeMods*

- **FieldName**   Defines the name of a field; must confirm to SQL Server identifier rules

- **FieldType**   Defines a SQL Server data type for a field

- **FieldTypeMods**   Defines a table column modifier for a field; must conform to T-SQL syntax

- **IndexSqlSchema**   Contains one or more *SqlStatement* elements used to create indexes on an event table

- **SqlStatement**   Contains a T-SQL statement used by Notification Services to create an index on an event table

---

**More Info**    This list contains only elements we'll be using in the sample application in this chapter. You can learn more about the other elements by locating the element name in SQL Server Books Online index, such as "FileGroup Element."

---

The definition of additional indexes to be created by Notification Services using the *IndexSqlSchema* and *SqlStatement* elements is optional. Notification Services creates indexes for the system fields *EventID* and *EventBatchID* that are automatically added to the event. Any custom indexes you define are added only to the view for the event class, which contains only current batches in the event class table for performance reasons.

---

**Note**    For more information about adding your own indexes to an event class, refer to the topic "Defining Indexes for an Event Class" in SQL Server Books Online.

---

If your application supports scheduled subscriptions or maintains a history of events, you can add an *event chronicle*. An event chronicle is a separate collection of tables, views, indexes, and stored procedures used to archive events. Archiving events is required for applications which do not send notifications on detection of events or when a new event needs to be compared to prior events because events are periodically deleted from the application database by the vacuuming process.

---

**Note**    For more information about working with event chronicles, see the topic "Defining Chronicles for an Event Class" in SQL Server Books Online.

---

Here is the syntax of an *EventClass* named *MyEventData* with a single field *MyField* to which an index on *MyField* is added:

```
<EventClasses>

    <EventClass>

        <EventClassName>MyEventData</EventClassName>

        <Schema>

            <Field>

                <FieldName>MyField</FieldName>

                <FieldType>nvarchar(35)</FieldType>

                <FieldTypeMods>not null</FieldTypeMods>

            </Field>

        <!-- Insert additional fields here -->
```

```
        </Schema>
        <IndexSqlSchema>
            <SqlStatement>
                CREATE TNDEX MyIndex ON MyEventData ( MyField );
            </SqlStatement>
        </IndexSqlSchema>
    </EventClass>
</EventClasses>
```

## Adding a Subscription Class

Subscription data describes the types of events that interest each subscriber and is stored, like event data, in the application database. Typically, a custom application is developed to allow subscribers to manage their own subscriptions. When you develop your Notification Services application, you need to plan the structure of the data captured by the subscription management application and determine whether to support multiple types of subscriptions. As an example, if your Notification Services application monitors information about customer sales, you could offer an event-driven subscription and a scheduled subscription. For the event-driven subscription, a subscriber could identify the specific customers triggering a notification when a sale is made. As an additional option, the subscriber could also create a scheduled subscription to receive a monthly sales activity report for the customers of interest.

You define a *subscription class* for each type of subscription in your application. The subscription class defines the properties of the tables, views, basic indexes, and stored procedures used to store and manage subscriptions in the application database. Like event classes, a subscription class has core elements that you must define in the ADF:

- **Subscriptionclasses**   Contains one or more *Eventclass* elements to define subscription classes

- **Subscriptionclass**   Contains several child elements to define a single subscription: Subscriptionclassname, Schema, Filegroup, Indexsqlschema, Eventrules, Scheduledrules, and Chronicles

- **Subscriptionclassname**   Defines the Name Of Table And View Objects in the application database related to a single subscription; must be unique and must conform to standard naming rules for database objects

- **Schema**   Contains *Field* elements used for a single subscription

- **Field**   Contains several elements defining a column in tables and views used for storing and displaying information about a subscription: *FieldName, FieldType,* and *FieldTypeMods*

- **FieldName**   Defines the name of a field; must confirm to SQL Server identifier rules

- **FieldType**   Defines a SQL Server data type for a field

- **FieldTypeMods**   Defines a table column modifier for a field; must conform to T-SQL syntax

- **EventRules**   Contains one or more EventRule elements to define how notifications are generated for a single subscription

- **EventRule**   Contains several child elements to define a notification rule: RuleName, EventClassName, ActionTimeout, and either Action or ConditionAction but not both

- **RuleName**   Defines a unique name for the notification rule within the application

- **EventClassName**   Associates an event class with the notification rule

- **Action**   Contains a T-SQL statement used by Notification Services to create a notification

---

**More Info**   This list contains only elements we'll be using in the sample application in this chapter. You can learn more about the other elements by locating the element name in SQL Server Books Online index, such as "ScheduledRules Element."

Most Notification Services applications also include a schema in the subscription class to enhance the default subscription fields with standard and custom fields. Each type of field is described in the following list:

- **Default subscription fields**   The following fields are always added as columns to the subscription table: *SubscriptionID, SubscriberID,* and *Enabled.* These fields are reserved and must not be duplicated elsewhere in the same subscription class schema. An additional default field, *ScheduleID,* is included when the subscription class has a scheduled rule.

- **Standard subscription fields**   The following fields are not required, but you can include them in the subscription class schema to use for formatting and delivering notifications: *DeviceName* and *SubscriberLocale.* If you omit these fields from the schema, you must provide static values for the device and the locale in the notification generation rule.

- **Custom subscription fields**  Fields that subscribers can use to further customize a subscription are added as columns to the subscription table. If you include custom subscription fields in the schema, you must also define the field's data type and any applicable field modifiers.

---

**Note**  For more information about defining fields in the subscription class schema, refer to the SQL Server Books Online topic "Defining the Subscription Schema."

---

In addition to a schema, most Notification Services applications also include at least one subscription rule to define the conditions under which a notification is generated. In principle, a subscription rule creates a notification record by joining an event with a subscription. There are two types of subscription rules:

- **Scheduled rule**  Generates a notification at a time specified by the subscription schedule

- **Event rule**  Generates a notification when a batch of events is collected

Regardless of the type of subscription rule you use, the rule includes an *action*, which is the T-SQL query used by Notification Services when it runs the rule. There are two types of actions you can create:

- **Action**  Accepts a parameter value defined by the subscriber for use as a limited filter in the query

- **Condition action**  Accepts a condition expression for use in the query for use as a more complex filter in the query

---

**Note**  If your query includes XML-reserved characters, you need to replace these characters with the corresponding entity reference. Each entity reference begins with an ampersand (&) and ends with a semicolon(;). Replace > with *&gt;*, replace < with *&lt;*, replace & with *&amp;*, and replace % with *&#37;*.

---

To improve application performance, you can add custom indexes to be created by Notification Services. By default, Notification Services creates an index for the system field *ScheduleID*. The custom indexes you define are added to the subscription table corresponding to the subscription class.

---

**Note**  For more information about adding a custom index to the subscription class, see the topic "Defining Indexes for a Subscription Class" in SQL Server Books Online.

You can optionally add a *subscription chronicle* to keep track of previous notifications. Your subscription rule can check the subscription chronicle before sending a new notification, for example, if your application has a requirement to limit the frequency of notifications. Each subscription class can have one or more chronicle tables.

---

**Note**    The SQL Server Books Online topic "Defining Chronicles for a Subscription Class" provides details about implementing subscription chronicles.

---

Here is the syntax of a *SubscriptionClass* named *MySubscription* with standard fields and a custom field *MyField* with an event rule and a basic action, with a comment as a placeholder for a T-SQL query:

```
<SubscriptionClasses>

    <SubscriptionClass>

<SubscriptionClassName>MySubscription</SubscriptionClassName>

        <Schema>

            <Field>

                <FieldName>DeviceName</FieldName>

                <FieldType>nvarchar(255)</FieldType>

                <FieldTypeMods>not null</FieldTypeMods>

            </Field>

            <Field>

                <FieldName>SubscriberLocale</FieldName>

                <FieldType>nvarchar(10)</FieldType>

                <FieldTypeMods>not null</FieldTypeMods>

            </Field>

            <Field>

                <FieldName>MyField</FieldName>

                <FieldType>nvarchar(35)</FieldType>

                <FieldTypeMods>not null</FieldTypeMods>

            </Field>

        </Schema>

        <EventRules>

            <EventRule>

                <RuleName>MyEventRule</RuleName>
```

```
          <EventClassName>MyEventData</EventClassName>
          <Action>
           <!-- Insert Transact-SQL Query here -->
          </Action>
        </EventRule>
      </EventRules>
    </SubscriptionClass>
</SubscriptionClasses>
```

> **Note**   An example of a T-SQL query as a basic action in an event rule is pro-
> vided later in this chapter in the section titled "Creating an Application Definition
> File by Using Visual Studio."

## Adding a Notification Class

The ADF for your application must include a *notification class* for each type of notification
to be generated. The notification class creates the tables, views, and stored procedures
used to store notifications in the application database. In addition, the notification class
defines the content formatters for notifications and the delivery protocols used to send
the notifications to subscribers. Core properties of the notification class are described in
the following list:

- **NotificationClasses**   Contains one or more NotificationClass elements to define
  notification classes

- **NotificationClass**   Contains several child elements to define a single notification:
  NotificationClassName, Schema, FileGroup, ContentFormatter, DigestDelivery,
  MulticastDelivery, NotificationBatchSize, Protocols, and ExpirationAge

- **NotificationClassName**   Defines the name of table and view objects in the application database related to a single notification; must be unique and must conform
  to standard naming rules for database objects

- **Schema**   Contains Field and optional ComputedField elements used for a single
  notification table

- **Field**   Contains several elements defining a column in tables and views used for
  storing and displaying information about a notification: FieldName, FieldType, and
  DigestGrouping

- **FieldName**   Defines the name of a field; must confirm to SQL Server identifier
  rules

- **FieldType**   Defines a SQL Server data type for a field

- **ContentFormatter**   Contains several child elements used by Notification Services to format the raw data of a notification as a user-friendly message: ClassName, AssemblyName, and Arguments

- **ClassName**   Defines the namespace and class that provides formatting functionality if you create a custom content formatter; specify *XlstFormatter* (without a namespace) to use the built-in content formatter

- **Arguments**   Contains one or more Argument elements to be passed by the distributor to the content formatter

- **Argument**   Defines a single argument for a content formatter

- **Protocols**   Contains one or more Protocol elements to be used with the notification class

- **Protocol**   Contains several child elements to define a delivery protocol: Protocol-Name, Fields, and ProtocolExecutionSettings

- **ProtocolName**   Defines a name for the delivery protocol which must be a built-in protocol (SMTP or File) or be specified in the ICF

---

**More Info**   This list contains only elements we'll be using in the sample application in this chapter. You can learn more about the other elements by locating the element name in SQL Server Books Online index, such as "DigestGrouping Element."

---

Optionally, the notification class defines the behavior of notifications, such as whether notifications are sent in individually or in digest mode and whether notifications can be multicast. You can also manage the size of notification batches to take advantage of parallel processing. Finally, you can specify a notification expiration age to end attempts to deliver a notification after a certain period of time.

When you define the schema for the notification class, you need to take care not to create custom fields that conflict with the default fields created by Notification Services. The following list describes the types of fields available to your notification class:

- **Default notification fields**   The following fields are always added as columns to the notification table: *NotificationID*, *NotificationBatchID*, *SubscriberID*, *DeviceName*, and *SubscriberLocale*. These fields are reserved and must not be duplicated elsewhere in the same notification class schema.

- **Custom notification fields**   Some fields are added as columns to the notification table for consolidating information as a notification. Custom fields must match data created by the subscription rule, and you must define each field's data type and any applicable field modifiers.

- **Default notification delivery fields**   The following fields are added to the notification table to track notification delivery: *DeliveryStatusCode*, *SentTime*, and *LinkNotificationID*. These fields are reserved and must not be duplicated elsewhere in the same notification class schema.

- **Computed fields**   These fields use T-SQL expressions to compute a value for a notification field immediately before formatting.

Here is the syntax of a *NotificationClass* named *MyAlerts* with standard fields and a single custom field *MyField* and the *File* delivery protocol defined in the ICF:

```
<NotificationClasses>

    <NotificationClass>

        <NotificationClassName>MyAlerts</NotificationClassName>

        <Schema>

            <Fields>

                <Field>

                    <FieldName>MyField</FieldName>

                    <FieldType>nvarchar(35)</FieldType>

                </Field>

                <!-- Insert additional fields here -->

            </Fields>

        </Schema>

        <ContentFormatter>

            <ClassName>XsltFormatter</ClassName>

            <Arguments>

                <Argument>

                    <Name>XsltBaseDirectoryPath</Name>

                    <Value>C:\TransformDirectory</Value>

                <Argument>

                <Argument>

                    <Name>XsltFileName</Name>

                    <Value>MyTransform.xsl</Value>

                <Argument>
```

```
            <Argument>
                <Name>DisableEscaping</Name>
                <Value>true</Value>
            <Argument>
        </Arguments>
    </ContentFormatter>
    <Protocols>
        <Protocol>
            <ProtocolName>File</ProtocolName>
        </Protocol>
    </Protocols>
</NotificationClass>
</NotificationClasses>
```

## Adding an Event Provider

An event provider collects data about events on a periodic basis by sending a query to the data source. If the query returns results, the result set is added to the event class view as an event batch. An event provider can be hosted or nonhosted. A hosted event provider is managed by the Notification Services engine. A nonhosted event provider is an external application that submits events.

If you use a hosted provider but your data sources are not accessible by the standard event providers included with Notification Services, you can develop a custom event provider to retrieve data from these sources. However, you should be able to use these standard event providers for most event collection scenarios:

- **File System Watcher Event**   Provider monitors a specified directory for new event files with an .xml extension, validates data in the file using a specified XML schema file, writes event data into the event table, and renames the event file to indicate the files has been processed

- **SQL Server Event**   Provider sends T-SQL queries to a relational data source and uses the event submission stored procedures to insert the selected events into the event table; optionally uses T-SQL queries to process events after collection

- **Analysis Services Event**   Provider sends an MDX query to an Analysis Services data source, maps the result set to the event class fields, and inserts the result set as events into the event table; uses either a static MDX query or a dynamic MDX query generated when the subscription rule fires

**Note**   Details for defining the properties of these event providers are provided in the topic "Standard Event Providers" and its subtopics in SQL Server Books Online.

Here is the syntax for a hosted SQL Server Event Provider named *MyProvider* that polls every 60 seconds for events to be added to the *MyEventData* event class:

```
<Providers>

    <HostedProvider>

        <ProviderName>MyProvider</ProviderName>

        <ClassName>SQLProvider</ClassName>

        <SystemName>%_DBEngineInstance_%</SystemName>

        <Schedule>

            <Interval>P0DT00H00M60S</Interval>

        </Schedule>

        <Arguments>

            <Argument>

                <Name>EventsQuery</Name>

                <Value>SELECT MyField FROM MyTable</Value>

            </Argument>

            <Argument>

                <Name>EventClassName</Name>

                <Value>MyEventData</Value>

            </Argument>

        </Arguments>

    </HostedProvider>

</Providers>
```

When you use a SQL Server event provider, you must provide values for the following required elements:

- **ProviderName**   Must be unique

- **ClassName**   Must be SQLProvider but do not provide an *AssemblyName* element as required when you define a content formatter

- **SystemName**   Name of server to run the event provider, name of virtual server if running on a failover cluster, or a parameter

- **Interval**  Frequency used to run event provider using the pattern PnYnMnDT-nHnMnS, where nY is the number of years, nM is the number of months, nD is the number of days, T is the date/time separator, nH is the number of hours, nM is the number of minutes, and nS is the number of seconds.

---

**Note**  You can optionally include a *ProviderTimeout* element using a value patterned like the *Interval* value, such as PT5M to specify a five minute timeout.

Each event provider has a set of elements for which you must provide values. The SQL Server event provider shown in this example uses only the two required elements, but accepts a total of three elements in any order. The following are the other acceptable elements:

- **EventClassName**  Name of the event class for which this event provider collects events

- **EventsQuery**  A T-SQL query or stored procedure used to gather events on the local server or a linked server; must return columns that map to the event class fields

- **PostQuery**  An optional T-SQL query or stored procedure used to process collected event data

---

**Note**  When using a stored procedure in either of the query arguments, be sure to include the EXECUTE statement in front of the stored procedure name.

## Adding a Generator

Each application has one generator, which is usually hosted by the Windows service running the Notification Services instance components. The generator is responsible for processing the rules defined in the application. Rules are processed in groups, beginning with event chronicle rules, followed by subscription event rules, and ending with subscription scheduled rules. Here is the basic syntax for a generator:

```
<Generator>
    <SystemName>%_DBEngineInstance_%</SystemName>
</Generator>
```

Notice the use of a parameter for the SystemName element. When you configure the instance, you provide a value for this parameter. The value is either the name of the server on which the generator runs or the name of the virtual server if the generator is on a failover cluster. Alternatively, you can use a parameter.

---

**Note**  By default, the generator thread pool size is 1, which limits processing to one rule at a time. The maximum thread pool size in Standard Edition is 1, but if you use Enterprise or Developer edition you can increase the thread pool size to allow more rules of the same type to process in parallel. All rules of a specific type must be processed before the next rule type can be processed. If you set the thread pool size to 0, Notification Services uses as many threads as possible up to a maximum of 25. To configure thread pool size, add the following code to the *Generator* section of the ADF.

```
<ThreadPoolSize>0</ThreadPoolSize>
```

## Adding a Distributor

Each application has at least one distributor. The distributor manages the formatting and delivery of notifications. If you have a scale-out configuration to run a Notification Services instance, you can run one distributor on each computer using the instance's Windows service if you are using Enterprise or Developer edition. Using multiple distributors is recommended when you have a high volume of notifications requiring complex formatting.

In the ADF, you define the time interval, called a *quantum*, used by the distributor to check for new notifications. If notifications are available, the distributor calls the content formatter defined in the ADF to format the data and sends the results to the delivery channel. If the notifications cannot be distributed and no expiration age is configured, the distributor tries again at the next interval.

Here is the basic syntax for a distributor with a quantum configured for 15 seconds.

```
<Distributors>

    <Distributor>

        <SystemName>%_DBEngineInstance_%</SystemName>

        <QuantumDuration>PT15S</QuantumDuration>

    </Distributor>

</Distributors>
```

The value for SystemName element is a parameter, as shown in this example, or the name of the server running the distributor. If the distributor is on a failover cluster, use the virtual server name. The QuantumDuration element defines a time interval in the formatPnYnMnDTnHnMnS, as described previously in this chapter in the section titled "Adding an Event Provider."

**Note**    By default, the distributor uses all available threads. If you use Enterprise or Developer edition, the thread pool size is unlimited and notifications can be processed in parallel. Notification Services will determine the optimal thread size if you don't configure a value. If you use Standard Edition, the default thread pool size is 3, but you can lower this value to 1 or 2 to limit parallel processing if your application produces a low volume of notifications or if you want to minimize the distributor's consumption of system resources. To configure thread pool size for 2 threads, add the following code to the *Distributor* section of the ADF.

```
<ThreadPoolSize>2</ThreadPoolSize>
```

## Configuring Application Execution Settings

Application execution settings can improve the performance of your application and manage the volume of data accumulated by the application. Although configuring application execution settings for your application is optional, you should at minimum configure the following elements:

- **ApplicationExecutionSettings**    Contains several optional child elements to configure execution settings for the application: *QuantumDuration, ChronicleQuantumLimit, SubscriptionQuantumLimit, ProcessEventsInOrder, PerformanceQueryInterval, EventThrottle, SubscriptionThrottle, NotificationThrottle, DistributorLogging,* and *Vacuum*

- **QuantumDuration**    Applies to the generator to define the frequency of firing event and subscription rules; independent of the distributor quantum duration

- **DistributorLogging**    Contains child elements used to log delivery information for all deliveries which consume database resources: *LogBeforeDeliveryAttempts, LogStatusInfo,* and *LogNotificationText*; enabled by default and should be disabled if your service level agreements don't require this information because all failed deliveries are already logged

- **LogBeforeDeliveryAttempts**    Indicates whether a row should be inserted into the distribution log before notification delivery

- **LogStatusInfo**    Indicates whether a row should be inserted into the distribution log for all deliveries or failed deliveries only

- **LogNotificationText**    Indicates whether notification text ix logged for all deliveries or failed deliveries only

- **Vacuum**    Contains child elements used to vacuum data from the event, notification, and distribution tables and related control tables in the application: RetentionAge and VacuumSchedule

- **RetentionAge**    Defines a minimum retention age for application data

- **VacuumSchedule**  Contains the Schedule element to define the vacuuming schedule to remove data that is older than the specified retention age

- **Schedule**  Contains the StartTime and Duration elements that are used to define the vacuuming schedule

- **StartTime**  Defines the start time in Universal Coordinated Time (UTC) format for daily vacuuming

- **Duration**  Defines the length of the vacuuming period in the format PnYn-MnDTnHnMnS

---

**Note**  For more information about these and other application execution settings, refer to the SQL Server Books Online topic, "Specifying Application Execution Settings."

---

Here is the syntax for the *ApplicationExecutionSettings* section to specify a quantum duration of 15 seconds, disable distributor logging for normal deliveries, and remove data older than one day beginning at 11 P.M. for a duration of two hours.

```
<ApplicationExecutionSettings>
    <QuantumDuration>PT15S</QuantumDuration>
    <DistributorLogging>
        <LogBeforeDeliveryAttempts>false</LogBeforeDeliveryAttempts>
        <LogStatusInfo>false</LogStatusInfo>
        <LogNotificationText>false</LogNotificationText>
    </DistributorLogging>
    <Vacuum>
        <RetentionAge>P1D</RetentionAge>
        <VacuumSchedule>
            <Schedule>
                <StartTime>23:00:00</StartTime>
                <Duration>P0DT02H00M00S</Duration>
            </Schedule>
        </VacuumSchedule>
    </Vacuum>
</ApplicationExecutionSettings>
```

## Creating an Application Definition File by Using Visual Studio

You can use your favorite XML editor or Visual Studio to create a new ADF, and you can edit an existing ADF by opening the file in SQL Server Management Studio. To begin a new ADF using Visual Studio, follow these steps:

1. Using Windows Explorer, create a folder for your Notification Services application, such as **C:\NS\TerritorySales,** for this example.

2. Create a folder for the file delivery of notifications, **Notifications,** in the C:\NS\TerritorySales folder.

3. In the Start menu, point to All Programs, point to Microsoft SQL Server 2005, and then click SQL Server Business Intelligence Development Studio. Despite its name in the Microsoft SQL Server 2005 program group, this item is actually a shortcut to Visual Studio.

4. Insert the companion CD provided with this book into your CD-ROM drive.

5. On the File menu, point to Open, and then select File.

6. In the Open File dialog box, navigate to the CD-ROM drive, open the Scripts\Chapter 24 folder, select the TerritorySalesADF.xml file, and then click Open. Here is the code in the file.

```xml
<?xml version="1.0" encoding="utf-8"?>.

<Application

    xmlns:xsd="http://www.w3.org/2001/XMLSchema"

    xmlns:xsi="http://www.w3.org/2001/XMLSchema-instance"

    xmlns="http://www.microsoft.com/MicrosoftNotificationServices/ApplicationDefinitionFileSchema">

    <EventClasses>

        <EventClass>

            <EventClassName>TerritorySalesData</EventClassName>

            <Schema>

                <Field>

                    <FieldName>Territory</FieldName>

                    <FieldType>nvarchar(50)</FieldType>

                    <FieldTypeMods>not null</FieldTypeMods>

                </Field>

                <Field>
```

```
                    <FieldName>CustomerName</FieldName>

                    <FieldType>nvarchar(100)</FieldType>

                    <FieldTypeMods>not null</FieldTypeMods>

                </Field>

                <Field>

                    <FieldName>OrderDate</FieldName>

                    <FieldType>datetime</FieldType>

                    <FieldTypeMods>not null</FieldTypeMods>

                </Field>

                <Field>

                    <FieldName>SalesOrderNumber</FieldName>

                    <FieldType>nvarchar(25)</FieldType>

                    <FieldTypeMods>not null</FieldTypeMods>

                </Field>

                <Field>

                    <FieldName>SalesAmount</FieldName>

                    <FieldType>money</FieldType>

                    <FieldTypeMods>not null</FieldTypeMods>

                </Field>

            </Schema>

            <IndexSqlSchema>

                <SqlStatement>

                    CREATE INDEX MyIndex ON

                        TerritorySalesData ( Territory );

                </SqlStatement>

            </IndexSqlSchema>

        </EventClass>

    </EventClasses>

<SubscriptionClasses>

    <SubscriptionClass>

        <SubscriptionClassName>

            SalesActivityTerritory
```

```
          </SubscriptionClassName>
          <Schema>
              <Field>
                  <FieldName>DeviceName</FieldName>
                  <FieldType>nvarchar(255)</FieldType>
                  <FieldTypeMods>not null</FieldTypeMods>
              </Field>
              <Field>
                  <FieldName>SubscriberLocale</FieldName>
                  <FieldType>nvarchar(10)</FieldType>
                  <FieldTypeMods>not null</FieldTypeMods>
              </Field>
              <Field>
                  <FieldName>Territory</FieldName>
                  <FieldType>nvarchar(50)</FieldType>
                  <FieldTypeMods>not null</FieldTypeMods>
              </Field>
          </Schema>
          <EventRules>
              <EventRule>
                  <RuleName>TerritoryEventRule</RuleName>
<EventClassName>TerritorySalesData</EventClassName>
                  <Action>
                      INSERT INTO TerritoryAlerts(SubscriberId,
                          DeviceName, SubscriberLocale, Territory,
                          CustomerName, OrderDate, SalesOrderNumber,
                          SalesAmount)
                      SELECT s.SubscriberId, s.DeviceName,
                          s.SubscriberLocale, e.Territory,
                          e.CustomerName, e.OrderDate,
                          e.SalesOrderNumber, e.SalesAmount
                      FROM TerritoryData e, SalesActivityTerritory s
```

```
                    WHERE e.Territory = s.Territory;
                </Action>
            </EventRule>
        </EventRules>
    </SubscriptionClass>
</SubscriptionClasses>
<NotificationClasses>
    <NotificationClass>
<NotificationClassName>TerritoryAlerts</NotificationClassName>
        <Schema>
            <Fields>
                <Field>
                    <FieldName>Territory</FieldName>
                    <FieldType>nvarchar(50)</FieldType>
                </Field>
                <Field>
                    <FieldName>CustomerName</FieldName>
                    <FieldType>nvarchar(100)</FieldType>
                </Field>
                <Field>
                    <FieldName>OrderDate</FieldName>
                    <FieldType>datetime</FieldType>
                </Field>
                <Field>
                    <FieldName>SalesOrderNumber</FieldName>
                    <FieldType>nvarchar(25)</FieldType>
                </Field>
                <Field>
                    <FieldName>SalesAmount</FieldName>
                    <FieldType>money</FieldType>
                </Field>
            </Fields>
```

```xml
            </Schema>
            <ContentFormatter>
                <ClassName>XsltFormatter</ClassName>
                <Arguments>
                    <Argument>
                        <Name>XsltBaseDirectoryPath</Name>
                        <Value>%_InstancePath_%\TerritorySales</Value>
                    </Argument>
                    <Argument>
                        <Name>XsltFileName</Name>
                        <Value>TerritoryTransform.xslt</Value>
                    </Argument>
                </Arguments>
            </ContentFormatter>
            <Protocols>
                <Protocol>
                    <ProtocolName>File</ProtocolName>
                </Protocol>
            </Protocols>
        </NotificationClass>
    </NotificationClasses>
    <Providers>
        <HostedProvider>
            <ProviderName>TerritoryProvider</ProviderName>
            <ClassName>SQLProvider</ClassName>
            <SystemName>%_DBEngineInstance_%</SystemName>
            <Schedule>
                <Interval>P0DT00H00M30S</Interval>
            </Schedule>
            <Arguments>
                <Argument>
                    <Name>EventsQuery</Name>
```

```
            <Value>
                SELECT t.Name AS Territory,
                c.LastName + ', ' + c.FirstName
                    AS CustomerName,
                OrderDate, SalesOrderNumber, SubTotal
                    AS SalesAmount
                FROM AdventureWorks.Sales.SalesOrderHeader so
                JOIN AdventureWorks.Sales.SalesTerritory t
                    ON so.TerritoryID = t.TerritoryID
                JOIN AdventureWorks.Person.Contact c
                    ON c.ContactID = so.CustomerID
                WHERE OrderDate = '2006-04-30'
            </Value>
        </Argument>
        <Argument>
            <Name>EventClassName</Name>
            <Value>TerritorySalesData</Value>
        </Argument>
    </Arguments>
  </HostedProvider>
</Providers>
<Generator>
  <SystemName>%_DBEngineInstance_%</SystemName>
</Generator>
<Distributors>
  <Distributor>
    <SystemName>%_DBEngineInstance_%</SystemName>
    <QuantumDuration>PT15S</QuantumDuration>
  </Distributor>
</Distributors>
<ApplicationExecutionSettings>
```

```
                    <QuantumDuration>PT15S</QuantumDuration>
                    <DistributorLogging>

        <LogBeforeDeliveryAttempts>false</LogBeforeDeliveryAttempts>
                        <LogStatusInfo>false</LogStatusInfo>
                        <LogNotificationText>false</LogNotificationText>
                    </DistributorLogging>
                    <Vacuum>
                        <RetentionAge>P1D</RetentionAge>
                        <VacuumSchedule>
                            <Schedule>
                                <StartTime>23:00:00</StartTime>
                                <Duration>P0DT02H00M00S</Duration>
                            </Schedule>
                        </VacuumSchedule>
                    </Vacuum>
                </ApplicationExecutionSettings>
            </Application>
```

In this example, the event class *TerritorySalesData* stores the following data collected about sales: *Territory, CustomerName, OrderDate, SalesOrderNumber* and *SalesAmount*. This data is collected by the hosted provider, *TerritoryProvider*, based on a query that captures information based on the last order date. This query would require modification in a production environment to collect only new events, but it suits our purposes here as an example. This query will fail as written unless you give the service account running the instance permissions to read the *AdventureWorks* database. In a production system, you might choose to implement an event chronicle and then select only source records with a *SalesOrderNumber* greater than the last one in the event chronicle. When the subscription rule fires, as defined in the subscription class, *SalesActivityTerritory*, event data is compared to subscription data, and a notification containing all fields is created for each subscriber and inserted into the view for the *TerritoryAlerts* notification class.

---

**Note**    Use a stored procedure instead of a query as the *EventsQuery* value to simplify maintenance of the business logic used to collect events.

7.  On the File menu, select Save TerritorySalesADF.xml as type **C:\NS\Territo-rySales\TerritorySalesADF.xml** in the File Name dialog box, and then click Save. Your ADF file is now complete.

## Creating an XSLT File

The Notification Services content formatter requires an XSLT file to transform the raw notification data into a nicely formatted message. You configure the application to use an XSLT in the *ContentFormatter* section of a notification class.

---

**On the CD**   You will find a complete sample XSLT file, TerritoryTransform.xslt, on the book's companion CD in the \Scripts\Chapter 24 folder.

To begin a new XSLT using Visual Studio, follow these steps:

1.  Click Start, point to All Programs, point to Microsoft SQL Server 2005, and then click SQL Server Business Intelligence Development Studio. Despite its name in the Microsoft SQL Server 2005 program group, this item is actually a shortcut to Visual Studio.

2.  Insert the companion CD provided with this book into your CD-ROM drive.

3.  On the File menu, point to Open, and then select File.

4.  In the Open File dialog box, navigate to the CD-ROM drive, open the Scripts\Chapter 24 folder, select the TerritoryTransform.xslt file, and then click Open. Here is the code in the file.

```
<?xml version="1.0" encoding="utf-8"?>

<xsl:stylesheet version="1.0"

    xmlns:xsl="http://www.w3.org/1999/XSL/Transform">

<xsl:template match="notifications">

    <html>

        <body>

            <xsl:apply-templates/>

            <i>AdventureWorks Territory Sales Notifications</i>

        </body>

    </html>

</xsl:template>

<xsl:template match="notification">
```

```
            On <xsl:value-of select="OrderDate" />,

            <b>

                <xsl:value-of select="CustomerName" />

            </b>

            <br/>

            placed order <xsl:value-of select="SalesOrderNumber" />

            for $<xsl:value-of select="SalesAmount" />

            in <b><xsl:value-of select="Territory" /></b>

            <br/>

        </xsl:template>

    </xsl:stylesheet>
```

---

> **Note**   For more information about using an XSLT file to format notifica-
> tions, see "Creating XSLT Files" in SQL Server Books Online.

5.  On the File menu, select Save TerritoryTransform.xslt as type **C:\NS\Territo-
    rySales\TerritoryTransform.XSLT** in the File Name dialog box, and then click Save.

# Using Notification Services Applications

If you built your Notification Services application using NMO, you can also use NMO to
deploy and manage your application, but this type of programmability is beyond the
scope of this book. In the following sections, we'll show you how to use SQL Server Management Studio to deploy Notification Services applications created based on ICF and
ADF files on a single server. We'll also show you how to simulate adding subscribers and
subscriptions and submitting events, so you can view notifications generated by the
application.

## Deploying a Notification Services Application

Once the ICF and ADF are prepared, you are ready to deploy your Notification Services
application. First, you create a new Notification Services instance to a server. When a
new instance is created or a new application is added to an instance, Notification Services creates databases and database objects according to the definitions in the ICF and
ADF. After the databases are created, you configure security for Notification Services to
manage data in these databases and grant permissions to directories on the file system

as needed. When the databases are created and security is configured, you can start the application.

## Installing a Notification Services Engine

The Notification Services engine is either a Windows service that you create when you register the instance on a computer or a process hosted by a custom application. You must install and run the Notification Services engine on each computer specified by the *SystemName* values in the ADF. When you start the Notification Services engine, it connects to the instance and application databases to determine which components are enabled and which enabled components are configured to run on the local server. Notification Services builds the instance and application databases and creates objects for the event, subscription, and notification classes. To follow this example, you must first complete all steps in the section "Developing Notification Services Applications." To install the Notification Services engine for the application created in the previous sections of this chapter, follow these steps:

1. Start SQL Server Management Studio. In the Connect To Server dialog box, select the name of the SQL Server 2005 server hosting the Notification Services instance in the Server Name drop-down list, select the applicable authentication mode, and provide credentials if required.

2. In Object Explorer, right-click Notification Services, and then click New Notification Services Instance.

3. Click Browse, navigate to the folder containing the instance configuration file, which in this example is C:\NS, and open the SalesActivityICF.xml file.

4. Type the name of your SQL Server instance in the Value box for the _DBEngineInstance_ parameter in the New Notification Services Instance dialog box, shown in Figure 24-1.

   Notice the _InstancePath_ value is provided automatically because the *ParameterDefaults* section of the ICF configured this value. If you saved the ICF and ADF files to a different folder, you can override the value for this parameter in the New Notification Services Instance dialog box by typing a new value.

5. Select the Enable Instance After It Is Created check box, and then click OK. Enabling an instance allows the instance and application components to run. You can choose to enable the instance manually later if you prefer. Once Notification Services builds the databases, the instance will start collecting events. You need to add subscribers and subscriptions before notifications can be generated, however.

6. When the instance is successfully created, click Close.

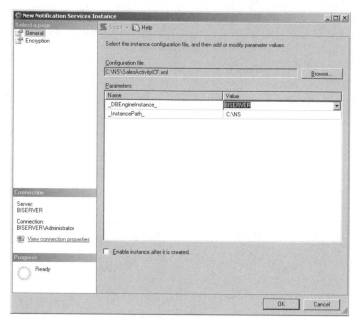

**Figure 24-1** The New Notification Services Instance dialog box.

## Creating a Windows Service Account for a Notification Services Instance

A Notification Services instance requires at least one user account available to perform the following functions:

- **Deploy Notification Services instances** To create an instance, you must log in using an account with membership in the local Administrators group in the operating system and membership in the SQL Server sysadmin role because this task creates databases and modifies the registry.

> **Note** Other administrative tasks can be performed using an account with lower privileges. For more information, refer to the topic "Permissions Required to Deploy and Administer Notification Services" in SQL Server Books Online.

- **Run the Windows service for the Notification Services Instance** This service, *NS$<instancename>*, runs the hosted event providers, generator, and distributors for applications associated with the instance. You can choose between a built-in account, a local user account, or a domain user account.

---

**Note** Microsoft discourages the use of NT AUTHORITY\Local Service, NT AUTHORITY\Network Service, or the Local System account for running a Notification Services instance because many services can use these accounts and gain access to network resources or SQL Server databases through Notification Services.

---

- **Log in to a SQL Server instance and access the instance and application databases** You must create a database account for the Windows service using either Windows or SQL Server authentication and grant permissions to each database used by the instance. If the instance runs on a single server, add the database account to the NSRunService role for each database. If components are distributed across multiple servers, you can add the database account on each server to a more restrictive role as appropriate to the component: NSEventProvider, NSGenerator, or NSDistributor.

- **Send notifications using the SMTP service** If your application sends notifications using SMTP, the Windows service running the Notification Services instance must be a member of the local Administrators group.

- **Read and write to the operating system** The Windows service running the Notification Services instance must be able to access the file system. When you register the instance, Notification Services grants the following permissions to the service account:

   - Read and execute in the Notification Services folder (<SQL Server install folder>\90\Notification Services\<n.n.nnn>) and subfolders

   - Read and write registry keys used by Notification Services

   - Write to the Windows application log

   - Read and write in folders used by the File System Watcher Event Provider

   - Read the folders used by the File Delivery protocol

   - Read the folders containing XSLT files used by the content formatter

To configure security for the application described in this chapter, we'll add a service account for running the Notification Services instance and for connecting to the databases used by this instance. To create the service account, follow these steps:

1. Click Start, point to Administrative Tools, and then click Computer Management.

2. Expand the Local Users And Groups node, right-click the Users folder, and then select New User.

3. Enter a user name: **NSSalesActivity**.

4. Add a description: **Account used for running the Notification Services Sales Activity instance**.

5. Provide a strong password.

6. Clear the User Must Change Password At Next Logon check box, select the User Cannot Change Password check box, select the Password Never Expires check box, and then click Create.

7. Click Close, and then close the Computer Management console.

## Granting Permissions to a Notification Services Instance

Your next step is to grant permissions to the Notification Services Windows service to access these databases. This Windows service needs permissions to log in to the SQL Server instance and to access the relevant databases so events can be added to the events table and notifications can be generated. In addition, you need to give the Windows account the appropriate permissions to the application folder to use the XSLT content formatter and to write to the notifications folder if you use the File Delivery protocol. To follow this example, you must first complete all steps in the section "Developing Notification Services Applications" and the previous two sections. To grant permissions for the NS$SalesActivity instance, follow these steps:

1. Start SQL Server Management Studio, and connect to the SQL Server 2005 server hosting the Notification Services.

2. In Object Explorer, expand Security, right-click Logins, and then click New Login.

3. If your SQL Server instance uses mixed mode authentication, type **<servername>\NSSalesActivity** in the Login Name dialog box, replacing <servername> with the name of your server. If your SQL Server instance uses SQL Server authentication, type **NSSalesActivity** in the Login Name dialog box, select SQL Server Authentication, and type a strong password in the Password and Confirm Password boxes.

4. Click the User Mapping page, select the check box to the left of the *AdventureWorks* database, then select db_datareader in the Database Role Membership list to give the application's event provider access to the source database.

5. Select the check box to the left of the *SalesActivityNSMain* database, and then select the NSRunService check box in the Database Role Membership list.

6. Select the check box to the left of the *SalesActivityTerritorySales* database, select the NSRunService check box in the Database Role Membership list, and then click OK.

7. Open Windows Explorer and navigate to the C:\NS folder.

8. Right-click the TerritorySales folder, select Sharing And Security, click the Security tab, and then click Add.

9. In the Enter the Object Names to Select box, type **<servername>\NSSalesActivity**, where <servername> is the name of your server, and then click OK.

10. With NSSalesActivity selected, clear all permissions in the Allow columns, select Write in the Allow column, and then click OK, as shown in Figure 24-2.

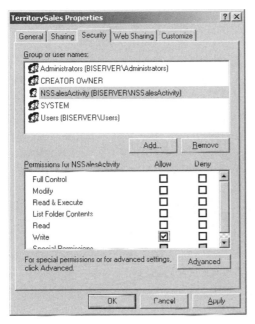

**Figure 24-2**  The TerritorySales Properties dialog box.

## Starting a Notification Services Instance

Registering the Notification Services instance creates registry entries and performance counters for the instance. If you are not hosting the Notification Services instance in a custom application, you create a Windows service when you register the instance and you associate a Windows user account with the service. Also, if you use SQL Server authentication on the server hosting the instance and application databases, you must provide the SQL Server login to associate with the service. To follow this example, you must first complete all steps in the section "Developing Notification Services Applications" and the previous three sections. To register the SalesActivity instance, follow these steps:

1. Start SQL Server Management Studio and connect to the SQL Server 2005 server hosting the Notification Services instance.

2. In Object Explorer, expand Notification Services, right-click SalesActivity, point to Tasks, and then click Register.

3. In the Register Instance – SalesActivity dialog box, select the Create Windows Service check box.

4. In the Account box, type **<servername>\NSSalesActivity,** where <servername> is the name of your server, and type the password for this account in the Password box, as shown in Figure 24-3.

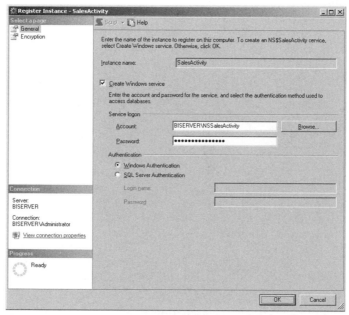

**Figure 24-3** The Register Instance — SalesActivity dialog box.

5. Skip this step if your SQL Server instance uses Mixed Mode authentication. Select SQL Server Authentication, type **NSSalesActivity** in the Login Name box, and type the password you created for this login in the Password box.

6. Click OK, and then click Close when the instance registers successfully.

7. Right-click SalesActivity, click Start to start the Windows service, and then click Close when the service starts successfully.

## Testing a Notification Services Application

Using a custom application, you add subscribers and subscription data, which are required to launch the event collection process. Because developing custom applications is beyond the scope of this book, we'll simulate the output of a custom application by using T-SQL statements to add subscribers, subscriptions, and events to your application. If your application is properly designed, the generator will create notifications for any events that match a subscription, format the notifications as defined by the content formatter, and send the notification to the delivery channel. In this section, we'll review each stage of this process in greater detail.

---

**More Info**   You can find details about the Notification Services subscription management API used to build your own custom application in the topic, "Developing Subscription Management Interfaces" in SQL Server Books Online.

---

## Adding Subscribers

The simplest possible method for adding subscribers to your application is using a T-SQL query. Rather than work directly with the *NSSubscribers* table in the instance database, you use the *NSSubscriber* view to add, change, or delete subscriber records. Before you can insert records into this view, subscribers must be enabled, which occurs automatically when you enable the Notification Services instance as described in the previous topic "Deploying a Notification Services Application." You can disable and enable subscribers manually when you right-click the instance in the Notification Services folder (such as *SalesActivity* to continue the example in this chapter), select Properties, click Subscribers, and then select or clear the Enable check box.

In addition, each subscriber requires one or more devices to which notifications will be sent. You use the *NSSubscriberDeviceView* to add, change, or delete subscriber device records. You must associate the device with a delivery channel configured for the instance.

Here is the T-SQL syntax to add a subscriber and a subscriber device to the *SalesActivity* instance described previously in this chapter:

```
USE SalesActivityNSMain;

INSERT INTO dbo.NSSubscriberView (SubscriberId, Enabled)

VALUES (N'TestUser1', 1);

INSERT INTO dbo.NSSubscriberDeviceView

(SubscriberId, DeviceName, DeviceTypeName,

    DeviceAddress, DeliveryChannelName)

VALUES (N'TestUser1', N'Work e-mail', N'e-mail',

    N'carol2@adventure-works.com', N'FileChannel');
```

## Adding Subscriptions

Notifications are generated only when events match a subscription, so you need to capture subscription information to make it available to your application. As with subscribers, the simplest way to do this is by using a T-SQL query to add, change, or delete subscription records in the *NS<SubscriptionClassName>View* view in the application database. Here is the syntax to add subscriptions to the *TerritorySales* application described previously in this chapter:

```
USE SalesActivityTerritorySales;

INSERT INTO NSSalesActivityTerritoryView

    (SubscriberId, Enabled, DeviceName, SubscriberLocale, Territory)

VALUES

    (N'TestUser1', N'Enabled', N'Work e-mail', N'en-US', N'Southeast');
```

---

**Note**   This example illustrates a conditional subscription. If your application supports scheduled subscriptions, the query to insert a subscription record omits a column for the condition and includes *ScheduleStart* and *ScheduleOccurrence* columns to assign a start date/time and frequency for the schedule. For more information about scheduled subscriptions, see the SQL Server Books Online topic "Adding a Subscription."

## Submitting Events

Once you have subscribers and subscriptions added to the instance and application databases, your application is up and running. As events are collected by the application's event provider, these events are compared to enabled subscriptions. Because we're working with a sample application, we don't have real events to trigger notifications. Instead, we'll simulate sales activity in the *AdventureWorks* database by submitting events directly to the stored procedures that manage event batches. In a production system, the event provider performs this task transparently. Here is the syntax to submit events to the *TerritorySales* application described previously in this chapter:

```
USE SalesActivityTerritorySales;

INSERT INTO dbo.TerritorySalesData (Territory, CustomerName,

    OrderDate, SalesOrderNumber, SalesAmount)

VALUES (N'Southeast', N'Price, Jeff', GetDate(), N'SO75160',42463.53);
```

To view the batch details, use this code:

```
USE SalesActivityTerritorySales;

DECLARE @LastBatch bigint;
```

```
SET @LastBatch = (SELECT max(EventBatchId) FROM dbo.NSEventBatchView);
EXEC dbo.NSEventBatchDetails
    @EventClassName = TerritorySalesData,
    @EventBatchId = @LastBatch;
```

## Viewing Notifications

When Notification Services finds a match between submitted events and subscriptions, the generator creates the notifications, sends the notifications to the content formatter configured for the application, and then sends them to the delivery channels specified in the subscriptions. When you first test an application, you should use the File Delivery protocol because it is the easiest to implement and you can easily view the results in a file first. Once you are certain the application is working correctly with this protocol, you can then introduce other delivery protocols into your application. To follow this example, you must first complete all steps in the section "Developing Notification Services Applications" and the previous six sections. To view notifications for the *TerritorySales* application, follow these steps:

1. Wait at least 30 seconds after submitting events to give Notification Services time to generate notifications.

2. Start Windows Explorer, navigate to C:\NS\TerritorySales\Notifications, and open FileNotifications.htm, which is shown in Figure 24-4.

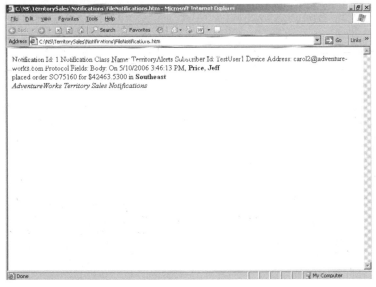

**Figure 24-4** The FileNotifications.htm file created by Notification Services.

When you use the File Delivery protocol, all notifications generated for a subscription class are added to one file. As additional events are submitted, any resulting notifications are appended to this file. Notice that there is a header for each notification that shows subscription information, such as subscriber ID and device address. The actual text and formatting of the notification is visible after *Body*.

3.  In SQL Server Management Studio, right-click the instance and then select Disable when you're finished testing the application to prevent unnecessary firings of the rules on your server.

### Real World    Troubleshooting Notification Services

If the notification file isn't created, first check to see if there are records in the *NS<applicationname>AlertsNotificationDistribution* view. If no records are in the *NS<applicationname>AlertsNotificationDistribution* view, make sure events are being collected properly. Check the queries in your ADF file in the event class and in the subscription class for logic or syntax errors. Verify there are records in the *NS<subscriptionclassname>View* view. Look to see whether events matching these subscriptions have been submitted in the *NSEventBatchView*.

If records exist in the *NS<applicationname>AlertsNotificationDistribution* view, check the *DeliveryStatusDescription* column. If you see notifications with a value "Delivery failed" in this column, check the Windows Event Viewer's Application log for more information. Also, check permissions on the folder to which the notifications file should be written. If the notification file is created, but is empty, check the XSLT file used for formatting for accuracy.

If you don't see a value for *DeliveryStatusDescription*, check to be sure the Windows service and Notification Services components are running. In SQL Server Management Studio, you can right-click the instance, click Properties, and select the application in the Application drop-down list to view whether the components are enabled. If enable is pending, try restarting the service. Until the components are enabled, notifications will not generate. Click Windows Services to verify the service and associated components are running. You can stop or start the service on this page.

Notification Services includes several diagnostic tools as stored procedures in both the instance and application databases. Look for stored procedures beginning with *NSDiagnostic*. You can find more information about these stored procedures by finding the corresponding topic in SQL Server Books Online, such as "NSDiagnosticDeliveryChannel (Transact-SQL)."

# What Is Service Broker?

Service Broker is a framework included in SQL Server 2005 you use to develop and manage asynchronous messaging applications. An asynchronous messaging application is a layer between an *initiator application*, a producer of information, and a *target application*, a consumer of information. Because these two applications may not be online at the same time or may not even be in the same network environment, asynchronous messaging is used to enable sharing information between them. To facilitate sharing, Service Broker uses *message queues* stored in a SQL Server 2005 database to temporarily store messages from the initiator application. In addition, Service Broker manages the sequence of multiple messages to ensure they are retrieved only once and in the correct order by the target application.

To use Service Broker, you must first have an initiator and a target application available. However, you don't integrate these applications with Service Broker using an API. Instead, you independently create Service Broker objects using T-SQL statements or stored procedures written in T-SQL or any .NET language. Then, you exchange messages between applications, also by using T-SQL statements. Typically, applications send these statements using Microsoft ADO .NET.

## Service Broker Fundamentals

Service Broker is not itself an application but rather a collection of components that work together to support external applications that need to exchange messages. In other words, you build applications that use Service Broker, but you don't build Service Broker into applications. The initiator application starts a *conversation*, a session that can be maintained indefinitely with a target application. The duration of this session might be very short-term, lasting only seconds, or very long-term, lasting over a year. Within the context of this conversation, the two applications share a *dialog* in which one participant creates a *message*, a file in binary or XML format, and the other participant receives it. Each participant application can be a sender or receiver at any time in the dialog. To send or receive messages, each application sends T-SQL commands to SQL Server and then responds to the results.

By leveraging the performance capabilities of SQL Server's database engine, Service Broker can efficiently manage messages in the queue without requiring a separate service to manage distributed transactions. Service Broker does not commit a message operation until the current transaction commits. In this way, Service Broker can prevent messages from being sent or received unless the participant commits the transaction. If the transaction rolls back, then the message operation is not completed. To take advantage of this feature, the participant applications must process messages and perform database updates in one transaction.

Service Broker is also able to use SQL Server's database security features. Another benefit of integration into the database engine is the ability to incorporate backups and restoration of the data into standard administrative routines established for SQL Server. Service Broker is also highly scalable because it can take advantage of multiple instances of SQL Server and can dynamically adapt its consumption of system resources according to demand.

Perhaps the most difficult tasks associated with messaging applications is the management of access to messages, including the sequence of message delivery and the delivery of the same message to multiple readers. Service Broker makes sure that each target application receives a particular message only once. If multiple messages in the same conversation are in the queue for the same target application, Service Broker ensures the messages are received in the order in which they were sent. Service Broker allows only one reader at a time to read messages in a conversation group.

## Service Broker Components Overview

There are three types of components used by Service Broker to support messaging between applications: conversation components, services components, and routing and security components. Conversation components are components that exist only at run-time. Service components are persisted database objects used in conversations. Routing and security components support the messaging infrastructure by managing the message exchange process and securing messages in transit.

The following list describes Service Broker's conversation components:

- **Message**  Data shared between two applications, such as XML or binary data
- **Dialog**  Bidirectional conversation between two Service Broker services
- **Conversation**  A session that persists over time
- **Conversation group**  A collection of conversations working together on the same task

The following list describes Service Broker's service components:

- **Message type**  Metadata describing a message and optionally validating the contents of the message
- **Contract**  Metadata describing which message types are allowed in a conversation
- **Queue**  SQL Server table used to store messages

- **Service**    An endpoint from which messages are received or to which messages are sent

The following list describes routing and security components of Service Broker:

- **Remote service bindings**    Dialog encryption and authorization for conversations with remote services

- **Route**    Location information for service to receive messages in a conversation

- **Service broker endpoint**    SQL Server object used to send and receive messages across a network using a specific TCP port number

# Implementing Service Broker Applications

The process of implementing a Service Broker application includes creating Service Broker objects and enabling participating applications to send and receive messages from Service Broker. Development of participating applications and preparing these applications to send and receive messages using Service Broker is not the focus of this book. However, you do need to understand how these applications will interact with Service Broker using T-SQL statements.

In this section, we'll explore how to implement a very simple Service Broker application that exchanges messages between two services. By separating the operations of the systems, the initiating system can simply hand off information and thereby scale to process more transactions because it doesn't need to wait for a response from the target system.

> **More Info**    You can learn much more about using Service Broker in *The Rational Guide to SQL Server 2005 Service Broker*, by Roger Wolter (Rational Press, 2006).

## Creating Service Broker Objects

When you implement a Service Broker application, you create at least two services as addressable names to perform specific tasks when a conversation between the services is started. Before you create the services, you create a contract and message types to control the content and direction of messages between the services, and a queue to store messages awaiting delivery to the target. If you need to configure routes between services or encrypt messages, you need to create two more Service Broker objects, routes and remote service bindings. When you are ready to implement your Service Broker application, you create all of these objects using Service Broker Data Manipulation Language (DML).

---

**Note** Space does not permit inclusion of a complete reference to Service Broker Data Manipulation Language in this chapter. Instead, the focus is on the general usage to provide an overview of using Service Broker. For more information about creating objects, refer to the applicable topic in SQL Server Books Online. As an example, to learn more about creating the message type object, refer to "CREATE MESSAGE TYPE (Transact-SQL)."

---

## Creating Message Types

Each service that will participate in conversations must include message type objects with the same name. Message type objects are used to validate messages on receipt. If the method of validation is not specified, any message will be accepted, which is generally not a good practice. To ensure an application sends or receives messages only of the proper type, you should specify the validation method to use when you create the message type object. Your options are to receive an empty message, a message with well-formed XML, or a message containing XML that conforms to a specified schema. If the contents of a received message do not validate correctly, Service Broker discards the message and returns an error message to the service sending the invalid message. Here is the syntax for creating a message to contain well-formed XML and an empty response message:

```
USE MyDatabase;

CREATE MESSAGE TYPE MyRequest

    VALIDATION = WELL_FORMED_XML;

CREATE MESSAGE TYPE MyRequestResponse

    VALIDATION = EMPTY;
```

---

**Note** *MyDatabase* is used here and throughout the sections covering Service Broker. Be sure to replace this database name with the existing database on your server in which you intend to execute Service Broker's T-SQL statements.

---

## Creating a Contract

After you define message types, you create a contract object to specify which message types can be used in a conversation between services and which participants in the conversation can send each message type. When the initiating service starts a conversation, the service also identifies the contract to govern conversation. Here is the syntax to create a contract defining the usage of the message types described in the previous section:

```
USE MyDatabase;

CREATE CONTRACT MyContract
```

```
(
    MyRequest                SENT BY INITIATOR,
    MyRequestResponse        SENT BY TARGET
);
```

## Creating a Queue

A queue is required to store a message until it can be received by a target application. You must identify the database and schema to store the database and provide a unique name for the queue. When you create the queue, you can specify whether it is available immediately. You might, for instance, prefer to make the queue unavailable until you have installed and tested the participating applications. Here is the basic syntax to create a queue available at creation:

```
USE MyDatabase;

CREATE QUEUE MyRequestQueue;
```

An *activation stored procedure* can be used to read a queue and process messages on arrival. You must create the activation stored procedure before you create the queue with which you associate it. Using a stored procedure for queue activation is called *internal activation*. Alternatively, you can use *external activation* by using Service Broker to produce an event as an indicator to a custom application to start reading the queue.

> **Note**   Some applications might not require any type of activation. See the SQL Server Books Online topic, "Service Broker Activation," for details concerning activation options.

## Creating a Service

You create a service for each task or set of tasks to be performed. This service is associated with a queue and a contract so that Service Broker knows which queue receives the message and how to enforce the contract. The queue must be in the same database as the service. If a service only initiates conversations, you can omit the contract. You can omit the contract specification if the service will be a target only. Here is the syntax for creating two services:

```
USE MyDatabase;

CREATE SERVICE MyRequestService
    ON QUEUE MyRequestQueue ( MyContract );

CREATE SERVICE MyResponseService
    ON QUEUE MyRequestQueue ( MyContract );
```

# Managing Conversations

While the specific implementation of Service Broker can vary according to application requirements, the general steps used to send and receive messages are similar. The initiator application starts a conversation and begins sending messages using extended T-SQL statements for Service Broker operations. The target message also sends statements to receive messages and to respond, if permitted. In this section, we'll look at the common statements used in a conversation.

## Starting a Conversation

An initiator application uses the BEGIN DIALOG CONVERSATION statement to define the endpoint services and the service contract to govern the conversation. First, you declare a variable for a system-generated conversation handle returned by this statement. You should start a transaction prior to starting the conversation as a best practice and end the transaction after sending a message to the queue, as described in the next section. Here is the syntax for starting a new conversation, which you should combine with the code for sending a message before executing:

```
USE MyDatabase;
DECLARE @MyRequestHandle uniqueidentifier;
BEGIN TRANSACTION;


    BEGIN DIALOG CONVERSATION @MyRequestHandle
        FROM SERVICE MyRequestService
        TO SERVICE 'MyResponseService'
        ON CONTRACT MyContract
        WITH ENCRYPTION = OFF;
```

If a conversation has already been started previously, you can use the BEGIN DIALOG statement, using the same syntax shown above, to continue the conversation. Recall that a conversation persists until it is explicitly ended, as described later in this chapter.

---

**Note**   By default, the dialog is encrypted. Adding With ENCRYPTION = OFF allows you to add messages to the queue without certificates in place. You can omit this argument if you add a certificate to the database. Dialog security is explained in more detail in the SQL Server Books Online topic "Service Broker Dialog Security."

## Sending a Message

You can send one or messages as part of the same dialog. You send a message using the SEND statement and defining the dialog handle, the message type, and the message data. After creating all messages, add a COMMIT statement to end the transaction. Here is the syntax for sending a simple message which should be included with the code for starting a conversation, as shown in the previous section before executing:

```
SEND ON CONVERSATION @MyRequestHandle

    MESSAGE TYPE MyRequest (N'Here is my request');

COMMIT;
```

When you send a message, Service Broker stores the message in the queue you created in the database. Until messages are received from the queue, you can view the metadata stored in the queue for sent messages as explained in the section "Querying a Queue" later in this chapter. The message itself is stored in binary format and cannot be viewed.

## Receiving a Message

You can wait indefinitely for messages to arrive in the queue, wait for a specified interval, or simply request receipt of available messages on demand. You have a variety of options for using the RECEIVE statement to retrieve only the messages you need at the time you need them. It is considered a best practice to begin a new transaction before receiving messages and to commit the transaction after messages have been successfully received. Here is the syntax for receiving all messages on arrival in the queue:

```
USE MyDatabase;
BEGIN TRANSACTION;
WAITFOR(
    RECEIVE * FROM MyRequestQueue
);
COMMIT;
```

## Ending Conversations

A conversation persists as long as needed until an END CONVERSATION statement is used by either the initiator or target application. When one participant receives a message containing END CONVERSATION, an END CONVERSATION message is sent back in response. When both participants have sent this type of message, the conversation ends. At that time, neither participant can send or receive messages using the ended conversation. If you don't maintain the conversation handle in the data store for your application, you can use the sys.conversation_endpoints and sys.services tables to locate the conversation handle. Here is the syntax for ending a conversation where conversation_handle is the applicable conversation handle.

```
USE MyDatabase;

END CONVERSATION conversation_handle;
```

# Managing Service Broker Applications

From time to time, you'll need to perform maintenance on Service Broker applications. In this section, we'll review the more commonly used commands for managing your applications.

## Stopping a Service Broker Application

When you stop a Service Broker application, the application prevents initiator applications from sending messages to the queue and target applications from receiving messages from the queue. You might need to do this when you need to make updates to the applications or to an activation stored procedures used by the application. Target applications that attempt to receive a message from the queue receive an error message. Incoming messages to the queue are held in the database transmission queue until the stopped queue becomes available, with no error sent to the initiating application. Here is the syntax to stop the queue in a Service Broker application:

```
USE MyDatabase;

ALTER QUEUE dbo.MyRequestQueue WITH STATUS = OFF;
```

## Starting a Service Broker Application

When you create a queue object for a Service Broker application, you may decide to create in an unavailable state to prevent messages from accumulating before all application objects are created, or you may have stopped an application using an activation stored procedure for maintenance reasons. In either case, the process to start the application is the same. If the queue has messages and has an activation stored procedure, the activation stored procedure starts immediately. Here is the syntax to restart a Service Broker application:

```
USE MyDatabase;

ALTER QUEUE dbo.MyRequestQueue WITH STATUS = ON ;
```

## Backing Up and Restoring a Service Broker Application

When you run backup and restore procedures for the database in which you created the Service Broker objects, these objects are automatically included with the other database objects. If your application uses other components that are not part of the database, then you need to establish a separate procedure for backing up and restoring those components. Be aware that some components used by Service Broker are stored on SQL Server independently of the application database. Specifically, the *msdb* database contains routes, while the *master* database contains Service Broker endpoints and transport security configuration.

In addition, Service Broker uses a unique identifier in each database for message delivery. If you restore a backup as a replacement for a database on the same server, make sure you don't change the identifier so that Service Broker applications can locate the database correctly. If you were to attempt to attach a database with the same identifier as another database in the same SQL Server instance, message delivery in the database you're attaching is disabled by SQL Server to prevent two databases from having the same identifier. To reactive Service Broker on a restored database and retain the existing identifier, use the following syntax:

```
ALTER DATABASE MyDatabase SET ENABLE_BROKER;
```

If you restore the database to a different instance, you need to change the identifier by using the NEW_BROKER option instead. Any existing conversations will be ended because those conversations will not be associated with the new identifier.

## Querying a Queue

You can use a SELECT statement to query a queue by using the queue name in the FROM clause as if it were a source table or view. Be sure to use the NOLOCK hint so applications attempting to read the queue are not blocked inadvertently. However, you cannot use an INSERT, UPDATE, DELETE, or TRUNCATE statement to modify the queue. Here is an example to query the queue described earlier in this chapter:

```
USE MyDatabase;

SELECT * FROM dbo.MyRequestQueue WITH (NOLOCK);
```

Of course, you need messages in the queue awaiting retrieval to see the results.

# Summary

After reading this chapter, you should have a general understanding of how Notification Services and Service Broker can be used to share information. Whether sending messages to subscribers when events of interest occur or exchanging messages asynchronously between applications, these technologies expand the potential of your SQL Server environment. The basic examples provided in this chapter are simply a starting point for the development of your skills with these messaging components. Be sure to read the recommended materials to gain a deeper understanding of Notification Services and Service Broker in preparation for developing production-ready systems for your organization.

# Part VI
# High Availability

# Chapter 25
# Disaster Recovery Solutions

Database administrators are constantly plagued with how to ensure that their business and mission critical databases are always available. Failure to ensure availability can adversely affect revenues and customer satisfaction. To protect the company's data resources, you must establish an architecture that can account for each component of the data infrastructure to provide high availability and recoverability. However, high availability and disaster recovery are not synonymous concepts, as they each provide a different level of database protection.

There are many types of protection that provide for many types of disaster scenarios. Disasters can take the form of a natural disaster such as Hurricane Katrina, or a man-made disaster such as the DBA deleting a table in the production database when it should have been deleted in the test database. Whether the disaster is major, such as the loss of a data center, or as minor as the loss of a single table, the effect can be just as devastating.

There is not one single solution that will protect you from all disasters. You should build upon a number of technologies to protect you from different failure scenarios. For example, you might choose to set up a standby database, which is very good. However, this should not preclude you from using a RAID I/O subsystem to protect you against a disk failure.

Creating a highly available, robust system involves many layers, starting with redundant components such as disk drives to protect you against disk failure, backups to protect you against user error, hardware failures and software failures, and redundant data centers to protect against a large-scale disaster such as the loss of the data center. No one solution will cover everything.

In addition, the disaster recovery components and plan must be thoroughly documented and tested. The person putting together the plan might not be available when it is necessary to put it into play; therefore, it must be well documented. The entire IT staff must be familiar with and able to implement this plan if necessary. A plan that is based on one person being available is doomed to fail.

So, how does a database administrator decide the level of protection required by the business and the methods that should be utilized? In this chapter, we will review how high availability and disaster recovery differ and what options are available to the Microsoft SQL Server DBA to implement these solutions.

---

**Note**   It has always been a good idea to implement a disaster recovery plan, but it hasn't always been a priority for companies because of the cost. Because it was not always a priority, the Sarbanes-Oxley Act of 2002 mandated certain minimum standards for disaster recovery, including testing. Many companies always had disaster recovery planning as a priority, but now they have no choice.

---

# What Are High Availability and Disaster Recovery?

High availability refers to the availability of a system's resources in the wake of component failures in that system. Assured system and data accessibility can be achieved by a combination of solutions that ensure redundancy of hardware and of custom or off-the-shelf software solutions. To achieve a highly available database system, all single points of failure must be addressed and a method for failing over to redundant components must be established. Disaster recovery, on the other hand, refers to the ability to continue to provide continuous data availability in the event of a disaster in which the primary database or the entire data center is unrecoverable. A major disaster scenario is a company located in a coastal town destroyed by a hurricane. Imagine that the company provides to customers nationwide a critical internet Web application that queried its database. It would be imperative to the business that this application and data continue to remain available, despite the fact that its primary site has been destroyed. How would you ensure this? With a disaster recovery plan.

As mentioned earlier, the key points to address are the single points of failure of your database system. A *single point of failure* refers to any component of your system and each component that, in a failed state, renders your data unavailable. These points can include computer hardware, software, and the network infrastructure. The most common point of failure in most computer systems is the hardware. Without redundant hardware, a failure can stop your database system in its tracks. In a typical server configuration, any component, including the CPU, memory, storage, and network interface card, can fail at any moment. Normally, when this happens, you have to replace the failed part, which can take as long as a few days, depending on the replacement part's availability. Typically, this is not an option with your business and mission critical database servers. Such a lengthy downtime can leave a business in ruins.

---

**Note** Many hardware vendors have redundancy built into their hardware to avoid a single point of failure. This is especially true of storage subsystems where there are redundant caches, redundant busses, redundant disk drives, and redundant cables. Since a disk drive is mechanical in nature, it is the most likely component to suffer a physical failure. Thus, if you have a limited budget and are interested in high availability, the I/O subsystem is a good place to start.

---

In addition to hardware failure, software can be a single point of failure as well. At some point in time, a database may become corrupt, or the operating system itself may need repair or reinstallation. Either can cause the system to be down for a significant amount of time. A software problem can, under certain conditions, be more devastating than a hardware problem. In cases where a power failure causes the system to go down for a short period of time, the system might be back very quickly. If the database were to become corrupt, a restore must be done, which can take many hours depending on where the backup is stored and the size of the database.

### Real World  Plan for the Worst

Consider this: Your datacenter, which hosts all of your mission-critical database servers, is located on the beautiful east coast of sunny Florida. One day, in early autumn, Florida's east coast is devastated by a hurricane. How will your company continue to do business? In this case, not only is redundant computer hardware and software necessary, but redundant sites are required as well. Obviously, there are many things to consider when planning for disaster recovery. Most of it truly depends on your company's needs and willingness to spend the money required to ensure availability. Thus, this involves a commitment all the way up to the CIO and maybe even the CEO.

# Fundamentals of Disaster Recovery and Disaster Survival

The most important part of implementing a disaster recovery plan is the plan itself. The many aspects to consider when designing your plan include these questions:

- What is the level of availability my business requires for this data?

- How much downtime can the business sustain before enduring loss?

- How much money do I have to spend to implement a disaster recovery plan?

- What are my risk factors?

You will most likely not be the person who needs to answer these questions, but you definitely need to be involved in the process and understand the answers in order to design a suitable solution. Behind the answers to these questions are things that many IT professionals do not consider when architecting IT solutions. Because many businesses are now dependent on technology, outages can have a great impact on the survival of a business (and your job).

There are other monetary costs incurred when mission-critical systems go down. Not only can your business lose potential revenue, but if systems and data aren't working, then neither are people. Moreover, if your company uses its data to provide service to external customers and your data is not available, then what does that do to your customer service scorecards? What is the cost to your organization of losing valuable customers? Remember, understanding the impact that system downtime has to your business is one of the most important things you can do.

Based upon the answers to the preceding questions, you will need to identify the level of redundancy that is required to assure you will meet your company's goals of availability. This needs to be done at the highest levels of the IT department and the highest levels of the company. If the CIO and CEO decide not to invest in disaster recovery, they need to be aware of the implications of that decision. Not all businesses are alike, and although each would like to have 100 percent uptime, executives need to be realistic about the company thresholds for acceptable downtime. For instance, organizations like NASA or your local Emergency Dispatch Center require higher levels of system uptime than, say, your local pizza online ordering system. Obviously, downtime for the fast food restaurant will not have consequences as dire as NASA mission control when trying to land a space shuttle.

Most organizations fall somewhere between these two examples. So, what I mean by level of redundancy is, what components of your system do you need to make redundant to meet the company requirements? Your company may have decided that it can afford to wait for that piece of hardware to be replaced or for the database to be restored from backup. However, you may find that you will need to ensure that every piece of hardware, including the CPU, memory, disk storage, network card, power supply, and server itself is duplicated. You may also need to provide redundant electrical circuits and environmental control units in your datacenter. In addition, you may need to establish a completely redundant system at a location that cannot be harmed by a hurricane that flattens your coastal datacenter.

Real-life disaster plans are greatly influenced by the level of funding available, and many companies cannot afford to build another location to accommodate a disaster recovery site. So, do as much as you can with the money you have. Thus, prioritization is extremely important. Gathering the numbers to show executives the negative impact of a disaster on business is a great tool for getting disaster plan budgets approved.

Assuming that you have designed your plan to include a separate disaster recovery site, what will you do if and when your primary site is back up and running? You must decide whether it is appropriate to fail back to the primary site to run in normal configuration. However, you may find it is not necessary. If you do decide to fail back to your primary database servers, you will need to have in place a process and the necessary bandwidth. The driving factors that will help you clarify your need to fail back are scalability, cost (how much is the standby site costing you), and resources (do you have the personnel available to fail back the system).

Scalability is important because most organizations cannot afford to set up disaster recovery sites with the same size hardware as their primary systems. Due to financial limitations, organizations more often than not will purchase the minimum required hardware configurations needed to provide database availability, with no room for scalability. Therefore, when the primary systems come back online, a fail back to the more powerful servers is necessary. Obviously, with all implementations, scalability and cost are always factors in deciding what will be your solution. If you can get away with less powerful servers in order to establish a disaster recovery site, then by all means, do.

If you have sufficient scalability at the disaster recovery site, you must then determine the costs of running at that site. This cost might be power, hotels for staff, and so on. The resources are also very important. Typically, the staff at the disaster recovery site is a skeleton crew that does not offer the same level of support as the primary site. However, once the primary site is up, the disaster recovery site can often be managed remotely.

---

**Note**   Many of the topics mentioned in this section are within the realm of the DBA, such as redundant systems, SQL Server backups, and so on. However, there are many topics mentioned that are not in the realm of the DBA, such as computer room backup generators, UPS power, and redundant network components. So, disaster recovery planning is a team effort that involves the database administrators, system administrators, network administrators, facilities, and management. Disaster recovery planning cannot be done on your own. The single point of failure concept must be applied to the IT staff as well. Multiple people must be involved in the disaster recovery planning and implementation process.

# Microsoft SQL Server Disaster Recovery Solutions

There are many disaster recovery solutions that can be used with SQL Server. Some of these solutions are SQL Server–specific, and other solutions are independent of SQL Server. Some solutions work regardless of the software involved in the system. Our discussion of the options assumes that waiting days for hardware replacement is unacceptable. You will see that each of the options varies in cost and recovery speed. Although the SQL Server 2005 features and other disaster recovery options provide high availability, your application code should be able to handle the failover to the disaster databases as well.

## Using Database Backups for Disaster Recovery

The most basic, and probably the most common disaster recovery method, is the use of existing database backups (as covered in Chapter 14, "Backup Fundamentals," and Chapter 15, "Restoring Data"). Database backups can be restored onto the same or different hardware in order to restore the database to the state that it was at the time of the backup. In conjunction with transaction log backups, the database can be restored to the point of failure (assuming that the system still exits). Database backups should be done on a regular basis, stored on a system other than the database system, and taken offsite as soon as possible. It is always a good idea to keep at least one set of database and transaction log backups on disk, if possible, for immediate restore if needed.

---

**Important**   If you are relying on database backups as your primary method of disaster recovery and your data center is destroyed or unavailable, you will be able to restore only up to the point of the last backup that was taken offsite. This backup could be very old.

---

Database backups can be considered a disaster recovery method, although it is not generally considered such because of the time needed to restore the backups. Database backups in conjunction with a remote system can be a somewhat effective disaster recovery solution even though the time needed to restore the backup can be excessive.

### Real World   Using Backups for Disaster Recovery

The following process was actually used by a well-known telecommunications company in the United States. Daily database backups were taken of all critical databases to network attached storage (NAS). The backup files were then backed up onto DLT tapes, which were transported over 800 miles to the disaster recovery location via courier, where another process restored the databases to a standby server farm, which mirrored the primary site. This disaster recovery process, as shown in Figure 25-1, occurred on a daily basis, and although it was extremely tedious, it was the only option due to existing financial and technological limitations. In actuality, the accumulated fees for the courier over the course of three years were enough to have purchased a sophisticated disaster recovery system. One of the key reasons for employing the courier for transport of the backup files to the disaster recovery site is the lack of network bandwidth across the WAN to copy them. Unfortunately, this process forced the potential for up to 24 hours of lost data in the event of an unexpected disaster.

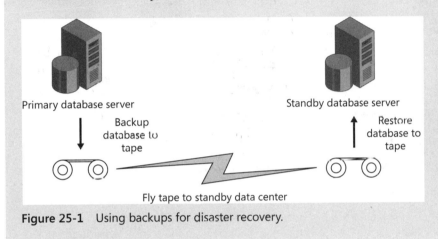

**Figure 25-1**   Using backups for disaster recovery.

The additional benefit of using backups as a disaster recovery solution is that once the backup has been restored on the disaster recovery system, you are certain that it is a good backup and that it can be used to restore the system in the event of a failure. It is always a good idea to test your backups.

---

**Best Practices**   Test your backups regularly (based on your standards and requirements). At the time it is needed, it is too late to find out that the backup or restore processes aren't working correctly.

---

Depending upon your infrastructure, you can set up variations of this process. As long as you can copy your backups and transaction logs to your disaster recovery site, you can use this method.

# Log Shipping

As discussed throughout the book, SQL Server 2005 contains features specifically designed for high availability and disaster recovery. Log shipping was an unsupported utility in SQL Server 2000, but Microsoft has incorporated it as a built-in feature in SQL Server 2005. Log shipping allows for automatic copying of transaction logs from a primary database to a secondary database to allow transactions to be duplicated on the secondary database, as shown in Figure 25-2. With this configuration, you will need to ensure that the primary and secondary database servers have mutual connectivity and that the pipe between them is large enough to handle the load.

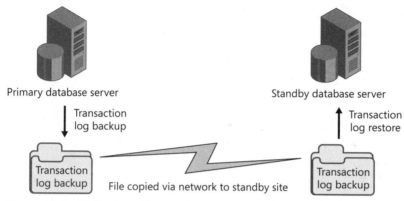

**Figure 25-2**   Using log shipping for disaster recovery.

> **Note**   Log shipping is not a dual write process. The transactions that occur on the secondary database are completely isolated from the transactions on the primary server.

Through the configuration options, you can identify how often you would like the transaction logs backed up and transferred. In a disaster scenario, the disaster recovery database will be as up-to-date as the last transaction log it received and applied, so there is a risk of some data loss. That loss will depend greatly on your shipping interval. Also, you will need to recover your database for use, and your applications will need to then point to your disaster recovery site. This re-mapping of servers can be done by changing the application or can be done at the DNS server or even with application logic.

### Real World   Disaster Recovery Architecture

There are several methods for configuring access from the application server to the primary and database server. Your choice is based on your specific budget, infrastructure, and needs. One option is to allow a failover of database servers and application servers independently. In this case, the mapping between the application server and the database server will have to change, so that the existing application server points to the standby database server. The other option is to configure and test the standby application server or servers and database server as a set. Thus, if a disaster occurs, only the mapping to the application server needs to change because the standby application server or servers are already pointing to the standby database server.

## Database Mirroring

A SQL Server 2005 feature that is designed for high availability and disaster recovery is database mirroring, which is covered in Chapter 27, "Log Shipping and Database Mirroring." Mirroring is a concept that is based largely on log shipping. However, there are a few important differences between the two technologies. Log shipping relies on transaction log backups in order to keep the secondary system in sync; thus, the secondary is always one log backup behind. Mirroring uses the transaction log itself, thus allowing more real-time mirroring of the databases. Mirroring also allows for automatic failover in the event of a system failure, thus requiring a witness. The three components of a comprehensive mirroring configuration are the principal, the mirror, and the witness, as shown in Figure 25-3.

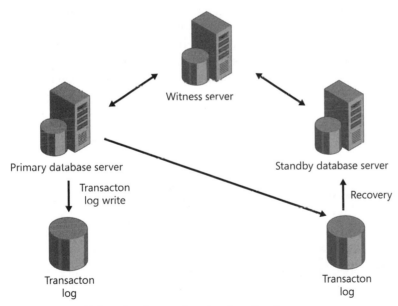

**Figure 25-3**  Using database mirroring for disaster recovery.

The *principal* is the server that is the source database, and the *mirror* is the target database. The *witness* is a server instance that performs no database transactions but instead allows for automatic failover to the mirrored server instance when running in synchronous mode. The three modes available to database mirroring are asynchronous, synchronous, and synchronous with automatic failover. *Asynchronous mode* configures all database transactions to commit changes on the principal database before sending the changes to the mirror. Conversely, *synchronous mode* will send the transaction to the mirror and await acknowledgement that the mirror had committed the transaction on its database before committing on the principal database.

With synchronous with automatic failover mode, the witness comes into play. If the witness notices any failures with the heartbeat of the principal server, it automatically fails over the active control of the database to the mirror. This is one of the key benefits that mirroring has over log shipping. With this type of failover, no code change is necessary for your client applications. The failover is transparent to the client. Moreover, the risk of data loss is decreased with database mirroring.

## Replication

Similar to the two previous features, which utilized some form of transactional processing on multiple databases, transactional replication, which is covered in Chapter 20, "Replication," is another way to ensure high availability and disaster recovery. An option that greatly distinguishes replication from log shipping and mirroring is the granularity for which transactions can be configured. While the previous two technologies allow for database level duplication, transactional replication can be configured for objects at the table or view level. Replication is also a little more difficult to configure, but the premise is the same. The log reader is a component of replication. Its function is to read the logs on the principal database and determine if any transactions need to be sent to the disaster recovery database, as shown in Figure 25-4. If the log contains transactions, then they are applied to the secondary database.

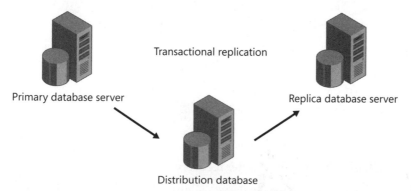

Transactional replication

Primary database server

Replica database server

Distribution database

**Figure 25-4**  Using replication for disaster recovery.

Because there is no validation of commit at the principal and secondary databases, there is also a risk of data loss. Just as with log shipping, there is no automatic failover to the disaster recovery site without some coding and/or DBA intervention.

---

**Important**    I do not recommend that you use replication as a disaster recovery solution. There is no guarantee that the secondary database is in sync with the principal database. Replication is not designed for disaster recovery.

---

## SQL Server Clusters

The next SQL Server 2005 option for high availability is failover clustering. Unlike the other technologies, implementing this feature is more costly and complicated. With failover clustering, your database system consists of two or more servers that are physically connected and share data storage and software resources to serve as a single unit. The technology is largely based upon Microsoft Clustering Services (MSCS), where the clustered servers are connected to shared disk devices via Fibre Channel or SCSI links, but reads and writes are arbitrated such that no two servers can access the disks simultaneously. A Microsoft cluster is shown in Figure 25-5.

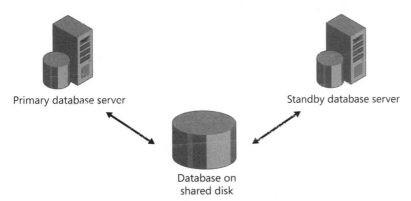

Primary database server                Standby database server

Database on
shared disk

**Figure 25-5**   Using clustering for high availability.

The most common clustered configuration, the clustered servers run in active/passive mode, which means one server owns all of the resources and data storage and performs all of the processing, while the other server node sits passive until it is needed. When any failure on the primary node occurs, the cluster software detects it and fails over the resources to the node on standby. Depending on the number of resources defined on your cluster system, it can take from 30 to 90 seconds for the failover to occur, so users may experience a brief outage.

> **Note**   A Microsoft cluster is a high-availability system designed to keep the database up as much as possible. It does this by resuming processing on the secondary server in the event of a failure on the principal server. Since the data resides on a shared disk, a Microsoft cluster will not survive a data corruption. This technology is high availability, not disaster recovery. All data resides in the same data center and on the same disk. A cluster can be used with other technologies, such as database mirroring.

Normally, there is only a single instance of any application running at a given time on a cluster system; however, clustering technology does allow for full use of hardware resources if distinct instances of an application are created. Individual cluster resources can be run on any node within the cluster, and as in the active/passive scenario, if any node fails, the resources are simply failed over to a running node.

In SQL Server 2005 clustering, the number of cluster nodes that are supported is dependent upon the operating system. With the 32-bit Microsoft Windows Server 2003 Datacenter version, up to eight cluster members are supported, while the 64-bit version supports only four members. The hardware requirements for clustering are not dictated by SQL Server requirements but, instead, by the clustering technology itself.

> **Note**   The best way to ensure that your cluster installation is supported by Microsoft is to refer to the Microsoft hardware compatibility list, or HCL, or the Windows Server 2003 Catalog, under the cluster solution category.

In addition, you will need to consider the level of redundancy within the cluster architecture. Not only will you have duplicate servers, but you can also duplicate your power distribution units (PDUs),UPSs, SCSI paths to disk storage, disks, network interfaces, and the cluster system itself. What I mean by a duplicate cluster is that you can try to separate the nodes of a cluster, but note that there are distance limitations. While Fibre Channel technology limitations are measured in miles, SCSI technology is supported only up to a few meters. Even in the Fibre Channel configuration, the distance separating the hardware may not suffice in a true disaster recovery plan. Instead, you can install a full cluster system at your primary site and duplicate the cluster at another location for the highest level of high availability and disaster recovery. Again, cost will be a huge issue.

> **Important**   One often overlooked component of the entire system is the cooling infrastructure. I have heard of several occasions where the computer room's air conditioning system has gone out, and it is not until servers begin failing that

the IT staff is alerted. At that point it is too late, and permanent damage might have been done to the servers. Similarly, a broken water pipe could cause the same problem. Environmental warning systems should be on your high availability and disaster recovery shopping list.

As I stated earlier, the installation and configuration of a failover cluster are slightly more complicated. Aside from the hardware requirements, there are software prerequisites for SQL Server 2005 clustering as well. The installation procedure for failover clustering is explained in Chapter 26, "Failover Clustering Installation and Configuration."

We have briefly discussed the various high availability and disaster recovery options offered by Microsoft and SQL Server 2005. However, there are other methods of implementing a disaster recovery solution that do not rely on Microsoft-specific technology at all. One such option is to apply trigger-based replication. This entails creating insert, update, and delete triggers on all pertinent tables which will, in effect, duplicate the transactions on the remote, disaster database. The problem with this option though is the increased overhead on database processing and the manageability of the data integrity. While the transactions are duplicated, there is not true acknowledgement that the remote updates were successful. Yet, this option provides you with a form of redundancy without excessive hardware and software cost. The only cost burden is the labor hours to support it.

Another disaster recovery solution that is not Microsoft based is SAN-based replication. SAN, or storage area network (as described in Chapter 4, "I/O Subsystem Planning and RAID Configuration," and Chapter 7, "Choosing a Storage System for Microsoft SQL Server 2005"), technology has matured greatly in the past five to ten years. Many SAN solutions now offer a block-level-based data replication in which the SAN handles the copying of data from the primary site to the disaster site. Most SAN solutions require a storage management system of some sort, whether it is vendor-supplied hardware or software to be installed on an existing server within your infrastructure, which can instigate and manage the replication of disk block changes real-time. In this configuration, SQL Server is connected to the SAN storage, where your actual database files are located. As SQL Server commits changes to disk, the data blocks on your SAN storage also change. The SAN technology can track and monitor these blocks and automatically send the changes to a duplicate SAN at the disaster recoery site. Basically, the data at your disaster site should mirror the data at the primary site, only in read-only mode. In the event of a failure at the primary site, you can switch the replicated data to read/write mode, attach the database files to the disaster SQL servers, and continue running. Yet again, the client applications will need to be able to point to the disaster site's database servers. This solution requires SAN expertise and the additional cost of the SAN software and hardware, but it can isolate the management of data duplication to only the storage. This technology has been gaining popularity in recent years and has been proven effective in production environments.

# Overview of High Availability and Disaster Recovery Technologies

The following table illustrates the types of technologies that are available and the pros and cons of each.

**Table 25-1   Comparison of SQL Server High Availability Technologies**

| Solution | Pros | Cons |
| --- | --- | --- |
| Database Backups | • Cheap and easy to do.<br>• No additional technologies needed.<br>• Should already be done. | • Must be taken offsite or they won't help in the event of a disaster.<br>• Slow to recover. |
| Log Shipping | • No single point of failure; separate disk and server usually.<br>• Databases can be in geographically dispersed areas.<br>• Secondary server can act as a reporting server.<br>• Simpler to administer; just another database in recovery mode.<br>• All objects in database are moved, not just the data.<br>• Recovery is fast.<br>• Protects against logical corruption; for example, DBA accidentally drops a table. | • Failover is not automatic.<br>• Higher latency because log has to be copied over and applied.<br>• All or nothing; cannot specify tables, and so on.<br>• Will not copy logins from master database over.<br>• When log is being restored, users cannot access the data.<br>• In the event of a failover, you could use an entire log's worth of data. |
| Mirroring | • Automatic fail over with witness in place.<br>• Data immediately applied after commit.<br>• All objects are moved over.<br>• Easy to administer.<br>• No single point of failure.<br>• Can use in conjunction with snapshots for reporting performance.<br>• Works over large geographic distances. | • Only one mirror allowed.<br>• Synchronous mirroring can be slow on a WAN.<br>• Does not protect against logical corruption. |

Table 25-1  **Comparison of SQL Server High Availability Technologies  (continued)**

| Solution | Pros | Cons |
|---|---|---|
| Replication | • Data moved to target server rapidly; less lag in access to it.<br>• Administrator controls exactly which data is moved between the systems.<br>• Access to data while the system is online. | • Typically used for a subset of tables, not whole databases.<br>• Administrative burden for anything more than a few tables.<br>• Solution is hand crafted. Not out of the box.<br>• Only data is moved between databases. Objects like stored procedures are not.<br>• Performance is adequate, but not as fast as a BACKUP/RESTORE operation.<br>• Failover is not automatic.<br>• Database server can take a performance hit on the CPU.<br>• Database is not guaranteed to be consistent with the publisher database. |
| Clustering | • Automatic failover.<br>• Data in sync, shared disk solution. | • Single point of failure; shared disk.<br>• Servers physically close to each other and prone to exposure to same disaster.<br>• More complex to administer; for example, patching.<br>• DBA needs additional training.<br>• Solution is more expensive due to extra hardware and redundancy. |

# Summary

The core of any business is its data and its ability to serve its customers. With most businesses moving to a "paperless" environment, they have turned to SQL Server as their primary storage of company data. As the database administrator, it is your job to ensure that this data is available at all times and can be recovered in the event of a disaster. However, ensuring both high availability and disaster recovery can be a daunting task. You must learn to understand the business impact of your data, and you must be able to provide an appropriate solution by balancing your infrastructure capabilities, business requirements, and cost. The options previously listed are only examples of how you can develop a disaster plan, and with some creativity, you can create a plan that will suit your organization's needs. Whatever you do, you need to ensure you have covered every possible disaster scenario. This undertaking should not be your responsibility on your own, but you are responsible for the database disaster recovery plan. Make sure your goals align with your company's, and you will have done your job. Just make sure you have a plan. You don't want to be caught by surprise without one.

# Chapter 26

# Failover Clustering Installation and Configuration

In recent years, computer systems have become more and more reliable. However, systems are still subject to failures. In order to speed the recovery from these failures and provide higher availability, Microsoft has developed the failover cluster. The failover cluster is designed to restart Microsoft Windows and Microsoft SQL Server quickly to resume normal operations as soon as possible. Failover clusters are useful for both hardware and software failures.

## What Is a Cluster?

A *cluster* is a group of computers that back up each other in the case of malfunction. In this chapter, you'll learn how Microsoft Cluster Services (MSCS) works and how to configure it, as well as how to plan for and recover from disasters. MSCS itself cannot make your system fault tolerant. You must combine this technology with careful planning to make your system capable of recovering from failures.

Microsoft Cluster Services is not a load balancing cluster technology. Microsoft Cluster Services is a failover cluster only. With MSCS, you do not get any more performance from a two-node cluster than you get from a single system. In fact, it is slightly slower because of the additional overhead incurred by the cluster. The benefit of a SQL Server cluster with MSCS is the creation of a system with a higher degree of high availability. High Availability and Disaster Recovery is covered in Chapter 25, "Disaster Recovery Solutions."

# Clustering Concepts

As a database administrator, your primary job is to keep the database up and running optimally during specific time periods, which are usually outlined in a service level agreement. This service level agreement probably specifies the amount of uptime your system must provide, as well as performance rates and recovery time in the event of a failure. Using MSCS can increase the amount of uptime and decrease recovery time. Although server hardware, Windows 2003, and SQL Server are usually stable and reliable, components sometimes fail. In fact, a variety of types of failures can occur in a complex computer system, including the following:

- **Disk drive failure**   Disk drive technology has improved, but a disk drive is still a mechanical device and, as such, is subject to wear. The disk drive is one of the most common areas of failure.

- **Hardware component failure**   Hardware failures can occur because of wear and tear on the components, primarily from heat. Even the best-made computer equipment can fail over time.

- **Software component failure**   Some software flaws are discovered only under rare conditions. Your system might run for months or years until a specific set of conditions uncovers a problem. In addition, adding applications to a stable environment might modify a critical library or file and cause problems.

- **External failure**   A system can fail because of external causes, such as power outages. Whether your system can survive such a failure depends on whether you are using an uninterruptible power supply (UPS) and redundant power sources.

- **Human error**   Clustering does not usually protect a system against failures caused by human error, such as accidentally deleting a table or a Windows 2003 file system partition.

Failures are unavoidable. How to best prepare for some of these failures will be our focus in this chapter.

# Overview of MSCS

MSCS is a built-in service of Windows 2003 Enterprise and Datacenter Editions. MSCS is used to form a server cluster, which, as mentioned earlier, is a group of independent servers working collectively as a single system. The purpose of the cluster is to preserve client access to applications and other resources in the event of a failure or planned outage. If one of the servers in the cluster is unavailable for any reason, the resources and applications move to another node in the cluster.

When we talk about clustered systems, we generally use the term "high availability" rather than "fault tolerant." Traditionally, the term "fault tolerant" refers to a specialized system that offers an extremely high level of redundancy, resilience, and recovery by reducing single points of failure. This type of system normally uses highly specialized software to provide a nearly instantaneous recovery (or in some cases, no loss of service whatsoever) from any single hardware or software failure. Fault-tolerant systems are significantly more expensive than systems without fault tolerance (although disk fault tolerance using RAID controllers is relatively inexpensive).

Clustered systems, which offer high availability, are not as costly as fault-tolerant systems. Clustered systems are generally composed of standard server hardware and a small amount of cluster-aware software in the operating system. As the availability needs of the installation increase, systems can be added to the cluster with relative ease. Though a clustered system does not guarantee continuous operation, it does provide greatly increased availability for most mission-critical applications.

A system running MSCS provides high availability and a number of other benefits. Some of the benefits of running MSCS are described here:

- **High availability**  System resources, such as disk drives and IP addresses, are automatically transferred from a failed server to a surviving server. This is called *failover*. When an application in the cluster fails, MSCS automatically starts the application on a surviving server, or it disperses the work from the failed server to the remaining nodes. Failover happens quickly, so users experience only a momentary pause in the service.

- **Failback**  When a failed server is repaired and comes back online, MSCS automatically rebalances the workloads in the cluster. This is called *failback*.

- **Manageability**  The Cluster Administrator software allows you to manage the entire cluster as a single system. You can easily move applications to different servers within the cluster by dragging the cluster objects in Cluster Administrator. You can move data in the same manner. These drag-and-drop operations can be used to manually balance server workloads or to "unload" a server to prepare it for planned downtime and maintenance. Cluster Administrator also allows you to monitor (from anywhere in the network) the status of the cluster, each node, and all the resources available. Figure 26-1 shows an example of the Cluster Administrator window.

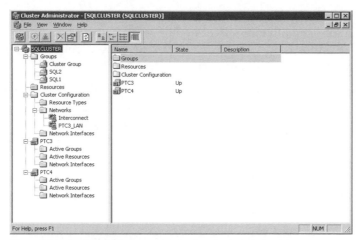

**Figure 26-1**    The Windows 2003 Cluster Administrator.

- **Scalability**    As the demands of the system increase, MSCS can be reconfigured to support the increase. Nodes can be added to the cluster when the overall load exceeds the capabilities of the cluster.

## Basic Concepts

MSCS reduces downtime by providing failover between multiple systems using a server interconnect and a shared disk system, as Figure 26-2 illustrates. The server interconnect can be any high-speed connection, such as an Ethernet network or other networking hardware. The server interconnect acts as a communication channel between the servers, allowing information about the cluster state and configuration to be passed back and forth. The shared disk system allows the database and other data files to be equally accessed by all of the servers in the cluster. This shared disk system can be SCSI, SCSI over Fibre Channel, or other proprietary hardware. The shared disks can be either stand-alone disks or a RAID system. (RAID systems are described in Chapter 4, "I/O Subsystem Planning and RAID Configuration," and Chapter 7, "Choosing a Storage System for Microsoft SQL Server 2005.")

---

**Important**    If the shared disk system is not fault tolerant and a disk subsystem fails, MSCS will fail over to another server, but the new server will still use the same failed disk subsystem. Be sure to protect your disk drives by using RAID because these mechanical devices are the components most likely to fail.

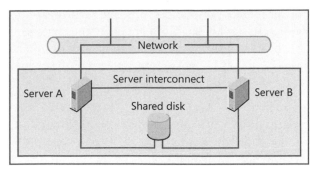

**Figure 26-2** The components of a cluster.

Once a system has been configured as a cluster server, it is transformed from a traditional server into a virtual server. A *virtual server* looks like a normal server, but the actual physical identity of the system has been abstracted away. Because the computer hardware that makes up this virtual server might change over time, the user does not know which actual server is servicing the application at any given moment. Therefore, the virtual server, not a particular set of hardware, serves user applications.

A virtual server exists on a network and is assigned an IP address used in TCP/IP. This address can switch from one system to another, enabling users to see the virtual server regardless of what hardware it is running on. The IP address actually migrates from one system to another to maintain a consistent presentation of the virtual server to the outside world. An application directed to a specific address can still access the address if a particular server fails, even though the address then represents a different server. The virtual server keeps the failover operations hidden from the user, so the user can keep working without knowing what's happening behind the scenes.

# Cluster Components

Several components are required to create a cluster: cluster management software, a server interconnect, and a shared disk system. These components must be configured in conjunction with cluster-aware applications to create a cluster. In this section, you'll learn about the various components and how they work together to create the cluster. In the section "SQL Server Cluster Configuration" later in this chapter, you'll learn how to configure a SQL Server cluster.

## MSCS Cluster Management Software

The *cluster management software* is actually a set of software tools used to maintain, configure, and operate the cluster. It consists of the following subcomponents, which work together to keep the cluster functioning and to perform failover if necessary:

- **Node Manager**   Maintains cluster membership and sends out "heartbeats" to members (nodes) of the cluster. *Heartbeats* are simply "I am alive" messages sent out periodically. If a node's heartbeats stop, another node will take steps to take over its functions. Node Manager is one of the most critical pieces of the cluster because it monitors the state of the cluster and its members and determines what actions should be taken.

- **Database Manager**   Maintains the cluster configuration database. This database keeps track of all of the components of the cluster, including the abstract logical elements (such as virtual servers) and physical elements (such as the shared disks). This database is similar to the Windows 2003 registry.

- **Failover Manager**   Starts and stops MSCS. Resource Manager/Failover Manager receives information (such as the loss of a node, the addition of a node, and so on) from Resource Monitor and Node Manager.

- **Membership Manager**   Monitors the cluster membership and the health of the nodes in the cluster. This component maintains a current list of which nodes are up and which are down.

- **Event Service**   Sends event messages to and from applications and to and from the cluster service components. This allows important event information to be disseminated within the cluster.

- **Event Log Replication Manager**   Replicates event information among components of the cluster.

- **Global Update Manager**   Communicates cluster state information (including information about the addition of a node to a cluster, the removal of a node, and so on) to all nodes in a cluster.

- **Resource Monitor**   Monitors the condition of the various resources in the cluster and provides statistical data. This information can be used to determine whether any failover action needs to be taken in the cluster.

- **Checkpoint Manager**   Saves application registry keys in a location on the shared quorum. This is to make sure that the cluster can survive a resource failure. When a resource is brought online, the checkpoint manager checks the registry keys. When a resource is taken offline, the checkpoint manager writes checkpoint data to the quorum.

- **Log Manager**   Writes changes to recovery logs on the quorum resource. The log manager and the checkpoint manager work together to assure recoverability in the event of a resource failure.

- **Backup/Restore Manager**  Works with the failover manager and database manager to back up the quorum log file and checkpoint files.

- **Time Service**  Ensures that all nodes in the cluster report the same system time. If Time Service was not present, events might seem to occur in the wrong sequence, resulting in bad decisions. For example, if one node reported that it was 2 P.M. and contained an old copy of a file and another node reported that it was 10 A.M. and contained a newer version of that file, the cluster would erroneously determine that the file on the first system was the most recent.

## Server Interconnect

The *server interconnect* is simply the connection between the nodes in the cluster. Because the nodes in the cluster need to be in constant communication (via Time Service, Node Manager, and so on), it is important to maintain this link, so the server interconnect must be a reliable communication channel between these systems.

In many cases, the server interconnect is an Ethernet network running TCP/IP. This setup is adequate. Because the interconnect is used only for status information, the bandwidth requirements are fairly low.

> **More Info**  A complete list of approved server interconnect devices is available from the hardware compatibility list on the Microsoft Windows Server Catalog Web site at *http://www.windowsservercatalog.com/*.

## Shared Disk System

Another key component of cluster creation is the shared disk system. If multiple computer systems can access the same disk system, another node can take over if the primary node fails. This shared disk system must allow multiple computer systems to have equal access to the same disks—in other words, each of the computers must be able to access all of the disks. In the current version of MSCS, only one system can access the disk at a time.

> **Note**  In the following sections, several different types of shared disk systems are introduced, including SCSI, Fibre Channel SAN, and iSCSI. New disk subsystems are being introduced which might work well with a Windows Server Cluster. Check the hardware matrix and check with your vendor to make sure that your hardware will work optimally in a clustered environment.

Several types of shared disk systems are available, as covered in Chapter 7, and new disk technology is always being developed. The SCSI disk subsystem has always supported multiple initiators. With multiple initiators, you can have multiple SCSI controllers on the same SCSI bus, which makes SCSI ideal for clustering. In fact, SCSI systems were the first disk subsystems to be used for clustering.

Technologies such as Fibre Channel and some proprietary solutions are designed to support clustering. Fibre Channel systems allow disks to connect over a long distance from the computer system. Most Fibre Channel systems support multiple controllers on the same Fibre Channel loop. Some RAID controllers are designed or have been modified to support clustering. Without modification or configuration changes, most disk controllers do not support clustering.

Whereas network attached storage was not previously supported with MSCS, the introduction of iSCSI technologies has changed this. With an iSCSI storage system or even a fileserver that supports iSCSI, you can now cluster to a disk subsystem across the network. The newly introduced Windows Storage Server can present its storage as iSCSI disk drives, thus making it a suitable candidate for MSCS.

Controller caches that allow writes to be cached in memory are also an issue with clustering when the cache is located on the controller itself, as shown in Figure 26-3. In this case, each node contains its own cache, and we say that the cache is "in front of" the disk sharing because two caches share the same disk drives. If each controller has a cache and a cache is located on a system that fails, the data in the cache might be lost. For this reason, when you use internal controller caches in a cluster configuration, they should be set as read-only. (Under some conditions, this setting might reduce the performance of some systems.)

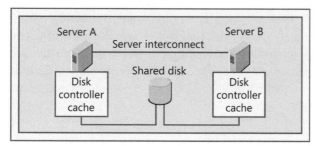

**Figure 26-3**   Controller caches in front of disk sharing.

Other solutions to the shared-disk problem involve RAID striping and caching in the disk system itself. In this configuration, the cache is shared by all nodes, and we say that the cache is "behind" the sharing, as shown in Figure 26-4. Here, the striping mechanisms and the cache are viewed identically by all of the controllers in the system, and both read caching and write caching are safe.

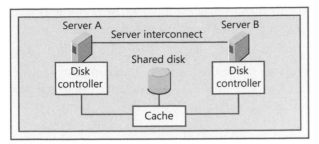

**Figure 26-4** Controller cache behind disk sharing.

Fibre Channel and iSCSI disk subsystems allow the RAID controller to be in the disk enclosure, rather than in the computer system. These systems offer good performance and fault tolerance. In fact, many RAID systems of this type offer fully redundant controllers and caches. Many of the newer RAID systems use this type of architecture. Let's look at some disk subsystems in detail:

- **I/O Subsystems** As mentioned, various types of I/O subsystems support clustering. The three main types of I/O subsystems are as follows:

  - **SCSI JBOD** This is a SCSI system with multiple initiators (controllers) on a SCSI bus that address JBOD (short for "just a bunch of disks"). In this setup, the disks are individually addressed and must be either configured into a stripe using Windows 2000 striping or addressed individually. This subsystem is not recommended.

  - **Internal RAID** A RAID controller is used in each server. The disadvantage of this subsystem is that the RAID logic is on the board that goes in the server and, thus, the controller caches must be disabled.

  - **External RAID** The RAID controller is shared by the systems in the cluster. The cache and the RAID logic are in the disk enclosure, and a simple host bus adapter (HBA) is used to communicate with the external controller. External RAID can be implemented either via a Storage Area Network (SAN) or Network Attached Storage (NAS) that includes iSCSI.

- **SAN** The Storage Area Network (SAN) is an ideal platform for clustering because of its robustness as well as the redundancy typically built into a SAN. In addition, SAN storage typically has significant capacity and is high performance.

- **iSCSI** The iSCSI storage subsystem is a new technology that uses the SCSI protocol encapsulated in an IP packet. iSCSI provides the flexibility and cost benefit of network storage while providing a robust and efficient transport layer that supports clustering.

The next two sections address only the two RAID solutions. The SCSI JBOD solution is not advisable unless the cluster is small and cost is a major issue.

### Internal RAID

Internal RAID controllers are designed such that the hardware that controls the RAID processing and the cache reside in the host system. With internal RAID, the shared disk system is shared behind the RAID striping, as shown in Figure 26-5.

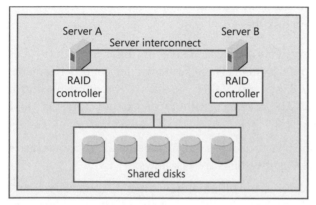

**Figure 26-5**   Internal RAID controller.

Because the cache is located on the controller, which is not shared, any data in the cache when the system fails will not be accessible. This is a big problem when a relational database management system (RDBMS) is involved. When SQL Server writes data to disk, that data has been recorded in the transaction log as having been written. When SQL Server attempts to recover from a system failure, these data blocks will not be recovered because SQL Server thinks that they have already been written to disk. In the event of a failure in this type of configuration, the database will become corrupted.

Therefore, vendors certify their caching RAID controllers for use in a cluster by disabling the cache (or at least the write cache). If the cache has been disabled, SQL Server is not signaled that a write operation has been completed until the data has actually been written to disk.

> **Note**   SQL Server performs all writes to disk in a nonbuffered, noncached mode. Regardless of how much file system cache is available, SQL Server will not use it. SQL Server completely bypasses the file system cache, as do most RDBMS products.

In certain situations, using the controller cache can provide a great performance benefit. This is particularly true when you are using a RAID-10 (aka RAID-0/1 or -1/0) or RAID-5 configuration because writes incur additional overhead with these RAID levels. To use a controller write cache in a cluster configuration, you must use an external RAID system so that the cache is shared and data is not lost in a failover.

### External RAID

In an external RAID system, the RAID hardware is outside the host system, as shown in Figure 26-6. Each server contains an HBA whose job is to get as many I/O requests as possible out to the RAID system as quickly as possible. The RAID system determines where the data actually resides. External RAID systems might be SAN or iSCSI NAS devices.

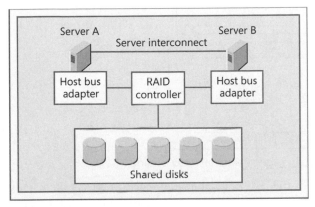

**Figure 26-6**   External RAID subsystem.

An external RAID subsystem is sometimes referred to as "RAID in the cabinet" or "RAID in the box" because RAID striping takes place inside the disk cabinet. The external RAID subsystem has many advantages. Not only is it an ideal solution for MSCS, but it's also a great solution overall. The advantages of the RAID-in-the-cabinet approach include the following:

- **Allows easier cabling**   Using internal RAID, you need multiple cables—one for each disk cabinet—coming from the RAID controller. With external RAID, you run one cable from the HBA to the RAID controller, and then you run cables from the controller to form a daisy chain connecting each of the disk cabinets, as illustrated in Figure 26-7. External RAID makes it easy to connect hundreds of drives.

- **Allows RAID redundancy**   Many of the external RAID solutions allow one storage controller to communicate with both a primary and a secondary RAID controller, allowing full redundancy and failover.

- **Allows caching in a cluster**   You can configure a caching RAID solution much more easily using external RAID. If you use external RAID, you can enable both caching and fault tolerance without having to worry about cache consistency between controllers because there is only one cache and one controller. In fact, using the write cache is safe if you use external RAID controllers. You still run some risks if you are caching RDBMS data, but you reduce those risks if you use external RAID controllers. Be sure that your external RAID system vendor supports mirroring of caches. Mirrored caches provide fault tolerance to the cache memory in case a memory chip fails.

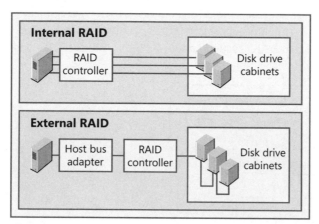

**Figure 26-7**   Internal RAID cabling versus external RAID cabling.

■ **Supports more disk drives**   In the case of large or high-performance systems, it is sometimes necessary to configure a large number of drives. The need for a large number of drives was illustrated in Chapter 4 and Chapter 6, "Capacity Planning," where you learned about RAID and how to size the system. External RAID devices let you connect hundreds of disks to a single HBA. Internal RAID systems are limited to a few dozen drives per controller, as are SCSI systems.

Of the disk subsystems available today that support clustering, external RAID cabinets are preferable for large clusters. Of course, cost might be a consideration, and some clusters are too small to justify using external RAID. However, in the long run, an external RAID solution provides the best performance, reliability, and manageability for your cluster.

## Cluster Application Types

Applications that run on systems running MSCS fall into one of four categories:

■ **Cluster-unaware applications**   Applications of this type do not have any interaction with MSCS. Although they might run adequately under normal conditions, they might not perform well if a failure occurs, forcing them to fail over to another node.

■ **Cluster-aware applications**   These applications are aware of MSCS. They take advantage of MSCS for performance and scalability. They react well to cluster events and generally need little or no attention after a component fails and the failover occurs. SQL Server 2005 is an example of a cluster-aware application.

- **Cluster management applications**  Applications of this type are used to monitor and manage the MSCS environment.
- **Custom resource types**  These applications provide customized cluster management resources for applications, services, and devices.

Figure 26-8 illustrates the application types and their interaction with MSCS.

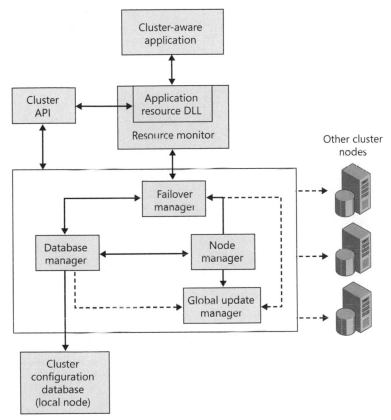

**Figure 26-8**  Application types and MSCS.

## MSCS Modes

You can run SQL Server 2005 cluster support and MSCS in different modes. In *active/passive mode*, one server remains in standby mode, ready to take over in the event of a system failure on the primary server. In *active/active mode*, each server runs a different SQL Server database. In the event of a failure on either of the servers, the other server takes over. In this case, one server ends up running two databases. In this section, we'll examine the advantages and the disadvantages of using each of these modes.

## Active/Passive Clusters

An active/passive cluster uses the primary node to run the SQL Server application, and the cluster uses the server in the secondary node as a backup, or standby, server, as illustrated in Figure 26-9.

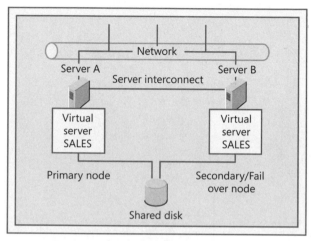

**Figure 26-9**   Active/passive cluster.

In this configuration, one server is essentially unused. This server might go for months without ever being called into action. In fact, in many cases, the backup server is never used. Because the secondary server is not being used, it might be seen as a costly piece of equipment that is sitting idle. Because this server is not available to perform other functions, other equipment might have to be purchased in order to serve users, making the active/passive mode potentially expensive.

Although the active/passive mode can be expensive, it does have advantages. With the active/passive configuration, if the primary node fails, all resources of the secondary node are available to take over the primary node's activity. This reliability can be important if you're running mission-critical applications that require a specific throughput or response time. If this is your situation, active/passive mode is probably the right choice for you.

It is highly recommended that the secondary node and the primary node have identical hardware (that is, the same amount of RAM, the same type and number of CPUs, and so on). If the two nodes have identical hardware, you can be certain that the secondary system will perform at nearly the same rate as the primary system. Otherwise, you might experience a performance loss in the event of a failover.

## Active/Active Clusters

In an active/active cluster, each server can run applications while serving as a secondary server for another node, as illustrated in Figure 26-10.

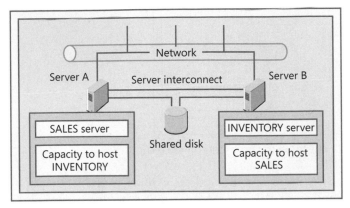

**Figure 26-10**   An active/active cluster.

Each of the two servers acts both as a primary node for some applications and as a secondary node for the other server's applications. This is a more cost-effective configuration because no equipment is sitting idle waiting for another system to fail. Both systems are actively serving users. In addition, a single passive node can act as a secondary node for several primary nodes.

One disadvantage of the active/active configuration is that, in the event of a failure, the performance of the surviving node will be significantly reduced because of the increased load on the secondary node. The surviving node now has to run not only the applications it was running originally but also the applications from the primary node. In some cases, performance loss is unacceptable, and the active/passive configuration is required.

# Examples of Clustered Systems

In this section, we'll look at four sample clustered systems that use MSCS. These examples will help you decide what type of cluster best suits your needs and environment.

## Example 1—High-Availability System with Static Load Balancing

This system provides high availability for multiple applications on the cluster. It does, however, sacrifice some performance when only one node is online. This system allows the maximum utilization of the hardware resources because each node is being accessed. Figure 26-11 illustrates the configuration of this cluster, which is an active/active cluster.

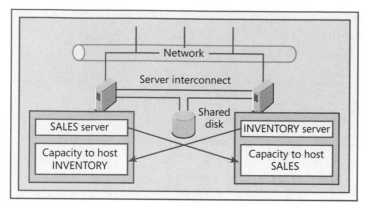

**Figure 26-11**    High-availability cluster with static load balancing.

Each node of this cluster advertises its own set of resources to the network in the form of virtual servers. Each node is configured with some excess capacity so that it can run the other node's applications when a failover occurs. Which client services from the failed node will be available depends on the resources and the server capacity.

## Example 2—Hot Spare System with Maximum Availability

This system provides maximum availability and performance across all the system resources. The downside to this configuration is the investment in hardware resources that, for the most part, are not used. One of the nodes acts as the primary node and supports all client requests. The other node is idle. This idle node is a dedicated hot spare and is accessed only when a failover occurs. If the primary node fails, the hot spare node immediately takes over all operations and continues to service the client requests. Figure 26-12 illustrates the configuration.

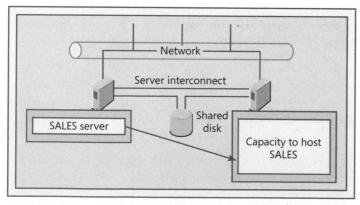

**Figure 26-12**    Hot spare system with maximum availability.

This configuration is best suited for the most mission-critical applications. If your company depends on sales over the Internet, your Web/commerce server could be run in this configuration. Because business depends on the system's being up and running, it is easier to justify the hardware expense associated with having an idle system.

## Example 3—Partial Server Cluster

The partial server cluster configuration demonstrates how flexible MSCS can be. In this system, only selected applications are allowed to fail over. As shown in Figure 26-13, you can specify that some applications will be available when their node is down but that others won't.

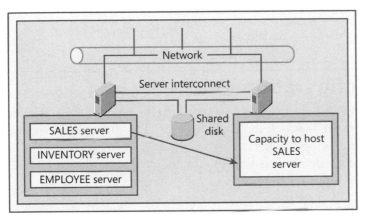

**Figure 26-13** Partial server cluster.

This configuration is ideal when you need to maximize hardware resource usage but still provide limited failover capability for mission-critical applications. In addition, this configuration supports applications that are not cluster aware while providing failover for applications that are cluster aware.

## Example 4—Virtual Server Only, with No Failover

Our final sample system is not a true cluster, but it does exploit MSCS and its support of virtual servers. This configuration, illustrated in Figure 26-14, is a way of organizing and advertising resources. The virtual server feature allows you to specify meaningful and descriptive names for resources, rather than the normal list of server names. In addition, MSCS automatically restarts an application or a resource after a server failure. This feature is useful with applications that do not provide an internal mechanism for restarting themselves. Implementing the configuration described in this example is also excellent preparation for true clustering. Once you have defined the virtual servers on a single node, you can easily add a second node without changing the server definitions.

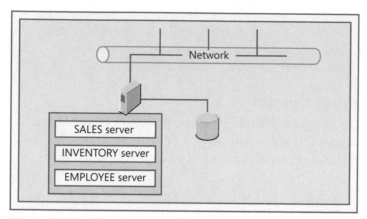

**Figure 26-14**   Virtual server only, with no failover.

# Planning Your Configuration

The first step in planning a SQL Server cluster is determining the type of hardware to be used and the mode of operation in which the cluster will run. The cluster can comprise systems with many hardware configurations, and it can operate in active/passive mode or active/active mode. The mode determines the amount and type of hardware you will need and should be used to justify the hardware costs to management.

Active/passive cluster configurations should consist of identical systems, each capable of handling the entire workload. Because the active/passive mode does not use the secondary system during normal operation, nor does it use the primary system after a failure has occurred, the performance of the virtual server will remain constant. Users will not experience any performance change if the primary system fails over to an identical secondary system.

Active/active cluster configurations should consist of two systems that are each running a specific workload. If a failure occurs, the surviving system will take over the workload of the failed system. In this case, two workloads will then be running on a single system, offering lower performance to all users. If you have planned carefully, the performance delivered by this system will still remain within acceptable limits, but that performance is not guaranteed. In planning the active/active cluster configuration, you must prepare for some performance loss by planning to eliminate some services or by warning users that performance will be degraded in the event of a failover.

The next step you must perform when you are configuring SQL Server for a cluster is to check and possibly change several SQL Server settings. The next three sections examine these settings.

## Setting the Recovery Time

In tuning SQL Server, you might have set the configuration parameter *recovery interval* to something other than the default value of 0. Changing this setting increases the time between checkpoints and improves performance but also increases recovery time. (The system must recover after it has failed over.) In a clustered system, the default value of 0, which specifies automatic configuration, should not be changed. (Having a system to which another system can fail over is the primary reason for using MSCS and should outweigh performance considerations.) This setting causes a checkpoint to occur approximately every minute, and the maximum recovery time is also about one minute.

> **More Info**    For more information, check the SQL Server Books Online index for "Recovery Interval Option."

> **Note**    A checkpoint operation causes all modified data in the SQL Server cache to be written to disk. Any modified data that has not been written to disk at the time of a system failure is cleaned up by SQL Server at startup by rolling forward committed transactions and rolling back noncommitted transactions.

## Configuring SQL Server for Active/Passive Clusters

To create an active/passive cluster configuration, you might have to change one setting in SQL Server. If your secondary server is identical to the primary server, no change is necessary. If the secondary server has fewer resources than the primary server, you should set the SQL Server configuration parameter *min server memory* to 0. This setting instructs SQL Server to allocate memory based on available system resources.

> **More Info**    For more information, check the Books Online index for "Min Server Memory Option" or "Server Memory Options."

## Configuring SQL Server for Active/Active Clusters

In an active/active cluster configuration, you must set the SQL Server configuration parameter *min server memory* to 0. If this configuration parameter is set to Manual, SQL Server might over-allocate memory after a failover. Because Windows 2003 is a virtual-memory system, it is possible to allocate more memory than is physically available. In fact, this problem frequently arises causing paging. For example, if each SQL Server system allocates 75 percent of the system's memory and a failover occurs, the combined SQL Server services would demand 150 percent of the available memory, essentially bringing the system to a standstill.

# Installing and Configuring Windows 2003 and SQL Server 2005 Clustering

## Creating the Windows Cluster

To create a SQL Server cluster, you must first create a Windows cluster. The Windows cluster in Microsoft Windows 2003 (Enterprise Edition and Datacenter Edition) is a built-in feature that does not require any additional software to be installed. Nodes in the cluster can have different hardware, but the operating system must be the same across all nodes in the cluster:

1. To create the cluster from the Start menu, select Administrative Tools and then select Cluster Administrator. This invokes the Cluster Administrator tool.

---

**Note**   Prior to creating the cluster, the shared disk and network interconnect should have been configured. The interconnect can be an Ethernet connection through a switch or a crossover cable (for two node clusters). The shared disk must be visible by both nodes in the cluster. You must have one partition for the Quorum and at least one partition for data.

---

2. Because there currently is not a cluster defined, the Open Connection to Cluster dialog box appears with the Open Connection to Cluster option selected in the drop-down list. Click the drop-down list and select Create New Cluster, as shown in Figure 26-15. This invokes the New Server Cluster Wizard.

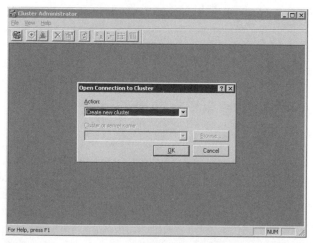

**Figure 26-15**   The Cluster Administrator.

3.  You are greeted with the typical Welcome to the Wizard page (not shown). Click Next to proceed to the Cluster Name And Domain page. Here you are prompted for the domain (usually already filled in) and the name of the new cluster to create. If you will have multiple clusters in your domain, it is useful to have a descriptive name. If you only have one SQL Server cluster, it is OK to name it something generic like SQLCLUSTER, as shown in Figure 26-16. Click Next to continue.

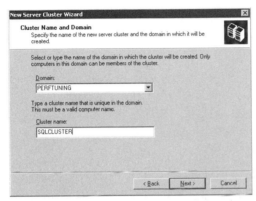

**Figure 26-16**   The Cluster Name And Domain page.

4.  On the Select Computer Name page, you must select the name of the system on which to create the cluster. You must have privileges on this system, and being part of an Active Directory domain is recommended. By default, you will get a full cluster installation. If you wish to select a minimal configuration, click the Advanced button. Enter the system name, as shown in Figure 26-17 (the system that you are on is defaulted). Select Next to continue.

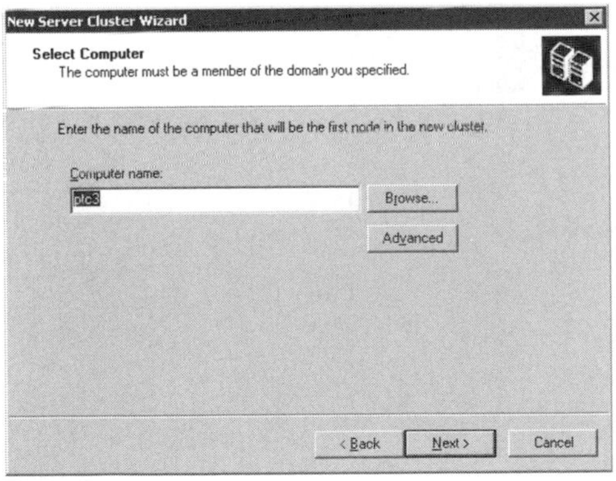

**Figure 26-17**   The Select Computer Name page.

5. Once you have selected the computer system, a check is made of the various components in the system. You will see the Analyzing Configuration window, shown in Figure 26-18, when the analysis has completed. If there is a problem, you are notified, and you should correct that problem before proceeding. Hopefully, the warnings and diagnostic information should be enough to help you locate and fix the problem.

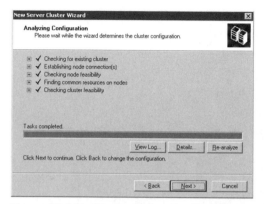

Figure 26-18    The Analyzing Configuration page.

Once the analysis is completed and successful (all green) you can proceed by clicking Next. If there are any warnings you should review and correct them.

6. You are now required to provide an IP address for the Windows cluster. This is a cluster-wide IP address that is used for communication to the cluster manager. Fill in the blanks (with information specific to your environment), as illustrated in Figure 26-19. Click Next to proceed.

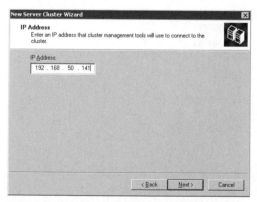

Figure 26-19    The Cluster IP Address page.

7. On the Cluster Service Account page, you are prompted to supply a username, password, and domain name for an account that will be used to run the cluster service. Depending on your corporate standards, the name and type of account might vary. This screen is shown in Figure 26-20. Click Next to continue.

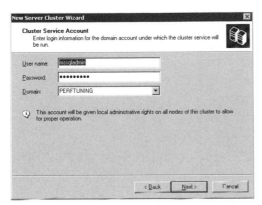

**Figure 26-20**   The Cluster Service Account page.

8. You are now presented with the Proposed Cluster Configuration page. Here you can review your settings before proceeding. This page is shown in Figure 26-21. Click Next to continue.

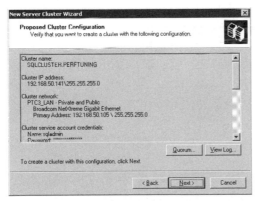

**Figure 26-21**   The Proposed Cluster Configuration page.

9. When you click Next to continue, the cluster creation process begins. The Creating the Cluster page shows you the progress of the cluster creation and notifies you when it has completed successfully. Even though it has completed successfully

there still might be warnings. If there are any issues, you should investigate and correct them. The completed Creating the Cluster page is shown in Figure 26-22.

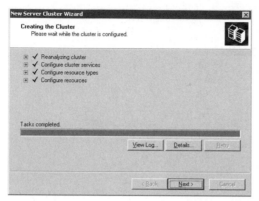

**Figure 26-22** The Creating The Cluster page.

10. You are finally presented with the Completing The New Server Cluster Wizard page (not shown). There should be no errors at this point, and you can click Finish to exit the wizard.

   Once the cluster has been configured you are brought back into the Cluster Administrator program, as seen in Figure 26-23. From this window, you can see that the cluster has one node and several resources.

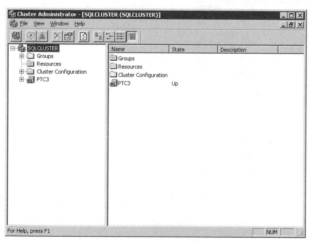

**Figure 26-23** The Cluster Administrator.

A cluster made up of one node is not much better than not having a cluster at all, so the next task is to add a second node to the cluster. Before proceeding, you should check the location of the quorum drive and the order of network interfaces to use for cluster communication by right-clicking the cluster and selecting Properties. If all of the properties are set the way you want them to be, you proceed with creating the second node of the cluster. If there are issues, such as the wrong IP address, Quorum drive, etc., you should correct them before proceeding:

1. To add a node to the cluster either select New, then Node from the File menu, or select the Open icon and choose Add Nodes To Cluster from the action menu. In either case you are greeted with the Welcome To The Add Nodes Wizard page. Click Next to begin adding a node to the cluster.

2. The Select Computers page prompts you to enter the name of one or more computers to add to the cluster, as shown in Figure 26-24. Type in or browse for the computer names and click Add to add them to the list. When you have added all of the nodes that you desire, click Next to continue.

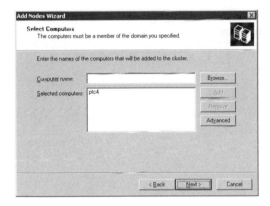

**Figure 26-24**   The Add Nodes wizard.

3. The Analyzing The Configuration page is used to check various components of the second node in the cluster to make sure that it is capable of joining the cluster. Once all of the conditions necessary to add a node to the cluster are satisfied, as shown in Figure 26-25, click Next to proceed.

---

**Important**   If there are errors, do not proceed. Make sure everything is compliant before proceeding.

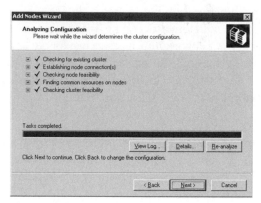

**Figure 26-25**   The Analyzing The Configuration page.

4. The Cluster Services Account page prompts for the password of the cluster account, as shown in Figure 26-26. The account name is the same as the one with which you originally created the cluster. Fill in the password, and click Next to proceed.

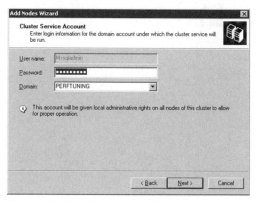

**Figure 26-26**   The Cluster Services Account page.

5. The Proposed Cluster Configuration page displays a summary of the cluster node addition as it will be added, as shown in Figure 26-27. Review this page and click Next to continue.

6. Once you have clicked Next, the Adding Nodes To A Cluster page appears and the node addition process commences. You will see the progress of the node addition while it is occurring by both the task completed bar and checkmarks next to the steps that have been run. If any errors occur, you are informed of it by

a red X next to the step and (depending on the severity) the progress bar turning red. When the successful node addition has completed, you are informed, as shown in Figure 26-28.

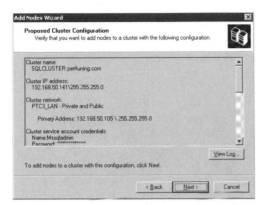

**Figure 26-27**   The Proposed Cluster Configuration page.

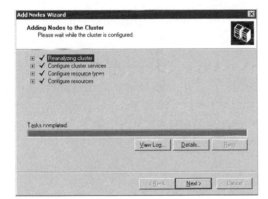

**Figure 26-28**   The Adding Nodes To The Cluster page.

7. The Completing The Add Nodes Wizard page (not shown) provides an opportunity to view the log that was generated by the cluster creation. When you are finished, click the Finish button to exit the wizard.

You are now returned to the cluster administrator again. However, this time you will see both systems in the cluster. This is shown in Figure 26-29.

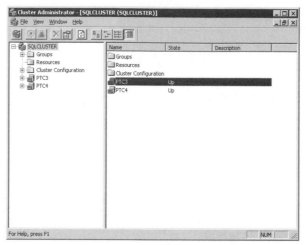

**Figure 26-29**   The Cluster Administrator.

Here you can view the properties of the cluster, such as the resources managed by the cluster, the cluster groups, and the configuration of the cluster. Before continuing on to creating the SQL Server cluster, make any necessary changes to the Windows cluster. These modifications might include:

- **Changing the network connectivity**   You can set network adapters to be either internal (cluster) communication only, public, or both.

- **Network priorities**   You can set the cluster up to favor one network over others.

- **Cluster Groups**   Cluster groups represent resources that work together. For example, if you have four cluster disks that will all be used for one SQL Server cluster, they should be moved to the same group. For example, the SQL Server instance and all the disks used by that instance should be put into the same group.

Once you have completed configuring and testing the cluster, you are ready to move on to the next step, creating the SQL Server cluster.

---

**Note**   In order to create an active/passive cluster, you must have one shared disk resource in addition to the Quorum disk. For an active/active cluster you must have two shared disk resources in addition to the Quorum.

## Creating the SQL Server Cluster

The SQL Server cluster is created as part of the installation process. Because installing SQL Server is covered in Chapter 8, "Installing and Upgrading Microsoft SQL Server 2005," it will not be repeated here. However, specifics involving clustering will be pointed out:

1. The SQL Server 2005 should be done on one node in the cluster. The installation process works exactly the same as the stand-alone installation. This includes the License Agreement window, the Installation of Prerequisites window, the Server Installation Wizard Welcome window, the System Configuration Check, and the Registration Information window.

2. The installation is no different from the stand-alone installation until the Components to Install page, as shown in Figure 26-30. Here there is now an option to create a SQL Server failover cluster and Analysis Services failover cluster (if you are installing Analysis Services). Check this box and the boxes of any other components that you want to install, and click Next.

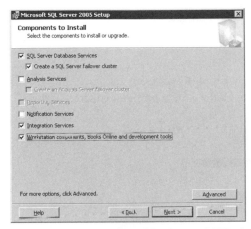

**Figure 26-30**   Installing SQL Server 2005.

3. On the Instance Name page, you should select a named instance if you intend to create an active/active cluster. If you are creating an active/passive cluster and have no intention of ever adding another instance, you can choose to use the Default instance. It is recommended that you use a named instance, just in case you ever want to add another instance. The Instance Name page is shown in Figure 26-31. Click Next to continue.

4. When creating a SQL Server 2005 cluster, you must provide a name and IP address for the SQL Server virtual server.

> **Note**   The virtual server name (and associated IP address) is the interface that the users will use to connect to SQL Server. In the event of a failover, this virtual name and IP address will fail over to another node in the cluster. Thus, the connection to SQL Server will always be the same, where the resources reside will change.

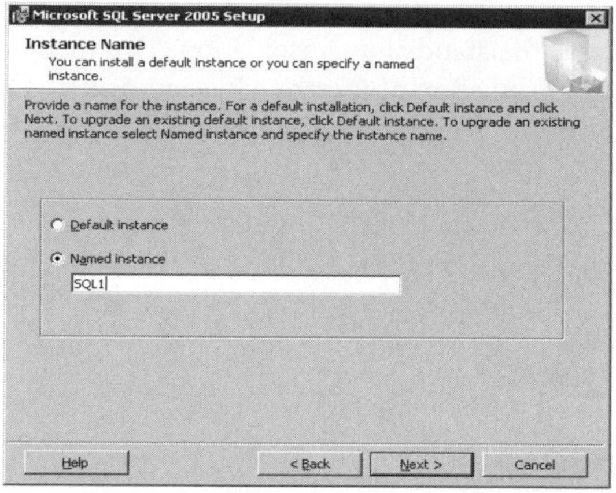

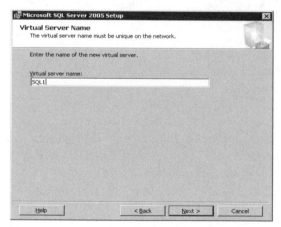

**Figure 26-31**    The Instance Name page.

On the Virtual Server Name page you must provide this name, as shown in Figure 26-32. This name can be the same as the instance name or different. Click Next to continue.

**Figure 26-32**    The Virtual Server Name page.

5.  On the Virtual Server Configuration page, as shown in Figure 26-33, you must select the proper network adapter and type the IP address of the SQL Server virtual server. The network adapter chosen is the one over which client traffic connects to the virtual server. Input the IP address, and click the Add button. When you are finished, click Next to continue.

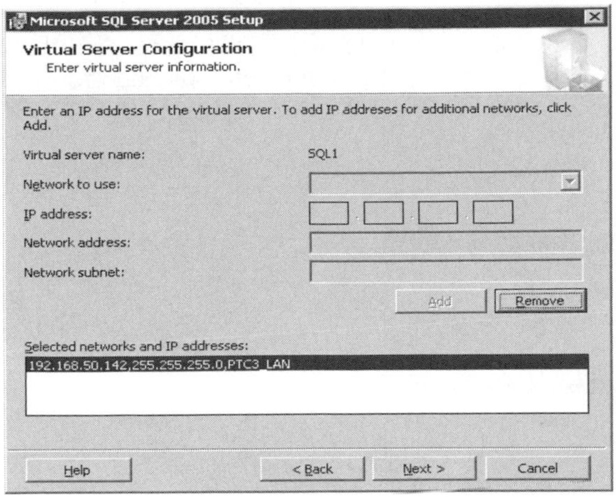

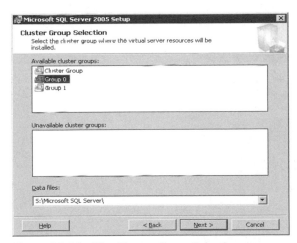

**Figure 26-33**   The Virtual Server Configuration page.

6. The Cluster Group Selection page is where you select the cluster group that will be used for this installation. Choose the group that contains the disks that you wish to use. If you are planning on using more than one shared disk, you will move those disks into this group later. You can also later rename this group to something more specific . This screen is shown in Figure 26-34. Click Next to continue.

**Figure 26-34**   The Cluster Group Selection page.

7. The Cluster Node Configuration page allows you to choose the nodes on which the SQL Server cluster can run. The node on which you are installing is required. In this walkthrough, the second node (ptc4) has already been selected.

> **Note**  If you are creating a multi-node cluster, select all of the nodes that you want to add. If you choose to add one at a time you will need to run the entire add-node process again later.

Click Next to continue.

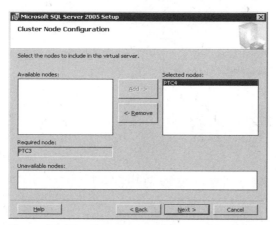

**Figure 26-35**    The Cluster Node Configuration page.

8. The Remote Account Information page is where you provide a password to the account that will be adding SQL Server to the cluster, as shown in Figure 26-36. Type the password for the pre-selected user, and click Next to continue.

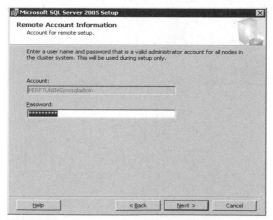

**Figure 26-36**    The Remote Account Information page.

9. As with the stand-alone configuration, you must provide a service account under which the SQL Server services run. It is recommended that an active directory

domain account is used, as shown here in Figure 26-37. Put in the account information for the SQL Server active directory domain account that the services will run under, and click Next to continue. This account can be the same as in the previous step, or can be different.

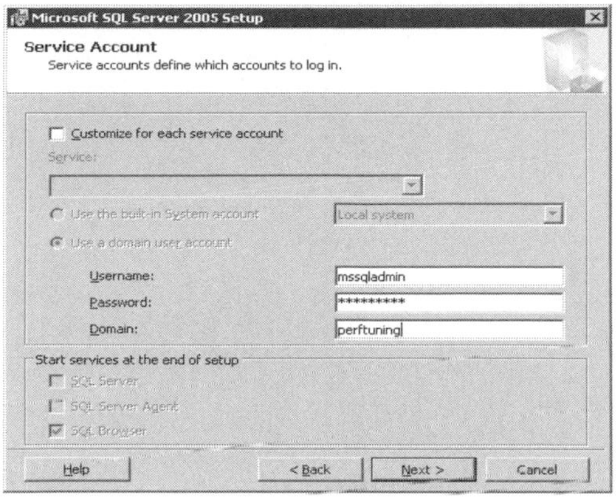

**Figure 26-37**   The Service Account page.

10.  The SQL Server service accounts must be made a member of an Active Directory security group in the Domain Groups For Clustered Services page. For each service account, specify the Security Group name, as shown in Figure 26-38. Click Next to continue.

> **Note**   The SQL Server security group that you intend to use must already be configured by your domain administrator.

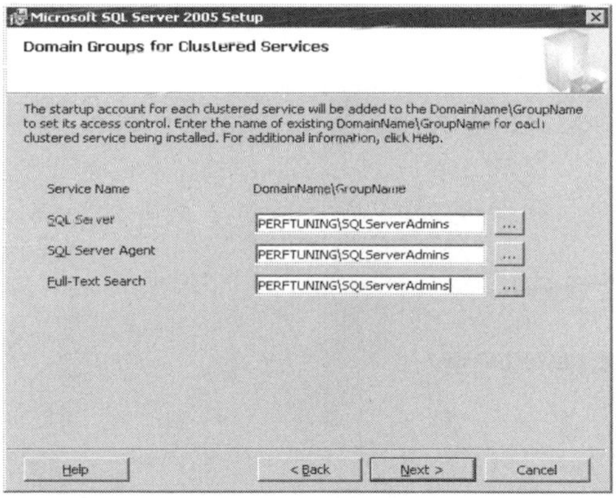

**Figure 26-38**   The Domain Groups For Clustered Services page.

11. From this step on you are back to the normal SQL Server installation process. The Authentication Mode page, as shown in Figure 26-39, lets you configure for Windows authentication (recommended) or SQL Server and Windows authentication. Make your selection, and click Next to continue.

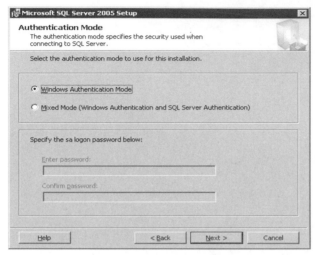

**Figure 26-39**   The Authentication Mode page.

12. The Collation Settings page is used to select the collation designator and sort order. The default is sufficient for most cases. This is shown in Figure 26-40. Click Next to continue.

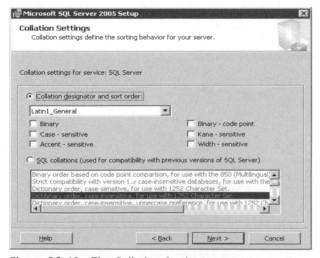

**Figure 26-40**   The Collation Settings page.

13. Next is the Error and Usage Report settings page. Here you can determine what information is sent to Microsoft on errors. This page is not shown. Click Next to Continue.

14. You are now at the Ready to Install page. Click Next to move to the Setup Progress page (not shown). The installation has now begun. You will see the installation progress screen and the status as it completes each step. You will notice that the Setup Progress page includes a drop-down list that includes each node in the cluster. You can select any node to view the progress of that node.

---

**Note** You might receive an error message when trying to install SQL Server 2005. This error message could be caused by the error described in the Microsoft Knowledge Base article 910851. To resolve this, make sure that you are not currently logged into the second node of the cluster, only the node that you are installing from.

---

15. When the installation has completed (on both nodes), you are informed of it in the Setup Progress page. Click Next to finish the setup process. The Completing the Microsoft SQL Server 2005 Setup page allows you to view the logs and review the setup. Click Finish to exit the wizard.

# Additional Steps

At this point, there are several additional steps that can be taken. They include modifying the cluster configuration, upgrading SQL Server 2005 to the latest service pack, and creating an Active-Active cluster. Each of these tasks are independent of each other and will be described here.

## Modifying the Cluster Configuration

There might be a few modifications to the cluster configuration that you will want to do. In addition, you should check and make sure that all of the names, IP addresses, and so on, are correct. Other things to validate include the following:

- **Install SQL Server Client Tools** By default, the SQL Server client and administration tools are installed only on the first node of the cluster. You might choose to install them on the second node as well. This depends on whether you administer your system locally or via a remote system. If you administer it remotely, the client and administrative tools are not really necessary on the server.

- **Cluster Group Name** I personally prefer to rename the cluster group to something descriptive, such as SQL1.

- **Failback**   If you prefer one node over another, you can set the cluster up to fail back to that node, either immediately upon that node returning to the cluster or during a certain time period that you specify.

- **Dependencies**   You might want to add dependencies for additional disk drives and so on.

- **Test the cluster**   Move the SQL Server resources from one node to another and verify that you can still connect to SQL Server from another system.

There usually are not significant modifications that you have to make to the cluster itself.

## Upgrading the Cluster

Upgrading SQL Server to the latest service pack does not raise any special considerations because you are on a cluster. Run the service pack on the node of the cluster that currently owns the resources. The service pack is automatically applied to all nodes in the cluster. To verify that the service pack has been properly applied, move the resources (by right clicking on the resource and selecting Move Resource) from one node to the other. Look at the startup messages in the SQL Server log in order to make sure that both nodes are running the same version of SQL Server. Each time SQL Server restarts, the following lines are placed into the SQL Server Error log:

```
2006-08-16 20:10:58.22 Server       Microsoft SQL Server 2005 - 9.00.1399.06
(Intel X86)
    Oct 14 2005 00:33:37
    Copyright (c) 1988-2005 Microsoft Corporation
    Developer Edition on Windows NT 5.2 (Build 3790: Service Pack 1)

2006-08-16 20:10:58.24 Server       (c) 2005 Microsoft Corporation.
2006-08-16 20:10:58.24 Server       All rights reserved.
```

Notice that the SQL Server 2005 build number is listed as 9.00.1399.06. In a later error log, after SP1 has been applied, the following is observed:

```
2006-08-17 09:21:34.30 Server       Microsoft SQL Server 2005 - 9.00.2047.00
(Intel X86)
Apr 14 2006 01:12:25
Copyright (c) 1988-2005 Microsoft Corporation
Developer Edition on Windows NT 5.2 (Build 3790: Service Pack 1)

2006-08-17 09:21:34.31 Server       (c) 2005 Microsoft Corporation.
2006-08-17 09:21:34.31 Server       All rights reserved.
```

The build number of SQL Server 2005 SP1 is 2047. Verify this for all nodes in the cluster.

### Real World   Trust Yet Verify

Even though it looks as if the service pack installations have succeeded, I always want to verify. On one of my very first SQL Server 2005 engagements, I configured an active/active cluster with database mirroring. After updating to SP1, I noticed an anomaly and discovered that SQL Server had been updated on only three of the four nodes. If a cluster failover were to occur, database mirroring would fail because that copy of SQL Server was not at SP1. So, make sure you verify that the upgrade has worked.

Before upgrading to the latest service pack, make sure to back up all of your databases.

### Create an Active/Active Cluster

An active/active cluster is simply two active/passive clusters using the same hardware. There is still only one quorum disk, but you must have a separate disk, name, and IP address resource for the second active node in the cluster. In addition, SQL Server resources must be configured such that the system can run properly even if both SQL Server instances are running on the same node in the cluster.

To install an active/active SQL Server cluster, simply install SQL Server again (preferable from the other node) and give it a different instance name. It is acceptable to install the second instance on the same node on which you installed the first time, but by using the second node, you get the additional advantage of the opportunity to install the SQL Server tools, such as SQL Server Management Studio, Profiler, and so on.

Once you have installed the second SQL Server instance, you must also upgrade that instance to the latest service pack. As before, verify that all nodes have been updated.

## Using a Three-Tier Application

Most applications establish a direct connection to a database. The application submits transactions, and the database responds to those transactions. In the event of a system failure, the transaction times out and the application fails. In many cases, this is the best setup—if the transaction is not completed, you want the application to fail. If you implement a failover cluster, however, the database soon becomes available and able to respond to transactions after a failure. By carefully designing a three-tier application, you can help ensure that the application takes advantage of this fast restoration of service.

In a three-tier application, the middle layer can detect that the server has stopped responding, wait a specified amount of time, and resubmit the transaction. The user will experience a longer delay waiting for the transaction to be completed, but the delay might be preferable to the transaction failing. To succeed, the application must be able to detect that the connection to the server has failed and must know to reconnect. In addition, the application should inform the end user that this process is taking place by displaying a message box or through some other means.

With a three-tier application, seamless failover is possible. The application must be cluster aware and must know that the virtual server will soon be up and functioning. Because the SQL Server cluster will soon fail over and be back up and running, the three-tier application must be coded such that upon a failure it will wait a designated amount of time and then retry. Remember that failing over a SQL Server cluster can take several minutes. Using a three-tier application framework in conjunction with MSCS can provide both application and data robustness.

## Summary

We've examined the basics of MSCS and how SQL Server works within that architecture. We've also seen how SQL Server can survive some types of catastrophic hardware and software failures and be back up and running transactions in a short time. To achieve this degree of fault tolerance, you must not only enable MSCS but also take other measures. Two important steps are performing regular and effective backups and preparing a disaster recovery plan. The procedures for backing up your system and preparing a disaster recovery plan are described in detail in Chapter 14, "Backup Fundamentals," and Chapter 15, "Restoring Data," as well as Chapter 27, "Log Shipping and Database Mirroring." Clustering servers and creating RAID storage are not alternatives to performing backups. In many cases, neither of these technologies can help you if your system crashes and you have not performed a backup. These situations can include the following types of failures:

- **Hardware failures**   In rare cases, hardware failures can corrupt data. If the primary system experiences a hardware failure that corrupts the database, the secondary server fails over to a corrupted database.

- **Software failures**   Regardless of how well software has been developed and tested, occasional bugs can sneak in. If one of these rare software bugs corrupts the database, failover to that database is of no avail. RAID technology simply offers a fault-tolerant copy of corrupted data.

- **Human error**   Users commonly delete their data by mistake. Neither clustering technology nor RAID solves this problem.

Chapter 25 explains more about planning for a disaster and enabling your system to survive one. The preceding examples simply illustrate the fact that clusters and failover serve specific purposes and are only two weapons in the battle to provide constant data access and data integrity.

# Chapter 27
# Log Shipping and Database Mirroring

Log shipping has been a method for creating a standby database since SQL Server 2000. In fact, if you count homemade methods, log shipping has been around even longer. In SQL Server 2005, log shipping is still available, but it has been enhanced with the addition of SQL Server mirroring. SQL Server mirroring builds on log shipping technology but allows the standby system to be completely in sync with the primary system.

In this chapter, you will learn how to configure and manage both log shipping and database mirroring. As you have seen in Chapter 25, "Disaster Recovery Solutions," both of these can be used as a *disaster recovery* solution designed to keep your company in business in the unfortunate event of a disaster.

> **Note** Database mirroring has been supported only since Service Pack 1 of SQL Server 2005. Service Pack 1 or later is required for database mirroring.

Log shipping is designed as a disaster recovery solution and is not intended as a high availability solution. Database mirroring can actually be used as a disaster recovery and/ or a high availability solution. In this chapter, you will learn how to configure mirroring for both. It is possible that at some point in the near future database mirroring will make SQL Server clusters obsolete.

Log shipping and database mirroring are designed to create a standby database that can be used in the event of a catastrophic failure that renders your production database unusable. Both log shipping and database mirroring can be used locally within the datacenter to provide protection against the loss of a system or can be configured in a remote location to protect against the loss of the entire data center. Because these products create a copy of the production database, they can protect you against many types of data loss.

## Types of Data Loss

In general, there are two types of data loss: physical and logical. Physical corruption of data typically happens when there is a hardware or software malfunction. For example, a hard drive crashes or a firmware/driver flips bits incorrectly and corrupts the data. Logical corruption is usually induced by end users. Examples of this include someone not putting a WHERE clause on a DELETE statement and accidentally deleting all the rows in a table instead of just a few or a DBA accidentally mistaking a table for a view and dropping it.

# Log Shipping

Log shipping is a technology that has been around for many years. It's stable, reliable, and easy to implement. Simply put, log shipping gives you the ability to have a warm standby database or databases running in case something bad happens. The standby database can be located physically close to the primary database or on another continent. You can have one standby or multiple standby databases geographically dispersed. Additionally, log shipping gives you a very granular level of control over the current state of the standby database.

On the surface, this may sound trivial—distance and chronological history—but in reality, these are very real concerns. For example, with clustering either at the server level or at the disk storage level, physical restraints are present in even the most expensive solutions. The constraints are usually limited to a few kilometers at best. What happens if there is an earth quake or flood in a city? If you have clustering in place, both sites could very easily be taken down. With regards to chronological history, what if a user accidentally deletes important data? Clustering is a shared disk solution that provides redundancy at the hardware level, not at the data level. A change on one node instantly is reflected in the other. Log shipping removes these two chief concerns.

Often in recovery, going to a tape backup is the last resort. If you can recover from a more immediate source, then you have more options available to you. There are a variety of different reasons for this logic. The primary reason that tape is a solution of last resort is because of performance. Tapes can take a long time to restore, and if the tape you need has been archived offsite, it can take even longer.

Often a consideration when recovering a database is the quality of the data itself, not necessarily the performance of the database server. In an OLTP environment, high throughput and many spindles are a chief consideration when architecting a solution. In recovery, you first and foremost want the data back—then you worry about performance. Log shipping gives you the ability to ship to a less powerful machine. For example, you can log ship to an older server with a few high capacity/low performance disk drives. This creates an inexpensive and quick recovery option while the primary server is being rebuilt. With other technologies, it is strongly recommended that like hardware be used for both the source and target systems.

---

**Important**   Although it is possible to log ship to a smaller, less powerful system, this decision should be made with care. In the event of a long-term outage, your performance could suffer for an extended period of time. This is a judgment that you must make.

---

At a high level, log shipping consists of a source database and a target database. Changes that are made on the source database are backed up, copied over to the target database, and then applied. These tasks can all be controlled via SQL Agent jobs that are created and scheduled through SQL Server Management Studio. In the following sections of this chapter, we'll explore each one in depth and examine the considerations you should make for them.

---

**Note**   Log shipping can be used only with either full- or bulk-logged recovery models enabled.

---

Log shipping technology is easy to configure and helps provides a strong database, high availability strategy. In principle, it's possible for you to log ship to the same SQL Server, but in reality, it should be on a separate physical server. The basic process involves backing up the primary database to the secondary system and constantly restoring transaction log backups. This is shown in Figure 27-1.

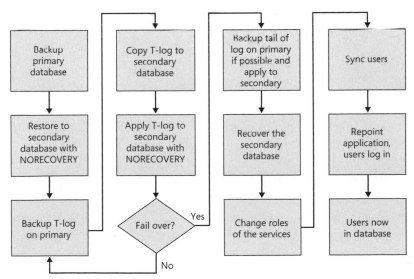

**Figure 27-1**   General overview of log shipping.

In order to configure log shipping (and database mirroring), it is first necessary to configure security.

# Configuring Security for Log Shipping and Database Mirroring

Prior to configuring log shipping or database mirroring, there are two steps that must be completed:

1. Surface area configuration

2. Service account configuration

For security reasons, SQL Server by default turns off remote access so hackers cannot get to the database. For example, if you try to connect from Server A to Server B and remote connections is not configured, then the connection is refused and the query does not run.

Enabling surface area communication allows the servers talk to each other. Ensuring proper service account permissions allows two SQL Servers access to each other's file systems and other resources. For example, Server B needs to copy over the transaction log backup from Server A. If the wrong account is used, then they are not able to access each other's directories to copy the files.

---

**Important**    If these features are not enabled, you will get errors saying it cannot find files and directories on the remote servers. For example, issuing the SQL command:

```
RESTORE FILELISTONLY
FROM DISK = '\\srvbox000fm\h$\sql\backup\prod.bak'
```

results in the following error message when a remote connection can be created to the remote server:

```
Msg 3201, Level 16, State 2, Line 3
Cannot open backup device
'\\srvbox000fm\h$\sql\backup\prod.bak'. Operating system error
5(Access is denied.).
Msg 3013, Level 16, State 1, Line 3
RESTORE FILELIST is terminating abnormally.
```

## Surface Area Configuration Process

Follow these steps to enable remote access:

1. Using SQL Server Management Studio or sqlcmd, confirm that the SQL Server parameter "remote access" is enabled. In SQL Server Management Studio, right-click the SQL Server instance and select Properties. In the Server Properties window, select the Connections page. On this page, make sure that the box is checked next to Allow Remote Connections to This Server.

2. From the Start menu, select All Programs, then select Microsoft SQL Server 2005, then select Configuration Tools, and finally select Surface Area Configuration Tool.

3. In the Service Area Configuration tool, select the Surface Area Configuration For Services And Connections option, and then select the Remote Connections component in the left pane. If you do not see the Remote Connections component listed, expand the Database Engine component under your server instance.

4. Select the Local And Remote Connections and Using Both TCP/IP And Named Pipes options, as shown in Figure 27-2.

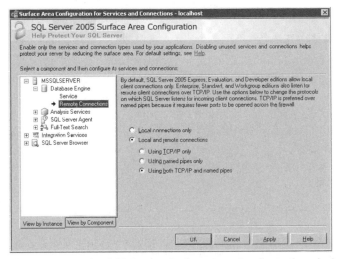

**Figure 27-2**   The SQL Server Surface Area Configuration choices.

5. Click OK to exit the SQL Server 2005 Surface Area Configuration tool.

## SQL Server Service Account Configuration

The SQL Server service configuration includes the user account under which this service will run. Often when you install SQL Server, you take the defaults and use the local system user account to start up the services. While this works in a local environment, it will fail to work properly in a larger landscape where communication and sharing of resources is needed between machines. There are several ways to solve this problem:

- Create local Windows accounts on both servers using the same account name and passwords on both machines.

- Use a domain account that both machines can share.

For administrative purposes, it's typically easier to have one domain account that is used for all SQL Servers. The primary reason is password management. When the password is changed on one machine, it's changed on all of them. Make sure the locally cached credentials get flushed and refreshed on each server.

---

**Note**    Set the user account and password on all dependent SQL Server services (on all participating systems) to be the same, preferably a domain account, for example, SQL Server service and SQL Server Agent service using the same account. This helps keep all the permissions in sync when exchanging data.

---

Finally, make sure that the appropriate firewall ports are open for the SQL Server instance, as well as any additional ports that may be needed for mirroring.

## Configuring Log Shipping

Configuring log shipping is done via the log shipping configuration tool. This tool creates SQL Agent jobs on both the primary and secondary database servers, which then perform log shipping tasks automatically. Log shipping can be configured from SQL Server Management Studio. In SQL Server Management Studio, expand the SQL Server instance, and then expand Databases. Right-click the source database, select Tasks, and then select Ship Transaction Logs. This invokes the Database Properties window in which you will configure log shipping. In the Database Properties window, perform the following steps:

1.  Make sure Transaction Log Shipping is selected in the left pane of the window.

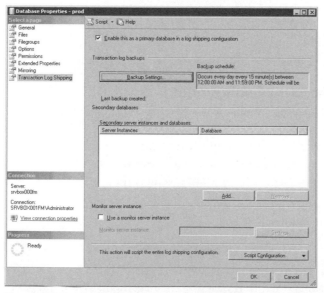

Figure 27-3    Database Properties—Transaction Log Shipping.

2. Select the Enable This As A Primary Database In A Log Shipping Configuration check box, and then click Backup Settings.

> **Note**  If the database is not currently using the full recovery model, you will get an error message and be required to set it up that way at this time.

3. From this window, you must define the network path to the backup folder. This path is used by the SQL Server agent to copy the backup file from the primary server to the standby server. This is a common directory to which both systems must have access. In addition to defining the network backup folder and local name, if applicable, you can also define the frequency of backups, the name of the job, and the frequency that the job is run. You can also disable the job from here. Once you have completed this page, click OK to continue. This returns you to the Database Properties window.

> **Note**  Before configuring the backup location in this window, make sure both systems service accounts have proper permissions to get to this location, as shown in Figure 27-4.

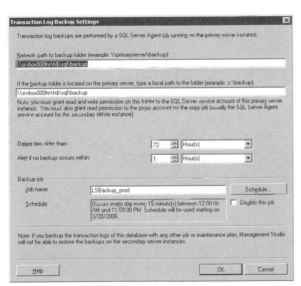

**Figure 27-4**   The Transaction Log Backup Settings window.

4. Once you have set up the initial backup, you must add a secondary server for SQL Server to which to log ship. In the Database Properties window, click Add.

This invokes the Secondary Database Settings window. Click Connect to open the Connect To Server window, and enter (or browse for) the name of the secondary database server. In this window, you will specify the credentials to connect to the secondary server. Once you have properly entered the server and authentication information, click Connect to return to the Secondary Database Settings window.

5. Three tabs in the Secondary Database Settings window define how the database is set up on the secondary server. The Initialize Secondary Database tab defines how the database is initially established, as shown in Figure 27-5. SQL Server can back up the database on the primary server and copy it over, or you can restore the database manually. It may be necessary to copy the database manually if you have a very large database and the copy/restore over a network will take too long. In this case, you might need to back up the database to tape, send this tape to the remote location, and restore it there.

---

**Note** If you are restoring a database manually, remember to use the NORECOVERY syntax, or else no transaction logs can be applied, for example:

```
RESTORE DATABASE prod
    FROM DISK= 'F:\sql\backup\prod.bak' WITH NORECOVERY;
```

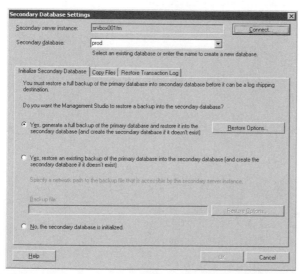

**Figure 27-5** The Initialize Secondary Database tab.

6.  The Copy Files tab specifies where the backups of the transaction logs and initial backup are put, as shown in Figure 27-6. Again, make sure the appropriate permissions are in place, or the copy job will not work after it has been configured. The Delete Copied Files After parameter controls how long the transaction log backup is saved after it has been sent to the secondary database server. This value should be determined by your backup schedule.

    The default schedule for the backup transaction log, copy files, and restore transaction log is every 15 minutes. This schedule is adjustable. See the "Advanced Log Shipping Strategies" section in this chapter for more information on strategies for changing these parameters. Generally, 15 minutes should be sufficient.

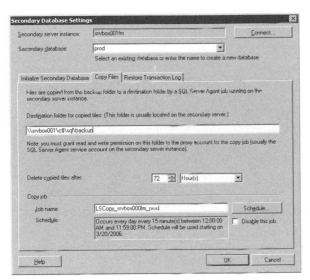

**Figure 27-6**   The Copy Files tab.

7.  Finally, the Restore Transaction Log tab defines the database on the secondary server to which the logs are applied, how the logs are applied, and the frequency with which they are applied, as shown in Figure 27-7. The default application of the log is set to zero, which means the log is applied as soon as the job is run. While on the surface this may sound obvious, there are reasons why you might not want this setting. For example, if someone accidentally deletes all the rows in a table and the application of the log on the secondary server is set to immediate, then the delete is also immediately propagated. If the latency of the application is delayed by an hour, then you have one hour to catch the error and recover the data on the secondary

server before it's deleted. As with the copy job, the defaults provided are usually good enough to get started with.

Remember, application of the log is in chronological time. The "real" time to apply the logs and catch up is usually very fast. For example, you might configure immediate copy of the transaction logs and a one-hour latency delay in the application of the log on the secondary database, but it will only take a few minutes to roll that hour of "chronological time" delay forward in case the database needs to be brought online immediately. Once you have configured the Secondary Database Settings appropriately, click OK to exit this window. You are now returned to the Database Properties window in the Ship Transaction Logs tab.

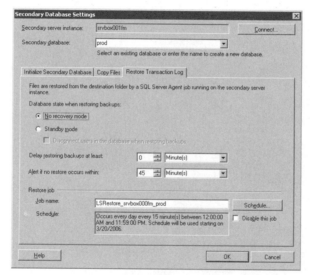

**Figure 27-7**    The Restore Transaction Log tab.

8.  Finally, configure the log shipping monitor. This tool helps you track statistics, status, and errors that could happen during log shipping, for example, if network connectivity goes down between the two servers and the copy job fails. Define where the log shipping monitor will reside. In large implementations, there may be one central server that tracks all log shipping.

Select the Use A Monitor Server Instance check box. Then click Settings. In the Log Shipping Monitor Settings window (see Figure 27-8), connect to a monitor instance as you did above with the secondary database instance, define the retention history as needed, and then click OK. This exits the Secondary Database Settings window, and you are now back in the Database Properties window in the Transaction Log Shipping tab.

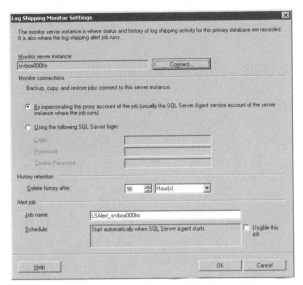

Figure 27-8    The Log Shipping Monitor settings.

9.  Click OK and SQL Server creates all the needed jobs on the primary and secondary servers, as shown in Figure 27-9.

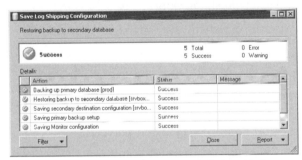

Figure 27-9    Log Shipping successfully installed.

The jobs can be seen when the SQL Server Agent is expanded on the primary and secondary servers. The primary has the backup and monitor jobs. The secondary has the copy and restore jobs.

# Monitoring Log Shipping

As with any mission critical application, you need to monitor log shipping. The process of monitoring log shipping is accomplished in three ways:

1.  Running the transaction log shipping status report

2. Looking at the SQL Server Agent job history

3. Checking the SQL Server log

## Running the Transaction Log Shipping Status report

To run the transaction log shipping status report, follow these steps. In the summary pane of SQL Server Management Studio, highlight the SQL Server instance, click the Report drop-down menu, and select the Transaction Log Shipping Status report.

This interrogates the job history in internal SQL Server tables and generates a report that provides information on when the last events occurred. A sample of the output is seen in Figure 27-10.

**Figure 27-10**   The Transaction Log Shipping Status report.

In the case of an alert, the report reads in red and shows which job failed and how far behind the job is.

## SQL Server Agent Job History

Checking the job history is an easy process. In the Object Explorer pane of SQL Server Management Studio, expand SQL Server Agent, and then expand the Jobs folder. The log shipping jobs are listed. Right-click the appropriate job and select View History.

This shows a listing of the jobs, their frequency, and whether any errors happened during the job run. This information is often useful for debugging errors, for example, when permissions have changed on a share and the job is no longer able to access it. It helps for also figuring out when something has broken and for root-cause analysis.

## Checking the SQL Server Log

The SQL Server Log can be viewed in SQL Server Management Studio by expanding the SQL Server instance, then expanding Management, and then expanding the SQL Server Logs folder. Select a log and double-click. Look for the last time that the log was backed up and when it was last applied. If any of these jobs are not running as scheduled, investigate the root cause by looking through the log. Additionally, the SQL

Server error log can be found in the %PROGRAM FILES%\Microsoft SQL Server\MSSQL.1\MSSQL\LOG directory (will be MSSQL.2 for second instance, etc.). When debugging issues, it's usually best to sort by date and time stamp. Typically, the problem you had last is written as the last entry in the last log. From a DOS command window, you can run the DIR /OD command in the LOG directory and get this listing.

### Real World    Problem Resolution

There can be any number of reasons that log shipping could fail. How to debug and solve the problem really depends on the problem itself. The log files are the best place to start, followed by the Windows event log and any other monitoring that you might have, such as MOM monitoring. Common problems affecting log shipping include network connectivity, space, and system problems. Follow the logs and look for the obvious.

## Metadata: Transact-SQL for Database Mirroring Information

The following is a list of system stored procedures for adding, removing, and monitoring log shipping on both the primary and secondary databases. These stored procedures require permissions from the sysadmin role. SQL Server Books Online provides a complete explanation of each.

Of particular interest are the following stored procedures:

- *sp_help_log_shipping_monitor*
- *sp_resolve_logins*

*sp_help_log_shipping_monitor* provides an overview of the log shipping landscape, and *sp_resolve_logins* is needed to resolve logins to users after secondary database post failover.

# Log Shipping Failover

Failing over the database in an emergency is a straight-forward process that involves several steps. As one would expect, there are different approaches based on whether the primary server is still available. For example, if a natural disaster strikes the primary datacenter on the East Coast, then the datacenter on the West Coast is not able to back up the tail of the transaction log, thereby exposing the company to loss of data that is in the final log. The recovery plan and business service level agreement need to factor this in when designing the overall high availability strategy and how often the transaction log on the primary server is backed up and copied to the secondary. The failover process includes the following steps:

1. Back up the master..syslogins Table to a text file. This file will be used to synchronize sysusers to syslogins on the secondary server when failover occurs. If you don't have this ready, you will have orphaned connections and users will not be able to properly log in to the secondary database after failover.

   To get this information, run the following command at a DOS command window. Alternately, you can script it into a SQL Agent job that runs nightly after your backup:

   ```
   C:\tmp>bcp master..syslogins out c:\tmp\syslogins.dat -N -S . -T
   ```

   > **Note**    The –T option specifies use of the trusted (windows) authentication. You can substitute –Usa –P**password** for –T if needed..

2. Disable log shipping on the primary if it's still available. Disabling log shipping on the primary requires going into the transaction log shipping configuration window, as described in "Configuring Log Shipping" previously in this chapter, and shown in Figure 27-3. Click the Backup Settings button in the center of the window. Next, select the Disable This Job check box, as seen in Figure 27-11. This keeps the log shipping jobs intact but suspends the database transaction log backup.

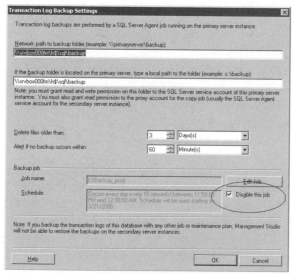

**Figure 27-11**    Log Shipping Backup Job.

3.  Back up the tail of the transaction log. If the primary server is still accessible, back up the tail of the transaction log. This contains the last few records prior to the database coming down. To back up the tail of the transaction log, run the following command:

```
USE master ;

BACKUP LOG prod

   TO DISK='\\srvbox000fm\h$\sql\backup\tail.trn' WITH NO_TRUNCATE,INIT ;
```

> **Note**    You can also back up the primary log file using the "NORECOVERY" syntax puts the primary database in a recovery state. This allows the secondary to repoint back to the primary once the failed server is fixed. However, this option requires the database to be in single user mode, thus requiring a restart before proceeding.

4.  Restore the tail to the secondary and recover the database manually. Now restore the last transactions from the tail of the transaction log to the secondary server and recover the database so users can access it:

```
USE master ;

RESTORE LOG prod

   FROM DISK='\\srvbox000fm\h$\sql\backup\tail.trn' WITh RECOVERY ;
```

5.  Resolve logins. Run the following stored procedure to resolve the logins between the primary and secondary databases (using your own database names):

```
EXEC sp_resolve_logins @dest_db = 'prod',

   @dest_path = '\\srvbox000fm\h$\',

   @filename = 'syslogins.dat'

GO
```

> **Note**    See the section titled "Failovers: Users, Logins" in this chapter for a complete explanation of syslogins and sysusers in the recovery process.

> **Note**    Substitute your database destination and path in this command.

At this point, users can now log into the database using their login and passwords that they use on the primary database server.

6.  Next point this application to the new database server IP address or change the ODBC DSN connection string and other specifications so the application can find

the new database server. Additionally, depending on the configuration, you may need to take the new primary database server (that was previously the secondary) and point to a new secondary server. This requires going through the configuration process again. All of this is application-dependent and dependent on how it fits into your site's high availability plan for business continuity.

While this may seem cumbersome, you should have all of this scripted out, and it should not take more than a few minutes to complete all of the steps during an emergency.

---

**Note**    The keys to successful failover are planning, documentation, and testing. Have all of the processes debugged and scripted well in advance. The last thing a DBA needs is to debug a recovery process in an emergency situation. In addition to documenting the system, also have a tape recall policy, support and account numbers, management escalation paths, hotels, and 24-hour food outlets documented.

---

## Removing Log Shipping

Removing log shipping is very easy. Simply go into the log shipping configuration window as discussed in the section "Configuring Log Shipping" and then clear the Enable This As A Primary Database In A Log Shipping Configuration check box, as shown in Figure 27-3, and click OK to continue. You are prompted that this will remove log shipping. Next, a window pops up that shows you the status of the log shipping jobs being removed.

## Tuning Log Shipping: Operations and Considerations

Log shipping can be planned in two basic configurations: one for data availability, and the other for performance and availability. In the former case, the company is looking for access to the data not for performance reasons but for recovery times and accessibility that are faster than going to a backup tape and rebuilding a system. The reasons for this might be an offline reporting server, staggered copies of the data for advanced recovery scenarios, or just having another option in their recovery choices. In this scenario, older systems are typically used. Performance is not a key consideration.

In the latter scenario, availability and performance, companies are planning on failing over a production environment to a secondary disaster database. In this case, the company needs a system that can handle as many users and batch processes on the database server as the primary server. The hardware requirements for this case are significantly different than having a system that is used as a reporting server.

With this in mind, tuning log shipping is really a function of several variables that are independent and yet act together. They consist of hardware, network speed, and log shipping configuration jobs, as mentioned throughout this book:

- Database server hardware
- Number of disks participating in the disk volumes and how they are configured (RAID level, and so on)
- Speed of the disk
- Speed of the LAN/WAN
- Frequency of the copy job
- Frequency of the apply job
- Frequency of size of the transaction log backups

## Hardware Considerations

As with any computer configuration, you can go only as fast as your slowest component, which tends to be a disk. If you are planning on a reporting or data-only configuration, older hardware can be used. However, this is not recommended. In the unfortunate event of a failover, the slower backup hardware will not be able to keep up with your current load, and your performance might suffer dramatically. It is recommended that sufficient hardware be allocated as the secondary server.

## Network Considerations

Network can be a significant bottleneck, depending on the location of the secondary database and the size of the transaction volume. Just as with a disk, you can go only as fast as your slowest network segment allows. For example, your network may be on a gigabit fabric switch, but your data may be going over a VPN connection where a router on a distant network is running very slowly. In this case, you can go only as fast as the slow router on the remote network even though your gear is highly optimized.

Networks tend to be tough issues to diagnose. At a rudimentary level, basic information can be attained by running a **tracert** command. This shows you how many hops the packets have to go over the routers and how long it takes for each hop to take place. With a disaster recovery site on the other side of the country, it's feasible to be hopping over 20 or 30 routers, each taking a significant amount of time. If the copy jobs are taking a long time, debug with the **tracert** command and try taking the database out of the equation by just **XCOPY** a file from one server to the other and measuring the times. If the network is too slow to keep up with copying the transaction log backups, the network must be enhanced or log shipping will not work for you.

## How Often Should the Transaction Log Be Backed Up?

This is a common question that we are often asked. The answer basically comes down to how much data the company can be exposed to if the transaction log device is lost. In a perfect world, the data is never lost. The next best scenario is that the risk of loss is mitigated through various high availability technologies such as RAID devices at the disk level, geospatial replication at the disk subsystem, log shipping, and database mirroring. The reality is that data loss does happen because disks are mechanical devices that can and do break.

Backing up the database transaction log once an hour is going to involve the same total amount of data as backing up the database multiple times during the same hour. For example, one 100 MB transaction log backup once an hour is going to take up the same disk space as four 25M transaction log backups done every 15 minutes during that same time frame. The only difference is that if the company lost the log device during that one hour backup, it could lose all 100M of data in it. If the company backed up once every 15 minutes, then data loss exposure could be 25M, hence limiting the exposure to loss of data.

On large mission-critical databases, such as an ERP system, backing up the transaction log is done more often than on data warehouses because data is updated more frequently in an ERP system. The more frequent the transaction log backups are done, the less effect it has on the system. However, performing transaction log backups too frequently can cause extra contention on the log disks.

## Log Shipping Job Configuration

There are two considerations to keep in mind when tuning the jobs: recovery time and size of transactional volume. If the company has a high transactional volume, then the failure to move the data over to the remote site in an expedited way means exposure to data loss. Conversely, if the transactional volume is low, then the need to move the data over could be less.

Within the context of moving the data over, the copy job of log shipping can be changed to reflect this concern. Typically, the company wants the data over to the remote site as soon as the transaction log is backed up. The default, 0, copies the data over as soon as the transaction log is backed up. There really are not that many reasons not to copy the data over to the remote server as soon as it's backed up—it mitigates the risk of a *single point of failure* on the primary server.

The application of the transaction log can be staggered based on the company's recovery strategy. This can be tuned by changing the Delay Restoring Backups option in the Restore Transaction Log tab on the Secondary Database Settings screen in the log shipping configuration window.  To reach this screen, select the database that is being log shipped in the Object Explorer by expanding databases. Right click the database and select Tasks, and then select Ship Transaction Logs. In the Transaction Log Shipping page, click the ellipses button next to the secondary database to invoke the Secondary Database Settings screen. From here, click the Restore Transaction Log tab.

### Real World    Why Delay?

The primary reason for keeping the secondary database up to date on the copy but delayed behind on the application of the transaction log, is to protect from logical corruption. Take this scenario, for example: The secondary database is backed up every 15 minutes, delayed by one hour, and the copy is immediate. A developer accidentally drops a table on the primary at 10 a.m. and discovered his error at 10:08 a.m. You could go to the secondary server, which would be at 9 a.m. in recovery, and you could stop the log shipping, apply all the transaction logs until 10 a.m., and then recover the table. If the copy and apply were immediate or if mirroring was used, then the data would have been dropped on both the primary and secondary databases, forcing you to go to tape for a restore on a server and then rolling forward many transaction logs until 10 a.m. Having the delay built in can protect the company and help on the recovery issues.

## Practical Log Shipping Advice

Log shipping in itself is a simple and strong strategy. This is not to be confused with being simplistic. It offers a robust and resilient tool in your high availability strategy. There are a variety of permutations to consider when implementing log shipping.

### Real World    Not Just "A" Database: Multiple Secondaries

Many environments require not just single redundancy, but multiple redundant systems. This provides a much higher degree of redundancy and thus a greater chance that a standby system is available. Log shipping provides that kind of coverage. You can configure multiple secondary servers as shown in Figure 27-12.

By having multiple standby servers, you can take advantage of the performance provided by having the standby system local and still provide for a standby system in another part of the country or world. Because of network speed and latency, the distant system might be further behind, but it will provide for redundancy in the event of a regional disaster.

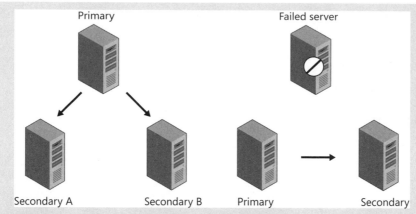

**Figure 27-12**   Multiple secondary database servers.

Log shipping has the ability to control the frequency of many of its components, for example, how often the transaction log is backed up, copied, and then restored. Take advantage of these parameters in creative ways. In my production support role, we backed up the transaction log every five minutes, copied it immediately, but applied the log with a one-hour delay. This gave us the following advantages:

- The ability to have all but five minutes of the data on the remote systems in case of recovery.

- A one hour delay to catch any catastrophic errors. For example, once a developer dropped what he thought was a view but was in reality a table. We were able to go to the secondary server and recover the data all the way up to the moment before the table was dropped.

- Even though we were behind one hour (12 transaction logs = 60 min./5 min. logs), rolling the logs forward in case of emergency was done in less than a few minutes. One hour of chronological time does not take very long to catch up. This time, of course, depends on the size of your transaction load.

Extending this idea further, one server could be 10 minutes behind, another server could be 30 minutes behind, and another one hour behind. Offering even more recovery options.

## Script Log Shipping

Log shipping also has the flexibility of scripting. All jobs that are run through the GUI can be generated into SQL scripts. This can help with standardizing deployments by ensuring that exactly the same script is run on all servers. When configuring log shipping, simply click the Script Configuration button, and then choose where to script it to.  You can select to script it to the clipboard, a new query window, or to a file.

## Using Mirroring and Log Shipping Together

Database mirroring and log shipping are two different technologies that can be deployed independently or together to mutually complement each other. The primary reason for using both technologies at the same time is the limitation that only one mirror server is definable per database. Hence, if your high availability strategy is in need of multiple standby databases for extra resiliency in your landscape, then you will need log shipping deployed, too. Additionally, log shipping gives you the ability to control the latency when applying a transaction log in log shipping, which cannot be controlled with mirroring. A typical landscape for this configuration can be seen in Figure 27-13. On the left, the landscape is up and running properly. On the right, the principal has failed, and the mirror has become the new principal and is now the log shipping.

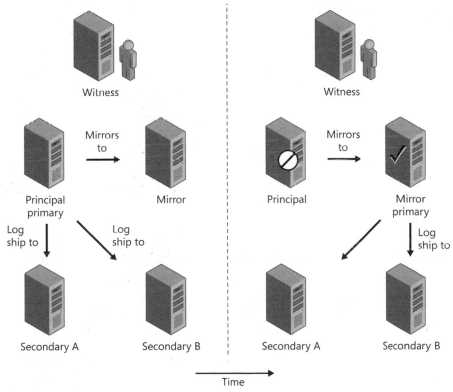

**Figure 27-13**   Log shipping and database mirroring deployed simultaneously.

## Test Failing Over

Arguably the most important concept that is often not performed is practice recoveries. Many times DBAs configure log shipping but don't actually test it. For example, you recover the database but do not have the user logins to sync, or the sync script does not work as expected. Now, you have a database, but users cannot log into it. Or, as in the above "not just a database," the failover is a bit more sophisticated. A secondary database is converted to a primary database and then is repointed to another secondary database. This is not difficult, but it needs to be documented and tested thoroughly. The bottom line is that at least once a year, if not more frequently, recoveries should be tested.

## Backups and Log Shipping

In a very indirect way, log shipping tests the validity of your transaction log files. For example, if you cannot restore a transaction log file in log shipping, chances are good that the file was corrupted, perhaps via a controller error or a bad block on the disk. Needless to say, this provides an early warning mechanism that it's time to do a full backup of your primary database due to the breaking of the log chain. Please note that this is not a substitute for testing your backups. SQL Server's development team mantra is "You are only as good as your last restore." They will not guarantee future restores. The simple reason is that backup media can go bad. In addition, tapes should be rotated and tested. This is covered in detail in Chapter 14, "Backup Fundamentals," and Chapter 15, "Restoring Data."

## What You Will Not Be Protected From

You can log ship a corrupted database. I have experienced a customer who had a very robust high availability solution which included clustering and log shipping to two remote sites and a SAN with triple mirroring. The problem was that the SAN firmware corrupted the database and log shipped the corruption to the remote locations. Additionally, they also backed up the corruption onto tape and overwrote their last good backup. The only element missing in their solution was running DBCC CHECKDB on their database, which would have caught the issue. Log shipping and mirroring do not protect you against such failures. A RESTORE command does not check the validity of the data structures on the restored pages.

## Backup Log Frequency

As pointed out in the log shipping tuning section above, minimize your data loss exposure by frequently backing up the transaction log. You will not save disk space by making fewer and larger backups. The only exposure you have is massive data loss if that one large file is corrupted or the log device is lost prior to backing it up. Shipping the log at many small points in time provides less chance for data loss by moving the data over to the log shipping server in more frequent intervals. Experiment on your hardware. Take tests and measurements. Figure out what your company's data loss exposure is. Talk with the managers to understand the service level agreement between IT and the business units. Reflect these realities in the scheduling of the transaction log backups and the overall database recovery strategy.

## Log Shipping Summary

Log shipping and mirroring are just technologies that help facilitate high availability. In and of themselves, they are not a substitute for a strategy. High availability is a goal, and how you get there is the strategy. Log shipping and mirroring fit in well and compliment each other in the array of choices a company has for deploying a high availability solution. They fit in well with clustering, replication at the SAN level (dark fiber), a robust backup solution, and so on. Take full advantage of them. They are a terrific out-of-the-box solution that will save you time and the company a lot of money, both in development hours and reduction in lost data.

# Database Mirroring

Database mirroring is a new high availability technology that was introduced in SQL Server 2005. Primarily, it is used as part of an overall high availability solution, but it can also be used as a database reporting solution. It can be used in a variety of ways: stand alone or in conjunction with log shipping, clustering, or database snapshots. Mirroring provides a hybrid solution: a copy of database like with log shipping, rapid failover capabilities like with clustering, and elimination of the issues associated with shared disk solutions.

Mirroring in a minimal configuration consists of two database servers: the principal and the mirror. The *principal* database is the primary database that is online and accessible to users. The *mirror* database is a copy of the principal that is in a restoring state and has the changes applied to it from the principal database as they occur. The failover method for this configuration is manual.

A more robust configuration consists of three database servers: principal, mirror, and the *witness*. The witness server is an active observer of the principal/mirror combination. If the principal goes down, the witness automatically fails over to the mirror and brings it online.

These configurations are explained in this chapter, in addition to practical uses of each and how they fit into an overall high availability solution.

## Configuring Database Mirroring

Like log shipping, database mirroring starts with a backup copy of the primary database, but unlike log shipping, the writes to the transaction log are transmitted to the standby system immediately, not when a log backup occurs. This allows the mirror system to remain in sync with the primary system. Because of this, it is much more flexible in terms of the protection it provides; however, the performance considerations of the network are more restrictive.

# Planning and Considerations for Database Mirroring

Designing a highly available system requires understanding of the technologies to be deployed, how they work together, and the advantages and disadvantages of each. Mirroring is no different. The solution offers compelling benefits and several options in the configuration of the solution that must be decided upon before implementation. The main considerations to take into account when designing database mirroring are the performance characteristics of the mirror and recovery method.

By considering these options prior to configuring database mirroring, you will end up with a more successful design.

> **Note**    To run database mirroring, the recovery model has to be set to FULL. For example, **ALTER DATABASE prod SET RECOVERY FULL** or via the database properties screen in the SQL Server Management studio.

The database mirroring solution is a high availability and disaster recovery solution that serves a specific purpose. It is not a substitute for database backups.

> **Note**    You cannot mirror system databases: *master*, *tempdb*, *msdb*, or *model*.

### Major Parts in a Mirror Pair

Database mirroring consists of several main components. They are the principal database, mirror database, the witness, and the endpoints. The various combinations of these help define how the operating modes of mirroring work in a highly available environment. First, let's start off by defining the basic components:

- **Principal**    The principal is the originating database in the mirror pair. There can be only one principal database, and it has to be on a separate SQL Server instance than the mirror database.

- **Mirror**    The mirror is the receiving database in the mirror pair. Every DML and DCL command that goes into the transaction log on the principal database is applied to the mirror database. There can be only one mirror for each principal database. The mirror needs to be on its own separate SQL Server instance, preferably on a separate physical server.

■ **Witness**   The witness (optional) provides the mechanism to ensure a highly available solution. It monitors the mirrored pair and ensures that both database servers are in proper operating order. The witness is a separate SQL Server instance, preferably on a separate physical server than the principal or mirror. One witness server can monitor multiple mirror pairs. If any of the servers go down (witness, principal, or mirror), the whole database landscape halts until either the down server becomes available and reconnects or the witness is disabled. This ensures the integrity of the entire mirroring environment. If a witness is not defined and either the principal or mirror goes down, the landscape stays up. You will just have to recover the mirror database and repoint the application in the case of the principal going down, or you repair the mirror database if it malfunctions and users will be running just on the principal as usual.

■ **Quorum**   A *quorum* is the relationship between the witness, the principal, and the mirror. Each operating mode has different quorum states and recovery scenarios depending on which node in the relationship is lost. This will be discussed later in this chapter.

■ **Mirrored Pair**   A principal and mirror operating together are called a *mirrored pair*. The changes on the principal database are reflected in the mirrored database.

■ **Endpoint**   An *endpoint* is the method that the SQL Server Database Engine uses to communicate with applications. Within the context of a database mirrored pair, the endpoint is the method that the principal uses to communicate with the mirror. The mirror listens on a port defined in the endpoint. The default is TCP port 5022. Each database mirror pair listens to its own unique port. To see a list of all database mirror endpoints, run:

```
SELECT * FROM sys.database_mirroring_endpoints ;
```

To see a list of all endpoints, run:

```
SELECT * FROM sys.tcp_endpoints ;
```

Defining the endpoints can be done in T-SQL or through the GUI tool when setting up the mirror. This is covered later in this chapter.

## Operating Modes

SQL Server provides three operating modes for database mirroring, as shown in Table 27-1. The differentiators between the operating modes is determined by whether a witness is present to handle automatic failover and the performance of the communication method between the principal and mirror databases. The communication method will help determine the performance characteristics of the overall application

Table 27-1    Database Mirroring Operating Modes

| Mode Name | Transaction Safety | Mirroring Method | Witness Required | Automatic Failover Possible? |
|---|---|---|---|---|
| High availability | Set to FULL | Synchronous | Yes | Yes |
| High protection | Set to FULL | Synchronous | No | No |
| High performance | Set to OFF | Asynchronous | No | No |

High availability mode provides the most robust coverage. It consists of a principal, a mirror, and a witness in synchronous communication. In this mode, SQL Server ensures that each transaction that is committed on the principal database is committed on the mirror database prior to continuing on to the next database operation on the principal. The costs for this configuration are the need for a witness database instance and the overhead of running in synchronous communication. If the network does not have bandwidth, a bottleneck could form, causing performance issues on the principal. If the principal database is lost, the mirror can automatically take over.

High protection mode consists of a principal and a mirror in synchronous communication. It offers transactional consistency without the need for a witness instance. As with high availability mode, it ensures that each transaction that is committed on the principal database is committed on the mirror database prior to continuing on to the next database operation on the principal. The protection it affords is guaranteed transactional consistency between the principal and the mirror. The cost for this configuration is the overhead of synchronous communication for the confirmation acknowledgement. There is no automatic failure to this mode.

High performance mode consists of only a principal and a mirror in asynchronous communication. It does not require a witness or the overhead of synchronous communication. The mirror database maintains transactional consistency but may not be real-time up-to-date because high performance mode uses asynchronous communication. Asynchronous communication guarantees that the databases remain transactional consistent but not necessarily real time. There may be an arbitrary small amount of time the mirror usually lags behind, but the lag can increase if the principal database is under heavy stress. The performance increase comes from the originating application not having to wait for confirmation of the log records being applied to the mirror server. The application can keep doing work while the principal database queues and applies the records to the mirror database as quickly as it can. High performance mode is recommended when the mirror is a significant distance away from the principal and the network latency can cause performance issues. There is no automatic failover in this mode.

## Synchronous and Asynchronous Explained

Mirroring offers two methods for exchanging data. The performance characteristics of each have tradeoffs. The two are:

- Synchronous

- Asynchronous

Synchronous mirroring requires that the mirror receive the data, confirm that the operation has been committed on the mirror database, and then send an acknowledgement, or ack, back to the principal confirming that the operation has been completed prior to committing on the principal and the client proceeding to the next operation. The key concept is that the client waits until the operation is complete on the remote mirror database.

If the network is fast, then there is not much penalty. If the network is slow, then the wait for the commit on the remote mirror can become a performance issue. This is the most secure method for assuring that data is absolutely correct on the principal and mirror combination, but it's also the slowest method due to the overhead of the principal having to wait for the ack to be sent back. The penalty of the waiting for an ack is directly proportional to the network speed and bandwidth available as illustrated in Figure 27-14. If the mirror is on a local gigabit Ethernet network, then the penalty may be minimal.

> **Important**   If the mirror is on the other side of the country, synchronous communication may be impractical to use due to network latency issues across a WAN connection. If the mirror is on the other side of the world, synchronous communication will definitely be impractical.

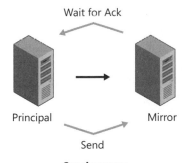

**Synchronous**

**Figure 27-14**   Synchronous: Waiting for acknowledgement.

Asynchronous mirroring is a "give and go" type method. The data is sent to the mirror server as resources are available, but the client does not wait for the ack to be sent back before continuing. The transactional consistency between the principal and the mirror is always maintained. The mirror database may receive the log records at some arbitrary time in the future. It may be immediately or 20 seconds from the commit on the principal, depending on how heavy the transactional volume. (This latency can be observed in the data mirroring monitor.)

The application and user do not wait for the ack to be sent back from the mirror, hence allowing more operations to go forward in a higher performance configuration. The "give and go" nature of asynchronous method allows the principal and mirror to be in physically different areas, still maintain the database integrity, and have high performance, even though it may be over a slower WAN connection as illustrated in Figure 27-15.

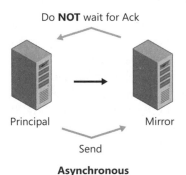

**Figure 27-15**   Asynchronous: Does not wait for acknowledgement.


## SQL Server Database Mirroring Version Support

Database mirroring is available on all versions of SQL Server in some method, whether as a full participant or as just a witness. The following matrix compares the different versions of SQL Server and the levels of support that are provided in a mirrored environment. For example, only the Developer and Enterprise Editions provide Different, the mechanism for asynchronous mirroring, thus enabling the High Performance mode.

**Table 27-2   SQL Server Database Mirroring Version Support Matrix**[*]

| Database Mirroring Feature | Enterprise Edition | Developer Edition | Standard Edition | Workgroup Edition | SQL Express |
|---|---|---|---|---|---|
| Partner | Yes | Yes | Yes | No | No |
| Witness | Yes | Yes | Yes | Yes | Yes |
| Safety = FULL | Yes | Yes | Yes | No | No |
| Safety = OFF | Yes | Yes | No | No | No |
| Available During UNDO After Failure | Yes | Yes | Yes | No | No |
| Parallel Redo | Yes | Yes | No | No | No |
| Database Snapshots | Yes | Yes | No | No | No |

*Source: Microsoft TechNet Web site paper:
*http://www.microsoft.com/technet/prodtechnol/sql/2005/dbmirror.mspx.*

# Tuning Database Mirroring

Much like log shipping, performance tuning in database mirroring is directly proportional to server speed, network bandwidth and speed, and disk drive characteristics. Performance is also strongly influenced by the safety model chosen and the underlying communication method it employs, as seen in the previous section. Specifically, high availability and high protection use synchronous mirroring, and high performance uses asynchronous. These decisions are usually taken in conjunction with the business users and are part of the service level agreement for acceptable recovery times, costs of the system being designed, and acceptable exposure levels.

## Failing Over with Database Mirroring

Failing over in a mirrored environment can happen in several different ways depending on the operating mode of the witness (optional) and mirror, and whether the principal database is available. In general, there are two types of failover: automatic and manual. For automatic to be in place, the high availability mode must be used. For high protection and high performance modes, the failover is manual.

The recovery path for each mode is dependent on which nodes in the quorum are available at any given time. For example, if the principal database in the high performance database is not accessible, then the tail of the transaction log cannot be backed up, and because the communication method in this mode is asynchronous, then all of the log records may not be on the mirror. Hence, data loss may occur. Conversely, in a high protection mode, this may not be the case because of synchronous communication ensuring that the log records were applied to the mirror. The role of the quorum in recovery can be seen in the following table.

Table 27-3    Quorum Scenarios in Database Mirroring

| State | Description | Role in Failover |
|---|---|---|
| Full Quorum | This is when the principal, mirror, and witness can all communicate with each other. | If principal is lost and witness is up and running, automatic failover to mirror. |
| Quorum | This state exists if the witness and either partner can communicate with it. | If mirror is lost, principal retains control. |
| | | If witness is lost and principal and mirror are up and running, then partner-to-partner quorum established. |
| Partner-to-Partner Quorum | When only the principal and mirror can communicate with each other. | In this case only the witness is missing and no failover occurs. |

The following diagrams illustrate the recovery paths when failing over in database mirroring, depending on the operating mode and quorum of available nodes.

## Highly Available

In the highly available mode, a full quorum is defined as the principal, mirror, and witness being available and communicating with each other. Figure 27-16 explains the recovery path depending on which server or servers are up and available. If the principal is lost and the witness and mirror are available, then failover is automatic.

## High Protection

In the high protection mode, a full quorum is defined as the principal, the witness and the mirror being available and communicating with each other. Figure 27-17 explains the recovery path depending on which server or servers are up and available. If the principal is lost and the mirror is available, then you have to manually fail the system over.

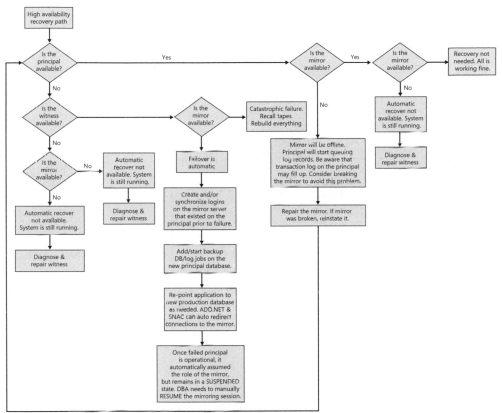

**Figure 27-16** Recovery tree for highly available mode.

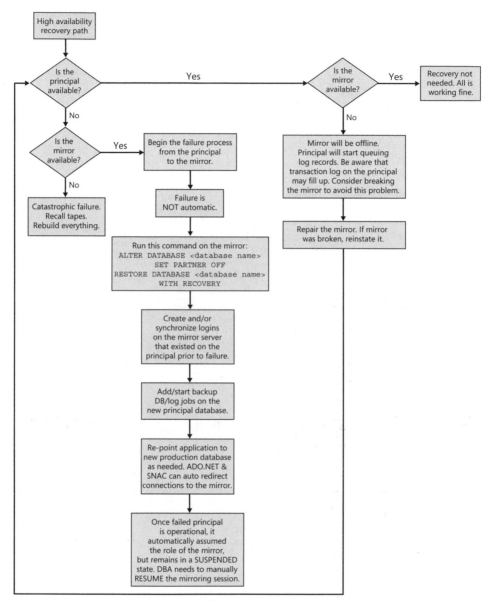

**Figure 27-17** Recovery tree for high protection mode.

## High Performance

In the high performance mode, a full quorum is defined as the principal and the mirror being available and communicating with each other. Figure 27-18 explains the recovery path depending on which server or servers are up and available. If the principal is lost and the mirror is available, then you have to manually fail the system over with possible data loss.

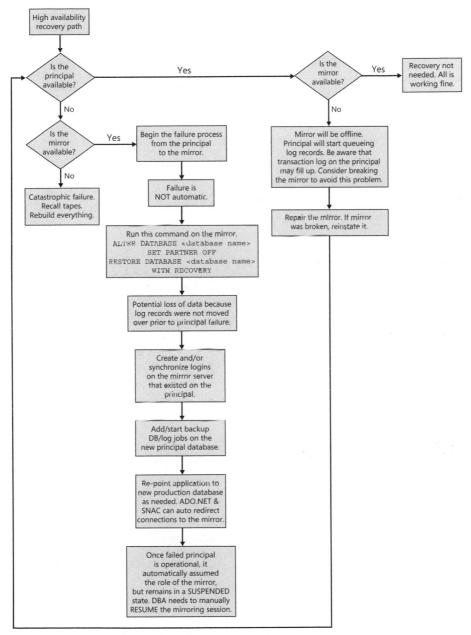

**Figure 27-18** Tree for high performance mode.

## Failover Scenario: High Performance

The following recovery scenario assumes that database mirroring is set up in high performance mode (i.e., the safety is off, and it's running asynchronously) and the principal database server is down:

1.  From the mirror, run the command ALTER DATABASE **<database_name>** SET PARTNER FORCE_SERVICE_ALLOW_DATA_LOSS. For example:

    ```
    ALTER DATABASE prod
      SET PARTNER FORCE_SERVICE_ALLOW_DATA_LOSS ;
    ```

    This causes the mirror to stop and become the new principal. When the original principal becomes available, it is marked as mirroring in a suspended state.

    > **Note**   If the principal is still up and the command **ALTER DATABASE prod** SET PARTNER FORCE_SERVICE_ALLOW_DATA_LOSS is run on the mirror, you will get an error that the database is not in the correct state to become the principal database.

2.  Ensure that the users and logins are in sync by, for example, running the *sp_resolve_logins* system stored procedure or restoring the master database from a previous backup of the original principal.

3.  Repoint to the new principal server any applications that pointed to the original principal.

## Failover Scenario: High Protection

The following recovery scenario assumes that database mirroring is set up in high protection mode (i.e., the safety is on, and it's running synchronously) and the principal database server is unavailable:

1.  From the mirror, run the command ALTER DATABASE **<database name>** SET PARTNER OFF **command.** At this point, the mirroring is broken and the database needs to be recovered.

2.  To recover the database, run the RESTORE DATABASE **<database name>** WITH RECOVERY command. As with the high performance recovery path, the users and logins must be synced and then the applications pointed to the standby server.

3.  Ensure that the users and logins are in sync by, for example, running the *sp_resolve_logins* system stored procedure or restoring the master database from a previous backup of the original principal.

4.  Repoint to the new principal server any applications that pointed to the original principal.

## Failovers: Users, Logins

An important and often overlooked concept is how SQL Server handles users and logins, especially during a failover. This happens in both log shipping and mirroring. The main idea is SQL Server has the concept that a person logs into a database server and then is a user in a specific database on that server. For example, an accountant logs into the database server but needs specific permissions to access the accounts payable database. It is very possible that a person could have a login into a database server and NOT be a user in any databases.

The following queries show the correlation between users and logins. In the first query, there is one login on the database server called frankmcband one user in the prod database called frankmcb. The login is stored in the syslogins table in the master database. The user is stored in the sysusers table in the user database. If a user logs into this database server, everything goes as expected. Note how the SID values are the same:

```
SELECT l.name 'syslogins name', l.sid 'syslogins sid',
  u.name 'sysusers name', u.sid 'sysusers sid'
FROM master..syslogins l JOIN prod..sysusers u ON
  l.name = u.name AND l.sid = u.sid;
```

```
syslogins name         syslogins sid
---------              ----------------------------------
frankmcb               0xC5E95662C3583A4CBCF39C459376AE9

sysusers name          sysusers sid
---------              ----------------------------------------
frankmcb               0xC5E95662C3583A4CBCF39C459376AE9

(1 row(s) affected)
```

If you failed over the database from principal to mirror and the logins and users had not been properly synchronized, running the same query will result in no rows being returned.

Note that the user ID exists in the user database but not in the logins for the new principal database server:

```
SELECT u.name 'sysusers name', u.sid 'sysusers sid'
FROM prod..sysusers u
WHERE u.name = 'frankmcb';
```

```
SELECT l.name 'sysusers name', l.sid 'sysusers sid'
FROM master..syslogins l
WHERE l.name = 'frankmcb';
```

```
sysusers name        sysusers sid
---------            ---------------------------------------------
frankmcb             0xC5E95662C3583A4CBCF39C459376AE9
```

(1 row(s) affected)

---

**Important**   If you try to log into the new principal prior to synchronizing the logins and users, you get an error message that the login failed.

---

As with log shipping mentioned earlier, to get around this issue, the logins and users must be synchronized on the database that was failed over to. This is the case regardless of whether it was manual or automatic failover. The process has two simple steps if the original principal database is still available:

1.  Run the BCP command to get the data from the syslogins table:

    ```
    C:\tmp>bcp master..syslogins out c:\tmp\syslogins.dat -N -S . -T ;
    ```

    ---

    **Note**   If you wish to use SQL Server authentication, substitute –Usa –Ppassword for –T (trusted authentication).

    ---

2.  Run the system stored procedure to import it into the new principal server:

    ```
    EXEC sp_resolve_logins @dest_db = 'prod',
      @dest_path = '\\srvbox000fm\h$\',
      @filename = 'syslogins.dat'
    GO
    ```

Alternately if the original principal database is not available, you have these two choices:

1.  Restore the master database to another server and extract the syslogins table there and then *sp_resolve_logins* to the new principal server.

2.  If the master database was not backed up, key the user logins by hand.

However you look at it, the database server logins (syslogins) and the database users (sysusers) must be in sync for the user to get data out of a SQL Server database. Plan for this as part of the recovery documentation, daily backup processes, and mock tests and recovery scenarios.

> **Note**   This is why it is very important to backup the *master* database every time you back up the principal database. Typically, the *master* database is less than 10 megabytes in size. It is also a very good idea to backup the *msdb* database because it contains all of the SQL Server job definition and history.

## Configuring Database Mirroring

Mirroring can be configured in three ways:

1.  High availability mode

2.  High protection mode

3.  High performance mode

As explained earlier in this chapter, each has its own advantages and disadvantages depending on the desired high availability needs and dependent hardware and networking capacity.

At the very minimum configuration (high performance and high protection), the mirror database serves as a hot standby. This means that the database is in a recovery state waiting for the last transactions to be applied either automatically via the mirroring definition, forced role switch, or manually when you back up the tail of the log (presuming it's available), and applies it to the mirror and then recovers the database for users to access it. When the landscape is configured in the high availability mode, there are more resilient features offered, such as automatic failover between the principal and mirror.

The following example shows how to configure two database servers in high performance mode. The steps are to define the servers, set up security, and establish endpoints:

1.  In the SQL Server Management Studio, expand the SQL Server instance and then expand Databases. Right-click the target database and select "Tasks," and then select "Mirror." This invokes the Database Properties window, from which mirroring will be configured.

2.  The Database Properties window for the database appears with Mirroring selected. Click the Configure Security button at the top right of the window, as seen in Figure 27-19.

3.  At this point, a configuration wizard pops up, walking you through the database mirroring security. The first screen you see is the introductory screen (not shown). Click the Next button to continue.

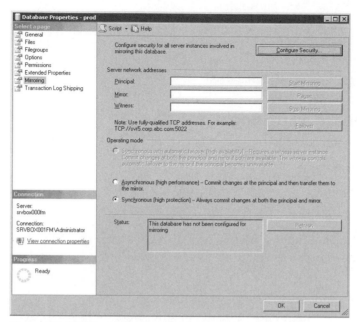

**Figure 27-19**    Database Properties—Configure Security.

4.  The first question asked is whether there is a witness server in the landscape. Remember that the witness server is what provides the automatic failover mechanism, but it also requires the dependency of running in synchronous communication. In this example, we are running in high performance mode, which does not require a witness server and runs in asynchronous communication mode as shown in Figure 27-20. In this example, "No" and "Next" are selected.

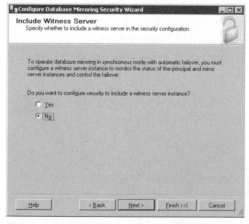

**Figure 27-20**    Include witness server.

5. Because we are already on the principal server, the option is grayed out, and we need to select the server that will be the mirror as shown in Figure 27-21. Select the Mirror Server Instance checkbox, and then click the Next button.

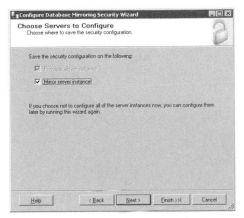

**Figure 27-21**   Server instance selection.

6. The next two pages ask for information about the principal and mirror server instances. This information is used to configure the endpoints. As discussed earlier, the endpoints are the ports to which SQL Server will listen when exchanging information. Specifically with mirroring, these are the ports in which the principal server sends over the log records to be applied to the mirror server and the acknowledgement of the application confirmed back to the principal. The following screens ask you to select the listener ports (default is 5022), whether the data transmitted is to be encrypted (default is yes), the name of the mirror server, and the name of the endpoint on each server itself, as shown in Figure 27-22, for the principal server.

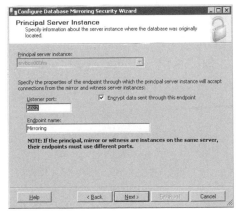

**Figure 27-22**   Principal server port and security configuration.

> **Note**    Make sure your various firewalls have port 5022 open or else communication between the servers will not be available for mirroring. Note that SQL Server's normal port for other communications is different than 5022, so just because you can run T-SQL against SQL Server does not ensure that mirroring will be available as well.

7. Repeat this for the mirror server as shown in Figure 27-23.

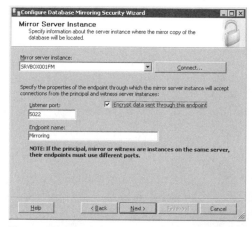

**Figure 27-23**    Mirror server port and security configuration.

8. If different account names are used, then supply them in the screen shown in Figure 27-24. If the servers use the same domain account and password or the same user account and password on the local servers, then you can leave the information blank and click the Next button.

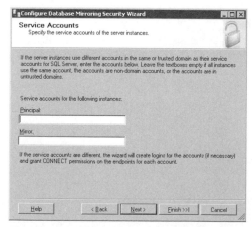

**Figure 27-24**    Service account configuration.

9.  At this point, all of the information for configuration of the endpoints and security has been defined. The Complete The Wizard screen gives an overview of all of the various data input (not shown). Click the Finish button.

10. If everything is set up correctly and the services can communicate properly, SQL Server establishes the endpoints on both the principal and mirror servers, as seen in Figure 27-25.

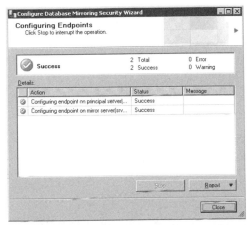

**Figure 27-25**  Successful endpoint configuration.

11. The following two windows after the endpoint configuration announce that mirroring has been configured but has not started. The Database Properties window for the database now shows that the "Server network addresses" show the principal and mirror configured and listening on TCP port 5022 as shown in Figure 27-26.

12. Prior to starting database mirroring, the mirror server must have a copy of the principal's database in a recovery state. If the database has been restored and is in a recovery state, then start mirroring in this pair by clicking the Start Mirroring button.

> **Note**  Prior to starting the mirror, make sure the database has been restored on the mirror. Additionally, make sure that at least one transaction log has been applied there, too.

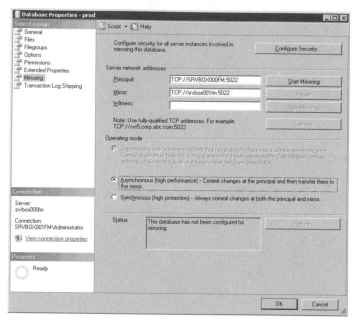

**Figure 27-26**   Database Properties window showing mirror definition populated.

If you do not have a database in recovery state on the mirror, you get an error instructing you to restore the principal database. The following scripts illustrate how to properly restore a database and transaction log and leave it in recovery state. This then allows you to click the Start Mirroring button and mirroring to start successfully.

The following script restores the database from a backup from the principal database's server share. Please note the final clause, "NORECOVERY." This keeps the database closed so that the transaction log can be applied:

```
RESTORE DATABASE prod
  FROM DISK = '\\srvbox000fm\h$\sql\backup\prod_mirror.bak'
  WITH MOVE 'data_file' TO 'c:\sql\data\data_file.mdf',
  MOVE 'log_file' TO 'c:\sql\log\log_file.ldf',
  NORECOVERY;
```

For mirroring to be properly initialized, one transaction log has to be applied to the mirror database. The following script applies one log, and as with the RESTORE, it leaves the database in NORECOVERY mode so that when mirroring is started, the log records from the principal can be applied properly.

```
RESTORE LOG prod
  FROM DISK = '\\srvbox000fm\h$\sql\backup\prod_mirror.trn'
  WITH NORECOVERY ;
```

Once you have clicked the Start Mirroring button and the mirror database has been properly restored, then mirroring will be running, as seen in the Status pane on the Database Properties window as shown in Figure 27-27.

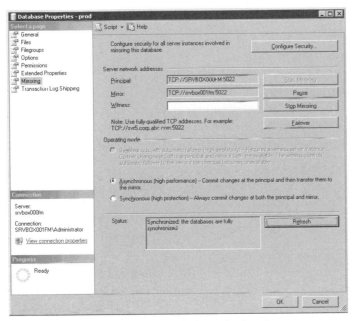

**Figure 27-27**   Successful completion of mirroring.

At this point, mirroring has been completed for the high performance mode configuration. As the Database Properties window options show, there are several options available at this point. You can monitor the status of the mirror, pause the mirrored pair, or instigate a failover from the principal database to the mirror database and change roles (presuming the principal database is still operational). If you go back into the Object Explorer in the SQL Server Management Studio, you can see that the principal database is in a synchronized state and that the mirror database is designated in working condition with a green arrow and also shown in a synchronized and restoring state.

# Monitoring Database Mirroring

SQL Server provides six methods to monitor database mirroring:

- The status screen in SQL Server Management Studio
- SQL Server errorlog
- Metadata with T-SQL
- Window's Performance Monitor (*perfmon.exe*)
- SQL Server Profiler
- Database Mirroring Monitor

The following sections describe each method.

## SQL Server Management Studio

SQL Server Management Studio provides a very rudimentary overview of the mirroring landscape. It displays whether the principal and mirror are in sync and up-to-date, and if not displays graphically that the nodes are not communicating properly or are offline.

Simply expand Databases on the principal and Database Snapshots on the mirror. A green upward pointing arrow on the mirror means all is running well. A red arrow indicates problems that need to be investigated.

## SQL Server errorlog

The SQL Server errorlog file is the chronological repository of all SQL Server notifications. When experiencing any mirroring issues, one of the first places you should look is here. The log is located in the LOG directory, typically under the MSSQL directory, for example:

```
%PROGRAM FILES%\Microsoft SQL Server\MSSQL.1\MSSQL\LOG>
```

The SQL Server log provides information on the establishment and status of mirroring. If an error occurs it will be logged in the SQL Server error log. In addition, errors will be logged in the Windows event log as well.

## Metadata: T-SQL for Database Mirroring Information

To look at the state of the mirror in real time using T-SQL, you can query the SQL Server metadata. This data provides the name, role, state, safety level, mirroring pair, and so on. This type of information is good for scripting out automatic notifications in jobs or reports that can be generated from SQL Agent.

The following are the most typical queries for this type of reporting. The first query shows the mirroring pair data:

```
SELECT d.name, d.database_id,
    dm.mirroring_role_desc, dm.mirroring_state_desc,
    dm.mirroring_safety_level_desc,
    dm.mirroring_partner_name, dm.mirroring_partner_instance,
    dm.mirroring_witness_name, dm.mirroring_witness_state_desc
FROM sys.database_mirroring dm, sys.databases d
WHERE dm.database_id = d.database_id AND
    dm.mirroring_state_desc IS NOT NULL ;
```

The second query displays information regarding the witness for the pair:

```
SELECT principal_server_name, mirror_server_name,
    database_name, safety_level_desc
FROM sys.database_mirroring_witnesses ;
```

The last query displays information regarding the endpoints:

```
SELECT  dme.name, dme.protocol_desc, dme.type_desc,
    dme.role_desc, dme.state_desc,
    te.port, dme.is_encryption_enabled, dme.encryption_algorithm_desc,
    dme.connection_auth_desc
FROM sys.database_mirroring_endpoints dme, sys.tcp_endpoints te
WHERE dme.endpoint_id = te.endpoint_id ;
```

## Performance Monitor

In addition to log files and metadata, you can also monitor mirroring using Window's Perfomance Monitor tool (perfmon). Perfmon can provide real-time information showing the status of multiple metrics in the pair concurrently, for example, the log send queue size and bytes sent per second. To run perfmon, simply click the Start button, then select All Programs, select Administrative Tools, and then select Performance.

Add the performance object "SQLServer:Database Mirroring" by clicking the plus button and choose the counters (such as Bytes Received/sec, Bytes Sent/sec, Transaction Delay, and so on) as needed in the window.

---

**Note**   Perfmon is typically used for diagnosing real-time issues as they are occurring. An overlooked benefit of perfmon is trending over time. Set up a perfmon trace to sample every 15 minutes and log it. Over time this can be used for performance trending, establishing base lines, estimating when networks need to be upgraded, and so on. This data can be used for projecting when new hardware will be needed in budget and capacity planning cycles.

---

**Note** Microsoft Operations Manager (MOM) is a good place to look for long-term perfmon data as described in Chapter 24, "Notification Services and Service Broker."

---

## SQL Server Profiler

Simply put, SQL Server Profiler gives the best view inside the database kernel of any tool available. One of the many events that SQL Server Profiler provides is the state of the database mirror. Use of the profiler is covered in detail in Chapter 30, "Using Profiler, Management Studio, and Database Tuning Advisor."

## Database Mirroring Monitor

Arguably, the best tool SQL Server 2005 provides is database mirror monitoring. The package shows you all of the statistics about where the log records are in both the principal and mirror databases. With this tool, you can see an overview of the entire mirroring landscape.

To invoke the Mirroring Monitor, follow these steps:

1.  In the SQL Server Management Studio in the navigation pane, expand Databases.

2.  Right-click on the principal database, select Tasks, and select Launch Database Mirroring Monitor.

3.  At this point, no databases are known to the monitor. Click Register Mirrored Database, and then select the drop-down item "Server Instance" and click the Connect button.

4.  Register the principal, mirror, and witness (if needed) into the monitor and click OK, as shown in Figure 27-28.

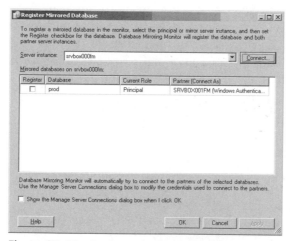

**Figure 27-28**   Registered mirror databases.

At this point, you will see the mirrored landscape and see the status of the pair. A quick overview is provided in this screen with a date and time showing the current state of both the principal and mirror, as shown in Figure 27-29.

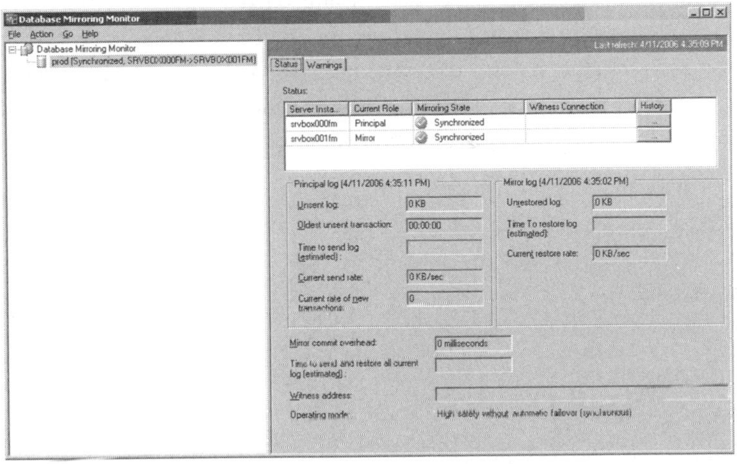

**Figure 27-29**   Overview of mirror landscape.

5. For more detailed information, click History to show the Database Mirroring History screen, as shown in Figure 27-30, and then select the filter criteria and choose the settings. This is good for seeing the overall health of the system over time. For example, if there were times when the network may not have been keeping up well with the database, and so on.

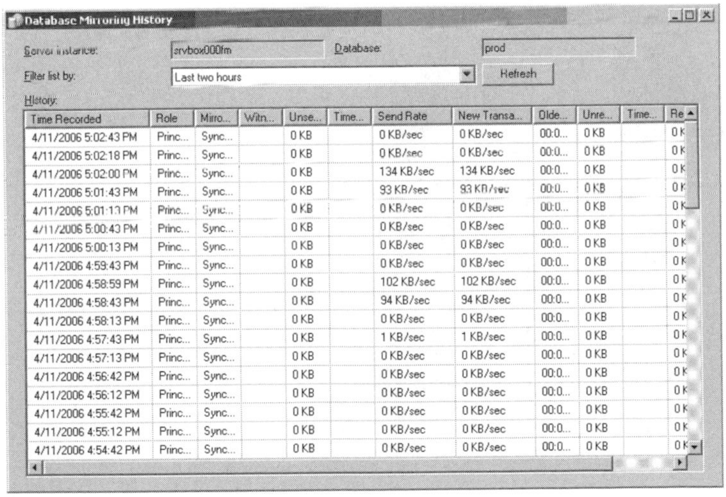

**Figure 27-30**   Detailed history of mirror.

# Using Mirroring and Snapshots for Reporting Servers

A basic issue is the conflict between high performance database needs and business requirements of large aggregating for reports. On the surface, it may sound trivial. Data is data, and just get it all from the same place. What materializes soon after this strategy is deployed is database gridlock. The online system for normal users consist of quick, short, and discrete transactions. The needs of the reporting server are long-running queries that grind out large amounts of disk I/O. Fundamentally, these two different requirements conflict. Hence, the need for a dedicated database just for reporting users.

SQL Server 2005 provides a technology called snapshots that provides a read-only copy of an OLTP database. It's easy to configure and deploy. The main issue is that by itself, a snapshot is on the local SQL Server as the production OLTP database. Hence, even though reporting users and OLTP users are on separate databases, they still share the same SQL Server instance memory, CPU, and probably disk subsystem.

Mirroring fixes this contention issue of OLTP and reporting on the same server. By itself, users cannot run queries against a mirror database because it's in a state of recovery. The solution is for you to snapshot copies off the mirror. These snapshots are read-only and let users access them directly for reporting. What's more, there is also the flexibility of having multiple snapshots of the same database. This is seen in Figure 27-31.

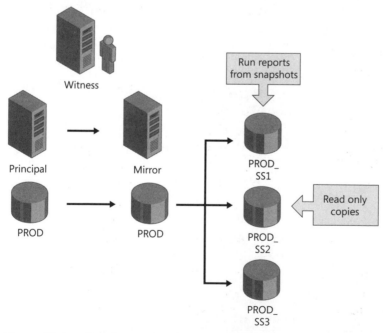

**Figure 27-31**   Database mirroring and snapshots.

Configuring the reporting snapshot consists of obtaining the description of the principal database's file names and then creating the snapshot with those descriptors. The following simple example shows the syntax and process for creating a snapshot:

```
CREATE DATABASE prod_ss4
    ON (NAME = 'data_file',
    FILENAME = 'c:\sql\data\prod_ss4.SNP')
    AS SNAPSHOT OF prod ;


USE prod_ss3;
SELECT COUNT(*) FROM from test_table;
```

If the user tries to drop the table in the snapshot, it fails because it's a read-only copy and changes are not allowed. This is seen in the following script:

```
USE prod_ss3;
DROP TABLE test_table ;
```

which generates the following error message:

```
Msg 3906, Level 16, State 1, Line 2
Failed to update database "prod_ss3" because the database is read-only.
```

To delete a snapshot that is not needed anymore, simply use the same syntax as you would if it was a normal database.

```
DROP DATABASE prod_ss4 ;
```

> **Note**    You need to run the *sp_helpdb* on the principal database. If you try to run *sp_helpdb* on the mirror database, you get a no permission to access database error due to the inaccessibility of the mirror during recovery:

The above is a simple example, but the premise is the same for databases of other sizes. Considerations of speed and space still exist—how much disk I have for snapshots and how fast are the disk themselves. The good news is that reporting can be offloaded onto slower, less expensive disk space and save money on the OLTP solution. The combination of mirroring as part of a high available solution and snapshots for reporting make a compelling technological solution at an economical price point that both DBAs and business users will like.

# Summary

Log shipping and database mirroring provide two key elements in the high available solution that Microsoft SQL Server offers. They are resilient and easy to set up, and offer a good price point in the overall choices you have. The key is that these are individual technologies that need to fit within the context of the overall SLA with the business units. Business users do not care how fast the database can failover if the overall ERP system does not come up at all in a catastrophe.

These technologies are just that; they provide parts of a solution and are not ends in themselves. Other parts of a highly available system are backups, clustering of the database server, redundancy in controllers, disk RAID levels, and so on. The recovery of the entire system needs to be planned as a whole, fully documented, and, most importantly, tested regularly for it to be considered adequate.

# Part VII
# Performance Tuning and Troubleshooting

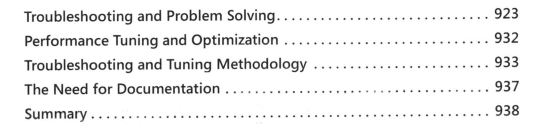

Chapter 28

# Troubleshooting, Problem Solving, and Tuning Methodologies

Problem solving is one of the most complex intellectual functions. *Problem solving* involves determining a way to achieve a goal where it is not obviously apparent. *Troubleshooting* is the systematic search for the source of a problem. One of the fundamental components of troubleshooting and problem solving is the need for a system or methodology. This is also a key component of Microsoft SQL Server tuning. This chapter provides methodologies and techniques for systematically finding problems and solving those problems. It is through a systematic approach that you will more easily determine the cause and solutions to any type of problem—not just SQL Server or hardware problems.

This chapter is separated into two main sections. The first section covers troubleshooting and problem solving, which share the goal of solving a particular problem or issue. The second section covers tuning, which is different in that you might or might not have a problem, and there might or might not be a solution.

---

## Troubleshooting and Problem Solving

Troubleshooting and problem solving both involve a number of personal characteristics that not everybody has, including patience, endurance, and a positive attitude.

# The Problem Solving Attitude

Of all of the tasks that a DBA performs, troubleshooting and problem solving typically involve the most pressure, the most skill, and the best attitude. I've personally found that those who are best at troubleshooting typically have the most positive attitude about it. Troubleshooting involves 50 percent skill, 50 percent experience, and 50 percent attitude. Yes, troubleshooting involves 150 percent of your effort. This section provides some tips and techniques for having a good and winning attitude that can help you be a successful troubleshooter.

## Don't Give Up or Get Discouraged

In order to be successful at troubleshooting, start with a "can do" attitude. Know that if you persist in your efforts, eventually you can succeed. Don't get me wrong—there are some things that simply won't work, but if you are attempting an achievable goal, don't give up. Stop and consider the problem. If it's something that should work, retrace your steps and try again.

### Real World    Even Simple Problems Are Difficult

Recently, I purchased a new notebook computer. In order to install SQL Server 2005, I copied the contents of the two CDs to my hard disk because I had plenty of space on the new notebook. I named the contents of the CDs Disk1 and Disk2 (not knowing any better). The installation of the SQL Server Database and Integration Services succeeded, but the client components and SQL Server Books Online failed. There was an error message about the installation failing, but it didn't provide enough information to lead me to the solution.

Since I have installed SQL Server 2005 before, I knew that the installation process worked. Therefore, I just had to troubleshoot this problem. It took several tries and multiple trips to the Microsoft Knowledge Base, but I eventually solved the problem. (The solution was that if you install from hard disk, the directories [for the CDs] must be named Server and Tools.)

The point of the previous example is that you must persist when you know that the end result is something achievable. However, a different problem is posed if you *do not* know whether the result is achievable.

## Strive for the Achievable

In order to be successful, you must take on tasks that are feasible and possible. There are times when the task presented to you does not have a solution, or at least not one that you can achieve in the allotted time frame or the allotted budget. In these cases, it is necessary to set expectations up front and, in some cases, you might have to decline the job:

> *You got to know when to hold 'em, know when to fold 'em,*
> *know when to walk away, and know when to run.*

> *Don Schlitz, as sung by Kenny Rogers*

My specialty is performance tuning and optimization. In rare cases, a performance problem can be solved in a very short time frame by miraculously rebuilding or creating indexes. However, this is very unlikely. Typically, there are multiple performance problems, and they are solved only by investigating all of them, analyzing the system, and making multiple changes.

Thus, when we get a client who wants a one-day-or-fewer performance tuning engagement, we usually turn it down because the goals cannot be met in such a short time frame. The consultant ends up frustrated, and the customer ends up disappointed in the results. Thus, you should not give up, but on the other hand, don't try to achieve the impossible.

## Success Comes from Enthusiasm

As I mentioned in the beginning of this chapter, successful troubleshooting has a lot to do with attitude and enthusiasm. If you don't have a good attitude, you won't be very good at troubleshooting. In addition, if you are not enthusiastic, your co-workers or clients might not have faith in your abilities. Personally, I really enjoy the challenge of tackling a tough problem and trying to solve it. When I have finished, I get a great deal of satisfaction and a feeling of a job well done.

It is often very difficult to remain enthusiastic and maintain a positive attitude when everything around you seems to be falling apart. This is when you have to dig in, keep up a good attitude, and give it another shot:

> *Now remember, things look bad and it looks like you're*
> *not gonna make it, then you gotta get mean. I mean plumb,*
> *mad-dog mean. 'Cause if you lose your head and you give*
> *up then you neither live nor win. That's just the way it is.*

> *Clint Eastwood, in* The Outlaw Josie Wales

A great attitude is crucial for the ability to properly troubleshoot a problem, but it is only one piece of the effort. You must also have skill and experience. In the next few sections, you will learn techniques (skill), and you will learn from some of our experiences.

### Stay Focused

When troubleshooting, it is easy to lose focus and stray from your goals. This often occurs when outside pressure is applied. In order to complete the task at hand, it is necessary to stay on target. Staying focused on the problem at hand means that you should always keep in mind what the problem is and not be distracted by other less important tasks.

### Take a Break

When troubleshooting a problem, especially one that involves downtime and loss of service, you should be careful not to become too fatigued. When too much time is spent on a problem without a break, you can begin to make mistakes. Sometimes, the mistakes can be worse than the original problem. Even when there is significant pressure to quickly fix an out-of-service system, it is important not to make things worse.

If you need a break, take it. Falling asleep at the keyboard does not help anything. Get some rest or a bit of fresh air to help clear your head.

### Ask For Help

There is nothing wrong with asking for help. There are many consultants with extensive experience in many different areas. By engaging an expert, you not only bring extensive experience to your problem, but you also have an excellent way to enhance your own skills. If your consultant is not willing to work with you, you should try to find another consultant. Bringing in additional expertise should be a learning experience for you.

### Learn Something New

Every troubleshooting task should also be a rewarding learning experience. It is also important to keep notes or records of what you have learned in a format that is easy to find and search. Otherwise, you might have to relearn the same thing over again.

## Troubleshooting Techniques

Now that you are motivated and enthusiastic, you are ready to learn some troubleshooting techniques. These techniques are helpful for developing a structured, scientific approach to troubleshooting and to performance tuning. These techniques are designed to help with defining a problem. Once you have defined the problem, then you can attempt to solve it.

The first step—or in some cases the only step—in troubleshooting a problem is to determine what the problem is. It may be that once you determine the problem, the solution is obvious. In other cases, determining the problem is only the beginning. In this section, a number of problem discovery techniques are presented. Often you must combine two or more of these techniques to ultimately define the problem, and sometimes the result of one technique leads you to another technique.

The troubleshooting techniques that are covered here include the following:

- **Splitting the problem**  This provides a choice for further investigation.
- **Finding the error logs**  Often they are not easy to find.
- **Interpreting the error logs**  Once you have the logs, you must decide whether they provide any useful information.
- **Retracing your steps**  This technique is good for determining where you went wrong.
- **Test for the sake of the problem**  Sometimes a change or test has nothing to do with improving the situation, but you do it only for the sake of learning something.

These are some of the techniques that can be very helpful in defining—or at least pointing you in the direction of—the problem.

## Splitting the Problem

Probably the most important technique involved in troubleshooting is to *split the problem*. This technique is used to make a binary decision between one problem area and another. For example, the problem can be split into network problems or SQL Server problems, or the problem can be split into memory or I/O problems. There may be many ways to split a problem.

Here are just a few examples to illustrate how to split a problem in order to eliminate issues that are not the cause of the problem. You must be careful to determine whether your understanding of the problem itself might be flawed.

### Example 1: Is network an issue?

In order to determine whether a problem is related to the network or to SQL Server, eliminate the network by running a test locally. If you are having problems running a query remotely but can run it locally, this tells you that the problem is probably in the network area. On the other hand, if it doesn't work locally, it doesn't necessarily mean that the network still isn't the problem.

### Example 2: Is I/O an issue?

If you are experiencing a performance problem that you think is I/O related, it might be difficult to split the problem without getting more disk drives, but there are a few things that you can try. Try reducing the data set so that all of the activity occurs in memory. If you see a reduction in I/O via perfmon but you still have the same problem, then you might not have an I/O problem.

### Example 3:  Is blocking an issue?

If you believe that a query or transaction is blocking, split the problem by running this query or transaction with nothing else on the system running. If it runs well, this is an indication that blocking may be a problem. If it runs poorly, this test might not be very useful because blocking still might be a problem being masked by something else. For example, if the program simulating the user community is the bottleneck, no changes that you make on the database will have any effect because the simulation program cannot go any faster.

### Splitting the Problem Summary

Splitting the problem into things that can be tested can be very useful for eliminating possibilities. Keep in mind that sometimes only one result provides useful data. For example, a positive reaction to a test might prove that your theory was right, but a negative reaction might be inconclusive. Be careful not to make the wrong conclusion.

## Finding the Error Logs

One of the first steps in tracking down a problem is to look in the error logs. In order to look in the error log, it is first necessary to find the error log. With SQL Server, this is easy. The error log is located in

```
C:\%PROGRAM FILES%\Microsoft SQL Server\MSSQL.1\MSSQL\LOG
```

Of course this will be different if you have multiple instances, but the SQL Server log is not the only log that you might need to be concerned with. The log is rotated, so you will see the files ERRORLOG, ERRORLOG.1, ERRORLOG.2, and so on. You should look through all error logs. There are also SQL Agent logs. You can also view the logs from within SQL Server Management Studio. In the navigation pane, expand the SQL Server instance, then expand Management, and then expand SQL Server Logs. Here you can open any of the SQL Server logs by right-clicking the log and selecting View SQL Server Log. This invokes the Log File Viewer.

It is recommended that SQL Server systems be used only for the database server and that the application tier should run on a separate system, but you might still have some components of the application that run on the database tier. Look for logs and take note of where they reside.

In addition to the SQL Server logs, the Windows event log is also a good place to look for error messages. These alerts can be very useful, but they often do not provide enough information to debug a problem. Also, don't forget that you can turn on additional logging for some applications, such as ODBC.

## Interpreting Error Logs

Interpreting the error log varies depending on what type of error log it is. If the error log is very large, as is often the case, you can search on error, err, or sql. If you are viewing the log with a text editor, use that editor's search function. If you are viewing the log with the SQL Server Management Studio, use the Search button in the Log File Viewer. Look for specific problems and work backwards in order to try to determine the original cause of the problem. The error log can often be the first and best place to look when trying to troubleshoot a problem.

## Help Desk Details

One area of troubleshooting that is often overlooked is the help desk. It is very important to analyze the data that you receive from the help desk in order to properly debug a problem. Often this data can be the key to solving the problem.

### Real World   Details Are Everything

Several years ago, I was working with a company that was experiencing severe performance problems. The help desk reported sporadic and random problem reports. Upon pressing the help desk for more information, we were able to piece together a list of user accounts that were reporting errors. Upon correlating that data with system information, we were able to determine that all of the users reporting problems were located in a satellite office. This indicated that the problem was a network problem and not a SQL Server problem. The problem was eventually solved by information we received from the help desk, but these details were not readily available. If the help desk had collected more details originally, we might have saved significant time piecing together the details on our own.

The DBA and the help desk should work together to determine what information should be logged in order to better debug problems and to collect good data that can aid in problem solving.

> **Note**   The help desk staff can't read your mind. Tell them what to look for, what questions to ask, and what to document. They will appreciate your input.

## Retracing Your Steps

If you have trouble performing a task that you've performed in the past but aren't able to determine the reason why it isn't working now, retrace your steps. It is often helpful to document your steps. By thinking through the problem and retracing your steps, you might be able to identify differences and therefore be better able to solve the problem.

> ### Real World   Talk It Over
>
> In a previous example, I described a situation in which I was having trouble installing SQL Server 2005, even though I had done it many times before. It was only by recounting my steps and thinking about each one and whether it differed from previous installations that I was able to determine that my problem had to do with not installing from CD. When I have a problem like this, I often talk it over with one of my co-workers, and before I finish explaining all of my steps, I discover the problem and the solution.

### Test for the Sake of the Problem

Sometimes it is necessary to perform tests that have no chance of improving the situation. These tests are done purely for the sake of trying to determine the cause of the problem. This is often related to splitting the problem. For example, removing the network from the test will not improve performance, because the network is necessary for functionality, but it can help point out the reason for your performance problem.

Don't be afraid to test for the sake of problem determination. This is often the only way to discover the root cause of your problem. However, once you have the results of this test, try to focus back on the problem and don't be distracted for too long.

## The Search for Knowledge

Once you have discovered the cause of your problem through exhaustive troubleshooting procedures, it still might be difficult to find the solution to this problem. Once you arrive at this stage, the search for knowledge has begun. This search can take on many forms and involve many mediums. Today, we are fortunate to have many different ways to search for knowledge.

> *The beginning of knowledge is the discovery of something that we do not understand.*
>
> *Frank Herbert*

We not only have magazines and books, such as this one, but now there are Internet sites that specialize in SQL Server. In addition, Microsoft has an excellent knowledge base that can assist with problem solving. In this section, you will learn a number of tips on how to find, retain, and absorb knowledge.

### Finding Knowledge Bases

There are many knowledge bases available today on the Internet. In fact, in the last few years, the number of SQL Server Web sites has increased dramatically. In addition to the

Microsoft Knowledge Base, there are a number of discussion forums on the Microsoft Forums site: *http://forums.microsoft.com*. Select SQL Server and choose the forum that you want to view.

---

**Note**    It is a good idea to find a knowledge base or bulletin board that you like and stick with it. By doing this, you will become used to the format and to other members, which makes it easer to ask questions and offer suggestions.

---

With all of the information available online today, you must be a little skeptical because not all of this information has been validated and is accurate. In the case of really leading edge problems, you may not find much information on the Internet, but as the problem becomes more commonplace, more solutions will be available online.

## Developing Your Own Knowledge Base

It is often useful to create your own knowledge base. This knowledge base can be as simple as a directory that contains documents and notes or as sophisticated as a knowledge base that is completely searchable and modifiable. You can use products such as Microsoft SharePoint or a bulletin board product. By using a bulletin board or notes board, you can insert information entries and then add to those entries as appropriate.

---

**Note**    I use a bulletin board, where I post notes with my personal experiences and with problems I have resolved. By using a bulletin board, I can organize my knowledge into various groups and grant access to it to my co-workers.

---

It is critical to keep records about what you've done in the past. If you do not properly document what you have learned, you will likely debug the same problem again a few years later. A little bit of documentation can help you easily and quickly solve some problems that you have previously encountered.

*Those who cannot learn from history are doomed to repeat it.*

*George Santayana*

## Learn from Others (Find a Mentor)

Troubleshooting is an acquired skill as well as a technique. It is often beneficial to work with someone who is an expert troubleshooter in order to learn his or her techniques and methods. Most good troubleshooters are willing to share their experiences and techniques with you.

*To acquire knowledge, one must study; but to acquire wisdom, one must observe.*

*Marilyn vos Savant*

If you can find a good mentor, you should consider yourself very fortunate. A mentor shares his or her experience and knowledge with you, and not only helps you to do your job better but can help to improve your career as well. You might find a mentor, or at least get to network with people of similar interests at user groups and conferences.

# Performance Tuning and Optimization

*Performance tuning* is the process of modifying a computer system or software in order to make the entire system or some aspect of that system run faster. *Optimization* is the process of modifying a computer system in order to maximize its efficiency. Performance tuning and optimization are a regular part of administering a SQL Server database. Let's look at some of the basics of performance tuning and optimization.

## Tuning and Optimization Basics

Unlike troubleshooting and problem solving, where you have a specific problem that needs to be uncovered and solved, tuning and optimization involves more gradual changes to the system. In some cases, the performance of the system can be optimized by making changes in the application or in the way SQL Server has been configured. In other cases, there is not much that you can do besides adding more hardware.

In order to create the most optimal system possible, you must complete many of the steps that you do when troubleshooting a problem. However, before you proceed, you must determine if there is an actual problem. This is not always easy. When tuning a SQL Server system, it is usually recommended that you take the approach to tune the application first and then tune the SQL Server instance.

### Tuning the Application

It is recommended that the application and SQL statements be tuned first and then the database system. This is to allow the possibility of reducing system resources by using more efficient indexes, partitioning, and hints. By reducing resources such as CPU utilization, memory, and I/Os, you can improve performance while at the same avoiding the need to increase hardware resources.

### Tuning the Instance

Tuning the SQL Server instance typically involves adding more hardware to allocate more memory to SQL Server or adding more disk drives to reduce I/O latencies. As you know, there aren't a lot of SQL Server parameters that can be modified. SQL Server instance tuning typically is done by adding more hardware, which can be costly. If the application is not optimal, you can easily add more and more hardware and still end up with a poorly performing system.

In order to properly troubleshoot or tune a system, you must follow a structured methodology. This methodology allows you to be scientific in your approach and to continually move forward in your tasks.

# Troubleshooting and Tuning Methodology

Now that you have some idea of the attitude and skills that are required for troubleshooting and performance tuning, it is time to look at some of the processes and methodologies for these tasks. Both troubleshooting and tuning benefit from using a standard methodology. So, what is a methodology?  A methodology is a set of rules, processes, and steps that you follow in order to perform a task in a scientific and repeatable manner.

## Developing a Methodology

In this section, you are introduced to performance tuning, optimization, and troubleshooting methodologies. This is the methodology that I have used for several years. You can take this methodology as a guideline and adapt it to your own needs. This methodology has several steps:

1. Make an initial assessment and establish a baseline.

2. Monitor the system.

3. Analyze the results.

4. Create a hypothesis.

5. Propose a solution.

6. Implement changes.

7. Test the solution.

8. If other problems still exist, return to Step 2; if not, exit.

These steps are covered in detail in the following sections.

### Step 1:  Initial Assessment

The first step in tuning and troubleshooting is to understand the environment. It is important to begin by gathering information in order to learn about the application and begin to understand what problems, if any, exist in the system. Some things that should be done and completely documented in this step are as follows:

- Learn about the application

- Ask about how it works and what it does

- Determine what the reported problem is
- Document database size, tuning parameters, and so on
- Look at the system as a whole
- Validate parameters

By performing these steps, you can get a feeling for where things are and how to approach the problem. This is a good time to talk with IT staff as well as end users, if possible, in order to learn from them about the issues. Inquire what they are doing when the problem occurs. Do some good investigative work to help you determine the problem.

## Step 2:  Monitor the System

Monitoring the system is the primary method of discovering the problem or tuning the system. Monitoring the system can take a number of forms, including viewing error logs, viewing perfmon data, and looking at application data. The goal of this step is to gather baseline information and to make an initial determination of the possible problems. Tools to monitor the system include the following:

- Operating system tools: perfmon, task manager, event viewer
- SQL Server tools: error log, sys tables
- Third-party tools
- Analyze operating system and SQL Server configuration parameters

Baseline information is important so that you can determine initial issues and see whether changes make an improvement. As with every step of the methodology, this step should be documented with great detail.

## Step 3:  Analyze Results

Once you have done an initial assessment and collected data, you must analyze and interpret this data. The analysis is important because it allows you to determine the problem and its cause. The analysis should be done carefully and deliberately and should include several areas of study:

- Analyze monitoring data
- Review error logs
- View customer performance data from their monitoring software

This assessment should be documented; it will be the basis of your report to your customer or management. As part of a full SQL Server assessment, this data should include the following data:

- CPU utilization

- I/O utilization and response time

- Memory utilization

- Errors reported in the error log

- Wait stats (if available)

By carefully analyzing performance data, you might immediately be able to determine the problem, or you might be able to formulate a theory about possible contributing factors of the problem. This step and the next can benefit from having more than one person participate in order to provide ideas, experience, and guidance.

## Step 4: Create a Hypothesis

Once you have analyzed the monitoring and log data, you are ready to postulate a theory about the cause of the problem. This might sound more complicated than it actually is. Formulating a hypothesis is as simple as formulating a theory and documenting it. If you don't document the hypothesis, it can be easy to stray from proper testing of this hypothesis. The goal is to determine what the problem is; components of this step include the following:

- Formulate a theory: I/O problem, locking problem, and so on

- Document your theory

- Back up that theory with data

Once you have developed the theory, you should be able to develop a solution or test.

## Step 5: Propose Solution

Once you have formulated the hypothesis, you are ready to develop a solution to the performance problem. In many cases, you will not be able to immediately solve the problem. You might instead have to develop a test to further narrow down the problem. Your test might be designed to split the problem or to improve some aspect of the system. Components of the solution include the following:

- Developing a solution

- Developing a validation plan

- Documenting expected results

Keep in mind that these tests often provide useful results only by providing either a positive or negative result, but not both—for example, if you believe that you have an I/O problem and propose a solution to solve this problem by changing the RAID level or adding more disk drives. Upon implementing this change, if performance improves, you have validated that I/O was a performance problem. If you implement a change and no improvement occurs, this does not prove that there was not an I/O problem. The I/O problem could still exist, but it might be masked by something else.

You must also determine the metrics of the results. With I/O problems, the result of the change might not be to improve query performance but to reduce I/O latencies. By anticipating the positive and negative outcome of your change, you will be better prepared to analyze and interpret the results of the tests.

## Step 6:  Implement Change

Once you have theorized the problem and developed a solution or test, it is time to implement change. These change implementations might take the following forms:

- A hardware change

- A configuration parameter change

- Adding an index

- Changing a query or using a hint

Implementing a change should be done very carefully. Changes should be categorized to no risk, moderate risk, and high risk. If at all possible, test the changes on a test system first before implementing a change on the production system. Follow the doctor's mantra of "do no harm."

## Step 7:  Test Solution

Of course, the final step is to actually run the test. If at all possible, perform this test in a nonproduction environment; however, low-risk changes such as indexes can be done on production systems. A few tips and best practices for changes are as follows:

- Change only one thing at a time

- Document the result of the change

- Compare performance after the test to the baseline metrics

- If possible, test the change in a nonproduction environment

- If possible, run load tests

The testing phase is a very important part of the troubleshooting and testing methodology. When tests are done too quickly and too many at a time, you often lose track of which ones actually helped and which ones actually hurt. Documentation is critical.

## Step 8: Go to Step 2.

Once you have started Step 7, you should return to Step 2; monitor the system in order to gather data about the state of the system while the test is going on. Follow the methodology until you run out of time, budget, or problems.

By documenting each step, you will not only get better results, but you will be better able to create professional and complete reports on the engagement, the problem, the solution, and the results.

# The Need for Documentation

Documentation is the most crucial component of performance tuning. If testing hasn't been documented, how can you reproduce it or even know what was done to improve the problem? On the other hand, documentation is the part of the job that we all dislike the most. It is tedious and a lot of work. Here are a few tips to ease the documentation burden:

- Create an outline of your report before you begin work on it. By outlining the report, all you have to do is fill in parts of it as you get results.

- Work on the report during the engagement or duration of the test. Don't wait until all of your testing is done before putting together the report. Work on it a little each day.

- Get feedback. Get someone else to look at it and provide feedback on the scope of the report and the outline that you have done.

- Editorial review. Have someone critique the final report before it is sent to the customer.

Documentation is no fun, but it is a necessary part of each tuning and troubleshooting exercise.

> **Note** In our company, no documentation goes to the client before it receives a thorough internal review. This improves quality and consultant efficiency. In addition, we keep a great deal of internal documentation that is used for training purposes and to improve our skills companywide.

A good document makes a good project, and poor documentation invalidates the entire project.

## Summary

Problem solving is considered one of the most complex of all intellectual functions. This chapter provides tips, techniques, and methods to more easily perform troubleshooting and tuning exercises. With all these tasks, process is very important. It is through a systematic approach that you can more easily determine the cause and solutions to any type of problem—not just SQL Server or hardware problems.

# Chapter 29
# Database System Tuning

As we saw in Chapter 3, "Roles and Responsibilities of the Microsoft SQL Server 2005 DBA," one of the responsibilities of the DBA is to tune the system monitor and performance tune the SQL Server solution. When deciding on a tuning methodology there are basically two approaches you can take:

- **Proactive approach** You monitor your SQL Server solution and tune the database system when you notice capacity reaching resource limits.

- **Reactive approach** You wait until events occur, such as users complaining about slow queries or batch processes failing and then tune the database system as required.

Realistically, a combination of both approaches is required because you usually do not have the resources required to monitor everything, nor can you forsee every problem that may occur because SQL Server is a complex, concurrent client-server architecture. The most important factors are typically the most difficult to predict: users and how they are using the database solution.

When tuning a complex, concurrent environment, you must be aware of the different components that might impact overall performance. These factors can be categorized the following way:

- **Hardware** Includes components such as the server, available memory, number of processors, and disk subsystem

- **Network infrastructure** Includes the network cards, switches, and the rest of your LAN or WAN

■ **Operating system**   Can have a major impact on the overall performance of your database solution. It is important to ensure that it has been optimally configured for running SQL Server.

---

**Note**   Do not overlook the importance of tuning the operating system. There is a lot that you can do to improve the performance, security, and stability of your SQL Server solution. For example, disabling all of the superfluous services is a very good start.

---

■ **Database engine**   Although SQL Server 2005 is self-tuning, there are still a number of tuning techniques that you can use to maximize performance. It is always ideal to know both the SQL Server architecture and your operational environment and requirements.

■ **Database**   There are a number of way in which you can tune the databases, from the layout of files to database options.

■ **Client application**   The way client applications connect and work with your SQL Server solution can impact dramatically the overall database solutions performance and functionality.

In this chapter we will concentrate on tuning the hardware and SQL Server instance.

### Real World   The Best Thing About SQL Server

I am often asked what I like best about SQL Server. For me, it's the ability to see how the underlying database engine and related technology can easily be monitored and consequently tuned through a variety of graphical tools and commands. Not only does this ability help to diagnose and troubleshoot performance problems, it offers a great way of teaching both Microsoft SQL Server and relational database theory because it combines the theoretical with the real world.

# Monitoring and Tuning Hardware

Although your primary duty as a DBA is to monitor your SQL Server solution, this does not mean that you should not pay attention to the hardware and operating system. I have always stressed to my students the importance of learning the underlying operating system and keeping abreast of hardware technology because this knowledge enables a DBA to diagnose performance problems more easily and optimally tune a SQL Server solution.

It also allows a DBA to recommend the appropriate hardware and software solution to meet a new SQL Server solution's requirements and allow for future growth.

# Tools for Monitoring and Tuning Hardware

The Windows operating system has many tools and commands that can be used to monitor and diagnose hardware issues so you can tune your SQL Server solution for optimal performance. It is important to use the tool most appropriate for the metrics you want to gather and your processing requirements. Commonly used tools used for monitoring and tuning hardware include the following:

- **Network Monitor Agent** Used to analyse network traffic and diagnose network-related problems

- **Performance Logs and Alerts** Used to gather performance-related metrics and to generate an alert when a gathered metric reaches a user-defined threshold

- **System Monitor (perfmon)** Tracks resource usage of various components of the operating system and installed applications, such as SQL Server, through an Object/Counter model

- **Task Manager** Can be used as a quick way to gather key metrics about which processes are running on the local SQL Server instance, the processor utilization, and network utlilization

The primary resources used by a DBA are the System Monitor and the Performance Logs and Alerts tools.

## System Monitor (PERFMON.EXE)

The System Monitor tool allows you to monitor the hardware and operating system resources on your SQL Server server. Through the System Monitor, you can collect performance-related data about the various performance objects and their corresponding counters. You typically use the System Monitor to perform benchmarks, monitor performance, or investigate performance-related issues.

Although we have encountered the System Monitor tool in earlier chapters, this chapter highlights and recommends some of the more important performance objects and counters that you should monitor when tuning both your hardware and SQL Server solution.

You can use System Monitor to view performance metrics from multiple servers simultaneously, which can be useful in a production and testing environment. You can also create charts and export the performance data.

---

**Note** Monitoring performance on a local computer through the System Monitor tool can add a performance overhead. This performance overhead can be reduced by monitoring fewer counters, increasing the sampling interval, or logging the collected data to another disk. More commonly though, DBAs monitor a SQL Server instance from a remote machine, an approach that has the least performance overhead, although it does generate additional network traffic.

■ **Using the System Monitor Tool**   To monitor your hardware or SQL Server instance using the System Monitor tool, follow these steps:

1. To start the System Monitor tool, click Start, then click Administrative Tools, and then click Performance. (If you do not see Administrative Tools from your Start menu, navigate to Control Panel first.) Ensure the System Monitor folder is selected.

   System Monitor supports a number of different ways in which you can view performance counter data. The toolbar at the top has three buttons representing the Graph, Histogram, and Report views. To the left are two buttons that allow you either to see the current activity or to open up performance data that has been previously saved in either a file or database table. Figure 29-1 shows the default chart view with no performance object counters added.

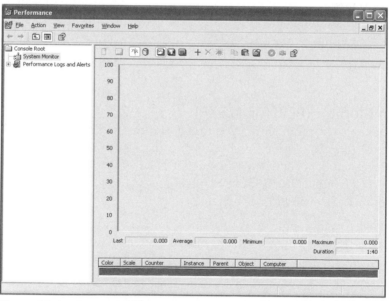

**Figure 29-1**   System Monitor.

2. To add performance object counters to the current activity view, click the plus sign button on the toolbar. This opens the Add Counters dialog box, as shown in Figure 29-2.  Notice that you can monitor performance object

counters on both the local and remote computers. Click to select the Use Local Computer Counters option to add performance objects counters from the computer on which you are running System Monitor, or click to select the Select Counters From Computer option and select or type the NetBIOS computer name or IP address of the SQL Server instance you want to monitor.

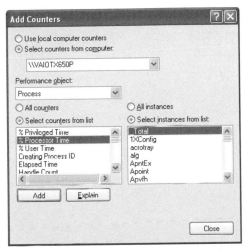

**Figure 29-2**   The Add Counters dialog box.

3. Click the Performance Object drop-down list, as shown in Figure 29-3. This shows the list of Windows and SQL Server performance objects that are available on the computer. The performance objects listed depend on the operating system and software installed on the monitored computer. Click the performance object, such as the Process performance object counter shown in Figure 29-3, which you want to monitor.

4. Once you have chosen the performance object, you can specify the performance object counter that you want to monitor in the scroll box below the Performance Object drop-down list, as shown in Figure 29-4. If you want to observe all of the performance objects counters, click the All Counters option. For specific counters, click the Select Counters From List option and then select the specific counter from the scroll box. You can select multiple counters by holding down the Ctrl key when selecting the counters. In some cases, as with the Processor\%Processor Time performance object counter being selected in Figure 29-4, you can further choose whether you want to monitor all instances of the performance object counter or a combination of specific instances. Click the All Instance option to select all instances, or click the Select Instances From List option and select the specific instances.

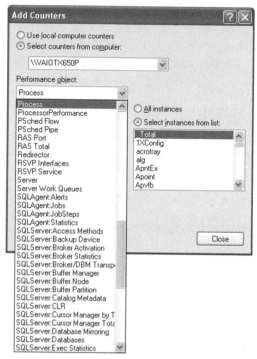

**Figure 29-3**    The Performance Object drop-down list.

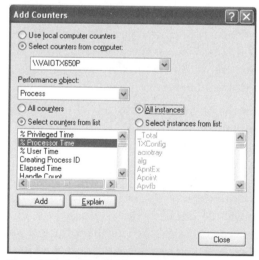

**Figure 29-4**    The Add Counters dialog box.

5. To read more information about what the performance object counter monitors, click the Explain button. The Explain Text dialog box opens with

explanatory information, as shown in Figure 29-5. This explanatory information can be very useful because there are hundreds of performance object counters in SQL Server 2005 alone, let alone the rest of the operating system.

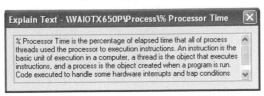

**Figure 29-5**   The Explain Text dialog box.

6. Click the Add button to add the combination of counters you have selected to the Performance window. You can continue to add more performance object counters by repeating the above process. When you are ready to return to the Performance window, click the Close button. The Performance Window starts to gather and display performance metrics at the default schedule, which is every one second. Figure 29-6 shows the System Monitor graph displaying performance metrics for a number of the SQL Server-related process instances using the Processor\%Processor Time performance object counter.

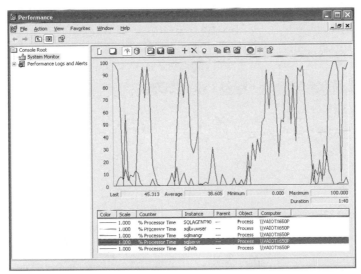

**Figure 29-6**   System Monitor graph view.

7. You can highlight performance object counters in System Monitor to help you more easily view and interpret the performance metrics being returned. To highlight a particular performance object counter, click its name in the bottom pane and press Ctrl+H. The performance object counter is highlighted, as showm in Figure 29-7.

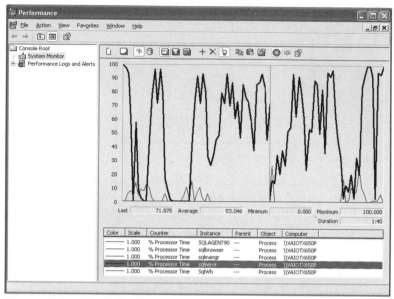

**Figure 29-7**   Highlighted performance monitor counter.

8. Alternatively, you might want to use the histogram view to help you more easily identify which performance monitor counter is consuming the most resources. Click the View Histogram button in the toolbar or press Ctrl+B. Figure 29-8 shows the histogram view in System Monitor.

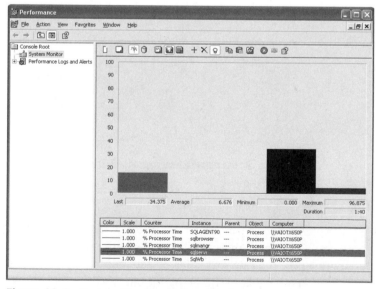

**Figure 29-8**   System Monitor histogram view.

## Performance Logs and Alerts

The Performance Logs and Alerts tool is used to log performance-related metrics and generate alerts when an event occurs or a user-defined threshold is met. The Performance Logs and Alerts tool can be configured to run as a service and collect performance data automatically, which means that it does not require user interaction.

The performance data can be displayed in a number of formats, including comma-separated, tab-separated, and a number of binary file formats. These files can be subsequently opened for analysis by the System Monitor tool, so they are a great way of sending performance data to other DBAs for analysis.

---

**Note**   You can also collect the performance data directly to a SQL Server database, which I particularly find useful because you can then use your querying skills to manipulate the collected data.

---

When configuring alerts, you can specify a number of actions to be triggered when the alert fires, including these:

- Sending a network message
- Starting a performance data log
- Running a program

---

**Note**   You should not use the Performance Logs and Alerts tool to generate alerts based on SQL Server 2005 performance object counters. The ability of SQL Server Agent in SQL Server 2005 to create alerts based on the same performance object counters is far superior. Creating SQL Server performance condition alerts through SQL Server Agent is covered in Chapter 30, "Using Profiler, Management Studio, and Database Engine Tuning Advisor."

---

- **Using the Performance Logs and Alerts Tool**   The ability to collect performance metrics for further analysis, for benchmarking, or for establishing a basline is a powerful capability of the Performance Logs and Alerts tool. To set up logging of performance counters using the Performance Logs and Alerts tool, follow these steps:

    1. Click Start, Administrative Tools, and Performance to start the System Monitor tool. (If you do not see Administrative Tools from your Start menu, navigate to Control Panel first.) Ensure the Performance Logs and Alerts folder is selected. Figure 29-9 shows the default Performance Logs and Alerts folder.

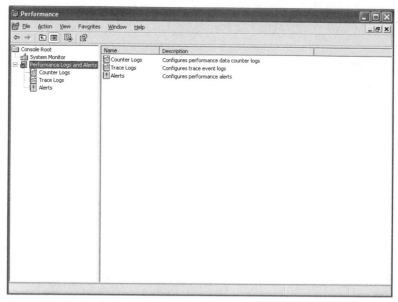

**Figure 29-9**    Performance Logs and Alerts.

2.  Expand the Performance Logs and Alerts folder in the left pane of the Performance window. Right-click the Counter Logs folder and select the New Log Setting menu option. Type an appropriate name for your log settings in the New Log Settings dialog box, shown in Figure 29-10. Click the OK button to continue.

**Figure 29-10**    New Log Settings dialog box.

3.  A window with the same name that you entered for your log file appears. The General tab, shown in Figure 29-11, allows you to add either performance objects or specific performance object counters from the local and remote computers. To add performance objects, click the Add Objects button. Alternatively, to add performance object counters, click the Add Counters button. Both buttons pop up the appropriate dialog box, allowing you to select the combination of performance monitor objects and counters you are interested in logging, as covered earlier.

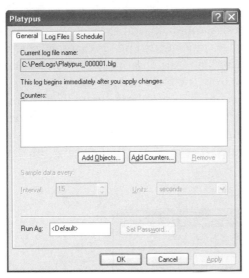

**Figure 29-11** Counter Log Properties dialog box.

4. Once you have chosen the combination of performance monitor objects and counters you want to monitor, confirm that the sampling interval is appropriate for your requirements. Figure 29-12 shows the Process, SQLServer:Databases, SQLServer:General Statistics and SQLServer:Locks performance objects being selected and the interval changed to 10 seconds.

**Figure 29-12** General tab of the Counter Log Properties dialog box.

5.  Click the Log File tab to set additional properties of the log file. Log files can either binary or text files. Additionally you can save the log to a SQL database. One of the advantages of using text files is that they can be opened in range of various tools. Configure the appropriate log file settings by choosing the appropriate type from the Log File Type drop-down list and configuring the location and name via the Configure button. Once you are back in the Log Files tab you can further configure the suffix properties for the file name and provide a comment if required. Figure 29-13 shows the log configured as a comma-delimited text with a suffix denoting the date. Click the Schedule tab.

**Figure 29-13**   The Log Files tab of the Counter Log Properties dialog box.

6.  The Schedule tab allows you to configure whether the log file will be automatically generated according to a schedule or manually controlled. To configure the log to be started and stopped manually choose the option buttons as shown in Figure 29-14 and click the OK button.

7.  Once configured, the log can be started and stopped manually in the Performance window. To start logging performance counters to a particular log, click the log and then click the Start button located in the toolbar. The log

should change color from red to green to indicate that it is running. Figure 29-15 shows a log running.

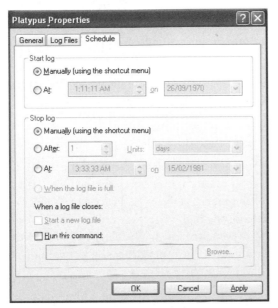

**Figure 29-14** The Schedule tab of the Counter Log Properties dialog box.

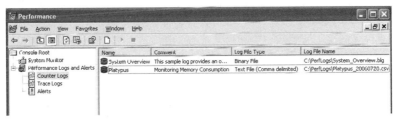

**Figure 29-15** Log running in the Performance Logs and Alerts tool.

## Determining Hardware Bottlenecks

Determing hardware *bottlenecks* and tuning your operating system environment can be a bit of an art form, which comes with experience and mastery of the skills discussed in Chapter 28, "Troubleshooting, Problem Solving, and Tuning Methodologies." You should never make assumptions by looking at one set of gathered metrics but try to corroborate it through correlated data. When determining hardware bottlenecks, you need to identify which hardware susbsytem you should be examining.

## Processor Subsystem

Identifying whether your processors are the bottleneck in your SQL Server solution is a relatively straightforward process. Use the following guidelines to determine if your processor subsystem represents the bottleneck:

- The Processor: %Processor Time counter should not be greater than 80 percent for a sustained period.

- The System: Processor Queue Length counter should not be greater than two for a sustained period.

- The Processor-Context Switches/sec counter should not be excessively high per processor. (Use 8,000 as a very rough threshold.)

The first step after identifying a processor bottleneck is to determine whether SQL Server or some other operating system or application process is responsible. This can be done by examining all the instances of the Process Object: % Processor Time counter. If your SQL Server instance is responsible for the high processor utilization, there are a number of techniques discussed later in this chapter for diagnosing and solving this problem. Otherwise, you will have to determine why the other process is consuming so much processor resources on your SQL Server solution.

Solving processor bottlenecks generally involves purchasing additional or faster processors. That is why you should try to purchase server hardware that can scale with your growing processor requirements.

## Memory Subsystem

Memory is probably the most important factor in SQL Server performance for most environments. I suppose you can never have enough memory, but SQL Server takes significant advantage of what it has been given through a complex caching architecture. Symptoms of bottleneck problems with the memory subsystem include generally poor performance, no available memory, and lots of I/O caused by either the lazywriter or checkpoint processes and operating system paging. Use the following guidelines to determine whether your memory subsystem is causing the bottleneck:

- Examine the Physical Memory and Commit Charge values in the Performance tab of the Task Manager.

- Examine the Memory: Available KBytes (or Memory: Available Mbytes) counter for a lack of available memory in System Monitor.

- Examine the Memory: Pages/sec and Memory: Page Faults/sec counters in System Monitor. Ideally they should be as close to zero as possible. Sustained values greater than two, for example, indicate a problem.

- You should always also examine the following set of performance counters in System Monitor for correlating metrics:

  ❑ The Memory: System Cache Resident Bytes, Memory: Committed Bytes, and Memory: Commit Limit counters.

  ❑ The Process: Working Set and Process: Private Bytes counters for all the processes running on your server.

Once you have determined that your SQL Server solution has a memory bottleneck, the first thing you must identify is whether this is due to external or internal memory pressures. Is it a problem at the operating system level? Or is it related to the way your SQL Server instance has been configured and is managing the memory allocated to it internally? This can be done only by gathering a number of performance metrics and analyzing this information.

Solving memory bottlenecks generally involves purchasing more memory. As with your processor subsystem, you should always try to purchase server hardware that has the capacity to grow with your growing memory requirements. You can also reduce the memory footprint of your operating system through a number of techniques, such as disabling unnecessary services and reconfiguring the registry. Additionally, you can reduce the amount of memory your SQL Server instance requires through appropriate indexing strategies and efficient queries. Inefficient queries tend to use tablescans and hash operators, which can consume a lot of memory.

## I/O Subsystem

The main I/O hardware bottleneck to look for is for your disk array subsystem as covered in Chapter 4, "I/O Subsystem Planning and RAID Configuration," and Chapter 7, "Choosing a Storage System for Microsoft SQL Server 2005." Unfortunately, disk drive technology has not improved exponentially over the last decade, unlike advances with processors, networking infrastructure, and, to a degree, memory. Ultimately, databases are stored on this slower secondary media. This is why SQL Server has such an extensive caching architecture and why memory is the most important performance-determining factor.

Unfortunately, memory is a finite and relatively expensive resource. Consequently, you can still experience bottlenecks in you I/O subsystem for a number of reasons, such as the operational environment. To determine if you have a bottleneck with your I/O susbsytem, use the following guidelines as a basis:

- The PhysicalDisk: %Disk Time counter should not be greater than 50 percent for a sustained period.

- The PhysicalDisk: Avg. Disk Queue Length counter should not be great than two for a sustained period.

- The PhysicalDisk: Avg. Disk Reads/Sec and PhysicalDisk: Avg. Disk Writes/Sec counters should consistently be less than 85 percent of your disk subsystem's capacity.

Use the following guidelines when monitoring your PhysicalDisk: Avg. Disk Sec/Read and PhysicalDisk: Avg. Disk Sec Write counters:

- <10 ms : Very good

- 10-20 ms : OK

- 20-50 ms : Slow, needs attention

- >50 ms : Serious I/O bottleneck

When monitoring these counters, you must look at your disk subsystem as a whole. If you are using a RAID array, for example, you must adjust the above values to account for your RAID array as follows:

| RAID Level | I/Os Per Disk |
| --- | --- |
| RAID-0 | (Reads+Writes)/Number of Disks |
| RAID-1 | [(Reads+(2×Writes)]/2 |
| RAID-5 | [(Reads+(4×Writes)]/Number of Disks |
| RAID-10 | [(Reads+(2×Writes)]/Number of Disks |

For example, you determine that your RAID-1 disk array has a Disk Reads/sec value of 60, a Disk Writes/sec value of 80, and an Avg. Disk Queue Length of 4. Taking into account the RAID-1, your disk array is experiencing 110 I/O operations per disk and your Avg. Disk Queue Length per disk is 2. This represents a borderline I/O bottleneck.

Solving I/O subsystem bottlenecks generally involves purchasing additional disk drives to separate out the I/O, redistributing the location of relevant database files, reconfiguring your RAID array, or changing/optimizing the type of SAN (see Chapter 7).

# Monitoring and Tuning SQL Server

As with monitoring and tuning your hardware, you need to know how SQL Server operates and what to look for when monitoring and tuning your SQL Server solution. You need to choose the appropriate tool that will allow you to gather the information you need to correctly analyze any existing problems and respond accordingly.

# Tools for Monitoring and Tuning SQL Server

SQL Server has a rich set of tools and command that can be used to monitor and tune your SQL Server instance. As a DBA, you need to identify the correct tool to use to solve your monitoring or tuning requirements. The more commonly used tools that come with SQL Server include the following:

- **DBCC Commands**   A set of commands used to perform administrative tasks and return various types of information useful to the DBA.

- **Dynamic Management Views**   Expose the internal workings of the SQL Server instance as views. The various DMVs supported by SQL Server 2005 are described in Chapter 31, "Dynamic Management Views."

- **SQL Server Profiler**   An external tool that allows you to trace user activity against your SQL Server instance.

- **SQL Server Management Studio**   The main tool used by DBAs to administer SQL Server instances and execute Transact-SQL commands and statements. SQL Server Managment Studio allows you to see the currenty activity.

- **System Stored Procedures**   SQL Server comes with a number of stored procedures written by Microsoft that can be used to monitor and tune your SQL Server instance.

- **SQL Trace**   Also allows you to trace user activity.

We will look at how to use SQL Server Profiler, SQL Server Management Studio environment, and Database Engine Tuning Advisor in more detail in Chapter 30.

## System Monitor

The System Monitor tool is covered in more detail earlier in this chapter. Although it is part of the operating system, a default installation of SQL Server installs a number of performance objects and their related counters that are specific to SQL Server. This set of counters is extremely useful for determining the cause of any performance bottlenecks that you might have within your SQL Server 2005 instance.

Some of the more commonly used SQL Server related counters for performance analysis include the following:

- **SQLServer:Access Methods–Full Scans/sec**   Collects the number of unrestricted full scans of base tables or indexes

- **SQLServer:Buffer Manager–Buffer Cache Hit Ratio**   Collects the percentage of pages found in the buffer pool without reading from disk

> **Note** The Cache Hit Ratio is calculated over time differently in SQL Server 2005 than in earlier versions of SQL Server. It is more accurate now.

- **SQLServer:Databases–Log Growths** Collects the total number of log growths for the selected database

- **SQLServer:Databases–Percent Log Used** Collects the percentage of space in the log that is in use for the selected database

- **SQLServer:Databases–Transactions/sec** Collects the number of transactions started for the selected database

- **SQLServer:General Statistics–User Connections** Collects the number of users connected to the system

- **SQLServer:Latches–Average Latch Wait Time** Collects the average latch wait time in milliseconds for latch requests that had to wait

- **SQLServer:Locks–Average Wait Time** Collects the average amount of wait time milliseconds for each lock request that resulted in a wait

- **SQLServer:Locks–Lock Waits/sec** Collects the number of lock requests that could not be satisfied immediately and required the caller to wait

- **SQLServer:Locks–Number of Deadlocks/sec** Collects the number of lock requests that resulted in a deadlock

- **SQLServer:Memory Manager–Memory Grants Pending** Collects the current number of processes waiting for a workspace memory grant

> **More Info** You can also define you own custom counters through SQL Server:User Settable performance objects. For more information, search for the "SQL Server, User Settable Object" topic in SQL Server 2005 Books Online.

## SQL Server Profiler

SQL Server Profiler, shown in Figure 29-16, is the main tool used to capture a trace, which basically represents the activity between client applications and a SQL Server instance. Not only does this trace potentially capture the T-SQL statements and stored procedure calls, it also captures "internal" database engine information, such as what locks were acquired and released, what security permissions where checked, and relevant deadlock information.

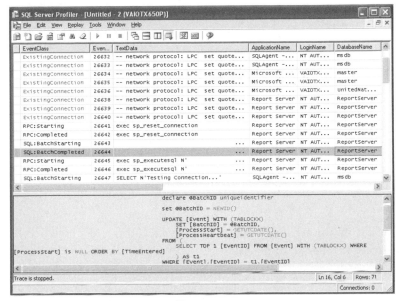

**Figure 29-16**    SQL Server Profiler.

With SQL Server 2005, SQL Server Profile can also be used to trace activity against an Analysis Services instance, as discussed in Chapter 22, "Analysis Services." You also have the ability to correlate your captured trace with your Windows performance log data to get a better picture of what is happening with your SQL Server instance. We will show you how to use SQL Server Profiler in Chapter 30.

As a DBA, it is typically up to you to determine whether a client application is at fault. Tools such as SQL Server Profiler can be extremely helpful in this case.

## Real World    United Nations

In 2001, I was consulting for the United Nations in East Timor. Specifically, I was asked to analyse a mission-critical database system for this emerging nation. The Civil Registry database was going to be used for elections and would act as the foundation for the country's civil services. Unfortunately, the design and implementation had been rushed due to various pressures, and there was a concern about it's efficacy, so I was asked to perform an audit and analysis.

There was no documentation for the database design, nor, more importantly, the various Visual Basic applications that had been written. In my opinion, the database design was not optimal, and there were a lot of custom software components used due to the obvious security requirements of a database solution that had collected data on the entire population of East Timor.

It is only through the use of SQL Server Profiler that I was able to reverse-engineer how the application and entire database solution worked. Importantly, it also provided me with the evidence required to justify my conclusions and recommendations to management.

Without SQL Server Profiler, there would have been a lot of guesswork and conjecture. I highly recommend you invest the energy and time in learning how to use this very powerful and important tool.

## SQL Trace

Another technique for tracing the activity between client applications and a SQL Server instance is to create traces through a set of system stored procedures instead of using SQL Server Profiler.

**Table 29-1   SQL Trace Stored Procedures**

| Stored Procedure | Description |
| --- | --- |
| fn_trace_geteventinfo | Returns information about events included in a trace. |
| fn_trace_getfilterinfo | Returns information about filters applied to a trace. |
| fn_trace_getinfo | Returns information about a specified trace. (Or all existing traces.) |
| sp_trace_create | Creates a trace definition |
| sp_trace_generateevent | Creates a user-defined event |
| sp_trace_setevent | Adds or removes an event class or column to a trace |
| sp_trace_setfilter | Applies a filter to a trace |
| sp_trace_setstatus | Closes, starts or stops a trace |

**More Info**   For more information on how to create traces manually, see the topic "Introducing SQL Trace" in SQL Server 2005 Books Online.

## Dynamic Management Views and Functions

Dynamic Management Views (DMV) and Functions are relational entities that expose SQL Server in memory structures and can be queried using your standard DML statements. They are quick to query and have a low overhead as they expose information that needs to be maintained by the database engine. This information is ideal for performance tuning and  troubleshooting your SQL Server instance. We will examine DMVs in more detail in Chapter 31.

---

**Note** DMVs are not exactly new, as they did exist in earlier versions of SQL Server. The sysprocesses "system table" is one such example.

---

# Determining SQL Server Performance Bottlenecks

Once you have determined that you have a performance bottleneck problem and that it is related to your SQL Server instance, you need to further drill down into the appropriate SQL Server subsystem to determine the cause of the bottleneck and hopefully be able to tune your SQL Server solution.

## Determining Processor Bottlenecks

Once you have identified that your SQL Server instance is consuming the processor resources, as explained above, you must identify the cause. The following DMVs can be queried to gather more metrics about how the SQL Server database engine is utilizing the processors:

- Look for high values in the runnable_tasks_count column of the sys.dm_os_schedulers DMV, that would indicate a processor bottleneck.

- Query the sys.dm_exec_query_stats DMV, as shown below, aggregating the total_worker_time and execution_count columns to help determine which queries are consuming the most processor resources. The plan_handle value can be passed to the dm_exec_query_plan dynamic management function to see the execution plan for further analysis.

```
SELECT plan_handle,
       SUM(total_worker_time) AS total_cpu_time,
       SUM(execution_count) AS total_execution_count,
       COUNT(*) AS  number_of_statements
FROM sys.dm_exec_query_stats AS QueryStats
GROUP BY plan_handle
ORDER BY sum(total_worker_time) DESC;
```

The main causes for high processor utilization for a SQL Server instance include the following:

- Excessive compilation or recompilation
- Inefficient query plan
- Intra-query parallelism

Otherwise, you will need to determine the cause of the high processor utilization of your SQL Server instance by determining the root cause.

### Excessive Recompilations

To determine whether excessive recompilations are the cause of your high processor utilization, examine the following metrics:

- SQL Server: SQL Statistics object in System Monitor. Examine the Batch Requests/sec, SQL Compilations/sec, and SQL Re-Compilations/sec counters. A high ratio of SQL Re-Compilations/sec to Batch Requests/sec would indicate excessive recompilations.

- The SP:Recompile and SQL:StmtRecompile events in SQL Trace.

- The optimizations and elapsed time counter values in the sys.dm_exec_query_optimizer_info DMV. The elapsed time counter is the average elapsed time (in seconds) per optimization of an individual query).

- The plan_generation_num, which returns the number of times the plan has been recompiled and the execution_count columns of the sys.dm_exec_query_stats DMV. To determine the query, you can use the sql_handle value to query the sys.dm_exec_sql_text(*sql_handle*) DMV, as demonstrated in Chapter 31.

If you have determined that your SQL Server instance is experiencing excessive recompilations, examine the T-SQL batches that are the cause. There are a number of techniques that your developers can use to reduce the excessive recompilation that you might be experiencing. It might also be caused by a problem with statistics or poor indexes. Consider running the Database Engine Tuning Advisor, discussed in Chapter 30, to see what it recommends.

---

**More Info**    For more information on recompilation issues, read the "Batch Compilation, Recompilation, and Plan Caching Issues in SQL Server 2005" white paper available at http://www.microsoft.com/technet/prodtechnol/sql/2005/recomp.mspx

---

### Inefficient Query Plans

Another potential cause of excessive processor utilization is a high number of compute-intensive query plans being generated. Use the sys.dm_exec_query_stats DMV, together with the sys.dm_exec_sql_text(*sql_handle*) DMV as shown below, to find these processor intensive queries by looking for queries that have consumed the most CPU resources (total_worker_time column).

```
SELECT *
FROM sys.dm_exec_query_stats AS QueryStats
CROSS APPLY sys.dm_exec_query_plan(QueryStats.plan_handle)
ORDER BY total_worker_time DESC ;
```

Another approach is to look for compute-intensive operators such as Hash Matches and Sorts in the sys.dm_exec_cached_plans DMV. This can be done by running the following query and filtering for either '%Hash Match%' or '%Sort%' on the query_plan column:

```
SELECT *
FROM sys.dm_exec_cached_plans AS CachedPlans
CROSS APPLY sys.dm_exec_query_plan(CachedPlans.plan_handle) ;
```

As with excessive recompilations, you will need to identify the poorly executing queries and present your findings to your developers. Again, the cause might be related to poor statistics or inappropriate indexes, so consider running the Database Engine Tuning Advisor. Otherwise, your developers will have to examine their queries and the indexing strategy of the database. They might have to use query hints to override the optimizer, but this should be considered a last resort.

### Intra-Query Parallelism

Queries that are executed using parallel execution plans can be expensive and can be the cause of your high processor utilization. Use the following techniques to identify whether your SQL Server instance is running a large number of parallel queries running:

- Look for where the CPU value is greater than the duration value in the RPC.Completed event class using SQL Trace.

- Look for cached execution plans that have the Parallelism operator indicating they will potentially run in parallel depending on the activity on your SQL Server instance:

```
SELECT *
FROM sys.dm_exec_cached_plans ASCachedPlans
CROSS APPLY sys.dm_exec_query_plan(CachedPlans.plan_handle) AS QueryPlan
CROSS APPLY sys.dm_exec_sql_text(CachedPlans.plan_handle) AS SQLText
WHERE CachedPlans.cacheobjtype = 'Compiled Plan'
AND QueryPlan.query_plan.value('declare namespace
ns="http://schemas.microsoft.com/sqlserver/2004/07/showplan";
max(//ns:RelOp/@Parallel)', 'float') > 0 ;
```

■  The      sys.dm_exec_requests,      sys.dm_os_tasks,      sys.dm_exec_sessions,
   sys.dm_exec_sql_text and sys.dm_exec_cached_plan DMVs can be queried, as
   shown below to, to determine whether any currently executing queries are running
   in parallel. For queries running in parallel, you will see multiple rows for the
   session_id and request_id columns of the sys.dm_os_tasks DMV. You can retrieve
   the Transact-SQL code via the sys.dm_exec_sql_text DMV and the execution plan
   from the sys.dm_exec_cached_plan through their respective handles.

```
SELECT Requests.session_id,
       Requests.request_id,
       MAX(ISNULL(exec_context_id, 0)) AS number_of_workers,
       Requests.sql_handle,
       Requests.statement_start_offset,
       Requests.statement_end_offset,
       Requests.plan_handle
FROM sys.dm_exec_requests AS Requests
JOIN sys.dm_os_tasks AS Tasks
ON Requests.session_id = Tasks.session_id
JOIN sys.dm_exec_sessions AS Sessions
ON Requests.session_id = Sessions.session_id
WHERE Sessions.is_user_process = 0x1
GROUP BY
    Requests.session_id,
    Requests.request_id,
    Requests.sql_handle,
    Requests.plan_handle,
    Requests.statement_start_offset,
    Requests.statement_end_offset
HAVING MAX(ISNULL(exec_context_id, 0)) > 0;
```

■  Where total_worker_time column value is greater than the total_elapsed_time column value for the sys.dm_exec_query_stats DMV as shown below. Not all  parallel
   queries will exhibit this behavior.

```
SELECT *
FROM sys.dm_exec_query_stats AS QueryStats
CROSS APPLY sys.dm_exec_sql_text(QueryStats.plan_handle) AS SQLText
WHERE total_worker_time > total_elapsed_time ;
```

Once you have identified the problem, use the same techniques as with inefficient query plans discussed above to reduce processor resource utilization. Alternatively, you can control how SQL Server 2005 uses parallel execution plans through the Cost Threshold for Parallelism SQL Server configuration option, discussed later.

## Determining Memory Bottlenecks

As discussed earlier in this chapter, the first step in analyzing a potential memory bottle neck is identifying whether it is due to external or internal pressue.

Because of the way SQL Server's dynamic buffer pool works, memory bottlenecks typically manifest themselves as specific memory-related error messages that are show in Table 29-2. Otherwise, your SQL Server solution should start exhibiting general slow performance and higher I/O utilization as Windows starts excessively paging.

**Table 29-2   Error Messages Indicating Memory Pressure**

| Error Number | Error Message |
| --- | --- |
| 701 | There is insufficient system memory to run this query. |
| 802 | There is insufficient memory available in the buffer pool. |
| 8628 | A timeout occurred while waiting to optimize the query. Rerun the query. |
| 8645 | A timeout occurred while waiting for memory resources to execute the query. Rerun the query. |
| 8651 | Could not perform the requested operation because the minimum query memory is not available. Decrease the configured value for the Min Memory Per Query server configuration option. |

Determining the cause of a memory bottleneck is probably the most difficult of all the bottlenecks because it requires a good knowledge of SQL Server, Windows, virtual and physical memory, the virtual address space (VAS), potentially AWE, and so on. Use the following guidelines to help you identifying the cause of your memory bottleneck:

- Examine the values of the Mem Usage and VM Size columns for the SQL Server process (sqlservr.cxe) in the Processes tab of the Windows Task Manager to see the amount of memory they are consuming relative to the amount of memory available on your server.

- You should see a drop in the value for SQL Server: Buffer Manager: Buffer Cache Hit Ratio performance object counter. The general rule of thumb used in the industry is around 90 percent, but you need to correlate that with other metrics because your SQL Server solution might never be able to achive 90 percent due to operational factors.

- Look for an increase in SQL Server: Buffer Manager: Checkpoint Pages/sec and SQL Server: Buffer Manager: Lazy Writes/sec performance object counters because SQL Server 2005 starts to flush pages out of the buffer pool cache under memory pressure.

- Examine the following set of performance counters in System Monitor:

    - The Process: Private Bytes counter should be close to the Process: Working Set for the SQL Server instance, indicating that there have not been a lot of memory paged out. A discrepancy would indicate some sort of external memory pressure.

    - SQL Server: Buffer Manager: Page Life Expectancy counter should not be too low.

- Examine the Buffer Distribution, Buffer Counts, Global Memory Objects, Query Memory Objects and Gateways values of the DBCC MEMORYSTATUS output to help determine if there is any internal memory pressure. Ideally the Target value in the Buffer Counts section will account for most of the memory consumed by your SQL Server instance. This Target value represents the target size of the buffer pool, as periodically recalculated by SQL Server 2005, represented by 8KB pages. Compare the amount of memory shown by the Target value (Target x 8KB) to the Process: Private Bytes performance object counter discussed above. If this amount is substantially less this would be indicative of internal memory pressure from components that are using memory from outside the buffer pool.

    > **More Info**   For more information on the DBCC MEMORYSTATUS command, read the "How to use the DBCC MEMORYSTATUS command to monitor memory usage on SQL Server 2005" *Knowledge Base* article located at *http://support.microsoft.com/kb/907877*.

- Examine the following DMVs, discussed in more detail in Chapter 31 for correlating metrics:

    - sys.dm_os_memory_cache_clock_hands
    - sys.dm_os_memory_cache_counters
    - sys.dm_os_memory_clerks,
    - sys.dm_os_ring_buffers
    - sys.dm_os_virtual_address_dump

The strategy for eliminating your memory bottleneck depends on the outcome of your analysis. You might have to correlate a lot of metrics to determine whether the bottleneck is due to external or internal memory pressures. You can obviously add more memory, but you can also control how SQL Server consumes the available memory through a number of configuration options discussed later in this chapter. Be aware that it might not be possible to eliminate a memory bottleneck if your SQL Server solution has outgrown the available resources.

## Determing I/O Subsystem Bottlenecks

Bottleneck problems with your I/O subsystem typically manifest themselves as timeout error messages and generally slow response times. The performance object counters discussed earlier should clearly indicate that the I/O subsystem is operating near its maximum capacity. Use the following guidelines to help you identify the cause of your I/O subsystem bottleneck:

- Query the sys.dm_os_wait_stats DMV shown below to see the statistics on the I/O latch waits, which basically indicate that a page requested was not found in the buffer pool and consequently a worker thread had to wait for the page to be fetched from disk.

```
SELECT *
FROM sys.dm_os_wait_stats
WHERE wait_type LIKE 'PAGEIOLATCH%' ;
```

- Examine the output of the sys.dm_io_pending_io_requests and sys.dm_io_virtual_file_stats(*db_id, file_id*) DMVs, as shown below, to see whether there are any currently pending I/O requests.

```
SELECT *
FROM sys.dm_io_pending_io_requests AS PendingIORequests
JOIN sys.dm_io_virtual_file_stats(NULL, NULL) AS VirtualFileStats
WHERE PendingIORequests.io_handle = VirtualFileStats.file_handle ;
```

- Examine the output of the sys.dm_exec_query_stats DMV to see which cached querie plans are generating the most I/O. Use the execution_count column in combination with the following columns to analyze the I/O operations being performed by these queries and the most expensive queries :

    - last_logical_reads
    - last_logical_writes
    - last_physical_reads
    - max_logical_reads
    - max_logical_writes
    - max_physical_reads

❑ min_logical_reads

❑ min_logical_writes

❑ min_physical_reads

❑ total_logical_reads

❑ total_logical_writes

❑ total_physical_reads

For example, to find the top 10 queries that generate the most amount I/O operations in a single execution, you would execute:

```
SELECT TOP 10 *
FROM sys.dm_exec_query_stats
ORDER BY (total_logical_reads + total_logical_writes)/execution_count ;
```

I/O subsystem bottlenecks are typically a result of SQL Server moving extents and pages between your memory and disks, so increasing the amount of memory made available to your SQL Server should obviously help alleviate the problem. Other causes include transaction log activity and *tempdb* system database activity, examined next.

Resolving I/O bottlenecks does not necessarily involve just improving your I/O subsystem with faster drives, faster controllers, more drives, or separating various database files. Inefficient queries that have to perform large tables scans can result in excessive I/O, as will a memory bottleneck. So you might also have to look at rewriting queries and reconfiguring how SQL Server utilizes the available memory to resolve a bottleneck.

## Determing *tempdb* System Database Bottlenecks

I will discuss the importance of, and how to tune the *tempdb* system database at the end of the chapter. It is sufficient at this stage to say that it plays a much more important role in SQL Server 2005 than in earlier versions and, consequently, can represent a potential bottleneck in your SQL Server solution. In earlier versions of SQL Server, it was difficult to determine whether your *tempdb* system database was a bottleneck in your SQL Server solution.

In SQL Server 2005, Microsoft has included a number of DMVs that can be used to see which users are accessing the *tempdb* system database, the internal objects being used, and version store sizes:

■ sys.dm_db_file_space_usage

■ sys.dm_db_session_space_usage

■ sys.dm_db_task_space_usage

---

**Note**  In SQL Server 2005, these DMVs apply only to the *tempdb* system database.

You can use SQL Server:Transactions object: Version Generation rate (KB/s) and SQL Server:Transactions object: Version Cleanup rate (KB/s) performance object counters to monitor the row versioning usage of your SQL Server solution.

The main way of reducing contention in your *tempdb* system database is to capacity plan and correctly size and configure the system database. However, inefficient queries can create excessive internal temporary objects, so you can also take advantage of the query tuning techniques discussed previously in this chapter.

## Tuning Microsoft SQL Server Configuration Options

Althought a lot of SQL Server 2005 configuration options are dynamic, responding to various software and hardware pressures automatically, you can still alter the way your SQL Server 2005 instance behaves through the modification of certain settings using the sp_configure system stored procedure or SQL Server Management Studio environment.

To configure the SQL Server 2005 options using T-SQL, use the sp_configure system stored procedure, which has the following syntax:

```
sp_configure 'option_name', value
```

When executing the sp_configure system stored procedure, you typically run the RECONFIGURE command afterwards, which updates the currently configured value to the new value stipulated. To enable the Common Language Runtime (CLR) in SQL Server 2005, execute the following:

```
EXEC sp_configure 'clr enabled', 1 ;
RECONFIGURE ;
GO
```

It is generally easier to change most options through SQL Server Managment Studio. To change the configuration options through SQL Server Management Studio, follow these steps:

1.  Start SQL Server Management Studio and connect to your SQL Server instance.

2.  Right-click your SQL Server instance in SQL Server Management Studio and select the Properties menu item.

3.  Click on the appropriate page in the pane located on the left side of the Server Properites dialog box. Figure 29-17 shows the Advanced page.

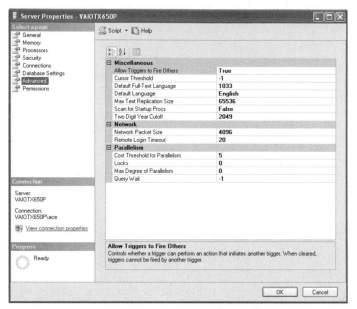

**Figure 29-17**   Changing SQL Server 2005 configuration options.

   4.   Change the desired SQL Server 2005 configuration option and click the OK button.

The following SQL Server configuration options can be used to fine tune your SQL Server solution.

## The Affinity I/O Mask (Affinity64 I/O Mask) Option

The Advanced Affinity I/O Mask option is new to SQL Server 2005 and controls which processors are used for processing SQL Server disk I/O threads. The default value is zero and uses all of the available processors. Internal SQL Server processes such as the lazy-writer and logwriter are impacted by this option. A binary bitmask is used to bind specific processors for I/O operations. Reconfiguring the affinity I/O mask option requires you to restart the SQL Server instance.

As an example, to reconfigure your SQL Server 2005 instance to only use the first (0) and third (2) processors for disk I/O threads and shutdown the SQL Server 2005 instance, you would execute the following:

```
EXEC sp_configure 'affinity I/O mask', 5
RECONFIGURE ;
GO
SHUTDOWN ;
GO
```

In most cases, the default affinity I/O mask provides the best performance. The affinity I/O mask is typically configured as a fine tuning mechanism for SQL Server instances where you want to separate I/O processing from computational processing.

## The Affinity Mask (Affinity64 Mask) Option

The Affinity Mask option dynamically binds which processors the SQL Server instance will use. Unlike earlier versions, changing the affinity mask option does not require a restart of the SQL Server instance. When this option is changed, SQL Server either enables a new scheduler or disables an existing scheduler. New schedulers are considerd for incoming batches. Current batches continue to execute on existing schedulers until the complete, when SQL Server deallocates that scheduler.

The Affinity Mask option is typically used as a fine-tuning mechanism where you have a multi-instance cluster or multiple instances of SQL Server installed on a multi-processor server and need to guarantee a certain level of performance, for example, to meet service level agreements, for example. It can also be used to fine tune performance SQL Server solutions that are experiencing heavy loads and, consequently, might have CPU caches repeatedly reloaded with data.

You also might want to affinitize your schedulers to only the physical processors, not the logical procesors, if you have determined that hyperthreading is having a detrimental affect on the performance of your SQL Server solution. Another alternative is to turn off hyperthreading at the BIOS level.

---

**Important**   When you configure the affinity mask and affinity I/O mask options, the RECONFIGURE command checks to ensure that the affinity settings are mutually exclusive. You can override this safety check via the RECONFIGURE WITH OVERRIDE option, but it is not recommended.

---

## The Cost Threshold for Parallelism Option

The Cost Threshold for Parallelism option dynamically controls the threshold at which SQL Server starts to consider parallel execution plans over serial execution plans. Parallel execution plans take longer to work out but execute more quickly on multi-processor servers. It does not apply to a uniprocessor server.The default value of five seconds indicates that SQL Server should use a parallel execution plan when it estimates that a serial plan will take longer than that threshold to execute on a specific hardware configuration.

The Cost Threshold for Parallelism option is considered a fine-tuning mechanism and typically left alone.

## The Lightweight Pooling Option

The Lightweight Pooling option controls whether SQL Server switches to fiber mode scheduling. A fiber is a lightweight thread that requires fewer processor resources because it avoids the need for context switching. The Lightweight Pooling option may reduce the system overhead associated with execessive context switching sometimes experienced in multiprocessor servers. Reconfiguring the Lightweight Pooling option requires you to restart the SQL Server instance.

Be careful with the lightweight pooling option because certain SQL Server 2005 components, such as the Common Language Runtime (CLR), are not supported under lightweight pooling.

You should consider evaluating the need of using the Lightweight Pooling option only if you are experiencing both high processor utilization and excessive context switching. You should monitor your SQL Server solution using System Monitor both before and after changing the Lightweight Pooling option to determine whether it is appropriate.

---

**Important** Microsoft has rewritten the way SQL Server 2005 works in fiber mode scheduling. The lightweight pooling option is not supported on Windows 2000 and Windows XP.

## The Locks Option

The Locks option controls the amount of memory allocated by SQL Server for managing locks; each lock consumes 96 bytes. The default value of zero allows SQL Server to dynamically allocate and deallocate memory used for managing locks. This dynamic lock pool does not exceed 60 percent of the memory allocated to the SQL Server instance. The Locks option also controls lock escalation. Reconfiguring the Locks option requires you to restart the SQL Server instance.

The Locks option is typically left alone and considered a fine-tuning mechanism. Consider changing the locks option if your SQL Server instance is generating lock errors.

## The Max Server Memory Option

The Max Server Memory option dynamically controls the upper limit of the amount of memory (in MB) that the SQL Server instance's buffer pool uses. The default value of zero allows the SQL Server instance to respond to external memory pressure and dynamically uses up to all of the available memory.

The Max Server Memory option is typically used as a fine-tuning mechanism where you have a multi-instance cluster, multiple instances of SQL Server, or other software running on your SQL Server solution, where you want to limit the amount of memory your SQL Server instance consumes.

## The Max Degree of Parallelism Option

The Max Degree of Parallelism option dynamically controls the number of processors the SQL Server instance uses for parallel execution plans. You can set the max degree of parallelism to one to prevent SQL Server from using parallel execution plans. The default value of zero uses all of the available processors, both physical and logical, taking into account the affinity mask setting.

The Max Degree of Parallelism option is typically used as a fine-tuning mechanism where you have a multi-instance cluster or multiple instances of SQL Server. It is recommended that you adjust the Max Degree of Parallelism option to match the number of physical processors in a hyperthreaded environment for optimal performance.

> **Note** Queries can override the max degree of parallelism option through the MAXDOP optimizer hint, which specifies the maximum number of processors that can be used for parallelism, when creating the query execution plan. For more information on the MAXDOP optimizer hint see "Query Hint (Transact-SQL)" topic in SQL Server 2005 Books Online.

## The Max Worker Threads Option

The advanced Max Worker Threads option dynamically controls the number of worker threads SQL Server uses for execution on the schedulers. Each worker thread consumes 512KB of stack space. Normally, each user connection consumes a worker thread; however, if you have more user connections than worker threads, SQL Server starts to share user connections between worker threads through a process known as thread pooling. The default value of zero allows SQL Server to automatically configure the number of worker threads at startup, depending on the number of processors available as seen in Table 29 3.

**Table 29-3  Default Automatic Configuration of Max Worker Threads by SQL Server 2005**

| Number of Processors | 32-bit Architecture | 64-bit Architecture |
|---|---|---|
| <= 4 | 256 | 512 |
| 8 | 288 | 576 |
| 16 | 352 | 704 |
| 32 | 480 | 960 |

In most cases, you should let SQL Server configure the max worker threads automatically. You can increase the number of worker threads to service more user connections concurrently, but you have to be careful not to saturate your processors. Conversely, if you have installed a multi-instance cluster or multiple instances of SQL Server, you might want to reduce the Max Worker Threads option.

**Important**    Microsoft recommends that you do not configure the Max Worker Threads option beyond 1,024 on a 32-bit architecture and 2,048 on a 64-bit architecture.

## The Min Memory Per Query Option

The Min Memory Per Query option controls the minimum amount of memory (in KB) that SQL Server allocates for the execution of any single query. The default is 1,024 KB.

The Min Memory Per Query option is typically left alone and considered a fine-tuning mechanism. Increasing the Min Memory Per Query option may improve performance for some small to medium-sized queries, but it could lead to internal memory pressure.

## The Min Server Memory Option

The Min Server Memory option dynamically controls the lower limit of the amount of memory (in MB) that the SQL Server instance's buffer pool uses. As with the Max Server Memory option, the default value of zero allows the SQL Server instance to respond to external memory pressure and dynamically decrease the amount of memory it uses until this lower limit is hit.

The Min Server Memory option is typically used as a fine-tuning mechanism to guarantee a SQL Server instance a certain amount of memory so as to guarantee a certain level of performance.

**Best Practices**    Typically DBAs either leave the Min Server Memory and Max Server Memory options alone or set them both to a predetermined value. Don't forget that you can also just adjust the min server memory to a level above the default but below the max server memory. As an example, you might have two SQL Server instances running on a server with 4 GB of memory. To guarantee that both SQL Server instances perform well, you configure both SQL Server instances to a min server memory setting of 1 GB and leave the max server memory at the default value. This guarantees that both SQL Server instances perform well because they will always have a minimum of 1 GB of memory to use. However, as users heavily utilize a particular SQL Server instance, or batch processes and large transactions run, that particular SQL Server instance can "grab" more of the remaining memory from the other SQL Server instance. This methodology allows you to guarantee a certain level of performance while maximizing your available memory.

## The Open Objects Option

The Open Objects option has no effect in SQL Server 2005 and has been included for backward compatibility only.

## The Priority Boost Option

The Priority Boost option increases the priority of SQL Server threads to High (13). This can improve performance because the SQL Server threads are not preempted by other applications running on the operating system. Conversely, other applications might be adversely affected because they do not have a high enough priority to preempt SQL Server's threads.

The priority boost option is typically left alone and considered a fine-tuning mechanism. You might also want to evaluate its use in a server environment where you have multiple instances of SQL Server running and certain instances have certain SLAs that need to be met.

## The Query Governor Cost Limit Option

The Query Governor Cost Limit option dynamically controls whether queries that the query optimizer estimates will take longer than the configured value will execute. The default value of zero turns off the query governor.

Configuring this option allows you to prevent run-away queries or expensive queries (such as Cartesian products), from executing and potentially having a detrimental impact on your SQL Server instance's performance. Be careful when configuring this option because SQL Server 2005's query optimizer compares its estimate of how many seconds it has predicted the query will take to execute, although the actual execution time taken might be less.

## The Recovery Internal Option

The Recovery Interval option dynamically controls how often the checkpoint process runs. This is probably one of the least-understood configuration options. The recovery interval value does not indicate how frequently the checkpoint process should run; it indicates the worst-time scenario in minutes for recovering a database. In other words, the frequency of how often the checkpoint process runs is based not on a time-based value but on an estimate made by SQL Server of how long it will take to write all data modifications that have occurred to the database since the last checkpiont. The default value of zero does not indicate that the checkpoint process runs every minute, as is commonly thought; it indicates that SQL Server checks every minute to see whether it should issue a checkpoint depending on a number of factors, including how many data modifications have occurred and how long it will take SQL Server to write them back to disk, how busy the SQL Server instance is at that moment, and what percentage of the transaction log is full. In practice, this typically translates to recovery time of less than a minute and a checkpoint that runs every minute for active databases.

The Recovery Interval option is typically left alone and considered a fine-tuning mechanism. You should consider changing the  Recovery Interval option only if you have determined that your SQL Server database solution's performance is being degraded by checkpoint.

### The Set Working Set Size Option

The Set Working Set Size option has no effect in SQL Server 2005 and has been included for backward compatibility only.

# Tuning the Database Layout

In Chapter 10, "Creating Databases and Database Snapshots," we examined creating databases in detail. We also also looked at disk I/O subsytems and the various levels of RAID in Chapter 4 and Chapter 7. There are a number of techniques that you can use to optimize performance at the database level.

## Database Layout

Perhaps one of the easieist techniques that a DBA can employ to tune his or her databases is to take advantage of the file and filegroup architecture supported by SQL Server databases. Don't forget that you can change your file and filegroup strategies once a database has been created.

---

**Note** Don't forget to put your transaction log onto a separate spindle for your OLTP databases to separate your sequential transaction log I/O from your random database I/O.

### Files

You can improve performance in a mulitprocessor server environment by using multiple data files in your database. By using multiple secondary data files, you can take advantage of SQL Server's multithreaded architecture because it will use one thread per database file to perform concurrent I/O operations. There is no point, from a performance point of view, in creating more files than the number of processors available on the server, taking into account any affinity settings, because SQL Server allocates only enough threads, up to the number of processors for the I/O operations.

So how large should database data files be? One tip I commonly suggest is limiting database file to the capacity of current CD/DVD technology. For example, if you limit your primary database file and secondary database file to 4.7 GB you can easily burn them onto DVDs for offsite backup purposes or for shipping databases to a remote site for attaching. With larger databases, you could obviously take advantage of new technology such as DVD+/-DL, Blue-Ray and HD-DVD.

## Filegroups

Another technique which requires more planning is taking advantage of file groups. As we saw in Chapter 10, filegroups allow you give a logical name to a set of strategically placed database files. You can then bind database objects, such as tables and indexes, to these database file sets using the logical name.

So, for example, you could create two files groups that consist of two sets of files located on separate disk drives. You could then create your tables on one filegroup and the non-clustered indexes on the other. The end result is a separation of your table I/O from your index I/O, which improves performance.

In another example, you could create two separate file groups for your Sales and Marketing departments and then create their respective tables on these two separate file groups. Again, you have improved performance by separating the I/O between the two departments at the disk drive level, potentially ensuring certain SLAs are met.

There are many examples of where to use file groups. Data archiving is yet another commonly used example.

I have always been a fan of keeping only the system tables on your primary file group, so for larger enterprise clients I recommend that databases always be created with a small primary data file and a secondary data file that is bound to a filegroup that has been configured as the default file group. It's an elegant separation of the system tables from the user data that has a number of benefits.

# Database Options

We examined various database options when we looked at how to create databases in Chapter 10. Although database options are normally functional in nature, the DBA can take advantage of a number of database options to potentially improve the performance of the database.

You can change the database options in SQL Server 2005 by using the ALTER DATABASE T-SQL statement. You should not use the *sp_dboption* system stored procedure that was predominantly used in earlier versions of SQL Server because it is being deprecated and will be removed in future versions of SQL Server. To change the *AdventureWorks* database to be read-only, execute the following statement:

```
ALTER DATABASE AdventureWorks SET READ_ONLY ;
```

**More Info**  For more information about the syntax of the ALTER DATABASE statement see the "ALTER DATABASE (Transact-SQL)" topic in SQL Server 2005 Books Online.

It is much easier, and more common, to change the database options through SQL Server Managment Studio. To change the configuration options through SQL Server Management Studio, follow these steps:

1. Start SQL Server Management Studio and connect to your SQL Server instance.

2. Expand the Database folder and right-click the database you want to configure. Select the Properties menu item.

3. Click on the Options page in the pane located on the left side of the Database Properites dialog box. Figure 29-18 shows the Options page.

**Figure 29-18** Changing the database options.

4. Change the desired database option(s) and click the OK button.

When tuning your databases through these database options, you should make sure you understand the implications of setting these options and monitor your database solution before and after the modification to ensure you have realized expected performance goals.

## AUTO_UPDATE_STATISTICS_ASYNC Database Option

SQL Server 2005 supports a new AUTO_UPDATE_STATISTICS_ASYNC database option that can be used to fine tune your database solution. Normally when an executing query triggers an automatic updating of statistics through the query optimizer, the query has to wait until the statistics are updated before continuing. In other words, it is a synchronous process. The AUTO_UPDATE_STATISTICS_ASYNC database option can be used to turn off the waiting that such queries have to perform. In other words, the query does not wait until the statistics are updated before continuing on with its execution. However, it will be using out of date statistics and consequently might not have an optimal execution plan generated, unlike subsequent queries.

> **Note** The AUTO_UPDATE_STATISTICS_ASYNC database option has no effect if the AUTO_UPDATE_STATISTICS database option is turned off.

## DATE_CORRELATION_OPTIMIZATION Database Option

The DATE_CORRELATION_OPTIMIZATION database option is another new database supported by SQL Server 2005 that can be used to fine tune your database solution. The DATE_CORRELATION_OPTIMIZATION database option can be used to improve equi-join performance between two tables that have a correlated datetime column. This datetime column must be part of the search argument. SQL Server 2005 keeps additional correlation statistics on the related columns between the two tables, which helps the query optimizer potentially determine more efficient query plans.

> **More Info** For more information on where to use the DATE_CORRELATION_OPTIMIZATION database option, see the topic "Optimizing Queries That Access Correlated datetime Columns" in SQL Server 2005 Books Online.

## PARAMETERIZATION Database Option

SQL Server 2005 supports another new PARAMETERIZATION database option that can be used to fine tune your database solution. You might improve performance in your database solution by turning on forced parameterization because you might reduce the frequency of compilations and recompilations in your OLTP database solution.

> **More Info** For more information about simple and forced parametrization, see the topics "Simple Parameterization" and "Forced Parameterization" in SQL Server 2005 Books Online.

### READ_ONLY Database Option

Setting the READ_ONLY database option prevents DML operations from being performed on the database. However, few DBAs realize that if you do set the option on, you can realize a performance benefit, as no locking needs to be managed within the database. This can translate to better query performance and less overhead on the Lock Manager of the Database Engine. So if your databases are read-only, turn on this option.

# Tuning the *tempdb* System Database

The *tempdb* system database plays a particularly important role in SQL Server 2005, which uses this temporary workspace for operations involving temporary tables, table variables, cusrors, hash-joins, and row versioning. Athough you might not be using any of these explicitly, your SQL Server instance might be implicity using *tempdb* for operations such as for DML after triggers, Multiple Active Result Sets (MARS), and online index operations, all of which use row-versioning in the background. DBCC checks also use row-versioning as a means of checking a consistent state of the tables or indexes.

Consequently, it is important to optimize performance of your *tempdb* system database, especially for an intensive OLTP environment. You can optimize the performance of the *tempdb* using a combination of the following recommendations:

- Capacity plan and pre-allocate adequate space.  By correctly capacity planning and pre-allocating adequate initial space to the *tempdb* system database, you are hopefully avoiding automatic growth which slows down performance because it represents a context switch. You should still consider leaving autogrow on to accommodate unexpected *tempdb* activity.

- Separate the log file. As with all databases, separating the log file or files from the database files or files realizes performance benefits because you have separated your random database I/O from your sequential transaction log I/O.

- Use multiple data files. By adding multiple secondary data files to the *tempdb* system database, you can take advantage of SQL Server's multithreaded architecture. SQL Server uses one thread per *tempdb* system database file to perform concurrent I/O operations. As discussed earlier in this chapter, SQL Server uses only as many threads for I/O opertations as there are schedulers.

- Use a faster disk. If your database solution heavily utilizes the *tempdb* system database, you should consider using faster disk drives for the the *tempdb* system database. For example, you could use 10,000 rpm disk drives to store the user databases, but use a more expensive 15,000 rpm disk drive to store the *tempdb* system database. You could also use solid-state drives, although they tend to be expensive.

- Use an appropriate RAID solution. The *tempdb* system database is typically write-intensive and can be heavily utilized. Consequently, RAID-5 and RAID-6 are not the best choices because they generally perform poorly compared to other RAID configurations. RAID-10 or RAID-0 are more appropriate. Remember, though, that RAID-0 does not provide any redundancy.

- Use the local disk subsystem. If you are using a SAN solution, you must decide whether the *tempdb* system database is stored on the local storage or the SAN solution. If your *tempdb* system database is heavily utilized, your SQL Server solution generates a lot of traffic between the server and the SAN. Therefore, it is recommended to store the *tempdb* system database locally.

# Summary

In this chapter, you learned how to monitor and detect both hardware and SQL Server-related performance problems through the various tools and commands available in both the Windows operating system and SQL Server 2005 environments.

You learned the major subsystems that exist and what specific performance metrics you should watch out for when trying to determine the causes of bottlenecks and to tune the performance of your SQL Server solution.

There are a number of configuration options that exist in SQL Server 2005 that you can modify to tune the performance of your SQL Server solution once you become more familiar with your operational environment.

The *tempdb* system database plays a more important role in SQL Server 2005 compared to earlier versions, so special attention should be given to maximize the performance of this system database.

## Chapter 30

# Using Profiler, Management Studio, and Database Engine Tuning Advisor

In this chapter, we will examine the main tools you use on a daily basis as a SQL Server 2005 database administrator. SQL Server Managment Studio and SQL Server Profiler are the most common tools that a DBA uses, so we will concentrate on these tools in this chapter. We will look at how you perform common DBA tasks using SQL Server Managment Studio and how to interpret the rich information embedded inside this powerful tool. We will also examine how you can capture a trace of activity against your SQL Server 2005 instance and use that information to iteratively tune your database solutions.

Remember that SQL Server 2005 uses a cost-based optimizer, which means that you should always base your performance tuning decisions on the actual usage patterns and data contained within your production databases. To help you with this, Microsoft has incorporated a powerful tuning utility called Database Engine Tuning Advisor, which we will examine at the end of the chapter.

## Overview of SQL Server Tools

Given the complexity of SQL Server 2005 and its various components, it is important to understand the different tools available, their locations, and their uses. Although we will concentrate on SQL Server Managment Studio and SQL Server Profiler, they will not suffice for certain configuration and administrative tasks. Microsoft has deliberately incorporated certain functionality into a set of separate, external tools for security reasons.

## Performance Tools

The following tools are located in the Performance Tools folder of the Microsoft SQL Server 2005 folder. They are primarily used to analyze and performance tune your SQL Server instances and related services. We will cover how to use these tools later in this chapter.

- **Database Engine Tuning Advisor** The Database Engine Tuning Advisor tool is used to analyze the uses of patterns against your database solution and make performance tuning recommendations.

- **SQL Server Profiler** SQL Server Profiler is a powerful utility that allows you to capture the network traffic between the client applications and your SQL Server instance.

## Configuration Tools

The following tools are located in the Configuration Tools folder of the Microsoft SQL Server 2005 folder. They are primarily used to configure your SQL Server instances and related services, so you typically will not be using them on a daily basis.

- **Notification Services command prompt** The Notification Services command prompt is used to configure your Notification Services instances.

- **Reporting Services Configuration** The Reporting Services Configuration tool is used to configure your Reporting Services (SSRS) instance. The Reporting Services Configuration tool allows you to control global settings such as the IIS configuration, what database to use, and what e-mail server SSRS is going to use. Figure 30-1 shows an SMTP gateway that has been configured for reporting services.

- **SQL Server Configuration Manager** SQL Server Configuration Manager's primary function is to allow you to control the individual services of the components installed for your SQL Server instance. SQL Server Configuration Manager allows you to control the security context and start mode of the individual services. It also controls which protocols can be used to connect to your SQL Server instance and what client protocols can be used. Another important feature of SQL Server Configuration Manager is the ability to configure aliases to your SQL Server instances.

Figure 30-2 shows a new SQL Server alias being created using SQL Server Configuration Manager.

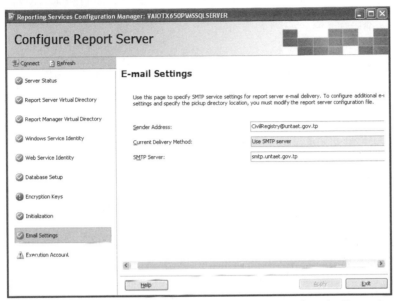

**Figure 30-1**   Configuring an SMTP Gateway for SSRS using the Reporting Services Configuration tool.

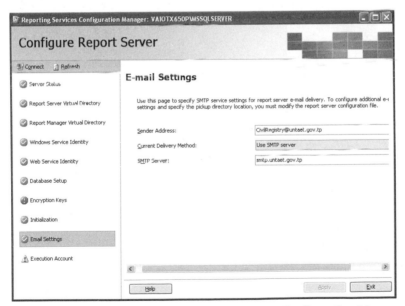

**Figure 30-2**   Creating an alias through SQL Server Configuration Manager tool.

**Note** SQL Server aliases can be a great way of abstracting your "SQL Server layer" from your "infrastructure layer." Removing dependencies on server names or IP addresses allows you to change your infrastructure layer with minimal impact on the client applications.

■ **SQL Server Error and Usage Reporting** SQL Server Error and Usage Reporting tool is a simple dialog box that allows you to send information about serious errors and the usage of SQL Server features to Microsoft. You can customize the error and usage reports on a component level of the installed SQL Server instances by selecting the appropriate check boxes, as shown in Figure 30-3.

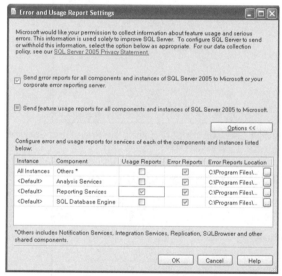

**Figure 30-3**    SQL Server Error and Usage Reporting tool.

■ **SQL Server Surface Area Configuration** SQL Server Surface Area Configuration tool allows you to control the security surface area of local and remote instances of SQL Server 2005. Use this tool to control which services, network protocols, and SQL Server components are enabled. Figure 30-4 shows the CLR integration being enabled for a SQL Server instance using the SQL Server Surface Area Configuration tool.

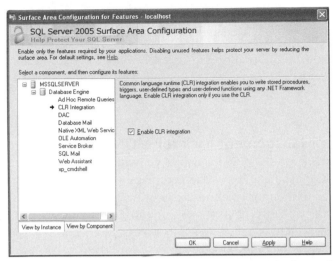

**Figure 30-4**    Enabling the CLR Integration using SQL Server Surface Area Configuration tool.

# External Tools

There are a number of useful tools that do not come with SQL Server 2005 that you might want to take advantage of, depending on your requirements. Always ensure that you have the latest version of the tools. These tools are all available at Microsoft download center (*http://www.microsoft.com/downloads*).

## Microsoft Security Baseline Analyzer

The Microsoft Security Baseline Analyzer (MBSA) tool is designed to ensure that your SQL Server instance and Windows operating system environment have the latest patches and have been configured securely. The MBSA can scan multiple computers on your network utilising the Windows Server Update Services.

> **Note**    At the time of this book's publication, Microsoft has not yet updated this tool to work with SQL Server 2005. Nevertheless, you can still use this powerful tool to check other security-related issues on your SQL Server 2005 instance.

## Microsoft SQL Server Best Practices Analyzer

Microsoft SQL Server Best Practices Analyzer (BPA) is a database management tool that lets you verify the implementation of common best practices. These best practices typically relate to the usage and administration aspects of SQL Server databases and ensure that your SQL Servers are managed and operated well.

---

**Note**   At the time of this book's publication, Microsoft has not yet updated this tool to work with SQL Server 2005.

---

## Microsoft SQL Server Management Pack for MOM 2005

SQL Server Management Pack for MOM 2005 enables you to monitor your SQL Server 2005 and SQL Server 2000 instances across the enterprise environment. It includes enterprise-level capabilities to monitor resource availability and configuration, collect performance data, and test default thresholds so that you can identify and manage issues before they become critical. MOM 2005 is designed to increase the security, availability, and performance of your SQL Server infrastructure.

## Microsoft SQL Server 2005 Upgrade Advisor

SQL Server 2005 Upgrade Advisor tool is designed to help facilitate the upgrade of SQL Server 7.0 and 2000 databases. It analyses your existing databases and SQL Server solution and makes the following recommendations:

- Upgrade issues that will block an upgrade from being successful.

- Upgrade issues that need to be fixed before the upgrade process.

- Upgrade issues that need to be addressed after the upgrade process.

Make sure you understand the limitations of SQL Server 2005 Upgrade Advisor: it does not analyze encrypted stored procedures, code in extended stored procedures, or source code in languages other than Transact-SQL. Because it analyses only the code in your database solutions, it does not detect any issues that you might have in client applications. Consequently, it is important to capture a trace of the traffic between your client applications and the databases solution using SQL Server Profiler to ensure that you pick up any additional issues that might arise during the upgrade process. Figure 30-5 shows the output of SQL Server 2005 Upgrade Advisor.

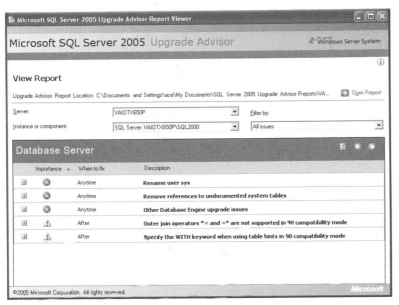

**Figure 30-5**   SQL Server 2005 Upgrade Advisor report.

# Using SQL Server Management Studio

SQL Server Management Studio is an integrated utility you use to manage the database engine, analysis services, integration services, reporting services, and SQL Server mobile. It is the main tool you use as a DBA to manage your SQL Server instances on a daily basis.

It replaces the myriad of tools that were available in early versions of SQL Server. Watch for future "add ons" such as the Microsoft Visual Studio 2005 Team Edition for Database Professionals, which will help develop databases in a managed project environment with support for deployment, off-line development, refactoring, unit testing and versioning.

## SQL Server Management Studio Environment

Since SQL Server Managment Studio environment is based on the Visual Studio IDE, it is highly customisable and modular. You should become a familiar with the following components of SQL Server Managment Studio:

- **Object Explorer**   Object Explorer is a hierarchical representation of the components and database objects that make up your SQL Server 2005 instance. It offers a rich visual environment and context-sensitive menus that allow you to perform your daily tasks as a DBA. We will look at how to use Object Explorer in more detail shortly. If it is not visible, you can use the F8 key as a shortcut to invoke Object Explorer.

■ **Summary Reports**    Summary Reports gives you an overview of how your SQL Server instance is currently performing. It can be used as a quick way of isolating any performance problems. We will look at Summary Reports in more detail as well. Use the F7 key as a short-cut to see Summary Reports.

■ **Registered Servers**    The Registered Servers pane, shown in Figure 30-6, allows you to register multiple SQL Server instances, reflecting all organizational hierarchy, so that you can manage multiple SQL Servers from the single SQL Server Managment Studio interface. Right-click within the Registered Servers pane to add new server groups and SQL Server registrations. Use the Ctrl-Alt-G key short-cut to see Registered Servers.

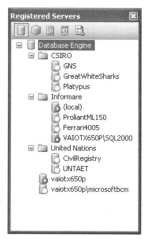

**Figure 30-6**    Registered Servers window.

■ **Template Explorer**    Template Explorer, shown in Figure 30-7, represents a rich set of T-SQL templates that have been predefined by Microsoft for both the developer and a DBA. You can add your own folders and templates to represent commonly used T-SQL scripts. To use a template, you simply drag it from Template Explorer to the query pane. Use the Ctrl-Alt-T key short-cut to see Template Explorer.

■ **Solution Explorer**    Solution Explorer, shown in Figure 30-8, allows you to build a hierarchy of your SQL Server connections, T-SQL scripts, and other miscellaneous files in a SQL Server scripts project. It's a great way of organizing scripts that you would commonly use on a daily basis.  You can incorporate other projects such as Analysis Services Scripts and SQL Mobile Scripts into the one solution. Use Ctrl+Alt+L shortcut to see the Solution Explorer.

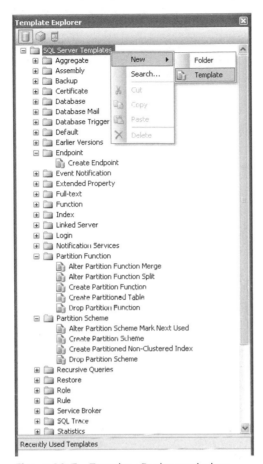

**Figure 30-7**   Template Explorer window.

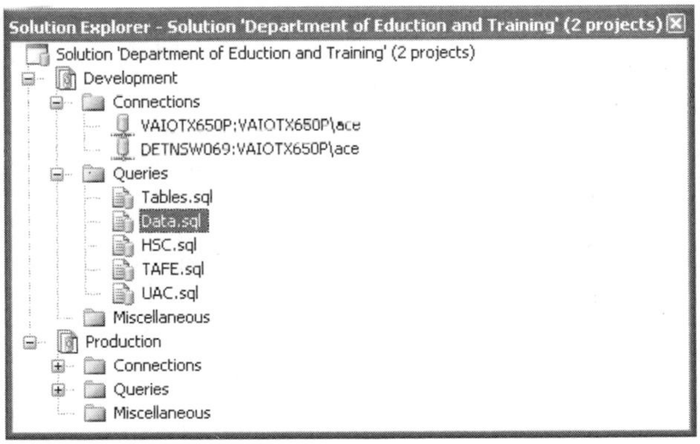

**Figure 30-8**   Solution Explorer window.

# Using Object Explorer

Object Explorer is a window in SQL Server Management Studio that allows you to visually explore and manage all of the database objects and SQL Server components that make up your SQL Server 2005 solution. The Databases folder contains your user databases and allows you to administer and develop your databases solutions. The Security folder allows you to configure global security objects such as logins. The Management folder contains important information such as SQL Server logs and Activity Monitor. The Server Objects, Replication, and Notification Services folders are used to configure those specific SQL Server components. The Object Explorer is shown in Figure 30-9.

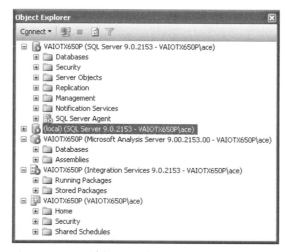

**Figure 30-9**   Object Explorer window.

The Databases folder contains the user databases installed on your SQL Server instance. System databases and database snapshots have their own respective folders. Object Explorer is context-sensitive, so once you navigate to the object of interest, right-click it to see what tasks can be performed and what properties are exposed. Figure 30-10 shows all of the tasks that can be performed at the database level.

To see what objects exist within your database, simply expand the appropriate database's folders. For example, to see what tables make up the *AdventureWorks* database, expand the databases folder, then the *AdventureWorks* database, and finally Tables. To see what columns make up the [dbo].[GlobalEmailList] table, you further expand the dbo.GlobalEmailList folder and finally the Columns folder, as shown in Figure 30-11.

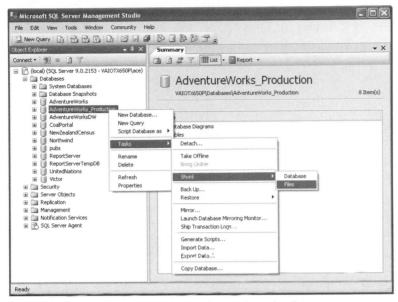

**Figure 30-10**   Tasks that can be performed on databases.

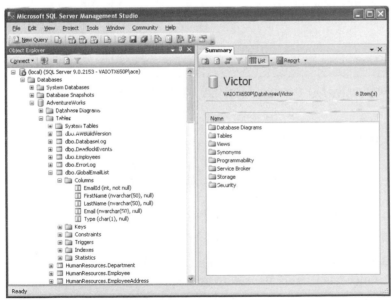

**Figure 30-11**   Viewing a table's columns in Object Explorer.

Having information about your databases objects so easily available inside SQL Server Management Studio makes it easier to write T-SQL queries and develop various database objects. Not only can you view information in Object Explorer, but you can also modify objects, drag-and-drop objects into the Query pane, and even script the creation and modification of database objects by right-clicking the folder or object of interest and navigating through the context-sensitive menu. Figure 30-12 shows an example of this context-sensitive menu. In this instance, an insert statement is being generated for the [dbo].[GlobalEmailList] table.

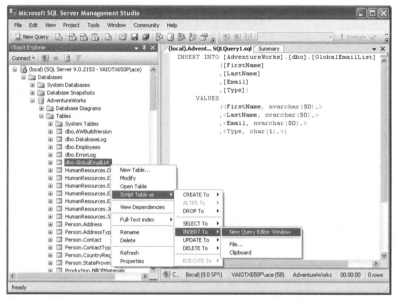

**Figure 30-12**   Scripting an INSERT statement through the context-sensitive menu in Object Explorer.

## Using the Summary Report Pane

The Summary Report pane was a late addition to SQL Server 2005 in the beta cycle. However, it provides potentially critical information in an easily accessible and readable fashion. As a DBA using SQL Server 2005, you should get used to looking at it first, before any other utilities or commands, because it might help you easily identify any performance issue.

There are a number of different summary reports available in the Summary Report pane:

- **Server Dashboard**   The Server Dashboard report provides overview data about SQL Server instance, such as configuration and activity details. It also provides summary information of CPU usage and logical I/O performed.

- **Configuration Changes History**   The Configuration Changes History report provides a history of all *sp_configure* and trace flag changes recorded by the default trace.

- **Schema Changes History**   The Schema Changes History report provides a history of all committed DDL statements recorded by the default trace.

- **Scheduler Health**   The Scheduler Health report provides detailed activity data on each Scheduler being used by SQL Server 2005.

- **Memory Consumption**   The Memory Consumption report provides detailed information on the consumption of memory by the various components of SQL Server 2005, as well as historical changes of the memory footprint. It also shows some important metrics, such as page life expectancy and the memory granted both outstanding and pending.

- **Activity**   There are several different Activity reports that show information about the various connections, sessions, cursors, and blocking transactions against the SQL Server 2005 instance. The All Blocking Transactions Activity report allows you to quickly identify any contention inside your SQL Server instance.

- **Top Transactions**   There are three different reports that report information about transactions, based on either their age, blocked transactions count, or locks count.

- **Performance**   There are several different performance reports that report batch execution statistics, object execution statistics, and top queries based on CPU time or I/O.

- **Service Broker Statistics**   The Service Broker Statistics report basic information on Service Broker activity, based primarily on performance object counters.

- **Transaction Log Shipping Status**   The Transaction Log Shipping Status report assures the status of your log shipping configuration, depending on whether your SQL Server instance is a primary, secondary, or monitor server.

To view these summary reports, follow these steps:

1. Click Start, then click All Programs, and then click Microsoft SQL Server 2005, and start SQL Server Management Studio. The Connect To Server dialog box should appear, as shown in Figure 30-13.

**Figure 30-13**   Connect To Server dialog box.

2. Type in your server name and authentication details, and then click Connect. Click the Report button that is available in the Summary pane. This displays a list of all available summary reports, as shown in Figure 30-14.

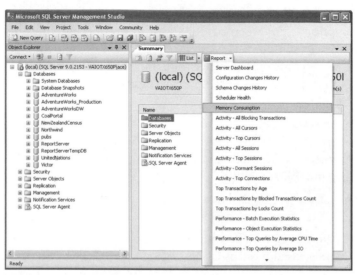

**Figure 30-14** Summary reports available in Object Explorer.

3. Choose the appropriate report by clicking it in the drop-down list. Figure 30-15 shows the Memory Consumption report.

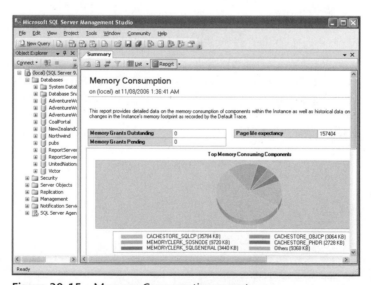

**Figure 30-15** Memory Consumption report.

Don't forget that these summary reports represent a snapshot at a particular time. To update the summary report with the latest information, click the Refresh button located in the toolbar.

## Analysing SQL Server Logs

Both the SQL Server 2005 database engine and SQL Server Agent have specific log files to which they write information about events, and importantly, error messages. When monitoring or troubleshooting your SQL Server instance, it is important to go to the correct log. It is common for DBAs to forget to examine SQL Server Agent Error Log when troubleshooting an administration problem. Figure 30-16 shows the location of both the SQL Server logs and the SQL Server Agent Error Logs in SQL Server Management Studio.

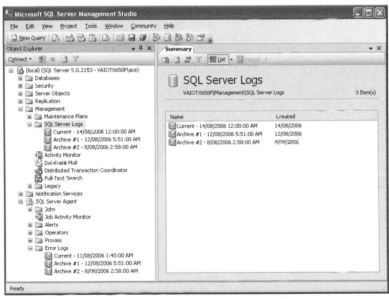

**Figure 30-16**   SQL Server Logs and SQL Server Agent Errors Logs.

SQL Server 2005 creates a new error log each time the instance is started. By default, the error log is located at %Program Files%\Microsoft SQL Server\MSSQL.*n*\MSSQL\ERROR-LOG, and SQL Server 2005 will archive six error logs before it starts to overwrite them. To configure the SQL Server Error Logs, right-click the SQL Server Logs folder located in the Management folder and click Configure. Figure 30-17 shows the various configurations options available for configuring the SQL Server Log.

---

**Note**    Because SQL Server 2005 creates a new error log only when the instance is started, the log file can grow to a very large size. This can be problematic when you need to read the error log and it takes a long time to load due to its size. You can use the *sp_cycle_errorlog* system stored procedure to cycle the error log files without having to restart the SQL Server instance. This stored procedure is typically run through a SQL Server Agent job that is scheduled to run periodically.

---

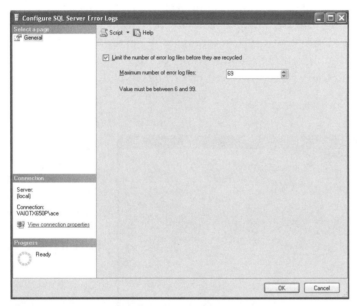

**Figure 30-17**    Configuring the SQL Server Log.

SQL Server Agent writes to its own separate log, again starting a new instance whenever the service starts. To configure the location, the amount of information written, and the location of the SQL Server Agent Error Log, right-click the Error Logs folder located in the SQL Server Agent folder and click Configure. Figure 30-18 shows the various configurations options available for configuring the SQL Server Agent Error Log.

By default, execution trace messages are not written to the SQL Server Agent Error Log. This is by design, as it can quite quickly fill up the SQL Server Agent Error Log. However, to troubleshoot a particular problem, you might need the additional information that the execution trace messages will provide, in which case it makes sense to temporarily turn on this feature. To configure SQL Server Agent to include execution trace messages in its error log, right-click SQL Server Agent in Object Explorer, and select the Properies option. Click on Include Execution Trace Messages check box on the General page, as shown in Figure 30-19.

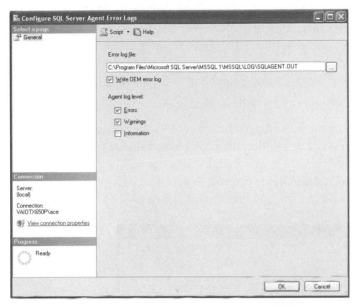

**Figure 30-18**   Configuring the SQL Server Agent Error Log.

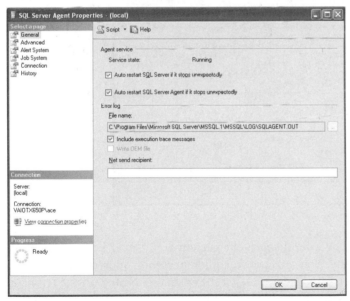

**Figure 30-19**   Including execution trace messages dialog box.

When troubleshooting a SQL Server issue, the DBA typically needs to look at a number of different log files to help him or her determine the cause of the problem. This typically involves looking at the SQL Server Logs and potentially the Windows NT Event logs for correlated information, which can be difficult. SQL Server Management Studio, however, has an integrated Log File Viewer that allows you to examine the Database Mail, SQL Server Agent, SQL Server, and Windows NT Event Logs simultaneously. Additionally, the Log File Viewer provides some basic filtering, searching, and exporting capabilities.

To view the SQL Server and Windows logs, follow these steps:

1. Start SQL Server Management Studio and connect to your SQL Server instance. Navigate to the SQL Server Logs folder, which is located under the Management folder. To open the Log File Viewer utility, right-click the SQL Server Logs folder, then choose View, and then SQL Server and Windows Logs from the context-sensitive menu. This launches the Log File Viewer utility, as seen in Figure 30-20.

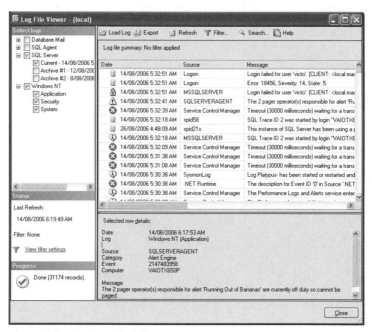

**Figure 30-20**    Log File Viewer.

2. By default, the Log File Viewer displays the current SQL Server Log and the three Windows NT Event Logs. You can choose a different combination of logs by checking the appropriate check boxes in the Select Logs pane located on the left-hand side of the Log File Viewer.

3. The log, as expected, contains a lot of detailed information. You can search for specific log entries by clicking the Search button and using the Search dialog box, as shown in Figure 30-21.

**Figure 30-21**   Log File Viewer Search dialog box.

4.  You also have some basic filtering capabilities. You can filter on the user, computer, start and end date, message, and source. To configure the filter settings, click the Filter button, located in the top toolbar, and use the Filter Settings dialog box, as shown in Figure 30-22.

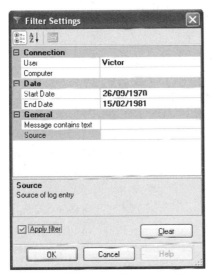

**Figure 30-22**   Log File Viewer Filter Settings dialog box.

The Log File Viewer also has the capability of exporting this rich information to a log file. This can prove useful for archiving important events or sending log events to remote DBAs or support staff for analysis.

## Viewing Current Activity

SQL Server Management Studio environment also allows the DBA to readily see what processes are currently running against the SQL Server instance, which can be useful when database users are complaining about poor query performance or unresponsive client applications.

There are a number of different techniques you can use to see what is happening on your SQL Server instance. The technique that you use depends on the level of information that you are after, your familiarity with the tool, and the overhead that it will have on a potentially stressed SQL Server instance.

Don't forget that contention may be the cause of perceived poor performance. When users are complaining about slow response times, it is not due to a lack of server resources such as memory or CPU resources, but other concurrent active transactions that are blocking the complainants. It is up to you to identify whether you have a contention problem or a true performance problem. If it is a contention problem, there are a number of strategies that your developers can employ to reduce the amount of locking contention experienced in your SQL Server solution, including optimizing the T-SQL statements, improving indexing strategies, or investigating the viability of read-committed snapshot isolation.

## Using the Activity Monitor

The Activity Monitor tool allows you to view what processes are currently running within your SQL Server instance, what database objects they are accessing, and what kind of locks are being either acquired or released. To view this information, follow these steps:

1.  Start SQL Server Management Studio and connect to your SQL Server instance. Expand the Management folder and right-click the Activity Monitor icon. This presents you with different ways of viewing which processes are currently running against your SQL Server databases.

2.  Click View Processes to launch the Activity Monitor, as shown in Figure 30-23. The Activity Monitor shows the system process IDs (SPID) of all the current user connections and which database they are using; their status (background, dormant, pending, rollback, runnable, running, sleeping, spinloop, or suspended); the host name; which application and command each user connection is running; the amount of time the connection has been waiting for a resource to become available; metrics about CPU, I/O, and memory usage; any transactions that are open; and, importantly, whether the user connection is being blocked or blocking someone else. Don't forget that the activity monitor represents a snapshot, so to get the latest information you have to click the Refresh button located on the top toolbar.

---

**Note**   In SQL Server 2005, you can change the refresh rate in Activity Monitor so that it is automatically refreshed. This can be done by clicking the Review Refresh Settings option in the Status pane, located on the left-hand side of the Activity Monitor.

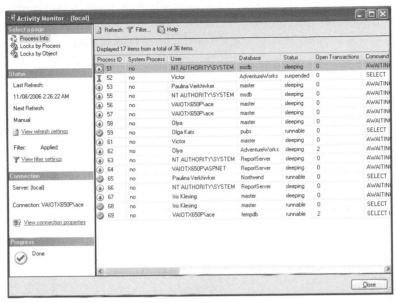

**Figure 30-23**   Activity Monitor.

3. To see the actual T-SQL batch that is being run by a user connection, double-click the process within Activity Monitor. The Process Details dialog box, shown in Figure 30-24, shows you the last T-SQL command batch that was executed by the SPID and allows you to kill the process. Note that the details of the Process Details dialog box will be different for you, depending on what T-SQL commands your users have executed.

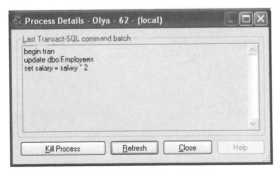

**Figure 30-24**   Process Details dialog box.

4. Select the Locks by Process page to see lock information for a particular SPID. Choose the appropriate SPID from the Selected Process drop-down list, as shown in Figure 30-25. The Activity Monitor shows locking information specific for this SPID, including the lock type, the lock mode, and the status of the lock.

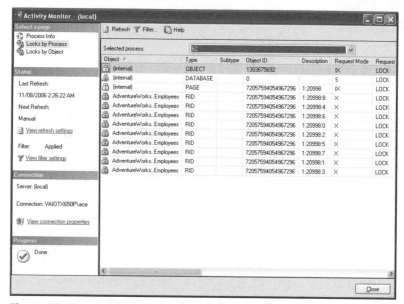

**Figure 30-25** Activity Monitor—Locks by Process.

The following are the different types of locks available in SQL Server 2005:

- ❏ **_TOTAL**   Information for all locks
- ❏ **ALLOCATION_ UNIT**   Allocation unit
- ❏ **APPLICATION**   Application-specific resource
- ❏ **DATABASE**   The entire database
- ❏ **EXTENT**   Eight contiguous pages (64 KB).
- ❏ **FILE**   Database file
- ❏ **HOBT**   Heap or B-tree; an allocation unit used to describe a heap or B-tree
- ❏ **KEY**   Row lock within an index used to protect key ranges in serializable transactions
- ❏ **METADATA**   Catalog information about an object
- ❏ **OBJECT**   Any database object (sys.all_objects)

- ❑ **PAGE**   Data or index page (8 KB)
- ❑ **RID**   Row identifier, that represents a single row within a table
- ❑ **TABLE**   Entire table, including the indexes

When examining page locks, you will see that the Description column has two integers separated by a colon that denote the file number and page number. Likewise, when working with RID locks, you will see three integers separated by colons that indicate the file number, page number, and slot number.

The following are the different types of request modes available in SQL Server 2005:

- ❑ **BU**   Bulk-Update lock
- ❑ **I**   Intent lock
- ❑ **IS**   Intent-Shared lock
- ❑ **IU**   Intent-Update lock
- ❑ **IX**   Intent-Exclusive lock
- ❑ **RangeS_S**   Shared Range-Shared resource lock
- ❑ **RangeS_U**   Shared Range-Update resource lock
- ❑ **RangeI_N**   Insert Range-Null resource lock
- ❑ **RangeI_S**   Insert Range-Shared resource lock
- ❑ **RangeI_U**   Insert Range-Update resource lock
- ❑ **RangeI_X**   Insert Range-Exclusive resource lock
- ❑ **RangeX_S**   Exclusive Range-Shared resource lock
- ❑ **RangeX_U**   Exclusive Range-Update resource lock
- ❑ **RangeX_X**   Exclusive Range-Exclusive resource lock
- ❑ **S**   Shared lock
- ❑ **Sch-M**   Schema-Modification lock
- ❑ **Sch-S**   Schema-Stability lock
- ❑ **SIU**   Shared Intent-Update lock
- ❑ **SIX**   Shared Intent-Exclusive lock
- ❑ **U**   Update lock
- ❑ **UIX**   Update Intent-Exclusive lock
- ❑ **X**   Exclusive lock

The status of a lock request in SQL Server 2005 can be one of the following:

❑ **GRANT.** Lock was granted to process.

❑ **WAIT.** Process is being blocked by another process.

❑ **CNVT.** Lock is being converted to another type of lock.

SQL Server 2005 has the following different types of entities that can request a lock from the lock manager:

❑ **CURSOR.** A cursor

❑ **EXCLUSIVE_TRANSACTION_WORKSPACE.** Exclusive part of the transaction workspace

❑ **TRANSACTION.** A transaction

❑ **SESSION.** A user session

❑ **SHARED_TRANSACTION_WORKSPACE.** Shared part of the transaction workspace

5. Select the Locks by Object page to see lock information for a specifc database object. Choose the appropriate object from the Selected Object drop-down list, as shown in Figure 30-26. The Activity Monitor shows the same locking information that we saw previously but from a different perspective.

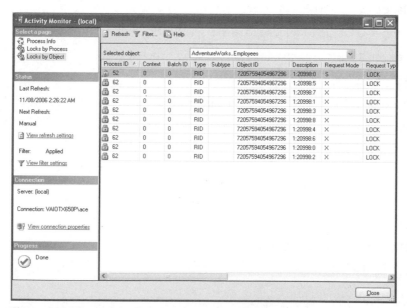

**Figure 30-26**   Activity Monitor—Locks by Object page.

> **More Info**   For more information on the different lock types and their request modes, search for the "Activity Monitor (Locks by Object Page)" and "Lock Modes" topics in SQL Server 2005 Books Online.

## Using System Stored Procedures

You can also view information about processes that are running on your SQL Server instance by using a number of stored procedures that have always been available with SQL Server:

- *sp_who*   The *sp_who* system stored procedure reports basic information very similar to what the Activity Monitor shows.

- *sp_who2*   The undocumented *sp_who2* system stored procedure reports richer information compared to the *sp_who* system stored procedure.

- *sp_lock*   The *sp_lock* system stored procedure returns basic information about locks.

> **Important**   The *sp_lock* system stored procdure is being deprecated in a future release of SQL Server, so you should try to avoid using it and use the sys.dm_tran_locks Dynamic Management View instead.

The *sp_who* system stored procedure generally executes very quickly because it returns such basic information. It represents a quick way of finding out whether a particular process is being blocked by another process. If users are complaining about slow transactions or unresponsive queries, try executing the following command in a query window in SQL Server Management Studio to determine whether their processes are being blocked by other transactions:

```
EXEC sp_who ACTIVE ;

GO
```

The ACTIVE parameter excludes sessions that are waiting for the next command from a user connection. Figure 30-27 shows sample results of this *sp_who* system stored procedure. Look for a SPID value in the [blk] column, which would indicate that that process is being blocked by that SPID.

## Using the sys.dm_tran_locks DMV

Another technique that you can use to view more detailed information about locks in SQL Server 2005 is to query the new sys.dm_tran_locks Dynamic Management View by executing the following T-SQL statement:

```
SELECT * FROM sys.dm_tran_locks;
```

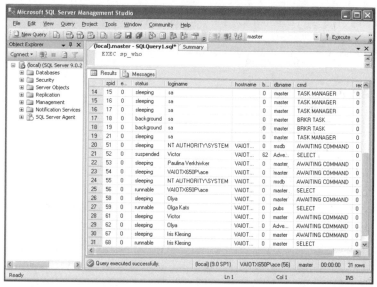

**Figure 30-27**    Output of the *sp_who* system stored procedure.

A sample resultset from running this statement in SQL Server Management Studio is shown in Figure 30-28. The output is very similar to what we have shown above, although there will be some more low-level locking information.

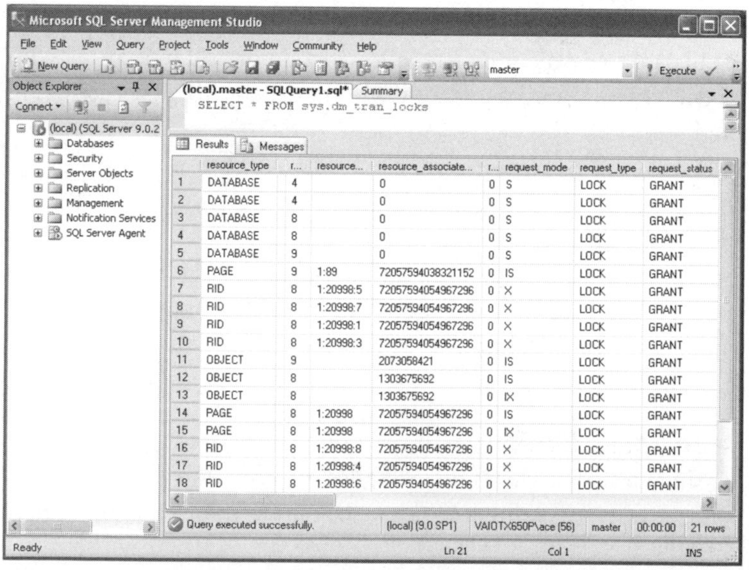

**Figure 30-28**    Output of the sys.dm_tran_locks Dynamic Management View.

We will cover Dynamic Management Views in more detail in Chapter 31, "Dynamic Management Views."

# Generating SQL Server Agent Alerts

It is the responsibility of a DBA to minimise the downtime of a SQL Server 2005 solution and provide a certain level of performance. Consequently, you will like to be notified when certain important events occur so that you can take corrective action or, better still, get SQL Server 2005 to automatically take the corrective action. SQL Server Agent and the alerts architecture allow you to create such a proactive SQL Server solution.

SQL Server Agent has the ability to generate alerts based on a number of different criteria within your database solution. Alerts are basically a response to an event that you identify, such as when a database's transaction log is full or, better still, over a certain threshold, such as 90 percent full. The event depends on the type of SQL Server Agent alert. SQL Server 2005 supports the following types of SQL Server Agent alerts:

- **SQL Server Event Alert**   SQL Server Event Alerts are based on the SQL Server error messages that are generated by SQL Server 2005 Database Engine. The error messages are stored in the sys.sysmessages system catalog. You need to be familiar with the various error messages that can be generated by SQL Server, their severity, and message text so you can define alerts for them. Database developers can add their own user-defined messages in using the *sp_addmessage* system stored procedure and generate them using the RAISERROR T-SQL statement.

- **SQL Server Performance Condition Alert**   SQL Server Performance Condition Alerts are based on SQL Server Performance Monitor Object Counters, a number of which were recovered in Chapter 29, "Database System Tuning."

- **WMI Event Alert**   Windows Management Instrumentation (WMI) event alerts are based on particular SQL Server-related events occuring that are being monitored by the WMI provider for server events, which SQL Server Agent monitors.

> **Note**   The WMI layer is Microsoft's Web-Based Enterprise Management (WBEM)-compliant implementation of the Common Information Model (CIM) initiative developed by the Distributed ManagementTask Force (DMTF). For information on the WMI, go to *http://msdn.microsoft.com/library/default.asp?url=/library/en-us/dnwmi/html/wmioverview.asp*.

The WMI provider for server events manages a WMI namespace for each instance of SQL Server 2005. The namespace has the \.\root\Microsoft\SqlServer\ServerEvents\*instance_name* format, with the default SQL Server 2005 instance using the MSSQLSERVER instance name. There are two categories of events that make up the programming model for the WMI provider for server events: the DDL and SQL trace events. The following list represents the set of DDL events:

**DDL_DATABASE_LEVEL_EVENTS**

  **DDL_ASSEMBLY_EVENTS**

- CREATE_ASSEMBLY, ALTER_ASSEMBLY, DROP_ASSEMBLY

  **DDL_DATABASE_SECURITY_EVENTS**

    **DDL_APPLICATION_ROLE_EVENTS**

- CREATE_APPLICATION_ROLE, ALTER_APPLICATION_ROLE, DROP_APPLICATION_ROLE

    **DDL_AUTHORIZATION_DATABASE_EVENTS**

- ALTER_AUTHORIZATION_DATABASE

    **DDL_CERTIFICATE_EVENTS**

- CREATE_CERTIFICATE, ALTER_CERTIFICATE, DROP_CERTIFICATE

    **DDL_GDR_DATABASE_EVENTS**

- GRANT_DATABASE, DENY_DATABASE, REVOKE_DATABASE

    **DDL_ROLE_EVENTS**

- CREATE_ROLE, ALTER_ROLE, DROP_ROLE

    **DDL_SCHEMA_EVENTS**

- CREATE_SCHEMA, ALTER_SCHEMA, DROP_SCHEMA

    **DDL_USER_EVENTS**

- CREATE_USER, DROP_USER, ALTER_USER

  **DDL_EVENT_NOTIFICATION_EVENTS**

- CREATE_EVENT_NOTIFICATION, DROP_EVENT_NOTIFICATION

  **DDL_FUNCTION_EVENTS**

- CREATE_FUNCTION, ALTER_FUNCTION, DROP_FUNCTION

  **DDL_PARTITION_EVENTS**

    **DDL_PARTITION_FUNCTION_EVENTS**

- CREATE_PARTITION_FUNCTION, ALTER_PARTITION_FUNCTION, DROP_PARTITION_FUNCTION

    **DDL_PARTITION_SCHEME_EVENTS**

- CREATE_PARTITION_SCHEME, ALTER_PARTITION_SCHEME, DROP_PARTITION_SCHEME

**DDL_PROCEDURE_EVENTS**

- CREATE_PROCEDURE, DROP_PROCEDURE, ALTER_PROCEDURE

## DDL_SSB_EVENTS

**DDL_CONTRACT_EVENTS**

- CREATE_CONTRACT, DROP_CONTRACT

**DDL_MESSAGE_TYPE_EVENTS**

- CREATE_MSGTYPE, ALTER_MSGTYPE, DROP_MSGTYPE

**DDL_QUEUE_EVENTS**

- CREATE_QUEUE, ALTER_QUEUE, DROP_QUEUE

**DDL_REMOTE_SERVICE_BINDING_EVENTS**

- CREATE_REMOTE_SERVICE_BINDING, ALTER_REMOTE_SERVICE_BINDING, DROP_REMOTE_SERVICE_BINDING

**DDL_ROUTE_EVENTS**

- CREATE_ROUTE, DROP_ROUTE, ALTER_ROUTE

**DDL_SERVICE_EVENTS**

- CREATE_SERVICE, DROP_SERVICE, ALTER_SERVICE

## DDL_SYNONYM_EVENTS

- CREATE_SYNONYM, DROP_SYNONYM

## DDL_TABLE_VIEW_EVENTS

**DDL_INDEX_EVENTS**

- CREATE_INDEX, DROP_INDEX, ALTER_INDEX, CREATE_XML_INDEX

**DDL_STATISTICS_EVENTS**

- CREATE_STATISTICS, UPDATE_STATISTICS, DROP_STATISTICS

**DDL_TABLE_EVENTS**

- CREATE_TABLE, ALTER_TABLE, DROP_TABLE

**DDL_VIEW_EVENTS**

- CREATE_VIEW, ALTER_VIEW, DROP_VIEW

## DDL_TRIGGER_EVENTS

- CREATE_TRIGGER, DROP_TRIGGER, ALTER_TRIGGER

## DDL_TYPE_EVENTS

- CREATE_TYPE, DROP_TYPE

**DDL_XML_SCHEMA_COLLECTION_EVENTS**

- CREATE_XML_SCHEMA_COLLECTION, ALTER_XML_SCHEMA_COLLECTION, DROP_XML_SCHEMA_COLLECTION

**DDL_SERVER_LEVEL_EVENTS**

- CREATE_DATABASE, ALTER_DATABASE, DROP_DATABASE

**DDL_ENDPOINT_EVENTS**

- CREATE_ENDPOINT, ALTER_ENDPOINT, DROP_ENDPOINT

**DDL_SERVER_SECURITY_EVENTS**

- ADD_ROLE_MEMBER, ADD_SERVER_ROLE_MEMBER, DROP_ROLE_MEMBER, DROP_SERVER_ROLE_MEMBER

**DDL_AUTHORIZATION_SERVER_EVENTS**

- ALTER_AUTHORIZATION_ SERVER

**DDL_GDR_SERVER_EVENTS**

- GRANT_SERVER, DENY_SERVER, REVOKE_SERVER

**DDL_LOGIN_EVENTS**

- CREATE_LOGIN, ALTER_LOGIN, DROP_LOGIN

The following list represents the set of SQL trace events:

**TRC_CLR**

- ASSEMBLY_LOAD

**TRC_DATABASE**

- DATA_FILE_AUTO_GROW, DATA_FILE_AUTO_SHRINK, DATABASE_MIRRORING_STATE_CHANGE, LOG_FILE_AUTO_GROW, LOG_FILE_AUTO_SHRINK

**TRC_DEPRECATION**

- DEPRECATION_ANNOUNCEMENT, DEPRECATION_FINAL_SUPPORT

**TRC_ERRORS_AND_WARNINGS**

- BLOCKED_PROCESS_REPORT, ERRORLOG, EVENTLOG, EXCEPTION, EXCHANGE_SPILL_EVENT, EXECUTION_WARNINGS, HASH_WARNING, MISSING_COLUMN_STATISTICS, MISSING_JOIN_PREDICATE, SORT_WARNINGS, USER_ERROR_MESSAGE

### TRC_FULL_TEXT

■   FT_CRAWL_ABORTED, FT_CRAWL_STARTED, FT_CRAWL_STOPPED

### TRC_LOCKS

■   DEADLOCK_GRAPH, LOCK_DEADLOCK, LOCK_DEADLOCK_CHAIN, LOCK_ESCALATION

### TRC_OBJECTS

■   OBJECT_ALTERED, OBJECT_CREATED, OBJECT_DELETED

### TRC_OLEDB

■   OLEDB_CALL_EVENT, OLEDB_DATAREAD_EVENT, OLEDB_ERRORS, OLEDB_PROVIDER_INFORMATION, OLEDB_QUERYINTERFACE_EVENT

### TRC_PERFORMANCE

■   SHOWPLAN_ALL_FOR_QUERY_COMPILE, SHOWPLAN_XML, SHOWPLAN_XML_FOR_QUERY_COMPILE, SHOWPLAN_XML_STATISTICS_PROFILE

### TRC_QUERY_NOTIFICATIONS

■   QN_DYNAMICS, QN_PARAMETER_TABLE, QN_SUBSCRIPTION, QN_TEMPLATE

### TRC_SECURITY_AUDIT

■   AUDIT_ADD_DB_USER_EVENT, AUDIT_ADDLOGIN_EVENT, AUDIT_ADD_LOGIN_TO_SERVER_ROLE_EVENT, AUDIT_ADD_MEMBER_TO_DB_ROLE_EVENT, AUDIT_ADD_ROLE_EVENT, AUDIT_APP_ROLE_CHANGE_PASSWORD_EVENT, AUDIT_BACKUP_RESTORE_EVENT, AUDIT_CHANGE_AUDIT_EVENT, AUDIT_CHANGE_DATABASE_OWNER, AUDIT_DATABASE_MANAGEMENT_EVENT, AUDIT_DATABASE_OBJECT_ACCESS_EVENT, AUDIT_DATABASE_OBJECT_GDR_EVENT, AUDIT_DATABASE_OBJECT_MANAGEMENT_EVENT, AUDIT_DATABASE_OBJECT_TAKE_OWNERSHIP_EVENT, AUDIT_DATABASE_OPERATION_EVENT, AUDIT_DATABASE_PRINCIPAL_IMPERSONATION_EVENT, AUDIT_DATABASE_PRINCIPAL_MANAGEMENT_EVENT

AUDIT_DATABASE_SCOPE_GDR_EVENT, AUDIT_DBCC_EVENT,
AUDIT_LOGIN, AUDIT_LOGIN_CHANGE_PASSWORD_EVENT,
AUDIT_LOGIN_CHANGE_PROPERTY_EVENT, AUDIT_LOGIN_FAILED,
AUDIT_LOGIN_GDR_EVENT, AUDIT_LOGOUT,
AUDIT_SCHEMA_OBJECT_ACCESS_EVENT,
AUDIT__SCHEMA_OBJECT_GDR_EVENT,
AUDIT_SCHEMA_OBJECT_MANAGEMENT_EVENT,
AUDIT_SCHEMA_OBJECT_TAKE_OWNERSHIP_EVENT,
AUDIT_SERVER_ALTER_TRACE_EVENT,
AUDIT_SERVER_OBJECT_GDR_EVENT,
AUDIT_SERVER_OBJECT_MANAGEMENT_EVENT ,
AUDIT_SERVER_OBJECT_TAKE_OWNERSHIP_EVENT,
AUDIT_SERVER_OPERATION_EVENT,
AUDIT_SERVER_PRINCIPAL_IMPERSONATION_EVENT,
AUDIT_SERVER_PRINCIPAL_MANAGEMENT_EVENT,
AUDIT_SERVER_SCOPE_GDR_EVENT

**TRC_SERVER**

■ MOUNT_TAPE, SERVER_MEMORY_CHANGE, TRACE_FILE_CLOSE

**TRC_STORED_PROCEDURES**

■ SP_CACHEINSERT, SP_CACHEMISS, SP_ CACHEREMOVE, SP_RECOMPILE

**TRC_TSQL**

■ SQL_STMTRECOMPILE, XQUERY_STATIC_TYPE

**TRC_USER_CONFIGURABLE**

■ USERCONFIGURABLE_0, USERCONFIGURABLE_1, USERCONFIGURABLE_2,
USERCONFIGURABLE_3, USERCONFIGURABLE_4, USERCONFIGURABLE_5,
USERCONFIGURABLE_6, USERCONFIGURABLE_7, USERCONFIGURABLE_8,
USERCONFIGURABLE_9

---

**More Info**   Notice you have 10 user-settable SQL trace events that you can
customize for your purposes. For more information on the how to implement
there user-settable objects search on the topic "SQL Server, User Settable Object"
topic in SQL Server 2005 Books Online.

To define a SQL Server Agent Alert, follow these steps:

1. Start SQL Server Management Studio and connect to your SQL Server instance. Expand the SQL Server Agent folder in Object Explorer, right-click the Alerts folder, and choose the New Alert option. The New Alert window appears, as shown in Figure 30-29. By default, it shows a SQL Server event alert. Give the new alert a unique name.

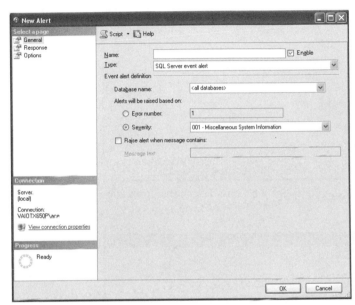

**Figure 30-29**   New Alert window.

2. As discussed above, SQL Server Agent supports three different types of alerts that can be configured on the General page. To generate a SQL Server event alert, select the database from the Database Name drop-down list against which the alert will fire. Select the criteria for the alert based on the error number, severity level, or particular string in the message text. Figure 30-30 shows an example of a SQL Server event alert that fires whenever the *AdventureWorks* database's transaction log is full. (An error number of 9002 is generated.)

   Alternatively, to generate a SQL Server performance condition alert, change the alert type to SQL Server performance condition alert. The General page should now allow you to type in the performance object, its counter, the particular instance, and the threshold of value. Figure 30-31 shows an example of a SQL Server performance condition alert that will fire whenever the *AdventureWorks* database's transaction log rises above 90 percent full.

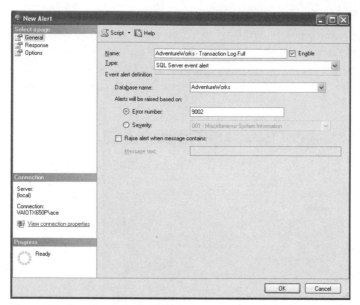

**Figure 30-30**   SQL Server Event Alert based on Transaction Log Full error message.

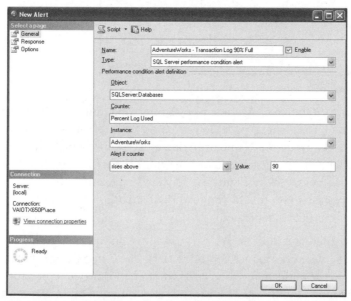

**Figure 30-31**   SQL Server Performance Condition Alert based on Transaction Log object counter rising above 90 percent threshold.

Alternatively, to generate a WMI event alert, change the alert type to WMI event alert. The General page should allows you to change the namespace to the appropriate SQL Server instance and the WQL query that will poll the WMI interface. Figure 30-32 shows an example of a WMI event alert that fires whenever there is a deadlock within the *AdventureWorks* database.

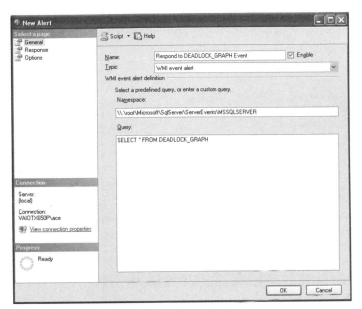

**Figure 30-32**   WMI Alert based on deadlock event.

> **Note**   The WMI Query Language (WQL) is a simple language based on SQL that is used to query the WMI layer of the Windows operating system.

3. Once you have defined the appropriate SQL Server Agent alert, you must configure the course of action SQL Server Agent should take. Click on the Response page, as shown in Figure 30-33. To execute a job whenever the alert fires, select the Execute Job check box and choose an existing job or define a new job. To notify someone whenever the alert fires, click the Notify Operators check box and select the appropriate operators.

4. To define a new operator, click the New Operator button. The New Operator window, shown in Figure 30-34, appears. Configure the operator's notification options at the details and click the OK button.

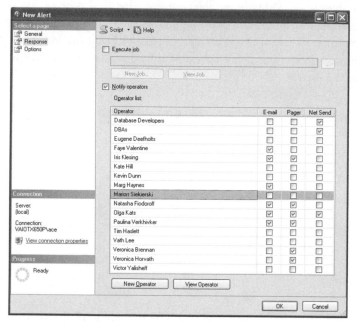

**Figure 30-33**    New Alert—Response page.

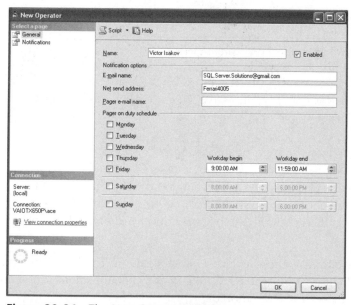

**Figure 30-34**    The New Operator window.

5. Once you have defined SQL Server Agent alert's response, click the Response page. The Options page appears, as shown in Figure 30-35. Configure whether you want the alert error message in the operator's notification, any additional message text, and the delay between responses.

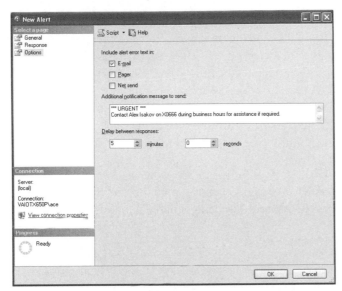

**Figure 30-35**    New Alert—Options page.

> **Note**    Note that you can configure the Delay Between Responses setting to an appropriate level, depending on either functional requirements or technical constraints, so that it does not overload SQL Server Agent alert engine. This can be particularly useful for alerts that will potentially fire rapidly in a short period of time. As this setting value can be very subjective, most DBAs leave the setting with the default value unless SQL Server Agent fires too many alerts for a given condition in a give space of time.

# Executing T-SQL Statements

SQL Server Managment Studio, supplied with SQL Server 2005, has replaced Query Analyzer as the tool to write T-SQL queries and develop database objects. It provides a rich environment for debugging, analyzing, and optimizing T-SQL code. To use SQL Server Managment Studio to execute T-SQL statements, follow these steps:

1. Start SQL Server Management Studio and connect to your SQL Server instance. Make sure the correct server is highlighted in Object Explorer and click the New

Query button on the top toolbar, or select the Query with Current Connection menu item from the File menu. A blank query pane should appear. In the database drop-down list at the top of the toolbar, select the database in which you want to run your T-SQL statements.

2.  Type in the T-SQL script you want to execute. Notice that SQL Server Managment Studio color-codes the T-SQL statements for you. You can check the syntax of your T-SQL script by clicking the Parse button (the blue tick mark) on the toolbar. To run your T-SQL script, click the Execute button (red exclamation mark followed by Execute) or press F5 (Alt-x also works). When executing your T-SQL script, you can direct the Results to either text, a grid, or a file. This is done by choosing either the Results to Text (Ctrl-T shortcut), Results to Grid (Ctrl-D shortcut), or Results to File (Ctrl+Shift+F shortcut) button on the toolbar. Figure 30-36 shows the Results of a T-SQL query output to text.

3.  You can save the resultset by right-clicking anywhere in the Results pane and choosing the Save Results As option. The type of file depends on the Results pane type.

---

**Note**   If you have executed your T-SQL query to a grid, you can also highlight cells of interest, copy them, and paste them into Microsoft Excel.

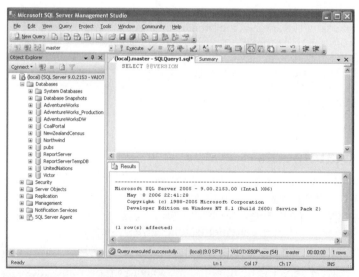

**Figure 30-36**   An executed T-SQL statement.

If you are unfamiliar or new to the T-SQL language, you can take advantage of the graphical Query Designer tool in SQL Server Managment Studio to build your T-SQL query graphically. To use the Query Designer, follow these steps:

1. Start SQL Server Management Studio and connect to your SQL Server instance. Navigate to the database and click on it in Object Explorer. Click the New Query button on the top toolbar, or select the Query with Current Connection menu item from the File menu. Right click on the Query pane in SQL Server Managment Studio and select the Design Query In Editor option. The Query Designer window appears with the Add Table dialog box to get you started. Figure 30-37 shows an example of the Add Table dialog box for the *AdventureWorks* database.

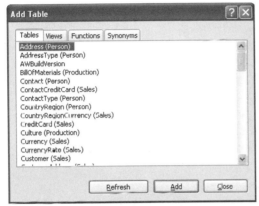

**Figure 30-37**   Add Table dialog box.

2. Add the tables, views, functions, and synonyms that your T-SQL query will be accessing through the Add button. Click the Close button when you're finished. The Query Designer should automatically link the tables together if foreign key constraints have been defined between the tables. You can make the window larger and resize the panes to fit the tables and get more details and select items graphically. You can link a tables together by dragging a field from the parent table to the child table. You can change the type of a join that your query will use by right clicking the links between the tables. Figure 30-38 shows an example of a query within the *AdventureWorks* database accessing the [HumanResources].[Employee], [HumanResources].[EmployeeAddress], [Person].[Address], [Person].[Contact] and [Person].[StateProvince] tables.

3. Select the fields that your query will use by checking the appropriate check boxes. The query designer automatically starts to construct the query for you in the bottom pane. Figure 30-39 shows an example based on the tables chosen in the previous step.

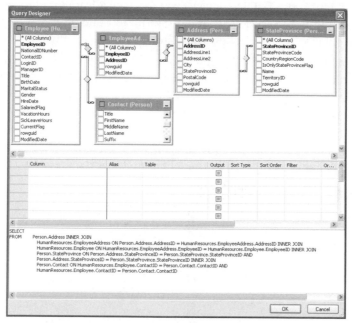

**Figure 30-38**   Query Designer windows with tables.

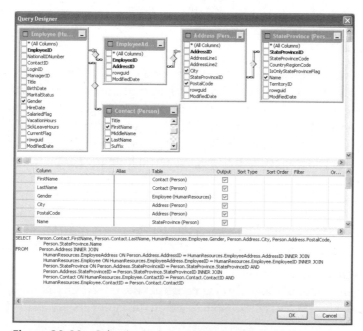

**Figure 30-39**   Selecting columns in Query Designer window.

4.  You can also type in column names or expressions into the Column column. To order the results, modify the Sort Type and Sort Order columns. To restrict the records to be returned, type in a value or expression into the Filter and subsequent Or columns. Sometimes, it is easier to modify the T-SQL statement directly in the bottom pane. Figure 30-40 shows an example of a completed query against the *AdventureWorks* database.

5.  Once you have completed your T-SQL statement, click the OK button to return to SQL Server Managment Studio environment.

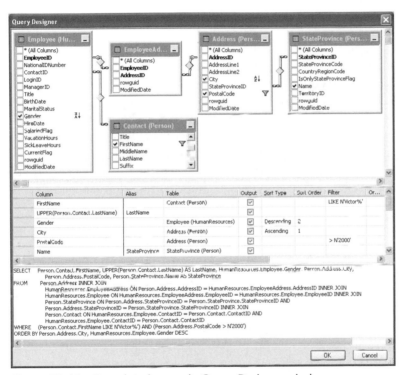

**Figure 30-40**   Completed query in Query Designer window.

# Viewing Execution Plans

SQL Server Management Studio environment has the ability to display the execution plan that SQL Server 2005's query optimizer chose when executing a particular T-SQL statement. This feature can help you determine whether your T-SQL statements are executing efficiently or whether corrective action is necessary. This typically involves either rewriting the query or redesigning your indexing strategy. In certain cases, however, you will have to resort to overriding the optimizer through optimizer hints. (Make sure you always document the reasons for overriding the optimizer for future reference.)

> **Note**    The execution plan describes how the query optimizer executed a T-SQL statement within a batch. The plan shows the different types of operations that needed to be performed, the order in which they were performed, and the data access method used to retrieve data from the tables (index scan, index seek, or table scan). It shows which steps consumed the most resources and/or time within both the T-SQL statement and batch. Watch out for expensive operations such as table scans and hash joins.

SQL Server Managment Studio has the ability to display both the estimated execution plan and the actual execution plan. With the *estimated* execution plan, your T-SQL script is only parsed and an execution plan estimated based on the best efforts of SQL Server Managment Studio. The *actual* execution plan, on the other hand, can be generated only when your T-SQL script is actually executed. Be careful of the estimated execution plan because SQL Server does not guarantee that it will be the same as the actual execution plan at runtime. Developers typically use the estimated execution plan as an indication of how their T-SQL query is going to perform without consuming the resources of the SQL Server instance, which could have a dramatic impact on performance in a production environment.

To use SQL Server Managment Studio to view the actual execution plan of a T-SQL statement, follow these steps:

1.  Start SQL Server Management Studio and connect to your SQL Server instance. Navigate to the database and click on it in Object Explorer. Click the New Query button on the top toolbar. Type the T-SQL statement you are interested in analyzing, click the Include Actual Execution Plan button (or press Ctl-M) on the top toolbar, and execute your T-SQL script. An execution plan, similar to that shown in Figure 30-41, should be seen in bottom pane of SQL Server Managment Studio.

> **Note**    There is a lot of rich information located in the graphical execution plan that can be easily overlooked. For example, the width of the arrows linking the various nodes together indicates the amount of the data that was passed from one operation to the other. Holding the mouse over one of these arrows actually shows you the actual number of rows generated amongst other information.

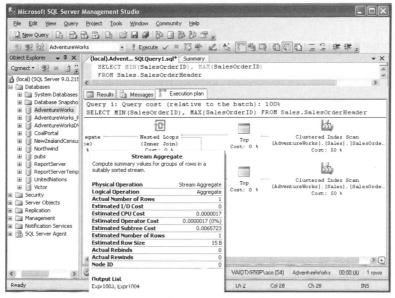

**Figure 30-41**   Examining the query execution plan.

2. To get more information about each individual step in the execution plan, hover your mouse over a particular operation. This causes a tool tip to appear, which will have more information about the operation as follows:

❑ **Physical Operation**   The physical operation performed by the query, such as a Bookmark Lookup, Hash Join, Nested Loop, and so on. Physical operators correspond to an execution algorithm and have costs associated with them.

---

**Note**   Watch for physical operators in the execution plan that are displayed in red, as this indicates some sort of a problem that the optimiser has detected, such as missing statistics.

---

❑ **Logical Operation**   The relational algebraic operation used that matches the physical operation; typically logical operation can be implemented by various physical operators.

❑ **Actual Number of Rows**   The actual number of rows returned by this operation.

❑ **Estimated I/O Cost**   The estimated cost of all I/O resources for this operation. (This should be as low as possible.)

❑ **Estimated CPU Cost**   The estimated cost of all CPU resources for this operation.

❑ **Estimated Operator Cost**   The estimated cost of performing this operation (This cost is also represented as a percentage of the overall cost of the query. in parentheses.)

❑ **Estimated Subtree Cost**   The estimated cost of performing this operation and all proceeding operations in its subtree.

❑ **Estimated Number of Rows**   The estimated number of rows returned by this operation.

---

**Note**   Watch out for a large discrepancy between the estimated number of rows value and actual number of rows value.

---

❑ **Estimated Row Size**   The estimated size of the Rovers, in bytes, retrieved by the operation.

❑ **Actual Rebinds/Actual Rewinds**   The number of times the physical operator needed to initialise itself and set up any internal data structures. A rebind indicates that the input parameters changed and a re-evaluation was done. The rewind indicates that existing structures were used.

❑ **Ordered**   Whether the rows returned by this operation are ordered.

❑ **Node ID**   A unique identifier for the node.

❑ **Object/Remote Object**   The database object that this operation accessed.

❑ **Output List**   The list of outputs for this particular operation.

---

**More Info**   For more information on the different types of logical operators that SQL Server's optimizer has available, search on the topic "Graphical Execution Plan Icons (SQL Server Management Studio)" in SQL Server 2005 Books Online.

---

3. SQL Server Managment Studio also has the capability to provide client statistics, which can also provide some important metrics when testing your T-SQL statements. It can also automatically average multiple executions of your T-SQL statement to get rid of any environmental anomalies and highlight whether there has been a decrease or an increase in the metrics returned. To view the client statistics,

click the Include Client Statistics button (which is located to the right of the Include Actual Execution Plan button), or press Shift+Alt+S. Figure 30-42 shows an example of two executions of the same T-SQL statement and the client statistics metrics returned.

---

**Note**   The client statistics are not automatically reset for a given user connection in SQL Server Managment Studio. So if you change your T-SQL query, you should also reset the cllient statistics. This can be done by clicking on the Query menu and selecting the Reset Client Statistics option.

---

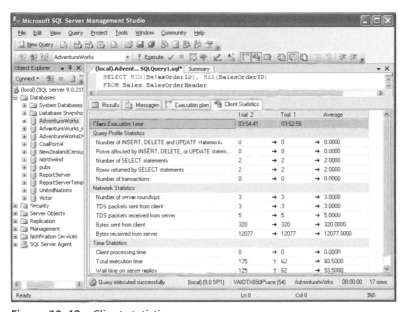

Figure 30-42   Client statistics.

---

# Using SQL Server Profiler

As you have seen, you can use SQL Server Management Studio to analyse and fine tune T-SQL statements. However, it will not help you to find which queries are potentially inefficient in your database solution. If you are interested in identifying the different types of queries and T-SQL statements that are being executed by various client applications inside your particular environment, you will have to use a tool such as SQL Server Profiler.

SQL Server Profiler is a very powerful utility that basically tries to capture the network activity between client applications and your SQL Server instance by listening in on the Tabular Data Stream (TDS). SQL Server Profiler can display this captured trace information in a very rich graphical environment, providing sorting and filtering capabilities that allow you to easily locate T-SQL statements of interest. It is particularly useful when working with third-party vendor applications over which you have no control, and you either want to learn more about how they work or perform-tune/troubleshoot them.

## Capturing a SQL Server Profile Trace

To start SQL Server Profiler and capture a trace, follow these steps:

1. Click Start, All Programs, Microsoft SQL Server 2005, and Performance Tools and start SQL Server Profiler. When SQL Server Profiler first starts, it is blank because there are no traces running. The first thing you'll have to do is connect to your SQL Server instance. Click on the File menu and then New Trace (or press Ctrl-N) to connect to your SQL Server instance. Type your server name and authentication details, and then click the Connect button.

2. The Trace Properties Windows appears, as shown in Figure 30-43. To start profiling you need to create a new trace. Although you can create your own trace from scratch, the easiest way to create a trace is to use one of the predefined templates created by Microsoft. This saves time because you don't have to set up traces from scratch all the time. Don't forget that you can further customize what information these pre-defined traces gather or create templates specific to your particular requirements as required. SQL Server Profiler comes with the following predefined trace templates:

   ❑ *SP_Counts*    Collects all stored procedures that have been issued. The trace returns the results grouped by the stored procedure name and includes the number of times the stored procedure was executed. The *SP_Counts* template captures information for the SP:Starting event class.

   ❑ **Standard**    Collects general information about all connections, stored procedures, and T-SQL batches that have been issued. Use the Standard template as a generic trace to monitor general activity. The Standard template captures information for the following event classes: Audit Login, AuditLogout, ExistingConnection, RPC:Completed, SQL:BatchCompleted, SQL:Batch-Starting. The *Standard* template is the default trace.

❑ **TSQL**   Collects all T-SQL statements that have been issued and the time issued. Use the TSQL template to debug client applications. The TSQL template captures information for the following event classes: Audit Login, Audit Logout, ExistingConnection, RPC:Starting, SQL:BatchStarting.

❑ **TSQL_Duration**   Collects all T-SQL statements that have been issued and their execution time (milliseconds), and groups them by this execution time. Use the TSQL_Duration template to identify slow queries. The TSQL_Duration template captures information for the following event classes: RPC:Completed, SQL:BatchCompleted.

❑ **TSQL_Grouped**   Collects information identical to the TSQL trace, but groups that information by either the users or client applications that issued the T-SQL statements. Use the TSQL_Grouped template to investigate users or client applications. The TSQL_Grouped template captures information for the following event classes: Audit Login, Audit Logout, ExistingConnection, RPC:Starting, SQL:BatchStarting.

❑ **TSQL_Replay**   Collects detailed information about the T-SQL statements that have been issued so that they can be replayed. Use the TSQL_Replay template for iterative tuning, benchmark, or unit testing. The TSQL_Replay template captures information for the following event classes: CursorClose, CursorExecute, CursorOpen, CursorPrepare, CursorUnprepare, Audit Login, Audit Logout, Existing Connection, RPC Output Parameter, RPC:Completed, RPC:Starting, Exec Prepared SQL, Prepare SQL, SQL:BatchCompleted, SQL:BatchStarting.

❑ **TSQL_SPs**   Collects detailed information about the stored procedures calls that have been issued. Use the TSQL_SPs template to analyze the individual statements within the stored procedures. The TSQL_SPs template captures information for the following event classes: Audit Login, AuditLogout, ExistingConnection, RPC:Starting, SP:Completed, SP:Starting, SP:StmtStarting, SQL:BatchStarting.

---

**Note**   Add the SP:Recompile event if you suspect that procedures are being recompiled.

---

❑ **Tuning**   Collects information about T-SQL statements and stored procedures that have been issued for tuning purposes. The Tuning template captures information for the following event classes: RPC:Completed, SP:StmtCompleted, SQL:BatchCompleted.

---

**Note**    Use the Tuning template to generate a workload file for the Database Engine Tuning Advisor when tuning your databases.

---

In the General tab, provide an appropriate name and select the appropriate template from the Use the Template drop-down list. You can choose whether you want to save the trace to a file or table, in which case you will have to provide the appropriate details. If neither of these is selected, the trace is automatically displayed. Additionally, you can specify time for the trace to finish, which can be useful in situations where you want to monitor activity for the remainder of the day and are not planning to be around to stop the trace.

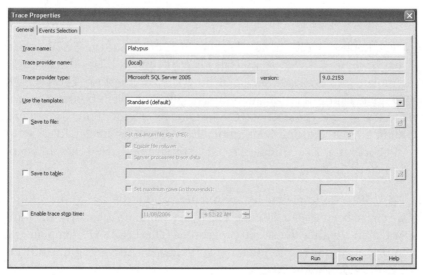

**Figure 30-43**    General tab of the Trace Properties window.

3. Click the Events Selection tab, shown in Figure 30-44. This tab allows you to further refine the events that you would like the trace to capture. Depending on the template chosen, there will be a number of events already ticked. You can add or remove event columns to trace by clicking the appropriate check box. You can click both the event or an event column to see their descriptions at the bottom of the Events Selection tab.

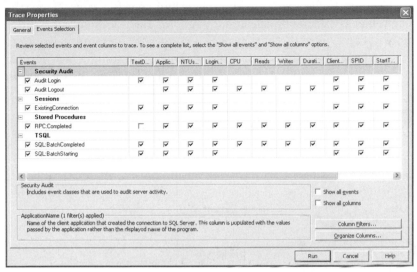

**Figure 30-44**   Events Selection tab of the Trace Properties window.

4.   To see the complete list of events and/or columns, click the Show All Events and Show All Columns check boxes, as displayed in Figure 30-45.

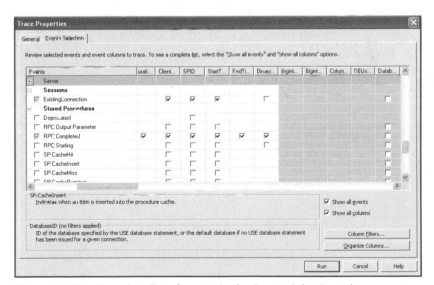

**Figure 30-45**   Complete list of events in the Events Selection tab.

5.   To further filter what information is going to be captured by SQL Server Profiler, click the Column Filters button. The Edit Filter dialog box appears, as shown in

Figure 30-46, and allows you to include or exclude specific events. Notice that SQL Server Profiler is excluded by default. By refining the trace definition through filtering, you can reduce the impact of SQL Server Profiler and make it easier to search and to read the trace after it has completed running. Once you have finished examining or configuring your column filters, click on the OK button.

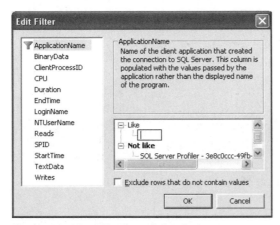

**Figure 30-46**   Edit Filter dialog box.

6. If you want to control how the trace will group events, click the Organize Columns button. The Organise Columns dialog box, shown in Figure 30-48, appears. Use the Up and Down button to change the order of the columns or their grouping. Once you have finished examining or organizing your column, click on the OK button.

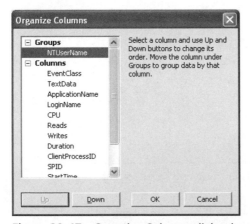

**Figure 30-47**   Organize Columns dialog box.

7. Once you have finished configuring your trace properties, click the Run button to start the trace. Once the trace has started, events will appear in real time. You can pause, start, and stop the trace through the appropriate buttons located in the top toolbar. Figure 30-48 shows SQL Server Profiler running a trace.

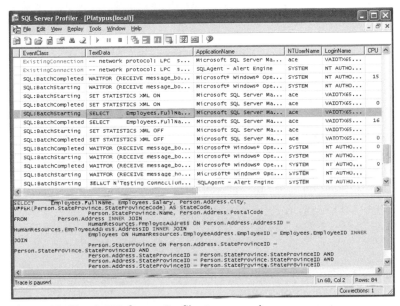

**Figure 30-48**  A SQL Server Profiler trace running.

8. Once you have captured a trace, you can save it to a file for further analysis or auditing purposes. To save your trace, click on the File menu and select the Save option. Once you have saved a trace file you can additionally save it to other formats, such as an XML file through the Save As option in the File menu.

---

**Note**  A saved SQL Server Profiler trace is commonly referred to as a workload file, as it represents the work done against your SQL Server instance. This workload file can be used to tune your database solution through the Database Engine Tuning Advisor, which we will be covering shortly.

---

SQL Server Profiler environment also has some rudimentary searching capabilities. Depending on the type of trace you have captured, you also can replay the trace as well, which can be particularly useful for advanced troubleshooting or testing purposes, in which case there are some nice features to step through a trace, pause a trace, set break-points, and run to the cursor location within the trace.

### Saving Traces to Database Tables

I particularly like saving a SQL Server Profiler trace to a table in a SQL Server data-base because it allows me then to use all of T-SQL language's powerful searching and aggregating capabilities. It also allows me to quite easily delete unwanted trace information, which can be very useful because there can be a lot of superfluous information captured in a trace at times.

## Correlating a SQL Profiler Trace with Performance Log Data

A new feature in SQL Server 2005 is the ability of SQL Server Profiler to correlate per-formance metrics collected with the Performance Logs and Alerts tool, as shown in Chapter 29, with SQL Server 2005 or Analysis Services 2005 events. This allows the DBA to easily see the impact of identified T-SQL statements on the operating system and hardware resources. To correlate a SQL Server Profiler trace with performance metrics, follow these steps:

1. Define and start a Counter log of the performance objects and/or counters you are interested in using the Performance Logs and Alerts tool, as shown in Chapter 29.

2. Define and start a trace of your SQL Server instance using SQL Server Profiler, as discussed above.

3. Stop the Counter log.

4. Stop SQL Server Profiler trace. Click the File menu and then the Save option (or press Ctrl-S) to save the captured trace to an appropriate location.

5. Open the saved SQL Server Profiler trace by clicking the File menu and then select-ing the Open, Trace File option (or press Ctrl-O).

6. To correlate the performance metrics from the counter log, click the File menu option and choose the Import Performance Data option. The Open File dialog box appears. Select the appropriate counter log and click the Open button.

7. The Performance Counters Limit dialog box appears, as shown in Figure 30-49. Check the name of your SQL Server instance and the appropriate performance monitor counters. Click the OK button.

**Figure 30-49**   Performance Counters Limit dialog box.

8.   SQL Server Profiler window should now look like Figure 30-50, showing both the captured T-SQL activity and the Counter log performance metrics across the timeline.

9.   You can show and hide the performance object counters by right clicking them and choosing the appropriate option in the menu, as shown in Figure 30-52. Notice you also have the capability of going to a minimum and a maximum value.

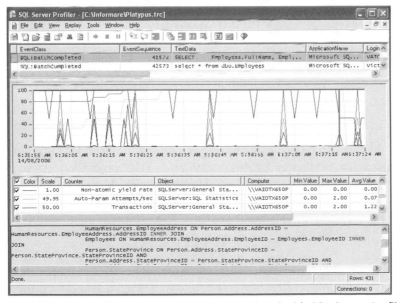

**Figure 30-50**   Performance Counter Log correlated with SQL Server Profiler trace.

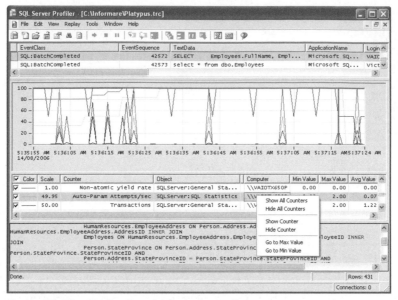

**Figure 30-51** Navigating through the Performance Log metrics.

# Using the Database Engine Tuning

The Database Engine Tuning Advisor, available with SQL Server 2005, has replaced the Index Tuning Wizard that was available in earlier versions of SQL Server. It can analyze trace activity captured through SQL Server Profiler or a T-SQL work load script against your database and recommend various performance tuning enhancements. These performance tuning enhancements can include creating and dropping indexes, or implementing indexed views or a partitioning strategy if you have the correct edition of SQL Server 2005.

The Database Engine Tuning Advisor can now recommend a number of performance enhancements across a number of databases simultaneously from a single trace or workload file. Although you can limit the amount of time you want the Database Engine Tuning Advisor to spend analyzing the workload, it is generally not recommended because the more time the Database Engine Tuning Advisor spends analyzing the workload, the quality of its recommendations increases.

The Database Engine Tuning Advisor analysis generates a list of recommendations that can be converted into it XML script or a series of T-SQL scripts. You can evaluate these recommendations and apply them as necessary. The various reports that are produced summarized different aspects of the workload and the results. Consider saving these reports as part of your change management routines.

---

**Note**   You should use the Database Engine Tuning Advisor in preference of the Index Tuning Wizard for tuning your SQL Server 2000 databases because it will do a superior job of recommending performance enhancements. The Database Engine Tuning Advisor is "SQL Server 2000 aware" and will make only recommendations that apply to SQL Server 2000.

---

To use the Database Engine Tuning Advisor, follow these steps:

1. Click Start, All Programs, Microsoft SQL Server 2005, and Performance Tools, and start Database Engine Tuning Advisor. Type your server name and authentication details, and then click the Connect button.

2. Type an appropriate session name. Type the details of the location of the workload file. Click the database you want to tune. Filter out any tables as appropriate using the drop-down list in the Selected Tables column. Figure 30-52 shows a tuning session being configured for the *AdventureWorks* database, including all its tables.

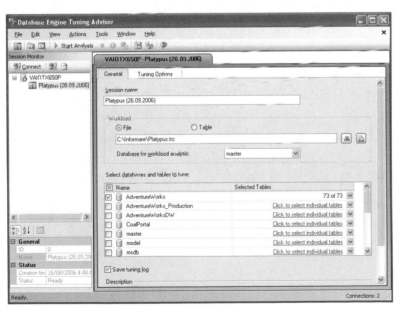

**Figure 30-52**   Database Engine Tuning Advisor.

3.  Click the Tuning Options tab. The Tuning Options tab, as shown in Figure 30-53, allows you to further refine the potential recommendations that the Database Engine Tuning Advisor makes. As indicated before, try not to limit the tuning time, as you might not get optimal recommendations. You can reduce the amount of time the Database Engine Tuning Advisor by reducing tuning options that you do not want it to consider. Select the appropriate combination of options. If in doubt as to what options to choose, leave the defaults alone.

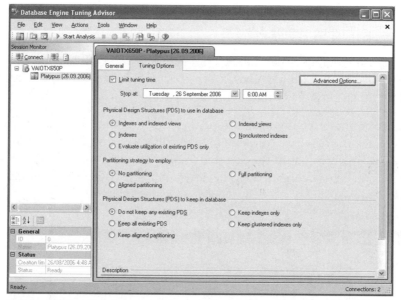

**Figure 30-53**    Database Engine Tuning Advisor Tuning Options.

4.  Click the Advanced Options button. The Advanced Tuning Options dialog box, shown in Figure 30-54, allows you to further refine the tuning options. Review and change these options as appropriate.  Click the OK button when you have finished.

5.  Click the Start Analysis button on the toolbar. Figure 30-55 shows the progress of the analysis.

6. Once the Database Engine Tuning Advisor has finished its analysis, it will generate a Recommendations window, as shown in Figure 30-56. You can choose to ignore a recommendation by deselecting the check box associated with it.

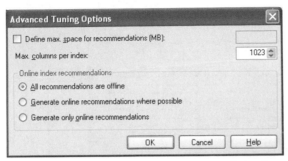

**Figure 30-54**   Advanced Tuning Options dialog box.

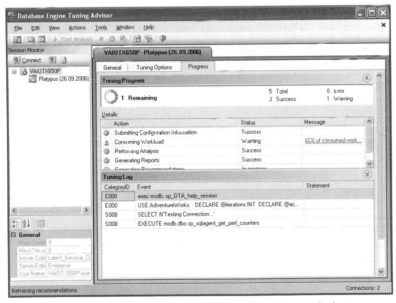

**Figure 30-55**   Database Engine Tuning Advisor Progress window.

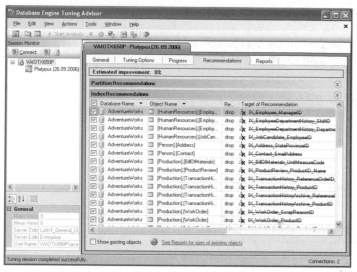

**Figure 30-56**    Database Engine Tuning Advisor Recommendations window.

7.  To see the T-SQL script that would be used to implement a recommendation, scroll to the right until you see the Definition column and click the recommendations hyperlink. The SQL Script Preview window, shown in Figure 30-57, is generated. You can copy the T-SQL script to the clipboard, if required. Click the Close button when you're finished.

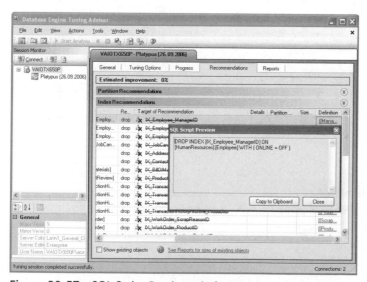

**Figure 30-57**    SQL Script Preview window.

8. Click the Reports tab. This tab provides a summary of the Database Engine Tuning Advisor session. A number of different tuning reports are also available in the bottom half of the window. You can click on the Select report drop-down list to see a list of the available reports that have been generated and view them individially. Figure 30-58 shows an example output of the "Index detail report (current)" report.

9. To save the results, click on the File menu and choose the Export Session Results option, specifying the location and name of the XML file.

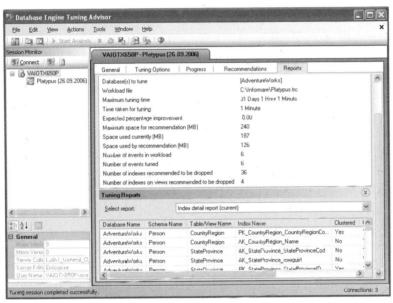

**Figure 30-58**   Database Engine Tuning Advisor Reports window.

# Summary

In this chapter, you learned about the various tools that SQL Server 2005 has to offer the DBA. You learned the various components of SQL Server Managment Studio and how to view the new summary reports to get a quick indication of how your SQL Server is performing, analyze the various logs, and view the current activity on your SQL Server instance.

In addition, you learned how to set up SQL Server alerts based either on error messages, performance monitor object counters, or WMI events.

You then learned how to use SQL Server Managment Studio to generate the execution plan for T-SQL queries for analysis, so as to be able to see how they are being executed by SQL Server's query optimizer.

Finally, you learned how to use SQL Server Profiler tool to capture the network traffic between the client applications and a SQL Server instance for analysis, and how to use this trace file with the Database Engine Tuning Advisor and optimise your database design.

# Dynamic Management Views

Analyzing and tuning database performance is more an art than a science. There can be many reasons why performance may be suboptimal—insufficient memory, incorrectly configured system parameters, disk bottlenecks, and poorly written queries being just a few of the more common causes. Understanding the operational details and the possible cause of the problem is often more difficult and time-consuming than actually taking the corrective actions. Anything that helps you get to the bottom of the problem quickly helps save time, effort, and cost. SQL Server 2005 introduces more than 80 new *Dynamic Management Views* (DMVs) which, as the name suggests, are views built on top of system tables to surface the dynamically changing information about the database engine. These views present the internal operational statistics of the various components of the engine in a meaningful and easily comprehendible way.

In this chapter, we'll take a look at the new DMV functionality and how it simplifies the tasks of performance tuning and analysis of the database operation as compared to earlier versions of SQL Server. We will also take a detailed look at each of the new DMVs and see for what each can be most effectively used. Lastly, we will take a look at creating a simple performance data warehouse that can be used to archive historical performance data for analysis at a later time.

## Understanding Dynamic Management Views

In earlier versions of SQL Server troubleshooting, a performance problem usually involved using tools like Windows System Monitor (perfmon.exe) and SQL Server Profiler, configured with the relevant set of counters and events, and waiting to capture a snapshot of the problem when it occurred. This was tedious and often invasive to the application performance, sometimes to a point where the overhead of the tools on the system and application would cause the problem to not reproduce. All in all, the entire process was somewhat trial-and-error based and was not always reliable. Those of you who have investigated performance problems with earlier versions of SQL Server will be able to relate to this and appreciate the powers and flexibility that DMVs offer.

DMVs are system views that surface the internal counters of the database engine and help present an easily comprehendible dashboard of the database engine performance that can be used to monitor the health of a server instance, diagnose problems, and tune performance. Unlike tools like Windows System Monitor (perfmon.exe) and SQL Server Profiler that need to be explicitly invoked and set up to collect the data events of interest, DMVs are always active and constantly collecting the performance data for the instance of SQL Server 2005. As the name suggests, DMVs are dynamic in nature, implying that the data they present represents the instantaneous state of the database engine. Because the state is constantly changing, successive queries to the same DMV usually produce different results. All dynamic management views and functions exist in the SYS schema and follow this naming convention: dm_*. When you use a dynamic management view or function, you must prefix the name of the view or function with the name of the schema. For example, the SELECT statement below uses a two-part name to reference the dm_exec_query_stats DMV:

```
SELECT * FROM sys.dm_exec_query_stats;
```

DMVs can only be referenced using two-part (for example, [sys].[dm_exec_query_stats]), three-part (for example, [master].[sys].[dm_exec_query_stats]), or four-part (for example, [HOTH\SS2K5].[master].[sys].[dm_exec_query_stats]) names. They cannot be referenced using one-part names (for example, [dm_exec_query_stats]). For the most part, DMVs report the absolute operational values of the underlying objects. These values can be correlated with values from other DMVs as well as computed on to derive more meaningful and easily comprehendible information. For example, the following statement uses the sys.dm_exec_query_stats and sys.dm_exec_sql_text DMVs to determine the hundred most frequently executed queries on the server in descending order:

```
SELECT TOP 100 execution_count,
    SUBSTRING(est.text, (eqs.statement_start_offset/2) + 1,
    ((CASE statement_end_offset
        WHEN -1
            THEN DATALENGTH(est.text)
        ELSE eqs.statement_end_offset
    END
```

```
        - eqs.statement_start_offset)/2) + 1) AS statement_text,

    creation_time, last_execution_time
FROM sys.dm_exec_query_stats as eqs

CROSS APPLY sys.dm_exec_sql_text(eqs.sql_handle) AS est

ORDER BY execution_count DESC;
```

All the DMVs are installed by default along with the database engine. You do not need to take any special steps to install or enable the functionality. DMVs are read-only views, implying that the data displayed by them cannot be modified.

All DMV counts are dynamic in nature and initialized to zero (0) when the instance of SQL Server 2005 is started. In addition, a few DMVs, such as sys.dm_os_latch_stats, have explicit commands (such as DBCC SQLPERF('sys.dm_os_latch_stats', CLEAR);) that can be used to manually reset the counts. In addition, other DMVs, such as sys.dm_exec_query_stats, have their counts dependent on the existence of the query plan in the database engine's plan cache. The counts are deleted when the respective plan is evicted from the plan cache, as explained in more detail later in this chapter.

There are two types of dynamic management views and functions: server-scoped, and database-scoped. Querying a dynamic management view or function requires SELECT permission on object plus the VIEW SERVER STATE permission for the server-scoped DMVs, or the VIEW DATABASE STATE permission for the database-scoped DMVs. This security mechanism lets you selectively restrict access of a user or login to DMVs and functions. The permissions can be set using the GRANT command. For example, the following command grants the VIEW SERVER STATE permission to Ben Smith whose login id is BenSmith:

```
USE master;
GRANT VIEW SERVER STATE TO [BenSmith];
```

# Using Dynamic Management Views

SQL Server 2005 groups the DMVs into twelve distinct categories based on the engine component to which they relate. These twelve categories are listed below:

1. Common language runtime
2. Database
3. Database mirroring

4. Execution

5. Full-text search

6. Input/output

7. Index

8. Query notifications

9. Replication

10. Service broker

11. SQL Server operating system

12. Transaction

In the sections below, the DMVs contained within each of these categories are explained in detail, along with example queries where applicable. Additional details about the DMVs can be found in the SQL Server Books Online.

---

**On the CD**   The sample DMV T-SQL statements in the sections below that are longer than four lines are provided on the CD. Look for the DMV_Example_Scripts.sql file in the \Scripts\Chapter 31 folder.

---

# Common Language Runtime–Related DMVs

There are four DMVs related to the newly introduced common language runtime (CLR) functionality in SQL Sever 2005. All four of these DMVs are server scoped and require you to have the VIEW SERVER STATE permission on the server in order to access.

## sys.dm_clr_appdomains

The sys.dm_clr_appdomains DMV returns a row for each application domain in the server. In Microsoft .NET Framework common language runtime (CLR) terminology, an application domain (appdomain) is a construct for the unit of isolation for an application.

## sys.dm_clr_loaded_assemblies

The sys.dm_clr_loaded_assemblies DMV returns a row for each managed user assembly loaded into the server address space.

## sys.dm_clr_properties

The sys.dm_clr_properties DMV returns a row for each property related to SQL Server 2005 common language runtime (CLR) integration, including the version and state of the hosted CLR. This DMV does not show whether execution of user CLR code has been enabled on the server. Execution of user CLR code can be enabled by using the sp_configure stored procedure (sp_configure 'clr enabled', 1) or via the surface area configuration utility.

### sys.dm_clr_tasks

The sys.dm_clr_tasks DMV returns a row for all common language runtime (CLR) tasks that are currently running on the server and displays details of the underlying SQL batch and the state of the task.

## Database-Related DMVs

There are four DMVs related to databases that present details about the database sizes, files used, and partition information, if present. All database DMVs except sys.dm_db_partition_stats are server scoped and require you to have the VIEW SERVER STATE permission on the server. The sys.dm_db_partition_stats DMV has a database wide scope and requires the VIEW DATABASE STATE permission on the server.

### sys.dm_db_file_space_usage

The sys.dm_db_file_space_usage DMV returns space usage information for each data file in the *tempdb* system database (database id = 2). This DMV is not currently applicable to any other user or system database.

This DMV is particularly useful when using the snapshot isolation level, explained in Chapter 18, "Transactions and Blocking," because it helps determine the total number of pages being used for the version store. For *tempdb* databases configured with more than one data file, the version_store_reserved_page_count counts reported for all the files need to be added to determine the total space being used. The following query can be used to determine the total number of pages used and the total space in megabytes (MB) used by the version store in *tempdb*:

```
SELECT SUM(version_store_reserved_page_count) AS [version store pages used],
    (SUM(version_store_reserved_page_count)*1.0/128)
    AS [version store space in MB]
FROM sys.dm_db_file_space_usage;
```

Another useful counter reported by the DMV is user_object_reserved_page_count. This counter helps determine the total number of pages being used by user objects such as user-defined tables and indexes, system tables and indexes, global temporary tables and indexes, local temporary tables and indexes, table variables, and tables returned in the table-valued functions. The following query can be used to determine the total number of pages used by user objects and the total space in megabytes (MB) used by user objects in *tempdb*:

```
SELECT SUM(user_object_reserved_page_count) AS [user object pages used],
    (SUM(user_object_reserved_page_count)*1.0/128)
    AS [user object space in MB]
FROM sys.dm_db_file_space_usage;
```

### sys.dm_db_session_space_usage

The sys.dm_db_session_space_usage DMV returns the number of pages allocated and de-allocated by each session in the *tempdb* system database (database id = 2). This DMV is not applicable to any other user or system database. All counters are initialized to zero (0) at the start of a session and are updated when a task ends. The counters do not reflect counts for tasks that are still running.

The user objects allocation and de-allocation counts report the number of pages reserved or allocated for user objects such as user-defined tables and indexes, system tables and indexes, global temporary tables and indexes, local temporary tables and indexes, table variables, and tables returned in the table-valued functions by the session. For example, you can use the following query to find the top user sessions that are allocating internal objects, including currently active tasks:

```
SELECT t1.session_id,
    (t1.internal_objects_alloc_page_count + task_alloc) AS allocated,
    (t1.internal_objects_dealloc_page_count + task_dealloc) AS deallocated
FROM sys.dm_db_session_space_usage AS t1,
    (SELECT session_id,
        SUM(internal_objects_alloc_page_count) AS task_alloc,
        SUM (internal_objects_dealloc_page_count) AS task_dealloc
    FROM sys.dm_db_task_space_usage
    GROUP BY session_id) AS t2
WHERE t1.session_id = t2.session_id
    AND t1.session_id > 50
ORDER BY allocated DESC;
```

### sys.dm_db_partition_stats

The sys.dm_db_partition_stats DMV returns page and row counts for every partition in the current database. One row is returned for each partition with information about the object ID and index ID of the table or indexed view of which the partition is a part of. For example, the query below returns all information for the partitions of the Employee table in the *AdventureWorks* database:

```
USE AdventureWorks;
SELECT * FROM sys.dm_db_partition_stats
WHERE object_id = OBJECT_ID(N'HumanResources.Employee');
```

### sys.dm_db_task_space_usage

The sys.dm_db_task_space_usage DMV returns page allocation and de-allocation activity by task for the *tempdb* system database (database id = 2). All the page counters are initialized to zero at the start of a request and aggregated at the session level when the request is completed. Similar to the sys.dm_db_session_space_usage, this DMV presents allocation and de-allocation counts for user and internal objects. For example, the query below reports the total allocation and de-allocation page count for the internal and user objects for all currently running tasks in *tempdb*:

```
SELECT session_id,
    SUM(internal_objects_alloc_page_count)
        AS 'Internal obj alloc pg count',
    SUM(internal_objects_dealloc_page_count)
        AS 'Internal obj dealloc pg count',
    SUM(user_objects_alloc_page_count)
        AS 'User obj alloc pg count',
    SUM(user_objects_dealloc_page_count)
        AS 'User obj dealloc pg count'
FROM sys.dm_db_task_space_usage
WHERE session_id > 50
GROUP BY session_id
ORDER BY session_id;
```

## Database Mirroring-Related DMV

There is only one DMV, sys.dm_db_mirroring_connections, related to the new database mirroring feature explained in Chapter 25, "Disaster Recovery Solutions." This DMV is server scoped, and accessing it requires you to have the VIEW SERVER STATE permission on the server.

### sys.dm_db_mirroring_connections

The sys.dm_db_mirroring_connections DMV returns a row for each connection established for database mirroring. The DMV presents details about the connection, current state, principal, login state, data sent and received, and the encryption algorithm used for each connection. The following command can be used to view all the details of all the database mirroring connections that are active on the server:

```
SELECT * FROM sys.dm_db_mirroring_connections;
```

## Execution-Related DMVs and Functions

SQL Server 2005 introduces 14 new execution-related DMVs. These DMVs provide insights into the query execution statistics and are very useful for analyzing and tuning performance. All execution-related DMVs are server scoped and require you to have the VIEW SERVER STATE permission on the server in order to access. In addition to the fourteen execution related DMVs, there is a 15th one, sys.dm_exec_query_transformation_stats, which is reserved for Microsoft internal use only and presents no useful data. This DMV is not covered in this chapter.

### sys.dm_exec_background_job_queue

The sys.dm_exec_background_job_queue DMV returns a row for each asynchronous update statistics job that is scheduled for execution on the server instance as a background task. Currently, only asynchronous update statistics jobs appear in the sys.dm_exec_background_job_queue DMV, but this may change in the future. The DMV presents information about the object on which the statistics are asynchronously being updated, the time the job was queued, the database id the object belongs to, the status of the job, and many other details.

### sys.dm_exec_background_job_queue_stats

The sys.dm_exec_background_job_queue_stats DMV returns a single row of data that provides aggregated statistics for asynchronous update statistics jobs submitted for execution as a background task. This DMV presents information about the length of the queue; the number of requests that have started, ended, and failed execution; and average and maximum elapsed times for the requests.

### sys.dm_exec_cached_plans

SQL Server 2005 caches query execution plans to avoid having to regenerate them for successive executions of the same query. This feature is explained in detail in Chapter 33, "Tuning Queries Using Hints and Plan Guides." The sys.dm_exec_cached_plans DMV returns information about all the query execution plans that are currently cached by SQL Server. A single row is returned for each plan; it presents information about the type of the cached object (compiled plan, executable plan, parse tree, extended stored procedure), the number of bytes used by the object, the number of times this plan has been used since it was cached, the type of object for which the plan was created, and the plan handle.

For example, the following query uses the sys.dm_exec_cached_plans DMV and the sys.dm_exec_query_plan DMV, explained later in this section, to present information about the usage count, size, object type, and XML showplan for all cached compiled plans residing in the plan cache in descending order of their usage counts:

```
SELECT usecounts, size_in_bytes, objtype,

    (SELECT query_plan FROM sys.dm_exec_query_plan(cp.plan_handle))

    AS QueryPlan

FROM sys.dm_exec_cached_plans cp

WHERE cacheobjtype = 'Compiled Plan'

ORDER BY usecounts DESC;
```

The sys.dm_exec_cached_plans DMV can also be used to analyze the reusability of the cached compiled plans using the following query:

```
SELECT TOP 100

    ecp.usecounts, ecp.cacheobjtype, ecp.size_in_bytes,

    SUBSTRING(eqt.text,eqs.statement_start_offset/2,

        (CASE

            WHEN eqs.statement_end_offset = -1

                THEN len(convert(NVARCHAR(MAX), eqt.text))*2

            ELSE eqs.statement_end_offset

        END - eqs.statement_start_offset)/2) AS statement,

    eqs.plan_handle

FROM sys.dm_exec_query_stats eqs

    CROSS APPLY sys.dm_exec_sql_text(eqs.sql_handle) AS eqt

    INNER JOIN sys.dm_exec_cached_plans AS ecp

        ON eqs.plan_handle = ecp.plan_handle

WHERE ecp.plan_handle = eqs.plan_handle

ORDER BY [usecounts] ASC;
```

This query lists the 100 least frequently used query plans and is useful for determining whether the objects held in the plan cache are being reused. A very high number of objects with a low usage count (usecounts) may signify a problem in the application, such as the existence of non-parameterized queries which result in the query plans not being reused effectively.

### sys.dm_exec_connections

The sys.dm_exec_connections DMV returns details about each connection currently established to the SQL Server 2005 instance. Some of the key information this DMV presents includes the session id (SPID), time at which the connection was established, the protocol used for the connection (Shared Memory, TCP, etc), the network packet size, the number of bytes read and written over the connection, the time the last read and write operation occurred, and the most recent SQL query handle. For example, the query below displays the SPID, the timestamp the connection was established, the number of bytes read over the connection, the number of bytes written over the connection, the timestamp of the last read and write, and the most recent SQL handle:

```
SELECT session_id, connect_time, num_reads, num_writes,

    last_read, last_write, most_recent_sql_handle

FROM sys.dm_exec_connections;
```

The SQL query handle is particularly useful because it helps identify the SQL query last executed on the connection. The SQL handle can be used to determine the most recent SQL statement that was executed on the connection by passing its value to the sys.dm_exec_sql_text DMV, which is explained later in the section. For example, the following query can be used to retrieve the SQL statement text associated with the SQL handle specified. (Note: the SQL handle specified below is for example purposes only and should be replaced with the SQL handle obtained from the previous query):

```
SELECT *

FROM sys.dm_exec_sql_text(0x02000000FEC7CB19E3AB91BD34F4A2654EEC3AE7DADD82C5);
```

### sys.dm_exec_cursors

The sys.dm_exec_cursors DMV returns information about the cursors that are currently open in the instance of SQL Server. You can either pass in the session id (SPID) to the DMV to have it display the cursors open for the particular SPID, or you can pass in 0 for it to display all open cursors for all databases. This is another highly useful DMV that presents detailed information about client-side cursors, also known as application programming interface (API) cursors, originating in packaged third-party application. Those of you who have worked with earlier versions of SQL Server probably know about the hardships associated with determining and tuning cursor-based queries and will appreciate this DMV the most. For example, the following query can be used to return information about all cursors that have been open on the server for more than a specified period of time (600 seconds in the example):

```
SELECT session_id, creation_time, cursor_id, name, properties, reads, writes
FROM sys.dm_exec_cursors(0)
WHERE DATEDIFF(s, creation_time, GETDATE()) > 600;
```

## sys.dm_exec_plan_attributes

The sys.dm_exec_plan_attributes DMV takes a plan handle as input and returns information about the attributes associated with the plan specified by the plan handle. This DMV returns one row for each attribute associated with the plan, listing the attribute's name, the value, and whether the attribute is used as part of the cache lookup key for the plan ("1" indicates that it is). For example, the following query returns the list of attributes for the particular plan handle, as shown in Figure 31-1:

```
SELECT *
FROM sys.dm_exec_plan_attributes
    (0x06000600BF820A0AB881CC05000000000000000000000000);
```

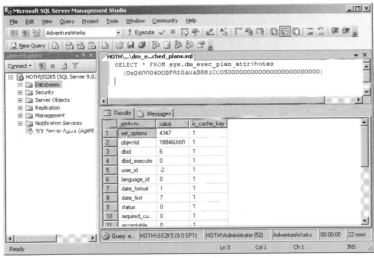

**Figure 31-1**   sys.dm_exec_plan_attributes—list of plan attributes.

## sys.dm_exec_query_memory_grants

The sys.dm_exec_query_memory_grants DMV returns information about the queries that have acquired a memory grant or that still require a memory grant to execute. Queries that do not have to wait on a memory grant will not appear in this view. Some of the key information this DMV presents includes the session id (session_id), a pointer to the sql statement (sql_handle), a pointer to the xml plan (plan_handle), the amount of memory requested (requested_memory_kb), the amount of memory granted (granted_memory_kb), and the amount of memory still required (required_memory_kb). It also lists the amount of time in milliseconds that the query has been waiting for the memory to be acquired (wait_time_ms). This DMV was made available in SQL Server 2005 Service Pack 1 (SP1); therefore, you need to have SP1 installed in order to be able to execute it.

### sys.dm_exec_query_optimizer_info

The sys.dm_exec_query_optimizer_info DMV returns detailed statistics about the internal operation of the SQL Server query optimizer. This DMV is very useful for determining what the optimizer is doing and where it is spending its time. For example, the following query displays the current average time in milliseconds the optimizer has taken to optimize queries. Taking two snapshots of this query and computing the difference between the values shows the time that is spent optimizing queries in the given time period:

```
SELECT ISNULL(value,0.0)*1000 AS MillisecondsPerOptimization

FROM sys.dm_exec_query_optimizer_info

WHERE counter = 'elapsed time';
```

All the counters are reset to 0 when SQL Server 2005 starts up and are incremented from there on. There is no way to reset the count while the instance of SQL Server is still running.

### sys.dm_exec_query_plan

The sys.dm_exec_query_plan dynamic management function takes a plan handle as input and returns the corresponding XML query plan for the SQL statement. For example, the following query displays the xml showplan for the specified plan handle:

```
SELECT *

FROM

sys.dm_exec_query_plan(0x06000100AABF4014B861DD030000000000000000000000000);
```

> **Note**  The XML schema (showplanxml.xsd) for the XML Showplan is available under the: %Program Files%\Microsoft SQL Server\90\Tools\Binn\schemas\sqlserver\2004\07\showplan directory.

## sys.dm_exec_query_resource_semaphores

The sys.dm_exec_query_resource_semaphores DMV returns information about general query execution memory status, enabling you to determine whether the system can access enough memory. This view complements memory information obtained from sys.dm_os_memory_clerks, explained later in this chapter, to provide a complete snapshot of server memory status. This DMV returns two rows, one for the regular resource semaphore (resource_semaphore_id=0) and one for the small-query resource semaphore (resource_semaphore_id=1). The sys.dm_exec_query_resource_semaphores DMV was made available in SQL Server 2005 Service Pack 1 (SP1); therefore, you need to have SP1 installed in order to be able to execute it.

## sys.dm_exec_query_stats

The sys.dm_exec_query_stats DMV returns aggregate performance statistics for each query plan that is currently cached by the instance of SQL Server. One row is returned for each query plan. The lifetime of the row is tied to the plan itself, implying that when a plan is evicted from the cache, the corresponding row is no longer reported by this DMV. This is one of the most important DMVs for performance tuning because it helps you quickly determine the details of the query execution. Some of the key information that the sys.dm_exec_query_stats DMV returns includes the sql handle (sql_handle), the plan handle (plan_handle), the time at which the plan was compiled (creation_time) and last executed (last_execution_time), the number of times that the plan has been executed (execution_count), the worker times, the physical reads, the logical reads, the logical writes, the common language runtime (CLR) times, and the elapsed times.

## sys.dm_exec_requests

The sys.dm_exec_requests DMV returns information about each request that is currently executing within the instance of SQL Server. One row is returned for every executing query. Once the request completes execution, it is no longer reported by the DMV. The sys.dm_exec_requests DMV is very useful to determine the operation of queries that take a long time to execute as it helps gain insight into the progress of the query while it is still executing. Those of you who have worked with earlier versions of SQL Server will quickly realize the value of this DMV because prior to the introduction of this DMV, it was not possible to get clear insight into the details about queries that were executing. Execution information was available only after a query completed execution. Some of the key attributes reported by this DMV include handle to the SQL statement (sql_handle) and the xml showplan (plan_handle), the time in milliseconds elapsed since the query started (total_elapsed_time), and the number of reads and writes. For example, the following query displays details about all user queries currently executing on the instance of SQL Server 2005:

```
SELECT session_id, command, total_elapsed_time, status,
    reads, writes, start_time, sql_handle
FROM sys.dm_exec_requests
WHERE session_id > 50
ORDER BY total_elapsed_time DESC;
```

> **Note**  If a user executing this DMV does not have the VIEW SERVER STATE permission on the server instance, the user will be able to see only queries executing in the current session.

### sys.dm_exec_sessions

The sys.dm_exec_sessions DMV returns one row for every authenticated session established on the instance of SQL Server 2005. This DMV is useful for quickly getting a summary of the attributes of the client applications connecting to the instance of SQL Server 2005. Some of the key information this DMV returns includes the session id, the time when the session was established, the client interface name and version, the number of reads and writes performed by all queries executed over this sessions, the number of rows by all queries executed over the connection, the transaction isolation level, and the connection properties. For example, the following query can be used to determine the client interface and version being used by all user connections. This is useful if you suspect that some clients are using client versions that are not recommended or supported by your organization:

```
SELECT session_id, client_interface_name, client_version,
    login_name, login_time
FROM sys.dm_exec_sessions
WHERE session_id > 50;
```

Another use could be to deterime the users who are currently connected to the SQL Server 2005 instance and how many connections each one of them has open. The following query can be used to extract this information:

```
SELECT login_name, count(session_id) AS session_count
FROM sys.dm_exec_sessions
GROUP BY login_name
ORDER BY login_name;
```

### sys.dm_exec_sql_text

The sys.dm_exec_sql_text DMV takes a sql_handle as an input parameter and returns the text of the corresponding sql statement. This DMV is a replacement for the fn_get_sql function that was available in earlier versions of SQL Server. The fn_get_sql function is planned to be deprecated in a future release of SQL Server, so you should switch to using sys.dm_exec_sql_text. This DMV also returns information about the database id, the object id, the number of the stored procedure, and whether the sql text is encrypted.

The sys.dm_exec_sql_text DMV can be executed directly by passing in a sql query handle, as shown in the following query:

```
SELECT text
FROM sys.dm_exec_sql_text(0x02000000AC1BE33A180F67ECE2C1AA08CCCBA9F5DF60268A);
```

Or, it can be cross applied with another DMV as shown here:

```
SELECT execution_count,
    total_worker_time, total_physical_reads, total_logical_writes,
    (SELECT TOP 1 SUBSTRING(s2.text,statement_start_offset / 2 + 1 ,
      ((CASE
          WHEN statement_end_offset = -1
              THEN (LEN(CONVERT(nvarchar(max),s2.text)) * 2)
          ELSE statement_end_offset
      END) - statement_start_offset) / 2 + 1))
    AS sql_statement,
    last_execution_time
FROM sys.dm_exec_query_stats AS s1
CROSS APPLY sys.dm_exec_sql_text(sql_handle) AS s2
WHERE s2.objectid is null
ORDER BY execution_count DESC, total_worker_time DESC;
```

## Full-Text Search–Related DMVs

SQL Server 2005 introduces five new full-text related DMVs that help gain insight into the full-text service. All full-text related DMVs are server scoped and require you to have the VIEW SERVER STATE permission on the server in order to access them.

### sys.dm_fts_active_catalogs

The sys.dm_fts_active_catalogs DMV returns information about the full-text catalogs that have some population activity in progress on the server. One row is returned for each full-text catalog that is active. Catalogs that are up-to-date are not reported by this DMV.

### sys.dm_fts_index_population

The sys.dm_fts_index_population DMV returns information about the full-text indexes that have some population activity in progress on the server. One row is returned for each full-text index that has population activity in progress. Full-text indexes that are up-to-date are not reported by this DMV. The query below can be used to determine the full-text index's database name, table name, description of the full-text index population, the status, and the start time for all full-text indexes that have some population activity in progress:

```
SELECT DB_NAME(database_id) AS database_name,
    OBJECT_NAME(table_id) AS table_name, population_type_description,
    status_description, start_time
FROM sys.dm_fts_index_population
ORDER BY start_time;
```

### sys.dm_fts_memory_buffers

The sys.dm_fts_memory_buffers DMV returns information about memory buffers belonging to a specific memory pool that are being used as part of a full-text crawl or a full-text crawl range.

### sys.dm_fts_memory_pools

The sys.dm_fts_memory_pools DMV returns information about the memory pools used as part of a full-text crawl or a full-text crawl range.

### sys.dm_fts_population_ranges

The sys.dm_fts_population_ranges DMV returns information about the specific ranges related to a full-text index population currently in progress.

## Input/Output Related DMVs and Functions

SQL Server 2005 introduces four new Input/Output (I/O)-related DMVs that help gain insight into I/O operations, I/O devices, and database file statistics. All I/O-related DMVs are server scoped and require you to have the VIEW SERVER STATE permission on the server in order to access them.

## sys.dm_io_backup_tapes

The sys.dm_io_backup_tapes DMV identifies the list of tape devices and the status of mount requests for backups. One row is returned for each device. This DMV can be used to determine details of the devices and is especially useful to determine their current status.

## sys.dm_io_cluster_shared_drives

The sys.dm_io_cluster_shared_drives DMV returns the name of the drive that represents an individual disk taking part in the cluster shared disk array if the current server is a clustered server. One row is returned for every single disk of that shared disk array that is used by the clustered SQL Server instance. If the current server instance is not clustered, an empty result set is returned.

## sys.dm_io_pending_io_requests

The sys.dm_io_pending_io_requests DMV returns information about pending I/O requests. One row is returned for each pending I/O request in the SQL Server instance.

## sys.dm_io_virtual_file_stats

The sys.dm_io_virtual_file_stats DMV takes the database id and file id as input parameters and returns information about the I/O statistics, such as the total number of I/Os performed on a file, for data and log files. For example, the statement below returns the file statistics for the AdventureWorks_Data file (file_id = 1) of the *AdventureWorks* database (db_id = 6).

```
SELECT *
FROM sys.dm_io_virtual_file_stats(DB_ID(N'AdventureWorks'),
    FILE_IDEX('AdventureWorks_Data'));
```

You can also use this DMV with NULL specified for the file_id parameter, in which case the I/O statistics for all the files in the specified database are returned:

```
SELECT * FROM sys.dm_io_virtual_file_stats(6, NULL);
```

This DMV is useful for identifying the amount of time users have to wait to read or write to a file, as well as which database files, if any, are being used heavily. For example, in the following query if the I/O stalls (io_stall_total_ms) is very high for any of the files, it may signify a disk bottleneck where a high number of reads and writes are occurring on that file. The average I/O waits per read (avg_io_stall_read_ms) and the average I/O waits per write (avg_io_stall_write_ms) can further help determine whether the bottleneck is being caused by read or write activity:

```
SELECT DB_NAME(database_id) AS database_name,
    FILE_NAME(file_id) AS filename, num_of_reads, io_stall_read_ms,
    CAST(io_stall_read_ms/(num_of_reads+1) AS NUMERIC(10,1))
```

```
        AS 'avg_io_stall_read_ms',
    num_of_writes, io_stall_write_ms,
    CAST(io_stall_write_ms/(num_of_writes+1) AS NUMERIC(10,1))
        AS 'avg_io_stall_write_ms',
    (num_of_reads+num_of_writes) AS 'total_num_of_ios',[[tab]]
    (io_stall_read_ms+io_stall_write_ms) AS 'io_stall_total_ms',
    CAST((io_stall_read_ms+io_stall_write_ms)/(num_of_reads+num_of_writes+1)
        AS NUMERIC(10,1)) AS 'avg_io_stall_total_ms'
FROM sys.dm_io_virtual_file_stats(NULL,NULL)
ORDER BY avg_io_stall_total_ms DESC;
```

This DMV replaces the fn_virtualfilestats function, which was available in earlier versions of SQL Server as well.

## Index Related DMVs and Functions

SQL Server 2005 introduces three new index related DMVs (sys.dm_db_index_operational_stats, sys.dm_db_index_physical_stats, sys.dm_db_index_usage_stats) that help gain insight into I/O operations, I/O devices, and database file statistics. In addition, SQL Server 2005 Service Pack 1 introduces four additional DMVs (sys.dm_db_missing_index_columns, sys.dm_db_missing_index_details, sys.dm_db_missing_index_group_stats, sys.dm_db_missing_index_groups) making the total for index-related DMVs seven. All index-related DMVs are server scoped and require you to have the VIEW SERVER STATE permission on the server in order to access them.

### sys.dm_db_index_operational_stats

The sys.dm_db_index_operational_stats DMV takes the database id, object id, index id, and partition number as input and returns current locking, latching, access method, and I/O activity for each partition of a table or index in the database. The DMV can also be invoked with NULL values for any of the four parameters, in which case all data related to the NULL parameter values is returned. For example, you can use the following command to view the operational index statistics of all the indexes for the Person.Address table in the *AdventureWorks* database:

```
SELECT *
FROM sys.dm_db_index_operational_stats(DB_ID(N'AdventureWorks'),
    OBJECT_ID(N'AdventureWorks.Person.Address'), NULL, NULL);
```

Each column in the sys.dm_db_index_operational_stats DMV is initialized to 0 when the metadata for the heap or index is brought into the metadata cache, which usually occurs when the heap or index is first accessed. Once cached, the database engine accumulates counts until the cache object is removed from the metadata cache. Because there is a high likelyhood of frequently accessed indexes and heaps remaining in the cache, there is a high likelyhood that the counts will be maintained and available. For example, you can use the following query to list tables and indexes in the current database with most blocking:

```
SELECT DB_NAME(database_id) AS 'db_name',
    OBJECT_NAME(ios.object_id) AS 'obj_name',
    i.name AS 'idx_name', i.index_id,
    row_lock_count, row_lock_wait_count,
    CAST(row_lock_wait_count/(row_lock_count+1)*100 AS NUMERIC(10,2))
        AS '% blocked',
    row_lock_wait_in_ms,
    CAST (row_lock_wait_in_ms/(row_lock_wait_count+1) AS NUMERIC(10,2))
        AS 'avg_row_lock_wait_in_ms'
FROM sys.dm_db_index_operational_stats (db_id(), NULL, NULL, NULL) ios,
    sys.indexes i
WHERE OBJECTPROPERTY(ios.object_id, 'IsUserTable') = 1
    AND i.object_id = ios.object_id
    AND i.index_id = ios.index_id
ORDER BY row_lock_wait_count DESC;
```

## sys.dm_db_index_physical_stats

The sys.dm_db_index_physical_stats dynamic management function takes a database id, object id, index id, partition number, and mode as input parameters and returns the fragmentation information and sizes for the data and indexes for the specified table or view. Sys.dm_db_index_physical_stats returns one row for each index in each partition, one row for each in-row data allocation unit of each partition for a heap and one row for each large object data allocation unit of each partition. For example, the following query returns the fragmentation information for all five indexes in the HumanResources.Employee table, as shown in Figure 31-2:

```
SELECT *
FROM sys.dm_db_index_physical_stats(DB_ID(N'AdventureWorks'),
    OBJECT_ID(N'AdventureWorks.HumanResources.Employee'),
        NULL, NULL, 'DETAILED');
```

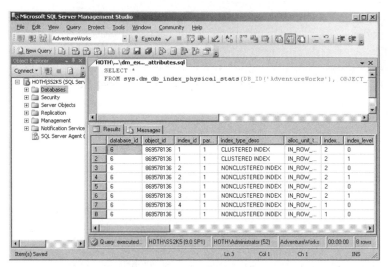

**Figure 31-2**   Sys.dm_db_index_physical_stats—query output.

---

**Important**   When using the DB_ID or OBJECT_ID functions as used in the previous example, you should make sure that they return the correct ids. If an invalid name is specified, the DB_ID and OBJECT_ID functions return a NULL, which in turn is interpreted by the DMV to request information for all databases or objects. A best practice is to always specify the object names in their corresponding three-part format, for example: 'AdventureWorks.HumanResources.Employee'.

---

This dynamic management function replaces the DBCC SHOWCONTIG command available in earlier versions of SQL Server which is planned to be deprecated in a future release of SQL Server.

## sys.dm_db_index_usage_stats

The sys.dm_db_index_usage_stats DMV returns the counts of different types of index operations and the time each operation was last performed. Each column in the DMV is initialized to 0 whenever the metadata for the index is brought into the metadata cache, which usually occurs when the index is first accessed. The database engine then increments the corresponding counter by one for every individual seek, scan, lookup, or update on the specified index.

In general, indexes are good and most of the time help speed up the execution of queries, as explained in Chapter 12, "Creating Indexes for Performance." However, the benefits come at a price. The database engine has to maintain all active indexes at all times, and the cost of this maintenance can often be significant, especially for heavily updated tables. Given this, the performance increase realized by the existence of an index should outweigh the cost overhead to maintain it in order to realize a net benefit. To ensure that the indexes in your database are all useful indexes, you can use the following query to determine which indexes in the current database are used least frequently and are possibly not really beneficial:

```
SELECT OBJECT_NAME(ios.object_id) AS 'obj_name',
    ios.object_id, i.name AS 'idx_name', i.index_id,
    (user_seeks + user_scans + user_lookups + user_updates)
        AS 'total_usage_count',
    user_seeks, user_scans, user_lookups, user_updates
FROM sys.dm_db_index_usage_stats ios, sys.indexes i
WHERE database_id = db_id()
    AND objectproperty(ios.object_id, 'IsUserTable') = 1
    AND i.object_id = ios.object_id
    AND i.index_id = ios.index_id
ORDER BY total_usage_count ASC;
```

> **Note**   The rarely used indexes will have a low total usage count (total_usage_count) and therefore appear towards the top of the listing in the query output.

You can also use the sys.dm_db_index_usage_stats DMV to determine the indexes in the current database that are not being referenced at all using the following query:

```
SELECT OBJECT_NAME(i.object_id) AS 'obj_name',
    i.name AS 'idx_name', i.index_id
FROM sys.indexes i, sys.objects o
WHERE OBJECTPROPERTY(o.object_id, 'IsUserTable') = 1
    AND o.object_id = i.object_id
    AND i.index_id NOT IN (
        SELECT s.index_id
        FROM sys.dm_db_index_usage_stats s
        WHERE s.object_id = i.object_id
```

```
        AND i.index_id=s.index_id

        AND database_id = db_id() )

ORDER BY obj_name, i.index_id ASC;
```

---

**Important** You should drop (or disable) any rarely used or unused indexes only after careful consideration because there could be queries existing in dormant jobs that have not been run in a while but which require the indexes in order to operate optimally. An example is a year-end financial application batch job that closes the annual accounts. This job may run only once a year at midnight on December 31, and therefore, if the database server was recycled, say in January, indexes used and required by this job may end up being reported as unused for the rest of the year.

---

## sys.dm_db_missing_index_columns

The sys.dm_db_missing_index_columns dynamic management function was introduced in SQL Server 2005 Service Pack 1. This dynamic management function takes an index handle returned by the sys.dm_db_missing_index_details or sys.dm_db_missing_index_groups DMVs, explained later in this chapter, as input and returns information about database table columns that are missing an index as shown in the following example query batch:

```
DECLARE @idx_handle INT;

SELECT @idx_handle = mid.index_handle

FROM sys.dm_db_missing_index_group_stats migs,

    sys.dm_db_missing_index_groups mig,

    sys.dm_db_missing_index_details mid

WHERE migs.group_handle = mig.index_group_handle

    AND mid.index_handle = mig.index_handle;

SELECT * FROM sys.dm_db_missing_index_columns(@idx_handle)

ORDER BY column_id;
```

The sys.dm_db_missing_index_columns dynamic management function is updated whenever a query is optimized.

## sys.dm_db_missing_index_details

The sys.dm_db_missing_index_details DMV was introduced in SQL Server 2005 Service Pack 1 and can be used to return detailed information about missing indexes. This dynamic management function is updated whenever a query is optimized.

### sys.dm_db_missing_index_group_stats

The sys.dm_db_missing_index_group_stats DMV was introduced in SQL Server 2005 Service Pack 1 and can be used to return summary information about groups of missing indexes. Unlike the sys.dm_db_missing_index_details DMV, explained previously, which presents details about a single missing index, the missing index group includes details of all missing indexes that should produce some performance improvement for a given query.

### sys.dm_db_missing_index_groups

The sys.dm_db_missing_index_groups DMV was introduced in SQL Server 2005 Service Pack 1 and can be used to return summary information about what missing indexes are contained in a specific missing index group. This DMV is updated whenever a query is optimized. For example, the following query uses the sys.dm_db_-missing_index_groups DMV, along with the sys.dm_db_missing_index_group_stats and sys.dm_db_missing_index_details DMVs, to present details about the missing indexes and computed benefit of the index (avg_user_impact), which is the estimated percentage improvement with the suggested index created:

```
SELECT mid.*, migs.avg_total_user_cost, migs.avg_user_impact,
    migs.last_user_seek, migs.unique_compiles
FROM sys.dm_db_missing_index_group_stats migs,
    sys.dm_db_missing_index_groups mig,
    sys.dm_db_missing_index_details mid
WHERE migs.group_handle = mig.index_group_handle
    AND mid.index_handle = mig.index_handle
ORDER BY migs.avg_user_impact DESC;
```

**Best Practices** Because the previous four DMVs potentially contain vital performance tuning information that is not persisted across SQL Server restarts, you should periodically make backup copies of the output of these DMVs. You can do this manually or automate the process using a methodology similar to that explained in the Performance Data Warehouse section later in this chapter. This historical data can be very useful for determining which indexes are missing and which will have the biggest positive impact when created.

## Query Notifications-Related DMVs

SQL Server 2005 introduces just one new query notification-related DMV that helps gain insight into active query notifications subscriptions in the server. This DMV is server scoped and requires you to have the VIEW SERVER STATE permission on the server in order to access it.

### sys.dm_qn_subscriptions

The sys.dm_qn_subscriptions DMV returns information about each active query notification subscriptions in the server, including the current status. One row is returned for each active query notification subscription. If the user does not have VIEW SERVER STATE permission, this view returns only information about subscriptions owned by current user.

## Replication-Related DMVs

SQL Server 2005 introduces four new replication-related DMVs that help gain insight into the workings of replication in the database. All four DMVs are database scoped and require you to have the VIEW DATABASE STATE permission on the publication database in order to access them.

### sys.dm_repl_articles

The sys.dm_repl_articles DMV returns information about database objects published as articles in a replication topology. Only information for those replicated database objects that are currently loaded in the replication article cache is reported.

### sys.dm_repl_schemas

The sys.dm_repl_schemas DMV returns information about table columns published by replication. Only information for those replicated database objects that are currently loaded in the replication article cache is reported.

### sys.dm_repl_tranhash

The sys.dm_repl_tranhash DMV returns information about transactions being replicated in a transactional publication. Only information for those replicated database objects that are currently loaded in the replication article cache is reported.

### sys.dm_repl_traninfo

The sys.dm_repl_traninfo DMV returns information on each replicated transaction. Only information for those replicated database objects that are currently loaded in the replication article cache is reported.

## Service Broker-Related DMVs

SQL Server 2005 introduces four new Service Broker-related DMVs that help gain insight into the workings of the service broker. These DMVs are server scoped and require you to have the VIEW SERVER STATE permission on the server in order to access them.

### sys.dm_broker_activated_tasks

The sys.dm_broker_activated_tasks DMV returns information about stored procedures activated by Service Broker. One row is returned for each stored procedure.

## sys.dm_broker_connections

The sys.dm_broker_connections DMV returns information about Service Broker network connections. One row is returned for each Service Broker network connection.

## sys.dm_broker_forwarded_messages

The sys.dm_broker_forwarded_messages DMV returns information about Service Broker messages that an instance of SQL Server is in the process of forwarding. One row is returned for every message.

## sys.dm_broker_queue_monitors

The sys.dm_broker_queue_monitors DMV is used to view information about the queue monitor, which manages activation for a queue, in the instance. One row is returned for each queue monitor. The following query can be used to retrieve the current status of all the message queues:

```
SELECT t1.name AS ServiceName, t3.name AS SchemaName, t2.name AS QueueName,

    CASE WHEN t4.state IS NULL THEN 'Not available'

        ELSE t4.state

    END AS [Queue_State],

    CASE WHEN t4.tasks_waiting IS NULL THEN '--'

        ELSE CONVERT(VARCHAR, t4.tasks_waiting)

    END AS tasks_waiting,

    CASE WHEN t4.last_activated_time IS NULL THEN '--'

        ELSE CONVERT(varchar, t4.last_activated_time)

    END AS last_activated_time,

    CASE WHEN t4.last_empty_rowset_time IS NULL THEN '--'

        ELSE CONVERT(varchar,t4.last_empty_rowset_time)

    END AS last_empty_rowset_time,

    (SELECT COUNT(*) FROM sys.transmission_queue t6

    WHERE (t6.from_service_name = t1.name)) AS TransMessageCount

FROM sys.services t1

    INNER JOIN sys.service_queues t2 ON (t1.service_queue_id = t2.object_id)

    INNER JOIN sys.schemas t3 ON (t2.schema_id = t3.schema_id)

    LEFT OUTER JOIN sys.dm_broker_queue_monitors t4

        ON (t2.object_id = t4.queue_id AND t4.database_id = DB_ID())

    INNER JOIN sys.databases t5 ON (t5.database_id = DB_ID());
```

## SQL Server Operating System-Related DMVs

SQL Server 2005 introduces 23 new SQL Server operating system (OS) related DMVs that help gain insight into the internal operations of the SQL Server OS. It also introduces five other operating system-related DMVs that are for Microsoft internal use and are not covered in this chapter. These DMVs are server scoped and require you to have the VIEW SERVER STATE permission on the server in order to access them.

### sys.dm_os_buffer_descriptors

The sys.dm_os_buffer_descriptors DMV returns information about the buffer pool descriptors that are being used by a database. This DMV returns information only about pages that have been successfully loaded into the buffer pool. Information about free or stolen pages and information about pages that had errors when they were read is not reported.

The following query can be used to return information about the buffer pool descriptors for the current database:

```sql
SELECT * FROM sys.dm_os_buffer_descriptors
WHERE database_id = DB_ID()
ORDER BY page_id ASC;
```

Figure 31-3 displays the output of the previous query run against the *AdventureWorks* database (Note: This is an example output only; the output you observe may be different.)

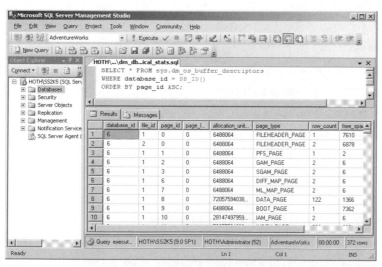

**Figure 31-3**    sys.dm_os_buffer_descriptors–query output.

---

**Note**   The rows corresponding to database_id 32767 in the sys.dm_os_buffer_descriptors output correspond to the pages that are being used by the SQL Server 2005 resource database, explained in Chapter 10, "Creating Databases and Database Snapshots."

## sys.dm_os_child_instances

The sys.dm_os_child_instances DMV returns information about the SQL Server Express user instances that have been created from the parent database. One row is returned for each user instance. *User instance* is a feature of SQL Server 2005 Express Edition that enables users who are not administrators to run a local version of SQL Server Express in their own account. With user instances, nonadministrators have database owner privileges over the instance running in their own account.

## sys.dm_os_cluster_nodes

The sys.dm_os_cluster_nodes DMV returns information about the nodes in the virtual server configuration. For clustered SQL Server instances, this DMV returns a list of nodes on which this virtual server has been defined. If the current server instance is not a clustered server, it does not return any rows.

## sys.dm_os_hosts

The sys.dm_os_hosts DMV returns information about the hosts currently registered in an instance of SQL Server 2005. SQL Server uses a host to keep track of and manage the resources used by these external components (for example, an OLE DB provider) that run inside its process. This DMV also returns the resources that are used by the hosts.

## sys.dm_os_latch_stats

The sys.dm_os_latch_stats DMV returns information about the latch waits for the different classes of latches. One row is returned for each class of latch. In SQL Server, a latch is a light-weight internal synchronization object used by internal engine components. A latch wait occurs when a latch request cannot be granted immediately. This DMV can be used to identify the source of latch contention by examining the relative wait counts and wait times for the different latch classes.

The counts returned by this DMV are cumulative from the time SQL Server instance was started, or they were manually reset. A manual reset of the counts can be done using the following command:

```
DBCC SQLPERF ('sys.dm_os_latch_stats', CLEAR);
```

### sys.dm_os_loaded_modules

The sys.dm_os_loaded_modules DMV returns information about the user and system modules (DLLs) loaded into the server address space. One row is returned for each module specifying the details of the module. For example, the following query can be used to determine all the details of the SQL Server Native Client being used by SQL Server instance:

```
SELECT * FROM sys.dm_os_loaded_modules
WHERE name LIKE '%sqlncli.dll%';
```

### sys.dm_os_memory_cache_clock_hands

The sys.dm_os_memory_cache_clock_hands DMV returns the status of each hand for a specific cache clock. SQL Server 2005 implements two clock hands that are used to sweep through the cache and purge the least recently used entries from caches. An internal clock hand is used to control the size of a cache relative to other caches. This clock hand starts moving when the cache is about to reach its capacity limit. A second, external clock hand is also used and starts to move when SQL Server as a whole gets into memory pressure. Movement of the external clock hand can be due to either external or internal memory pressure. The movement of these clock hands helps determine whether SQL Server is under memory pressure. For example, if the values for the rounds_count and removed_all_rounds_count counters are increasing between successive executions of the following query, then SQL Server is under internal or external memory pressure:

```
SELECT * FROM sys.dm_os_memory_cache_clock_hands
WHERE rounds_count > 0
    AND removed_all_rounds_count > 0;
```

### sys.dm_os_memory_cache_counters

The sys.dm_os_memory_cache_counters DMV provides run-time information about the cache entries allocated for each cache store. This DMV can be used to help determine how the cache is being utilized and by which cache store. This can be particularly useful for database servers that host multiple databases. For example, the following statement can be used to determine the number of entries in the cache, the number of entries in the cache that are currently being used, the amount of single and multi-page memory allocated, and the amount of single and multi-page allocated memory that is currently being used by the cache store associated with the *AdventureWorks* database:

```
SELECT name, entries_count, entries_in_use_count, single_pages_kb,
    multi_pages_kb, single_pages_in_use_kb, multi_pages_in_use_kb
FROM sys.dm_os_memory_cache_counters
WHERE name = 'AdventureWorks';
```

## sys.dm_os_memory_cache_entries

The sys.dm_os_memory_cache_entries DMV returns information about all entries in all the caches. One row is returned for each entry. This DMV can be used to obtain statistics on cache entries and to trace cache entries to their associated objects.

## sys.dm_os_memory_cache_hash_tables

The sys.dm_os_memory_cache_hash_tables DMV returns information about each active cache in the instance of SQL Server 2005. One row is returned for each active cache.

## sys.dm_os_memory_clerks

The sys.dm_os_memory_clerks DMV returns information about the set of all memory clerks that are currently active in the instance of SQL Server. SQL Server components create their corresponding clerks at the time SQL Server is started. Every component that allocates a significant amount of memory must create its own memory clerk and allocate all its memory by using the clerk interfaces. For example, you can use the sys.dm_os_memory_clerks in the following query to find out how much memory SQL Server has allocated through the AWE (Address Windowing Extensions) mechanism:

```
SELECT SUM(awe_allocated_kb)/1024 AS 'AWE_allocated_mem_Mb'

FROM sys.dm_os_memory_clerks;
```

## sys.dm_os_memory_objects

The sys.dm_os_memory_objects DMV returns information about memory objects that are currently allocated by SQL Server. This DMV is useful in analyzing memory use and identifying possible memory leaks. For example, the following query can be used to determine the amount of memory in kilo bytes (KB) used by each memory object type:

```
SELECT type, SUM(pages_allocated_count * page_size_in_bytes)/1024

    AS 'KB_Used'

FROM sys.dm_os_memory_objects

GROUP BY type

ORDER BY KB_Used DESC;
```

## sys.dm_os_memory_pools

The sys.dm_os_memory_pools DMV returns information about each object store in the instance of SQL Server. This DMV can be used to monitor cache memory usage and help identify suboptimal caching patterns.

### sys.dm_os_performance_counters

The sys.dm_os_performance_counters DMV returns information about the performance counters maintained by the instance of SQL Server 2005. One row is returned for each performance counter maintained by the server. These are the same counts that are reported by Windows System Monitor (perfmon), the only difference being that this DMV reports the absolute counts and leaves to the user the task of converting them into more meaningful data. For example, to determine the buffer cache hit ratio percentage, you must divide the Buffer cache hit ratio by the Buffer cache hit ratio base, as shown in the following query batch:

```
DECLARE @Numerator FLOAT, @Denominator FLOAT;

SET @Numerator = (

    SELECT cntr_value

    FROM sys.dm_os_performance_counters

    WHERE counter_name = 'Buffer cache hit ratio');

SET @Denominator = (

    SELECT cntr_value

    FROM sys.dm_os_performance_counters

    WHERE counter_name = 'Buffer cache hit ratio base');

SELECT (@Numerator/@Denominator)*100 AS 'Cache_Hit_Ratio (%)';
```

### sys.dm_os_schedulers

The sys.dm_os_schedulers DMV returns information about the internal SQL Server OS schedulers. One row is returned for each scheduler that is mapped to an individual processor. This DMV can be used to monitor the condition of a scheduler or to identify situations where there might be runaway tasks. For example, the following query can be used to determine the current workload on the scheduler:

```
SELECT scheduler_id, cpu_id, current_tasks_count,

    runnable_tasks_count, work_queue_count

FROM sys.dm_os_schedulers

WHERE scheduler_id < 255

ORDER BY work_queue_count DESC, scheduler_id ASC;
```

The current_task_count presents the number of tasks that are currently assigned to the scheduler, and the runnable_tasks_count presents the number of tasks that are ready to run. A nonzero value for runnable_tasks_count indicates that tasks have to wait for their time slice to run. Continuously high values for this counter are a symptom of a processor bottleneck. A high work_queue_count value indicates multiple tasks waiting on a scheduler.

### sys.dm_os_stacks

The sys.dm_os_stacks DMV returns internal stack information for SQL Server. This DMV can be used to keep track of debug data such as outstanding allocations or validate logic that is used by SQL Server components in places where the component assumes that a certain call has been made. The sys.dm_os_stacks DMV requires the matching version of the debug symbols (sqlservr.pdb) for SQL Server (sqlservr.exe) and the other components to be installed in the correct path on the server in order to display the information correctly. This DMV is of limited use for normal performance analysis and tuning activities.

### sys.dm_os_sys_info

The sys.dm_os_sys_info DMV returns a single row of a set of miscellaneous information about the computer and resources available to and consumed by the SQL Server instance. For example, you can use the query below to determine the number of physical processors and the amount of memory available in mega bytes (MB) to the SQL Server instance:

```
SELECT (cpu_count/hyperthread_ratio) AS NumberOfPhysicalProcessors,
    (physical_memory_in_bytes/1024/1024) AS MemoryAvailableInMB
FROM sys.dm_os_sys_info;
```

### sys.dm_os_tasks

The sys.dm_os_tasks DMV returns information about the tasks that are active in the instance of SQL Server. One row is returned for each task. For queries that are executed with a parallel query execution plan on a multi-processor system, one row is returned for every parallel query execution thread. For example, the query below returns information about all the currently active OS tasks with tasks belonging to the same session (session_id) grouped together:

```
SELECT * FROM sys.dm_os_tasks
WHERE session_id IS NOT NULL
ORDER BY session_id, request_id;
```

### sys.dm_os_threads

The sys.dm_os_threads DMV lists all the SQL Server OS threads that are running under the instance of SQL Server 2005, including ones that have been started by external components such as SQL Server extended stored procedures.

## sys.dm_os_virtual_address_dump

The sys.dm_os_virtual_address_dump DMV returns information about the range of pages in the virtual address space of the calling process. One row is returned for each range. This DMV is of limited use for normal performance analysis and tuning activities.

## sys.dm_os_wait_stats

The sys.dm_os_wait_stats DMV returns information about the wait statistics encountered by all threads that are in execution. One row is returned for each of the 195 different wait types. The counts reported by this DMV are cumulative across the entire instance of SQL Server. They are initialized to 0 when the SQL Server 2005 instance is started and then incremented. You can manually initialize the counters at any time by executing the following command. However, all the counters are always initialized together; there is no way to selectively initialize only a subset of the counters:

```
DBCC SQLPERF ('sys.dm_os_wait_stats', CLEAR);
```

This DMV can be used to help tune overall performance. For a well-optimized system, the waiting_tasks_count and wait_time_ms counts should be low. A high value for any of the wait types indicates a resource bottleneck. The following query can be used to list all the wait types that have a wait time associated with them:

```
SELECT * FROM sys.dm_os_wait_stats

WHERE wait_time_ms > 0;
```

It is normal for some of the resources, such as LAZYWRITER_SLEEP and SQLTRACE-_BUFFER_FLUSH, to have high wait times associated with them. To use this DMV effectively, you should establish a baseline of the counters during normal activity and then look for significant deviations from this baseline to determine the resources that may be possible bottlenecks.

## sys.dm_os_waiting_tasks

The sys.dm_os_waiting_tasks DMV returns information about the wait queue of tasks that are waiting on some resource. One row is returned for every waiting task. The following query can be used to list details of all user tasks that are waiting on some resource:

```
SELECT * FROM sys.dm_os_waiting_tasks

WHERE session_id >= 51

ORDER BY session_id;
```

---

**Note**   Session_ids less than 51 are related to system processes and often display high wait times. This is normal and usually not indicative of a problem.

### sys.dm_os_workers

The sys.dm_os_workers DMV returns information about the worker in the instance of SQL Server 2005. One row is returned for every worker thread, or *fiber*, in the system.

## Transaction-Related DMVs and Functions

SQL Server 2005 introduces ten new transaction-related DMVs that help gain insight into the operations of active transactions. These DMVs are particularly useful when using the new snapshot isolation levels. These DMVs are server scoped and require you to have the VIEW SERVER STATE permission on the server in order to access them.

### sys.dm_tran_active_snapshot_database_transactions

The sys.dm_tran_active_snapshot_database_transactions DMV returns information about all active user transactions that generate, or potentially access, row versions. One row of data is returned for each of the following:

- A transaction that is running under snapshot isolation level or read-committed isolation level that is using row versioning

- A transaction that causes a row version to be created in the current database

- A transaction under which a trigger is fired

- A transaction that is creating an index as an online operation

- A transaction that is accessing row versions when *Multiple Active Results Sets* (MARS) session is enabled.

Nested transactions always return only one row of data regardless of the nesting level. This DMV can be very useful for investigating the operation of the system when the snapshot isolation level is being used. For example, the following query can be used to determine long-running transactions in the instance of SQL Server:

```
SELECT * FROM sys.dm_tran_active_snapshot_database_transactions
WHERE elapsed_time_seconds > 0
ORDER BY elapsed_time_seconds DESC;
```

### sys.dm_tran_active_transactions

The sys.dm_tran_active_transactions DMV returns information about all active user and system transactions for the SQL Server instance. One row is returned for each transaction. Nested transactions always return only one row of data regardless of the nesting level.

### sys.dm_tran_current_snapshot

The sys.dm_tran_current_snapshot DMV returns information about all transactions that are active at the time the current snapshot transaction starts. No rows are returned if the current transaction is not a snapshot transaction.

### sys.dm_tran_current_transaction

The sys.dm_tran_current_transaction DMV returns a single row of data presenting the state information of the transaction in the current session.

### sys.dm_tran_database_transactions

The sys.dm_tran_database_transactions DMV returns information about transactions at the database level. For example, the following command can be used to view information about all transactions in the current database:

```
SELECT * FROM sys.dm_tran_database_transactions
WHERE database_id = DB_ID();
```

Nested transactions always return only one row of data regardless of the nesting level.

### sys.dm_tran_locks

The sys.dm_tran_locks DMV returns information about lock manager resources. One row is returned for each currently active request to the lock manager for a lock that either has been granted or is waiting to be granted. This DMV provides information about the resource on which the lock request is being made and the request which describes the lock request itself. The sys.dm_tran_locks DMV can be very useful for quickly getting a holistic view of the current locking and blocking situation on the SQL server instance. For example, the following query can be used to display the blocking information:

```
SELECT DB_NAME(resource_database_id) AS database_name,
    resource_type, request_mode, request_session_id,
    blocking_session_id, resource_associated_entity_id
FROM sys.dm_tran_locks AS dtl
INNER JOIN sys.dm_os_waiting_tasks AS dowt
    ON dtl.lock_owner_address = dowt.resource_address;
```

**Note** The resource_database_id returned by the sys.dm_tran_locks DMV is the database id corresponding to the database to which the particular resource belongs and is in no way related to the SQL Server 2005 Resource database explained in Chapter 10.

### sys.dm_tran_session_transactions

The sys.dm_tran_session_transactions DMV returns correlation information mapping currently active associated transactions to their respective sessions. One row is usually displayed for every active transaction. However, sys.dm_tran_session_transactions displays multiple rows for bound sessions, distributed transactions, and queries executed in autocommit mode using multiple active result sets (MARS).

### sys.dm_tran_top_version_generators

The sys.dm_tran_top_version_generators DMV returns information about objects that are producing the most versions in the version store. This DMV lists the top 256 aggregated record lengths that are grouped by the database_id and rowset_id. The sys.dm_tran_top_-version_generators can be used to determine the largest consumers of the version store when the snapshot isolation database options (READ_COMMITTED_SNAPSHOT or ALLOW_SNAPSHOT_ISOLATION) are enabled. You may want to be selective in using this DMV because it queries the entire version store, which can be a costly operation that is intrusive to system performance.

### sys.dm_tran_transactions_snapshot

The sys.dm_tran_transactions_snapshot DMV returns the sequence_number of transactions that are active when each snapshot transaction starts. This DMV can be used to find the number of currently active snapshot transactions and to identify data modifications that are ignored by a particular snapshot transaction.

> **Note** For a transaction that is active when a snapshot transaction starts, all data modifications by that transaction, even after that transaction commits, are ignored by the snapshot transaction.

### sys.dm_tran_version_store

The sys.dm_tran_version_store DMV returns a virtual table that displays all version records in the version store. Each versioned record is stored as binary data together with some tracking or status information. This DMV can be used to find the previous versions of the rows in binary representation as they exist in the version store. You may want to be selective in using this DMV because it queries the entire version store, which can be a costly operation that is intrusive to system performance.

# Creating a Performance Data Warehouse

As we've seen in this chapter, DMVs present a very powerful means for gaining insights into the operations of the server and analyzing performance problems. However, the dynamic nature of DMVs can limit their usefulness in certain situations. Consider a case where the users of an application complain of occasional poor transaction response times that occur at random and especially after midnight. You, the database administrator, know that SQL Server is possibly not performing optimally but cannot effectively investigate the problem because by the time the users encounter the problem and tell you about it the next morning, the problem has stopped occurring. Now, given that the problem has resolved itself by morning and the information presented by DMVs is transient in nature, the data does not accurately represent the state of the server when the problem occurred, rendering it of limited use in investigating the problem the following morning.

To address this issue, you can consider creating a performance data warehouse. A performance data warehouse is essentially a historical archive of periodic snapshots of the DMV data of interest. You can archive the data from as many DMVs as you want, at the required frequency, and in a level of detail you believe will be most useful for analyzing the performance of your workload. For example, you can choose to capture the data of all DMVs every 60 minutes, or you can capture the information for just a few columns of a handful of DMVs every 60 seconds.

Now, let's take a look at creating a simple but very useful performance data warehouse. The purpose of this performance data warehouse is to archive key elements of query execution details so that the information can be used to analyze query performance in any interval of time. We can achieve this by capturing the top few (say, 10) longest-running queries using the sys.dm_exec_query_plans DMV and archiving the data into a database.

Let's start by creating a performance database called PerfDB that we will use to archive the performance data:

---

**On the CD**   The code for the example below is provided on the CD in the file Performance_Data_Warehouse_Example.sql in the \Scripts\Chapter 31 folder.

---

```
CREATE DATABASE PerfDB
ON (NAME = PerfDB_dat,
    FILENAME = 'C:\PerfDB_dat.mdf', SIZE = 100, FILEGROWTH = 10)
LOG ON (NAME = PerfDB_log,
    FILENAME = 'C:\PerfDB_log.ldf', SIZE = 10, FILEGROWTH = 10);
```

---

**Note**   You should change the database file location, size, and growth parameters to best suit your usage model. Additional information about the database creation command can be found in Chapter 10.

Next, let's create a table (ExecQueryStats) to store the query execution information. Because we will be extracting and storing information from the sys.dm_exec_query_stats DMV, we will create a table very similar to the output of that DMV, the only two changes being the addition of a datetime column (to store information about the time the query information was archived) and the replacement of the sql_handle and associated offsets with the actual SQL text. The create DDL statement for this table is listed here:

```
USE PerfDB;
CREATE TABLE ExecQueryStats(
    current_datetime DATETIME,
    sql_text NVARCHAR(MAX),
    plan_generation_num BIGINT,
    plan_handle VARBINARY(64),
    creation_time DATETIME,
    last_execution_time DATETIME,
    execution_count BIGINT,
    total_worker_time BIGINT,
    last_worker_time BIGINT,
    min_worker_time BIGINT,
    max_worker_time BIGINT,
    total_physical_reads BIGINT,
    last_physical_reads BIGINT,
    min_physical_reads BIGINT,
    max_physical_reads BIGINT,
    total_logical_writes BIGINT,
    last_logical_writes BIGINT,
    min_logical_writes BIGINT,
    max_logical_writes BIGINT,
    total_logical_reads BIGINT,
    last_logical_reads BIGINT,
    min_logical_reads BIGINT,
    max_logical_reads BIGINT,
    total_clr_time BIGINT,
    last_clr_time BIGINT,
```

```
        min_clr_time BIGINT,
        max_clr_time BIGINT,
        total_elapsed_time BIGINT,
        last_elapsed_time BIGINT,
        min_elapsed_time BIGINT,
        max_elapsed_time BIGINT
);
```

Now that we have the infrastructure in place, all we need to do is extract the query execution information using the DMV and insert it into this table at some predetermined interval (say, every 10 minutes). We can achieve this using the following INSERT statement:

```
USE PerfDB;

INSERT ExecQueryStats
    SELECT TOP 10 GETDATE(),
        (SELECT SUBSTRING(text, statement_start_offset/2,
            (CASE WHEN statement_end_offset = -1
                THEN LEN(CONVERT(nvarchar(max), text)) * 2
            ELSE statement_end_offset
            END - statement_start_offset)/2 + 1)
        FROM sys.dm_exec_sql_text(sql_handle)),
        plan_generation_num,
        plan_handle,
        creation_time,
        last_execution_time,
        execution_count,
        total_worker_time,
        last_worker_time,
        min_worker_time,
        max_worker_time,
        total_physical_reads,
        last_physical_reads,
        min_physical_reads,
        max_physical_reads,
```

```
        total_logical_writes,

        last_logical_writes,

        min_logical_writes,

        max_logical_writes,

        total_logical_reads,

        last_logical_reads,

        min_logical_reads,

        max_logical_reads,

        total_clr_time,

        last_clr_time,

        min_clr_time,

        max_clr_time,

        total_elapsed_time,

        last_elapsed_time,

        min_elapsed_time,

        max_elapsed_time

    FROM sys.dm_exec_query_stats AS eqs

    ORDER BY eqs.last_worker_time DESC;
```

This statement extracts the relevant details of the 10 longest-running queries in the particular interval of time from the sys.dm_exec_query_stats DMVs and inserts that into the ExecQueryStats table created above. Along with this, it also inserts the timestamp and the SQL text extracted using the sys.dm_exec_sql_text DMV.

The last task in creating the performance data warehouse is to set up a mechanism through which the data collection can be automated to occur every 10 minutes. While you can use any scheduler tool to do this, I've found the SQL Agent, which is installed along with the database engine, the easiest to use. The following steps list the procedure you can use to create a SQL Agent job to automate the execution of the previous query:

1.  Make sure that the SQL Server Agent service is running and that it is set to auto start when the server is started. You can do this using SQL Server Configuration Manager, as explained in Chapter 9, "Configuring Microsoft SQL Server 2005 on the Network."

2.  In Object Explorer view, connect to the server instance of your choice, and then expand the server's Databases folder.

3.  Expand the Server node and then the SQL Server Agent node by clicking on the + sign, as shown in Figure 31-4.

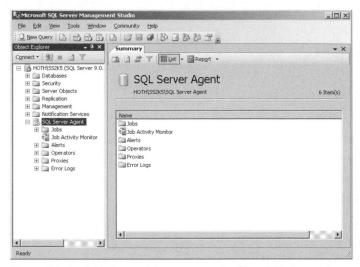

**Figure 31-4**    SQL Server Management Studio—SQL Server Agent view.

4. Right-click Jobs and select New Job.

5. Type in a name for the job and a description in the New Job window that appears, as shown in Figure 31-5.

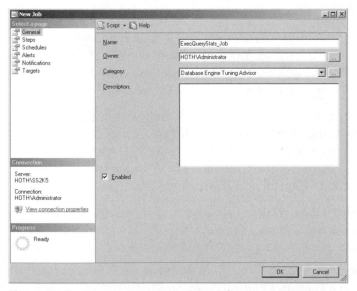

**Figure 31-5**    SQL Server Agent—New Job.

6. Click the Steps page and then click the New button at the bottom left-side of the window.

7. In the New Job Step window that appears, type in a name for the step, change the database to be PerfDB from the drop-down list, and add the SQL text for the step presented in the INSERT statement above, as shown in Figure 31-6. Click OK to continue. This will put you back in the New Job window.

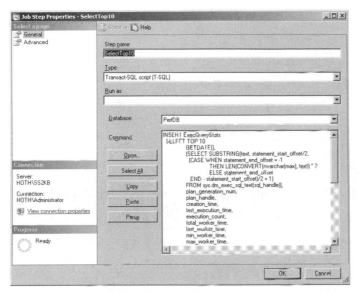

**Figure 31-6**   New Job—New Job Step.

8. In the New Job window, click the Schedules page and then click the New button at the bottom left-side of the window.

9. In the New Job Schedule window that appears, type in a name for the schedule, and change the Frequency to Occurs Daily from the drop-down list. In the Daily Frequency section, select the radio button next to Occurs Every, type **10** in the text box next to it, and then select Minute(s) from the drop-down list adjacent to that, as shown in Figure 31-7. Click OK to continue.

10. In the New Job window, click OK to create the job.

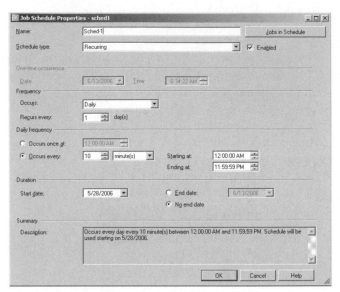

**Figure 31-7**    New Job—New Job Schedule.

## Real World    Identifying the Cause and Source of Performance Problems Using a Performance Data Warehouse

A customer with whom I work closely recently adopted the procedure of creating a performance data warehouse very similar to the example presented previously and in just a few days of capturing the data was able to identify and resolve some significant performance issues with their in-house financials application.

The process used to identify the issues was fairly simple. After having accumulated a couple of days of performance data snapshots, they selected the top 1,000 queries for the particular 24-hour period in descending order of the amount of time the query had taken to execute (using the last_worker_time column). When analyzing the data, they observed that there were only 4 unique SQL statements, and all of them had very high processor utilization (total_worker_time) and high reads (total_physical_reads) associated with them. The customer also observed that three of the four queries were always executed only near the start of the hour. This fact helped them easily link the queries back to a batch job they had scheduled to run every hour at the start of the hour. After further analysis of the queries, they tuned three of them by creating two additional indexes, while the fourth one had to be rewritten in order to eliminate an expensive wildcard search operation predicate (SELECT ... FROM ...WHERE ... AND ColA LIKE 'BU028%').

> After completing this exercise the customer observed order of magnitude improvement in its batch job and also significantly lower utilization on its back-end SAN disk subsystem.

While this example presents the archiving of the snapshots of a single DMV, the same mechanism can be extended to archive snapshots of multiple DMVs in the same data warehouse, or possibly even different data warehouses. Depending on the number of DMVs you archive and the frequency of the archiving, your performance data warehouse can grow to be significantly large pretty quickly. For example, the sample performance data warehouse we created will have 1,440 rows archived in every 24-hour period and, assuming that each row spans about 4 kilobytes (KB) on average, up to 6 MB of data can be added to the table in the corresponding period. If you capture multiple DMV outputs in your performance data warehouse or have a higher frequency, you can quickly end up with several gigabytes of data. To ensure that you do not run out of disk space, you should closely monitor the disk drive on which you've created your performance data warehouses and have a policy in place to periodically backup and purge the old data.

# Summary

Understanding the operation of an application and tuning performance usually requires insights into the internal operation of the database engine components. While this was generally possible in earlier versions of SQL Server, SQL Server 2005 dramatically simplifies the process of surfacing this information with the introduction of dynamic management views and functions.

In this chapter, we described the new DMV functionality and took a detailed look at each of the new DMVs. We also covered several example scenarios where DMVs were used very effectively to investigate application performance and understand the workings of the database engine. Lastly, we stepped through the process of creating a sample performance data warehouse to archive a log of slow running queries.

## Chapter 32
# Microsoft SQL Server 2005 Scalability Options

Your database solution's response time and, more importantly, the level of its throughput have a direct impact on the productivity and revenue of your organization. Performance and throughput are a measure of not only your underlying hardware platform but also how well your database solution has been designed.

Although hardware performance has significantly improved even as cost has dropped dramatically during the last decade, organizations and database users demand more from their database solutions as databases increase in both size and the number of concurrent users. The research and development costs of improving the performance of hardware for vendors, especially in the microprocessor sector, have likewise increased significantly. Moore's law is under strain and various laws of physics are becoming a real issue in microprocessor, disk drive, and memory design.

Consequently, software companies like Microsoft have introduced features into their operating systems and database solutions that can better utilize the available hardware resources. In this chapter, we'll look at the various technologies offered by SQL Server 2005 to realize better performance and throughput.

> **Note**   As a database architect, I think it is great to have such a massive range of options in SQL Server 2005 for scaling your database solution. But make sure you don't confuse scalability and high availability, which is quite common. Although the two concepts may seem related, they are not. With high availability, you are trying to guarantee a certain level of a up-time, or availability, whereas scalability is primarily concerned with getting better performance through utilization of more resources. The fact that certain SQL Server 2005 technologies can be used both to scale your database solution and to provide high availability probably does not help this confusion.

When evaluating the various available SQL Server scalability options, don't forget that you can also combine certain options to get a best-of-breed solution. Ultimately, as always, it depends on a thorough understanding of your business requirements and technical constraints.

# Scalability Options

Once your database design and database application have been optimized, there are two main methods of improving response time and increasing throughput: scaling up or scaling out your SQL Server 2005 solution. Typically, you scale up your SQL Server 2005 solution because it is generally cheaper to "throw more hardware at it," but eventually you will reach some limit, in which case you need to start looking at your scale-out options. Remember to explore all options for scaling up to understand how they can best be used for your particular SQL Server 2005 solution. A lot of these options have already been discussed in earlier chapters, such as Chapter 4, "I/O Subsystem Planning and RAID Configuration," and other chapter references.

# Scaling Up

Scaling up means maximizing the performance capabilities of your existing SQL Server 2005 instance's hardware resources by adding more processors, memory, and storage capacity, or by replacing your existing hardware resources with faster versions.

Let's examine these hardware subsystems and the options for scaling up their hardware resources. Be sure to purchase the appropriate hardware, operating system, and SQL Server 2005 edition to allow for future growth as your database solution's requirements grow.

## Processor Subsystem

Although most SQL Server instances are I/O-bound rather than compute-bound, scaling up your processor susbsystem generally results in better performance and allows for more capacity. There are a number of considerations available when scaling up your processor subsystems:

- Using a 32-bit x86 processor from AMD or Intel
- Using a 64-bit x64 processor from AMD or Intel
- Using a 64-bit IA64 (Itanium-based) processor from Intel
- Using hyperthreading technology

- Using a multiprocessor-based server

- Using a multicore-based processor

Ideally, your organization purchases server hardware that allows for future growth. Generally speaking, it is recommended that you use a 64-bit server for any new SQL Server 2005 solutions, primarily due to the amount of addressable memory that is available. We'll get into more detail about that shortly.

Another important consideration is whether to use a x64 or IA64 instruction set based processor. A detailed discussion is beyond the scope of this book, so you will need to investigate this further through your hardware vendor, but keep a couple of points in mind. x64 processors offer the *fastest* performance at the processor level today with generally faster clock speeds than the IA64 processors. The battle between AMD and Intel in the x64 marketplace is continually bringing the release of increasingly fast processors at decreasing prices, relative to performance. The IA64 processors generally offer better floating point arthimetic, and their architecture scales much better where your workload requires more than eight processors.

In short, you should keep up-to-date with hardware vendors to ensure that you have the latest information so that you can make correct recommendations for purchasing hardware within your budgetary constraints. Although it may have a minimal impact on your decision-making process when designing your database solution, you might still want to check out the various performance benchmarks for relational database engines at *http:/ /www.tpc.org/* to see how well SQL Server 2005 will scale and what kind of hardware is required.

---

**Note**   Whether SQL Server 2005 will run faster on a 64-bit platform compared to a 32-bit platform depends on a number of factors, such as whether memory is the bottleneck, whether the database solution is CPU-bound, whether there are pointers in the working set data, whether the processors are instruction set-bound, and whether your database solution is floating-point intensive.

Microsoft has found that SQL Server 2005 solutions that are not memory-constrained on a 32-bit platform may run about 10 percent less efficiently using the 64-bit edition than the 32-bit edition on the same server. Additionally, you may see the processors busier on a 64-bit platform than on a 32-bit one when you perform an equivalent workload.

## Multiple Processors

The Windows operating system uses a Symmetric multiprocessing (SMP) architecture to allow multiple processes to run concurrently. This multitasking is done at the thread level, so if an application is multithreaded, as is the case with SQL Server 2005, it can perform tasks concurrently.

A recent trend in hardware is scaling out the processors by supporting multiple cores per processor because it is more cost effective to shrink and use multiple cores on a processor than to increase the speed of processors. Modern operating systems and business applications, such as SQL Server 2005, are multithreaded and, consequently, can take advantage of this technology.

The best multitasking performance is achieved through multiprocessor servers versus equivalent multicore uniprocessor servers. With the advent of multicore processors, discussions can get a bit confusing, so it is common to refer to the sockets on the motherboard, as opposed to the processors. The number of sockets that a server supports depends on the hardware vendor, but eight-way socket servers are now commonplace. Using more than eight sockets tends to substantially increase the hardware cost due to the complexity of designing appropriate motherboard technology.

An interesting trend, as shown in Figure 32-1, is how dual-socket servers catch up with four-socket within 12 to 24 months based on Intel Xeon processor-based servers over the past decade. So when purchasing your hardware remember to plan for future growth. This might involve purchasing additional processors or upgrading to faster processors. So talk to your hardware vendor.

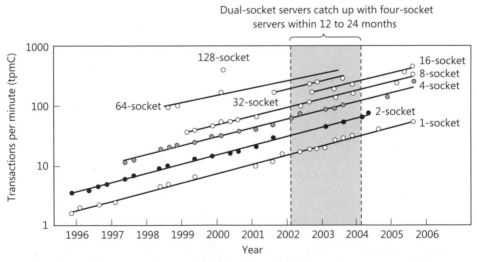

**Figure 32-1**   How dual socket servers catch up with four-socket servers within 12 to 24 months.

---

**More Info**   For more information on right-sizing your server and cutting system costs through dual-socket server, you should read the "Server Rightsizing:

Dual-socket Systems Cut Costs" article located at *http://www.intel.com/it/pdf/ server-rightsizing.pdf*.

---

## Multicore Processors

Multicore processor solutions available from AMD and Intel represent a great way of scaling your processor susbsystem. Processors with multiple cores can execute multiple jobs simultaneously (multitask) compared to single-core processors, although an application has to be multithreaded to take advantage of the architecture. SQL Server 2005 can take advantage of multiple cores because it allocates a scheduler to each core as if it were a separate processor. SQL Server 2005 licensing is based on the processor (or socket) and not how many cores the processor has, so multicore processors represent a lower total cost of ownership (TCO).

Multicore processors scale very effectively, although AMD and Intel have taken different approaches with the design of their Opteron/Athlon and Xeon/Pentium processors, respectively. When deciding on a multicore processor server, don't forget to look at the the multicore architecture, the Front Side Bus (FSB) speed, the memory controller, related I/O chipsets and power usage/efficiency. In other words, it is a holistic look at the entire server, as opposed to concentrating on any particular hardware component.

At the time of writing this book, Intel just released quad-core processors in the last quarter of 2006, and AMD is planning to release their re-engineered quad-core processors in mid 2007. I would not be surprised to see eight-core processors being released as early as 2008 as both AMD and Intel shift to 65nm fabrication for their processor lines.

## Hyperthreading

Intel's hyperthreading technology has the potential to yield good performance gains on a number of applications by effectively allowing the CPU to remain less idle. However, hyperthreading does not guarantee the same performance as a server with two processors or a multicore processor.

Microsoft's conservative testing has shown 10 to 20 percent improvements in certain SQL Server workloads, but the application patterns have a significant impact on these metrics. You might find that your SQL Server 2005 solution does not receive an increase in performance by taking advantage of hyperthreading. If the physical processor is already saturated with multiple concurrent scheduler tasks, using these logical processors can actually reduce the workload because you end up thrashing the CPU cache.

---

**More Info**    For more information on SQL Server and hyperthreading, you should read the Microsoft Knowledge Base article located at *http://support.microsoft.com/kb/322385/*.

---

## Memory Subsystem

Most SQL Server 2005 instances are I/O-bound, not CPU-bound. The best way to improve your I/O performance is by adding more memory to your SQL Server 2005 solution because the database engine will then be able to cache more data in its buffer pool. The amount of memory SQL Server 2005 can address depends on the underlying operating system. Standard 32-bit addresses can map a maximum of 4 GB of memory. Therefore, standard address spaces of 32-bit processes are limited to 4 GB. By default, 32-bit Microsoft Windows operating systems reserve 2 GB for the operating system, leaving 2 GB for any application. However, you can specify the /3GB parameter in the BOOT.INI file of Windows 2000 Advanced Server or above, so that the operating system reserves only 1 GB of the address space for itself, effectively allowing the application to access up to 3 GB.

If you are running 32-bit SQL Server 2005, you are generally limited to 4 GB of virtual address space (VAS), depending on the underlying operating system. However, due to the design of the Windows operating system, 32-bit SQL Server 2005 can only access 2GB of the VAS on 32-bit Windows because of the user-mode address space limit, unless you have enabled 3 GB tuning, in which case 32-bit SQL Server can access the 3 GB. This was covered in more detail in Chapter 2, "Microsoft SQL Server 2005 Editions, Capacity Limits, and Licensing."

However, 32-bit SQL Server 2005 can take advantage of the full 4 GB of VAS if you are running it on Windows Server 2003 x64 using the WOW64 (Windows On Windows) layer. The address space limit for SQL Server 2005 is summarized in Table 32-1. With 64-bit SQL Server 2005, the VAS depends on the hardware platform and is probably going to be restricted by the vendor's hardware limitations.

**Table 32-1    Address Space Limit for 32-Bit and 64-Bit SQL Server 2005**

| Windows Server 2003 | SQL Server 2005 | Virtual Memory Limits | Physical Memory Limits |
|---|---|---|---|
| 32-bit | 32-bit | 2 GB<br><br>(3 GB with 3 GB BOOT.INI switch) | 64 GB |
| 64-bit (x64) | 32-bit | 4 GB | 64 GB |

**Table 32-1   Address Space Limit for 32-Bit and 64-Bit SQL Server 2005** (continued)

| Windows Server 2003 | SQL Server 2005 | Virtual Memory Limits | Physical Memory Limits |
|---|---|---|---|
| 64-bit (x64) | 64-bit (x64) | 8 TB | 1 TB <br> (Operating System Dependant) |
| 64-bit (IA64) | 64-bit (IA64) | | 32 TB |

*Address Windowing Extensions* (AWE) is a set of extensions to Windows memory manager that is designed to work around the 32-bit 4 GB VAS limit, thereby allowing an application to utilize more than 4 GB of memory. Although the 32-bit address space is limited to 4 GB, the nonpaged memory can be much larger. So AWE allows an application to acquire physical memory and then dynamically map views of the nonpaged memory to the 32-bit address space. This enables memory-intensive applications, such as large database systems, to address more memory than can be supported in a 32-bit address space. Applications need to be written specifically to take advantage of AWE, and there is some overhead incurred.

SQL Server 2005 can use AWE only for its data cache. Not all SQL Server 2005 components are AWE aware, so SQL Server Analysis Services, SQL Server Integration Services, SQL Server Reporting Services, and CLR components cannot take advantage of AWE.

> **Note**   You cannot use the /3GB switch in BOOT.INI if your server has more than 16 GB of memory as the Windows operating system needs the full 2 GB to manage the AWE memory.

The advantages of using the flat address space of 64-bit Windows are numerous, and it is recommended that you follow this path instead of using AWE, although SQL Server 2005 has improved the use of AWE memory over SQL Server 2000.

> **More Info**   SQL Server 2005 handles AWE differently on Windows Server 2003 from Windows Server 2000 in a number of ways. The major difference is that SQL Server 2005 supports dynamic allocation of AWE memory on Windows Server 2003. For more information on these differences search for the "Enabling AWE Memory for SQL Server" topic in SQL Server 2005 Books Online.

# I/O Subsystems

Another technique to improve the throughput of your SQL Server 2005 instance is to scale up the I/O subsystem. Unfortunately, disk drive technology and networks have not had the same dramatic improvements in performance as processors have had over the last decade. Nevertheless, there are a number of techniques that you can employee.

The main technique for improving your disk I/O subsystem is through an appropriate RAID array or SAN solution. The various levels of RAID and their respective performances and levels of protection were covered in Chapter 4. You should read that chapter before implementing your RAID subsystem to ensure you have chosen the appropriate level of RAID for your SQL Server 2005 instance.

I/O performance of your SAN performance can be improved through both faster Host Bus Adapters (HBA) and and a dedicated/ faster network infrastructure. Another technique of improving your I/O subsystem, one that is often overlooked, is through Network Interface Card (NIC) teaming. NIC teaming allows you to group multiple physical NICs into a single logical network device called a bond. The main advantage of NIC teaming is that it allows you to load balance or scale out your network traffic through a single IP address to provide high bandwidth. Another advantage is that NIC teaming effectively provides fault tolerance.

Most hardware vendors offer a NIC teaming solution. Make sure you read your vendor's documentation and generally ensure that you are running the latest firmware and NIC drivers.

# Scaling Out

Scaling out generally involves the addition of extra SQL Servers to provide increased scalability. When a SQL Server 2005 instance for a particular database solution is at its maximum potential and unable to meet performance demands, you should consider scaling out. SQL Server 2005 allows you to scale out both the database storage solution and the hardware solution. Chapter 19, "Data Partitioning," covered how you can use data partitioning to scale out your database solution. In this chapter, I will examine the following technologies for potentially scaling out your SQL Server solution:

- SQL Server instances
- Clustering
- Database mirroring
- Log shipping
- Replication
- Shared scalable databases

These various SQL Server 2005 technologies have not necessarily been designed to scale out your SQL Server solution, so make sure you understand what the technology was designed to do and its correct implementation so that you can leverage any scale-out capabilities.

## Multiple SQL Server Instances

Remember to consider taking advantage of SQL Server 2005's ability to run multiple instances on the same server. This ability provides an effective technique of taking advantage of modern multiprocessor hardware, especially with latest generation of multicore processors that are currently available and are planned for release in the next coming years.

This technique involves installing multiple SQL Server 2005 instances on the same server and deploying database solutions on these separate instances. Each database solution get its own database engine with its own allocation of processor and memory resources. Furthermore, through the separate database engine, each database gets its own lock manager, set of worker threads, and *tempdb* system database.

> **Note**   Licensing for SQL Server 2005 is based on the processor (sockets) and not the number of cores the processor has. Furthermore, the number of processors a SQL Server instance can use is likewise based on the processor and not the number of cores it supports.

You can further compartmentalize each SQL Server 2005 instance, thus guaranteeing a certain level of performance and resources, by taking advantage of some of the configuration options, such as the affinity mask, that is covered in Chapter 29, "Database System Tuning."

### Real World   SQL Server 2005 Express Edition

I am particularly excited by the potential of SQL Server 2005 Express Edition for a number of my clients. For these clients, the features supported by Express Edition of SQL Server 2005 are sufficient for their needs. Given the multicore processors available and the 64-bit address space of Windows Server 2003 x64, it allows me to install multiple instances of SQL Server 2005 Express Edition on the same server and deploy a database solution per instance, guaranteeing both performance and reliability at the instance level at a phenomenal price.

> **Note**   SQL Server 2005 supports 50 instances on a stand-alone server and 25 instances on a failover cluster.

# Clustering

The failover clustering technology available in SQL Server 2005 does not inherently provide any scalability advantages. The failover clustering is used to provide a high-availability solution by protecting against server failure, including the hardware, operating system, and SQL Server 2005 instance. Chapter 26, "Failover Clustering Installation and Configuration," covered how to install, configure, and test a SQL Server 2005 failover cluster.

Although SQL Server 2005 does not support load-balancing clustering, you can still take advantage of SQL Server 2005 clustering technology to scale out your database solution by taking advantage of the spare hardware available through the passive node. This might not be possible if you have cross-database dependencies, but you can host stand-alone database solutions on separate virtual servers. You will also need to purchase additional SQL Server 2005 licences.

When designing a clustering topology to scale out your database solutions, it is important to take into account several considerations, including any existing service level agreements (SLAs), availability requirements, failover policies, and risk assessments. It is important to capacity plan your hardware resources correctly in case a failover occurs.

## Multiinstance Cluster

A multiinstance cluster typically has two virtual servers installed in a cluster. The database data and log files for each virtual server are typically installed on a shared storage resource that is dedicated to that virtual server. The primary node for each virtual server runs on separate hardware, as shown in Figure 32-2. Because there are multiple instances of SQL Server 2005 running on each instance, a separate SQL Server 2005 license is required for each virtual server.

You can use a multinstance cluster to scale out database solutions to separate hardware resources. It is more cost-effective than a single-instance cluster because it utilizes all of your existing hardware. The *HR* and *Sales* databases shown in Figure 32-2 effectively run on separate hardware resources and are therefore able to individually fully utilize the memory and processor resources available.

---

**Note**    In case of a failover, you need to ensure that each node has the required memory and processor resources to maintain any existing SLAs, as one node will now be running two instances of SQL Server 2005. You can take advantage of SQL Server 2005's dynamic configuration options to allocate resources appropriately in case a failover occurs.

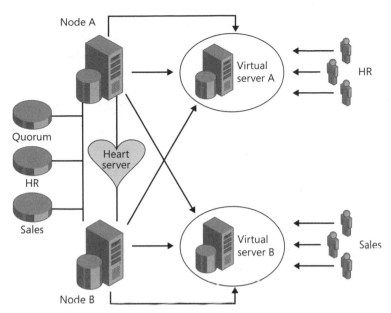

**Figure 32-2**   Multiinstance cluster used to scale out the *HR* and *Sales* databases.

## N+1 Cluster

An N+1 cluster has two or more virtual servers installed in a cluster along with one passive node (+1). The database data and log files for each virtual server are installed on a shared storage resource that is dedicated to that virtual server. A separate SQL Server 2005 license is required for each virtual server.

In the case of a primary node for a virtual server failing or being taken offline, the passive node takes control of the shared storage resource for that virtual server. The other virtual servers, those using the previously passive node, are not affected by this failover.

An N+1 cluster can be more cost-effective than configuring multiple single-instance clusters, as fewer servers are required. N+1 clusters allow you to better scale out database solutions on existing servers while still guaranteeing a level of performance due to the spare passive node.

---

**Note**   The most important consideration when designing an N+1 cluster is calculating the resource capacity in the case of more than one node failing at the same time. Your passive node might need to handle the entire load caused by multiple node failures.

### N+M Cluster

An N+M cluster has two or more virtual servers installed in a cluster together with two or more passive nodes (M). Again, the database data and log files for each virtual server are installed on a shared storage resource that is dedicated to that virtual server. Again, a separate SQL Server 2005 license is required for each virtual server.

The advantage of an N+M cluster is that you have multiple passive nodes that can be utilized in case of multiple failovers, so the load of multiple primary node failures can be spread across the passive nodes.

N+M clusters are typically used when it is important to gurantee levels of performance. Alternatively, they are used where your passive nodes do not have the appropriate level of hardware to handle multiple failovers.

**Note**   It is most common to see an N+M cluster used in an eight-node configuration as either a 6+2 or 5+3 cluster.

## Database Mirroring

As you learned in Chapter 27, "Log Shipping and Database Mirroring," database mirroring is a new technology to SQL Server 2005 that delivers a high-availability solution by providing redundancy at the database level. With database mirroring, transaction log records are sent directly from the principal database to the mirror. This technique keeps the mirror database up-to-date with a principal database with no loss of committed data. If the principal server fails, the secondary server can take over. The failover process can be automatic only when a witness server has been configured, to solve the "split-brain" problem as discussed in Chapter 27; otherwise it has to be initiated manually.

As with clustering, database mirroring is primarily designed to provide fault tolerance, but at the database level. As database mirroring is implemented at the SQL Server engine level through software, there is no need for the specialized hardware that clustering requires.

**Note**   Database mirroring relies heavily upon reliable network infrastructure, so it is not suited to WAN links that are unreliable or have low bandwidth.

Database mirroring allows only one mirror database per principal database, and normally your users are not able to access the mirror database. Nevertheless, you can still use SQL Server's database mirroring technology to scale out your database solution and realize some performance benefits by offloading reporting activity from the principal server, as shown in Figure 32-3.

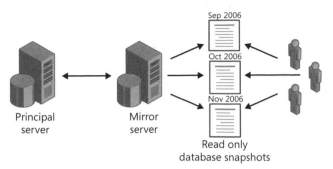

**Figure 32-3**   Offloading reporting activity through database mirroring.

To use a database mirroring for reporting, you must create a database snapshots on the mirror database, as shown in Chapter 10, "Creating Databases and Database Snapshots," and then redirect client applications to the appropriate snapshot. Client applications are then able to access this static, read-only, transactionally consistent snapshot of the mirror database, although the mirror database itself is inaccessible.

> **Note**   The mirrored database must be in a SYNCHRONIZED database state for you to be able to create a database snapshot.

Due to the point-in-time nature of the database snapshot, new or updated data in the mirrored database is not available until you create a new database snapshot. Consequently, you will have to create a new database snapshot as required and have your client applications reconnect to the latest database snapshot. This might introduce a latency, that you will need to analyze to see whether it is acceptable or not, depending on your business requirements. Use any existing SLAs for guidance.

Another import consideration is to correctly size and plan the capacity of your database snapshot(s). Although a database snapshot is initially almost empty, it can grow very quickly depending on the amount of data that changes within your database, so you need to ensure you have enough capacity to store the database snapshot. The database snapshot can easily take up as much space as the database itself if enough of the data has changed.

Although you can have multiple database snapshots, they might decrease the performance on the principal database, depending on the configuration of the principal and mirror server. Consequently, Microsoft recommends that you keep only a few relatively recent database snapshots on your mirror databases. In most cases, you will need to keep only the most recent database snapshot and will be able to drop all earlier ones.

> **Note**   You will not be able to drop any database snapshots until after any current queries accessing those database snapshots finish executing.

Because each principal is restricted to having only one mirror database, the read-only nature of database snapshots, and the potential latency arising due to the time between database snapshots, database mirroring is not commonly used as a means of scaling out your database solution. It probably works best for organisations that have already decided to use database mirroring and would like to take advantage of offloading reporting from the production system.

## Log Shipping

Although enhanced in SQL Server 2005, log shipping has been available in one form or another in all versions of SQL Server. It relies on proven technologies, such as transaction log backups, file copying, and SQL Server Agent. Chapter 27 provides an overview of log shipping and shows how to configure and tune a SQL Server 2005 log shipping solution. Remember that log shipping does not automatically failover from the primary server to the secondary server when the primary database fails. However, it does guarantee a transactionally consistent version of the primary database on a secondary SQL Server 2005 instance. The main issue with log shipping is the degree of latency you can afford between the primary and secondary servers. This data latency depends mainly on the backup, copy, and restore schedule, although environmental considerations such as your network infrastructure are important.

As the secondary databases of the secondary server are accessible by users only for read-only purposes, log shipping represents an excellent way of scaling out your reporting requirements because you have removed query processing from the primary server to one or more secondary servers, thus freeing up the resources on the primary server. Otherwise, you have achieved better data availability by providing your data closer to the user.

The main advantage of log shipping over database mirroring is that you can have multiple secondary servers to which you have log-shipped your primary database's transaction logs. Nor is there the dependency on the network infrastructure, as with database mirroring, so you can schedule your transaction logs to be shipped periodically throughout the business day or after hours, as required. Consequently, log shipping works particularly well with geographically dispersed SQL Server instances, as seen in Figure 32-4.

In this example, we're log shipping our customer database from the head office located in Sydney to satellite offices in East Timor, Perth, and Wellington. Because both Perth and Sydney are in Australia and have a fast reliable network connection, log shipping has been scheduled at an hourly frequency. East Timor has an expensive WAN link and only has a small operation, so it is sufficient to configure log shipping to occur once a week as they do not need the latest information from the Sydney office. As Wellington is behind in time relative to Sydney, it is sufficient to replicate once daily after the close of business in the Sydney office. By the time the employees in Wellington come in to work, they should see the latest version of the customer database. The main point here is that log-shipping can be highly customized to suit the business requirements and infrastructure available. It is a completely asynchronous solution.

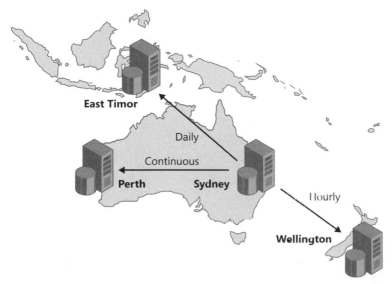

**Figure 32-4**   Scaling out reporting requirements geographically with log shipping.

The log shipping was designed primarily as a warm standby solution. Consequently, the secondary database on the secondary server is configured by default in NORECOVERY mode, which allows additional transaction logs to be loaded while preventing users from accessing the secondary database. In this example, you must configure the secondary database in STANDBY mode, which allows read-only access to the database but also allows additional transaction logs to be loaded. There are two configuration choices for the STANDBY mode:

- The default does not disconnect users from the secondary database when the next shipped log is ready to be loaded. Shipped transaction logs accumulate until all users are disconnected. This can obviously be problematic if you have a very busy database solution in which your users are running reports continually throughout the day.

- You can select the Disconnect Users In The Database When Restoring Backups check box, as shown in Figure 32-5, which disconnects users from the secondary database whenever the next shipped transaction log is ready to be loaded. The disconnection occurs based on the schedule that you have configured for the restore job.

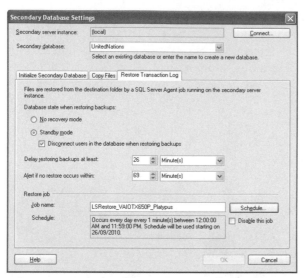

**Figure 32-5**   The Disconnect Users In The Database
When Restoring Backups check box.

You will have to decide upon an appropriate schedule for shipping the logs, and how to respond to connected users based on your business requirements, acceptable degree of latency, and operational behaviour.

---

**Note**   Don't forget that the restore jobs can have a different frequency than the transaction log backups and shipping jobs. The transaction logs accumulate until they are ready to be loaded.

---

A log shipping solution can be particularly effective at scaling out your reporting requirements to different departments. Each department has its own version of a secondary database on a SQL Server instance against which they can report. One department's queries do not adversely affect another department's query performance. You have also provided a layer of fault tolerance, so if one department's secondary database crashes other departments will still be able to report with their secondary databases.

Alternatively, for a true fault tolerance layer at the secondary database level, you can use Microsoft's Network Load Balancing (NLB) technology to provide both fault tolerance and load balancing. NLB allows client applications to connect to a single, virtualized IP address configured on the NLB cluster. The NLB cluster is responsible for automatically redirecting the client application to one of the physical IP addresses of the secondary databases that make up the NLB cluster, as shown in Figure 32-6. An additional benefit of implementing an NLB cluster is that it allows you to take your secondary

SQL Server instances offline to perform maintenance tasks without having to a reconfigure client applications.

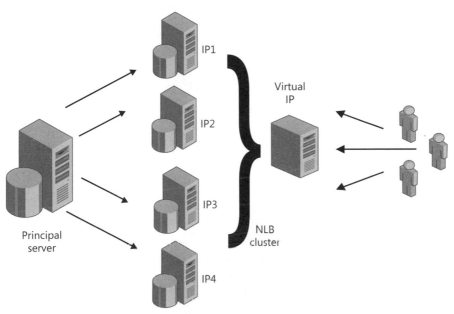

**Figure 32-6**   A log shipping solution using an NLB cluster.

# Replication

SQL Server's replication technology has proven to be powerful, reliable, and flexible during the last decade, representing a great way of scaling out your database solution. Chapter 20, "Replication," covers the fundamentals of replication and the different replication types for configuring, managing, and tuning replication.

When considering SQL Server 2005's replication technology, make sure you understand how the technology works to determine the appropriate replication topology for your scale-out solution. The two main considerations are the latency that your database solution can afford, whether database users will need to modify data, and, if so, whether you need to deal with update conflicts.

Environmental and operational factors influence the performance of your replication topology, so it is a good idea to set up a testbed environment to see how it performs within your organization and set correct expectations for all stakeholders.

## Merge Replication

With merge replication, data modifications are kept tracked via triggers on both the publisher and the subscriber. When the publisher and subscriber try to synchronize, they send each list of modified rows and attempt to merge the changes to get a consistent view of the data. In this type of replication, data modification conflicts can occur, so you need to configure some form of conflict resolution.

Merge replication is typically used between a SQL Server instance and a client computer that is not constantly connected to the network, such as in the case of traveling sales staff. When they are back in the office (or connect remotely potentially), they can synchronise their new orders and customers back with the publisher, while the publisher sends them the latest products, pricelists, and any other updated data.

However, you can still use merge replication as a means on scaling out your database solution to multiple SQL Server 2005 instances. Although you could use merge replication rather than transaction replication when you have a slower network infrastructure between the publisher and subscribers, the main reason for using merge replication as a scale-out solution is when you need to modify data at all SQL Server 2005 instances.

When designing a merge replication topology, define the conflict resolution rules, as discussed in Chapter 20, as separate database users can modify the "same data" that is located on their instance of the database. However, merge replication works best where data modifications tend to be mutually exclusive. Figure 32-7 shows an example of merge replication being used to scale out a sales database to multiple offices within Australia. The Brisbane, Melbourne, Perth, and Darwin offices all merge replicate their new orders and customers with the head office in Sydney. Sydney then merge replicates this information to all of the offices. Because Sydney is responsible for the ordering, delivery, and consignment of requested products from overseas, it maintains the product catalog and the status of overseas' orders, which it merge replicates with the various offices. This sort of a scale-out solution does not need to work in real-time, so merge replication is the perfect technology.

## Transactional Replication

With transactional replication, you stream all the DML operations as required from the publisher to the subscriber. Transactional replication has a hierarchy, with transactions being replicated from the publisher to the subscriber.

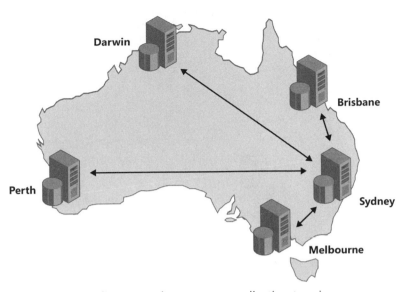

Figure 32-7   Scaling out using a merge replication topology.

Because transactional replication assumes a hierarchical structure, with "read-only" subscribers it works well as a scale-out solution where you want to distribute data to multiple SQL Server 2005 instances for reporting purposes, as shown in Figure 32-8. Database users can connect to any one of the subscribers to generate reports, although there will be some latency between data being modified on the publisher and it being replicated to the subscribers, which depends on your hardware and network infrastructure. Because the HR, Marketing and Sales department are all located at the  Head Office in Sydney on the same LAN continous replication has been configured. Consequently those departments should only experience a minor latency of a few seconds. For the branch office located in Darwin, which is connected via a WAN link, it is sufficient to replicate every hour as a degree of latency is acceptable.

If one of your subscribers goes offline, the transactional replication technology does not automatically switch database users to another available subscriber. You perform the switch at the application level by adding code that automatically redirects a connection if a particular database isn't available.

---

**Note**   Alternatively, you can use the NLB clustering technology, as discussed previously, to virtualize your subscriber layer.

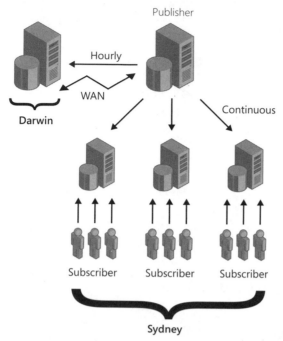

**Figure 32-8**   Scaling out using a transactional replication topology.

Due to transactional replication's hierarchy, you typically do not modify data at the subscriber because your data modifications can be overwritten or cause data conflict errors. Consequently, transactional replication has limited use in a scale-out scenario in which you want your data to be modified at the subscribers. However, you have the ability to update subscriptions without data conflicts by using one of the following options:

- **Immediate updating**   With immediate updating subscriptions, the subscriber and publisher are updated in a single distributed transaction using the Microsoft Distributed Transaction Coordinator DTC. There is a minimal chance of a conflict with this option, but it requires reliable network connections.

- **Queued updating**   With queued updating subscriptions, you queue the DML operations, which means a potential conflict because you effectively allow for simultaneous modification of the same data. Consequently, you have to configure some conflict resolution; the options are as follows:

    - ❑  Publisher wins (default)
    - ❑  Publisher wins, and subscription is reinitialized
    - ❑  Subscriber wins

Figure 32-9 shows a transactional replication with immediate updating subscriber topology in a trading environment. Because all the SQL Server 2005 instances are located on the same fast, reliable LAN, we can take advantage of the (DTC) technology. In this scenario, a user making a change to the "back office" subscriber's database invokes a distributed transaction with the "front office" publisher. This transaction then remains to be replicated to the "middle office" subscriber.

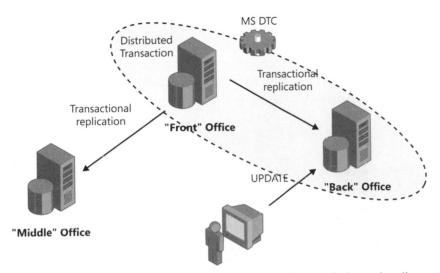

**Figure 32-9**   Transactional replication with immediate updating subscribers.

## Peer-to-Peer Transactional Replication

The new peer-to-peer transactional replication technology is available only in SQL Server 2005 Enterprise Edition. Based on transactional replication, peer-to-peer transactional replication takes advantage of SQL Server 2005's existing transactional replication technology, providing a number of wizards that help you manage the setup and configuration of your peer-to-peer transactional replication solution.

With peer-to-peer transactional replication, you need to ensure that the database schemas on all of the peers are identical. Because peer-to-peer transactional replication uses the same continuous synchronization technique available in existing transactional replication technology, there is some inherent latency. If one of your SQL server 2005 instances goes down, it is possible that not all of its transactions will make it to the other servers. As peer-to-peer transactional replication operates in near real-time, the amount of latency and potential data loss is relatively low.

---

**Note**    Peer-to-peer transactional replication has no built-in conflict detection and resolution technology, as with merge replication. The technology is designed to work so that DML operations for any given data are made only at one database, which is then synchronized with its peers.

Peer-to-peer transactional replication works best where your DML operations are mutually exclusive to each site and is designed to scale out your geographic workload by automatically replicating data between these remote sites, as shown in Figure 32-10. In this scenario, you have help desks based in Sydney, Florence, and Seattle that are used to service your organization globally. If each help desk site operates in a window of time mutually exclusive from the other two, there is no DML conflict as help desk operators add and resolve customer problems. (This scenario would also work, irrespective of the time window, if each help desk site services only its region's customers because all DML operations will also be mutually exclusive.)

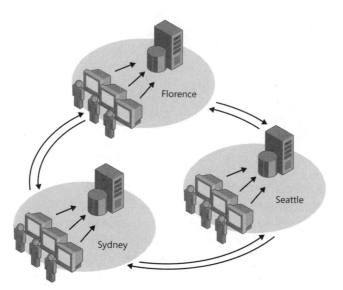

**Figure 32-10**   Using peer-to-peer transactional replication to scale out a database solution geographically.

Figure 32-11 shows an alternative implementation of peer-to-peer transactional replication in which an application server is used to load balance DML operations between two SQL Server 2005 instances. In this scenario, the data can be read from either SQL Server 2005 instance, which improves performance.

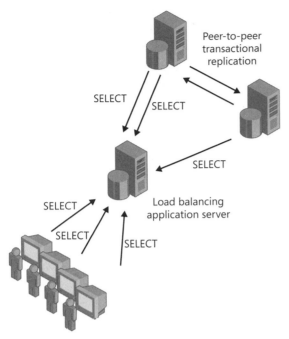

**Data Read Operations**

**Figure 32-11**   Reading data through an application server in a peer-to-peer transactional replication solution used to scale out a database.

However, for DML operations, as seen in Figure 32-12, the application server has to modify only one of the SQL Server 2005 instances for any given DML operation through either data partitioning or some other load-balancing or queuing mechanism.

When deploying peer-to-peer transactional replication, it is important to understand the network traffic that is generated between the peers because this can have a negative impact on your network infrastructure. Understanding the network traffic and it's impact also allows you to set correct performance expectations for all stakeholders. Remember that each SQL Server 2005 instance needs to replicate its transactions to every other SQL Server 2005 instance. Figure 32-13 shows the network traffic that will be generated between five SQL Server 2005 instances in a Peer-to-Peer Transactional Replication topology.

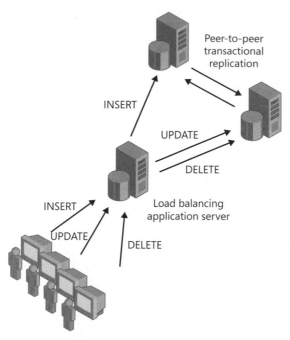

**Data Modification Operations**

**Figure 32-12**    Modifying data through an application server in a peer-to-peer transactional replication solution used to to scale out a database.

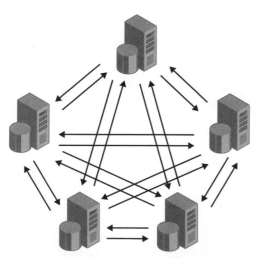

**Figure 32-13**    Peer-to-peer transactional replication network traffic between five peers.

---

**Best Practices**   It can be very difficult to predict the amount of network traffic that will be generated in your peer-to-peer transactional replication topology, and its impact on your network infrastructure. The best way to determine this impact is to set up a testbed environment that simulates a typical day's database activity. This can easily be done through SQL Server Profiler, which was discussed in Chapter 30, "Using Profiler, Management Studio, and Database Engine Tuning Advisor."

---

## Shared Scalable Databases

Shared scalable databases (SSD) are a new feature available with SQL Server 2005 Enterprise Edition only that allows you scale out a read-only database built solely for reporting purposes. The shared scalable database must reside on a read-only volume accessible over a storage area network. After building the reporting database on a set of volumes, you mark the volumes as read only and then mount them on multiple reporting servers, as shown in Figure 32-14.

---

**Note**   The reporting servers used to access the shared database must be running Windows Server 2003 Service Pack 1 or later installed with SQL Server 2005 Enterprise Edtion (or later).

---

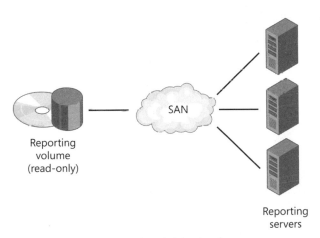

Reporting
volume
(read-only)

SAN

Reporting
servers

**Figure 32-14**   A shared scalable database.

Shared scalable databases allow you to scale out your reporting workload because you are using multiple SQL Server instances to access the same database files, but using each server's processor, memory, and *tempdb* system database resources. Thererfore, you are isolating queries that are running on different servers from each other. This prevents inefficient or expensive queries running on one SQL Server instance from degrading performance globally (although the reporting volume can be a potential bottleneck). Shared scalable databases are a great way to guarantee any SLA for a particular set of users or department because you can compartmentalise your server resources accordingly.

---

**Note**   It is recommended that you limit your scalable shared databases to eight SQL Server instances of the shared scalable database.

---

To implement shared scalable databases, start off by mounting your SAN volumes on your production SQL Server, and build your reporting database by using any of the tools provided by SQL Server 2005, such as the Database Copy wizard, to copy your production database on to the mounted volumes. Once your production database has been copied across, the volumes are dismounted from your production SQL Server, and these volumes are marked as read-only. This build phase is shown in Figure 32-15.

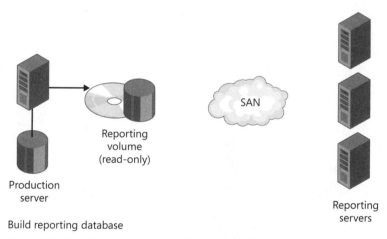

Production
server

Reporting
volume
(read-only)

SAN

Reporting
servers

Build reporting database

**Figure 32-15**   Build phase of a shared scalable database.

Once built, the read-only database has to be attached to the various reporting servers. First, you must attach the read-only volumes to the SQL Server instances across the SAN. You then attach the database files to your SQL Server instance using SQL Server Managment Studio or *sp_attach_db* system stored procedure, as discussed in Chapter X. This process is repeated on all of the SQL Server instances that require this read-only database. Figure 32-16 shows this attach phase.

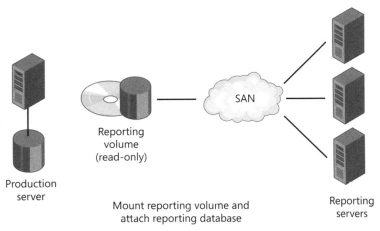

Production
server

Reporting
volume
(read-only)

Mount reporting volume and
attach reporting database

Reporting
servers

**Figure 32-16** Attach phase of a shared scalable database.

If you need to refresh the data in your shared scalable database, you will need to perform the following steps:

- **Detach shared scalable database** Before the shared scalable database can be refreshed on the SAN, all instances of SQL Server using the database must be detached from the database files.

- **Refresh shared scalable database** Once detached, the shared scalable database needs to be refreshed from the production SQL Server instance. This process is similar, if not identical, to the one used to create the initial database.

- **Attach shared scalable database** Once refreshed, the shared scalable database can be mounted back on to the various SQL Server instances as required.

Shared scalable databases are not appropriate for every environment, but they represent a great way of scaling out read-only information, such as census or other reference data. They even work for data that is periodically refreshed, such as civil registries or market data, which tend to change infrequently but at well-defined intervals over time. This type of data tends to consume a lot of storage space, so you probably do not want to have it replicated throughout your enterprise. Shared scalable databases represent a great way of scaling out this data without paying the storage cost.

**Note** Shared scalable databases, unlike normal databases in SQL Server 2005, support NTFS compression. When deciding whether to compress your shared scalable databases, as with all forms of compression, you need to weigh the savings in storage against the CPU cost to uncompress the data, which heavily depends on the type and quantity of data stored in your SSD.

# Summary

In this chapter, you learned about the two main approaches you can use to improve the performance and throughput of your database solution: scaling up and scaling out. Scaling up involves the addition of more or faster hardware resources. Scaling out involves the addition of more SQL Server 2005 instances to distribute the load on your database solution.

Various techniques of scaling up were discussed. You learned how to scale up the main hardware subsytems of your SQL Server 2005 solution.

The chapter concluded with an examination of the various scaling out technologies available with SQL Server 2005. When considering a SQL Server 2005 scale out technology, you learned to consider the potential latency and any other data issue to see if it would be appropriate for your database solution.

# Chapter 33
# Tuning Queries Using Hints and Plan Guides

In this chapter, we build on the performance tuning methodology and concepts presented in earlier chapters. We will take a look at tuning queries in somewhat extraordinary conditions where the common performance tuning methods, such as tuning system resources, creating the optimal indexes, and ensuring accurate table statistics, do not resolve the problem and a more brute force approach of specifying explicative directives to the query, called hints, is required.

We start by taking a detailed look at the three different types of hints: join hints, query hints, and table hints, along with examples of how to use them and where they are most applicable. We will also take a look at the new plan guides feature introduced in Microsoft SQL Server 2005 and how it can be used to effectively tune queries originating from applications that cannot be modified, as well as restrictions and recommended best practices. We conclude the chapter by going through several typical usage scenarios for plan guides and query hints.

## Understanding the Need for Hints

SQL Server 2005 uses the *cost-based optimizer* (CBO) to dynamically generate query execution plans. The CBO probes several system-wide resource states and employs many complex algorithms to optimize and generate the best possible execution plan for a query. The optimization and query plan generation process is often costly, especially for complex queries. Once generated, query plans are cached in the SQL Server plan cache to avoid repeating the optimization task when the identical query is re-executed. You can view the query plans cached by SQL Server by querying the syscacheobjects table. For example the following query can be used to list all the compiled plans in the instance of SQL Server:

```
SELECT * FROM sys.syscacheobjects
WHERE cacheobjtype = 'Compiled Plan';
```

Since the query plans are optimized for the specific data present in these tables, the SQL Server engine constantly monitors changes to the underlying tables and triggers a recompile of the query plan when it estimates that the data has changed significantly enough to justify a re-optimization. Once a query plan is recompiled, the old plan is discarded from the plan cache and replaced with the new plan.

This targeted optimization and caching mechanism works perfectly well for most queries most of the time. However, it is occasionally (though rarely) necessary to force a particular query plan based on experience with the operation of the application, insights into idiosyncrasies in the application schema, or to force a better query execution plan than the one generated by the optimizer. This can be done very easily in SQL Server by using hints.

*Hints* are directives that influence the behavior of the CBO but do not change the semantics of the query or the results in any way. During the optimization phase, the optimizer weighs the benefits among the various possible query plans to select the one that is best suited for the particular situation. Hints provided in the query bias this selection process.

While query hints present a powerful method of manually controlling the behavior of the optimizer and give you control over how query plans are generated, they should be used sparingly only as a last resort by experienced database administrators. The reason for this is simple: Once a query hint is specified, the optimizer is always biased toward choosing the query plan directed by the hint. This selection may be good for the situation at hand, but it may prevent the optimizer from choosing a possibly better plan at a later time when the shape of the underlying data or some other condition changes and the hint is no longer optimal.

# Microsoft SQL Server 2005 Hints

In addition to the hints available in earlier SQL Server versions, SQL Server 2005 introduces many new hints, such as USE PLAN, FORCED PARAMETERIZATION, and so on. These hints can be used in all editions of SQL Server 2005.

SQL Server 2005 classifies hints broadly into three categories: join hints, query hints, and table hints. The entire list of hints included in these categories is explained in the sections below.

## Join Hints

*Join hints* are used to enforce a join strategy between the joined tables. When no join hint is specified (the default case for a majority of the queries), the optimizer automatically selects the join type that is best suited for the query. With SQL Server 2005, you can use join hints to force nested loop joins, hash joins, merge joins, and remote joins for SELECT, UPDATE, and DELETE statements. These hints are mutually exclusive, implying that only one of them can be specified for any query:

- **LOOP**   This hint specifies a nested loop join. In a nested loop join, every row in the inner table is checked using the join criteria to see whether the values of specified fields are equal to those in each corresponding row in the outer table. Nested loop joins are by far the most commonly used and are particularly well-suited for cases where a small number of rows from a table are joined to a large number of rows in another table.

- **HASH**   This hint specifies a hash join. In a hash join, one table is reorganized as a hash table. The other table is scanned one row at a time, and the hash function is used to search for equalities.

- **MERGE**   This hint specifies a merge join. In a merge join, each table is first sorted and then one row at a time from each table is compared with the corresponding row in the other table in descending order.

- **REMOTE**   This hint specifies a remote join. A remote join is when at least one of the participating tables is remote. When this hint is specified, the join operation is performed on the site of the right table. This hint is useful when the left table is a local table (a table on the database where the query is executed) and the right table is a remote table (table on a remote database server). The REMOTE hint should be used only for inner joins when the left table has fewer rows than the right table.

Let's take a look at an example where a join hint is specified to force a merge join for a query executed against the *AdventureWorks* sample database:

```
SELECT EmployeeID, FirstName, LastName, EmailAddress, Phone
FROM HumanResources.Employee e, Person.Contact c
WHERE e.ContactID = c.ContactID
OPTION (MERGE JOIN);
```

Join hints can also be specified when you use the SQL-92 standard syntax for joins. When using the SQL-92 syntax, the merge join hint can be specified as shown in the following example:

```
SELECT EmployeeID, FirstName, LastName, EmailAddress, Phone
FROM HumanResources.Employee AS e
INNER MERGE JOIN Person.Contact AS c
ON e.ContactID = c.ContactID;
```

---

**Note**   If a joint hint is also specified for any particular pair of joined tables in the FROM clause, it takes precedence over a join hint specified in the OPTION clause.

---

There are no real rules of thumb concerning when to use join hints. If you suspect that a particular join type will yield better results, the best way to test it is to force it using a join hint and see whether it results in better performance. However, as mentioned earlier, you should not use hints unless you are absolutely certain that the hint you specify will be beneficial to all users in all cases and should monitor performance to make sure that the join hint stays relevant and provides the intended performance benefits. If you're not sure about using a join hint, I recommend you just let the query optimizer select the best join type.

## Query Hints

Query hints are specified using the OPTION clause at the end of the query and help indicate to the optimizer that the directive indicated by the query hint should be used throughout the query. Multiple (comma delimited) query hints can be specified using a single OPTION clause, as in this example:

```
SELECT EmployeeID, FirstName, LastName, EmailAddress, Phone
FROM HumanResources.Employee e, Person.Contact c
WHERE e.ContactID = c.ContactID
OPTION (RECOMPILE, MAXDOP 1, FAST 80);
```

If any of the hints cause the query optimizer to be unable to generate a valid plan, SQL Server reports an error with error code 8622.

Query hints can be specified for INSERT, SELECT, UPDATE, and DELETE statements and are supported in all editions of SQL Server 2005. The list below explains the different query hints:

- **HASH GROUP or ORDER GROUP**   This hint specifies that aggregations described in the GROUP BY, DISTINCT, or COMPUTE clause of the query should be done using hashing (HASH GROUP) or ordering (ORDER GROUP).

- **CONCAT UNION or HASH UNION or MERGE UNION**   This hint specifies that all UNION operations in the query should be performed by concatenating (CONCAT UNION), hashing (HASH UNION), or merging (MERGE UNION) the union sets. If more than one UNION hint is specified, the query optimizer selects the least expensive strategy from the hints specified.

- **LOOP JOIN or HASH JOIN or MERGE JOIN**   This hint specifies that all join operations in the entire query should be performed by a nested loop join (LOOP JOIN), hash join (HASH JOIN) or merge join (MERGE JOIN). If more than one JOIN hint is specified, the query optimizer selects the least expensive strategy from the hint specified.

- **FAST number_rows**   This hint specifies that the query is optimized for fast retrieval of the first *number_rows* rows. When specified, SQL Server returns the first *number_rows* as quickly as possible. After the first *number_rows* are returned, the query continues execution and produces the full result set. The number specified has to be a non-negative integer, otherwise the query will report a syntax error.

  This hint is often useful for online transaction processing-type applications that present the result set to the user via multiple screens and for which retrieving the set of rows for the first screen is crucial to the perceived response time. For example, in a customer relationship management (CRM) application, the customer search capability, where the results are displayed in multiple screens of 40 results per screen, may require that the first 40 rows of the result set be served back to the client system as quickly as possible. This can be achieved by appending the OPTION (FAST 40) query hint to the SELECT statement:

  ```
  SELECT FirstName, LastName, Phone, EmailAddress
  FROM Person.Contact WHERE Phone LIKE '617%'
  OPTION (FAST 40);
  ```

- **FORCE ORDER**   This hint specifies that the join order during query optimization should be kept the same as the order in which the tables are specified in the query. You can use this hint for situations where you want to control the exact order in which the tables are joined. This can be achieved by specifying the tables in the particular order in which you want them joined and then appending the OPTION (FORCE ORDER) hint to the query. You should use this hint for queries only where you're sure that the particular order being forced is guaranteed to help the query execution, and you should always verify using SQL Server Management Studio or SQL Server Profiler that the query execution plan is what you expected it to be.

- **MAXDOP number_of_processors** SQL Server has an instance-wide setting called max degree of parallelism (set using SQL Server Management Studio or the sp_configure stored procedure) which is used to control the extent to which a query execution is parallelized (intra-query parallelism). The MAXDOP query hint permits you to override this instance-wide setting and use a different degree of parallelism value for a particular query. This hint only specifies the maximum number of processors that can be used; it does not necessarily force a parallel execution plan across the processors.

- **OPTIMIZE FOR ( @variable_name = literal_constant [ ,...n ] )** As explained earlier, SQL Server 2005 probes the query parameter values to generate the most optimized query plan for a query and then caches that plan for use when the same query is re-executed. This can sometimes lead to undesirable effects for cases where the underlying table data is highly skewed and the parameter value for the first execution of the query does not represent the majority case in the underlying table data. Since the query is cached, the successive executions of the query with the more common data value may result in suboptimal performance.

  In such situations, the OPTIMIZE FOR query hint can be used to direct the optimizer to optimize the query for the particular parameter value. The parameter value is used only during query optimization and not during execution. @variable_name is the name of a local variable used in the query to which a literal_constant value should be assigned during optimization. The data types for literal_constant should be the same as the @variable_name parameter, or at least implicitly convertible. You can specify multiple comma-separated pairs of @variable_name = literal_constant values in the OPTIMIZE FOR query hint, for example: OPTION (OPTIMIZE FOR (@P1=28,@P2='ABC', @P3=9.99)).

- **PARAMETERIZATION SIMPLE or PARAMETERIZATION FORCED** *Parameterization* is a process by which a query consisting of literal values (for example, PartNumber = 1234) is automatically changed to use parameters (for example, PartNumber = @P1, where @P1 is set to 1234 prior to the query execution) such that the cached query plan can be reused more effectively. The PARAMETERIZATION option specifies the parameterization rules that the SQL Server query optimizer applies to the query when it is compiled. PARAMETERIZATION SIMPLE instructs the query optimizer to attempt simple parameterization, while PARAMETERIZATION FORCED instructs the optimizer to attempt forced parameterization. The PARAMETERIZATION query hint can be specified only inside a plan guide, which is explained later in this chapter. Unlike the other query hints, it cannot be specified directly within a query. When this option is specified, it overrides the default database-wide parameterization setting set via SQL Server Management Studio or the ALTER DATABASE command.

**More Info**   For more information about simple and forced parameterization, search for "simple parameterization" and "forced parameterization" in SQL Server Books Online.

- **RECOMPILE**   The RECOMPILE hint instructs SQL Server to discard the generated query plan after the query completes execution, forcing the query optimizer to recompile a plan the next time the same query is executed. This query hint is useful for cases where the same query is executed with very different parameter values or different values will be passed to stored procedures and the performance is suboptimal when the query plan is reused across the different parameter values. Query recompilation can be an expensive operation, especially for complex queries, and therefore should be used selectively only for cases where the overall benefits for recompiling the query plan each time outweighs the cost of the recompilation.

- **ROBUST PLAN**   When a query is processed, intermediate tables and operators may have to store and process rows that are wider than any one of the input rows. The rows may be so wide that sometimes a particular operator is unable to process the row. If this occurs, an error is returned during query execution. The ROBUST PLAN query hint forces the query optimizer to try to generate a plan that works for the maximum potential row size, possibly at the expense of performance, and not consider any query plans that may encounter this problem. If such a plan is not possible, the query optimizer returns an error instead of deferring error detection to when the query is executed.

- **KEEP PLAN**   As explained earlier, SQL Server caches the query execution plans and recompiles them only when the auto update statistics is enabled and the underlying data has changed sufficiently by the execution of UPDATE, DELETE, or INSERT statements, warranting a recompile. The KEEP PLAN query hint forces the query optimizer to relax the estimated recompile threshold for a query and ensures that a query will not be recompiled as frequently when there are multiple updates to a table.

- **KEEPFIXED PLAN**   This query hint forces the query optimizer to not recompile a query due to changes in statistics of the underlying tables. Specifying KEEPFIXED PLAN ensures that a query will be recompiled only if the schema of the underlying tables is changed or if the *sp_recompile* stored procedure is executed against the tables used by the query.

- **EXPAND VIEWS**   A view is considered to be expanded when the view name is replaced by the view definition in the query text. The EXPAND VIEWS hint specifies that indexed views are not used by the query optimizer for any part of the query. This query hint virtually disallows direct use of indexed views and indexes on indexed views in the query plan. The one exception to this is when the WITH (NOEXPAND) table hint is also specified for the query. Only the views in the SELECT part of statements, including those contained in INSERT, UPDATE, and DELETE statements are affected by this hint.

- **MAXRECURSION *number*** This MAXRECURSION query hint is used to specify the maximum number of recursions allowed for a query. *Number* is a non-negative integer between 0 and 32,767 (0 implies infinite recursion). If this option is not specified, the default limit is 100. When the specified or default number of recursions is reached, the query is terminated with an error and all effects of the statement are rolled back. When this error is encountered, it may yield in a incomplete result set, and it's therefore best to discard the results.

- **USE PLAN N'*xml_plan*'** In SQL Server 2005, a query execution plan can be represented in XML format, as explained in Chapter 31, "Using Dynamic Management Views." The USE PLAN query hint, which is new in SQL Server 2005, can be used to force the query optimizer to select a query plan that is specified by '*xml_plan*'. The *xml_plan* specified has to be one that the optimizer would normally consider during its selection process. This implies that you cannot create any arbitrary XML showplan and expect the optimizer to use it. It is not advisable to hand code or modify the XML showplan that is specified in the USE PLAN query hint. The XML showplan is a lengthy and complex listing, and any change that would make this not identically match one of the query optimizer-generated plans, results in the USE PLAN hint being ignored.

---

**More Info**    For an example of how to capture the xml_plan and specify it in a query, search for "Plan Forcing Scenario: Create a Plan Guide That Uses a USE PLAN Query Hint" in SQL Server 2005 Books Online.

---

This query hint provides you with a brute-force method to force a query plan and, in a way, eliminates the trial-and-error approach associated when using the query hints. The *xml_plan* should always be specified as a Unicode literal by adding the N prefix, for example, N'*xml_plan*'. Doing this makes sure that any characters in the plan specific to the Unicode standard are not lost when the SQL Server interprets the string. Only query plans for SELECT and SELECT INTO statements can be forced. Query plans for UPDATE, DELETE, or INSERT statements cannot be forced.

The USE PLAN hint is designed primarily for ad-hoc performance tuning and test purposes and for use with the plan guides feature. You should avoid embedding this query hint directly into your application code because this makes the maintenance of the application across query plan and SQL Server version changes almost impossible to manage.

## Table Hints

Similar to join and query hints, table hints help influence the behavior of the SQL Server optimizer. One or more table hints can be specified using the WITH clause for a query and help control whether the query optimizer use a table scan, one or more indexes, a particular locking method, and so on when executing the query. The table hints are ignored if the table is not accessed by the query plan. For example, the optimizer may choose not to access a table because an indexed view is accessed instead. While earlier versions of SQL Server permitted a table hint to be specified without a WITH clause (Example: SELECT Col1 FROM Table1 NOLOCK WHERE Col1=1), SQL Server 2005 requires the WITH clause to be specified for most of the table hints.   In my experience, this is one of the most common causes that applications employing table hints break when migrated to SQL Server 2005. While SQL Server 2005 Books Online has a detailed list of the hints that can be used without the WITH clause, I'd strongly recommend that you not waste your time figuring this out. Instead, always specify the WITH clause when using table hints. It is also recommended that you separate the table hints with commas instead of spaces. Separating the hints using spaces is supported only for backward compatibility purposes. Here is an example of a query specifying multiple table hints that can be executed against the *AdventureWorks* sample database:

```
SELECT ContactID, FirstName, LastName, EmailAddress
FROM Person.Contact WITH (NOLOCK, INDEX(PK_Contact_ContactID), FASTFIRSTROW)
WHERE ContactID < 15;
```

The various table hints are described here:

- **NOEXPAND**   The NOEXPAND hint specifies that any indexed views are not expanded to access underlying tables when the query optimizer processes the query. This hint applies only to indexed views.

- **INDEX ( index_val [ ,...n ] )**   This hint is used to specify the index name or index identifier number to be used by the query optimizer when it processes the statement.   Multiple, comma-separated index names or identifiers can be specified in the INDEX hint directing the optimizer to use the indexes specified for retrieving the rows of the table. When multiple indexes are specified in the hint, the order of the indexes is significant. The maximum number of indexes in the table hint is 250 nonclustered indexes, but you should never even come close to specifying this many indexes in the hint. An error is returned if the index specified in the hint does not exist.

The INDEX hint is one of the more commonly used ones for optimizing query performance. For example, the index hint in the following query forces the optimizer to select index PK_Vendor_VendorID when processing the query:

```
SELECT Name FROM Purchasing.Vendor
WITH (INDEX(PK_Vendor_VendorID))
WHERE VendorID = 10 ;
```

- **FASTFIRSTROW**   This hint is equivalent to OPTION (FAST 1) query hint explained in the previous section.

- **NOWAIT**   This hint instructs SQL Server 2005 to return an error message 1222 (Lock request time-out period exceeded) as soon as a lock is encountered on the table. The NOWAIT hint is equivalent to specifying SET LOCK_TIMEOUT 0 for a specific table.

- **ROWLOCK**   This hint specifies that row locks be taken on the table instead of page or table locks.

- **PAGLOCK**   This hint specifies that page locks be taken on the table instead of row or a table locks.

- **TABLOCK**   This hint specifies that a shared table lock be taken on the table and held until the end of the statement.

> **Note**   The ROWLOCK, PAGLOCK, and TABLOCK are mutually exclusive, and only one of them can be specified against a table. Specifying more than one conflicting hint results in an error.

- **TABLOCK**   This hint specifies that an exclusive lock be taken on the table and held until the end of statement.

- **NOLOCK**   This hint is equivalent to the READUNCOMMITTED hint explained in an up coming paragraph.

- **HOLDLOCK**   This hint is equivalent to the SERIALIZABLE hint explained below and applies only to the table or view for which it is specified. Starting with the query statement in which it appears, the HOLDLOCK hint remains effective for the remainder of the transaction in which the query appears. This hint cannot be used in a SELECT statement that includes the FOR BROWSE option.

- **UPDLOCK**   This hint specifies that update locks should be acquired on the table and held until the end of the transaction. When used in combination with the ROWLOCK, PAGLOCK, or TABLOCK hints, the exclusive locks are acquired at the specified level of granularity.

- **XLOCK**   This hint specifies that exclusive locks should be acquired on the table and held until the end of the transaction. When used in combination with the

ROWLOCK, PAGLOCK, or TABLOCK hints, the exclusive locks are acquired at the specified level of granularity.

■ **READPAST**   When the READPAST hint is specified, SQL Server 2005 skips reading rows or pages that are locked by other transactions, effectively "reading past" and not blocking on them. When READPAST is specified, both row-level and page-level locks are skipped. This hint can be specified only for transactions operating at the READ COMMITTED or REPEATABLE READ isolation levels.

■ **READUNCOMMITTED**   This hint specifies that no shared locks be issued to prevent other transactions from modifying data read by the current transaction, and exclusive locks set by other transactions do not block the current transaction from reading the locked data. This hint should be used only in cases where uncommitted ('("dirty'dirty") reads are acceptable because allowing dirty reads can possibly lead you to a situation where you read data that does not exist because you read a transient state that was or is being rolled back. I would recommend you use this hint only after understanding all the implications. This hint cannot be specified for tables modified by insert, update, or delete operations.

■ **READCOMMITTED**   This hint specifies that read operations comply with the rules for the READ COMMITTED isolation level by using either locking or row versioning. If the READ_COMITTED_SNAPSHOT database option is disabled, SQL Server 2005 acquires shared locks as data is read and releases those locks when the read operation is completed. If the READ_COMMITTED_SNAPSHOT database option is enabled, SQL Server does not acquire locks but uses row versioning instead.

■ **READCOMMITTEDLOCK**   This hint is new in SQL Server 2005 and specifies that read operations comply with the rules for the READ COMMITTED isolation level by using locking. SQL Server acquires shared locks as data is read and releases those locks when the read operation is completed, regardless of the setting of the READ_COMMITTED_SNAPSHOT database option.

■ **REPEATABLEREAD**   This hint specifies that read operations comply with the rules for the REPEATABLE READ isolation level in which a statement cannot read data that has been modified but not yet committed by other transactions, and no other transactions can modify data that has been read by the current transaction until the current transaction completes.

■ **SERIALIZABLE**   This hint makes shared locks more restrictive by holding them until a transaction is completed instead of releasing the shared lock as soon as the required table or data page is no longer needed, whether or not the transaction has been completed. This hint is equivalent to the HOLDLOCK hint.

- **KEEPIDENTITY**   This hint is used to specify that identity values in the imported data file should be used for the identity column. If KEEPIDENTITY is not specified, the identity values for this column are verified but not imported. This hint is applicable only in an INSERT statement when the BULK option is used with OPEN-ROWSET.

- **KEEPDEFAULTS**   This hint is used to specify to insert a table column's default value (if any) instead of inserting NULL values when the data record does not contain a value for the column. This hint is applicable only in an INSERT statement when the BULK option is used with OPENROWSET.

- **IGNORE_CONSTRAINTS**   This hint is used to specify that any constraints on the table are ignored by the bulk-import operation. However, you cannot use this hint to disable UNIQUE, PRIMARY KEY, FOREIGN KEY, or NOT NULL constraints. This hint is applicable only in an INSERT statement when the BULK option is used with OPENROWSET.

- **IGNORE_TRIGGERS**   This hint is used to specify that any triggers defined on the table are ignored by the bulk-import operation. This hint is applicable only in an INSERT statement when the BULK option is used with OPENROWSET.

---

**Important**   Table hints should be used only as a last resort by experienced users who fully understand the effects of specifying the hints.

---

# Plan Guides

As we've seen so far, hints provide a powerful option for influencing the behavior of the SQL Sever database engine and, in a way, give you almost full control over how a query is executed. While a powerful option, the hints are of little use for queries originating in applications which you do not have the code and therefore cannot modify the query to add the hints. For example, you could have the following query that originates in a third-party CRM application and exhibits poor performance due to an incorrect selection of the join type by the optimizer:

```
SELECT pc.ContactID, FirstName, LastName, EmailAddress, CreditCardID
FROM Person.Contact pc, Sales.ContactCreditCard ccc
WHERE pc.ContactID = ccc.ContactID
AND pc.ContactID < 15;
```

For this query, say you know that it operates much better when a MERGE JOIN hint is specified as follows:

```
SELECT pc.ContactID, FirstName, LastName, EmailAddress, CreditCardID
FROM Person.Contact pc, Sales.ContactCreditCard ccc
WHERE pc.ContactID = ccc.ContactID
AND pc.ContactID < 15
OPTION (MERGE JOIN);
```

However, since this query may be dynamically formulated in the application and you do not have access to the application code, there is no way for you to specify the query hint. This is where the new plan guides feature introduced in SQL Server 2005 can be of great use.

The *plan guides* feature offers users a mechanism to inject hints into the original query without having to modify it. Any of the query hints explained above can be applied to a SELECT, UPDATE, DELETE, or INSERT...SELECT statement using a plan guide.

The plan guide mechanism utilizes an internal look-up system table (based on information stored in the *sys.plan_guides* catalog view) to map the original query to a substitute query or to a template, as explained later in this chapter). In this mechanism, every query statement or batch is first compared against the optimizer's cached plan store to check for a match. If a query plan already exists in the cache, it is used to execute the query. If not, the query or batch is checked against the set of existing plan guides in the current database for a match. If an active plan guide exists for the statement and its context, the original matching statement is substituted with the one from the plan guide; otherwise, the original statement is used. The query plan is then compiled and cached, and the statement or batch executed.

### Real World   Plan Guides Save the Day

I recently consulted on a customer case where the customer was migrating an enterprise resource planning (ERP) application from SQL Server 2000 to SQL Server 2005 and simultaneously performing other application changes as well.

After migrating the database to SQL Server 2005 and doing their usual tuning, the customer observed that there was one frequently executed query that consistently performed poorly and was responsible for significantly slowing down one of their jobs. Moreover, the usual tuning procedures such as ensuring optimal indexes had no effect on the performance. This is when the database administrator was forced to look into alternatives. There was a dire need to resolve the problem as quickly as possible to stay on schedule for their go-live date.

The problematic query was very complex and not particularly well written. After much experimenting, the DBA discovered that specifying an OPTION (LOOP JOIN) query hint on the query sped it up significantly. Since this was a packaged application and the query itself could not be changed, the DBA created a plan guide to temporarily work around the problem and contacted the application vendor the next week to request a fix for the particular query. This saved the day for the customer and helped them go-live on schedule.

# Creating and Administering Plan Guides

SQL Server 2005 introduces two new stored procedures to create, drop, enable, and disable plan guides. The sections below explain the procedure of creating and administering plan guides.

### sp_create_plan_guide

The *sp_create_plan_guide* stored procedure is used to create a plan guide. This stored procedure can be used only on SQL Server 2005 Standard Edition, Enterprise Edition, and Developer Edition and is not available for use in any of the other editions. The format for this command and the description of the command arguments is as follows:

```
sp_create_plan_guide     [ @name = ] N'plan_guide_name'
    , [ @stmt = ] N'statement_text'
    , [ @type = ] N' { OBJECT | SQL | TEMPLATE }'
    , [ @module_or_batch = ]
    { N'[ schema_name.]object_name'
        | N'batch_text' | NULL }
    , [ @params = ] { N'@parameter_name data_type [,...n ]' | NULL }
    , [ @hints = ] { N'OPTION ( query_hint [,...n ] )' | NULL }
```

- **@name (type: navrchar(128))**  Specifies the name of the plan guide. Because plan guides have a database-wide scope, @name is required to be unique within a database and cannot begin with a hash (#) character.

- **@stmt (type: navrchar(max))**  Specifies the SQL statement, or batch.

- **@type (type: nvarchar(60))**  Specifies the type of entity against which this plan guide will be matched. @type can be "N'OBJECT'," "N'SQL'," or "N'TEMPLATE'."

- **N'OBJECT'**  Indicates that the statement_text appears in the context of a stored procedure, scalar function, a multi-statement table-valued function, or a DML trigger.

- **N'SQL'**  Indicates that the given statement_text appears in the context of a stand-alone statement or batch.

- **N'TEMPLATE'**   Indicates that the plan guide applies to any query that parameterizes to the form indicated in statement_text.

- **@module_or_batch (type: nvarchar(max))**   Specifies the module name or batch text. If @module_or_batch is NULL (default value) and @type = "N'SQL'," then @module_or_batch is set to @stmt. If @type = 'TEMPLATE', then @module_or_batch must be NULL. The batch text cannot include a USE 'database' statement.

- **@params (type: nvarchar(max))**   Specifies a string containing the definitions of all parameters for a statement or batch to be matched by the plan guide. You can specify multiple parameter value pairs by separating them with commas. Each parameter definition consists of a parameter name and a data type. @params is applicable only when @type = N'SQL' or N'TEMPLATE' and cannot be set to NULL when @type = N'TEMPLATE'. If the statement or batch does not contain parameters, @params must be set to NULL (default value).

- **@hints (type: nvarchar(max))**   Specifies the OPTION clause text to attach to query that matches @stmt which can be used to specify any valid sequence of query hints.

All arguments for the *sp_create_plan_guide* stored procedure must be either constants of the designated type or variables that can be implicitly converted to the designated type, as in this example:

```
sp_create_plan_guide
N'MyPlanGuide',
@stmt = N'
    UPDATE [HumanResources].[Employee]
        SET [NationalIDNumber] = @NationalIDNumber
            ,[BirthDate] = @BirthDate
            ,[MaritalStatus] = @MaritalStatus
            ,[Gender] = @Gender
        WHERE [EmployeeID] = @EmployeeID;',
@type = N'OBJECT',
@module_or_batch = N'HumanResources.uspUpdateEmployeePersonalInfo',
@params = NULL,
@hint = N'OPTION (KEEPFIXED PLAN)';
```

> **Best Practices**   For readability and consistency purposes, it is best to specify the parameter names (for example, @stmt) and parameter values (for example, N'MyPlanGuide') for all the parameters of the *sp_create_plan_guide* procedure. Alternatively, you can specify the parameter values only for all the parameters.

> However, once you specify a parameter with a parameter name in the form "@name = value," all subsequent parameters must be passed in the same form, and specifying a parameter without the parameter name results in an error. For example, in the query above, specifying the hint without "@hints =" results in an error because "@name =" has not been specified for the first parameter.

When creating a plan guide, you should be sure to specify the @stmt and @params parameters exactly as they are formatted in the application, including any spaces, tab characters, line-feeds, or carriage returns; otherwise, the plan guide will not match the original statement. The best way to achieve this is to capture the batch or statement text using SQL Profiler.

---

**More Info**   For additional information on how to create and test a plan guide, search for "Using SQL Server Profiler to Create and Test Plan Guides" in SQL Server Books Online.

---

Plan guides cannot be created against stored procedures, functions, or DML triggers that have been encrypted using the WITH ENCRYPTION clause. Also, once a plan guide has been created, the function, stored procedure, or DML trigger that is referenced by the plan guide cannot be modified or deleted. Trying to do so results in an error. In addition, the plan guide name and the combination of @stmt and @module_or_batch should be unique within the database. Trying to create a plan guide with similar values for either of these attributes results in an error.

---

**Note**   Plan guides cannot be specified for DDL triggers; only DML triggers are supported.

---

### sp_control_plan_guide

The *sp_control_plan_guide* is used to enable, disable, or drop a plan guide. The format for this command and the description of the command arguments is as follows:

```
sp_control_plan_guide
    [ @operation = ] N'<control_option>'
    [ , [ @name = ] N'plan_guide_name' ]
```

- **@operation (type: nvarchar(max))**   N'DISABLE' Used to disable the plan guide specified by plan_guide_name. Once a plan guide is disabled, successive executions of the query are not influenced by the actions originally specified in the plan guide.

- **N'DISABLE ALL'** Used to disable all plan guides in the current database. No plan_guide_name can be specified when this option is used. Once the plan guides are disabled, successive executions of the queries are not influenced by the actions originally specified in the plan guides.

- **N'DROP'** Used to drop the plan guide specified by plan_guide_name. Once a plan guide is dropped, successive executions of the query are not influenced by the actions originally specified in the plan guide.

- **N'DROP ALL'** Used to drop all plan guides in the current database. No plan_guide_name can be specified when this option is used. Once all the plan guides are dropped, successive executions of the queries are not influenced by the actions originally specified in the plan guides.

- **N'ENABLE'** Used to enable the plan guide specified by plan_guide_name. Plan guides are enabled by default. This command is used to enable a previously disabled plan guide.

- **N'ENABLE ALL'** Used to enable all plan guides in the current database. No plan_guide_name can be specified when this option is used. Plan guides are enabled by default. This command enables all disabled plan guides in the database.

- **@name (type: nvarchar(max))** Specifies the name of the plan guide.

For example, the following command can be used to drop the plan guide created in the previous section:

```
sp_control_plan_guide N'DROP', N'MyPlanGuide';
```

A plan guide can be created, enabled, or disabled only in SQL Server 2005 Standard Edition, Enterprise Edition and Developer Edition; however, it can be dropped in all editions.

---

**Important** The parameters passed in to the *sp_control_plan_guide* stored procedure have to be specified as Unicode strings using the N prefix (for example, N'MyPlanGuide'). Executing the statement with parameters specified as non-Unicode results in an error.

---

## Creating Template-Based Plan Guides

As explained in Chapter 10, "Creating Databases and Database Snapshots," SQL Server 2005 introduces two new options to parameterize queries: FORCED PARAMETERIZATION and SIMPLE PARAMETERIZATION. The FORCED PARAMETERIZATION option is particularly powerful because it forces a nonparameterized query to be autoparameterized at the database without actually having to change the original query. This, in turn, enables the query plan to be reused for successive invocations of the same query with differing parameter values. For example, in the following nonparameterized query the Sales.Store.Name is being passed in as a literal of N'Brakes and Gears':

```
SELECT DISTINCT Sales.Customer.CustomerID, Sales.Store.Name
FROM Sales.Customer JOIN Sales.Store ON
     ( Sales.Customer.CustomerID = Sales.Store.CustomerID)
WHERE Sales.Store.Name = N'Brakes and Gears';
```

The same query in its parameterized form would have the parameter value set before the query executes (for example, @P1 = N'Brakes and Gears') and then have the query modified to the following:

```
SELECT DISTINCT Sales.Customer.CustomerID, Sales.Store.Name
FROM Sales.Customer JOIN Sales.Store ON
     ( Sales.Customer.CustomerID = Sales.Store.CustomerID)WHERE Sales.Store.Name = @P1;
```

This can be achieved by changing the query itself; however, this is not always possible. An alternate solution is to specify the PARAMETERIZATION FORCED query hint for the particular query using a plan guide.

Specifying the correct form of the parameterize query and the parameter types can often be challenging. The example query presented in this section is intentionally kept simple to clearly present the concept. Real-world application queries can be many tens, and in some cases even hundreds, of lines long with many parameters. To simplify the process of determining the parameterized form of a query, SQL Server 2005 introduces a new stored procedure *sp_get_query_template* that helps determine the parameterized form of a query. The *sp_get_query_template* stored procedure uses the nonparameterized form of a query as an input parameter and returns the parameterized form of the query and the parameters as output, as shown in the following code fragment:

```
DECLARE @templatetext nvarchar(max);
DECLARE @parameters nvarchar(max);

EXEC sp_get_query_template N'
    SELECT Name, ProductNumber, OrderQty, ReceivedQty, ReorderPoint
    FROM Purchasing.PurchaseOrderDetail pod, Production.Product p
    WHERE pod.ProductID = p.ProductID
       AND ReceivedQty <= 550.00
       AND Name = ''Spokes'';',
@templatetext OUTPUT,
@parameters OUTPUT;

SELECT @templatetext;
SELECT @parameters;
```

This code fragment returns the parameterized form of the query and the parameter value as the following:

```
select Name , ProductNumber , OrderQty , ReceivedQty , ReorderPoint
from Purchasing . PurchaseOrderDetail pod , Production . Product p
where pod . ProductID = p . ProductID and ReceivedQty < = @0 and Name = @1

@0 numeric(38,2),@1 varchar(8000)
```

The *sp_get_query_template* stored procedure can be used directly as input to *sp_create_plan_guide* to create a template-based plan guide for the query. For example, a plan guide can be created for the above query to specify the forced parameterization query hint as follows:

```
DECLARE @templatetext nvarchar(max)
DECLARE @parameters nvarchar(max)
EXEC sp_get_query_template N'
    SELECT Name, ProductNumber, OrderQty, ReceivedQty, ReorderPoint
    FROM Purchasing.PurchaseOrderDetail pod, Production.Product p
    WHERE pod.ProductID = p.ProductID
        AND ReceivedQty <= 550.00
        AND Name = ''Spokes'';',
@templatetext OUTPUT,
@parameters OUTPUT
EXEC sp_create_plan_guide N'TemplatePG',
@stmt = @templatetext,
@type = N'TEMPLATE',
@module_or_batch = NULL,
@params = @parameters,
@hints = N'OPTION(PARAMETERIZATION FORCED)';
```

> **Note**   In the example above, the literal value has been delimited by double single-quotation marks ("Spokes").

Once created, this plan guide template matches all executions of queries with this format irrespective of the literal values compared with ReceivedQty and Name, thereby enabling query plan reuse and a reduced number of query compilations. The plan guide created above matches only ReceivedQty decimal values that have a scale of two (for example, 550.00). Values received in a different scale will not match even though the numeric value is actually the same (for example, 550.0 and 550.000). This should be a rare occurrence; however, if you need to address multiple scale values for the same query, an easy way to achieve this is to create plan guides to match each different scale value.

# Best Practices

One of the most important best practices is to use hints and plan guides sparingly and only for cases where the conventional query tuning options have been tried exhaustively yet failed to produce the desired results. It is also recommended that you attempt to use hints only for a small fraction of the workload. If you find yourself forcing more than a few dozen queries, you may want to check whether there are other issues with the configuration such as inadequate resources (memory, processor, disks, and so on), incorrect configuration settings, missing indexes, or poorly written queries that are limiting performance.

Only experienced DBAs who understand the full implications and long-term ramifications of forcing query plans using hints should use these options because once a query plan has been forced, the query optimizer can no longer dynamically adapt to changing data shapes, new indexes, or improved query execution algorithms in future SQL Server releases, SQL Server service packs (SPs), or SQL Server engineering fixes, also known as hot-fixes or QFEs.

Once created, plan guides are stored in the sys.plan_guides table within a user database. This system table can be queried to access details about the plan guide such as the name, query text, date it was created, date modified, enabled/disabled status, parameters, hints, and so on. The sys.plan_guides table should never be modified directly; instead, you should use the *sp_create_plan_guide* and *sp_control_plan_guide* stored procedures to manage it. Figure 33-1 shows a database with five plan guides, two of which have been disabled, as can be determined via the is_disabled flag.

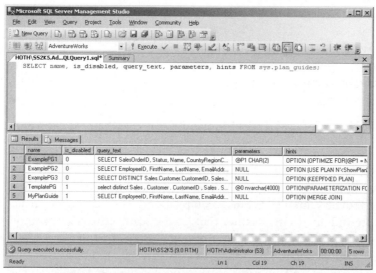

**Figure 33-1**    List of plan guides in a database.

It is recommended that the plan guides created in a database be well-documented, as they constitute an integral part of performance tuning. In addition, it is advisable to save the content of the sys.plan_guides in your database regularly, by using: SELECT * FROM (*sys.plan_guides*).

Doing so helps you capture and archive the details of the plan guides you've created for the particular application, including their status (enabled/disabled).

## Verifying Plan Guides Usage

Once created, a plan guide should always be thoroughly tested to make sure that it is being applied to the intended queries and that the actions being taken are in line with your expectation. This can be done easily by verifying that the showplan XML listing, produced by the "Showplan XML" event in the "Performance" group in SQL Server Profiler as explained in Chapter 30, "Using Profiler, Management Studio, and Database Engine Tuning Advisor," or the SET SHOWPLAN_XML ON output, contains the PlanGuideDB and PlanGuideName attributes for the plan guide that you expected the query to match. For example, in the XML showplan fragment below, the PlanGuideDB="Adventure-Works" and PlanGuideName="ExamplePG1" indicate that the ExamplePG1 plan guide within the AdventureWorks database was used for the query:

```
<ShowPlanXML
xmlns="http://schemas.microsoft.com/sqlserver/2004/07/showplan"
    Version="1.0" Build="9.00.1399.06">
    <BatchSequence>
        <Batch>
            <Statements>
                <StmtSimple PlanGuideDB="AdventureWorks"
                    PlanGuideName="ExamplePG1">
                    ...
                </StmtSimple>
            </Statements>
        </Batch>
    </BatchSequence>
</ShowPlanXML>
```

## Example Usage Scenarios for Plan Guides

This section presents three example scenarios where plan guides are used to influence the query optimizer behavior by injecting hints without actually changing the original query itself. The scenarios are provided for example purposes only and may not actually exhibit any performance issues or gains.

1. **Optimizing for a particular parameter value** As explained earlier, there are times when the SQL Server 2005 compile and cache mechanism may result in a query plan that may not necessarily be optimal for the majority case parameter values being cached, thereby resulting in suboptimal overall performance. For example, consider the case where the sales order table has a majority of the rows (say, 100 million rows) where country equals "US" and very few rows (say, 10 rows) where country equals "GB". In this case, if the first invocation of the query was with parameter value "GB," it may result in suboptimal performance for queries that are executed with the "US" parameter value. To avoid the case where the cached query plan is not dependent on the value of the country parameter with which the statement is first executed, you can use the OPTIMIZE FOR hint. Assuming that the query originates in an application where the query cannot be modified, you can create a plan guide using the following command to achieve the desired behavior:

```
sp_create_plan_guide N'ExamplePG1',
N'
    SELECT SalesOrderID, Status, Name, CountryRegionCode
    FROM Sales.SalesOrderHeader h, Sales.Customer c, Sales.SalesTerritory t
    WHERE h.CustomerID = c.CustomerID AND c.TerritoryID = t.TerritoryID
        AND CountryRegionCode = @P1',
N'SQL',
NULL,
N'@P1 CHAR(2)',
N'OPTION (OPTIMIZE FOR(@P1 = N''US''))';
```

2. **Forcing a query plan using the USE PLAN hint** Another common hint for use with plan guides is the USE PLAN query hint. This query hint is useful when you already know of a query plan that performs better. The USE PLAN hint forces SQL Server 2005 to use the particular query plan specified explicitly in the hint syntax when executing the query, as long as it is one of the query plans the optimizer would normally have considered in its selection process. For example, a specific query plan for the query above can be forced as follows. (The full XML showplan listing is several pages long and therefore been replaced with the ellipses.):

```
sp_create_plan_guide
@name = N'ExamplePG2',
@stmt = N'
    SELECT EmployeeID, FirstName, LastName, EmailAddress, Phone
    FROM HumanResources.Employee e, Person.Contact c
    WHERE e.ContactID = c.ContactID;',
@type = N'SQL',
@module_or_batch = NULL,
@params= NULL,
@hint = N'OPTION (USE PLAN N''
```

```
<ShowPlanXML

xmlns="http://schemas.microsoft.com/sqlserver/2004/07/showplan"
    Version="1.0" Build="9.00.1399.06">
    <BatchSequence>
        <Batch>
            <Statements>
                ...
            </Statements>
        </Batch>
    </BatchSequence>
</ShowPlanXML>'')';
```

3. **Locking down a particular query plan** There may be situations where you would like to lock down the execution plan for a particular query and prevent it from recompiling due to changes in statistics of the underlying tables. As explained earlier, the KEEPFIXED PLAN hint can help achieve this. For example, consider the following query for which you'd like to lock down the query plan:

```
SELECT DISTINCT Sales.Customer.CustomerID, Sales.Store.Name
FROM Sales.Customer JOIN Sales.Store ON
    ( Sales.Customer.CustomerID = Sales.Store.CustomerID)
WHERE Sales.Customer.TerritoryID = 1;
```

Assuming that this query originates in an application that cannot be modified, the only way to enforce the query hint is to create a plan guide, as shown below, and specify the hint within that:

```
sp_create_plan_guide
@name = N'ExamplePG3',
@stmt = N'
SELECT DISTINCT Sales.Customer.CustomerID, Sales.Store.Name
FROM Sales.Customer JOIN Sales.Store ON
    ( Sales.Customer.CustomerID = Sales.Store.CustomerID)
WHERE Sales.Customer.TerritoryID = 1;',
@type = N'SQL',
@module_or_batch = NULL,
@params= NULL,
@hint = N'OPTION (KEEPFIXED PLAN)';
```

**Important** The query specified in the *sp_create_plan_guide* command's @stmt parameter must match the original query character for character. This includes any space characters that appear at the start or the end of a line, line feeds, or carriage returns. If the statement specified does not match the original statement, the plan guide will not match.

# Summary

While SQL Server 2005 does a great job of automatically optimizing queries and creating the best possible query execution plans, there may be times when you need to manually control the way a query plan is created. SQL Server 2005 presents more than thirty-five query hints to enable you to fine tune and control different attributes of a query plan generation.

In this chapter, we took a detailed look at the three different categories of hints—join, query, and table—along with examples of where they are most useful. We also learned about the new plan guides feature that has been introduced in SQL Server 2005, along with a detailed look at the commands used to create and administer plan guides, best practices, and some common usage examples.

# Glossary

**ACID**  An acronym for atomicity, consistency, isolation, and durability, the four properties required for a valid transaction.

**Action, Notification Services**  A T-SQL query used by Notification Services when firing a subscription rule.

**activation stored procedure**  A stored procedure used to read a Service Broker queue and process messages on arrival.

**active/active cluster**  Two active/passive clusters that share the same hardware, each acting as the standby server for the other.

**active/passive cluster**  *See* failover cluster.

**ad hoc report**  A report developed by a business user using a single data source and applying limited formatting.

**Address Windowing Extension (AWE)**  The software component that allows SQL Server to access more than 4 GB of memory.

**aggregation**  Precalculated summarized values derived from detailed source data and stored on the server.

**alternate keys**  After a PRIMARY KEY is selected from the candidate keys, the remaining candidate keys are then known as alternate keys.

**annotation**  Text added to a package to document workflow and data flow paths.

**API**  *See* application programming interface.

**application definition file (ADF)**  An XML file used by Notification Services describing the structure of database objects related to events, subscribers, notifications, and other components used to run the application.

**application programming interface (API)**  A set of routines, protocols, and tools for building software applications.

**article**  A table or subset of a table that is being replicated.

**attribute**  An object defined in a report model corresponding to a relational table column or an expression to be used in an ad hoc report.

**AWE**  *See* Address Windowing Extension.

**benchmark**  A performance test used to compare the performance of different hardware or software.

**bit**  The fundamental unit of computing that has two states: on (1) and off (0).

**blocking**  A situation in which one SQL Server process is held in a wait state while waiting to acquire a lock on a resource that is not compatible with a lock currently being held by another process on that same resource. Once the lock is available, the process continues execution.

**bookmark lookup**  A cluster key index lookup resulting from the values retrieved from a nonclustered index lookup.

**bottleneck**  A component of a system that limits the performance or throughput of the entire system. The term is a metaphor drawn from the narrow neck of a bottle that restricts the flow of liquid as it is poured out.

**bound sessions**  Sessions in which two or more sessions share the same transaction and locks and can work on the same data without lock conflicts. They ease the coordination of actions across multiple sessions on the same server. Bound sessions can be created from multiple sessions within the same application or from multiple applications with separate sessions.

**branch node** Intermediate pages in an index.

**breakpoint** An instruction to the control flow engine or data flow engine to pause execution for debugging.

**byte** Equal to 8 bits.

**cache** Small but fast memory used to store data that is immediately going to be used.

**CAL** *See* client access license.

**candidate keys** A column or set of columns that each could serve as the PRIMARY KEY. (Only one will be used as the PRIMARY KEY.)

**capacity planning** The act of determining the additional resources required for your existing system to meet future load requirements.

**Central Processing Unit (CPU)** The brains of the computer, used to control all aspects of the system. A computer system must have one or more CPUs.

**CHECK constraints** Used to enforce domain integrity by restricting the values allowed in a column to specific values. They contain a logical (Boolean) expression, similar to the WHERE clause of a query.

**checkpoint** A SQL Server operation (and the name of the SQL Server background process that performs checkpoint operations) that synchronizes the physical data and log files with the current state of the buffer cache by writing out all modified data pages in the buffer cache to disk.

**client access license (CAL)** A legal document granting a device or user access to the SQL Server software. A single-user CAL can grant access to multiple servers for one user. Similarly, a single-device CAL can grant access to multiple servers for one device.

**cluster** *See* failover cluster.

**cluster manager software** A set of software tools used to maintain, configure, and operate the cluster.

**clustered index** An index where the table data is stored in the leaf node.

**collation** Determines the rules by which character data is sorted and compared.

**composite index** An index that has more that one key column.

**container** A control flow component used to group tasks and other containers for the purpose of controlling the order in which each component executes.

**control flow** The run-time support managing connections, committing transactions, supporting debugging, logging, event handling, managing variables, and controlling the sequence of executables during package execution.

**conversation** A persistent Service Broker session that is maintained indefinitely by initiator and target applications.

**cost-based optimizer** An internal component of the SQL Server database engine that analyzes object statistics to determine the most optimal execution plan for a query. The cost-based optimizer isn't directly accessible by a user.

**covering index** An index that includes enough information so that it is not necessary to perform the bookmark lookup.

**CPU** *See* central processing unit.

**cube** A multidimensional structure in which each intersection of unique dimension members contains a data value.

**DAS** *See* direct attached storage.

**data flow** The path used to extract data from a source, transform data in-memory, and load results into a destination, as well as the engine that manages these activities.

**data mining** In general, the automated discovery of hidden patterns in large volumes of data.

**data modeling**    The logical layout of the database including table relationships and referential integrity constraints.

**data partitioning**    The process of dividing a table into smaller, more manageable pieces.

**data pipeline**    Another phrase for data flow.

**data region**    A report layout structure that contains data, such as a table, matrix, chart, or list.

**data source**    A file that contains the connection string and credentials used by Integration Services to connect to a data store.

**data source view**    A file that contains a description of database objects, their relationships, and custom expressions used by a data source adapter to filter or manipulate data to extract from a source.

**Data Transformation Services (DTS)**    A product used for movement of data in SQL Server 2000 that has been replaced by SQL Server Integration Services in SQL Server 2005.

**data viewer**    An object placed between two data flow components to capture and display information about the data currently in the pipeline.

**database**    An organized repository of data. Databases in SQL Server are stored as operating system files.

**database administrator (DBA)**    The title given to the person responsible for the upkeep and stability of the SQL Server database.

**database snapshot**    A read-only, static view of a database (the source database) that is explicitly created using DDL.

**dataset**    A collection of items including a pointer to a data source, a query defining data to be retrieved for a report, and a set of fields describing each column returned by the query.

**DBA**    *See* database administrator.

**deadlock**    A situation in which two SQL Server processes become blocked waiting on lock resources that the other holds, and neither can continue execution. SQL Server chooses one process as a deadlock victim, and that process is rolled back and must be run again.

**DEFAULT definitions**    Provides automatic entry of a default value for a column when an INSERT statement does not specify the value for that column.

**delivery channel**    A Notification Services endpoint for the delivery of notifications using a specified protocol.

**designer**    A collection of design tools, including a workspace, toolbox, dialog boxes, and various windows, used to build a Visual Studio project.

**DHCP**    Dynamic Host Configuration Protocol.

**dialog**    A bi-directional conversation between two Service Broker services.

**dimension**    Labels that add context to numerical data

**dimension table**    A relational database table containing columns with descriptive information about each member of a dimension, including a unique name and other specific characteristics for that member.

**direct attached storage (DAS)**    Disk drive storage that is contained within the computer or is directly attached to the computer for direct data access, without involving any type of network device as with NAS or SAN.

**dirty page**    A data page residing in the SQL Server buffer cache (in memory) that has been modified but has not yet been written out to disk.

**disaster recovery** The ability of the system or company to remain working in the event of a catastrophic failure of the data center or database server or servers.

**disk volume** An entity that appears to the OS as a disk drive, but is actually made up of a piece of one or more disk drives in a RAID set.

**distributed partitioned view** A view that joins horizontally partitioned data from a set of tables that reside in distinct instances of SQL Server on two or more servers.

**distributor** The replication system responsible for managing replication; contains the distribution database.

**DMV** *See* Dynamic Management View.

**domain integrity** Also known as column integrity; enforces that values inserted or updated into a table comply with a specified set of data values that are valid for a column. Enforced through the use of CHECK, DEFAULT, NULL, and NOT NULL constraint types.

**drilling** Navigating from summarized data to detailed data.

**DTS** *See* Data Transformation Services.

**Dynamic Management View (DMV)** A view that returns server state information that can be used to monitor the health of a server instance, to diagnose problems, and to tune performance.

**EM64T** EM64T refers to Intel Extended Memory 64 Technology (Intel EM64T). This technology allows platforms to access larger amounts of memory using 64-bit addressing while maintaining compatibility with today's 32-bit applications and operating systems.

**EM64T processor** The Intel processor that runs both 64-bit and 32-bit programs natively.

**endpoint** The method that the SQL Server Database Engine uses to communicate with applications.

**enterprise report** A report that presents formatted data from one or more data sources in one or more data regions and is stored in a centralized location for access by many users in an organization or distributed via e-mail or other methods.

**Enterprise Resource Planning** (ERP) Management information systems that integrate and automate many of the business practices associated with the operations or production aspects of a company.

**entity** An object in a report model corresponding to a table in a data source view.

**entity integrity** Also known as table or row integrity; requires that all the rows in a table have a unique identifier; enforced through the use of PRIMARY KEY or UNIQUE constraints.

**equijoin** A join operation with a join condition containing an equality operator; combines rows that have equivalent values for the specified columns.

**ETL (Extract, Transform, and Load)** The process of taking data from one system, converting it, and loading it into another system.

**event** A message raised by an executable that indicates the current conditions, such as the start of the executable or failure of the executable.

**event chronicle** A history of events collected by Notification Services.

**event class** A set of properties used by Notification Services to create tables, views, basic indexes, and stored procedures for the storage and management of events in an application database.

**Event, Notification Services**   An occurrence of interest to subscribers, such as a change in a key performance indicator or the availability of new data in a transactional database.

**event provider**   A Notification Services component that collects events on a periodic basis by sending a query to a specified data source.

**exabyte (EB)**   $2^{60}$ bytes, or 1,152,921,504,606,846,976 bytes.

**executables**   A container or task in the package control flow.

**external activation**   Use of an external application notified by an event to process messages in a Service Broker queue.

**fact table**   A relational database table containing columns for one or more measures at the lowest level of detail for one or more dimensions.

**failback**   The act of resources moving back to the original node in a cluster upon its resumption of service or at a scheduled time.

**failover**   The act of resources moving to the remaining node of a cluster in the event of a failure.

**failover cluster**   Two or more computer systems that run the same database, one active and the other in standby mode, ready to take over in the event of a failure of the primary system.

**failover clustering**   Failover clustering is a process through which the operating system and application software work together to provide continuous availability in the event of an application, hardware, or operating system failure.

**FASMI**   *See* Fast Analysis of Shared Multidimensional Information.

**Fast Analysis of Shared Multidimensional Information (FASMI)**   A term introduced by The OLAP Report to describe OLAP.

**FAT**   A file system used with DOS and some versions of Windows; stands for File Allocation Table, the main feature of this file system.

**FC (Fibre Channel)**   A high-speed data transport technology used to build storage area networks (SANs); primarily used to transfer SCSI commands between servers and disk arrays.

**FCP (Fibre Channel Protocol)**   A protocol that serializes SCSI commands into FC frames for transfer over Fibre Channel.

**fiber**   A lightweight thread that is managed by SQL Server and can switch context when in user mode, thereby requiring fewer resources than a Windows thread. A single Windows thread can be mapped to many fibers.

**filegroup**   A named grouping of data files used primarily for manageability and allocation purposes.

**forced parameterization**   An option to force the query optimizer to automatically parameterize all queries that pass in predicate values as literals.

**FOREIGN KEY**   A column or set of columns whose value matches the value of a PRIMARY KEY or UNIQUE KEY in another table.

**fully redundant**   The ability of multiple I/O system components to take over functions so that the system can continue transferring data if a component fails, allowing the system to continue transferring data.

**gigabyte (GB)**   $2^{30}$ bytes, or 1,073,741,824 bytes.

**group**   A set of detail rows related to a common field returned in a query result set or to an expression.

**HBA**   *See* Host Bus Adapter.

**heartbeat**    A message sent between nodes in a cluster to verify that the node is still up and running properly.

**hierarchy**    A navigation path that allows the user to move from summarized values for one attribute to summarized values for another attribute.

**high availability**    The availability of the system's resources in the wake of a component failure.

**hint**    An optional clause you can make to a SQL Server statement to direct the query optimizer to construct the query execution plan a particular way. Hints can be specified for SELECT, INSERT, UPDATE, or DELETE statements.

**HOLAP**    An OLAP storage mode in which detail data is stored in a relational database and aggregated values are stored in a multidimensional structure.

**horizontal filter**    A filter used to create a subset of rows.

**horizontal partitioning**    The splitting of a table with a large number of rows into multiple partitions, each with the same number of columns but fewer rows.

**Host Bus Adapter (HBA)**    Also called a controller or host adapter, it is an expansion card that plugs into the computer bus to connect one or more peripheral units to the computer. As related to SAN, a HBA provides I/O transfer capability between the host computer and the disk array.

**hyperthreading**    Hyperthreading is a processor technology that provides thread-level parallelism on each processor, resulting in more efficient use of processor resources, higher processing throughput, and improved performance primarily for multithreaded software.

**I/O**    Input/Output. I/O typically refers to the reading from and writing to disk drives.

**index key**    The column in the table that is to be indexed.

**Index width**    The size of the index key; a wide index has many large columns in the index key; a narrow index has one or few small columns in the index key.

**indexed view**    A view that has a unique clustered index created on it. The results of the clustered index are stored permanently on disk at the time the index is created. Indexed views are used in certain cases to increase performance. Nonclustered indexes can also be created on the same view once the clustered index is created.

**initiator application**    An application which sends a Service Broker message to a target application.

**instance configuration file (ICF)**    An XML file used by Notification Services describing an instance used to run applications, the SQL Server hosting the instance, the path to files used by the application, and parameters used by the application.

**Instance, Notification Services**    A host service for one or more notification applications.

**interconnect**    To attach one device to another; the physical method used to connect two devices.

**intermediate report**    A version of a report created after query execution but before rendering that may be stored permanently as a snapshot or temporarily as a cached instance.

**internal activation**    Use of a stored procedure to process messages on arrival in a Service Broker queue.

**IOPS**    (I/O Operations Per Second) The number of reads and/or writes to the device per second.

**iSCSI (Internet SCSI)**   A protocol that serializes SCSI commands and converts them to TCP/IP for transfer over an IP network, also sometimes referred to as IP SAN.

**Itanium**   Itanium refers to the Intel Itanium 2 Processor, Intel's highest-performing and most reliable server platform.

**key performance indicator (KPI)**   A measurement of business operations used to compare a value at a point in time to a predefined goal.

**kilobyte (KB)**   $2^{10}$ bytes or 1,024 bytes.

**latency**   In general, a period of time spent waiting for an event to complete or the time between the end of one event and the beginning of another, most commonly used to refer to latencies involved in transferring data.

**lazy writer**   A SQL Server operation (and the name of the SQL Server background process that performs lazy writer operations) that periodically checks to ensure that the free buffer list does not fall below a specific size. If the free list has fallen below that size, the lazy writer scans the cache, reclaims unused pages, and frees dirty pages so those pages can be reused for other data.

**leaf level**   The most detailed level of data.

**leaf node**   The bottom pages in an index.

**level**   A group of related dimension members typically associated with a hierarchy; members on the same level usually come from the same column in a dimension table.

**linked report**   A virtual copy of a report definition which has its own execution, parameter, security, and subscription properties.

**load test**   The practice of modeling the characteristics of a program or system by simulating a number of users accessing that system or program.

**logical disk**   An entity that appears to the OS as a disk drive, but is actually made up of a piece of one or more disk drives in a RAID set.

**login**   Used to allow a user to connect into the database. A login can use either SQL Server or Windows authentication.

**measure**   A numeric value that can be summarized.

**measure group**   A collection of measures derived from the same fact table.

**megabyte (MB)**   $2^{20}$ bytes or 1,048,576 bytes.

**member**   A single item in a dimension that usually corresponds to a single row in a dimension table.

**merge replication**   Type of replication that uses triggers for two-way replication.

**message queue**   Temporary storage for messages exchanged using Service Broker.

**metadata**   Data that is used to describe other data, for example, table, column, index, view, and statistic definition.

**Microsoft Data Access Components (MDAC)**   A group of Microsoft technologies that interact together as a framework allowing programmers a uniform and comprehensive way of developing applications for accessing data; made up of various components: ActiveX Data Objects (ADO), OLE DB, and Open Database Connectivity (ODBC).

**mirror**   The receiving database in the mirror pair.

**mirrored pair**   A principal and mirror operating together.

**MOLAP**   A proprietary OLAP storage mode that is highly efficient and enables fast retrieval.

**multicore**   A processor technology in which a single physical processor consists of two or more complete execution units, known as cores. All of the cores run at the same frequency and are plugged into a single processor socket. Multicore processors can perform multiple tasks in parallel in each clock tick.

**multipath I/O**   Refers to having more than one physical path for data transfer between a computer and a disk storage device, and software to manage the paths so that if one path fails, the I/O will be handled by the remaining path.

**multiple active result sets (MARS)**   A new feature in SQL Server 2005 that allows applications to have more than one pending request per connection, and in particular, to have more than one active default result set per connection.

**multiprocessor**   A computer with multiple processors. The term is based on the number of sockets supported by the motherboard and not the number of cores on the die.

**named pipes**   A protocol developed for local area networks with which a portion of memory is used by one process to pass information to another process, so that the output of one is the input of the other.

**named query**   A SQL query used in place of a table to construct a specific logical view of the underlying data source for use in a data source view.

**narrow index**   An index that is created on one or a few columns.

**NAS**   *See* network attached storage.

**natural key**   A column or set of columns already existing in the table that meet the conditions for a PRIMARY KEY.

**network attached storage (NAS)**   A specialized file server/storage device that connects to an IP network to process only I/O requests supporting file sharing protocols such as NFS (Unix) and SMB/CIFS (Windows). It appears as another node on the network. Computers transfer data to and from the device by connecting to the network using the traditional Ethernet access method and the TCP/IP protocol.

**network bandwidth**   The amount of data that a network can transmit in a specified amount of time.

**network interface card (NIC)**   An expansion board you insert into a computer so the computer can be connected to a network; most are designed for a particular type of network, protocol, and media, although some are designed to serve multiple networks.

**New Technology File System (NTFS)**   The disk file structure used by Windows NT and Windows 2000, Windows XP, and Windows 2003 operating systems; uses a Master File Table instead of a file allocation table.

**NIC**   *See* network interface card.

**nonclustered index**   An index where the table data is not stored in the leaf node.

**normalization**   The standard RDBMS practice of taking redundancy out of rows in a table by storing redundant data once and then referencing that data in a lookup table.

**notification**   A message, typically in the form of an e-mail message or a file, delivered to a subscriber by Notification Services.

**notification application**   An application that delivers a notification to a subscriber.

**notification class**   A set of properties used by Notification Services to create tables, views, and stored procedures for the storage and management of notifications in an application database.

**NTFS** *See* New Technology File System.

**NULL / NOT NULL constraints** Used on a column in a table definition to allow or prevent NULL values from being inserted into that column.

**nullability** Refers to the ability of a column to accept NULL as a value or not.

**OLAP** *See* Online Analytical Processing.

**OLTP** *See* Online Transaction Processing.

**Online Analytical Processing (OLTP)** A type of database designed specifically to support analysis for decision-making.

**Online Transaction Processing (OLTP)** A type of computer workload computer in which the computer responds immediately to user requests. Each request is considered to be a transaction.

**Opteron processor** The AMD processor that runs both 64-bit and 32-bit programs natively.

**optimization** The process of modifying a computer system in order to maximize its efficiency.

**package** An executable unit of work that encapsulates the objects connecting to data sources, performing tasks, transforming data, and managing workflows.

**PAE** *See* Page Address Extension.

**Page Address Extension (PAE)** Hardware and software modifications that allow 32-bit processors to address more than 4 GB of memory.

**parameterization** The process of modifying a statement so that the predicate values are passed in as parameters (example: @P1) and not specified directly as literals (for example, "123").

**partition** A cube structure used to optimize physical storage, aggregations, query performance, and processing.

**partition column** The column that defines the partition values.

**partition key** The column that partitioning is defined on (similar to an index key column).

**partitioned view** A view that joins horizontally partitioned data from a set of tables that reside in one instance of SQL Server on one server. This is also known also as a local partitioned view to distinguish from a distributed partitioned view. For SQL Server 2005, partitioned views are supported for backward compatibility as the new partitioned tables feature is replacing them.

**partitioning, horizontal** *See* horizontal partitioning.

**partitioning, vertical** *See* vertical partitioning.

**partitions** The piece of a table that has been divided out via SQL Server partitioning.

**PC** Personal computer.

**performance tuning** The process of modifying a computer system or software in order to make the entire system or some aspect of that system run faster.

**permission** Approvals to perform specific tasks or access specific objects.

**persistent storage** Storage that survives even when power is removed.

**petabyte (PB)** $2^{50}$ bytes or 1,125,899,906,842,624 bytes.

**physical memory** Hardware used to store data in a computer.

**pivot** Switch labels on rows and columns.

**PK** *See* PRIMARY KEY.

**plan guides** A feature introduced in SQL Server 2005 that helps you specify hints on statements without having to modify the text of the statement directly. Plan guides are very useful for tuning queries that originate in applications that cannot be modified.

**precedence constraint**   A package object defining the sequence of operations of two tasks in the control flow and the conditions which determine whether the second task will execute.

**PRIMARY KEY**   A column or set of columns that uniquely identifies a row in a table. There can only be one PRIMARY KEY per table.

**principal database**   The originating database in the mirror pair. There can only be one principal database, and it has to be on a SQL Server instance separate from the mirror database.

**principals**   Entities that can request access to SQL Server resources and consist of their own hierarchy.

**proactive caching**   Processing updates to database objects only when source data changes.

**process**   Load data from a relational source into dimension or measure group partition structures.

**protocol**   A format and procedure that governs the transmission and receipt of data.

**publication**   A collection of articles that is defined to be replicated.

**publisher**   The replicated system from which data is replicated and the originator of the replication.

**QA**   Quality assurance.

**quantum**   An interval of time used by Notification Services to check for new notifications.

**query execution plan**   A representation of the exact sequence of operations the SQL Server database engine performs in order to execute a SQL statement.

**queue time**   The time that the action that you are measuring waits on all of the jobs ahead of it to complete.

**queuing theory**   The mathematics that governs the effects of multiple entities each using the same resources.

**quorum**   The relationship between the witness, the principal, and the mirror.

**RAID**   Redundant Array of Inexpensive Disks. RAID disk controllers create a large logical disk drive by striping multiple disk drives together.

**random I/O**   Requests to read and write data from and to random places on the disk drive.

**random seek**   The time it takes on average for data to move from one track to another randomly.

**recovery**   The process of rolling data back (roll back is also known as undo) and bringing the data online.

**recovery path**   Any complete sequence of data and log backups that can be restored to bring a database to a point in time.

**referential integrity**   Ensures that the relationships between tables with associated data are maintained; enforced through the use of FOREIGN KEY constraints that reference a UNIQUE or PRIMARY KEY constraint.

**replication**   A feature of SQL Server that allows you to enable the automatic creation of copies of SQL Server objects or subset of objects on a system and the propagation of the objects to other systems. Replication comes in three forms: snapshot, transactional, and merge.

**report definition**   A description of a report's data, layout, and properties.

**report item**   An item used to display text or graphical elements in a report, such as a textbox, table, chart, or image.

**report model**   A logical view of a relational database describing the database's tables and columns and the relationships between them; used to build ad hoc reports.

**reporting life cycle**   A three-stage process that includes tasks for report authoring, report management, and report delivery.

**response time**   The sum of the service time and the queue time.

**restore**   The process of copying data and rolling data forward (roll forward is also known as redo) as needed.

**restore sequence**   A set of restore statements used to perform the restore steps: data copy, roll forward, roll back, and bring data online.

**ROLAP**   An OLAP storage mode in which data is stored in a relational database.

**role**   A pseudo-entity; a holder of permissions that can be assigned to logins and/or users. In a report model, an object defining a relationship between entities. In a security system, a group of functionally related activities to which a Windows group or user is assigned.

**role assignment**   Assignment of a specific user or a group to a role for a specific item on the report server.

**role definition**   An association of roles and tasks in the Reporting Services security system.

**root node**   The first page in an index.

**rotational latency**   The time it takes for a disk drive to spin to the desired sector.

**row splitting**   The practice of dividing rows into two or into different storage areas with a one-to-one row equivalency.

**RPM**   Revolutions per minute.

**sac**   Surface area configuration command-line utility used to import and export surface area configuration settings.

**SAN**   *See* storage area network.

**scale out**   A system that is distributed in order to provide a higher degree of performance.

**scale up**   To add more and bigger hardware to a system in order to achieve a higher degree of performance.

**schema**   An entity that owns a securable. A schema is like a user but doesn't necessarily have logins associated with it.

**SCSI**   Small Computer System Interface. A hardware interface that allows for the connection of up to 15 peripheral devices to a single PCI board called a "SCSI host adapter" that plugs into the motherboard. Connects computers to disk drives as well as other peripheral devices such as printers and tape drives. Pronounced "skuzzy."

**securables**   Resources that the SQL Server database engine regulates access to, or secures.

**seek time**   The time it takes for a disk head to move from one track to another.

**semiadditive measure**   A measure that can be summed along some, but not all, dimensions, such as an inventory count.

**sequential I/O**   Requests to read and write data from and to adjacent locations on the disk drive.

**server interconnect**   The connection between the nodes in the cluster.

**service level agreement (SLA)**   A contract, either formal or informal, between the IT organization and the customer that defines the level of service that will be provided to them.

**service time**   The time that the action that you are measuring takes to complete.

**SGAM**   *See* Shared Global Allocation Map.

**Shared Global Allocation Map (SGAM)**
Pages used to record which extents are being used as mixed extents and have free pages for allocation.

**simple index**    An index that has been defined with only one key column.

**simple parameterization**    An option to permit the query optimizer to choose to parameterize the queries as appropriate.

**single point of failure**    A component whose failure will cause the failure of the entire system.

**sizing**    The act of determining the resources required for a new system.

**SLA**    *See* service level agreement.

**slice and dice**    To cross-tabulate data.

**SMP**    *See* Symmetric Multi Processor.

**SNAC**    SQL Native Access Client. A data access technology new in Microsoft SQL Server 2005; a stand-alone data access application programming interface that combines the SQL OLE DB provider and the ODBC driver into one native dynamic-link library (SQLNCLI.DLL).

**snapshot replication**    Type of replication that creates an entire copy of the publication.

**split the problem**    The technique of devising a test to determine whether a problem is of one type or another.

**SQL Server Active Directory Helper**    Service used to publish and manage SQL Server services in Windows active directory.

**SQL Server Agent**    Service used for automating administrative tasks, executing jobs, alerts, and so on.

**SQL Server Analysis Services**    Online analytical processing (OLAP) and data mining functionality for Business Intelligence (BI) applications.

**SQL Server Browser**    Name resolution service that provides SQL Server connection information for client computers.

**SQL Server Full Text Search**    Service that enables fast linguistic searches on content and properties of structured and semistructured data by using full-text indexes.

**SQL Server Integration Services**    Provides management support for Integration Services package storage and execution.

**SQL Server Notification Services**    Platform for developing and deploying applications that generate and send notifications.

**SQL Server Reporting Services**    SQL Server 2005 component used to manage, execute, render, schedule, and deliver reports.

**SQL Server Surface Area Configuration**    Tool used to enable, disable, start, or stop the features, services, and remote connectivity of SQL Server 2005 installations.

**SQL Server Upgrade Advisor**    Tool you can use to prepare for upgrades to SQL Server 2005.

**SQL Server VSS Writer**    Service used to allow backup and restore applications to operate in the Volume Shadow-copy Service (VSS) framework.

**statistics**    A histogram and associated density groups created over a column or set of columns of a table or indexed view.

**storage area network (SAN)**    A network of disks that allows multiple computers to connect to a pool of disks. The SAN contains its own I/O controller(s) such that the computer hosts transfer data via an HBA, rather than via an Ethernet card as with a NAS device.

**subcube** A subset of a cube created by a CREATE SUBCUBE MDX statement to focus subsequent analysis on a smaller set of data for improved query performance.

**subscriber** The replicated system to which data is replicated and the recipient of the replication.

**subscription** A rule that defines the conditions for sending a notification to a subscriber.

**subscription chronicle** A history of notifications maintained by Notification Services.

**subscription class** A set of properties used by Notification Services to create tables, views, basic indexes, and stored procedures for the storage and management of subscriptions in an application database.

**surrogate key** An artificial identifier that is unique. This is most often a system-generated sequential number.

**Symmetric Multi Processor (SMP)** A type of server where two or more similar processors are connected via a high-bandwidth link and managed by one operating system. Each processor has equal access to memory and the I/O devices.

**system role assignment** An association of a Windows user or group with a system role to define who can perform administrative tasks on the Report Server.

**system tables** A set of built-in tables used to store system metadata; store information and definitions of all objects in a database

**table** A collection of cells organized into a fixed number of columns with a variable number of detail and group rows.

**target application** An application which receives a Service Broker message from an initiator application.

**task** A control flow component performing a specific function, such as executing a SQL statement.

**TCP/IP** Transmission Control Protocol/Internet Protocol; a suite of communications protocols used to connect hosts on the Internet; uses several protocols, the two main ones being TCP and IP.

**terabyte** $2^{40}$ bytes, or 1,099,511,627,776 bytes.

**trace flag** A database switch used to temporarily set specific server characteristics or to switch off a particular behavior.

**track-to-track seek** The time the heads take to move between adjacent tracks.

**transaction** 1. A logical unit of work. 2. In relation to the SQL Server transaction log specifically, a transaction is a modification to data in the database. For example, a transaction can be an insertion, update, or deletion of data, or a schema change. Transactions are recorded in the transaction log.

**transaction log** A database file in which all database modifications are recorded.

**transactional replication** Type of replication that uses the transaction log to keep the subscriber in sync with the publisher.

**transfer time** The time it takes to move the data from the disk drive electronics to the I/O controller.

**transformation** A data flow component manipulating data in a data flow, such as sorting rows.

**troubleshooting** The systematic search for the source of a problem.

**T-SQL** Transact-Structured Query Language, the language used to define the database objects, manipulate data, and administer the SQL Server instance.

**Unified Dimension Model (UDM)** The measure groups and dimensions as well as related analysis objects that collectively provide access to business intelligence data.

**Uniprocessor**   A computer with a single processor. The term is based on the number of sockets supported by the motherboard and not the number of cores on the die.

**UNIQUE KEY**   A column or set of columns that uniquely identifies a row in a table and is defined within a UNIQUE constraint. The difference from a PRIMARY KEY constraint is that a UNIQUE constraint will accept NULL as a value, and there can be multiple UNIQUE constraints per table.

**user**   Allows permissions to be assigned to a login in a specific database. Typically a login has a corresponding user ID in each database.

**user hierarchy**   A collection of attributes placed into a hierarchy structure to enable navigation from one attribute to another.

**user instance**   A SQL Server Express feature that enables nonadministrators to run a local version of SQL Server in their own accounts. With user instances, nonadministrators have database owner privileges over the instance running in their own accounts.

**user-defined integrity**   Lets the user defined business rules that do not fall under one of the other integrity categories, including column-level and table-level constraints.

**UserID**   *See* user.

**vacuuming**   A process to periodically remove stale data from a Notification Services application database.

**vertical filter**   A filter used to create a subset of columns.

**vertical partitioning**   The splitting of a table with a large number of columns or very large columns into multiple partitions, each with the same number of rows but fewer columns.

**VIA**   Virtual Interface Adapter. A high performance communication protocol.

**view**   A virtual table whose contents are defined by a SELECT statement; the resulting rows and columns of the view are not stored on disk, but are dynamically produced when the view is referenced.

**virtual memory**   A technique by which a process in a computer system can address memory whose size and addressing is not coupled to the physical memory of the system

**virtual server**   A server on which the actual physical identity of the system has been abstracted away.

**wide index**   An index with many key columns.

**witness**   Monitors the mirrored pair and ensures that both database servers are in proper operating order.

**XML showplan**   The XML-based representation of the query execution plan.

**yottabyte (YB)**   $2^{80}$ bytes, or 1,024 zettabytes.

**zettabyte (ZB)**   $2^{70}$ bytes, or 1,024 exabytes.

# Index

# N

# About the Authors

**Edward Whalen** is the founder of Performance Tuning Corporation (*www.perftuning.com*), a consulting company specializing in database performance, administration, and backup/recovery solutions. He has extensive experience in database system design and tuning for optimal performance. His career has consisted of hardware, operating system, and database development projects for many different companies. He has written four other books on the Microsoft SQL Server RDBMS and has also written four books on Oracle. In addition to writing, he has worked on numerous benchmarks and performance tuning projects with both Microsoft SQL Server and Oracle. He is recognized as a leader in database performance tuning and optimization on both SQL Server and Oracle. He can be reached at *ewhalen@perftuning.com*.

**Marcilina (Marci) Garcia** is director of consulting operations and senior database consultant for Performance Tuning Corporation (*www.perftuning.com*). She has worked as a consultant for more than nine years, specializing in troubleshooting and tuning Microsoft SQL Server database systems, system and storage architecture, database benchmarks, load test development, and sizing and capacity planning. She has previously co-authored four technical books for Microsoft Press on SQL Server administration and performance tuning.

**Burzin Patel** is currently a program manager in the SQL Server team at Microsoft Corporation. He is responsible for managing the relationship with strategic Independent Software Vendors (ISVs) as well as large-scale customers. Prior to Microsoft, he consulted at IBM Corporation as lead performance engineer for four years, where he specialized in end-to-end system performance and configuration. He has authored several papers and lectured on a variety of topics around the world. He currently holds two U.S. patents, plus others that are pending approval, for inventions pertaining to performance and optimizations. You can contact him via e-mail at *burzinp@microsoft.com* or telephone (650) 867-7314.

**Stacia Misner** is the founder of Data Inspirations, where she delivers business intelligence consulting and education services. She is a consultant, educator, mentor, and author specializing in business intelligence and performance management solutions using Microsoft technologies. Stacia has more than 22 years of experience in IT and has focused exclusively on business intelligence since 1999. She wrote both *Microsoft SQL Server 2005 Reporting Services Step by Step* and *Microsoft SQL Server 2005 Reporting Services Step by Step*, and wrote *Microsoft SQL Server 2005 Analysis Services Step by Step and Business*

*Intelligence: Making Better Decisions Faster*. She currently lives in Las Vegas, Nevada, with her husband, Gerry, and their flock of parrots. She can be contacted at *smisner@datain-spirations.com*.

**Victor Isakov** is a database architect and Microsoft Certified Trainer based in Sydney, Australia. He holds the following certifications/credentials: LLB/BSc (Computer Science), CTT, MCT, MCSE, MCDBA, MCTS: *SQL Server 2005, MCTS: SQL Server 2005 Business Intelligence, MCITP: Database Developer, MCITP: Database Administrator, MCITP: Business Intelligence Developer*. Although he has a strong operating system and networking background, he specializes in SQL Server, providing consulting and training services to various organizations in the public, private, and NGO sectors globally. He runs the SQL Server User Group in Sydney and has a Web site dedicated to SQL Server (*http://www.SQLServerSessions.com*) and SQL Server training (*http://www. SQLServerLounge.com*). He regularly presents at various international events and conferences, such as Microsoft TechEd and SQL PASS. He has written a number of books about SQL Server and worked closely with Microsoft to develop the new generation of SQL Server 2005 certification and Microsoft official curriculum for both instructor-led training and e-learning courses. He also writes articles regularly for *http://www.devx.com* and *http://searchsqlserver.com*. You can reach him at *SQL.Server.Solutions@gmail.com*.

# Additional SQL Server Resources for Administrators

*Published and Forthcoming Titles from Microsoft Press*

## Microsoft® SQL Server™ 2005 Reporting Services *Step by Step*
Hitachi Consulting Services • ISBN 0-7356-2250-7

SQL Server Reporting Services (SRS) is Microsoft's customizable reporting solution for business data analysis. It is one of the key value features of SQL Server 2005: functionality more advanced and much less expensive than its competition. SRS is powerful, so an understanding of how to architect a report, as well as how to install and program SRS, is key to harnessing the full functionality of SQL

Server. This procedural tutorial shows how to use the Report Project Wizard, how to think about and access data, and how to build queries. It also walks the reader through the creation of charts and visual layouts to enable maximum visual understanding of the data analysis. Interactivity (enhanced in SQL Server 2005) and security are also covered in detail.

## Microsoft SQL Server 2005 Administrator's Pocket Consultant
William R. Stanek • ISBN 0-7356-2107-1

Here's the utterly practical, pocket-sized reference for IT professionals who need to administer, optimize, and maintain SQL Server 2005 in their organizations. This unique guide provides essential details for using SQL Server 2005 to help protect and manage your company's data—whether automating tasks; creating indexes and views; performing backups and recovery; replicating transactions; tuning performance; managing server

activity; importing and exporting data; or performing other key tasks. Featuring quick-reference tables, lists, and step-by-step instructions, this handy, one-stop guide provides fast, accurate answers on the spot, whether you're at your desk or in the field!

## Microsoft SQL Server 2005 Administrator's Companion
Marci Frohock Garcia, Edward Whalen, and Mitchell Schroeter • ISBN 0-7356-2198-5

*Microsoft SQL Server 2005 Administrator's Companion* is the comprehensive, in-depth guide that saves time by providing all the technical information you need to deploy, administer, optimize, and support SQL Server 2005. Using a hands-on, example-rich approach, this authoritative, one-volume reference book provides expert advice, product information, detailed solutions, procedures, and real-world troubleshooting tips from experienced SQL Server 2005 professionals. This expert guide shows you how to design high-availability database systems, prepare for installation, install and configure SQL Server 2005, administer services and features, and maintain and troubleshoot your database system. It covers how to configure your system for your I/O system and model and optimize system capacity. The expert authors provide details on how to create and use defaults, constraints, rules, indexes, views, functions, stored procedures, and triggers. This guide shows you how to administer reporting services, analysis services, notification services, and integration services. It also provides a wealth of information on replication and the specifics of snapshot, transactional, and merge replication. Finally, there is expansive coverage of how to manage and tune your SQL Server system, including automating tasks, backup and restoration of databases, and management of users and security.

## Microsoft SQL Server 2005 Analysis Services *Step by Step*
Hitachi Consulting Services • ISBN 0-7356-2199-3

One of the key features of SQL Server 2005 is SQL Server Analysis Services—Microsoft's customizable analysis solution for business data modeling and interpretation. Just compare SQL Server Analysis Services to its competition to understand/grasp the great value of its enhanced features. One of the keys to harnessing the full functionality of SQL Server will be leveraging Analysis Services for the powerful tool that it is—including creating a cube, and deploying, customizing, and extending the basic calculations. This step-by-step tutorial discusses how to get started, how to build scalable analytical applications, and how to use and administer advanced features. Interactivity (which is enhanced in SQL Server 2005), data translation, and security are also covered in detail.

---

**Microsoft SQL Server 2005 Express Edition**
*Step by Step*
Jackie Goldstein • ISBN 0-7356-2184-5

**Inside Microsoft SQL Server 2005:**
**The Storage Engine**
Kalen Delaney • ISBN 0-7356-2105-5

**Inside Microsoft SQL Server 2005:**
**T-SQL Programming**
Itzik Ben-Gan • ISBN 0-7356-2197-7

**Inside Microsoft SQL Server 2005:**
**Query Processing and Optimization**
Kalen Delaney • ISBN 0-7356-2196-9

---

*For more information about Microsoft Press® books and other learning products,*
*visit:* **www.microsoft.com/mspress** *and* **www.microsoft.com/learning**

# Microsoft Windows Server 2003 Resource Kit
# The *definitive* resource
## for Windows Server 2003!

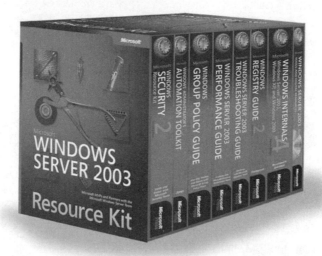

Get the in-depth technical information and tools you need to manage and optimize Microsoft® Windows Server™ 2003—with expert guidance and best practices from Microsoft MVPs, leading industry consultants, and the Microsoft Windows Server team. This official *Resource Kit* delivers seven comprehensive volumes, including:

- **Microsoft Windows® Security Resource Kit, Second Edition**
- **Microsoft Windows Administrator's Automation Toolkit**
- **Microsoft Windows Group Policy Guide**
- **Microsoft Windows Server 2003 Performance Guide**
- **Microsoft Windows Server 2003 Troubleshooting Guide**
- **Microsoft Windows Registry Guide, Second Edition**
- **Microsoft Windows Internals, Fourth Edition**

You'll find 300+ timesaving tools and scripts, an eBook of the entire *Resource Kit*, plus five bonus eBooks. It's everything you need to help maximize system performance and reliability—and help reduce ownership and support costs.

**Microsoft Windows Server 2003 Resource Kit**
Microsoft MVPs and Partners with the Microsoft Windows Server Team
**ISBN:** 0-7356-2232-9

*For more information about Microsoft Press® books, visit:* **www.microsoft.com/mspress**

*For more information about learning tools such as online assessments, e-learning, and certification, visit:* **www.microsoft.com/learning**

**Microsoft**
*Press*

# Prepare for Certification with Self-Paced Training Kits

## *Official Exam Prep Guides—*
### *Plus Practice Tests*

Ace your preparation for the skills measured by the MCP exams—and on the job. With official *Self-Paced Training Kits* from Microsoft, you'll work at your own pace through a system of lessons, hands-on exercises, troubleshooting labs, and review questions. Then test yourself with the Readiness Review Suite on CD, which provides hundreds of challenging questions for in-depth self-assessment and practice.

- **MCSE Self-Paced Training Kit (Exams 70-290, 70-291, 70-293, 70-294): Microsoft® Windows Server™ 2003 Core Requirements.** 4-Volume Boxed Set. ISBN: 0-7356-1953-0. (Individual volumes are available separately.)
- **MCSA/MCSE Self-Paced Training Kit (Exam 70-270): Installing, Configuring, and Administering Microsoft Windows® XP Professional, Second Edition.** ISBN: 0-7356-2152-7.
- **MCSE Self-Paced Training Kit (Exam 70-298): Designing Security for a Microsoft Windows Server 2003 Network.** ISBN: 0-7356-1969-7.
- **MCSA/MCSE Self-Paced Training Kit (Exam 70-350): Implementing Microsoft Internet Security and Acceleration Server 2004.** ISBN: 0-7356-2169-1.
- **MCSA/MCSE Self-Paced Training Kit (Exam 70-284): Implementing and Managing Microsoft Exchange Server 2003.** ISBN: 0-7356-1899-2.

*For more information about Microsoft Press® books, visit*: **www.microsoft.com/mspress**

*For more information about learning tools such as online assessments, e-learning, and certification, visit:*
**www.microsoft.com/mspress** *and* **www.microsoft.com/learning**

# Additional Windows (R2) Resources for Administrators

*Published and Forthcoming Titles from Microsoft Press*

## Microsoft® Windows Server™ 2003 Administrator's Pocket Consultant, Second Edition

William R. Stanek • ISBN 0-7356-2245-0

Here's the practical, pocket-sized reference for IT professionals supporting Microsoft Windows Server 2003—fully updated for Service Pack 1 and Release 2. Designed for quick referencing, this portable guide covers all the essentials for performing everyday system administration tasks. Topics include managing workstations and servers, using Active Directory® directory service, creating and administering user and group accounts, managing files and directories, performing data security and auditing tasks, handling data back-up and recovery, and administering networks using TCP/IP, WINS, and DNS, and more.

## MCSE Self-Paced Training Kit (Exams 70-290, 70-291, 70-293, 70-294): Microsoft Windows Server 2003 Core Requirements, Second Edition

Holme, Thomas, Mackin, McLean, Zacker, Spealman, Hudson, and Craft • ISBN 0-7356-2290-6

The Microsoft Certified Systems Engineer (MCSE) credential is the premier certification for professionals who analyze the business requirements and design and implement the infrastructure for business solutions based on the Microsoft Windows Server 2003 platform and Microsoft Windows Server System—now updated for Windows Server 2003 Service Pack 1 and R2. This all-in-one set provides in-depth preparation for the four required networking system exams. Work at your own pace through the lessons, hands-on exercises, troubleshooting labs, and review questions. You get expert exam tips plus a full review section covering all objectives and sub-objectives in each study guide. Then use the Microsoft Practice Tests on the CD to challenge yourself with more than 1500 questions for self-assessment and practice!

## Microsoft Windows® Small Business Server 2003 R2 Administrator's Companion

Charlie Russel, Sharon Crawford, and Jason Gerend • ISBN 0-7356-2280-9

Get your small-business network, messaging, and collaboration systems up and running quickly with the essential guide to administering Windows Small Business Server 2003 R2. This reference details the features, capabilities, and technologies for both the standard and premium editions—including Microsoft Windows Server 2003 R2, Exchange Server 2003 with Service Pack 1, Windows SharePoint® Services, SQL Server™ 2005 Workgroup Edition, and Internet Information Services. Discover how to install, upgrade, or migrate to Windows Small Business Server 2003 R2; plan and implement your network, Internet access, and security services; customize Microsoft Exchange Server for your e-mail needs; and administer user rights, shares, permissions, and Group Policy.

## Microsoft Windows Small Business Server 2003 R2 Administrator's Companion

Charlie Russel, Sharon Crawford, and Jason Gerend • ISBN 0-7356-2280-9

Here's the ideal one-volume guide for the IT professional administering Windows Server 2003. Now fully updated for Windows Server 2003 Service Pack 1 and R2, this *Administrator's Companion* offers up-to-date information on core system administration topics for Microsoft Windows, including Active Directory services, security, scripting, disaster planning and recovery, and interoperability with UNIX. It also includes all-new sections on Service Pack 1 security updates and new features for R2. Featuring easy-to-use procedures and handy work-arounds, this book provides ready answers for on-the-job results.

---

## MCSA/MCSE Self-Paced Training Kit (Exam 70-290): Managing and Maintaining a Microsoft Windows Server 2003 Environment, Second Edition

Dan Holme and Orin Thomas • ISBN 0-7356-2289-2

## MCSA/MCSE Self-Paced Training Kit (Exam 70-291): Implementing, Managing, and Maintaining a Microsoft Windows Server 2003 Network Infrastructure, Second Edition

J.C. Mackin and Ian McLean • ISBN 0-7356-2288-4

## MCSE Self-Paced Training Kit (Exam 70-293): Planning and Maintaining a Microsoft Windows Server 2003 Network Infrastructure, Second Edition

Craig Zacker • ISBN 0-7356-2287-6

## MCSE Self-Paced Training Kit (Exam 70-294): Planning, Implementing, and Maintaining a Microsoft Windows Server 2003 Active Directory® Infrastructure, Second Ed.

Jill Spealman, Kurt Hudson, and Melissa Craft • ISBN 0-7356-2286-8

---

*For more information about Microsoft Press® books and other learning products,*
*visit:* **www.microsoft.com/mspress** *and* **www.microsoft.com/learning**

**Microsoft** *Press*

# What do you think of this book?
# We want to hear from you!

Do you have a few minutes to participate in a brief online survey? Microsoft is interested in hearing your feedback about this publication so that we can continually improve our books and learning resources for you.

To participate in our survey, please visit:

## www.microsoft.com/learning/booksurvey

And enter this book's ISBN, 0-7356-2198-5. As a thank-you to survey participants in the United States and Canada, each month we'll randomly select five respondents to win one of five $100 gift certificates from a leading online merchant.* At the conclusion of the survey, you can enter the drawing by providing your e-mail address, which will be used for prize notification *only*.

Thanks in advance for your input. Your opinion counts!

Sincerely,

Microsoft Learning

**Microsoft** | Learning

*Learn More. Go Further.*